Cost Accounting
A Managerial Emphasis

Cost

Accounting

A Managerial Emphasis

FOURTH EDITION

CHARLES T. HORNGREN
Ph.D., C.P.A.
Stanford University

PHI
Prentice/Hall International, Inc., London

Prentice-Hall International, Inc., *London*
Prentice-Hall of Australia Pty. Ltd., *Sydney*
Prentice-Hall of Canada, Ltd., *Toronto*
Prentice-Hall of India (Private) Ltd., *New Delhi*
Prentice-Hall of Japan, Inc., *Tokyo*
Prentice-Hall of Southeast Asia Pte. Ltd., *Singapore*
Whitehall Books Limited, Wellington, *New Zealand*
Prentice-Hall, Inc., Englewood Cliffs, *New Jersey*

Cost Accounting: A Managerial Emphasis CHARLES T. HORNGREN FOURTH EDITION

Printed in the United States of America

10 9 8 7 6 5 4 3

ISBN: 0-13-180000-0

To Professor William J. Vatter

Contents

2

An Introduction to Cost Terms and Purposes 19

3

Cost-Volume-Profit Relationships 44

4

Job-Order Accounting: An Illustration of Systems Design 74

SECTION TWO

Multiple Purpose Systems for Management Control

SECTION THREE

Special Topics for Further Study

Preface

Cost accounting provides data for three major purposes: (1) planning and controlling routine operations; (2) nonroutine decisions, policy making, and long-range planning; and (3) inventory valuation and income determination. This volume gives abundant consideration to all three of these, but emphasis is placed on the first two. In short, the major theme is "different costs for different purposes."

The topics emphasized from the outset are those that challenge the student and spur his curiosity. Because the emphasis is on costs for planning and control, the following topics of prime managerial significance are introduced early: the role of the accountant in the organization; cost behavior and volume-profit relationships; responsibility accounting; standard costs; flexible budgets; cost structures for control and motivation; and relevant costs of nonroutine decisions. The favorable reaction to the format of previous editions is evidence that cost accounting courses can be enriched, relieved of drudgery, and broadened from coverage of procedures alone to a full-fledged treatment of concepts, analyses, and procedures that pays more than lip-service to accounting as a managerial tool.

This flexible treatment of cost accounting and management accounting presupposes just a one-term introduction to basic accounting. Ample material is provided for a two-semester or two-quarter course, especially if it is supplemented with outside readings. The need for supplementation may be diminished with this edition because it has more substance (especially in the latter half) than previously. The first eleven chapters provide the essence of a one-term course. Because instructors may disagree about what constitutes a proper sequence, this book has been designed to permit a maximum degree of flexibility with a minimum of discontinuity.

Cost accounting courses now cover a wider range of topics than ever. Some instructors prefer to concentrate on developing a solid comprehension of the uses and limitations of formal cost accounting systems as they exist. Others prefer a normative approach, focusing on how cost systems should be designed —or on how cost information should be provided for various classes of decisions. This book attempts to satisfy both needs: the order of chapters provided is only one of many possible sequences.

A major objective of this revision has been to promote flexibility by using a modular approach. The material has been arranged to allow instructors—who are working with students having different backgrounds and within curricula having various overlaps—the greatest latitude in picking and choosing chapters. For example, if the courses in finance emphasize cash budgeting and capital budgeting, Chapters 5, 12, and 13 might be omitted. If the instructor wishes to cover product-costing systems in depth, Chapters 18 and 19 on process costing (except for the portions on standard costing) and Chapter 20 on payroll accounting might be assigned immediately after Chapter 4 on job-order costing. The standard costing in Chapters 18 and 19 might then be assigned immediately after Chapter 9.

changes in this edition

In this edition changes have been made in both content and organization. Most chapters have been thoroughly rewritten. In addition, many new problems and cases have been provided. Major changes include:

1. A cost-benefit approach toward judging alternative cost accounting systems is used as a frame of reference throughout the book.

2. The role of costs in relation to making decisions under uncertainty is introduced in Chapter 3 via sensitivity analysis. This approach is illustrated for cost-volume-profit models and in later chapters for capital-budgeting models, inventory-control models, regression models, and linear-programming models.

3. The role of income taxes in cost-volume-profit analysis is introduced in Chapter 3.

4. More attention is paid to cost accounting in non-manufacturing and not-for-profit organizations, primarily via the use of illustrations and problems.

For example, see the section, "Job and Process Costing: A Matter of Averaging," in Chapter 4 and Problems 4-24 and 4-25. Also see the section, "Applicability to Nonprofit Organizations" in Chapter 12.

5. Chapters 7 through 10 have taken a fresh approach to flexible budgets and standard costs. Variance analysis is comprehended more easily, and its relation to management decisions is more sharply delineated.

6. Chapter 10 introduces a new section that provides an overview of variance analysis and ties it to the original master budget of net income.

7. Chapter 12 on cost allocation has been divided into two chapters and moved to become Chapters 15 and 16. This edition contains a more extensive discussion of the various purposes of cost allocation.

8. Chapter 12 has a new section and problems on capital budgeting and inflation. For example, see Problems 12-27 and 13-16.

9. Chapter 13 employs a new table that eases discounted cash-flow computations for sum-of-the-years-digits depreciation.

10. The role of the Cost Accounting Standards Board is discussed in a new appendix at the end of the book and in Chapters 15 and 16.

11. The material on joint products and by-products is now in Chapter 17. It contains a new discussion of by-product accounting.

12. Chapters 18 and 19 contain a completely revised approach to process accounting and the computation of equivalent units.

13. The two-chapter treatment of accounting in relation to decentralized operations is rewritten so that the material on transfer pricing is introduced in the first instead of the second of the two chapters.

14. Chapter 24 (formerly 23) is a thoroughly rewritten treatment of decision theory and uncertainty.

15. Chapter 25 (formerly 24) is a complete revision of the coverage of cost behavior patterns and regression analysis. More emphasis is given to the interpretation of regression results.

16. Chapter 26 is a revision and combination of former Chapters 25 and 26. There is a completely new and simpler discussion of mix and yield variances.

17. Chapter 27 is a deeper analysis of the accounting implications of linear programming models.

18. As with previous editions, the problems are designed to stress key points. Many new ones have been added; for instance, consider problems 2-22 through 2-26, 2-31, 3-10 through 3-15, 3-28, 4-14, 4-19, 4-23 through 4-25, 6-21, 6-26, 6-29, 7-18 through 7-20, 7-24, 7-25, 8-13, 8-15, 8-16, 8-27, 8-28, 9-7, 9-8, 9-13, 9-18, 9-20 through 9-23, 10-6, 10-7, 10-11, 10-17, 10-21, 10-22, 10-25, through 10-30, 11-9, 12-24 through 12-28, 13-15 and 13-28 through 13-30. Others are apparent for each chapter.

The placement of Chapter 6 (responsibility accounting and motivation) continues to be a particularly troublesome decision. This chapter provides a perspective on management control systems. It is debatable whether it is most advantageous to provide this perspective before the details in Chapters 7 through 9; therefore, the instructor may choose to cover Chapters 7, 8, and 9 before 6.

Another alternative might be to cover the chapters in the order presented but assign one problem from Chapter 6 with each succeeding assignment from Chapters 7 through 9.

Another consideration in preparing this revision was the extent to which a quantitative approach should be included. If more quantitative material is added, should it be interwoven with appropriate topics or considered separately? The choice was to add more quantitative material but to confine it to Chapters 24-27, again because it allows maximum flexibility. Those instructors wanting to integrate such material with earlier chapters may do so; suggestions as to how are provided in the solutions manual. Those who prefer to concentrate on other matters will not be hampered by the necessity to omit portions of chapters.

Various parts of this book may be packaged to provide a cost accounting course with a heavy quantitative emphasis (Chapters 1, 24, 3, 4, 25, 10, 11, 27, 12–14, 6–9, 26) or a heavy behavioral emphasis (Chapters 1–4, 6–11, 22–23). **The front section of the solutions manual contains profuse suggestions regarding various course outlines and choices of problem material.**

acknowledgments

I am indebted to many for ideas and assistance. The acknowledgments in the three previous editions contain a long list of my creditors. My primary obligation is to Professor William J. Vatter to whom this book is dedicated. For those who know him, no words are necessary; for those who do not know him, no words will suffice.

Professor Dudley W. Curry has aided me immensely with his detailed review of the manuscript of this edition. **Moreover, he has prepared the quiz and examination material and a student's study guide that is available as supplementary material.** The reviews of various chapters by Joel Demski, Joseph Greco, Hiroyuki Itami, and James Patell have also been significantly helpful. Joel Demski has been particularly generous with his comments and problem material for Chapter 25.

The following professors influenced this edition by their preparation of reviews of the preceding edition: Andrew Bailey, Jr., David Buehlman, James Caldwell, Emily Chang, William Crum, Joseph Curran, Leon Ennis, Jr., Donald Gorton, David Green, Robert Hamilton, Gary Holstrum, Yow-Min Lee, Chris Luneski, Donald Madden, Patrick McKensie, James Montgomery, Hugo Nurnberg, Anthony Pustorino, Gayle Rayburn, C. Stevenson Rowley, Leopold Schachner, Hadley Schaefer, Mary Strecker, and Robert West. In addition, I have received helpful suggestions by mail from many users, too numerous to mention here.

Many students have read the manuscript and worked the new problems to insure that they are as error free as possible. They have also contributed ideas and material for revising chapters and preparing new problems. Particular thanks go to Randall Bolten, Christopher Canellos, Alfred Castino, Elizabeth Davila, Curtis Fitzgerald, Sherryl Hossack, Joyce Kaneda, Peter Kent, Kathleen McPherson, Sarah Supplee, Robert Thompson, and especially Robert Bickerton and Jules Goins.

A special note of gratitude is extended to Christiane Jose for her skillful typing of much material in syllabus form.

Also, I thank the people at Prentice-Hall: Garret White, Eleanor Paige, Marvin Warshaw, Judy Winthrop, Robert Boyle, and Ken Cashman.

Appreciation also goes to the American Institute of Certified Public Accountants, The National Association of Accountants, The Institute of Management Accounting, the Society of Industrial Accountants of Canada, the Certified General Accountants' Association of Canada, the Financial Executives Institute of America, and to many other publishers and companies for their generous permission to quote from their publications. Problems from the Uniform CPA Examinations are designated (CPA); problems from the Certificate in Management Accounting examinations are designated (CMA); problems from the Canadian examinations administered by the Society of Industrial Accountants' Association are designated (SIA); problems from the Certified General Accountants' Association are designated (CGAA). Many of these problems are adapted to highlight particular points.

I am grateful to the professors who contributed assignment material for this edition. Their names are indicated in parentheses at the start of their specific problems; for example, (W. Crum) indicates a contribution by William F. Crum.

Comments from users are welcome.

CHARLES T. HORNGREN

Cost Accounting
A Managerial Emphasis

Cost Accounting Fundamentals

SECTION ONE

The Accountant's Role in the Organization

1

As this chapter is being written, former accountants are the top executives in many large companies, including Chrysler Corporation, General Motors Corporation, and General Electric Company. Accounting duties played a key part in their rise to the management summit. Accounting cuts across all facets of the organization; the management accountant's duties are intertwined with executive planning and control.

The study of modern cost accounting yields insight and breadth regarding both the accountant's role and the manager's role in an organization. How are these two roles related? Where may they overlap? How can accounting help managers? This book tries to answer these questions. In this chapter, we[1] shall try to get some perspective on where the accountant should fit in the organization. Then we shall have a framework for studying the rest of the chapters.

[1] Should an author use "I," "we," "the author," or "this writer" in contexts such as these? Each mode of expression has its weaknesses, but I prefer "we." As used in this book, "we" denotes a mutual exploration of the subject by the author and the readers. Incidentally, for conciseness "he" and "his" are usually used in this book rather than "he or she" or "his or hers" or "person." If you prefer, substitute "she" or "hers" where appropriate.

focus of cost accounting and management accounting

emphasis on internal decisions

The accounting system is the major quantitative information system in almost every organization. How does "cost accounting" fit into this overall accounting system? Originally, the label *cost accounting* referred to ways of accumulating historical costs and tracing them to units of output and to departments, primarily for purposes of providing the inventory valuations used in balance sheets and income statements. Although cost accounting continues this important role today, its boundaries extend far beyond the major financial statements. Cost accounting is generally indistinguishable from so-called *management accounting* or *managerial accounting;* its fundamental aim is to assist the manager in making a host of decisions.

The essence of the management process is decision making—the purposeful choosing from among alternative courses of action to achieve some objective. These decisions range from the routine (for example, whether to schedule a job on machine one or two) to the nonroutine (for example, whether to launch a new product line).

Sometimes the field of accounting is divided into two major parts: financial accounting and managerial (cost) accounting. The major distinction between them is their use by two different classes of decision makers. The field of financial accounting is concerned mainly with how accounting can serve *external* decision makers, such as stockholders, creditors, governmental agencies, and others. The field of managerial (cost) accounting is concerned mainly with how accounting can serve *internal* decision makers, such as managers.

relation to decisions

The manager has a method for deciding among courses of action, often called a *decision model,* which is a conceptual representation that measures the effects of alternative actions. Whether a decision maker uses a very informal decision model (such as a final pricing decision made by hunch) or a well-defined mathematical model (such as linear programming for scheduling production) is not important to our perspective. We are mainly concerned with choosing what accounting information to provide, *given* either a plain or fancy decision model.

Consider an example of a decision concerning the rearrangement of a production line and facilities in order to save operating labor costs. Assume the only alternatives are to "do nothing" or "rearrange." At this point, study the analysis of this example in Exhibit 1-1, which puts the role of accounting information in perspective.

The historical labor costs of $2.00 per unit of output are the starting point for *predicting* the labor costs under both of the alternatives. The prediction under the "do nothing" alternative is $2.00 because the prediction method, used here for simplicity, assumes that the past will exactly repeat itself, although a different prediction method might well have been appropriate. The labor cost under

EXHIBIT 1-1

ACCOUNTING INFORMATION AND THE DECISION PROCESS

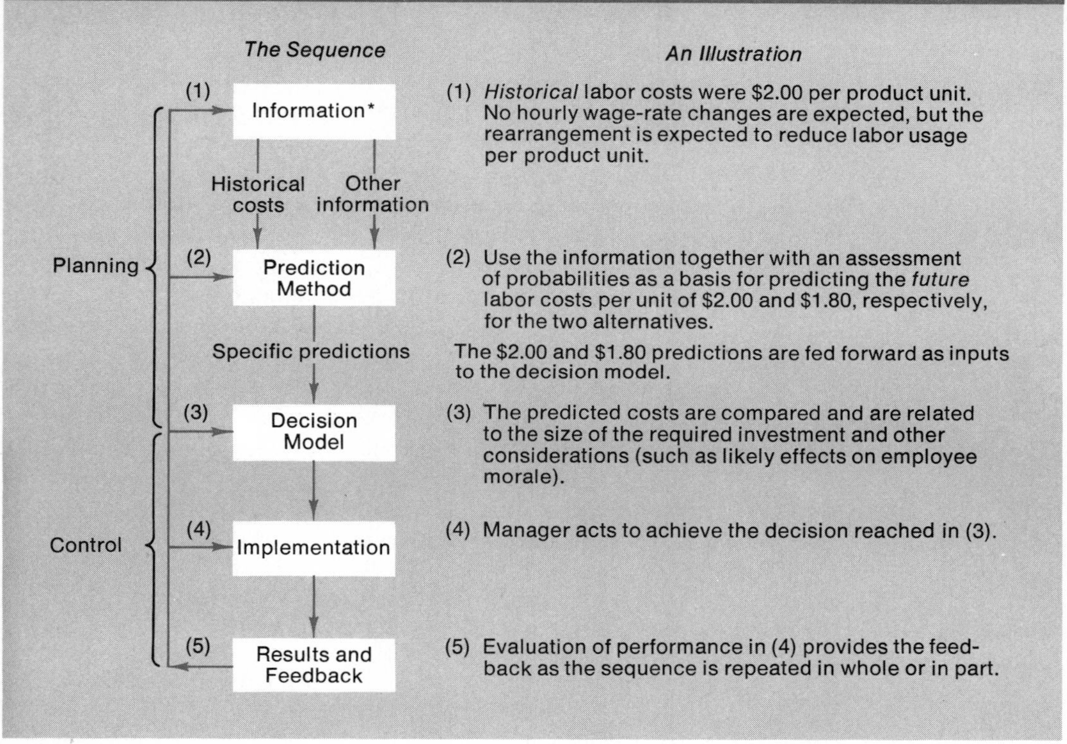

The Sequence
An Illustration
(1)
Information*
Historical costs
Other information
(2)
Prediction Method
Specific predictions
(3)
Decision Model
(4)
Implementation
(5)
Results and Feedback
Planning
Control
(1) Historical labor costs were $2.00 per product unit. No hourly wage-rate changes are expected, but the rearrangement is expected to reduce labor usage per product unit.
(2) Use the information together with an assessment of probabilities as a basis for predicting the future labor costs per unit of $2.00 and $1.80, respectively, for the two alternatives.
The $2.00 and $1.80 predictions are fed forward as inputs to the decision model.
(3) The predicted costs are compared and are related to the size of the required investment and other considerations (such as likely effects on employee morale).
(4) Manager acts to achieve the decision reached in (3).
(5) Evaluation of performance in (4) provides the feed-back as the sequence is repeated in whole or in part.

* The words *information* and *data* have a variety of meanings in both the popular and technical literature. In most cases, data is a more general term; that is, data consist of both information and non-information. For example, *information* is often regarded as that subset of data that is likely to alter a decision maker's prediction.

the "rearrange" alternative is $1.80 per product unit because of expected reductions in labor usage.

The specific predictions are fed forward as inputs to a decision model, which might consist of a comparison of the total predicted labor savings against the required additional investment, if any. If the total predicted labor savings were sufficiently high to warrant the investment, the rearrangement would be implemented. The actual results would become the *feedback* that might influence subsequent information, predictions, decisions, and implementation methods.

planning and control There are countless definitions of planning and control. Here we define *planning* as a delineation of goals and a formulation of a decision model for selecting means of achieving them. In our illustration, the goal might be to maximize corporate net income and the decision model might be a comparison of the total labor savings with any required additional investment under each alternative, indicating the alternative with the least net cost.

Control is the implementation of the decision and the use of feedback so that the goals are attained. This definition is comprehensive and flexible. Control is concerned with the successful *implementation* of any chosen course of action, but it is also concerned with *feedback* that might change any or all of the future predictions, the prediction method, the decision model itself, or the implementation.

In our illustration, the actual results of the plant rearrangement may show that the new labor costs are \$2.50 per product unit rather than the \$1.80 originally predicted. This feedback may lead to better implementation (step 4 in Exhibit 1-1), such as a change in supervisory behavior, in employee training, or in personnel, so that the \$1.80 target is achieved. On the other hand, the feedback may convince the decision maker that the prediction method, rather than the implementation, was faulty. Perhaps the prediction method for similar decisions in the future should be modified to allow for worker training or learning time.

Another illustration like Exhibit 1-1 is the typical budgeting process for, say, material usage in a manufacturing operation:

1. The initial information may be the historical cost of materials during the year just ended.
2. The prediction method may consist of taking the historical-cost measure and modifying it by the expected change in unit prices for the forthcoming year to show a predicted (budgeted) material cost.
3. The decision may be to (a) continue using the same type of material or (b) replace it with some alternative material. Note that often this first type of decision is implicit; that is, the same material continues in use because it is "obviously" the most attractive choice—no formal decision model is used. Nevertheless, "do nothing" or "repeat the same procedures" are always decision alternatives.
4. The manager implements the budgeted choice.
5. The feedback consists of a comparison of the budget with the actual results. Note that this feedback may be used for (1) making the same type of specific predictions again, (2) changing the method of making predictions, (3) changing the decision model that was used to choose this material, (4) changing the means of attaining the desired outcomes, or (5) measuring and rewarding performance.

To recapitulate, although at first glance it may appear awesome, Exhibit 1-1 is a simplified description of the role of accounting information in the planning (prediction and decision-making) and control (implementation and feedback) processes. Also, Exhibit 1-1 illustrates the interactive nature of the processes. To keep perspective, we should view these processes in total, not as separable subparts.

cost-benefit approach An accounting information system is a commodity, an economic good just like butter, eggs, or smog-control devices. We should habitually ask the question: **How much would we be willing to pay for one information system versus another? The cost-benefit method can be related to Exhibit 1-1. It basically involves the accountant, the manager, or both in predicting the relationships among the accounting measures or systems, the manager's decision models, and the results.** The optimal accounting measure or system is the one that produces the greatest benefit nėt of the costs of obtaining the information.

Admittedly, the measurement of these costs and benefits is an imposing, complex undertaking that may often be infeasible. Nevertheless, this conceptual approach[2] is a powerful, intuitively appealing foundation for resolving accounting issues. It represents a major theme of this entire textbook.

Even though these cost-benefit decisions are most often made implicitly, the underlying philosophy here should not be overlooked. For example, we often see opinions about what data are "needed" for making assorted decisions with only passing reference (at most) to the associated "costs" and "benefits."

To illustrate this point, you may encounter arguments from time to time that one way is better than a second way of computing the cost of a product, that Method 1 is "needed" because it provides a "more accurate" or a "truer" approximation of "economic reality." The cost-benefit approach to such an issue does not use "need" or "truth" or "accuracy" as the fundamental method of resolving the dispute. **Instead, its method is to ask whether the decisions affected by these costs will differ if Method 1 is used rather than Method 2.** If the decisions will be unaffected, then the less costly alternative is preferable. If the decision will be affected differently, then the preferable alternative is that which is expected to produce the greatest benefit after deducting the costs of getting the data. The choices of how to design management accounting systems are inherently dependent on specific circumstances.[3] Sweeping generalizations across contexts are alien to the cost-benefit philosophy.

For example, in Exhibit 1-1 the compilation of labor costs may be a valueless exercise—an economic waste—for purposes of the plant-rearrangement decision if the manager has other reasons for favoring the rearrangement. Therefore, any elaborate cost-finding scheme that would provide "more accurate"

[2] The cost-benefit way of thinking is widely applicable even if the costs and benefits defy precise measurement. As a motto in the System Analysis Office of the Department of Defense says, "It is better to be roughly right than precisely wrong." For example, if two methods of accomplishing the same disease cure are available, the least costly is preferable. Similarly, if two proposals have equal costs, the proposal that is perceived to yield more benefits is preferable. This judgment can be achieved without a numerical measurement of the levels of benefits. For example, will \$100,000 spent on teachers' salaries produce more benefits than \$100,000 spent on teaching machines? See R. Anthony and R. Herzlinger, *Management Control in Nonprofit Organizations* (Homewood, Ill.: Richard D. Irwin, Inc.), p. 194.

[3] A rigorous description of this *information-evaluation approach* is J. Demski and G. Feltham, *Cost Determination: A Conceptual Approach* (Ames, Iowa: Iowa State University Press, 1976).

labor data would be a squandering of resources. On the other hand, a detailed measure of historical costs and a careful prediction may be central to the rearrangement decision. In short, "what difference does it make" is a good question to ask in resolving cost accounting questions.

accountant as a decision maker

Exhibit 1-1 has another decision-making implication that is perhaps not obvious. Note that the decision maker must not only make an *action* choice (to rearrange or not); he must also make an *information* choice (what information to buy). The decision maker frequently delegates this information decision to a specialist, such as an accountant. So the accountant as well as the manager is often in a decision-making role. Hence, we frequently have at least two decision makers and two decisions, and each must be aware of the problems of the others.

The relationship of accounting to decisions may sometimes seem far-fetched and murky. Nevertheless, every dispute about accounting can be ultimately related to some decision by the user of the data. We are not considering abstractions for their own sake here. On the contrary, we are laying the groundwork—formulating a point of view—that will help the ensuing details fall into place.

the pervading duties of the management accountant

line and staff relationships

Most entities have the production and sale of goods or services as their basic objectives. Line managers are *directly* responsible for attaining these objectives as efficiently as possible. Staff elements of organizations exist because the scope of the line manager's responsibility and duties expands so that he needs specialized help to operate effectively. When a department's primary task is that of advice and service to other departments, it is a *staff* department.

Except for exerting line authority over his own department, the chief accounting executive generally fills a staff role in his company, as contrasted with the line roles of sales and production executives.[4] This includes advice and help in the areas of budgeting, controlling, pricing, and special decisions. The accounting department does not exercise direct authority over line departments. Uniformity of accounting and reporting is often acquired through the delegation of authority regarding accounting procedures to the chief management accountant, the controller, by the top line management. Note carefully that when the controller prescribes the line department's role in supplying account-

[4] Management literature is hazy on these distinctions, and we shall not belabor them here. For example, some writers distinguish among three types of authority: line, staff, and functional. Line authority is exerted downward over subordinates. Staff authority is the authority to *advise* but not command others; it is exercised laterally or upward. Functional authority is the right to *command* action laterally and downward with regard to a specific function or specialty.

ing information, he is speaking for top line management—not as the controller, a staff man. The uniform accounting procedure is authorized by the president and is installed for him by the controller.

Theoretically, the controller's decisions regarding the best accounting procedures to be followed by line people are transmitted to the president. In turn, the president communicates these procedures through a manual of instructions that comes down through the line chain of command to all people affected by the procedures.

Practically, the daily work of the controller is such that his face-to-face relationships with the production manager or foreman may call for his directing how production records should be kept or how work tickets should be completed.[5] The controller usually holds delegated authority from top line management over such matters.

Exhibit 1-2 illustrates the general organizational relationships described above. Note the distinction between producing departments and service departments. The primary purpose of a factory is to produce goods. Therefore, the production-line manufacturing departments are usually termed *producing* or *operating departments.* To facilitate production, most plants also have *service departments,* which exist to facilitate the tasks of the producing departments.

the controller: the chief management accountant

The word *controller* is applied to various accounting positions. The stature and duties of the controller vary from company to company. In some firms he is little more than a glorified bookkeeper who compiles data primarily for conventional balance sheets and income statements. In other firms—for example, General Electric—he is a key executive who aids management planning and control in over 170 subdivisions. In most firms his status is somewhere between these two extremes. For example, his opinion on the tax implications of certain managerial decisions may be carefully weighed, yet his opinion on the other aspects of these decisions may not be sought. Whatever his title, he is viewed in this book as the chief management accounting executive. The point of terminology here is that the modern controller does not do any controlling in terms of line authority, except over his own department. Yet the modern concept of controllership maintains that the controller *does* control in a special sense. That is, by reporting and interpreting relevant data, the controller exerts a force or influence that impels management toward logical decisions consistent with objectives.

distinctions between controller and treasurer

Many people confuse the offices of controller and treasurer. The position of Vice-President—Finance has evolved in many organizations. This executive typically oversees both the con-

[5] According to some writers, this would be exercising the *functional authority* described in the previous footnote.

EXHIBIT 1-2

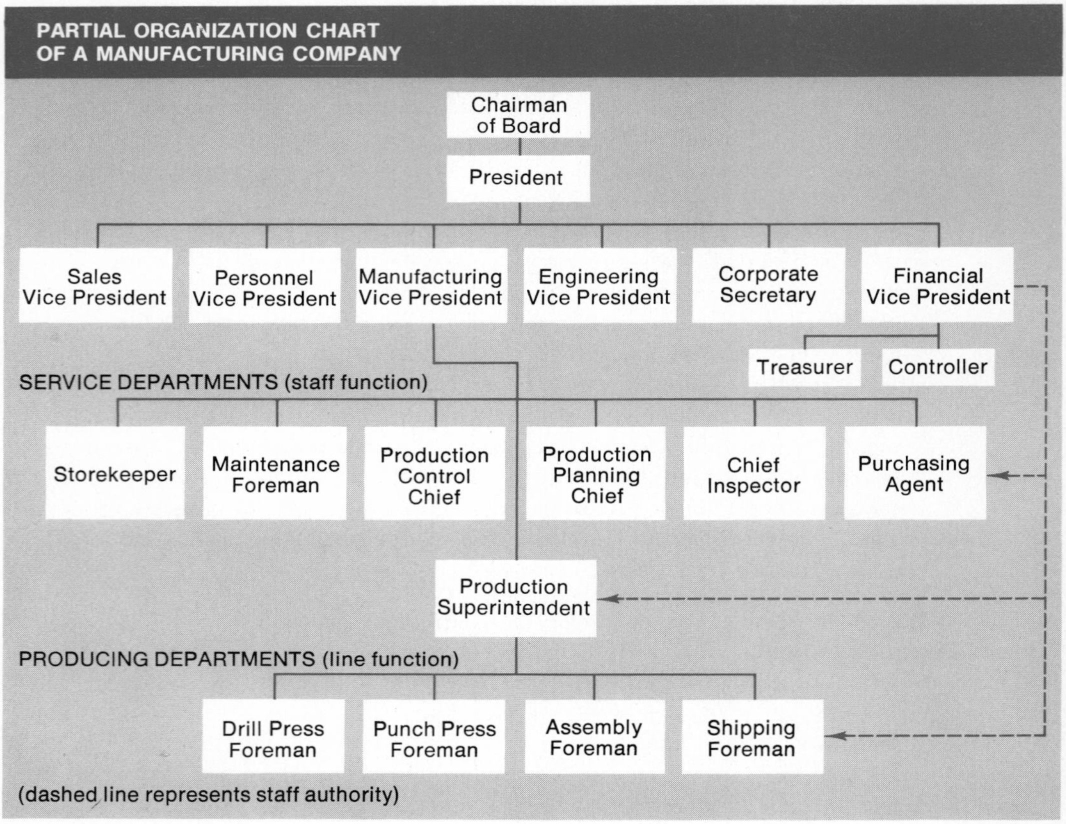

trollership and treasurership functions. The Financial Executives Institute, an association of corporate treasurers and controllers, distinguishes their functions as follows:

Controllership	Treasurership
1. Planning for control	1. Provision of capital
2. Reporting and interpreting	2. Investor relations
3. Evaluating and consulting	3. Short-term financing
4. Tax administration	4. Banking and custody
5. Government reporting	5. Credits and collections
6. Protection of assets	6. Investments
7. Economic appraisal	7. Insurance

Note how managerial cost accounting is the controller's primary *means* of implementing the first three functions of controllership.

We shall not dwell at length on the treasurer's functions. As the seven points indicate, he is concerned mainly with financial, as distinguished from operating, problems. The exact division of various accounting and financial duties obviously varies from company to company.

The controller has been compared to the ship's navigator. The navigator, with the help of his specialized training, assists the captain. Without the navigator, the ship may flounder on reefs or miss its destination entirely, but the captain exerts his right to command. The navigator guides and informs the captain as to how well the ship is being steered. This navigator role is especially evident in points 1 through 3 of the seven functions.

division of duties

Accountants often face a dilemma because they are supposed to fulfill two conflicting roles simultaneously. First, they are seen as watchdogs for top managers. Second, they are seen as helpers for all managers. The watchdog role is usually performed via the scorekeeping task of accumulating and reporting to all levels of management. The helper role is usually performed via the tasks of directing managers' attention to problems and of assisting managers in solving problems.[6]

The sheer volume of the watchdog or scorekeeping task is often overwhelming; the day-to-day routines and endless deadlines shunt the helper role into the background and often into oblivion. To prevent the helper role from falling by the wayside, many organizations deliberately split the accountants' duties in ways similar to those in Exhibit 1-3.

The attention-directing and problem-solving tasks improve mutual understanding if a member of the controller's staff personally explains and interprets reports as they are presented to line managers. This attention-directing role (for example, explaining the differences between budgeted and actual performance) is often performed by experienced accountants who, at least to some degree, can talk the line manager's language. Indeed, the interpreters are the individuals who will establish the status of the controller's department in the company. Close, direct contacts between accountants and operating managers usually instill confidence in the reliability of the financial reports, which are the measuring devices of performance.

Many companies deliberately rotate their young accountants through scorekeeping, attention-directing, and problem-solving posts. In this way, accountants are more likely to appreciate the decision-maker's viewpoint and are thus prone to keep the accounting system tuned to the needs of the users.

[6] H. A. Simon, H. Guetzkow, G. Kozmetsky, and G. Tyndall, *Centralization vs. Decentralization in Organizing the Controller's Department* (New York: Controllership Foundation, Inc.). This perceptive study is much broader than its title implies.

EXHIBIT 1-3

ORGANIZATION CHART OF A CONTROLLER'S DEPARTMENT

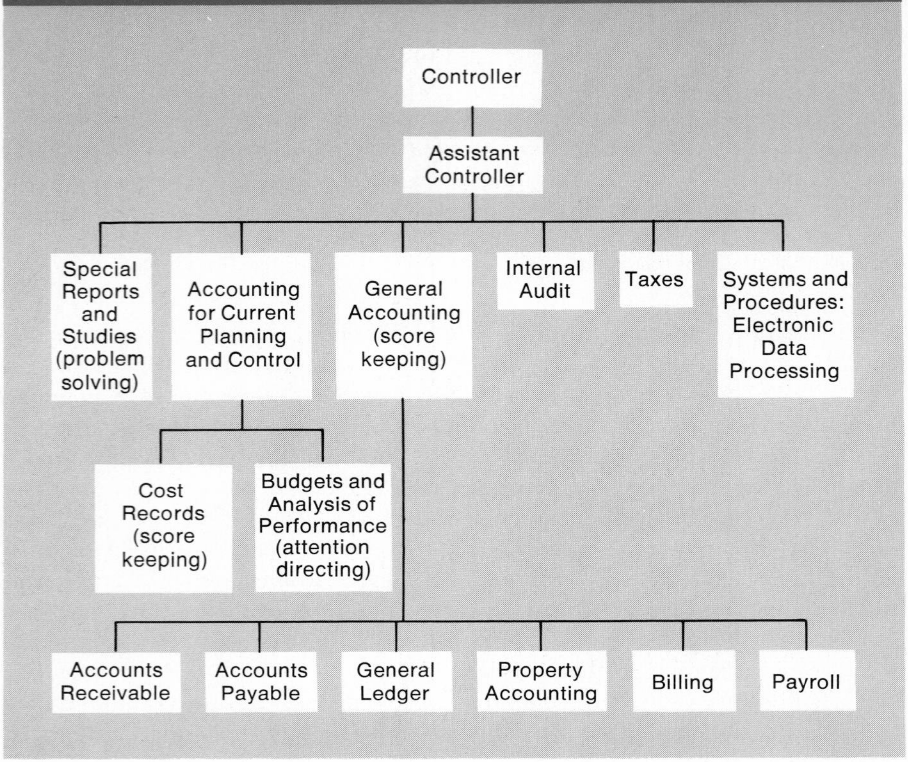

SUMMARY

This chapter stressed the interrelationship of accounting information and management decisions. The first major part of this chapter provided a conceptual overview. The second major part described how accountants fit into typical organizational settings.

Accounting information is an important input to many decision makers. In turn, the accountant frequently must choose what and how much information to provide. The choices among accounting measures and systems are aimed at facilitating an optimal ultimate action by some decision maker.

The cost-benefit approach is a major theme of this book. In a most fundamental sense, the question of what accounting data, report, or system to buy must focus on how decisions (and resulting benefits) are going to be affected. The method of analysis is to ask what decisions will ensue upon the receipt of each possible set of accounting data (or no accounting data) and what outcomes will follow from these decisions.

PROBLEMS FOR SELF-STUDY

(Try to solve these problems before examining the solutions that follow.)

PROBLEM 1

Reexamine the plant-rearrangement decision in Exhibit 1-1.

a. Give an example of (1) a prediction method for direct-labor costs under the "do nothing" alternative that is more specific than using the historical costs indicated in the exhibit; and (2) a decision model that is more specific than described in the exhibit.

b. What steps in Exhibit 1-1 are often described as planning? As control?

SOLUTION 1

a. (1) One possibility is a method that explicitly recognizes a constantly decreasing unit cost caused by the increased speed and skill of employees as they become more familiar with their tasks. Other possibilities would include the use of various formulas that incorporate expected operating improvements through time.

(2) A simple model would be to sum the predicted costs over the life of both alternatives and choose the alternative with the least cost. Another decision model would explicitly divide the predicted annual cost savings by the required investment to obtain a rate of return on the investment. If the rate was above the desired minimum, the investment would occur.

b. Planning encompasses steps (1), (2), and (3), whereas controlling entails steps (4) and (5), including the feedback process.

PROBLEM 2

Using the organization charts in this chapter (Exhibits 1-2 and 1-3), answer the following questions:

a. Do the following have line or staff authority over the assembly foreman: maintenance foreman, manufacturing vice-president, production superintendent, purchasing agent, storekeeper, personnel vice-president, president, chief budgetary accountant, chief internal auditor?

b. What is the general role of service departments in an organization? How are they distinguished from operating or producing departments?

c. Does the controller have line or staff authority over the cost accountants? The accounts-receivable clerks?

d. What is probably the *major duty* (scorekeeping, attention directing, or problem solving) of the following?

1. Payroll clerk	7. Budgetary accountant
2. Accounts-receivable clerk	8. Cost analyst
3. Cost-record clerk	9. Head of special reports and studies
4. Head of general accounting	10. Head of accounting for planning and control
5. Head of taxes	
6. Head of internal auditing	11. Controller

A sad commentary on many existing accounting systems is that they fulfill their scorekeeping tasks admirably—but they stop there. With minimal additional cost, immense benefit could be generated if the attention-directing and problem-solving functions were also performed.

SOLUTION 2

a. The only executives having line authority over the assembly foreman are the president, the manufacturing vice-president, and the production superintendent.

b. A typical company's major purpose is to produce and sell goods or services. Unless a department is directly concerned with producing or selling, it is called a service or staff department. Service departments exist only to help the production and sales departments with their major tasks: the efficient production and sale of goods or services.

c. The controller has line authority over all members of his own department, all those shown in the controller's organization chart (Exhibit 1-3).
d. The major duty of the first five is typically scorekeeping. Attention directing is probably the major duty of the next three. Problem solving is probably the primary duty of the head of special reports and studies. The head of accounting for planning and control and the controller should be concerned with all three duties: scorekeeping, attention directing, and problem solving. However, there is a perpetual danger that day-to-day pressures will emphasize scorekeeping. Therefore, accountants and managers should constantly see that attention directing and problem solving are also stressed. Otherwise, the major management benefits of an accounting system may be lost.

QUESTIONS, PROBLEMS, AND CASES

Special note about the assignment material **No attempt has been made to distinguish among questions, problems, and cases, because distinctions among them are so often artificial. Many problems are based on actual business situations. To aid selection, most problems have individual short titles that describe their subject matter.**

1-1 Why do the controller and his staff have to understand the company organization structure?

1-2 As a new controller, answer this comment by a factory superintendent: "As I see it, our accountants may be needed to keep records for stockholders and Uncle Sam—but I don't want them sticking their noses in my day-to-day operations. I do the best I know how; no pencil-pusher knows enough about my responsibilities to be of any use to me."

1-3 "The way these modern controllers put themselves on a pedestal, you may as well give them the title of President and be done with it. Look at the first three points in their functions of controllership. With the change of a word or two, these points could be a job description for the company president." Discuss.

1-4 Define *decision making.*

1-5 Define *planning.* Distinguish it from control.

1-6 "Planning is really much more vital than control." Do you agree? Why?

1-7 "We need to record replacement costs because they are more accurate approximations of economic reality." How would an advocate of cost-benefit analysis react to this statement?

1-8 "The controller is both a line and a staff executive." Do you agree? Why?

1-9 "The modern concept of controllership maintains that the controller *does* control in a special sense." Explain.

1-10 What are some common causes of friction between line and staff executives?

1-11 How is cost accounting related to the concept of controllership?

1-12 Distinguish among line, staff, and functional authorities.

1-13 *Role of the Accountant in the Organization: Line and Staff Functions*

1. Of the following, who have line authority over a cost-record clerk: budgetary accountant; head of accounting for current planning and control; head of general accounting; controller; storekeeper; production superintendent; manufacturing vice-president; president; production-control chief?

2. Of the following, who have line authority over an assembler: stamping foreman; assembly foreman; production superintendent; production-control chief; storekeeper; manufacturing vice-president; engineering vice-president; president; controller; budgetary accountant; cost-record clerk?

1-14 *Scorekeeping, Attention Directing, and Problem Solving* For each of the following, identify the function the accountant is performing: i.e., scorekeeping, attention directing, or problem solving. *Also* state whether the departments mentioned are service or production departments.

1. Processing the weekly payroll for the maintenance department
2. Explaining the welding foreman's performance report
3. Analyzing the costs of several different ways to blend raw materials in the foundry
4. Tallying sales, by branches, for the sales vice-president
5. Analyzing, for the president, the impact on net income of a contemplated new product
6. Interpreting why a branch did not meet its sales quota
7. Interpreting variances on a machining foreman's performance report
8. Preparing the budget for research and development
9. Adjusting journal entries for depreciation on the personnel manager's office equipment
10. Preparing a customer's monthly statement

1-15 *Draw an Organization Chart* Draw an organization chart for a company that has the following positions:

Vice-president, controller and treasurer
Chief designer
Receiving and stores superintendent
Branch A sales manager
Production superintendent
Chief of finished stockroom
Shipping-room head
Chief of cost accumulation
Maintenance superintendent
Employment manager
Welding and assembly superintendent
Machining superintendent
Vice-president, manufacturing
Finishing-department superintendent
Vice-president, chief engineer
Foundry superintendent
Head of job evaluation
Vice-president, personnel
Head of general accounting
Budget director
Tool-room superintendent
Chief purchasing agent
Head of cost analysis
Inspection superintendent
Stamping superintendent
Head of research
President
Head of production control
Vice-president, sales

1-16 *Responsibility for Analysis of Performance* John Phillipson is the new controller of a huge company that has just overhauled its organization structure. The company is now decentralized. Each division is under an operating vice-president who, within wide limits, has responsibilities and authority to run his division like a separate company.

Phillipson has a number of bright staff members, one of whom, Bob Garrett, is in charge of a newly created performance-analysis staff. Garrett and his fellow staff members prepare monthly divisional performance reports for the company president. These reports are divisional income statements, showing budgeted performance and actual performance, and are accompanied by detailed written explanations and appraisals of variances. Each of Garrett's staff members had a major responsibility for analyzing one division; each consulted with divisional line and staff executives and became generally acquainted with the division's operations.

After a few months, Bill Whisler, vice-president in charge of Division C, has stormed into the controller's office. The gist of his complaint follows:

"Your staff is trying to take over part of my responsibilities. They come in, snoop around, ask hundreds of questions, and take up plenty of our time. It's up to me, not you and your detectives, to analyze and explain my division's performance to central headquarters. If you don't stop trying to grab my responsibilities, I'll raise the whole issue with the president."

required

1. What events or relationships may have led to Whisler's outburst?
2. As Phillipson, how would you answer Whisler's contentions?
3. What are some alternative actions that Phillipson can take to improve future relationships?

1-17 *Accountant's Role in Planning and Control* Dick Victor has been president of Sampson Company, a multidivision textile company, for ten months. The company has an industry reputation as being conservative and having average profitability. Previously, Victor was associated with a very successful company that had a heavily formalized accounting system, with elaborate budgets and effective uses of performance reports.

Victor is contemplating the installation of a formal budgetary program. To signify its importance, he wants to hire a new vice-president for planning and control. This fellow would report directly to Victor and would have complete responsibility for implementing a system for budgeting and reporting performance.

required

If you were controller of Sampson Company, how would you react to Victor's proposed move? What alternatives are available to Victor for installing his budgetary program? In general, should figure specialists all report to one master figure expert, who in turn is responsible to the president?

1-18 *Organization of Accounting Department: Centralization or Decentralization*[7] The following quotation is from an address made by an officer of the Ford Motor Company:

> We can all, I think, take pride in the way cost accounting has kept pace with industrial development in this country. Tremendous strides have been made during the last quarter of a century, and I'm sure that much more progress will be made in the future. In fact, progress will *have* to be made if we are to keep the science of cost accounting abreast of the times. The whole of industry is now operating on a different level than we have known before—a higher plateau, on which cost accounting appears in a new light, becomes more and more significant as a factor in business management.
>
> It is my experience that the function of cost determination is basic to every other function of a modern business. Cost factors thread their way through every phase of a business and to a large extent influence the makeup of the entire enterprise—its products, its markets, and its methods of operation.
>
> We must, of necessity, have rather complex and extensive costing organizations, but the principle according to which they work is the same—finding out what each of the operations costs before it is too late to avoid doing the wrong thing.
>
> I am sure you would be interested in knowing that the accounting office at Ford was formerly almost completely centralized and that we have begun to install a decentralized system. . . .
>
> It is planned that after the decentralized and the local organizations are prepared to assume the responsibilities involved, these accounting offices will be placed under the direct jurisdiction of the managers of the operations which they serve. . . .

[7] From the *N.A.C.A. Bulletin,* Vol. 29, No. 7, Sec. II.

> Under the decentralized system, each division has its own complete accounting service. . . . Each separate activity, such as each assembly plant, has been provided with an accounting office to compile its own internal operating reports for its own use, and to forward the financial statements required by the central office.

required

1. Under the decentralized organization of the accounting work, would it be better for the controller of the Ford Motor Company to have direct authority or functional authority over the branch and divisional accounting offices? Discuss.
2. Will the decentralized system, in your opinion, make the cost accounting activities more significant in business management? In other words, is the change to a decentralized system in keeping with the trend that is outlined in the first three quoted paragraphs? Explain your answer, stating and illustrating advantages and disadvantages of the decentralized system in this case.
3. As a newly hired business school graduate in the plant controller's department, would you prefer that the plant controller's line responsibility be to the plant manager or to the company controller? Why?

1-19 *Scorekeeping, Attention Directing, and Problem Solving* Internal (management) accounting tends to emphasize the attention-directing and problem-solving functions of accounting. However, there are many companies with accounting systems that are oriented almost exclusively to scorekeeping. For example, one critic has stated:

> Very few people in business have had the opportunity to reflect on the way in which the accounting model developed, particularly on how an instrument well adapted to detect fraud and measure tax liability has gradually been used as a general information source. Having become accustomed to information presented in this form, business people have adapted their concepts and patterns of thought and communication to it rather than adapting the information to the job or person. When one suggests the reverse process, as now seems not only logical but well within economic limits, he must expect a real reluctance to abandon a pattern of behavior that has a long history of working apparently quite well.[8]

Considering the introductory material in this chapter, comment on this quotation, particularly on the meaning and implications for today's and tomorrow's controllers of the last sentence quoted.

1-20 *Preview of Coming Attractions* David Colhane, an able electrical engineer, was informed that he was going to be promoted to assistant factory manager. David was elated but uneasy. In particular, his knowledge of accounting was sparse. He had taken one course in "financial" accounting but had not been exposed to the "management" accounting that his superiors found helpful.

Colhane planned to enroll in a management accounting course as soon as possible. Meanwhile, he asked Susan Hansley, an assistant controller, to state three or four of the principal distinctions between financial and management accounting, including some concrete examples.

As the assistant controller, prepare a written response to Colhane.

1-21 *Evolution of Accounting Systems* You recently opened a bicycle repair shop, using the family garage as your place of business.

required

1. You are self-employed. You buy parts for cash and render service for cash. How much accounting data would you collect?

[8] William R. Fair, "The Next Step in Management Controls," in Donald G. Malcom and Alan J. Rowe, eds., *Management Control Systems* (New York: John Wiley & Sons, Inc., 1960), pp. 229–30.

2. You buy parts on credit and you extend credit to some customers. How much accounting data would you collect?
3. You wonder how business is progressing this month versus last month and this year versus last year. How much data would you collect?
4. You wonder how well you have done this year versus what you budgeted for this year. How much data would you collect? Why might you prefer the approach in (4) to the approach in (3)?

1-22 *Value of Information* You own a shop that sells and services bicycles. Your partner wants your approval for adding a line of bicycles that will retail for $100.

required

1. Will you add the line? What data would be particularly important to you to help you decide?
2. What is the value of the data regarding your prospective unit purchase cost of bicycles? How accurate must the data be? For instance, suppose you know that the purchase cost does not exceed $60, but you are unsure whether the purchase cost is really $48, $54, or $60. If the minimum acceptable gross profit per unit is $40, how much would you be willing to pay for a cost estimate that is more accurate than "cost does not exceed $60"?

2 An Introduction to Cost Terms and Purposes

Now we turn to the language—what cost means. We usually do not decide to buy a commodity without some idea of its makeup or characteristics. Similarly, if we acquire knowledge of the composition of cost data and systems, we will be in a better position to decide what types to "buy" in what situations. In this chapter we shall learn some basic terminology, the jargon that every technical subject seems to possess. More important, we shall see quickly that there are different costs for different purposes. When it is economically feasible, cost accounting systems are usually designed to serve multiple purposes.

This chapter contains several widely recognized cost concepts and terms. They are sufficient to demonstrate the multiple purposes that will be stressed throughout the book. There are many other types of costs, but you will not be swamped by them in this chapter. It will be more efficient if we ease into the subject matter of cost accounting, and so a discussion of many costs is being deliberately postponed. For example, the idea of controllable and uncontrollable costs is covered at length in Chapter 6, and opportunity cost is covered in Chapter 11.

cost objectives Accountants usually define *costs* as resources sacrificed or foregone to achieve a specific objective. For now, consider costs as being measured in the conventional accounting way, as monetary units (dollars) that must be paid for goods and services.

To guide his decisions, the manager wants data pertaining to a variety of purposes. He wants the cost *of something.* This something may be a product, a group of products, a service rendered to a hospital patient or a bank customer, a machine-hour, a social-welfare project, a mile of road, or any conceivable activity. We call this a *cost objective* and define it as *any activity for which a separate measurement of costs is desired.*[1]

cost systems *Cost accumulation* is the collection of cost data in an organized way via an accounting system. The word *system* implies regularity—for example, the routine compilation of historical data in an orderly fashion. Other cost data may be gathered on occasion as desired (for example, replacement costs of certain equipment). Of course, continuous compilation is more expensive than occasional compilation; the relative elaborateness of systems is fundamentally a cost-benefit decision as to what data to "buy" on a regular basis.

Cost objectives are chosen not for their own sake but to facilitate decisions. The most economically feasible approach to the design of a cost system is typically to assume some common classes of decisions (for example, inventory control and labor control) and to choose cost objectives (for example, products and departments) that relate to those decisions. Nearly all systems at least accumulate *actual costs,* which are amounts determined on the basis of costs incurred (historical costs), as distinguished from predicted or forecasted costs. The relationships are exemplified as follows:

Years ago many cost accounting systems emphasized one cost objective—product costing for inventory valuation and income determination—as if it were an end in itself. Consequently, many systems failed to collect the data in a form suitable for other purposes. However, modern systems have a more balanced approach; obtaining the inventory cost of finished product units is regarded as

[1] George J. Staubus, *Activity Costing and Input-Output Accounting* (Homewood, Ill.: Richard D. Irwin, Inc., 1971), p. 1, stresses that we must recognize that in essence we are determining the cost of an activity or action:

"Costing is the process of determining the cost of doing something, e.g., the cost of manufacturing an article, rendering a service, or performing a function. The article manufactured, service rendered, or function performed is known as the object of costing. . . . Objects of costing are always activities. We want to know the cost of doing something. We may, however, find ourselves speaking of the cost of a product as an abbreviation for the cost of acquiring or manufacturing that product. . . ."

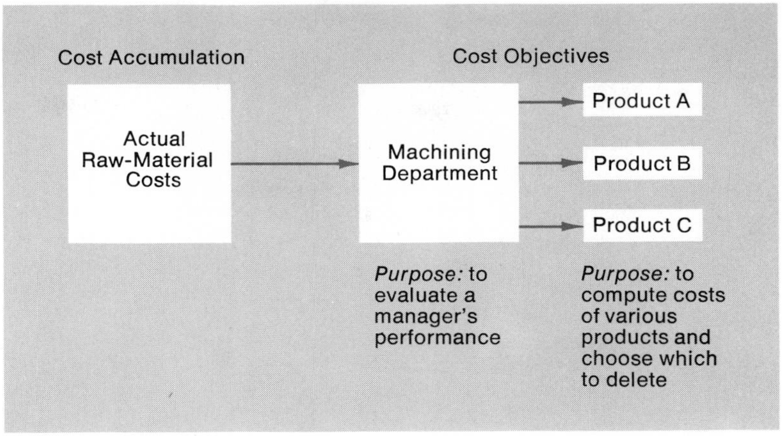

only one purpose. Other purposes include getting a reliable basis for predicting the economic consequences of a host of decisions, including:

1. Which products should we make? Delete?
2. Should we manufacture a product component or should we acquire it outside?
3. What prices should we charge?
4. Should we buy the proposed equipment?
5. Should we change our manufacturing methods?
6. Should we promote this manager?
7. Should we expand the department?

variable costs and fixed costs

costs and changes in activity

Variable and fixed costs are usually defined in terms of how a *total* cost changes in relation to fluctuations in the activity (often called *volume*) of a chosen cost objective. The activity or volume of the cost objective may be measured in units of product manufactured or sold, hours worked, miles driven, gallons consumed, patients seen, payroll checks processed, lines typed, sales dollars, or any other index of volume. **If a given cost changes in total in proportion to changes in activity, it is *variable;* if a cost remains unchanged in total for a *given time period* despite *wide fluctuations in activity,* it is *fixed.* Consider two examples:**

1. If Massive Motors Company buys one type of fuel filter at $1 each for its M-1 model car, then the total cost of fuel filters should be $1 times the number of cars produced. This is an example of a variable cost, a cost that is uniform *per unit* so that it fluctuates in total in direct proportion to changes in the total activity

EXHIBIT 2-1

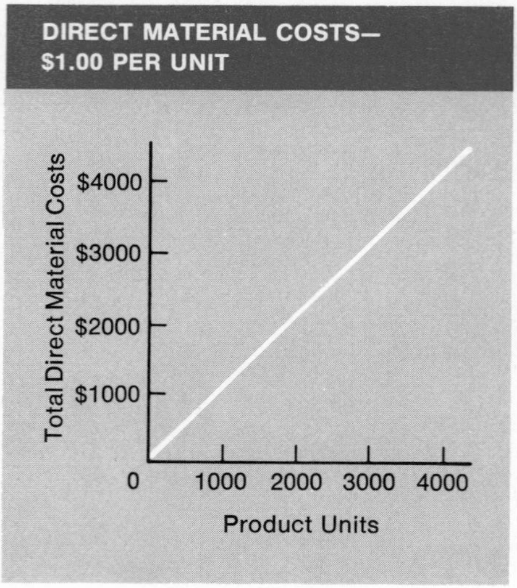

EXHIBIT 2-2

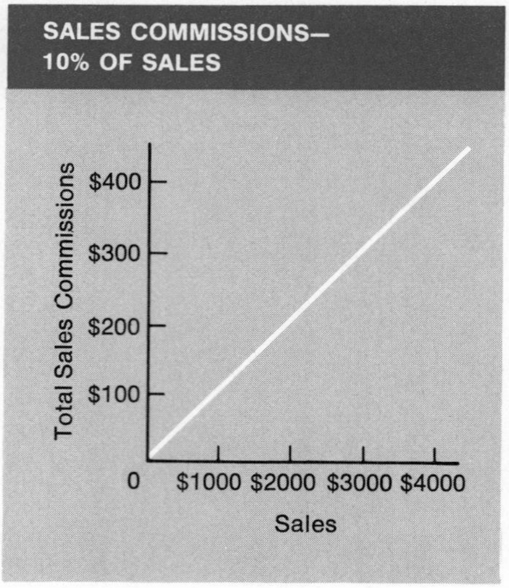

(volume). Examples include most materials and parts, many types of assembly labor, sales commissions, and certain supplies.

Variable cost behavior may be plotted graphically. Exhibit 2-1 shows the relationship between direct material costs and units produced; Exhibit 2-2 shows the relationship between total commissions and dollar sales.

2. Massive Motors may incur $100 million in a given year for property taxes, executive salaries, rent, insurance, and depreciation. These are examples of fixed costs, costs that do not fluctuate in total over a wide range of volume during a given time span, but that become progressively smaller on a *per unit* basis as production increases.

fixed costs and shutdown costs

A fixed cost is fixed only in relationship to a given period of time and a given, though wide, range of activity, called the "relevant range." Thus, a company's fixed costs may be unchanged for a given year, although property-tax rates and executive salaries may be higher the next year. In addition, the fixed-cost level may be applicable to, say, a range of 30,000 to 95,000 hours of activity per month. But a prolonged strike or economic recession may cause executive salary cuts, layoffs, or shutdowns. Therefore, fixed costs may be reduced substantially if activity levels fall drastically. In some cases, an entire plant may be shut down, virtually eliminating the need for executive and service personnel.

These relationships are shown in Exhibit 2-3. The likelihood of activities being outside the relevant range is usually slight, so $50,000 becomes the fixed-cost level. The three-level refinement in Exhibit 2-3 is not usually shown, because

EXHIBIT 2-3

TOTAL MONTHLY FIXED COSTS—CONCEPTUAL ANALYSIS

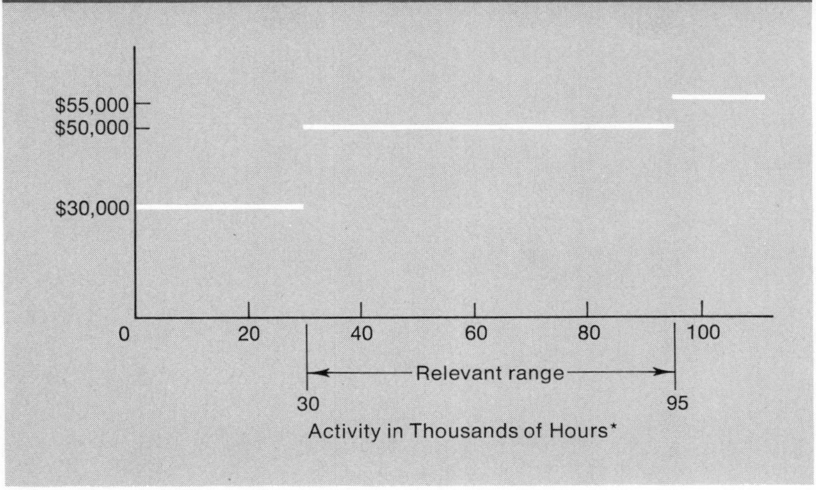

* $50,000 level between 30,000 and 95,000 hours.
$55,000 level in excess of 95,000 hours: hiring of additional supervision.
$30,000 level from shutdown (zero hours) to 30,000 hours: laying-off of supervision.

the chances are very remote that activity will be less than 30,000 hours or more than 95,000 hours. Exhibit 2-4 shows how this $50,000 figure is usually plotted in practice.

cost behavior patterns Nearly every organization has costs that may be classified as either variable or fixed. Throughout this book we shall see why the accountant and the manager find this distinction helpful. Variable and fixed costs are just two of an assortment of cost behavior patterns that are often useful to recognize. For the time being, we shall assume that all costs may be placed in one of these two classifications. In practice, of course, the task of classification is exceedingly difficult and nearly always necessitates some simplifying assumptions.

One basic simplification is the widespread assumption that cost behavior patterns are linear rather than curvilinear; that is, when plotted on simple graph paper they appear as unbroken straight lines instead of curves. Moreover, in practice, activity is inevitably assumed to be unidimensional: units of product, or labor-hours, or machine-hours, or sales dollars, and so on. The relationships between a given cost incurrence and changes in related activity levels may be vastly oversimplified and misleading because many costs are clearly affected by

EXHIBIT 2-4

TOTAL MONTHLY FIXED COSTS AS PLOTTED IN PRACTICE

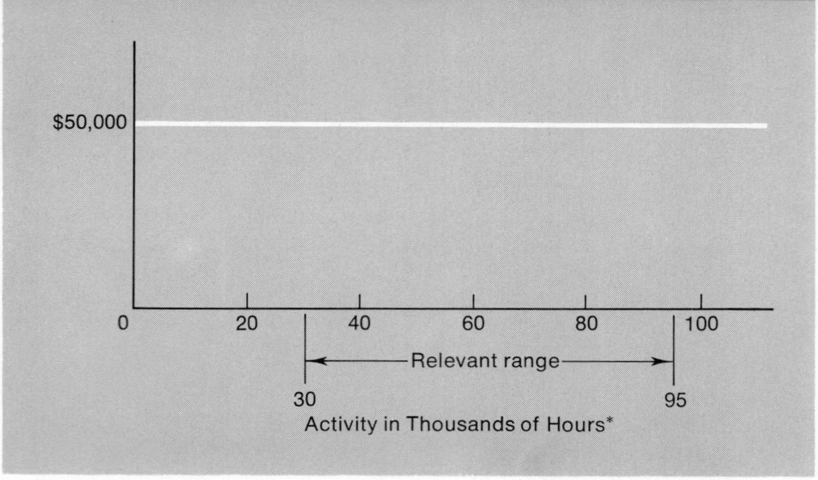

*$50,000 level between 30,000 and 95,000 hours.
$55,000 level in excess of 95,000 hours: hiring of additional supervision.
$30,000 level from shutdown (zero hours) to 30,000 hours: laying-off of supervision.

more than one factor. These ideas are explored more fully in Chapters 7, 8, and 25.

unit costs and total costs

The preceding section concentrated on the behavior patterns of total costs in relation to chosen activity levels of the cost objective. Generally, the decision maker should take a straightforward analytical approach by thinking in terms of total costs rather than unit costs. As we shall see momentarily, unit costs must be interpreted cautiously. Nevertheless, their use is essential in many decision contexts. For example, the chairman of the social committee of a fraternity may be trying to decide whether to hire a prominent musical group for a forthcoming party. The total fee may be predicted with certainty at $1,000. This knowledge is helpful for the decision, but it may not be enough.

Before a decision can be reached, the decision maker must predict both the total cost and the probable number of persons who will attend. Without knowledge of both, he cannot decide intelligently on a possible admission price or even on whether to have a party at all. So he computes a unit cost by dividing the total cost by the expected number of persons who will attend. If 1,000 people attend, the unit cost is $1; if 100 attend, the unit cost soars to $10 per person.

Unless the total cost is "unitized," the $1,000 cost is difficult to interpret; so the unit cost combines the total cost and the number of persons in a handy communicative way.

In management accounting, different cost objectives may be used as units, depending on the circumstances. Generally, unit costs are expressed in terms most meaningful to people who are responsible for incurring the costs. The unit in question is not always a physical product; the unit is often that objectively definable statistic of activity that is most closely correlated with cost incurrence. Thus, the unit may differ among departments of a given company; it may be machine-hours in a factory department, pounds handled in the shipping department, and number of invoices processed or lines billed in the billing department.

The unit cost of making a finished good is sometimes computed by accumulating manufacturing costs and then dividing the total by the number of units produced. For example:

Total costs of manufacturing 1,000 units	$3,800
Divided by the number of units produced	÷ 1,000
Equals a cost per unit	= $3.80

Suppose that 800 units are sold and 200 units remain in ending inventory. The unit-cost idea facilitates the assignment of a total cost to various accounts:

Cost of goods sold, 800 units × $3.80	= $3,040
Ending inventory of finished goods, 200 units × $3.80 =	760

Unit costs are averages, and they must be interpreted with caution. For example, what does it mean to say that the unit cost for the musicians is $1 if 1,000 persons attend? In this case of fixed costs, the *total* cost of $1,000 is unaffected by the activity level, the size of the denominator. But the *unit* cost is strictly a function of the size of the denominator; it would be $1,000 per unit if one person attended, $1.00 per unit if 1,000 persons attended, and $.10 per unit if 10,000 persons attended.

In contrast, assume that the musicians agreed to perform for $1.00 per person. Then we would have a variable-cost situation. If one person attended, the *total* cost would be $1.00; if 1,000 attended, $1,000; if 10,000 attended, $10,000.

Note that for decision purposes the unit fixed cost must be distinguished from the unit variable cost. A common mistake is to regard all unit costs indiscriminately—as if all costs were variable costs. Changes in activity will affect *total* variable costs but not *total* fixed costs. In our first example, the chairman could use the $1.00 unit variable cost to predict the total costs. But using a $1.00 unit fixed cost to predict the total costs would be perilous. His prediction would be correct if, and only if, 1,000 persons attended—total fixed costs would be $1,000 regardless of the number attending. The moral is: unit costs are often useful, but they should be interpreted with extreme caution.

These relationships are summarized below:

	BEHAVIOR AS VOLUME FLUCTUATES	
	Total Cost	Cost Per Unit
Variable cost	Change	No change
Fixed cost	No change	Change

product costs and period costs

manufacturing and nonmanufacturing activities

Some form of cost accounting is applicable to any entity that has a goal, including manufacturing companies, railroads, retail stores, insurance companies, advertising agencies, government units, hospitals, and nearly all other organizations, whether or not they are operated for a profit goal. We shall consider both manufacturing and nonmanufacturing companies throughout this book, but we shall begin with the manufacturing company because it provides the most general case—embracing production, marketing, and general administration functions. This will develop a completely general framework of cost accounting that you can readily apply to any organization.

Historically, accounting techniques for planning and control arose in conjunction with manufacturing rather than nonmanufacturing because the measurement problems were less imposing and external factors such as economic conditions, customer reactions, and competitor activity were generally less influential. However, the basic concepts of planning and control are equally applicable to both manufacturing and nonmanufacturing activities. At the moment, we will examine manufacturing and nonmanufacturing from the viewpoint of inventory costing and income determination—the product-costing purpose, when the cost objective is the unit of product.

Manufacturing is the transformation of materials into other goods through the use of labor and factory facilities. Merchandising is the selling of goods without changing their basic form. For example, assume that Jack Nentlaw wants to make hairdressing and sell it directly to retailers. He may buy certain oils and fancy containers, purchase a factory and equipment, hire some workers, and manufacture thousands of units of finished product. This is his manufacturing function. But in order to persuade retailers to buy his hairdressing, Nentlaw will have to convince the ultimate consumer that this product is desirable. This means advertising, including the development of a sales appeal, the selection of a brand name, the choice of media, and so forth. To maximize his success, Nentlaw must effectively manage both manufacturing and merchandising functions.

three manufacturing cost elements

Notice the basic difference between the conventional income statements of Nentlaw's business and Crump's Department Store in Exhibit 2-5. In the cost-of-goods-sold section, the

EXHIBIT 2-5

COMPARISON OF INCOME STATEMENTS

NENTLAW (A manufacturer)

Income Statement
For the Year Ended December 31, 19_2

Sales		$210,000
Less cost of goods sold:		
Finished goods, December 31, 19_1	$ 22,000	
Cost of goods manufactured (see schedule)	104,000	
Cost of goods available for sale	$126,000	
Finished goods, December 31, 19_2	18,000	
Cost of goods sold		108,000
Gross margin (or gross profit)		$102,000
Less selling and administrative expenses (detailed)		80,000
Net income*		$ 22,000

CRUMP'S (A retailer)

Income Statement
For the Year Ended December 31, 19_2

Sales		$1,500,000
Less cost of goods sold:		
Merchandise inventory, December 31, 19_1	$ 95,000	
Purchases	1,100,000	
Cost of goods available for sale	$1,195,000	
Merchandise inventory, December 31, 19_2	130,000	
Cost of goods sold		1,065,000
Gross margin (or gross profit)		$ 435,000
Less selling and administrative expenses (detailed)		315,000
Net income		$ 120,000

NENTLAW

Schedule of Cost of Goods Manufactured†

Direct materials:		
Inventory, December 31, 19_1	$11,000	
Purchases of direct materials	73,000	
Cost of direct materials available for use	$84,000	
Inventory, December 31, 19_2	8,000	
Direct materials used		$ 76,000
Direct labor		18,000
Factory overhead:		
Indirect labor	$ 4,000	
Supplies	1,000	
Heat, light, and power	1,500	
Depreciation—Plant building	1,500	
Depreciation—Equipment	2,500	
Miscellaneous	500	11,000
Manufacturing costs incurred during 19_2		$105,000
Add work-in-process inventory, December 31, 19_1		6,000
Manufacturing costs to account for		$111,000
Less work-in-process inventory, December 31, 19_2		7,000
Cost of goods manufactured† (to Income Statement)		$104,000

* In practice, the term *net income* is usually used to describe the final residual after deducting all expenses, including income taxes, from all revenue of any kind. The term "operating income" is usually used to describe the result after deducting "operating" expenses from the normal major sources of revenue. In situations like this example, the term *net income* is used frequently in place of "operating income," because for convenience other income and other expenses, including income taxes, are ignored. In short, in this text sometimes you will encounter the terms operating income and net income being used interchangeably because it is either expressed or implied that their amounts are identical.

† Note that the term *cost of goods manufactured* refers to the cost of goods brought to completion (finished) during the year, whether they were started before or during the current year. Some of the manufacturing costs incurred are held back as costs of the ending work in process; similarly, the costs of the beginning work in process become a part of the cost of goods manufactured for 19_2. **Note too that this schedule can become a Schedule of Cost of Goods Manufactured and Sold simply by including the opening and closing finished-goods inventory figures in the supporting schedule rather than directly in the body of the income statement.**

Nentlaw statement has a "cost of goods manufactured" line instead of the "purchases" line found in the Crump statement. The details of the cost of goods manufactured appear in the separate supporting schedule.

There are three major elements in the cost of a manufactured product:

1. *Direct materials.* All materials that are physically observable as being identified with the finished good and that may be traced to the finished good in an economically feasible manner. Examples are sheet steel and subassemblies for an automobile company. Direct materials often do *not* include minor items such as glue or nails, because the costs of tracing insignificant items do not seem worth the possible benefits of having more accurate product costs. Such items are considered *supplies* or *indirect materials.*
2. *Direct labor.* All labor that is physically traceable to the finished good in an economically feasible manner. Examples are the labor of machine operators and assemblers. Much labor, such as that of material handlers, janitors, and plant guards, is considered *indirect labor* because of the impossibility or economic infeasibility of tracing such activity to specific products via physical observation.
3. *Indirect manufacturing costs.* All costs other than direct materials and direct labor that are associated with the manufacturing process. Other terms describing this category include *factory overhead, factory burden, manufacturing overhead,* and *manufacturing expenses.* The term *indirect manufacturing costs* is a clearer descriptor than *factory overhead,*[2] but the latter will be used throughout this book because it is briefer. Two subclassifications of factory overhead are:
   a. *Variable factory overhead.* The two main examples are supplies and most indirect labor. Whether the cost of a specific subcategory of indirect labor is variable or fixed depends on its behavior pattern in a given company. In this book, unless we specify otherwise, indirect labor will be considered a variable rather than a fixed cost.
   b. *Fixed factory overhead.* Examples are rent, insurance, property taxes, depreciation, and supervisory salaries.

Two of the three major elements are sometimes combined in cost terminology as follows: *Prime cost* consists of (1) + (2), direct materials plus direct labor. *Conversion cost* consists of (2) + (3), direct labor plus factory overhead.

product costs (inventoriable costs)

The scope of the term *cost* is extremely broad and general. When used, the word *cost* is usually linked with some adjective in order to avoid ambiguity. For example, costs may be *unexpired* or *expired.* Unexpired costs are all costs, including inventory costs and miscellaneous deferred or prepaid costs, that are associated with ("matched" with) the revenue of future periods. Unexpired costs are measures of assets. In contrast, expired costs are measures of expenses—they are all costs, including the manufacturing cost of goods sold, that are associated with the revenue of the current period in question. Expired costs are costs that cannot be justifiably carried

[2] The term *overhead* is peculiar; its origins are unclear. Some accountants have wondered why such costs are not called "underfoot" rather than "overhead" costs. The answer probably lies in the organization chart. Lower departments ultimately bear all costs, including those coming from over their heads.

forward to future periods either because they do not represent future benefits or because the future benefits are so uncertain as to defy measurement.

A major objective of accounting is income measurement. In their efforts to refine the measure of income, accountants have developed certain practical classification techniques for distinguishing between assets and expenses. This distinction is accomplished to a large extent by viewing manufacturing costs as inventoriable costs.

If costs can be looked upon as "attaching" or "clinging" to units produced, they are classified as *inventoriable costs,* also commonly called *product costs.* These costs are measures of assets until the goods to which they relate are sold; then the costs are released as expenses and matched against sales. All costs in the schedule of cost of goods manufactured in Exhibit 2-5 are called product costs. Direct-material, direct-labor, and factory-overhead items are inventoriable costs because they are costs of services utilized in forming the product. Thus, in general, all the costs of operating the factory—the manufacturing costs—are classified as product costs.

Two decisions are made about costs with regard to income determination. Decision 1: Which costs apply to the current accounting period? Decision 2: Which of those under Decision 1 are inventoriable? For example, a three-year $300 insurance premium may be charged originally to an asset account, *unexpired insurance.* The subsequent accounting for this cost will hinge on (a) the amount applicable to the current period—say, $100 for the first year—and (b) the purpose of the insurance coverage. Insurance on factory machinery is inventoriable and is therefore transferred from unexpired insurance to an inventory account. Insurance on a sales office is not inventoriable and is therefore transferred from unexpired insurance to an outright expense account.

Let us review the terminology by examining Exhibit 2-6. In manufacturing accounting, many unexpired costs (assets) are transferred from one classification of unexpired costs to another before becoming expired costs (expenses). Examples are factory insurance, depreciation on plant, and wages of production workers. These items are held back as product costs (inventory costs); they are released later to expense as part of cost of goods sold (an expense). Distinguish sharply between the merchandising accounting and the manufacturing accounting for such costs as insurance, depreciation, and wages. In merchandising accounting, such items are generally treated as expired costs (expenses); whereas in manufacturing accounting, most of such items are related to production activities and thus are inventoriable costs—costs that do not expire (become expenses) until the goods to which they relate are sold. This point is demonstrated by the factory-overhead breakdown in Exhibit 2-5 and the diagram at the bottom of Exhibit 2-6.

effect on the balance sheet

As Exhibit 2-6 shows, balance sheets of manufacturers and merchandisers differ with respect to inventories. The merchandise inventory account is supplanted in a manufacturing con-

EXHIBIT 2-6

RELATIONSHIPS OF PRODUCT COSTS AND PERIOD COSTS

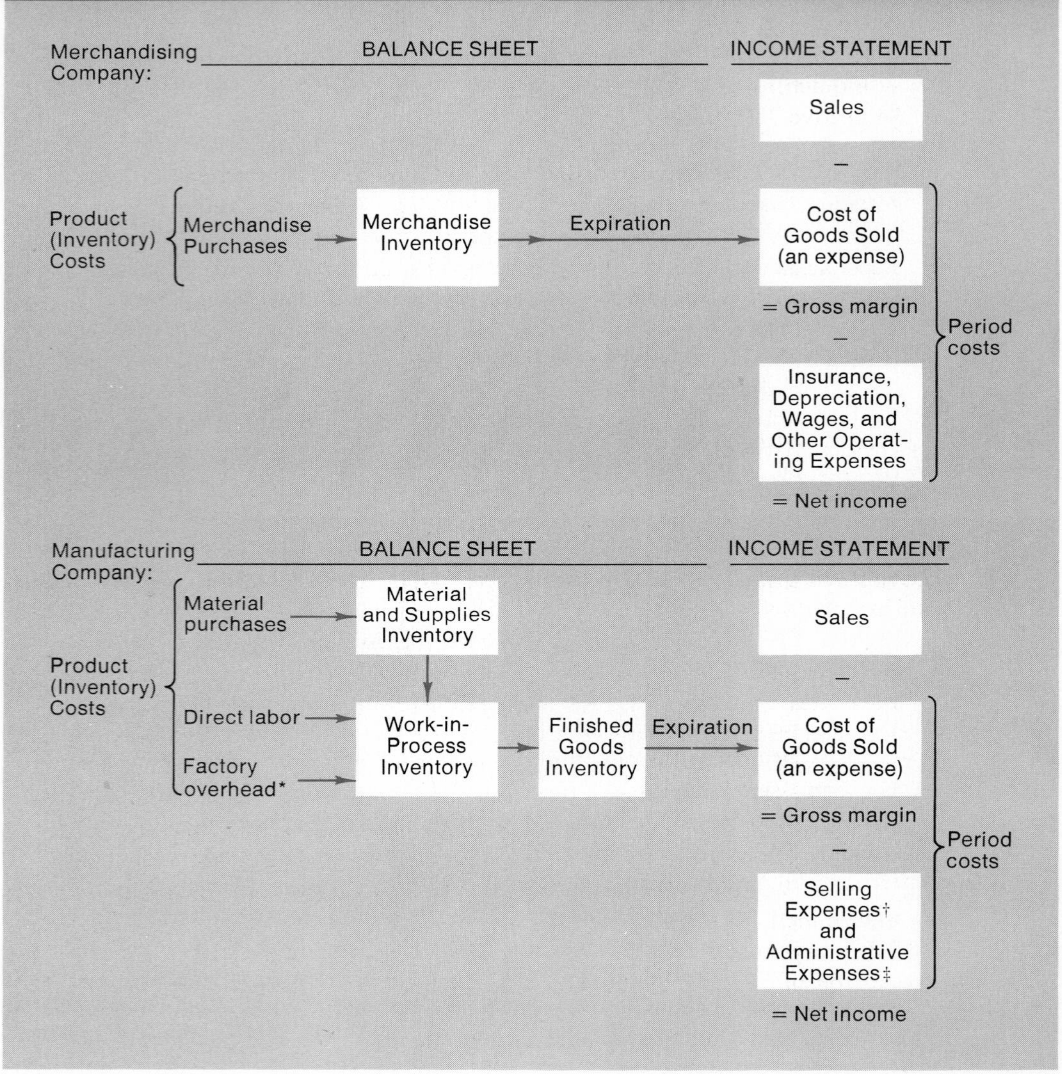

* Examples: see Exhibit 2-5.

† Examples: insurance on salesmen's cars, depreciation on salesmen's cars, salesmen's salaries.

‡ Examples: insurance on corporate headquarters building, depreciation on office equipment, clerical salaries.

Note particularly that where insurance and depreciation relate to the manufacturing function, they are inventoriable; but where they relate to selling and administration, they are not inventoriable.

cern by three inventory classes: *materials and supplies inventory; work-in-process inventory* (cost of uncompleted goods still on the production line containing appropriate amounts of the three major manufacturing costs: direct material, direct labor, and factory overhead); and *finished goods* (fully completed goods). The only essential difference between the structure of the balance sheet of a manufacturer and that of the balance sheet of a retailer would appear in their respective current-asset sections:

CURRENT-ASSET SECTIONS OF BALANCE SHEETS

MANUFACTURER			*RETAILER*	
Cash		$ 4,000	Cash	$ 30,000
Receivables		5,000	Receivables	70,000
Finished goods	$12,000			
Work in process	2,000			
Materials and supplies	3,000			
Total inventories		17,000	Merchandise inventories	100,000
Prepaid expenses		1,000	Prepaid expenses	3,000
Total current assets		$27,000	Total current assets	$203,000

perpetual and periodic inventories

There are two fundamental ways of accounting for inventories: perpetual and periodic. The *perpetual inventory method* requires a continuous record of additions to or reductions in materials, work in process, and cost of goods sold on a day-to-day basis. Such a record facilitates managerial control and preparation of interim financial statements. Physical inventory counts are usually taken at least once a year in order to check on the validity of the clerical records.

The *periodic inventory method* does not require a day-to-day record of inventory changes. Instead, costs are recorded by natural classifications, such as Material Purchases, Freight In, and Purchase Discounts. Costs of materials used or costs of goods sold cannot be computed accurately until ending inventories, determined by physical count, are subtracted from the sum of the opening inventory, purchases, and other operating costs. See Exhibit 2-7 for a comparison of perpetual and periodic inventory methods.

some cost accounting language

troublesome terminology

There are many terms that have very special meanings in accounting. The meanings often differ from company to company; each organization seems to develop its own distinctive and extensive accounting language. This is why you will save much confusion

EXHIBIT 2-7

SUMMARY COMPARISON OF PERIODIC AND PERPETUAL INVENTORY METHODS

(Figures from Exhibit 2-5)

PERIODIC METHOD		PERPETUAL METHOD	
Beginning inventories (by physical count)	$ 22,000	Cost of goods sold (kept on a day-to-day basis rather than being determined periodically)*	$108,000
Add: Manufacturing costs (direct materials used, direct labor, factory overhead)	104,000		
Cost of goods available for sale	126,000		
Less ending inventories (by physical count)	18,000		
Cost of goods sold	$108,000		

* Such a condensed figure does not preclude the presentation of a supplementary schedule showing details of production costs similar to that in Exhibit 2-5.

and wasted time if you always find out the exact meanings of any strange jargon that you encounter.

For example, the term *manufacturing expenses,* which is often used to describe factory overhead, is a misnomer. Factory overhead is not an expense. It is part of product cost and will funnel into the expense stream only when the product costs are released as cost of goods sold.

Also, *cost of goods sold* is a widely used term that is somewhat misleading when you try to pin down the meaning of *cost.* Cost of goods sold is an *expense* because it is an expired cost; it is every bit as much an expense as are salesmen's commissions. Cost of goods sold is also often called *cost of sales.*

subdivisions of labor costs

The terminology for labor costs is usually the most confusing, because each organization has seemingly developed its own interpretation of various labor-cost classifications. Let us consider some commonly encountered labor terminology.

All factory-labor costs other than direct labor are usually classified as *indirect labor,* a major component of indirect manufacturing costs. The term has many subsidiary classifications to facilitate appraisal of these costs. Thus, wages of fork-lift truck operators are generally not commingled with janitors' salaries, although both are regarded as indirect labor.

Costs are classified in a detailed fashion primarily in the attempt to associate a specific cost with its specific cause or reason for incurrence. Two classes of indirect labor need special mention. *Overtime premium* paid to factory workers is usually considered a part of overhead. If a lathe operator gets $6.00 per hour for straight time, and time and one-half for overtime, his *premium* would be \$3.00 per overtime hour. If he works forty-four hours, including four overtime hours, in one week, his gross earnings would be classified as follows:

Direct labor	44 hours × \$6.00	\$264.00
Overtime premium (factory overhead):		
	4 hours × \$3.00	12.00
	Total earnings	\$276.00

Another subsidiary classification of indirect labor is *idle time.* This typically represents wages paid for unproductive time caused by machine breakdowns, material shortages, sloppy production scheduling, and the like. For example, if the lathe operator's machine broke down for three hours, his earnings would be classified as follows:

Direct labor:	41 hours × \$6.00	\$246.00
Overtime premium (factory overhead):		
	4 hours × \$3.00	12.00
Idle time (factory overhead):		
	3 hours × \$6.00	18.00
	Total earnings	\$276.00

Why is overtime premium usually considered an indirect cost rather than direct? After all, it can usually be traced to specific batches of work. It is usually not considered a direct charge because the scheduling of production jobs is generally random. For example, assume that Jobs 1 through 5 are scheduled for a specific workday of ten hours, including two overtime hours. Each job requires two hours. Should the job scheduled during hours 9 and 10 be assigned the overtime premium? Or should the premium be prorated over all the jobs? The latter approach does not penalize a particular batch of work solely because it happened to be worked on during the overtime hours. Instead, the overtime premium is considered to be attributable to the heavy overall volume of work, and its cost is thus regarded as factory overhead, which is borne by all units produced.

payroll fringe costs The classification of factory-payroll fringe costs, such as employer contributions to Social Security, life insurance, health, pension, and miscellaneous other employee benefits, differs from company to company. In most companies, these are classified as factory overhead. For instance, a direct laborer such as a lathe operator, whose gross paycheck is computed on the basis of a \$6.00 straight-time hourly rate, may enjoy payroll fringe benefits totaling, say, \$1.00 per hour. Most companies tend to classify the \$6.00 as direct labor and the \$1.00 as factory overhead. In some companies, however, the fringe benefits related to direct labor are charged as an additional direct-labor cost; these companies would classify the entire $7.00 as direct labor. The latter approach is conceptually preferable because these costs are also a fundamental part of acquiring labor services.

classifications of cost

This chapter has merely hinted at the vast number of classifications of cost that have proven useful for various purposes. Among other categories, classifications can be made by:

1. Time when computed
   a. Historical costs
   b. Budgeted or predetermined costs (via cost "prediction")
2. Behavior in relation to fluctuations in activity
   a. Variable cost
   b. Fixed cost
   c. Other cost
3. Degree of averaging
   a. Total costs
   b. Unit costs
4. Management function
   a. Manufacturing costs
   b. Selling costs
   c. Administrative costs
5. Ease of traceability
   a. Direct costs
   b. Indirect costs
6. Timing of charges against revenue
   a. Product costs
   b. Period costs

SUMMARY

Accounting systems should serve multiple decision purposes, and there are different measures of cost for different purposes. A frequent distinction that is made concerning cost-accounting systems is between the purpose of providing costs for inventory valuation and that of providing costs for other purposes.

The most economically feasible approach to designing a management accounting system is to assume some common wants for a variety of decisions and choose cost objectives for routine data accumulation in light of these wants.

PROBLEM FOR SELF-STUDY

(Try to solve this problem before examining the solution that follows.)

PROBLEM Consider the following data of the Laimon Company for the year 19_1:

Sandpaper	$ 2,000	Depreciation—Equipment	$ 40,000
Material handling	40,000	Factory rent	50,000
Lubricants and coolants	5,000	Property taxes on equipment	4,000
Overtime premium	20,000	Fire insurance on equipment	3,000
Idle time	10,000	Direct materials purchased	400,000
Miscellaneous indirect labor	40,000	Direct materials, 12/31/_1	50,000
Direct labor	300,000	Sales	1,200,000
Direct materials, 12/31/_0	40,000	Sales commissions	60,000
Finished goods, 12/31/_1	150,000	Sales salaries	100,000
Finished goods, 12/31/_0	100,000	Shipping expenses	70,000
Work in process, 12/31/_0	10,000	Administrative expenses	100,000
Work in process, 12/31/_1	14,000		

required

1. Prepare an income statement with a separate supporting schedule of cost of goods manufactured. For all items except sales, purchases of direct materials, and inventories, indicate by "V" or "F" whether each is basically a variable or a fixed cost. If in doubt, decide on the basis of whether the total cost will fluctuate substantially over a wide range of volume.
2. Suppose that both the direct-material and rent costs were related to the manufacturing of the equivalent of 900,000 units. What is the unit cost for the direct materials assigned to those units? What is the unit cost of the factory rent? Assume that the rent is a fixed cost.
3. Repeat the computation in part 2 for direct materials and factory rent, assuming that the costs are being predicted for the manufacturing of the equivalent of 1,000,000 units next year. Assume that the implied cost behavior patterns persist.
4. As a management consultant, explain concisely to the president why the unit costs for materials and rent differed in parts 2 and 3.

SOLUTION

1.

LAIMON COMPANY

Income Statement
For the Year Ended December 31, 19_1

Sales		$1,200,000
Less cost of goods sold:		
Finished goods, December 31, 19_0	$ 100,000	
Cost of goods manufactured (see schedule below)	900,000	
Cost of goods available for sale	$1,000,000	
Finished goods, December 31, 19_1	150,000	
Cost of goods sold		850,000
Gross margin		$ 350,000
Less selling and administrative expenses:		
Sales commissions	$ 60,000 (V)	
Sales salaries	100,000 (F)	
Shipping expenses	70,000 (V)	
Administrative expenses	100,000*	330,000
Operating income		$ 20,000

* Probably a mixture of fixed and variable items.

LAIMON COMPANY

Schedule of Cost of Goods Manufactured
For the Year Ended December 31, 19_1

Direct materials:		
Inventory, December 31, 19_0		$ 40,000
Purchases of direct materials		400,000
Cost of direct materials available for use		$440,000
Inventory, December 31, 19_1		50,000
Direct materials used		$390,000 (V)
Direct labor		300,000 (V)
Indirect manufacturing costs:		
Sandpaper	$ 2,000 (V)	
Lubricants and coolants	5,000 (V)	
Material handling (Example: wages of fork-lift truck operators)	40,000 (V)	
Overtime premium	20,000 (V)	
Idle time	10,000 (V)	
Miscellaneous indirect labor	40,000 (V)	
Factory rent	50,000 (F)	
Depreciation—Equipment	40,000 (F)	
Property taxes on equipment	4,000 (F)	
Fire insurance on equipment	3,000 (F)	214,000
Manufacturing costs incurred during 19_1		$904,000
Add work in process, December 31, 19_0		10,000
Manufacturing costs to account for		$914,000
Less work in process, December 31, 19_1		14,000
Cost of goods manufactured (to Income Statement)		$900,000

2. Direct-material unit cost = Direct materials used ÷ Units produced
   = $390,000 ÷ 900,000 = $.4333
   Factory-rent unit cost = Factory rent ÷ Units produced
   = $50,000 ÷ 900,000 = $.0556
3. The material costs are variable, so they would increase in total. However, their unit costs would be unaffected:

   Direct materials = $433,333 ÷ 1,000,000 units = $.4333

   In contrast, the factory rent is fixed, so it would not increase in total. However, if the rent is assigned to units produced, the unit costs would decline from $.0556 to $.05:

   Factory-rent unit cost = $50,000 ÷ 1,000,000 = $.05
4. The explanation would begin with the answer to part 3. The accountant should stress that the unitization of costs having different behavior patterns can be misleading. A common error is to assume that a total unit cost, which is often a sum of some variable unit costs and some fixed unit costs, is an indicator that *total* costs change in a wholly variable way as activity fluctuates. The next chapter demonstrates the necessity for distinguishing between cost behavior patterns.

As already mentioned, in information gathering the elementary want is for a set of signals that will facilitate the prediction of how the costs of the total organization will be affected under each decision alternative. The total costs assigned to a cost objective are essentially an estimate of how the total costs of the organization have been affected by a particular action. That is, if the cost objective (e.g., unit of product) had not been present, the total costs assigned thereto would not have been incurred. In practice, this ideal is rarely attainable. Above all, the user must be wary about unit fixed costs. Too often, unit fixed costs are erroneously regarded as indistinguishable from variable costs.

QUESTIONS, PROBLEMS, AND CASES

2-1 What two major purposes of cost accounting were stressed in this chapter?

2-2 Distinguish between *manufacturing* and *merchandising.*

2-3 What are the three major elements in the cost of a manufactured product?

2-4 Define the following: *direct materials, direct labor, indirect materials, indirect labor, factory overhead, prime cost, conversion cost.*

2-5 Give at least four terms that may be substituted for the term *factory overhead.*

2-6 Distinguish among *direct labor, indirect labor, overtime premium,* and *idle time.*

2-7 What is the major difference between the balance sheets of manufacturers and merchandisers?

2-8 Distinguish between *unexpired costs* and *expired costs.* How are manufacturing costs classified in relation to the problem of income measurement?

2-9 "For purposes of income determination, insurance, depreciation, and wages should always be treated alike." Comment.

2-10 Why is the term *manufacturing expenses* a misnomer?

2-11 "Cost of goods sold is an expense." Do you agree? Explain.

2-12 Why is the unit-cost concept helpful in accounting?

2-13 Define: *variable cost, fixed cost, relevant range.*

2-14 Give three examples of variable factory overhead.

2-15 Distinguish between *costing for inventory valuation* and other purposes.

2-16 Give three examples of fixed factory overhead.

2-17 "Fixed costs are really variable. The more you produce, the less they become." Do you agree? Explain.

2-18 "An action once taken cannot be changed by subsequent events." What implications does this have for the cost accountant?

2-19 Why is overtime premium usually considered an indirect cost rather than direct?

2-20 *Periodic or Perpetual Inventory Methods* (SIA) The terms *periodic* and *perpetual inventories* are referred to frequently in presenting the accounting procedures that are followed by businesses in recording their business transactions in any given period of their operations. Discuss the difference between periodic and perpetual inventory procedures and indicate the advantages and disadvantages of each method.

2-21 *Unit Manufacturing Cost* (SIA, adapted) The Toronto Manufacturing Company incurred the following costs for the month of May:

Materials used:		
Direct materials	$6,600	
Indirect materials	1,200	
Payroll costs incurred:		
Direct labor	6,000	
Indirect labor	1,700	
Salaries—production	2,400	
administration	5,100	
sales	3,200	
Others:		
Building rent (production uses 1/2 of building)	1,400	
Rent for molding machine	400	per month plus 50¢ per unit produced
Royalty paid for use of patents (calculation based on units produced, 80¢ per unit)		
Indirect miscellaneous costs:		
Production	2,700	
Sales and administration	1,800	

The company produced 1,000 units.

required | Determine the unit cost of goods manufactured.

2-22 *Straightforward Manufacturing Statement* The following data pertain to the XY Company (in millions):

	INVENTORIES	
	12/31/_3	12/31/_4
Direct materials	$ 9	$ 7
Work in process	4	3
Finished goods	10	13

MANUFACTURING COSTS INCURRED DURING 19_4		
Direct materials used		$20
Direct labor		13
Indirect manufacturing costs:		
Indirect labor	$ 5	
Utilities	2	
Depreciation—Plant and equipment	3	
Other	6	16
Total		$49

required

1. Prepare a statement of cost of goods manufactured and sold.
2. Compare your statement with those in Exhibit 2-5. How does your statement differ from the Schedule of Cost of Goods Manufactured in Exhibit 2-5?
3. Compute the prime costs incurred during 19_4. Compute the conversion costs incurred during 19_4.
4. What is the difference in meaning between the terms "total manufacturing costs incurred in 19_4" and "cost of goods manufactured in 19_4"?
5. Even though no T-accounts were shown in the chapter, draw a T-account for Work in Process. Enter the amounts shown on your financial statement

into the T-account as you think they might logically affect Work in Process, assuming that the account was kept on a perpetual inventory basis. Use a single summary number of $16 million for entering any effects of the indirect manufacturing costs rather than entering the four individual amounts.

2-23 *Statement of Cost of Goods Manufactured* The Mondale Corporation has the following accounts (in millions of dollars):

Selling and administrative expenses	$100
Work in process, December 31, 19_1	10
Factory supplies used	10
Direct materials, December 31, 19_2	20
Factory utilities	30
Finished goods, December 31, 19_2	55
Indirect labor	60
Work in process, December 31, 19_2	5
Purchases of direct materials	125
Direct labor	200
Depreciation—factory building and equipment	80
Factory supervisory salaries	5
Miscellaneous factory overhead	35
Sales	700
Finished goods, December 31, 19_1	70
Direct materials, December 31, 19_1	15

required

Income statement and a schedule of cost of goods manufactured for the year ended December 31, 19_2. (For additional questions regarding these facts, see the next problem.)

2-24 *Interpretation of Statements* Refer to the preceding problem.

required

1. How would the answer to the preceding problem be modified if you were asked for a schedule of cost of goods manufactured and sold instead of a schedule of cost of goods manufactured? Be specific.
2. Examine Exhibit 2-6. Would the sales manager's salary be accounted for any differently if the Mondale Corporation were a merchandising company instead of a manufacturing company? Using the boxes in the exhibit, describe how an assembler's wages would be accounted for in this manufacturing company.
3. Factory supervisory salaries are usually regarded as indirect manufacturing costs. When might some of these costs be regarded as direct costs? Give an example.
4. Suppose that both the direct materials and the depreciation were related to the manufacture of the equivalent of one million units of product. What is the unit cost for the direct materials assigned to those units? For depreciation? Assume that yearly depreciation is computed on a straight-line basis.
5. Assume that the implied cost behavior patterns in (4) persist. That is, direct material costs behave as a variable cost and depreciation behaves as a fixed cost. Repeat the computations in part (4), assuming that the costs are being predicted for the manufacture of the equivalent of 1.2 million units of product. How would the total costs be affected?
6. As a management accountant, explain concisely to the president why the unit costs differed in parts (4) and (5).

2-25 *Statement of Cost of Goods Manufactured* The following items pertain to Sorter Corporation (in dollars):

		FOR YEAR 19_2	
Work in process, Dec. 31, 19_2	2,000	Selling and administrative expenses (total)	70,000
Finished goods, Dec. 31, 19_1	40,000	Direct materials purchased	80,000
Accounts receivable, Dec. 31, 19_2	30,000	Direct labor	70,000
Accounts payable, Dec. 31, 19_1	40,000	Factory supplies	6,000
Direct materials, Dec. 31, 19_1	30,000	Property taxes on factory	1,000
Work in process, Dec. 31, 19_1	10,000	Factory utilities	5,000
Direct materials, Dec. 31, 19_2	5,000	Indirect labor	20,000
Finished goods, Dec. 31, 19_2	12,000	Depreciation—Plant and equipment	9,000
Accounts payable, Dec. 31, 19_2	20,000	Sales	350,000
Accounts receivable, Dec. 31, 19_1	50,000	Miscellaneous factory overhead	10,000

required

Prepare an income statement and a supporting schedule of cost of goods manufactured. (For additional questions regarding these facts, see the next problem.)

2-26 *Interpretation of Statements* Refer to the preceding problem.

required

1. How would the answer to the preceding problem be modified if you were asked for a schedule of cost of goods manufactured and sold instead of a schedule of cost of goods manufactured? Be specific.
2. Examine Exhibit 2-6. Would the sales manager's salary be accounted for any differently if the Sorter Corporation were a merchandising company instead of a manufacturing company? Using the boxes in the exhibit, describe how an assembler's wages would be accounted for in this manufacturing company.
3. Factory supervisory salaries are usually regarded as indirect manufacturing costs. When might some of these costs be regarded as direct costs? Give an example.
4. Suppose that both the direct materials and the depreciation were related to the manufacture of the equivalent of 1,000 units of product. What is the unit cost for the direct materials assigned to those units? For depreciation? Assume that yearly depreciation is computed on a straight-line basis.
5. Assume that the implied cost behavior patterns in (4) persist. That is, direct material costs behave as a variable cost and depreciation behaves as a fixed cost. Repeat the computations in part (4), assuming that the costs are being predicted for the manufacture of the equivalent of 1,500 units of product. How would the total costs be affected?
6. As a management accountant, explain concisely to the president why the unit costs differed in parts (4) and (5).

2-27 *Answers from Incomplete Data* The following accounts of a manufacturing company appeared in the balance sheets of December 31, 19_1, and December 31, 19_2:

	DECEMBER 31, 19_1	DECEMBER 31, 19_2
Raw-material inventory	$30,000	$46,000
Goods-in-process inventory	17,500	19,000
Finished-goods inventory	23,000	18,200
Accrued factory payroll	3,100	2,400
Accrued interest on notes receivable	120	80

The following amounts appeared in the income statement for 19_2:

Raw material used	$300,000
Cost of goods sold	920,000
Factory labor	275,000
Interest income	400

required

1. Raw material purchased in 19_2.
2. Cost of goods manufactured for 19_2.
3. Factory labor paid in 19_2.
4. Interest received on notes in 19_2.

2-28 *Finding Unknown Balances* For each of the cases in the list below, find the unknowns designated by letters.

	CASE 1	CASE 2	CASE 3	CASE 4
Finished-goods inventory, 1/1	$ 5,000	$ 4,000	$ 7,800	$ G
Direct material used	8,000	6,000	3,600	5,000
Direct labor	13,000	11,000	8,000	6,000
Factory overhead	7,000	D	13,000	7,000
Purchases of direct material	9,000	7,000	8,000	8,000
Sales	42,000	31,800	E	40,000
Accounts receivable, 1/1	2,000	1,400	3,000	400
Accounts receivable, 12/31	6,000	2,100	3,000	2,800
Cost of goods sold	A	22,000	28,000	15,000
Accounts payable, 1/1	3,000	1,700	1,600	300
Accounts payable, 12/31	1,800	1,500	1,800	1,200
Finished-goods inventory, 12/31	B	5,300	F	7,600
Gross profit	11,300	C	10,000	25,000
Work in process, 1/1	-0-	800	1,300	2,000
Work in process, 12/31	-0-	3,000	300	2,500

2-29 *Fire Loss; Computing Inventory Costs* A distraught employee, Fang W. Arson, put a torch to a factory on a blustery February 26. The resulting blaze completely destroyed the plant and its contents. Fortunately, certain accounting records were kept in another building. They revealed the following for the period December 31, 19_1–February 26, 19_2:

Prime costs average 70 percent of the cost of goods manufactured.
Gross profit percentage based on net sales, 20 percent.
Cost of goods available for sale, $450,000.
Direct material purchased, $160,000.
Work in process, 12/31/_1, $34,000 (have same cost proportions as finished goods).
Direct material, 12/31/_1, $16,000.
Finished goods, 12/31/_1, $30,000.
Factory overhead, 40 percent of conversion costs.
Sales, $500,000.
Direct labor, $180,000.

The loss was fully covered by insurance. The insurance company wants to know the approximate cost of the inventories as a basis for negotiating a settlement, which is really to be based on replacement cost, not historical cost.

required

Calculate the cost of:

1. Finished-goods inventory, 2/26/_2.

2. Work-in-process inventory, 2/26/_2.
3. Direct-material inventory, 2/26/_2.

2-30 *Different Cost Classifications for Different Purposes* A machining department has a number of cost accounts. Some accounts selected at random are reproduced below.

Use two columns to classify each account in two ways:

Direct or Indirect Product Costs	D or I
Variable or Fixed Costs*	V or F

An example would be Foreman's salary, I, F.

1. Cutting tools
2. Lubricants
3. Patterns
4. Nails, rivets, etc.
5. Factory rent
6. Repairs
7. Castings
8. Freight in on castings
9. Material handling
10. 25 percent of superintendent's salary
11. Direct labor
12. Idle time
13. Overtime premium
14. Employer payroll taxes
15. Compensation insurance
16. Fire insurance on equipment
17. Depreciation—Equipment
18. Property taxes on equipment
19. Blueprints prepared by drafting department

2-31 *Overtime and Fringe Costs* A city printing department had a flurry of work during a particular week. The printers' labor contract provided for payment to workers at a rate of 150 percent of the regular hourly wage rate for all hours worked in excess of 8 per day. Anthony Bardo worked 8 hours on Monday through Wednesday, 10 hours on Thursday, and 9 hours on Friday. His regular pay rate is $12.00 per hour.

required

1. Suppose that the printing department works on various jobs. All costs of the jobs are eventually allocated to the users, whether the consumers be the property-tax department, the city hospital, the city schools, or individual citizens who purchase some publications processed by the department. Compute Bardo's wages for the week. How much, if any, of Bardo's wages should be classified as indirect costs of particular printing jobs. Why?
2. The city pension plan provides for the city to contribute to an employee pension fund for all employees at a rate of 20 percent of gross wages (not considering pension benefits). How much, if any, of Bardo's retirement benefits should be classified as direct costs of particular printing jobs? Why?

For an expansion of this problem, see Problem 4-22.

* If in doubt, select on the basis of whether the item will vary over wide ranges of activity.

2-32 *Comprehensive Problem on Unit Costs, Product Costs, Variable and Fixed Costs, and Budgeted Income Statement* The Fancher Company makes a single product. Costs are as follows (V stands for variable; F, for fixed):

Production in units	*100,000*
Costs incurred:	
Direct material used	$100,000 V
Direct labor	70,000 V
Power	5,000 V
Indirect labor	10,000 V
Indirect labor	20,000 F
Other factory overhead	8,000 V
Other factory overhead	20,000 F
Selling expenses	30,000 V
Selling expenses	20,000 F
Administrative expenses	50,000 F
Work-in-process inventory, December 31, 19_1	—
Direct-material inventory, December 31, 19_1	2,000 lbs.
Finished-goods inventory, December 31, 19_1	$ 20,970

Dollar sales were $318,500 in 19_1. There were no beginning inventories in 19_1. The company's ending inventory of finished goods was carried at the average unit cost of production for 19_1. Direct material prices have been stable throughout the year. Two pounds of direct material are used to make a unit of finished product.

required

1. Direct-material inventory, total cost, December 31, 19_1.
2. Finished-goods inventory, total units, December 31, 19_1.
3. Unit sales price, 19_1.
4. Net income, 19_1. Show computations.

(For an additional question regarding these facts, see the next problem.)

2-33 *Budgeted Income Statement* This problem is more difficult than previous ones. Refer to the preceding problem. Management has asked that you prepare a budgeted income statement for 19_2, assuming that all unit prices for sales and variable costs will not change. Assume that sales will be 102,000 units and that ending inventory of finished goods, December 31, 19_2, will be 12,000 units. Assume that fixed costs will remain the same. Show supporting computations, and include a schedule of cost of goods manufactured. The ending inventory of finished goods is to be carried at the average unit cost of production for 19_2.

Cost-Volume-Profit Relationships

3

The previous chapter distinguished sharply between two major purposes of cost accounting systems: (a) decision making for planning and control, and (b) product costing for inventory valuation and income determination. This chapter and the next will examine these two purposes in more depth. Cost-volume-profit analysis is a subject inherently appealing to most students of management, because it gives a sweeping overview of the planning process and because it provides a concrete example of the importance of understanding cost behavior—the response of costs to a variety of influences. That is why we consider this subject now, even though it could just as easily be studied later.

Managers are constantly faced with decisions about selling prices, variable costs, and fixed costs. Basically, managers must decide how to acquire and utilize economic resources in light of some objective. Unless they can make reasonably accurate predictions about cost and revenue levels, their decisions may yield undesirable or even disastrous results. These decisions are usually short run: How many units should we manufacture? Should we change our price? Should we spend more on advertising? However, long-run decisions such as buying plant and equipment also hinge on predictions of the resulting cost-volume-profit relationships.

At the outset, remember that we will be considering simplified versions of the real world. Are these simplifications justifiable? The answer depends on the facts in a particular case. The simplifications are warranted even if they lead to worse decisions than more complex models, as long as the decrease in benefit from a poorer decision is less than the increased savings arising from "buying" the cheaper decision model.

the breakeven point

First, we obtain an overview by examining the interrelationships of changes in costs, volume, and profits—sometimes too narrowly described as breakeven analysis. The breakeven point is often only incidental in these studies. **Instead, the focus is on the impact upon operating income or net income of various decisions that affect sales and costs.** The breakeven point is that point of activity (sales volume) where total revenues and total expenses are equal; that is, there is neither profit nor loss.

Consider the following example:

> A person plans to sell a toy rocket at the state fair. He may purchase these rockets at 50¢ each with the privilege of returning all unsold rockets. The booth rental is $200, payable in advance. The rockets will be sold at 90¢ each. How many rockets must be sold to break even? (Ignore income taxes, which we consider in the appendix to the chapter.)

equation method

The first solution method for computing the breakeven point is the *equation method.* Every income statement may be expressed in equation form, as follows:

$$\text{Sales} - \text{Variable Expenses} - \text{Fixed Expenses} = \text{Net Income}$$

or

$$\text{Sales} = \text{Variable Expenses} + \text{Fixed Expenses} + \text{Net Income}$$

This equation provides the most general and easy-to-remember approach to any breakeven or profit-estimate situation. For the example above:

$$\begin{aligned}
\text{Let } X &= \text{Number of units to be sold to break even} \\
\$.90X &= \$.50X + \$200 + 0 \\
\$.40X &= \$200 + 0 \\
X &= \frac{\$200 + 0}{\$.40} \\
X &= 500 \text{ units (or \$450 total sales at 90¢ per unit)}
\end{aligned}$$

contribution-margin method

A second solution method is the *contribution-margin* or *marginal-income* method. *Contribution margin* is equal to sales minus *variable* expenses. Sales and expenses are analyzed as follows:

1. *Unit contribution margin* to coverage of fixed expenses and desired net income

$$= \text{Unit Sales Price} - \text{Unit Variable Expense} = \$.90 - \$.50 = \$.40$$

2. *Breakeven point* in terms of units sold

$$= \frac{\text{Fixed Expenses} + \text{Desired Net Income}}{\text{Unit Contribution Margin}} = \frac{\$200 + 0}{\$.40} = 500 \text{ units}$$

Stop a moment and relate the contribution-margin method to the equation method. The key calculation was dividing \$200 by \$.40. Look at the third line in the equation solution. It reads:

$$\$.40X = \$200 + 0$$
$$X = \frac{\$200 + 0}{\$.40},$$

giving us a general formula:

$$\text{Breakeven Point in Units} = \frac{\text{Fixed Expenses} + \text{Desired Net Income}}{\text{Contribution Margin per Unit}}$$

The *contribution-margin* method is merely a restatement of the *equation* in different form. Use either technique; the choice is a matter of personal preference.

graphic approach

The relationships in this example are graphed in Exhibit 3-1. The graph in Exhibit 3-1 used the following building blocks:

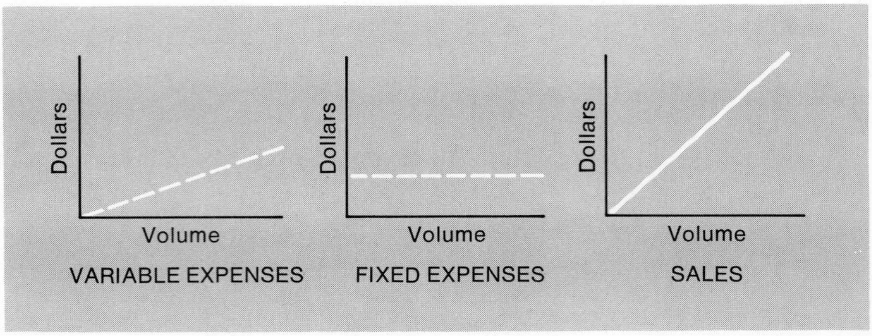

Note that total sales and total variable expenses fluctuate in direct proportion to changes in physical volume, whereas fixed expenses are the same in total over the entire volume range.

Now combine the fixed and variable expenses in a single graph:

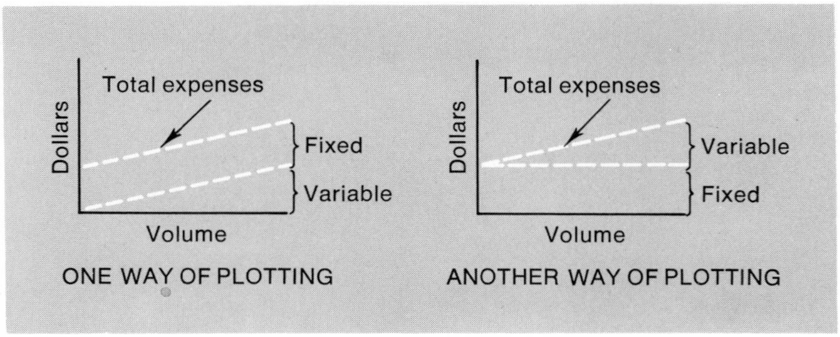

Note that the "total expenses" line is the same under either method. The graph that plots fixed expenses above the variable expenses is preferred by many accountants because it emphasizes the contribution margin notion. (See Exhibit 3-1.) Both the sales and variable-cost lines start at the origin; the vertical distance between them is the contribution margin. When operations are below the breakeven point, the vertical distance between the sales line and the variable-cost line measures the total amount of the "contribution" that sales volume is making to fixed expenses.

Finally, introduce the sales line:

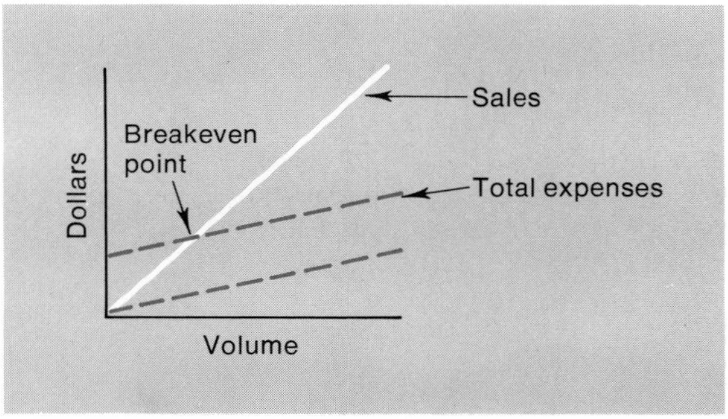

Exhibit 3-1 shows the complete breakeven chart. The *breakeven point* is the point where the total-sales line and total-expense line intersect. But note further that this graph shows the profit or loss outlook for a wide range of volume. The confidence we place in any particular breakeven chart is naturally a consequence of the relative accuracy of the cost-volume-profit relationships depicted.

EXHIBIT 3-1

COST-VOLUME-PROFIT CHART

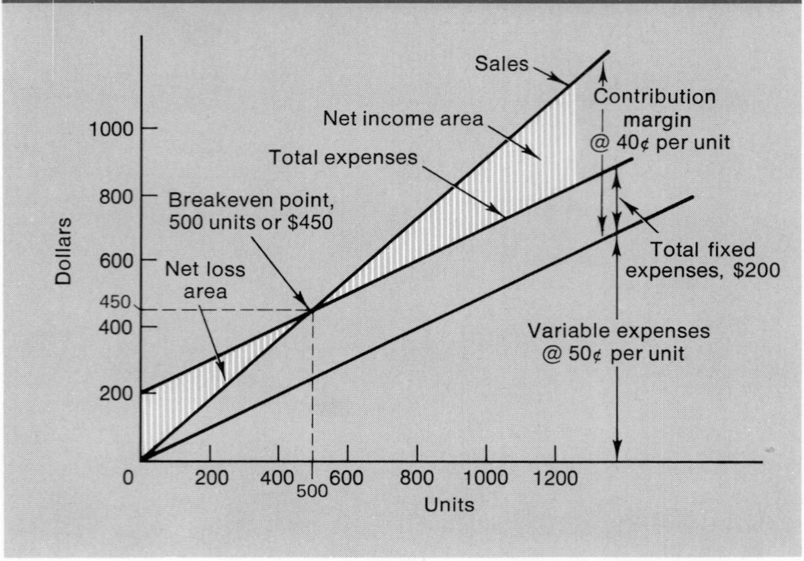

target net income Let us introduce a profit element by asking, *How many rockets must be sold to yield a net income of 20 percent of sales?* The same basic approach may be used. The equation method follows:

Let X = Number of units to be sold to yield desired net income

Sales = Variable Expenses + Fixed Expenses + Desired Net Income

$$\$.90X = \$.50X + \$200 + .20(\$.90X)$$
$$\$.90X = \$.50X + \$200 + \$.18X$$
$$\$.22X = \$200$$
$$X = 909 \text{ units}$$

Proof:			
	Sales = 909 × $.90	$818.10	100.00%
	Variable expenses = 909 × $.50	454.50	55.56
	Contribution margin	$363.60	44.44%
	Fixed expenses	200.00	24.44
	Net income	$163.60	20.00%

Find the 909-unit volume on the graph in Exhibit 3-1. The difference between sales and total expenses at that volume is the $164 net income.

Alternatively, the contribution-margin method could be used:

$$X = \frac{\text{Fixed Expenses} + \text{Desired Net Income}}{\text{Unit Contribution Margin}}$$

$$X = \frac{\$200 + .20(\$.90X)}{\$.40}$$

$$\$.40X = \$200 + \$.18X$$

$$\$.22X = \$200$$

$$X = 909 \text{ units}$$

cost-volume-profit assumptions

relevant range

In a real-life company situation, the breakeven chart may be drawn as shown in Exhibit 3-1. However, the many assumptions that underlie the chart are subject to change if actual volume falls outside the relevant range that was the basis for drawing the chart. It would be more realistic if the lines on these charts were not extended back to the origin, as follows:

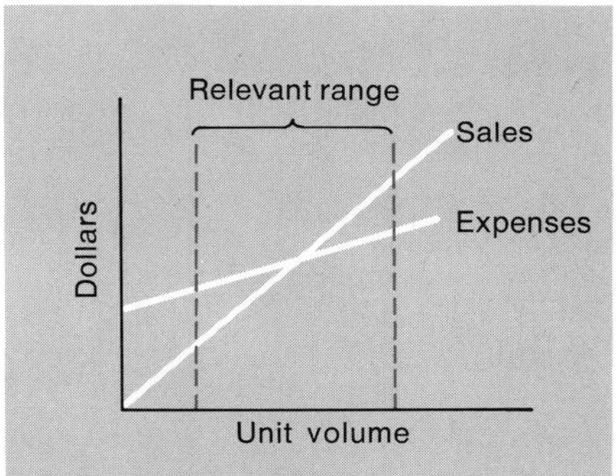

CONVENTIONAL CHART
(As shown in Exhibit 3-1)

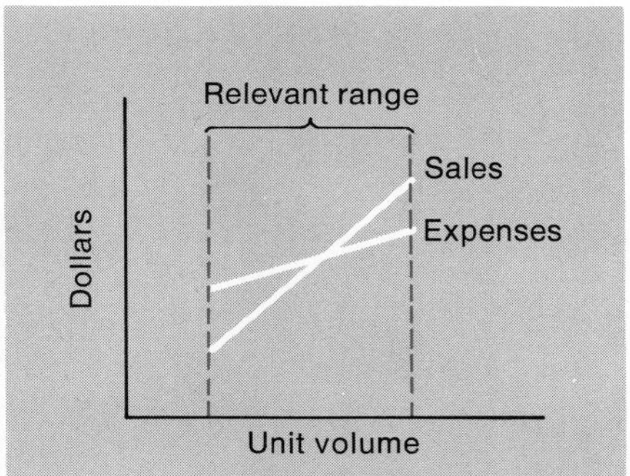

MODIFIED CHART

The modified chart highlights the fact that tenuous, static assumptions underlie a graph of cost-volume-profit relationships. The sales and expense relationships may be valid within a band of activity called the *relevant range.* The relevant range is usually a range in which the firm has had some recent experience. But the same relationships are unlikely to persist if volume falls outside the limits of the relevant range. For example, as shown in the previous chapter, some fixed costs may be avoided at low volume levels.

the economist's breakeven chart

Two principal differences between the accountant's and the economist's breakeven charts are:

1. The accountant usually assumes a constant *unit* variable cost instead of a unit variable cost that changes with the rate of production. In other words, the accountant assumes linearity, but the economist does not.
2. The accountant's sales line is drawn under the assumption that price does not change with the rate of production or sale, but the economist assumes that price changes may be needed to spur sales volume. Therefore, the economist's chart is nonlinear.

The differences can be graphed as follows:

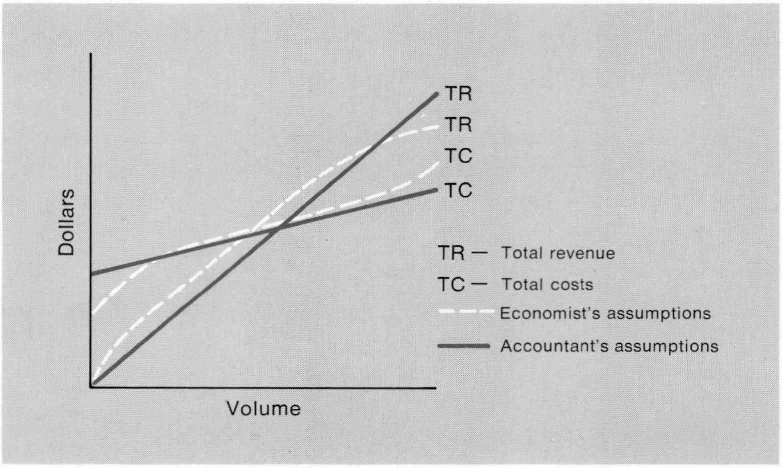

The economist's assumptions are undoubtedly more valid; the accountant's simplifications may or may not lead to less profitable decisions. The point is that obtaining more accurate cost functions is often difficult and expensive. Managers and accountants are aware of the simplifications introduced by the assumptions of linearity, but generally they have decided that the value of any additional information that might be gained from more accurate data would not exceed the additional costs of obtaining the data. They also take comfort in knowing that most of their decisions are made within the relevant range of volume, where the linearity assumption is likely to be more accurate.

limitations of assumptions

Cost behavior is affected by the interplay of a number of factors. Physical volume is only one of these factors; others include unit prices of inputs, efficiency, changes in production technology, wars, strikes, legislation, and so forth. Any breakeven analysis is based on assumptions made about the behavior of revenue, costs, and volume. A change in expected behavior will alter the breakeven point; in other words, profits are affected by changes in other factors *besides volume.* A breakeven chart must be interpreted in the light of the limitations imposed by its underlying assumptions. *The real benefit of preparing breakeven charts is in the enrichment of understanding of the interrelationships of all factors affecting profits, especially cost behavior patterns over ranges of volume.*

In summary, the following typical underlying assumptions will limit the precision and reliability of a given breakeven analysis:

1. The behavior of costs and revenues has been reliably determined and is linear over the relevant range.
2. All costs may be divided into fixed and variable elements.
3. Fixed costs remain constant over the relevant volume range of the breakeven analysis.
4. Variable costs are proportional to volume.
5. Selling prices are to be unchanged.
6. Prices of cost factors are to be unchanged.
7. Efficiency and productivity are to be unchanged.
8. The analysis either covers a single product or it assumes that a given sales mix will be maintained as total volume changes. *Sales mix* may be defined as the relative combination of quantities of a variety of company products that compose total sales. If the mix changes, overall sales targets may be achieved, but the effects on profits depend on whether low-margin or high-margin goods predominate in the sales mix. For additional discussion, see Chapter 26.
9. Revenue and costs are being compared on a common activity base (for example, sales value of production or units produced).
10. Perhaps the most basic assumption of all is that volume is the only relevant factor affecting cost. Of course, other factors also affect costs and sales. Ordinary cost-volume-profit analysis is a crude oversimplification when these factors are unjustifiably ignored.
11. Changes in beginning and ending inventory levels are insignificant in amount. (The impact of inventory changes on cost-volume-profit analysis depends on what inventory pricing method is used. This complexity is discussed in Chapter 10.)

Business is dynamic, not static. The user of cost-volume-profit analysis must constantly challenge and reexamine his assumptions in the light of changes in business conditions, prices, cost factors, sales mixes, cost mixes, and the like. Moreover, cost-volume-profit analysis need not adhere rigidly to the traditional assumptions of linearity and unchanging prices.

interrelationships of cost, volume, and profits

uncertainty and sensitivity analysis

Throughout this book we almost always work with single-number "best estimates" in order to emphasize and simplify various important points. For example, our cost-volume-profit models, budget models, and capital-investment models make strong assumptions regarding such critical items as the levels of variable costs, fixed costs, volume attainable, and so on. In short, for purposes of introducing and using many decision models, we often conveniently assume a world of certainty.

Obviously, our estimates and predictions are subject to varying degrees of uncertainty, which is defined here as the possibility that the actual amount will deviate from the expected amount. How do we cope with uncertainty? There are many complex models available that formally analyze expected values in conjunction with probability distributions.[1] But the application of *sensitivity analysis* to the certainty model is the most widely used approach.

Sensitivity analysis is a "what-if" technique that measures how the expected values in a decision model will be affected by changes in the critical data inputs. In the context of cost-volume-profit analysis, sensitivity analysis answers questions such as: "What will my net income be if the unit variable costs or the sales prices change by some amount from the original prediction?"

The major benefit of sensitivity analysis is its provision of an immediate financial measure of the consequences of possible prediction errors. It helps focus on those aspects that are very sensitive indeed, and it eases the manager's mind regarding those predictions that have little impact on decisions.

The advantages of using certainty models coupled with sensitivity analysis are their relative simplicity and economy. The major disadvantage is the possible overlooking of "better" actions that might be forthcoming if more formal models that include uncertainty were used.

cost of prediction error

Sensitivity analysis can be either a calming influence or a signal to buy more data before reaching a decision. Examples of such buying include getting more samples of how costs have behaved at various levels of volume, or scrapping the linear cost-volume model and replacing it with a more elaborate model.

If formal decision models (for example, the cost-volume-profit model in this chapter) are used, often it is feasible to measure sensitivity by estimating the *cost of prediction errors.* The procedure follows:

1. Predict the value of the critical parameter[2] and solve the decision problem by computing the optimal decision (action) given this original prediction.
2. Select an alternative possible value for the critical parameter and again solve the decision problem. Compute both the optimal decision (given the new parameter value) and the expected financial results of this action.
3. Compute the expected financial results of using the decision determined in step (1) under the alternative parameter value in step (2).
4. The cost of the prediction error is (2) minus (3).

[1] Examples are the Monte Carlo model and the decision-tree model. For an exploration of the role of uncertainty in cost-volume-profit analysis, see Problems 24-26 through 24-28.

[2] A *parameter* is a constant or the coefficient of some variable in a model or system of equations. Examples are the total fixed costs, the demand, the unit variable cost, and the unit selling price.

In a complete sensitivity analysis, steps (2) through (4) would be repeated for a range of possible parameter values. To determine the cost of a prediction error *after the actual outcome* value of the parameter is known, the actual value would be used in steps (2) and (3).

Suppose that the person in our example has been selling toy rockets for ten years during his vacations from his regular occupation. He has predicted a sales volume of 1,000 units at a selling price of 90¢ each. Unforeseen competition reduced sales to 600 units. What was the cost of his prediction error—that is, his failure to predict demand accurately?

1. Initial predicted sales = 1,000 units. Optimal original decision: purchase 1,000 units. Expected net income = $200 [(1,000 units × $.40 contribution) − $200 fixed costs = $200]	
2. Alternative parameter value (actual sales) = 600 units. Optimal decision: purchase 600 units Expected net income [(600 units × $.40 contribution) − $200 fixed costs = $40)]	$40
3. Results of original decision under alternative parameter value Expected net income [(600 units × $.40 contribution) − $200 fixed costs + 400 units returned at no cost = $40)]	40
4. Cost of prediction error, (2) − (3)	$ 0

In a complete sensitivity analysis, steps (2) through (4) would be repeated for a range of possible demand values. This would reveal that for an actual demand above 500 units, the financial results are insensitive to any predicted sales level above 500 units. If predicted demand is less than 500 units (the break-even volume), the optimal decision is to avoid renting the booth.

Now assume that the manager did not have the privilege of returning any unsold rockets. Instead, because of their souvenir markings, they became worthless. He had acquired 1,000 units. What was the cost of his prediction error?

1. Initial predicted sales = 1,000 units. Optimal decision: purchase 1,000 units. Expected net income = $200	
2. Alternative parameter value = 600 units Optimal decision: purchase 600 units Expected net income (as above)	$ 40
3. Results of original decision under alternative parameter value Expected net income: Revenue (600 units × $.90) − Cost of rockets (1,000 units × $.50) − $200 other costs =	− 160
4. Cost of prediction error, (2) − (3)	$200

The cost of prediction error can be used for sensitivity analysis either before or after the decision to order the rockets. In these examples we have the vantage point of knowing the actual value of the parameter, and we can therefore compute how much the poor prediction has cost. Of course, the entire sensitivity analysis could have been conducted for a number of demand values before any decision was made. The decision maker could then appraise the possible magnitude of various potential prediction errors and their effects on decisions. **The focus is on the relationship of data to decisions.** (For a further discussion of the role of uncertainty, see Chapter 24,)

changes in variable costs

Both the contribution margin and the breakeven point are altered by changes in unit variable costs. Thus, in the toy-rocket example, if the cost of a toy rocket is raised from 50¢ to 70¢ and the sales price is unchanged at 90¢, the unit contribution falls from 40¢ to 20¢, and the breakeven point increases from 500 to 1,000 units ($200 fixed expenses divided by $.20). A decrease in rocket cost from 50¢ to 30¢ would change the unit contribution from 40¢ to 60¢. The new breakeven point would become 333 units ($200 fixed expenses divided by $.60).

Variable costs are subject to various degrees of control at different volumes because of psychological as well as other factors. When business is booming, management tends to be preoccupied with the generation of volume "at all costs." When business is slack, management tends to ride herd on costs. Decreases in volume are often accompanied by increases in selling expenses and lower selling prices; at the same time labor turnover falls, labor productivity changes, and raw-material prices change. This is another illustration of the limitations of a breakeven chart; conventional breakeven charts assume proportional fluctuations of variable costs with volume. This implies adequate and uniform control over costs, whereas in practice such control is often erratic.

changes in fixed costs

Fixed costs are not static year after year. They may be deliberately increased in order to obtain more profitable combinations of production and distribution; these affect the three major profit determinants: revenue, variable costs, and fixed expenses. For example, a sales force may be established to reach markets directly instead of through wholesalers, thereby obtaining increased unit sales prices. More complicated machinery may be bought so as to reduce unit variable costs. Increases in labor rates are likely to make it desirable for a firm to invest in labor-saving equipment. In some cases, on the other hand, it may be wise to reduce fixed costs in order to obtain a more favorable combination. Thus, direct selling may be supplanted by the use of manufacturers' agents. A company producing stoves may find it desirable to dispose of its foundry if the resulting reduction in fixed costs would more than counterbalance increases in the variable costs of purchased castings over the expected volume range.

When a major change in fixed costs is proposed, management uses forecasts of the effect on the targeted net income and the contribution margin as a guide toward a wise decision. The management accountant makes continuing analyses of cost behavior and redetermines breakeven points periodically. He keeps management informed for the cumulative effect of major and minor changes in the company's cost and revenue patterns.

Fixed costs are constant only over a contemplated range of activity for a given time period. The volume range rarely extends from shutdown levels to 100 percent capacity. Thus, when a radical reduction in volume is foreseen, many fixed costs are "jarred loose" by managerial action. The slashing of fixed costs lowers the breakeven point and enables the firm to endure a greater decrease in volume before losses appear.

the P/V chart Exhibit 3-1 can be recast in simpler form as a so-called P/V chart (a profit-volume graph). This form is preferred by many managers who are interested mainly in the impact of changes in volume on net income. The first graph in Exhibit 3-2 illustrates the chart, using the data in our example. The chart is constructed as follows:

1. The vertical axis is net income in dollars. The horizontal axis is volume, which may be expressed in units or in sales dollars.
2. At zero volume, the net loss would be approximated by the total fixed costs—$200 in this example.
3. A net-income line will slope upward from the −$200 intercept at the rate of the unit contribution margin of 40¢. The line will intersect the volume axis at the breakeven point of 500 units. Each unit sold beyond the breakeven point will add 40¢ to net income.

EXHIBIT 3-2

P/V CHART

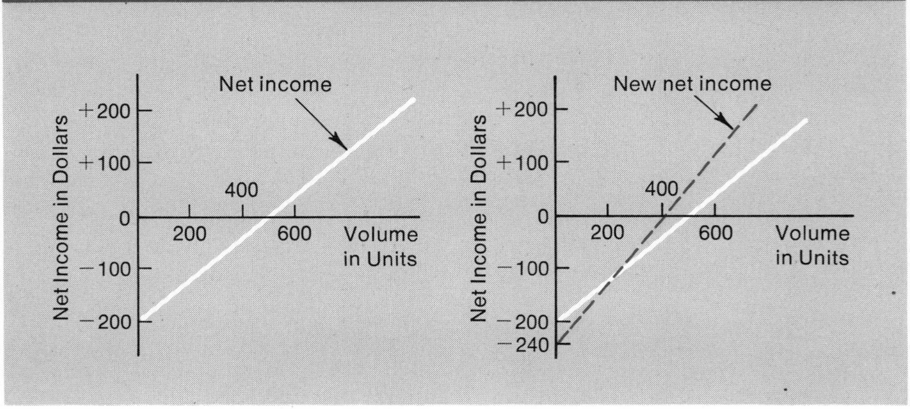

The P/V chart provides a quick condensed comparison of how alternatives on pricing, variable costs, or fixed costs may affect net income as volume changes. For example, the second graph in Exhibit 3-2 shows how net income and the breakeven point would be affected by a decrease in rocket cost from 50¢ to 30¢ and an increase in rent from \$200 to \$240. The unit contribution would become 60¢, and the breakeven point would fall from 500 units to 400 units:

$$\begin{aligned}\text{New Breakeven Point} &= \$240 \div \$.60 \\ &= 400 \text{ units}\end{aligned}$$

Note also the steeper slope of the net-income line, which means that the net income will increase at a faster rate as volume increases.

measuring volume

In our examples so far, we have used units of product as a measure of volume. But "volume" is a general term for activity levels that may be measured in several ways. For example, the volume of a hospital is often expressed in patient-days (number of patients multiplied by the average number of days each patient remained in the hospital). As another example, the volume of the teaching activity of a university is often expressed in terms of total student credit hours taken, not number of students enrolled.

Reconsider our initial toy-rocket example. If we wished to express breakeven volume in sales dollars, we could easily multiply the breakeven volume of 500 units by \$.90 to obtain a breakeven volume in sales dollars of \$450. Our breakeven computation could also be expressed in a seemingly more cumbersome manner:

$$\begin{aligned}\text{Let } X &= \text{Total Sales Dollars to Break Even} \\ X &= \text{Variable Cost Percentage times } X + \text{Fixed Expenses} \\ &\quad + \text{Net Income} \\ X &= \frac{\$.50}{\$.90}X + \$200 + 0 \\ X &= \$.5556X + \$200 + 0 \\ X - .5556X &= \$200 + 0 \\ .4444X &= \$200 + 0 \\ X &= \frac{\$200 + 0}{.4444} = \$450\end{aligned}$$

or

$$X = \frac{\text{Fixed Expenses} + \text{Desired Net Income}}{\text{Contribution Margin Ratio}}$$

The term *contribution margin* will be used frequently in this book. It may be expressed as a total, as an amount per unit, or as a percentage of sales. In our examples, the *total contribution margin* is 500 units × $.40, or $200; the *unit contribution margin* is $.40; and the *contribution margin percentage* or *ratio* is $.40 ÷ $.90, or 44.44 percent of sales. Moreover, the *variable-cost percentage* is $.50 ÷ $.90, or 55.56 percent of sales.

This measuring of volume in dollars rather than in units is more cumbersome in single-product situations. However, as soon as multiple products are encountered, their sales values are used as a common denominator for aggregation and interpretation of overall results.

The most widely encountered aggregate measure of the volume of activity is sales dollars, a monetary rather than a physical calibration of activity. Nearly all companies have more than one product. Although apples and oranges can be aggregated in physical units, such a sum is harder to interpret than their sales values in *dollars*. Similarly, it would be nonsense to aggregate in *units* for a company such as Sears that sells thousands of different products. Chapter 26 discusses the implications of cost-volume-profit analysis in multiproduct organizations.

contribution approach to income statements

contribution approach versus traditional approach

The traditional income statement classifies expenses primarily by *management function*, such as manufacturing, selling, and administrative expenses:

Sales	xx
Less manufacturing cost of goods sold (including fixed manufacturing overhead)	xx
Gross profit	xx
Less selling and administrative expenses	xx
Net income	xx

In contrast, the contribution approach stresses cost *behavior* as the primary classification scheme:

Sales		xx
Less variable expenses		
Manufacturing	xx	
Selling	xx	
Administrative	xx	xx
Contribution margin		xx
Less fixed expenses		
Manufacturing	xx	
Selling	xx	
Administrative	xx	xx
Net income		xx

Note that the traditional statement does not show any contribution margin. This raises analytical difficulties in the computation of the impact on net income of changes in sales. Fixed manufacturing overhead, under traditional procedures, is unitized and assigned to products. Hence, as we will see often in later chapters, unit costs and gross-profit figures include fixed overhead that must be removed for a short-run cost-volume-profit analysis.

The contribution approach stresses the lump-sum amount of fixed expenses to be recouped before net income emerges. This highlighting of total fixed expenses helps to attract management attention to fixed-expenses behavior and control when both short-run and long-run plans are being made. Keep in mind that advocates of this contribution approach *do not maintain that fixed expenses are unimportant or irrelevant,* but they do stress that the distinctions between behaviors of variable and fixed costs are crucial for certain decisions.

comparison of contribution margin and gross margin

Avoid confusing the terms *contribution margin* and *gross margin* (which is often also called *gross profit*). As the preceding financial statements show, *contribution margin* is the excess of sales over *all* variable expenses, including variable manufacturing, selling, and administrative categories.

In contrast, *gross margin* or *gross profit* is the excess of sales over the inventory cost of the goods sold. Therefore, in a manufacturing company, the manufacturing cost of goods sold (including *fixed* indirect manufacturing costs) is deducted from sales to obtain the gross margin.

Both the contribution margin and the gross margin may be expressed as *totals,* as amounts *per unit,* or as *percentages of sales* in the form of ratios. For example, a *contribution-margin ratio* is the total contribution margin divided by the total sales. Similarly, the *variable-cost ratio* is the total variable costs divided by the total sales.

advantages of contribution margins and ratios

The advantages of knowing the contribution margins and ratios of divisions and product lines include:

1. *Contribution-margin ratios* often help management decide on which products to push and which to deemphasize or to tolerate only because of the sales benefits that relate to other products.

2. *Contribution margins* are essential for helping management to decide whether a product line should be dropped. In the short run, if a product recovers more than its variable costs, it is making a contribution to overall profits. This information is provided promptly by the contribution approach. Under the traditional approach, the relevant information is not only difficult to gather, but there is a danger that management may be misled by reliance on unit costs that contain an element of fixed overhead.

3. Contribution margins may be used to appraise alternatives that arise with respect to price reductions, special discounts, special advertising campaigns, and the use of premiums to spur sales volume. Decisions such as these are really determined by a comparison of the added costs with the prospective additions in sales revenue. Ordinarily, the higher the contribution-margin ratio, the better the potential net benefit from sales promotion; the lower the ratio, the greater the increase in volume that is necessary to recover additional sales-promotion costs.

4. When desired profits are agreed upon, their attainability may be quickly appraised by computing the number of units that must be sold to secure the wanted profits. The computation is easily made by dividing the fixed costs plus desired profits by the contribution margin per unit.

5. Decisions must often be made as to how to utilize a given set of resources (for example, machines or materials) most profitably. The contribution approach furnishes the data for a proper decision, because the latter is determined by the product that makes the largest total contribution to profits. (However, the solution to the problem of calculating the maximum contribution is not always intuitively obvious. This point is amplified in Chapters 11 and 27.

6. The contribution approach is helpful where selling prices are firmly established in the industry, because the principal problem for the individual company is how much variable cost is allowable (a matter most heavily affected in many companies by design of products) and how much volume can be obtained.

7. Advocates of a contribution approach maintain that the compilation of unit costs for products on a contribution basis helps managers understand the relationships among costs, volume, prices, and profits and hence leads to wiser pricing decisions. Ultimately, maximum prices are set by customer demand. Minimum short-run prices are sometimes determined by the variable costs of producing and selling. Pricing is discussed at greater length in Chapter 11.

SUMMARY

The modern multiproduct company's performance is influenced by so many factors that the attempt to portray all of them on a breakeven chart by making assumptions is an ambitious one. The breakeven chart may be compared to the use of a meat-ax, not a scalpel. The chart is useful as a frame of reference for analysis, as a vehicle for expressing overall performance, and as a planning device.

Whenever the underlying assumptions of cost-volume-profit analysis do not correspond to a given situation, the limitations of the analysis must be clearly recognized. A single breakeven graph is static, because it is a picture of relationships that prevail under only one set of assumptions. If conditions change, a different set of cost-volume-profit relationships is likely to appear. The fluid nature of these relationships must be kept uppermost in the minds of executives and accountants if the breakeven tool is to be useful and educational.

Properly used, cost-volume-profit analysis offers essential background for important management decisions regarding distribution channels, outside contracting, sales-promotion expenditures, and pricing strategies. It offers an overall view of costs and sales in relation to profit planning, and it provides clues to possible changes in management strategy. It is also the springboard for a different type of income statement, which emphasizes cost behavior patterns. This is often called the "contribution" income statement.

PROBLEMS FOR SELF-STUDY

PROBLEM 1 Reconsider the toy-rocket problem in the chapter. Suppose you want to obtain a net income of $250. How many rockets must be sold?

SOLUTION 1 The equation method follows:

Let X = Number of units to be sold to yield desired net income

$\$.90X = \$.50X + \$200 + \$250$

$\$.40X = \$450$

$X = 1{,}125$ units

PROBLEM 2 Here is the income statement of C Company:

Net sales		$500,000
Less expenses:		
Variable	$350,000	
Fixed	250,000	600,000
Net loss		($100,000)

Assume that variable expenses will always remain the same percentage of sales.

a. If fixed expenses are increased by $100,000, what amount of sales will cause the firm to break even?

b. With the proposed increase in fixed expenses, what amount of sales will yield a net income of $50,000?

SOLUTION 2 This problem differs from the example in the text because all data are expressed in dollars; no information is given on the number of units:

a. Let S = Breakeven sales in dollars

$$S = \text{Variable Expenses} + \text{Fixed Expenses} + \text{Desired Net Income}$$

$$S = \frac{\$350{,}000}{\$500{,}000}S + (\$250{,}000 + \$100{,}000)$$

$$S = .70S + \$350{,}000$$

$$.30S = \$350{,}000$$

$$S = \$1{,}166{,}667$$

b. Let S = Sales needed to earn $50,000

$$S = .70S + \$350{,}000 + \$50{,}000$$

$$.30S = \$400{,}000$$

$$S = \$1{,}333{,}333$$

Note that 30 percent of each sales dollar is available for the coverage of fixed expenses and the making of *net income.* This *contribution-margin ratio* (*variable income ratio* or *contribution percentage*) is computed by subtracting the variable expense percentage, 70 percent, from 100 percent. This relationship is the foundation for the following commonly used formulas:

a. $$\text{B.E.} = \frac{\text{Fixed Expenses} + \text{Desired Net Income}}{1 - \dfrac{\text{Variable Expenses}}{\text{Sales}}}$$

$$\text{or} \quad \frac{\text{Fixed Expenses} + \text{Desired Net Income}}{\text{Contribution-Margin Ratio}}$$

$$\text{B.E.} = \frac{\$350{,}000}{1 - \dfrac{\$350{,}000}{\$500{,}000}} \quad \text{or} \quad \frac{\$350{,}000}{.30}$$

$$\text{B.E.} = \$1{,}166{,}667$$

$$\text{b. Required Sales } (RS) = \frac{\text{Fixed Expenses} + \text{Desired Net Income}}{\text{Contribution-Margin Ratio}}$$

$$RS = \frac{\$400{,}000}{.30}$$

$$RS = \$1{,}333{,}333$$

PROBLEM 3 Using the following data (in millions) for 19_3 for the Sprouse Company, prepare a contribution income statement and a traditional income statement. Assume that there are no beginning or ending inventories. (The problem of changes in inventory levels and how they affect these statements is discussed in Chapter 10.)

Sales	$150	Variable factory overhead	$ 5
Variable selling expenses*	15	Direct labor	20
Variable administrative expenses	12	Direct materials used	50
Fixed selling expenses	20	Fixed administrative expenses	5
Fixed factory overhead	10		

* These and other expenses would be detailed.

SOLUTION 3

SPROUSE CO.
Contribution Income Statement
For the Year Ending Dec. 31, 19_3
(In millions of dollars)

Sales		$150
Less variable expenses:		
Direct materials used	$50	
Direct labor	20	
Variable factory overhead	5	
Total variable manufacturing costs	$75	
Variable selling expenses	15	
Variable administrative expenses	12	
Total variable expenses		102
Contribution margin		$ 48
Less fixed expenses:		
Fixed factory overhead	$10	
Fixed selling expenses	20	
Fixed administrative expenses	5	
Total fixed expenses		35
Net income		$ 13

SPROUSE CO.
Traditional (Functional) Income Statement
For the Year Ending Dec. 31, 19_3
(In millions of dollars)

Sales			$150
Less manufacturing cost of goods sold:			
Direct material used		$50	
Direct labor		20	
Variable factory overhead		5	
Fixed factory overhead		10	85
Gross profit or gross margin			$ 65
Selling expenses:			
Variable	$15		
Fixed	20	$35	
Administrative expenses:			
Variable	$12		
Fixed	5	17	
Total selling and administrative expenses			52
Net income			$ 13

appendix: role of income taxes

Income taxes are most often computed as some percentage of income before income taxes. Therefore, the breakeven equation in our basic example would have to be modified accordingly. Suppose we are asked to compute the number of rockets that must be sold to yield a net income after taxes of \$164, the same amount calculated earlier in the "target net income" section of this chapter. Assume an income tax rate of 30 percent. The equation would be:

$$\$.90X = \$.50X + \$200 + \frac{\text{Target After-Tax Net Income}}{1 - \text{Tax Rate}}$$

$$\$.90X = \$.50X + \$200 + \frac{\$164}{1 - .30}$$

$$\$.90X = \$.50X + \$200 + \$234$$

$$\$.40X = \$434$$

$$X = 1{,}085 \text{ units}$$

Proof:	Sales = 1,085 × \$.90 =	\$976.50
	Variable expenses = 1,085 × \$.50 =	542.50
	Contribution margin	\$434.00
	Fixed expenses	200.00
	Income before income taxes	\$234.00
	Income taxes @ 30%	70.20
	Net income	\$163.80, or \$164

Note that the only change in the general equation approach is to modify the target net income to allow for the impact of income taxes. Our previous equation approach was:

$$\text{Sales} = \text{Variable Expenses} + \text{Fixed Expenses} + \text{Income Before Taxes}$$

We now have to introduce income tax effects:

$$\text{Let } y = \text{Income Before Taxes}$$

$$.3 = \text{Income Tax Rate}$$

$$z = \text{Income After Taxes}$$

Then

$$z = y - .3y$$

$$z = y(1 - .3)$$

$$y = \frac{z}{1 - .3} = \frac{\text{Target After-Tax Net Income}}{1 - \text{Tax Rate}}$$

Reexamine our solution. Using those numbers, a recapitulation of the relationships follows:

Income before taxes	\$234	100%
Income taxes	70	30
Net income	\$164	70%

Note that:

$$\text{Income Before Taxes} = \frac{\text{Target After-Tax Net Income}}{1 - \text{Tax Rate}}$$

$$\$234 = \frac{\$164}{1 - .30}$$

QUESTIONS, PROBLEMS, AND CASES

3-1 Why is it more accurate to describe the subject matter of this chapter as *cost-volume-profit relationships* rather than as *breakeven analysis?*

3-2 Why is it often more desirable to plot fixed costs above the variable costs on a breakeven chart?

3-3 What are the principal differences between the accountant's and the economist's breakeven charts?

3-4 Define: *contribution margin, variable-cost ratio, contribution-margin ratio.*

3-5 "This breakeven approach is great stuff. All you need to do is worry about variable costs. The fixed costs will take care of themselves." Discuss.

3-6 A lithographic company follows a policy of high pricing each month until it reaches its monthly breakeven point. After this point is reached, the company tends to quote low prices on jobs for the rest of the month. What is your opinion of this policy? As a regular customer, and suspecting this policy, what would you do?

3-7 *Relationships in Chapter Illustration* Refer to the initial toy-rocket example in the chapter.

required

1. Suppose the unit purchase cost of rockets rises from 50¢ to 60¢, but the sales price is unchanged. What is the new breakeven point in units?
2. Suppose the unit purchase cost of rockets declines from 50¢ to 40¢, but the sales price is unchanged. What is the new breakeven point in units?

3-8 *Governmental Price Controls* Governments periodically exert controls over maximum allowable selling prices. The MN Motorbike Company had achieved the following average operating figures for each of the three years preceding a war that restricted the MN output for consumer markets:

	IN MILLIONS		
Sales, 100,000 units @ $2,000		$200	100%
Variable costs, 100,000 units @ $900	$90		
Fixed costs	30	120	
Gross profit		$ 80	40%

During the first war year, variable costs had remained fairly steady per motorbike, but the output had fallen to 50,000 units. Total fixed costs were unchanged at $30 million.

required

1. Compute the gross profit in dollars *and* in percent of sales for a volume of 50,000 units.
2. The company applied for permission to raise its prices so as to provide the same gross profit percent on sales as before. Compute the new selling price that the company requested.

3-9 *Exercises in Cost-Volume-Profit Relationships* The Fresh Buy Grocers Corporation owns and operates twelve supermarkets in and around Chicago. You are given the following corporate budget data for next year:

Sales	$10,000,000
Fixed expenses	1,650,000
Variable expenses	8,200,000

required

Compute expected profit for each of the following deviations from budgeted data. (Consider each case independently.)

a. 10 percent increase in total contribution margin
b. 10 percent decrease in total contribution margin
c. 5 percent increase in fixed costs
d. 5 percent decrease in fixed costs
e. 8 percent increase in sales volume
f. 8 percent decrease in sales volume
g. 10 percent increase in fixed costs and 10 percent increase in sales volume
h. 5 percent increase in fixed costs and 5 percent decrease in variable costs

3-10 *Basic Cost-Volume-Profit Analysis* The Look Rite Company operates a chain of rented stores and departments within larger stores. The chain features a variety of "packs" of men's shirts, ties, and accessories that are sold at a price of $5 per pack. Therefore, all sales are at $5 per unit, where the pack is defined as one unit. Depending on quality, a "pack" might contain a single tie or several ties. Another pack might contain a single shirt or a matching tie and shirt. The chain operates on a relatively low margin and uses a sales commission to encourage its sales personnel to be more than mere order takers. Look Rite is trying to determine the desirability of opening another store that would possess the following expense and revenue relationships:

	PER PACK
Selling price	$5.00
Invoice cost of a pack	$4.00
Sales commissions	.25
	$4.25
Annual fixed expenses:	
Rent	$ 5,500
Wages	17,600
Utilities	2,100
Other fixed expenses	4,800
	$30,000

required

Consider each question independently:

1. What is the annual breakeven point in dollar sales and in unit sales?
2. If 35,000 packs were sold, what would be the store's net income (loss)?
3. If the store manager were paid 5¢ per pack as additional commission, what would be the annual breakeven point in dollar sales and in unit sales?
4. Refer to the original data. If sales commissions were discontinued in favor of an $8,000 increase in fixed salaries, what would be the annual breakeven point in dollars and in unit sales? Is this a desirable change? Why?
5. Refer to the original data. The regular $.25 commission is still in force. If the store manager were paid 10¢ per pack as commission on each pack sold in excess of the breakeven point, what would be the store's net income if 50,000 packs were sold?

3-11 *Extension of 3-10* Refer to part 4 of Problem 3-10.

required

1. Compute the point of indifference between a fixed-salary plan and a commission plan. That is, calculate the volume level in units where the profit under each plan would be equal. Above that volume level one plan would be more profitable than the other; below that level the reverse would occur.
2. Compute the net income or loss under each plan at volume levels of 25,000 units and 50,000 units.
3. Suppose the target net income is $6,000. How many units must be sold to reach the target under (a) the commission plan and (b) the salary plan?

3-12 *Sensitivity, Prediction Errors, and Inflation* Refer to Problem 3-10. As president of Look Rite, you are concerned that inflation may squeeze your profits. Specifically, you feel committed to the five-dollar selling price and fear that diluting the quality of the packs in the face of rising costs will be an unwise marketing move. You expect cost prices of the packs to rise by 10 percent during the forthcoming year. Therefore, you are tempted to avoid the price rise by placing a noncancellable order with a large supplier that would provide 50,000 packs of a specified quality for each store at $4 per pack. (To simplify this analysis, assume that all stores will face identical demands.)

These packs could be acquired and paid for as delivered throughout the year. However, all packs must be delivered to the stores by the end of the year.

As a shrewd merchandiser, you can foresee some risks in the sense that you deal exclusively in high-fashion goods that are subject to rapid obsolescence. If sales were less than 50,000, you feel that markdowns of the unsold merchandise would be necessary to move the goods. You predict that the average selling price of the leftover packs would be $3. The regular sales commission of 5 percent of sales would be paid.

required

1. Suppose that the actual demand for the year is 48,000 packs and that you contracted for 50,000 packs. What is the net profit for the store?
2. If you had had perfect knowledge, you would have contracted for 48,000 rather than 50,000 packs. What would the net profit have been if you had ordered 48,000 packs? Having ordered 50,000 instead, what was the cost of your prediction error?
3. Given an actual volume of 48,000 units, by how much would the average purchase cost of the pack have had to rise before you would have been indifferent between having the contract for 50,000 packs and not having the contract?

3-13 *Cost of Prediction Errors* Reconsider the toy-rocket illustration in the section on "Cost of Prediction Errors." Suppose the manager does not have the privilege of returning any unsold rockets. Instead, because of their souvenir markings, they are worthless. He acquired 1,000 units, but unforeseen competition reduced sales to 800 units.

required

1. What was the cost of the prediction error?
2. Suppose that demand was unusually heavy. He sold all 1,000 units, but he was sure that he could have sold a total of 1,200 units if he had not run out of stock. What was the cost of the prediction error?

3-14 *Cost of Prediction Errors* A company set a price for its product at $20 per unit. Predicted variable costs were $14 per unit. Expected sales were 100,000 units. Fixed costs for the year were expected to be $400,000.

required

Compute the cost of the prediction error if:

1. All of the forecasts were accurate, except that the actual variable costs were \$15 per unit. (Given a \$15 variable cost, the \$20 price would not be changed.)
2. Actual variable costs were \$15 per unit. Sales could have been 110,000 units if enough stock were available. However, only 100,000 units were acquired and sold.

3-15 *Prediction Error, Channels of Distribution* Through the end of 19_3, Mavis Company, a television manufacturer, had always sold its products through distributors. In 19_3 its sales were \$50,000,000 and its net income was 10 percent of sales. Total fixed expenses (manufacturing and selling) were \$10,000,000.

During 19_3 a number of Mavis' competitors had begun selling their units through discount houses and huge outlets. Mavis' marketing research group was asked to predict the effects of eliminating distributors from Mavis' channels of distribution and selling directly to retailers. The group was instructed to predict both changes in sales volume and changes in selling expenses, under the provision that the *selling price per unit would remain unchanged.*

The marketing analysis yielded the following predictions. Total sales dollars in 19_4 would *drop* 20 percent from the 19_3 figures, but net income for 19_4 would rise to \$5,200,000 owing to savings in selling expenses. This net savings in selling expenses from eliminating the "middleman" was impressive, since total fixed expenses (manufacturing and selling) would *increase* to \$10,800,000 because of the additional warehouse and delivery facilities required. If the 19_3 distribution system were continued, however, 19_4 results would replicate 19_3.

required

1. What was the breakeven point (in sales dollars) under the original situation prevailing in 19_3?
2. What would be the breakeven point (in sales dollars) under the proposed situation for 19_4?
3. On the basis of this analysis, Mavis adopted the new direct-distribution plan for 19_4, and reduced 19_4 production to the 40,000,000-sales-dollar level. Unfortunately, it became clear by early December of 19_4 that sales would reach only \$38,000,000, and Mavis cut back production so that no ending inventory remained. Variable costs *per unit* and total fixed costs were as predicted. Compute the cost of Mavis' prediction error.

3-16 *Effects of Size of Machines* The Dore Foods Company is planning to manufacture doughnuts for its chain of coffee shops throughout the city. Two alternatives have been proposed for the production of the doughnuts—use of a semiautomatic machine, or a fully automatic machine.

The shops now purchase their doughnuts from an outside supplier at a cost of 5¢ per doughnut.

	SEMIAUTOMATIC	AUTOMATIC
Annual fixed cost	\$3,000	\$5,000
Variable cost per doughnut	\$ .02	\$ .015

required

The president has asked for the following information:

1. For each machine, the minimum annual number of doughnuts that must be sold in order to have the total annual costs equal to outside purchase costs
2. The most profitable alternative for 300,000 doughnuts annually
3. The most profitable alternative for 600,000 doughnuts annually
4. The volume level that would produce the same net income regardless of the type of machine owned

3-17 *Effects of Sales Forecast* The Fragile Company has just been incorporated and plans to produce a product that will sell for $10 per unit. Preliminary market surveys show that demand will be less than 10,000 units per year, but it is not as yet clear how much less.

The company has the choice of buying one of two machines, each of which has a capacity of 10,000 units per year. Machine A would have fixed costs of $30,000 per year and would yield a profit of $30,000 per year if sales were 10,000 units. Machine B has a fixed cost per year of $16,000 and would yield a profit of $24,000 per year with sales of 10,000 units. Variable costs behave linearly for both machines.

required

1. Breakeven sales for each machine
2. The sales level where both machines are equally profitable
3. The range of sales where one machine is more profitable than the other

3-18 *Effect on Profits of Change in Price* (SIA) The Canadian Zinc Diecasting Company is one of several suppliers of part X to an automobile manufacturing firm. Orders are distributed to the various diecasting companies on a fairly even basis; however, the sales manager of Canadian Zinc believes that with a reduction in price he could secure another 30 percent increase in units sold.

The general manager has asked you to analyze the sales manager's proposal and submit your recommendation.

The following data are available:

	PRESENT	PROPOSED
Unit price	$2.50	$2.00
Unit sales volume	200,000 units	Plus 30%
Variable cost (total)	$350,000	Same unit variable cost
Fixed cost	$120,000	$120,000
Profit	$ 30,000	?

required

1. Net profit or loss based on the sales manager's proposal
2. Unit sales required under the proposed price to make the original $30,000 profit

3-19 *Influence of Relevant Range on Cost Behavior* The Charne Company's cost behavior is as follows:

PRODUCTION RANGE IN UNITS	FIXED COSTS
0– 20,000	$160,000
20,001– 65,000	190,000
65,001– 90,000	210,000
90,001–100,000	250,000

At an activity of 70,000 units per year, variable costs total $280,000. Full capacity is 100,000 units per year.

required

(Each case given below is independent of any other and should be considered individually.)

1. Production is now set at 50,000 units per year with a sales price of $7.50 per unit. What is the minimum number of additional units needed to be sold in an unrelated market at $5.50 per unit to show a total net profit of $3,000 per year?
2. Production is now set at 60,000 units per year. By how much may sales-promotion costs be increased to bring production up to 80,000 units and still earn a net profit of 5 percent of total sales if the selling price is held at $7.50?

3. If net profit is currently $10,000, with fixed costs at $160,000, and a 2 percent increase in price will leave units sold unchanged but increase profits by $5,000, what is the present volume in units?

3-20 *Comparison of Two Companies* (SIA, adapted) Black and White are the owners of the Modern Processing Company and the Oldway Manufacturing Company, respectively. These companies manufacture and sell the same product, and competition between the two owners has always been friendly. Cost and profit data have been freely exchanged. Uniform selling prices have been set by market conditions.

Black and White differ markedly in their management thinking. Operations at Modern are highly mechanized and the direct labor force is paid on a fixed-salary basis. Oldway uses manual hourly paid labor for the most part and pays incentive bonuses. Modern's salesmen are paid a fixed salary, whereas Oldway's salesmen are paid small salaries plus commissions. Mr. White takes pride in his ability to adapt his costs to fluctuations in sales volume and has frequently chided Mr. Black on Modern's "inflexible overhead."

During 19_2, both firms reported the same profit on sales of $100,000. However, when comparing results at the end of 19_3, Mr. White was startled by the following results:

	MODERN		OLDWAY	
	19_2	19_3	19_2	19_3
Sales revenue	$100,000	$120,000	$100,000	$150,000
Costs and expenses	90,000	94,000	90,000	130,000
Net income	$ 10,000	$ 26,000	$ 10,000	$ 20,000
Percent on sales	10%	21⅔%	10%	13⅓%

On the assumption that operating inefficiencies must have existed, White and his accountant made a thorough investigation of costs but could not uncover any evidence of costs that were out of line. At a loss to explain the lower increase in profits on a much higher increase in sales volume, they have asked you to prepare an explanation.

You find that fixed costs and expenses recorded over the two-year period were as follows:

Modern	$70,000 each year
Oldway	$10,000 each year

required

1. Prepare an explanation for Mr. White showing why Oldway's profits for 19_3 were lower than those reported by Modern despite the fact that Oldway's sales had been higher. Show relevant calculations to clarify the issue.
2. Indicate the volume of sales Oldway would have to have had in 19_3 to achieve the profit of $26,000 realized by Modern in 19_3.
3. Comment on the relative future positions of the two companies when there are reductions in sales volume.

3-21 *Margin of Safety* The *margin of safety* is the excess of budgeted or actual sales over the breakeven sales volume. It shows the amount by which sales may decrease before losses occur. This concept may be expressed as a percentage through dividing the dollar margin of safety by budgeted or actual sales (M/S). The validity of such a margin depends on the accuracy of cost estimates at the contemplated breakeven point. Often any drastic decrease in sales is accompanied by severe slashes in costs; the margin of safety is an approximation that presupposes given cost relationships.

The Axel Swang Company has the following data:

BUDGET (300,000 UNITS)		
Sales	$930,000	(100%)
Variable costs	325,500	(35%)
Contribution margin	$604,500	(65%)
Fixed costs	520,000	
Net income	$ 84,500	

Since management is not satisfied with the projected net income, it is considering four independent possibilities: (1) increase unit volume 10 percent; (2) increase unit selling price 10 percent; (3) decrease unit variable costs 10 percent; or (4) decrease fixed costs 10 percent.

required

1. Compute the breakeven sales and the margin of safety as a percentage of sales.
2. Rank the four action possibilities in terms of net income. Show computations. Are the four possibilities likely to be independent? Why?

3-22 *Role of Income Taxes* Reconsider the toy-rocket problem as described in Problem 1 for Self-Study at the end of the chapter. Also study the appendix. Suppose you want to obtain a net income of $250 after taxes. How many rockets must be sold? Assume an income-tax rate of 40 percent.

3-23 *Role of Income Taxes* Reconsider Problem 2 for Self-Study at the end of the chapter. Also study the appendix. With the proposed increase in fixed expenses, what amount of sales will yield a net income of $50,000 after taxes? The income tax rate is 40 percent.

3-24 *Cost-Volume Relationships, Income Taxes* (CMA) R. A. Ro and Company, maker of quality handmade pipes, has experienced a steady growth in sales for the past five years. However, increased competition has led Mr. Ro, the president, to believe that an aggressive advertising campaign will be necessary next year to maintain the company's present growth.

To prepare for next year's advertising campaign, the company's accountant has prepared and presented Mr. Ro with the following data for the current year, 19_2:

Variable costs (per pipe):	
Direct labor	$ 8.00
Direct materials	3.25
Variable overhead	2.50
Total variable costs	$13.75
Fixed costs	
Manufacturing	$ 25,000
Selling	40,000
Administrative	70,000
Total fixed costs	$135,000
Selling price, per pipe:	$25.00
Expected sales, 19_2 (20,000 units):	$500,000
Tax Rate: 40%	

Mr. Ro has set the sales target for 19_3 at a level of $550,000 (or 22,000 pipes).

required

1. What is the projected after-tax net income for 19_2?
2. What is the breakeven point in units for 19_2?
3. Mr. Ro believes an additional selling expense of $11,250 for advertising in 19_3, with all other costs remaining constant, will be necessary to attain the

sales target. What will be the after-tax net income for 19_3 if the additional $11,250 is spent?

4. What will be the breakeven point in dollar sales for 19_3 if the additional $11,250 is spent for advertising?
5. If the additional $11,250 is spent for advertising in 19_3, what is the required sales level in dollar sales to equal 19_2's after-tax net income?
6. At a sales level of 22,000 units, what maximum amount can be spent on advertising if an after-tax net income of $60,000 is desired?

3-25 *Miscellaneous Alternatives; Contribution Income Statement* The income statement of the Hall Company appears below on this page. Commissions are based on sales dollars; all other variable expenses vary in terms of units sold.

The factory has a capacity of 150,000 units per year. The results for 19_1 have been disappointing. Top management is sifting a number of possible ways to make operations profitable in 19_2.

required

(Consider each situation independently.)

1. Recast the income statement into a contribution format. There will be three major sections: sales, variable expenses, and fixed expenses. Show costs per unit in an adjacent column. Allow adjacent space for entering your answers to part 2.
2. The sales manager is torn between two courses of action.
   a. He has studied the market potential and believes that a 15 percent slash in price would fill the plant to capacity.
   b. He wants to increase prices by 25 percent, to increase advertising by $150,000, and to boost commissions to 10 percent of sales. Under these circumstances, he thinks that unit volume will increase by 50 percent.

   Prepare the budgeted income statements, using a contribution margin format and two columns. What would be the new net income or loss under each alternative? Assume that there are no changes in fixed costs other than advertising.

HALL COMPANY

Income Statement
For the Year Ended December 31, 19_1

Sales (90,000 units @ $4.00)				$360,000
Cost of goods sold:				
Direct materials			$90,000	
Direct labor			90,000	
Factory overhead:				
Variable		$18,000		
Fixed		80,000	98,000	278,000
Gross margin				$ 82,000
Selling expenses:				
Variable:				
Sales commissions*	$18,000			
Shipping	3,600	$21,600		
Fixed:				
Advertising, salaries, etc.		40,000	$61,600	
Administrative expenses:				
Variable		$ 4,500		
Fixed		20,400	24,900	86,500
Net loss				$ (4,500)

* Based on sales dollars, not physical units.

3. The president does not want to tinker with the price. How much may advertising be increased to bring production and sales up to 130,000 units and still earn a target profit of 5 percent of sales?
4. A mail-order firm is willing to buy 60,000 units of product "if the price is right." Assume that the present market of 90,000 units at $4 each will not be disturbed. Hall Company will not pay any sales commission. The mail-order firm will pick up the units directly at the Hall factory. However, Hall must refund $24,000 of the total sales price as a promotional and advertising allowance for the mail-order firm. In addition, special packaging will increase manufacturing costs on these 60,000 units by 10¢ per unit. At what unit price must the mail-order chain business be quoted for Hall to break even on total operations in 19_2?
5. The president suspects that a fancy new package will aid consumer sales and ultimately Hall's sales. Present packaging costs per unit are all variable and consist of 5¢ direct materials and 4¢ direct labor; new packaging costs will be 30¢ and 13¢, respectively. Assuming no other changes in cost behavior, how many units must be sold to earn a net profit of $20,000?

3-26 *Hospital Breakeven* (CPA) The Columbus Hospital operates a general hospital but rents space and beds to separate entities for specialized areas such as pediatrics, maternity, psychiatric, and so on. Columbus charges each separate entity for common services to its patients such as meals and laundry and for administrative services such as billings, collections, and so on. All uncollectible accounts are charged directly to the entity. Space and bed rentals are fixed for the year.

For the entire year ended June 30, 1973, the Pediatrics Department at Columbus Hospital charged each patient an average of $65 per day, had a capacity of 60 beds, operated 24 hours per day for 365 days, and had revenue of $1,138,800.

Expenses charged by the hospital to the Pediatrics Department for the year ended June 30, 1973, were as follows:

	BASIS OF ALLOCATION	
	Patient Days	Bed Capacity
Dietary	$ 42,952	
Janitorial		$ 12,800
Laundry	28,000	
Laboratory, other than direct charges to patients	47,800	
Pharmacy	33,800	
Repairs and maintenance	5,200	7,140
General administrative services		131,760
Rent		275,320
Billings and collections	40,000	
Bad debt expense	47,000	
Other	18,048	25,980
	$262,800	$453,000

The only personnel directly employed by the Pediatrics Department are supervising nurses, nurses, and aides. The hospital has minimum personnel requirements based on total annual patient days. Hospital requirements beginning at the minimum, expected level of operation follow.

ANNUAL PATIENT DAYS	AIDES	NURSES	SUPERVISING NURSES
10,000–14,000	21	11	4
14,001–17,000	22	12	4
17,001–23,725	22	13	4
23,726–25,550	25	14	5
25,551–27,375	26	14	5
27,376–29,200	29	16	6

The staffing levels above represent full-time equivalents, and it should be assumed that the Pediatrics Department always employs only the minimum number of required full-time equivalent personnel.

Annual salaries for each class of employee follow: supervising nurses—$18,000, nurses—$13,000, and aides—$5,000. Salary expense for the year ended June 30, 1973, for supervising nurses, nurses, and aides was $72,000, $169,000, and $110,000, respectively.

The Pediatrics Department operated at 100 percent capacity during 111 days for the past year. It is estimated that during 90 of these capacity days, the demand averaged 17 patients more than capacity and even went as high as 20 patients more on some days. The hospital has an additional 20 beds available for rent for the year ending June 30, 1974.

required

1. Calculate the **minimum** number of patient days required for the Pediatrics Department to break even for the year ending June 30, 1974, if the additional 20 beds are not rented. Patient demand is unknown, but assume that revenue per patient day, cost per patient day, cost per bed, and employee salary rates will remain the same as for the year ended June 30, 1973. Present calculations in good form.
2. Assuming for purposes of this problem that patient demand, revenue per patient day, cost per patient day, cost per bed, and employee salary rates for the year ending June 30, 1974 remain the same as for the year ended June 30, 1973, should the Pediatrics Department rent the additional 20 beds? Show the annual gain or loss from the additional beds. Present calculations in good form.

3-27 *Review of Chapters 2 and 3* For each of the following independent cases, find the unknowns, designated by letters.

	CASE 1	CASE 2	CASE 3
Sales	$100,000	$ *M*	$100,000
Direct material used	29,000	55,000	40,000
Direct labor	10,000	25,000	15,000
Variable selling and administrative expenses	16,000	70,000	*T*
Fixed manufacturing overhead	30,000	*Q*	20,000
Fixed selling and administrative expenses	9,000	*R*	10,000
Gross profit	*A*	*P*	20,000
Finished-goods inventory, 1/1	-0-	-0-	5,000
Finished-goods inventory, 12/31	-0-	-0-	5,000
Contribution margin (dollars)	*E*	40,000	*V*
Direct-material inventory, 1/1	1,000	*N*	50,000
Direct-material inventory, 12/31	10,000	15,000	*W*
Variable manufacturing overhead	*C*	10,000	*X*

	CASE 1	CASE 2	CASE 3
Work in process, 1/1	-0-	-0-	9,000
Work in process, 12/31	-0-	-0-	9,000
Purchases of direct material	*D*	60,000	10,000
Breakeven point (in dollars)	*F*	*S*	*Y*
Cost of goods manufactured	*B*	110,000	*U*
Net income (loss)	1,000	5,000	(5,000)

3-28 *Review of Chapters 2 and 3* The Cook Co. makes deluxe kitchen cabinets to special order. The controller has given you, his newly hired assistant, the task of constructing a so-called contribution income statement for the year ended December 31, 19_5. You are troubled because all the data produced by the routine accounting system do not distinguish between variable and fixed costs.

After laboring with statistical regressions you have identified various cost behavior patterns to your satisfaction. You have determined a breakeven point of $550,000; your computations were relatively easy because Cook's policy is not to carry any inventories. Instead, the company finishes pending orders sometime in December and gives all employees vacations that end in early January.

The traditional income statement included a gross profit of $70,000, sales of $500,000, direct labor of $140,000, and direct material used of $210,000.

The contribution margin was $100,000 and the variable manufacturing overhead was $30,000.

required

You need not work these in sequence:

1. Fixed manufacturing overhead
2. Variable selling and administrative expenses
3. Fixed selling and administrative expenses

Job-Order Accounting: An Illustration of Systems Design

4

This chapter examines a general approach to accounting for costs in a multiple-purpose accounting system. Two major cost objectives are discussed: departments and units of product. The former illustrates the control purpose of the system; the latter illustrates the product-costing purpose.

Here we must dwell heavily on techniques, because they are an essential part of the accounting function. Equally important, there is an opportunity to become familiar with many terms and fundamental ledger relationships that will aid visualization and comprehension of the key subjects covered in Chapters 5 through 11.

If you have never worked in a factory, you will need to study this chapter and its appendix with care. The chapter was written to be understood by the student with little business background. If you have had some business experience, you will probably be able to skip the appendix to this chapter. If you want a more complete study of the bookkeeping aspects of cost accounting, refer to Chapter 20 and the appendix to Chapter 21.

In any event, you should study the section on overhead accounting very carefully.

job-order approach to costing products

product-costing and control purposes

Ultimately, all costs are accumulated to facilitate someone's decisions. But all these decisions cannot be foreseen, so systems are designed to fulfill predetermined general desires that are commonplace among managers. **We will frequently distinguish between the *product-costing* purpose of a system and all other purposes. For convenience, we will sometimes refer to all other purposes as *planning and control purposes, budgetary-control purposes* or, for brevity, as the *control purpose.***

Aside from meeting the obvious external reporting demands for inventory valuation and income determination, managers want product costs for guiding their decisions regarding pricing and product strategies. In addition, managers want departmental costs (or costs of other components of the organization) for judging the performance of their subordinates and the subunits of the organization as economic investments.

Management accounting systems fulfill these general planning and control purposes by choosing *organizational subunits* as cost objectives. The aim is to compile costs by responsibility or accountability center. For example, costs are often routinely traced to a *cost center,* the smallest segment of activity or area of responsibility for which costs are accumulated. Typically, cost centers are departments, but in some instances a department may contain several cost centers. For example, although a machining department may be under one foreman, it may contain various groups of machines, such as lathes, punch presses, and milling machines. Each group of machines is sometimes regarded as a separate cost center with its own assistant foreman.

Another major cost objective is product costing for purposes of inventory valuation and income determination. **Therefore, the system must trace costs to these two major cost objectives: departments and products. This tracing is frequently accomplished in two steps: (1) *accumulation* of costs by departments and (2) *application* of the department costs to the physical units (or other measures of output) that pass through the departments. This second step is sometimes called cost *absorption* rather than cost *application.***

job and process costing: a matter of averaging

The two polar extremes of product costing are usually labeled as *job-order costing* and *process costing. Job-order* (or *job-cost* or *production-order*) accounting methods are used by companies whose products are readily identified by individual units or batches, each of which receives varying degrees of attention and skill. Industries that commonly use job-order methods include construction, printing, aircraft, furniture, and machinery.

Although a manufacturing situation is illustrated in this chapter, the job-costing approach is used in nonmanufacturing organizations too. Examples include auto repair, auditing and consulting engagements, hospital cases, social-welfare cases, and research projects.[1]

Process costing is most often found in such industries as chemicals, oil, textiles, plastics, paints, flour, canneries, rubber, lumber, food processing, glass, mining, cement, and meat packing. In these there is mass production of like units, which usually pass in continuous fashion through a series of uniform production steps called *operations* or *processes.* This is in contrast to the production of tailor-made or unique goods, such as special-purpose machinery or printing.

Where manufacturing is conducted by continuous operations, costs are accumulated by departments (sometimes also called *operations* or *processes*). The center of attention is the total department costs for a given time period in relation to the units processed. Accumulated department costs are divided by quantities produced during a given period in order to get broad, average unit costs. Then unit costs are multiplied by units transferred to obtain total costs applied to those units. These details of *process costing* are discussed in Chapter 18, *which may be studied immediately after Chapter 4, if preferred.*

The process-costing approach is used in nonmanufacturing too. Examples include check clearing in banks, mail sorting in post offices, food preparation in fast-food outlets, and premium handling in insurance companies. In practice, there are often no clear lines between job-order and process costing. Instead, many hybrid methods are found.

The distinction between the job-cost and the process-cost methods centers largely around how product costing is accomplished. Unlike process costing, which deals with broad averages and great masses of like units, the essential feature of the job-cost method is the attempt to apply costs to specific jobs, which may consist of either a single physical unit (such as a custom sofa) or a few like units (such as a dozen tables) in a distinct batch or job lot.

The most important point is that product costing under both cost methods is an *averaging* process. The unit cost used for inventory purposes is the result of taking some accumulated cost and dividing it by some measure of production. The basic distinction between job-order costing and process costing is the size of the denominator: in job-order costing, it is small (for example, one painting, 100 advertising circulars, or one special packaging machine); but in process costing, it is large (for example, thousands of pounds, gallons, or board feet).

[1] In nonprofit organizations the "job order" or class of services is often called a *program,* an identifiable segment of activities that often result in outputs in the form of services rather than goods. Examples are an alcoholic rehabilitation program, a drug-addict rehabilitation program, a safety program, and so on. Often various departments work on a multitude of programs, so the cost accounting challenge is to apply intelligently the various departmental costs to the various programs. Then more knowledgeable management decisions can be made regarding how to allocate limited resources among competing programs.

The evaluation of nonprofit programs entails special difficulties. The problem of cost measurement is similar to that in commercial enterprises. But there are only scattered messages from the marketplace to help managers estimate benefits, particularly for such activities as saving lives, curing the ill, and educating the handicapped. Because market prices are seldom available, indirect measurements of value are employed.

Again one must distinguish between costs for control and product costs. Whether a process-cost or a job-cost approach is used, costs must be accumulated by cost centers or departments for *control* purposes because control is also the responsibility of one or more managers.

source documents The basic document used by a job-order system to accumulate *product costs* is called the *job-order* or *job-cost sheet*. The file of uncompleted job orders makes up the subsidiary ledger for Work-in-Process Control the major product-costing account. Exhibit 4-1 illustrates a job-cost sheet.

Job shops usually have several jobs passing through the plant simultaneously. Each job typically requires different kinds of materials and department effort. Thus, jobs may have different routings, different operations, and different times required for completion. *Stores requisitions* (Exhibit 4-2) are used to charge job-cost sheets for direct materials used. *Work tickets* (Exhibit 4-3) are used to charge jobs for direct labor used. This work ticket (sometimes called *time ticket* or *time card*) indicates the time spent on a specific job. An employee who is paid an hourly wage and who operates a lathe will have one *clock card* (Exhibit 4-4), which is used as a basis for determining his individual earnings; but he will also fill out or punch several *work tickets* each day as he starts and stops work on particular jobs or operations. Many auto mechanics must account for their time in a similar way. (Of course, all the illustrated source documents might be in the form of punched cards to facilitate data processing.)

responsibility and control The department responsibility for usage of direct materials and direct labor is clearly drawn. Copies of direct-material requisitions and direct-labor work tickets are used for two purposes. One copy is used to post to job-cost sheets; another copy is used for fixing responsibility by departments. The department heads are usually kept informed of their direct-material and direct-labor performance by daily or weekly classified summaries of requisitions and work tickets charged to their departments.

The job-cost sheets also serve a control function. Comparisons are often made between predictions of job costs and the costs finally applied to the job. Deviations are investigated so that their underlying causes may be discovered.

illustration of job-order accounting

Because each job order often contains different materials and gets a different routing through departments, the time, costs, and attention devoted by departments to any given job may vary considerably. It is desirable, therefore, to keep

EXHIBIT 4-1

JOB-COST SHEET

SAMPLE COMPANY Job Order No.__________

For stock __________ Customer______________________________

Product __________ Date started__________ Date completed__________

Department A							
Direct Material			Direct Labor			Overhead	
Date	Reference	Amount	Date	Reference	Amount	Date	Amount
	(stores requisition number)			(work ticket number)		(based on predetermined overhead rate)	

Department B							
Direct Material			Direct Labor			Overhead	
Date	Reference	Amount	Date	Reference	Amount	Date	Amount

Summary of Costs

	Dept. A	Dept. B	Total
Direct material	xx	xx	xxx
Direct labor	xx	xx	xxx
Factory overhead applied	xx	xx	xxx
Total	xxx	xxx	xxx

a separate account for inventory purposes and another account, or other accounts, for department responsibility purposes. In practice, a Work-in-Process account, supported by a subsidiary ledger of individual job orders, is widely used for product-costing purposes. However, practice differs greatly as to the general-ledger accumulation of costs for department responsibility purposes.

EXHIBIT 4-2

STORES REQUISITION

Job No. 41
Department B
Debit Account WORK IN PROCESS
Authorized by GL

Date 2/22

Description	Quantity	Unit Cost	Amount
AF 462 BRACKETS	80	$2.50	$ 200.00

Consider a specific example. Assume that a factory has two departments and uses the job-cost system. Department A is the machining department; Department B is the assembly department. Exhibit 4-5 shows T-account relationships and relationships between the general and subsidiary ledgers. Typical general-journal entries for a job-cost system follow. **(Please be sure to trace each entry, step by step, to the accounts in Exhibit 4-5.)** Special points are included in the explanation for each entry.

EXHIBIT 4-3

WORK TICKET

Employee No. 741	Date 2/22	Job No. 41
Operation drill	Account Work in Process	Dept. A
Stop 4:45 P.M.	Rate $6.00	Pieces: Worked 15
		Rejected —
Start 4:00 P.M.	Amount $4.50	Completed 15

EXHIBIT 4-4

CLOCK CARD

Name FRANK YOUNG Employee Number 741

Department A Week ending 2/26

Date	AM In	AM Out	PM In	PM Out	Excess Hours In	Excess Hours Out	Total Hours
2/22	7:58	12:01	1:00	5:01			8
2/23	7:55	12:00	1:00	5:02			8
2/24	8:00	12:02	12:58	5:00	6:00	9:00	11
2/25	7:58	12:02	12:59	5:03			8
2/26	7:56	12:01	12:59	5:01			8

Regular Time 43 hrs. @ $6.00 $258.00

Overtime Premium 3 hrs. @ $3.00 $ 9.00

Gross Earnings $267.00

1. Stores control*	60,000	
Accounts (or vouchers) payable		60,000
To record purchases of materials and supplies.		

* The word "control," as used in journal entries and general-ledger accounts, has a narrow bookkeeping meaning. As contrasted with "control" in the management sense, "control" here means that the control account in question is supported by an underlying subsidiary ledger. To illustrate: In financial accounting, Accounts Receivable-Control is supported by a subsidiary customers' ledger, with one account for each customer. The same meaning applies to the "Stores" account here.

All purchases of materials and supplies are charged to Stores as purchased because the storekeeper is accountable for them. The subsidiary records for Stores Control would be perpetual-inventory records called *stores cards.* As a minimum, these cards would contain quantity columns for receipts, issues, and balance. Exhibit 4-6 is an illustration of a stores card.

2. Work-in-process control	48,000	
Factory department overhead control (supplies)	4,000	
Stores control		52,000
To record materials and supplies issued.		

Responsibility is fixed by using *stores requisitions* (sometimes called *material requisitions*) as a basis for charging departments. A stores requisition was shown in Exhibit 4-2.

Direct materials are charged to job orders; indirect materials (supplies) are charged to individual department-overhead cost sheets, which form a subsidiary ledger for Factory Department Overhead Control. In job-cost accounting, a single Factory Department Overhead Control account may be kept in the general ledger. The detail of factory overhead is charged to departments and recorded in subsidiary department-overhead ledgers (department-overhead cost sheets). (See Exhibit 4-7.) In turn, the overhead is applied to jobs, as will be described later.

3. Work-in-process control (direct labor)	39,000	
Factory department overhead control (indirect labor)	5,000	
Accrued payroll		44,000
To record incurrence of factory payroll costs.		

Payroll withholdings from employees are ignored in this example. Responsibility is fixed by using work tickets (Exhibit 4-3) or individual time summaries as a basis for tracing direct labor to jobs and direct and indirect labor to departments. Clock cards (Exhibit 4-4) are widely used as attendance records and as the basis for computation of payroll.

4. Accrued payroll	44,000	
Cash		44,000
To record payment of payroll.		

Actual payments and entries may be made weekly, even though entry 3 is made monthly. The reason for this is that paydays seldom coincide with the conventional accounting period (the month) for which costs are accumulated in the general ledger.[2] Thus, the Accrued Payroll account appears as follows:

ACCRUED PAYROLL

Payments	Gross Earnings
	Balance represents wages earned but unpaid.

5. Factory department overhead control	18,000	
Accounts payable		11,000
Unexpired insurance		1,000
Allowance for depreciation—Equipment		6,000
To record incurrence of other factory-overhead costs:		

Utilities, repairs, etc.	$11,000
Depreciation	6,000
Insurance	1,000
	$18,000

[2] For a detailed treatment of the mechanics of payroll accounting, see Chapter 20, which may be studied now if desired without losing continuity.

EXHIBIT 4-5

JOB-COST SYSTEM, DIAGRAM OF LEDGER RELATIONSHIPS

(Circled numbers refer to journal entries described more thoroughly in text.)

① Purchases

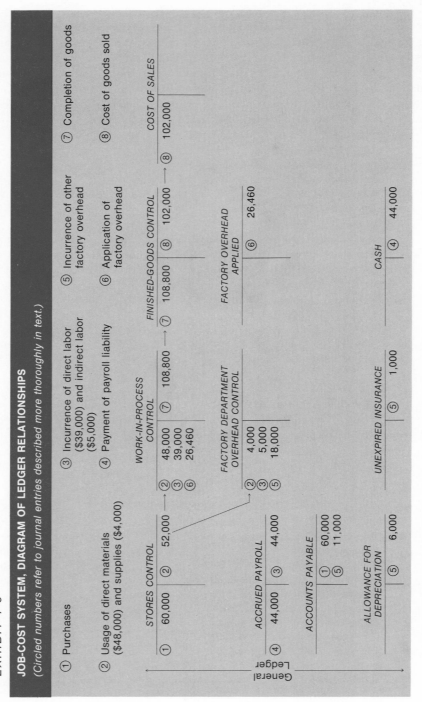

② Usage of direct materials ($48,000) and supplies ($4,000)

③ Incurrence of direct labor ($39,000) and indirect labor ($5,000)

④ Payment of payroll liability

⑤ Incurrence of other factory overhead

⑥ Application of factory overhead

⑦ Completion of goods

⑧ Cost of goods sold

General Ledger

STORES CONTROL

①	60,000	②	52,000 →

WORK-IN-PROCESS CONTROL

②	48,000	⑦	108,800 →
③	39,000		
⑥	26,460		

FINISHED-GOODS CONTROL

⑦	108,800	⑧	102,000 →

COST OF SALES

⑧	102,000		

FACTORY DEPARTMENT OVERHEAD CONTROL

②	4,000		
③	5,000		
⑤	18,000		

FACTORY OVERHEAD APPLIED

		⑥	26,460

ACCRUED PAYROLL

④	44,000	③	44,000

ACCOUNTS PAYABLE

		①	60,000
		⑤	11,000

ALLOWANCE FOR DEPRECIATION

		⑤	6,000

UNEXPIRED INSURANCE

		⑤	1,000

CASH

		④	44,000

EXHIBIT 4-5 (Cont.)

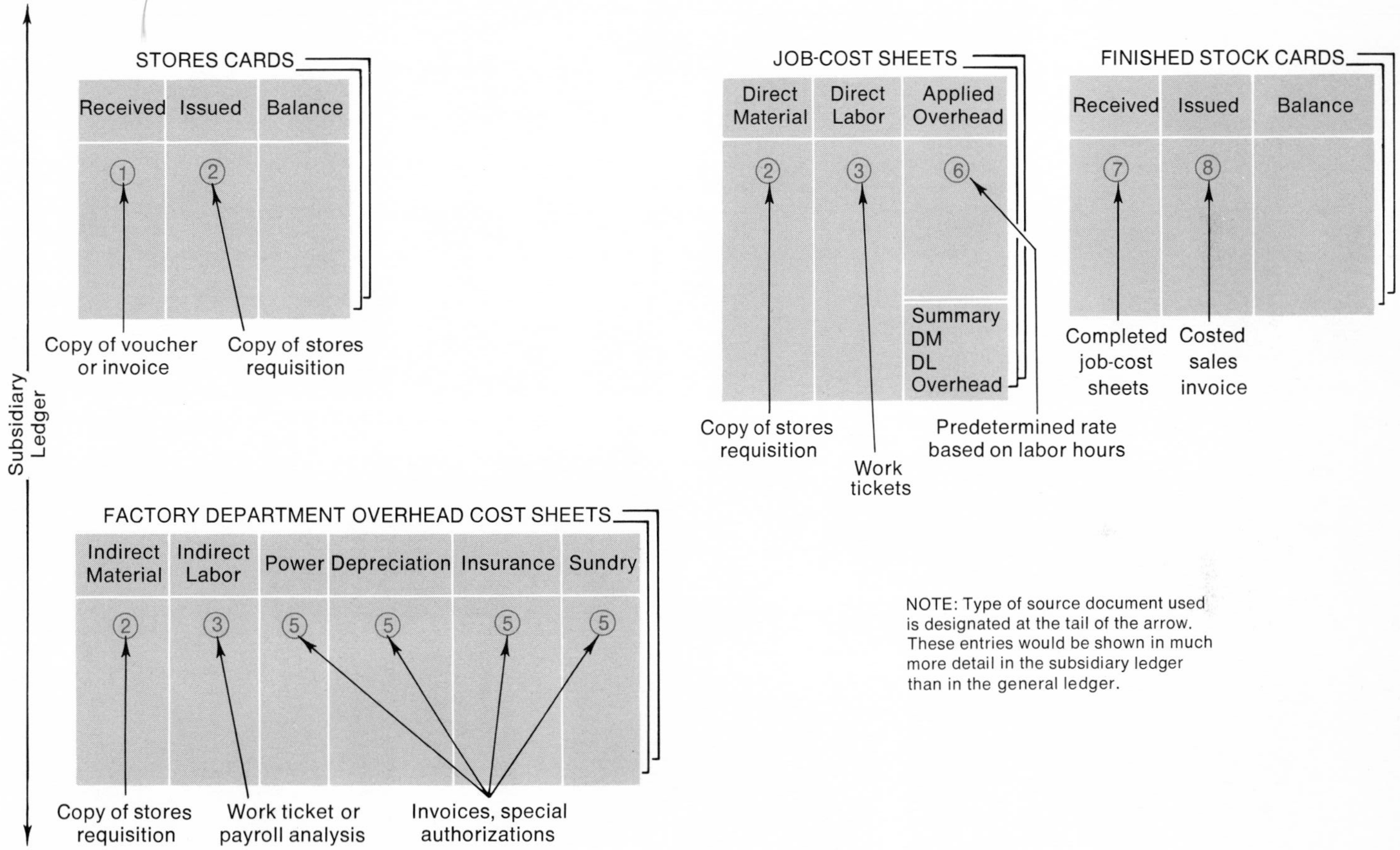

NOTE: Type of source document used is designated at the tail of the arrow. These entries would be shown in much more detail in the subsidiary ledger than in the general ledger.

EXHIBIT 4-6

STORES CARD

Item AF 462 Brackets

		Received			Issued			Balance		
Date	Reference	Quantity	Unit Cost	Total Cost	Quantity	Unit Cost	Total Cost	Quantity	Unit Cost	Total Cost
2/10	V 1014	300	2.50	750				300	2.50	750
2/22	R41				80	2.50	200	220	2.50	550

The detail of these costs is distributed to the appropriate columns of the individual department-overhead cost sheets that make up the subsidiary ledger for Factory Department Overhead Control. The basic documents for these distributions may be vouchers, invoices, or special memos from the responsible accounting officer.

6. Work-in-process control	26,460	
Factory overhead applied		26,460
To record application of factory overhead to job orders.		

EXHIBIT 4-7

FACTORY DEPARTMENT OVERHEAD COST SHEET

Date	Source Document	Lubricants	Other Supplies	Material Handling	Idle Time	Overtime Premium	Other Labor	Utilities	Insurance	Depr.
	Requisitions	xx	xx							
	Labor recap.			xx	xx	xx	xx			
	Invoices							xx		
	Special memos from chief accountant on accruals, pre-payments, etc.							xx	xx	xx

The predetermined overhead rate used here is $2.70 per direct-labor hour. Thus, the amount of overhead applied to a particular job is dependent on the amount of direct-labor hours used on that job. It is assumed here that 9,800 direct-labor hours were used for all jobs, resulting in a total overhead application of $26,460. This entry is explained further in a subsequent section of this chapter.

7. Finished-goods control	108,800	
Work-in-process control		108,800
To record completion of Job Nos. 101–108.		

As job orders are completed, the job-cost sheets are totaled. Some companies use the completed job-cost sheets as their subsidiary ledger for finished goods. Other companies use separate finished-stock cards to form a subsidiary ledger.

8. Cost of sales	102,000	
Finished-goods control		102,000
To record cost of goods sold.		

The eight summary entries are usually made monthly. The biggest share of clerical time is devoted to compiling the day-to-day details that are recorded in subsidiary ledgers. There is a mass of daily detail that finds its way to subsidiary ledgers, in contrast to the summaries of the detail that are posted monthly to the general ledger. Incidentally, these "ledgers" are increasingly being stored on a computer rather than on loose-leaf pages.

At this point please pause and reexamine this entire illustration, step by step.

the conceptual approach to accounting for prime costs

The general-ledger treatment of prime costs—direct materials and direct labor—differs extensively among companies. The method illustrated in our example is probably the easiest to learn because it uses the fewest journal entries and accounts. However, the conceptual treatment ought to be examined so that the short-cut treatment may be viewed as a less costly expedient rather than as the best theoretical design. See Exhibit 4-8 for a comparison of the conceptual notion with a treatment common in practice.

Exhibit 4-8 shows that direct materials and direct labor conceptually are (a) charged to departments and (b) then applied to jobs. But note that the department account becomes a clearing account for direct materials and direct labor. For example, the debit to Department Responsibility Cost Control in 2(a) is immediately offset by the credit in 2(b). A common practical treatment is to charge these items directly to the Work-in-Process account and not use the Department Responsibility account for either direct materials or direct labor.

EXHIBIT 4-8

JOURNAL ENTRIES FOR DIRECT MATERIALS AND DIRECT LABOR—JOB-ORDER SYSTEM

CONCEPTUAL TREATMENT			*PRACTICAL TREATMENT*		
Direct materials and direct labor are (a) charged to the department and (b) applied to product.			Direct materials and direct labor are charged directly to product. Accounting records are kept outside the general ledger to fix department responsibility for material and labor usage. Analysis sheets that summarize material usage and labor usage by departments are used for performance reports. These reports may be made weekly, daily, or sometimes even hourly. Furthermore, the direct-material usage and labor usage may be reported separately.		
DIRECT-MATERIAL USAGE					
2(a). Department-responsibility cost control	xx		2. Work-in-process control	xx	
Stores control		xx	Stores control		xx
2(b). Work-in-process control	xx				
Department-responsibility cost control		xx			
DIRECT-LABOR USAGE					
3(a). Department-responsibility cost control	xx		3. Work-in-process control	xx	
Accrued payroll		xx	Accrued payroll		xx
3(b). Work-in-process control	xx				
Department-responsibility cost control		xx			

This simplifies the general ledger and, as we shall see, highlights the intricate problem of overhead accounting. Make no mistake—accounting records are kept of department responsibility for direct materials and direct labor, but they are material- and labor-usage summaries and reports, which are maintained apart from the general ledger itself.

These reports, plus the report on department-overhead costs, may easily have different timing. Depending on their relative importance, direct-material usage may be reported daily; direct-labor usage, weekly; and department-overhead incurrence, monthly. In such cases, there is little need for keeping a subsidiary multicolumn department-cost sheet for direct-material, direct-labor, and overhead items. **Instead, the department cost sheet is usually kept only for overhead items, whereas direct-material-usage and direct-labor-usage reports are automatically produced in summaries of requisitions and work tickets. Thus, source documents for direct materials and direct labor are used directly as a basis for control without necessarily having them formally summarized by department in either the subsidiary ledgers or the general ledger.**

limitations of general ledger

We cannot overemphasize the fact that many appropriate accumulations of costs for planning and control are too broad and too deep to be fitted into a general ledger. The scope of management accounting extends far beyond ledger bookkeeping. Because most general ledgers are traditionally oriented toward product costing, especially in accounting for materials and labor, be on guard to avoid being preoccupied with the product-costing purpose while losing sight of the major purpose of management accounting: that of aiding decisions for planning and control. The position here is that costing for control is a day-to-day task that is primarily accomplished by source documents and daily or weekly summaries. Although the control devices may be fully integrated into the general ledger, the resulting complexities are more cumbersome and costly than the benefits derived.

overhead application

tracing overhead to product

Entry 6 (see page 84) in our master illustration used a predetermined overhead rate to apply factory overhead to product. Direct materials and direct labor may be traced to physical units worked on through requisitions and work tickets. But, by its very nature, factory overhead cannot be specifically identified with physical units. Yet the making of goods would be impossible without the incurrence of such overhead costs as depreciation, material handling, janitorial services, repairs, property taxes, heat, light, and so on.

Overhead is applied to products because of management's desire for a close approximation of costs of different products. If such product costs are to be helpful to management for product pricing, income determination, and inventory valuation, they must be timely as well as accurate. If the purpose were to apply all actual overhead to actual production for the year, the most accurate application of overhead could be made only at the end of the year, after actual results were determined. However, this would be too late. Managers want product-cost information throughout the year. Therefore, overhead application rates are computed in advance of production.

Accountants have chosen an averaging process for identifying overhead with product. Overhead items are often classified into variable and fixed categories. The behavior of individual overhead items is forecast for the forthcoming year. The total forecast overhead is related to some common denominator or base, such as expected total machine-hours, direct-labor hours, or direct-labor dollars for the ensuing year. A predetermined overhead rate is obtained by dividing the expected overhead costs by the chosen base. This rate is used to apply overhead to specific jobs as they are manufactured.

To illustrate, a company may budget its factory overhead for a forthcoming year as shown in Exhibit 4-9. Assume that the forecast is based on a

EXHIBIT 4-9

BUDGET OF FACTORY OVERHEAD FOR THE YEAR ENDING 19_1

	DEPARTMENT A	DEPARTMENT B	TOTAL
Overhead expected:			
Variable items:			
Lubricants	$ 5,000	$ 3,000	$ 8,000
Other supplies	19,000	21,000	40,000
Material handling[a]	9,000	12,000	21,000
Idle time[b]	2,000	2,000	4,000
Overtime premium	3,000	5,000	8,000
Other labor	30,000	35,000	65,000
Utilities and other variable overhead	34,000	24,000	58,000
Total variable overhead	$102,000	$102,000	$204,000
Fixed items:			
Insurance	$ 2,000	$ 3,000	$ 5,000
Depreciation	30,000	35,000	65,000
Supervision	16,000	15,000	31,000
Other fixed overhead	12,000	7,000	19,000
Total fixed overhead	$ 60,000	$ 60,000	$120,000
Total budgeted overhead	$162,000	$162,000	$324,000
Divided by:			
Expected direct-labor hours	60,000	60,000	120,000
Predetermined overhead rate per hour	$ 2.70	$ 2.70	$ 2.70

[a] Labor costs of moving materials and supplies.
[b] Labor costs incurred for employee time not devoted to production. Causes include equipment failure, poor scheduling, material shortages, and the like.

volume of activity expressed in direct-labor hours. Then, if detailed forecasts result in a prediction of total overhead of $324,000 for the forthcoming year at an anticipated 120,000-direct-labor-hour level of activity, the predetermined overhead rate would be:

$$\frac{\text{Total budgeted overhead}}{\text{Total budgeted volume expressed in direct labor hours}} = \frac{\$324{,}000}{120{,}000}$$
$$= \$2.70 \text{ per hour}$$

(This example assumes that the same overhead rate is appropriate for Departments A and B. This is an oversimplification. There are usually different overhead rates for different departments. These are illustrated and explained in Chapter 15, which can be studied now if desired.)

The $2.70 rate would be used for costing job orders. For example, during 19_1, a job-cost sheet for Job 323 included the following information:

Direct-material cost	\$100
Direct-labor cost	\$280
Direct-labor hours	40

The overhead to be applied to Job 323 would be: 40 hours times \$2.70, or \$108. The total cost of Job 323 would be: \$100 plus \$280 plus \$108, or \$488.

If actual results for the year conform to the prediction of the \$324,000 overhead cost and the 120,000-direct-labor-hour level of activity, total overhead costs will have been exactly applied to products worked on during the year. The basic idea of this approach is to use an annual average overhead cost per hour without changing this annual overhead rate in costing jobs from day to day and from month to month. The resultant product costs are more properly called *normal costs* rather than *actual costs,* because they include an average or normalized chunk of overhead.

annualized rates

Should overhead rates be set on the basis of weekly, or monthly, or yearly activity? There are two major conditions that have prompted the use of an annualized basis for predetermined rates:

1. To overcome volatility in computed unit costs that would result because of fluctuations in the volume of activity (the denominator reason) from month to month. This is the dominant reason.

2. To overcome the volatility in computed unit costs that would result because of seasonal, calendar, and other peculiar variations in the total level of overhead costs (the numerator reason) incurred each month.

THE DENOMINATOR REASON: FLUCTUATIONS IN MONTHLY ACTIVITY Some overhead costs are variable (for example, supplies and indirect labor), whereas others are fixed (for example, property taxes, rent, and depreciation). If production fluctuates from month to month, total variable overhead cost incurrence should change in close proportion to variations in production, whereas total fixed overhead will remain unchanged. This means that overhead rates based on monthly activity may differ greatly from month to month *solely because of fluctuations in the volume of activity over which fixed overhead is spread.*

Exhibit 4-10 gives an example of a company that gears production of its single product to a highly seasonal sales pattern. Few people support the contention that an identical product should be inventoried with an \$11.00 or \$51.00 overhead rate at the end of July or August and only a \$2.25 or \$2.00 overhead rate at the end of March or April. These different overhead rates are not representative of typical, normal production conditions. Management has committed itself to a specific level of fixed costs in the light of foreseeable needs far beyond a mere thirty days. Thus, where production fluctuates, monthly overhead rates may be volatile. An average, annualized rate based on the relationship of total annual overhead to total annual activity is more representative of typical relationships between total costs and volume than a monthly rate.

EXHIBIT 4-10

MONTHLY VERSUS ANNUAL OVERHEAD RATES

MONTH	TOTAL FACTORY OVERHEAD BUDGETED ($50,000 per month plus $1 per hour)	DIRECT-LABOR HOURS	MONTHLY RATE PER HOUR*	ANNUAL RATE PER HOUR†
January	$ 70,000	20,000	$ 3.50	$3.715
February	80,000	30,000	2.67	3.715
March	90,000	40,000	2.25	3.715
April	100,000	50,000	2.00	3.715
May	65,000	15,000	4.33	3.715
June	60,000	10,000	6.00	3.715
July	55,000	5,000	11.00	3.715
August	51,000	1,000	51.00	3.715
September	55,000	5,000	11.00	3.715
October	60,000	10,000	6.00	3.715
November	65,000	15,000	4.33	3.715
December	70,000	20,000	3.50	3.715
	$821,000	221,000	—	3.715

* Note that the fluctuation here is based solely on the presence of fixed overhead. By definition, variable overhead rates would be $1.00 regardless of whether monthly or annual rates were used.

† Can be subdivided as follows:

$$\text{Variable-overhead portion} = \frac{\$821{,}000 - (\$50{,}000 \times 12)}{221{,}000} = \$1.000$$

$$\text{Fixed-overhead portion} = \frac{\$600{,}000}{221{,}000} = 2.715$$

$$\text{Combined-overhead rate} = \$3.715$$

THE NUMERATOR REASON: PECULIARITIES OF SPECIFIC OVERHEAD ITEMS Fluctuation in monthly volume rather than fluctuation in monthly costs incurred is the dominant reason for using an annualized overhead rate. Still, certain costs are incurred in different amounts at various times of the year. If a month's costs alone were considered, the heating cost, for example, would be charged only to winter production and the air-conditioning cost only to summer production.

Typical examples of erratic behavior include repairs, maintenance, and certain supplies requisitioned in one month that will last two or more months. These items may be charged to a department on the basis of monthly repair orders or requisitions. Yet the benefits of such charges may easily extend over a number of months' production. It would be illogical to load any single month with costs that are caused by several months' operations.

The calendar itself has an unbusinesslike design; some months have twenty workdays while others have twenty-two or more. Is it sensible to say that a product made in February should bear a greater share of overhead like depreciation and property taxes than it would if it were produced in March?

Other erratic items that distort monthly overhead rates are vacation and holiday pay, professional fees, subscriptions that may fall due in one month, extra costs of learning, idle time connected with the installation of a new machine or product line, and the employer's share of Social Security taxes—which is lightest late in the year, after employee wages exceed the taxable maximum.

All the costs and peculiarities mentioned above are collected in the annual-overhead pool along with the kinds of overhead that do have uniform behavior patterns (for example, many supplies and indirect labor). In other words, the accountant throws up his hands and says, "We have to start somewhere, so let's pool the year's overhead and develop an annual overhead rate regardless of month-to-month peculiarities of specific overhead costs." **Such an approach provides a *normal* product cost that is based on an annual average instead of a so-called "actual" product cost that is affected by month-to-month fluctuations in production volume and by erratic or seasonal behavior of many overhead costs.** Such a normal cost is often used as a point of departure for setting and appraising product selling prices.

ledger procedure for overhead

Let us see how the notions above affect general-ledger procedure. For some reason, students have great trouble in understanding this phase of product costing; therefore, **special study of this section is warranted.**

As overhead costs are incurred by departments from month to month, these "actual" costs are charged in detail to department-overhead cost sheets (the subsidiary ledger) and in summary to Factory Department Overhead Control. These costs are accumulated weekly or monthly without regard to how factory overhead is applied to specific jobs. This ledger procedure serves the purpose of managerial control of overhead. These actual costs are compared with budgeted amounts in performance reports.

Because a predetermined overhead rate (at $2.70 per direct-labor hour) is an average used to apply costs to products, the daily, weekly, or monthly costing of *inventory* is independent of the actual incurrence of overhead costs by *departments.* For this reason, at any given time during the year, the balance in Factory Department Overhead Control is unlikely to coincide with the amount applied to product. Thus, managerial control can be exercised by comparing, say, actual lubricants used with the budget for lubricants. The actual lubricants used are accumulated on the department-overhead cost sheet. For product costing, all overhead items are pooled together, a predetermined overhead rate is computed, and this average rate is used on job orders for costing Work in Process. The use of an annual average results in inventories bearing a normalized share of factory overhead.

Most accountants stress this peculiarity of overhead accounting by confining Factory Department Overhead Control to the accumulation of "actual" overhead charges incurred and by setting up the credit side in a separate account called *Factory Overhead Applied* (sometimes called Factory Overhead *Absorbed*), much as Allowance for Depreciation is the separate credit side of, say, a Machinery account. To illustrate:

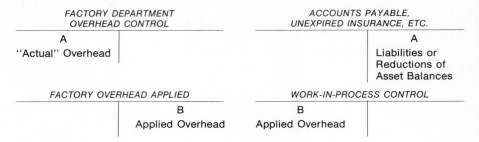

FACTORY DEPARTMENT OVERHEAD CONTROL	
A "Actual" Overhead	

ACCOUNTS PAYABLE, UNEXPIRED INSURANCE, ETC.	
	A Liabilities or Reductions of Asset Balances

FACTORY OVERHEAD APPLIED	
	B Applied Overhead

WORK-IN-PROCESS CONTROL	
B Applied Overhead	

underapplied or overapplied overhead

The workings of the ledger accounts for overhead may be more clearly understood if we pursue our master illustration. Let us assume that the month's entries are for January, the first month of the company's year. Postings would appear as follows:

FACTORY DEPARTMENT OVERHEAD CONTROL		
Jan. 31(2)	4,000	
Jan. 31(3)	5,000	
Jan. 31(5)	18,000	
Jan. 31 Balance	27,000	

FACTORY OVERHEAD APPLIED		
	Jan. 31(6)	26,460

The monthly debits to Factory Department Overhead will never equal the monthly credits to Factory Overhead Applied except by coincidence. In January, for example, there is a $540 difference between the two balances. This $540 amount is commonly referred to as *underapplied* (or *underabsorbed*) *overhead.* **Overhead is underapplied when the applied balance is less than the incurred (actual) balance; it is overapplied when the applied balance exceeds the incurred balance.**

Although the month-end balances may not coincide, the final year-end balances should be nearly equal. Experienced budgetary accountants can predetermine rates with astounding accuracy (with 1 percent error). Of course, the accuracy of predetermined overhead rates depends largely on the skill of those who do the predicting and on the nature of the business. Assume that the year's overhead costs incurred are $326,000, while only $324,000 has been applied to product. The year-end balances are closed out against one another; any insignificant difference between the final balances is generally carried to Cost of

EXHIBIT 4-11

ANALYSIS FOR PRORATION OF UNDERAPPLIED OVERHEAD

		Ending Balance in Accounts					Correction for Underapplied Overhead	
		Overhead	%	Total Product Cost	%	Account		
Jobs worked on:	101 — 150						Based on Overhead Applied (first choice)	Based on Total Costs in Accounts (second choice)
Sold:	101 — 140	$275,400	85	$900,000	90	Cost of sales	$1,700	$1,800
Finished:	141 — 146	32,400	10	70,000	7	Finished goods	200	140
In process:	147 — 150	16,200	5	30,000	3	Work in process	100	60
		$324,000	100%	$1,000,000	100%		$2,000	$2,000

Sales as an adjustment of that figure. Several bookkeeping techniques may be used. One simple way is:

Cost of sales	2,000	
Factory overhead applied	324,000	
Factory department overhead control		326,000

To close and to charge underapplied overhead to Cost of Sales. If overhead is overapplied, the overapplication would be credited to Cost of Sales.

Conceptually, the disposition of underapplied or overapplied overhead should require correction of the costs of jobs worked on during the year. These jobs were costed by using a predetermined overhead rate instead of the actual overhead rate, which can be determined only at year-end. Ideally, a clerk would get all the job orders worked on during the year and would adjust their final costs. Thus, the most defensible way to convert job orders to "actual" costs would appear as in Exhibit 4-11.

Assume that the year-end analysis is as shown in Exhibit 4-11. Ideally, the $2,000 underapplied overhead should be spread over the three accounts that contain the job costs. This proration should theoretically be in proportion to the unadjusted overhead component in each account. The journal entry would appear as follows:

Cost of sales	1,700	
Finished goods	200	
Work in process	100	
Factory overhead applied	324,000	
Factory department overhead control		326,000
To close and to prorate underapplied overhead among the three relevant accounts.		

Some companies will prorate in proportion to total product costs. This method is theoretically valid only when the proportions of direct material, direct labor, and overhead costs are constant among jobs. To illustrate, if leather is used for making 100 purses (Job A) and imitation fine leather is used for making 100 identical purses (Job B), the respective total job costs will differ markedly because of the large difference in material costs; yet their overhead components are unlikely to differ, because the labor-hours on each job should be about the same. In this case, to adjust for underapplied overhead on the basis of total product costs would be misleading, because conceptually a different base is used for year-end adjustments from what was used for overhead application during the year. Despite these objections, many companies will prorate on the basis of total product costs because the increase in accuracy is not significant enough to warrant the additional effort. For example, examine the small difference in the results of the two methods as shown in Exhibit 4-11.

Despite the theoretical superiority of the foregoing kinds of adjustments, *adjusting Cost of Sales for all the under- or overapplied overhead is the most widely practiced treatment.* It is valid as long as final results are not misleading. Exhibit 4-11 shows that more refined calculations that result in proration may not affect final costs enough to be significant. However, if under- or overapplied overhead is large enough to indicate some significant error in the overhead rate, the under- or overapplied overhead should be spread over the three accounts that contain the jobs bearing the faulty rate.

interim financial statements

The closing process for under- and overapplied overhead ordinarily takes place only at the end of the year. But what happens from month to month when interim financial statements must be prepared?[3]

We have already seen that month-to-month balances in the incurred and applied accounts do not agree. Look at these two accounts again:

[3] For a thorough, provocative discussion of these problems, see David Green, Jr., "Towards a Theory of Interim Reports," *Journal of Accounting Research,* Vol. 2, No. 1, pp. 35–49. Also see Alfred Rappaport, "Towards a Theory of Interim Reports: A Modification and an Extension," *Journal of Accounting Research,* Vol. 4, No. 1, pp. 121–26.

FACTORY DEPARTMENT OVERHEAD CONTROL		
Jan.	$27,000	
Feb.	26,000	
Together	$53,000	

FACTORY OVERHEAD APPLIED		
	Jan.	$26,460
	Feb.	26,810
	Together	$53,270

Statements for January (not for the two months together) may be prepared on one of two basic options:

OPTION ONE

Partial Income Statement

Sales (assumed)		$150,000
Cost of sales (per account)	$102,000	
Add:		
Underapplied factory overhead*	540	
Adjusted cost of sales		102,540
Gross margin		$ 47,460

* Difference between January 31 balances in Factory Department Overhead Control and Factory Overhead Applied.

Balance Sheet

(Prepared on usual basis)

OPTION TWO

Partial Income Statement

Sales	$150,000
Cost of sales	102,000
Gross margin	$ 48,000

Balance Sheet

Assets			*Equities*	
Current assets:				
Cash	$ xx		Liabilities	$xx
Receivables	xx		Ownership equity	xx
Inventories	xx			
Underapplied overhead	540	$xx		
Other assets		xx		
Total		$xx	Total	$xx

Option One treats underapplied overhead as if it were immediately chargeable to the period. Option Two treats underapplied overhead as a cost that will benefit the rest of the year's production. Top-management preference would dictate which of the two options is to be used for reporting purposes. This author prefers Option Two for internal purposes because it allows Cost of Sales to be stated at average or representative amounts; it also recognizes the fact that overhead cost incurrence should not necessarily mean such cost should be immediately written off to expense. For example, a repair will benefit the entire year's production, not just one month's. Furthermore, the central idea of overhead application is the use of a predetermined annual average rate. There are bound to be random month-to-month under- or overapplications that should come near to offsetting one another by the end of the year. The most frequent causes of these month-to-month deviations are (a) operations at different levels of activity; and (b) the presence of seasonal costs, such as heating, that are averaged in with other overhead items in setting an annual overhead rate.

January and February results taken together show a net overapplied balance of $270. Option One's approach would deduct this amount from Cost of Sales on the income statement for the two months ending February 28, 19_1. Option Two's approach would show the $270 either as a deferred credit on the right-hand side of the balance sheet or as an offset to inventory.

There can be a variety of reasons and explanations for the existence of under- or overapplied overhead. This complex subject is discussed fully in Chapters 9 and 10. At this stage, the reader should concentrate on terminology and ledger relationships.

external interim reporting

For external reporting purposes, "planned" underapplied or overapplied overhead would be deferred and not charged or credited to interim income. Why? Because such amounts are expected to disappear by the end of the year via the use of averaging as costs are applied to product. However, "unplanned" or unanticipated under- or overapplied overhead should be reported "at the end of an interim period following the same procedures used at the end of a fiscal year."[4] This approach represents a compromise between Options One and Two because "unplanned" and "planned" under- or overapplied overhead are accounted for differently.

The whole area of external interim reporting has been receiving increasing attention, although there continues to be a wide range of generally accepted practice. Many costs that are regarded as period costs for annual reporting purposes might be accrued or deferred among interim periods because they can be systematically related to operations, activities, or time periods within the fiscal year. Examples are property taxes, vacation pay, and audit fees.

SUMMARY

The job-cost system described in this chapter illustrates how historical costs are compiled for evaluation of performance and for facilitating predictions of how various departments and managers will perform in forthcoming periods and of how various

[4] Accounting Principles Board Opinion No. 28, *Interim Financial Reporting,* Paragraph 14(d). Also see the latest pronouncements of the Financial Accounting Standards Board.

future jobs should be priced. Job-order costing is an expensive accounting system because of the detailed underlying recordkeeping required for each job. The number of departments and the number of overhead application rates utilized in this system depend on the perceived improvements in decisions in relation to the extra costs of more elaborate record keeping.

Scorekeeping for the purpose of planning and control consists largely of *accumulating* costs by departments; for the product-costing purpose, it consists largely of *applying* costs to products in order to obtain a representative indication of the relative costs of resources devoted to various physical units of product. As in most phases of accounting, the bulk of clerical time is spent on basic source documents and subsidiary ledgers rather than on the general ledger itself. However, the general-ledger relationships of job costing offer a bird's-eye view of an entire system.

There are two widely used approaches to assigning costs to manufactured goods: job-order costing and process costing. In practice, each company's approach is tailored to its needs and is usually some sort of hybrid. Job-order costing was discussed at length in this chapter. Chapter 18, which can be studied now if desired, discusses process costing and compares it with job-order costing.

Many companies apply overhead at predetermined rates. The resultant product cost consists of "actual" direct materials, "actual" direct labor, and overhead applied using "predetermined" rates. Thus, this total product cost should be called a *normal* cost rather than an *actual* cost. **Therefore, a given product-costing system can properly be called an *actual-cost* system (where no costs are predetermined) or a *normal-cost* system (where predetermined rates are used to apply overhead).** Within a given system, either a job-order-costing approach or a process-costing approach or some hybrid approach is tailored to needs.

Some thoughtful solving of homework at this stage will strengthen your understanding of basic relationships and terminology.

PROBLEM FOR SELF-STUDY

Restudy the illustration of job-order accounting in this chapter. Then try to solve one or two straightforward job-order problems such as Problems 4-8 and 4-11. Then try to solve the following problem, which requires consideration of most of this chapter's important points.

PROBLEM

You are asked to bring the following incomplete accounts of a plant in a foreign country up to date through January 31, 19_2. Also consider the data that appear after the T-accounts.

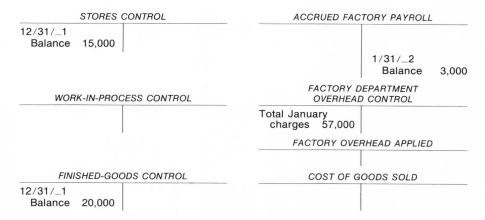

STORES CONTROL

12/31/_1 Balance 15,000	

ACCRUED FACTORY PAYROLL

	1/31/_2 Balance 3,000

WORK-IN-PROCESS CONTROL

FACTORY DEPARTMENT OVERHEAD CONTROL

Total January charges 57,000	

FACTORY OVERHEAD APPLIED

FINISHED-GOODS CONTROL

12/31/_1 Balance 20,000	

COST OF GOODS SOLD

Additional Information

1. The overhead is applied using a predetermined rate that is set every December by forecasting the following year's overhead and relating it to forecast direct-labor costs. The budget for 19_2 called for $400,000 of direct labor and $600,000 of factory overhead.
2. The only job unfinished on January 31, 19_2, was No. 419, on which total labor charges were $2,000 (1,000 direct-labor hours) and total direct-material charges were $8,000.
3. Total materials placed into production during January totaled $90,000.
4. Cost of goods completed during January was $180,000.
5. January 31 balances on stores cards totaled $20,000.
6. Finished-goods inventory as of January 31 was $15,000.
7. All factory workers earn the same rate of pay. Direct man-hours for January totaled 20,000. Indirect labor and supervision totaled $10,000.
8. The gross factory payroll paid on January paydays totaled $52,000. Ignore withholdings.
9. All "actual" factory overhead incurred during January has already been posted.

required

a. Materials purchased during January
b. Cost of goods sold during January
c. Direct-labor costs incurred during January
d. Overhead applied during January
e. Balance, Accrued Factory Payroll, Decmeber 31, 19_1
f. Balance, Work in Process, December 31, 19_1
g. Balance, Work in Process, January 31, 19_2
h. Overapplied or underapplied overhead for January

SOLUTION

a. Materials purchased: $90,000 + $20,000 − $15,000 = $95,000.
b. Cost of goods sold: $20,000 + $180,000 − $15,000 = $185,000.
c. Direct-labor rate: $2,000 ÷ 1,000 hours = $2 per hour (see 2).
Direct-labor cost: 20,000 hours × $2 = $40,000 (see 7).
d. Overhead rate: $600,000 ÷ $400,000 = 150%.
Overhead applied: 150% × $40,000 = $60,000.
e. Accrued factory payroll, Dec. 31: $52,000 + $3,000 − $40,000 − $10,000 = $5,000.
f. Work in process, Dec. 31: $180,000 + $13,000 − $90,000 − $40,000 − $60,000 = $3,000.
g. Work in process, Jan. 31: $8,000 + $2,000 + 150% of $2,000 = $13,000.
h. Overapplied overhead: $60,000 − $57,000 = $3,000.

Entries in T-accounts are numbered in accordance with the "additional information" in the problem and lettered in accordance with the amounts required to be determined.

STORES CONTROL

(given)	12/31/_1 Bal.	15,000		
	(a)	95,000*	(3)	90,000
1/31/_2 Bal.	(5)	20,000		

WORK-IN-PROCESS CONTROL

12/31/_1 Bal.	(f)	3,000*	(4)	180,000
Direct materials	(3)	90,000		
Direct labor	(2) (7) (c)	40,000		
Overhead	(7) (1) (d)	60,000		
1/31/_2 Bal.	(2) (g)	13,000		

FINISHED-GOODS CONTROL

(given)	12/31/_1 Bal.	20,000			
	(4)	180,000	(6)	(b)	185,000
1/31/_2 Bal.	(6)	15,000			

ACCRUED FACTORY PAYROLL

(8)	52,000	12/31/_1	(e)	5,000*
		(7)		40,000 10,000
		1/31/_2 Bal. (given)		3,000

FACTORY DEPARTMENT OVERHEAD CONTROL

January charges (given)	57,000	

FACTORY OVERHEAD APPLIED

		(7) (1) (d)	60,000

COST OF GOODS SOLD

(6) (b)	185,000	

* Can be computed only after all other postings in the account have been found, so (g) must be computed before (f).

appendix: supplementary description of ledger relationships

This appendix explains some of the paper work that underlies the general-ledger relationships described in this chapter. It also contains an exhibit that summarizes sample accounting entries for job costing.

subsidiary ledgers and general ledger

The general ledger is a summary device. Postings are made to it from totals and subtotals of underlying transactions. For example, the balance of the Stores Control may be supported by a voluminous file of stores cards. Postings to the debit side of the Stores Control may be made from the Stores column in a special journal, such as a purchases journal or a voucher register. But the specific stores card in the subsidiary ledger is posted from a copy of a voucher or an invoice.

The general ledger gives a bird's-eye view of cost-accounting relationships; the subsidiary ledgers contain the underlying details—the worm's-eye view. In turn, source documents, such as voucher copies, stores requisitions, work tickets, clock cards, and other memoranda, are the primary means of recording business events. In a sense, the source documents are the everyday tools for systematically recording operating activities. They are vital because all subsequent accounting classifications and reports are dependent on source documents.

direct-material-usage reports

A multicopy stores requisition may be made out by a foreman. For example, separate copies may serve as follows:

Copy 1—Kept by storekeeper
Copy 2—Used by job-order cost clerk to post to job-cost sheet
Copy 3—Used by accounting department as a basis for a summary of requisitions

This summary is the support for the general-ledger entry:

Work-in-process control	xx	
Stores control		xx

This entry is usually made monthly, although it can be made more frequently if desired.

Copy 4—Used by department cost clerk as a basis for material-usage reports to departments. If these reports are to prove useful for control, they must typically be prepared more often than once a month. Stale, month-old reports concerning major costs are not helpful. Daily or weekly reports are common. This is another reason why the general ledger is oriented toward product costing rather than toward costing for control. The reports for control are needed before formal postings can be made.

Copy 5—Retained by foreman. He can use these as a cross-check against the usage reports sent to him by the accounting department.

The accounting department may use punched cards as requisitions. These may be sorted in many ways. For example:

DIRECT-MATERIAL REQUISITION SUMMARY

Requisition Number	Job Order	Department	Amount	Job-Order Subtotals	Department Subtotals
501	1415	26	$ 32.00		
502	1415	27	51.00	$83.00	
503	1408	26	204.00		
504	1414	26	19.00		$255.00
505	1409	28	101.00		

Machine or computer accounting facilitates the accumulation and tabulation of data so that they may be classified, reclassified, summarized, and resummarized to provide the specific information needed by management. Thus, a material-usage report like that on page 101 may be submitted to the foreman of Department 26 on a daily, weekly, or monthly basis.

direct-labor-cost recapitulation

Similar analysis can be applied to the sorting of direct-labor costs, using the work ticket as the source document. Producing departments may have their labor classified by operations as well as by jobs. For example, the machining department may perform one or

Department 26 DIRECT-MATERIAL USAGE For the week ending ________		
Requisition Number	Job Order	Amount
501	1415	$ 32.00
503	1408	204.00
504	1414	19.00
510	1408	55.00
511	1412	122.00

more of the following operations: milling, cleaning, grinding, and facing. Thus, work tickets may be recapitulated as follows:

DIRECT LABOR COST RECAPITULATION								
Work Ticket Number	Employee Identification Number	Job Number	Department Number	Operation Number	Amount	Job Subtotals	Operation Subtotals	Department Subtotals
14	49	1410	26	6500	$20.00		$20.00	
15	49	1410	26	6501	6.00		6.00	$26.00
16	52	1410	27	7520	19.00		19.00	
17	53	1410	27	7522	16.00	$61.00		
18	30	1411	25	5298	30.00	30.00	30.00	30.00
19	61	1409	28	8414	24.60		24.60	24.60
20	52	1409	27	7522	9.75	34.35	25.75	44.75

This labor recapitulation can be used as a basis for the general-ledger entry that charges direct labor to product:

Work in process	xx	
Accrued payroll		xx

This entry is usually made monthly, although it can be made more frequently if desired.

The recapitulation also supplies the information for daily, weekly, or monthly usage reports to the department foreman. These reports may be broken down by jobs or operations to suit the wants and needs of the foreman.

Work tickets may also be used for idle time (for example, caused by machine breakdowns or shortages of material), overtime premium, material handling, and so forth. A clerk or timekeeper may have the duty of preparing a daily reconciliation of employee clock cards with individual work tickets to see that all clock-card time is accounted for as direct labor, idle time, overtime premium, and so forth.

sample entries Exhibit 4-12 summarizes the accounting entries for job costing.

QUESTIONS, PROBLEMS, AND CASES

4-1 Distinguish between producing departments and service departments.

4-2 Give two definitions of *control* as the word may be used by an accountant.

4-3 What is the purpose of a *department cost sheet?*

4-4 What is the principal difference between job-cost and process-cost accounting systems?

4-5 Distinguish between a *clock card* and a *work ticket.*

4-6 What are the limitations of the general ledger as a cost accounting device?

4-7 What is a *normal product cost?*

4-8 *T-Accounts* The following data relate to operations of the Donnell Printing Company for the year 19_5 (in millions):

Stores control, December 31, 19_4	$ 12
Work-in-process control, December 31, 19_4	3
Finished-goods control, December 31, 19_4	6
Materials and supplies purchased on account	150
Direct materials issued to the producing departments for production	145
Supplies issued to various departments	10
Labor used directly on production	90
Indirect labor incurred by various departments	30
Depreciation—Plant and equipment	19
Miscellaneous factory overhead incurred by various departments (ordinarily would be detailed as repairs, utilities, etc.)	9
Factory overhead applied at 70 percent of direct-labor cost	?
Cost of goods manufactured and transferred to finished stock	294
Sales	400
Cost of goods sold	292

required

1. Use T-accounts to analyze all transactions. Number your entries. What is ending balance of Work-in-Process Control?
2. Sketch how the subsidiary ledger would appear for Factory Department Overhead Control, assuming that there are four departments. You need not show any numbers.
3. Show the journal entry for disposing of over- or underapplied overhead directly as a year-end adjustment to Cost of Goods Sold. Post the entry to T-accounts.

For more details concerning these data, see Problem 4-9.

4-9 *Journal Entries and Source Documents* Refer to Problem 4-8. Prepare journal entries. For each entry, (a) indicate the most likely name of the source documents that would authorize the entry, and (b) give a description of the entry into the subsidiary ledgers affected, if any.

4-10 *Journal Entries* The H Company uses a job-order cost system. The following relate to the month of March:

1. Raw materials issued to production, $96,000
2. Direct-labor analysis, $78,000
3. Manufacturing overhead is applied to production on the basis of $4.00 per direct-labor hour. There were 13,000 direct-labor hours incurred.
4. Total manufacturing overhead for the month was $54,000.
5. Production orders that cost $200,000 were completed during the month.
6. Production orders that cost $190,000 were shipped and invoiced to customers during the month at a profit of 20 percent based on cost.

required

The beginning inventory of work in process was $20,000. Prepare the general-journal entries required to record this information. What is the ending balance of work in process?

4-11 *Accounting for Overhead* The Lynn Company has made the following predictions for 19_4:

	MACHINING	ASSEMBLY
Factory overhead	$ 600,000	$ 800,000
Direct-labor cost	1,000,000	1,600,000
Direct-labor hours	100,000	200,000
Machine-hours	50,000	200,000

The company uses a predetermined overhead rate for applying overhead to production orders on a machine-hour basis in Machining and on a direct-labor-cost basis in Assembly.

required

1. Compute the predetermined overhead rate for each department.
2. During February the cost sheet for job #494 contained the following:

	MACHINING	ASSEMBLY
Direct materials requisitioned	$ 5,000	$15,000
Direct-labor cost	10,000	12,000
Direct-labor hours	1,000	1,500
Machine-hours	2,000	1,000

   Compute the total overhead cost of job #494.
3. At the end of 19_4, the actual factory overhead costs were $680,000 in Machining and $725,000 in Assembly. Compute the over- or underapplied overhead for each department, assuming that the machine-hours and direct-labor costs were precisely as predicted.
4. Repeat the computations in part (3), assuming that 55,000 actual machine-hours were incurred in Machining and actual direct-labor cost in Assembly was $1,800,000.

4-12 *Manufacturing Statement* (CPA) The Helper Corporation manufactures one product and accounts for costs by a job-order-cost system. You have obtained the following information for the year ended December 31, 19_3, from the Corporation's books and records:

Total manufacturing cost added during 19_3 (sometimes called cost to manufacture) was $1,000,000 based on actual direct material, actual direct labor, and applied factory overhead on actual direct-labor dollars.

Cost of goods manufactured was $970,000 also based on actual direct material, actual direct labor, and applied factory overhead.

EXHIBIT 4-12

JOB-ORDER-SYSTEM SAMPLE ENTRIES

Transaction	General-Ledger Effects	Subsidiary Ledgers	Source Documents	Explanatory Comments
1. Purchases of materials or supplies	Stores control Accounts payable	Dr. Stores card, "Received" column	Approved invoice	
2. Issuance of direct materials	Work in process control Stores control	Dr. Job order Cr. Stores card, "Issued" column	Stores requisition	Requisitions are summarized and classified by department for hourly, daily, weekly, or monthly direct material usage reports
3. Issuance of supplies	Factory department overhead control Stores control	Dr. Department overhead cost sheets, appropriate columns Cr. Stores card, "Issued" column	Stores requisition	
4. Distribution of labor costs	Work-in-process control Factory department overhead control Accrued payroll	Dr. Job orders Dr. Department overhead cost sheets, appropriate columns for various classes of indirect labor	Summary of work tickets or daily time analyses. This summary is sometimes called a labor cost distribution summary or a payroll recapitulation	
5. Payment of payroll (for a complete description, see Chapter 20)	Accrued payroll Withholdings payable Cash		Summary of clock cards and individual withholdings as shown on payroll sheets	This entry is usually made weekly, while the cost distribution (the prior entry) is not necessarily made at the same time
6. Payment of withholdings	Withholdings payable Cash			Withholdings are usually broken down by type rather than lumped in one account
7. Employer payroll taxes	Factory department overhead control Employer payroll taxes payable	Dr. Department overhead cost sheets, appropriate columns	Accrual memoranda from accounting officer	

(Continued on next page)

Transaction	General Ledger Effects	Subsidiary Ledgers	Source Documents	Explanatory Comments
8. Utilities	Factory department overhead control Accounts payable or Accrued utilities	Dr. Department overhead cost sheets, appropriate columns	Approved invoices or accrual memoranda	
9. Depreciation on factory equipment	Factory department overhead control Allowance for depreciation—Equipment	Dr. Department overhead cost sheets, appropriate columns	Depreciation schedule	
10. Factory insurance write-off	Factory department overhead control Unexpired insurance	Dr. Department overhead cost sheets, appropriate columns	Insurance register or memoranda from accounting officer	
11. Application of overhead to product	Work-in-process control Factory overhead applied	Dr. Job order	Predetermined overhead rate computed by using overhead budget	
12. Transfer completed goods to finished stock	Finished-goods control Work-in-process control	Dr. Finished stock card, "Received" column Cr. Job order	Production report	Sometimes the completed job order serves as a finished stock card.
13. Sales	Accounts-receivable control Sales	Dr. Customers' accounts	Copy of sales invoice	
14. Cost of sales	Cost of sales Finished-goods control	Dr. Cost of sales record (optional) Cr. Finished stock cards	Copy of sales invoice plus costs as shown on finished stock cards	
15. Yearly closing of overhead accounts	Factory overhead applied Factory department overhead control Cost of sales (cr. if overhead is overapplied; dr. if overhead is underapplied)		General ledger balances	

Factory overhead was applied to work in process at 75 percent of direct-labor dollars. Applied factory overhead for the year was 27 percent of the total manufacturing cost.

Beginning work-in-process inventory, January 1, was 80 percent of ending work-in-process inventory, December 31.

required Prepare a formal statement of cost of goods manufactured for the year ended December 31, 19_3, for Helper Corporation. Use actual direct material used, actual direct labor, and applied factory overhead. Show supporting computations in good form.

4-13 The Burke Company has budgeted the following performance for 19_4:

Beginning inventories	None
Sales	$10,000,000
Net income	800,000
Factory overhead:	
Variable	1,000,000
Fixed	2,000,000
Selling and administrative expenses:	
Variable	1,000,000
Fixed	1,000,000
Plant and equipment, net	4,000,000

It is now the end of 19_4. A factory overhead rate of $1.00 per unit was used throughout the year for costing product. Total actual factory overhead incurred was $3,300,000.

Overapplied factory overhead was $200,000. There is no work in process. How many units were produced in 19_4?

4-14 *Incomplete Data* The Fullerton Company uses perpetual inventories and a normal cost system. Balances from selected accounts were:

	BALANCES DECEMBER 31, 19_1	BALANCES DECEMBER 31, 19_2
Factory department overhead control		$ 56,000
Finished goods	$50,000	40,000
Cost of goods sold		180,000
Direct-materials stores	?	20,000
Factory overhead applied at 60% of direct-labor cost		72,000
Work in process	?	130,000

The cost of direct materials requisitioned for production during 19_2 was $100,000. The cost of direct materials purchased during 19_2 was $90,000.

required Before considering any year-end adjustments for over- or underapplied overhead, compute:

1. Direct-materials stores, December 31, 19_1.
2. Work in process, December 31, 19_1.

4-15 *Journal Entries, Year-End Disposition of Overhead* Tuttle Company uses a job-order cost system. Factory overhead is applied at a rate of $2.50 per direct-labor hour. Both beginning and closing balances in work in process and finished goods are zero. You are given the following data for 19_4, and the fact that all goods manufactured are sold.

Direct-labor hours used	50,000
Direct materials used	$ 50,000
Direct labor used	100,000
Indirect labor used	25,000
Indirect supplies used	10,000
Rent—Plant and equipment	50,000
Miscellaneous overhead	50,000
Cost of goods sold	275,000

All under- or overapplied overhead is allocated wholly to cost of goods sold at the end of the year.

required

1. Factory overhead applied.
2. Factory overhead incurred.
3. Prepare journal entries to record all the facts above, including all necessary entries to adjust for over- or underapplied overhead.

4-16 *Accounting for Overhead* On December 30, 19_2, the Mitchell Company has completed all jobs in process except for Job # 447; the job cost sheet through that date showed direct materials of $40,000 and direct labor of $30,000. Total factory overhead incurred through December 30 was $900,000. The labor-cost recapitulation for the December 31 working day was: direct labor $8,000, indirect labor $2,000. In addition, miscellaneous factory overhead incurred on December 31 was $3,000. Direct materials of $2,000 were added to Job # 447.

The company's charges to Work in Process during 19_2 included direct labor for 19_2 of $720,000, excluding the December 31 working day described above. The factory overhead is applied to jobs at 120 percent of direct labor.

The balance in Finished-Goods Inventory, December 31, 19_2, was $112,000 and in Cost of Goods Sold was $2,000,000.

required

1. Compute the *normal cost* of ending inventory, Work in Process, December 31, 19_2.
2. What is the under- or overapplied factory overhead for 19_2?

4-17 *Overhead Application and Year-End Disposition* (D. Jacque Grinnell) A manufacturing company is divided into three producing departments, A, B, and C. All production is to customer's order. Budgeted manufacturing costs for 19_1 are as follows:

	DEPT. A	DEPT. B	DEPT. C	TOTAL
Direct material				$170,000
Direct labor	$40,000	$20,000	$60,000	120,000
Manufacturing overhead	10,000	40,000	30,000	80,000

The actual material and labor cost of producing a particular order (order #162) during 19_1 was as follows:

Direct material			$1,500
Direct labor:			
	Dept. A	$200	
	Dept. B	190	
	Dept. C	240	630

Manufacturing overhead is applied to product on the basis of direct-labor cost. Overhead rates are predetermined at the beginning of the year using annual budget data.

required

1. Determine the total manufacturing cost associated with order #162 assuming (a) a factorywide manufacturing overhead rate is used to apply cost to product and (b) departmental rates are used to apply cost to product.
2. *Actual* manufacturing costs for 19_1 were as follows:

	DEPT. A	*DEPT. B*	*DEPT. C*	*TOTAL*
Direct material				$180,000
Direct labor	$44,000	$19,000	$72,000	135,000
Manufacturing overhead	12,000	36,000	39,000	87,000

Determine the under- or overapplied overhead for the year assuming:
a. The use of the factorywide overhead rate.
b. The use of the departmental overhead rates.

3. Consider the information provided in requirement (2) above. Assume the firm chose to use departmental rates to apply overhead to product. Also assume that at the beginning of 19_1 there were no work-in-process or finished-goods inventories. At the end of 19_1 the work-in-process and finished-goods inventories were represented by the following balances:

Work in process	$19,500
Finished goods	60,500

The balances include actual direct-material costs, actual direct-labor costs, and applied overhead costs; that is, no year-end adjustments have been made for under- or overapplied overhead. Assuming the company desires to prorate under- or overapplied overhead between ending inventories and cost of goods sold in proportion to their unadjusted balances, compute the correct prorated amount to be assigned to cost of goods sold.

4-18 *Overview of General-Ledger Relationships* The Blakely Company uses a job-order cost system. The total debits and credits in certain accounts at year-end are:

	DECEMBER 30, 19_6	
	Total Debits	Total Credits
Direct-material control	$100,000	$ 70,000
Work-in-process control	320,000	305,000
Factory department overhead control	85,000	—
Finished-goods control	325,000	300,000
Cost of goods sold	300,000	—
Factory department overhead applied	—	90,000

Note that "total debits" in the inventory accounts would include beginning inventory balances, if any.

The above accounts *do not* include the following:

(a) The labor-cost recapitulation for the December 31 working day: direct labor, $5,000, and indirect labor, $1,000.
(b) Miscellaneous factory overhead incurred on December 30 and December 31: $1,000.

Additional Information

Factory overhead has been applied as a percentage of direct labor through December 30.
Direct material purchases during 19_6 were $90,000.
There were no returns to suppliers.
Direct labor costs during 19_6 totaled $150,000, not including the December 31 working day described above.

required

1. Beginning inventories of direct material, work in process, and finished goods. Show T-accounts.
2. Prepare all adjusting and closing journal entries for the above accounts. Assume that all under- or overapplied overhead is closed directly to Cost of Goods Sold.
3. Ending inventories, after adjustments and closing, of direct material, work in process, and finished goods.

4-19 *Proration of Overhead* The Invincible Company has commercial and defense contracting business. A contracting officer for the United States Air Force has insisted that underapplied overhead should no longer be written off directly as an adjustment of Cost of Defense Goods Sold for a given year. His insistence was prompted by the fact that $40 million of underapplied overhead was added to the $400 million of unadjusted Cost of Goods Sold in 19_4. There were no beginning inventories.

Overhead is applied as a percentage of direct labor as contracts are produced. The Air Force had a large cost-plus-fixed-fee contract representing $300 million of the $400 million of defense production started and sold during 19_4; it had no other contracts pending with Invincible. An analysis of (before considering the $40 million) costs showed (in millions):

	DEFENSE BUSINESS		
	Contracts in Progress	Finished-Goods Inventory	Cost of Goods Sold
Direct material	$380	$20	$200
Direct labor	90	10	100
Factory overhead applied	90	10	100
	$560	$40	$400

required

1. As a judge trying to settle a dispute on the disposition of the overhead, what position would you favor? Why? Show computations and, assuming your answer would be formally recorded in the books of account, show a journal entry for the proration.
2. As the contracting officer, what proration of the underapplied overhead would you favor? Why? Show computations.

4-20 *General-Ledger Relationships; Incomplete Data* You are asked to bring the following incomplete accounts up to date through May, 19_1. Also consider the additional information that follows the T-accounts.

STORES CONTROL

5/31/_1 Balance 18,000	

ACCOUNTS PAYABLE

	4/30/_1 Balance 10,000

WORK-IN-PROCESS CONTROL

4/30/_1 Balance 2,000	

DEPARTMENT FACTORY OVERHEAD CONTROL

Total charges for May 15,000	

FACTORY OVERHEAD APPLIED	

FINISHED-GOODS CONTROL	
4/30/_1 Balance 25,000	

COST OF GOODS SOLD	

Additional Information

a. The overhead is applied by using a predetermined rate that is set at the beginning of each year by forecasting the year's overhead and relating it to forecasted direct-labor hours. The budget for 19_1 called for a total of 150,000 hours of direct labor and $225,000 of factory overhead.
b. The accounts payable are for direct materials only. The balance on May 31 was $5,000. Payments of $35,000 were made during May.
c. The finished-goods inventory as of May 31 was $22,000.
d. The cost of goods sold during the month was $65,000.
e. On May 31 there was only one unfinished job in the factory. Cost records show that $1,000 (400 hours) of direct labor and $2,000 of direct material had been charged to the job.
f. A total of 9,400 direct man-hours were worked during the month of May. All factory workers earn the same rate of pay.
g. All "actual" factory overhead incurred during May has already been posted.

required

1. Materials purchased during May.
2. Cost of goods completed during May.
3. Overhead applied during May.
4. Balance, Work in Process, May 31, 19_1.
5. Materials used during May.
6. Balance, Stores Control, April 30, 19_1.
7. Over- or underapplied overhead for May.

4-21 *Underapplied Overhead on Interim Income Statements* The following data are available for ABC Company covering the month of January 19_4.

Sales	$100,000
Cost of sales (per account)	75,000
Factory overhead incurred	25,500
Factory overhead applied	22,100
Selling and administrative expenses	10,000

You are to prepare interim income statements for the month of January:

required

1. Assuming underapplied overhead is immediately chargeable to the period.
2. Assuming underapplied overhead as a cost that will benefit the rest of the year's production.

4-22 *Classification of Overtime Costs* This is an expansion of Problem 2-31. Suppose that the printing department gathers all of its indirect costs and applies them via a single overhead rate on the basis of, say, 300 percent of the direct-labor cost of individual jobs. If overtime premium and some pension costs were regarded as direct-labor costs rather than overhead, would the overhead rate be higher or lower than 300 percent? Why?

4-23 *Overview of General-Ledger Relationships* Frantic Publishing Company has its own printing facilities. Frantic uses a job-order accounting system and normal costing. Its president has interviewed you recently. As a graduate of a correspondence school in accountancy, he has a long-standing suspicion of accounting courses as being too general. He commented, "Most students learn high-blown theory, but when they are confronted by a few basic facts produced by an accounting system, they can't piece them together. If they don't understand such fundamental relationships, they can't possibly use the data intelligently."

Because of his suspicions he has prepared an entrance examination for all prospective employees who seek a Frantic management position. He provides them with the following data for the year 19_2 (in thousands of dollars):

Accounts receivable 1/1	65	Plant depreciation cost	130
Accounts receivable 12/31	100	Direct labor	420
Accounts payable 1/1	35	Factory heat and light cost	40
Accounts payable 12/31	40	Gross profit*	350
Stores inventory 1/1	70	Indirect labor	100
Stores inventory 12/31	60	Purchases of direct materials and supplies	400
Finished goods 1/1	50	Sales	1,230
Finished goods 12/31	250	Supplies used	30
Accrued payroll 1/1	20	Work in process inventory 12/31	110
Accrued payroll 12/31	70		

* This is after a separate correction (after cost of goods sold) has been made for overapplied factory overhead of 20.

required

The president asks you to compute the following. He says, "Use any technique you wish, but leave an audit trail so I can follow your work." You may use T-accounts if you wish.

1. Direct-material usage.
2. Cost of goods sold (at normal cost).
3. Cost of goods completed and transferred to finished goods (at normal cost).
4. Factory overhead applied.
5. Work in process, January 1, 19_2.

4-24 *Program Budgeting and Job Costing* Nonprofit institutions such as health centers and colleges continually face decisions concerning how to allocate their limited resources. A technique called program budgeting has been developed to help in the making of these decisions. The "program" is an activity or set of activities with a particular goal such as placing children for adoption, helping ex-convicts on parole, aiding disabled veterans, or educating students of management.

Program budgeting is a philosophy or state of mind rather than a rigid set of procedures. Questions such as the following are raised: (1) What are the organization's objectives or goals? Program categories sometimes cut across organizational lines so that two or more departments work together toward a common goal. (2) How much does each program cost? Costs typically include specifically traceable costs such as direct labor plus applied overhead. (3) How is each program funded? Are cash receipts from donations, tuition, or government grants earmarked specifically for one purpose? Sometimes raising money for a specific program can dislodge general funds for other purposes.

As 19_5 began, Muriel Clayton, director of the Uppervale Health Center, faced a decision. She had talked recently with Theodore Rosenberg, an administrator in the State Health Department. He told her that the state might be able to increase its support to the Center by $30,000. Ms. Clayton had to determine which of two activities, drug-addict rehabilitation or alcoholic rehabilitation, was more effective so she could write a formal request for the additional funds.

For purposes of cost analysis, the Center's activities were divided into four programs: (1) alcoholic rehabilitation, (2) drug-addict rehabilitation, (3) children's clinical services, and (4) after-care (counseling and support of patients after release from a mental hospital).

Ms. Clayton felt that costs per program would help her decide where to invest additional funds. Of course, such costs would give her some idea of the inputs devoted to each program. The measure of outputs is far more troublesome. Should it be patients treated, patients cured, patients not requiring further treatment for two years, or what measure? Ms. Clayton decided that cost per patient per year would be a helpful statistic for making her decision. She felt that it would be too expensive and too difficult to develop a more elegant measure of effectiveness. The Center's board and staff agreed that if the cost per drug patient per year was not more than 20 percent higher than for the alcoholic patient, the drug program would receive the additional funds.

The Center's simplified budget was typical for a nonprofit institution in the sense that it was a line-item budget, a mere listing of various costs classified by so-called "natural" descriptions:

Professional salaries:		
6 physicians @ $37,500	$225,000	
19 psychologists @ $25,000	475,000	
24 nurses @ $12,500	300,000	$1,000,000
Medical supplies		150,000
General overhead (administrative salaries, rent, utilities, etc.)		500,000
		$1,650,000

The budget and the accounting system did not show how the costs related to the four programs. Ms. Clayton decided to ask the professional staff to fill out a form indicating what percentage of time each devoted to the four programs. This was a critical form, and Clayton, who had earned uniformly high respect from the professional staff, stressed that it be filled out conscientiously.

Costs of medical supplies were to be allocated on the basis of physician hours spent in each program. General overhead would be allocated on the basis of direct-labor cost (where direct labor is defined to include the time of doctors, psychologists, and nurses multiplied by the salary rate of each.)

Clayton compiled the following data concerning allocations from individual time allocation forms:

		DRUG				
	Alcohol	Counseling	Clinical	Children	After-Care	Total
Physicians			2	4		6
Psychologists	6	4			9	19
Nurses	4	4	2	4	10	24

At any point in time, an average of 30 patients are in residence in the alcohol program, each staying about a half-year. Thus, the clinic processed 60 patients, but provided only 30 patient-years of service. Similarly, an average of 40 patients were involved in the drug program for about a half-year each; they received both counseling and clinical services.

required

What is the cost of the alcohol and drug programs, using the Clayton approach to cost analysis? What action should be taken?

4-25 *Job Costing in a Service Industry* Howe and Halling, Certified Public Accountants, use a form of job-costing system. In this respect they are similar to many professional service firms, such as management consulting firms, law firms, and professional engineering firms.

An auditing client may be served by various staff who hold professional positions in the hierarchy from partners to managers to senior accountants to assistants. In addition, there are secretaries and other employees.

Suppose that Howe and Halling have the following budget for 19_2:

Compensation of professional staff	$4,000,000
Other costs	2,400,000
Total budgeted costs	$6,400,000

Each professional staff member must submit a weekly time report, which is used to assign costs to jobs. An example is the time report of a senior accountant:

WEEK OF JANUARY 8	*S*	*M*	*T*	*W*	*T*	*F*	*S*	*TOTAL*
Chargeable hours:								
Client A		8	8	5				21
Client B				3		4		7
Etc.								
Nonchargeable hours:								
Professional development (attending seminar on computer auditing)					8			8
Unassigned time						4		4
Total	0	8	8	8	8	8	0	40

In turn, these time reports are used for charging hours to a client job-order sheet, summarized as follows for client A:

	WEEK OF				
Employees Charged	Jan. 8	Jan. 15	Total Hours	Billing Rates	Total Billed
Partners	4	4	8	$100	$ 800
Managers	4	4	8	60	480
Seniors	21	30	51	40	2,040
Assistants	48	70	118	20	2,360
Total hours	77	108	185		$5,680

In many cases these job-cost sheets bear only a summary of the *hours* charged. Each class of labor is billed at an appropriate hourly rate, so that the job-cost sheet is the central basis for billing the client.

required

1. Suppose that this firm had a policy of charging overhead to jobs at a predetermined percentage of the salaries charged to the job. The experience of the firm has been that chargeable hours average 80 percent of available hours for all

categories of professional personnel. The nonchargeable hours are regarded as additional overhead. What is the overhead rate as a percentage of the "direct labor," the chargeable professional compensation cost?

2. Compute the *total cost* of the Client A job for the two weeks that began January 8. Be as specific as possible. Assume that the average weekly compensation (based on a 40-hour week) of the personnel working on this job is: partners, $2,000; managers, $1,200; seniors, $800; assistants, $400.
3. As the tabulation for Client A implies, the job order often consists of only the time and no costs. Instead, the revenue is computed via multiplying the time by the billing rates. Suppose the partners' profit objective is 20 percent of the total costs budgeted. What predetermined percentage of the salaries charged to the jobs would be necessary to achieve a total billing that would ultimately provide the profit objective? That is, what is the billing rate as a percentage of "direct labor"?
4. In addition to billing, what use might you make of the data compiled on the job orders?

4-26 *Comprehensive Review Problem—Job-Order Costs* This problem is intended to provide a summary of general-ledger and subsidiary-ledger relationships for factory costs under a job-order cost system. The facts are unrealistic because, in order to save student time, the tremendous detail and number of accounts in a real situation are not reproduced here. However the solving of this problem should provide the student with a comprehensive view of the basic ledger framework.

Assume that the Mafco Company has been in business in Hong Kong for many years. The company rents its factory building. It also uses a job-order cost system because it has a wide variety of products that receives varying attention and effort in the two factory departments. Machining and Assembly.

Mafco has the following trial balance as of December 31, 19_0.

Cash	$ 15,000	
Accounts receivable	40,000	
Stores control	29,600	
Work-in-process control	4,000	
Finished-goods control	20,000	
Unexpired insurance	12,000	
Office equipment	15,000	
Accumulated depreciation—Office equipment		$ 5,000
Factory equipment	950,000	
Accumulated depreciation—Factory equipment		220,000
Accounts payable		23,000
Accrued payroll		1,000
Accrued utilities		2,000
Accrued property taxes		3,000
Capital stock		100,000
Retained earnings		731,600
	$1,085,600	$1,085,600

DETAIL ON SUBSIDIARY RECORDS AS OF DECEMBER 31, 19_0

Stores:

CODE	*QUANTITY*	*UNIT COST*	*AMOUNT*
A	5,000	$2.00	$10,000
B	10,000	1.50	15,000
C	400	8.00	3,200
Supplies	Various	—	1,400
			$29,600

Work in Process:

JOB-ORDER NUMBER	*DEPARTMENT*	*DIRECT MATERIALS*	*DIRECT LABOR*	*FACTORY OVERHEAD*	*TOTAL*
100	Machining	$1,800	$800	$900	$3,500
	Assembly	200	200	100	500
					$4,000

Finished goods:

STOCK NO.	*REFERENCE*	*QUANTITY*	*UNIT COST*	*AMOUNT*
X-1	Job 97	100	$80	$ 8,000
X-2	Job 99	1,000	12	12,000
				$20,000

The following factory-overhead budget has been prepared for the coming year, 19_1:

FACTORY OVERHEAD
BUDGET FOR YEAR ENDING DECEMBER 31, 19_1

	Machining	Assembly	Total
Factory overhead:			
Controllable:			
Supplies	$ 14,400	$ 5,400	$ 19,800
Indirect labor	22,800	16,800	39,600
Utilities	30,000	9,000	39,000
Repairs	24,000	6,000	30,000
Miscellaneous	22,800	12,000	34,800
	$114,000	$ 49,200	$163,200
Uncontrollable:			
Insurance	$ 7,200	$ 2,400	$ 9,600
Depreciation	114,000	14,400	128,400
Rent	24,000	16,800	40,800
Property taxes	4,200	1,200	5,400
Supervision	14,400	19,200	33,600
	$163,800	$ 54,000	$217,800
Total factory overhead	$277,800	$103,200	$381,000

This budget has been prepared after careful consideration of the sales outlook for the coming year. The production schedules are geared to the forecast sales pattern.

In order to cost jobs as they are worked on, a predetermined overhead rate is computed as follows:

	YEAR 19_1	
	Machining	Assembly
Factory overhead	$277,800	$103,200
Machine-hours	69,450	
Direct-labor cost		$206,400
Rate per machine-hour	$ 4.00	
Rate per direct-labor dollar		50%

These overhead rates will be used throughout the year to cost various jobs as they are worked on by each department. All overhead will be applied to all jobs worked on during the year in proportion to the machine-hour or direct-labor cost factor devoted to each job. If management predictions are accurate, total overhead applied to the year's jobs through the use of predetermined rates should be equal to the total overhead costs actually incurred.

January data:

1. Purchases for stores (credit Accounts Payable):

	QUANTITY	UNIT COST	JANUARY
A	7,500	$2.00	$15,000
B	14,000	1.50	21,000
C	2,125	8.00	17,000
Supplies			2,000
			$55,000

2. Returns (debit Accounts Payable): 50 units of Material B.
3. The direct-material requisitions were summarized, and the following data were shown on a material-usage report. These reports were submitted weekly to department foremen, although monthly data are shown here.

MACHINING DEPARTMENT

Direct-Material Usage
For the Month Ending January 31, 19_1

Requisition	Type	Job Order	Quantity	Unit Cost	Amount
M89	B	101	1,500	$1.50	$ 2,250
M90	A	102	3,000	2.00	6,000
M91	A	103	1,000	2.00	2,000
M92	B	103	1,000	1.50	1,500
M93	B	102	3,000	1.50	4,500
M94	B	101	200	1.50	300
M95	A	104	2,000	2.00	4,000
					$20,550

ASSEMBLY DEPARTMENT

Direct-Material Usage
For the Month Ending January 31, 19_1

Requisition	Type	Job Order	Quantity	Unit Cost	Amount
A301	C	100	5	$8.00	$ 40
A302	C	103	200	8.00	1,600
A303	C	101	800	8.00	6,400
A304	C	102	1,500	8.00	12,000
A305	C	103	20	8.00	160
					$20,200

4. A summary of payroll costs incurred follows. Compare with item (g) below. Payments (settlements) are independent of recognition of cost incurrence. In other words, costs may be summarized monthly while settlements are made weekly.

		LABOR HOURS		COST		
Work Ticket*	Job Order	Machining	Assembly	Machining	Assembly	Total
ML480	101	20		$ 50	$	$ 50
ML481	101	1,500		3,750		3,750
ML482	103	1,000		2,500		2,500
ML483	102	1,200		3,000		3,000
ML484	104	500		1,250		1,250
ML485	103	100		250		250
AL 60	100		20		40	40
AL 61	102		7,000		14,000	14,000
AL 62	101		500		1,000	1,000
AL 63	103		1,000		2,000	2,000
AL 64	102		200		400	400
Total direct labor		4,320	8,720	$10,800	$17,440	$28,240
Indirect labor				2,000	1,500	3,500
Supervision				1,200	1,600	2,800
Total factory labor				$14,000	$20,540	$34,540
Selling and administrative wages						6,000
Total payroll costs						$40,540

* In practice, there would be many more of these. Often they are recapitulated daily and posted to each job in groups rather than as individual tickets.

5. Apply overhead to jobs. Rates as calculated when overhead budget was prepared: Machining, $4.00 per machine-hour; Assembly, 50 percent of direct-labor cost. See data for entry 6 to obtain machine-hours worked.
6. Production and sales data:

JOB	UNITS COMPLETED	FINISHED	FINISHED STOCK NO.	UNITS SOLD	SOLD FOR	JANUARY MACHINE-HOURS WORKED IN MACHINING DEPT.
97	100	19_0	X-1	100	$ 9,000	
98	—	—	—	—	—	
99	1000	19_0	X-2	1000	16,000	
100	50	Jan. 5, 19_1	X-1	20	1,800	
101	1750	Jan. 12, 19_1	X-2	900	14,400	3,000
102	1000	Jan. 19, 19_1	X-3	950	55,000	2,000
103	100	Jan. 30, 19_1	X-4	50	6,500	150
104	Unfinished					800
					$102,700	5,950

7. Gross payroll paid in cash during month, $39,000.
8. The following additional overhead costs were incurred during January:

		DEPARTMENT			
Item	Total	Machining	Assembly	Selling and Administrative	General-Ledger Account To Be Credited
Supplies requisitioned	$ 2,000	$ 1,500	$ 400	$ 100	?
Utilities (cost recognized on basis of usage estimates for month rather than on basis of invoices, which may cover other dates than a current calendar month)	4,000	2,700	800	500	Accrued Utilities Payable
Repairs by outsiders (parts and labor)	3,000	2,350	600	50	Accounts Payable
Miscellaneous	3,000	2,000	900	100	Accounts Payable
Insurance	1,000	600	200	200	?
Depreciation on equipment	11,000	9,500	1,200	300	?
Rent	4,000	2,000	1,400	600	Accounts Payable
Property taxes	500	350	100	50	Accrued Property Taxes
	$28,500	$21,000	$5,600	$1,900	

9. Utility bills received, $2,900 (dr. Accrued Utilities).
10. Utility bills paid, $2,525 (dr. Accounts Payable).
11. Other selling and administrative expenses, $15,000 (cr. Accounts Payable).
12. Payments on accounts payable, other than the $2,525 in (10), $65,300.
13. Collections on accounts receivable, $99,000.

required

1. Enter beginning balances in general-ledger T-accounts.
2. Draw up stores cards, job-cost sheets, and finished-goods stock cards. Be sure to put in "reference" columns so that appropriate requisitions and work tickets, as well as dollar amounts, may be entered in the subsidiary ledger. A sample stores card and job-cost sheet appear on page 119.

   Finished-stock cards would be similar in design to stores cards.

   The factory-overhead cost sheets have columns for: date, reference, supplies, indirect labor, utilities, repairs, miscellaneous, insurance, depreciation on equipment, rent, property taxes, and supervision.

   Post beginning balances to subsidiary records.
3. Journalize and post entries for January.
4. Prepare a trial balance as of January 31, 19_1. Also prepare schedules of subsidiary-ledger balances.
5. Prepare an income statement for January and a balance sheet as of January 31, 19_1. Underapplied overhead is treated as a balance-sheet item on interim financial statements.
6. Prepare factory-overhead performance reports for January, one for Machining and one for Assembly. Show actual overhead, budgeted overhead, and variances. Assume arbitrarily that budget figures for January are one-twelfth of those shown in the annual overhead budget.

STORES CARD

Material A

Reference	Received			Issued			Balance			
	Quantity	Unit Cost	Amount	Quantity	Unit Cost	Amount	Date	Quantity	Unit Cost	Amount
Vouchers, Invoices or Requisitions							12/31/x0	5,000	$2.00	$10,000

Job Order No. 100

MACHINING DEPARTMENT

Direct Material				Direct Labor				Overhead	
Reference	Quantity	Unit Cost	Amount	Reference	Quantity	Unit Cost	Amount	Machine Hours Worked	Amount
Req. #A88	900	$2.00	$1800	Work tickets	320 hrs	$2.50	$800	225	$900

ASSEMBLY DEPARTMENT

Direct Material				Direct Labor				Overhead	
Reference	Quantity	Unit Cost	Amount	Reference	Quantity	Unit Cost	Amount	Reference	Amount
Req. #A300	25	$8.00	$200	Work tickets	100 hrs	$2.00	$200	50% of direct labor	$100

Summary

	Machining	Assembly	Total
Direct material	$ ______	$ ______	$ ______
Direct labor	______	______	______
Factory overhead applied	______	______	______
Total cost	$ ______	$ ______	$ ______

7. Assume that operations continue for the remainder of 19_1. Certain balances at December 31, 19_1 follow:

Stores	$ 30,000	
Work in process	10,000	
Finished goods	30,000	
Cost of sales	960,000	
Factory-overhead control	400,000	
Factory overhead applied		$385,000

Prepare journal entries to close the factory-overhead accounts, assuming that:

a. Underapplied overhead is treated as a direct adjustment of Cost of Sales.

b. Underapplied overhead is spread over appropriate accounts in proportion to their unadjusted ending balances.

Multiple Purpose Systems for Management Control

SECTION TWO

Budgeting in General: Profit Planning

5

Previous chapters have stressed that the essence of management is decision making and that the methods for making decisions are increasingly being called *decision models.* For example, Chapter 3 introduced cost-volume-profit analysis, which provides models for making decisions on prices, quantities, mix, and so on. Now we take an overview of the entire network of these decisions. This comprehensive view is expressed in the form of a master budget that encompasses and summarizes the expected impact of all the operating and financing decisions on income, financial position, and cash flows.

This chapter examines the master budget as a planning and coordinating device. The succeeding three chapters examine some detailed aspects of the budgeting decisions and their implementation.

major features of budgets

definition and role of budgets

A budget is a quantitative expression of a plan of action and an aid to coordination and implementation. Budgets may be formulated for the organization as a whole or for any subunit.

The master budget summarizes the objectives of all subunits of an organization—sales, production, distribution, and finance. It quantifies the expectations regarding future income, cash flows, financial position, and supporting plans. These are the culmination of a series of decisions resulting from a careful look at the organization's future. In most cases, the master budget is the best practical approximation to a formal model of the total organization: its objectives, its inputs, and its outputs.

Budgets are designed to carry out a variety of functions: planning, evaluating performance, coordinating activities, implementing plans, communicating, motivating, and authorizing actions. The last-named role seems to predominate in government budgeting and not-for-profit budgeting, where budget appropriations serve as authorizations and ceilings for management actions.

This book emphasizes how accounting helps the manager make *operating decisions,* those concerning the acquisition and utilization of scarce resources. However, we cannot ignore the importance of *financing decisions,* which concern the obtaining of funds for acquisition of resources. The master budget embraces the impact of both kinds of decisions; that is why this chapter examines cash budgets as well as operating budgets. Incidentally, the leading organizations are usually marked by both impressive operating management and excellent financial management. Business failures are often attributable to weaknesses in one or the other of these responsibilities.

wide use of budgets

Budgetary systems are more common in larger companies, where formalized and sophisticated techniques are developed to serve management. Still, the usefulness of budgeting to very small concerns should not be overlooked. Many deaths (and unwarranted creations) of small businesses could have been circumvented by an early attempt to quantify the dreams of headstrong but sloppy-thinking entrepreneurs who never directly faced the uncertainties of their venture.

For example, a small business moved into a lush market for school equipment with lofty hopes. However, failure to quantify the long collection periods, to forecast a maximum sales potential, and to control costs from the outset resulted in disaster within a year. Budgets for small businesses need not be as elaborate as those outlined in budgeting textbooks, but some budgeting is useful to an enterprise of any size. In fact, many companies have implicit budgets without even realizing their existence; that is, every businessman considers the future as he makes decisions.

Many managers claim that the uncertainties peculiar to their business make budgets impractical for them. Yet one can nearly always find at least some companies in the same industry that use budgets. Such companies are usually among the industry leaders, and they regard budgets as indispensable aids. The point is that managers must grapple with uncertainties, either with a budget or without one. The advocates of budgeting maintain that the benefits from budgeting nearly always exceed the costs. Some budget program, at least, will be helpful in almost every organization.

When administered wisely, budgets (a) compel management planning, (b) provide definite expectations that are the best framework for judging subsequent performance, and (c) promote communication and coordination among the various segments of the organization.

These advantages of budgets will be discussed more fully in the next chapter. **For now, the uppermost point is that budgets provide a discipline that brings planning to the forefront as a key management responsibility.**

types of budgets

time coverage

Budgets may span a period of one year or less—or, in cases of capital budgeting for plant and product changes, up to ten or more years. More and more companies are using budgets as essential tools for long-range planning. The usual planning-and-control budget period is one year. The annual budget is often broken down by months for the first quarter and by quarters for the remainder of the year. The budgeted data for a year are often revised as the year unfolds. For example, at the end of the first quarter, the budget for the next three quarters is changed in light of new information. *Continuous budgets* are increasingly used, whereby a twelve-month forecast is always available by adding a month or quarter in the future as the month or quarter just ended is dropped. Continuous budgets are desirable because they force management constantly to think concretely about the forthcoming twelve months, irrespective of whether the month at hand is May or October. Arizona Public Service Co. has a budget that looks ahead two years but is updated every month. The choice of budget periods largely flows from the objectives, uses, and dependability of the budget data.

classification of budgets

Budgets are basically forecasted statements. They are sometimes called *pro-forma* statements. Various descriptive terms for budgets have arisen. The difficulties of terminology are not insurmountable, but the reader should remember that terms vary among firms.

There are countless forms of budgets. Many special budgets are prepared, including:

Comparisons of planning budgets with actual performance (performance reports)
Reports for specific managerial needs—for example, breakeven projections
Long-term budgets, often called "capital" or "facilities" budgets (see Chapter 12)
Flexible overhead budget (see Chapter 8)

The following is a simplified subclassification of the *master budget,* the comprehensive plan. Many subsidiary budget schedules are necessary in actual practice.

MASTER BUDGET, CONSISTING OF:	
Operating Budget, Consisting of:	Financial Budget, Consisting of:
Budgeted income statement	Cash budget
Sales budget	Receipts
Production budget	Disbursements
Materials	Budgeted balance sheet
Direct labor	Budgeted statement of sources and applications of funds
Factory overhead	
Inventory levels	
Cost-of-goods-sold budget	
Selling-expense budget	
Administrative-expense budget	

illustration of master budget

Try to take the following basic data and prepare the required budgets before glancing at the solution. A step-by-step approach to formulating a master budget is described after the basic data are given. This illustration is largely mechanical, but remember that the master-budget process generates key top-management decisions regarding pricing, product lines, production scheduling, capital expenditures, research and development, management assignments, and so on. For instance, the first draft of the budget almost always leads to decisions that prompt further drafts before a final budget is chosen.

basic data and requirements

The M Company in Hong Kong uses a normal cost system. The company is ready to prepare its master budget for the year 19B. Having carefully examined all relevant factors, the executives expect the following for 19B:

Materials:	
Material 111	$1.20 per unit
Material 112	$2.60 per unit
Direct labor	$2.05 per hour
Overhead is applied on the basis of direct-labor hours.	

	Product F, Special Widgets	*Product G, De Luxe Widgets*
Finished products (content of each unit):		
Material 111	12 units	12 units
Material 112	6 units	8 units
Direct labor	14 hours	20 hours

The balance sheet for the year just ended is given below:

M COMPANY

Balance Sheet
December 31, 19A

Assets

Current assets:		
Cash	$ 10,000	
Accounts receivable	25,000	
Materials	19,000	
Finished goods	14,480	
		$ 68,480
Fixed assets:		
Land	$ 50,000	
Building and equipment	380,000	
Accumulated depreciation	(75,000)	355,000
Total assets		$423,480

Equities

Current liabilities:		
Accounts payable	$ 8,200	
Income taxes payable	5,000	$ 13,200
Stockholders' equity:		
Common stock, no-par—25,000 shares outstanding	$350,000	
Retained income	60,280	410,280
Total equities		$423,480

Additional information regarding the year 19B:

	Finished Product	
	F	G
Expected sales in units	5,000	1,000
Selling price per unit	$ 105.40	$ 164.00
Desired ending inventory in units	1,100	50
Beginning inventory in units	100	50

	Direct Materials	
	111	112
Beginning inventory in units	5,000	5,000
Desired ending inventory in units	6,000	1,000

(Work in process is negligible and may be ignored.)

At anticipated volume levels, the following costs will be incurred:

Factory overhead:	
Supplies	$ 30,000
Indirect labor	70,000
Payroll fringe costs	25,000

Power—variable portion	8,000
Maintenance—variable portion	20,000
Depreciation	25,000
Property taxes	4,000
Property insurance	500
Supervision	20,000
Power—fixed portion	1,000
Maintenance—fixed portion	4,500
	$208,000

Selling and administrative expenses:	
Sales commissions	$ 20,000
Advertising	3,000
Sales salaries	10,000
Travel	5,000
Clerical wages	10,000
Supplies	1,000
Executive salaries	21,000
Miscellaneous	5,000
	$ 75,000

Budgeted cash flows are:

	QUARTERS			
	1	2	3	4
Collections from customers	$125,000	$150,000	$160,000	$221,000
Disbursements:				
For materials	20,000	35,000	35,000	54,200
For other costs and expenses	25,000	20,000	20,000	17,000
For payroll	90,000	95,000	95,000	109,200
For income taxes	5,000	—	—	—
For machinery purchase	—	—	—	20,000

(The quarterly data are given for your convenience. The figures are based on the cash effects of the operations formulated in Schedules 1 through 8 in the solution.)

The company desires to maintain a $15,000 minimum cash balance at the end of each quarter. Money can be borrowed or repaid in multiples of $500 at an interest rate of 10 percent per annum. Management does not want to borrow any more cash than is necessary and wants to repay as promptly as possible. In any event, loans may not extend beyond four quarters. Interest is computed and paid when the principal is repaid. Assume that borrowings take place at the beginning and repayments at the end of the quarters in question. Compute interest to the nearest dollar.

required

Prepare a master budget for the year 19B. Include the following detailed schedules:

1. Sales budget
2. Production budget

3. Direct-material-purchases budget
4. Direct-labor budget
5. Factory-overhead budget
6. Ending-inventory budget
7. Cost-of-goods-sold budget
8. Selling and administrative expense budget

and

I. Budgeted income statement (Assume income taxes for 19B to be $20,000.)
II. Budgeted statement of cash receipts and disbursements by quarters, including details of borrowings, repayments, and interest
III. Budgeted balance sheet

basic approach to formulating master budget

This chapter provides a review of the technical material covered in the previous chapters, because the master budget (the overall business plan) is basically nothing more than the preparation of the familiar financial statements. The major technical difference is that the accountant is dealing with expected future data rather than with historical data.

The following techniques are basic to the study of budgeting. First, the steps in preparation are presented. Second, some condensed, illustrative budget reports are shown in the solution to the problem.

The basic steps in preparing budgeted statements follow. Use the steps to prepare your own schedules. Check each detailed schedule, one-by-one, before proceeding to the next step.

1. **The sales forecast is the starting point for budgeting,** because inventory levels and production (and hence costs) are generally geared to the rate of sales activity.[1] The sales budget (Schedule 1 in the solution) is the result of a series of management decisions reached through a process that is described more fully in a separate section near the end of this chapter.

2. After sales are budgeted, the production budget (Schedule 2) may be prepared. The total units needed will be the sum of the desired ending inventory plus the amount needed to fulfill budgeted sales. The total need will be partially met by the beginning inventory; the remainder must come from planned production. Therefore, production is computed as follows:

$$\begin{pmatrix}\text{Units to be}\\ \text{Produced}\end{pmatrix} = \begin{matrix}\text{Desired Ending Inventory of Finished Goods}\\ + \text{ Budgeted Sales} - \text{Beginning Inventory of Finished Goods}\end{matrix}$$

Note that the production budget is stated in physical units. As the calculation indicates, production is affected by both inventory levels and the sales budget. Frequently, production is stabilized throughout the year despite seasonal fluctu-

[1] Occasionally, limits to productive capacity result in sales being geared to production rather than vice versa. Examples are shortages of machinery, manpower, or materials because of wars, strikes, or other imbalances in supply and demand.

ations in sales. Therefore, inventory serves as a coordinating link between manufacturing and sales by providing a cushion that satisfies the marketing need for goods when demand is unusually heavy and that also satisfies a production aim of stable utilization of manpower and facilities.

3. When the level of production activity has been determined, the following budget schedules may be constructed:

a. Material usage and purchases (Schedule 3). Usage will depend upon the level of production activity determined in step 2 above (Note A to Schedule 3). The purchases are influenced by both expected usage and inventory levels. The computation is Purchases in Units = Desired Ending Material Inventory Quantities + Usage − Beginning Inventory Quantities.
b. Direct-labor costs (Schedule 4). These depend upon the type of products produced and the labor rates and methods that must be used to obtain desired production.
c. Factory-overhead costs (Schedule 5). These depend upon the behavior of costs of the individual overhead items in relation to the anticipated level of production.
d. Inventory levels (Schedule 6). These are the desired ending inventories. This information is required for the construction of budgeted financial statements.

4. Cost-of-goods-sold budget (Schedule 7). This budget depends upon the information gathered in step 3.

5. Budget of selling, administrative, and other expenses (Schedule 8).

6. Budgeted income statement (Exhibit I). Steps 1 through 5 will provide enough information for this statement.

7. Cash budget (Exhibit II), predicting effects on cash position of the levels of operation above. The illustrative cash budget is presented by quarters to show the impact of cash-flow timing on bank loan schedules. In practice, monthly—and sometimes weekly—cash budgets are very helpful for cash planning and control. Cash budgets aid in avoiding unnecessary idle cash and unnecessary cash deficiencies. The astute mapping of a financing program keeps cash balances in reasonable relation to needs. Ordinarily, the cash budget (Budgeted Statement of Cash Receipts and Disbursements) has the following main sections:

a. The beginning cash balance plus cash receipts yield the total cash available for needs, before financing. Cash receipts depend on collections of accounts receivable, cash sales, and miscellaneous recurring sources such as rental or royalty receipts. Studies of the prospective collectibility of accounts receivable are needed for accurate predictions. Key factors include bad-debt experience and average time lag between sales and collections.
b. Cash disbursements:
   (1) Material purchases—depends on credit terms extended by suppliers and bill-paying habits of the buyer.
   (2) Direct labor and other wage outlays—depends on payroll dates.
   (3) Other costs and expenses—depends on timing and credit terms. **Note that depreciation does not entail a cash outlay.**
   (4) Other disbursements—outlays for fixed assets, long-term investments.

c. Financing requirements depend on how the total cash available for needs, keyed as (a) in Exhibit II, compares with the total cash needed. Needs include disbursements, keyed as (b), plus the ending cash balance desired, keyed as (d). The financing plans will depend on the relationship of cash available to cash sought. If there is an excess, loans may be repaid or temporary investments made. The pertinent outlays for interest expenses are usually shown in this section of the cash budget.

d. The ending cash balance. The effect of the financing decisions on the cash budget keyed as (c) in Exhibit II, may be positive (borrowing) or negative (repayment), and the ending cash balance, (d), equals (a) + (c) − (b).

The cash budget in Exhibit II shows the pattern of short-term "self-liquidating cash loans." Seasonal peaks of production or sales often result in heavy cash disbursements for purchases, payroll, and other operating outlays as the products are produced and sold. Cash receipts from customers typically lag behind sales. The loan is self-liquidating in the sense that the borrowed money is used to acquire resources that are combined for sale, and the proceeds from the sale are used to repay the loan. This cycle (sometimes called the *working-capital, cash,* or *operating cycle*) moves from cash to inventories to receivables and back to cash.

Cash budgets help managers avoid having unnecessary idle cash, on the one hand, and unnecessary nerve-racking cash deficiencies on the other.

8. Budgeted balance sheet (Exhibit III). Each item is projected in the light of the details of the business plan as expressed in the previous schedules. For example, the ending balance of Accounts Receivable would be computed by adding the budgeted sales (from Schedule 1) to the beginning balance (given) and subtracting cash receipts (given and in Exhibit II).

SOLUTION

M COMPANY

Sales Budget
For the Year Ending December 31, 19B

Schedule 1

	Units	Selling Price	Total Sales
Product F (deluxe)	5,000	$105.40	$527,000
Product G (super deluxe)	1,000	164.00	164,000
Total			$691,000

M COMPANY

Production Budget,* in Units
For the Year Ending December 31, 19B

Schedule 2

	Products F	Products G
Planned sales (Schedule 1)	5,000	1,000
Desired ending finished-goods inventory	1,100	50
Total needs	6,100	1,050
Less beginning finished-goods inventory	100	50
Units to be produced	6,000	1,000

* Work in process is negligible and is ignored.

M COMPANY

Direct-Material-Purchases Budget
For the Year Ending December 31, 19B

Schedule 3

	Material 111	Material 112	Total
Desired ending direct-material inventory in units	6,000	1,000	
Units needed for production (Note A)	84,000	44,000	
Total needs	90,000	45,000	
Less beginning direct-material inventory in units	5,000	5,000	
Units to be purchased	85,000	40,000	
Unit price	$ 1.20	$ 2.60	
Purchase cost	$102,000	$104,000	$206,000

Note A to Schedule 3—Usage of Direct Materials in Units and Dollars

	Production				
Direct Materials	Product F (6,000 Units)	Product G (1,000 Units)	Total Direct-Material Usage	Material Unit Cost	Cost of Materials Used
111 (12 units per finished product)	72,000	12,000	84,000	$1.20	$100,800
112 (6 units per Product F, 8 units per Product G)	36,000	8,000	44,000	2.60	114,400
					$215,200

M COMPANY

Direct-Labor Budget
For the Year Ending December 31, 19B

Schedule 4

	Units Produced	Direct Labor Hours per Unit	Total Hours	Total Budget @ $2.05 per Hour
Product F	6,000	14	84,000	$172,200
Product G	1,000	20	20,000	41,000
Total			104,000	$213,200

M COMPANY

Factory-Overhead Budget
For the Year Ending December 31, 19B

Schedule 5

At anticipated activity of 104,000 direct labor hours:		
Supplies	$30,000	
Indirect labor	70,000	
Payroll fringe costs	25,000	
Power—variable portion	8,000	
Maintenance—variable portion	20,000	
Total variable overhead		$153,000
Depreciation	$25,000	
Property taxes	4,000	
Property insurance	500	
Supervision	20,000	
Power—fixed portion	1,000	
Maintenance—fixed portion	4,500	
Total fixed overhead		55,000
Total factory overhead: ($208,000 ÷ 104,000 is $2.00 per direct-labor hour)		$208,000

M COMPANY

Ending-Inventory Budget
December 31, 19B

Schedule 6

	Units	Unit Cost	Total Amount	
Direct materials:				
111	6,000*	$ 1.20	$ 7,200	
112	1,000*	2.60	2,600	$ 9,800
Finished goods:				
F	1,100**	$ 86.70***	95,370	
G	50**	116.20***	5,810	101,180
Total				$110,980

* From top line in Schedule 3
** From second line in Schedule 2
*** Computation of unit costs:

		Product F		Product G	
	Unit Cost	Units	Amount	Units	Amount
Material 111	$1.20	12	$14.40	12	$ 14.40
Material 112	2.60	6	15.60	8	20.80
Direct labor	2.05	14	28.70	20	41.00
Factory overhead	2.00	14	28.00	20	40.00
Total			$86.70		$116.20

M COMPANY

Cost-of-Goods-Sold Budget
For the Year Ending December 31, 19B

Schedule 7

	From Schedule		
Direct materials used	3		$215,200
Direct labor	4		213,200
Factory overhead	5		208,000
Total manufacturing costs			$636,400
Add finished goods, December 31, 19A	Given	$ 14,480	
Less finished goods, December 31, 19B	6	101,180	
Inventory increase for year			(86,700)
Total			$549,700

M COMPANY

Selling and Administrative Expense Budget
For the Year Ending December 31, 19B

Schedule 8

Sales commissions	$20,000	
Advertising	3,000	
Sales salaries	10,000	
Travel	5,000	
Total selling expenses		$38,000
Clerical wages	$10,000	
Supplies	1,000	
Executive salaries	21,000	
Miscellaneous	5,000	
Total administrative expenses		37,000
Total selling and administrative expenses		$75,000

M COMPANY

Budgeted Income Statement
For the Year Ending December 31, 19B

Exhibit I

	From Schedule		
Sales	1		$691,000
Cost of goods sold	7		549,700
Gross margin			$141,300
Selling and administrative expenses	8	$75,000	
Interest expense	Exhibit II	1,775	76,775
Net income before income taxes			$ 64,525
Income taxes	Assumed		20,000
Net income after income taxes			$ 44,525

M COMPANY

Budgeted Statement of Cash Receipts and Disbursements
For the Year Ending December 31, 19B

Exhibit II

		Quarters 1	Quarters 2	Quarters 3	Quarters 4	For the Year as a Whole
	Cash balance, beginning	$ 10,000	$ 15,000	$ 15,000	$ 15,325	$ 10,000
	Add receipts:					
	Collections from customers	125,000	150,000	160,000	221,000	656,000
(a)	Total available before current financing	$135,000	$165,000	$175,000	$236,325	$666,000
	Less disbursements:					
	For materials	$ 20,000	$ 35,000	$ 35,000	$ 54,200	$144,200
	For other costs and expenses	25,000	20,000	20,000	17,000	82,000
	For payroll	90,000	95,000	95,000	109,200	389,200
	For income tax	5,000	—	—	—	5,000
	For machinery purchase	—	—	—	20,000	20,000
(b)	Total disbursements	$140,000	$150,000	$150,000	$200,400	$640,400
	Minimum cash balance desired	15,000	15,000	15,000	15,000	15,000
	Total cash needed	$155,000	$165,000	$165,000	$215,400	$655,400
	Excess of total cash available over total cash needed before current financing (deficiency)	$ (20,000)	$ —	$ 10,000	$ 20,925	$ 10,600
	Financing:					
	Borrowings (at beginning)	$ 20,000	$ —	$ —	$ —	$ 20,000
	Repayments (at end)	—	—	(9,000)	(11,000)	(20,000)
	*Interest (at 10% per annum)	—	—	(675)	(1,100)	(1,775)
(c)	Total effects of financing	$ 20,000	$ —	$ (9,675)	$ (12,100)	$ (1,775)
(d)	Cash balance, end (a + c − b)	$ 15,000	$ 15,000	$ 15,325	$ 23,825	$ 23,825

* The interest payments pertain only to the amount of principal being repaid at the end of a given quarter. Note that the remainder of the $20,000 loan must be repaid by the end of the fourth quarter. Also note that depreciation does not necessitate a cash outlay. The specific computations regarding interest are: $9,000 × .10 × 3/4 = $675 and $11,000 × .10 = $1,100.

M COMPANY

Budgeted Balance Sheet
December 31, 19B

Exhibit III

Assets			
Current assets:			
Cash (from Exhibit II)		$ 23,825	
Accounts receivable (1)		60,000	
Materials (2)		9,800	
Finished goods (2)		101,180	$194,805
Fixed assets:			
Land (3)		$ 50,000	
Building and equipment (4)	$400,000		
Accumulated depreciation (5)	100,000	300,000	350,000
Total assets			$544,805
Equities			
Current liabilities:			
Accounts payable (6)		$ 70,000	
Income taxes payable (7)		20,000	90,000
Stockholders' equity:			
Common stock, no-par, 25,000 shares outstanding (8)		$350,000	
Retained income (9)		104,805	454,805
Total equities			$544,805

Notes:
Beginning balances are used as a start for most of the following computations:
(1) $25,000 + $691,000 sales − $656,000 receipts = $60,000.
(2) From Schedule 6.
(3) From beginning balance sheet.
(4) $380,000 + $20,000 purchases.
(5) $75,000 + $25,000 depreciation.
(6) $8,200 + ($206,000 purchases, $213,200 direct labor, $183,000 factory overhead,* $75,000 selling and administrative expenses) − ($144,200 materials, $82,000 other costs and expenses, and $389,200 payroll) = $70,000.
(7) $5,000 + $20,000 current year − $5,000 payment.
(8) From beginning balance sheet.
(9) $60,280 + $44,525 net income.

* $208,000 from Schedule 5 minus depreciation of $25,000.

sales forecasting—a difficult task

factors in sales forecasting

Incurrence of cost is necessarily keyed to production activity. Activity, in turn, depends on predicted sales. The sales prediction is the foundation for the quantification of the entire business plan.[2]

[2] The term *sales forecast* is sometimes distinguished from *sales budget* as follows: The forecast is the estimate—the prediction—that may or may not become the sales budget. The forecast becomes the budget only if management accepts it as an objective. Often, the forecast leads to adjustments of managerial plans, so that the final sales budget differs from the original sales forecast.

The chief sales officer has direct responsibility for the preparation of the sales budget. The task of preparation forces him to crystallize his plans.

The sales forecast is made after consideration of the following factors:

1. Past sales volume
2. General economic and industry conditions
3. Relationship of sales to economic indicators such as gross national product, personal income, employment, prices, and industrial production
4. Relative product profitability
5. Market research studies
6. Pricing policies
7. Advertising and other promotion
8. Quality of sales force
9. Competition
10. Seasonal variations
11. Production capacity
12. Long-term sales trends for various products

forecasting procedures An effective aid to accurate forecasting is to approach the same goal by several methods; each forecast acts as a check on the others. The three methods described below are usually combined in some fashion that is suitable for a specific company.

SALES STAFF PROCEDURES As is the case for all budgets, those responsible should have an active role in sales-budget formulation. If possible, the budget data should flow from individual salesmen or district sales managers upward to the chief sales officer. A valuable benefit from the budgeting process is the holding of discussions, which generally result in adjustments and which tend to broaden participants' thinking.

Previous sales volumes are usually the springboard for sales predictions. Sales executives examine historical sales behavior and relate it to other historical data such as economic indicators, advertising, pricing policies, and competitive conditions. Current information is assembled, production capacity is considered, and then the outlook is derived for the ensuing months (years, in long-run sales budgets).

One of the common difficulties in budgeting sales is the widespread aversion of sales executives to figures. The usefulness of budgeting must be sold to salesmen. The best sales executives may not particularly enjoy working with figures, but they realize that intelligent decisions cannot be made without concrete information. Market research is a sales executive's tool that helps to eliminate hunches and guessing. The market research group is a major staff department in many corporations.

STATISTICAL APPROACHES Trend, cycle projection, and correlation analysis are useful supplementary techniques. Correlations between sales and economic indicators help make sales forecasts more reliable, especially if fluctuations in certain economic indicators precede fluctuations in company sales. However, no firm should rely entirely on this approach. Too much reliance on statistical evidence is dangerous, because chance variations in statistical data may completely upset a program. As always, statistical analysis can provide help but not outright answers.

GROUP EXECUTIVE JUDGMENT All top officers, including production, purchasing, finance, and administrative officers, may use their experience and knowledge to project sales on the basis of group opinion. This quick method dispenses with intricate statistical accumulations; however, it muddles responsibility for sales predictions and ignores the need for a tough-minded approach to this important task.

It is beyond the scope of this book to give a detailed description of all phases of sales-budget preparation, but its key importance should be kept in mind. The Suggested Readings at the end of this chapter list some references on sales forecasting.

planning models and simulation

A master budget can be regarded as a comprehensive planning model for the organization. As the budget is formulated, it is frequently altered via a step-by-step process as executives exchange views on miscellaneous aspects of expected activities and ask "what-if" questions. Such alterations are cumbersome by hand, but they are facilitated by the computer.

Computer-based simulation models often use the master budget as their structural base. These models are often called *financial planning models* or *total models.* They are mathematical statements of the relationships among all operating and financial activities, as well as other major internal and external factors that may affect decisions.[3] The models are used for budgeting, for revising budgets with little incremental effort, for conducting sensitivity analysis, and for comparing a variety of decision alternatives as they affect the entire organization.

[3] See Thomas J. Gorman, "Corporate Financial Models in Planning and Control," *The Price Waterhouse Review,* XV, No. 2, 41–53. Another provocative approach is to look upon the budgetary process as a linear programming model. One experimental model has an objective of maximizing net additions to retained earnings subject to a host of constraints, including limits on cash balances and production capacity. See Y. Ijiri, F. K. Levy, and R. C. Lyon, "A Linear Programming Model for Budgeting and Financial Planning," *Journal of Accounting Research,* Vol. I, No. 2, 198–212. An easy-to-read summary of practice in corporate planning models is "Piercing Future Fog in the Executive Suite," *Business Week* (April 28, 1975), pp. 46–54. Examples include Ralston Purina Co., where a one percent change in the price of a prime commodity causes a change in company's cost models and a possible change in the whole corporate plan. At Dow Chemical Co., 140 separate cost inputs, constantly revised, are fed into the model. Such factors as major raw-material costs and prices by country and region are monitored weekly. Multiple contingency plans, rather than a single, master plan, are used more widely than before.

Simulations have various degrees of sophistication and usefulness, depending on how much an organization is willing to pay.[4] Rudimentary general-purpose simulators can be rented from consultants or software firms. These usually entail gathering specific firm data as input; the output consists of the conventional financial statements and supporting schedules. At the other extreme, management can have a special-purpose simulator designed that includes interactive capabilities, integrates detailed activities of all subunits of an organization, encompasses internal and external data, and permits probabilistic analyses.

As in all aspects of systems design, cost-benefit approaches must be applied in deciding whether to use computer-based simulation models. Some benefits were enumerated above, and the costs of using general-purpose models continue to decline. For example, some credit departments of banks now find it worthwhile to use a general-purpose simulator to monitor the progress of their borrowers. The borrowers' data are the input, which is updated periodically. The prospects of more widespread use of simple general-purpose models is excellent, but the costs of complex models are still too imposing to warrant predictions of their rapid adoption.[5]

SUMMARY

Comprehensive budgeting is the expression of management's master operating and financing plan—the formalized outlining of company objectives and their means of attainment. When administered wisely, budgets (a) compel management planning, (b) provide definite expectations that are the best framework for judging subsequent performance, and (c) promote communication and coordination among the various segments of the business.

The foundation for budgeting is the sales forecast. Inventory, production, and cost incurrence are generally geared to the rate of sales activity.

SUGGESTED READINGS

PYHRR, PETER A., *Zero-Base Budgeting.* New York: Wiley-Interscience, 1973.

WELSCH, G., *Budgeting: Profit Planning and Control,* 4th ed. Englewood Cliffs, N.J.: Prentice-Hall, Inc., 1976.

[4] George W. Gershefski, "Building a Corporate Financial Model," *Harvard Business Review,* Vol. 47, No. 4, 61–72. Also see R. C. Murphy, "A Computer Model Approach to Budgeting," *Management Accounting,* Vol. LVI, No. 12 (June, 1975), 34–38.

[5] "Piercing Future Fog," *op. cit.,* p. 48, reports that in a survey of 346 corporations, 73 percent were either using or developing a corporate planning model. The chief reason was to explore more alternatives in planning. Most corporations concentrate their attention on the eight to twelve variables most crucial to their industry—rate of inflation, consumer spending on non-durables, interest rates, and so on.

The following references pertain especially to the difficult problem of sales forecasting:

GREEN, PAUL E., and Donald S. Tull, *Research for Marketing Decisions,* 2nd ed. Englewood Cliffs, N.J.: Prentice-Hall, Inc., 1970. Chapter 16 covers sales forecasting.

WHEELWRIGHT, STEVEN C., and SPYROS MAKRIDAKIS, *Forecasting Methods for Management.* New York: Wiley-Interscience, 1973.

PROBLEM FOR SELF-STUDY

Before trying to solve the homework problems, review the illustration in this chapter.

QUESTIONS, PROBLEMS, AND CASES

5-1 What are the two major features of a budgetary program? Which feature is more important? Why?

5-2 What are the elements of the budgetary cycle?

5-3 Define: *continuous budget, pro-forma statements.*

5-4 "The sales forecast is the cornerstone for budgeting." Why?

5-5 Enumerate four common duties of a budget director.

5-6 What is the function of a *budget committee? A budget manual?*

5-7 "Budgets are half-used if they serve only as a planning device." Explain.

5-8 *Budgeting Material Purchases* The X Company has prepared a sales budget of 42,000 finished units for a three-month period. The company has an inventory of finished goods on hand at December 31 and desires a finished-goods inventory at the end of the succeeding quarter as follows:

	UNITS	
	Dec. 31	March 31
Finished product	22,000	24,000

It takes three units of direct materials to make one unit of finished product. The company has an inventory of units of raw material at December 31 and desires an ending raw-material inventory as follows:

	UNITS	
	Dec. 31	March 31
Direct materials	100,000	110,000

How many units of direct materials should be purchased during the three months ending March 31?

5-9 *Budgeting Material Costs* The Maxwell Company uses a single raw material to make its product; for each unit of product, three pounds of this material are required. The price of this material is $10 per pound. The company follows a purchasing policy of placing orders on or before the fifth of each month to cover that month's requirements. It plans its inventory position in advance, to cover expected situations.

The inventory of material at June 30, 19_1 was	9,000 pounds
The inventory level planned for July 31 was	15,000 pounds
The inventory level planned for August 31 was	35,000 pounds
The inventory level planned for September 30 was	20,000 pounds

Production scheduled for the three-month period was:

During July,	10,000 units of product
During August,	12,000 units of product
During September,	15,000 units of product

Suppose that this set of plans is carried out. What will be the total cost of materials purchased for the month of July? August? September?

5-10 *Budgeting Material Quantities* (SIA) A sales budget for the first five months of 19_3 is given for a particular product line manufactured by Arthur Guthrie Co. Ltd.

	SALES BUDGET IN UNITS
January	10,800
February	15,600
March	12,200
April	10,400
May	9,800

The inventory of finished products at the end of each month is to be equal to 25 percent of the sales estimate for the next month. On January 1, there were 2,700 units of product on hand. No work is in process at the end of any month.

Each unit of product requires two types of materials in the following quantities:

Material A:	4 units
Material B:	5 units

Materials equal to one-half of the next month's production are to be on hand at the end of each month. This requirement was met on January 1, 19_3.

Prepare a budget showing the quantities of each type of material to be purchased each month for the first quarter of 19_3.

5-11 *Budgeted Manufacturing Costs* The Bridget Company has budgeted sales for 100,000 units of its product for 19_1. Expected unit costs, based on past experience, should be $60 for direct materials, $40 for direct labor, and $30 for manufacturing overhead. Assume no beginning or ending inventory in process. Bridget begins the year with 40,000 finished units on hand but budgets the ending finished-goods inventory at only 10,000 units. Compute the budgeted costs of production for 19_1.

5-12 *Cash Budget* Using the information below, prepare a cash budget showing expected cash receipts and disbursements for the month of May, and balance expected at May 31, 19_1.

Planned cash balance, May 1, 19_1: $60,000.

Sales for May: $800,000, half collected in month of sale, 40 percent in next month, 10 percent in third month.

Customer receivables as of May 1: $70,000 from March sales; $450,000 from April sales.

Merchandise purchases for May: $500,000, 40 percent paid in month of purchase, 60 percent paid in next month.
Payrolls due in May: $88,000.
Three-year insurance policy due in May for renewal: $2,000 to be paid in cash.
Other expenses for May, payable in May: $41,000.
Depreciation for month of May: $2,000.
Accrued taxes for May, payable in December: $6,000.
Bank note due May 15: $175,000, plus $10,000 interest.
Accounts payable (from merchandise purchases), May 1: $240,000.

5-13 *Cash Budget* (SIA, adapted) The directors of TUV Company Limited, of which you are accountant, decide that in the future a short-term cash budget should be prepared for each quarter. Your company sells directly to the public for cash and through trade outlets on credit terms of 2/10, n/30. The accounts receivable have been analyzed and show the following record of collection:

70 percent of credit sales collected within the discount period
20 percent collected at the end of the 30-day period
Balance collected at the end of a 60-day period

At the end of any month, 25 percent of sales on which the cash discounts will be taken are still uncollected. Estimated sales for your first quarterly cash budget are as follows:

	19_1		
	January	February	March
Cash sales	$30,000	$38,000	$45,500
Credit sales	74,000	79,000	85,000

TUV Company Limited makes purchases of goods for resale by paying for goods as delivered. By so doing they obtain a cash discount of 3 percent.

The markup on sales presently in effect provides a gross margin of 50 percent on gross cost (before cash discounts).

The minimum inventory required for efficient operation is $100,000 at retail prices.

Expenses are estimated as follows:

	SELLING	GENERAL
Fixed expenses	$6,000 per month	$10,000 per month
Variable expenses	10% of sales	5% of sales

Expenses are paid monthly as they arise.

Ten percent of fixed expenses represents depreciation and amortization of deferred charges.

A piece of land priced at $30,000 is under option. Your cash budget will indicate to the directors whether or not they can purchase the land for cash on March 31, 19_1. Cash must be available to pay a quarterly dividend of $7,500 on preferred shares on March 31. The purchase of land must not affect the general current position of the company.

The following information is from the December 31, 19_0, Balance Sheet:

Cash	$29,000
Accounts receivable	20,000*
Inventory at gross cost	70,000

* Credit sales for December were $31,580, of which $15,000 is still outstanding. November sales still outstanding are $4,000. $1,000 is uncollectible.

required

1. Schedule of collections on accounts for each month of January, February, and March.
2. Schedule of cash required for purchases for each month of January, February, and March.
3. Cash budget for each of the three months ended January 31, February 28, and March 31, 19_1.
4. Brief comments for directors on the significance of the cash budget.

5-14 *Budget of Cash Requirements* (C.G.A., adapted) Based on a sales forecast for the season, the Singapore department of a manufacturing company has prepared the following production schedule for the coming month: 30,000 units of Product A and 20,000 units of Product B. The manufacturing specifications for the products are as follows:

PRODUCT A	PRODUCT B
2 lbs. material X @ $.30	3 lbs. material W @ $.80
1/2 lb. material Y @ $.20	3/4 lb. material Y @ $.20
2 hours direct labor @ $2.00	1.5 hours direct labor @ $2.00

To the direct-labor hours, a 5 percent allowance for idleness (accounted for as overhead) should be added. Indirect-labor time is estimated to be 5 percent of direct-labor hours (excluding idleness), and the wage rate for indirect labor is $1.50. The overhead estimate (not shown above) is as follows:

FIXED COSTS PER MONTH		VARIABLE COSTS
Depreciation	$ 6,900	$.80 per direct-labor hour.
Expired insurance	800	*NOTE:* This rate includes the costs of idle time and indirect labor.
Superintendence	3,000	
	$10,700	

It is planned to increase the inventory of raw material X by 4,000 lbs. and to decrease the inventory of raw material W by 2,000 lbs. as of the beginning of the next month.

Prepare a prediction of the amount of cash necessary for the manufacturing operations of the coming month. Assume that materials and payroll costs are paid for in the month of purchase.

5-15 *Comprehensive Budget; Fill in Schedules* Following is certain information relative to the position and business of the Newport Store:

Current assets as of Sept. 30:	
Cash on deposit	$ 12,000
Inventory	63,600
Accounts receivable	10,000
Fixed assets—net	100,000
Current liabilities as of Sept. 30:	None
Recent and anticipated sales:	
September	$ 40,000
October	48,000
November	60,000
December	80,000
January	36,000

Credit sales: Sales are 75 percent for cash, and 25 percent on credit. Assume that credit accounts are all collected within 30 days from sale. The accounts receivable on Sept. 30 are the result of the credit sales for September (25 percent of $40,000).

Gross profit averages 30 percent of sales. Purchase discounts are treated on the income statement as "other income" by this company.

Expenses: Salaries and wages average 15 percent of sales; rent 5 percent; all other expenses, excluding depreciation, 4 percent. Assume that these expenses are disbursed each month. Depreciation is $750 per month.

Purchases: There is a basic inventory of $30,000. The policy is to purchase each month additional inventory in the amount necessary to provide for the following month's sales. Terms on purchases are 2/10, n/30. Assume that payments are made in the month of purchase, and that all discounts are taken.

Fixtures: In October, $600 is spent for fixtures, and in November, $400 is to be expended for this purpose.

Assume that a minimum cash balance of $8,000 is to be maintained. Assume that all borrowings are effective at the beginning of the month and all repayments are made at the end of the month of repayment. Interest is paid only at the time of repaying principal. Interest rate is 6 percent per annum.

On the basis of the facts as given above:

required

1. Complete Schedule A.

SCHEDULE A
BUDGETED MONTHLY DOLLAR RECEIPTS

ITEM	*SEPTEMBER*	*OCTOBER*	*NOVEMBER*	*DECEMBER*
Total sales	$40,000	$48,000	$60,000	$80,000
Credit sales	10,000	12,000	____	____
Cash sales	____	____	____	____
Receipts:				
Cash sales		$36,000		
Collections on accounts receivable		10,000	____	____
Total		$46,000	____	____

2. Complete Schedule B. Note that purchases are 70 percent of next month's sales.

SCHEDULE B
BUDGETED MONTHLY CASH DISBURSEMENTS FOR PURCHASES

ITEM	*OCTOBER*	*NOVEMBER*	*DECEMBER*	*TOTAL*
Purchases	$42,000			
Less 2% cash discount	840	____	____	____
Disbursements	$41,160	____	____	____

3. Complete Schedule C.

SCHEDULE C
BUDGETED MONTHLY CASH DISBURSEMENTS FOR OPERATING EXPENSES

ITEM	*OCTOBER*	*NOVEMBER*	*DECEMBER*	*TOTAL*
Salaries and wages	$ 7,200			
Rent	2,400			
Other expenses	1,920	____	____	____
Total	$11,520	____	____	____

4. Complete Schedule D.

SCHEDULE D
BUDGETED TOTAL MONTHLY DISBURSEMENTS

ITEM	OCTOBER	NOVEMBER	DECEMBER	TOTAL
Purchases	$41,160			
Operating expenses	11,520			
Fixtures	600			
Total	$53,280			

5. Complete Schedule E.

SCHEDULE E
BUDGETED CASH RECEIPTS AND DISBURSEMENTS

ITEM	OCTOBER	NOVEMBER	DECEMBER	TOTAL
Receipts	$46,000			
Disbursements	53,280			
Net cash increase				
Net cash decrease	$ 7,280			

6. Complete Schedule F (assume that borrowings must be made in multiples of $1,000).

SCHEDULE F
FINANCING REQUIRED BY NEWPORT STORE

ITEM	OCTOBER	NOVEMBER	DECEMBER	TOTAL
Opening cash	$12,000	$ 8,720		
Net cash increase				
Net cash decrease	7,280			
Cash position before financing	4,720			
Financing required	4,000			
Interest payments				
Financing retired				
Closing balance	$ 8,720			

7. What do you think is the most logical means of arranging the financing needed by Newport Store? Explain.
8. Prepare a pro forma income statement for the fourth quarter and a balance sheet as of December 31.
9. Certain simplifications have been introduced in this problem. What complicating factors would be met in a typical business situation?

5-16 *Cash Budget for Month* (SIA) The treasurer of the Househall Company states, "Our monthly financial budget shows me our cash surplus or deficiency and assures me that an unexpected cash shortage will not occur."

The following revenue and cost information is available for the month of May, 19_5:

Sales forecast (terms, 2%, 10 days, net 30)		$650,000
Production requirements:		
Raw materials	$301,000	
Direct labor	85,000	386,000

Overhead and other charges:		
Indirect labor	$ 34,000	
Real estate taxes	1,500	
Depreciation	25,000	
Utilities	1,500	
Wage benefits	9,000	
Fire insurance	1,500	
Amortization of patents	5,000	
Spoilage of materials	1,500	79,000
Sales salaries		45,000
Administrative salaries		15,000

Raw-materials inventory will increase by $6,000; other inventories are not expected to change.

Monthly charges for wage benefits include:

Unemployment insurance (payable monthly)	$1,350
Canada pension plan (payable monthly)	820
Holiday pay (May holidays will require $2,040)	1,100
Company pension fund (includes one-twelfth of a $10,800 adjustment paid in January, 19_5)	5,000
Group insurance (payable quarterly with a payment due in February)	730

Raw-material purchases are paid net 30 days, and $320,000 was outstanding at the end of April, 19_5.

Accrued wages on April 30, 19_5, were $11,000. All May payroll amounts will be paid within the month of May.

Customer discounts on sales (2% ten days) are normally given on 50% of the collections from the prior month's sales. Freight-out included in April sales amounted to $1,000 and is payable the next month.

Fire insurance premiums are payable in January in advance.

Real estate taxes are paid in August each year.

Utilities are billed and paid within the month.

Accounts receivable on April 30, 19_5 were made up of:

April sales ($550,000 from sales of $550,000)
March sales ($47,000 from sales of $470,000)
February sales ($31,800 from sales of $530,000)
January sales ($8,500 from sales of $340,000)

Bad debts are negligible. All January sales outstanding will have been collected by the end of May, and the collection pattern since time of sale will be the same as in previous months.

required

1. Prepare a cash forecast in good form for the month of May 19_5 showing the net cash surplus or deficiency for the month. Ignore income taxes.
2. Comment briefly on the treasurer's statement quoted at the beginning of the question.

5-17 *Quarterly Cash Budget* (SIA) As part of the company's overall planning program, the controller of the So Good Blueberry Packing Co. Ltd. prepares a cash budget by quarters each year.

The company's operations consist solely of processing and canning the yearly crop of blueberries. As this is a seasonal commodity, all manufacturing operations take place in the quarter of October through December. Sales are made throughout the year and the company's fiscal year ends on June 30.

The sales forecast for the coming year indicates (all figures in thousands):

1st quarter	(July–September 19_1)	$ 780
2nd quarter	(October–December 19_1)	1,500
3rd quarter	(January–March 19_2)	780
4th quarter	(April–June 19_2)	780

All sales are on account. The beginning balance of receivables is expected to be collected during the first quarter. It is anticipated that subsequent collections will follow the pattern of two-thirds collected in the quarter of sales, the remaining one-third in the quarter following.

Purchases of blueberries are scheduled as follows: $240,000 in the 1st quarter and $720,000 in the 2nd quarter. Payment is made in the quarter of purchase.

Direct labor of $700,000 is incurred and paid in the second quarter.

Factory overhead cost (paid in cash during quarter it is incurred) is $860,000 in the second quarter. The standby (fixed) amount in each of the other three quarters is $200,000.

Selling and administrative expenses, incurred and paid, amount to $100,000 per quarter during the year.

To finance its seasonal working-capital needs, the company has obtained a line of short-term credit with the Royal Toronto Bank. The company maintains a minimum cash balance of $8,000 and borrows and repays only in multiples of $5,000. It repays as soon as it is able without impairing the minimum cash balance. Interest is at 8 percent and is paid at time of loan repayment. It is assumed that all borrowing is made at the beginning of a quarter, and the repayments are made at the end of a quarter. (Round interest calculations to nearest $1,000.)

The company plans to spend the following amounts on fixed assets:

3rd quarter	$150,000
4th quarter	50,000

Account balances as of July 1, 19_1 were:

Cash	$ 8,000
Accounts receivable	25,000

required

1. Prepare a schedule to show the cash budget and financing requirements for each quarter and for the year ended June 30, 19_2.
2. Comment briefly on the nature and purpose of cash budgets for managerial planning.

5-18 *Cost Forecast Model* (CMA) Over the past several years the Programme Corporation has encountered difficulties estimating its cash flows. The result has been a rather strained relationship with its banker.

Programme's controller would like to develop a means by which he can forecast the firm's monthly operating cash flows. The following data were gathered to facilitate the development of such a forecast.

1. Sales have been increased and are expected to increase at .5 percent each month.

2. Thirty percent of each month's sales are for cash; the other 70 percent are on open account.
3. Of the credit sales, 80 percent are collected in the first month following the sale and the remaining 20 percent are collected in the second month. There are no bad debts.
4. Gross margin on sales averages 25 percent.
5. Programme purchases enough inventory each month to cover the following month's sales.
6. All inventory purchases are paid for in the month of purchase at a 2 percent cash discount.
7. Monthly expenses are: payroll—$1,500; rent—$400; depreciation—$120; other cash expenses—1 percent of that month's sales. There are no accruals.
8. Ignore the effects of corporate income taxes, dividends, and equipment acquisitions.

required

Using the data above, develop a mathematical model the controller can use for his calculations. Your model should be capable of calculating the monthly operating cash inflows and outflows for any specified month.

5-19 *Cash Budgeting* On Dec. 1, 19_1, the XYZ Wholesale Co. is attempting to project cash receipts and disbursements through Jan. 31, 19_2. On this latter date, a note will be payable in the amount of $10,000. This amount was borrowed in September to carry the company through the seasonal peak in November and December.

The trial balance on Dec. 1 shows in part:

Cash	$ 1,000	
Accounts receivable	28,000	
Allowance for bad debts		$1,580
Inventory	8,750	
Accounts payable		9,200

Sales terms call for a 2 percent discount if paid within the first ten days of the month after purchase, with the balance due by the end of the month after purchase. Experience has shown that 70 percent of the billings will be collected within the discount period, 20 percent by the end of the month after purchase, and 8 percent in the following month, and that 2 percent will be uncollectible.

The unit sales price of the company's one product is $10. Actual and projected sales are:

October actual	$ 18,000
November actual	25,000
December estimated	30,000
January estimated	15,000
February estimated	12,000
Total estimated for year ending June 30	150,000

All purchases are payable within fifteen days. Thus, approximately 50 percent of the purchases in a month are due and payable in the next month. The unit purchase cost is $7. Target ending inventories are 500 units plus 25 percent of the next month's unit sales.

Total budgeted selling and administrative expenses for the year are $40,000. Of this amount, $15,000 is considered fixed (includes depreciation of $3,000). The remainder varies with sales. Both fixed and variable selling and administrative expenses are paid as incurred.

required

Prepare a columnar statement of budgeted cash receipts and disbursements for December and January.

5-20 *Cash Budgeting* For a problem dealing with cash budgeting under uncertainty, see Problem 25-24.

Systems Design, Responsibility Accounting, and Motivation

6

Recall that Exhibit 1-1 (page 5) presented a diagram of the role of accounting in decision making. The focus there is on the accountant in relation to a single decision maker; until now little has been said about accounting in multiperson settings. In this chapter we obtain perspective on the critical factors that deserve attention when executives and accountants choose an accounting system that affects more than a lone individual.

This chapter has a heavy behavioral emphasis. Some readers may prefer to study this material after dealing with the technicalities of budgets and standards that are covered in the subsequent chapters.[1] In any event, the behavioral problems raised now are absolutely central to cost or management accounting. The choice of a particular system is not made in the abstract. Sooner or later, behavioral problems must be identified and confronted, although there are no pat answers or even a systematic method for solving the problems. Therefore, you may want to review some parts of this chapter as you peruse succeeding chapters.

[1] For example, you may wish to cover this chapter through the section, "Responsibility Accounting." Then complete your study of Chapter 6 after you have finished Chapter 9.

We consider goal congruence, incentives, responsibility accounting, controllable costs, and the effects of systems on motivation. The human aspects cannot be overemphasized.

motivation and systems design

This section stresses the problems of obtaining goal congruence and providing incentives, which can be tied together in one word, *motivation.* Psychologists have defined motivation as the perception of some want or goal together with the resulting drive toward achieving the want. There is a strong link between the seemingly foreign ideas of motivation and the design of accounting systems, even though the relationship may initially appear far-fetched.

goal congruence: the first motivational problem

Essentially, the management process is a series of *decisions* aimed at some objectives. Accounting *systems* for management decision making and implementation are often called *management accounting systems* or *management control systems* or, more briefly, *control systems.* They are the rules and repetitive procedures that provide for data accumulation and communication aimed at facilitating decisions.

In control systems, performance criteria are set via a plan: behavior (e.g., actions or inputs) is monitored, actual performance (e.g., results or outputs) is compared to planned performance, and rewards are given for desired behaviors or outputs. After adjustments to the system are made, the cycle is repeated. Thus, feedback is a key element of control.

Note that top management may express or imply a set of objectives for the organization as a whole. Whether the *top-management objectives* are achieved usually depends on whether *individual* and *group* objectives within the organization harmonize with those of the organization as a whole. The first question to ask in appraising a system is: *Does goal congruence exist?* That is, does the system provide a global emphasis so that all major goals and their interrelationships are considered as carefully as possible when managers act? Expressed another way, does the system specify goals and subgoals to encourage behavior such that individuals accept top-management goals as their personal goals? Of course, before answering the question of goal congruence, we must identify goals or objectives.

incentive: the second motivational problem

Goal congruence occurs when two or more persons aim toward the same objective, while *incentive* is a reason for *striving* toward an objective, whatever it may be. Incentive is concerned with getting subordinates to run rather than walk toward the desired goals. Note that goal congruence can exist without much incentive, and that

many managers can have plenty of incentive aimed at undesirable goals. Although goal congruence and incentive are intertwined, each warrants separate attention when one is appraising or designing a control system.

The distinction between goal congruence and incentive might be clarified by an example. Division managers may accept top-management goals as their personal goals regarding sales, costs, quality control, research, or other items. So goal congruence may exist, but the incentive problem still remains. A major means of providing incentive is the *evaluation of performance.* Clearly, the manager is influenced by how his or her performance is appraised. The choices of the content, format, timing, and use of performance reports are heavily affected by their probable influence on incentives. For instance, top managers may want to predict the incentive effects of alternative accounting measures of performance. Should we set extremely tough targets? Should we tie executive bonuses specifically to productivity achievements?[2]

A summary of our general approach to management accounting follows. The task of the formal control system is to help provide goal congruence and incentive through the use of technical tools (e.g., budgets, standards, formal measures of performance) that provide information and feedback. **The systems designer usually considers various technical proposals (usually as modifications of an existing system) in a cost-benefit sense. Will the new data or configurations promote a benefit of more congruence and incentive that offsets the cost of such a system?** This is the central question that should be raised, even though the answers may not be precise. Keep in mind that this approach implies a cost-benefit framework—and as a fundamental approach, not as an afterthought.

explaining the evolution of systems

The application of cost-benefit analysis and the identification of problems of goal congruence and incentives provide an explanation for the evolution of management accounting systems in many organizations. The sequence frequently is:

1. Physical observation
2. Historical records
3. Static budgets
4. Flexible budgets and standards
5. Profit centers and investment centers

[2] There is little theory or research available regarding the relationships between management incentives and the evaluation of performance. Kenneth J. Arrow, "Control in Large Organizations," *Management Science,* Vol. 10, No. 3 (April 1964), observes: "There are (at least) two problems in devising incentive systems: (1) an effective incentive system creates new demands for information; the reward is a function of performance, so top management must have a way of measuring performance; (2) even if the [performance] index is appropriate, the relationship between the reward and the index remains to be determined." Also see E. E. Lawler, *Pay and Organizational Effectiveness* (New York: McGraw-Hill, Inc., 1971) and Anthony Hopwood, *Accounting and Human Behavior* (London: Haymarket Publishing Limited, distributed by Prentice-Hall International, 1974), pp. 100–101.

As the sequence occurs, the system tends to become more elaborate and costly because the earlier facets of the system are nearly always retained.

A scenario may occur as follows. A proprietor (or two partners such as Hewlett and Packard) may begin a modest enterprise in a garage. The manager's physical observations may provide the sole planning and control system for a day or two. But the simple tracking of cash will require a modicum of historical records. Furthermore, no formal cost-benefit analysis is necessary to convince the manager that sufficient documentation must be kept to satisfy the Internal Revenue Service; the benefits are keeping the business as a going concern and staying out of jail.

Historical records may be compared from year to year as a basis for evaluating performance and planning. But often such a comparison fails to focus on the right question. The question is not: "How did we do in 19B compared with 19A?" Instead, the question is: "How did we do in 19B compared with what we *should have done* in 19B? In other words, did we reach our goals?" To answer the latter question, budgets were developed. Managers found that investing in a formal budgeting system was a cost-effective way to promote goal congruence and improve incentive. Managers often begin budgeting with relatively simple static budgets and, as the net benefits become apparent, gradually develop flexible budgets and standards. (Static and flexible budgets will be explained in Chapter 8.)

advantages of budgets

Budgets are a major feature of most control systems. When administered intelligently, budgets (a) compel planning, (b) provide performance criteria, and (c) promote communication and coordination.

compelled planning

"Plan ahead" is a redundant watchword for business managers and for any individual as well. Yet too often, everyday problems interfere with such planning; operations drift along until the passage of time catches the firms or individuals in undesirable situations that should have been anticipated and avoided.

Budgets formulate expected performance; they express managerial targets. Without such targets, operations lack direction, problems are not foreseen, results lack meaning, and the implications for future policies are dwarfed by the pressure of the present. The planning role of all levels of management should be accentuated and enlarged by a budgetary system. Managers will be compelled to look ahead and will be ready for changing conditions. This forced planning is by far the greatest contribution of budgeting to management.

Budgets have direct or indirect influence on strategies. Strategies are relatively general and permanent plans that change as conditions or objectives change—for example, when new products are added, old products are dropped, organizations are revamped, or production methods are changed. Budgets affect the formulation of overall organization strategies and then help to implement such strategies. These strategy changes are often affected either directly by budgetary information or indirectly by the thinking that evolved from dealing with budgets.

framework for judging performance

Despite the existence of complex computers and automation, individuals still run organizations, from the president down to the foreman of the smallest department. Employees do not like to fumble along not really knowing what their superiors anticipate or to see such expectations vary with, for example, the conditions of the superior's sinus trouble. The budget helps meet this difficulty by letting employees know what is expected of them.

As a basis for judging actual results, budgeted performance is generally viewed as being a better criterion than past performance. The fact that sales are better than last year's, or that direct-labor costs are lower than last year's, may be encouraging—but it is by no means conclusive as a measure of success. For example, the news that a company sold 100,000 units this year as compared with 90,000 units in the previous year may not necessarily be greeted with joy. Perhaps sales should have been 112,000 units this year. A major weakness of using historical data for judging performance is that inefficiencies may be buried in the past performance. Furthermore, the usefulness of comparisons with the past may be hampered by intervening changes in technology, personnel, products, competition, and general economic conditions.

communication and coordination

Coordination is the meshing and balancing of all factors of production and of all the departments and functions of the organization so that its objectives are attained—that is, the interests of the individual managers are subordinated for the benefit of the organization as a whole.

The concept of coordination implies, for example, that purchasing officers integrate their plans with production requirements, and that production officers use the sales budget as a basis for planning personnel needs and utilization of machinery.

Budgets help management to coordinate in several ways:

1. The existence of a well-laid plan is the major step toward achieving coordination. Executives are forced to think of the relationships among individual operations, and the company as a whole.
2. Budgets help to restrain the empire-building efforts of executives. Budgets broaden individual thinking by helping to remove unconscious biases on the part of engineers, sales, and production officers.

3. Budgets help to search out weaknesses in the organizational structure. The formulation and administration of budgets isolate problems of communication, of fixing responsibility, and of working relationships.

The idea that budgets improve coordination and communication may look promising on paper, but it takes plenty of intelligent administration to achieve in practice. For instance, the use of budgets to judge performance may cause managers to wear blinders and concentrate more than ever on their individual worlds. We shall examine this problem in more detail later in the chapter.

The cost-conscious, cooperative attitudes toward budgetary control must permeate all levels of management. A skeptical top-management attitude will trickle down to the detriment of the entire company. *Top management must understand and enthusiastically support the budget and all aspects of the control system.*

Administration of budgets must not be rigid. Changed conditions call for changes in plans. The budget must receive respect, but it does not have to be so revered that it prevents a manager from taking prudent action. A department head prepares and accepts his budget; he commits himself to the outlined performance. But if matters develop so that some special repairs or a special advertising outlay will best serve the interests of the firm, the manager should feel free to request permission for such outlays, or the budget itself should provide enough flexibility to permit a manager reasonable discretion in deciding how best to get his job done.

human aspect Budgeting is too often looked upon from a purely mechanistic viewpoint. The human factors in budgeting are more important than the accounting techniques. The success of a budgetary system depends upon its acceptance by the company members who are affected by the budgets.

Budgets place managers in the spotlight. The natural reaction to restriction, to criticism, and to control is resistance and self-defense. *The job of education and selling is overwhelmingly important here.* Too many department heads think that budgets represent a penny-pinching, negative brand of managerial presssure.[3] To them, the word *budget* is about a popular as, say, *layoff, strike,* or *pay decrease.* Ideally, company personnel should understand and accept the role of budgets as positive vehicles for company improvement, department improvement, and individual improvement. The budget is not a heinous means of squeezing the last drop of sweat out of employees. Properly used, it is simply a systematic tool for establishing standards of performance, for providing motivation, for gauging results, and for helping management advance toward its objectives. The budget technique in itself is free of emotion; its administration, however, is

[3] Pressure, in varying amounts, is a part of almost every job responsibility. Used with care, pressure motivates toward goals and is thus desirable. However, the word *pressure* has unappealing connotations and usually indicates unreasonable, unbearable stress.

often packed with trouble. The budget's major role is to communicate the various motivations that basically already exist among the management personnel, so that everybody sees, understands, and coordinates the goals, means, and drives of the organization.

The importance of these human aspects cannot be overemphasized. Without a thoroughly educated and cooperative management group at all levels of responsiblity, budgets are a drain on the funds of the business and are a hindrance instead of a help to efficient operations. A budgetary program per se is not a remedy for weak managerial talent, faulty organization, or a poor information system.

responsibility accounting

systems and organization changes

Ideally, the organization itself and its processes must be thoroughly appraised, understood, and altered, if necessary, before a system is constructed. That is, the design of a system and the design of an organizational structure are really inseparable and interdependent. The most streamlined system is not a cure-all or a substitute for basic organizational ills or management ineptitude. On a practical level, there may be a powerful temptation to separate the design of system from the design of organizational processes by assuming that the organizational structure is given and therefore not subject to change. But some sad experiences with the hasty installation of computers demonstrate the weakness of such an approach.

To work optimally, top managers subdivide processes and stipulate an organizational hierarchy of managers, each of whom is expected to oversee a sphere of responsibility and ordinarily has some degree of latitude to make decisions within that sphere. The sphere of responsibility may be called a cost center; or, if the manager must also make decisions about sales or investments, the responsibility sphere may be called a profit center or investment center. Some form of responsibility accounting system usually accompanies this subdivision of decision making.

definition of responsibility accounting

Responsibility accounting, profitability accounting, or *activity accounting* systems recognize various decision centers throughout an organization and trace costs (and revenues, assets, and liabilities, where pertinent) to the individual managers who are primarily responsible for making decisions about the costs in question.

The impact of the responsibility accounting approach is described in the following:

> The sales department requests a rush production. The plant scheduler argues that it will disrupt his production and cost a substantial though not clearly determined amount of money. The answer coming from sales is: "Do you want to take the responsi-

bility of losing the X Company as a customer?" Of course the production scheduler does not want to take such a responsibility, and he gives up, but not before a heavy exchange of arguments and the accumulation of a substantial backlog of ill feeling. Analysis of the payroll in the assembly department, determining the costs involved in getting out rush orders, eliminated the cause for argument. Henceforth, any rush order was accepted with a smile by the production scheduler, who made sure that the extra cost would be duly recorded and charged to the sales department—"no questions asked." As a result, the tension created by rush orders disappeared completely; and, somehow, the number of rush orders requested by the sales department was progressively reduced to an insignificant level.[4]

Ideally, revenues and costs are recorded and automatically traced to the individual at the lowest level of the organization who shoulders primary day-to-day decision responsibility for the item. He is in the best position to evaluate and to influence a situation—to implement decisions.

Note the philosophy implied in the above quotation. Top management has delegated the freedom to make decisions to a lower level. Instead of having to check with somebody before accepting a rush order, the manager has full discretion. Thus, the manager is not subject to day-to-day monitoring of his behavior (decisions). However, he is accountable for the results via responsibility accounting. So responsibility accounting is a mechanism that supplies the desired balance to the greater freedom of action that individual executives are given.

illustration of responsibility accounting

The simplified organization chart in Exhibit 6-1 will be the basis for our illustration. We will concentrate on the manufacturing phase of the business. The lines of responsibility are easily seen in Exhibit 6-2, which is an overall view of responsibility reporting. Starting with the supervisor of the machining department and working toward the top, we shall see how these reports may be integrated through three levels of responsibility.

Note that each of three responsibility reports furnishes the department head with figures on only those items subject to his control. Items not subject to his control are removed from these performance reports; he should not receive data that may clutter and confuse his decision making. For example, a fixed cost such as depreciation on the factory building is excluded.

Trace the $72,000 total from the machining department report in Exhibit 6-2 to the production vice-president's report. The vice-president's report merely summarizes the reports of the three individuals under his jurisdiction. He may also want copies of the detailed statements of each supervisor responsible to him.

[4] Raymond Villers, "Control and Freedom in a Decentralized Company," *Harvard Business Review*, Vol. XXXII, No. 2, p. 95. Another example is National City Bank's responsibility accounting system for a check-processing department. On any given day, for every $1 million that is not delivered to the Federal Reserve Bank on time, the department is "fined" $167, the amount the parent company loses in potential interest. See *Wall Street Journal*, June 6, 1975, p. 17.

EXHIBIT 6-1

CURRY CO.: SIMPLIFIED ORGANIZATION CHART

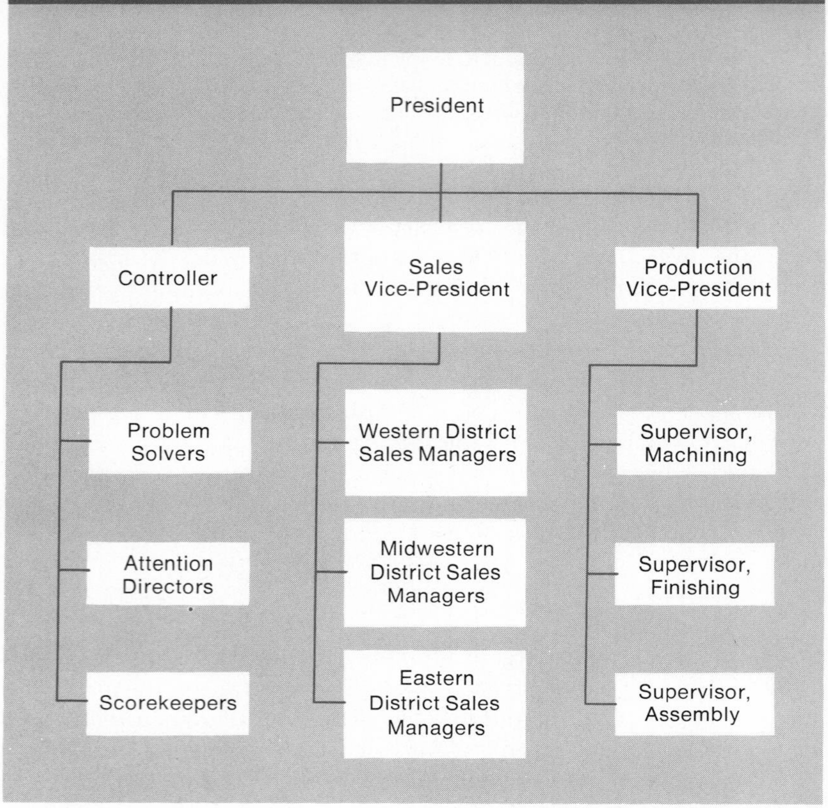

Also trace the $116,000 total from the production vice-president's report to the president's report. His summary report includes data for his own office plus a summarization of the entire company's current cost-control performance.

format of feedback reports This set of illustrative reports shows only the budgeted amount and the variance, which is defined as the difference between the budgeted and the actual amounts. This places the focus on the variances and illustrates *management by exception,* which means that the executive's attention is concentrated on the important deviations from budgeted items. In this way, managers do not waste time on those parts of the reports that reflect the smoothly running phases of operations.

EXHIBIT 6-2

CURRY CO.

President's Monthly Responsibility Performance Report

	BUDGET		VARIANCE: FAVORABLE, (UNFAVORABLE)	
	This Month	Year to Date	This Month	Year to Date
President's office	$ 6,000	$ 20,000	$ 100	$ 400
Controller	4,000	13,000	(200)	(1,000)
Production vice-president	→ 116,000	377,000	(8,950)	(20,600)
Sales vice-president	40,000	130,000	(1,000)	(4,000)
Total controllable costs	$166,000	$540,000	$(10,050)	$(25,200)

Production Vice-President's Monthly Responsibility Performance Report

	BUDGET		VARIANCE: FAVORABLE, (UNFAVORABLE)	
	This Month	Year to Date	This Month	Year to Date
Vice-president's office	$ 9,000	$ 29,000	$ (1,000)	$ (1,000)
Machining department	→ 72,000	236,000	(2,950)	(11,600)
Finishing department	15,000	50,000	(2,000)	(3,000)
Assembly department	20,000	62,000	(3,000)	(5,000)
Total controllable costs	$116,000	$377,000	$ (8,950)	$(20,600)

*Machining Department Supervisor's Monthly Responsibility Performance Report**

	BUDGET		VARIANCE: FAVORABLE, (UNFAVORABLE)	
	This Month	Year to Date	This Month	Year to Date
Direct materials	$ 40,000	$140,000	$ (1,000)	$ (4,000)
Direct labor	25,000	75,000	(2,000)	(7,000)
Setup	4,000	12,000	400	100
Rework	2,000	6,000	(200)	(300)
Supplies	200	600	(40)	(100)
Small tools	300	900	(50)	(100)
Other	500	1,500	(60)	(200)
Total controllable costs	$ 72,000	$236,000	$ (2,950)	$(11,600)

* He receives an itemized report of his performance. Totals are carried to the report of his immediate superior, whose results are, in turn, reported upward.

Of course, this illustration is only one possible means of presenting a report of performance. Another common reporting method shows three sets of dollar figures instead of two sets. Moreover, the variances could also be expressed in terms of percentages of budgeted amounts. For example, direct labor in the machining department could appear as follows:

	BUDGET		ACTUAL RESULTS		VARIANCE: FAVORABLE, (UNFAVORABLE)		VARIANCE: PERCENT OF BUDGETED AMOUNT	
	This Month	Year to Date	This Month	Year to Date	This Month	Year to Date	This Month	Year to Date
Direct labor	$25,000	$75,000	$27,000	$82,000	$(2,000)	$(7,000)	(8.0%)	(9.4%)

The full performance report would contain a similar line-by-line analysis of all items. The exact format adopted in a particular organization depends heavily on user preferences.

controllable and uncontrollable costs

definition of controllable costs

Responsibility accounting has a natural appeal because it specifies a boundary of operations and distinguishes between controllable and uncontrollable costs. It is easy to say that a manager's performance should be judged on the basis of only those items subject to his control. But experienced cost accountants and managers will testify that it is far from easy to decide whether an item is controllable or uncontrollable. Moreover, there are shades of influence—an item may be controllable in whole or in part. Therefore, do not expect to get a crystal-clear, practical concept of a controllable cost. It does not exist. Still, accountants must grapple with this problem, even though their approaches are often coarse.

Controllable costs are defined as those that are directly influenced by a *given manager* within a *given time span.* The definition has two important ingredients. First, we cannot distinguish controllable from uncontrollable costs without specifying a level and scope of management authority. That is, we must circumscribe the activity or organizational unit that is under the direction of the manager. For example, insurance costs on machinery may not be controllable by the manager of a producing department. However, such costs may indeed be controllable by the manager of the insurance department.

Second, the time-period assumption is important. If the time period were long enough, virtually all costs would be controllable by somebody in the organization. On the other hand, as the time period shortens, very few costs may be controllable. In the insurance example, note that the cost of a one-year insurance policy might not be controllable, even by the insurance manager, if the time period for evaluation were a week or a month instead of a year. In contrast, the rent on a building having a thirty-year lease could be viewed as controllable by the building and facilities manager if the time period used for evaluation were thirty years.

determining controllability or responsibility

The main trouble for the designer of a responsibility accounting system is that controllability is a matter of degree: (a) there are usually few costs that are clearly the *sole* responsibility of one person; and (b) the time-period problem is almost impossible to solve for many costs. Although controllability may often be difficult to pinpoint, responsibility accounting nevertheless clings to a tough-minded approach. It asks, Who is the one person in the organization with the most decision-making power over the item in question? This is usually the executive who most closely supervises the day-to-day activities that influence that cost. He typically has the authority to accept or reject the material or service in question. Therefore, he must bear the responsibility, and so must his superiors.

If the manager is responsible for both the acquisition and the use of the service, the cost should be deemed as controllable by him. However, the diffusion of control throughout the organization complicates the task of collecting data by responsibility centers. For example, raw-material *prices* may be most affected by the decisions of the purchasing officer, whereas raw-material *usage* may be most strongly influenced by the production supervisor.

As the next chapter will show in detail, the management accountant approaches this problem by charging the production department for raw materials at predetermined unit prices rather than actual unit prices. In this way, month-to-month price fluctuations do not affect the performance of the production supervisor. Predetermined prices (most often called *budgeted* or *standard* prices) are frequently utilized so that performance measures may exclude the possible misleading effects of changes in unit prices.

The whole complex problem of allocating indirect costs to departments, territories, products, and other cost objects, as we shall see in Chapter 16, illustrates how messy the idea of fixing responsibility or controllability can become. There are many instances where a manager can indirectly influence the amount of cost incurred. For instance, if a repair and maintenance department renders service to many departments, the level of repair costs borne by any production supervisor for nonroutine repairs can be affected by the wage rates in the repair department, the efficiency of the repair work force, the supervisory skills of the repair foreman, the efficiency of the production workers, the timing and care of the ordinary repairs done by regular production personnel, and so on.

reporting controllable and uncontrollable items

In a given situation, therefore, some costs may be regarded as controllable with various degrees of influence and others as uncontrollable. Most advocates of responsibility accounting favor excluding the uncontrollable items from a performance report. For example, the report for a shop foreman's department would contain only his controllable costs. Such items as property taxes and rent would not appear on his report; from his standpoint, these are uncontrollable costs.

The countervailing view is that uncontrollable items that are indirectly caused by the existence of the foreman's department should be included in his report. In this way, managers become aware of the whole organization and its costs. The behavioral implication of this idea is that some managers who have *no* direct control may nevertheless be spurred to influence the manager who has primary control over the cost.

example

A president of a large corporation insists that central basic research costs be fully allocated to all divisions despite objections about uncontrollability. His goal is to force division managers' interests toward such research activity. Accountants and managers disagree about the desirability of the president's practice. The basic question is whether the accounting system is the best vehicle for reaching such an objective. Indiscriminate cost allocations may undermine the confidence of the managers in the entire accounting system.

But there is also a pitfall in responsibility accounting. There can be overdependence on an accounting system as being the prime means of motivation and the final word on the appraisal of performance. Although the system may play a necessary role in coordination and motivation, its many limitations deserve recognition, too, particularly in matters of cost allocations. A common complaint of managers, often marked by tones of discouragement, is that they are being unfairly charged with uncontrollable costs. In any event, if management insists that both controllable and uncontrollable costs appear on the same report, these costs should not be mingled indiscriminately.

the time period and control

The influence of the time period on determining whether a cost is controllable is a vexing problem. Too often, managers are inclined to oversimplify by assuming that variable costs are controllable and fixed costs are uncontrollable. Such thinking may lead to erroneous conclusions. For example, rent is uncontrollable by the assembly foreman, but it may be controllable by, say, the executive vice-president, who is assigned the responsibility of choosing plant facilities and of deciding whether to own or rent. Moreover, managers frequently have the option of trading off variable for fixed costs—for example, by purchasing labor-saving machinery.

Some of the most severe analytical difficulties arise because of the existence of long-run costs like depreciation. How, for example, should depreciation be regarded in a situation where (a) a department already has all its needed equipment, (b) the current department manager has inherited the equipment from his predecessor, and (c) the life of the equipment is long? In such a situation, the main control must be exerted at the time of acquisition of the equipment; once incurred, the level of cost may be hard to influence for many years. Chapter 16 shows a possible way to report costs so that these long-run committed costs are sharply differentiated from other fixed and variable costs that are subject to short-run decisions.

feedback and fixing blame

Budgets coupled with responsibility accounting provide systematic help for managers, particularly if the feedback is interpreted carefully. **Discussions among managers, accountants, and students have repeatedly disclosed a tendency to "fix the blame"—as if the variance arising from a responsibility accounting system should pinpoint**

misbehavior and provide answers. However, no accounting system or variances can provide answers, ipso facto. But variances can suggest questions about possible causes of the variances or can direct attention to persons who should be asked to explain the variances. **In associating costs or variances with individuals, we should inquire *who should be asked* in a specific situation—*not* who should be blamed.**

subunit performance and manager performance

Distinguish between the performance of the *manager* and the performance of the *subunit.* To the extent feasible, the manager should be evaluated on the basis of his controllable performance. Furthermore, this evaluation often extends far beyond the measurements generated by an accounting system. Examples may include his performance in product quality, labor relations, and community relations.

In contrast, the performance of the subunit may be gauged so that top management can decide on whether it is a wise investment, on whether to change it or delete it. In such cases, some costs that are uncontrollable by the manager (e.g., rents, property taxes) may be logically assigned to the subunit.

effect of systems on human behavior

alternative views of organizations

A "rationalistic" model of organizations has been advocated *as a point of departure* here, whereby organizational objectives or goals are specified, alternatives systematically identified, consequences weighed, and actions chosen. Of course, in real life things are messier. For instance, some authors have maintained that a "garbage-can" model is more descriptive: ". . . organizations can be viewed for some purposes as collections of choices looking for problems, issues and feelings looking for decision situations in which they might be aired, solutions looking for issues to which they might be an answer, and decision makers looking for workers."[5]

This is not a book on organizations or on behavioral science, so we will not study alternative behavioral models here. Nevertheless, some cautionary words are warranted. First, *goal* congruence may be elusive in many organizations because the goals are unknown or not explicit. Thus, it may be better to think of *behavior* congruence;[6] that is, employee behavior (actions) congruent with top-management wants should be a major concern.

[5] Michael D. Cohen, James G. March, and Johan P. Olsen, "A Garbage Can Model of Organizational Choice," *Administrative Science Quarterly,* Vol. 17, No. 1 (March 1972). For good discussions of alternative models, see Hopwood, *Accounting and Human Behavior,* and Edwin H. Caplan, *Management Accounting and Behavioral Science* (Reading, Mass.: Addison-Wesley Publishing Company, 1971). For a fascinating description of how different models lead to different conceptions and interpretations of the same phenomena, see Graham T. Allison, *Essence of Decision* (Boston: Little, Brown and Company, 1971), a description of the Cuban missile crisis.

[6] Thomas Dyckman, "A Critique" in *Management Accounting and Control,* Proceedings of Beyer Symposium (Madison: University of Wisconsin, School of Business, 1975), p. 40.

EXHIBIT 6-3

THREE TYPES OF INTERDEPENDENT CONTROL

Type	Goals	Performance Criteria	Feedback	INCENTIVES: Rewards or Reinforcements	Punishments or Sanctions
Organization	Profits, share of market, quality of service	Budgets, standard costs, past performance	Quantitative variances	Commendation, promotions, salary raises	Condemnation, dismissal, salary cuts
Informal group	Mutual commitment, group ideals	Group norms	Deviant behavior	Peer-approval, membership, leadership	Kidding, hostility, ostracism
Individual	Personal goals, aspirations	Expectations, interim targets	Reaching or missing targets	Self-satisfaction, elation	Disappointment, self-hatred

SOURCE: Adapted from G. W. Dalton and P. R. Lawrence, eds., *Motivation and Control in Organizations* (Homewood, Ill.: Richard D. Irwin, Inc., 1971), p. 15.

Second, many researchers stress that there is no dominant organizational goal such as profit maximization. Instead of conducting exhaustive searches for alternatives, managers aim at "satisfactory" profits and focus on individual or subunit goals that frequently conflict.

Third, the organization controls (such as budgetary controls) are only one means of control, as the next section shows.

three types of control

Various authors[7] have identified three major types of control in organizations: organization, informal group, and individual. These are compared in Exhibit 6-3.

The organization controls usually consist of formal rules and standard operating procedures plus the informal procedures that are also communicated throughout the organization. The informal group controls "emerge from the shared values and the mutual commitments of members of a group to one another."[8] Individual controls are described in the next section.

These three types of controls are obviously interdependent. The challenge to accountants and managers is to (a) recognize their existence, (b) assess their potential conflicts, and (c) aim at increasing the acceptance of organizational controls by the affected groups and individuals. For example, the organizational controls may be designed to reward increases in productivity, but they may have

[7] G. W. Dalton and P. R. Lawrence, eds., *Motivation and Control in Organizations* (Homewood, Ill.: Richard D. Irwin, Inc., 1971), pp. 1–35, and Hopwood, *Accounting and Human Behavior,* pp. 21–37.

[8] Hopwood, *op. cit.,* p. 30.

little influence if the employees have developed their own group controls that restrict productivity improvements. The ultimate influence of budgets and performance measurements depends on how they affect and, in turn, are affected by the informal group controls and individual controls of managers and employees.[9] At this stage, the dimensions of the problem are reasonably clear, but no pat answers or sweeping generalizations are available.

system goals and individual goals

Clearly, it is not enough for the control system simply to specify subgoals so that they harmonize with top-management goals. Ideally, management should also design the system to lead the individual managers toward *acceptance* of those subgoals as their own personal goals. For example, how important is conformance to a budget prediction? If conformance is accepted by the manager as being important, and the accounting feedback is regarded as the most important source of information regarding his own appraisal of self-worth (for example, it tells him, "I am competent"), then the budget will be a crucial part of the control system.

Of course, the accounting system is only one of many control systems that influence an individual's behavior. Society as a whole can be viewed as a control system, and various institutions can impinge on an individual's values and reactions. For example, a person can be affected by his family, religion, profession, company, department, and so forth. This point may be obvious, but it is not trivial.

senior-manager support

The manager may try to influence the individual's acceptance of goals. However, his influence may be overwhelmed by the values of society and the feedback information from other sources. Furthermore, in practice it is very hard to detect and allow for the variations in perceived individual self-worths. For example, the design of budget systems for professional personnel, such as research scientists, is often particularly difficult. This is undoubtedly partially attributable to the phenomenon that perceived self-worth may be little affected by the formal control system per se. In short, propositions such as "It's important to adhere to budget" may be relatively unimportant to a researcher. Moreover, his feedback sources are more likely to be informal than formal. The opinions of co-workers and external critics may count heavily.[10]

The point is that the motivational effects of accounting systems are often

[9] *Ibid.*, pp. 35 and 37.

[10] John L. Neuman, "Make Overhead Cuts That Last," *Harvard Business Review*, Vol. 53, No. 3 (May-June 1975), p. 118, observes, "Organizations hire professionals to run and staff their service-performing departments. Typically, these people march to a different drummer. They measure themselves against their professional colleagues in other organizations, and they tend to get so absorbed in the technical aspects of their jobs that they lose sight of the overall value of their work to their employers."

weighty; however, in some parts of the organization they may simply be unimportant. **Personal goals, to the extent that acceptance of goals (such as budget goals) can be affected by formal systems within the organization, are likely to be heavily influenced by how higher executives support the system. Without massive top-management backing, the goals specified by the system, which should aim at goal congruence, are less likely to gain acceptance as group goals or as personal goals.** Note too that acceptance is the key; acceptance may be best achieved in some cases by participatory processes and in other cases by authoritative processes.[11]

illustrations of behavioral focus

This section reinforces the preceding sections by describing some behavioral problems that frequently arise in conjunction with control systems. Some attempts to solve such problems are also described.

general difficulties of goal congruence

The design of a management accounting system should begin with an identification of top-management objectives and subobjectives. The latter have been expressed in many forms and details. For example, subobjectives may be labeled as *critical success factors* or *key result areas.* Thus, a company might have a major objective of maximizing long-run income. The critical success factors or key result areas might be quality of product and production efficiency in one company, and they might be cost estimation and pricing strategy in another company.

The aim of a system is to obtain subgoal congruence, and this requires direction and balance. It is fairly easy to assess the direction of each subgoal by itself; the trouble is that they are interdependent. Moreover, the selection of

[11] Two polar types of management processes are *authoritative* and *participative.* For example, an authoritative way to prepare a budget is to have top management impose it on all managers without consulting them. In contrast, a participative way to prepare a budget is to have all responsible executives hammer out budget goals in a democratic fashion. R. J. Swieringa and R. H. Moncur, *Some Effects of Participative Budgeting on Managerial Behavior* (New York: National Association of Accountants, 1975), studied the use of participative budgeting in four production companies and examined the reactions of a sample of 137 managers. As might be expected, they found no magic guidelines. Instead, they concluded (p. 103) that "different variables may be important for predicting different aspects of how managers use budgeting." Many writers maintain that participative budgeting is better than authoritative budgeting. They also stress that budget-goal setting is highly individualistic. For example, a difficult budget may be perceived by a high achiever, to whom it represents an acceptable aspiration level, as a challenge, or by the low achiever as impossible. A. Buckley and E. McKenna, "Budgeting Control and Business Behavior," *Accounting and Business Research,* Spring 1972, p. 149, conclude that "managers like to achieve budget, since in doing so they fulfill esteem and achievement needs." For appraisals of the implications of behavioral science on accounting see T. Hofstedt, "Behavioral Accounting Research: Pathologies, Paradigms and Prescriptions," *Accounting, Organizations and Society* (1976), Vol. 1, No. 1, and T. Dyckman, M. Gibbins, and R. Swieringa, "Experimental and Survey Research in Financial Accounting: A Review and Evaluation" (Durham, N.C.: Duke University Graduate School of Business, 1976).

subgoals is essentially based on a series of assumptions regarding optimization that must be made at the strategic-planning level. For example, the General Electric Company[12] has stressed multiple goals by stating that organizational performance will be measured in the following eight areas:

1. Profitability
2. Market position
3. Productivity
4. Product leadership
5. Personnel development
6. Employee attitudes
7. Public responsibility
8. Balance between short-range and long-range goals

General Electric's efforts basically try to juggle two conflicting tendencies in goal setting. First, the overemphasis on multiple goals may lead to diffusion of efforts and the failure to perform as well as expected in any one area. Second, the overemphasis on a single goal may lead to success in one area but failure to attain other goals.

General Electric, despite citing eight separate goals, has found managers stressing one goal above all others: profitability. When several executives of General Electric were cited by the Justice Department for price fixing, one of the strongest arguments mustered in their defense was that a sense of internal pressure for profits had led toward this action, even though, in addition to being illegal, it was clearly opposed to the company's longer-run interests.[13]

The lesson is that the accounting system is still dominant as a means for setting goals and influencing management behavior in most organizations. Goals outside the accounting system, even though meritorious, are regarded as supplementary unless top management follows through and acts as if they are indeed as important as short-run financial performance.

example

The Soviet Union provides many cases where overstress on one or two aspects of the measurement system may lead to uneconomical behavior that focuses on a subgoal without considering overall organizational goals. To illustrate, taxi drivers were put on a bonus system based on mileage. Soon the Moscow suburbs were full of empty taxis barreling down the boulevards to fatten their bonuses. In response to bonuses based on tonnage norms, a Moscow chandelier factory produced heavier and heavier chandeliers, until they started pulling ceilings down.

The most common instance of overemphasis is the short-run maximization of net income or sales that hurts long-run results. There are many questionable ways to improve short-run performance—stinting, for example, on

[12] See E. Kirby Warren, *Long-Range Planning: The Executive Viewpoint* (Englewood Cliffs, N.J.: Prentice-Hall, Inc., 1966), Chapter 5. Market share as a goal has been receiving increasing general attention because it frequently goes hand-in-hand with increased profitability. A study of 57 companies revealed that "on the average, a difference of 10 percentage points in market share is accompanied by a difference of about 5 points in pretax return on investment." See R. D. Buzzell, B. T. Gale, and R. G. M. Sultan, "Market Share—A Key to Profitability," *Harvard Business Review,* Vol. 53, No. 1 (January-February 1975), p. 97.

[13] For this and other examples, see Warren, *Long-Range Planning,* Chapter 5.

repairs, quality control, advertising, research, or training. A manager may successfully exert pressure on employees for more productivity for short spurts of time. This may have some unfavorable long-run overtones.

As we explore various facets of systems design and techniques, we will see the importance of goal congruence in example after example. Top management must explicitly face the job of goal setting and coordination; it should not be a product of chance or a by-product of the day-to-day extinguishing of business brush fires. Financial-planning models and master budgets plus feedback reporting are probably the most widely used techniques for coordinating goals.[14]

human-resource accounting

Despite the efforts of some top managements to have systems designed to stress other goals in addition to the goal of profitability, the accounting system remains the most pervasive formal device for measuring performance. In the eyes of many, this has led to a short-run bias on the part of many managers, because accounting conventions (a) lead to immediate write-offs as expenses of outlays that should really be carried forward as assets, and (b) adhere to historical costs and ignore changes in the "real values" of many assets.

A notable example of this criticism is the research conducted on human-resource accounting. For many years, critics have stressed that accounting systems encourage the misuse of human resources; that managers tend to ignore the need for more employee participation in decision making and for more training of subordinates; and moreover, that pressures for short-run profits lead to unnecessary and uneconomical layoffs and discharges. The short-run increases in profit are illusory, because increases in employee turnover and later additional spending for hiring and training more than offset the immediate savings. Likert[15] advocates incorporating "human-resource" accounting as part of the formal accounting system. As a minimum measure, this would entail recording as assets the outlays for recruiting and training managers. These costs would be amortized over the expected useful lives of the employees.

Regardless of your reaction to these ideas, you should recognize that—after decades of research on the utilization of human resources—Likert apparently feels that the major formal performance-measurement system (the accounting system) is the best way to accomplish his ends. Other means, such as reporting measures of employee turnover and conducting attitude surveys, have generally

[14] The term "management by objectives" (MBO) has often been used to describe a formal program for implementing a philosophy of managing that presumes that a multiplicity of total organizational goals and personal goals are achieved through participation and commitment by all managers. MBO clearly stipulates goals, emphasizes the development of long- and short-range plans to achieve the goals, and stresses the use of measurements and feedback. See George S. Odiorne, *Management Decisions by Objectives* (Englewood Cliffs, N.J.: Prentice-Hall, Inc., 1970).

[15] See Rensis Likert, *The Human Organization, Its Management and Value* (New York: McGraw-Hill Book Company, 1967). Also see E. H. Caplan and S. Landekich, *Human Resource Accounting: Past, Present, and Future* (New York: National Association of Accountants, 1974), and E. Flamholtz, *Human Resource Accounting* (Belmont, Calif.: Dickenson Publishing Co., Inc., 1974).

been unsatisfactory because they have been regarded as supplementary and secondary in importance to accounting measures of income or costs. Consequently, to avoid its being given little attention, some kind of accounting for human resources must be incorporated within the accounting system. Likert is intrigued by human-asset accounting because he wants to repair what he perceives to be the motivational errors of existing formal control systems. He wants the system to change so that managers will make different decisions.

Much of the literature on human resources focuses on whether they can qualify in an accounting framework as assets and how they should be valued. **But the fundamental question is whether this more costly system will have the desired impact on decisions.** As usual, the answer may differ from organization to organization.

slack: a universal behavioral problem

The budgetary process entails the setting of goals. If the budget is overemphasized or viewed as a rigid monitor of performance, managers and employees are induced toward behavior that is not usually consonant with the typical goals of the organization as a whole. For example, budgets in not-for-profit organizations usually stipulate a top spending limit. This reinforces a philosophy of "We'd better spend it or we'll lose it," which does not lead to long-range cost reduction. Similarly, managers in industry are often disinclined to reduce costs because this leads to cuts in budget allowances for future periods. In other words, cost-cutting performance now may generate temporary praise or rewards but will make the job tougher later because the future budget will not be as easy to attain.

The personal goals of managers (personal income, size of staff, esteem, power) will often lead to a "bargained" budget, whereby managers intentionally create *slack* as a protective device.[16] Slack can be defined in a cost context as the difference between the minimum necessary costs and the actual costs of the firm. (Slack may be called *padding* in some organizations.) This seeking of slack permeates all budgeting in every conceivable sort of organization. Little has been done to counteract it.

An example of the attempt to reduce slack is the widespread use of lump-sum rewards to managers and other employees for "permanent" cost-savings. Another example is allowing the manager to "keep" the saving, in the form of not tightening the budget for a specified subsequent span of one to three years. Therefore, even though the old cost budget of $100,000 should be decreased to $90,000 because of the discovery of a new production method, the cut may be postponed for a year or more. Despite these attempts at counteraction, slack remains as one of the major unsolved problems in budgetary control.

[16] M Schiff and A. Lewin, "Where Traditional Budgeting Fails," *Financial Executive,* Vol. XXXVI, No. 5, pp. 51–62; and "The Impact of People on Budgets," *The Accounting Review,* Vol. XLV, No. 2 (April 1970), pp. 259–69.

cooperation versus competition

A fragile balance must be struck between careful delineation of responsibility, on the one hand, and a too-rigid separation of responsibility, on the other hand. Buck passing is a pervasive tendency that is supposedly minimized when responsibility is fixed unequivocally.

example

> A large utility used to hire college graduates and rotate them among all departments in the company during a two-year training program. Their salaries were not assigned to the departments, and individual managers took little interest in the trainees. But now it assigns the trainee to a definite department that fits his primary interest, where he is given direct responsibility as soon as possible. Both the trainees and the managers are much more satisfied with the new responsibility arrangement.

But often the motivational impact boomerangs; too much falls between the chairs. Managers often wear blinders and concentrate more than ever on their individual worlds. Family cooperation is replaced by intracompany competition. When departments are truly interdependent in many of their important decisions, serious consideration is often given to merging them into a single department for responsibility-accounting purposes.

importance of formal systems

In countless organizations, informal information systems are dominant in decision making. There is widespread use of little black books and special memorandums. In addition, many executives, including top managers, rely on rules of thumb and accumulated experience rather than on the output of formal systems such as accounting reports. This method often proves satisfactory because such executives are evaluating the information wisely and making decisions that keep their companies competitive.

As companies grow, managers become more dependent on formal rather than informal information systems. Professor Richard Vancil has observed that the formal system provides a crutch for the orderly succession of management. Large companies, with mobile executives who typically move frequently, must have such a system; after all, most managers do not have thirty years of experience on which to base their decisions. The introduction of formal decision models in business is an example of the response to the need for more crutches. For instance, the blending of various ingredients in sausage was once the task of some wise individual with a good feel for the critical variables. Now the blending decision is made by a computer program that resulted from the formalization of a previously informal process.

A prime challenge for systems designers is to discover whether some or all of the informal information system is leading to successful decisions. If so, the designer should attempt to formalize those parts of the informal system. For example, the formal system should aim at incorporating the key numbers or events that a manager may be keeping informally. Consider the pricing decision. The data compiled by the formal system may be ignored by the manager when he is setting prices because his experience and readings of industry or economic data are the keys to his decisions. The designer should then try to crystallize the manager's decision model explicitly, so that the critical data may be supplied by the formal system. In this way, the formal system can become the key information system, can engender sincere management support, and can ease the tasks of management succession as managers are promoted or transferred.

accurate scorekeeping Textbooks do not devote much space to the problems of obtaining accurate source documents. Yet this is easily one of the most pervasive, everlasting problems in collecting information. An accounting system cannot help managers predict and make decisions if its scorekeeping is haphazard.

Pressures may spur managers to encourage their subordinates to record time erroneously or to tinker with scrap or usage reports.

example

> The maintenance crews of one telephone company regularly performed recurring short-term maintenance and repair work on various projects. At other times, the same crews would be concerned with huge construction projects—installing or building plant and equipment. The company had weekly reports on performance of the regular maintenance work, but had only loose control over the construction projects. An investigation disclosed that the foremen were encouraging the workmen to boost the time on the construction projects and to understate the time on the regular maintenance projects. Thus the foremen's performance on the latter always looked good. The situation was corrected when the emphases on maintenance and on construction were balanced so that both were currently budgeted and controlled.

Hopwood[17] takes a dim view of what he calls a *budget-constrained style* of performance evaluation, which appraises managers primarily on the basis of whether they meet the short-term budget. Such a style induces undesirable filtering and falsifying of records. Thus, when a manager chooses to overemphasize a short-run budget, or when a manager misuses data when analyzing subordinates' performance, there are costly implications for accounting systems. For example, there is a higher probability of falsifying source documents. Either the costs of internal audits and other internal controls will rise, or the reliability of the accounting system will fall.

Accurate record keeping is essentially a problem of motivation. The accountant and manager should be more sensitive to possible errors, more aware of the futility of trying to get usage of time and materials reported accurately in small increments, and more conscious of the natural tendency of individuals to report their activities so as to minimize their personal bother and maximize

[17] A. Hopwood, "Leadership Climate and the Use of Accounting Data in Performance Evaluation," *Accounting Review,* Vol. XLIX, No. 3 (July 1974).

their own showing.[18] The hazard of trying to get extremely detailed reports extends not only to lack of confidence in individual reports themselves but to the likelihood of generating monumental contempt for the entire system.

Top managers can induce accurate scorekeeping if they can persuade subordinates that the documents are important for decision making. Again we see the desirability of active management support:

example

> A firm of civil engineers has surveying jobs throughout California that are largely obtained by firm price quotations. A key to profitability is the ability to predict how much time will be required for the various subtasks on the job. The president of the firm feels so strongly about the need for feedback that his field crew managers must mail daily time reports to the central office. If they are not received on the day expected, the president immediately phones to find out why.

intelligent analysis of relevant data

The accounting system should produce information that leads managers toward correct decisions regarding either evaluation of performance or selection among courses of action. Intelligent analysis of costs is often dependent on explicit distinctions between cost behavior patterns, which is more likely to be achieved via the contribution approach than via traditional methods. The general tendency toward indiscriminate full-cost allocations raises analytical dangers.

example

> A bakery distributed its products through route salesmen, each of whom loaded a truck with an assortment of products in the morning and spent the day calling on customers in an assigned territory. Believing that some items were more profitable than others, management asked for an analysis of product costs and sales. The accountants to whom the task was assigned allocated all manufacturing and marketing costs to products to obtain a net profit for each product. The resulting figures indicated that some of the products were being sold at a loss, and management discontinued these products. However, when this change was put into effect, the company's overall profit declined. It was then seen that, by dropping some products, sales revenues had been reduced without commensurate reduction in costs because the joint manufacturing costs and route-sales costs had to be continued in order to make and sell remaining products.[19]

SUMMARY

The choice of management accounting systems is as closely related to the behavioral sciences as it is to economics and the decision sciences. The task of the formal control system is to help provide goal congruence and incentives through the use of accounting techniques that provide information and feedback.

[18] Also see Sam E. Scharff, "The Industrial Engineer and the Cost Accountant," *NAA Bulletin*, Vol. XLII, No. 7, Sec. 1, for more examples.

[19] Walter B. McFarland, "The Field of Management Accounting," *NAA Bulletin*, Vol. XLV, No. 10, Sec. 3, p. 19.

A key question is: Will the costs of modifying the system be exceeded by the prospective benefits of increased congruence and incentive? Budgets, responsibility accounting, and performance measurements are major tools for obtaining goal congruence and incentive.

The systems designer and senior managers must try to harmonize three major types of controls: organization, group, and individual. Top-management support is a key to getting groups and individuals to accept organization goals as their own.

Illustrations of behavioral problems that arise in conjunction with control systems include: overemphasis on short-run goals, presence of slack, failure to pinpoint responsibility, cooperation versus competition, inaccurate source documents, and faulty cost analysis.

SUGGESTED READINGS

In addition to the items footnoted in the chapter, the following references provide an overview of behavioral research in accounting. Much current attention is being given to the areas of human information processing and contingency theories of organizational behavior. Most of these books contain extensive bibliographies:

AMERICAN ACCOUNTING ASSOCIATION, Reports of various Committees on Behavioral Sciences, Human Resource Accounting, and Management Information Systems are published in the annual *Accounting Review Supplements,* 1968 to date.

ANTHONY, ROBERT N., *Planning and Control Systems: A Framework for Analysis,* Boston: Harvard Business School, 1965.

BURNS, THOMAS J., ed., *The Behavioral Aspects of Accounting Data for Performance Evaluation.* Columbus, O.: College of Administrative Science, Ohio State University, 1970. This is a collection of six papers, seven critiques, and proceedings of an accounting symposium.

CAPLAN, EDWIN H., *Management Accounting and Behavioral Science.* Reading, Mass.: Addison-Wesley Publishing Co., Inc., 1971.

HODGE, B., and H. JOHNSON, *Management and Organizational Behavior.* New York: John Wiley & Sons, Inc., 1970.

HOFSTEDE, G. H., *The Game of Budget Control.* New York: Van Nostrand-Wiley, 1967.

LAWLER, E., and J. RHODE, *Information and Control in Organizations.* Pacific Palisades, Ca.: Goodyear Publishing Co., Inc., 1976.

LIKERT, RENSIS, *The Human Organization, Its Management and Value.* New York: McGraw-Hill Book Company, 1967.

LIVINGSTONE, J. L., ed., *Managerial Accounting: The Behavioral Foundations.* Columbus, O.: Grid, Inc., 1975.

SCHIFF, M., and Y. LEWIN, eds., *Behavioral Aspects of Accounting.* Englewood Cliffs, N.J.: Prentice-Hall, Inc., 1974.

SIMON, H. A., H. GUETZKOW, G. KOSMETSKY, and G. TYNDALL, *Centralization vs. Decentralization in Organizing the Controller's Department.* New York: The Controllership Foundation, Inc., 1954. This book is incisive and readable. Its title is deceiving because the book covers the entire range of management accounting. Unfortunately, it is out of print, so you may have difficulty in getting a copy.

STEDRY, ANDREW C., *Budget Control and Cost Behavior.* Englewood Cliffs, N.J.: Prentice-Hall, Inc., 1960.

PROBLEM FOR SELF-STUDY

PROBLEM Construct a chart with the following headings:

	Product Cost	Variable Cost	CONTROLLABLE COST By Sales Vice-President	By Assembly Supervisor	By Production Vice-President
Salesmen's commissions					
Direct materials					
Machining department—direct labor					
Finishing department—supplies					
Sales vice-president's salary					
Straight-line depreciation—equipment in assembly department					
Management consulting fee for improving labor methods in assembly department					

Assume the same organization chart as shown in Exhibit 6-1. For each account, answer "yes" or "no" as to whether the cost is a product cost, a variable cost, and a cost controllable by the three officers indicated. Thus, you will have five answers, entered horizontally, for each account.

SOLUTION Note particularly how the concepts of variable/fixed and controllable/uncontrollable costs differ. A variable cost is not necessarily a controllable cost. Controllability is dependent on a manager's responsibility within a given time period. Note, too, that all costs that are controllable by a manager are also regarded as being controllable by his superior line executive.

	Product Cost	Variable Cost	CONTROLLABLE COST By Sales Vice-President	By Assembly Supervisor	By Production Vice-President
Salesmen's commissions	No	Yes	Yes	No	No
Direct materials	Yes	Yes	No	Yes	Yes
Machining department—direct labor	Yes	Yes	No	No	Yes
Finishing department—supplies	Yes	Yes	No	No	Yes
Sales vice-president's salary	No	No	No	No	No
Straight-line depreciation—equipment in assembly department	Yes	No	No	No	No*
Management consulting fee for assembly dept.	Yes	No	No	Yes†	Yes

* Note that the time element is important here. Although depreciation may not be controllable in the short run, the production vice-president's policies on selection and timing of equipment purchases influence depreciation costs.

† Note that this is a fixed cost because it will be unaffected by fluctuations in production activity. Still, it is a controllable cost because either the assembly supervisor or one of his superiors decided to incur the cost in order to reduce labor costs. This is an example of a cost that is fixed but that may be controllable by the assembly supervisor. Of course, if he has no voice in the decision, the cost may be uncontrollable by him but controllable by one of his superiors.

QUESTIONS, PROBLEMS, AND CASES

6-1 Define *responsibility accounting.*

6-2 Define *controllable cost.* What two major factors help an evaluation of whether a given cost is controllable?

6-3 What guides are available in deciding the appropriate costs to be charged to a person?

6-4 "An action once taken cannot be changed by subsequent events." What implications does this have for the cost accountant?

6-5 List five common complaints about control budgets.

6-6 "Budgets are wonderful vehicles for communication." Comment.

6-7 Define *motivation.* How does it differ from *need?*

6-8 Give an example of how a control system can motivate a manager to behave against the best interests of the company as a whole.

6-9 "I'm majoring in accounting. This study of human relations is fruitless. You've got to be born with a flair for getting along with others. You can't learn it!" Do you agree? Why?

6-10 "Interpretation is essential for understanding accounting reports." Suggest how the accounting function may be organized to emphasize interpretation.

6-11 *Budgets as Motivators* "Budgets and responsibility accounting and other modern accounting techniques foster a policed, departmental orientation rather than a positive, overall organizational orientation." Do you agree? Explain.

6-12 *Budgets as Pressure Devices* Sord and Welsch have stated: "It should be recognized that pressure on supervisors need not come from control techniques, assuming that standards of performance are not unfair or too high. Pressure on supervisors comes from the responsibilities inherent in the supervisor's job." Do you agree? Why?

6-13 *Budgets as Motivators* "To accept budgets as motivators is to imply that supervisors do not have adequate interest in their job. This is seen as an insult to a man's integrity, and the factory supervisors resent it strongly." Do you agree? Why?

6-14 *Attitudes Toward the Accountant* A prominent financial analyst, who became very successful with his Wall Street investments, once commented:

"My experience with the accountant is that for him everything has equal importance. He is like the Lord in the Bible, where it is written that 'a thousand years are in His sight as yesterday' when it is past—except that it is just the other way around with the accountant: 10 cents in the balance sheet is just as important as a million dollars. The main thing for him is that every figure should be correct."

Elbert Hubbard, a philosopher popular in the twentieth century, made the following remarks:

"The typical auditor is a man past middle age, spare, wrinkled, intelligent, cold, passive, non-committal, with eyes like a codfish, polite in contact, but at the same time unresponsive, cold; calm and damnably composed as a concrete post or a plaster-of-paris cast; a human petrification with a heart of feldspar and without charm of the friendly germ, minus bowels, passion, or a sense of humour. Happily, they never reproduce and all of them finally go to Hell."

In general, do you agree with the remarks above? Why?

6-15 *Auto Dealership Profit Centers* Many automobile dealers divide their businesses into two major divisions: (a) parts and service and (b) vehicle sales. The gross profit of the parts and service activity is looked upon as the amount that is supposed to "cover" all parts and service overhead plus all general overhead of the dealership. If this goal can be achieved, the gross profit of the vehicle division can be regarded as "gravy"—as net profit. In other words, the contribution margin of the parts and service activity is looked upon as a cost recovery, whereas the vehicle sales are regarded as the profit-making mechanism.

required

Evaluate the merits of this approach. If you were managing an automobile dealership, would you view your operations any differently? How?

6-16 *Computation of Gross Profits on Car Sales* Many auto dealers use the "washout" concept. *Washout* is the method for computing gross profits on a series of deals starting with the sale of a new unit and ending with the straight (no trade-in) sale of the last vehicle in the series. The gross profit on the sale of the new unit and used units is totaled and stated in terms of gross profit per new unit retailed.

required

Evaluate the washout concept in terms of assigning responsibility to profit centers. How else could gross profit be computed?

6-17 *Controllable-Cost Concepts; Fill in Blanks* Assume the same organization chart as shown in Exhibit 1-2. For each item listed, indicate by "Yes" or "No" whether it would be classified as a product cost, variable cost, and controllable cost. If you are in doubt about whether an item has strictly variable or strictly fixed cost behavior, decide on the basis of whether the total cost will fluctuate substantially over a wide range of volume.

			CONTROLLABLE COST			
	Product Cost	Variable Cost	By Sales Vice-President	By Drill-Press Foreman	By Production Superintendent	By Manufacturing Vice-President
Assembly department—Polishing material	______	______	______	______	______	______
Secretary-Treasurer's salary	______	______	______	______	______	______
Chief inspector's department—Supplies	______	______	______	______	______	______
Straight-line depreciation—Equipment in drill-press department	______	______	______	______	______	______
Salesmen's travel expenses	______	______	______	______	______	______
Drill-press department—Direct materials	______	______	______	______	______	______

6-18 *Responsibility for Downtime* Two of several departments performed successive operations in the manufacture of automobile frames. The frames were transported from department to department via an overhead conveyor system that was paced in accordance with budgeted time allowances. Each department manager had responsibility for the budgeted costs and budgeted output of his department.

On Tuesday morning Department D had some equipment failure that caused the manager to ask the manager of Department C to stop the conveyor system. The Department C manager refused, so workers in Department D had to remove the frames, stack them, and return the frames to the conveyor later when production resumed.

The manager of Department D was bitter about the incident and insisted that the manager of Department C should bear the related labor and overhead costs of $1,770. In contrast, the manager of Department C said, "I was just doing my job as specified in the budget."

required

As the controller, how would you account for the $1,770? Why?

6-19 *Responsibility of Purchasing Agent*[20] Richards had just taken a new job as purchasing agent for The Hart Manufacturing Company. Sampson is head of the production planning and control department. Every six months, Sampson gives Richards a general purchasing program. Richards gets specifications from the engineering department. He then selects suppliers and negotiates prices.

When he took this job, Richards was informed very clearly that he bore responsibility for meeting the general purchasing program once he accepted it from Sampson.

During Week No. 24, Richards was advised that Part No. 1234—a critical part—would be needed for assembly on Tuesday morning, Week No. 32. He found that the regular supplier could not deliver. He called everywhere, finally found a supplier in the Middle West, and accepted the commitment.

He followed up by mail. Yes, the supplier assured him, the part would be ready. The matter was so important that on Thursday of Week No. 31, Richards checked by phone. Yes, the shipment had left in time. Richards was reassured and did not check further. But on Tuesday of Week No. 32, the part was not in the warehouse. Inquiry revealed that the shipment had been misdirected by the railroad company and was still in Chicago.

required

What department should bear the costs of time lost in the plant? Why? As purchasing agent, do you think it fair that such costs be charged to your department?

6-20 *A Study in Responsibility Accounting* The David Machine Tool Company is in the doldrums. Production volume has fallen to a ten-year low. The company has a nucleus of skilled tool-and-die men who could find employment elsewhere if they were laid off. Three of these men have been transferred temporarily to the building and grounds department, where they have been doing menial tasks such as sweeping, washing walls, and so on for the past month. These men have earned their regular rate of $8 per hour. Their wages have been charged to the building and grounds department. The supervisor of building and grounds has just confronted the controller as follows: "Look at the cockeyed performance report you pencil pushers have given me. The helpers' line reads:

	BUDGET	*ACTUAL*	*DEVIATION*	
Wages of helpers	$1,764	$4,704	$2,940	Unfavorable

"This is just another example of how unrealistic you bookkeepers are! Those tool-and-die guys are loafing on the job because they know we won't lay them off. The regular hourly rate for my three helpers is $3. Now that my regular helpers are laid off, my work is piling up, so that when they return

[20] Adapted from Raymond Villers, "Control and Freedom in a Decentralized Company," *Harvard Business Review*, Vol. XXXII, No. 2, pp. 89–96.

they'll either have to put in overtime or I'll have to get part-time help to catch up with things. Instead of charging me at $8 per hour, you should charge about $2—that's all those tool-and-die slobs are worth at their best."

required

As the controller, what would you do *now?* Would you handle the accounting for these wages any differently?

6-21 *Fixing Responsibility* (Adapted from a description by Harold Bierman, Jr.) The City of Mountainvale had hired its first city manager four years ago. She favored a "management by objectives" philosophy and accordingly had set up many profit responsibility centers, including a sanitation department, a city utility, and a repair shop.

For many months, the sanitation manager had been complaining to the utility manager about wires being too low at one point in the road. There was barely clearance for large trucks. The sanitation manager asked the repair shop to make changes in the clearance. The repair shop manager asked, "Whom should I charge for the $2,000 cost of making the adjustment, the sanitation or the utility department?" Both departments refused to accept the charge, so the repair department refused to do the work.

Late one day the top of a truck caught the wires and ripped them down. The repair department made an emergency repair at a cost of $2,600. Moreover, the city lost $1,000 of utility revenue (less variable costs) because of the disruption of service.

Investigation disclosed that the truck had failed to clamp down its top properly. The extra two inches of height caused the catching of the wire.

Both the sanitation and utility managers argued strenuously about whether they should bear the $3,000 cost. Moreover, the utility manager demanded reimbursement from the sanitation department of the $1,000 of lost contribution.

required

As the city controller in charge of the responsibility accounting system, how would you favor accounting for these costs? Specifically, what would you do next? What is the proper role of responsibility accounting in determining the blame for this situation?

6-22 *Budgets and Incentives* You are working as a supervisor in a manufacturing department that has substantial amounts of men and equipment. You are paid a "base" salary that is actually low for this type of work. The firm has a very liberal bonus plan, which pays you another $1,000 each time you "make the budget" and 2 percent of the amount you are able to save.

Your past experiences have been as follows:

PERIOD	1	2	3	4	5	6
Budget	$40,000	$40,000	$39,000	$36,000	$36,000	$36,250
Actual	41,000	39,500	37,000	37,000	36,500	36,000
Variance	$ 1,000 U	$ 500 F	$ 2,000 F	$ 1,000 U	$ 500 U	$ 250 F

required

1. What would you do as a "rational man" if you were starting the job all over again from period 1 with the above information?
2. What would you recommend, if anything, be done to the system if you are now promoted to a higher job in management and required to handle the "bonus system" in this department?

6-23 Billie Jean Prince operates a chain of health centers. One of the largest is in the heart of Chicago. Prince used the services of three managers, Dave, Nick, and Sid. Each had charge of a group of exercise and apparatus rooms similar in all regards. She offered three methods of weekly payment to the men:

Method X. A base rate of $6 per hour and 30 percent of all reductions in expenses below a "norm" of $600 per week.

Method Y. A flat wage of $7 per hour.

Method Z. No base rate, but a bonus of $300 for meeting the "norm," plus 10 percent of all reductions in expenses below the norm.

The men chose their method of compensation before starting employment. Assume a 40-hour week. The record for the past six weeks for the three areas follows (all data are in dollars):

	WEEKS					
	1	*2*	*3*	*4*	*5*	*6*
Dave:						
Utilities	250	250	250	250	250	250
Supplies	180	20	20	260	100	20
Repairs & misc.	305	250	220	265	260	200
Total	735	520	490	775	610	470
Nick:						
Utilities	250	250	250	250	250	250
Supplies	100	100	100	100	100	100
Repairs & misc.	250	200	265	220	260	305
Total	600	550	615	570	610	655
Sid:						
Utilities	250	250	250	250	250	250
Supplies	100	100	100	100	100	100
Repairs & misc.	250	250	250	250	250	250
Total	600	600	600	600	600	600

required

Which payment methods were most likely chosen by Dave, Nick, and Sid? Base your answer on an analysis of cost behavior patterns. Assume that each man picked a different plan. (Giving your final answer is not enough; briefly explain your choices.)

6-24 *Sales Incentives* (CMA) The Parsons Co. compensates its field sales force on a commission and year-end bonus basis. The commission is 20 percent of budgeted gross margin (planned selling price less cost of goods sold) contingent upon collection of the account. Customer's credit is approved by the company's credit department. Price concessions are granted on occasion by the top sales management, but sales commissions are not reduced by the discount. A year-end bonus of 15 percent of commissions earned is paid to salesmen who equal or exceed their annual sales target. The annual sales target is usually established by applying approximately a 5 percent increase to the prior year's sales.

required

1. What features of this compensation plan would seem to be effective in motivating the salesmen to accomplish company goals of higher profits and return on investment. Explain why.
2. What features of this compensation plan would seem to be countereffective in motivating the salesmen to accomplish the company goals of higher profits and return on investment? Explain why.

6-25 *Objectives of Public Accounting Firm* All personnel, including partners, of public accounting firms must usually turn in biweekly time reports, showing how many hours were devoted to their various duties. These firms have traditionally looked unfavorably on idle or unassigned staff time. They have looked favorably on heavy percentages of chargeable (billable) time because this maximizes revenue. What effect is such a policy likely to have on the behavior of the firm's personnel? Can you relate this practice to the problem of harmony of goals that was discussed in the chapter? How?

6-26 *Multiple Goals and Profitability*[21] The following are the multiple goals of the General Electric Company:

1. Profitability
2. Market position
3. Productivity
4. Product leadership
5. Personnel development
6. Employee attitudes
7. Public responsibility
8. Balance between short-range and long-range goals

General Electric is a Goliath corporation with sales of about $15 billion and assets of $11 billion in 1977. It had approximately 170 responsibility centers called "departments," but that is a deceiving term. In most other companies, these departments would be called divisions. For example, some GE departments have sales of over $300 million.

Each department manager's performance is evaluated annually in relation to the specified multiple goals. A special measurements group was set up in 1952 to devise ways of quantifying accomplishments in each of the areas. In this way, the evaluation of performance would become more objective as the various measures were developed and improved.

required

1. How would you measure performance in each of these areas? Be specific.

2. Can the other goals be encompassed as ingredients of a formal measure of profitability? In other words, can profitability per se be defined to include the other goals?

6-27 *Divisional Responsibility and Performance* (CMA) George Johnson was hired on July 1, 19_9, as Assistant General Manager of the Botel Division of Staple, Inc. It was understood that he would be elevated to general manager of the division on January 1, 19_1, when the then current general manager retired, and this was duly done. In addition to becoming acquainted with the division and the general manager's duties, Mr. Johnson was specifically charged with the responsibility for development of the 19_0 and 19_1 budgets. As general manager in 19_1, he was, obviously, responsible for the 19_2 budget.

The Staple Company is a multiproduct company that is highly decentralized. Each division is quite autonomous. The corporation staff approves division prepared operating budgets but seldom makes major changes in them. The corporate staff actively participates in decisions requiring capital investment (for expansion or replacement) and makes the final decisions. The division management is responsible for implementing the capital program. The major method used by the Staple Corporation to measure division performance is Contribution Return on Division Net Investment. The budgets presented below were approved by the corporation. Revision of the 19_2 budget is not considered necessary even though 19_1 actually departed from the approved 19_1 budget.

[21] Adapted from a problem originally appearing in R. H. Hassler and Neil E. Harlan, *Cases in Controllership* (Englewood Cliffs, N.J.: Prentice-Hall, Inc.).

BOTEL DIVISION (000'S OMITTED)

Accounts	Actual			Budget	
	19_9	19_0	19_1	19_1	19_2
Sales	1,000	1,500	1,800	2,000	2,400
Less Division variable costs:					
Material and labor	250	375	450	500	600
Repairs	50	75	50	100	120
Supplies	20	30	36	40	48
Less Division fixed costs:					
Employee training	30	35	25	40	45
Maintenance	50	55	40	60	70
Depreciation	120	160	160	200	200
Rent	80	100	110	140	140
Total	600	830	871	1,080	1,223
Division net contribution	400	670	929	920	1,177
Division investment:					
Accounts receivable	100	150	180	200	240
Inventory	200	300	270	400	480
Fixed assets	1,590	2,565	2,800	3,380	4,000
Less: Accounts and wages payable	(150)	(225)	(350)	(300)	(360)
Net Investment	1,740	2,790	2,900	3,680	4,360
Contribution return on net investment	23%	24%	32%	25%	27%

required

1. Identify Mr. Johnson's responsibilities under the management and measurement program described above.
2. Appraise the performance of Mr. Johnson in 19_1.
3. Recommend to the president any changes in the responsibilities assigned to managers or in the measurement methods used to evaluate division management based upon your analysis.

6-28 *Responsibility Accounting and Control of Costs* The Sharp Company develops, manufactures, and markets several product lines of low-cost consumer goods. Top management of the company is attempting to evaluate the present method and a new method of charging the different production departments for the services they receive from one of the engineering departments, which is called Manufacturing Engineering Services (MES).

The function of MES, which consists of about thirty engineers and ten draftsmen, is to reduce the costs of producing the different products of the company by improving machine and manufacturing process design, while maintaining the required level of quality. The MES manager reports to the engineering supervisor, who reports to the vice-president, manufacturing. The MES manager may increase or decrease the number of engineers under him. He is evaluated on the basis of several variables, one of which is the annual incremental savings to the company brought about by his department in excess of the costs of operating his department. These costs consist of actual salaries, a share of corporate overhead, the cost of office supplies used by his department, and a cost of capital charge. An individual engineer is evaluated on the basis of the ratio of the annual savings he effects to his annual salary. The salary range of an engineer is defined by his personnel classification; there are four classifications, and promotion from one classification to another depends on the approval of a panel that includes both production and engineering personnel

Production department managers report to a production supervisor, who reports to the vice-president, manufacturing. The production department for each product line is treated as a profit center, and engineering services are provided at a cost, according to the following plan. When a production department manager and an engineer agree on a possible project to improve production efficiency, they sign a contract that specifies the scope of the project, the estimated savings to be realized, the probability of success, and the number of engineering man-hours of each personnel classification required. The charge to the particular production department is determined by the product of the number of man-hours required times the "classification rate" for each personnel classification. This rate depends on the average salary for the classification involved and a share of the engineering department's other costs. An engineer is expected to spend at least 85 percent of his time on specific, contracted projects; the remainder may be used for preliminary investigations of potential cost-saving projects or self-improving study. A recent survey showed that production managers have a high degree of confidence in the MES engineers.

A new plan has been proposed to top management, in which no charge will be made to production departments for engineering services. In all other respects the new system will be identical to the present. Production managers will continue to request engineering services as under the present plan. Proponents of the new plan say that under it, production managers will take a greater advantage of existing engineering talent. Regardless of how engineering services are accounted for, the company is committed to the idea of production departments being profit centers.

required

Evaluate the strong and weak points of the present and proposed plans. Will the company tend to hire the optimal quantity of engineering talent? Will this engineering talent be used as effectively as possible?

6-29 *Evaluation of Control System* Laser Products Inc. is a manufacturer of lasers, laser systems, and related optical products. While its annual sales of $10 million and its 300 employees classify it as a small business, it is a major factor in the industry. The company has an international reputation for being both a leader in technology and a dependable quality producer.

After several years of existence, the last two producing slight losses and a severe drop in stock price, the company president stated survival as the primary corporate objective for the next fiscal year. Survival meant showing a profit of $600,000 in order to make peace with the investment community. Additionally, he wanted to concentrate on finding new commercial applications for existing technology: this strategy, as opposed to developing new technology, had been adopted as the best means by which to initiate and sustain growth in sales and profit.

To achieve these goals, a reorganization was undertaken. The organization chart was redrawn from a functional to a marketing orientation, with 90 percent of research and development (R&D) now tied directly to the marketing divisions. Six divisions reported directly to the president: Manufacturing, Administration, Advanced Product Development, and the three marketing divisions, Optical Products, Laser Products, and Engineered Laser Systems.

Concurrently, a budgeting process for internal use was adopted. Each of the marketing divisions submitted a sales forecast and then, in discussions with the president, settled on a sales figure (item 1 of the budget below), marketing costs (item 3), product R&D costs (item 4), and division overhead expenses (item 5). From the sales figure the manufacturing manager prepared budgets using standard costs, and the resulting manufacturing costs were incorporated in the marketing divisions' budgets (item 2). The corporate allocations (items 6 and 7) were determined by multiplying the ratio of the divisions' forecasted sales dollars to the corporation's forecasted total sales by the budgeted corporate expense. The marketing divisions then received budgets of the form:

(1) Forecasted Sales Dollars		xxx
Less:		
(2) Manufacturing Costs at standard	xxx	
(3) Marketing Costs	xxx	
(4) Product R&D	xxx	
(5) Division Overhead	xxx	
(6) Corporate Allocated R&D	xxx	
(7) Corporate Allocated G&A	xxx	xxx
Profit Target		xxx

Following this budgeting procedure, the company established a $600,000 corporate profit target.

In addition, it was decided that the three marketing-division managers would be paid a bonus based on their performance relative to the profit target of their division. This bonus would be calculated as follows:

ACTUAL PROFIT AS A PERCENT OF TARGET	BONUS AS A PERCENT OF FIXED ANNUAL SALARY
90	0
91	1
92	2
.	.
.	.
.	.
99	9
100	10
101	12
102	14
103	16
.	.
.	.
.	.
109	28
110	30
.	.
.	.
.	.

The manufacturing manager, the president, and the treasurer would be similarly rewarded based on the joint profit target of the three marketing divisions—i.e. the corporate profit target.

During the year the marketing divisions were charged with the actual costs, including actual manufacturing costs. The corporate allocations were made as a fixed percent, based on forecasted sales, times actual corporate R&D and G&A expenses.

Halfway through the year sales were good and it was clear that the profit targets would be met by all three marketing divisions. The four major division managers were questioned about the effect they thought the incentive system had on their performance. One remarked that he was a major stockholder and a one-point rise in the stock price would exceed any incentive bonus he might receive. Another stated that the budget and incentive program was a nice addition, but he didn't follow it closely because he knew that if he "did the right things" the bottom line would respond. The third marketing division manager stated that he had successfully tried to meet his target, trading off R&D and marketing expenses, and so on, but as yet had not found the time to look at new market opportunities.

Most concerned about the system was the manufacturing manager. He said things were great for him this year, since his bonus was based on corporate profits and things had picked up. But he was worried that in lean years, when cost control was emphasized, he would not be rewarded, and perhaps more importantly, the marketing-division managers would spend their time worrying about his costs rather than their sales. It was also his belief that the new system caused the marketing managers to focus on this year's results and to neglect the crucial search for new products and new markets. Lastly, he was concerned that the system might endanger the teamwork and informal structure that had characterized the company and made it a good place to work.

When questioned about the new budgeting and incentive system the president stated that he knew it wasn't the theoretically pure answer but his concern was to focus everyone on the bottom-line profit so that it didn't disappear this year. He admitted there might be some problems with it and seemed willing to modify it for the subsequent years.

required

Write a memo evaluating the system and proposing any modifications you feel deserve serious consideration.

6-30 *Human Resources Accounting* The body of the chapter referred to experimentation with human-resource accounting. Exhibit 6-4 is an excerpt from the Barry Corporation's annual report for 1973. The Barry Corporation is a manufacturer of leisure footwear in Columbus, Ohio. The data in Exhibit 6-4 are *supplementary* to the usual audited financial statements that are also presented in the annual report.

Many variations in human-resource accounting are possible, such as using some approximation of current values, but the Barry Corporation has confined its records to historical costs. The annual report explains:

"Human resource accounting is an attempt to identify, quantify and report investments made in recruiting, acquiring, training, familiarizing and developing people. Outlay costs connected with these activities are accumulated and capitalized where they are expected to have value beyond the current accounting period. The basic outlays in connection with acquiring and integrating new people are amortized over their expected tenure with the company. Investments made for training or development are amortized over a much shorter period of time. Total write-off of an individual's account occurs upon his departure from the company."

required

1. Were there more write-offs of human assets during 1973 than new investments? Explain, using the numbers given in Exhibit 6-4.
2. Why do you think that advocates of human resource accounting prefer such a formal approach instead of less formal measures like employee-attitude surveys, employee-turnover measures, absenteeism, and similar measures?
3. Do you support the use of human-resource accounting? Explain your position.

EXHIBIT 6-4

R. G. BARRY CORPORATION AND SUBSIDIARIES
PRO-FORMA
(Conventional and Human Resource Accounting)

BALANCE SHEET	*1973 CONVENTIONAL AND HUMAN RESOURCE*	*1973 CONVENTIONAL ONLY*
Assets		
Total current assets	$18,311	$18,311
Net property, plant, and equipment	3,500	3,500
Excess of purchase price over net assets acquired	1,285	1,285
Deferred financing costs	173	173
Net investments in human resources	**1,964**	—
Prepaid income taxes and other assets	213	213
	$25,448*	$23,484
Liabilities and Stockholders' Equity		
Total current liabilities	$ 3,909	$ 3,909
Long-term debt, excluding current installments	6,970	6,970
Deferred compensation	143	143
Deferred income tax based upon full tax deduction for human resource costs	**982**	—
Stockholders' equity:		
Capital stock	1,902	1,902
Additional capital in excess of par value	5,676	5,676
Retained earnings:		
Financial	4,883	4,883
Human resources	**982**	—
	$25,448	$23,484

INCOME STATEMENT		
Net sales	$43,161	$43,161
Cost of sales	28,621	28,621
Gross profit	$14,540	$14,540
Selling, general and administrative expense	10,783	10,783
Operating income	3,756	3,756
Interest expense	598	598
Income before income taxes	$ 3,157	$ 3,157
Net increase in human resource investment	**184**	—
Adjusted income before income taxes	$ 3,342	$ 3,157
Income taxes	1,615	1,523
Net income	$ 1,726	$ 1,634

* (000's deleted, so totals may appear slightly inaccurate.)

Standard Costs: Direct Material and Direct Labor

7

Standard costs are the building blocks of a budgeting and feedback system. The cost accounting literature often mistakenly divides product cost accounting systems into three systems, as if they were mutually exclusive: job costing, process costing, and standard costing. Such a three-way classification is erroneous, because standard costs can be used in a wide variety of organizations and in conjunction with any kind of product costing, whether it be job-order costing, process costing, or some hybrid product costing.

standard costs as feedback aids

distinction between budgets and standards

Standard costs are carefully predetermined costs; they are target costs, costs that should be attained. Standard costs help to build budgets, gauge performance, obtain product costs, and save bookkeeping costs.

A set of standards outlines how a task should be accomplished and how much it should cost. As work is done, actual costs incurred are compared with standard costs to reveal variances. This feedback helps discover better ways of adhering to standards, of altering standards, and of accomplishing objectives.

What is the difference between a standard amount and a budget amount? As they are most widely used, the term *standard cost* is a *unit* concept and the term *budgeted cost* is a *total* concept. It may be helpful to think of a standard as a budget for the production of a single unit of output. However, keep in mind that in practice the terms budgets and standards are used loosely and often interchangeably.

standards as basis for feedback

Consider the following facts concerning the manufacture of 10,000 finely crafted, heavy ash trays made of a special alloy bearing a unique color and luster:

	STANDARDS	*BUDGET FOR 10,000 UNITS OF OUTPUT**
Direct materials	Four pounds of input allowed @ $5, $20 per unit of output	$200,000
Direct labor	Two hours of input allowed @ $8, $16 per unit of output	160,000

* Also expressed as *total standard costs allowed,* based on 10,000 × 4, or 40,000 lbs. of materials and 10,000 × 2, or 20,000 hours of direct labor.

In addition to the preceding data, the following data were compiled regarding *actual* performance:

Good units produced	10,000
Direct-material costs	$270,000
Pounds of input	50,000
Price per pound	$5.40
Direct-labor costs	$171,600
Hours of input	22,000
Labor price per hour	$7.80

The foregoing data could be analyzed in many ways. For example, the standard-cost approach would begin with the following feedback:

	TOTAL ACTUAL COSTS	*BUDGET: TOTAL STANDARD COSTS ALLOWED**	*BUDGET VARIANCE*
Direct materials	$270,000	$200,000	$70,000 U
Direct labor	171,600	160,000	11,600 U

U = Unfavorable

* Based on a standard allowance for good output. Note that the total is computed by (1) measuring the good *output* produced and (2) compiling what it *should have cost* by multiplying the output by the number of pounds or hours allowed and then multiplying by their standard unit prices. **(Please reread this—it is important.)**

By definition, an unfavorable variance exists when actual costs exceed budgeted or standard costs; a favorable variance exists when actual costs are less than the budgeted or standard costs.

price and efficiency variances

The summary data in the foregoing comparison do not give a revealing story. The manager usually wants a few clues to help explain why actual results differ from original plans. The division of the budget variance into two primary subdivisions, price and efficiency, often is helpful:

Price variance: difference between actual unit prices and standard unit prices *multiplied by the actual inputs:*

$$\begin{pmatrix}\text{Difference in}\\ \text{unit price}\\ \text{of inputs}\end{pmatrix} \times \begin{pmatrix}\text{Actual}\\ \text{inputs}\\ \text{used}\end{pmatrix} = \begin{pmatrix}\text{Price}\\ \text{variance}\end{pmatrix}$$

Direct materials: (\$5.40 − \$5.00) × 50,000 = \$20,000 Unfavorable (U)
Direct labor: (\$7.80 − \$8.00) × 22,000 = \$4,400 Favorable (F)

Efficiency variance: Efficiency is a relative measure; it is often expressed as the ratio of inputs to outputs. For any given level of output (e.g., units produced) the efficiency variance is the difference between the inputs that should have been used and the inputs that were actually used—holding unit prices constant at the standard unit price:[1]

$$\begin{pmatrix}\text{Inputs} & & \text{Inputs that}\\ \text{actually} & - & \text{should have}\\ \text{used} & & \text{been used}\end{pmatrix} \times \begin{pmatrix}\text{Standard}\\ \text{unit}\\ \text{price}\end{pmatrix} = \begin{pmatrix}\text{Efficiency}\\ \text{variance}\end{pmatrix}$$

$$\begin{pmatrix}\text{Actual} & & \text{Standard allowed}\\ \text{pounds or} & - & \text{pounds or hours}\\ \text{hours used} & & \text{for good output}\end{pmatrix} \times \begin{pmatrix}\text{Standard}\\ \text{unit}\\ \text{price}\end{pmatrix} = \begin{pmatrix}\text{Efficiency}\\ \text{variance}\end{pmatrix}$$

substitute terminology

To underscore their basic similarity, the two primary variances are designated here as price and efficiency variances for both direct material and direct labor. In practice, however, be alert for a variety of terms that are sometimes used to designate these variances. For example, the price variance is often called a *rate* variance when it is used in conjunction with direct labor. The efficiency variance is often called a *usage* or *quantity* variance when it is used in conjunction with either direct materials or direct labor.

[1] Expressed algebraically, these variances are $V_p - (AP - SP) \times AQ$ and $V_e = (AQ - SQ) \times SP$.

V_p = price variance, V_e = efficiency variance, AP = actual unit price of inputs, SP = standard unit price of inputs, AQ = actual quantity of inputs, SQ = standard quantity of inputs allowed for good output.

measuring and expressing output

Exhibit 7-1 is a graphical representation of the analysis of direct labor. The cost function is linear, sloping upward at a standard price of $8.00 per hour. At any quantity of output you can read the total standard costs that would be allowed for any given output. Note that quantity is expressed in hours rather than in physical units of product. *This is commonly done because most departments have an assortment of products; hours become a useful common denominator for measuring the total level of all production.*

Standard costs systems frequently do not express output as, say, 10,000 ash trays. Instead, output is expressed as 20,000 *standard hours allowed* (also called *standard hours earned, standard hours worked,* or, most accurately, *standard hours of input allowed for good output produced*). This is a key concept in standard costs, so be sure you grasp it before reading on.

evolution of standard-cost system

the flexible budget

Consider the options available in interpreting the meaning of the word "budget." Chapter 5 introduced the idea of the static budget in the form of a master budget. That is, an original plan is constructed that serves as a target for the forthcoming period. The period unfolds and the resulting inputs and outputs achieved may deviate considerably from the static or master budget. The "flexible budget" idea evolved (a) to facilitate the explanation of deviations of volume from the original plans in the master budget and (b) to pinpoint price and efficiency variances.

Suppose that the master budget called for 12,000 units of output, which would require 24,000 standard direct-labor hours allowed. The budget line in Exhibit 7-1 can provide three budget figures for direct labor:

Master budget for 24,000 standard hours allowed @ $8.00/hour (visualize its appearance on the exhibit)	$192,000
Flexible budget for 20,000 standard hours allowed @ $8.00/hour	160,000
Flexible budget for 22,000 actual hours of input @ $8.00/hour	176,000
Actual costs for 22,000 actual hours @ $7.80/hour	171,600

Of course, many managers would be satisfied with a performance report that merely subtracted actual costs from the master budget to provide a variance of $192,000 − $171,600, or $20,400. But the master (static) budget provides an unsatisfactory benchmark for most analysis because the resulting variance of $20,400 combines too many factors—price, efficiency, and volume—in a single number:

Actual Inputs at Actual Prices	Master (Static) Budget
22,000 × $7.80 = $171,600	24,000 × $8.00 = $192,000

↑ Master or static budget variance, $20,400 F ↑

EXHIBIT 7-1

GRAPHICAL ANALYSIS OF DIRECT LABOR

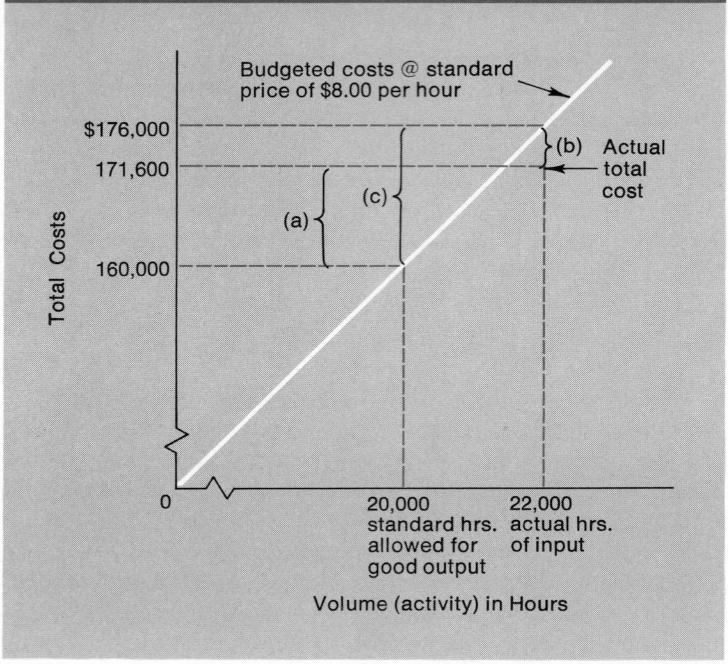

(a) Budget variance = Actual costs—Budgeted costs
= $11,600 U, as subdivided in (b) and (c).

(b) Price variance = Difference in price × Actual hours
= $4,400 F

(c) Efficiency variance = Difference in hours × Standard price
= $16,000 U

The graphic relationships can also be analyzed as follows:

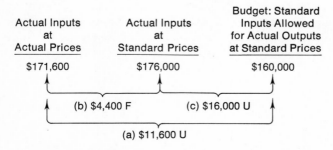

Actual Inputs at Actual Prices	Actual Inputs at Standard Prices	Budget: Standard Inputs Allowed for Actual Outputs at Standard Prices
$171,600	$176,000	$160,000

(b) $4,400 F (c) $16,000 U

(a) $11,600 U

U = Unfavorable; F = Favorable

two versions of flexible budget

A second analysis could use the flexible-budget idea by introducing an "adjusted" budget based on actual inputs:

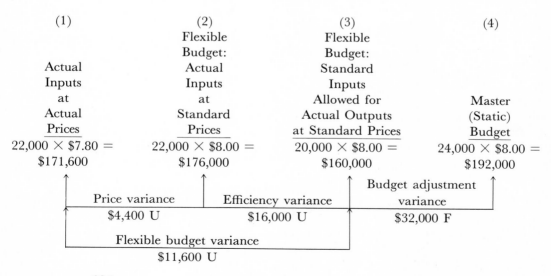

Actual Inputs at Actual Prices	Flexible Budget: Actual Inputs at Standard Prices	Master (Static) Budget
	22,000 × \$8.00 =	
\$171,600	\$176,000	\$192,000

Price variance, \$4,400 F — Budget adjustment variance, \$16,000 U

Note that the production manager's adjusted budget is "flexible" because it is determined by the actual volume of inputs, no matter what they may be. Surely, this altered budget provides an analytical improvement over the first comparison, because it does isolate price effects and it does recognize (via the budget adjustment variance) that volume levels deviated from the original target. But note that a flexible budget based on *actual inputs* is troublesome because (a) the manager's budget will be more generous as he becomes more inefficient (by using too many labor hours) and (b) there is no way to measure the degree of efficiency attained unless actual inputs are compared with *the inputs that should have been used to attain the outputs.*

The next analysis is more informative than the preceding two:

(1) Actual Inputs at Actual Prices	(2) Flexible Budget: Actual Inputs at Standard Prices	(3) Flexible Budget: Standard Inputs Allowed for Actual Outputs at Standard Prices	(4) Master (Static) Budget
22,000 × \$7.80 =	22,000 × \$8.00 =	20,000 × \$8.00 =	24,000 × \$8.00 =
\$171,600	\$176,000	\$160,000	\$192,000

Price variance \$4,400 U — Efficiency variance \$16,000 U — Budget adjustment variance \$32,000 F

Flexible budget variance \$11,600 U

Now the manager's flexible budget is geared to output (column 3) rather than input (column 2). His budget will not become more generous because of inefficiency, nor will it become tighter because of superefficient performance. Note that the use of column (3), the flexible budget based on outputs, permits the analyst (a) to isolate efficiency variances and isolate the volume effects of the budget adjustment variance for additional analysis as desired. The budget adjustment variance is the change in total budgeted costs because of deviations in the *output* from the original static level.[2]

Chapter 10 will discuss the analysis of these budget adjustment effects that represent an explanation of the deviations of the original master (static) budget from the flexible budget. After all, executives often begin with a static budget and later want to trace the actual results all the way back to the original static budget. Chapters 7, 8, and 9 will concentrate on the first three columns and will use the following terms consistently throughout these chapters:

For brevity, unless stated otherwise, *budget* will be used to denote the column (3) version, a *flexible budget* based on standard inputs allowed for actual outputs achieved. Similarly, the term *budget variance* will denote the difference between column (1), the actual inputs at actual prices, and the budget in column (3).

The term *flexible budget based on actual inputs* will be used to denote the column (2) idea. However, remember that, *when used alone,* the term *budget* will always represent the column (3) idea.

steps in evolution

The evolution of a control system in most organizations takes the following steps:

1. *Physical observations*—no records used for control. Sole dependence is placed on direct supervision.
2. *Historical records*—comparison of the actual costs of this month with the actual costs of last month or with the actual costs of the corresponding month of last year. System provides an unsatisfactory benchmark because inefficiencies are encompassed in prior costs.
3. *Static budgets*—comparison of the actual costs of this month with a single target of the budgeted costs for a specific predetermined level of output. System provides an unsatisfactory benchmark for judging efficiency if ensuing output deviates from the single original target. Thus, although a static budget provides a better benchmark than historical records, more refined benchmarks or criteria are often desired so that the financial impacts of price changes and efficiency changes are sharply pinpointed.

[2] Some readers may find the oft-made two-way distinction between *efficiency* and *effectiveness* helpful here. Efficiency compares inputs and outputs, whereas effectiveness is defined as the attainment of a predetermined fixed target. One can exist without the other. As a colleague has pointed out, the killing of a housefly with a sledge hammer may be effective, but it is inefficient. The above data show that performance was both inefficient and ineffective—ineffective because of the failure to reach the original target of 12,000 units of output.

4. *Standard costs and flexible budgets*—comparison of the actual costs of this month with a "flexible" or "variable" budget that is built up by using standard costs per unit. Note that this budget is tailored to the output achieved rather than the master or static budget. Thus, it *is based on a knowledge of how costs behave over a range of activity.* Essentially, a flexible budget is adjusted to the level of output attained.

Note that each step of this evolution is usually accompanied by a more complex and costly system that incorporates the major features of the preceding systems. Thus, a system of standard costs and flexible budgets will have physical observation, historical records, and static budgets too.

types of standards

How demanding should standards be? Should they express perfection, or should they allow for the various factors that prevent perfect performance? Accounting writers have coined a variety of names for different kinds of standards. Standards are often classified into three types:

1. *Basic cost standards* are unchanging standards. They provide the base for comparing actual costs through the years with the same standard. Thus the accounting reports spotlight trends. Price effects and changes in efficiency are gauged by comparison with the prices and efficiency that prevailed when standards were determined. Basic standard costs are seldom used because frequent changes in products and methods necessitate changes in standards. Thus, the trends lose their significance because of the short time that elapses between changes in products and methods.

2. *Perfection, ideal, maximum efficiency, or theoretical standard costs* reflect industrial engineers' dreams of a "factory heaven." Perfection standard costs are the absolute minimum costs that are possible under the best conceivable operating conditions, using existing specifications and equipment. Ideal standards, like other standards, are used where the management feels that they provide psychologically productive goals.

3. *Currently attainable standard costs* are the costs that should be incurred under forthcoming efficient operating conditions. They are difficult but possible to achieve. Attainable standards are looser than ideal standards because of allowance for normal spoilage, ordinary machine breakdowns, and lost time. However, attainable standards are usually set tight enough so that the operating people will consider the achievement of standard performance to be a satisfying accomplishment. In other words, variances are more likely to be slightly unfavorable than favorable—but favorable variances may be attained by a little more than expected efficiency.

In sum, most accountants and executives would probably agree with the following observations:

> Interview results show that a particular figure does not operate as a norm in either a score-card or attention-directing sense simply because the controller's department calls it a standard. It operates as a norm only to the extent that the executives and supervisors whose activity it measures accept it as a fair and attainable yardstick of their performance. Generally, operating executives were inclined to accept a standard to the extent that they were satisfied that the data were accurately recorded, that the standard level was reasonably attainable, and that the variables it measured were controllable by them.[3]

Terminology difficulties should also be kept in mind. Thus, *perfection standard* may be a *currently attainable standard* in some cases. For example, the outside purchases of expensive subassemblies such as tires or picture tubes should result in no waste in the assembly of a finished product. The standard here would be both *ideal* and *currently attainable.* As you might imagine, ideal or perfection standards are more likely to be used for material specifications than for labor control.

presence of expected variances

A major benefit from using *currently attainable standards* is the multipurpose use of the resultant standard costs. They may be used simultaneously for product costing, master budgets, and motivation. Throughout the illustrations and problems in this book, unless otherwise stated, currently attainable standards are assumed to be in use.

If standards are not currently attainable because they are perfection standards, the amount budgeted for financial (cash) planning purposes has to differ from the standard. Otherwise, projected income and cash disbursements will be forecast incorrectly. In such cases, perfection standards may be used for compiling performance reports, but expected variances are stipulated in the master budget for cash planning. For example, if unusually strict labor standards are used, the standard cost per finished unit may be \$16 even though top management anticipates an unfavorable performance variance of, say, \$1.60 per unit. In the master budget the total labor costs allowed would be \$17.60 per unit: \$16.00 plus an expected variance of \$1.60. In our example, a master budget could conceivably include the following item:

Direct labor:	
Budget allowance shown on departmental performance report	\$160,000
Expected variance that will appear on master budget for cash planning	16,000
Total budget allowance for cash planning	\$176,000

[3] H. A. Simon, H. Guetzkow, G. Kozmetsky, and G. Tyndall, *Centralization vs. Decentralization in Organizing the Controller's Department* (New York: The Controllership Foundation, Inc.), p. 29. For a discussion of budgets as targets, see Anthony Hopwood, *Accounting and Human Behavior* (London: Prentice-Hall, International, 1974), pp. 57–69.

responsibility for developing standards

The standard-setting and budget-setting process in an organization often is primarily the responsibility of the line personnel directly involved. The relative tightness of the budget is the result of face-to-face discussion and bargaining between the manager and his immediate superior. The budgetary accountants, the industrial engineers, and the market researchers should extend all desired technical assistance and advice, but the final decisions ordinarily should not be theirs. The line manager is the person who is supposed to accept and live with the budget or standard.

The job of the accounting department is (a) to price the physical standards—that is, to express the physical standards in the form of dollars and cents; and (b) to report operating performance in comparison with standards.

responsibility for price variance

Cost control is aided by measuring variances in terms of responsibilities. Typically, usage is the major responsibility of one department head (a foreman), whereas price may be the major responsibility of a different department head (a purchasing officer). Therefore, the dollar measure of the efficiency variance should not be influenced by changes in unit prices. Price is held constant at standard, and the resultant efficiency variance is attributable solely to off-standard usage by the foreman's department. In the case of the price variance, because the purchasing office does not influence the quantity used, the difference in unit price is said to be applicable to all quantities used. The responsibility of the purchasing manager is deemed to include buying for *all* needs regardless of whether the materials are used efficiently.

A chart of the relationship of price and efficiency variances may be helpful. Exhibit 7-2 shows a graphic analysis that demonstrates variance computations in rectangular terms. Theoretically, as shown in the graph, the price variance should be subdivided into two variances:

1. Pure Price Variance = Difference in Price × Standard Quantity (instead of Actual Quantity)
2. Combined or Joint Price–Efficiency Variance = Difference in Price × Difference in Quantity

The importance of this refinement depends on the significance and usefulness of isolating the joint variance. Where executive bonuses depend on variances, this refinement may be necessary. For example, an unfavorable total-price variance, as ordinarily computed, could be partially attributable to inefficient usage. Thus, a part of the price variance in our example would not have arisen if quantities used had not exceeded standard: (50,000 lbs. − 40,000 lbs.) ($5.40

EXHIBIT 7-2

GRAPHIC ANALYSIS OF VARIANCES

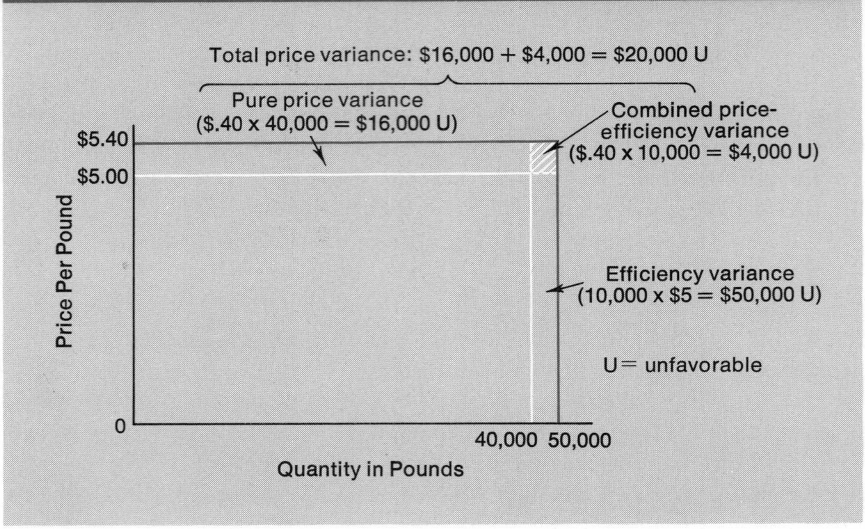

− $5.00) = $4,000. In this book, we shall not refine our analysis this far; all of the $20,000 is called price variance. That is, we shall consider the price variance to be the sum of the pure price variance and the combined price-efficiency variance.

Analysis of variances may be further subdivided beyond price and efficiency variances. For example, the efficiency variance may be partially explained by inferior quality; by faulty workmanship, such as sloppy trimming or careless cutting; by use of substitute materials; by improper mix of materials; or for some other reason. The specific reasons are sought to pin down responsibility for control purposes.

The key questions in deciding how variances should be collected and analyzed are: *Why* do we wish to identify this particular variance? What will we *do* with it? If we cannot make practical use of the variance, then we should not incur the cost of computing it.

trade-offs among variances

Managers often have opportunities to take advantage of bargain purchases or to combine available resources in a way that will save overall costs. For example, a quantity of a raw material having a few inferior characteristics (perhaps a different grade of lumber or shade of color) might be consciously acquired at an unusually low price. This material might lead to unusually heavy spoilage or excessive labor times in order to produce a finished product that will meet the standard quality specifications. Nevertheless, the manager may have enough discretion to proceed. The aim would be to reduce the total costs of manufacturing by trading off favorable price variances against expected unfavorable efficiency variances.

A standard-cost system should not be a straitjacket that prevents the manager from looking at the overall company objectives. Too often, each unfavorable variance is regarded as, ipso facto, bad; and each favorable variance is regarded as, ipso facto, good. If the manager guesses wrong, and the unfavorable efficiency variances exceed the favorable price variance, the decision to make the bargain purchase was unfavorable despite the favorable label pinned on the price variance. Similarly, if the manager guesses correctly, so that the favorable price variance exceeds the unfavorable efficiency variances, the decision was favorable despite the unfavorable label pinned on the efficiency variances. The point is that there are too many interdependencies among activities; an "unfavorable" or a "favorable" label should not lead the manager to jump to conclusions about what happened. By themselves, such labels merely raise questions and provide clues. They are attention directors, not answer givers.

physical standards and improvement of operations

Physical standards are the foundation of a standard-cost system. Ideally, they should represent reliable engineering or physical estimates, which may be expressed in tons or gallons produced and in minutes or hours of labor. These standards are often constructed from systematic observation, measurement, and controlled experiment. Analyses of the kinds and amounts of materials, labor time and methods, and necessary overhead items lead to these so-called engineered standards. The entire productive process is divided into various operations or activities, and the proper material and labor requirements are rigorously estimated.

Standard costs are developed by multiplying the physical standards by appropriate price factors. The use of price factors allows all standards in the company to be expressed in a common denominator—dollars. Furthermore, the pricing of physical standards calls attention to the more costly items that tend to deserve more managerial attention.

Textbooks generally give the impression that standard costs are always based on technical engineering studies and rigorous specifications. Accurate measurement is indeed the foundation for control. However, although a rigorous approach is desirable, it should be remembered that less scientific standards may still provide a useful way of presenting information in order to stimulate corrective action.

material-price standards

timing of material-price standards

Our chapter illustration showed how the price and efficiency variances for materials were computed simultaneously as production took place. This approach is adequate where material prices are not too volatile, or where large raw-material inventories are not carried, or where the purpose is solely to remove influences of price from efficiency reports. However, when current control of purchasing activities is also a major objective of isolating price variances, the approach should be modified, as we shall see.

Material-price standards are usually based either on expected prices for the period in question (sometimes as short as a week) or on prices prevailing at the time that standards are set. Price variances for purposes of *feedback* are computed at the time of *purchase* by taking the difference between actual and standard unit price times the actual quantity acquired. To delay the computation of the price variance until the time the quantity is *issued* (as we did in our illustration) usually defeats the usefulness of the information for control, because corrective action is then seldom possible.

Ideally, if the costs of running the system are ignored, where price variances are used for *feedback* purposes, they should be computed when the original purchase order is sent to the supplier. Practically, such variances are usually not computed until the invoice is received, because the latter event triggers entry into the formal accounting records, whereas the sending of the purchase order does not.

In most companies, the acquisition and the usage of raw materials require different decisions. The purchasing officer worries about getting the specified materials in the correct quantities at the right time and at the right price. The production officer concentrates on using the materials efficiently. The assessment of a manager's performance is facilitated by separating the factors that are directly subject to his decisions from those that are not. A popular way to achieve this separation is to isolate price variances so that they do not affect the measured performance of the production manager. Efficiency can then be judged without being mingled with unit-price effects that may be confusing.

who sets material-price standards?

If any one person is responsible for material-price variances, it is probably the purchasing officer. Therefore, he should have a strong role in setting price standards. Nevertheless, many companies have the accounting department and the purchasing department work out the task jointly. Responsibility for price standards is twofold:

1. Because prices are often set by external influences, setting price standards is mostly a task of accurate predicton. Thus, price variances are probably more a measure of forecasting ability than of failure to buy at predetermined standard prices.
2. Some control may be exerted over prices by getting numerous quotations, purchasing in optimum lots, hunting for bargains, selecting the most economical means of transportation, and taking advantage of cash discounts. Effective price standards help reduce the tendency of many purchasing people to play favorites among suppliers. Some check is desirable on the purchasing officer's setting of price standards. He should have to submit evidence in support of the standards to a standards committee or to the accounting department.

Failure to meet price standards may often be due to external factors mentioned previously or to departments other than the purchasing department. For example, sudden rush orders or unexpected volume changes in production may upset material price standards. In such cases, the major responsibility for variances may rest with the sales manager because of his faulty forecasting or with the head of production planning because of his sloppy production scheduling. The intelligent analysis of the variances will help pinpoint responsibility in these situations. The reports of price variances are often the starting point for management's finding substitute materials, changing methods or specifications, and altering selling prices.

material-efficiency standards

nature of efficiency standards

Although material prices are frequently difficult to control, the quantity of direct materials used is subject to closer regulation.

Most companies rely on engineering studies as a basis for determining quantity standards for material. Blueprints, product specifications, normal spoilage, unavoidable waste, and production methods are considered in preparing the *standard bill of materials* (Exhibit 7-3), which is the formal expression of material-efficiency standards. Note that we are considering physical standards; price factors are not relevant when the types and quantities of materials are determined. An efficiency variance may be expressed in dollars by merely multiplying the standard unit price by the physical quantity variance.

In addition to formal engineering studies, sample runs under regulated conditions or historical studies of material usage in a specific product may be

EXHIBIT 7-3

STANDARD BILL OF MATERIALS

Assembly No. b Description TV Table

Part Number	Number Required	Description
A 1426	4 sq. ft.	Plastic sheet — Pearl grey
455	1/8 lb.	Adhesive
642	1	Table top
714	4	Steel legs
961	1	Nut and bolt kit

used in setting efficiency standards. Of course, care must be exercised when relying on past performance because it may have been inefficient. Depending on specific materials or plant conditions, companies may use engineering studies, sample runs, historical studies, or some combination thereof.

setting efficiency standards Efficiency standards are usually set by the engineering department with the aid of the production department and the cost-accounting department. Although the production executive responsible for meeting the standards should participate, he should not have the final authority in setting the standards. But at least he should understand the standards and accept them as his targets.

control of usage Control over usage of material is best exerted when the foreman has timely comparisons of actual results with standards. When they are very important, these comparisons may be made continuously, or at least hourly. The exact control procedure depends on several factors, such as the following (*N.A.A. Research Series No. 12,* p. 908):

1. The nature and value of materials
2. The type of accounting plan used
3. The methods used for detecting and measuring losses of material in production

THE NATURE AND VALUE OF THE MATERIALS Usage of subassemblies and expensive parts can be predicted easily and can be accurately accounted for. Predictions of usage of bulk materials such as iron ore, alcohol, and coal are based on average consumption. Variances for these materials are aggregated as totals for given periods.

THE TYPE OF ACCOUNTING PLAN USED Where process costing is used, quantity variances are often determined periodically. Where job-order costing is used, quantity variances may be determined for each order if desired.

THE METHODS USED FOR DETECTING AND MEASURING LOSSES OF MATERIAL IN PRODUCTION When a department is expected to turn out a given job, batch, or specified number of product units, a standard bill of materials or stores requisition may be submitted to stores for withdrawal of the standard amount of direct materials needed. *As production takes place, any additional materials needed may be obtained from stores only by submitting an excess-materials requisition, which is usually of a distinct color.* Thus, the foreman is immediately informed of off-standard performance because he must sign the excess-materials requisition. A periodic summary of these requisitions provides the total unfavorable efficiency variance. If performance is better than standard, special returned-materials forms are used to compute favorable efficiency variances.

Other control methods are necessary when a given amount of output results from varying levels of input. A comparison of good production with input of direct materials is needed in order to judge performance, the key question being whether the standard amount of materials was used to obtain the given output. The difficulty here is that computation of variances is delayed until production is completed. To better achieve control in these cases, procedures have been developed to detect some variances prior to completion of work. These procedures include inspection at key operation points while work is in process, so that spoilage and other losses may be measured before full completion of the product.

Daily and weekly reports of variances are often expressed in physical terms only—gallons used, pounds consumed, and so on. The bases for these reports are usually the original source documents, such as excess-materials requisitions, scrap reports, inspection reports, and the like.

labor-price standards

Price factors are usually not subject to as much control as are efficiency factors. Department heads' control of labor rates is usually limited, because the rates are the result of union negotiations or local conditions of labor supply and demand. The cost department computes standard costs by applying the rates to the physical labor standards. Most companies change labor-price standards as specified by labor contracts.

If price standards are kept up to date, the price variances should be relatively small. Such variances are regarded as the responsibility of the foreman. He must match the men and the machines to the tasks at hand by using the proper grade of labor. Variances usually arise from (a) the use of a person with a wrong rate for a specific operation, (b) use of excess individuals per machine, or (c) paying expensive hourly rates instead of prescribed piece rates because of low productivity.

If price standards are not kept in line with changes in actual labor rates, the resulting variances cannot be considered the foreman's responsibility.

To develop standard unit costs, a single average labor rate may be used for a given operation. The rates of individual workers performing this operation may vary slightly from the average rate because of seniority or inexperience. Also, different products require different mixes of labor skills. This must be taken into account unless there are subheadings under "direct labor" for each of the separate skills and jobs.

Price variances generally are not large and consequently do not get the managerial attention that efficiency variances get. In companies where price variances are small, little formal reporting of variances takes place. In companies where price variances are important, variance reports are submitted to the executives responsible for the controllable variances.

labor-efficiency standards

general characteristics

The human element makes the setting of labor-efficiency (also called *labor-performance, labor-time,* and *labor-quantity*) standards a complicated task. As may be expected, disputes over proper standards are much more likely to arise over labor-efficiency standards than over material-efficiency standards.

Time and motion study is the most widely used method of setting operation-time standards. To be effective, it must consider the conditions prevailing around the labor operation as well as the operation itself. This means thorough consideration of such factors as equipment, material handling and availability, routing, and instructions for the worker. Properly trained and experienced methods engineers, acting in a staff capacity, usually set efficiency standards. Time standards are typically set for each individual operation. In turn, *master operations lists,* such as the one in Exhibit 7-4, may be compiled for scheduling and routing a variety of individual products.

What factors are usually considered in setting time standards? Some allowance is usually made for fatigue, rest time, and faulty material. Because the purpose of time standards is to measure efficiency, variances not caused by variations in individual efficiency are isolated and often are treated as part of factory overhead. Examples are machine breakdowns, idle time spent awaiting materials, rework, and vacation time.

Time standards are usually set tight enough to provide incentives and yet not so tight as to be unattainable. Thus, time variances generally are unfavorable. Favorable variances are usually caused by exceptionally efficient performance or loose standards. The latter exist because of failure to have standards reflect changes in operating methods or failure to have uniform working conditions. For cost-control purposes, time standards should be reviewed for change whenever operation methods have changed.

Foremen are held responsible for efficiency variances under their control. Variance reports are regularly submitted to foremen, often on a daily or weekly basis. The source documents for such reports are usually some type of work ticket. These work tickets are analyzed and variances are coded and classified. The classifications are almost always by responsibility (that is, by cost center), and often by operations, products, orders, and causes. Thus, a work ticket may have a number designating departmental responsibility and another number designating the cause of the variance. Causes may include machinery breakdowns, rework, faulty material, use of nonpreferred equipment, and so forth.

When variance reports are submitted, major variances are discussed by the interested executives. Investigations of possible operating improvements may be conducted by either line executives or staff experts on standards, or both.

setup time

Machines and accessory equipment often must be adjusted and "made ready" before a particular operation or job can

EXHIBIT 7-4

OPERATIONS ROUTING SHEET

MASTER OPERATIONS LIST

Part Name: Fuel pump body with bushings — Part Number: B-489

Stock Specifications: Grey iron casting — Standard Quantity: 200

Operation Number	Department Number	Standard Time Allowed in Minutes		Description of Operation
		Setup	Operation Per Unit	
20	27	90	10.2	Drill, bore, face, chamfer and ream
25	29	18	.7	Face and chamfer hub
30	29	12	1.5	Mill eng. fit pad
35	31	18	8.0	Drill and tap complete
40	29	12	1.5	Mill clearance
45	29	—	1.8	Clean and grind hose connection
50	29	12	2.3	Press in 2 bushings G-98 and face flange on mandrel
	13			Inspect
	21			To stockroom

commence. This setup time is easily traceable to an operation or a job, yet its total cost is seldom affected by whether 100 pieces of 2,000 pieces are subsequently processed. The question then is whether setup costs should be treated as direct labor or as a part of factory overhead. No categorical answer can be given. It seems clear that if production runs fluctuate wildly, setup costs should not ordinarily be regarded as direct labor, because the cost *per unit* of product would fluctuate solely because of the length of production run.

For analytical purposes and for cost-control follow-up, setup costs should not be commingled and averaged with the regular direct-labor costs even if it seems desirable to trace setup costs to specific jobs or operations. Most standard-cost systems have standard lot sizes for production runs. Often setup costs are allowed for in the standard direct-labor cost per unit by allocating the setup labor for each operation over the quantity in the standard lot. This practice may be suitable for product-costing purposes; but it has drawbacks for cost-control purposes, especially where standard lot sizes are seldom adhered to, because it mixes together two dissimilar elements that are subject to different control features. As a minimum, then, setup costs should always be coded so that they may be sharply distinguished from operating-labor costs. In this book, we shall assume that setup costs are classified as a part of overhead.

general-ledger entries

entries for illustration General-ledger entries for standard-cost systems are usually monthly summaries of detailed variances that were isolated from day to day. Using the data of our earlier illustration, suppose materials are carried in Stores at actual prices. All variances are isolated when Work in Process is charged at standard quantities allowed times standard unit prices:

1. Work in process	200,000	
Direct-material price variance	20,000	
Direct-material efficiency variance	50,000	
Stores		270,000
To record direct materials used. Note that unfavorable variances are always debits and favorable variances are always credits.		
2. Work in process	160,000	
Direct-labor efficiency variance	16,000	
Direct-labor price variance		4,400
Accrued payroll		171,600
To record liability for and allocation of direct labor costs.		

variations in systems There is a wide variety of general-ledger approaches to standard-cost systems. An excellent approach is that which isolates price variances most quickly. To do so, variances are recorded when *purchases* are made rather than when materials are *issued* to Work in Process. Reconsider our illustration by assuming that 90,000 pounds were purchased during the month, although only 50,000 pounds were issued:

1. Stores (90,000 lbs. @ $5.00)	450,000	
Direct-material price variance (90,000 lbs. @ $.40)	36,000	
Accounts payable (90,000 lbs. @ $5.40)		486,000
To record direct-material purchases.		
2. Work in process (40,000 lbs. @ $5.00)	200,000	
Direct-material efficiency variance (10,000 lbs. @ $5.00)	50,000	
Stores (50,000 lbs. @ $5.00)		250,000
To record direct materials used. An excess-material requisition would be the basis for isolating this variance.		

T-accounts would appear as follows:

STORES	
1. Actual quantity purchased × standard price, 450,000	2. Actual quantity requisitioned × standard price, 250,000

DIRECT-MATERIAL-PRICE VARIANCE	
1. Actual quantity purchased × difference in price, 36,000	

WORK IN PROCESS	
2. Standard quantity requisitioned × standard price, 200,000	

DIRECT-MATERIAL-EFFICIENCY VARIANCE	
2. Difference in quantity used × standard price, 50,000	

The major advantage of this system is its stress on the control feature of standard costs, whereby all variances are isolated as early as is economically feasible. Another advantage is the economical simplicity of carrying all inventories at standard prices. It avoids the problems and extra clerical costs of making cost-flow assumptions such as first-in, first-out, or last-in, first-out.

disposition of variances

Like the disposition of under- or overapplied overhead discussed in Chapter 4, price and efficiency variances are either written off immediately or prorated among the inventories and cost of goods sold. A full discussion is found in Chapter 10.

costs of data gathering

At first glance, it may appear that standard-cost systems would always be more costly to operate than other systems. Obviously, a startup investment must be made to develop the standards; but the ongoing costs can be even less than so-called "actual-cost" systems.

Of course, standard-cost systems will be more costly if they are run in complete parallel with an actual-cost system or normal-cost system (see Chapter 4). For instance, if actual direct-material costs and direct-labor costs continue to be traced to individual products even though a standard-cost system is in use, the costs of record keeping will increase.

On the other hand, many standard-cost systems have been adopted for the *major* purpose of saving record-keeping costs. A standard-cost system can be designed so that:

1. No "actual" costs of stores, work in process, and finished goods are traced to batches of product on a day-to-day basis. Only records of physical counts are kept.
2. Actual consumption of material and labor can be totaled by operation or department for, say, a month without tracing such consumption to jobs. Feedback on performance can be based on these actual totals of input compared to the total standard allowed inputs for the physical output during the month. However, the major advantage of this procedure is its clerical simplicity.

when to investigate variances

rules of thumb

When should variances be investigated? Frequently the answer is based on subjective judgments, hunches, guesses, and rules of thumb. The most troublesome aspect of feedback is deciding when a variance is significant enough to warrant management's attention. For some items, a small deviation may prompt follow-up. For other items, a minimum dollar amount or 5, 10, or 25 percent deviations from budget may be necessary before investigations commence. Of course, a 4 percent variance in a $1 million material cost may deserve more attention than a 20 percent variance in a $10,000 repair cost. Therefore, rules such as "Investigate all variances exceeding $5,000, or 25 percent of standard cost, whichever is lower" are common.

Variance analysis is subject to the same cost–benefit test as other phases of an information system. The trouble with the foregoing rules of thumb is that they are too frequently based on subjective assessments, guesses, or hunches. The field of statistics offers tools to help reduce these subjective features of variance analysis. These tools help answer the cost–benefit question, and they help separate variances caused by random events from variances that are controllable.

Accounting systems have traditionally implied that a standard is a single acceptable measure. Practically, the accountant (and everybody else) realizes that the standard is a *band* or *range* of possible acceptable outcomes. Consequently, he expects variances to fluctuate randomly within some normal limits.

By definition, a random variance per se is within this band or range. It calls for no corrective action to an existing process; random variances are attributable to chance rather than to management's implementation decisions. For a further discussion, see Chapter 26.

timing and aggregation

Another difficulty is that the accounting system compiles variances for a particular period of time. A cost-conscious management will follow up variances quickly—sometimes daily, or even hourly. But delayed reports and everyday work often allow variances to accumulate, so that it becomes too late to find out what caused them. Furthermore, favorable and unfavorable variances are frequently combined, so that significant variances may be offset in accounts and in management reports. Each overtime authorization, for example, is an incremental decision and should not be related to average rates of overtime allowances. This combination of delayed reporting and of cost accumulations that represent a conglomeration of different operations makes it difficult to find the causes of variances and to trace the causes in an economical way below the foreman level to individual machines, employees, and materials.

learning curves and accounting

effects of learning on productivity

When new products or processes are initiated, a learning or familiarity phenomenon occurs. As experience is gained, productivity heightens. The effect of learning on output per labor-hour or machine-hour is usually depicted by a learning curve, which helps managers to predict how costs will change as the process matures. Case studies have shown that the time needed per unit of product should be progressively smaller at some constant percentage rate as experience is gained. The applicable percentage of the previous time usually varies from 60 to 85 percent, but 80 percent is common. For example, as cumulative quantities double, average time per unit may fall to only 80 percent of the previous time. Exhibit 7-5 demonstrates an 80 percent learning curve, using the following data:

QUANTITY		*TIME IN MINUTES*	
Per Lot	Cumulative	Cumulative	Cumulative Average Per Unit
10	10	300	30.0
10	20	480	24.0 (30.0 × 80%)
20	40	768	19.2 (24.0 × 80%)
40	80	1,232	15.4 (19.2 × 80%)
80	160	1,968	12.3 (15.4 × 80%)

As Exhibit 7-5 indicates, as production quantities increase, the average time per unit starts to level off; so if total production were large enough, the time per unit would become quite stable.

The learning curve is applicable only to setting standards during the learning or start-up phases of production.[4] If production life is sufficiently long, or if the operations are relatively routine, a steady-state phase eventually occurs whereby no increases in productivity are predicted. Exhibit 7-5 shows the learning phase and the steady-state phase. Indices of productivity may be expressed, depending on the industry, as tons per machine-hour or finished units per labor-hour, or some other measure.

setting budgets or standards Predictions of costs should allow for the effects of learning. The costs most likely to be affected include labor, power, and other related overhead. Costs that may be unaffected typically include many materials, supplies, packing, selling, and nearly all fixed costs. Learning effects are more pronounced when the production process entails dexterity, sequential manual steps, and physical and mental adaptabilities of workers; learning has little application to automated or push-button operations.

[4] For an expanded discussion, see E. L. Summers and G. A. Welsch, "How Learning Curve Models Can Be Applied to Profit Planning," *Management Services,* Vol. 7, No. 2, pp. 45–50; and N. Baloff and J. W. Kennelly, "Accounting Implications of Product and Process Startups," *Journal of Accounting Research,* Vol. 5, No. 2, pp. 131–43. The learning-curve model is a power function:

$$y = ax^b$$

where y = productivity
x = cumulative output
a = parameter value, the productivity during the first unit of output
b = parameter value, the index of the rate of increase in productivity during learning

EXHIBIT 7-5

EIGHTY PERCENT LEARNING CURVE*

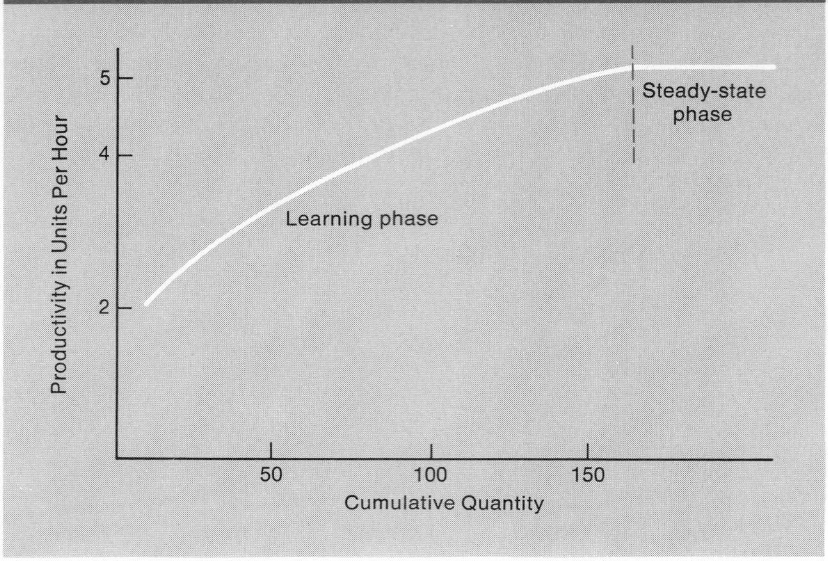

* In practice, these curves are plotted on log-log graph paper, so that they appear as straight lines for ease of use. Also, some learning curves express productivity in terms of average time or average cost per unit, which would be expected to fall as learning increases.

The learning curve has many ramifications for business strategies. For example, competitive bidding in defense contracting would be affected by the predicted learning effects. The expected volume could have a dramatic influence on the unit price.[5] The cost per airplane is much less if 500 are manufactured than if 50 are manufactured.

[5] Some observers maintain that learning efforts apply to all costs. The Boston Consulting Group has detected a widely applicable *experience curve,* which shows that overall unit costs decline in constant dollars by 20 to 30 percent with each doubling of experience. Experience is defined as the combined effects of learning, specialization, investment, and scale. If such an experience curve exists for any given company, it has enormous implications for strategic decisions regarding cost control, make or buy, pricing, growth, and so on. See "Selling Business a Theory of Economics," *Business Week,* September 8, 1973.

William J. Abernathy and Kenneth Wayne, "Limits of the Learning Curve," *Harvard Business Review,* Vol. 52, No. 5 (September-October 1974), pp. 109–19, admit that the pursuit of the learning curve can reap great benefits. They state that total costs decline by a constant and predictable percentage in terms of constant dollars each time volume doubles. But there is a practical limit. This limit is not reached because the manager has exhausted means of cutting costs; rather, it is determined by the market's demand for product change, the rate of technological innovation in the industry, and competitors' ability to segment the market via a superior product or customized options. Then the company on the learning curve must either "abandon the all-important volume bases of scale or introduce a major product improvement. Either step, or both, ends the cost-reduction sequence."

Standards during the learning phase are often erroneously based on stable or steady-state conditions. That is, anticipated standards are being applied from the start. Using these standards to plan and to judge performance may have undesirable consequences. Among the dangers are faulty cash planning and production scheduling because of failure to allow for the unusually high costs and time consumption of startups.

In addition, the inapplicable standards may have an unfavorable motivational impact. If the unfavorable discrepancy between the steady-state standard and actual performance is large and persistent, the goal may be rejected as unattainable.

Of course, the opposite effect may also occur. That is, the learning curve might be ignored, resulting eventually in outdated standards that are not stringent enough.

SUMMARY

Standard costs are used for building a budgeting and feedback system. They aid management predictions and provide a framework for judging performance. Actual costs are compared with standard costs to obtain variances. Variances raise questions; they do not provide answers. The variances are investigated to decide (a) how to improve the implementation of a given decision model or set of plans, or (b) how to change objectives, methods, or standards.

Currently attainable standards are the most widely used because they usually have the most desirable motivational impact and because they may be used for a variety of accounting purposes, including financial planning, as well as for monitoring departmental performance.

When standards are currently attainable, there is no real difference between standards and budgets. A standard is a *unit* concept, whereas a budget is a *total* concept. In a sense, the standard is the budget for one unit.

Material and labor variances are primarily divided into two categories: (a) price or rate, and (b) efficiency or usage. Price or rate variances are computed by multiplying differences in price by actual quantities. Efficiency or usage variances remove influences of price changes; they are computed by multiplying differences in quantities by a standard price.

General-ledger treatments for standard costs vary considerably. The method advocated in this book stresses isolation of variances as quickly as possible.

It is extremely important to personalize variances so that each variance is assignable to the person primarily responsible. Otherwise, the investigative follow-ups of reported variances—where the real payoff lies—will be fruitless. There is also a need to have some objective way to decide when a given variance is significant enough to warrant investigation.

PROBLEMS FOR SELF-STUDY

PROBLEM 1 The Chester Company uses standard costs. The purchasing manager is responsible for material-price variances, and the production manager is responsible for material-efficiency variances and direct-labor price and efficiency variances.

The standard price for metal used as a principal raw material was \$2 per pound. The standard allowance was six pounds per finished unit of product.

The standard rate for direct labor was \$7 per hour. The standard allowance was one hour per finished unit of product.

During the past week, 10,000 good finished units were produced. However, labor trouble caused the production manager to use much nonpreferred personnel. Actual labor costs were \$78,000 for 13,000 actual hours. 80,000 pounds of metal were acquired for \$1.80 per pound. 71,000 pounds of metal were consumed during production.

required

1. Compute the material purchase-price variance, material-efficiency variance, direct-labor price variance, and direct-labor efficiency variance.
2. As a supervisor of both the purchasing manager and the production manager, how would you interpret the feedback provided by the computed variances?
3. What are the budget allowances for the production manager for direct materials and direct labor? Would they be different if production were 7,000 good finished units?
4. Prepare a condensed responsibility performance report for the production manager for the 10,000 units produced. Show three columns: budget, actual, and variance.

SOLUTION 1

1. The format for the solution (Exhibit 7-6) may seem awkward at first, but upon review you will discover that it provides perspective and insight.
2. The variances direct attention and prompt investigation about the following possibilities at first glance. The purchasing manager made an advantageous purchase, but the favorable variance may be attributable to a number of causes.

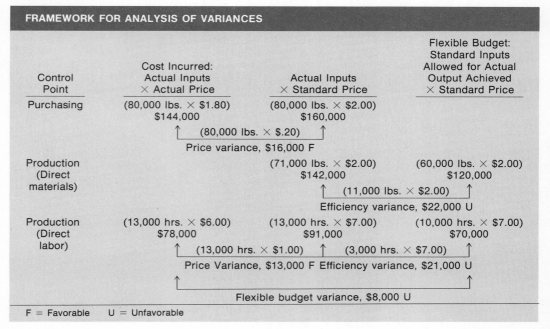

EXHIBIT 7-6

FRAMEWORK FOR ANALYSIS OF VARIANCES

Control Point	Cost Incurred: Actual Inputs × Actual Price	Actual Inputs × Standard Price	Flexible Budget: Standard Inputs Allowed for Actual Output Achieved × Standard Price
Purchasing	(80,000 lbs. × \$1.80) \$144,000	(80,000 lbs. × \$2.00) \$160,000	
	(80,000 lbs. × \$.20) Price variance, \$16,000 F		
Production (Direct materials)		(71,000 lbs. × \$2.00) \$142,000	(60,000 lbs. × \$2.00) \$120,000
		(11,000 lbs. × \$2.00) Efficiency variance, \$22,000 U	
Production (Direct labor)	(13,000 hrs. × \$6.00) \$78,000	(13,000 hrs. × \$7.00) \$91,000	(10,000 hrs. × \$7.00) \$70,000
	(13,000 hrs. × \$1.00) Price Variance, \$13,000 F	(3,000 hrs. × \$7.00) Efficiency variance, \$21,000 U	
	Flexible budget variance, \$8,000 U		

F = Favorable   U = Unfavorable

The manager may have predicted prices incorrectly so that the standard of $2 is inaccurate, or he may have made a bargain purchase through his own special skills, or some combination thereof. Moreover, if the quality were less than normal, the savings in unit purchase cost may be more than offset by excessive usage or may have contributed to excessive usage. (Note too that the facts are unclear as to whether the material used came from the units purchased currently or from previous stockpiles, or both.)

The production manager probably had abnormal troubles. Among the possible causes are the use of inferior materials or of nonpreferred workmen, or some combination of both. Assume that the materials were of normal quality. The trade-off of lower-rate labor for more inefficiency apparently led to net higher costs of direct-labor and direct-material usage. In short, less-skilled workers probably used too much time and too much materials to produce the 10,000 units of output.

3. The chapter made the point that standard costs can be thought of as the budget allowance for one unit of output. That is, the standard is a *unit* concept and the budget is a *total* concept. Viewed in this way, the budget allowances for the production manager would be:

Direct materials, 60,000 lbs. × $2.00	$120,000
Direct labor, 10,000 hrs. × $7.00	70,000

Note that the budget allowance is the same as (is equal to) the total standard quantity allowed for the good units produced times the standard price.

If 7,000 units were produced, the budget allowance would be lowered accordingly:

Direct materials, 7,000 × 6 lbs. × $2.00	$84,000
Direct labor, 7,000 × 1 hr. × $7.00	49,000

4.

	BUDGET	*ACTUAL*	*VARIANCE*
Direct materials			
(at standard unit prices)	$120,000	$142,000*	$22,000 U
Direct labor	70,000	78,000	8,000 U

* This "actual" charge of $142,000 illustrates the basic nature of responsibility accounting. The $142,000 is not an actual cost in the usual sense, because materials are charged to the production manager at a predetermined standard unit price. In this way, fluctuations in material *prices,* which are supposed to be the primary responsibility of the purchasing manager, do not affect the production manager's performance report. In contrast, because the production manager is deemed to be responsible for both labor rates and labor efficiency, actual labor cost is assigned in full to him.

PROBLEM 2

Consider the following for April, when 2,000 finished units were produced:

Direct materials used, 4,400 pounds. The standard allowance per finished unit is two pounds at $5 per pound. Six thousand pounds were purchased at $5.50 per pound, a total of $33,000.

Actual direct-labor hours were 6,500 at a total cost of $40,300. The standard labor cost per finished unit was $18. Standard labor time allowed is three hours per unit.

required

1. Journal entries for a "normal"-cost system as described in Chapter 4. That is, "actual" charges for direct materials and direct labor are charged to Work in Process.
2. Journal entries for a "standard-cost" system.
3. Show an alternate approach, including journal entries, to the way you quantified the material-price variance in requirement 2. Which way is better? Explain.

SOLUTION 2

1. *NORMAL-COST SYSTEM*

Stores or direct-material inventory	$33,000	
Accounts payable		$33,000
Work in process (4,400 @ $5.50)	24,200	
Stores		24,200
Work in process (6,500 @ $6.20)	40,300	
Accrued payroll		40,300

2. *STANDARD-COST SYSTEM*

Stores or direct-material inventory (6,000 @ $5.00)	$30,000	
Direct-material purchase-price variance	3,000	
Accounts payable		$33,000
Work in process (4,000 @ $5.00)	20,000	
Direct-material efficiency variance	2,000	
Stores (4,400 @ $5.00)		22,000
Work in process (2,000 @ $18.00)	36,000	
Direct-labor price variance	1,300	
Direct-labor efficiency variance	3,000	
Accrued payroll		40,300

Actual Inputs × Actual Price	Actual Inputs × Standard Price	Flexible Budget: Actual Outputs × Standard Price
(6,500 × $6.20)	(6,500 × $6.00)	(2,000 × $18.00) or (6,000 × $ 6.00)
$40,300	$39,000	$36,000

6,500 × $.20 — Price variance $1,300 U

500 @ $6.00 — Efficiency variance $3,000 U

Flexible budget variance, $4,300 U

3. An alternate standard-cost approach to that shown in 2 (Approach in 2 is better because it isolates variances earlier, when something is more likely to be done about the variances):

Stores	$33,000	
Accounts payable		$33,000
Work in process (4,000 @ $5.00)	20,000	
Direct-material price variance (4,400 @ $.50)	2,200	
Direct-material efficiency variance	2,000	
Stores (4,400 @ $5.50)		24,200

The direct-labor entries would be the same as under requirement 2.

QUESTIONS, PROBLEMS, AND CASES

7-1 What are standard costs? Why is their use superior to comparisons of actual data with past data?

7-2 What are the key questions in deciding how variances should be collected and analyzed?

7-3 List and briefly describe three different types of standards.

7-4 "Cost control means cost reduction." Do you agree? Why?

7-5 List four common causes of material-price variances.

7-6 List the major factors that affect control procedures for material quantities.

7-7 Define: *standard bill of materials, excess materials, requisition, operations list.*

7-8 "Setup costs are easily traceable to specific jobs. Therefore, they should be classified as direct-labor costs." Do you agree? Why?

7-9 "Standard costing is O.K. for big companies that can afford such an elaborate system. But our company relies on an 'actual' system because it saves clerical costs." Comment.

7-10 How does management decide when a variance is large enough to warrant investigation?

7-11 List five purposes of standard costs.

7-12 Who should ordinarily be responsible for the extra costs arising from rush sales orders? Why?

7-13 Define *learning curve.* Name four of its uses.

7-14 Who is responsible for developing standards?

7-15 Why do budgeted variances arise?

7-16 When will budgets differ from standards? When will they be the same?

7-17 *Inefficiency and Product Costing* (CPA) Discuss the following quotation from the standpoint of:

1. The places in the accounting procedure at which wastes may be most readily recognized, measured, and analyzed.
2. The accounting techniques available to aid in isolating these wastes:

> Gradually, the older belief that every expense incurred in the factory must be considered a cost of the products of the factory is giving way to the more logical one that recognizes that some of the expenditures . . . are costs of goods and some are costs of idleness, of wasted time and materials, and of general inefficiency. . . .

7-18 *Material Variances* Assume that a table manufacturer uses plastic tops. Plastic is purchased in large sizes, cut down as needed, and then glued to the tables. A given-sized table will require a specified amount of plastic. If the amount of plastic needed per Type-F TV table is 4 square feet and the cost per square foot is 65¢, then the standard cost of plastic for a single TV table would be $2.60. But a certain production run of 1,000 tables results in usage of 4,300 square feet at 70¢ per square foot, a total cost of $3,010.

required — Compute the price variance and the efficiency variance.

7-19 *General Journal Entries for Materials* Consider the following data compiled by the manufacturer of 1,000 television tables:

Standard price per square foot	$.65
Actual price per square foot	$.62
Standard quantity allowed	4,000 square feet
Actual quantity used	4,300 square feet
Actual quantity purchased	5,000 square feet

required

1. The manager of purchasing wants early monitoring of price variances, and the manager of production wants early detection of efficiency variances. Prepare journal entries that would most closely reflect the timing of the isolation of each variance. Price variances are isolated upon purchase of materials, and efficiency variances upon the use of excess-materials requisitions.
2. Another company has the same process, but its managers are less concerned about early isolation of variances. Instead, price variances are isolated upon

material requisitions by the producing departments. In this way, the production department's efficiency can still be measured because price volatility will not affect the efficiency variance. This company does not isolate efficiency variances until after production is completed. Prepare journal entries that would most closely reflect the timing of the isolation of each variance. Show T-accounts.

7-20 *Journal Entries for Direct Labor* The AB Company had a standard rate (price) of $8.00 per direct-labor hour. Actual hours in July were 20,526 at an actual price of $7.90 per hour. The standard direct-labor hours allowed for the output achieved were 20,000.

required

Prepare general-journal entries that isolate price and efficiency variances. Prepare one entry whereby Work in Process is carried at standard hours allowed times standard prices. Then prepare a second set of entries whereby (a) price variances are isolated as labor costs are originally journalized and (b) efficiency variances are isolated as units are transferred from Work in Process to Finished Goods.

7-21 *Choosing Labor Standards* (CMA) The Alton Company is going to expand its punch-press department. It is about to purchase three new punch presses from Equipment Manufacturers, Inc. Equipment Manufacturers' engineers report that their mechanical studies indicate that for Alton's intended use, the output rate for one press should be 1,000 pieces per hour. Alton has very similar presses now in operation. At the present time, production from these presses averages 600 pieces per hour.

A study of the Alton experience shows the average is derived from the following individual outputs.

WORKER		DAILY OUTPUT
L. Jones		750
J. Green		750
R. Smith		600
H. Brown		500
R. Alters		550
G. Hoag		450
	Total	3,600
Average		600

Alton management also plans to institute a standard cost accounting system in the very near future. The company engineers are supporting a standard based upon 1,000 pieces per hour, the accounting department is arguing for 750 pieces per hour and the department foreman is arguing for 600 pieces per hour.

required

1. What arguments would each proponent be likely to use to support his case?
2. Which alternative best reconciles the needs of cost control and the motivation of improved performance? Explain why you made that choice.

7-22 *Comparison of General-Ledger Entries for Direct Materials and Direct Labor* The Sweeney Co. has the following data for the month of March, when 1,100 finished units were produced:

Direct materials used, 3,600 pounds. The standard allowance per finished unit is 3 pounds at $3.00 per pound. Five thousand pounds were purchased at $3.25 per pound, a total of $16,250.

Direct labor, actual hours, was 2,450 hours at a total cost of $9,800. The standard labor cost per finished unit was $7.60. Standard time allowed is 2 hours per unit.

required

1. Prepare journal entries for a "normal"-cost system.
2. Prepare journal entries for a "standard"-cost system. Support your entries with a detailed variance analysis, using the columnar analytical format illustrated in the chapter.
3. Show an alternate approach, including journal entries, to the way you quantified the material price variance in 2. Which way is better, and why?

7-23 *Journal Entries for Standard Costs* Here is a summary of certain Hong Kong data for a job shop that uses standard costs for direct materials and direct labor.

MATERIALS	PURCHASES	PURCHASE COST	STANDARD PRICE PER POUND	USAGE
A	2,000 lbs.	$10,200	$5.00	1,800 lbs.
B	4,000 lbs.	26,800	7.00	3,500 lbs.

The company produced a wide variety of job orders, two of which required all the A and B materials used above. The standard quantities allowed for the output on which A and B were used were:

		PER UNIT OF FINISHED PRODUCT	
Finished Product	Job. Nos.	Material A	Material B
800 widgets	101, 104, 109	1.1 lbs.	3 lbs.
200 gidgets	103, 105	5.0 lbs.	6 lbs.

Four basic operations were used in the shop, but not all operations are used uniformly on all jobs.

	OPERATIONS				FINISHED UNITS
	1	2	3	4	
Standard hours per unit	1	2	4	3	
Standard labor rate per hour	$5.50	$2	$4	$3	
Operations performed:					
Job. No. 101	√	√	√	√	400
103	√		√	√	150
104		√	√	√	200
105	√	√	√		50
109	√	√		√	200

Summary of actual direct-labor usage on the jobs above:

	HOURS	ACTUAL DIRECT-LABOR COSTS INCURRED
Operation 1	850	$ 4,590
Operation 2	1,670	3,340
Operation 3	3,300	13,860
Operation 4	2,800	8,540
		$30,330

required

1. Journal entries, assuming that material-price variances are isolated upon purchase. Also assume that Stores Control is the general-ledger account for all materials. Support all journal entries with detailed analyses of variance computations.

2. What are the relative merits of isolating material-price variances upon purchase rather than upon withdrawal from the storeroom?
3. In terms of clerical costs, compare a standard-cost system with a regular job-order cost system.

7-24 *Elementary Variance Analysis and Graph* Consider the following data regarding the manufacture of 20,000 units (pairs) of boots:

	STANDARDS
Direct materials	Two pounds of input at $4 per pound, or $8 per unit of output
Direct labor	One half hour of input at $10 per hour, or $5 per unit of output

The following data were compiled regarding actual performance: good units produced, 20,000; pounds of input acquired and used, 37,000; price per pound, $4.10; direct-labor costs, $88,200; actual hours of input, 9,000; labor rate per hour, $9.80.

required

1. Show computations of price and efficiency variances for direct materials and for direct labor. Prepare a plausible explanation of why the variances arose.
2. Sketch a graphical analysis of the direct-labor variance, using the vertical axis for total costs and the horizontal axis for volume or activity in hours. Indicate what vertical distances represent the flexible budget variance, price variance, and efficiency variance.
3. Suppose 60,000 pounds of materials were purchased even though only 37,000 pounds were used. Suppose further that variances are identified with their most likely control point; accordingly, direct-material purchase-price variances are isolated and traced to the purchasing department rather than to the production department. Compute the price and efficiency variances under this approach.

7-25 *Flexibility in Budgets* Refer to Problem 7-24. Suppose that the original budget was for 24,000 units of output. The general manager is gleeful about the following report:

	ACTUAL COSTS	ORIGINAL BUDGET	VARIANCE
Direct materials	$151,700	$192,000	$52,000 F
Direct labor	$ 88,200	$120,000	$31,800 F

required

Is the manager's glee warranted? Prepare a report that might provide a more detailed explanation of why the original budget was not achieved. Good output was 20,000 units.

7-26 *Journal Entries and T-Accounts* Prepare journal entries and T-accounts for all transactions in the Problem 7-24, including part 3. Summarize how these journal entries differ from the normal costing entries as described in Chapter 4.

7-27 *Analysis of Variances* (SIA, adapted) The Alpha Co. Ltd. produces toys for national distribution. The management has recently established a standard-cost system to control costs. Established standard costs are:
(a) Materials: 12 pieces per unit at 56¢ per piece
(b) Labor: 2 hours per unit at $2.75 per hour
During the month of December 1966, the company produced 1,000 units of finished goods. Production information for December is as follows:
(a) Materials: 14,000 pieces at a total cost of $7,140
(b) Labor costs: $8,000

(c) Direct-labor hours worked were 2,500
(d) Inventories: December 1, nil
December 31, nil

required

1. Computation of material price and efficiency variances and labor-price and efficiency variances.
2. A brief explanation to management giving the significance of each variance.

7-28 *Analysis of Variances* (CPA, adapted) Ross Shirts, Inc., manufactures short- and long-sleeve men's shirts for large stores. Ross produces a single-quality shirt in lots to each customer's order and attaches the store's label to each. The standard costs for a dozen long-sleeve shirts include:

Direct materials	24 yards @ \$ .55	\$13.20
Direct labor	3 hours @ 2.45	7.35

During October 19_9, Ross worked on three orders for long-sleeve shirts. Job-cost records for the month disclose the following:

LOT	UNITS IN LOT	MATERIALS USED	HOURS WORKED
30	1,000 dozen	24,100 yards	2,980
31	1,700 Dozen	40,440 yards	5,130
32	1,200 dozen	28,825 yards	2,890

The following information is also available:

(a) Ross purchased 95,000 yards of material during the month at a cost of \$53,200. The material-price variance is recorded when goods are purchased, and all inventories are carried at standard cost.

(b) Direct labor incurred amounted to \$27,500 during October. According to payroll records, production employees were paid \$2.50 per hour.

(c) There was no work in process at October 1. During October, lots 30 and 31 were completed, and all material was issued for lot 32, which was 80 percent completed as to labor.

required

1. Prepare a schedule computing the material-price variance for October 19_9 and indicate whether the variance is favorable or unfavorable.
2. Prepare schedules computing, and indicating whether favorable or unfavorable, for each lot produced during October 19_9:
   a. Material-efficiency variance in yards
   b. Labor-efficiency variance in hours
   c. Labor-price variance in dollars

7-29 *Combined or Joint Price-Efficiency Variances and Incentives* The MTT Company had a long history of using bonuses that were specifically tied to performance. Minimal inventories of any kind were kept. The purchasing manager was given a bonus of 5 percent of the favorable purchase-price variance for the year. The production manager was given a bonus of 5 percent of the favorable direct-material efficiency variance for the year plus additional bonuses regarding labor and overhead variances.

In 19_4, the performance regarding Material A, an important chemical ingredient, was:

Standard pounds allowed @ \$1.00, one per finished unit
Actual pounds consumed, 500,000
Actual production, 520,000 finished units
Actual unit purchase price, \$.90

required

1. Compute the material price and efficiency variances.
2. Split the price variance into a "pure" price variance and a combined price-efficiency variance. As the purchasing manager, would you be pleased by the favorable efficiency variance? Why? Would your attitude change if the actual unit price were $1.10?
3. As the production manager, what would be your attitude toward the bonus system?
4. Given that top management is committed to a bonus system based on variances, what modifications in the bonus system would you favor? Why?

7-30 *Analysis of Labor* The City of San Francisco has a maintenance shop where all kinds of truck repairs are performed. Through the years, various labor standards have been developed to judge performance. However, during a March strike, some labor records vanished. The actual hours of input were 2,000. The direct-labor flexible-budget variance was $1,500, favorable. The standard labor price was $7.00 per hour; however, a recent labor shortage had necessitated using higher-paid workers for some jobs and had produced a labor-price variance for March of $600, unfavorable.

required

1. Actual labor price per hour.
2. Standard hours allowed for output achieved.

7-31 *Budgets and Expected Variances* The Werelius Manufacturing Company uses standard costs and budgets for planning and controlling current production of its two products, F and G. Schedules for the year ending December, 19_1, call for the production of 6,000 units of F and 1,000 units of G.

The standards set for direct labor call for 14 direct-labor hours per unit for F and 20 direct-labor hours for G. However, these standards have been deliberately made tight so as to encourage better performance. Management expects that direct-labor performance will fall short of these goals by one direct-labor hour per unit for each product.

The standard rate for direct labor is $6 per hour. However, negotiations are under way with the union for a new contract. Although the results of these negotiations are uncertain, management expects the rate for direct labor to rise to $6.30 per hour.

Develop the budget for direct labor, showing both standard cost and expected cost, and show any expected or budgeted variances.

7-32 *Learning Curve and Cost Estimation* The Smyth Company, a subcontractor for the aircraft and missile industry, has been asked to bid on a prospective contract for 900 units of a precision missile part. Two months ago, the Smyth Company had produced 300 of these parts at the following total costs:

Direct materials	$12,000
Direct labor (6,000 hours @ $4.00)	24,000
Tooling cost[a]	3,000
Variable overhead[b]	3,000
Other overhead[c]	6,000
Total costs	$48,000

[a] Tooling can be reused, even though all of its cost was assigned to the original order of 300 parts.

[b] Variable-overhead incurrence is directly affected by direct-labor hours.

[c] Other overhead is assigned at a flat rate of 25 percent of direct-labor cost for purposes of bidding on contracts.

The Smyth Company has used an 80 percent learning curve as a basis for forecasting what pertinent costs should be.

required | Prepare a prediction of the total expected costs for bidding on a contract of 900 units.

7-33 *Learning Curve, Cost Predictions, and Pricing* The Boeheed Corporation is a large, multidivision company with annual sales in excess of one billion dollars. One of Boeheed's divisions, the Spriggs Division, manufactures aircraft. The division is currently developing a new type of aircraft that will determine the success of the division for the next few years.

Spriggs has already spent $200 million on developing and testing the new technology that the aircraft will utilize. It is also constructing a new $20 million specialized-production facility, which would become totally obsolete after production of the planes was completed. The engineering department has predicted that an additional $20 million will have to be spent on further development and testing before the aircraft is ready for production. Boeheed's accounting policy was to capitalize all development and equipment costs until production actually started.

The division is presently attempting to determine a price for the aircraft. A price is necessary now because of the long production-schedule lead time of about twelve months, which results from the limited production capacity of ten aircraft per month.

Orders will be made on the basis of this established price, even though deliveries will not be made for one or two years.

The marketing department has forecast that demand for the aircraft will range between 200 and 300 units. The actual demand will be determined by both the ultimate aircraft characteristics and, more important, the aircraft price.

The division has made detailed predictions of the aircraft's production costs. These predictions have proven to be extremely accurate on previous projects of this type. All the aircraft parts requirements are subcontracted for fabrication. Spriggs has already contracted for parts for 200 aircraft, which will cost $3 million per aircraft. These contracts have a provision for parts for an additional 100 aircraft but at a 10 percent decrease in cost per aircraft.

Direct labor is the most significant element of the production costs. Labor costs are substantial in an absolute sense, but large reductions are possible because of the "learning curve" that affects the labor costs during the production period. The learning curve applicable to the new aircraft is based on ten-unit production lots, with the following cost-reduction schedule based on an initial Lot 1 having labor costs of $8 million:

LOT NO.	LEARNING CURVE (% OF INITIAL COSTS)	COST PER AIRCRAFT (MILLIONS)
1	100%	$8.0
2	80	6.4
4	64	5.1
8	51	4.0
12	44	3.5
16	41	3.2
24	35	2.8
32	32	2.5

For example, the overall direct-labor cost per plane for the seventy-first through the eightieth planes produced should be $4 million per plane, or a total direct-labor cost for Lot No. 8 of $40 million.

The general manager and the controller, naturally concerned about setting a unit price for the aircraft, decided to view the new aircraft program as a single job order. They prepared a graph of the predicted direct-labor costs (see Exhibit 7-7). They segmented the graph to develop total direct-labor costs for each segment. They analyzed segments as follows:

SEGMENTS IN EXHIBIT 7-7	AVERAGE DIRECT-LABOR COST PER UNIT IN SEGMENT
0–40	82% of initial unit cost
41–100	55%
101–200	42%
201–300	34%

Combined applicable general, administrative, and indirect production costs are estimated at $50 million annually. Historically, these costs have been applied on the basis of direct-labor costs.

They decided that the fixed costs applicable to the program that must be recovered included $240 million plus whatever indirect production costs and general and administrative costs were incurred. Their prediction of the latter was $100 million if 200 units were produced and sold (2 years × $50 million) and $150 million if 300 units were produced and sold (3 years × $50 million).

required

1. What price must be set to break even, assuming 200 units are sold? Assuming 300 units are sold?
2. Suppose that Spriggs sets a price of $8.6 million. This price has produced orders for 250 planes. The marketing department now reports that a potential new customer will purchase 50 planes, but only if the price is $8.1 million or less. This price reduction would have to be made retroactive and applied to all customers. Should Spriggs accept the new order?

EXHIBIT 7-7

EFFECT OF "LEARNING CURVE" ON DIRECT-LABOR COST

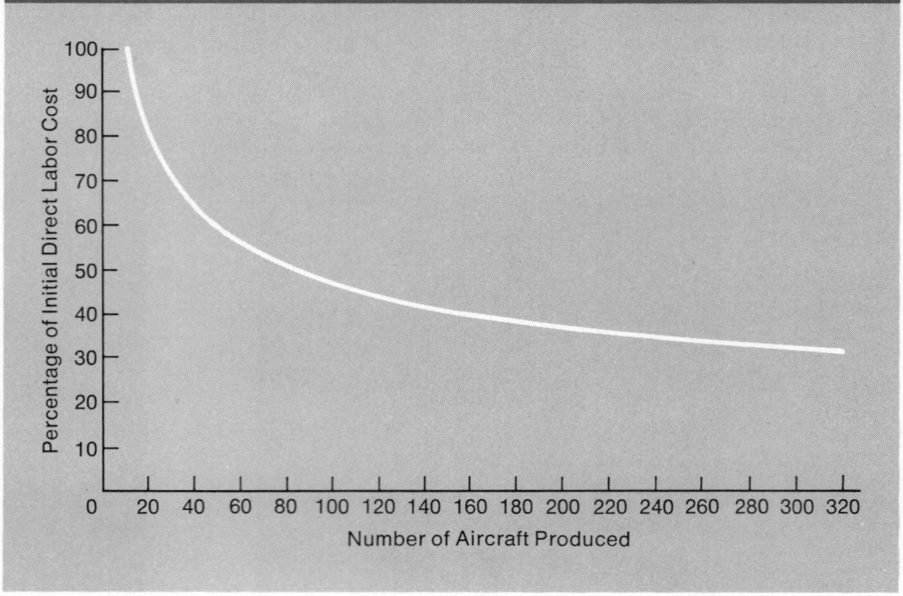

Flexible Budgets and Overhead Control

8

This chapter concentrates on the flexible budget and work measurement as tools for decisions and feedback. It extends the ideas of the previous chapter.

flexible budgets

the variety of control techniques

The cost-benefit approach to the design of a control system leads to a variety of detailed techniques within every organization. Each organization has individual costs that are relatively major. In a service organization, salaries are usually the most prominent cost. In a wholesaling or retailing business, the purchase cost of merchandise is usually the most significant item. In a manufacturing business, the costs of direct materials and direct labor are usually both important. The distinct significance of such individual items generates elaborate formal techniques for decisions and feedback regarding them.

Total factory overhead, as well as selling and administrative overhead, is usually a major part of total costs. Yet *individual* overhead items generally are not large in comparison with direct materials and direct labor. Therefore, although the ideas underlying the control of overhead are basically the same, the techniques differ because the size of individual overhead costs often does not justify costly control systems that routinely produce exhaustive analyses of variances in individual items.

In practice, direct materials and direct labor are said to be controlled with the help of *standard costs,* whereas factory overhead is usually said to be controlled with the help of *department-overhead budgets.* The distinction probably arises because the timing and the techniques for controlling direct materials, direct labor, and overhead differ. For example, in a paper mill, direct-material usage may be closely watched on an hour-to-hour basis, direct-labor efficiency may be followed on a day-to-day basis, and department overhead may be scrutinized on a month-to-month basis. Conceptually, however, *all* factory costs—direct materials, direct labor, and overhead—can properly be included in a single flexible budget for individual factory departments. The notion of a flexible budget may also be applied to administrative and selling functions. The key point is not what items are in a particular flexible budget; it is rather the flexibility that is incorporated in the budget.

basic approach of the flexible budget

Recall in Exhibit 7-1 that the flexible-budget allowances were a function of the good output produced. Furthermore, good output may be expressed either in terms of (a) the physical units of production achieved or (b) the standard allowed inputs for that given output. That is, if two standard direct-labor hours are allowed per unit of output, 1,000 units of output achieved may be equivalently expressed as 2,000 "standard hours allowed."

The flexible-budget approach is based on an adequate knowledge of cost behavior patterns. It is essentially a means for constructing a budget tailored to *any* level of activity. In a company using a flexible-budget technique, a budget for variable overhead might resemble Exhibit 8-1.

Note that the budget would not necessarily have to be shown for the 4,600 to 5,200 activity levels. *The essential ingredient is the budget formula, which may be used in constructing a total budget for any given activity level.* For example, the performance report prepared at the *end* of June (Exhibit 8-2) shows the application of the budget formula to the 4,700-unit level of output actually achieved. The flexible budget is often used to present a more meaningful comparison of a department foreman's day-to-day overhead-cost control, because the level of activity underlying the comparison is the same. On the other hand, the flexible-budget performance report would not ordinarily show the foreman's deviation from his scheduled production *volume.* The ideal combination, therefore, is a flexible budget for measuring efficient use of input factors, accompanied by information, perhaps expressed in units only, such as that shown at the top of Exhibit 8-2,

EXHIBIT 8-1

MACHINING DEPARTMENT FLEXIBLE BUDGET, VARIABLE OVERHEAD

For the Month of June 19_1

	*BUDGET FORMULA**	*VARIOUS LEVELS OF ACTIVITY*			
Units produced		4,600	4,800	5,000	5,200
Indirect labor	42¢ per unit	$1,932	$2,016	$2,100	$2,184
Supplies	10¢ per unit	460	480	500	520
Repairs	8¢ per unit	368	384	400	416
Total variable overhead	60¢ per unit	$2,760	$2,880	$3,000	$3,120

* The budget formulas used here assume proportionately variable behavior. Flexible budgets can often encompass other costs also.

about the foreman's ability to meet any single production schedule (or, in the case of a sales manager, his sales target).

how should activity be budgeted? Our example measured activity or volume in terms of units of product. In practice, the measurement of budgeted volume is not so easy, except in the rare instance of a department that produces only one uniform product. When there is a variety of products or operations, the following criteria should help in selecting a measure of volume.

1. *Cause of Cost Fluctuation.* An individual cost should be related to some activity that causes that cost to vary. Common measures include hours of labor, machine-hours, weight of materials handled, miles traveled, number of calls

EXHIBIT 8-2

MACHINING DEPARTMENT VARIABLE OVERHEAD PERFORMANCE REPORT

For the Month of June 19_1

Units originally scheduled	5,000			
Units produced	4,700			
	ACTUAL	*BUDGET**	*VARIANCE*	*EXPLANATION*
Indirect labor	$2,080	$1,974	$106 U	Idle time due to storm
Supplies	480	470	10 U	None offered
Repairs	400	376	24 U	Extra repairs due to storm
Total variable overhead	$2,960	$2,820	$140 U	

* For 4,700 units produced.

made by salesmen, number of beds in a hospital, number of lines billed, number of credit investigations, and so forth.

2. *Independence of Activity Unit.* The activity unit should not be greatly affected by variable factors other than output volume. For example, the use of total direct-labor dollars or total dollar sales as a measure of volume is subject to the basic weakness of being changeable by labor-rate or price fluctuations. The use of machine-hours or labor-hours eliminates the unwanted influence of fluctuations in the purchasing power of the dollar. Then, if physical volume does not change, a change in wage rates does not necessarily mean a change in other costs. The effects of price changes should not affect the unit by which activity is budgeted; this is usually accomplished by using standard wage rates or uniform sales prices.

3. *Ease of Understanding.* Units for budgeted activity should be easily understandable and should be obtainable at a minimum clerical expense. Complicated indexes are undesirable.

4. *Adequacy of Control over Base.* The common denominator that serves as a measure of budgeted activity must be under adequate control. As was explained in Chapter 7, *because it is not affected by variations in performance, the standard direct-labor hours allowed (or machine-hours allowed) for units produced is a better basis for performance evaluation than actual direct-labor hours.* A department head should not enjoy a more generous overhead budget allowance because of his inefficiency simply because the budget was based on actual hours instead of standard hours allowed.

If standard allowances are developed for all the factors of production, one factor may be tied to the other so that all factors may be related to a common base. For example, if it takes one pound of direct materials, one grinding wheel, one machine-hour, and one direct-labor hour to produce one finished unit, usage may be related to the standard direct-labor hour as follows: If 1,000 standard direct-labor hours are used, the use of 1,000 units of each of the other factors may be anticipated. These relationships may be expedient and meaningful even though use of grinding wheels, repairs, and the like is more closely related than direct-labor hours to finished units produced or even to an assortment of casual factors. It is because of the latter phenomenon that we have stressed the need for an item-by-item analysis of variances.

To summarize, an index of activity based on *actual* hours fluctuates with efficiency; it is a measure of inputs, not outputs. The use of *standard hours allowed* or of some base built on standard hours allowed (for example, standard direct-labor dollars) is a measure of outputs. Flexible budgets based on such measures of outputs permit the inefficient usage of inputs to appear as efficiency variances instead of becoming additional budgetary allowances.

spending and efficiency variances

The preceding section stressed the point that performance should be measured in terms of outputs, rather than inputs, for determining flexible-budget allowances. Consider an example where activity is measured in standard direct-labor hours allowed; this is simply a way of expressing *output.* That is, unless the units of output are known, the standard hours allowed to produce that output cannot be calculated. In contrast, the actual direct-labor hours utilized is an *input* concept.

Assume that a department is scheduled to produce 10,000 units of product in 10,000 standard direct-labor hours. However, it has taken 12,000 actual direct-labor hours to produce the 10,000 units. The variable overhead items are as follows:

	BUDGET FORMULA PER STANDARD DIRECT-LABOR HOUR ALLOWED	ACTUAL COSTS INCURRED
Indirect labor	$1.00	$11,700
Maintenance	.10	1,150
Lubricants	.05	600
Cutting tools	.08	1,500
	$1.23	$14,950

The actual direct-labor rate is $8.10 per hour; the standard rate is $8.00. You are asked to:

1. Prepare a detailed performance report, with two major sections: direct labor and variable overhead.
2. Explain the similarities and differences between the direct-labor and the variable-overhead variances.

One version of the performance report would be highly condensed, as shown at the top of Exhibit 8-3. The budget column is based on the standard hours allowed for the given output. The budget variance is merely the difference between the numbers in the first two columns.

Another version is shown at the bottom of Exhibit 8-3. It begins with an analysis of the direct-labor variance, which is divided between a price variance and an efficiency variance in the identical way described in the preceding chapter. The subdivision (see Exhibit 8-3) of the budget variance for variable overhead into *spending variance* and *efficiency variance* is analogous to the split of the total direct-labor variance into *price variance* and *efficiency variance.*

The fundamental assumption underlying the usual efficiency-variance computation for variable overhead is simple but fragile: Variable-overhead costs should fluctuate in direct proportion to changes in standard direct-labor hours. Therefore, the efficiency variance for variable *overhead* is a measure of the extra overhead (or savings) that would be expected *solely* because *direct-labor* usage exceeded (or was less than) the standard direct-labor hours allowed for the output achieved:

$$\text{Overhead Efficiency Variance} = (\text{Actual Hours} - \text{Standard Hours Allowed}) \times \text{Standard Overhead Rate}$$

EXHIBIT 8-3

TWO VERSIONS OF A DEPARTMENT PERFORMANCE REPORT: DIRECT LABOR AND VARIABLE OVERHEAD

For the Month of October 19_1

Actual hours, 12,000 Standard hours allowed, 10,000 Excess hours, 2,000

CONDENSED VERSION	*ACTUAL RESULTS*	*FLEXIBLE BUDGET*	*FLEXIBLE-BUDGET VARIANCE*
Direct labor	$ 97,200*	$80,000	$17,200 U
Indirect labor	11,700	10,000	1,700 U
Maintenance	1,150	1,000	150 U
Lubricants	600	500	100 U
Cutting tools	1,500	800	700 U
Total	$112,150	$92,300	$19,850 U

DETAILED VERSION	*(1)*	*(2)*	*(3)*	*(4)*	*ANALYSIS OF (4)*	
	ACTUAL INPUTS AT ACTUAL PRICES	*FLEXIBLE BUDGET BASED ON 12,000 ACTUAL DIRECT HOURS OF INPUTS*	*FLEXIBLE BUDGET BASED ON 10,000 STANDARD DIRECT HOURS OF INPUTS ALLOWED FOR ACTUAL OUTPUT ACHIEVED*	*(1) − (3) FLEXIBLE-BUDGET VARIANCE TO BE ANALYZED*	*(1) − (2) SPENDING VARIANCE*	*(2) − (3) EFFICIENCY VARIANCE*
Direct labor	$97,200	$96,000	$80,000	$17,200 U	$1,200 U†	$16,000 U
Variable overhead:						
Indirect labor	$11,700	$12,000	$10,000	$ 1,700 U	$ 300 F	$ 2,000 U
Maintenance	1,150	1,200	1,000	150 U	50 F	200 U
Lubricants	600	600	500	100 U	—	100 U
Cutting tools	1,500	960	800	700 U	540 U	160 U
Total variable overhead	$14,950	$14,760	$12,300	$ 2,650 U	$ 190 U	$ 2,460 U

* 12,000 hours @ $8.10

† This $1,200 variance is a direct-labor price variance. The term *spending variance* pertains to overhead items only.

Note the similarity between the efficiency variances for direct labor and for variable overhead. Both are differences between actual hours and standard hours allowed, multiplied by a standard price. For instance, the budget variance for lubricants in Exhibit 8-3 was $100, unfavorable. Under this approach, the entire variance is attributed to the inefficiency of a related factor, direct labor. That is, because direct labor was inefficiently used by 2,000 hours, or 20 percent of the 10,000 standard hours allowed, we would expect the related usage of lubricants to be proportionately excessive *solely* because of *labor* inefficiency.

Although the spending variance for variable factory overhead is similar to the price variance for the direct labor, its causal factors encompass more than price changes alone—that is why it is not called a price variance. Other causes include poor budget estimates for one or more individual overhead items; variation in attention to and control of individual costs; and erratic behavior of individual overhead items that have been squeezed for convenience into a budget formula with only one base (that is, hours of labor). The cost of indirect labor for handling materials, for example, may be closely related to the number of units *started* during a period and have nothing directly to do with the standard direct-labor hours allowed for output achieved. Also, the usage of cutting tools may be more closely related to machine-hours than to labor-hours. In these days of automation, one laborer may operate several machines simultaneously.

To recapitulate, suppose you investigate why there was a $700 unfavorable variance in Exhibit 8-3 for cutting tools. The performance report implies:

Actual costs		$1,500
Efficiency variance—This is the amount that would be expected to be incurred *because of the inefficient use of direct labor.* Since variable-overhead costs generally fluctuate in relation to corresponding fluctuations in direct-labor costs, the excess use of direct labor would be expected to cause a corresponding increase in the cost of cutting tools of 2,000 × $.08 =	$160 U	
Spending variance—This is the amount unexplained by the efficiency-variance analysis above. It could arise, say, from a unit *price* change for cutting tools. But it could also arise simply from general waste and inefficient use of such materials. In short, this too could be partially or solely traceable to *more inefficiency,* even though it is labeled as a spending variance.	540 U	
Flexible-budget variance		700 U
Budgeted amount in flexible budget		$ 800

The primary limitation of the analyses of variances should be underscored. The *only* way to discover why variable-overhead performance did not agree with the budget is to investigate possible causes, item by item, from Indirect Labor to Maintenance to Lubricants to Cutting Tools. However, the summary analysis yields an overall view that may be used as a springboard for a more rigorous analysis.

use of standard hours as a budget base

Note that the budget in Exhibit 8-3 is based on standard hours allowed (output) rather than actual hours (input). If it were based on actual hours, the *only* variance that would be produced would be the spending variance, column (1) minus column (2). *There would be no efficiency variances.* The manager would get only a partial size-up of performance; he would have a focus only on input relationships (given the inputs, how much cost should I have incurred?). By basing the budget on standard hours of inputs allowed for the output achieved, he focuses on input *and* output relationships (given the outputs, how many inputs should I have incurred?). The standard-hour budget base generates both spending and efficiency variances.

the scope of flexible budgets

Earlier in this chapter, the point was made that the term *flexible budget* is often used to describe a department-overhead budget. Moreover, the earlier exhibits were confined to only a few overhead items to illustrate the essential idea that flexible budgets are tailored to cover a relevant range rather than merely one level of activity.

Flexible budgets may be broadened to include all cost (*and revenue*) items if desired. For example, Exhibit 8-3 showed a first step in that direction by including direct labor as well as variable overhead. Consider Exhibit 8-4. It differs from Exhibit 8-3 in only one respect: It shows how a performance report might appear when fixed costs are included. The portion of the budget attributable to fixed costs will remain constant regardless of fluctuations in production volume, but the variable costs will be affected. Therefore, the budget in such cases could be expressed by the following overall formula: a static portion of $35,000 per month plus variable portions of $8.00 per hour for direct labor and $1.23 per hour for variable overhead. Note that it is the variable-cost portion of the formula that injects the flex into the flexible budget.

In summary, a flexible budget need not be confined to variable costs alone. It may also refer to revenue or to fixed costs. Of course, the flexible budget for fixed costs, when considered alone, would show the same total amount regardless of the fluctuations of volume over a relevant range. However, in practice the flexible budget most often includes both variable- and fixed-cost elements. Therefore, the flexible budget for total costs would indeed change over the relevant range. Exhibit 8-5 shows these points for overhead, where the formula would be $35,000 per month plus $1.23 per hour.

mixed costs

cost functions and simplifications

Unfortunately for cost analysts, the world cannot be neatly divided between variable and fixed costs. In most organizations, the behavior of each cost item is predicted on a line-by-

EXHIBIT 8-4

CONDENSED DEPARTMENT-PERFORMANCE REPORT
CONVERSION COSTS
For the Month of October 19_1

Actual hours, 12,000 | Standard hours allowed, 10,000 | Excess hours, 2,000

	ACTUAL COSTS INCURRED	*FLEXIBLE BUDGET*	*FLEXIBLE-BUDGET VARIANCE*
Direct labor	$ 97,200	$ 80,000	$17,200 U
Indirect labor	$ 11,700	$ 10,000	$ 1,700 U
Maintenance	1,150	1,000	150 U
Lubricants	600	500	100 U
Cutting tools	1,500	800	700 U
Total variable overhead	$ 14,950	$ 12,300	$ 2,650 U
Total variable costs	$112,150	$ 92,300	$19,850 U
Fixed costs:			
Supervision	$ 14,400	$ 14,000	$ 400 U
Rent	5,000	5,000	—
Depreciation	15,000	15,000	—
Property taxes	1,000	1,000	—
Total fixed costs	$ 35,400	$ 35,000	$ 400 U
Total conversion costs	$147,550	$127,300	$20,250 U

line basis. Sometimes this is an easy chore, but often careful studies are needed. Therefore, the budget formulas for some individual costs will not be flatly stated as \$.80 per hour or as \$1,000 per month. Instead, a variety of prediction equations might be utilized.

Accountants and managers constantly use simplified models in coping with complicated phenomena. Two common simplifications are used in the estimation of cost functions: (1) cost behavior can be sufficiently explained by one independent variable (such as labor-hours) instead of more than one (such as hours *and* pounds handled); (2) linear approximations to cost behavior are sufficiently accurate even though nonlinear behavior is widespread.

It is usually cost-effective to study direct material and direct labor intensively and develop a tailored approach to these major items. In contrast, the behavior of overhead costs, almost by definition, is harder to pinpoint. Given an assumption of linearity between x (some measure of volume) and y (some measure of total cost), the problem of cost estimation can be expressed as trying to approximate some underlying relation for the expected value, $E(y)$, in the form

$$E(y) = A + Bx$$

EXHIBIT 8-5

GRAPH OF FLEXIBLE BUDGET OF FACTORY OVERHEAD

Data are from Exhibit 8-4

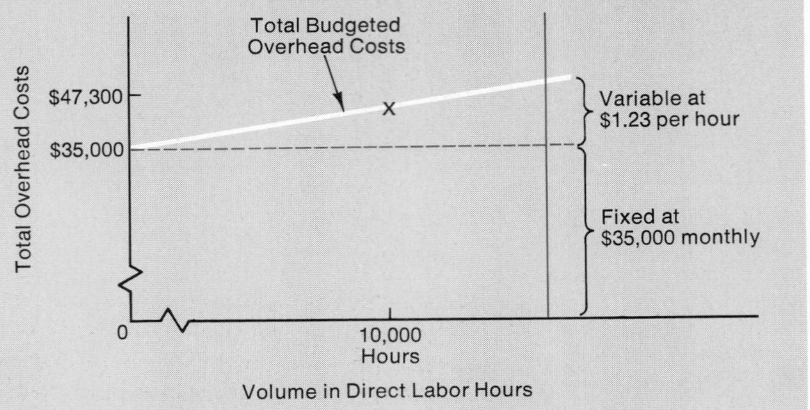

where A and B are the true (but unknown) parameters of a linear cost function. (A *parameter* is a constant, such as A, or a coefficient, such as B, in a model or system of equations.)

Working with historical data, the accountant usually develops an approximation of the underlying relationship in the formula form

$$y' = a + bx$$

where y' is the calculated value as distinguished from the observed value y, and a and b are the approximations of the true A and B.

Again, the simplifications are justified if more elaborate assumptions are too costly to implement in light of expected benefits. But never lose sight of the enormity of these simplifications. Chapter 25 explores in more detail the entire problem of measuring cost functions.

nature of mixed costs As the name implies, a mixed cost (sometimes called *semivariable cost*) has both fixed and variable elements (see Exhibit 8-6). The fixed element represents the minimum cost of supplying a service. The variable element is that portion of the mixed cost that is influenced by changes in activity. An example of a mixed cost is the rental of a delivery truck for a fixed cost per month plus a variable cost based on mileage.

EXHIBIT 8-6

MIXED COST

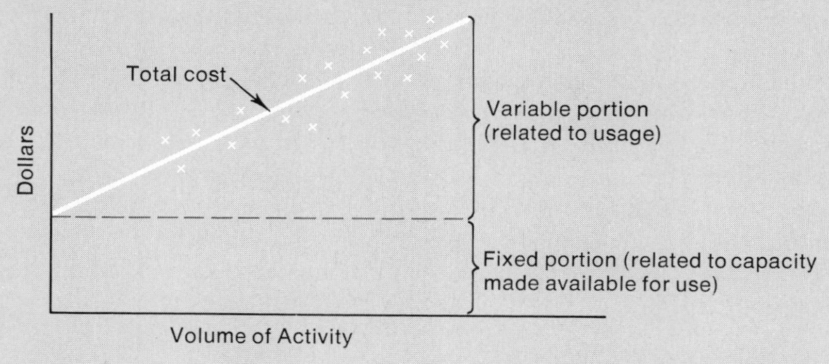

Ideally, there should be no accounts for mixed costs. All such costs should be subdivided into two accounts, one for the variable portion and one for the fixed portion. In practice, these distinctions are rarely made in the recording process because of the difficulty of analyzing day-to-day cost data into variable and fixed sections. Costs such as power, indirect labor, repairs, and maintenance are generally accounted for in total. It is typically very difficult to decide, as such costs are incurred, whether a particular invoice or work ticket represents a variable or fixed item. Moreover, even if it were possible to make such distinctions, the advantages might not be worth the additional clerical effort and costs. Whenever cost classifications are too refined, the perpetual problem of getting accurate source documents is intensified.

In sum, mixed costs are merely a blend of two unlike cost behavior patterns; they do not entail new conceptual approaches. Anybody who obtains a working knowledge of the planning and controlling of variable and fixed costs, separately, can adapt to a mixed-cost situation when necessary.

budgeting mixed costs How should mixed costs be budgeted? Ideally, of course, their variable and fixed elements should be isolated and budgeted separately. One widely practiced method is a budget formula that contains both a fixed and a variable element. For example, repairs for delivery trucks might be budgeted at $45 per month plus 1¢ per mile.

The estimation of mixed-cost behavior patterns should preferably begin with a scatter chart of past cost levels, a graph on which dots are plotted to show various historical costs, as shown in Exhibit 8-6. A line is fitted to the points, either visually or by the statistical method of least squares (described in Chapter 25). The intersection of the line with the vertical axis is often labeled as the amount of the fixed-cost component.

As Chapter 25 explains in more detail, the major purpose of determining cost behavior patterns is to estimate how costs behave as volume changes over a relevant range of activity levels, which seldom encompasses zero volume. Thus, the emphasis is on determining the slope of the line—the rate of change of the total cost as volume fluctuates—*the behavior of the variable-cost component over the relevant range.* Consequently, it is more fruitful to think of the fixed-cost component as merely the y-intercept (that is, the total cost at zero volume) in an estimate of total cost that consists of $y' = a + bx$, where y' is the estimate of the total mixed cost, a is the total cost at zero volume, b is the variable-cost rate (the slope of the line), and x is the measure of volume (for example, miles, hours, or units produced).

high-low method Exhibit 8-6 shows a straight line fitted through a mass of dots. What procedure is used to draw the line? As already mentioned, least squares and visual fitting are widely used procedures. A *high-low* method is also used occasionally. It is a relatively crude procedure because it entails choosing only two points, one a *representative* highest cost and one a *representative* lowest cost, within the relevant range. (Note that the haphazard choice of high and low points is avoided.) The line connecting the high and low costs becomes the best estimate of the cost behavior.

Consider the example in Exhibit 8-7. The graphical technique shows how the line is extended back to zero volume. The algebraic computation of the mixed cost is based on the equation for a straight line:

$$y' = a + bx$$

$$b = \frac{y_H - y_L}{x_H - x_L} = \frac{\text{Change in mixed cost}}{\text{Change in machine-hours}}$$

$$= \frac{\$1{,}600 - \$1{,}200}{2{,}000 - 1{,}200} = \frac{\$400}{800} = \$.50 \text{ per machine-hour}$$

$$a = y' - bx = \text{Total mixed cost less variable component}$$

At 1,200-hour level of activity:

$$= \$1{,}200 - \$.50(1{,}200) = \$1{,}200 - \$600 = \$600$$

To check, at 2,000-hour level of activity:

$$= \$1{,}600 - \$.50(2{,}000) = \$1{,}600 - \$1{,}000 = \$600$$

Cost formula = \$600 per month plus \$.50 per machine-hour

EXHIBIT 8-7

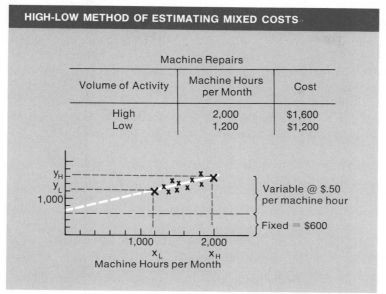

HIGH-LOW METHOD OF ESTIMATING MIXED COSTS

Machine Repairs

Volume of Activity	Machine Hours per Month	Cost
High	2,000	$1,600
Low	1,200	$1,200

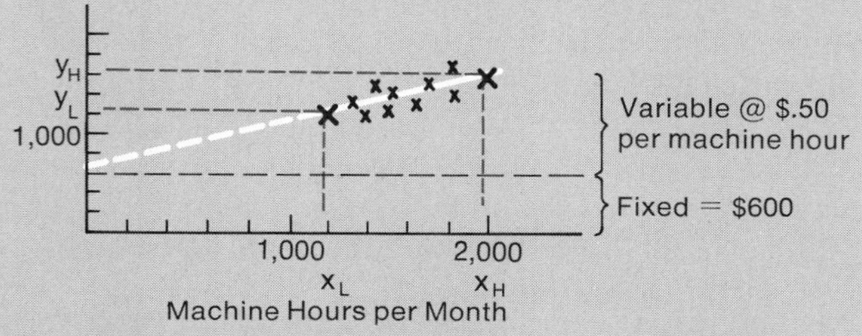

Such cost formulas are only the first step in the budgetary process. The budgeted figures are expected *future* data, so cost formulas must be altered to reflect anticipated changes in prices, efficiency, technology, and other influential factors.

committed, discretionary, and engineered costs

A threefold classification of costs into committed, discretionary, and engineered is increasing in popularity. Such a classification stresses the characteristics of the different decisions that give rise to costs.

committed fixed costs In general, few day-to-day or month-to-month decisions affect fixed costs, so a company's performance is somewhat locked in by far-reaching decisions concerning fixed costs. Thus, for planning and control, fixed costs may be usefully subdivided into committed and discretionary costs. *Committed fixed costs* consist largely of those fixed costs that arise from the possession of plant, of equipment, and of a basic organization. Examples are depreciation, property taxes, rent, insurance, and the salaries of key personnel. These costs are affected primarily by long-run sales forecasts that, in turn, indicate the long-run capacity needs.

The behavior of committed fixed costs may best be viewed by assuming a zero volume of activity in an organization that fully expects to resume normal activity (for example, during a strike or a shortage of materials that forces a complete shutdown of activity). The committed fixed costs are all those organization and plant costs that continue to be incurred and that cannot be reduced without injuring the organization's competence to meet long-range goals. Committed fixed costs are the least responsive of the fixed costs, because they tend to be less affected by month-to-month and year-to-year decisions.

In planning, the focus is on the impact of these costs over a number of years. Such planning usually requires tailoring the capacity to future demand for the organization's products in the most economical manner. For example, should the store size be 50,000 square feet, or 80,000, or 100,000? Should the gasoline station have one, or two, or more bays for servicing automobiles? Such decisions usually involve selecting the point of optimal trade-off between present and future operating costs. That is, constructing excess capacity now may save costs in the long run, because construction costs per square foot may be much higher later. On the other hand, if the forecasted demand never develops, the organization may own facilities that remain idle.

These decisions regarding capital expenditures are generally shown in an annual budget called the *capital budget* or *capital-spending budget.* As you recall, the *master budget* is based primarily on the annual sales forecast, the cornerstone of budgeting. Similarly, all capital-spending decisions are ultimately based on long-range sales forecasts. Capital budgeting is discussed in Chapter 12.

Once buildings are erected and equipment is installed, little can be done in day-to-day operations to affect the *total level* of committed costs. From a control standpoint, the objective is usually to increase current utilization of facilities, because this will ordinarily increase net income.

There is another aspect to the control problem, however. A follow-up, or audit, is needed to find out how well the ensuing utilization harmonizes with the decision that authorized the facilities in the first place. The latter approach helps management to evaluate the wisdom of its past long-range decisions and, in turn, should improve the quality of future decisions.

discretionary fixed costs

Discretionary fixed costs (sometimes called *managed* or *programmed costs*) are fixed costs that arise from periodic (usually yearly) appropriation decisions that directly reflect top-management policies. Discretionary costs may have no particular relation to volume of activity. Examples are research and development, advertising, sales promotion, donations, management consulting fees, and many employee training programs. Conceivably, these costs could be reduced almost entirely for a given year in dire times, whereas the committed costs would be much more difficult to reduce.

Discretionary fixed costs are decided upon by management at the start of the budget period. Goals are selected, the means for their attainment are chosen, the maximum expense to be incurred is specified, and the total amount to be spent is appropriated. For example, a company may appropriate $5 million for an advertising campaign. The company's advertising agency is unlikely to exceed that amount, nor is it likely to spend much less than $5 million in trying to attain the company goals. In the give-and-take of the process of preparing the master budget, the discretionary costs are the most likely to be revised.

Discretionary fixed costs represent an assortment of manufacturing, selling, administrative, and research items. As in the case of committed costs, the resources acquired should be carefully planned and fully utilized if net income is to be maximized. Unlike committed costs, discretionary costs can be influenced more easily from period to period. It is also harder to measure the utilization of resources acquired via discretionary costs, principally because the results of services like creative personnel, advertising, research, and training programs are much more difficult to isolate and quantify than the results of utilizing plant and equipment to make products.

The behavior of some discretionary fixed costs is easy to delineate. Advertising, research, donations, and training programs, for example, are usually formulated with certain objectives in mind. The execution of such projects is measured by comparing total expenditures with the appropriation. Because the tendency is to spend the entire appropriation, the resulting dollar variances are generally trivial. But planning is far more important than this kind of day-to-day control. The perfect execution of an advertising program—in the sense that the full amount authorized was spent in the specified media at the predetermined times—will be fruitless if the advertisements are unimaginative and lifeless or if they reach the wrong audience.

comparing inputs and outputs

The most noteworthy aspect of discretionary fixed costs is that, unlike most other costs, they are not subject to ordinary engineering input–output relationships. For example, an optimum relationship between inputs and outputs can be specified for direct materials because it takes three pounds or five gallons or two square feet to make a finished product. *In contrast, we are usually unsure of the "correct" amount of advertising, research, management training, industrial relations, legal, accounting, and management consulting costs.* Furthermore, only highly subjective appraisals are available about the quality of the service in question.

Top management often has a difficult time contending with the natural desires of service-department managers to build individual empires that can provide a wide variety of services almost instantly. But such desires may not be congruent with top-management goals of running a cost-effective organization.[1]

[1] John L. Neuman, "Make Overhead Cuts That Last," *Harvard Business Review,* Vol. 53, No. 3 (May-June 1975), p. 118, points out that professionals "perform their services at a quality level out of proportion to actual need, and they tend to encourage requesters of these services to demand more of the same." Later, p. 122, he comments, "A reduction in service is almost never in the receivers' interests, particularly if they are not charged for the services. Nor will the suppliers normally be happy to see demand for their services reduced." This is an example of the oft-heard criticism that service departments and nonprofit organizations aim at building up their budgets. They rarely must meet market tests and they attempt to please *all* markets within the organization, so that their goals are too diffuse. Some organizations are using "zero-based budgeting" as a means of planning and controlling discretionary costs. In essence, such budgets must be justified from the ground up instead of on the traditional incremental basis. See G. Minmier and R. Hermanson, "A Look at Zero-Base Budgeting—The Georgia Experience," *Atlanta Economic Review,* Vol. 26, No. 4 (July–August, 1976), pp. 5–12.

Some organizations ask their managers to indicate the specific programs they would add or subtract if they received an appropriation of, say, 10 percent more or less than the requested budgetary amount. In this way, more concrete attention is given to decisions at the margin.

engineered variable costs

Although it is rarely done, variable costs could be divided into "engineered" and "discretionary" categories. Most types of variable costs have an explicit "engineered," or physical, relationship with volume. An engineered variable cost exists when an optimum relationship between inputs and outputs is closely specified. For example, an automobile may have exact specifications: one battery, one radiator, two fan belts, and so forth. In short, there is a clear-cut cause-and-effect interdependence between sales (or production) levels and many variable costs. The term "discretionary" is usually linked with a class of fixed costs because their behavior tends to be fixed. However, sometimes a few discretionary costs take on a variable-cost behavior pattern. Depending on management policy, costs may go up and down with sales (or production) merely because management has predetermined that the organization can afford to spend a certain percentage of the sales dollar for items such as research, donations, and advertising. For example, a manufacturer may grant an advertising allowance to a regional distributor of 10 cents per case of beer sold. These costs would have a pattern of variability, but not for the same reasons as direct materials or direct labor. An increase in such costs may be due to management's authorization to spend "because we can afford it" rather than because there is an obvious cause-and-effect relationship between such costs and sales.

nonmanufacturing work measurement

measurement is needed for control

There are two management approaches to cost control. The first, most widespread approach is informal and is heavily dependent on human supervision for successful control. The second approach is more formal and is dependent on work measurement as well as on human supervision for successful control; it is getting more attention from organizations as they seek to improve their efficiency. This approach is based on a fundamental premise: Permanent improvement in any performance is impossible unless the work is measured.

To portray cost behavior as it responds to volume, we need to measure volume (the horizontal axis) as well as cost (the vertical axis). Industrial engineers and others concerned with cost control stoutly maintain that control is impossible without careful measures of work loads and capability. Work measurement began in the factory but has extended into selling and administrative areas in recent years.

Work measurement is the careful analysis of a task, its size, the methods used in its performance, and its efficiency. Its objective is to determine the work load in an operation and the number of workers needed to perform that work efficiently. The techniques used include time and motion study, observation of a random sample of the work (that is, work sampling), and the estimation, by a work-measurement analyst and a line supervisor, of the amount of time required for the work (that is, time analysis). The work load is expressed in *control-factor units,* which are used in formulating the budget.

For example, the control-factor units in a payroll department might include operations performed on time cards, on notices of change in labor rate, on notices of employee promotion, on new employment and termination reports, and on routine weekly and monthly reports. All of these would be weighed. The estimated work load would then be used to determine the required labor force and budgetary allowance.

other examples of measurement

The activity measure used as a budget base may be sales dollars, product units, cases, tons, or some other unit that best reflects cost influence:

OPERATION	*UNIT OF MEASURE (CONTROL-FACTOR UNIT)*
Billing	Lines per hour
Warehouse labor	Pounds or cases handled per day
Packing	Pieces packed per hour
Posting accounts receivable	Postings per hour
Mailing	Pieces mailed per hour

Standards for certain order-filling activities, such as packing or driving a truck, may necessarily be less refined than for such manufacturing activities as assembly work, but they still provide the best available formal tool for planning and control. For example, short-interval scheduling has been attempted; this technique routes all work through a supervisor, who batches the work in hourly lots. This develops standards, controls backlogs, and provides close follow-up.[2]

The measurement of work often spurs controversy, because employees do not usually welcome more stringent monitoring of their productivity. Despite some delicate problems of human relations, there is an increasing tendency for work measurement to be applied in office, transportation, and other nonmanufacturing activities.

Note that all of these examples entail nonmanufacturing activities. The long-held belief is slowly fading that it is somehow acceptable to subject manufacturing activities to work measurement while exempting nonmanufacturing activities. The most obvious candidates for work measurement are high-volume, repetitive tasks. For example, Citibank's Operating Group uses assembly-line tactics for bookkeeping, clearing and filing checks, and preparing bank state-

[2] Vincent Melore, "Cutting Payroll Costs in Manufacturing Staffs," *Management Service,* Vol. 1, No. 3, p. 24.

ments for customers. Each job has a standard.[3] Forecasts are made and performance is measured—annually, monthly and, in many instances, daily or hourly. A 2 percent variance is considered significant.

The Citibank experience with work measurement was highly successful. In a span of five years, work-force turnover dropped from 50 to 10 percent annually, employment fell from 10,000 to 6,500, and costs per unit processed fell remarkably.

budgeting of nonmanufacturing costs

There is much disagreement about how some nonmanufacturing costs should be controlled. Advocates of work measurement favor a more rigorous approach, which essentially regards these costs as engineered variable costs. In contrast, a discretionary-cost approach, which basically regards these costs as fixed, is more often found in practice.

Assume that ten payroll clerks are employed, and that each clerk's operating efficiency *should be* the processing of the pay records of 500 employees per month. In the month of June, 4,700 individuals' pay records were processed by these ten clerks. Each clerk earns $600 per month. The variances shown by the engineered-cost approach and the discretionary-cost approach are tabulated below and graphed in Exhibit 8-8.

THE ENGINEERED VARIABLE-COST APPROACH: PERFECTION STANDARDS The engineered-cost approach to this situation is to base the budget formula on the unit cost of the individual pay record processed, $600 ÷ 500 records, or $1.20. Therefore, the budget allowance for payroll-clerk labor would be $1.20 × 4,700, or $5,640. Assume that the ten employees worked throughout the month. The following performance report would be prepared:

	ACTUAL COST	*FLEXIBLE BUDGET: TOTAL STANDARD COST ALLOWED FOR GOOD UNITS PRODUCED*	*BUDGET VARIANCE*
Payroll-clerk labor	$6,000 (10 × $600)	$5,640 (4,700 × $1.20)	$360 U

A graphic representation of what has occurred (Exhibit 8-9) may yield insight.

Essentially, two decisions must be made in this operation. The first is a policy decision. How many clerks do we desire? How flexible should we be? How divisible is the task? Should we use part-time help? Should we hire and fire as the volume of work fluctuates? The implication of these questions is that once the hiring decision is made, the total costs incurred can be predicted easily—$6,000 in our example.

The second decision concentrates on day-to-day control, on how efficiently and effectively the given resources are being utilized. The work-measurement

[3] *Wall Street Journal,* June 6, 1975, p. 1.

EXHIBIT 8-8

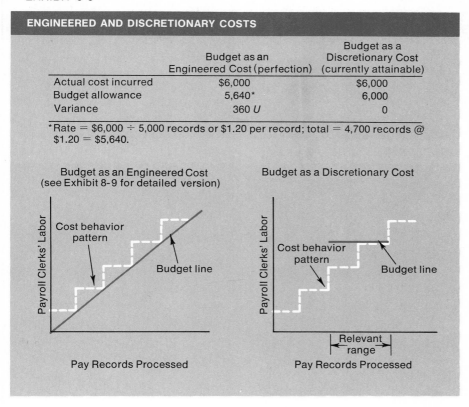

ENGINEERED AND DISCRETIONARY COSTS

	Budget as an Engineered Cost (perfection)	Budget as a Discretionary Cost (currently attainable)
Actual cost incurred	$6,000	$6,000
Budget allowance	5,640*	6,000
Variance	360 *U*	0

*Rate = $6,000 ÷ 5,000 records or $1.20 per record; total = 4,700 records @ $1.20 = $5,640.

Budget as an Engineered Cost (see Exhibit 8-9 for detailed version) | Budget as a Discretionary Cost

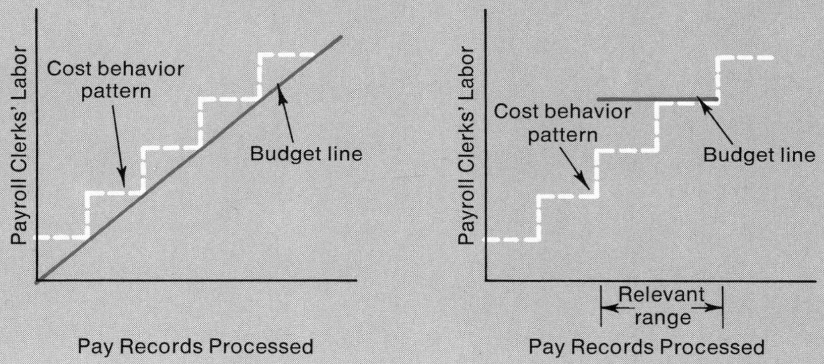

approach is an explicit and formal attempt to measure the utilization of resources by:

1. Assuming a proportionately variable-cost budget and the complete divisibility of the work load into small units. Note that the *budget line* on the graph in Exhibit 8-9 is variable, despite the fact that the costs are really incurred in steps.
2. Generating a budget variance that assumes a comparison of actual costs with a perfection standard—the cost that would be incurred if payroll-clerk labor could be turned on and off like a faucet. In this case, the variance of $360 informs management that there was overstaffing (that is, the tenth step was only partially utilized). The work-load capability was 5,000 pay records, not the 4,700 actually processed. $360 is the extra cost that resulted from operating in a way that does not attain the lowest possible cost, even though this may not be the result of a conscious decision but merely the effect of producing the volume that satisfies the total monthly demand. Advocates of work measurement maintain that such a variance shows where the managers should be alert for cost reduction opportunities, because options may be available. Such an approach provides a measure ($360) of the amount that management is currently investing to provide stability in the work force.

EXHIBIT 8-9

STEP-VARIABLE COSTS AND VARIANCES

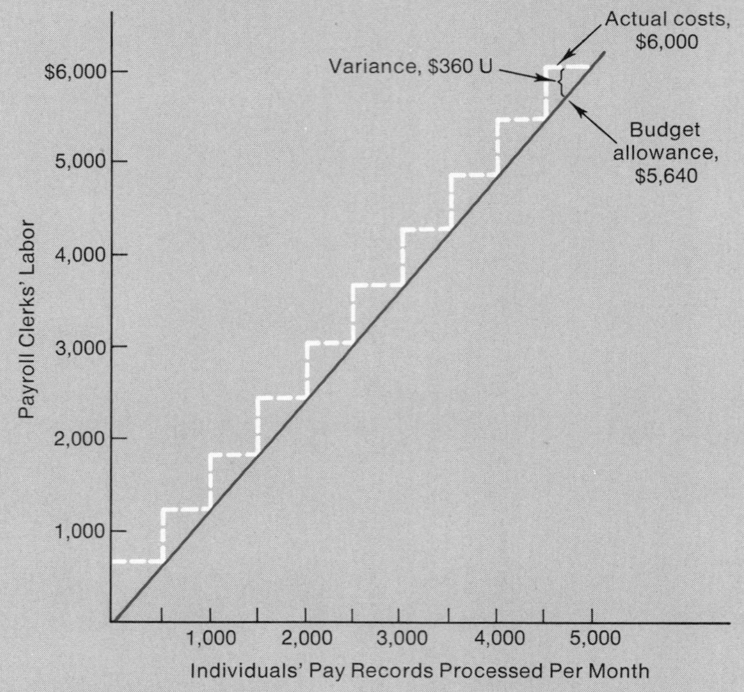

The use of a tight budget based on perfection standards generates variances that upon investigation will reveal either or both of the following: (a) inefficient use or underutilization of available personnel (for instance, perhaps 5,000 individual payroll records had to be processed, and other clerks or supervisors had to pitch in to get all the work done); (b) the cost of a management policy of deliberately retaining personnel to service long-run needs even though the volume of the current work load is insufficient (for instance, the maximum work available for payroll clerical labor may be 4,700 individual payroll records and the individual work may have been performed with complete efficiency).

THE DISCRETIONARY FIXED-COST APPROACH: CURRENTLY ATTAINABLE STANDARDS Work-measurement techniques are not used in the vast majority of organizations. Consequently, the tendency is to rely on the experience of the department head and his superior for judging the size of the work force needed to carry out the department's functions. There is a genuine reluctance to over-hire because there is a corresponding reluctance to discharge or lay off people when volume slackens. As a result, temporary peak loads are often met by hiring temporary workers or by having the regular employees work overtime.

In most cases, the relevant range of activity during the budget period can be predicted with assurance, and the work force needed for the marketing and administrative functions can be readily determined. If management refuses, consciously or unconsciously, to control costs rigidly in accordance with short-run fluctuations in activity, these costs become discretionary. That is, their total amount is relatively fixed and unresponsive to short-run variations in volume.

Hence, there is a conflict between common practice and the objective of work measurement, which is to treat most costs as engineered and so subject them to short-range management control. *The moral is that management's attitudes and its planning and controlling decisions often determine whether a cost is fixed or variable. A change in policy can transform a fixed cost into a variable cost and vice versa.*

Moreover, management may regard a cost as a discretionary fixed cost for *cash-planning purposes* in the preparation of the master budget, but may use the variable-cost approach for *control purposes* in the preparation of flexible budgets for performance evaluation. These two views may be reconciled within the same overall system. In our example, a master budget conceivably could include the following items:

Payroll-clerk labor:	
Flexible-budget allowance for control	$5,640
Expected flexible-budget variance (due to deliberate overstaffing)	360
Total budget allowance for cash planning	$6,000

FOLLOW-UP ANALYSIS UNDER DISCRETIONARY FIXED COSTS Thus, we see that control may be exercised (a) in the commonly accepted sense of the day-to-day follow-up that is associated with engineered costs; and (b) in the special sense of periodically evaluating an expenditure, relating it to the objectives sought, and carefully planning the total amount of the cost for the ensuing period. The latter approach does not mean that day-to-day follow-up is neglected; follow-up is necessary to see that the resources made available are being used fully and efficiently. It does mean that perceptive planning is stressed and that daily control *via a formal measurement system* is de-emphasized. Reliance is placed more on hiring capable people and less on frequent checking up.

The practical effects of the discretionary fixed-cost approach are that the budgeted costs and the actual costs tend to be very close, so that resulting budget variances are small. Follow-ups to see that the available resources are being fully and efficiently utilized are regarded as the managers' responsibility, a duty that can be achieved by face-to-face control and by records of physical quantities (for example, pounds handled per day in a warehouse, pieces mailed per hour in a mailing room) that do not have to be formally integrated into the accounting records in dollar terms. However, some benchmarks are still utilized even if such "standards" are not explicit.

difficulties in applying work measurement

The success of the work-measurement, engineered variable-cost approach to some nonmanufacturing costs is limited by the nature of the work being performed. Attempts have been made to measure the work of legal personnel and claims adjusters in insurance companies, of economists in a Federal Reserve Bank, and of stock clerks in retail stores. Such attempts have achieved only limited success because of either (a) the inability to develop a satisfactory control-factor unit, (b) the diversity of tasks and objectives of such personnel, or (c) the difficulty of measuring the output of lawyers or economists.

For example, consider the attempt to measure the work of clerks and stock helpers in a food store. Their tasks are routine and repetitive, but they are often fragmented. Attempts at measuring employee work have shown volatile results. The trouble is that each employee usually performs a variety of tasks on a variety of items. He may unpack, price-mark, stock shelves, operate a cash register, bag groceries, cart groceries to automobiles, sweep floors, and watch for shoplifters.[4]

To recapitulate, work measurement has proven helpful in both nonmanufacturing and manufacturing. Its use is becoming more widespread. However, please keep this textbook presentation in perspective. It is not a sales pitch for work measurement. Instead, it has merely described two general approaches to a problem. Whether the engineered-cost approach is "better" than the discretionary-cost approach must be decided on a case-by-case basis, *using a cost-benefit approach that focuses on how much operating decisions will be improved.* Of course, the consultants who want to install work-measurement systems will typically try to demonstrate that their more costly formal systems will generate net benefits in the form of cost savings and better customer service.

SUMMARY

A flexible budget is a budget that may be tailored to any level of activity, so that the evaluation of efficiency (the relation of inputs to outputs) is not contaminated by comparing a budget for one level of activity with results for another level of activity. Although they are most often associated with the control of overhead, flexible budgets may also include direct materials and direct labor. Flexible budgets are based on careful studies of cost behavior patterns; therefore, they may be fitted to a particular volume—before or after the fact.

Flexible budgets tell how much cost should be incurred for any level of *output,* which is usually expressed in product units or standard direct-labor hours. Because it provides an efficiency variance, standard direct-labor hours allowed for actual output achieved is a better yardstick than actual direct-labor hours for evaluating performance.

When variable overhead is closely associated with direct-labor costs, the efficiency variance for variable-overhead items might be better labeled as a "labor efficiency" variance This is because the efficiency variance is an estimation of how much more (or less)

[4] *The Economics of Frozen Food,* McKinsey-Birds Eye Study, General Foods Corporation (White Plains, N.Y.: 1964), p. 37.

variable overhead would be expected *solely* because of inefficiency (or extra efficiency) of direct labor.

The most important aspect of intelligent cost planning is an understanding of cost behavior patterns and influences. The behavior patterns may be roughly divided between variable and fixed. However, there are proportionately variable, mixed, committed fixed, discretionary fixed costs, and other types of costs. Moreover, there are curvilinear as well as linear behavior patterns. The accountant tends to oversimplify these behavior patterns. Whether this simplification is justified depends on how sensitive the manager's decisions are to the errors that the simplifications might generate. In some cases, additional accuracy may not make any difference; in other cases, it may be significant.

The job of cost analysis is quickly complicated in the real world by a variety of causal factors that underlie any particular result. Modern cost accounting offers useful techniques, although they sometimes seem too crude for the task at hand. Measurement frequently seems to be performed with a yardstick rather than with a micrometer. But a yardstick is sufficient for many measurement problems for which a micrometer is too expensive.

SUGGESTED READINGS

BEYER, ROBERT and D. TRAWICKI, *Profitability Accounting for Planning and Control,* 2nd ed. New York: The Ronald Press Company, 1972. Particularly strong in the area of flexible budgeting.

PROBLEMS FOR SELF-STUDY

PROBLEM 1 The Rank Company had scheduled production of 1,000 units of product in 1,000 hours. However, it has taken 1,100 hours to manufacture the 1,000 units. The variable-overhead items are:

	EXPECTED COST BEHAVIOR PER STANDARD DIRECT-LABOR HOUR	*COSTS INCURRED*
Rework and inspection	$ .60	$ 720
Cleanup time	.20	250
Oilers and cleaners	.10	120
Maintenance	.10	130
	$1.00	$1,220

required

1. Prepare a detailed performance report for the foreman, showing:

(1) INCURRED	*(2) BUDGET BASED ON 1,100 ACTUAL HOURS*	*(3) BUDGET BASED ON 1,000 STANDARD HOURS ALLOWED*	*(4) (1) − (3) FLEXIBLE BUDGET VARIANCE*	*ANALYSIS OF (4): (1) − (2) SPENDING VARIANCE*	*ANALYSIS OF (4): (2) − (3) EFFICIENCY VARIANCE*

2. The analysis in part 1 basically assumed that the budget allowances were based on the standard hours allowed for good *output.* Repeat part 1, but assume that budget allowances are based solely on actual hours worked (inputs). What would be the total budget variance? Could it be subdivided for further analysis?

SOLUTION 1

1.

	(1) INPUTS: INCURRED	(2) INPUTS BUDGET BASED ON 1,100 ACTUAL HOURS OF WORK DONE	(3) OUTPUTS: BUDGET BASED ON 1,000 STANDARD HOURS OF WORK ALLOWED FOR UNITS PRODUCED	(4) (1) − (3) FLEXIBLE BUDGET VARIANCE	ANALYSIS OF (4): (1) − (2) SPENDING VARIANCE	ANALYSIS OF (4): (2) − (3) EFFICIENCY VARIANCE
Rework and inspection	$ 720	$ 660	$ 600	$120 U	$ 60 U	$ 60 U
Cleanup time	250	220	200	50	30	20
Oilers and cleaners	120	110	100	20	10	10
Maintenance	130	110	100	30	20	10
Total variable overhead	$1,220	$1,100	$1,000	$220 U	$120 U	$100 U

2. A performance report based solely on actual hours worked would have three columns. The first two would coincide with columns (1) and (2) in requirement 1. The third would coincide with the Spending Variance column in requirement 1, but now it would be labeled as the Total Budget Variance, $120. As a total budget variance, this variance could not be subdivided for further analysis in a manner similar to requirements 1 and 2.

   Think carefully about the differences in approach. Ideally, a performance report based on *both* bases, such as the one in requirement 1, would be most informative. If one base is to be used, standard hours is the better base because the overhead budget will not be influenced by the variations in usage of the labor hours (inputs) that formulate the base. In other words, an unchanging yardstick based on good output is used to judge cost incurrence. The amount of overhead that a department head should incur is not increased because the usage (input) of direct labor has been excessive. Furthermore, the use of standard hours (*output-oriented*) as a budget base generates two subvariances, *efficiency* and *spending,* whereas the use of actual hours as the budget base generates only the *spending* variance.

PROBLEM 2

The Alic Co. has many small accounts receivable. Work measurement of billing labor has shown that a billing clerk can process 2,000 customers' accounts per month. The company employs 30 billing clerks at an annual salary of $9,600 each. The outlook for next year is for a decline in the number of customers, from 59,900 to 56,300 per month.

required

1. Assume that management has decided to continue to employ the 30 clerks despite the expected drop in billings. Show two approaches, the engineered-cost approach and the discretionary fixed-cost approach, to the budgeting of billing labor. Show how the *performance report* for the year would appear under each approach.
2. Some managers favor using tight budgets as motivating devices for controlling operations. In these cases, the managers really expect an unfavorable variance and must allow, in cash planning, for such a variance so that adequate cash will be available as needed. What would be the budgeted variance, also sometimes called expected variance, in this instance?
3. Assume that the workers are reasonably efficient. (a) Interpret the budget variances under the engineered-cost approach and the discretionary fixed-cost approach. (b) What should management do to exert better control over clerical costs?

SOLUTION 2

1. Engineered-cost approach:

Standard Unit Rate = \$9,600 ÷ 2,000 = \$4.80 per customer per year
or = \$ .40 per customer per month

	ACTUAL COST	FLEXIBLE BUDGET: TOTAL STANDARD INPUTS ALLOWED FOR GOOD UNITS PRODUCED × STANDARD UNIT PRICE	FLEXIBLE BUDGET VARIANCE
Billing-clerk labor	(30 × \$9,600) \$288,000	(56,300 × \$.40 × 12 months) \$270,240	\$17,760 U

Discretionary fixed-cost approach:

	ACTUAL COST	FLEXIBLE BUDGET[5]	FLEXIBLE BUDGET VARIANCE
Billing-clerk labor	\$288,000	\$288,000	—

2. The budgeted variance would be \$17,760 unfavorable. The master budget for financial planning must provide for labor costs of \$288,000; therefore, if the engineered cost approach were being used for control, the master budget might specify:

Billing-clerk labor:	
Control-budget allowance	\$270,240
Expected control-budget variance	17,760
Total budget allowance for cash planning	\$288,000

3. As the chapter explains, management decisions and policies are often of determining importance in categorizing a cost as fixed or variable. If management refuses, as in this case, to control costs rigidly in accordance with short-run fluctuations in activity, these costs are discretionary. The \$17,760 variance represents the price that management, consciously or unconsciously, is willing to pay currently in order to maintain a stable work force geared to management's ideas of "normal needs."

Management should be given an approximation of such an extra cost. There is no single "right way" to keep management informed on such matters. Two approaches were demonstrated in the previous parts of this problem. The important point is that clerical work loads and capability must be measured before effective control may be exerted. Such measures may be formal or informal. The latter is often achieved through a supervisor's regular observation, so that he knows how efficiently work is being performed.

QUESTIONS, PROBLEMS, AND CASES

8-1 Why do techniques for overhead control differ from techniques for control of direct materials and direct labor?

8-2 When can't the terms *budgeted performance* and *standard performance* be used interchangeably?

8-3 What two basic questions must be asked in approaching the control of overhead?

8-4 Define *semivariable cost.*

[5] Note that a "flexible" budget for fixed costs is really static in the sense that the total budget allowance would not change even though volume changed.

8-5 "For practical purposes, curvilinear variable costs almost always may be treated as if they had straight-line behavior." Why?

8-6 What factors must management consider in the year-to-year planning of fixed costs?

8-7 "There are different types of fixed costs." Explain.

8-8 "The idea of comparing performance at one activity level with a plan that was developed at some other activity level must be pertinent in judging the effectiveness of planning and control." Comment.

8-9 Why is the title "flexible budget" a misnomer?

8-10 "If only one budget base is to be used for appraising performance, *standard* direct-labor hours is a better base than *actual* direct-labor hours." Do you agree? Why?

8-11 List four criteria for selecting a volume base.

8-12 List six factors besides volume that cause costs to vary.

8-13 The Burling Company had the following performance report for the month ended June 30, 19_1:

	ACTUAL	MASTER (STATIC) BUDGET	VARIANCE	BUDGET FORMULA PER UNIT
Variable costs:				
Direct material	$ 21,350	$ 27,000	$ 5,650 F	$ 3.00
Direct labor	61,500	72,000	10,500 F	8.00
Labor to transport materials internally and provide general support	11,100	14,400	3,300 F	1.60
Idle time	3,550	3,600	50 F	.40
Cleanup time	2,500	2,700	200 F	.30
Other indirect labor	800	900	100 F	.10
Miscellaneous supplies	4,700	5,400	700 F	.60
Variable manufacturing costs	$105,500	$126,000	$20,500 F	$14.00*
Fixed costs:				
Factory supervision	$ 14,700	$ 14,400	$ 300 U	
Rent of factory	5,000	5,000	—	
Depreciation of factory equipment	15,000	15,000	—	
Other fixed factory costs	2,600	2,600	—	
Fixed manufacturing costs	$ 37,300	$ 37,000	$ 300 U	
Total manufacturing costs	$142,800	$163,000	$20,200 U	

F = Favorable cost variances occur when actual costs are less than budgeted costs.
U = Unfavorable

* Note that the budget formula for fixed costs is $37,000 per month. Therefore, the budget formula for total costs is $14.00 per unit plus $37,000 per month.

The general manager was unhappy about not achieving the original production target of 9,000 units, which was the basis for the master (static) budget. Actual production was only 7,000 units. However, she was pleased that all variable manufacturing costs had favorable budget variances.

required

1. Prepare a performance report that might provide a better explanation of what has happened. Indicate whether each variance is favorable or unfavorable.
2. Some managers would contend that the fixed costs do not belong in this report. Do you agree? Why?

8-14 *Fundamentals of Flexible Budgets* The Carey Company produces one uniform product. The assembly department encounters wide fluctuations in activity levels from month to month. However, the following department-overhead budget depicts expectations of currently attainable efficiency for an "average" or "normal" level of activity of 20,000 units of production per month:

	BUDGET—NORMAL MONTH	INCURRED "ACTUAL" COSTS IN JUNE
Indirect labor—variable	$20,000	$19,540
Supplies—variable	1,000	1,000
Power—variable	1,000	980
Repairs—variable	1,000	880
Other variable overhead	2,000	1,800
Depreciation—fixed	10,000	10,000
Other fixed overhead	5,000	5,000
	$40,000	$39,200

required

1. Prepare a columnar flexible budget at 16,000-, 20,000-, and 24,000-unit levels of activity.
2. Express requirement 1 in formula form.
3. In June, the department operated at a 17,600-unit level of activity. Prepare two performance reports, comparing actual performance with (a) budget at normal activity and (b) budget at a 17,600-unit level of activity.
4. Which comparison, 3(a) or 3(b), would be more helpful in judging the foreman's efficiency? Why?
5. Sketch a graph (not necessarily to exact scale) of how the flexible-budget total behaves over the 16,000- to 24,000-unit range of activity. Sketch a graph of how the variable-overhead items behave and of how the fixed-overhead items behave. Why is the "flex" in the flexible budget confined to variable overhead?

8-15 *Spending and Efficiency Variances* Refer to Problem 8-14. Suppose that it actually took 19,000 hours of input to obtain the 17,600 units of output achieved. The standard direct-labor allowance is one hour per unit of product manufactured.

required

1. Prepare a performance report showing five columns: (a) actual inputs at actual prices, (b) spending variance, (c) flexible budget based on actual hours of input times budgeted or standard unit prices, (d) efficiency variance, and (e) flexible budget based on standard hours allowed for the actual output achieved.
2. Sketch a graph of how the total overhead behaves. Indicate where the total spending variance and the total efficiency variance would appear on the graph.
3. Suppose that a new worker wasted an extra $300 of supplies during the month, so that the actual cost of supplies was $1,300. The unit cost of supplies was unaffected. Would the $300 appear as an additional efficiency variance or as an additional spending variance? Explain fully.

8-16 *Fundamentals of Flexible Budgets* Joan Eastman, the manager of a medical testing laboratory, has been under pressure from the director of the large clinic,

Dr. Elvira Coleman, to get more productivity from her employees. New government rules for reimbursement of medical charges had resulted in the disallowance of many costs in the clinic as being too high in relation to standard fees charged elsewhere. In particular, the costs of various blood tests were deemed "outrageous" by one government auditor.

Eastman had been provided with some industry standards for various tests and had compiled a budgeted cost behavior pattern for direct labor and indirect costs. Some selected variable-cost items for a recent four-week period were:

	BUDGETED COST BEHAVIOR PATTERN PER DIRECT-LABOR HOUR	BUDGET BASED ON 4,000 ACTUAL LABOR HOURS	ACTUAL	VARIANCE	
				AMOUNT	PERCENTAGE OF BUDGET
Direct labor	$8.00	$32,000	$32,000	—	—
Supplies	2.00	8,000	6,400	1,600	20%
Indirect labor	1.00	4,000	3,000	1,000	25%
Miscellaneous	2.00	8,000	6,000	2,000	25%

Eastman was pleased with her budgetary performance, but Coleman was not happy. She asked you to reconstruct the performance report, saying, "This report seems incomplete. I want a better pinpointing of the degree of basic efficiency in that department."

Your investigation of the industry literature and your discussion with a management consultant in health care revealed that standard times have been developed for these clinical procedures. Although the standard times were open to criticism if examined on an hour-by-hour or day-by-day basis, in the aggregate over a week they provided a fairly reliable benchmark for measuring outputs against inputs. Your study of the output showed that about 2,600 standard direct-labor hours should have been allowed for the output actually achieved by the laboratory.

required

For the chosen items, prepare a better performance report for Dr. Coleman. Why is your report better? Be specific.

8-17 *Price and Spending Variances* The GH Company used a flexible budget and standard costs. In March the company produced 7,000 units of its finished product. Assume that 15,000 actual hours were used at an actual hourly rate of $4.10. Two direct-labor hours is the standard allowance for producing one unit. The standard-labor rate is $4 per hour. The flexible budget for miscellaneous supplies is based on a formula of 60¢ per unit, which can also be expressed as 30¢ per direct-labor hour. The actual cost of supplies was $4,700.

required

1. Compute the "price" and "efficiency" variances for direct labor and for supplies.
2. The "price" variance for supplies is rarely labeled as such. Instead, it is often called a spending variance. The plant manager has asked, "I have been troubled by the waste of supplies for months. I know that the prices are exactly equal to the budgeted prices for every supply item, because a two-year stock of supplies was bought a year ago in anticipation of prolonged inflation. Consequently, we used known prices for preparing our budgets. Given these facts, please explain how a price or spending variance can arise for miscellaneous supplies. Why doesn't all waste appear as an efficiency variance?" Respond to the manager's comments. Be clear and specific; the manager is impatient with muddled explanations, and your next pay raise will be affected by her appraisal of your explanation.

8-18 *Direct Labor and Variable Overhead Variances* (SIA, adapted) The Schock Manufacturing Company uses a standard cost system. The standards are set before January 1, each year and remain unchanged until December 31.

The standard costs set for the next year are:

Direct materials	$10.00 per unit
Direct labor	7.50 per unit
Overhead	6.00 per unit

The labor standard above includes a methods change from 2 hours to $1\frac{1}{2}$ hours per unit, effective January 1, and a change in labor rates from $4.00 to $5.00 per hour effective February 28.

Overhead will be applied on the basis of standard labor hours. The standard overhead rate per hour is $4.00 ($1\frac{1}{2}$ hrs. $\times$ 4 = $6.00 per unit). The variable portion is $2.00 per hour. The original budgeted production volume for January was 5,000 units. The actual cost data for January are:

Units produced, 6,000
Direct materials used, $62,000
Direct labor, 11,000 hours costing $46,000

Actual overhead incurred:

Variable	$23,000
Fixed	$14,000

required

1. Prepare a Production statement for the month of January, showing:
   (a) actual costs,
   (b) budgeted production costs on a flexible-budget basis,
   (c) budget variances.
2. Prepare detailed variance analyses for direct labor and variable overhead.
3. Comment on the January production performance—e.g., efficiency, reason for variances, and so on.

8-19 *Flexible Budget* (CMA, adapted) The Melcher Co. produces farm equipment at several plants. The business is seasonal and cyclical in nature. The company has attempted to use budgeting for planning and controlling activities, but the variable nature of the business has caused some company officials to be skeptical about the usefulness of budgeting to the company. The accountant for the Adrian plant has been using a system he calls "flexible budgeting" to help his plant management control operations.

The company president asks him to explain what the term means, how he applies the system at the Adrian plant, and how it can be applied to the company as a whole. The accountant presents the following data as part of his explanation.

Budget data for 19_3			
Normal monthly activity of the plant in direct-labor hours			10,000 hours
Material costs	6 lbs. @ $1.50		$9.00 unit
Labor costs	2 hours @ $3.00		$6.00 unit
Overhead estimate at normal monthly activity:			
Variable (controllable):			
Indirect labor		$ 6,650	
Indirect materials		600	
Repairs		750	
Total variable		$ 8,000	

Fixed (noncontrollable):	
Depreciation	$ 3,250
Supervision	3,000
Total fixed	$ 6,250
Total fixed and variable	$14,250
Planned units for January 19_3	4,000
Planned units for February 19_3	6,000
Actual data for January 19_3	
Actual hours of input	8,400
Units produced	3,800
Costs incurred:	
Material (24,000 lbs.)	$36,000
Direct labor	25,200
Indirect labor	6,000
Indirect materials	600
Repairs	1,800
Depreciation	3,250
Supervision	3,000
Total	$75,850

required

1. Prepare a master (static) budget for January.
2. Prepare a report for January comparing actual and budgeted costs for the actual activity for the month.
3. Can flexible budgeting be applied to the nonmanufacturing activities of the company? Explain your answer.

8-20 *Flexible Budget, Selection of Appropriate Activity Base, and Analysis of Variable-Overhead Variances* The Selkirk Company has produced 10,000 units of product. The *standard direct-labor hours allowed* (also called *standard hours earned* or *standard hours worked*) were 2 hours per unit, or a total of 20,000 hours. The actual direct-labor hours worked were 21,000. The standard direct-labor rate is $3 per hour. Actual direct-labor costs totaled $65,100. Variable overhead was divided into the following categories:

INCURRED	*TYPE OF OVERHEAD ITEM*	*STANDARD COST BEHAVIOR PATTERN**
$14,700	Indirect labor—variable	$ .70
2,000	Supplies—variable	.10
2,200	Repairs—variable	.10
2,100	Power—variable	.10
$21,000	Total variable overhead	$1.00

* Per standard direct-labor hour.

required

1. Standard costs applied to production have sometimes been referred to as a function of *outputs,* whereas actual costs incurred have sometimes been called a function of *inputs.* Analyze the variances for direct labor and then comment on your analysis in relation to the outputs-inputs distinction and to the terminology distinction between *standard hours worked* and *actual hours worked.*[6]

[6] An example of the distinction between actual hours worked and standard hours worked is as follows: A lathe operation may require a standard of 10 pieces to be turned per hour. If the necessary operation is performed on 100 pieces in 11 hours, the actual hours worked would be 11 but the standard hours worked (sometimes called *standard hours earned* or *standard hours allowed*) would be 100 ÷ 10, or only 10 hours.

2. Prepare a detailed performance report for the foreman, showing:

(1) INCURRED	(2) BUDGET BASED ON 21,000 HOURS	(3) BUDGET BASED ON 20,000 HOURS	(4) (1) − (3) TOTAL BUDGET VARIANCE	ANALYSIS OF (4): (1) − (2) SPENDING VARIANCE	ANALYSIS OF (4): (2) − (3) EFFICIENCY VARIANCE

3. Prepare a summary analysis of the total variance for total variable overhead.
4. The analysis in parts 2 and 3 basically assumed that the budget allowances were based on the standard hours allowed for good *output.* Repeat parts 2 and 3, but assume that budget allowances are based solely on actual hours worked (inputs). What would be the total budget variance? Could it be subdivided for further analysis?
5. Compare and contrast the price and efficiency variances of direct labor with the spending and efficiency variances of variable overhead.

8-21 *Standard Costs and Responsibility* (CMA) The Carberg Corporation manufactures and sells a single product. The cost system used by the company is a standard-cost system. The standard cost per unit of product is shown below:

Material—one pound plastic @ $2.00	$ 2.00
Direct labor 1.6 hours @ $4.00	6.40
Variable overhead cost	3.00
Fixed overhead cost	1.45
	$12.85

The overhead cost per unit was calculated from the following annual overhead-cost budget for a 60,000-unit volume.

Variable overhead cost:	
Indirect labor 30,000 hours @ $4.00	$120,000
Supplies—Oil 60,000 gallons @ $.50	30,000
Allocated variable service-department costs	30,000
Total variable overhead cost	$180,000
Fixed overhead cost:	
Supervision	$ 27,000
Depreciation	45,000
Other fixed costs	15,000
Total fixed overhead cost	$ 87,000
Total budgeted annual overhead cost at 60,000 Units	$267,000

The charges to the manufacturing department for November, when 5,000 units were produced, are given below:

Material: 5,300 pounds @ $2.00	$10,600
Direct labor: 8,200 hours @ $4.10	33,620
Indirect labor: 2,400 hours @ $4.10	9,840
Supplies—Oil: 6,000 gallons @ $.55	3,300
Other variable overhead costs	3,200
Supervision	2,475
Depreciation	3,750
Other	1,250
Total	$68,035

The purchasing department normally buys about the same quantity as is used in production during a month. In November 5,200 pounds were purchased at a price of $2.10 per pound.

required

1. Calculate the following variances from standard costs for the data given:
   a. materials purchase price
   b. materials efficiency
   c. direct-labor wage price
   d. direct-labor efficiency
   e. overhead budget
2. The company has divided its responsibility such that the purchasing department is responsible for the price at which materials and supplies are purchased. The manufacturing department is responsible for the quantities of materials used. Does this division of responsibilities solve the conflict between price and efficiency variances? Explain your answer.
3. Prepare a report which details the overhead budget variance. The report, which will be given to the manufacturing department manager, should display only that part of the variance that is the responsibility of the manager and should highlight the information in ways that would be useful to that manager in evaluating departmental performance and when considering corrective action.
4. Assume that the department manager performs the timekeeping function for this manufacturing department. From time to time analysis of overhead and direct-labor variances have shown that the department manager has deliberately misclassified labor hours (e.g., listed direct-labor hours as indirect-labor hours and vice versa) so that only one of the two labor variances is unfavorable. It is not feasible economically to hire a separate timekeeper. What should the company do, if anything, to resolve this problem?

8-22 *Control of Discretionary Costs* The manager of a Singapore warehouse for a mail-order firm is concerned with the control of his fixed costs. He has recently applied work-measurement techniques and an engineered-cost approach to the staff of order clerks and is wondering if a similar technique could be applied to the workers who collect merchandise in the warehouse and bring it to the area where orders are assembled for shipment.

The warehouse foreman contends that this should not be done, because the present work force of twenty men should be viewed as a fixed cost necessary to handle the normal volume of orders with a minimum of delay. These men work a forty-hour week at $2.50 per hour.

Preliminary studies show that it takes an average of twelve minutes for a worker to locate an article and take it to the order-assembly area, and that the average order is for two different articles. At present the volume of orders to be processed is 1,800 per week.

required

1. For the present volume of orders, develop a discretionary-cost and an engineered-cost approach for the weekly performance report.
2. Repeat 1 for volume levels of 1,600 and 1,400 orders per week.
3. What other factors should be compared with the budget variances found in 1 and 2 in order to make a decision on the size of the work force?

8-23 *Work Measurement* The Hayward Company has installed a work-measurement program for its billing operations. A standard billing cost of $.50 per bill has been used, based on hourly labor rates of $4.00 and an average processing rate of 8 bills of 10 lines each per hour. Each clerk has a 7½-hour workday and a 5-day workweek.

The supervisor has received the following report of performance from his superior—the office manager, Mr. Davis—for a recent 4-week period regarding his clerks:

			VARIANCE	
	ACTUAL	BUDGET	AMOUNT	EQUIVALENT PERSONS
Billing labor (5 clerks)	$3,000	$1,850 (3,700 bills × $.50)	$1,150 U	1.9

The supervisor knows that he must explain the unfavorable variance and offer suggestions regarding how to avoid such an unfavorable variance in the future. Because of a recession, the office manager is under severe pressure to cut staff. In fact, he had penciled a question on the report: "Looks as if we can get along with two less clerks?"

Anticipating the pressures, the supervisor had taken a random sample of 400 of the 3,700 bills that were prepared during the period under review. His count of the lines in the sample totaled 5,200.

required | As the supervisor, prepare a one-page explanation of the $1,150 unfavorable variance, together with your remedial suggestions.

8-24 *Ford Motor Company's Flexible-Budget Control over Clerical Costs Through Work Measurement* This case illustrates a method by which flexible-budget controls have been adapted to a nonmanufacturing operation to control costs that might normally be classed as fixed labor and operating expense. It is possible and practical to control many expenses of this nature by the use of "standard" processing rates for work performed.

The following information is presented as background material to outline the control approach followed by this company:

The parts and accessories division of the Ford Motor Company controls and evaluates the performance of its branch-warehouse operations by the use of "flexible labor and expense budgets." These budgetary controls are in use in both the warehousing and the accounting activities of these operations and are used for both weekly and monthly analysis.

Primarily, variable-labor functions and controllable-expense classifications are supervised in this manner. Fixed costs that are not controllable by local management, such as supervision, taxes, and depreciation, are administered by the use of fixed (static) budget allowances.

All variable functions of the warehousing and accounting activities have been analyzed and standardized and related to some measurable work output. By maintaining daily control of these functional productivities and related daily labor charges, the required operating reports are prepared and submitted to the general office for analysis, consolidation, and comparison to national operating-budget levels.

A primary source of output statistics is obtained from a record of actual daily shipments made by the warehouse, as many accounting-function productivities are based on this measurement. The determinable output measurements are compared to the predetermined functional-budget rate to calculate "budget hours generated" during the budget period under review. The operating variances are determined by comparing generated budget hours to actual functional-labor charges during the same period. These variances are expressed both in hours of variance and equivalent-persons variance. The latter variance is calculated by comparing the hourly variance amounts to the forty shift-hours available in the budget period under review.

For a recent normal workweek of five operating days, the following output information and labor-distribution detail have been accumulated for certain selected accounting-department functions. The complete budget review is actually applied to approximately fifty separate and distinct activities in this operation.

OUTPUT STATISTICS

1. Number of orders shipped	8,640
2. Number of line items* shipped	99,280
3. Number of line items backordered in warehouse	2,720
4. Number of checks written for merchandise received	3,290
5. Number of line items on shipments received	4,960
6. Number of credit adjustments approved	975

* Represents a single part number shipped or received, regardless of quantity.

FUNCTIONAL BUDGET RATES AND LABOR DISTRIBUTION

FUNCTION	BUDGET RATE PER HOUR	ACTUAL HOURS WORKED
Invoice scheduling	135 orders shipped	68.0
Keypunch†	680 line items processed	142.0
Keyverification†	1,360 line items processed	71.0
IBM machine operator†	1,020 line items printed	108.0
Proofreading†	510 line items proofread	208.0
Accounts payable:		125.0‡
Invoice matching	80 line items received	
Check auditing	70 payments made	
Credit adjustments	15 adjustments issued	69.0
Budgeted hourly labor rate—$5.00 per hour		
Actual payroll costs —$2,256.00		

† To determine the output allowance, the 2,720 line items backordered should be added to the 99,280 items shipped.

‡ The 125.0 represents the combined actual hours worked on accounts payable; no sub-division is available for invoice matching and check auditing.

required

1. Determine labor variance by function. Express variance in both hours and equivalent persons.
2. Calculate total labor variance in dollars.
3. Analyze the total dollar variance as determined in part 2. What portion of this variance was attributable to a labor-price variance and a labor-efficiency variance?

8-25 *Guaranteed Minimum Wages and Cost Behavior Patterns* (Prepared by the author and adapted for use in a CPA examination) The Lavin Company had a contract with a labor union that guaranteed a minimum wage of $500 payable monthly to direct laborers with at least 12 years' service. One hundred workers currently qualified for such coverage. All direct-labor employees are paid $5 per hour.

The budget for 19_1 was based on the usage of 400,000 hours of direct labor, a total of $2,000,000. Of this amount, $600,000 (100 workers × $500 × 12 months) was regarded as fixed.

Data on performance for the first three months of 19_1 follow:

	JANUARY	FEBRUARY	MARCH
Direct-labor hours actually worked	22,000	32,000	42,000
Standard direct-labor hours allowed*	22,000	32,000	42,000
Direct-labor costs budgeted	$127,000	$162,000	$197,000
Direct-labor costs incurred	110,000	160,000	210,000
Variance (U = unfavorable; F = favorable)	17,000 F	2,000 F	13,000 U

* Note that perfect efficiency is being assumed.

The factory manager was perplexed by the results, which showed favorable variances when production was low and unfavorable variances when production was high. He felt that his control over labor costs was consistently good.

required

1. Why did the variances arise? Use amounts and diagrams, as necessary, to explain.
2. Assume that only 5,000 standard and actual hours were utilized in a given month and that all the most senior workers were used. Does this direct-labor budget provide a basis for evaluating direct-labor performance? What variances would arise under the approach used in 1? What variances would arise under the approach you recommend?
3. Suppose that 5,500 actual hours were used, but that only 5,000 standard hours were allowed for the work accomplished. What variances would arise under the approach used in 1? Under the approach you recommend?

8-26 *Division of Mixed Costs Into Variable and Fixed Components* The controller of the Ijiri Co. wants you to approximate the fundamental variable- and fixed-cost behavior of an account called Maintenance from the following:

MONTHLY ACTIVITY IN MACHINE-HOURS	MONTHLY MAINTENANCE COSTS INCURRED
4,000	$3,000
7,000	3,900

8-27 *Nonlinear Cost Behavior* The MNO Company has assumed that its total manufacturing overhead cost is most heavily affected by only one variable, direct-labor hours. The company used a linear approximation, as shown in the following graph, as a basis for determining its flexible-budget allowances at various volumes:

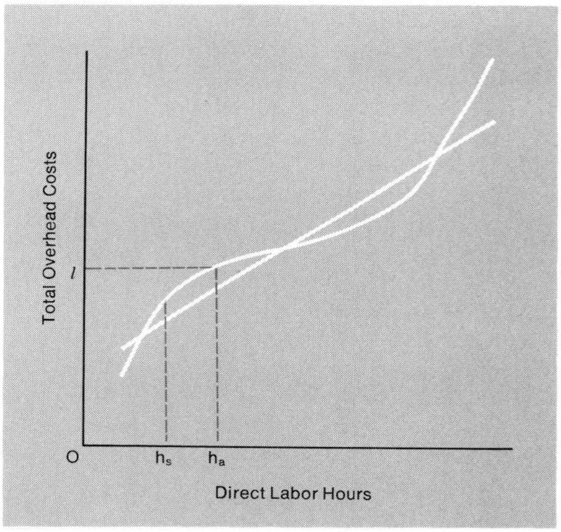

The actual cost behavior pattern is the nonlinear function represented by the curve in the graph.

Suppose that manager Charles is responsible for the whole plant, manager Baker for overhead spending variances, and foreman Able for overhead efficiency variances. At the end of the period, actual hours are Oh_a and standard hours are Oh_s. Actual overhead is Ol.

required

1. Suppose that the flexible budget was based on the linear approximation. Use the graph to measure the amount of the spending variance (call it hl), the efficiency variance (call it gh), and the flexible-budget variance (call it gl).
2. Suppose the budget was based on the curve. How would your answers in 1 be different? Be specific.
3. Compare your answers in 1 and 2. If the linear approximation in 1 is used as a basis for flexible budgeting, what are the likely effects on the attitudes of each of the three managers?

8-28 *Work Measurement* Some management consultants have developed standards for the clerical work force in a large local hospital. Some estimates of overhead behavior also were developed. The standard variable overhead rate per billing in the billing department was $.12. Five bills per hour is regarded as standard productivity per billing clerk. The actual total overhead incurred was $97,000, of which $70,000 was fixed. There were no variances for fixed overhead. The variable-overhead spending variance was $3,000, favorable. The variable-overhead budget variance was $600, favorable. Compute (1) variable-overhead efficiency variance, (2) actual hours of input, and (3) standard hours allowed for output achieved.

8-29 *Nonlinear Costs* See the preceding problem. Suppose that cost studies had developed the following approximation for relating overhead to labor hours (L):

$$\text{Total Overhead} = \$68{,}000 + \$.40L + \$30\sqrt{L}$$

If this cost function was used as a flexible-budget formula (instead of the linear budget used in the preceding problem), what would be the efficiency variance in this case? (Round your square root to the nearest hour.)

8-30 *Reformulating a Performance Report* The Touche Manufacturing Company produces and sells instruments for the aircraft industry. Material and labor standards and overhead budgets have been developed for each of the departments. The assembly department budget for 19_4 appears in Exhibit 8-10.

Monthly reports are prepared comparing actual department costs with budgeted department costs. The June report for the assembly department is shown in Exhibit 8-11.

"You're trying to tell me I spent too much," the department foreman shouted when he saw the report, "and I deny it! I've got control over my costs. Look at Fringe Benefits. How can I spend too much? It's a fixed percent of the wages. And direct-labor wages are set by the union contract, so the only way I can spend too much is to work overtime. There were 320 hours of overtime, but that only costs $800, not $2,300.

"I'm being charged for costs I can't control," he complained again. "You know those rush orders Sales keeps bringing us? When we complain we don't have time to do them, they argue that we will be responsible for losing business. So we do them. And they run up the costs.

"There were two special orders this month. One was for #720 thermostats, and the other for #4 altimeters. We usually do up to 1,000 thermostats at a time, and we're allowed 1,100 hours. That 1,100 includes 20 hours of setup

EXHIBIT 8-10

TOUCHE MANUFACTURING COMPANY ASSEMBLY DEPARTMENT 19_4 CONVERSION-COST BUDGET

Expected Volume—40,000 Direct-Labor Hours

	FIXED COSTS	*VARIABLE COSTS*	*TOTAL COSTS*	*VARIABLE RATE PER STANDARD DIRECT-LABOR DOLLAR*
Standard direct-labor cost	$ —	$200,000	$200,000	—
Overhead:				
Indirect labor	$24,000	$ 32,000	$ 56,000	.160
Supplies	1,800	6,000	7,800	.030
Tools	5,400	5,200	10,600	.026
Power	4,800	8,000	12,800	.040
Maintenance	13,200	15,000	28,200	.075
Fringe benefits	12,000	32,000	44,000	.160
Scrap	—	24,000	24,000	.120
Depreciation and taxes	36,000	—	36,000	—
Total overhead	$97,200	$122,200	$219,400	.611
Total conversion costs	$97,200	$322,200	$419,400	

EXHIBIT 8-11

TOUCHE MANUFACTURING COMPANY ASSEMBLY DEPARTMENT PERFORMANCE

June, 19_4

	BUDGET	*ACTUAL*	*VARIANCE: FAVORABLE (UNFAVORABLE)*
Standard direct-labor cost	$15,500	$17,800[a]	$(2,300)
Overhead:			
Indirect labor	$ 4,480[b]	$ 4,735	$ (255)
Supplies	615	660	(45)
Tools	853	904	(51)
Power	1,020	1,087	(67)
Maintenance	2,263	2,382	(119)
Fringe benefits	3,480	3,848	(368)
Scrap	1,860	2,042	(182)
Depreciation and taxes	3,000	3,000	—
Total overhead	$17,571	$18,658	$(1,087)
Total conversion costs	$33,071	$36,458	$(3,387)

[a] There were no deviations from standard labor rates.

[b] The basic cost behavior pattern is revealed in Exhibit 8-10: $2,000 per month + .16($15,500) = $4,480.

time and 20 hours of tear-down time. We need that much time no matter how many we do. They wanted only 500 thermostats. I had to spend 590 hours to complete it and only 50 hours were overtime.

"We usually do 1,000 altimeters and have 1,500 hours[7] to complete them, including 30 hours each of setup time and tear-down time. They wanted 400 altimeters, and it took us 636 hours to do them. We had to work 40 hours overtime on that one. Then, we wasted another 40 hours sitting around waiting for materials that Purchasing should have had in the plant. And that preventive maintenance didn't prevent one of the machines from breaking down. We sat around for 100 hours waiting for that to be fixed.

"How do you expect me to keep my costs down when all of this is going on? Just tell me that!"

The production manager told the controller about the foreman's complaint and asked for a different report, which would be more meaningful to the foreman.

required

1. Prepare the revised report to show how the foreman is really doing. Use the June 19_4 data. (*Hint:* One way to approach a solution to part 1 would be to expand Exhibit 8-11 by adding two rows. Insert a row at the top for "Direct-labor hours." Change the line "Standard direct-labor cost" to "Standard direct-labor cost of hours above." Add another row after "Standard and direct-labor cost" labeled "Overtime premium," removing that amount from the total now in the "Standard direct-labor cost" row. Then add seven columns with the overall label "Analysis of Variances," including two columns for special orders, two for unavoidable wait time, one for "Balance to be explained," one for spending and one for efficiency. This problem is more detailed than any in this chapter, but careful study will pay off in added understanding of standards and budgets.)
2. For which of these costs can the foreman really be held accountable? Comment.

[7] Therefore apparently the original allowed hours included in the budget in Exhibit 8-11 for the smaller runs were 110% × 500 and 150% × 400, respectively.

Standard Absorption Costing: Overhead Variances

9

This chapter is very important, because it integrates, contrasts, and compares the control and product-costing purposes of cost accounting. It also gives you a chance to consolidate and crystallize your study of the previous two chapters. You will then have a solid grasp of flexible budgets and standard costs.

The objective of this chapter is to examine the relationships of overhead control and overhead application, with particular emphasis on the variances between incurrence and application. Although the ideas presented here are simple, the analysis of overhead variances becomes confusing if the two purposes of overhead accounting—control and product costing—are overlooked or misunderstood.

Chapter 4 contained a discussion of the necessity for using predetermined overhead rates in applying overhead to products.[1] Now we shall consider this problem in more detail.

[1] Several important intricacies of overhead accounting are being skipped temporarily. They include (a) factors to be considered in selecting the appropriate base for product costing, (b) department versus plantwide overhead rates, and (c) reapportionment of service-department costs to producing departments before setting rates. These issues are discussed in Chapters 10, 15, and 16.

Because of the differences in behavior and controllability of costs, management has found that the distinction between variable costs and fixed costs is useful in budgeting and in product costing. Where feasible, it is desirable to classify overhead items into variable and fixed categories, even though the danger of oversimplification exists. The variable-fixed distinction should probably improve the comprehension of the decision maker concerning the uses and limitations of the cost measures.

In this chapter we introduce the term *absorption costing* for the first time; it refers to the common product-costing practice of *applying fixed factory overhead* to the goods produced. Of course, you have already studied absorption costing in Chapters 2 and 4, even though the term was not used there. The following comparison summarizes what we have covered previously in product costing:

	CHAPTER 2 APPROACH, CALLED ACTUAL ABSORPTION COSTING: *WORK-IN-PROCESS INVENTORY*	*CHAPTER 4 APPROACH, CALLED* NORMAL ABSORPTION COSTING: *WORK-IN-PROCESS INVENTORY*	*CHAPTER 9 APPROACH, CALLED* STANDARD ABSORPTION COSTING: *WORK-IN-PROCESS INVENTORY*
Direct materials	actual costs	actual	standard inputs allowed for actual output achieved × standard prices (applies to all four items)
Direct labor	actual	actual	
Variable factory overhead	actual	actual inputs × predetermined overhead rates (applies to variable and fixed overhead)	
Fixed factory overhead	actual		

variable-overhead rate

developing the rate

As we saw in Chapter 8, the flexible budget covers a range of anticipated activity. On a monthly basis, the flexible budget may appear as in Exhibit 9-1.

For purposes of computing standard unit costs of products, detailed studies of usage of direct materials and direct labor are made in order to trace these costs to the physical units produced. If overhead costs have been properly classified, variable overhead may be assigned to products with assurance, because the hourly or product rate used is valid at any level of production over wide ranges. Thus, a standard-cost sheet may contain the following:

M COMPANY

Standard Cost Sheet
Product X (Per Unit)

Direct materials, 40 pounds @ 50¢	$20.00
Direct labor, 3 hours @ $7.00	21.00
Variable overhead, 3 hours @ $1.70	5.10
Fixed overhead, 3 hours @ ? (to be discussed later)	?
Total standard cost per unit	$?

By definition, total variable-overhead costs fluctuate in proportion to changes in activity levels. A variable-overhead rate is often developed with labor-hours as the base. This rate is merely multiplied by the number of standard hours allowed to produce a product; the result is the variable-overhead component of the total standard cost per unit of product (3 hours × $1.70, or $5.10 per unit of product, in the example).

Consider these additional facts concerning one month's operations:

Variable overhead incurred for 7,900 actual direct-labor hours of input	$14,250	
Variable overhead applied to product:		
Standard hours allowed for output achieved, 8,000 × $1.70 (or may be computed as units produced, 2,666-2/3 × $5.10)	13,600	
Variable-overhead variance	$ 650	Unfavorable

general-ledger entries The summary general-ledger treatment of the facts above would be:

Variable factory-overhead control	14,250	
Accounts payable, Accrued payroll, etc.		14,250
To record actual variable overhead incurred. Detailed postings of variable-overhead items, such as material handling, supplies, and idle time, would be made to the department-overhead sheets in the subsidiary ledger for Variable Factory-Overhead Control.		
Work in process (at standard)	13,600	
Variable factory overhead applied		13,600
To apply overhead at the predetermined rate times work done as expressed in *standard hours allowed* (often called *standard hours worked* or *standard hours earned*). This would be $1.70		

EXHIBIT 9-1

M COMPANY
MACHINING DEPARTMENT
Simplified Flexible Factory-Overhead Budget for Anticipated Monthly Activity Range

Standard direct-labor hours allowed	8,000	9,000	10,000	11,000
Variable factory overhead:				
Material handling	$ 8,000	$ 9,000	$10,000	$11,000
Idle time	800	900	1,000	1,100
Rework	800	900	1,000	1,100
Overtime premium	400	450	500	550
Supplies	3,600	4,050	4,500	4,950
Total	$13,600	$15,300	$17,000	$18,700
Variable-overhead rate, $1.70 per DLH.				
Fixed factory overhead (To be considered in Exhibit 9-4)				

× 8,000 standard hours. Note that this calculation coincides with the flexible-budget total for this level of activity expressed in standard hours. The budget total would be $1.70 × 8,000 hours, or $13,600.

The only change in general-ledger procedure in this chapter is the replacement of a single Department Factory-Overhead Control account with two new accounts, one for variable overhead and another for fixed overhead. Also, *there will be two Applied accounts instead of the single Applied account used in Chapter 4.*

At this point, note that the total variable-overhead variance is not in a separate variance account, whereas direct-material and direct-labor variances are commonly isolated in separate accounts as general-ledger entries are made. However, the total variable-overhead variance may be readily computed by taking the difference between the debit balance of the Variable Factory-Overhead Control account and the credit balance of the Variable Factory-Overhead Applied account.

The general-ledger treatment practiced in standard-cost systems is not at all uniform. However, the reader who really understands the features of standard costs can easily adapt himself to any given bookkeeping system. Differences in general-ledger treatment usually center around (a) the number of detailed variance accounts desired, and (b) the timing of isolation of variances in the ledger.

analysis of variable-overhead variances

The previous chapter (specifically, Exhibit 8-3) demonstrated how variances in variable overhead were analyzed, so there is no need for repetition here. However, a few points deserve emphasis.

Exhibit 9-2 contains four columns. The first three should be familiar; they are the same as those used in Chapters 7 and 8 when we concentrated on the *budgetary-control purpose* of standard cost accounting. Now we consider the *product-costing purpose* and introduce column (4), which shows the overhead applied to product.

1. **As Exhibit 9-2 shows, the variable overhead applied to product in the general ledger ($13,600) coincides *exactly* with the amount provided in the flexible budget. Therefore, there is no conflict between the information generated for product-costing purposes and that developed for control purposes.**
2. The budget variance to be explained, $650, is often called the *flexible-budget* variance, because it is the difference between the actual amount incurred and the amount of variable cost provided for in the flexible budget.
3. Many companies refrain from subdividing the variable-overhead variance beyond the *flexible-budget variance* stage. This simplifies reports, but it does not yield as much information. Such an approach, which was originally illustrated at the top of Exhibit 8-3 in the preceding chapter, would yield an itemized report as follows:

EXHIBIT 9-2

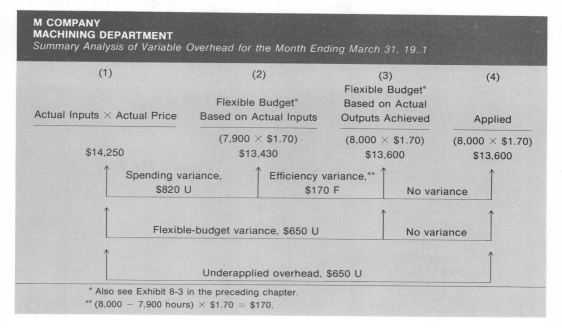

M COMPANY
MACHINING DEPARTMENT
Summary Analysis of Variable Overhead for the Month Ending March 31, 19_1

(1)	(2)	(3)	(4)
Actual Inputs × Actual Price	Flexible Budget* Based on Actual Inputs	Flexible Budget* Based on Actual Outputs Achieved	Applied
	(7,900 × $1.70)	(8,000 × $1.70)	(8,000 × $1.70)
$14,250	$13,430	$13,600	$13,600

Spending variance, $820 U (between columns 1 and 2); Efficiency variance,** $170 F (between columns 2 and 3); No variance (between columns 3 and 4)

Flexible-budget variance, $650 U (between columns 1 and 3); No variance (between columns 3 and 4)

Underapplied overhead, $650 U (between columns 1 and 4)

* Also see Exhibit 8-3 in the preceding chapter.
** (8,000 − 7,900 hours) × $1.70 = $170.

DETAILED ANALYSIS	*ACTUAL*	*FLEXIBLE BUDGET— 8,000 STANDARD HOURS ALLOWED*	*FLEXIBLE-BUDGET VARIANCE*	*EXPLANATION*
Variable factory overhead:				
Material handling	$ 8,325	$ 8,000	$325 U	High-rate workers used
Idle time	850	800	50 U	Machine #1 breakdown
⋮	⋮	⋮	⋮	
Total variable overhead	$14,250	$13,600	$650 U	

4. The budget variance is always equal to the underapplied (or overapplied) variable overhead because there is never any difference between columns (3) and (4).

fixed overhead and standard absorption costing

developing a unit cost By definition, *total* fixed-overhead costs do not change over wide ranges of activity. However, unit costs do change; the higher the level of activity, the lower the unit cost. A costing difficulty arises here, because management desires a single representative standard cost for a *product* despite month-to-month changes in production volume. What level of activity should be used in developing a single application rate for applying fixed overhead to product? Consider this illustration:

M COMPANY Standard Cost Sheet Product X (Per Unit)	
Direct materials, 40 pounds @ 50¢	$20.00
Direct labor, 3 hours @ $7.00	21.00
Variable overhead, 3 hours @ $1.70	5.10
Fixed overhead, 3 hours @ ?	?
Total standard cost per unit	$?

Now consider the budget for fixed overhead (the bottom half of the flexible budget in Exhibit 9-3).

Total fixed overhead is $10,000. Although Exhibit 9-3 indicates an 8,000- to 11,000-hour range, monthly volume expressed in standard labor-hours might fluctuate even more widely, from 5,000 up to a maximum of 15,000. Thus, the hourly cost of fixed overhead could fluctuate from $2.00 down to $66\frac{2}{3}$¢, with a consequent effect on standard product costs. This problem does not arise with

EXHIBIT 9-3

M COMPANY
MACHINING DEPARTMENT
Simplified Flexible Factory-Overhead Budget for Anticipated Monthly Activity Range

Standard direct-labor hours allowed	8,000	9,000	10,000	11,000
Variable factory overhead:				
Material handling	$ 8,000	$ 9,000	$10,000	$11,000
Idle time	800	900	1,000	1,100
Rework	800	900	1,000	1,100
Overtime premium	400	450	500	550
Supplies	3,600	4,050	4,500	4,950
Total	$13,600	$15,300	$17,000	$18,700
Variable-overhead rate, $1.70 per DLH				
Fixed factory overhead:				
Supervision	$ 1,700	$ 1,700	$ 1,700	$ 1,700
Depreciation—Plant	2,000	2,000	2,000	2,000
Depreciation—Equipment	5,000	5,000	5,000	5,000
Property taxes	1,000	1,000	1,000	1,000
Insurance—Factory	300	300	300	300
Total	$10,000	$10,000	$10,000	$10,000

Fixed-overhead rate based on denominator application level of 10,000 hours, $1.00 per DLH

variable overhead, because by definition, anticipated total variable overhead would be $8,500 at a 5,000-hour level of activity and $25,500 at a 15,000-hour level of activity—a constant hourly rate of $1.70 no matter what the volume.

fixed-overhead application and the denominator

To obtain a single standard product cost for pricing and inventory uses, a selection of an appropriate activity (often called *volume*) level is necessary. A predetermined rate for applying fixed overhead is computed as follows:

$$\left(\begin{array}{c}\text{Predetermined fixed}\\ \text{factory-overhead rate for}\\ \text{applying costs to product}\end{array}\right) = \frac{\text{Budgeted fixed factory overhead}}{\text{Some preselected activity level for the year}}$$

In Exhibit 9-3, the 10,000-hour level is merely an expression in monthly terms of the following plans for the year:

$$\text{Fixed-overhead rate} = \frac{\$120{,}000 \text{ (the budget for the year)}}{120{,}000 \text{ hours (the chosen denominator level of activity for the year)}}$$

$$= \$1.00 \text{ per direct-labor hour}$$

Note that Exhibit 9-3 expresses expectations in "average" monthly terms, but that the predetermination and choice of overhead rate is usually done annually. Therefore, the preselected activity level may be expressed as either 120,000 hours for the year or as an average of 10,000 hours per month. This preselected activity level will be referred to as the *denominator level.*

If fixed costs are important, the choice of the denominator level can have a significant effect on standard unit costs. For example, consider the data in Exhibit 9-3. Note how unit costs would change if a different denominator level were chosen:

(1) VARIOUS MONTHLY LEVELS OF ACTIVITY	*(2) TOTAL BUDGETED FIXED OVERHEAD FOR THE YEAR ($10,000 × 12 MONTHS)*	*(3) TOTAL VOLUME FOR THE YEAR (MONTHLY LEVEL × 12)*	*(2) ÷ (3) PREDETERMINED FIXED-OVERHEAD RATE FOR PRODUCT COSTING*
8,000	$120,000	96,000	$1.25
9,000	120,000	108,000	1.11
10,000	120,000	120,000	1.00
11,000	120,000	132,000	.91

selecting the denominator level

The selection of an appropriate denominator level for the predetermination of fixed-overhead rates is a matter of judgment; a dozen independent accountants or engineers would probably decide on a dozen different denominator levels based on the same set of available facts. Thus, the standard product cost would differ, depending on who sets the rate for fixed overhead. The problem of choosing the "best" denominator level is discussed more fully in the next chapter.

Exhibit 9-3 also indicates that the applications to product of both variable and fixed overhead are based on standard direct-labor hours allowed. Ideally, separate criteria may be used in selecting a base for a variable-overhead rate, as opposed to those used in selecting a different base for a fixed-overhead rate. The variable-overhead rate would be related to the activity base that is most logically linked to fluctuations in variable-overhead costs. On the other hand, fixed overhead does not vary in relation to any base; therefore, the preferred base for applying fixed overhead is one that best expresses the production capability of the plant. One of the purposes of fixed-overhead application is to obtain some measurement of the utilization of capacity. Where there are a variety of products, this capacity measure is often fundamentally expressed as labor-hours or machine-hours.

Although fixed-overhead rates are important for product costing and long-run pricing, such rates *have limited significance for control purposes.* At the lower levels of supervision, almost no fixed costs are under direct control; even at higher levels of supervision, few fixed costs are controllable within wide ranges of anticipated activity.

general-ledger entries

Consider the following facts as an example of the monthly treatment of fixed overhead in the general ledger:

Fixed overhead budgeted (this total is the same over wide ranges of activity)	$10,000
Denominator level, expressed in standard hours allowed for good output	10,000
Predetermined overhead rate per hour	$ 1.00
Actual fixed overhead incurred	$10,200
Fixed overhead applied (computed by multiplying $1.00 × 8,000, the good output expressed in standard hours allowed)	$ 8,000
Underapplied fixed overhead, $10,200 − $8,000	$ 2,200
Actual hours of input	7,900

The summary general-ledger treatment of the facts above would be:

Fixed factory-overhead control	10,200	
Accrued payroll, Allowance for depreciation, etc.		10,200
To record actual fixed overhead incurred. Detailed postings of fixed-overhead items, such as salaries, depreciation, property taxes, and insurance, would be made to the department-overhead sheets in the subsidiary ledger for Fixed Factory-Overhead Control.		
Work in process (at standard)	8,000	
Fixed factory overhead applied		8,000
To apply overhead at the predetermined rate times work done as expressed in standard hours allowed. Note that this total differs from the fixed-overhead budget for this level of activity. The budget total for fixed overhead is $10,000 at any level of activity.		

analysis of fixed-overhead variance The first step in analyzing overhead is to calculate the under- or overapplied overhead. In this example, the underapplied overhead is $2,200, the difference between $10,200 incurred and $8,000 applied. This $2,200 may be broken down into two subvariances, the *budget variance* and the *denominator variance.* A variance report may take the form of Exhibit 9-4.

EXHIBIT 9-4

M COMPANY
MACHINING DEPARTMENT
Analysis of Variance in Fixed Overhead for the Month Ending March 31, 19_1

ITEM[a]	*ACTUAL*	*BUDGET*	*VARIANCE*	*EXPLANATION*
Supervision	$ 1,700	$ 1,700	$ —	
Depreciation—Plant	2,000	2,000	—	
Depreciation—Equipment	5,000	5,000	—	
Property taxes	1,150	1,000	150 U	Increased assessment
Insurance—Factory	350	300	50 U	Increased coverage
	$10,200[a]	$10,000	$200 U	

Summary analysis. The denominator activity for setting the rate is 10,000 standard hours. Standard hours allowed for output were 8,000.

(1) ACTUAL INPUTS × ACTUAL PRICES	*(2)* FLEXIBLE BUDGET BASED ON ACTUAL INPUTS	*(3)* FLEXIBLE BUDGET BASED ON ACTUAL OUTPUTS ACHIEVED	*(4)* APPLIED
	Same regardless of volume level	Same regardless of volume level	(8,000 × $1.00)
$10,200	$10,000	$10,000	$8,000

Between (1) and (2): Spending variance, $200 U[b]
Between (2) and (3): No variance[c]
Between (3) and (4): Denominator variance, $2,000 U[d]

Between (1) and (3): Budget variance, $200 U[b]
Between (3) and (4): Denominator variance, $2,000 U

Between (1) and (4): Underapplied overhead, $2,200 U

[a] To simplify the example, not all possible fixed-overhead items are included here.

[b] The *budget variance* for fixed overhead is the difference between the amount incurred and the budget figure. Keep in mind that the budget figure would be the same regardless of the actual level of activity. Note that the *spending variance* and the *budget variance* are always equal.

[c] There is no efficiency variance for fixed overhead, as is explained later in the text.

[d] The *denominator variance* is also called the *volume variance,* the *utilization variance,* the *activity variance,* and the *capacity variance. It is the difference between fixed overhead applied and budgeted. It can also be expressed as the fixed-overhead rate times the difference between the denominator hours used for determining the rate and standard hours allowed for the outputs achieved.*

Unless otherwise stated, hereafter the terms *flexible-budget variance* and *budget variance* will be used interchangeably. That is, the use of a flexible budget will be implied whenever a budget is used. Moreover, the flexible-budget concept will pertain to all costs, variable and fixed, even though the fixed portion of any flexible budget will be the same regardless of the fluctuations in activity within the relevant range.

nature of fixed-overhead variances

The major difficulty in analyzing fixed-overhead variances arises from the fundamental behavior of fixed costs in relation to the dual purposes (control and product costing) of cost accounting. For control purposes, each overhead item is studied in relation to changes in activity. Budgets are devised, and results are compared with the budget. The deviations from budget are known as *flexible-budget variances.* Although these fixed-overhead variances are often beyond immediate managerial control, this information at least calls attention to changes in price factors. For example, property insurance rates may rise unexpectedly.

Think about the flexible budget once again. How flexible is it, really? The flex in the flexible budget is confined to the variable costs. The fixed- overhead component is really static for a wide range of anticipated activity. Thus, the typical flexible budget for overhead is really composed of two separate budgets: a really flexible budget for variable overhead plus a static budget for fixed overhead. This point is important. The analysis of fixed-overhead variance differs from the analysis of variable-overhead variance **because fixed costs do not behave in the same way, nor do they have the same control features.**

Exhibit 9-5 compares the general behavior patterns of variable and fixed overhead. Costs are plotted on the vertical axis (the y-axis) while volume is plotted on the horizontal axis (the x-axis). First, concentrate on the budget lines. Note that the budget line for variable overhead extends diagonally upward, although the budget line for fixed overhead is horizontal.

Now concentrate on the graph for variable overhead. At zero volume, no variable overhead is incurred, nor is any variable overhead applied to production—there is no production. The cost line slopes upward at the rate of $1.70 per standard direct-labor hour. Slope is the amount by which y increases when x increases by one unit, or the variable-overhead cost per unit of product. The equation for this budget is $y = bx$ ($y = \$1.70x$); the same equation holds for overhead application, so a single line portrays *both* budgeted amounts for control and overhead application for product costing. **Conceptually, there are really two lines on the graph—the budget line and the applied line—but they are superimposed on one another.**

If actual costs lie above the budget and overhead-applied line, the budget variance is unfavorable, and vice versa.

EXHIBIT 9-5

COMPARISON OF CONTROL AND PRODUCT-COSTING PURPOSES, VARIABLE AND FIXED OVERHEAD

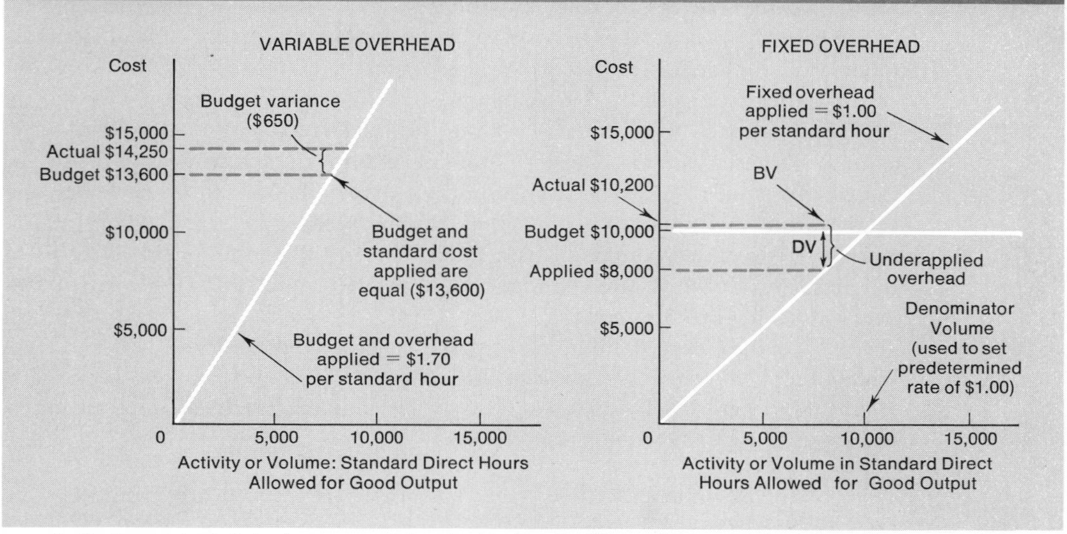

For fixed overhead, note that under-or overapplied overhead is always the difference between actual costs incurred and costs applied. An analysis of this variance may then be made:

Underapplied overhead = Budget variance + Denominator variance
= BV ($200) + DV ($2,000)

Now examine fixed overhead. For product-costing purposes, it is necessary to apply fixed overhead by using a predetermined rate that is usually based on standard hours allowed at some denominator level of activity. This predetermined rate is used to cost production regardless of the actual activity levels encountered. A *denominator* variance ($2,000, in the example above) arises whenever production expressed in standard hours allowed for the output achieved deviates from the activity level selected as the denominator for computing the product-costing rate. *The denominator variance is a conventional measure of the cost of failure to operate at the denominator activity (or the benefit of operating at above the denominator activity.)*[2]

Most companies consider denominator variances to be beyond immediate control—although sometimes the top sales executive has to do some explaining

[2] *Denominator variance* is a term being introduced here to supplant *volume variance*, a term that is most often used to describe the denominator variance. The reason for using denominator variance is that it more clearly describes the nature of the variance, which arises from the choice of some denominator and is measured by deviations from that denominator. In contrast, volume variance is used loosely in practice. For example, it is frequently used to describe two different types of variances: the denominator variance as explained here plus a true volume variance arising from not having sales or production reach the original targets in a master budget. For a fuller discussion, see the final section of Chapter 10.

or investigating, because denominator volume is often geared to anticipated sales. Sometimes, failure to reach denominator volume is caused by idleness due to poor production scheduling, unusual machine breakdowns, shortages of skilled workers, strikes, storms, and the like.

There is no denominator variance for variable overhead. The concept of denominator variance arises for fixed overhead because of the conflict between accounting for control (by budgets) and accounting for product costing (by application rates). Note carefully that the fixed-overhead budget serves the control purpose, whereas the development of a product-costing rate results in the treatment of fixed overhead *as if it were* a variable cost. In other words, the applied line in Exhibit 9-5 is artificial in the sense that, for product-costing purposes, it seemingly transforms a fixed cost into a variable cost. This bit of magic forcefully illustrates the distinction between accounting for control and accounting for product costing.

To summarize, denominator variance arises because the activity level encountered (expressed as *standard hours allowed*) frequently does not coincide with the activity level used as a basis for selecting a predetermined product-costing rate for fixed factory overhead.

1. When denominator activity and standard hours allowed are identical, there is no denominator variance.
2. When standard hours allowed are less than denominator activity, the denominator variance is unfavorable. It is measured in Exhibit 9-5 as follows:

$$(\text{Denominator activity} - \text{Standard hours allowed}) \times \text{Predetermined fixed overhead rate} = \text{Denominator variance}$$

$$(10{,}000 \text{ hours} - 8{,}000 \text{ hours}) \times \$1.00 = \$2{,}000$$

or

$$\text{Budget minus Applied} = \text{Denominator variance}$$
$$\$10{,}000 - \$8{,}000 = \$2{,}000$$

3. When standard hours allowed exceed denominator activity, the denominator variance is favorable, because it is an index of better-than-denominator utilization of facilities.

weaknesses and dangers in fixed-overhead analysis

Above all, we should recognize that fixed costs are simply not divisible like variable costs; they come in lump sums and they are related to the provision of big chunks of production or sales capability rather than to the production or sale of a single unit of product.

There are conflicting views on how fixed-overhead variances are best analyzed. These views are discussed in Chapter 28. Obviously, the "best" way is the one that provides management in a particular company with the most insight. Consequently, overhead analysis varies from company to company. In many companies, variances are most usefully expressed in physical terms only. For instance, a denominator variance could be expressed in machine-hours or kilowatt-hours.

The position in this chapter has been to distinguish between fixed and variable overhead as separate management problems. This contrasts with the tendency among many accountants to analyze variable costs and fixed costs in a parallel manner. For instance, an efficiency variance for fixed overhead is often computed, just as it is for the other variable costs:[3]

$$\text{Efficiency variance} = (\text{Actual hours} - \text{Standard hours allowed}) \times \text{Hourly fixed-overhead rate}$$

However, the resulting variance is very different from the efficiency variances for materials, labor, and variable overhead. Efficient usage of these three factors can affect actual cost, but short-run fixed-overhead cost is not affected by efficiency. Furthermore, the managers responsible for inefficiency will be aware of its existence through reports on variable-cost control, so there is little to gain from expressing ineffective utilization of facilities in historical dollar terms.

Finally, what is the economic significance of unit fixed costs? Unlike variable costs, total fixed costs do not change in the short run as production or sales fluctuate. *Management would obtain a better measure of the cost of underutilization of physical facilities by trying to approximate the related lost-contribution margins instead of the related historical fixed costs.* Fixed-cost incurrence often involves lump-sum outlays based on a pattern of expected recoupment. But ineffective utilization of existing facilities has no bearing on the amount of fixed costs currently incurred. The economic effects of the inability to reach target volume levels are often directly measured by lost-contribution margins, even if these have to be approximated. The historical-cost approach fails to emphasize the distinction between *fixed-cost incurrence,* on the one hand, and the objective of *maximizing the total contribution margin,* on the other hand. These are separable management problems, and the utilization of existing capacity is more closely related to the latter.[4]

[3] Some accountants favor computing denominator variance on the basis of the difference between the fixed-overhead budget ($10,000) and (*actual* hours worked × fixed-overhead rate). In this example, the denominator variance would then become $10,000 − (7,900 × $1), or $2,100 unfavorable. The remaining variance of $100 favorable [(actual hours − standard hours) × $1 overhead rate] is sometimes called the fixed-overhead *efficiency* or *effectiveness* variance—the measure of the ineffective use or waste of facilities because of off-standard labor performance. This breakdown of the denominator variance really attempts to separate the cost of *misused* facilities from the cost of *unused* facilities.

The author thinks this refinement is unnecessary in most cases, because (a) in the short run, total fixed costs incurred are *not* changed by efficiency changes, and (b) if the budget uses standard hours as a base, the denominator variance is more logically calculated by comparing standard hours achieved with the denominator volume that was used as a basis for setting the predetermined overhead rate. For an elaboration, see Chapter 28.

[4] For an elaboration of these ideas, see Charles T. Horngren, "A Contribution Margin Approach to the Analysis of Capacity Utilization," *The Accounting Review,* Vol. XLII, No. 2, pp. 254–64.

For instance, in our example the variance was computed at $2,000 by multiplying a unit fixed cost of $1.00 by the 2,000-hour difference between the 10,000 hours of denominator activity and 8,000 standard hours allowed. This $2,000 figure may be helpful in the sense that management is alerted in some crude way to the probable costs of failure to use 10,000 hours. But the more relevant information is the lost-contribution margins that pertain to the 2,000 hours. This information may not be so easy to obtain. The lost-contribution margins may be zero in those cases where there are no opportunities to obtain any contribution margin from alternative uses of available capacity; in other cases, however, the lost-contribution margins may be substantial. For example, if demand is high, the breakdown of key equipment may cost a company many thousands of dollars in lost-contribution margins. Unfortunately, in these cases, existing accounting systems would show denominator variances based on the unitized fixed costs and entirely ignore any lost-contribution margins.

combined-overhead rate and two-way and three-way analysis

combined rate

Many companies, while separating variable overhead and fixed overhead for control purposes, combine them for product-costing purposes and use a single predetermined overhead rate. In the example in this chapter, such a rate would be $2.70, which is the variable-overhead rate of $1.70 plus the fixed-overhead rate of $1.00. (See Exhibit 9-3.) In such cases, the overhead-variance analysis would merely be sums of what we computed earlier. Do not attempt the study of this section until you are thoroughly familiar with the earlier material in this chapter.

The easiest way to grasp these relationships is to examine Exhibit 9-6, which is really a combination of the two graphs in Exhibit 9-5. You can readily see that what we are about to study is **nothing more than a simultaneous consideration of the variable and fixed components, where the flexible-budget formula is expressed as $10,000 per month plus $1.70 per hour.**

Exhibit 9-7 provides a comprehensive analysis of all relationships among the combined-overhead analysis and its variable and fixed parts. Study it slowly, step by step.

Even when the actual overhead costs cannot be separated into variable and fixed components, it is still possible to generate almost all of the flexible-budget analysis illustrated in the chapter. The only variances that could not be derived are the separate variable-overhead spending variance and the separate fixed-overhead budget variance.

two-way and three-way analysis

Note that Exhibit 9-7 distinguishes between the so-called two-way and three-way overhead analysis. The three-way analysis is the method that was used earlier in the chapter,

EXHIBIT 9-6

COMBINED VARIABLE- AND FIXED-OVERHEAD BUDGET AND APPLICATION OF VARIOUS MONTHLY PRODUCTION VOLUMES

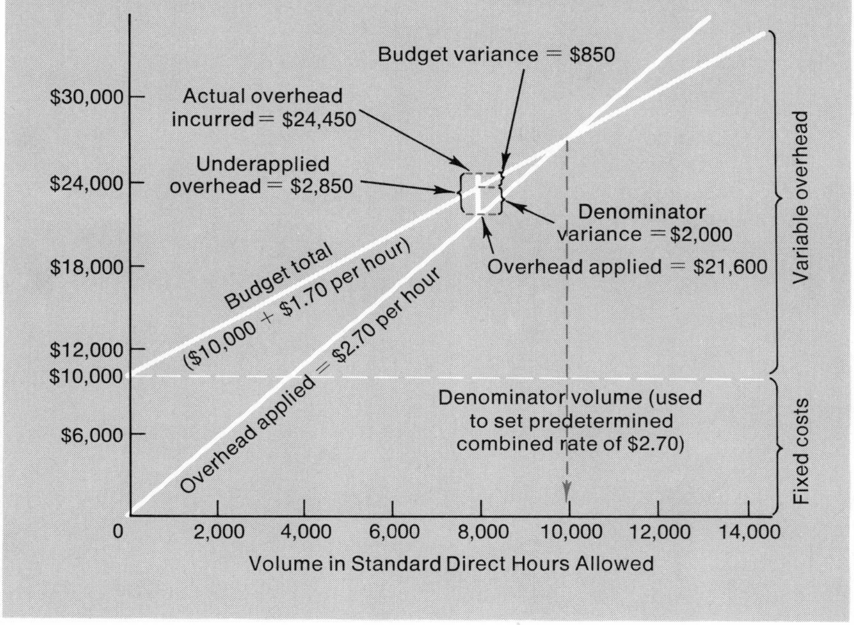

where three different variances were computed: spending, efficiency, and denominator variances. The two-way analysis computes only two: budget (sometimes called the *controllable variance*) and denominator variances. The budget variance, as is clear in Exhibit 9-7, is simply the difference between actual costs and the budget allowance based on standard hours allowed. The two-way analysis stops there; it does not subdivide the budget variance into spending and efficiency variances.

SUMMARY

Thorough study of the contents of this chapter should be rewarding, because analysis of overhead variances must consider two major frames of reference: the flexible budget for control and the use of predetermined overhead rates for product costing. The budget variance is considered to be controllable, at least to some degree. The denominator variance is considered uncontrollable in most instances. Thus, this chapter has highlighted and contrasted the many purposes that must be served in accounting for overhead. The general ledger is designed mainly to serve purposes of product costing.

EXHIBIT 9-7

WORKSHEET SUMMARY OF RELATIONSHIPS OF COMBINED-OVERHEAD ANALYSIS AND ITS VARIABLE AND FIXED PARTS

	(1) ACTUAL INPUTS × ACTUAL PRICES	(2) FLEXIBLE BUDGET* BASED ON ACTUAL INPUTS	(3) FLEXIBLE BUDGET* BASED ON ACTUAL OUTPUTS ACHIEVED	(4) APPLIED
V	14,250	(7,900 × $1.70) 13,430	(8,000 × $1.70) 13,600	(8,000 × $1.70) = 13,600
F	10,200	Lump-sum 10,000	Lump-sum 10,000	(8,000 × $1.00) = 8,000
Combined	24,450	23,430	23,600	(8,000 × $2.70) = 21,600

3-way Analysis

	Spending Variance (1) − (2)	Efficiency Variance (2) − (3)	Denominator Variance (3) − (4)
V	820 U	170 Fav.	(not applicable)
F	200 U	(not applicable)	2,000 U
Combined	1,020 U	170 Fav.	2,000 U

2-way Analysis

	Flexible-Budget Variance (1) − (3)	Denominator Variance (3) − (4)
V	650 U	(not applicable)
F	200 U	2,000 U
Combined	850 U	2,000 U

	Underapplied Overhead (1) − (4)
V	650 U
F	2,200 U
Combined	2,850 U

U = Unfavorable Fav. = Favorable V = Variable F = Fixed

* Budget Formula: $10,000 per month + $1.70 per hour.

Note: See footnote 3 in this chapter for a discussion of an alternative way to compute the denominator variance.

Yet management's major purpose, that of control, is aided by using flexible-budget figures, which are not highlighted in general-ledger balances. As is often the case, conventional general-ledger bookkeeping for overhead often provides only a minimum of the information needed for control.

This chapter covered only some of the many methods of budgeting overhead, applying overhead, and analyzing overhead variances. How overhead is budgeted, applied, analyzed, and reported is really determined by the individual managements concerned. For further consideration of alternative versions of overhead analysis, see Chapter 28.

Note that the general-ledger entries in this chapter sharply distinguish between fixed and variable overhead. This treatment is more effective for management than combining the two because it emphasizes the basic differences in cost behavior of these two kinds of overhead. Such basic differences are often important in influencing managerial decisions. The final section demonstrates that these distinctions can be maintained even if a combined overhead rate is used for product costing.

The worksheet analysis illustrated in Exhibit 9-7 provides a useful approach to the analysis of overhead variances. The first step is to obtain the under- or overapplied overhead—the difference between overhead incurred and overhead applied. Then any further variance breakdowns can be added algebraically and checked against the total variance.

PROBLEM FOR SELF-STUDY

PROBLEM

The McDermott Furniture Company has established standard costs for the cabinet department, in which one size of a single four-drawer style of dresser is produced. The standard costs are used in evaluating actual performance. The standard costs of producing one of these dressers are shown below:

STANDARD-COST CARD

Dresser, Style AAA

Materials: Lumber—50 board feet @ \$.20	\$10.00
Direct labor: 3 hours @ \$6.00	18.00
Indirect costs:	
Variable charges—3 hours @ \$1.00	3.00
Fixed charges—3 hours @ \$.50	1.50
Total per dresser	\$32.50

The costs of operations to produce 400 of these dressers during January are stated below (there were no initial inventories):

Materials purchased:	25,000 board feet @ \$.21	\$5,250.00
Materials used:	19,000 board feet	
Direct labor:	1,100 hours at \$5.90	6,490.00
Indirect costs:		
Variable charges		1,300.00
Fixed charges		710.00

The flexible budget for this department at the monthly activity level used to set the fixed-overhead rate called for 1,400 direct-labor hours of operation. At this level, the variable indirect cost was budgeted at \$1,400, and the fixed indirect cost at \$700.

required

All journal entries. Compute the following variations from standard cost. Label your answers as *favorable* (F) or *unfavorable* (U).

1. Material purchase price, isolated at time of purchase.
2. Material efficiency.
3. (a) Direct-labor price;
   (b) Direct-labor efficiency.
4. (a) Variable-overhead budget variance;
   (b) Fixed-overhead budget variance;
   (c) Fixed-overhead denominator variance.
5. (a) Variable-overhead spending variance;
   (b) Variable-overhead efficiency variance.

SOLUTION

Journal entries are supported by pertinent variance analysis.

1. Stores control (25,000 @ $.20)	5,000	
Material purchase-price variance (25,000 @ $.01)	250	
Accounts payable (25,000 @ $.21)		5,250
2. Work-in-process control (400 units × 50 board feet × $.20)	4,000	
Material-efficiency variance (1,000 × $.20)		200
Stores control (19,000 × $.20)		3,800
3. Work-in-process control (400 units × $18.00)	7,200	
Direct-labor price variance (1,100 hrs. × $.10)		110
Direct-labor efficiency variance (100 hrs. × $6.00)		600
Accrued payroll (1,100 hrs. × $5.90)		6,490
For analysis of variances, see Exhibit 9-8.		
4. Variable-overhead control	1,300	
Accounts payable and other accounts		1,300
Work-in-process control	1,200	
Variable overhead applied (400 × 3 × $1.00)		1,200
5. Fixed-overhead control	710	
Accounts payable and other accounts		710
Work-in-process control	600	
Fixed overhead applied (400 × 3 × $.50)		600

The analysis of variances in Exhibit 9-8 summarizes the characteristics of different cost behavior patterns. The approaches to direct labor and variable overhead are basically the same. Furthermore, there is no fundamental conflict between the budgetary-control and product-costing purposes; that is, the applied amounts in column (4) also equal the flexible-budget allowances. In contrast, the behavior patterns and control features of fixed overhead require a different analytical approach. The budget is static, not flexible. There is no efficiency variance for fixed factory overhead because short-run performance cannot ordinarily affect incurrence of fixed factory overhead. Finally, there will nearly always be a conflict between the budgetary-control and product-costing purposes because the applied amount in column (4) for fixed overhead will differ from the static budget allowance. The latter conflict is highlighted by the denominator variance, which measures the effects of working at other than the volume used to set the product-costing rate.

EXHIBIT 9-8

McDERMOTT FURNITURE COMPANY

Analysis of Manufacturing Costs

Direct Materials

	(1) Actual Inputs × Actual Price		(2) Actual × Standard Price: Purchases	(2) Actual × Standard Price: Usage		(3) Flexible Budget* Based on Actual Outputs Achieved
Direct Materials	(25,000 @ \$.21) \$5,250		(25,000 @ \$.20) \$5,000	(19,000 @ \$.20) \$3,800		(20,000 @ \$.20) \$4,000
		(25,000 × \$.01) Price Variance, \$250 U			(1,000 × \$.20) Efficiency Variance, \$200 F	

Direct Labor, Variable Overhead, Fixed Overhead

	(1)		(2) Flexible Budget Based on Actual Inputs		(3)		(4) Applied
Direct Labor	(1,100 × \$5.90) \$6,490		(1,100 × \$6.00) \$6,600		(400 × 3) × \$6.00 \$7,200		
		(1,100 × \$.10) Price Variance, \$110 F		(100 × \$6.00) Efficiency Variance, \$600 F			
	Flexible-Budget Variance, \$710 F						
Variable Overhead	(1,100 × \$1.1818) \$1,300		(1,100 × \$1.00) \$1,100		(1,200 × \$1.00) \$1,200*		(1,200 × \$1.00) \$1,200
		(1,100 × \$.1818) Spending Variance, \$200 U		(100 × \$1.00) Efficiency Variance, \$100 F		No Variance	
	Flexible-Budget Variance, \$100 U					No Variance	
	Underapplied Overhead, \$100 U						
Fixed Overhead	\$710	Lump-sum	\$700	Lump-sum	\$700†		1,200 × \$.50 \$600
		Spending, \$10 U		No Variance		Denominator Variance, \$100 U	
	Flexible-Budget Variance, \$10 U					(1,400 − 1,200) × \$.50 Denominator Variance, \$100 U	
	Underapplied Overhead, \$110 U						

U = Unfavorable F = Favorable *See next page. †See next page.

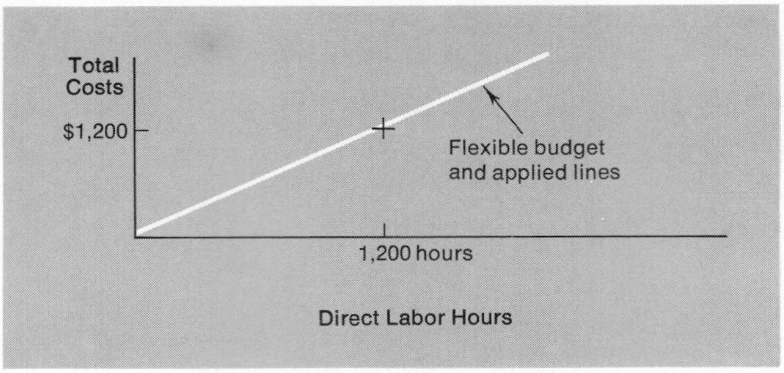

* Graphically, the flexible budget line for variable costs and the applied line for variable costs are superimposed. Example above is for variable overhead.

† Graphically, the flexible budget line for fixed costs is not really flexible because it is horizontal (the total budgeted fixed overhead is the same over a wide range of volume). Hence the budget amount will differ from the applied amount when activity is not at the level (hence called denominator activity) used to set the fixed overhead rate for product costing.

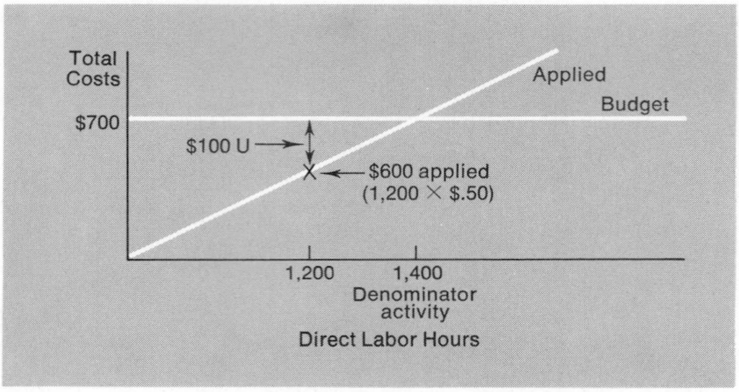

In sum, the accountant is faced with a special problem with regard to fixed overhead, which has very different cost behavior characteristics and cost control features than variable overhead. In trying to apply fixed overhead to product, he must develop a predetermined costing rate. In so doing, he has to select a level of activity as the denominator in his formula:

$$\text{Fixed overhead rate} = \frac{\text{Budget}}{\text{Denominator activity}} = \frac{\$700}{1{,}400 \text{ hours}} = \$.50 \text{ per hour}$$

Therefore, a denominator variance will arise when ensuing activity differs from denominator activity. Denominator variance arises only in connection with fixed overhead. There is no denominator variance for variable overhead. The budget and the applied amounts for fixed overhead will usually not be equal, in contrast to the equality of the amounts for variable costs.

The following is a summary of variances:

1. Material purchase price	$250 U
2. Material efficiency	200 F
3. (a) Direct-labor price	110 F
(b) Direct-labor efficiency	600 F
4. (a) Variable-overhead budget variance	100 U
(b) Fixed-overhead budget variance	10 U
(c) Fixed-overhead denominator variance	100 U
5. (a) Variable-overhead spending variance	200 U
(b) Variable-overhead efficiency variance	100 F

overhead variances in the ledger

There are several ways of accounting for overhead variances. The easiest way is probably to allow the department-overhead control accounts and applied accounts to cumulate month-to-month postings until the end of the year. Monthly variances would not be isolated formally in the accounts, although monthly variance reports would be prepared. Assume that the data in the self-study problem are for the *year* rather than for the *month*. At the year-end, isolating and closing entries could be made as follows:

6. Variable factory overhead applied	$1,200	
Variable-overhead spending variance	200	
Variable-overhead efficiency variance		$ 100
Variable factory-overhead control		1,300
To isolate variances for the year.		
7. Fixed factory overhead applied	600	
Fixed-overhead budget (or spending)[4] variance	10	
Fixed-overhead denominator variance	100	
Fixed factory-overhead control		710
To isolate variances for the year.		
8. Income summary (or Cost of goods sold)	100	
Variable-overhead efficiency variance	100	
Variable-overhead spending variance		200
To close.		
9. Income summary (or Cost of goods sold)	110	
Fixed-overhead budget variance		10
Fixed-overhead denominator variance		100
To close.		

If desired, the isolation entries for the monthly variances could be made monthly, although the closing entries are usually confined to the year-end.

Of course, rather than being closed directly to the Income Summary or Cost of Goods Sold, in certain cases the overhead variances may be prorated at the year-end, as is shown in the next chapter.

QUESTIONS, PROBLEMS, AND CASES

9-1 What is the essential difficulty in applying fixed overhead to product?

9-2 "There should be an efficiency variance for fixed overhead. A foreman can inefficiently use his fixed resources." Comment.

9-3 *Fundamentals of Overhead Variances* The Allen Company has a standard absorption costing and flexible budgeting system. The standard costs of its two products differ slightly because the direct materials are $9.00 higher per unit for Product B. The standard costs for Product A include:

Direct materials, 3 pounds @ $20.00	$60.00
Direct labor, 5 hours @ $10.00	50.00

For budgetary-control purposes, production is expressed in standard hours allowed. Denominator activity is expressed as 20,000 standard direct-labor hours per month. Fixed factory overhead is budgeted at $120,000 per month.

[4] Under this approach, you will sometimes encounter the terms fixed-overhead *budget variance* and *spending variance* being used interchangeably to denote the same variance. Also, our approach provides no efficiency variance for fixed overhead.

The predetermined fixed overhead rate for product costing is not changed from month to month or within months.

required

1. All factory overhead is applied to product on the basis of standard direct-labor hours allowed per finished unit. The variable factory overhead rate is $4.00 per direct-labor hour. Compute the standard absorption cost per unit of Product A. What is the variable factory overhead per unit of Product A? Fixed factory overhead per unit?
2. Graph (a) the budgeted variable overhead and (b) the applied variable overhead from 16,000 to 26,000 hours.
3. Graph (a) the budgeted fixed overhead and (b) the applied fixed overhead from 16,000 to 26,000 hours.
4. Assume that 17,000 standard direct-labor hours are allowed for all output during a given month. Input was 17,900 actual hours used. Actual overhead incurred was: variable $80,000 and fixed, $125,000. What is the variable-overhead flexible-budget variance? Spending and efficiency variances? Fixed-overhead flexible-budget variance? Denominator variance? Show how you obtained your answers.
5. Repeat part 4, but assume that 24,000 standard direct-labor hours are allowed for all output during a given month. Input was 22,800 actual hours used. Actual overhead incurred was: variable, $100,000 and fixed, $116,000.

9-4 *Journal Entries* Refer to Problem 9-3. Prepare the necessary journal entries to record the overhead transactions described in requirement 4.

9-5 *Variance Analysis and Journal Entries for Overhead* The Starr Company uses a standard-cost system. Denominator output per month is 5,000 units.

Standard Costs:	
Direct labor, 3 hrs. @ $5.00	$15.00
Direct materials, 20 lbs @ $.30	6.00
Overhead, 20% of direct labor	3.00
Total cost per finished unit	$24.00

The following production data are for the month of July 19_0:

Work in process, July 1	-0-
Units completed by July 31	4,500
Work in process, July 31	-0-
Materials purchased, 120,000 lbs. @ $.31	$ 37,200
Materials used	105,000 lbs.
Variable overhead incurred	$ 8,500
Direct-labor use, 13,750 hrs. @ $5.10 per hr.	$ 70,125
Fixed overhead incurred	$ 6,000

The overhead flexible-budget formula has a variable cost component of 60¢ per standard direct-labor hour.

required

1. Prepare complete analyses of variances for materials, labor, variable overhead, and fixed overhead.
2. Prepare journal entries for the overhead incurrence and application. You may omit the entries for materials and labor.

9-6 *Comprehensive, Straightforward Problem on a Standard-Cost System* The Brandon Company uses a standard cost system. The month's data regarding its lone product follows:

Fixed-overhead costs incurred, $6,150
Variable overhead applied at $.90 per hour
Standard direct-labor cost, $4.00 per hour
Standard material cost, $1.00 per pound
Standard pounds of material in a finished unit, 3
Denominator production per month, 2,500 units
Standard direct-labor hours per finished unit, 5
Materials purchased, 10,000 lbs., $9,500
Materials used, 6,700 lbs.
Direct-labor costs incurred, 11,000 hours, $41,800
Variable-overhead costs incurred, $9,500
Fixed-overhead budget variance, $100, favorable
Finished units produced, 2,000

required

Prepare journal entries. Prepare schedules of all variances, using the worksheet approach described in this chapter. Material price variances are isolated as materials are purchased.

9-7 *Straightforward Overhead Analysis* The Crum Company uses a standard-cost system. Its standard cost of Product Y, based on a denominator activity of 40,000 units per year, included six hours of variable overhead at $.80 per hour and six hours of fixed overhead at $1.50 per hour. Actual output achieved was 44,000 units. Actual variable factory overhead was $240,000. Actual hours of input were 284,000. Actual fixed overhead was $368,000.

Prepare journal entries. Prepare a worksheet analysis for all variable-overhead and fixed-overhead variances, using the approach illustrated in the chapter.

9-8 *Characteristics of Fixed-Overhead Variances* The Clive Company is preparing revised standards for the forthcoming year, 19_5. The standard time allowed for manufacturing one unit of product is thirty minutes. Expected production for 19_5 is 400,000 units of product. Expected fixed factory overhead is $600,000; expected variable overhead is $2 per standard direct-labor hour.

required

1. If denominator activity is 200,000 standard hours allowed, what is the fixed factory overhead rate per hour? Graph the budgeted and the applied fixed factory overhead for a volume of 100,000 to 300,000 hours.
2. It is the end of 19_5. Compare the effects of three different assumptions regarding actual production:

ASSUMPTION	ACTUAL UNITS OF PRODUCT MANUFACTURED
(a)	300,000
(b)	400,000
(c)	500,000

What is the denominator variance for each assumption? Show how the denominator variance would appear on a graph for each assumption. In your own words, define a denominator variance. Why does it arise? Can a denominator variance exist for variable overhead? Why?
3. Assume that the actual fixed overhead for 19_5 was $630,000. What is the budget variance? Are the denominator variances in part 2 affected by this additional information? If so, how? If not, why?
4. Return to part 1. What would be the fixed factory-overhead rate per hour if the denominator volume were 100,000 hours? If the denominator volume were 300,000 hours? Draw a graph showing three applied lines for denominator volumes of 100,000, 200,000, and 300,000 hours; indicate the fixed-overhead rate

represented by each line. Tabulate the denominator variances that would arise for each of these denominator volumes if actual production were 400,000 units. What are the implications of this part regarding the setting of product-costing rates for fixed overhead?

9-9 *Analysis of Fixed Overhead; Choice of Denominator* The fixed overhead items of the lathe department of The Clancy Company include, for the month of January, 19_4:

ITEM	ACTUAL	BUDGET
Supervision	$ 900	$ 800
Depreciation—Plant	750	750
Depreciation—Equipment	1,750	1,750
Property taxes	350	400
Insurance—Factory	400	300
	$4,150	$4,000

Expected activity for the lathe department is 1,000 standard hours per month. Maximum capacity is 1,600 standard hours per month. Standard hours allowed for good units actually produced were 1,250.

required

1. Prepare a summary analysis of fixed-overhead variances, using expected activity as the denominator base.
2. Prepare a summary analysis of fixed-overhead variances, using maximum capacity as the denominator base.
3. Explain why the budget variances in parts 1 and 2 are identical whereas the denominator variances are different.

9-10 *Find the Unknowns* Consider each of the following situations independently. Data refer to operations for a week in April. For each situation assume a standard product-cost system. Also assume the use of a flexible budget for control of variable and fixed overhead based on standard direct-labor hours.

	CASES		
	A	B	C
(1) Actual fixed overhead	—	$ 9,900	$12,550
(2) Actual variable overhead	$ 7,500	12,000	9,500
(3) Denominator activity in hours	10,000	—	6,000
(4) Standard hours allowed for good output	11,000	12,000	—
Flexible-budget data:			
(5) Fixed factory overhead	5,000	—	—
(6) Variable factory overhead (per standard hour)	70¢	—	75¢
(7) Budgeted fixed factory overhead	5,000	—	—
(8) Budgeted variable factory overhead*	—	—	—
(9) Total budgeted factory overhead*	—	a	21,000
(10) Standard variable overhead applied	—	—	9,000
(11) Standard fixed overhead applied	—	—	—
(12) Denominator variance	—	600F	—
(13) Variable-overhead spending variance	—	—	100F
(14) Variable-overhead efficiency variance	—	—	—
(15) Fixed-overhead budget variance	300U	—	—
(16) Actual hours of input	11,200	11,700	—

[a] $21,200 at 10,000 hours; $27,800 at 16,000 hours.

* For standard hours allowed for output achieved.

required

Fill in the blanks under each case. Prepare your answer by (a) listing the numbers that are blank for each case and (b) putting the final answers next to the numbers. Prepare supporting computations on a separate sheet. For example, your answer to Case A would contain a vertical listing of the numbers 1, 8, 9, 10, 11, 12, 13, and 14, with answers next to the appropriate numbers.

9-11 *Standard Times* The Smith Company manufactures electronic equipment. The president, Catherine Smith, heavily supports the use of a flexible budget and standard costs. Overhead is applied on the basis of standard labor-hours. The assembly department has concentrated on one product, a transformer, during the past week. The following standard rates were applicable: direct-labor rate, $9.00 per hour; combined overhead rate, $12.00 per hour; copper and other materials, $20.00 per unit.

The production schedule for the past week called for 3,750 direct-labor hours, $26,250 variable-overhead costs, and $25,000 fixed-overhead costs. The flexible budget indicates that total overhead is linear over a wide range and would amount to $49,500 and $56,500 at production levels of 700 units and 900 units weekly, respectively.

What is the standard time for assembling a transformer?

9-12 *Overhead Analysis* (SIA, adapted) The Ballentine Company produces a single product—spaghetti. The product unit is 100 pounds (cwt.) of spaghetti.

Monthly flexible-budget data follow:

Volume in units of product	15,000	25,000
Material costs	$ 30,000	$ 50,000
Direct labor	45,000	75,000
Factory overhead:		
Indirect material	15,000	25,000
Indirect labor	30,000	50,000
Supervision	26,250	33,750
Heat, light, and power	15,250	22,750
Depreciation	63,000	63,000
Insurance and taxes	8,000	8,000
Total overhead	$157,500	$202,500
Total manufacturing costs	$232,500	$327,500

Other information:

The standard time for one unit of product is 1.5 direct-labor hours.
The denominator activity is 30,000 direct-labor hours.
Actual data during June, 19_1:

Units produced	22,000
Actual direct-labor hours of input	32,000
Overhead incurred	$191,000

Standard factory overhead rates are based on direct-labor hours.

required

1. Prepare a summary factory-overhead variance analysis (using three variances) for June, 19_1. Show all computations.
2. What possible courses of action are open to management to investigate the variances?

9-13 *Combined Overhead Rate* The Wright-Peterson Air Force Base contained an extensive repair facility for jet engines. It had developed standard costing and flexible budgets for this activity. Budgeted *variable* overhead at a 16,000 standard monthly direct-labor-hour level was $64,000; budgeted *total* overhead at a 20,000 standard direct-labor-hour level was $197,600. The standard cost applied to repair output included a combined overhead rate of 120 percent of standard direct-labor cost.

Total actual overhead for October was $250,000. Direct-labor costs actually incurred were $202,440. The direct-labor price variance was $9,640, unfavorable. The di.ect-labor budget variance was $14,440, unfavorable. The standard labor price was $8.00 per hour. The denominator variance was $14,000, favorable.

required

Direct-labor efficiency variance. Combined overhead spending, efficiency, and denominator variances. Also compute the denominator volume. (Hint: See Exhibit 9-7.)

9-14 *Controllable Variances and Bonus* (SIA, adapted) At Stephens' Limited all departmental standard cost variances are classified as being controllable or noncontrollable by the department foreman in addition to being favorable or unfavorable. Controllable variances are totaled for each department and if the net amount is favorable, the foreman receives a bonus of 5 percent of the net favorable controllable variance. Of course, if unfavorable controllable variances are larger, no bonus is paid. The departmental foreman has no control over wage rates or volume of production, but he does control all overhead costs in relation to a flexible budget.

For Department XY, the budgeted overhead is $48,000 per month plus $2 per direct-labor hour. Material-cost variances are negligible for the month. The actual direct-labor cost for April was $69,000 (15,000 hours @ $4.60 per hour). Actual factory overhead for April was $77,500. The department's output for April had a standard cost of:

Labor	15,500 hours @ $4.50	=	$ 69,750
Overhead	15,500 hours @ $5.00	=	$ 77,500
			$147,250

required

1. Compute all the variances that can be computed from the above data presenting the details of all calculations. Indicate whether each variance is controllable or noncontrollable and favorable or unfavorable.
2. Calculate the foreman's bonus, if any.
3. What are the advantages and disadvantages of this system?

9-15 *Normal Costing and Overhead Analysis* The Blaney Company had *budgeted* the following performance for 19_4:

Units	10,000
Sales	$120,000
Total variable production costs, including variable factory overhead of $5,000	60,000
Total fixed production costs	25,000
Gross margin	35,000
Beginning inventories	None

It is now December 31, 19_4. The factory-overhead rate that was used throughout the year was $3 per unit. Total factory overhead incurred was $30,000. Underapplied factory overhead was $900. There is no work in process.

required

1. How many units were produced during 19_4?
2. Nine thousand units were sold at regular prices during 19_4. Assuming that the predicted cost behavior patterns implicit in the budget above have conformed to the plan (except for variable factory overhead), and that underapplied factory overhead is written off directly as an adjustment of cost of goods sold, what is the gross margin for 19_4? How much factory overhead should be assigned to the ending inventory if it is to be carried at "normal" cost?
3. Explain *why* overhead was underapplied by $900. In other words, analyze the variable- and fixed-overhead variances as far as the data permit.

9-16 *Variance Analysis; Find Standard Time per Unit* The Mahon Electrical Company manufactures special electrical equipment in Kowloon. The management has established standard costs for many of its operations and uses a flexible budget. Overhead is applied on a basis of standard labor-hours. The Transformer Assembly Department operates at the following standard rates:

STANDARD COSTS	
One Multiplex Transformer TR-906	
Materials:	
4 sheets soft iron, 9 × 16 in.	@ $1.12 ea.
2 spools copper wire	@ $2.39 ea.
Direct-labor rate	$2.50 per hour
Combined-overhead rate	$2.10 per direct-labor hour

The flexible budget indicates that total overhead would amount to $4,489 and $4,989 at production levels of 500 and 600 units, respectively. The production budget for the past month called for 2,340 direct-labor hours, $2,925 variable-overhead costs, and $1,989 fixed-overhead costs. Only 550 transformers were produced, at the costs listed below:

Materials purchased:
- 3,000 sheets soft iron, $3,300
- 1,500 spools copper wire, $3,600

Materials used:
- 2,215 sheets soft iron
- 1,106 spools copper wire

Direct labor:
- 2,113 hours, $5,409.28

Overhead:
- Variable costs, $2,769
- Fixed costs, $2,110

required

1. What is the standard time for assembling a transformer?
2. What is the standard unit cost?
3. What was the material-price variance during the past month?
4. The material-efficiency variance?
5. The direct-labor price variance?
6. The direct-labor efficiency variance?
7. Variable-overhead spending variance?
8. Variable-overhead efficiency variance?
9. Fixed-overhead budget variance?
10. Fixed-overhead denominator variance?

9-17 *Multiple Choice* (CMA adapted) The Organet Stamping Company manufactures a variety of products made of plastic and aluminum components. During the winter months substantially all of the production capacity is devoted to the production of lawn sprinklers for the following spring and summer season. Other products are manufactured during the remainder of the year. Because a variety of products are manufactured throughout the year, factory volume is measured by production labor-hours rather than units of product.

Production and sales volume have grown steadily for the past several years, as can be seen from the following schedule of standard production labor content of annual output expressed in hours:

19_3	32,000
19_2	30,000
19_1	27,000
19_0	28,000
19_9	26,000

The company has developed standard costs for its several products. Standard costs for each year are set in the preceding October. The standard cost of a sprinkler for 19_4 was $2.50, computed as follows:

Direct materials:			
Aluminum	.2 lbs.	@ $ .40 per lb.	$ .08
Plastic	1.0 lbs.	@ .38 per lb.	.38
Production labor	.3 hrs.	@ 4.00 per hr.	1.20
Overhead (calculated using 30,000 production labor-hours as denominator capacity):			
Variable	.3 hrs.	@ 1.60 per hr.	.48
Fixed	.3 hrs.	@ 1.20 per hr.	.36
Total			$2.50

During February 19_4, 8,500 good sprinklers were manufactured. The following costs were incurred:

Materials requisitioned for production:			
Aluminum	1,900 lbs.	@ $ .40 per lb.	$ 760
Plastic:			
Regular grade	6,000 lbs.	@ .38 per lb.	2,280
Low grade*	3,500 lbs.	@ .38 per lb.	1,330
Production labor:			
Straight time	2,300 hrs.	@ 4.00 per hr.	9,200
Overtime	400 hrs.	@ 6.00 per hr.	2,400
Overhead:			
Variable			5,200
Fixed			3,100
Total costs charged to manufacturing departments			$24,270

Material-price variations are not charged to production but to a material-price-variation account at the time the invoice is entered. All materials are carried in inventory at standard prices. Material purchases for February were:

Aluminum	1,800 lbs.	@ $ .48 per lb.	$ 864
Plastic:			
Regular grade	3,000 lbs.	@ .50	1,500
Low grade*	6,000 lbs.	@ .29	1,740

* Owing to plastic shortages, the company was forced to purchase lower-grade plastic than called for in the standards. This increased the number of sprinklers rejected on inspection.

Every item below is related to the above facts and should be answered on the basis of those facts. Show your computations. Choose the best answer:

1. The total variation from "standard cost applied" of the costs charged to manufacturing departments for February 19_4 is (a) $3,080 unfavorable, (b) $3,020 unfavorable, (c) $3,140 favorable, (d) $3,020 favorable, (e) some other amount.
2. The standard material quantities already include an allowance for acceptable material scrap loss. In this situation the material efficiency variations would most likely be caused by (a) defective aluminum, (b) improper processing by labor, (c) inadequate allowance for scrap loss, (d) substitute plastic, (e) none of these reasons.
3. The spending or budget variation for the fixed portion of the overhead costs is (a) $100 unfavorable, (b) $60 favorable, (c) zero, (d) not calculable from the problem, (e) not listed above.
4. The labor-efficiency variation is the difference between standard labor-hours allowed for output achieved and (a) 2,300 hours, (b) 2,700 hours, (c) 2,900 hours, (d) 2,500 hours, (e) some other amount.
5. The production labor-price variation is (a) $0, (b) $600 unfavorable, (c) $800 unfavorable, (d) $1,400 unfavorable (e) $2,400 unfavorable.
6. The manufacturing overhead denominator variation is (a) the result of inadequate cost-control effort, (b) the result of sales volume exceeding production volume, (c) the result of actual production hours exceeding standard production hours of output, (d) the result of the overapplication of fixed cost to output, (e) not the result of any of these reasons.
7. The variable-overhead-budget variation is (a) $1,120 unfavorable, (b) $1,220 unfavorable, (c) $1,160 unfavorable, (d) $1,280 unfavorable, (e) none of these.
8. The variations of material prices from standard would (a) best be reported as materials-price variations—$36 favorable, (b) best be reported as materials-price variations—aluminum, $144 unfavorable; plastic, $180 favorable, (c) best be reported as materials-price variations—aluminum, $144 unfavorable; plastic, $360 unfavorable; material substitution, $540 favorable, (d) best be reported as materials-price variations—aluminum, $144 unfavorable; plastic, $360 unfavorable; price difference due to plastic substitution not reported (e) not be reported because material prices are uncontrollable.

9-18 *Working Backwards* Reliance, Inc., utilizes a standard-cost system for budget and control purposes. Flexible budgets are determined, and all indirect costs are assigned on the basis of standard direct-labor hours.

The following standard cost per unit was determined on the basis of a projected monthly denominator activity for 19_6.

Direct materials: 3 lbs. @ $6.00	$18.00
Direct labor: 2 hours @ $6.00	12.00
Variable indirect costs: 2 hours @ $1.50	3.00
Fixed indirect costs: 2 hours @ $1.00	2.00
Total	$35.00

You have just received this condensed performance report for February 19_7.

	Standard Costs Applied	VARIANCE ANALYSIS Price or Rate	Efficiency	Denominator
Direct materials used	$162,000	$14,000 F	$6,000 U	—
Direct-labor costs	108,000	18,200 U	1,200 U	—
Variable indirect costs	27,000	5,250 U	300 U	—
Fixed indirect costs	18,000	1,500 U*	—	4,000 U

* 1,500 U is entire flexible-budget variance for fixed indirect costs.

required

1. Number of units produced.
2. Actual number of direct labor-hours of input.
3. Actual wage rate.
4. Actual fixed indirect costs.
5. Denominator activity (monthly) expressed in units.
6. Actual price paid per pound of direct materials.
7. Actual pounds of direct material used.

9-19 *Effects of Choice of Denominator* (SIA, adapted) In setting up the annual factory budget at the Talisman Company, the production manager and the sales manager spent much time discussing the volume level. As a result, the factory manager prepared two estimates of factory overhead:

VOLUME	TOTAL FACTORY OVERHEAD
150,000 units	$540,000
170,000 units	$564,000

At the last moment however, the sales manager obtained another order, which prompted management to set the predetermined overhead rate per unit at the 180,000-unit level; this rate was applied during the year.

During the latter part of the year sales dropped unexpectedly. Production was reduced immediately; however, 60,000 units of the annual production remained unsold in finished-goods inventory. Actual overhead amounted to $560,000. When the overhead variances were being analyzed, an unfavorable idle-capacity variance of $40,000 was determined.

required

1. Calculate the predetermined overhead rate used during the year and compute the over- (under-) application of overhead at year-end.
2. The company writes off overhead variances to cost of goods sold. What would have been the effect on the annual income statement and the year-end balance sheet, had the company used the actual overhead rate (as discovered at year-end), throughout the year, instead of the predetermined rate?

9-20 *Combined Overhead Variances* (SIA, adapted) The Weser Company uses a predetermined total overhead rate of $4.00 per unit based on a denominator capacity of 600,000 units a year or 50,000 units a month.

During October, the company produced 52,000 units and experienced the following combined overhead variances:

Overhead budget variance	$1,500 unfavorable
Overhead denominator variance	$5,000 favorable

During November, unit production was 49,000 units and the actual overhead cost incurred was $2,000 less than October's overhead.

Determine the overhead budget and denominator variances for the month of November.

9-21 *Hospital Cost Control* The Sharon Hospital, a large metropolitan health-care complex, has had much trouble in controlling its accounts receivable. Bills for patients, for various government agencies, and for private insurance companies have frequently been inaccurate and late. This has led to intolerable levels of bad debts and investments in receivables.

You were employed by the hospital as a consultant on this matter. After conducting a careful study of the billing operation, you developed some currently attainable standards that were implemented in conjunction with a flexible budget four weeks ago. You had divided costs into fixed and variable categories. You regarded the bill as the product, the unit of output.

You have reasonable confidence that the underlying source documents for compiling the results have been accurately tallied. However, the bookkeeper has had some trouble summarizing the data. He has provided the following:

Variable costs, including all billing operators, whose compensation is regarded as variable, allowance per standard hour	$ 10
Fixed overhead budget variance, favorable	200
Combined budgeted costs for the bills produced	22,500
Denominator variance, favorable	900
Variable-cost "spending" variance, unfavorable	2,000
Variable-cost efficiency variance, favorable	2,000
Standard hours allowed for the bills produced, 1,800	

required

1. Actual hours of input
2. Fixed-overhead budget
3. Standard fixed overhead applied
4. Denominator activity in hours

9-22 *Overhead Variances* In 19_4 the Howard Company used a predetermined *total* factory overhead rate of $7 per standard direct-labor hour allowed for product costing. Prior to 19_4 the company had used a normal denominator activity of 80,000 hours (based on average usage over four years) for developing an overhead rate for product costing. In 19_4 this budgetary practice changed, and management decided to use the expected annual activity of 70,000 standard allowed hours as the denominator volume for 19_4. No other changes in cost estimates were anticipated.

Management was conscious that this chosen denominator would incorporate an hourly amount of $.50, which represented a charge for idle capacity. That is, if the previous normal denominator activity of 80,000 hours had been used, the hourly total overhead application rate would have been lower by $.50.

The company used a flexible budget for control. The *total* factory overhead applied for the year 19_4 was $504,000, and the *total* overhead was overapplied by $6,000.

required

Compute:

1. Flexible-budget variance for *total* overhead.
2. Denominator variance.

9-23 *Variance Analysis from Fragmentary Evidence* Being a bright young person, you have just landed a wonderful job as assistant controller of Gyp-Clip, a new and promising division of Croding Metals Corporation. The Gyp-Clip Division has been formed to produce a single product, a new-model paper clip. Croding Laboratories has developed an extremely springy and lightweight new alloy, Clypton, which is expected to revolutionize the paper-clip industry.

Gyp-Clip has been in business one month; it is your first day on the job. The controller takes you on a tour of the plant and explains the operation in detail: Clypton wire is received on two-mile spools from the Croding mill at a fixed price of $40 a spool, which is not subject to change. Clips are bent, cut, and shipped in bulk to the Croding packaging plant. Factory rent, depreciation, and all other items of fixed factory overhead are handled by the home office at a set rate of $100,000 per month. Ten thousand tons of paper clips have been produced, but this is only 75 percent of denominator activity, since demand for the product must be built up.

The controller has just figured out the month's variances; she is looking for a method of presenting them in clear, logical form to top management at the home office. You say that you know of just the method, and promise to have the analysis ready the next morning.

Filled with zeal and enthusiasm, feeling that your future as a rising star in this growing company is secure, you decide to take your spouse out to dinner to celebrate the trust and confidence that your superior has placed in you.

Upon returning home, with the flush of four martinis still upon you, you are horrified to discover your dog happily devouring the controller's figure sheet. You manage to salvage only the following fragments:

Miles used...................... 5,300
Variable overhead incurred..$50,000

Overhead efficiency variance...$8,500 U

variance...$35,000 U

dard Costs per ton:

bor hours....6
age rate.........$2

al overhead........$12.60
Clypton wire...........1/2 mile

You remember that the $35,000 variance did not represent the grand total of all variances. You also recall that variance analysis was easier to tackle by expressing items in terms of hours rather than units.

required Don't let the controller think you're a knucklehead; go ahead and make up your analysis of all variances.

9-24 *Review of Chapters 8 and 9* (H. Schaefer) The manager of the Victory Division received the following report for the year 19_4:

Sales (100,000 units)		$3,000,000
Manufacturing cost of sales (at standard)		
Beginning inventory (10,000 units)	$ 270,000	
Production (150,000 units)	4,050,000	
Available for sale (160,000 units)	$4,320,000	
Ending inventory (60,000 units)	1,620,000	2,700,000

Gross margin before variances	$ 300,000
Manufacturing variances—favorable	50,000
Gross margin	$ 350,000
Nonmanufacturing expenses	150,000
Net income	$ 200,000

Note A: Manufacturing costs incurred during 19_4:

Material	$ 760,000
Labor	1,525,000
Overhead	1,715,000
	$4,000,000

Note B: Standard manufacturing costs per unit:

Material	$ 5.00
Labor	10.00
Overhead	12.00
	$27.00

The overhead cost is based upon an annual denominator activity of 110,000 units and annual fixed costs of $330,000.

The division manager is delighted with the income number—but suspicious. In 19_3 he also sold 100,000 units but produced only 110,000 units and had a much lower income number. He asks you to do some "costly" analysis.

First, he wants to know more about the $50,000 favorable variance in manufacturing costs. How much is attributable to material? Labor? Overhead? Did it result from spending less?

Second, he wants to know why 19_4 is better than 19_3—aside from possible differences in efficiency and input prices. That is, for this part assume that there were zero price and efficiency variances for both 19_3 and 19_4. Compute the difference between 19_3 and 19_4 net income. Give a specific explanation of why it occurred.

9-25 *Two Plants and Standard Costs* The Orose Glass Company is organized into three divisions. The Industrial Glass Division, headed by Bill Carder, general manager, has seven plants, located in various parts of the United States. The plants are located near the ultimate customers, because competition is very intense. A manufacturer that has to add long-haul freight costs into a bid stands little chance of getting profitable business.

On this particular morning, Bill was talking to two of his plant managers, who supplied adjacent geographical locations in the western part of the country. "A new technique has been developed that will impregnate glass with a special material, AlN. Glass impregnated with this material effectively filters 99.9 percent of harmful rays from the sun, at the same time allowing an observer to determine the color and quantity of the material in the bottle.

"Market research on the product indicates that Orose Glass would not be able to pass on any added cost of this product to the industrial consumer. However, the research did show that if containers made of the new material were sold at the same price as present containers ($295 per batch), the demand would be heavy. The market forecast is 500 batches. (A batch is 10,000 bottles.)

"We want to convert a part of one plant to the new process. We would like it to be one of your plants because of the similarity of your activities. Since you share a common sales force, your sales are just about equal. The operating costs for this product for your two plants are very similar." (Exhibit 9-9.)

EXHIBIT 9-9

(Because of the similarities of the two plants, one operating statement for this product is applicable to both plants.)

Sales: 350 batches			
Total revenue (350 × $295)			$103,250.00
Cost of sales:			
Direct labor at standard	$ 8,575.00		
Direct materials at standard	61,250.00		
Total prime costs		$69,825.00	
Overhead costs at flexible budgeted amounts;			
Indirect labor	$ 4,700.00		
Power	2,375.00		
Maintenance and repair	1,605.00		
Supplies	387.50		
Supervision	4,000.00		
Division administrative expense	2,500.00		
Home-office burden	3,500.00		
Depreciation*	13,000.00		
Total overhead costs		32,067.50	
Total cost			101,892.50
Plant profit before variances			$ 1,357.50
Spending and price variances		$1,000 F	
Efficiency variances		1,000 U	0
Plant profit			$ 1,357.50

* Does not include allowance for new equipment.

Bill went on to say, "Because of the density of the liquid glass when it contains AlN, a new glass-blowing machine will have to be purchased. However, the rest of the production process can use existing equipment. The cost of the new machine is $50,000, and it has an expected life of 20 years. Straight-line depreciation will be used for internal control and evaluation. The cost of the AlN will be $15 a batch.

"Well, boys, that's the story," said Bill. "Why don't you take a look at the figures and let me know which of you thinks he can make a profit on the new process."

Jim Cline took one look at the numbers and said, "This baby will cost me a lot of money. Take a look. The full cost to produce a batch is $280.30 (Exhibit 9-10). If we add $15 to that, I am going to lose 30¢ a batch plus the added cost of depreciation. Besides, my denominator variance was unfavorable by $3,787.50 last year, which means my batch cost must be more than $280.30. No thanks; I don't want that new process."

George Atkins pondered the numbers a little longer and said, "I haven't had time to check all the numbers, but I think this might be a money maker. Let me work on this a while, Bill, and I'll let you know if I want to use it."

required

1. Who is right, Jim or George?
2. If the process is used, how much will profits increase or decrease?
3. Explain the $3,787.50 variance that Jim mentioned. Why is it not in Exhibit 9-9? Show computations.

EXHIBIT 9-10

Denominator volume:	400 batches (4,000,000 units)	
Practical capacity:	600 batches (6,000,000 units)	
Average volume last three years:	350 batches (3,500,000 units)	

Standard costs based on denominator volume of 400 batches:

	TOTAL COST (400 BATCHES)	*STANDARD COST PER BATCH*
Direct labor	$ 9,800	$ 24.50
Direct materials	70,000	175.00
Indirect labor	4,800	12.00
Power	2,500	6.25
Maintenance and repair	1,620	4.05
Supplies	400	1.00
Supervision	4,000	10.00
Division administrative expense	2,500	6.25
Home-office burden	3,500	8.75
Depreciation	13,000	32.50
Total cost at standard	$112,120	$280.30

Standard cost per batch = $280.30

4. Given your answer to 2, assume that the material AlN could go up or down in price over the next few months. At what AlN price would the new process be exactly as profitable as the old (given that sales would be at 500 batches a year)?

Note 1: Old glass-blowing machines are fully depreciated and have no salvage value. The cost of removal is very small.

Note 2: Inventories of products are not maintained. Production is done on a job-order basis in batches of 10,000. Standard costs are determined for batches of 10,000.

Note 3: If one of the plants is converted, all of its current production will be replaced by the new product. That is, there will be no possibility of producing the two different products in one plant.

Income Effects of Alternative Product-Costing Methods

10

When an accounting system is designed, managers and accountants must choose an inventory-valuation method. This decision is vital for many reasons, including its effects on reported income in any given year, on the evaluation of a manager's performance, and on pricing decisions.

The major purposes of this chapter are to *examine and compare the effects of some costing alternatives on the measurements of product costs and income.* Other decision implications of these alternatives are also mentioned, but they are discussed more fully in subsequent chapters.

We consider four major topics: (a) the contribution approach to income measurement, often called direct costing; (b) the role of various activity levels in absorption costing; (c) standard-cost variances and the income statement; and (d) an overview of budgetary control, which recapitulates Chapters 5 through 10 in summary form. These topics are related sufficiently to warrant their being considered in a single chapter. *However, they may be studied independently.* Consequently, each of the four Problems for Self-Study in this chapter is placed at the end of the appropriate major section. You will benefit by pausing at the end of each section and solving the pertinent Problem for Self-Study.

contribution approach to income measurement

absorption costing and direct costing

Chapter 9 described the absorption-costing approach, whereby fixed manufacturing overhead was unitized and became absorbed as a cost of product along with the variable manufacturing overhead.

Before continuing, study Exhibit 10-1 and consider some terminology. There are two opposing ideas, commonly labeled as *absorption costing* and *direct costing.* Absorption costing (the traditional approach) signifies that **fixed factory overhead is inventoried.** In contrast, direct costing signifies that **fixed factory overhead is not inventoried.** These terms may be coupled with either of two major product-costing systems you have learned in this book—normal costing and standard costing—depending **solely** on whether a particular system inventories **fixed** overhead:

1. *Normal absorption costing.* Includes actual prime costs (direct materials and direct labor) plus variable and fixed manufacturing overhead applied by using predetermined rates times actual hours of input.
2. *Standard absorption costing.* Includes predetermined prime costs plus predetermined variable and fixed overhead.
3. *Normal direct costing.* Includes actual prime costs plus variable manufacturing overhead applied by using predetermined rates times actual hours of input; excludes fixed manufacturing overhead.
4. *Standard direct costing.* Includes predetermined prime costs plus predetermined variable manufacturing overhead; excludes fixed manufacturing overhead.

Absorption costing is much more widely used than direct costing, although the growing use of the contribution approach in performance measurement and cost analysis has led to increasing use of direct costing for *internal* purposes.

Direct costing is more accurately called *variable* or *marginal* costing, because in substance it applies only the *variable* production costs to the cost of the product. Direct costing has an impact on net income different from that of absorption costing, because fixed manufacturing overhead is regarded as a period cost (charged against revenue immediately) rather than as a product cost (assigned to units produced, which equals units sold only by coincidence).

Direct costing has been a controversial subject among accountants—not so much because there is disagreement about the need for delineating between variable- and fixed-cost behavior patterns for management planning and control, but because there is a question about its theoretical propriety for *external* reporting. Proponents of direct costing maintain that the fixed part of factory overhead is more closely related to the *capacity* to produce than to the production of specific units. Opponents of direct costing maintain that inventories should carry a fixed-cost component, because both variable and fixed costs are necessary to produce goods; both these costs should be inventoriable, regardless of their differences in behavior patterns. Neither the public accounting profession nor the Internal Revenue Service has approved of direct costing as a generally acceptable method of inventory valuation.

The notion of direct costing blends easily with the contribution-margin approach described in this text. Exhibit 10-1 illustrates the principal differences between direct costing and absorption costing. Note the following points about the exhibit:

1. Under absorption costing, fixed production costs are applied to the product, to be subsequently released to expense as a part of Cost of Goods Sold. Under direct costing, fixed production costs are regarded as period costs and are immediately released to expense along with the selling and administrative expenses.
2. Under direct costing, only the variable manufacturing costs are regarded as product costs. Variability with manufacturing volume is the criterion used for the classification of costs into product or period categories.
3. In direct costing, the *contribution margin*—the excess of sales over *all* variable costs—is a highlight of the income statement. Other terms for *contribution margin* include *marginal income, marginal balance, profit contribution,* and *contribution to fixed costs.*
4. The absorption-costing statement in Exhibit 10-1 differentiates between the variable and fixed costs only to aid your comparison. Costs are seldom classified as fixed or variable in absorption-costing statements, although such a classification is possible. Managers who are accustomed to looking at operations from a breakeven-analysis and flexible-budget viewpoint find that the absorption income statement fails to dovetail with cost-volume-profit relationships. They are then forced to take time for an attempt to reconcile and interpret two or more sets of figures that portray a single operating situation. Direct-costing proponents say that it is more efficient to present important cost-volume-profit relationships as integral parts of the major financial statements.
5. If inventories increase during a period, the direct-costing method will generally report less net income than absorption costing; when inventories decrease, direct costing will report more net income than absorption costing. The differences in net income, as the note at the bottom of Exhibit 10-1 indicates, are due *solely* to the difference in accounting for *fixed* manufacturing costs as related to inventory valuation.[1]

In formula form, if the fixed-overhead product-costing rate is unchanged, the difference between net incomes (profits) under absorption and direct costing may be shown as follows:

$$\begin{pmatrix}\text{Profit}\\ \text{Computed by}\\ \text{Absorption}\\ \text{Costing}\end{pmatrix} - \begin{pmatrix}\text{Profit}\\ \text{Computed}\\ \text{by Direct}\\ \text{Costing}\end{pmatrix} = \frac{\begin{pmatrix}\text{Total Fixed}\\ \text{Factory Overhead}\end{pmatrix}}{\begin{pmatrix}\text{Denominator Used}\\ \text{for Unitizing}\\ \text{Fixed Overhead}\end{pmatrix}} \times \begin{pmatrix}\text{Volume}\\ \text{Produced}\\ \text{minus}\\ \text{Volume}\\ \text{Sold}\end{pmatrix}$$

or

$$\text{Difference in Profits} = \begin{pmatrix}\text{Fixed Factory}\\ \text{Overhead}\\ \text{per Unit}\end{pmatrix} \times \begin{pmatrix}\text{Change in}\\ \text{Inventory}\\ \text{Units}\end{pmatrix}$$

[1] Also see Yuji Ijiri, Robert K. Jaedicke, and John L. Livingstone, "The Effect of Inventory Costing Methods on Full and Direct Costing," *Journal of Accounting Research,* Vol. III, No. 1, pp. 63–74.

EXHIBIT 10-1

COMPARISON OF ABSORPTION AND DIRECT COSTING

B Company

Income Statements for the Year Ending Dec. 31, 19 1

(Data assumed; there is no beginning inventory; the unit *variable* manufacturing cost is $6.00.)

ABSORPTION COSTING

	UNIT COST	TOTAL	
Sales, 1,000 units @ $10.00			$10,000
Cost of goods sold:			
Variable manufacturing costs: 1,100 units	$6.00	$6,600*	
Fixed manufacturing costs	2,00	2,200	
Cost of goods available for sale	$8.00	$8,800	
Less ending inventory: 100 units	8.00	800	8,000
Gross margin			$ 2,000
Less total selling and administrative expenses, including $400 of variable expenses			900
Net income			$ 1,100†

DIRECT COSTING

Sales		$10,000
Variable manufacturing cost of goods produced	$6,600*	
Less ending inventory: 100 units @ $6.00	600	
Variable manufacturing cost of goods sold	$6,000	
Add variable selling and administrative expenses	400	
Total variable costs charged against sales		6,400
Contribution margin		$ 3,600
Less fixed costs:		
Fixed manufacturing costs	$2,200	
Fixed selling and administrative expenses	500	2,700
Net income		$ 900*

* Composed of:

	Unit Cost	*Total*
Direct materials	$3.00	$3,300
Direct labor	2.00	2,200
Variable overhead	1.00	1,100
	$6.00	$6,600

† The $200 difference in net income is caused by the $200 ($800 × $600) difference in ending inventories. Under absorption costing $200 of the $2,200 fixed manufacturing costs is held back in inventory, whereas under direct costing the $200 is released immediately as a charge against sales.

Application of the formula on page 296 to Exhibit 10-1 is shown as follows:

$$\$1{,}100 - \$900 = \$2.00 \text{ per unit} \times (1{,}100 - 1{,}000) \text{ units}$$
$$\$200 = \$200$$

Whether direct costing should be acceptable for external reporting need not be of paramount importance to accountants or managers. Company systems can accommodate either method; the important point is that it may be cost effective if internal reports use the contribution approach as a technique for evaluation and control.

the central issue: a question of timing

Nearly all accountants agree that distinctions between variable and fixed costs are helpful for a wide variety of managerial decisions. The traditional view recognizes this possibility, but takes the position that such information may be supplied without changing the conventional methods of income determination. Adherents of direct costing maintain that the importance of variable- and fixed-cost behavior should be spotlighted not only by changing the format of the financial statements but also by changing the basic principles or concepts, whereby fixed factory overhead would be written off in the period incurred rather than funneled into inventory as an integral part of inventory costs. Thus, the central question becomes, What is the proper *timing* for release of fixed factory overhead as expense: at the time of incurrence, or at the time that the finished units to which the fixed overhead relates are sold? The focus must be upon relating fixed overhead to the definition of an asset.[2]

Absorption costing is far from uniform in its application. There are different inventory methods, such as first-in, first-out; last-in, first-out; and weighted average.[3] There are different assumptions as to overhead application, such as the inclusion of some administrative costs in inventory and the classification of packaging costs. However, these problems remain, whether direct costing or absorption costing is used. The issue thus narrows to the propriety of excluding fixed costs from inventory.

PROBLEM FOR SELF-STUDY

PROBLEM

The Blazek Company had the following operating characteristics in 19_4 and 19_5:

Basic production data at standard cost:		
Direct materials	$1.30	
Direct labor	1.50	
Variable overhead	.20	$3.00
Fixed overhead ($150,000 ÷ 150,000 units of denominator volume)		1.00
Total factory cost at standard		$4.00

[2] See G. H. Sorter and C. T. Horngren, "Asset Recognition and Economic Attributes—The Relevant Costing Approach," *The Accounting Review,* Vol. XXXVII, No. 3, for a discussion of the role of fixed overhead in the valuation of inventory.

[3] For a discussion, see Chapter 14.

Sales price, $5.00 per unit.

Selling and administrative expense is assumed for simplicity as being all fixed at $65,000 yearly, except for sales commissions at 5% of dollar sales.

	19_4	*19_5*
In units:		
Opening inventory	—	30,000
Production	170,000	140,000
Sales	140,000	160,000
Closing inventory	30,000	10,000

There were no variances from the standard variable costs, and fixed overhead incurred was exactly $150,000 per year. Any denominator variance is written off directly at year-end as an adjustment to Cost of Goods Sold.

required

1. Income statements for 19_4 and 19_5 under direct costing and absorption costing.
2. A reconciliation of the difference in operating income for 19_4, 19_5, and the two years as a whole.

SOLUTION

1.

BLAZEK COMPANY

Comparative Income Statements (in thousands of dollars) for the Years 19_4 and 19_5

		19_4	*19_5*
Direct Costing:			
Sales	(1)	700	800
Opening inventory—at variable standard cost		—	90
Add variable cost of goods manufactured		510	420
Available for sale		510	510
Deduct ending inventory—at variable standard cost		90	30
Variable manufacturing cost of goods sold		420	480
Variable selling expenses—at 5% of dollar sales		35	40
Total variable expenses	(2)	455	520
Contribution margin	(3) = (1) − (2)	245	280
Fixed factory overhead		150	150
Fixed selling and administrative expenses		65	65
Total fixed expenses	(4)	215	215
Operating income	(3) − (4)	30	65
Absorption Costing:			
Sales		700	800
Opening inventory—at standard absorption cost		—	120
Cost of goods manufactured		680	560
Available for sale		680	680
Deduct ending inventory		120	40
Cost of goods sold—at standard		560	640
Denominator variance*		(20)	10
Adjusted cost of goods sold		540	650
Gross margin or gross profit—at "actual"		160	150
Selling and administrative expenses		100	105
Operating income		60	45

* Computation of denominator variance based on denominator volume of 150,000 units:

19_4	$20,000	overapplied (170,000 − 150,000) × $1.00
19_5	10,000	underapplied (150,000 − 140,000) × $1.00
Two years together	$10,000	overapplied (310,000 − 300,000) × $1.00

2. Reconciliation of differences in operating income:

	19_4	19_5	TOGETHER
Operating income under:			
Absorption costing	$60,000	$ 45,000	$105,000
Direct costing	30,000	65,000	95,000
Difference to be explained	$30,000	$−20,000	$ 10,000
The difference can be reconciled by multiplying the fixed-overhead rate by the *change* in the total inventory units:			
Fixed-overhead rate	$1.00	$1.00	$1.00
Change in inventory units:			
Beginning inventory	—	30,000	—
Ending inventory	30,000	10,000	10,000
Change	30,000	20,000	10,000
Difference in operating income explained	$30,000	$−20,000	$ 10,000

role of various activity levels in absorption costing

Chapter 9 pointed out that product costs and income can be significantly affected by the choice of a particular activity level as a denominator in the computation of fixed-overhead rates. We now study how various alternative levels of activity can affect operating income under absorption costing. As fixed costs become a more prominent part of an organization's total costs, the importance of this choice becomes greater.

characteristics of capacity

The choice of a capacity size is usually the result of capital-budgeting decisions, which are reached after studying the expected impact of these capital outlays on operations over a number of years. The choice may be influenced by a combination of two major factors, each involving trade-off decisions and each heavily depending on long-range forecasts of demand, material costs, and labor costs:

1. Provision for seasonal and cyclical *fluctuations* in demand. The trade-off is between (a) additional costs of physical capacity and (b) the costs of inventory stockouts and/or the carrying costs of inventory safety stocks of such magnitude to compensate for seasonal and cyclical variations, the costs of overtime premium, subcontracting, and so on.
2. Provision for upward *trends* in demand. The trade-off is between (a) the costs of constructing too much capacity for initial needs and (b) the later extra costs of satisfying demand by alternative means. For example, should a factory designed to make color television tubes have an area of 100,000, 150,000, or 200,000 square feet?

Although it can be defined and measured in a particular situation, capacity is an illusive concept. Consider, for example, the following:

> Capacity planning requires definition and measurement of capacity in a manner relevant to questions which arise in the planning process. This problem has two aspects. First, it is necessary to specify capacity in terms of how much the company should be prepared to make and to sell. Second, the capacity of specific facilities available or to be acquired must be determined. . . . A variety of alternative combinations of capacity and operating patterns is usually possible.[4]

There is much fluidity in the quotation above. To most people, the term *capacity* implies a constraint, an upper limit. We sometimes hear, "I'm working to capacity now. I simply can't do more." This same notion of capacity as a constraint is commonly held in industry.

Although the term *capacity* is usually applied to plant and equipment, it is equally applicable to other resources, such as people and materials. A shortage of direct labor, executive time, or raw materials may be critical in limiting company production or sales.

The upper limit of capacity is seldom absolutely rigid, at least from an engineering viewpoint. That is, ways—such as overtime, subcontracting, or paying premium prices for additional raw materials—can usually be found to expand production. But these ways may be totally unattractive from an economic viewpoint. Hence, the upper limit of capacity is *specified* by management for current planning and control purposes after considering engineering *and* economic factors. In this way, the upper limit is usually imposed by management, not by external forces.

In our subsequent discussion, let us consider the word *capacity* as representing *practical capacity* (sometimes called *practical attainable capacity*), the maximum level at which the plant or department can operate efficiently. Practical capacity often allows for unavoidable operating interruptions such as repair time or waiting time (downtime).

Two commonly used[5] levels of capacity utilization are:

1. *Normal activity,* which is the level of capacity utilization (which is some percentage of practical capacity) that will satisfy average consumer demand over a span of time (often five years) that includes seasonal, cyclical, and trend factors; and
2. *Expected annual activity,* which is the anticipated level of capacity utilization for the coming year.

There are apt to be differences in terminology between companies, so be sure to obtain an understanding of terms in a given situation.

[4] "Accounting for Costs of Capacity," *N.A.A. Research Series Report No. 39* (New York: National Association of Accountants), p. 10.

[5] It is difficult to make sweeping generalizations about how companies apply overhead to product. Studies of practice show conflicting results about whether actual or predetermined rates are used. In the latter cases, there are no clear patterns as to how normal activity, expected annual activity, or some other basis for application is selected in a particular company. See Charles R. Purdy, "Industry Patterns of Capacity or Volume Choice: Their Existence and Rationale," *Journal of Accounting Research,* Vol. III, No. 2, pp. 228–41. Also see various publications of the Cost Accounting Standards Board (Washington, D.C.) for descriptions of overhead practices.

normal activity versus expected annual activity

Expected annual activity, which may also be called *master-budgeted activity,* is the basis for applying all fixed overhead to products on a year-to-year basis, while the overhead rate based on *normal activity* attempts to apply fixed overhead by using a *longer-run* average expected activity. Conceptually, the *normal rate* results in overapplications in some years that are offset by underapplications in other years.

We shall deal with fixed overhead only, because variable overhead fluctuates with changes in activity, and fixed overhead does not. *Thus, the entire problem of using expected annual activity or normal activity is raised by the presence of fixed overhead.* (If you will recall, the denominator variance in Chapter 9 was confined to fixed overhead.) Consider the following data:

Fixed factory overhead	$500,000
Practical capacity per year	100,000 standard direct-labor hours
Normal activity	90,000 standard direct-labor hours
Expected annual activity for specific year	(Fluctuates from year to year)
Normal overhead rate, $500,000 ÷ 90,000 hours	$5.55
Expected annual overhead rate	(Varies from year to year)

Exhibit 10-2 shows that if normal activity is the base, the overhead rate of $5.55 would be used for costing inventory. In the second year, there would be an underapplied fixed-overhead balance of $5.55 times 20,000 hours, or

EXHIBIT 10-2

COMPARISON OF EXPECTED ANNUAL AND NORMAL ACTIVITY FOR OVERHEAD APPLICATION

		EXPECTED ANNUAL ACTIVITY BASIS			NORMAL ACTIVITY BASIS		
YEAR	STANDARD LABOR-HOURS ALLOWED*	OVERHEAD RATE	TOTAL APPLIED	UNDER- (OVER-) APPLIED*	OVERHEAD RATE	TOTAL APPLIED	UNDER- (OVER-) APPLIED†
1	90,000	$5.55	$500,000	$ —	$5.55	$500,000	$ —
2	70,000	7.15	500,000	—	5.55	389,000	111,000
3	100,000	5.00	500,000	—	5.55	555,000	(55,000)
4	80,000	6.33	500,000	—	5.55	445,000	55,000
5	100,000	5.00	500,000	—	5.55	555,000	(55,000)
6	100,000	5.00	500,000	—	5.55	555,000	(55,000)
				$ —			$ -0-‡

* For illustrative purposes, we assume that expected annual activity in terms of standard labor-hours allowed is equal to actual output achieved.

† Debit underapplied or credit overapplied overhead directly to Income Summary as a measure of gain or loss from under- or overutilization of capacity. Note that this is simply the denominator variance.

‡ Rounded

$111,000. This unfavorable denominator variance would be considered the measure of the cost of *not* producing—the loss from idle capacity. Inventories would be costed with a $5.55 rate instead of a $7.15 rate. Under the expected-annual-activity method, if volume fluctuates from year to year, product and inventory costs will vary solely because of differences in utilization of facilities. Using a normal rate will avoid capricious changes in unit costs and will also provide a yearly and monthly measure of the cost of idle capacity.

Note carefully that Exhibit 10-2 is designed to stress only the computation of overhead rates under different activity bases. It deliberately avoids introducing changes in budgeted fixed-overhead costs; instead, it assumes that total fixed costs are constant from year to year. Actually, year-to-year changes in the prices paid for fixed-overhead items and services can affect the overhead rate, regardless of whether expected annual activity, normal activity, or some other activity base is used to set the rate.

selection of activity base

The activity base to be used depends largely on its effect on decisions. Fixed costs measure the capacity to make and sell. They usually include at least depreciation and a core of salaried payroll costs. The total fixed-cost commitment is influenced by the long-run sales outlook. The conventional view is that all products should receive some "equitable" portion of fixed overhead.

If the total sales volume does not change greatly from year to year, *expected annual activity* for each year is a rational base, because expected annual activity and normal activity coincide. In these cases, even if the companies have seasonal sales patterns, all fixed factory overhead is exactly applied to product by the end of the year. See Exhibit 10-2.

Many accountants reject the normal-activity notion and maintain that each year must stand by itself; that is, each year's overhead must be applied to each year's production, written off as a loss, or both. This attitude arises from (a) the widespread conviction that the year is the key time period, and (b) adherence to the idea that overhead costs for a given year generally must cling or attach to the units produced during that year regardless of the relationship of that year's activity to average long-run activity.

A more convincing reason for using expected annual activity as a base is the overwhelming measurement problem that accompanies the determination of normal activity. Sales not only fluctuate cyclically, but they have trends over the long run. In effect, the use of normal activity implies an unusual talent for accurate long-run forecasting. Many accountants and executives who reject the normal-activity idea as a base claim that the nature of their company's business precludes accurate forecasts beyond one year.

Where companies use normal activity, the objective is to choose a period long enough to average out sizable fluctuations in volume and to allow for trends in sales. The uniform rate for applying fixed overhead supposedly provides for "recovery" of fixed costs over the long run. General Motor's pricing policy uses this approach. Companies expect that overapplications in some years will be offset by underapplications in other years.

Conceptually, when *normal activity* is the base, the yearly over- or under-applied overhead should be carried forward on the balance sheet. Practically, however, year-end balances are closed directly to Income Summary, because the accounting profession (and the Internal Revenue Service) generally views the year as being the terminal time span for allocation of under- or overapplied overhead. In year 2 in Exhibit 10-2, the year-end journal entry for closing the fixed Factory Overhead accounts may appear as follows:

Fixed factory overhead applied	389,000	
Denominator variance, unfavorable (to income summary)	111,000	
Fixed factory overhead control		500,000

The journal entry for the end of year 3 would appear as follows:

Fixed factory overhead applied	555,000	
Denominator variance, favorable		55,000
Fixed factory overhead control		500,000

The logical question that should arise at this point is: Why use normal activity at all if the yearly over- or underapplications are written off at year-end anyway? Are the yearly results not the same, whether expected annual activity or normal activity is used? The Problem for Self-Study shows the fundamental answer: "There is still a difference, because inventory costs are different."

practical capacity Many managements want to keep running at full capacity, which really means practical capacity. Their "normal activity" for applying fixed costs is "practical capacity"; anything less reduces profits and is undesirable. Where product costs are used as guides for pricing, some managers say that this policy results in more competitive pricing, which maximizes both volume and profits in good times and bad. Of course, profits also depend on factors other than physical volume—for example, the elasticity of demand. The accounting effects of such a policy are lower unit costs for inventory purposes and the almost perpetual appearance of an unfavorable denominator variance, sometimes described on the income statements as loss from idle capacity.

significance of activity base for product costing and control Obviously, the activity base for product costing is largely a matter of opinion. The selection of a base probably becomes crucial where product costs heavily influence managerial decisions. For example, in a cyclical industry, the use of expected annual activity rather than normal activity as a base would tend to cause a company to quote low prices in boom years and high prices in depression years—in obvious conflict with good business judgment. That is why normal activity makes more sense as an overhead base when there are wide swings in business volume through the years, even though the yearly over- and underapplied overhead is not carried forward in the balance sheet from year to year.

In the realm of current planning and control, however, normal activity is an empty concept. Normal activity is used as a basis for long-range plans. It depends on the time span selected, the forecasts made for each year, and the weighting of these forecasts. In Exhibit 10-2, a comparison in year 2 of the 70,000-hour expected annual activity with the 90,000-hour normal activity might be suggested as the best basis for auditing long-range planning. However, normal activity is an average that has no particular significance with respect to a follow-up for a particular year. The pertinent comparison is a particular year's expected annual activity with that year's activity level used in the authorization for the acquisition of facilities. This comparison may be done project by project. It need not be integrated in the accounting system on a routine basis. Furthermore, attempting to use normal activity as a reference point for judging current performance is an example of misusing a long-range measure for a short-range purpose.

The expected annual activity, rather than normal activity or practical capacity, is more germane to the evaluation of current results. Expected annual activity is the basis for the year's master budget—the principal short-run planning and control tool. Managers feel much more obligated to reach the levels stipulated in the master budget, which should have been carefully set in relation to the maximum opportunities for sales in the current period. In contrast, normal activity and practical capacity are not so pertinent to current operating problems, because they are not usually incorporated in the comprehensive or master budget—the focus of attention.[6]

PROBLEM FOR SELF-STUDY

PROBLEM

The Shane Co. incurs fixed manufacturing overhead of $500,000 annually. Practical capacity is 100,000 standard direct-labor hours allowed; normal activity, 90,000 hours; and expected annual activity, 70,000 hours. In 19_1, 70,000 units were produced (in 70,000 standard hours) and 60,000 units were sold. Standard hours allowed were 70,000. There was no beginning inventory.

required

1. Prepare a three-column comparison of the various methods of applying fixed overhead to product. Designate which methods would result in the highest and the lowest net income. For each method, show the amounts that would be charged to:

   Cost of sales (expense)
   Loss from idle capacity, denominator variance (loss)
   Ending inventory

[6] Also see Charles T. Horngren, "A Contribution Margin Approach to the Analysis of Capacity Utilization," *The Accounting Review,* Vol. XLII, No. 2, pp. 254–64.

2. Why is expected annual activity better than either practical capacity or normal activity for judging current operating performance?

SOLUTION

1. Exhibit 10-3 shows that the use of different activity bases for developing product-costing overhead rates results in different *inventory valuations* and different net incomes. Further, the measure of utilization of facilities, the denominator variance, will differ markedly. In Exhibit 10-3, income is lowest where practical capacity is the overhead base and highest when expected annual activity is the overhead base, because a smaller portion of overhead is held back as an asset in inventory when a lower overhead rate is used.

   The exhibit also indicates that the accounting effects of using practical capacity are lower unit costs for inventory purposes and the steady appearance of "Loss from idle capacity" on the income statement.
2. As is explained more fully in the chapter, expected annual activity is more pertinent to current operating problems because it is usually the notion of activity that is incorporated in the master budget. Therefore, it has more current meaning to the department managers who must live with the budget.

standard-cost variances and the income statement

proration to achieve actual costs

Managers and accountants tend to think of "actual" costs as somehow representing absolute truths. Therefore, "normal" or "standard costs" produce valuations that are somehow untrue unless month-end or year-end variances are prorated among the affected accounts to get corrected valuations that better approximate "actual" costs.[7] Of course, in all cases immaterial variances (however defined) can be written off against income immediately.

To see how these prorations occur in the realm of standard costs, consider the following problem. Try to solve the problem before examining the solution.

PROBLEM

The Bridget Company began operations on January 2, 19_4. Results for 19_4 are:

Direct labor incurred, 85,000 hours @ $6.05 per hour	$514,250
Sales	$660,000
Factory overhead incurred	$161,000
Selling and administrative expenses	$ 70,000
Purchase of direct materials, 100,000 lbs. @ $1.10. Standard price is $1.00. Purchases are charged to Stores at standard prices. The standard allowance per unit of finished output is one pound.	
Pounds of material consumed	90,000
Production in units	80,000
Sales in units	60,000

Direct-labor standards are one hour per unit at $6 per hour. Factory overhead is applied at a rate of $2 per standard hour allowed.

required

1. Using standard absorption costing, prepare an income statement. Assume that all variances, including under- or overapplied overhead, are written off at year-end as separate deductions after the gross profit (at standard) is computed.
2. Prepare an income statement based on a proration of all variances. Include

[7] For example, see Standard #407, "Use of Standard Costs for Direct Material and Direct Labor," of the Cost Accounting Standards Board, Washington, D.C.

EXHIBIT 10-3

SOLUTION TO SELF-STUDY PROBLEM, PART 1

Income-Statement Effects of Using Various Activity Bases for Overhead Application

	EXPECTED ANNUAL ACTIVITY[a]		NORMAL ACTIVITY[b]		PRACTICAL CAPACITY[c]	
	USING A $7.15 OVERHEAD RATE		USING A $5.55 OVERHEAD RATE		USING A $5.00 OVERHEAD RATE	
Sales		$ xxx		$ xxx		$ xxx
Production costs:						
Direct materials, direct labor, variable overhead	$ xxx		$ xxx		$ xxx	
Fixed overhead applied to product	500,000		389,000		350,000	
Total production costs—70,000 units	$ xxx		$ xxx		$ xxx	
Ending inventory—fixed-overhead component—10,000 units	71,500		55,555		50,000	
Total fixed-overhead component of cost of sales		428,500		333,445		300,000
Loss from idle capacity (shown separately on income statements)—the denominator variance, unfavorable		None		111,000		150,000
Total fixed overhead charged to the period's sales		$428,500		$444,445		$450,000
Net income		Highest		Middle		Lowest
Recapitulation:						
Total overhead to account for		$500,000		$500,000		$500,000
Accounted for as follows:						
Charged to Cost of Sales (expense)		$428,500		$333,445		$300,000
Charged to Loss from Idle Capacity, denominator variance		None		111,000		150,000
Charged to Ending Inventory (asset)		71,500		55,555		50,000
Overhead accounted for		$500,000		$500,000		$500,000

[a] $500,000 ÷ 70,000 hours allowed = $7.15 (rounded)

[b] $500,000 ÷ 90,000 hours normal activity = $5.55

[c] $500,000 ÷ 100,000 hours practical capacity = $5.00

a schedule showing the proration to Direct-Material Efficiency Variance, Finished Goods, Cost of Goods Sold, and Stores.

3. Explain why operating income in requirement 2 differs from that in 1.

SOLUTION 1.

BRIDGET COMPANY

Income Statement for the Year Ending December 31, 19_4

Sales	$660,000
Cost of goods sold—at standard cost of $9 per unit*	540,000
Gross profit—at standard	$120,000
Deduct unfavorable variances (see schedule)	55,250
Gross profit—at actual	$ 64,750
Selling and administrative expenses	70,000
Operating income (loss)	$ (5,250)

* $1 + $6 + $2 = $9 per unit

SCHEDULE OF VARIANCES

Direct-material pruchase price, 100,000 lbs. @ $.10	$ 10,000
Direct-material efficiency, 10,000 lbs. @ $1.00	10,000
Direct-labor price, 85,000 hrs. @ $.05	4,250
Direct-labor efficiency, 5,000 hrs. @ $6.00	30,000
Total overhead variance	1,000
Total variances (to income statement)	$ 55,250

2.

BRIDGET COMPANY

Income Statement for the Year Ending December 31, 19_4

Sales	$660,000
Cost of goods sold (see schedule)	580,688
Gross profit	$ 79,312
Selling and administrative expenses	70,000
Operating income	$ 9,312

SCHEDULE OF PRORATION OF VARIANCES

	TOTAL BEFORE PRORATION	DIRECT-MATERIAL EFFICIENCY	TO STORES	TO FINISHED GOODS	TO COST OF GOODS SOLD
Standard costs of materials	$100,000	$10,000	$10,000	$20,000	$ 60,000
Prorations of variances:					
Purchase price	$ 10,000	$ 1,000	$ 1,000	$ 2,000	$ 6,000
Direct-material efficiency:					
Unadjusted balance	10,000	10,000			
Adjusted balance		$11,000		2,750	8,250
Direct-labor price	4,250			1,062	3,188
Direct-labor efficiency	30,000			7,500	22,500
Total overhead variance	1,000			250	750
Final prorations	$ 55,250		$ 1,000	$13,562	$ 40,688
Standard cost of goods sold					540,000
"Actual" cost of goods sold					$580,688

Note: The material-purchase price variance was prorated in proportion to the standard costs of materials in each account. The remaining variances should also be allocated in proportion to the related standard costs in each account. For example, direct labor would be prorated in proportion to the standard direct-labor components of Work in Process, Finished Goods, and Cost of Goods Sold. Because we are dealing with a uniform product here, we merely allocate 20/80, or 1/4, to Finished Goods and 60/80, or 3/4, to Cost of Goods Sold.

3. The $14,562 difference, $9,312 − ($−5,250), in operating income is explained by the holding back of variances of $14,562 as inventory ($13,562 in Finished Goods and $1,000 in Raw-Material Stores). Note that even though variances may be small in relation to total standard costs incurred, they may be large in relation to operating income.

proration of material-price variance

The general rationale is to prorate variances in proportion to their related standard costs, over whatever accounts the standard costs might be in. This logic leads to straightforward prorations for direct labor and overhead; check their prorations in the above schedule.

The most difficult proration to comprehend is the material-price variance. To be most accurate, the proration should be traced at 10 cents per pound to wherever the 100,000 pounds have been charged at standard prices: 10,000 pounds have been wasted, so they are in the Direct-Material Efficiency Variance account; 10,000 are in Stores; 20,000 are in Finished Goods; and 60,000 are in Cost of Goods Sold. As the next step, the now-adjusted Material-Efficiency Variance should be prorated to Work in Process, Finished Goods, and Cost of Goods Sold, as shown in the above schedule of proration of variances.[8]

the case against proration

Some accountants, industrial engineers, and managers reject the idea that actual costs represent absolute truth. Instead, they claim that currently attainable standard costs are the "true costs" in the sense that such costs are the only costs that may be carried forward as assets or unexpired costs. They contend that variances are measures of inefficiency or abnormal efficiency. Therefore, variances are not inventoriable and should be completely charged or credited against revenue of the period instead of being prorated among inventories and cost of sales. In this way, inventory valuations will be more representative of desirable and attainable costs. In particular, there is no justification for carrying costs of inefficiency as assets, which is what proration accomplishes.

varieties of proration

Variations of these proration methods may be desirable under certain conditions. For instance, efficiency variances may be

[8] In practice, this refinement is often omitted. If so, the proration would be:

	TOTAL	*TO STORES*	*TO FINISHED GOODS*	*TO COST OF GOODS SOLD*
Purchase price	$10,000	$1,111	2,222	$6,667
Direct-material efficiency	10,000		2,500	7,500

If you prepared your solution in this way, be sure you understand why it is a cruder approximation than the one that first prorates the purchase-price variance to the direct-material-efficiency variance account. For instance, note that it results in a $1.111 "actual" unit cost for Stores instead of the $1.10 calculated in the first solution.

viewed as being currently avoidable and price variances as being unavoidable and therefore proratable. Conceptually, this is superior to the other methods because the costs of avoidable inefficiency are written off, whereas unavoidable costs are not. This is correct because the costs of avoidable inefficiency do not qualify as assets under any economic test.

The author believes that unfavorable variances do not have to be inventoried as long as standards are currently attainable. However, if standards are not up to date, or if they reflect perfection performance rather than expected performance under reasonably efficient conditions, then conceptually the variances should be split between the portion that reflects departures from currently attainable standards and the portion that does not. The former should be written off as period charges; the latter should be prorated to inventories and cost of sales. For example, assume that an operation has a perfection standard time allowed of 50 minutes, which is reflected in a formal standard-cost system. The currently attainable standard is 60 minutes. Now if it takes, say, 75 actual minutes to perform the operation, the conceptual adjustment would call for writing off 15 minutes of the 25-minute variance as a period cost and for treating the remaining 10-minute variance as a product cost.

PROBLEM FOR SELF-STUDY

Review the Bridget example in this section.

an overview of budgetary control

a variance threesome

This section attempts to place in perspective the budgets, variances, and product-costing methods described in Chapters 5 through 10. From a control viewpoint, the world of variances can be divided into three major parts: price, efficiency, and volume. Of course, we encounter countless labels and combinations regarding these variances. But the threesome of price, efficiency, and volume provides the most basic distinctions for the analysis of performance in all settings, manufacturing and nonmanufacturing, profit and nonprofit, and so on.

To see this approach, suppose a hospital prepared a budget for its X-ray department that was based on standard costs of direct material and direct labor as well as a flexible-budget formula for overhead. The master (static) budget for a given year was for 60,000 X-rays at an average revenue of $20 each and average variable costs of $11 each. The fixed costs were budgeted at $330,000.

A comparison of actual results for 50,000 X-rays with the original budget for 60,000 X-rays showed that income was $185,000 below the static budget:

	ACTUAL	*ORIGINAL MASTER (STATIC) BUDGET*	*VARIANCE*
Physical quantity	50,000	60,000	10,000 U
Revenue	$950,000	$1,200,000	$250,000 U
Variable costs	595,000	660,000	65,000 F
Contribution margin	$355,000	$ 540,000	$185,000 U
Fixed costs	330,000	330,000	—
Operating income	$ 25,000	$ 210,000	$185,000 U

As a hospital administrator you probably would find the preceding tabulation only moderately helpful. If a flexible budget were "inserted" or "dropped in" between columns one and two, you would obtain a better idea of the financial effects of changes in volume, efficiency, and prices. This drop-in becomes column (4) in Exhibit 10-4. Study the exhibit, including its footnotes, carefully; it demonstrates how the flexible-budget idea facilitates a sharper explanation, bridging from the original plan to the actual results. In summary:

Original targeted operating income was		$210,000
It was not reached because of unfavorable:		
Volume variances	$90,000	
Efficiency variances	55,000	
Price and spending variances	40,000	185,000
Actual operating income		$ 25,000

This approach provides a complete explanation that follows a trail from the master budget to the actual results. Note especially that the *volume variance,* as introduced and used here, represents the changes in *budgeted* costs and revenue that arose *solely* because volume differed from the original plan. All intervening price and efficiency changes are held constant and do not affect the computation of the volume variance.

role of denominator variance

In practice, the term *volume variance* is used loosely, so again be alert for the exact meaning of variance terminology in a particular organizational setting. The denominator variance used in Chapter 9 is frequently called a volume variance, but in this book volume variance does not mean denominator variance.

Denominator variance is a specialized variance arising solely out of the product-costing purpose of applying factory fixed overhead when absorption costing is used. There is no denominator variance when direct (variable) costing is used, because no fixed overhead is applied to product. Furthermore, the denominator variance has little economic meaning for planning and control; it is very difficult to interpret and explain to managers.

In contrast, the volume variance as used here is easy to explain and has straightforward economic significance. Thus, in Exhibit 10-4, if prices and efficiency had remained as originally planned, the unfavorable volume variance for revenue tells the manager that the 10,000-unit deviation from the 60,000-unit master budgeted amount should have resulted in $200,000 less revenue.

relationship of volume and denominator variances

Consider another example that involves inventories. Suppose that ABC Company has the following master budget:

Sales 100 units @ $10		$1,000
Variable manufacturing and administrative selling costs @ $5	$500	
Variable selling and administrative costs @ $1	100	600
Contribution margin		$ 400
Fixed indirect manufacturing costs		300
Net income (or operating income)		$ 100

Ignore all other costs.

EXHIBIT 10-4

OVERVIEW OF BUDGETARY CONTROL

	(1) ACTUAL	(2) PRICE AND SPENDING VARIANCES	(3) EFFICIENCY VARIANCES	(4) FLEXIBLE BUDGET	(5) (6) − (4) VOLUME VARIANCES[a]	(6) MASTER (STATIC) BUDGET
Physical quantity	50,000			50,000	10,000 U	60,000
Revenue	$950,000	$50,000 U[d]	$ —	$1,000,000[b]	$200,000 U	$1,200,000
Variable costs	595,000	10,000 F[e]	55,000 U[e]	550,000[c]	110,000 F	660,000
Contribution margin	$355,000	$40,000 U	$55,000 U	$ 450,000	$ 90,000 U	$ 540,000
Fixed costs	330,000	—	—	330,000[f]	—	330,000[f]
Operating income	$ 25,000	$40,000 U[g]	$55,000 U	$ 120,000	$ 90,000 U	$ 210,000

U—Unfavorable F—Favorable

[a] The volume variances for revenue and variable costs show the reductions that would be expected to accompany the decline in volume of activity—assuming price and efficiency factors as constant.

[b] 50,000 X-rays at $20 average revenue each.

[c] 50,000 X-rays at $11 average variable costs each.

[d] The average actual selling price was $19 instead of the $20 budgeted price; thus, there was a $50,000 unfavorable price variance for 50,000 X-rays.

[e] Assume here that several technicians were new so that inputs of both labor and material were 10 percent in excess of the standard allowed. Therefore, variable-cost inefficiencies would be .10 × $550,000, or $55,000. The remaining variances would be price and spending variances: $595,000 − $550,000 − $55,000 = $10,000 F.

[f] The predicted fixed costs of $330,000 remain the same regardless of the output produced.

[g] Another column could be inserted between columns (2) and (3); it would be the flexible budget based on actual inputs at standard prices.

Actual results had no flexible-budget variances, but sales volume was only 80 units. An analysis follows:

	ACTUAL	FLEXIBLE-BUDGET VARIANCES	FLEXIBLE BUDGET	VOLUME VARIANCE	MASTER BUDGET
Sales @ $10	$800	—	$800	$200 U	$1,000
Variable costs @ $6	480	—	480	120 F	600
Contribution margin	$320	—	$320	$ 80 U	$ 400
Fixed costs	300	—	300	—	300
Net income (loss)	$ 20		$ 20	$ 80 U	$ 100

Thus far the analysis has assumed variable (direct) costing. There is no volume variance for fixed costs, because their total does not fluctuate with volume.

How can this approach be reconciled with the denominator variance used under absorption costing? Suppose there is no beginning inventory, but production of 100 units occurred. Also suppose that the denominator volume was 100 units, resulting in a fixed overhead rate of $300 ÷ 100, or $3.00 per unit. An analysis follows:

	ACTUAL	FLEXIBLE-BUDGET VARIANCES	FLEXIBLE BUDGET	VOLUME VARIANCE	MASTER BUDGET
Sales	$800		$800	$200 U	$1,000
Variable costs	480		480	120 F	600
Fixed costs:*					
Budgeted			300		300
Applied to goods sold	240				
Applied to inventory, $60					
Denominator variance	0				
Total costs charged against sales	720		780		900
Net income	$ 80	—	$ 20	$ 80 U	$ 100
	↑	$60	↑		

* Fixed costs accounted for, $240 + $60 = $300.

The $60 difference is explained by the $60 increase in fixed overhead in inventory.

This example of absorption costing showed the case where the denominator volume coincided with the master budgeted volume. How would the analysis change if the denominator volume were, say, 150 units? Then the fixed overhead rate would be $300 ÷ 150, or $2.00 per unit. The denominator variance would be (150 − 100) × $2.00, or $100. An analysis follows, assuming that the denominator variance affects income immediately rather than being prorated among inventory and cost of goods sold:

	ACTUAL	FLEXIBLE-BUDGET VARIANCES	FLEXIBLE BUDGET	VOLUME VARIANCE	MASTER BUDGET
Sales	$800		$800	$200 U	$1,000
Variable costs	480		480	120 F	600
Fixed costs:*					
Budgeted			300		300
Applied to goods sold @ $2	160				
Applied to inventory, $40					
Denominator variance	100				
Total costs charged against sales	740	—	780		900
Net income	$ 60		$ 20	$ 80 U	$ 100

↑——— $40 ———↑ (between Actual net income $60 and Flexible budget net income $20)

* Fixed costs accounted for, $160 + $40 + $100 = $300.

The $40 difference is explained by the $40 increase in fixed overhead in inventory.

The point of this analysis is to stress that the volume variance, as described here, has significance for budgetary-control purposes. There is no volume variance for fixed overhead. The denominator variance is a peculiarity of absorption costing that complicates the analysis but basically has no relation to the basic threefold analysis of variances: price, efficiency, and volume.

These relationships may be tied back to Exhibit 9-7. Reconsider the facts there. Assume that the master (static) budget volume was 11,000 standard hours allowed. A new column (5) would be added for this master budget. No variances in the original exhibit would be affected, except that a final set of variances could be added at the bottom. Then, the volume variance would span from column (3) to the new column (5). The relationships among all overhead variances may be summarized:

(1)	(2)	(3)	(4)	(5) MASTER (STATIC) BUDGET
		V 13,600		V (11,000 × 1.70) = 18,700
		F 10,000		F = 10,000
24,450	23,430	23,600	21,600	28,700

↑ Spending ↑ Efficiency ↑ Denominator ↑

↑ Flexible budget ↑ Denominator ↑

↑ Under- or overapplied overhead ↑

↑ Spending ↑ Efficiency ↑ Volume ↑

Spending		Efficiency		Volume	
V	820 U	V	170 F	V	5,100 U
F	200 U	F (not applicable)		F (not applicable)	
Combined	1,020 U	Combined	170 F	Combined	5,100 U

↑ Master or static budget variance ↑

The bottom two sets of brackets demonstrate how the basic threefold analysis of variances (price or spending, efficiency, and volume) provides an explanatory trail. The path proceeds from column (1), actual results at actual prices, to column (5), the master (static) budget that is so often the original point of departure in the minds of managers.

PROBLEM FOR SELF-STUDY

PROBLEM

1. Suppose that the average unit selling price in Exhibit 10-4 had been actually $20. What would the volume variance have been?
2. In addition to the above, assume that the new technicians caused labor and material inputs to be 15 percent in excess of the standard allowed. What would have been the (a) total efficiency variances and (b) total price and spending variances?

SOLUTION

1. The volume variance would be unaffected because its computation is based on the assumption that all price and efficiency factors are held constant.
2. (a) .15 × $550,000 = $82,500 efficiency variance (unfavorable).
   (b) There is no price variance in revenue. The $45,000 unfavorable variance in variable costs has been partially explained by the $82,500 unfavorable efficiency variance. Therefore, the remainder must be a favorable price and spending variance of $82,500 − $45,000, or $37,500.

SUMMARY

Many varieties of product costing are in use. For years, manufacturing companies have regularly used absorption costing, which includes fixed factory overhead as a part of the cost of product. In contrast, direct costing, which is more accurately called *variable costing,* charges fixed factory overhead to the period immediately; that is, fixed overhead is excluded from inventories. Absorption costing continues to be much more widely used than direct costing, although the growing use of the contribution approach in performance measurement has led to increasing use of direct costing for internal purposes.

Three commonly used activity bases for developing product-costing fixed-overhead rates are (a) expected annual activity, (b) normal activity over three to five years, and (c) practical capacity. The selection is essentially a matter of opinion. The choice will influence inventory valuations and resultant timing of income recognition.

The advocates of currently attainable standard costs for product costing maintain that the results are conceptually superior to the results under "actual" or "normal" product-costing systems. They contend that the costs of inefficiency are not inventoriable.

There are essentially three basic types of variances that provide perspective for budgetary control: price, efficiency, and volume. All other variances are subparts or combinations of these three.

SUGGESTED READINGS

GERMAIN BOER, *Direct Cost and Contribution Accounting: An Integrated Management Accounting System* (New York: John Wiley & Sons, Inc., 1974.)

W. B. MCFARLAND, *Concepts for Management Accounting* (New York: National Association of Accountants, 1966).

There are literally hundreds of articles on direct costing or the contribution approach in accounting periodicals, most notably *Management Accounting.*

QUESTIONS, PROBLEMS, AND CASES

10-1 Why is *direct costing* a misnomer?

10-2 List four alternate terms for *contribution margin.*

10-3 "The central issue in direct costing is *timing.*" Explain.

10-4 "The main trouble with direct costing is that it ignores the increasing importance of fixed costs in modern business." Do you agree? Why?

10-5 "The depreciation on the paper machine is every bit as much a part of the cost of the manufactured paper as the cost of the raw pulp." Do you agree? Why?

10-6 *Straightforward Direct-Costing Income Statement* (W. Crum) Admiral Company wants an income statement prepared from the following information, using the direct-costing (variable-costing) approach. No beginning inventories of work in process or finished goods; no ending inventories of work in process. Production was 500,000 units, of which 400,000 were sold for $30 each. Unit direct-material cost was $6; unit direct-labor cost was $8; variable manufacturing cost was $1 per unit; fixed manufacturing cost was $2,000,000. Variable selling and administrative cost was $1 per unit sold; fixed selling and administrative cost was $1,500,000. Ignore income taxes.

10-7 *Comparison of Actual Costing Methods* The AX Company sells its product at $2 per unit. The company uses a first-in, first-out, actual costing system. That is, a new fixed factory overhead application rate is computed each year by dividing the actual fixed factory overhead by the actual production. The following data relate to its first two years of operation:

	YEAR 1	*YEAR 2*
Sales	1,000 units	1,200 units
Production	1,400 units	1,000 units
Costs		
Factory—Variable	$700	$500
—Fixed	700	700
Selling—Variable	100	120
Administrative—Fixed	400	400

required

1. Income statements for each of the years based on absorption costing.
2. Income statements for each of the years based on direct or variable costing.
3. A reconciliation or explanation of the differences in the reported profits for each year resulting from the use of the methods required above.

10-8 *Income Statements* (SIA) The Mass Company manufactures and sells a single product. The following data cover the two latest operating years:

	19_3	*19_4*
Selling price per unit	$ 40	$ 40
Sales in units	25,000	25,000
Opening inventory in units	1,000	1,000
Closing inventory in units	1,000	5,000
Fixed manufacturing costs	120,000	120,000
Fixed selling and administrative costs	90,000	90,000

Standard variable costs per unit:

Materials	$10.50	Variable selling and administrative	$1.20
Direct labor	9.50		
Variable overhead	4.00		

The denominator activity is 30,000 units a year. Mass Company accounting records produce direct-costing information, and year-end adjustments are made to produce external reports showing absorption-costing data. Any variances are charged to cost of sales.

required

1. Ignoring income taxes, prepare two income statements for 19_4, one under the direct-costing method and one under the absorption-costing method. Present your answer in good format.
2. Explain briefly why the net income figures computed in part (a) agree or do not agree.
3. Give two advantages and two disadvantages of using direct costing for internal reporting.

10-9 *Direct Costing and Cost-Volume-Profit Relationships* (Prepared by the author and adapted for use in a CPA examination.) The Fleer Company has a maximum capacity of 210,000 units per year. Normal activity is regarded as 180,000 units per year. Standard variable manufacturing costs are $11 per unit. Fixed factory overhead is $540,000 per year. Variable selling costs are $3 per unit, while fixed selling costs are $252,000 per year. Sales price is $20 per unit.

required

(Assume no variances from standard variable manufacturing costs in parts 1 through 3)

1. What is the breakeven point expressed in *dollar* sales?
2. How many *units* must be sold to earn a target net income of $60,000 per year?
3. How many units must be sold to earn a net income of 10 percent of sales?
4. Assume the following results for a given year:

   Sales, 150,000 units. Net variance for standard variable manufacturing costs, $40,000, unfavorable. Production, 160,000 units. Beginning inventory, 10,000 units.

   All variances are written off as additions to (or deductions from) Standard Cost of Sales.

   a. Prepare income statements for the year under:
      (1) Absorption costing
      (2) Direct costing
   b. In fifty words or less, explain the difference in net income between the two statements.

10-10 *Multiple-Choice Absorption-Direct Costing* (CPA) The following annual flexible budget has been prepared for use in making decisions relating to product X.

	100,000 UNITS	150,000 UNITS	200,000 UNITS
Sales volume	$800,000	$1,200,000	$1,600,000
Manufacturing costs:			
Variable	$300,000	$ 450,000	$ 600,000
Fixed	200,000	200,000	200,000
	$500,000	$ 650,000	$ 800,000
Selling and other expenses:			
Variable	$200,000	$ 300,000	$ 400,000
Fixed	160,000	160,000	160,000
	$360,000	$ 460,000	$ 560,000
Income (or loss)	$ (60,000)	$ 90,000	$ 240,000

The 200,000-unit budget has been adopted and will be used for allocating fixed manufacturing costs to units of product X; at the end of the first six months the following information is available:

	UNITS
Production completed	120,000
Sales	60,000

All fixed costs are budgeted and incurred uniformly throughout the year and all costs incurred coincide with the budget.

Over- and underapplied fixed manufacturing costs are deferred until year-end. Annual sales have the following seasonal pattern:

	PORTION OF ANNUAL SALES
First quarter	10%
Second quarter	20
Third quarter	30
Fourth quarter	40
	100%

required

1. The amount of fixed factory costs applied to product during the first six months under absorption costing would be (a) overapplied by $20,000, (b) equal to the fixed costs incurred, (c) underapplied by $40,000, (d) underapplied by $80,000, (e) none of the above.
2. Reported net income (or loss) for the first six months under absorption costing would be (a) $160,000, (b) $80,000, (c) $40,000, (d) ($40,000), (e) none of the above.
3. Reported net income (or loss) for the first six months under direct costing would be (a) $144,000, (b) $72,000, (c) $0, (d) ($36,000), (e) none of the above.
4. Assuming that 90,000 units of product X were sold during the first six months and that this is to be used as a basis, the revised budget estimate for the total number of units to be sold during this year would be (a) 360,000, (b) 240,000, (c) 200,000, (d) 120,000, (e) none of the above.

10-11 *Direct versus Absorption Costing* The Davis Company uses an absorption-costing system based on the "normal costing" procedures described in Chapter 4. Variable manufacturing costs, including material costs, were $3.00 per unit; the actual production rate was ten units per hour. Fixed factory overhead was applied at $5.00 per hour ($300,000 ÷ 60,000 hours of denominator activity). Sales price is $5.00 per unit. Variable selling and administrative costs, which are related to units sold, were $1.00 per unit. Fixed selling and administrative costs were $120,000. Beginning inventory in 19_1 was 30,000 units; ending inventory was 40,000 units. Sales in 19_1 were 540,000 units. The same unit costs persisted throughout 19_0 and 19_1.

required

1. Prepare an income statement for 19_1, assuming that all under- or overapplied overhead is written off directly at year-end as an adjustment to Cost of Goods Sold.
2. The president has heard about direct costing. He asks you to recast the 19_1 statement as it should appear under direct costing.
3. Explain the difference in net income as calculated in parts 1 and 2.
4. Prepare a freehand graph of how *fixed factory* overhead was accounted for under absorption costing. That is, there will be two lines—one for the budgeted fixed

overhead (which happens to also be the actual fixed factory overhead) and one for the product application rate. Show how the over- or underapplied overhead might be indicated on the graph.

10-12 *Breakeven Points Under Absorption Costing* Refer to Problem 10-11. Assume the same facts except that sales were 420,000 units.

required

1. What is the breakeven point under direct costing?
2. Compute the net income under (a) direct costing and (b) absorption costing.
3. What is the breakeven point under absorption costing? Explain the difference in net income as calculated in part 2.
4. What would be the net income under (a) direct costing and (b) absorption costing if production were 600,000 units and sales were 540,000 units?

10-13 *The All-Fixed Company in 1996* (R. Marple, adapted) It is the end of 1996. The All-Fixed Company began operations in January 1995. The company is so named because it has no variable costs. All its costs are fixed; they do not vary with output.

The All-Fixed Company is located on the bank of a river and has its own hydroelectric plant to supply power, light, and heat. The company manufactures a synthetic fertilizer from air and river water, and sells its product at a price that is not expected to change. It has a small staff of employees, all hired on an annual-salary basis. The output of the plant can be increased or decreased by adjusting a few dials on a control panel.

The following are data regarding the operations by the All-Fixed Company:

	1995	*1996**
Sales	10,000 tons	10,000 tons
Production	20,000 tons	—
Selling price	$30 per ton	$30 per ton
Costs (all fixed):		
Production	$280,000	$280,000
General and administrative	$ 40,000	$ 40,000

* Management adopted the policy, effective January 1, 1996, of producing only as the product was needed to fill sales. During 1996, sales were the same as for 1995 and were filled entirely from inventory at the start of 1995.

required

1. Prepare three-column income statements for 1995, 1996, and the two years together, using
   a. Absorption costing,
   b. Direct (variable) costing.
2. What is the breakeven point under (a) absorption costing and (b) variable costing?
3. What inventory costs would be carried on the balance sheets at December 31, 1995 and 1996, under each method?
4. Comment on the results in 1 and 2. Which costing method appears more useful?

10-14 *The Semi-Fixed Company in 1996* The Semi-Fixed Company began operations in 1995 and differs from The All-Fixed Company (described in Problem 10-13) in only one respect: It has both fixed and variable production costs. Its variable costs are $7 per ton and its fixed production costs $140,000 a year. Normal activity is 20,000 tons per year.

required

1. Using the same data as in Problem 10-13, except for the change in production-cost behavior, prepare three-column income statements for 1995, 1996, and the two years together, under
   a. Absorption costing,
   b. Variable costing.
2. Why did the Semi-Fixed Company earn a profit for the two-year period while the All-Fixed Company in Problem 10-13 suffered a loss?
3. What inventory costs would be carried on the balance sheets at December 31, 1995 and 1996, under each method?
4. How may the variable-costing approach be reconciled with the definition of an asset as being "economic service potential"?

10-15 *Inventory Techniques and Management Planning* It is November 30, 19_4. Given the following for a company division's operations for January through November, 19_4:

DIVISION G

Income Statement for Eleven Months Ending November 30, 19_4

	UNITS	*DOLLARS*	
Sales @ $1,000	1,000		1,000,000
Less cost of goods sold:			
Beginning inventory, December 31, 19_3, @ $800	50	40,000	
Manufacturing costs @ $800, including $600 per unit for fixed overhead	1,100	880,000	
Total standard cost of goods available for sale	1,150	920,000	
Ending inventory, November 30, 19_4, @ $800	150	120,000	
Standard cost of goods sold*	1,000		800,000
Gross margin			200,000
Other expenses:			
Variable, 1,000 units @ $50		50,000	
Fixed, @ $10,000 monthly		110,000	160,000
Net operating income			40,000

* There are absolutely no variances for the eleven-month period considered as a whole.

Production in the past three months has been 100 units monthly. Practical capacity is 125 units monthly. In order to retain a stable nucleus of key employees, monthly production is never scheduled at less than 40 units.

Maximum available storage space for inventory is regarded as 200 units. The sales outlook for the next four months is 70 units monthly. Inventory is never to be less than 50 units.

The company uses a standard absorption-costing system. Denominator production activity is 1,200 units annually. All variances are disposed of at year-end as an adjustment to Standard Cost of Goods Sold.

required

1. The division manager is given an annual bonus that is geared to net operating income. Given the data above, assume that the manager wants to maximize the company's net income for 19_4. How many units should he schedule for production in December? Note carefully that you do not have to (*nor should you*) compute the exact net income for 19_4 in this or in subsequent parts of this question.

2. Assume that standard direct costing is in use rather than standard absorption costing. Would direct-costing net income for 19_4 be higher, lower, or the same as standard absorption-costing net income, assuming that production for December is 80 units and sales are 70 units? Why?
3. If standard direct costing were used, what production schedule should the division manager set? Why?
4. Assume that the manager is interested in maximizing his performance over the long run, and that his performance is being judged on an after-income-tax basis. Given the data in the beginning of the problem, assume that income tax rates will be halved in 19_5, and assume that the year-end write-offs of variances are acceptable for income tax purposes. Assume that standard absorption costing is used. How many units should be scheduled for production in December? Why?

10-16 *Some Additional Requirements to Problem 10-15; Absorption Costing and Denominator Variances* Refer to Problem 10-15.

1. What net operating income will be reported for 19_4 as a whole, assuming that the implied cost behavior patterns will continue in December as they did in January through November, and assuming—without regard to your answer to requirement 1 in Problem 10-15—that production for December is 80 units and sales are 70 units?
2. Assume the same conditions as in requirement 1, except that practical capacity was used in setting fixed-overhead rates for product costing throughout 19_4. What denominator variance would be reported for 19_4?

10-17 *Comparison of Variable Costing and Absorption Costing* Consider the following data:

MELDER COMPANY

Income Statement for the Year Ended December 31, 19_4

	VARIABLE COSTING	ABSORPTION COSTING
Sales	$7,000,000	$7,000,000
Costs applied to goods sold (at standard)	$3,660,000	$4,575,000
Fixed manufacturing overhead	1,000,000	—
Manufacturing variances (all unfavorable):		
Direct material	50,000	50,000
Direct labor	60,000	60,000
Variable overhead	30,000	30,000
Fixed overhead:		
Spending or Budget	100,000	100,000
Denominator	—	400,000
Total selling expenses	1,000,000	1,000,000
Total administrative expenses	500,000	500,000
Total expenses	$6,400,000	$6,715,000
Operating income	$ 600,000	$ 285,000

The inventories, carried at standard costs, were:

	VARIABLE COSTING	ABSORPTION COSTING
December 31, 19_3	$1,320,000	$1,650,000
December 31, 19_4	60,000	75,000

required

1. Malcolm Melder, president of the Melder Company, has asked you to explain why the income for 19_4 is less than that for 19_3, despite the fact that sales have increased 40 percent over last year.
2. At what percentage of denominator activity was the factory working during 19_4?
3. Prepare a numerical reconciliation and explanation of the difference between the operating incomes under absorption costing and variable costing.

10-18 *Executive Incentives; Relevant Costing* The data below pertain to the B. E. Company:

	YEAR 19_1
Selling price per unit	$ 2.00
Total fixed costs—production	$ 8,400,000.00
Total fixed costs—selling and administrative	$ 600,000.00
Variable cost per unit—selling and administrative	$ .50
Sales in units	17,000,000
Production in units	17,000,000
Normal activity in units (based on three- to five-year demand)	30,000,000
Operating loss	$ 500,000.00

No opening or closing inventories.

The board of directors has approached a competent outside executive to take over the company. He is an optimistic soul and he agrees to become president at a token salary, but his contract provides for a year-end bonus amounting to 10 percent of net operating profit (before considering the bonus or income taxes). The annual profit was to be certified by a huge public accounting firm.

The new president, filled with rosy expectations, promptly raised the advertising budget by $3,500,000, stepped up production to an annual rate of 30,000,000 units ("to fill the pipelines," the president said). As soon as all outlets had sufficient stock, the advertising campaign was launched, and sales for 19_2 increased—but only to a level of 25,000,000 units.

The certified income statement for 19_2 contained the following data:

Sales, 25,000,000 × $2.00		$50,000,000
Production costs:		
Variable, 30,000,000 × $1.00	$30,000,000	
Fixed	8,400,000	
Total	$38,400,000	
Inventory, 5,000,000 units (1/6)	6,400,000	
Cost of goods sold		32,000,000
Gross margin		$18,000,000
Selling and administrative expenses:		
Variable	$12,500,000	
Fixed	4,100,000	
		16,600,000
Net operating profit		$ 1,400,000

The day after the statement was certified, the president resigned to take a job with another corporation having difficulties similar to those that B. E. Company had a year ago. The president remarked, "I enjoy challenges. Now that B. E. Company is in the black, I'd prefer tackling another knotty difficulty." His contract with his new employer is similar to the one he had with B. E. Company.

required

1. As a member of the board, what comments would you make at the next meeting regarding the most recent income statement? Maximum production capacity is 40,000,000 units per year.
2. Would you change your remarks in 1 if (consider each part independently):
   a. Sales outlook for the coming three years is 20,000,000 units per year?
   b. Sales outlook for the coming three years is 30,000,000 units per year?
   c. Sales outlook for the coming three years is 40,000,000 units per year?
   d. The company is to be liquidated immediately, so that the only sales in 19_3 will be the 5,000,000 units still in inventory?
   e. The sales outlook for 19_3 is 45,000,000 units?
3. Assuming that the $140,000 bonus is paid, would you favor a similar arrangement for the next president? If not, and you were outvoted, what changes in a bonus contract would you try to have adopted?

10-19 *Overhead Rates and Cyclical Business* It is a time of severe business depression throughout the capital-goods industries. A division manager for a large corporation in a heavy-machinery industry is confused and unhappy. He is distressed with the controller, whose cost department keeps feeding the manager costs that are of little use because they are higher than ever before. At the same time, the manager has to quote lower prices than before in order to get any business.

required

1. What activity base is probably being used for application of overhead?
2. How might the overhead be applied in order to make the cost data more useful in making price quotations?
3. Would the product costs furnished by the cost department be satisfactory for the costing of the annual inventory?

10-20 *Argument About Proper Activity Base* The president, the controller, and the assistant controller have studied possible alternative activity bases for overhead application to products. Until now, the company has applied all actual overhead to products on a month-to-month basis. The three executives have different views as to the most appropriate base. They briefly summarized their thinking as follows:

President: "The only time I'm satisfied is when we are operating at peak capacity. If we're not, our profits are less than what they should be. As I understand it, the use of practical capacity as a base will result in lower product costs. This will allow us to price more competitively, and at the same time we'll have some idea of the loss from our inability to utilize full capacity."

Controller: "The only proper base for overhead application is expected activity for the year. Each year's costs are borne to benefit each year's production. The only sensible way to track yearly overhead costs is to pool them and then use an annual average rate to funnel them to products as they are manufactured. Any major year-end over- or underabsorbed overhead should be prorated over the year's production by an adjusting entry."

Assistant Controller (who plans to resign next week): "You're both wrong! Anybody who thinks this matter through realizes that the core of the question is the sticky, almost unalterable behavior of fixed overhead. Commitments like fixed assets, research costs, and executive salaries not only do not change from month to month; they do not even change materially from year to year.

These commitments are made to sustain a level of operations for three or four years ahead. We should use normal activity as a base. Furthermore, major year-end under- or overabsorbed overhead should be carried forward on the balance sheet from year to year. Over a three- or four-year period, such overhead will be largely counterbalanced."

Pertinent data on factory overhead for this company follow:

	YEAR	VARIABLE OVERHEAD	FIXED OVERHEAD	TOTAL OVERHEAD	STANDARD DIRECT-LABOR HOURS
Past data:					
	1	$ 500,000	$1,000,000	$1,500,000	500,000
	2	1,000,000	1,100,000	2,100,000	1,000,000
	3	800,000	1,200,000	2,000,000	800,000
Future estimates:					
	4	880,000	1,300,000	2,180,000	800,000
	5	1,100,000	1,300,000	2,400,000	1,000,000
	6	1,320,000	1,400,000	2,720,000	1,200,000

As a management consultant who specializes in cost-accounting difficulties, write a concise report supporting the most proper overhead activity base to be used in this case. As an appendix, write a brief answer to each of the contentions of the president, controller, and assistant controller. Assume that practical capacity is 1,300,000 hours.

10-21 *Income Taxes and Practical Capacity* In the United States there is nothing illegal or immoral about keeping multiple sets of accounting records, one to satisfy income tax reporting requirements, one to satisfy investor reporting requirements, one to satisfy manager decision requirements, and so on. Nevertheless, real or imagined costs versus benefits lead most companies to have one or, at most, two sets of records. Income tax regulations have heavy effects on accounting systems because records must be kept to satisfy tax laws.

For years the Internal Revenue Service was liberal regarding the tendency of companies to write off many indirect manufacturing costs, particularly depreciation on equipment, as charges against income immediately. However, in 1975 new income tax regulations (see the Regulations 1.471-11) forced industry to hold back more indirect costs as "inventoriable" costs. In short, the regulations came down hard against the variable- or direct-costing approach to inventory valuation and in favor of absorption costing.

The regulations insist that any significant under- or overapplied overhead be prorated among the appropriate inventory accounts and cost of goods sold. However, the regulations explicitly approve a "practical capacity concept." This permits the immediate write-off (rather than proration) of the denominator variance that results from using a fixed overhead rate based on a practical capacity denominator volume level.

Corporation X operates a stamping plant with a theoretical capacity of 50 units per hour. The plant is actually open 1,960 hours per year based on an 8-hour day, 5-day week and 15 shut-down days for vacations and holidays. A reasonable allowance for down-time (the time allowed for ordinary and necessary repairs and maintenance) is 5 percent of theoretical capacity. The latter is defined as the level of production that the manufacturer could reach if all machines and departments were operated continuously for the 1,960 hours at peak efficiency.

required

1. Compute practical capacity in units per year. Assume no loss of production during starting up, closing down, or employee work breaks.
2. Assume that 74,480 units are produced for the year and that budgeted and actual fixed indirect production costs totaled $9,310,000. Also assume that 7,448 units are on hand at the end of the taxable year and that there were no beginning inventories. Compute the amount of fixed indirect costs that would have been applied to production during the year. What amount will be allowed as a deduction in the computation of income taxes for the year? Label your computations.

10-22 *Effects of Denominator Choice* The Armstrong Company installed standard costs and a flexible budget on January 1, 19_3. The president had been pondering on how fixed manufacturing overhead should be applied to product. He decided to wait for the first month's results before making a final choice of what denominator volume should be used from that day forward.

In January, the company operated at an activity of 70,000 standard hours allowed for the good units actually produced. If the company had used practical capacity as a denominator volume, the budget variance would have been $10,000, unfavorable, and the denominator variance would have been $36,000, unfavorable. If the company had used "normal" activity as a denominator volume, the denominator variance would have been $20,000, favorable. Budgeted fixed overhead was $120,000 for the month.

required

1. Denominator volume, assuming "normal" activity as the denominator.
2. Denominator volume, assuming practical capacity as the denominator.

10-23 *Choice of Activity Base and Proration of Variances* (CPA, adapted) Last year the Crowley Corporation adopted a standard-cost system. Labor standards were set on the basis of time studies and prevailing wage rates. Material standards were determined from material specifications and prices then in effect. In determining its standard for overhead, Crowley estimated that a total of 6,000,000 finished units would be produced during the next five years to satisfy demand for its product. The five-year period was selected to average out seasonal and cyclical fluctuations and allow for sales trends. By dividing the annual average of 1,200,000 units into the total annual budgeted overhead, a standard cost was developed for manufacturing overhead.

At June 30, 19_9, the end of the current fiscal year, a partial trial balance revealed the following:

	DEBITS	CREDITS
Material-price variance		$25,000
Material-quantity variance	$ 9,000	
Labor-price variance	30,000	
Labor-efficiency variance	7,500	
Controllable-overhead variance	2,000	
Noncontrollable (capacity) overhead variance	75,000	

Standards were set at the beginning of the year and have remained unchanged. All inventories are priced at standard cost.

required

1. What conclusions can be drawn from each of the six variances shown in Crowley's trial balance?
2. The amount of nonvariable manufacturing-overhead cost to be included in product cost depends on whether or not the allocation is based on: (a) ideal

(or theoretical) capacity, (b) practical capacity, (c) normal activity, or (d) expected annual activity. Describe each of these allocation bases and give a theoretical principal argument for each.

3. Give the theoretical justification for each of the following methods of accounting for the net amount of all standard-cost variances for year-end financial reporting:
   a. Presenting the net variance as an income or expense on the income statement
   b. Allocating the net variance among Inventories and Cost of Goods Sold
   c. Presenting the net variance as an adjustment to Cost of Goods Sold

10-24 *Proration of Variances, Multiple Choice* (CPA) Tolbert Manufacturing Company uses a standard-cost system in accounting for the cost of production of its only product, product A. The standards for the production of one unit of product A are as follows:

Direct materials: 10 feet of item 1 at $.75 per foot and 3 feet of item 2 at $1.00 per foot.
Direct labor: 4 hours at $3.50 per hour.
Manufacturing overhead: applied at 150 percent of standard-direct-labor costs.

There was no inventory on hand at July 1, 19_2. Following is a summary of costs and related data for the production of product A during the year ended June 30, 19_3.

100,000 feet of item 1 were purchased at $.78 per foot.
30,000 feet of item 2 were purchased at $.90 per foot.
8,000 units of product A were produced which required 78,000 feet of item 1, 26,000 feet of item 2, and 31,000 hours of direct labor at $3.60 per hour.
6,000 units of product A were sold.

At June 30, 19_3, there are 22,000 feet of item 1, 4,000 feet of item 2, and 2,000 completed units of product A on hand. All purchases and transfers are "charged in" at standard.

required

Choose the best answers:

1. For the year ended June 30, 19_3, the total debits to the raw-materials account for the purchase of item 1 would be (a) $75,000, (b) $78,000, (c) $58,500, (d) $60,000.
2. For the year ended June 30, 19_3, the total debits to the work-in-process account for direct labor would be (a) $111,600, (b) $108,500, (c) $112,000, (d) $115,100.
3. Before allocation of standard variances the balance in the material-efficiency-variance account for item 2 was (a) $1,000 credit, (b) $2,600 debit, (c) $600 debit, (d) $2,000 debit.
4. If all standard variances were prorated to inventories and cost of goods sold, the amount of material-efficiency variance for item 2 to be prorated to raw-materials inventory would be (a) $0, (b) $333 credit, (c) $333 debit, (d) $500 debit.
5. If all standard variances were prorated to inventories and cost of goods sold, the amount of material-price variance for item 1 to be prorated to raw-materials inventory would be (a) $0, (b) $647 debit, (c) $600 debit, (d) $660 debit.

10-25 *Comparison of Actual Costing, Normal Costing, and Standard Costing* The Vatner Company began business on January 1, 19_1. It manufactured a single product that was easy to standardize, so a standard-cost system was adopted.

Price variances for raw material were isolated upon purchase, and Work in Process, Finished Goods, and Cost of Goods Sold were carried at standard cost. The standard cost per finished unit was based on one pound of raw material usage, one hour of direct-labor time, and an overhead rate as related to labor time.

The standard price for raw material was $1 per pound; for direct labor, $4 per hour. The factory overhead budget for 19_1 was $200,000; 100,000 units were scheduled for production during 19_1. Any predetermined overhead rates were to be based on a denominator activity of 100,000 hours.

The following are the actual results for 19_1:

Sales	$1,000,000
Material purchases, 160,000 pounds @ $1.10	176,000
Material inputs, 110,000 pounds	
Direct-labor inputs, 120,000 hours	480,000
Factory overhead incurred	215,000
Nonmanufacturing expenses	300,000
Finished units produced, 100,000	
Finished units sold, 70,000	

Amy Vatner, the president, decided to use some form of absorption costing. She realized that because hers was a new company she had some latitude in deciding how to report the results of operations to investors and to the Internal Revenue Service. Moreover, she also realized that her choice would set a precedent regarding the method of reporting in subsequent years. Finally, she recognized that she could continue to use standard costing for internal reporting purposes without being obliged to use it for external purposes.

required

(T-accounts may be helpful)

1. Vatner has asked you to prepare three comparative income statements in columnar form. The columns would be based on the following assumptions: (a) actual costing, (b) normal costing, and (c) standard costing. All variances are to be written off against revenue.
2. By how much do the net incomes in columns (b) and (c) differ from column (a)? Fully explain each difference.
3. Which of the three alternatives should Vatner choose for reporting to investors? For reporting to the Internal Revenue Service? Why?

10-26 *Proration Comparisons* Stin Company has the following results for the year:

Purchases of direct materials (charged to Stores at standard prices)	$100,000
Purchase-price variance	10,000
Direct labor—applied at standard rate	40,000
Direct-labor price variance	1,000
Direct-labor efficiency variance	4,000
Direct-material efficiency variance	4,000
Direct-materials—applied at standard prices	80,000
Manufacturing overhead applied—at standard rate	40,000
Manufacturing overhead incurred	45,000
Sales	135,000
Selling and administrative expenses	20,000

Assume that there is no ending work in process. Assume that one uniform product is made and that 60 percent of the production has been sold. There were no beginning inventories.

required

A comparative analysis of the effects on net income of the following assumptions:

1. Actual historical costing. That is, no predetermined costs are used.
2. Normal costing with proration of underapplied overhead.
3. Normal costing without proration of underapplied overhead.
4. Standard costing with proration of all variances.
5. Standard costing without proration of any variances.

10-27 *Relating Results to Master Budget* The Argon Company, a one-department firm, produced and sold a type of carry-on flight luggage that required several hand operations. The product had some variations, but it was essentially visualized as a single product bearing one selling price. The master budget for the forthcoming month included the condensed income statement below:

	ACTUAL RESULTS AT ACTUAL PRICES	MASTER (STATIC) BUDGET	VARIANCE	BUDGET FORMULA PER UNIT
Units	7,000	9,000	2,000	—
Sales	$168,000	$216,000	$48,000 U	$24.00
Variable costs	112,500	133,200	20,700 F	14.80
Contribution margin	$ 55,500	$ 82,800	$27,300 U	$ 9.20
Fixed costs	70,300	70,000	300 U	
Operating income (loss)	$ (14,800)	$ 12,800	$27,600 U	

F = Favorable U = Unfavorable

The budget formula for fixed costs is $70,000 per month.

The president wants a performance budget that better pinpoints some major variances between the actual results and the master budget. For example, she is displeased by the report above because it indicates favorable variances for variable costs despite her suspicions that day-to-day control was unsatisfactory.

required

1. Prepare a summary of performance that provides an overview for the president. That is, prepare a five-column report: actual results at actual prices, flexible-budget variances, flexible budget, volume or activity variance, and master budget. Have six rows: physical units, sales, variable costs, contribution margin, fixed costs, and operating income.
2. Assume that the monthly denominator volume is 10,000 units. Compute the denominator variance. Show how your tabulation in part 1 would be changed if absorption costing were used instead of direct (variable) costing.
3. Repeat part 2. However, assume that production was 8,800 units and inventories have risen by 1,800 units. For simplicity, assume that the dollar amounts of the variable-cost variances are still $8,900, unfavorable, and that the fixed-cost budget variance is still $300, unfavorable. Assume that the denominator variance affects income immediately rather than being prorated between inventory and cost of goods sold.

10-28 *Extension of Problem 10-27* Repeat part 3 of the problem, except assume that production was 6,000 units and inventories had declined by 1,000 units. Also assume that the level of fixed costs, the denominator volume, and the fixed overhead rate had not changed over two years.

10-29 *Volume and Denominator Variances* Reconsider the final example in the section, "Relationship of Volume and Denominator Variances." Suppose that the denominator volume were 200 units instead of 150 units. Compute the denominator variance. How much fixed costs would be applied to ending inventory? What would be the difference between the net income under absorption costing and direct costing?

10-30 *Analysis of Airline Operations* The Carruthers Airline had the following data for 19_2 (in thousands of dollars):

	MASTER BUDGET	RESULTS AT ACTUAL PRICES	VARIANCE
Revenue	100,000	84,000	16,000 U
Variable expenses	60,000*	51,600	8,400 F
Contribution margin	40,000	32,400	7,600 U
Fixed expenses	35,000	35,000	0
Operating income	5,000	(2,600)	7,600 U

* Includes $45 million of wages, meals, and fuel.

You discover that a midyear airfare increase of 9 percent had resulted in a 5 percent increase in average revenue per passenger mile flown for the year. Wage, meal, and fuel increases and various inefficiencies had exceeded the pace of the fare increases and averaged 10 percent for the year. Other price and efficiency effects were minor and can be ignored.

required

Prepare an analytical tabulation as an explanation for the president. Begin with actual results at actual prices and end with the master budget. Show the variances attributable to (a) combined price and efficiency and (b) volume effects.

10-31 *Difficult Comparison of Volume and Denominator Variances* Given for *combined* variable and fixed overhead, using the definitions of denominator variance and volume variance employed in this course:

Underapplied overhead	$48,000	Standard hours allowed for output achieved	102,000
Spending variance	$54,000 U	Variable overhead rate per hour	$1
Efficiency variance	$6,000 U	Master budget in terms of standard hours allowed	110,000
Budgeted overhead at denominator volume	$392,000	Actual overhead incurred	$456,000

required

Assume that a flexible budget and standard absorption-costing system is in use. Compute (1) the denominator volume used to set the overhead rate, (2) volume variance, (3) master-budget variance. Indicate whether your variances in (2) and (3) are unfavorable or favorable by using U or F.

10-32 *Difficult Comparison of Absorption and Direct Costing; Volume and Denominator Variances* Salvation Industries, a not-for-profit charity, has an extensive profit-seeking activity that repairs old furniture and appliances for resale. Through the years, experience has led to the development of a standard absorption-costing system for controlling activities. As donated goods are received, decisions are made regarding which items to repair, which items to sell untouched, and which items to discard altogether. The profit from the repair activity is used to help cover other organizational overhead.

The manager of a centralized Chicago repair center, Susan Zingler, decides what items should be repaired and uses a form of standard-cost analysis. She tries to maximize profit in relation to total available hours. However, despite her contribution approach to work scheduling, she has been forced to use an absorption-costing system that was installed with the help of a CPA firm in 1923.

For the year 19_4, the budgeted and actual fixed costs were both equal in the manufacturing ($100,000) and nonmanufacturing ($25,000) phases of the activity. The sum of the spending, price, and efficiency variances was $50,000, unfavorable. On an absorption-costing basis, the fixed manufacturing overhead had been applied to various products on the basis of the denominator volume level in hours used in the master budget. There was an unfavorable denominator variance for fixed manufacturing overhead of $20,000. Production and sales were expressed in terms of equivalent standard hours earned; 40,000 standard hours were produced and sold at an average selling price of $30 per hour during 19_4. The budgeted average selling price was also $30 per hour.

required

You have been asked to prepare a comparative statement of the original budgeted income statement for the year and the actual results. No variances were anticipated in the original budget. Even though the organization has kept records on an absorption-costing basis, you have decided to prepare a statement on the direct-costing basis. You have determined that the standard contribution margin was $10 per hour. Please present a neat, fully labeled statement.

SPECIAL REVIEW MATERIAL FOR CHAPTERS 7 THROUGH 10

10-33 *Comparison of Alternative Income Statements* (J. March, adapted) Alternative income statements for the same company for a given year follow:

	A	B	C
Sales	$100,000	$100,000	$100,000
Cost of goods sold	40,000	30,000	42,000
	$ 60,000	$ 70,000	$ 58,000
Variances:			
Direct material	(1,500)	(1,500)	—
Direct labor	(500)	(500)	—
Factory overhead	(4,000)	—	(4,000)
	$ 54,000	$ 68,000	$ 54,000
Other operating expenses (all fixed)	40,000	54,000	40,000
Operating income	$ 14,000	$ 14,000	$ 14,000

required

Write a brief explanation for each of your answers:

1. Which cost system: (1) actual cost, (2) standard absorption cost, (3) standard variable cost, or (4) historical cost with predetermined overhead rates was used for *A*? For *B*? For *C*?
2. Did the inventory: (1) increase, (2) decrease, (3) remain unchanged for *A*? For *B*? For *C*?
3. What was the selling and administrative expense for the year?

4. What would you expect the net operating income to be if sales volume increased 10 percent and selling prices remained the same? Assume that all variable costs will be at standard—in other words, no variances are to be budgeted for material, labor, or variable overhead for any production.
5. Was the production volume for the year higher than, lower than, or equal to the predetermined volume?
6. What was the fixed factory overhead for the year?
7. Was the variable factory overhead for the year more than, less than, or equal to the budget?

10-34 *Comprehensive Review of Absorption Costing and Direct Costing* A fire destroyed most of the assets and records of the Salinas Division of a large corporation on December 31, 19_2. The division manufactured a single product and used a standard-cost system together with a flexible budget. Salinas must try to reconstruct its records to help establish the amount of an insurance claim and its loss for income tax purposes. Unfortunately, the records are in chaos. Moreover, the division manager had been thinking of switching from an absorption (full) costing to variable (direct) costing. As an experiment, parallel records were being kept throughout 19_2 on both the absorption-costing and direct-costing basis.

You have been asked to collect the known data in one place. You have compiled the following:

(a) direct-material purchases, at standard prices, $90,000;
(b) actual and budgeted selling and administrative expenses (all fixed), $20,000; there are no variable selling and administrative costs;
(c) notes receivable from Gilroy Division, $8,000;
(d) sales, $300,000;
(e) cash on hand, December 31, 19_2, $6,000;
(f) standard variable manufacturing costs per unit, $2.00;
(g) variances from standard of all variable manufacturing costs, $20,000, unfavorable;
(h) total notes payable December 31, 19_2, $57,000;
(i) unfavorable budget variance, fixed manufacturing costs, $3,000;
(j) contribution margin, at standard (before deducting any variances), $120,000;
(k) direct material used, at standard, $108,000;
(l) actual fixed manufacturing costs, $73,000;
(m) operating (or net) income, absorption-costing basis, $6,200;
(n) accounts receivable December 31, 19_2, $47,000;
(o) gross profit, absorption costing at standard (before deducting variances), $48,000;
(p) all standard *unit* costs have remained unchanged throughout 19_1 and 19_2.

required

Ignore income taxes. Solve for the following items. Various alternative approaches might be taken to obtain some of the items, so the items need not be solved in any particular order. Double-check your arithmetic. The avoidance of arithmetic errors is crucial and checks are available; therefore, an arithmetic error here is a more serious transgression than in an ordinary case or problem. Your work will be used to help establish the amount of insurance claim and the amount of income taxes. Compute:

1. Operating income on a variable-costing (direct-costing) basis.
2. Variable manufacturing cost of goods sold, at standard prices.

3. Number of units sold.
4. Manufacturing cost of goods sold at standard prices, absorption costing.
5. Number of units produced.
6. Number of units used as the denominator to obtain fixed indirect manufacturing-cost application rate per unit on an absorption-costing basis.
7. Did inventory (in units) increase or decrease? Explain.
8. By how much in dollars did the inventory level change (a) under absorption costing; (b) under direct costing?

10-35 *Comprehensive Review of Flexible Budgets and Standard Product Costs* (W. Warrick) "It's darn tough for an old dog like me to have to keep learning new tricks!" exclaimed Mr. Walter Warrick in some exasperation. Mr. Warrick, president of Kowloon Manufacturing Co., explained that he had given his son full responsibility for the operations of one branch of the business a few months previously. "Since then," he said, "it's been one dad-blamed thing after another!"

The most recent cause for complaint was the latest monthly income statement received from the plant run by his son:

INCOME FOR MONTH ENDING APRIL, 30, 19_1

Sales:			
14,000 X frames @ $7.50	$105,000		
12,000 H frames @ $8.00	96,000		$201,000
Standard cost of goods sold:			
26,000 × $4.50			117,000
Standard gross profit			$ 84,000
	LOSS	*GAIN*	
Material variance		$1,500	
Labor variance	$3,100		
Burden and overhead variance		3,700	
	$3,100	$5,200	2,100
Gross profit			$ 86,100
Selling and administrative expenses			40,000
Income before income tax			$ 46,100

Mr. Warrick explained that at the beginning of the year his son had prepared a "Profit-Graph" (Exhibit 10-5), which showed for various levels of volume what his plant sales, various categories of expense, and profit should be. "As nearly as I can figure out that thing, he should have shown a profit of just under $50,000 even at our regular price of $7.50 per frame. Since it looks as if he got a better rate on his H frames this month, doesn't it look to you as if he should have cleared almost $56,000?" demanded Mr. Warrick.

Further investigation disclosed that the plant under consideration made two types of metal frames that were used in the construction industry. The X frame, although larger than the H frame, was less complex and required less welding than did the H frame. At the beginning of the year when standards were set, it so happened that the extra material cost of the X frame was exactly offset by the extra labor cost of the H frame, so that the prime cost (direct labor plus materials) of each frame was $3.00. This greatly facilitated the preparation of volume-cost-profit estimates such as the Profit-Graph.

At that time, it was estimated that each X frame required two units of metal stripping and one unit of welding supplies. The H frame, on the other hand, required one unit of metal stripping and two units of welding supplies. Metal stripping normally cost $1.00 per unit and the welding supplies cost 60¢ per unit.

The direct-labor requirement was the opposite of that for the raw materials. The X frame required approximately half the time to fabricate than the H frame did. It was estimated that under normal working conditions, five H frames per man-hour could be assembled and one welder could keep up with two assemblers. That is, H frames could be welded at the rate of ten per welder-hour. Assemblers normally received $2.50 per hour and welders $3.00 per hour, Failure to schedule work properly and failure to provide adequately for absenteeism sometimes resulted in overtime or night work, which, of course, was paid for at premium rates. For purposes of variance computation, such extra pay was shown as a labor cost, not a burden cost, since it was felt that this placed the responsibility more nearly where it belonged.

The term "plant overhead" was used to describe a series of costs actually incurred at the plant where the frames were manufactured. Indirect labor consisted mainly of the wages paid to several material handlers employed at the plant. At the time the standards were set, power was purchased at the rate of $.008 per kwh. Since that time, the rate had gone up to $.009, although no change had been made in the standards. For control purposes it was assumed that the power requirements would vary directly with the total number of frames produced. Supervision and inspection made up a fairly expensive item that tended to be reasonably constant over quite a wide range of output. Depreciation was computed on a straight-line basis and naturally depended upon the cost of the production facilities of the part of the firm under consideration.

An examination of the general burden revealed that this cost was an assigned cost. It was the practice of Kowloon Manufacturing Co. to assign the general administration burden (the cost of such departments as accounting, engineering, etc., which were grouped at a central location) to the various operating branches of the firm. It was the policy of the company to anticipate this category of expense and assign a fixed sum monthly to each of the operating plants. However, when, as occasionally happened, the expenses of these central departments exceeded the amount anticipated, larger sums were assigned to the operating branches in order that such costs might be fully allocated by the end of the year.

Selling and administrative expense was budgeted at a fixed sum per month, since this expense was regarded as a direct result of management decision making and did not vary in direct relation with any of the standard parameters by which business activity might be judged.

Mr. Warrick pointed out that in general, apart from the change in power rate noted above, only one change from standard had been made in the base rate paid for any input to the plant. He explained that the plant was now paying less than formerly for their supply of welding rod. "I'm really tickled at the interest the boy has taken in every part of the operation," he confided. "As you can see, he has managed to raise the price we are getting for H frames. Not only that, he looked around until he found a fellow who would sell us welding rod at a lower price. Rod that used to cost us sixty cents we are now getting for only fifty. I guess we have to burn a little more, but you can see from that material variance that we are money ahead in the long run."

"Not only that," he continued, "a couple of months ago he talked me into buying some portable conveyors, which he put in the plant and which cut the cost of material handling quite a bit. They were not cheap, but they will

EXHIBIT 10-5

MONTHLY "PROFIT-GRAPH"

(Based on January 19_1 estimates)

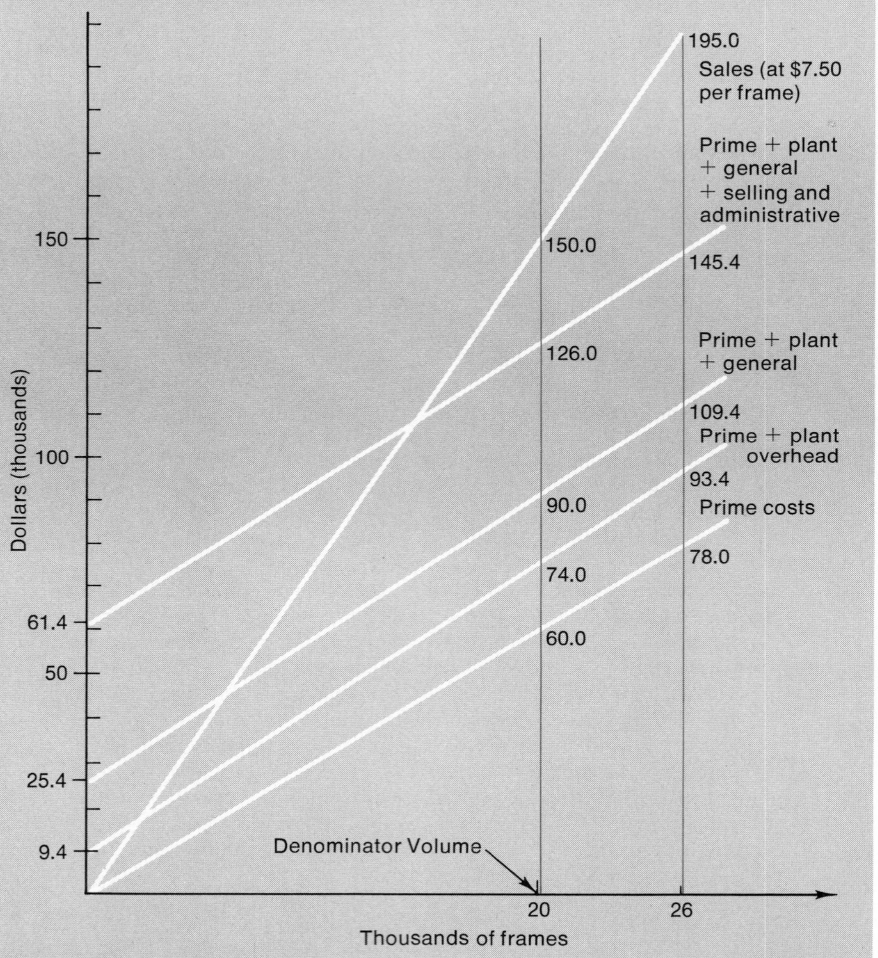

STANDARD COSTS AT DENOMINATOR VOLUME OF 10,000 UNITS OF EACH FRAME:

Prime costs at standard		$3.00
Plant overhead:		
Indirect labor	$ .20	
Power	.03	
Supervision and inspection	.27	
Depreciation	.20	
Sub-total plant overhead		.70
General burden:		.80
Total standard cost per frame		$4.50

last ten years and I expect they will pay for themselves several times over before that."

"Still and all," Mr. Warrick grumbled, resuming the earlier trend of his conversation, "I wish I could get a little more accurate estimate of how well he is doing. When I got lost on that income statement, I asked for a little more dope; here are the actual figures for his April operations."

Raw materials consumed:		
Metal stripping	36,300 units	$ 36,300
Welding supplies	39,600 units	19,800
Direct labor:		
Assemblers	3,450 hours	9,000
Welders	2,160 hours	8,500
Plant overhead:		
Supervision and inspection		5,400
Power		900
Depreciation		7,000
Indirect labor		1,000
General burden		18,000
Total		$105,900

Production: 12,000 X frames; 12,000 H frames

"In spite of the fact that his income statement does not show him making as much as he ought to from the Profit-Graph, it looks to me as if the actual cost for the average frame he has turned out this month is only $4.41—almost a dime less than standard. It is all pretty confusing," concluded Mr. Warrick. "I would like you to explain a few things to me in plain English. First of all, how come the income statement does not agree with the Profit-Graph? Is it only because of the rate changes from standard? Is there some less confusing (and not too expensive) way of reporting on how well he's making out? Second, how well is he doing? Is he making progress or is he just making changes? Third, he says because of the changes he has made, some of our standards should be changed. What does he mean by that?"

required

Answer Mr. Warrick's questions as completely and simply as possible. Include your supporting computations.

Relevant Costs and the Contribution Approach to Decisions

11

We have already seen how the contribution approach, with its emphasis on cost behavior patterns, helps cost analysis and the evaluation of performance. Our study has had two purposes: product costing and costing for routine control of operations. In this chapter we turn to a third purpose: costing for special non-routine decisions, such as the addition or deletion of a product line, the manufacture or purchase of direct materials (make or buy), the acceptance or rejection of a special order, the replacement of equipment, and countless others. Teamwork among executives is commonly used in reaching these decisions, which are often fusions of the thinking of engineers, economists, production managers, sales managers, mathematicians, and accountants. Cost analysis is nearly always helpful, and that is why the cost accountant plays an important role in these special decisions.

Before the mid-1960s, the word "relevant" was not overused. Now it seems to be applied in every context imaginable. Nevertheless, "relevant" is particularly apt for our purposes, so we will stress the word in this chapter. When is an item relevant to a particular management decision? When is it irrelevant? These distinctions are crucial to the making of intelligent decisions. The contribution approach, combined with the ability to distinguish relevance from irrelevance, enables accountants and managers to reach correct conclusions in this challenging area.

meaning of relevance

historical costs and predictions

Please refer to Exhibit 1-1 in Chapter 1, where a manager is trying to decide about a plant rearrangement that would reduce labor costs. The discussion there showed that every decision deals with the future—whether it be ten seconds ahead (the decision to adjust a dial) or eighty years ahead (the decision of where to locate a factory). A decision always involves a prediction. Therefore, the function of decision making is to select courses of action for the future. There is no opportunity to alter the past.

Recall in Exhibit 1-1 that the decision model concentrated on a comparison of *expected future* costs that will *differ* among alternatives. If all other considerations are a standoff, and the objective is to minimize costs, then rearrangement is the more desirable alternative. The $2 predicted direct-labor charge may be the same as in the past, and the past records may have been extremely helpful in preparing the $2 forecast. Most accountants and managers view the $2 past cost as the future cost. However, the crucial point is that the $2 is an expected future cost, not a past cost. *Historical costs in themselves are irrelevant to the decision, although they may be the best available basis for predicting future costs.*

Now suppose that past direct-materials costs of $5 per unit should not change under either alternative. Thus, our prediction becomes $5 per unit. Yet these future costs are irrelevant, because they will not differ under alternatives.[1] Of course, there is no harm in preparing a comparative analysis that includes both the relevant direct-labor-cost forecast and the irrelevant direct-material-cost forecast:

	COST COMPARISON PER UNIT	
	Do Not Rearrange	Rearrange
Direct materials	~~$5.00~~	~~$5.00~~
Direct labor	2.00	1.80

However, as the above cancellation marks show, we can safely ignore the direct-material cost, because it is not an element of difference between the alternatives. Concentrating solely on relevant costs may eliminate bothersome irrelevancies and may sharpen both the accountant's and the manager's thinking regarding costs for decision making. A key question in determining relevance is "What difference will it make?" (Of course, irrelevant costs may be

[1] The time value of money is discussed in the next chapter. When interest factors are introduced, expected future costs and revenues with the same magnitude but different timing can be relevant.

included in cost comparisons for decisions, provided that they are included properly and do not mislead the decision maker.)

In summary, relevant costs for decisions are expected future costs that will differ under alternatives. Historical costs, although helpful in predicting relevant costs, are always irrelevant costs per se.

The definition of relevance is the major conceptual lesson in this chapter. This idea of relevance, coupled with the contribution approach, arms the manager and the accountant with a powerful general weapon for making special decisions. The rest of this chapter will show how to apply these notions to some commonly encountered decisions. Note particularly that the analytical approach is consistent regardless of the particular decision encountered.

qualitative and quantitative factors

The consequences of each alternative may be divided into two broad categories, *qualitative* and *quantitative.* Qualitative factors are those whose measurement in dollars and cents is difficult and imprecise; yet a qualitative factor may easily be given more weight than the measurable cost savings. For example, a militant union that opposes the introduction of some labor-saving machinery may cause an executive to defer or to reject completely the contemplated installation. Or the chance to manufacture some product components at a cost below supplier quotations may be rejected because of a long-run dependency on the supplier for other important subassemblies. Quantitative factors are those that may more easily be reduced to terms of dollars and cents, such as projected alternative costs of materials, direct labor, and overhead. The accountant, statistician, and mathematician increasingly try to express as many decision factors as possible in quantitative terms. This approach tends to reduce the number of qualitative factors to be judged.

illustration of relevance: choosing activity levels

Decisions that affect activity levels are made under a given set of conditions, including existing plant capacity, equipment, and basic operating conditions. Such decisions are essentially short-run in nature; but they have long-run overtones that should never be overlooked.

the special order

Management is sometimes faced with the problem of price quotations on special orders when there is idle capacity.

example

X Company manufactures overshoes. The current operating level, which is below full capacity of 110,000 pairs per year, will probably show the results for the year as contained in Exhibit 11-1. (Note that these are predictions.)

A mail-order chain offers to buy 20,000 pairs at $7.50, for a total of $150,000. The buyer will pay for the shipping expenses. The acceptance of this special

EXHIBIT 11-1

PREDICTED INCOME STATEMENT FOR THE YEAR
Absorption Format

		PER UNIT
Sales—80,000 pairs @ $10.00	$800,000	$10.000
Manufacturing cost of goods sold*	650,000	8.125
Gross profit or gross margin	$150,000	$ 1.875
Selling expenses†	120,000	1.500
Operating income	$ 30,000	$ .375

* Includes fixed costs of $250,000. The remaining $400,000 is for variable costs of $5.00 per pair.

† Includes fixed costs of $80,000. The remaining $40,000 consists only of shipping expenses of $.50 per pair.

order will not affect regular sales. The president is reluctant to accept that order because the $7.50 price is below the $8.125 factory unit cost. Should the offer be accepted?

Exhibit 11-2 shows a report based on the contribution approach that might be presented as a guide for decision making. The relevant costs are those that will be affected by taking the special order—the variable *manufacturing* costs. The fixed manufacturing costs and all of the selling expenses are irrelevant in this case. Therefore, the only relevant items here are sales and variable manufacturing costs.

fixed expenses and unit costs

Exhibit 11-2 also illustrates the frequent relevance of fixed costs in a decision of this kind. If the fixed costs remain the same under each alternative (acceptance or rejection), then the $330,000 is irrelevant. You may substitute $1 or $1,000,000 wherever the $330,000 fixed-cost amount is shown without changing the net difference in result.

Note also that the full factory unit cost at the 80,000-unit activity level was $8.125. If such a cost were used as a guide in deciding, the offer might be unwisely rejected, on the grounds that the $7.50 prospective selling price is well below the $8.125 unit cost. In most cases (as demonstrated here) it is safer to compare *total* costs and revenues rather than the *unit* amounts. The spreading of the $250,000 fixed manufacturing cost over 100,000 units instead of 80,000 units will lower the average *unit cost* for all units produced. But how fixed costs are applied to units of product has no bearing on this decision because the *total* fixed costs are unaffected.

EXHIBIT 11-2

COMPARATIVE PREDICTED INCOME STATEMENTS FOR THE YEAR
Contribution Format, Two Decision Alternatives

	WITHOUT SPECIAL ORDER, 80,000 UNITS		WITH SPECIAL ORDER, 100,000 UNITS	
	PER UNIT	TOTAL	TOTAL	DIFFERENCE
Sales	$10.000	$800,000	$950,000	$150,000*
Variable costs:				
Manufacturing	$ 5.000	$400,000	$500,000	$100,000†
Selling	.500	40,000	40,000	—
Total variable costs	$ 5.500	$440,000	$540,000	$100,000
Contribution margin	$ 4.500	$360,000	$410,000	$ 50,000
Fixed costs:				
Manufacturing	$ 3.125	$250,000	$250,000	—
Selling	1.000	80,000	80,000	—
Total fixed costs	$ 4.125	$330,000	$330,000	—
Operating income	$ .375	$ 30,000	$ 80,000	$ 50,000

* 20,000 @ $7.50
† 20,000 @ $5.00

short run and long run *Do not jump to the conclusion that all variable costs are relevant and all fixed costs are irrelevant.* This preconceived attack may be handy, but it is far from being foolproof. For instance, in this special-order example, although the selling costs are variable, they are irrelevant because they are not affected by this special order. Moreover, fixed costs are often affected by a decision. For example, plans to buy a second car for family use should be most heavily influenced by the new set of fixed costs that would be encountered. Moreover, if the total family mileage were unaffected, the variable costs could conceivably be wholly irrelevant.

Economists and accountants agree that if the length of time under consideration is long enough, no type of cost is fixed. Yet management is faced with the task of making decisions when the length of time under consideration is short enough so that many conditions and costs are fixed. What role should fixed costs play in decision making? No categorical answer may be given to this question. About the most useful generalization is that fixed costs should be considered when they are expected to be altered, either immediately or in the future, by the decision at hand. If activity levels change so that additional supervision, plant, equipment, insurance, and property taxes are needed, these new fixed costs are relevant. For example, sales or production may expand to the point where a new delivery truck must be bought.

reports for decision making

Frequently, the decision alternatives are compared as in Exhibit 11-2 by preparing a separate income statement for each alternative, as well as by showing the differences. But shortcut reports may emphasize *differences* in order to spotlight only the relevant factors that influence the final results. A shortcut analysis would be confined to the "difference" column in Exhibit 11-2.

Concentration on the revenues and costs that make a difference in analyzing data does not necessarily mean that the final reports submitted to the decision-making executives should contain only these differential items. The final reports should be tailored to managerial quirks and wants. There is no single way to present reports. However, the contribution approach tends to facilitate understanding.

contribution approach to pricing

The special-order decision is merely one example of a pervasive difficulty that confronts managers: the pricing decision. This decision is the subject of an extensive literature in economics, so we will concentrate on only a few aspects here. The major purpose is to put the role of costs in perspective with regard to the pricing decision.

superiority of the contribution approach

When used intelligently, the contribution approach offers equal or better help than the absorption-costing approach to guiding a pricing decision.

First, the contribution approach offers more detailed information than the absorption-costing approach, because variable- and fixed-cost behavior patterns are delineated. Because the contribution approach is sensitive to cost-volume-profit relationships, it is a better, easier basis for developing pricing formulas.

Second, a "normal" or "target" pricing formula can be as easily developed under the contribution approach as under absorption costing for the "usual" or "nonincremental" situations. Consider the data in the absorption format of Exhibit 11-1. The target markup percentage is often expressed as a percentage of manufacturing cost: $1.875 ÷ $8.125 = 23.1 percent. In contrast, consider the data in the contribution format of Exhibit 11-2. The target markup percentage might be expressed as a percentage of variable costs: $4.50 ÷ $5.50 = 81.8 percent. Under *either* approach, the pricing-decision maker will have a formula that will lead toward the *same* target price. If he is unable to obtain such a price consistently, the company will not achieve its $30,000 income objective or its desired operating-income percentage of sales.

Third, as the preceding example shows, the contribution approach offers insight into short-run versus long-run effects of cutting prices on special orders.

Generally, a manager can weigh such decisions by asking whether the expected long-run benefits of not cutting the price are worth a present "investment" equal to the immediate contribution to operating income ($50,000 in Exhibit 11-2) that will be otherwise sacrificed. Under absorption costing, he must ordinarily conduct a special study to find the immediate effects; under the contribution approach, he has a system that will routinely provide such information.

the contribution approach or absorption costing?

A major criticism leveled at the contribution approach is that it will result in underpricing and ultimate company disaster. Such a criticism implies that full manufacturing cost is a safer guide because it does not ignore fixed factory overhead and will therefore lead to better long-run pricing decisions.

There are at least four basic weaknesses in that argument. First, full manufacturing cost also ignores some costs—the selling and administrative costs, which are often substantial. Under absorption costing, pricing decisions are often guided by unit gross profit rather than by unit net profit.[2] Second, even when absorption costing is used, there is no single unit cost that may be used as a guide as long as volume is a variable. Third, cost accountants and businessmen give excessive emphasis to costs as a guide to pricing. That is, they say and perhaps think that costs influence pricing decisions, but their actions show that *customer demand* and *competitor behavior* greatly overshadow costs as price-influencing factors.[3] Fourth, a N.A.A. survey (*Report No. 37,* p. 55) of 38 companies that use direct costing reported:

> No instance of unprofitable pricing attributable to direct costing was reported, but, on the contrary, opinion was frequently expressed to the effect that direct costing had contributed to better pricing decisions. However, companies restrict product cost and margin data to individuals qualified to interpret such data and responsible for pricing policy decisions.

Our general theme of different costs for different purposes also extends into the area of pricing. To say that either contribution costing or absorption costing provides the best guide to pricing decisions is a dangerous oversimplification of one of the most perplexing problems in business. Lack of understanding and judgment can lead to unprofitable pricing regardless of the kind of cost data available or cost accounting system used.

need for clear information

Pricing decisions almost inevitably have long-run implications and thus require acute ability for proper weighting of short-run and long-run impacts. Because of the bewildering number of influencing factors, many managers are content with "satisfactory" returns

[2] *Current Application of Direct Costing, N.A.A. Research Report No. 37,* p. 43.

[3] For an expanded discussion, see the second appendix to this chapter.

rather than "maximum" returns—primarily because they are rarely sure of what the latter amounts may be. The contribution-margin approach will help clarify some factors that are not easily brought out by the conventional approach. *N.A.A. Research Report No. 37* (page 55) cited the following cases, which took place before the contribution approach was adopted:

> Instances were cited in which management had unknowingly continued selling products below out-of-pocket cost or had decided to withdraw from the market when a substantial portion of the [fixed] costs could have been recovered. . . .
>
> In one interview . . . when direct costing was introduced, analysis demonstrated that contracts which would have contributed to [fixed] costs had often been refused at times when the company had a large amount of idle capacity.

the robinson-patman act

Another major factor that influences pricing decisions is the Robinson-Patman Act. This legislation forbids quoting different prices to competing customers unless such price discrimination is justified by differences in costs of manufacturing, sales, or delivery. Decisions of courts and the Federal Trade Commission have been based on full-costing allocations rather than on direct or differential costing.

Most of these price differentials are justified by differences in distribution costs like advertising, warehousing, and freight, rather than in manufacturing costs. That is why companies with flexible pricing policies need to keep careful records of distribution costs to answer any government inquiries. However, cost justification is only one aspect of these cases. In most instances, it has been overshadowed by the issues of lessening competition and price cutting in good faith.[4]

impact on behavior

The examples in this chapter also relate to the various potential impacts of alternative cost analyses on human motivation and decisions. For example, in pricing decisions, managers face the difficult task of predicting how total costs will be affected. These predictions will obviously affect decisions.

The dilemma is often to choose between (1) and (3) as a guide to pricing:

(1) Total "incremental" or variable costs	xxx
(2) Add: allocation of fixed costs	xxx
(3) Total "full" or absorption cost	xxx

In practice, most managers maintain that variable costs provide understatements of the "real" additions to costs caused by a decision alternative in question. At the same time, most managers will admit that "full" cost is also an

[4] Herbert G. Whiting, "Cost Justification of Price Differences," *Management Services,* Vol. 3, No. 4, pp. 31–32. Also see the "Legal Developments" sections of *The Journal of Marketing* for summaries of court cases.

inaccurate approximation. Still, the latter tends to be regarded as a safer basis for an ongoing pricing policy. In short, in coping with uncertainty, managers tend to be more comfortable with the "full-cost" simplification than the "variable-cost" simplification as a routine approximation of the unknown "real-cost" functions that might measure additions to costs. In this way, managers contend with a fact of life: As more activities are undertaken, costs inevitably creep upward at a rate higher than indicated by the variable or incremental costs identified with particular decisions, analyzed one at a time.

costs as substitutes for the market

Market prices frequently do not exist or are unobtainable in any feasible way. The defense-contracting industry offers numerous examples. In these cases, costs become *the* means for establishing a "fair" price—that is, a price that is regarded as mutually acceptable by both buyer (the government) and seller.

When costs are used for determining a "fair," "equitable," or "satisfactory" price, keep in mind that the resulting price may or may not coincide with the "true" underlying costs. For instance, in government contracting some costs are deemed allowable for recovery in the price and some are unallowable (for example, the premium paid for first-class airfare).

Thus, when costs are viewed as substitutes for the market in government contracting, or in allocating costs to service departments, or elsewhere, disputes may arise about how underlying costs "truly" behave. Settling such arguments on the basis of probable cost behaviors is sometimes hopeless. In these cases, certitude is a dream. It may be helpful to recognize that cost allocations are being used to obtain a mutually acceptable price and not necessarily to portray cause-and-effect relationships of cost incurrence. (For additional discussion, see Chapter 15.)

other illustrations of relevance and the contribution approach

contribution per unit of constraining factor

When a multiproduct plant is being operated at capacity, decisions must often be made as to which orders to accept. The contribution approach supplies the data for a proper decision, because the latter is determined by the product that makes the largest *total* contribution to profits. This does not necessarily mean that the products to be pushed are those with the biggest contribution-margin *ratios* per unit of product or per sales dollar. The objective is to maximize total profits, which depends on getting the highest contribution margin per unit of the *constraining* (that is, *scarce, limiting,* or *critical*) *factor.* The following example may clarify the point. Assume that a company has two products:

	PRODUCT (PER UNIT)	
	A	B
Selling price	$10	$15
Variable expenses	7	9
Contribution margin	$ 3	$ 6
Contribution-margin ratio	30%	40%

At first glance, B looks more profitable than A. However, if you were the division manager, had 1,000 hours of capacity available, and knew that you could turn out 3 units of A per hour and only 1 unit of B per hour, your choice would be A, because it contributes the most margin *per hour,* the constraining factor in this example:

	A	B
Units per hour	3	1
Contribution margin per hour	$ 9	$ 6
Total contribution for 1,000 hours	$9,000	$6,000

The constraining factor is the item that restricts or limits the production or sale of a given product. Thus, *the criterion for maximum profits, for a given capacity, is the greatest possible contribution to profit per unit of the constraining factor.* The constraining factor in the example above may be machine-hours or labor-hours. It also may be cubic feet of display space. The success of the suburban discount department stores illustrates the concept of the contribution to profit per unit of constraining factor. These stores have been satisfied with subnormal markups because they have been able to increase turnover and thus increase the contribution to profit per unit of space. Exhibit 11-3 demonstrates this point and assumes that the same total selling space is used in each store.

As you can imagine, in most cases there will be many constraining factors that must be utilized by each of a variety of products. The problem of formulating the most profitable production schedules and the mixes of raw materials is essentially that of maximizing the contribution in the face of *many* constraints. These complications are solved by linear programming techniques, which are discussed in Chapter 27.

EXHIBIT 11-3

	REGULAR DEPARTMENT STORE	DISCOUNT DEPARTMENT STORE
Retail price	$4.00	$3.50
Cost of merchandise	3.00	3.00
Contribution to profit per unit	$1.00(25%)	$ .50(14 + %)
Units sold per year	20,000	44,000
Total contribution to profit	$20,000	$22,000

make or buy, and idle facilities

Manufacturers are often confronted with the question of whether to make or buy a product—whether, that is, to manufacture their own parts and subassemblies or to buy them from vendors. The qualitative factors may be of paramount importance. Sometimes the manufacture of parts requires special know-how, unusually skilled labor, rare materials, and the like. The desire to control the quality of parts is often the determining factor in the decision to make them. On the other hand, companies hesitate to destroy mutually advantageous long-run relationships by the erratic order-giving that results from making parts during slack times and buying them during prosperous times. They may have difficulty in obtaining any parts during boom times, when there are shortages of materials and workers and no shortage of sales orders.

What are the quantitative factors relevant to the decision of whether to make or buy? The answer, again, depends on the context. A key factor is whether there are idle facilities. Many companies make parts only when their facilities cannot be used to better advantage.

Assume that the following costs are reported:

COST OF MAKING PART NO. 300

	Total Costs for 10,000 Units	Costs Per Unit
Direct materials	$ 10,000	$ 1
Direct labor	80,000	8
Variable overhead	40,000	4
Fixed overhead applied	50,000	5
Total costs	$180,000	$18

Another manufacturer offers to sell B Company the same part for $16. Should B Company make or buy the part?

Although the figures above seemingly indicate that the company should buy, the answer is rarely obvious. The key question is the difference in future costs between the alternatives. Consider the fixed overhead. The total applied to the part is $50,000. Perhaps $30,000 of this fixed overhead represents those costs (for example, depreciation, property taxes, insurance, and allocated executive salaries) that will continue regardless of the decision. If so, the entire $30,000 becomes irrelevant, which is $3 per unit for a 10,000-unit volume.

Again it is risky to say categorically that only the variable costs are relevant. Perhaps, as we assume here, $20,000 of the fixed costs will be saved if the parts are bought instead of made. In other words, fixed costs that may be avoided in the future are relevant.

For the moment, let us assume that the capacity now used to make parts will become idle if the parts are purchased. The relevant computations follow:

	TOTAL COSTS			PER-UNIT COSTS		
	Make		Buy	Make		Buy
Direct materials	$ 10,000			$ 1		
Direct labor	80,000			8		
Variable overhead	40,000			4		
Fixed overhead that can be avoided by not making	20,000			2		
Total relevant costs	$150,000		$160,000	$15		$16
Difference in favor of making		$10,000			$1	

essence of make or buy: utilization of facilities The choice in our example is not really whether to make or buy; it is how best to utilize available facilities. Although the data above indicate that making the part is the better choice, the figures are not conclusive—primarily because we have no idea of what can be done with the manufacturing facilities if the component is bought. Only if the released facilities are to remain idle are the figures above valid.

If the released facilities can be used advantageously in some other manufacturing activity or can be rented out, these alternatives also may merit consideration. The two courses of action have become four (figures are in thousands):

	MAKE	BUY AND LEAVE FACILITIES IDLE	BUY AND RENT	BUY AND USE FACILITIES FOR OTHER PRODUCTS
Rent revenue	$ —	$ —	$ 5	$ —
Contribution from other products	—	—	—	19
Obtaining of parts	(150)	(160)	(160)	(160)
Net relevant costs	$(150)	$(160)	$(155)	$(141)

The analysis indicates that buying the parts and using the vacated facilities for the production of other products should yield best results.

beware of unit costs Unit costs should be analyzed with care in decision making. There are two major ways to go wrong: (a) the inclusion of irrelevant costs, such as the $3 allocation of fixed costs in the make-or-buy comparison, which would result in a unit cost of $18 instead of the relevant unit cost of $15; and (b) comparisons of unit costs not computed on the same basis. Generally, it is advisable to use total costs rather than unit costs. Then, if desired, the total may be unitized. Machinery salesmen, for example, often brag about the low unit costs of using their new machines. Sometimes they neglect to point out that the unit costs are based on outputs far in excess of the volume of activity of their prospective customer. The unitization of fixed costs in this manner can be particularly misleading. The lesson here is to use total costs, not unit costs, in relevant cost analysis when possible. This approach has been called "McNamara's First Law of Analysis: always start by looking at the grand total. Whatever problem you are studying, back off and look at it in the large."[5]

irrelevance of past costs

As defined earlier, a relevant cost is (a) an expected future cost (b) that will differ among alternatives. The contribution aspect of relevant-cost analysis has shown that those expected future costs that will not differ among alternatives are irrelevant. Now we return to the idea that all past costs are also irrelevant.

obsolete inventory A company has 100 obsolete missile parts that are carried in inventory at a manufacturing cost of $100,000. The parts can be: (a) remachined for $30,000, and then sold for $50,000; or (b) scrapped for $5,000. Which should be done?

This is an unfortunate situation; yet the $100,000 cost is irrelevant to the decision to remachine or scrap. The only relevant factors are the expected future revenue and costs:

	REMACHINE	*SCRAP*	*DIFFERENCE*
Expected future revenue	$ 50,000	$ 5,000	$45,000
Expected future costs	30,000	—	30,000
Relevant excess of revenue over costs	$ 20,000	$ 5,000	$15,000
Accumulated historical inventory costs*	100,000	100,000	—
Net overall loss on project	$ (80,000)	$ (95,000)	$15,000

* Irrelevant because it is not an element of difference as between the alternatives.

We could completely ignore the historical cost and still arrive at the $15,000 difference, the key figure in the analysis.

regular inventory Note another important point. Although this example dealt with obsolete parts, the idea that past costs are irrelevant per se applied to the historical cost of *any* inventory, whether obsolete or fully merchantable. The replacement cost of additional units of inventory is a future

[5] A. Enthoven and K. Wayne Smith, *How Much Is Enough? Shaping the Defense Program 1961–1969,* (New York: Harper & Row, Publishers, 1971), p. 54, referring to Robert S. McNamara, former U.S. Secretary of Defense.

cash outflow that is likely to be common to nearly all alternatives under consideration. However, it is a separate outflow; it should not be confused with the question of what to do with the units on hand. This point may be clarified by an example.

Suppose a company uses copper as an input. At the beginning of the period, there are 1,000 units in copper inventory that were acquired for $110 per unit. Assume further that if the company decides not to use the 1,000 units on hand, it is possible to sell them to a salvage yard for $95 per unit. Another salvage yard has offered $90. There are many alternative end-product uses for the copper. Another alternative would be to throw the units in the city dump. A "total-alternatives" approach to the analysis follows (in thousands of dollars):

	CHOICES						
	USE COPPER IN PRODUCT				SALVAGE		THROW AWAY
	A	B	C	D	1	2	
Expected future revenue	220	204	186	170	95	90	—
Expected future costs:							
Labor and overhead	90	70	60	100	—	—	—
Excess of revenue over costs	130	134	126	70	95	90	—
		Best					

opportunity cost Note that all alternatives are listed and analyzed in the same systematic way under the total-alternatives approach. Ideally, the decision maker should be able to make an exhaustive list of alternatives and then compute the expected results under each, giving full consideration to interdependent and long-run effects. Practically, the decision maker sifts among the possible alternatives, discards many out of hand as being obviously unattractive, undoubtedly overlooks some attractive possibilities, and concentrates on a limited number.

The idea of an opportunity cost has arisen because some alternatives are excluded from formal consideration. For example, suppose that the total alternatives under formal consideration are described by choices A through D above but that the salvage and throw-away alternatives will not be analyzed in the same format. Then an opportunity approach is desirable. **Opportunity cost is the maximum contribution that is foregone by using limited resources for a particular purpose.** The use of opportunity cost is a practical means of reducing the alternatives under consideration; the solution reached is still the same as that given by a more complete "total-alternatives" approach. The decision maker says, "There are many alternatives that I want to reject without conducting a thorough analysis. Therefore, I shall take the *best* of these, compute its contribution, and use that as the cost of the scarce resource [copper in the example] when I explicitly analyze the remaining alternatives." The decision maker would then organize his analysis of the remaining alternatives as follows (in thousands of dollars):

	CHOICES			
	USE COPPER IN PRODUCT			
	A	*B*	*C*	*D*
Revenue	220	204	186	170
Relevant costs:				
Opportunity cost of copper	95	95	95	95
Outlay costs: Labor and overhead	90	70	60	100
Total relevant costs	185	165	155	195
Net advantage	35	39	31	(25)

Note that the *best* of the excluded alternatives is included in the formal comparison as an opportunity cost. The other two (or more) excluded alternatives are not in this analysis. The possible uses of the copper in Products A, C, and D may also eventually become excluded alternatives, but they are excluded after formal consideration in the decision model used.

Suppose the copper could be sold for a scrap price of $195 instead of $95. Then all the results for the alternatives formally included above would be negative. This would indicate that the best excluded alternative, the scrap sale at $195, is in fact optimum.

Note that an opportunity cost is not ordinarily incorporated in formal external accounting systems.[6] Such costs represent contributions *foregone* by rejecting the next-best alternative; therefore, opportunity costs do not entail cash receipts or disbursements. Accountants usually confine their systematic recording of costs to the *outlay costs* requiring exchanges of assets. Accountants confine their history to alternatives selected rather than those rejected, primarily because of the infeasibility of accumulating meaningful data on what might have been.

book value of old equipment

Assume that there is a machine, with a cost of $120,000, two-thirds depreciated on a straight-line basis, with a book value of $40,000, and with a remaining useful life of four years. The old machine has a $4,000 disposal value now; in four years, its disposal value will be zero. A new machine is available that will dramatically reduce operating costs. Annual revenue of $100,000 will not change regardless of the decision. The new machine will cost $60,000 and have zero disposal value at the end of its four-year life. The new machine promises to slash variable operating costs from $80,000 per year to $56,000 per year. Many managers and accountants would not replace the old machine because it would entail recognizing a $36,000 "loss on disposal," whereas retention would allow spreading the $40,000 over

[6] However, an argument can be made that the issuance of capital stock by a corporation for noncash assets is accounted for on the basis of opportunity costs. That is, such assets may be recorded at the market value of the stock under the reasoning that the company's best foregone opportunity was the issuance of the stock for cash. This is one of a few applications of the opportunity-cost idea to external accounting.

four years in the form of "depreciation expense" (a more appealing term than "loss on disposal"). See Exhibit 11-4.

Under our definition of relevant costs, book value of old fixed assets is always irrelevant in making decisions. This proposition is by far the most difficult for managers and accountants alike to accept. The real concept of importance here is that *all* historical costs are irrelevant. At one time or another, we all like to think that we can soothe our wounded pride arising from having made a bad purchase decision by using the item instead of replacing it. The fallacy here is in erroneously thinking that a current or future action can influence the long-run impact of a past outlay. All past costs are down the drain. *Nothing* can change what has already happened.

We can apply our definition of relevance to four commonly encountered items:

1. *Book value of old equipment.* Irrelevant, because it is a past (historical) cost.
2. *Disposal value of old equipment.* Relevant (ordinarily), because it is an expected future inflow that usually differs between alternatives.
3. *Gain or loss on disposal.* This is the algebraic difference between 1 and 2. It is therefore a meaningless combination of book value, which is always irrelevant, and disposal value, which is usually relevant. The combination form, *loss* (or *gain*) *on disposal,* blurs the distinction between the irrelevant book value and the relevant disposal value. Consequently, it is best to think of each separately.[7]
4. *Cost of new equipment.* Relevant, because it is an expected future outflow that will differ between alternatives.

Exhibit 11-4 should clarify the above assertions. Book value of old equipment is irrelevant regardless of the decision-making technique used. The Difference columns in Exhibit 11-4 show that book value of old equipment is not an element of difference between alternatives and could be completely ignored without changing the $10,000 difference in average annual net income. No matter what the *timing* of the charge against revenue, the *amount* charged is still $40,000 regardless of any available alternative. In either event, the undepreciated cost will be written off with the same ultimate effect on profit.[8] The $40,000 creeps into the income statement either as a $40,000 offset against the $4,000

[7] For simplicity, we ignore income tax considerations and the effects of the time value of money in this chapter. But book value is irrelevant even if income taxes are considered, because the relevant item is then the tax cash flow, not the book value. Using the approach in Exhibit 1-1, the book value is essential information for the *prediction method,* but the expected future income tax cash outflows are the relevant information for the *decision model.* The prediction method would be: Disposal value, $4,000 − Book value, $40,000 = Loss on disposal, $36,000. If the income tax rate is 50 percent, the income tax cash saving would be $18,000. This $18,000 would be the expected future cash flow that is relevant input to the decision model. For elaboration, see Chapter 24.

[8] We are deliberately ignoring income tax factors for the time being. If income taxes are considered, the *timing* of the writing off of fixed-asset costs may influence income tax payments. In this example, there will be a small real difference: the present value of $40,000 as a tax reduction now versus the present value of a $10,000 tax deduction each year for four years. But this difference in *future* income tax flows is the *relevant* item—not the book value of the old fixed asset per se. See Chapter 13.

EXHIBIT 11-4

COST COMPARISON—REPLACEMENT OF MACHINE, INCLUDING RELEVANT AND IRRELEVANT ITEMS

(In Thousands of Dollars)

	FOUR YEARS TOGETHER			*ANNUALIZED (DIVIDED BY 4)*		
	KEEP	*REPLACE*	*DIFFERENCE*	*KEEP*	*REPLACE*	*DIFFERENCE*
Sales	$400	$400	$ —	$100	$100	$ —
Expenses:						
Variable	320	224	96	80	56	24
Old machine (book value):						
Periodic write-off	40		—	10		—
or						
Lump-sum write-off		40*			10	
Disposal value		−4*	4	—	−1	1
New machine, written off periodically as depreciation	—	60	−60	—	15	−15
Total expenses	$360	$320	$ 40	$ 90	$ 80	$ 10
Operating income	$ 40	$ 80	$ 40	$ 10	$ 20	$ 10

The advantage of replacement is $40,000 for the four years together; the *average* annual advantage is $10,000.

* In a formal income statement, these two items would be combined as "loss on disposal" of $36,000.

proceeds to obtain the $36,000 *loss on disposal* in one year or as $10,000 depreciation in each of four years. But how it appears is irrelevant to the replacement decision. In contrast, the $15,000 annual depreciation on the new equipment *is* relevant because the total $60,000 depreciation may be avoided by not replacing.

Note the motivational factors here. A manager may be reluctant to replace simply because the large loss on disposal will severely harm his perceived profit performance in the first year. This demonstrates how overemphasis on the measurement of short-run income may conflict with the objective of maximizing income over the long run.

examining alternatives over the long run

The foregoing is the first example that has looked beyond one year. A useful technique is to view the alternatives over their entire lives and then to compute annual average results. In this way, peculiar nonrecurring items (such as loss on disposal) will not obstruct the long-run view that must necessarily be taken in almost all special managerial decisions.

EXHIBIT 11-5

COST COMPARISON—REPLACEMENT OF MACHINE: RELEVANT ITEMS ONLY
(In Thousands of Dollars)

	FOUR YEARS TOGETHER			*ANNUALIZED (DIVIDED BY 4)*		
	KEEP	*REPLACE*	*DIFFERENCE*	*KEEP*	*REPLACE*	*DIFFERENCE*
Variable expenses	$320	$224	$ 96	$80	$ 56	$ 24
Disposal value of old equipment	—	−4	4		−1	1
Depreciation—new equipment	—	60	−60		15	−15
Total relevant expenses	$320	$280	$ 40	$80	$ 70	$ 10

Exhibit 11-5 concentrates on relevant items only. Note that the same answer (the $40,000 net difference) will be produced even though the book value is completely omitted from the calculations. The only relevant items are the variable operating costs, the disposal value of the old equipment, and the depreciation on the new equipment.

the problem of uncertainty

It is vitally important to recognize that throughout this chapter and the next, dollar amounts of future sales and operating costs are assumed in order to highlight and to simplify various important points. In practice, the forecasting of these key figures is generally the most difficult aspect of decision analysis. For elaboration, see Chapter 24.

SUMMARY

The accountant's role in special decisions is basically that of a technical expert on cost analysis. His responsibility is to see that the manager is supplied with relevant data for guiding decisions.

The ability to distinguish relevant from irrelevant items and the use of the contribution approach to cost analysis are twin foundations for tackling many decisions.

To be relevant to a particular decision, a cost must meet two criteria: (a) it must be an expected *future* cost; and (b) it must be an element of *difference* between alternatives. The key question is, "What difference does it make?" If the objective of the decision maker is to maximize long-run net income, all *past* (*historical*) costs are irrelevant to any *decision* about the future.

The role that past costs play in decision making is an auxiliary one; the distinction here should be definitive, not fuzzy. Past (irrelevant) costs are useful because they provide empirical evidence that often helps sharpen *predictions* of future relevant costs. But the expected future costs are the *only* cost ingredients in any decision model per se.

For a given set of facilities or resources, the key to maximizing net income is to obtain the largest possible contribution per unit of constraining factor.

Generally, in cost analysis it is advisable to use total costs, not unit costs, because unitized fixed costs are often erroneously interpreted as if they behaved like variable costs. A common activity or volume level must underlie the comparison of equipment.

The book value of old equipment is always irrelevant in replacement decisions. Disposal value, however, is usually relevant.

Incremental or differential costs are the differences in total costs under each alternative.

Cost reports for special decisions may concentrate on relevant items only (Exhibit 11-5), or they may encompass both relevant and irrelevant items (Exhibit 11-4). The best format depends on individual preferences. The shortcut approach concentrates only on the Difference column, because it summarizes the relevant items. The problem of uncertainty, which is discussed in Chapter 24, complicates prediction and is easily the gravest practical difficulty.

PROBLEM FOR SELF-STUDY

PROBLEM

The San Carlos Company is an electronics company having eight product lines. Income data for one of the products for the year just ended follow (in millions):

Sales—200,000 units @ average price of $100		$20
Variable costs:		
Direct materials @ $35	$7	
Direct labor @ $10	2	
Variable factory overhead @ $5	1	
Sales commissions @ 15 percent of selling price	3	
Other variable costs @ $5	1	
Total variable costs @ $70		14
Contribution margin		$ 6
Fixed costs:		
Discretionary (See Chapter 8) @ $15	$3	
Committed (See Chapter 8) @ $10	2	
Total fixed costs		5
Operating income		$ 1

required

1. The electronics industry had severe price competition throughout the year. Near the end of the year, Abrams Co., which was experimenting with various components in its regular product line, offered $80 each for 3,000 units. The latter would have been in addition to the 200,000 units actually sold. The acceptance of this special order by San Carlos would not affect regular sales. The salesman hoped that the order might provide entrance into a new application, so he told George Holtz, the product manager, that he would accept a flat commission of $6,000 if the order were accepted. Holtz pondered for a day, but he was afraid of the precedent that might be set by cutting the price. He said, "The price is below our full costs of $95 per unit. I think we should quote a full price, or Abrams Co. will expect favored treatment again and again if we continue to do business with them." If Holtz had accepted the offer, what would operating income have been?
2. The Gregorio Company had offered to supply San Carlos Company with a key part (M-I-A) for $20 each. One M-I-A is used in every finished unit. The

San Carlos Company had made these parts for variable costs of $18 plus some additional fixed costs of $200,000 for supervision and other items. What would operating income have been if San Carlos purchased rather than made the parts? Assume that the discretionary costs for supervision and other items would have been avoided if the parts were purchased.

3. The company could have purchased the M-I-A parts for $20 each and used the vacated space for the manufacture of a different electronics component on a subcontracting basis for Hewlett-Packard, a much larger company. Assume that 40,000 special components could have been made for Hewlett-Packard (and sold in addition to the 200,000 regular units through regular channels) at a unit variable cost of $150, exclusive of parts. Part M-I-A would be needed for these components as well as for the regular production. No sales commission would have to be paid. All the fixed costs pertaining to the M-I-A parts would have continued, including the supervisory costs, because they related mainly to the facilities used. What would operating income have been if San Carlos had made and sold the components to Hewlett-Packard for $170 per unit and bought the M-I-A parts?

SOLUTION

1. Analysis of special order:

Additional sales of 3,000 units @ $80		$240,000
Direct materials—3,000 units @ $35	$105,000	
Direct labor—3,000 units @ $10	30,000	
Variable factory overhead—3,000 units @ $5	15,000	
Other variable costs—3,000 units @ $5	15,000	
Sales commission	6,000	
Total variable costs		171,000
Contribution margin		$ 69,000

Note that the variable costs, except for commissions, are affected by physical units of volume, not dollar revenue.

Operating income would have been $1,000,000 plus $69,000, or $1,069,000, if the order had been accepted. In a sense, the decision to reject the offer means that San Carlos is willing to invest $69,000 in immediate gains foregone (an opportunity cost) to preserve the long-run selling-price structure.

2.

	MAKE	PURCHASE
Purchase cost @ $20		$4,000,000
Variable costs @ $18	$3,600,000	
Avoidable discretionary costs	200,000	
Total relevant costs	$3,800,000	$4,000,000

Operating income would have fallen by $200,000, or from $1,000,000 to $800,000, if San Carlos had purchased the parts.

3.

Sales would increase by 40,000 units @ $170		$6,800,000
Additional costs to the company as a whole:		
Variable costs exclusive of M-I-A parts would increase by 40,000 units @ $150	$6,000,000	

Effects on overall costs of M-I-A parts:			
Cost of 240,000 parts purchased @ $20	$4,800,000		
Less cost of making 200,000 parts @ $18 (only the variable costs are relevant because fixed costs continue)	3,600,000		
Additional cost of parts		1,200,000	7,200,000
Disadvantage of making components			$ (400,000)

Operating income would decline by $400,000, from $1,000,000 to $600,000.

appendix a: cost terms used for different purposes

Because costs must be tailored to the decision at hand, many terms (too many!) have arisen to describe different types of cost. The author believes that the variety of terms is more confusing than illuminating; yet the varying usage of such terms necessitates a familiarity with them. Whenever you are confronted by these terms in practice, you will save much confusion and wasted time if you find out their exact meaning in the given case. For that matter, this word of caution applies to all the weird accounting terms used from company to company. Individual companies frequently develop their own extensive and distinctive accounting language. This language is not readily understood by accountants outside the company. The following terms will be related to other terms used previously in this book.

An *imputed cost* is the result of a process that recognizes a cost as it pertains to a particular situation, although the cost may not be routinely recognized by ordinary accounting procedures. Imputed costs attempt to make accounting better dovetail with economic reality.

Imputed costs may be either opportunity costs or outlay costs. A common example of an opportunity cost is the inclusion among divisional or departmental expenses of "interest expense" on ownership equity. Some outlay costs are also imputed costs, but not all outlay costs are imputed costs. For example, if $3,000 is paid for labor, it is an outlay cost but not an imputed cost, because it would be routinely recognized by ordinary accounting processes. By itself, the $3,000 measures the economic impact of that particular event.

On the other hand, suppose $100,000 is loaned to a supplier at simple interest of 2 percent when loans of comparable risk in the free market are being made at 10 percent. Such a loan may be partial consideration under a purchase contract for supplier products at lower than the prevailing market prices. An accurate accounting would require recognizing that a part of the $100,000 loan is really an additional cost of the products purchased during the contract term. This would create an initial loan discount, which would be amortized as interest income over the life of the note. Thus, this transaction illustrates the imputation of part of an outlay of $100,000 as a cost of product.

In sum, imputation applies to both outlay costs and opportunity costs. The aim is to get better recognition of the economic impact of a particular event or decision and not to take things at face value.

Out-of-pocket costs, a short-run concept, are those costs that entail current or near-future outlays for the decision at hand. For example, the acceptance of an order so that otherwise idle facilities may be used would entail a compilation of the out-of-pocket costs that otherwise could be avoided by not accepting the order; the depreciation on the machinery and equipment used for production would be irrelevant, because it does not entail out-of-pocket outlays as a result of the decision.

Joint cost is that term most often applied to the costs of two or more kinds of manufactured goods that are produced simultaneously by a single process and are not identifiable as individual types of products until a certain stage of production known as the *split-off point* (point of separation) is reached. Examples of such products are soap and glycerin, kerosene and gasoline, chemicals, and lumber. Joint costs are total costs incurred up to the point of separation. Inasmuch as joint costs by their very nature cannot be directly traced to units worked on, any method of apportioning such costs to various units produced is essentially arbitrary. The usefulness of joint-cost apportionment is limited to purposes of inventory costing and income measurement. Such apportionment is generally regarded as useless for cost-planning and control purposes.

Viewed broadly, joint costs plague the accountant throughout his work. Few costs are not joint in relation to some other factor, such as time or facilities. The entire problem of allocating the costs of fixed assets to months, years, departments, and products is essentially that of joint costing. Sometimes the term *common cost* is used instead of *joint cost* to describe another aspect of joint costing, such as the problem of determining unit cost of such services as bank accounts. Any allocation method is arbitrary, because many facilities and services are shared by many revenue-producing activities. The entire problem of reapportioning service-department costs among producing departments is really one of joint cost.

Postponable costs are those that may be shifted to the future with little or no effect on the efficiency of current operations. The best example of these is maintenance and repairs. Railroads sometimes go on an economy binge and cut their sizable maintenance budgets. But it is really a matter of deferral and not avoidance. Eventually some overhauls must be made and tracks must be repaired.

Avoidable costs are those that may be saved by not adopting a given alternative. For example, by not adopting a new product line, additional direct-material, direct-labor, and overhead costs could be avoided. The criterion here is the question: Which costs can be saved by not adopting a given alternative?

Sunk cost is another term for a past cost that is unavoidable because it cannot be changed no matter what action is taken. The author dislikes this term because it often beclouds the distinction between historical and future costs. However, *sunk cost* is discussed here because it is one of the most widely used terms in special-decision making.

To illustrate, if old equipment has book value of $600,000 and scrap value of $70,000, what is the sunk cost? There are two ways of looking at the $600,000 book value of old equipment. This author agrees with a minority view maintaining that the entire $600,000 is sunk because it represents an outlay made in the past that cannot be changed; the $70,000 scrap value is a future factor, to be considered apart from the $600,000 sunk cost. The majority view maintains that $530,000 of the $600,000 is sunk, whereas $70,000 is not sunk because it is immediately recoverable through scrapping. Thus, the sunk part of a historical cost is what is irrecoverable in a given situation. The latter view is that the two factors (book value and present scrap value) are complementary in replacement decisions; that is, book value minus scrap value equals sunk cost.

In the author's opinion, the term *sunk cost* should not be used at all. It muddles the task of collecting proper costs for decision making. Because all past costs are irrelevant, it is fruitless to introduce unnecessary terms to describe past costs. The issue of what part of past cost is sunk need not arise. The essence of the distinction between costs, past and future, irrelevant and relevant, was described earlier in this chapter. These distinctions are all that are needed for approaching special decisions. The term *sunk cost* is often more befuddling than enlightening. If it is going to be used, *sunk cost* should have the same meaning as *past cost.*

appendix b: cost-plus for setting prices

Professional economists, self-styled economists, and businessmen have been arguing for centuries about the cause-and-effect relationships between costs and prices. The problems here are intricate because of the interplay of long-run and short-run factors.

Many businessmen maintain that they use cost-plus pricing. They say that they figure their average unit costs and tack on a "fair" margin that will yield an adequate return on investment. This entails circular reasoning, because price, which influences sales, depends upon full cost, which in turn is partly determined by the *volume* of sales. Also, this "plus" in cost-plus is bothersome. It is rarely a rigid "plus." Instead, it is flexible, depending on the behavior of competitors and customers. There are at least three major influences on pricing decisions: customers, competitors, and costs.

CUSTOMERS The businessman must always examine his pricing problems through the eyes of his customers. He cannot level a shotgun at his customers and say, "Buy, or else!" Customers can reject a company's product and turn to competitors' products or, perhaps, to a completely different industry for a substitute product. When coffee prices are high, many people drink one cup instead of two; others switch to tea. If a company's prices get too high, the immediate reaction of the customer is to check with competitors, who welcome such inquiries. Perhaps the customer makes its own product or tries to find a different product that will serve just as well (aluminum instead of copper). For example, buyers of welding equipment are often most heavily influenced by the way the product affects their costs. The buyer not only has alternate sources of supply within the welding-equipment industry, he may not buy at all, but may keep using his existing equipment. He may substitute some other kind of equipment to accomplish his tasks; or he may manufacture the needed equipment himself.

COMPETITORS Rivals' reactions or lack of reactions will influence pricing decisions. In guessing a competitor's reactions, one must speculate on what the competitor's costs are, rather than be concerned with his own costs. Of course, one's own costs may be helpful in guessing, but it is the rival's costs that are relevant. Knowledge of the rival's technology, plant size, and operating policies help sharpen estimates of his costs. Companies within industries that loathe price competition have been known to swap detailed cost information for mutual benefit. Where there is no collusion, rivals' reactions and price quotations must be guessed when pricing decisions are made.

COSTS The maximum price that may be charged is the one that does not drive the customer away. The minimum price is zero. Companies occasionally will give or virtually give their products away in order to enter a market or to obtain a profitable long-run relationship with a customer. A more practical guide is gleaned from our study of cost-volume-profit relationships. In the short run, the minimum price to be quoted should be the additional costs from accepting the order or segment of available business. Any amount in excess of those additional costs directly increases income.

Where a company has some discretion in price setting, customer demand at various price levels determines the sales volume. In these situations, study must be given to differential cost-volume-profit relationships; in turn, these relationships are dependent on market conditions, elasticity of industry demand, concentration of capacity, and rivals' reactions.

Where a company has little discretion, it accepts the price that competition has set. Then under given economic conditions, the company ordinarily selects the level of production and sales that maximizes profits.

QUESTIONS, PROBLEMS, AND CASES

11-1 Distinguish briefly between *quantitative* and *qualitative* factors in decision making.

11-2 Define *relevant cost* as the term is used in this chapter. Why are historical costs irrelevant?

11-3 What is a *differential cost?* Distinguish it from a relevant cost.

11-4 "All future costs are relevant." Do you agree? Why?

11-5 Theater prices are usually lower for matinees than for evening performances. Why? As a movie-theater manager, what factors would influence your decision as to conducting matinees? To what degree are operating costs affected by the size of the audience?·

11-6 *Questions on Disposal of Assets*

1. A company has an inventory of 1,000 assorted missile parts for a line of missiles that has been junked. The inventory cost $100,000. The parts can be either (a) remachined at total additional costs of $30,000 and then sold for a total of $35,000, or (b) scrapped for $2,000. What should be done?
2. A truck, costing $10,000 and uninsured, is wrecked the first day in use. It can be either (a) disposed of for $1,000 cash and replaced with a similar truck costing $10,200, or (b) rebuilt for $8,500 and be brand-new as far as operating characteristics and looks are concerned. What should be done?

11-7 *The Careening Bookkeeping Machine* (From W. A. Paton, "Restoration of Fixed Asset Values to the Balance Sheet," *Accounting Review,* Vol. XXII, No. 2, pp. 194–210.) A young lady in the accounting department of a certain business was moving a bookkeeping machine from one room to another. As she came alongside an open stairway, she carelessly slipped and let the machine get away from her. It went careening down the stairs with a great racket and wound up at the bottom in some thousands of pieces, completely wrecked. Hearing the crash, the office manager came rushing out, and turned rather white when he saw what had happened. "Someone tell me quickly," he yelled, "if that is one of our fully amortized units." A check of the equipment cards showed that the smashed machine was, indeed, one of those which had been written off. "Thank God!" said the manager.

required

Explain and comment on the point of Professor Paton's anecdote.

11-8 *Determination of Relevant Costs* The Frel Company makes a standard line of gauges. A large aircraft company has asked for competitive bids on an order of 10,000 special gauges for use in the manufacture of aircraft parts. Frel Company wants to know the minimum price to bid that will insure at least a $5,000 increase in net income.

The operating picture, as it will appear for the year if the extra order is not landed, is as follows:

FREL COMPANY

Income Statement
for the Year Ending December 31, 19_1

Sales (40,000 gauges)		$600,000
Cost of sales:		
Direct materials	$100,000	
Direct labor	200,000	
Variable overhead (varies with direct-labor hours)	50,000	
Fixed overhead	100,000	450,000
Gross margin		$150,000
Selling and administrative expenses:		
Variable (including shipping costs of 40¢ per unit)	$ 30,000	
Fixed	80,000	110,000
Net income		$ 40,000

Assume that the cost behavior patterns will not be changed by the additional order, except as follows:

a. Shipping costs, which are ordinarily borne by the Frel Company, will be paid for and borne by the aircraft company.
b. Special setup costs and the cost of special tools (that will not be reusable) will total $5,000.
c. Direct-labor charges on these gauges will be 20 percent higher because of more time needed per unit.

required

1. Prepare a new income statement, assuming that the order is landed after the minimum price has been quoted. Set up your solution in the following manner:

	COLUMN		
	(A) *OLD INCOME STATEMENT*	*(B)* *CHANGE*	*(C)* *NEW INCOME STATEMENT*
Sales			
Cost of sales:			
Direct materials			
Direct labor			
(and so forth)			

2. Examine the format of your answer to requirement 1. How else could the information be presented?

11-9 *Replacement of Equipment* You are the manager in charge of the Y Division of Gigantic Enterprises, Ltd., a huge diversified corporation. On January 2, 19_4, you invested $600,000 cash for some special-purpose molding machinery that was installed immediately and that will produce a new product. The machinery and the product will have a useful life of three years with zero terminal value. Your budgeted income statement for the product for 19_4 is:

Revenue		$2,000,000
Cash operating expenses	$1,260,000	
Straight-line depreciation	200,000*	1,460,000
Operating income		$ 540,000

* Assume that the only depreciation is on this machinery.

Today (January 3) you were visited by an old friend, Jose Garcia, who used to sell lots of equipment to you that proved to be reliable. Garcia had been transferred to a different territory two years ago. His successor was less competent, and Garcia's firm had not sold any equipment to Gigantic since his transfer.

Garcia was shocked to learn about yesterday's purchase. His company had some new equipment that could be delivered within five days for $750,000 cash and that would bring total cash operating costs down to $1,000,000 per year for the next three years. The machine would consume less power, reduce spoilage, require less maintenance, and require less labor. It would have a zero terminal value.

You discover that the special-purpose nature of the equipment acquired yesterday will mean that its cash disposal value in five days will be only $120,000. Garcia will not accept any trade-ins.

The Gigantic performance evaluation system gives responsibility to each division manager for divisional income after deducting all charges, including losses on equipment.

required

1. Assume that it is a world of zero interest. (The interest implications of this problem are covered in Problem 12-11.) Prepare statements of cash receipts and disbursements for each of the three years under both alternatives. What is the cumulative difference in cash flow for the three years?
2. Prepare statements of income as they would appear in each of the three years under both alternatives. Assume straight-line depreciation. What is the cumulative difference in net income for the three years?
3. What are the irrelevant items in each of your presentations for requirements 1 and 2? Why are they irrelevant?
4. Suppose that the cost of the "old" equipment was $100 million rather than $600,000. Its disposal value in five days will also be $120,000. Would the net difference in requirements 1 and 2 change? Explain.
5. Your controller says, "Keeping the old equipment avoids a loss. We should keep it at least until we recoup our investment." Do you agree? Why? What action do you prefer? Why?
6. Change the setting. Suppose that as the mayor of a medium-sized city you had purchased voting machines yesterday. New machines could be acquired now for $750,000 that would save $260,000 yearly for each of the next three years. The "old" machines cost $600,000 and would entail total operating costs of $300,000 annually. Would any of your answers to requirements 1 through 5 change? How? Why?

11-10 *Costs of Operating an Automobile* Here are typical costs of operating a salesman's car for 30,000 miles in a year:

Gasoline—1,000 gallons @ 80¢	$ 800
Oil changes and lubrication—5 @ $10	50
Tire wear (based on life of 20,000 miles; a new set of 4 costs $100)	150
Regular maintenance and repair	210
Auto insurance	290
Washing and waxing	100
Licenses	100
Garage rent and parking fees	300
Depreciation—($4,800 − $2,800) ÷ 2-year life	1,000
	$3,000

Unit cost is $3,000 ÷ 30,000 miles, or 10¢ per mile.

required

1. If the salesman drove 20,000 miles per year, what would be the average unit cost per mile? If he drove 40,000 miles?
2. He takes his car on a 200-mile journey with a friend who agrees to share the cost of the trip. How much should the friend pay?
3. The salesman's wife wants a similar car for shopping and other errands that the husband now performs. If he buys the second car, it will be driven 4,000 miles per year; but suppose the total mileage of the two cars taken together will still be 30,000 miles. What will the annual cost of operating the second car be? The average unit cost? What costs are relevant? Why?
4. List other possible costs of car ownership that are not included in the tabulation above.
5. What costs are relevant to the question of selling the car at the end of one year (market value, $3,500) and using other means of transportation?
6. Assume that the salesman has no car. What costs are relevant to the question of buying the car described versus using other means of transportation?

11-11 *Relevance of Inventory Costs to a Business Investment Decision* Assume that a wealthy investor is contemplating buying a paper-manufacturing company. Certain inventory of the paper company is carried at $100,000, including $40,000 of variable production costs and $60,000 of fixed factory overhead.

required | How much should the investor pay for the inventory? Why?

11-12 *An Argument About Pricing* A column in a newspaper contained the following:

Dear Miss Lovelorn: My husband and I are in constant disagreement because he drives 10 miles to work every day, and drives a mile in the opposite direction to pick up and deliver the man who rides with him. For this service the man pays $2 every other week toward gas. Bus fare would cost $5 each week. I say this fellow should pay at least $3 each week, which would be one-half the cost for the week's gas. But my husband says he can't just ask him for the money, so he settles for this arrangement month after month. We have three children and are in debt for several hundred dollars, and even this $3 a week would really help, as we live on a very tight budget. Am I reasonable to think the gas expense should be split 50-50?

required | As Miss Lovelorn, write a reply.

11-13 *Contribution Approach to Pricing* A company has a budget for 19_2; the absorption-costing approach follows (figures assumed):

Sales	$100,000	100%
Factory cost of goods sold, including $20,000 fixed costs	60,000	60
Gross profit	$ 40,000	40%
Operating expenses, including $20,000 fixed costs	30,000	30
Net income target	$ 10,000	10%

Normal or target markup percentage:
$40,000 ÷ $60,000 = 66.7% of absorption cost

required |

1. Recast the income statement in a contribution format. Indicate the normal or target markup percentage based on total variable costs.
2. Assume the same cost behavior patterns as above. Assume further that a customer offers $540 for some units that have a factory cost of goods manufactured of $600 and total variable costs of $500. Should the offer be accepted? Explain.
3. Under what circumstances would you adopt a contribution approach to pricing as a part of your usual accounting system? That is, the system would routinely provide data using the contribution format.

11-14 *Costs and pricing* (CMA) E. Berg and Sons build custom-made pleasure boats that range in price from $10,000 to $250,000. For the past 30 years, Mr. Berg, Sr., has determined the selling price of each boat by estimating the costs of material, labor, a prorated portion of overhead, and adding 20 percent to their estimated costs.

For example, a recent price quotation was determined as follows:

Direct materials	$ 5,000
Direct labor	8,000
Overhead	2,000
	$15,000
Plus 20 percent	3,000
Selling price	$18,000

The overhead figure was determined by estimating total overhead costs for the year and allocating them at 25 percent of direct labor.

If a customer rejected the price and business was slack, Mr. Berg, Sr., would often be willing to reduce his markup to as little as 5 percent over estimated costs. Thus, average markup for the year is estimated at 15 percent.

Mr. Ed Berg, Jr., has just completed a course on pricing, and believes the firm could use some of the techniques discussed in the course. The course emphasized the contribution-margin approach to pricing, and Mr. Berg, Jr. feels such an approach would be helpful in determining the selling prices of their custom-made pleasure boats.

Total overhead, which includes selling and administrative expenses for the year, has been estimated at $150,000, of which $90,000 is fixed and the remainder is variable in direct proportion to direct labor.

required

1. Assume the customer in the example rejected the $18,000 quotation and also rejected a $15,750 quotation (5 percent markup) during a slack period. The customer countered with a $15,000 offer.
   a. What is the difference in company net income for the year between accepting or rejecting the customer's offer?
   b. What is the minimum selling price Mr. Berg, Jr. could have quoted without reducing or increasing company net income?
2. What advantages does the contribution-margin approach to pricing have over the approach used by Mr. Berg, Sr.?
3. What pitfalls are there, if any, to contribution-margin pricing?

11-15 *Product Deletion* (W. Crum.)

	NOX	*POX*	*ROX*
Sales	5,000 at $20	12,000 at $12	16,000 at $10
Variable costs	$12 each	$6 each	$4 each
Fixed costs	$50,000	$40,000	$50,000

These products are made in competition with each other; the company believes that by an advertising outlay of $20,000 it could get 80 percent of the users of Nox to buy Pox or Rox, thus permitting the firm to drop the Nox line, owing to its unprofitability. Analysis reveals $20,000 of the Nox fixed cost is separable and would stop with the dropping of that line. Assume continuing fixed costs of Nox will be divided 3/4 to Pox and 1/4 to Rox.

Would you advise the company to do this if a market survey concluded sales of Pox would go up by 3,000 with the remainder of the Nox Customers turning to Rox (those that would not go to competitors)? Show figures in support of your answer.

11-16 *Make-or-Buy Decision* (CPA) When you had completed your audit of The Scoopa Company, management asked for your assistance in arriving at a decision whether to continue manufacturing a part or to buy it from an outside supplier. The part, which is named Faktron, is a component used in some of the finished products of the Company.

From your audit working papers and from further investigation you develop the following data as being typical of the Company's operations:

1. The annual requirement for Faktrons is 5,000 units. The lowest quotation from a supplier was $8.00 per unit.
2. Faktrons have been manufactured in the Precision Machinery Department. If Faktrons are purchased from an outside supplier, certain machinery will be sold and would realize its book value.

3. Following are the total costs of the Precision Machinery Department during the year under audit when 5,000 Faktrons were made:

Materials	$67,500
Direct labor	50,000
Indirect labor	20,000
Light and heat	5,500
Power	3,000
Depreciation	10,000
Property taxes and insurance	8,000
Payroll taxes and other benefits	9,800
Other	5,000

4. The following Precision Machinery Department costs apply to the manufacture of Faktrons: material, $17,500; direct labor, $28,000; indirect labor, $6,000; power, $300; other, $500. The sale of the equipment used for Faktrons would reduce the following costs by the amounts indicated: depreciation, $2,000; property taxes and insurance, $1,000.
5. The following additional Precision Machinery Department costs would be incurred if Faktrons were purchased from an outside supplier: freight, $.50 per unit; indirect labor for receiving, materials handling, inspection, etc., $5,000. The cost of the purchased Faktrons would be considered a Precision Machinery Department cost.

required

1. Prepare a schedule showing a comparison of the total costs of the Precision Machinery Department (1) when Faktrons are made, and (2) when Faktrons are bought from an outside supplier.
2. Discuss the considerations in addition to the cost factors that you would bring to the attention of management in assisting them to arrive at a decision whether to make or buy Faktrons. Include in your discussion the considerations that might be applied to the evaluation of the outside supplier.

11-17 *Discontinuing a Department; Make or Buy* (CPA) The Ace Publishing Company in Hong Kong is in the business of publishing and printing guidebooks and directories. The board of directors has engaged you to make a cost study to determine whether the company is economically justified in continuing to print, as well as publish, its books and directories. You obtain the following information from the company's cost-accounting records for the preceding fiscal year:

	DEPARTMENTS			
	PUBLISHING	PRINTING	SHIPPING	TOTAL
Salaries and wages	$275,000	$150,000	$25,000	$ 450,000
Telephone and telegraph	12,000	3,700	300	16,000
Materials and supplies	50,000	250,000	10,000	310,000
Occupancy costs	75,000	80,000	10,000	165,000
General and administrative	40,000	30,000	4,000	74,000
Depreciation	5,000	40,000	5,000	50,000
	$457,000	$553,700	$54,300	$1,065,000

Additional Data

1. A review of personnel requirements indicates that if printing is discontinued, the publishing department will need one additional clerk at $4,000 per year to handle correspondence with the printer. Two layout men and a

proofreader will be required, at an aggregate annual cost of $17,000; other personnel in the printing department can be released. One mailing clerk, at $3,000, will be retained; others in the shipping department can be released. Employees whose employment was being terminated would immediately receive, on the average, three months' termination pay. The termination pay would be amortized over a five-year period.

2. Long-distance telephone and telegraph charges are identified and distributed to the responsible department. The remainder of the telephone bill, representing basic service at a cost of $4,000, is allocated in the ratio of 10 to publishing, 5 to printing, and 1 to shipping. The discontinuance of printing is not expected to have a material effect on the basic service cost.
3. Shipping supplies consist of cartons, envelopes, and stamps. It is estimated that the cost of envelopes and stamps for mailing material to an outside printer would be $5,000 per year.
4. If printing were discontinued, the company would retain its present building but would sublet a portion of the space at an annual rental of $50,000. Taxes, insurance, heat, light, and other occupancy costs would not be significantly affected.
5. One cost clerk would not be required ($5,000 per year) if printing is discontinued. Other general and administrative personnel would be retained.
6. Included in administrative expenses is interest expense on a 5 percent mortgage loan of $500,000.
7. Printing and shipping-room machinery and equipment having a net book value of $300,000 can be sold without gain or loss. These funds in excess of termination pay would be invested in marketable securities earning 5 percent.
8. The company has received a proposal for a five-year contract from an outside printer, under which the volume of work done last year would be printed at a cost of $550,000 per year.
9. Assume continued volume and prices at last year's level.

required

Prepare a statement setting forth in comparative form the costs of operation of the printing and shipping departments under the present arrangement and under an arrangement in which inside printing is discontinued. Summarize the net saving or extra cost in case printing is discontinued.

11-18 *Order-Filling Costs and Minimum Order Size* The Independent Wholesale Drug Co. has made a time study of the cost of filling orders, with the following results:

SIZE OF ORDERS IN DOLLARS	AVERAGE TIME REQUIRED
.00 to 2.00	.10 hour
2.01 to 5.00	.12 hour
5.01 to 15.00	.16 hour
15.01 to 25.00	.20 hour
Over 25.00	.25 hour

Order-filling costs totaled $4,480 for the month in which the study was made, and 1,600 man-hours were worked in the Order-Filling Department. During the same period, the costs of receiving orders and of billing and posting the customers' accounts were calculated at a minimum of 16¢ per order. Gross margin (profit) on the company's merchandise averages 20 percent.

Ignoring all considerations other than these cost data, should the company adopt a rule that it will accept orders only above some minimum size? If so, what minimum order size would you recommend?

11-19 *Different Cost Terms* (CPA) *Instructions:* You are to match each of the nine numbered "items" that follow with the *one* term listed immediately below (A through R) that *most specifically* identifies the cost concept indicated parenthetically. (*Caution:* An item of cost may be classified in several ways, depending on the purpose of the classification. For example, the commissions on sales of a proposed new product line might be classified as *direct, variable,* and *marginal,* among others. However, if such costs are being considered specifically as to the amount of *cash outlay* required in making a decision concerning adoption of the new line, the commissions are *out-of-pocket costs.* That would be the *most* appropriate answer in the context.) The same term may be used more than once.

Indicate your choice of answer for each item by printing beside the item numbers the capital letter that identifies the term you select.

Terms

A. By-product cost
B. Common or joint cost
C. Controllable cost
D. Direct cost
E. Estimated cost
F. Fixed cost
G. Historical cost
H. Imputed cost
I. Differential cost
J. Indirect cost
K. Opportunity cost
L. Original cost
M. Out-of-pocket cost
N. Prime cost
O. Replacement cost
P. Standard cost
Q. Sunk cost
R. Variable cost

Items

1. The management of a corporation is considering replacing a machine that is operating satisfactorily with a more efficient new model. Depreciation on the cost of the existing machine is omitted from the data used in judging the proposal, because it has little or no significance with respect to such a decision. (*The omitted cost.*)
2. One of the problems encountered by a bank in attempting to establish the cost of a commercial-deposit account is the fact that many facilities and services are shared by many revenue-producing activities. (*Costs of the shared facilities and services.*)
3. A company declined an offer received to rent one of its warehouses and elected to use the warehouse for storage of extra raw materials to insure uninterrupted production. Storage cost has been charged with *the monthly amount of the rental offered.* (*This cost is known as?*)
4. A manufacturing company excludes all "fixed" costs from its valuation of inventories, assigning to inventory only *applicable portions of costs that vary with changes in volume of product.* (*The term employed for the variable costs in this context by advocates of this costing procedure.*)
5. The sales department urges an increase in production of a product and, as part of the data presented in support of its proposal, indicates the total

additional cost involved for the volume level it proposes. (*The increase in total cost.*)

6. A CPA takes exception to his client's inclusion, in the cost of a fixed asset, of an "interest" charge based on the client's own funds invested in the asset. The client states that the charge was intended to obtain a cost comparable to what would have been the case if funds had been borrowed to finance the acquisition. (*The term that describes such interest charges.*)
7. The "direct" production cost of a unit includes those portions of factory overhead, *labor,* and *materials* that are obviously traceable directly to the unit. (*The term used to specify the last two of the named components.*)
8. Calling upon the special facilities of the production, planning, personnel, and other departments, a firm estimated its future unit cost of production and used this cost (analyzed by cost elements) in its accounts. (*The term used to specify this scientifically predetermined estimate.*)
9. A chemical-manufacturing company produces three products originating in a common initial material mix. Each product gains a separate identity partway through processing and requires additional processing after the "split." Each contributes a significant share of revenue. The company plans to spread the costs up to the "split" among the three products by the use of relative market values. (*The term used to specify the costs accumulated up to the point of the split.*)

11-20 *Selection of Most Profitable Product* The Flabbo Co. produces two basic types of reducing equipment, G and H. Pertinent data follow:

	PER UNIT	
	G	H
Sales price	$100.00	$70.00
Expenses:		
Direct materials	$ 28.00	$13.00
Direct labor	15.00	25.00
Variable factory overhead*	25.00	12.50
Fixed factory overhead*	10.00	5.00
Selling expenses (all variable)	14.00	10.00
	$ 92.00	$65.50
Net margin	$ 8.00	$ 4.50

* Applied on the basis of machine-hours.

The reducing craze is such that enough of either G or H can be sold to keep the plant operating at full capacity. Both products are processed through the same production centers.

required

Which product should be produced? If more than one should be produced, indicate the proportions of each. Briefly explain your answer.

11-21 *Product Choice* (R. Jaedicke.) The Borg Company manufactures a type of raw sheet metal that can be sold at this stage or that can be processed more and sold as a type of alloy used in manufacturing high-grade control systems of various types. The raw-sheet-metal market is such that the entire output can be sold at the market price, which at the present time is $100 per ton. The processed selling price has been about $180 per ton for several years, but recently the market has been weak and on several occasions the price has dropped as low as $140. This has caused the sales manager to suggest that the alloy is no longer profitable and should be dropped. He feels that the entire capacity should be used to produce the raw metal. His suggestion is prompted by the following data:

	COST PER TON OF RAW SHEET METAL	COST PER TON OF ALLOY
Raw materials	$ 50	
Direct labor	10	
Overhead	30	
Cost per ton	$ 90	$ 90
Selling value	100	
Profit	$ 10	
Processing cost:		
Additional materials		20
Direct labor		10
Overhead		30
Cost per ton of alloy		$150
Selling value of alloy		140
Loss		($ 10)

The sales manager argues that, because of a $10 loss per unit of alloy, the product should be dropped any time the price per ton falls below $150.

In the cost calculations, the raw materials and the labor costs are variable. The overhead rate per unit is calculated by estimating the total overhead for the coming year and dividing this total by the total hours of capacity available. The total overhead is, for the most part, a fixed cost.

required

1. Should the alloy be dropped and the entire production facility be used to produce raw metal if the price per ton of alloy for the coming year is estimated to be $140? Support your conclusion with an appropriate analysis.
2. Prepare an analysis to aid the sales manager in determining the lowest alloy price that would be acceptable to the company.
3. Assume that the total overhead for the company is about 50 percent fixed, 50 percent variable. Would you accept the $140 offer for alloy? Why? What would be the lowest acceptable price for the alloy?

Note: You may find it helpful to assume that the total hours of capacity available are 1,000,000. It takes one hour to make a ton of raw sheet metal and one hour of additional processing to make a ton of alloy. The total available capacity is interchangeable.

11-22 *Production Scheduling* (R. Jaedicke.) A paperboard manufacturing company has two plants, one in Washington and one in California, producing equivalent grades of "cardboard." The Washington plant has been operating at 75 percent of plant capacity, producing 2,700 tons of cardboard per month, and the California plant has been operating at 60 percent of plant capacity and producing 3,600 tons per month.

The major raw material used in producing the cardboard is waste paper. For each 100 tons of product, 80 tons of waste paper are required. At the Washington plant the local waste-paper costs are $18.75 per ton of waste paper but the supply is limited to 1,440 tons per month. At the California plant local waste paper costs $20.00 per ton and is limited to 4,000 tons. Additional waste paper must be purchased through brokers at $27.50 per ton (delivered at either plant).

The cost schedules for a typical month's production are given below.

WASHINGTON PLANT	
Raw materials (2,160 tons input)	$ 46,800
Fixed cost (per month)	59,400
Variable cost	102,600*
Total cost ($77.33 per ton output)	$208,800

CALIFORNIA PLANT	
Raw materials (2,800 tons input)	$ 57,600
Fixed cost	108,000
Variable cost	140,400*
Total cost ($85.00 per ton output)	$306,000

* Variable costs are constant per ton of output.

required

(Disregard any marketing costs in your answer to the questions):

1. If the total combined production of both plants is to be continued at the present rate of 6,300 tons per month, would there be any apparent advantage to shifting part of the scheduled production from one of the plants to the other? If so, which plant's production should be increased and by how much? What is the amount of the cost savings as a result of this switch?
2. If production requirements increased to 9,100 tons per month, how much would you recommend be produced at each plant? (Show calculations.)

11-23 *Relationship of Disposal Value, Book Value, and Net Loss on Old Equipment* Scott Harshaw is the president of a small plastics company. He wants to replace an old special-purpose molding machine (original cost, $18,700; eight years old; book value, $9,100; straight-line depreciation, $1,200 per year; residual value at end of useful life, $700) with a new, more efficient machine. The new machine has an expected useful life of only seven years, but it promises savings in cash operating costs of $2,257 per year. Operating costs with the new machine are $30,000; with the old machine, $32,257. The cost of the new machine is $8,800. The old machine can be sold outright for $2,300, less $200 removal cost. It is estimated that the old machine would have a net disposal value of $700 seven years from now; the new machine, a value of $750 seven years from now.

Vladimar Galoot, controller, opposes replacement because no advantage is apparent. His analysis shows:

Cost of new investment:	
Outlay	$ 8,800
Loss on old machine ($9,100 minus $2,100)	7,000
Total cost	$15,800
Savings: $2,257 per year × 7 years	15,800 (rounded)
Net advantage of replacement	$ 0

He also adds, "I can't ever see disposing of fixed assets at a loss before their useful life expires. Plant and equipment are bought and depreciated with some useful life in mind. We are in business to maximize income (or minimize loss). It seems to me that the alternatives are clear: (a) disposal of a fixed asset before it diminishes to zero or residual book value often results in a loss; (b) keeping and *using* the same fixed asset avoids such a loss. Now, any sensible person will have brains enough to avoid a loss when his other alternative is recognizing a loss. It makes sense to use a fixed asset till you get your money out of it."

Yearly sales are $90,000, and cash expenses, excluding the data given above, are $50,000.

required

(Ignore income tax effects.)

1. How will net income be affected if the old machine is scrapped and the new machine is purchased? Show computations for the seven years taken together and on an average annual basis.
2. Prepare columnar income statements for years 1 through 7 under both alternatives, as follows:

YEAR 1	EACH YEAR, 2–7	7 YEARS TOGETHER

3. Generalize as to the role of disposal value on old equipment in these decisions.
4. Generalize as to the role of (a) book value in these decisions and (b) net loss on disposal of old fixed assets.
5. Criticize Galoot's schedule and his comments.
6. What important cost factor has been ignored in your answers to 1 and 2?

11-24 *Multiple Choice; Comprehensive Problem on Relevant Costs* The following are the Class Company's *unit* costs of making and selling a given item at a level of 20,000 units per month:

Manufacturing:	
Direct materials	$1.00
Direct labor	1.20
Variable indirect cost	.80
Fixed indirect cost	.50
Selling and other:	
Variable	1.50
Fixed	.90

The following situations refer only to the data given above—there is *no connection* between the situations. Unless stated otherwise, assume a regular selling price of $6 per unit.

Choose the answer corresponding to the most nearly acceptable or correct answer in each of the nine items. Support each answer with summarized computations.

1. In presenting an inventory of 10,000 items on the balance sheet, the unit cost conventionally to be used is (a) $3.00, (b) $3.50, (c) $5.00, (d) $5.90, (e) $2.20.
2. The unit cost relevant to setting a *normal* price for this product, assuming that the implied level of operations is to be maintained, is (a) $5.00, (b) $4.50, (c) $3.50, (d) $3.00, (e) $5.90.
3. This product is usually sold at the rate of 240,000 units per year (an average of 20,000 per month). At a sales price of $6.00 per unit, this yields total sales of $1,440,000, total costs of $1,416,000, and a net margin of $24,000, or 10¢ per unit. It is estimated by market research that volume could be increased by 10 percent if prices were cut to $5.80. Assuming the implied cost behavior patterns to be correct, this action, if taken, would:
   a. Decrease profits by a net of $7,200.
   b. Decrease profits by 20¢ per unit, $48,000, but increase profits by 10 percent of sales, $144,000; net, $86,000 increase.

c. Decrease unit fixed costs by 10 percent or 14¢ per unit and thus decrease profits by 20¢ − 14¢, or 6¢ per unit.
d. Increase sales volume to 264,000 units, which at the $5.80 price would give total sales of $1,531,200; costs of $5.90 per unit for 264,000 units would be $1,557,600, and a loss of $26,400 would result.
e. None of these.

4. A cost contract with the government (for 5,000 units of product) calls for the reimbursement of all costs of production plus a fixed fee of $1,000. This production is part of the regular 20,000 units of production per month. The delivery of these 5,000 units of product increases profits from what they would have been, were these units not sold, by (a) $1,000, (b) $2,500 (c) $3,500, (d) $300, (e) none of these.
5. Assume the same data as in 4 above, except that the 5,000 units will displace 5,000 other units from production. The latter 5,000 units would have been sold through regular channels for $30,000 had they been made. The delivery to the government increases (or decreases) net profits from what they would have been, were the other 5,000 units sold by (a) $4,000 decrease, (b) $3,000 increase, (c) $6,500 decrease, (d) $500 increase, (e) none of these.
6. The company desires to enter a foreign market, in which price competition is keen. An order for 10,000 units of this product is being sought on a minimum unit-price basis. It is expected that shipping costs for this order will amount to only 75¢ per unit but the fixed costs of obtaining the contract will be $4,000. Domestic business will be unaffected. The minimum basis for breakeven price is (a) $3.50, (b) $4.15, (c) $4.25, (d) $5.00, (e) $3.00.
7. The company has an inventory of 1,000 units of this item left over from last year's model. These must be sold through regular channels at reduced prices. The inventory will be valueless unless sold this way. The unit cost that is relevant for establishing the minimum selling price would be (a) $4.50, (b) $4.00, (c) $3.00, (d) $1.50, (e) $5.90.
8. A proposal is received from an outside supplier who will make and ship this item directly to the Class Company's customers as sales orders are forwarded from Class's sales staff. Class's fixed selling costs will be unaffected, but its variable selling costs will be slashed 20 percent. Class's plant will be idle, but its fixed factory overhead would continue at 50 percent of present levels. To compare with the quotation received from the supplier, the company should use a unit cost of (a) $4.75, (b) $3.95, (c) $2.95, (d) $5.35, (e) none of these.
9. Assume the same facts as in 8 above, except that if the supplier's offer is accepted, the present plant facilities will be used to make a product whose unit costs will be:

Variable manufacturing costs	$5.00
Fixed manufacturing costs	1.00
Variable selling costs	2.00
Fixed selling costs (new increment)	.50

Total fixed factory overhead will be unchanged, while fixed selling costs will increase as indicated. The new product will sell for $9. This minimum desired net profit on the two products taken together is $50,000 per year. What is the maximum purchase cost per unit that the Class Company should be willing to pay for subcontracting the old production?

Special Topics for Further Study

SECTION THREE

Cost Analysis and Capital Budgeting

12

Should we add a product? Should we buy the new equipment? Should we close a division? Managers often use information provided by accountants to guide nonrecurring decisions having a long-range impact on the organization. These are frequently called capital-budgeting decisions. In recent years new decision models have been used for capital budgeting. These models have incorporated the time value of money; they represent a sharp departure from the accrual accounting models so widely used previously.

The manager and the accountant should understand the uses and limitations of the various decision models for capital budgeting. Most important, managers should particularly recognize the basic incompatibility between the discounted cash-flow models for *decisions* and the accrual accounting models so often used for the *evaluation of the results* of those decisions. Let us examine and compare these models.

contrasts in purposes of cost analysis

At this stage we again focus on purpose. Income determination and the planning and controlling of operations primarily have a *current time-period* orientation. Special decisions and long-range planning primarily have a *project* or *program* orientation with a far-reaching time span.

The project and time-period orientations of Exhibit 12-1 represent two distinct cross sections of the total corporate assets. The vertical dimension signifies the total investment (assets) of the company, which is a portfolio, a collection of resources, that may be subdivided into divisions, product lines, departments, buildings, a fleet of trucks or machines. These parts of an organization's resources are individual *projects* or *programs* that result from investment decisions. The horizontal dimension represents successive years in a company's life.

The black horizontal rectangle shows that a project can entail commitments over a prolonged span of time, not just one year. The focus is on a single cross section, a lone investment venture, throughout its life. The interest income that can be earned over a period of time (that is, the time value of money) often looms large in special decisions and in long-range planning.

The black vertical rectangle illustrates the focus of income determination and current planning and control. The cross-sectional emphasis is upon the company's overall performance and status for a year or less. The time period is relatively short, and the interest value of money is usually not directly involved.

The point of all this is that our ordinary accounting systems and techniques have been designed to determine the cost and income of products for

EXHIBIT 12-1

THE PROJECT ORIENTATION OF CAPITAL BUDGETING

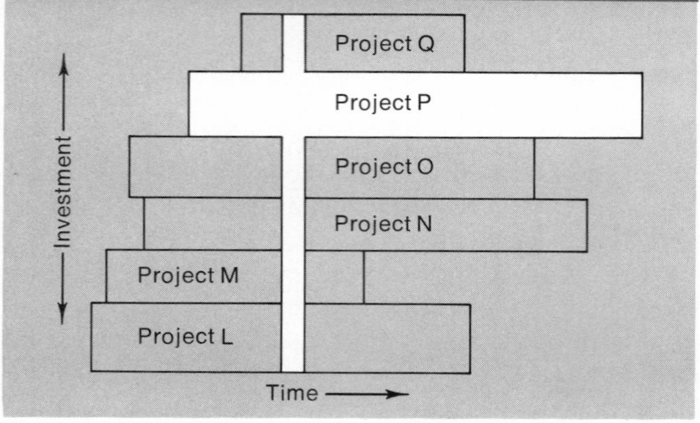

current planning and control. There is a great danger of using the existing general-purpose accounting system incorrectly—that is, of using data indiscriminately for solving special problems.

So in this chapter, we shift gears. We shall take a fresh look at the purpose of the special decision, and then we shall decide what models seem best for achieving that purpose.

definition of capital budgeting

Capital budgeting is the making of long-term planning decisions for investments and their financing. The profitability of an investment decision depends on two vital factors: (a) future net increases in cash inflows or net savings in cash outflows; and (b) required investment. Thus, a chance to receive an annual return of $5,000 for a given number of years on a bond or stock can be judged only in relationship to how much money need be committed to obtain the $5,000. Depending on risk and available alternatives, individuals and corporate investors usually have some notion of a minimum rate of return that would make various projects desirable investments.

The quantitative approach to the selection of projects generally compares predicted cash flows to the required investments. Thus, all projects having rates of return in excess of the minimum rate of return would be desirable, and vice versa. The problem of choosing the minimum acceptable rate of return (more a problem of finance than of accounting) is extremely complex.

There are several different models for the capital-budgeting decision. Although we shall discuss (a) urgency and persuasion, (b) discounted cash flow,[1] (c) payback, and (d) the accrual accounting rate of return, we shall concentrate on discounted cash flow because it is conceptually superior to the others.[2]

[1] Although discounted cash-flow models were used in financial markets for many years, the models did not come into wide use by business managers until the 1950s. As might be expected, the companies making large capital expenditures were the first to search for improved decision models. The leaders in adopting discounted cash flow were petroleum companies and public utilities. Keep in mind that the switching to "better" decision models is a cost-benefit decision. Many companies have viewed discounted cash-flow models as too costly to use (in particular, costly in the sense of educating personnel) in relation to the expected benefits of more profitable decisions. But the trend toward wider use of such models is unmistakable.

[2] Thomas Klammer, "Empirical Evidence of the Adoption of Sophisticated Capital Budgeting Techniques," *The Journal of Business,* Vol. VL, No. 3 (October 1972), surveyed 369 large firms and received 184 responses. Fifty-seven percent of the firms responding indicated that they used discounted cash-flow techniques in 1970, as compared with only 19 percent in 1959:

	PERCENTAGE USING IN:		
	1970	*1964*	*1959*
Discounting	57	38	19
Accounting rate of return	26	30	34
Payback	12	24	34
Urgency	5	8	13
	100	100	100

urgency and persuasion

Many phases of business operations are managed in the same manner in which many individuals care for their cars. How many of us keep cars going until that bald tire becomes suddenly useless, the old battery refuses to perform, or the sticky valves keep the car from starting in cold weather? Then what happens? Stop-gap action may be taken so that the car can be put back in service quickly. When a machine part fails, a belt breaks, or a generator wears out, routine replacements are made to avoid disruption in production. If the old machine on the assembly line suddenly disintegrates, there may be a fast but uneconomic replacement so that down time is minimized. Ideally, all repairs, maintenance, and replacements should be implementations of an overall equipment policy that considers future-cost comparisons and timing.

Often the urgent action taken is correct on logical grounds. But it is correct by coincidence rather than by methodical analysis. The pressures of the moment lead to quick remedial action. When a contemplated outlay is large and far-reaching in its effects, urgency should not be a convincing influence.

The individual manager's power of persuasion is a key factor where urgency or postponability is paramount in influencing the spending decisions of top management. The managers who are best at selling their own projects to the decision maker get the lion's portion of the available money, whereas the rest of the managers either get nothing or wait, and then wait some more. Economic considerations become secondary as individual managers war with words and with impressive operating performance that may or may not be relevant to the capital-budgeting problem at hand.

discounted cash flow

time value of money

The discounted cash-flow (DCF) model for capital-budgeting decisions recognizes that the use of money has a cost (interest), just as the use of a building or an automobile may have a cost (rent). A dollar in the hand today is worth more than a dollar to be received (or spent) five years from today. For instance, in the interim a dollar can be invested in a savings institution; the dollar would grow markedly during a five-year span because of the interest it would earn. *Because the discounted cash-flow model explicitly and routinely weighs the time value of money, it is usually the best model to use for long-range decisions.*

Another major aspect of DCF is its focus on *cash* inflows and outflows rather than on *net income* as computed in the conventional accounting sense. Cash is invested now with the hope of receiving cash in a greater amount in the future. As we shall see, the student without a strong accounting background has an advantage here. He does not have to unlearn the accrual concepts of accounting, which the accounting student often wrongly tries to inject into discounted cash-flow analysis.

There are two main variations of DCF: (a) *internal rate of return* (also often called *time-adjusted rate of return*), and (b) net present value. A brief summary of the tables and formulas used is included in Appendix B at the end of this book. **Before reading on, be sure you understand this appendix.**

internal rate of return

The internal rate of return may be defined as "the maximum rate of interest that could be paid for the capital employed over the life of an investment without loss on the project."[3] This rate corresponds to the effective rate of interest so widely computed for bonds purchased or sold at discounts or premiums.

example 1

> A manager is considering buying a new special-purpose machine, which is expected to have a five-year useful life, have zero disposal value, and result in cash operating savings of $1,000 annually. If the machine will cost $3,791 now, what is the internal rate of return on this project?

Note in Exhibit 12-2 that $3,791 is the present value, at a rate of return of 10 percent, of a five-year stream of inflows of $1,000 in cash per year. Ten percent is the rate that equates the amount invested ($3,791) with the present value of the cash inflows ($1,000 per year for five years). In other words, *if* money were borrowed at an effective interest rate of 10 percent, the cash inflow produced by the project would exactly repay the hypothetical loan plus interest over the five years. If the minimum desired rate of return[4] is less than 10 percent, the project will be profitable. If the minimum desired return exceeds 10 percent, the cash inflow will be insufficient to pay interest and repay the principal of the hypothetical loan. Therefore, 10 percent is the internal rate of return for this project.

explanation of compound interest

The internal rate of return is computed on the basis of the funds in use from period to period instead of on the original investment. See Exhibit 12-3. The return in that exhibit is

[3] *Research Report 35, Return on Capital as a Guide to Managerial Decisions,* National Association of Accountants, p. 57. *Rate of return* may alternatively be defined as the discounting rate that makes the gross present value of a project equal to the cost of the project. That is, the net present value is zero, as Exhibit 12-2 shows.

[4] Minimum desired rate of return (cost of capital) is discussed in Chapter 13. For now, we assume the cost of capital as given; it is the minimum desired rate of return. Any project with a rate of return exceeding the cost of capital is desirable. Cost of capital is usually a long-run weighted average based on both debt and equity. Cost of capital is *not* typically a piecemeal computation based on the market rate of interest; that is, it is not "interest expense" on borrowed money as the accountant usually conceives it to be. For example, a mortgage-free house still has a cost of capital—the amount that could be earned with the proceeds if the house were sold.

EXHIBIT 12-2

TWO PROOFS OF INTERNAL RATE OF RETURN

Original investment	$3,791
Useful life	5 years
Annual cash inflow from operations	$1,000
Internal rate of return	10%[a]

Proof 1: Discounting Each Year's Cash Inflow Separately[b]

	PRESENT VALUE OF $1, DISCOUNTED AT 10P	*TOTAL PRESENT VALUE*	*SKETCH OF CASH FLOWS*					
End of Year			0	1	2	3	4	5
Cash flows:								
Annual cash savings	.909	$ 909		$1,000				
	.826	826			$1,000			
	.751	751				$1,000		
	.683	683					$1,000	
	.621	621						$1,000
Present value of future inflows		$3,791[c]						
Initial outlay	1.000	(3,791)	$(3,791)					
Net present value (the zero difference proves that the rate of return is 10%)		$ 0						

Proof 2: Using Annuity Table[d]

			0	1	2	3	4	5
Annual cash savings	3.791	$3,791		$1,000	$1,000	$1,000	$1,000	$1,000
Initial outlay	1.000	(3,791)	$(3,791)					
Net present value		$ 0						

[a] The rate of return would be computed by trial-and-error methods; this is explained later in the chapter.

[b] Present values from Table 2, Appendix B at the end of the book.

[c] Sum is really $3,790, but is rounded.

[d] Present values of annuity from Table 4, Appendix B at the end of the book.

10 percent of the capital invested during each year. The cash flows in excess of the 10 percent "rent" on the invested capital are regarded as recoveries of the original investment. In this example, the five-year cash inflow just recovers the original investment plus annual interest at a rate of 10 percent on the as yet unrecovered capital.

EXHIBIT 12-3

RATIONALE UNDERLYING INTERNAL RATE-OF-RETURN MODEL

(Same data as in Exhibit 12-2)

Original investment	$3,791
Annual cash inflow from operations	1,000
Useful life	5 years
Internal rate of return	10%

	(1)	(2)	(3)	(4)	(5)
YEAR	UNRECOVERED INVESTMENT AT BEGINNING OF YEAR	ANNUAL CASH INFLOW	INTEREST AT 10% PER YEAR (1) × 10%	AMOUNT OF INVESTMENT RECOVERED AT END OF YEAR (2) − (3)	UNRECOVERED INVESTMENT AT END OF YEAR (1) − (4)
1	$3,791	$1,000	$ 379	$ 621	$3,170
2	3,170	1,000	317	683	2,487
3	2,487	1,000	249	751	1,736
4	1,736	1,000	173	827	909
5	909	1,000	91	909	0
		$5,000	$1,209	$3,791	

Assumptions: Unrecovered investment at beginning of each year earns interest for whole year. Annual cash inflows are received at the end of each year. For simplicity in the use of tables, all operating cash inflows are assumed to take place at the *end* of the years in question. This is unrealistic because such cash flows ordinarily occur uniformly throughout the given year, rather than in lump sums at the end of the year. Compound-interest tables especially tailored for these more stringent conditions are available, but we shall not consider them here. See J. Bracken and C. Christenson, *Tables for Use in Analyzing Business Decisions* (Homewood, Ill.: Richard D. Irwin, Inc.).

depreciation and discounted cash flow

Students are often perplexed by the seeming exclusion of depreciation from DCF computations. A common homework error is to discount cash flows less depreciation. This tendency betrays a lack of understanding of a basic idea of the internal rate of return. Because the DCF approach is fundamentally based on inflows and outflows of *cash* and not on the *accrual* concepts of revenues and expenses, no adjustments should be made to the cash flows for the periodic allocation of the asset cost called depreciation expense (which is not a cash flow). In the DCF approach, the initial cost of an asset is usually regarded as a *lump-sum* outflow of cash at time zero. **Therefore, it is wrong to deduct depreciation from operating cash inflows before consulting present value tables.** To deduct periodic depreciation would be a double-counting of a cost that has already been considered as a lump-sum outflow.

net present-value model Another type of DCF model is called the net present-value model. Computing the exact internal rate of return entails trial and error and, sometimes, cumbersome hand calculations and interpolations using a compound interest table. In contrast, the net present-value model assumes some minimum desired rate of return that is often called the *hurdle rate* or *cut-off rate.* All expected cash flows are discounted to the present, using this minimum desired rate. If the result is positive, the project is desirable because its return exceeds the desired minimum. If the result is negative, the project is undesirable.

Example 1 will also be used to demonstrate the net present-value model. The new machine will cost $3,791. Exhibit 12-4 indicates a net present value of

EXHIBIT 12-4

NET PRESENT-VALUE MODEL

Original investment	$3,791
Useful life	5 years
Annual cash inflow from operations	$1,000
Hurdle rate of return	8%

Approach 1: Discounting each year's cash inflow separately[a]

	PRESENT VALUE OF $1, DISCOUNTED @ 8%	TOTAL PRESENT VALUE	SKETCH OF CASH FLOWS					
End of Year			0	1	2	3	4	5
Cash flows:								
Annual cash savings	.926	$ 926		$1,000				
	.857	857			$1,000			
	.794	794				$1,000		
	.735	735					$1,000	
	.681	681						$1,000
Present value of future inflows		$3,993						
Initial outlay	1.000	(3,791)	$(3,791)					
Net present value		$ 202						

Approach 2: Using Annuity Table[b]

			0	1	2	3	4	5
Annual cash savings	3.993	$3,993		$1,000	$1,000	$1,000	$1,000	$1,000
Initial outlay	1.000	(3,791)	$(3,791)					
Net present value		$ 202[c]						

[a] Present values from Table 2, Appendix B.
[b] Present annuity values from Table 4.
[c] Rounded.

$202, assuming a hurdle rate of 8 percent; therefore, the investment is desirable. The manager would be able to invest $202 more, or a total of $3,993 (that is, $3,791 + $202), and still earn 8 percent on the project.

The higher the hurdle rate, the less the manager would be willing to invest in this project. At a rate of 12 percent, the net present value would be $−186 (that is, $1,000 × 3.605, the present-value factor from Table 4, = $3,605, which is $186 less than the required investment of $3,791). When the hurdle rate is 12 percent, rather than 8 percent, the machine is undesirable at its selling price of $3,791.

assumptions of model Before reading on, reflect on the meaning of the net present-value model. First, the model assumes a world of certainty. That is, you are absolutely sure that the predicted cash flows will be forthcoming at the times indicated. Second, the model assumes that the original amount of investment funds can be viewed as either borrowed by you or loaned by you at the specified minimum desired interest rate.

Thus, the net present value of $202 in Exhibit 12-4 tells you that if you borrowed $3,791 from a bank at 8 percent per annum, invested in the project, and repaid the loan with the project cash flows, you would accumulate the same net amount of money as if you deposited $202 in a bank at 8 percent interest. Exhibit 12-5 demonstrates these relationships. Suppose somebody approached you at time zero and offered you $202 for the project that you had invested in ten seconds before. Also suppose that he would assume the obligation to repay the bank loan. You accept and invest the $202 in the bank at an interest rate of 8 percent. In our assumed world of certainty, you would be completely indifferent regarding whether you (a) kept the original investment or (b) accepted the person's offer and invested the $202 in the bank.

comparison of net present-value and internal-rate models

As we have seen, there are two major DCF models: internal rate of return and net present value. Compare them and also review what this chapter has covered so far.

example 2

The Block Company is thinking of buying, at a cost of $22,000, some new material-handling equipment that is expected to save $5,000 in cash operating costs per year. Its estimated useful life is ten years, and it will have zero disposal value. Compute:

1. Internal rate of return.
2. Net present value if the hurdle rate is 16 percent.

SOLUTION

1. Internal rate: $22,000 = P.V. of annuity of $5,000 at X percent for 10 years, or what factor (F) in the table of present values of an annuity (Table 4 in Appendix B at the end of the book) will satisfy the following equation:

EXHIBIT 12-5

RATIONAL UNDERLYING NET PRESENT-VALUE MODEL
(Same Data as in Exhibit 12-4)

Alternative One: Invest and hold the project

	(1)	(2)	(3)	(4)	(5)
YEAR	LOAN BALANCE AT BEGINNING OF YEAR	INTEREST AT 8% PER YEAR	(1) + (2) ACCUMULATED AMOUNT AT END OF YEAR	CASH FOR REPAYMENT OF LOAN	(3) − (4) LOAN BALANCE AT END OF YEAR
1	$3,791	$303	$4,094	$1,000	$3,094
2	3,094	248	3,342	1,000	2,342
3	2,342	187	2,529	1,000	1,529
4	1,529	122	1,651	1,000	651
5	651	52	703	1,000	(297)*

* After repayment of the final $703 loan installment, the investor would have $297 left over from the $1,000 cash provided by the project at the end of the fifth year; he would be $297 wealthier at the end of five years.

Alternative Two: Invest, Sell the Project for $202 an Instant Later, and Deposit the $202 in a Bank.

	(1)	(2)	(3)
YEAR	INVESTMENT BALANCE AT BEGINNING OF YEAR	INTEREST AT 8% PER YEAR	(1) + (2) ACCUMULATED AMOUNT AT END OF YEAR
1	$202	$16	$218
2	218	17	235
3	235	19	254
4	254	20	274
5	274	22	296†

† The investor would have the same amount of wealth at the end of five years as in Alternative One. (The $1 difference between the $296 and the $297 in Alternative One is a rounding error.) Note that stating the net present value at $202 at time zero is *equivalent* to stating the future amount at $296; the investor is indifferent to whether he has $202 today or $296 five years hence.

$$\$22{,}000 = \$5{,}000\ (F)$$
$$F = \$22{,}000/\$5{,}000 = 4.400$$

Now, on the ten-year line in the table for the present value of an annuity (Table 4), find the column that is closest to 4.400. You will find that 4.400 lies somewhere between a rate of return of 18 percent and one of 20 percent. Interpolate as follows:

	18%	4.494	4.494
True rate ⟶			4.400
	20%	4.192	
	Difference	.302	.094

True rate: 18% plus (.094/.302)(2%)
18% plus .31 (2%)
18% plus .62%, or 18.62%

The internal rate (18.62 percent) is the rate that equates the amount invested ($22,000) with the present value of the cash inflows ($5,000 per year for ten years). In other words, if money were borrowed at an effective interest rate of 18.62 percent, the cash inflow (or savings) produced by the project would exactly repay the loan and interest over the ten years. If the hurdle rate is less than 18.62 percent, the project will be profitable at a rate measured by the difference between the hurdle rate and the rate earned by the investment (18.62 percent). If the hurdle rate exceeds 18.62 percent, the cash inflow (or savings) will not be enough to pay interest and repay the principal of the hypothetical loan.

2. Net present value:
This model takes the same basic equation used in 1:

$$\$22{,}000 = \text{P.V. of annuity of } \$5{,}000 \text{ at } X \text{ percent for 10 years}$$

However, this time we shall replace the $22,000 with an unknown and replace X percent with the hurdle rate (assumed to be 16 percent):

$$X = \text{P.V. of annuity of } \$5{,}000 \text{ at 16 percent for 10 years}$$

Consult the table for the present worth of an annuity. Find the 16-percent column and the 10-year row. The factor is 4.833. Substitute in the equation:

$$X = \$5{,}000(4.833)$$
$$X = \underline{\underline{\$24{,}165}}$$

$$\text{Net present value} = \$24{,}165 \text{ minus } \$22{,}000 = \underline{\underline{\$2{,}165}}$$

The computed gross present value is compared to the required investment. If the gross present value exceeds the required investment, the project is desirable. The *gross* present value of the future cash flows minus the initial investment is referred to as the *net* present value.

We can summarize the decision rules offered by these two models as follows:

INTERNAL RATE OF RETURN	*NET PRESENT VALUE*
1. Using present-value tables, compute the internal rate of return by trial-and-error interpolation.	1. Calculate the net present value, using the hurdle rate of return as the discount rate.
2. If this rate equals or exceeds the hurdle rate, accept the project; if not, reject the project.	2. If the net present value is zero or positive, accept the project; if negative, reject the project.

We emphasize the net present-value model in this text because it has distinct advantages over the internal rate of return. The net present-value approach does not entail scouring tables and solving for the "true" rate of return by trial and error. It can be applied to any situation, regardless of whether there is uniform cash flow (present value of annuity) or some uneven cash flows. The internal-rate-of-return model is more tedious, as the self-study problem will demonstrate, because it calls for taking the future cash flows for *each* year separately in the contemplated project and discounting them to the present. (See the next chapter for a more detailed comparison.)

In practice, the internal rate of return is used more widely than the net present-value measure. Most accountants and managers seem to be able to interpret the internal rate more easily; moreover, with this method they are not forced to specify a hurdle rate as a prerequisite to discounted cash-flow computations. Awkward trial-and-error calculations of the internal rate, which students must frequently perform by hand, can be performed swiftly by electronic computers. Canned computer programs are commonly available for such computations.

dealing with uncertainty

To emphasize and simplify various important points in this and other chapters, we almost always work with the expected values of cash flows: single dollar amounts (sometimes called *certainty equivalents*) that represent several possible cash flows. These cash flows are subject to varying degrees of risk or uncertainty, defined here as the possibility that the actual cash flow will deviate from the expected cash flow. Nevertheless, as a minimum, a manager must make some prediction of the probable outcome of various alternative projects. These expected values really should be analyzed in conjunction with probability distributions, as we see in Chapter 24. However, to stress the fundamental differences among various decision models, in this chapter we deal only with the expected values.

As was explained in Chapter 3, *sensitivity analysis* is a widely used approach to the problem of uncertainty. In the context of capital budgeting, sensitivity analysis answers the question, "How will my rate of return or net present value be changed if the useful life or the cash flows that I used for its computation are inaccurate?"

Sensitivity analysis may be approached by computing the cost of prediction errors.[5] Suppose that in Exhibit 12-4 the cash inflows were $800 annually instead of $1,000. What would be the cost of the prediction error?

1. Original decision, given original prediction of cash flows of $1,000: invest.		
2. Results of optimal decision, given alternative parameter:		
Gross present value, $800 × 3.993 (the factor from Exhibit 12-4)	$ 3,194	
Required investment	−3,791	
Net present value	$ −597	
Optimal decision: do not invest		
Financial results		$ 0
3. Results of original decision, given alternative parameter value		−597
4. Cost of prediction error, (2) − (3)		$ 597

[5] See the section, "Cost of Prediction Error," in Chapter 3 for a fuller description.

Negative signs or parentheses are used to denote cash outflows. The cost of prediction error will always be zero or have a positive sign because step 2 above will always have a financial result that is at least as attractive as the result in step 3.

Of course, sensitivity analysis may take a variety of forms. For instance, management may want to know how far cash inflows will have to fall to break even on the investment. Here "break even" means arrive at the point of indifference, the point where the net present value is zero:

Let X = annual cash inflows and let net present value = 0. Then

$$3.993(X) - \$3{,}791 = 0$$
$$3.993(X) = \$3{,}791$$
$$X = \$3{,}791 \div 3.993 = \$950$$

Thus, the amount by which annual cash inflows can drop before they reach the point of indifference regarding the investment is \$1,000 − \$950 = \$50.

Another critical factor is useful life. If useful life were only four years, the gross present value would be \$1,000 times 3.312 (from the period-4 row in Table 4), or \$3,312, again producing a negative net present value, \$3,312 − \$3,791, or a cost of prediction error of \$479.

These calculations are also applicable to testing the sensitivity of rates of return. A fall in the annual cash inflow from \$1,000 to \$900 reduces the internal rate of return from 10 percent (which was proven in Exhibit 12-3) to 6 percent:

Investment = P.V. of annuity of \$900 at X percent for 5 years, or what factor (F) in Table 4 will satisfy the following equation:

$$\$3{,}791 = \$900(F)$$
$$F = 4.212$$

Examine the five-year line in Table 4. Find the column closest to 4.212. In this instance, you do not have to interpolate; the rate is exactly 6 percent.

Of course, sensitivity analysis works both ways. It can measure the potential increases in net present value or rate of return as well as the decreases. The major contribution of sensitivity analysis is that it provides an immediate financial measure of the possible errors in forecasting. Therefore, it can be very useful because it helps focus on those decisions that may be very sensitive indeed, and it eases the manager's mind about those decisions that are not so sensitive.[6]

In addition, sensitivity analysis is applicable to the comparison of various capital-budgeting decision models. That is, as Appendix B at the end of this chapter explores in more detail, the results under the DCF models may be compared to the results, using the same basic data, generated under simpler models such as payback and accounting rate of return.

[6] For a fuller discussion, see Chapter 13. Also see Alfred Rappaport, "Sensitivity Analysis in Decision Making," *The Accounting Review*, Vol. XLII, No. 3, pp. 441–56.

applicability to nonprofit organizations

Discounted cash-flow analysis is applicable to both profit-seeking and nonprofit-seeking organizations. For example, almost all organizations must decide which fixed assets will accomplish various tasks at the least cost. Moreover, all organizations, including governments, have to bear costs of money.[7]

As practiced in the U.S. Department of Defense, uncertainties in quantitative analyses have often been contended with by using sensitivity analysis. In addition, in many analyses three estimates have been used in a procedure called "bop" estimates (for *b*est or most likely estimate, *o*ptimistic, and *p*essimistic). Bop estimates are also frequently used in profit-seeking organizations.

inflation and capital budgeting

Inflation, the decline in the general purchasing power of the monetary unit, is a commonly encountered risk. Discounted cash-flow models can be adjusted for inflation in two basic ways:

1. The discount rate is raised to incorporate an element attributable to inflation, and the predicted monetary flows are similarly raised. For example, the hurdle rate is sometimes portrayed as consisting of a "pure" risk-free base plus elements attributable to inflation and other risks. In addition, the predicted cash flows are adjusted, using either the expected changes in the general price level or, preferably, more specific indexes such as industry indexes or wage indexes. For instance, if wages were expected to rise 10 percent per year, predicted labor costs would be increased accordingly. These predicted indexes may be varied from year to year. A common error is to adjust the discount rate upward for inflation without altering predictions of the future cash flows. *Both should be adjusted.*[8]
2. The discount rate excludes the element attributable to inflation and the predicted monetary flows are all expressed in terms of their 19_0 monetary units. For instance, if inflation is 10 percent and if 19_0 wages are $1 million and 19_1 wages are predicted at $1.1 million, the latter would be restated in "real" dollar terms at $1 million and then discounted to the present using the discount rate that excludes inflation.

Properly used, both ways yield the same net present values.[9] However, method 1, which is preferred here, tends to be more easily understood. It also

[7] A discussion of the appropriate interest rate to use as a hurdle rate is beyond the scope of this book. Nearly all U.S. Departments must use 10 percent; it is a crude approximation of the opportunity cost to the economy of having investments made by public agencies instead of by private organizations. See H. Bierman and S. Smidt, *The Capital Budgeting Decision,* 4th ed. (New York: The Macmillan Company, 1976), Chap. 16. Also see R. Anthony and R. Herzlinger, *Management Control in Nonprofit Organizations* (Homewood, Ill.: Richard D. Irwin, Inc., 1975), pp. 200–202.

[8] For a fuller discussion, see James C. Van Horne, "A Note on Biases in Capital Budgeting Introduced by Inflation," *Journal of Financial and Quantitative Analysis,* Vol. VI (January 1971), pp. 653–58.

[9] Bierman and Smidt, *The Capital Budgeting Decision,* Chap. 13.

expresses predictions in terms of the monetary units that the accounting system is most likely to use at any given time (for example, the then current dollars). In this way, the subsequent auditing or follow-up of the capital-budgeting decision becomes less cumbersome.

analysis of typical items under discounted cash flow

1. FUTURE DISPOSAL VALUES The disposal value at the date of termination of a project is an increase in the cash inflow in the year of disposal. Errors in forecasting disposal value are usually not crucial because the present value is usually small.

2. CURRENT DISPOSAL VALUES AND REQUIRED INVESTMENT In a replacement decision, how should the current disposal value affect the computations? For example, suppose that the current disposal value of old equipment is $5,000 and that new equipment is available at $40,000. There are a number of correct ways to analyze these items, all of which will have the same ultimate effect on the decision. Generally, the required investment is most easily measured by offsetting the current disposal value of the old assets against the gross cost of the new assets ($40,000) and by showing the net cash outgo at $35,000.

3. CURRENT ASSETS Additional investments in plant and equipment or in sales promotions of product lines are invariably accompanied by additional investments in the cash, receivables, and inventories required to support these new activities. In the discounted cash-flow model, *all* investments at time zero are alike, regardless of how they may be accounted for by the accrual accounting model. That is, the initial outlays are entered in the sketch of cash flows at time zero. At the end of the useful life of the project, the original outlays for machines may not be recouped at all or may be partially recouped in the amount of the salvage values. In contrast, the entire original investments in receivables and inventories are usually recouped when the project is terminated. **Therefore, except for their expected "disposal" values being different from the initial outlays, all investments are typically regarded as outflows at time zero, and their terminal disposal values are regarded as inflows at the end of the project's useful life.**

4. BOOK VALUE AND DEPRECIATION Depreciation is a phenomenon of accrual accounting that entails an allocation of cost, not a specific cash outlay. Depreciation and book value are ignored in discounted cash-flow approaches for the reasons mentioned earlier in this chapter.

5. INCOME TAXES In practice, comparison between alternatives is best made after considering tax effects, because the tax impact may alter the picture. (The effects of income taxes are considered in Chapter 13 and may be studied now if desired.)

6. OVERHEAD ANALYSIS In the relevant cost analysis of overhead, only the overhead that will differ between alternatives is pertinent. There is need for careful study of the fixed overhead under the available alternatives. In practice, this is an extremely difficult phase of cost analysis, because it is difficult to relate the individual costs to any single project.

7. UNEQUAL LIVES Where projects have unequal lives, comparisons may be made either over the useful life of the longer-lived project or over the useful life of the shorter-lived project. For our purposes, let us predict what the residual values will be at the end of the longer-lived project and assume a reinvestment at the end of the shorter-lived project. This makes sense primarily because the decision maker should extend his time horizon as far as possible. If he is considering a longer-lived project, he should give serious consideration to what actually could be done in the time interval between the termination dates of the shorter-lived and longer-lived projects.

8. MUTUALLY EXCLUSIVE PROJECTS When the projects are mutually exclusive, so that the acceptance of one automatically entails the rejection of the other (for example, buying Dodge or Ford trucks), the project that maximizes wealth measured in net present value in dollars should be undertaken.

9. A WORD OF CAUTION The foregoing material has been an *introduction* to the area of capital budgeting, which is, in practice, complicated by a variety of factors: unequal lives; mutually exclusive investments; major differences in the size of alternative investments; pecularities in internal rate-of-return computations; various ways of allowing for uncertainty (see Chapter 24); changes over time, in desired rates of return; the indivisibility of projects in relation to a fixed overall capital-budget appropriation; and more. These niceties are beyond the scope of this introductory chapter, but the next chapter will help you pursue the subject in more depth.

payback

Payback, sometimes called *payout* or *payoff,* is a rough-and-ready model that is looked upon with disdain by many academic theorists. Yet payback is a widely used decision model, and it certainly is an improvement over the criterion of urgency or postponability. Furthermore, it is a handy device (a) where precision in estimates of profitability is not crucial and preliminary screening of a rash of proposals is necessary; (b) where a weak cash-and-credit position has a heavy bearing on the selection of investment possibilities; and (c) where the contemplated project is extremely risky.

Assume that $4,500 is spent for a machine that has an estimated useful life of ten years. It promises cost savings of $1,000 a year in *cash flow from operations* (depreciation is ignored). The payback calculations follow:

$$P = I/O_c$$
$$P = \$4{,}500/\$1{,}000 = 4.5 \text{ years}$$

P is the payback time, I is the initial incremental amount invested; and O_c is the uniform annual incremental cash inflow from operations.

Essentially, payback is a measure of the *time* it will take to recoup in the form of cash from operations only the original dollars invested. Given the useful life of an asset and *uniform cash flows,* the less the payout period, the greater the profitability; or, given the payback period, the greater the useful life of the asset, the greater the profitability.

Although the payback method may often yield clues to profitability, it should not be used blindly. Note that payback does *not* measure profitability; it does measure how quickly investment dollars may be recouped. An investment's main objective is profitability, not recapturing the original outlay. If a company wants to recover its investment outlay rapidly, it need not bother spending in the first place. Then the payback time is zero; no waiting time is needed.

The major weakness of the payback model is its neglect of profitability. The mere fact that a project has a satisfactory payback does not mean that it should be selected in preference to an alternative project with a longer payback time. To illustrate, consider an alternative to the $4,500 machine mentioned earlier. Assume that this other machine requires only a $3,000 investment and will also result in gross earnings of $1,000 per year before depreciation. Compare the two payback periods:

$$P_1 = \$4{,}500/\$1{,}000 = 4.5 \text{ years}$$
$$P_2 = \$3{,}000/\$1{,}000 = 3.0 \text{ years}$$

The payback criterion would favor buying the $3,000 machine. However, one fact about this machine has been purposely withheld. Its useful life is only three years. Ignoring the complexities of compound interest for the moment, one finds that the $3,000 machine results in zero profits, whereas the $4,500 machine yields profits for five and one-half years beyond its payback period. Despite these criticisms, a form of the payback model, called the *payback reciprocal,* discussed in Appendix B to this chapter, is useful in many situations.[10]

accounting rate of return: conflict of models

the basic computation

The *accounting rate of return* is also known as the *unadjusted rate of return,* the *book-value rate of return,* and the *approximate rate of return.* In its simplest form, the accounting rate of return is the following fraction:

[10] Also see Alfred Rappaport, "The Discounted Payback Period," *Management Services,* Vol. 2, No. 4, pp. 30–35.

$$\frac{\text{Increase in expected future average annual stated net income}}{\text{Initial increase in required investment}}$$

Sometimes the denominator is the average increase in investment, rather than the initial increase.

The facts in our payback illustration would yield the following accounting rate of return ($4,500 cost, 10-year life, $1,000 cash inflow from operations):

$$R = \frac{\$1{,}000 - \$450 \text{ average depreciation}}{\$4{,}500} = 12.2\%$$

If the denominator is the "average" investment, which is often assumed for equipment as being the average book value over the useful life, or $4,500 ÷ 2, the rate would be doubled.

Note that the accounting rate of return is based on the familiar financial statements prepared under accrual accounting. Unlike the payback model, the accounting-rate-of-return model at least has profitability as an objective. However, its most serious drawback is its ignoring of the time value of money. Appendix A to this chapter explores the accounting rate in more detail.

evaluation of performance

The use of the conventional accrual accounting models for evaluating performance is a stumbling block to the implementation of DCF models for capital-budgeting decisions. To illustrate, the manager of a division of a huge company took a course in management accounting in an executive program. He learned about discounted cash flow. He was convinced that such a model would lead to decisions that would better achieve the long-range profit goals of the company.

When he returned to his company, he was more frustrated than ever. Top management used the overall rate of return of his division to judge his performance. That is, each year divisional net income was divided by average divisional assets to obtain his rate of return on investment (ROI). Such a measure usually inhibits investments in plant and equipment that might be clearly attractive using the DCF models. Why? Because a huge investment often boosts depreciation inordinately in the early years under accelerated-depreciation methods, thus reducing the numerator in the ROI computation. Also, the denominator is increased substantially by the initial cost of the new assets. As one manager said, "Top management is always giving me hell about my new flour mill, even though I know it is the most efficient we've got regardless of what the figures say."

Obviously, there is an inconsistency between citing DCF models as being best for capital-budgeting decisions and then using quite different concepts for monitoring subsequent performance. **As long as such practices continue, man-**

agers will frequently be tempted to make decisions that may be suboptimal under the present-value criterion but optimal, at least over short or intermediate spans of time, under accrual accounting models of evaluating operating performance. Such temptations become more pronounced when managers are subject to regular transfers and promotions. For a deeper exploration of this issue, see Chapter 23.

administration of capital budgets

Although ordinary budget procedures are well entrenched in many companies, formal capital budgeting is still quite undeveloped, largely because it has flowered fairly recently.

The first feature of effective capital-budgeting administration is the awareness on the part of all managers that long-run expenditures are generators of long-run profits. This engenders a constant search for new methods, processes, and products.

Approval of overall capital budgets is usually the responsibility of the board of directors. Depending on the amounts involved, individual projects receive approval at various managerial levels. Requests are usually made semiannually or annually. They are reviewed as they pass upward through managerial levels until they reach a committee that examines capital-budget requests and submits recommendations to the president. In turn, the president submits final recommendations to the board of directors.

Of course, most companies will have a set of forms and a timetabled, uniform routine for processing capital budgets.

When projects are authorized, there is a need for follow-up on two counts. First, control is needed to see that spending and specifications conform to the plan as approved. Second, the very existence of such follow-up will cause capital-spending requests to be sharply conceived and honestly estimated.

Systematic procedures are needed not only to implement capital budgets but to audit the profitability performance of projects. This is *vital* to a successful capital budgeting program. The comparison of performance with original estimates not only better insures careful forecasts but also helps sharpen the tools for improving future forecasts.

SUMMARY

Capital budgeting is long-term planning for proposed capital outlays and their financing. Projects are accepted if their rates of return exceed a minimum desired rate of return.

Because the discounted cash-flow (DCF) model explicitly and automatically weighs the time value of money, it is the best model to use for long-range decisions. The overriding goal is maximum long-run net cash inflows.

The DCF model has two variations: internal rate of return and net present value. Both approaches take into account the timing of cash flows and are thus superior to other methods.

The payback model is a widely used approach to capital-spending decisions. It is simple and easily understood, but it neglects profitability.

The accounting rate of return model (discussed more fully in Appendix A to this chapter) is also widely used, although it is much cruder than DCF models. It fails to recognize explicitly the time value of money. Instead, the accrual accounting model depends on averaging techniques that may yield inaccurate answers, particularly when cash flows are not uniform through the life of a project. The accounting model is adequate where the return plainly far exceeds the minimum desired rate or where projects are not subject to close competition for funds from other projects.

The prediction of cost savings (different cash flows) is the key measurement for capital budgeting. Factors that must be considered in these calculations include income taxes and different capacities of plant and equipment, as well as the usual recurring operating costs. The use of sensitivity analysis and probability theory can help approach and measure the uncertainty that plagues this work.

A serious practical impediment to the adoption of DCF models is the widespread use of accrual accounting models for evaluating performance. Frequently, the optimal decision under discounted cash flow will not produce a good showing in the early years, when performance is computed under accrual accounting methods. For example, heavy depreciation charges and the expensing rather than capitalizing of initial development costs will hurt reported income for the first year.

The difficult forecasting problem makes capital budgeting one of the most imposing tasks of management. Although judgment and attitudes are important ingredients of capital budgeting, the correct application of the techniques described here should crystallize the relevant factors and help management toward intelligent decision making.

Special difficulties in relevant costs and capital budgeting, including income tax factors, are discussed in Chapter 13. A suggested reading list appears at the end of Chapter 13.

PROBLEM FOR SELF-STUDY

PROBLEM The mechanics of compound interest may appear formidable to those readers who are encountering them for the first time. However, a little practice with the interest tables should easily clarify the mechanical aspect. More important, we shall now blend some relevant cost analysis with the discounted cash-flow approach.

A company owns a packaging machine that was purchased three years ago for \$56,000. The machine has a remaining useful life of five years but will require a major overhaul at the end of two more years of life, at a cost of \$10,000. Its disposal value now is \$20,000; in five years its disposal value is expected to be \$8,000, assuming that the \$10,000 major overhaul will be done on schedule. The cash operating costs of this machine are expected to be \$40,000 annually.

A salesman has offered a substitute machine for \$51,000, or for \$31,000 plus the old machine. The new machine will slash annual cash operating costs by \$10,000, will not require any overhauls, will have a useful life of five years, and will have a terminal disposal value of \$3,000.

required

Assume that the hurdle rate of return is 14 percent. Using the net present-value technique, show whether the new machine should be purchased using (a) a total-project approach; (b) an incremental approach. Try to solve before examining the solution.

SOLUTION A difficult part of long-range decision making is the structuring of the data. We want to see the effects of each alternative on future cash flows. The focus here is on bona fide *cash* transactions, not on opportunity costs. Using an opportunity-cost approach may yield the same answers, but repeated classroom experimentation with various analytical methods has convinced the author that the following steps are likely to be the clearest:

Step 1. Arrange the relevant cash flows by project, so that a sharp distinction is made between total-project flows and incremental flows. The incremental flows are merely algebraic differences between two alternatives. (There are *always* at least two alternatives. One is the status quo, the alternative of doing nothing.) Exhibit 12-6 shows how the cash flows for *each* alternative are sketched.

Step 2. Discount the expected cash flows and choose the project with the least cost or the greatest benefit. Both the total-project approach and the incremental approach are illustrated in Exhibit 12-6. Which approach you use is a matter of preference. However, to develop confidence in this area, you should work with both at the start. In this example, the $8,425 net difference in favor of replacement is the ultimate result under either approach.[11]

appendix a: the accrual accounting rate-of-return model

fundamental model

Discounted cash-flow approaches to business decisions are being increasingly used. However, there are other techniques with which the accountant and manager should be at least somewhat familiar, because they are entrenched in many businesses.

Because the technique we are about to discuss is conceptually inferior to DCF approaches, why do we bother studying it? Changes in business practice occur slowly. If older models, such as payback or the accounting rate, are used despite the availability of better tools, they should be used correctly. Many managers use the accounting rate because they regard it as satisfactory for their particular decisions. In other words, the costs (including the costs of educating managers) of more sophisticated models would exceed the benefit from making a sufficient number of more profitable decisions. In such cases, care should be taken so that the cruder tool is used properly. The situation is similar to using a pocket knife instead of a scalpel for removing a person's appendix. If the pocket knife is used by a knowledgeable and skilled surgeon, the chances for success are much better than if it is used by a bungling layman.

The label for the *accrual accounting model* is not uniform. It is also known as the *financial-statement method*, the *book-value method*, the *rate-of-return on assets method*, the *approximate rate-of-return method*, and the *unadjusted rate-of-return method*. Its computations supposedly dovetail most closely with conventional accounting models of calculating income and required investment. However, the dovetailing objective is not easily attained, because the purposes of the computations differ. The

[11] The internal rate of return on the investment of $31,000 is 26 percent. See Appendix C to this chapter for the computations, using trial-and-error methods.

EXHIBIT 12-6

TOTAL PROJECT VERSUS INCREMENTAL APPROACH TO NET PRESENT VALUE

(Data from Self-study Problem)

END OF YEAR	PRESENT-VALUE DISCOUNT FACTOR, @ 14%	TOTAL PRESENT VALUE	SKETCH OF CASH FLOWS 0	1	2	3	4	5
TOTAL PROJECT APPROACH								
A. *Replace*								
Recurring cash operating costs, using an annuity table*	3.433	$(102,990)		($30,000)	($30,000)	($30,000)	($30,000)	($30,000)
Disposal value, end of Year 5	.519	1,557						3,000
Initial required investment	1.000	(31,000)	($31,000)					
Present value of net cash outflows		$(132,433)						
B. *Keep*								
Recurring cash operating costs, using an annuity table*	3.433	$(137,320)		($40,000)	($40,000)	($40,000)	($40,000)	($40,000)
Overhaul, end of Year 2	.769	(7,690)			(10,000)			
Disposal value, end of Year 5	.519	4,152						8,000
Present value of net cash outflows		$(140,858)						
Difference in favor of replacement		$ 8,425						
INCREMENTAL APPROACH								
A–B *Analysis Confined to Differences*								
Recurring cash operating savings, using an annuity table*	3.433	$ 34,330		$10,000	$10,000	$10,000	$10,000	$10,000
Overhaul avoided, end of Year 2	.769	7,690			10,000			
Difference in disposal values, end of Year 5	.519	(2,595)						(5,000)
Incremental initial investment	1.000	(31,000)	($31,000)					
Net present value of replacement		$ 8,425						

* Table 4, Appendix B, at the end of the book.

most troublesome aspects are depreciation and decisions concerning capitalization versus expense. For example, advertising and research are usually expensed, even though they may often be viewed as long-range investments.

The equations for the accounting rate of return are:

$$\begin{pmatrix}\text{Accounting}\\ \text{rate of return}\end{pmatrix} = \frac{\text{Increase in future average annual net income}}{\text{Initial increase in required investment}} \tag{1}$$

$$R = \frac{O_c - W + S}{I} \tag{2}$$

where R = Average annual rate of return on initial incremental investment
O_c = Average annual incremental cash inflow from operations
W = Average annual write-off of incremental investment (akin to depreciation except that salvage value is handled separately)
S = Average annual incremental effects of salvage values
I = Initial increase in required investment

Assume the same facts as in our payback illustrations: cost of machine, \$4,500; useful life, ten years; estimated terminal disposal value, zero; and expected annual cash inflow from operations, \$1,000. Substitute these amounts into Eq. (2):

$$R = \frac{\$1{,}000 - \$450 + 0}{\$4{,}500} = 12.2\%$$

the denominator: investment base Many advocates of the accrual accounting model would not use \$4,500 in the denominator. Instead, they would halve the original investment, because only about half the \$4,500, or \$2,250, is the average amount invested in the machine over its ten-year life. Their reasoning is that depreciable assets do not require a permanent investment of the original amount. The funds are gradually recovered as the earnings are realized.[12] Under this approach, the rate of return would obviously be doubled, as follows:

$$R = \frac{\$1{,}000 - \$450 + 0}{\$2{,}250} = 24.4\%$$

[12] The measure of funds recovered in the example above is \$450 a year, the amount of the annual depreciation. Consequently, the average funds committed to the project would decline at a rate of \$450 per year from \$4,500 to zero; hence, the average investment would be the beginning balance plus the ending balance (\$4,500 + 0) divided by 2, or \$2,250.

initial investment as a base Although our examples in this appendix will use the initial-investment base, practice is not uniform as to whether initial investment or average investment in fixed assets should be used in the denominator. Companies defend the use of the initial-investment base because it does not change over the life of the investment; therefore, follow-up and comparison of actual rate of return against predicted rate of return is facilitated. This follow-up is crucial for control and for improving future capital planning and comparison on a year-to-year, plant-to-plant, and division-to-division basis. The initial base is not affected by depreciation methods.

In most cases, the rankings of competing projects will not differ regardless of whether the gross or average investment base is used. Of course, using the average base will show substantially higher rates of return; however, the desirable rate of return used as a cut-off for accepting projects should also be higher.

current assets as a part of investment base Current assets, such as cash, receivables, and inventories, often are expanded in order to sustain higher activity levels. In our example, if a $1,000 increase in current assets is required, the denominator will be $4,500 plus $1,000, or $5,500. This $1,000 increase in current assets will be fully committed for the life of the project; so, under the average-investment method, the average base would be $3,250 ($2,250 average investment in equipment plus $1,000 average investment in current assets).

danger of understating investment The gross or initial investment in the project should include the following: all additional required current assets, fixed assets, research costs, engineering costs, market-testing costs, start-up costs, initial costs of sales promotion, and so forth. The omission of any of these items from the base can give misleading results.

Although the *accrual accounting model* for investment decisions tries to approximate the figures as they will eventually appear in financial statements, there is not always an exact agreement between figures on conventional statements and figures used for decision making. The tendency in accounting practice is to write costs off to expense quickly. Thus the assembly of figures for special decisions requires care to see that investment is not understated. Often the investment base for decision making should include items, such as research and sales-promotion costs, that the accountant ordinarily writes off immediately as expenses.

accounting model is an averaging technique The accounting model ignores the time value of money. Expected future dollars are unrealistically and erroneously regarded as equal to present dollars while the discounted cash-flow model explicitly allows for the force of interest and the exact timing of cash flows. In contrast, the accounting model is based on *annual averages.*

Compare the internal rate of return in Example 2, 18.62 percent, with the accounting rate of return:

Based on intitial investment:

$$R = \frac{O_c - W + S}{\text{Initial } I} = \frac{\$5{,}000 - \$2{,}200 + 0}{\$22{,}000} = 12.727\%$$

Based on average investment:

$$R = \frac{O_c - W + S}{\text{Average } I} = \frac{\$5{,}000 - \$2{,}200 + 0}{.5(\$22{,}000)} = 25.455\%$$

Note how the accounting rate of return, however calculated, can produce results that differ markedly from the internal rate of return.

To demonstrate how the accounting method is basically an averaging technique that ignores the time value of money, reexamine the problem for self-study (Exhibit 12-6).

INCREMENTAL EFFECTS	*FIVE YEARS TOGETHER*	*ANNUAL AVERAGE*
Recurring cash operating savings	$50,000	$10,000
Overhaul avoided, end of year 2	10,000	2,000
Average annual incremental cash inflow from operations		$12,000 = O_c
Incremental initial investment ($51,000 − $20,000)	31,000	= I
Average annual write-off of incremental investment		6,200 = W
Difference in disposal values: new equipment, $3,000; old equipment, $8,000	5,000	
Average annual incremental effects of disposal values		1,000 = S

$$R = \frac{O_c - W + S}{I} = \frac{\$12{,}000 - \$6{,}200 + (-\$1{,}000)}{\$31{,}000} = \frac{\$4{,}800}{\$31{,}000} = 15.48\% \text{ or } 15\%^*$$

* Because we deal with uncertainty about expected future data, computations to the nearest whole percent should be satisfactory.

Note in the illustration that the current disposal value of old assets should be offset against the gross cost of new assets in computing the *incremental* (additional) initial-investment base. *One of the most frequent mistakes in the accounting model is to fail to relate the proper investment base to the proper operating figures.* The $4,800 net annual advantage should be related to the $31,000 *additional* investment, not the $51,000 total investment.

conflict of concepts and purposes

The DCF model is more objective because its answer is not directly influenced by decisions as to depreciation methods, capitalization-versus-expense decisions, and conservatism.

(These decisions do influence income tax cash flows, however.) Erratic flows of revenue and expense over the project's life are directly considered under DCF but are "averaged" under the accounting method. "The [accounting model] utilizes concepts of capital and income which were originally designed for the quite different purpose of accounting for periodic income and financial position."[13] Thus, in the accounting model, the initial capital may be computed differently, the force of interest may be ignored, and the approximation of the average rate of return may be far from the real mark. The degree of error often becomes larger where the cash inflows do not have a uniform pattern. Equipment becomes much more desirable where cash savings are bigger in early years than where they are spread evenly throughout the useful life. Yet the accounting model would not make this distinction in computing average annual effects.

uneven cash flows DCF models can more readily compare projects having different lives and having different timings of cash inflows because discounting allows comparisons to be made at the same point in time. See Exhibit 12-7 for an illustration of the effect of different timings of cash flows. Some projects, such as mines and oil wells, have heavy earnings in early years. Other projects, like new product lines and new stores, take more time to produce maximum earnings.

postaudit The accounting model usually facilitates follow-up, because the same numbers are used in the forecast as are used in the accounts. Yet exceptions to this ideal situation often occur. The most common exceptions arise from the inclusion in the forecast of some initial-investment items that are not handled in the same manner in the subsequent accounting records. For example, the accounting for trade-ins and disposal values varies considerably. In practice, test checks are frequently used on key items. An interesting suggestion on the problem of postaudit follows:

> When a major project is undertaken, it seems desirable to prepare project cost and income budgets employing the usual accounting classifications, so that subsequent actual figures drawn from the accounts can be compared directly with estimates. Rates of return can also be computed by the [accounting method], using the budgeted and actual data. Thus . . . the discounted cash-flow method would be used as a basis for project selection, and rate of return based upon a financial budget for the project would be used as a goal against which to compare subsequent performance.[14]

understandability There is general agreement that the accounting model is easier to understand and apply than the discounted cash-flow model.

[13] *N.A.A. Research Report 35, Return on Capital as a Guide to Managerial Decisions,* p. 64.
[14] *N.A.A. Research Report 35, op cit.,* pp. 72–73.

EXHIBIT 12-7

COMPARISON OF RATES OF RETURN BY ACCOUNTING MODEL AND DISCOUNTED CASH-FLOW MODEL*

	PROJECT A	PROJECT B	PROJECT C
Amount invested	$ 75,000	$ 75,000	$ 75,000
Cumulative† cash inflow from operations:			
Years 1–5	$160,000	$ 80,000	$ 40,000
6–10	100,000	80,000	80,000
11–15	80,000	80,000	120,000
16–20	40,000	80,000	100,000
21–25	20,000	80,000	60,000
Totals	$400,000	$400,000	$400,000
Average annual cash flow	$ 16,000	$ 16,000	$ 16,000
Less depreciation ($75,000 ÷ 25)	3,000	3,000	3,000
Average annual net income	$ 13,000	$ 13,000	$ 13,000
Rate of return on original investment ($13,000 ÷ $75,000)	17.3%	17.3%	17.3%
Rate of return on average investment ($13,000 ÷ $37,500)	34.7%	34.7%	34.7%
Internal rate of return by discounted cash-flow method‡	40.5%	21.4%	16.6%

* Source: *N.A.A. Research Report 35, Return on Capital as a Guide to Managerial Decisions,* p. 67.

† For example, Project A's cash inflow is $32,000 annually for the first five years, $20,000 annually for the next five years, and so forth.

‡ These time-adjusted rates could be computed by trial-and-error methods. As you can imagine, this is a tedious process if you use hand calculations. In this case, the N.A.A. used tables that assumed cash inflows to be forthcoming *throughout* the year rather than at the *end* of the year. Table 4 in Appendix B at the end of this book assumes the latter; this would produce slightly lower rates. (Why?)

Yet proponents of DCF maintain that its difficulty is overestimated, that reluctance to use it is based more on unfamiliarity than on inherent complexity. (Experience in the author's classes indicates that the student has far more difficulty understanding the accounting model than the DCF model.) Tables and shortcuts are available to reduce the pencil pushing. Also, the prediction of cash flows does not require a knowledge of the intricacies of accounting concepts and conventions.

The choice of model is ultimately dependent on personal preference and on the danger of making wrong decisions by using the less precise accounting model. *In any event, the isolation and prediction of relevant revenue and cost factors are usually more important than which decision model is used.* Because we are dealing only with future costs, all the compiled figures are necessarily clouded by varying degrees of uncertainty;[15] any intricate compound-interest techniques applied to these estimates are useful only insofar as the basic data are reliable.

[15] See Chapter 24 for an extended discussion of how to deal with uncertainty. Also see the suggested readings in Chapter 13, particularly the Hertz articles. Hertz uses a simulation approach that yields an expected value together with a range of minimum and maximum probable values.

appendix b: comparison of decision models

The sensitivity analysis described in the chapter is also applicable to a comparison of various capital-budgeting decision models. This appendix will discuss some additional aspects of the payback model; it will then show how the results of the payback model and the accounting rate-of-return models compare with the results of the internal rate-of-return model.

nonuniform cash inflows

The payback formula is designed for uniform cash inflows. When cash inflows are not uniform, the payback computation takes a cumulative form. That is, each year's net cash inflows are accumulated until the initial investment is recovered. For example, assume that the $4,500 machine produces a total cash savings of $10,000 over ten years, but not at a rate of $1,000 annually. Instead, the inflows are as follows:

YEAR	*CASH SAVINGS*	*ACCUMULATED*	*YEAR*	*CASH SAVINGS*	*ACCUMULATED*
1	$2,000	$2,000	6	$800	$ 8,300
2	1,800	3,800	7	600	8,900
3	1,500	5,300	8	400	9,300
4	1,200	6,500	9	400	9,700
5	1,000	7,500	10	300	10,000

The payback time is slightly beyond the second year. Straight-line interpolation within the third year reveals that the final $700 (that is, $4,500 − $3,800) needed to recover the investment would be forthcoming in 2.47 years—that is,

$$\frac{\$700}{\$1{,}500} \times 1 \text{ year} = .47 \text{ year}$$

the bail-out factor: a better approach to payback

The typical payback computation tries to answer the question, "How soon will it be before I can recoup my investment *if operations proceed as planned?*" However, a more fundamental question is, "Which of the competing projects has the best bail-out protection if things go wrong? In other words, which has the least risk?" To answer such a question, we must consider the salvage value of the equipment throughout its life, an item that is ignored in the usual payback computations.

For instance, salvage values of general-purpose equipment far exceed those of special-purpose equipment. These salvage values can be incorporated in a bail-out approach to payback as follows:

Assume that Equipment A (general-purpose) costs $100,000 and that Equipment B (special-purpose) costs $150,000. Each has a ten-year life. A is expected to produce uniform annual cash savings of $20,000; B, of $40,000. A's salvage value is expected to be $70,000 at the end of year 1; it is expected to decline at a rate of $10,000 annually thereafter. B's salvage value is expected to be $80,000 at the end of year 1; it is expected to decline at a rate of $20,000 annually. Note the difference in results under the traditional payback and the bail-out payback methods. The "bail-out payback time" is reached when the cumulative cash operating savings plus the salvage value at the end of a particular year equal the original investment:

TRADITIONAL PAYBACK

If operations go as expected:

A: $P = \dfrac{I}{O_c} = \dfrac{\$100{,}000}{20{,}000} = 5$ years

B: $P = \dfrac{I}{O_c} = \dfrac{\$150{,}000}{40{,}000} = 3.75$ years

BAIL-OUT PAYBACK

If the project fails to meet expectations:

	AT END OF	*CUMULATIVE CASH OPERATING SAVINGS*		*SALVAGE VALUE*		*CUMULATIVE TOTAL*
A:	Year 1	$ 20,000	+	$70,000	=	$ 90,000
	Year 2	40,000	+	60,000	=	100,000

Therefore, payback is 2 years.

B:	Year 1	$ 40,000	+	$80,000	=	$120,000
	Year 2	80,000	+	60,000	=	140,000
	Year 3	120,000	+	40,000	=	160,000

Therefore, payback is 2.75 years, assuming that the salvage value would also be $40,000 at the end of that time.

The analysis above demonstrates how different interpretations of the payback method can produce different results. If the objective is to measure risk (in the sense of how to avoid loss), the bail-out method is better than the traditional method.

annuity formula and payback reciprocal

The much-maligned traditional payback method has received increasing attention[16] and approval as being useful for a wide number of situations.

The major argument in favor of payback is based on the equation for the present value of an annuity.

General formula for present value of annuity:

$$P_N = O_c\left(\frac{1 - \dfrac{1}{(1+R)^N}}{R}\right) \tag{1}$$

Restated:

$$P_N = \frac{O_c}{R} - \left(\frac{O_c}{R}\,\frac{1}{(1+R)^N}\right) \tag{2}$$

Multiply by R:

$$RP_N = O_c - \left(O_c\,\frac{1}{(1+R)^N}\right) \tag{3}$$

[16] Myron Gordon, "Payoff Period and Rate of Profit," *Journal of Business*, Vol. XXVIII, No. 4, pp. 253–60.

Solve for R: $$R = \frac{O_c}{P_N} - \frac{O_c}{P_N}\left(\frac{1}{(1+R)^N}\right) \tag{4}$$

P_N = investment; O_c = annual *cash* savings or cash inflow from operations; R = rate of return; N = life of investment in years.

Note in equation (4) that the first right-hand term is the reciprocal of the payback period. The second right-hand term is the same reciprocal multiplied by $1/(1 + R)^N$. Now, if either R or N is large, this second term becomes small; therefore, *in these cases,* the rate of return will be closely approximated by the payback reciprocal. (Will the payout reciprocal be larger or smaller than the true rate of return?)

limitations of payback reciprocal

A project with an infinite life would have a rate of return exactly equal to its payback reciprocal, because the second right-hand term, in equation (4), becomes zero. Thus, in practice, the payback reciprocal is a helpful tool in quickly estimating the true rate of return where the project life is *at least twice the payback period.*

The payback reciprocal has wide applicability as a meaningful though rough tool. But its major limitations should be kept in mind:

1. It is valid only when the useful life of the project is at least twice the payback period. In any event, the payback reciprocal will always exceed the true rate of return.
2. It assumes that earnings or savings are constant over the investment's life.

relationships of payback reciprocal to rate of return

Exhibit 12-8 shows the relationships of the payback reciprocal to the rate of return for a project with a five-year payback period (payback reciprocal is 20 percent) and various useful lives. Note that the payback reciprocal gives a reasonable approximation of the internal rate of return only if the useful life of the project is at least ten years—twice the payback period. Otherwise, the regular time-adjusted computations must be made.

The table in Exhibit 12-9 shows various combinations of payback periods and internal rates of return. The table is based on one used by a company that uses the payback period in approximating the rate of return. Examples of how to use the table are included in Exhibit 12-9.

Returning to Example 2, discussed earlier in this chapter:

$$\text{Payback reciprocal} = O_c/I = \frac{\$5{,}000}{\$22{,}000} = \underline{\underline{22.73\%}}$$

EXHIBIT 12-8

RECIPROCAL OF PAYBACK PERIOD COMPARED WITH RATE OF RETURN

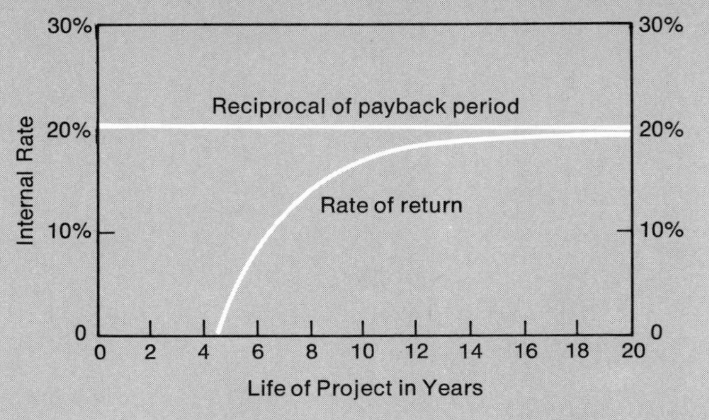

Source: *N.A.A. Research Report 35, Return on Capital as a Guide to Managerial Decisions,* p. 78.

Note that this rate is closer to the internal rate (18.62 percent) of return than is either answer provided by the accounting method, discussed in Appendix A.

Note also that the table in Exhibit 12-9 would be used as follows:

$$\text{Payback period} = \frac{\$22{,}000}{\$5{,}000} = 4.400 \text{ or } 4\tfrac{1}{2} \text{ years}$$

The useful life is ten years. The table's ten-year row and $4\frac{1}{2}$-year column indicate an internal rate of return of 19 percent, a very accurate approximation.

Payback is widely used in industry. Prudent use of the device shows that it may be very helpful:

> This company uses the rate of return on "book investment" [i.e., the accounting method], exclusively for projects costing over $25,000. For smaller projects, it uses the payback period. The controller stated that, as a general guide, the company "should get its money back in no more than half the expected life of the project" and that furthermore this payback period should be a relatively short period of years. Apparently he realized that, where the life of the project is substantially in excess of the payback period, the payback period varies inversely with rate of return and, by keeping the payback period short, the company insures a fairly high rate of return.[17]

[17] For this and other examples of company uses of payback methods, see *N.A.A. Research Report 35, op. cit.,* pp. 80–81.

EXHIBIT 12-9

TABLE FOR APPROXIMATING RATE OF RETURN

USEFUL LIFE IN YEARS	*INTERNAL RATE OF RETURN (PERCENT)*										
3	0										
4	15	11	7	3	0						
5	23	19	15	12	9	6	4	2	0		
6	27	23	20	17	15	12	10	8	6	3	0
7	29	26	23	20	18	15	13	11	10	7	4
8	30	27	25	22	20	18	16	14	12	10	8
9	31	28	26	23	21	19	18	16	15	12	10
10	32	29	27	24	22	21	19	18	16	14	11
15	33	30	28	25	25	23	22	20	19	16	15
20	33	30	28	26	25	23	22	20	19	18	16
Over 20	33	31	29	27	25	24	23	21	20	19	17
Payback period in years	3	3¼	3½	3¾	4	4¼	4½	4¾	5	5½	6

Source: Adapted from *N.A.A. Research Report 35, Return on Capital as a Guide to Managerial Decisions*, p. 76.

Example 1. (Same facts as plotted in graph in Exhibit 12-8.) Project savings expected to last ten years; computed payback period is five years (a payback reciprocal of 20%). Enter table at ten-year row and five-year column. Table shows 16% internal rate of return. (The relationships on the graph in Exhibit 12-8 can also be found in the five-year column of this table.)

Example 2. Project savings expected to last 12 years. Computed payback period is 4.7 years. Enter table using nearest values; that is, use 10 years for savings and 4¾ years for payback period. Table shows 18% internal rate of return. For more accurate computations, interpolation may be used.

accounting rates and internal rates

As the payback reciprocal demonstrated, the accuracy of a shortcut model as an approximation of the internal rate of return is a function of two variables: the economic life of the investment proposal (N) and the time-adjusted rate (R). As Exhibit 12-10 shows, the payback reciprocal is a better approximator than the accounting methods when the economic life is long and the internal rate is large. The comparisons for the earlier illustration (investment, \$4,500; life, 10 years; annual operating inflow, \$1,000) follow:

Internal rate of return:

$$\$4{,}500 = \$1{,}000(F)$$
$$F = 4.500$$

EXHIBIT 12-10

SETS *R* AND *N* FOR WHICH EACH ALTERNATIVE MODEL PROVIDES THE CLOSEST APPROXIMATION TO THE INTERNAL RATE OF RETURN

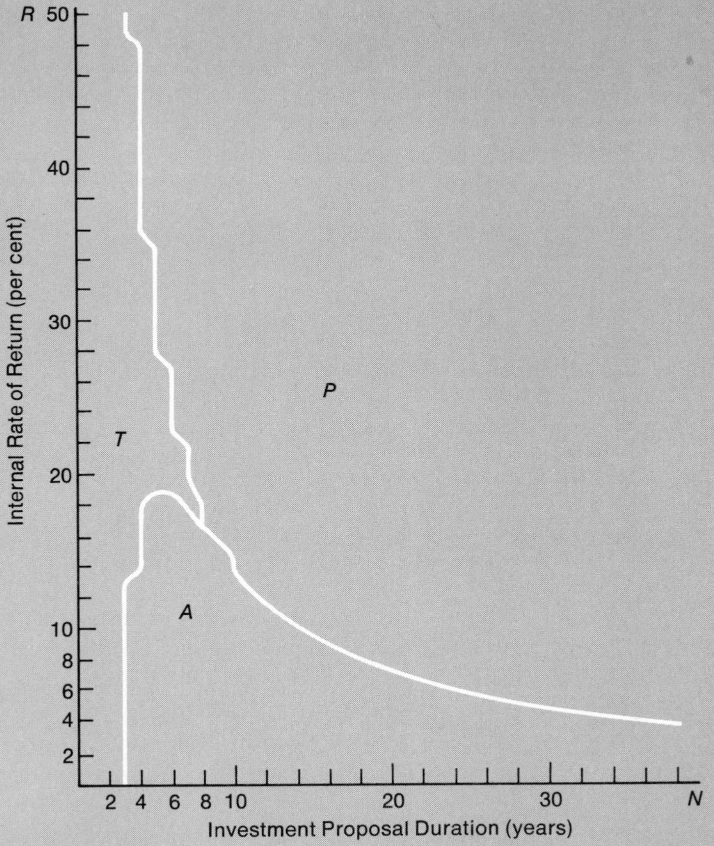

Key:

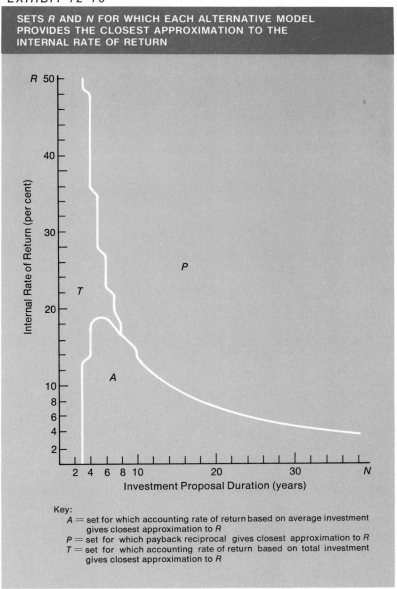

A = set for which accounting rate of return based on average investment gives closest approximation to *R*

P = set for which payback reciprocal gives closest approximation to *R*

T = set for which accounting rate of return based on total investment gives closest approximation to *R*

Source: Marshall Sarnat and Haim Levy. "The Relationship of Rules of Thumb to the Internal Rate of Return: A Restatement and Generalization." *Journal of Finance,* Vol. XXIV, No. 3 (June 1969), p. 486.

Therefore, 10-year line in Table 4 indicates internal rate is 18.0%

$$\text{Payback reciprocal} = \$1{,}000 \div \$4{,}500 = 22.2\%$$

$$\text{Accounting rate based on total investment} = \frac{\$1{,}000 - \$450}{\$4{,}500} = 12.2\%$$

$$\text{Accounting rate based on average investment} = \frac{\$1{,}000 - \$450}{.5(\$4{,}500)} = 24.4\%$$

Note that the *P* set in Exhibit 12-10 gives a more accurate approximation than the two variants of the accounting rate of return for an investment with a life of ten years and an internal rate above 14 percent.

Now suppose that the investment is $6,710 instead of $4,500. The internal rate of return is

$$\$6{,}710 = \$1{,}000(F)$$
$$F = 6.710$$

Therefore, 10-year line in Table 4 indicates time-adjusted rate is 8.0%.

$$\text{Payback reciprocal} = \$1{,}000 \div \$6{,}710 = 14.9\%$$

$$\text{Accounting rate based on total investment} = \frac{\$1{,}000 - \$671}{\$6{,}710} = 4.9\%$$

$$\text{Accounting rate based on average investment} = \frac{\$1{,}000 - \$671}{.5(\$6{,}710)} = 9.8\%$$

Note that the *A* set in Exhibit 12-10 gives a more accurate approximation than the other two sets for investment proposals with economic lives longer than three years and with time-adjusted rates of 19 percent and lower as the life lengthens.[18]

This comparison of models illustrates how managers and accountants often may intuitively use simple models (rules of thumb, shortcuts, or crude approximations) that they perceive as "good enough" in particular circumstances. The point is that our increasing knowledge of decision models now often permits us to use sensitivity analysis to test whether the simpler models are indeed leading to optimal decisions.

appendix c: internal rate of return using trial-and-error methods

The data are from Exhibit 12-6, the incremental approach. Trial-and-error methods must be used to calculate the rate of return that will equate future cash

[18] The Sarnat and Levy article cited in Exhibit 12-10 stresses that the relationships among the alternative models shown in the exhibit remain invariant for any level of taxation. Thus, all the general properties of the relationships hold for both the before-tax and after-tax cases.

flows with the incremental initial investment of $31,000. If there were only an annuity of $10,000 per year, the factor for the true rate would be $31,000 ÷ 10,000 = 3.100, which is between 18 and 20 percent on the 5-year line of Table 4 in Appendix B at the end of the book. Because there is an additional benefit at the end of year 2, you may want to try a higher rate, say 20 percent. Apply this rate to all flows, year by year; use Table 2, because the flows are not uniform:

		FIRST TRIAL: 20 PERCENT		*SECOND TRIAL: 22 PERCENT*	
YEAR	*NET CASH INFLOWS*	*PRESENT-VALUE FACTOR*	*TOTAL PRESENT VALUE*	*PRESENT-VALUE FACTOR*	*TOTAL PRESENT VALUE*
1	$10,000	.833	$ 8,330	.820	$ 8,200
2	20,000	.694	13,880	.672	13,440
3	10,000	.579	5,790	.551	5,510
4	10,000	.482	4,820	.451	4,510
5	5,000	.402	2,010	.370	1,850
			$34,830		$33,510

At 20 percent, the total present value of the future cash flows *exceeds* the initial investment. This means that the "true" rate must be higher than 20 percent. You are trying to find a rate that will make the total present value exactly *equal* to $31,000. A second trial shows that 22 percent is also too low. The third trial, at 26 percent, produces an answer so close that interpolation is not needed. The internal rate is 26 percent:

		THIRD TRIAL: 26 PERCENT	
YEAR	*NET CASH INFLOWS*	*PRESENT-VALUE FACTOR*	*TOTAL PRESENT VALUE*
1	$10,000	.794	$ 7,940
2	20,000	.630	12,600
3	10,000	.500	5,000
4	10,000	.397	3,970
5	5,000	.315	1,575
			$31,085

Note that a much cruder approach might be used. For example, we may think with some assurance that the rate is surely above 14 percent and below 30 percent. We compute, using these widely different rates, and interpolate:

		TRIAL: 14 PERCENT		*TRIAL: 30 PERCENT*	
YEAR	*NET CASH INFLOWS*	*PRESENT-VALUE FACTOR*	*TOTAL PRESENT VALUE*	*PRESENT-VALUE FACTOR*	*TOTAL PRESENT VALUE*
1	$10,000	.877	$ 8,770	.769	$ 7,690
2	20,000	.769	15,380	.592	11,840
3	10,000	.675	6,750	.455	4,550
4	10,000	.592	5,920	.350	3,500
5	5,000	.519	2,595	.269	1,345
			$39,415		$28,925

The true rate is somewhere between 14 and 30 percent. It can be crudely approximated by straight-line interpolation even though the present-value tables are not based on linear relationships:

	TOTAL PRESENT VALUES	
14%	$39,415	$39,358
True rate		31,000
30%	28,925	
Difference	$10,490	$ 8,358

$$\text{Therefore:}\quad \text{True rate} = 14\% + \frac{\$8{,}358}{\$10{,}490}(30\% - 14\%)$$
$$= 14\% + .8\,(16\%)$$
$$= 14\% + 12.75\%$$
$$= 26.75\%$$

Note that 26.8 percent is a fairly good approximation of the true rate, even though straight-line interpolation was used between widely separated trial rates.

QUESTIONS, PROBLEMS, AND CASES

Special note For all problems, ignore income taxes. The effects of income taxes are considered in Chapter 13.

12-1 Define *capital budgeting*.

12-2 What is the payback method? What is its main weakness?

12-3 Define *internal rate of return*.

12-4 "The payback reciprocal has wide applicability as a meaningful approximation of the time-adjusted rate of return. But it has two major limitations." What are the two limitations?

12-5 "The trouble with discounted cash-flow techniques is that their use ignores depreciation costs." Do you agree? Why?

12-6 "Accelerated depreciation provides higher cash flows in early years." Do you agree? Why?

12-7 "A project with a useful life of sixty years would have an internal rate of return practically exactly equal to its payback reciprocal." Why?

12-8 *Exercises in Compound Interest* To be sure that you understand how to use the tables in Appendix B at the end of this book, solve the following exercises. Do the exercises on your own before checking your answers. The correct answers rounded to the nearest dollar are printed after the last problem in this chapter.

1. You have just won $5,000. How much money will you have at the end of ten years if you invest it at 6 percent compounded annually? Ignore income taxes in this and other parts of this problem.
2. Ten years from now, the unpaid principal of the mortgage on your house will be $8,955. How much do you have to invest today at 6 percent interest compounded annually just to accumulate the $8,955 in ten years?

3. You plan to save $500 of your earnings each year for the next ten years. How much money will you have at the end of the tenth year if you invest your savings compounded at 6 percent per year?
4. If the unpaid mortgage on your house in ten years will be $8,955, how much money do you have to invest annually at 6 percent to have just this amount on hand at the end of the tenth year?
5. You hold an endowment insurance policy that will pay you a lump sum of $20,000 at age 65. If you invest the sum at 6 percent, how much money can you withdraw from your account in equal amounts each year so that at the end of ten years there will be nothing left?
6. You have estimated that for the first ten years after you retire, you will need an annual income of $2,720. How much money must you invest at 6 percent at age 65 to just realize this annual income?
7. The table below shows two schedules of prospective operating cash inflows, each of which requires the same initial investment:

		ANNUAL CASH INFLOWS	
YEAR		*PLAN A*	*PLAN B*
0		$ 1,000	$ 5,000
1		2,000	4,000
2		3,000	3,000
3		4,000	2,000
4		5,000	1,000
	Total	$15,000	$15,000

The minimum desired rate of return is 6 percent compounded annually. In terms of present values, which plan is more desirable? Show computations.

12-9 *Compare Two Projects* (SIA, adapted) The management of Dilex Diversified must decide between two proposals. The following information is available:

	INVESTMENT	*NET CASH INFLOWS*		
PROPOSAL	*NOW*	*PERIOD 1*	*PERIOD 2*	*PERIOD 3*
A	$ 80,000	$95,400	$39,000	$12,000
B	100,000	35,000	57,500	80,000

Assuming that the company can earn 12 percent on projects of this type and that the cash inflows are received at the end of each period, advise management regarding the proposal that should be selected. Submit computations of net present values. Ignore income tax considerations.

12-10 *Payback Period* A manager is considering three mutually exclusive investment projects, A, B, and C, each promising a cash flow of $20,000 per year for an initial investment of $100,000. Useful lives are as follows:

PROJECT	*YEARS*
A	5
B	6
C	7

required

1. Compute the payback period for each project. If payback time is the sole criterion for the decision, which project is most desirable?
2. Which project offers the highest rate of return?

12-11 Refer to Problem 11-9. Assume that the new machinery will cost $750,000 in cash, and that the old machinery cost $600,000 and can be sold now for $120,000 cash.

required

1. Compute the net present value of the proposed investment in new equipment, assuming that the minimum desired rate of return is 10 percent. Compute the solution in the two ways illustrated in the chapter, the "incremental" way and the "total-project" way.
2. Compute the internal rate of return and the payback period on the incremental investment.

12-12 *Comparison of Approaches to Capital Budgeting* The Gehrig Company estimates that it can save $2,800 a year in cash operating costs for the next ten years if it buys a special-purpose machine at a cost of $11,000. No residual value is expected. The company's minimum desired rate of return is 14 percent.

required

(Round all computations to the nearest dollar. Ignore income taxes.) Compute:

1. Payback period
2. Using discounted cash flow:
   a. Internal rate of return
   b. Net present value
3. Payback reciprocal

12-13 *Golf Course* (W. Crum) Gotrocks offers you a chance to buy a miniature golf course he has built near a resort area. It would cost you $50,000 cash. For this you would get an operating golf course built on leased property at a cost of $30,000, with lease payments of $10,000 per year, payable at end of the year. Assume a salvage value of $5,000 for the equipment on the course at end of the lease. Operating costs per year for the golf course are $40,000, disregarding depreciation. Income per year, all in cash, is $60,000. You wish to use a 10 percent interest rate in your evaluation. The lease expires in 10 years.

required

1. Does this appear to be a good investment for you? Show all figures.
2. Compute the payback period for this investment.

12-14 *Sensitivity Analysis, Payback Reciprocal* The All Directions Railroad is considering the replacement of an old power jack tamper used in the maintenance of track with a new improved version that should save $5,000 per year in net cash operating costs.

The old equipment has zero disposal value, but it could be used indefinitely. The estimated useful life of the new equipment is 12 years and it will cost $20,000.

required

1. Payback time.
2. Internal rate of return.
3. Management is unsure about the useful life. What would be the internal rate of return if the useful life were (a) 6 years instead of 12, and (b) 20 years instead of 12?
4. Suppose the life will be 12 years, but the savings will be $3,000 per year instead of $5,000. What would be the rate of return?
5. Suppose the annual savings will be $4,000 for 6 years. What would be the rate of return?
6. Professor Myron Gordon has pointed out that the payback reciprocal can be a crude approximation of the true rate of return where (a) the project life

is at least twice the payback period, and (b) the cash earnings or savings are uniformly received in equal amounts throughout the investment's life. The payback reciprocal, using the original data, will be $5,000 ÷ $20,000, or 25 percent.

a. How close is this to the internal rate of return?
b. Compute the payback reciprocals for 3(a) and 3(b). How close are they to the internal rates of return?
c. Compute the payback reciprocals for (4) and (5). How close are they to the internal rates of return?

12-15 *Different Approaches to Capital Budgeting; Proper Investment Base* The Ruth Company has been operating a small lunch counter for the convenience of employees. The counter occupies space that is not needed for any other business purpose. The lunch counter has been managed by a part-time employee whose annual salary is $3,000. Yearly operations have consistently shown a loss as follows:

Receipts		$20,000
Expenses for food, supplies (in cash)	$19,000	
Salary	3,000	22,000
Net loss		$ (2,000)

A company has offered to sell Ruth automatic vending machines for a total cost of $13,000, less $1,000 trade-in allowance on old equipment (which was carried at zero book value and which could be sold outright for $1,000 cash) now used in the lunch-counter operation. Sales terms are cash on delivery. The old equipment will have zero disposal value ten years from now.

The predicted useful life of the equipment is ten years, with zero scrap value. The equipment will easily serve the same volume that the lunch counter handled. A catering company will completely service and supply the machines. Prices and variety of food and drink will be the same as those that prevailed for the lunch counter. The catering company will pay 5 percent of gross receipts to the Ruth Company and will bear all costs of foods, repairs, and so forth. The part-time employee will be discharged. Thus, Ruth's only cost will be the initial outlay for the machines.

required

Consider only the two alternatives mentioned.

1. Prospective annual income statement under new plan. What is the annual income difference between alternatives?
2. Compute the payback period.
3. Compute:
   a. Present value under discounted cash-flow method if relevant cost of company capital is 20 percent.
   b. Rate of return under discounted cash-flow method.
4. Compute the payback reciprocal. Compare your answer with the result in 3(b).
5. Management is very uncertain about the prospective revenue from the vending equipment. Suppose that the gross receipts amounted to $14,000 instead of $20,000. Repeat the computation in part 3(a).
6. What would be the minimum amount of annual gross receipts from the vending equipment that would justify making the investment? Show computations.
7. What other considerations may influence the decision?

12-16 *Compute Minimum Desired Rate of Return* The Strubel Company has used the net present-value method in making capital-investment decisions. The company rejected an offer of a machinery salesman who had convincing evidence that his $12,500 lifting equipment would save the company $3,000 in cash operating costs per year for ten years. The disposal value of the machine was $2,000 at the end of ten years. In applying the net present-value method, the company computed a negative net present value of $457. What was the minimum desired rate of return? Show computations.

12-17 *Replacement of Machine* The Maris Company is considering the purchase of a vertical milling machine to replace an obsolete milling machine. The machine currently being used for the operation is in good working order and will last, physically, for at least ten years. However, the proposed machine will perform the operations so much more efficiently that Maris Company engineers predict that labor, materials, and other direct costs of the operation will be reduced $2,000 a year if the proposed machine is installed. The proposed milling machine costs $10,000 delivered and installed. The company requires a minimum of 20 percent on all investments. Taxes are to be disregarded. The new machine's useful life is ten years.

Note: The present value of $1 received annually for ten years at various interest rates is:

15%	16%	18%	20%	22%	25%
5.019	4.833	4.494	4.192	3.923	3.571

required

1. Assuming that the present machine is being depreciated at a rate of $800 per year, that it has a book value of $8,000 (cost, $18,000; accumulated depreciation, $10,000), and that it has zero net salvage value today, what action should be taken? What internal rate of return would be earned on the investment in the new machine?
2. Data of part 1, except that the net salvage value of the old machine today is $2,000, and if retained for ten years its salvage value will be zero. How is your answer to part 1 altered?

12-18 *Equipment Replacement, Sensitivity Analysis* A toy manufacturer who specializes in making fad items has just developed a $50,000 molding machine for automatically producing a special toy. The machine has been used to produce only one unit so far. It is planned to depreciate the $50,000 original cost evenly over four years, after which time production of the toy will be stopped.

Suddenly a machine salesman appears. He has a new machine that is ideally suited for producing this toy. His automatic machine is distinctly superior. It reduces the cost of materials by 10 percent and produces twice as many units per hour. It will cost $44,000 and will have zero disposal value at the end of four years.

Production and sales would continue to be at a rate of 25,000 per year for four years; annual sales will be $90,000. The scrap value of the toy company's machine is now $5,000 and will be $2,600 four years from now. Both machines will be useless after the 100,000-unit total market potential is exhausted.

With its present equipment, the company's annual expenses will be: direct materials, $10,000; direct labor, $20,000; and variable factory overhead, $15,000. Fixed factory overhead, exclusive of depreciation, is $7,500 annually, and fixed selling and administrative expenses are $12,000 annually.

required

1. Assume that the hurdle rate of return is 18 percent. Using discounted cash-flow techniques, show whether the new equipment should be purchased. Use a total-project approach and an incremental approach. What is the role of the book value of the old equipment in the analysis?
2. What is the payback period for the new equipment?
3. As the manager who developed the $50,000 molding machine, you are trying to justify not buying the new $44,000 machine. You question the accuracy of the expected cash operating savings. By how much must these cash savings fall before the point of indifference, the point where net present value of the project is zero, is reached?

12-19 *Capital Investment in a Baseball Player* William Voock, president of the Chicago Chartreuse Sox, is currently considering a player deal in which he will acquire Bill Blue, a great gate attraction, from the New York Confederates in exchange for $500,000 cash plus George Bumble, a regular Sox outfielder who is currently receiving a salary of $15,000 a year. Blue is to be Bumble's replacement in the regular outfield. Voock and his fellow executives have assembled the following data:

Estimated useful life of Blue	5 years
Estimated residual value of Blue	$20,000
Estimated useful life of Bumble	5 years
Estimated residual value of Bumble	None
Current cash offer for Bumble received from the Atlanta Carpetbaggers Baseball Club	$50,000
Applicable minimum desired rate of return	10%

Other data:

YEAR	BLUE'S SALARY	ADDITIONAL CLUB GATE RECEIPTS BECAUSE OF BLUE	ADDITIONAL EXPENSES OF HANDLING HIGHER VOLUME
1	$60,000	$330,000	$33,000
2	70,000	300,000	30,000
3	80,000	200,000	20,000
4	80,000	100,000	10,000
5	72,000	40,000	4,000

required

(Ignore income taxes.)

1. Based on the data as given, should the Sox buy Blue? Use the following present value factors for $1 at 10 percent:

	FOR END OF YEAR				
	1	2	3	4	5
Factor	.91	.83	.75	.68	.62

2. What other factors should be considered before making the decision? How much confidence do you have in the available data?

12-20 *Purchase of New Furnace: Different Capacities, Different Useful Lives* The Glen University is using a single gas-fired furnace at present, but owing to expected increases in consumption, it is considering the following alternatives:

a. Purchase a new electric furnace with double the capacity of the present furnace, and sell the present furnace.

b. Purchase a new gas furnace similar to the present one, and operate the two gas furnaces.

The following information is available to aid in making the decision:

1. All furnaces are assumed to have a ten-year life with zero salvage value at the end of that time.
2. The old furnace had a cost of $4,000 four years ago. It can be sold outright for $2,400 cash.
3. The price of a new gas furnace is $4,680. This price is expected to increase at a rate of 4 percent compounded annually.
4. Repair and maintenance costs for a gas furnace used regularly during the year are $1,400 per year.
5. The price of a new electric furnace is $22,400; annual repair and maintenance costs are expected to be $1,200.
6. Comparative variable costs per charge (the unit of heating) are:

	GAS	*ELECTRIC*
Purchased power source	$ 6.80	$12.40
Supplies	2.60	1.20
Labor	10.60	4.40
	$20.00	$18.00

7. Property taxes are estimated to be $150 per gas furnace and $700 per electric furnace per year.
8. Minimum desired rate of return is 6 percent.
9. It is estimated that machine usage over the next ten years will be at the rate of 700 units (charges) per year.

required

To ease computations, round off all factors from the compound-interest tables to two decimal places.

1. The "payout" or "payback" time. The payback reciprocal. What can you conclude from the reciprocal?
2. The net present value of the electric furnace.
3. Indicate for *each* of the following whether the use of the *gas*-furnace system would become more or less desirable. Justify your answer by a *one*-sentence explanation.
   (1) Property tax rates advance.
   (2) New labor contract raises wage rates.
   (3) Interest rates advance.
   (4) Demand for product increases, so that machine usage is increased to 800 units.
   (5) The Federal Power Commission authorizes an increase in natural-gas rates.

12-21 *Deferred Annuity* (SIA, adapted) Lewis Stanfield is considering the acquisition of a business enterprise. To purchase this business he would have to pay $130,000 now. Stanfield wants to retire in 20 years' time. He predicts that the net cash receipts from this business will be $25,000 per year for the first 15 years and $20,000 per year for the last five years. He believes that the business could be sold at the end of the 20-year period for $30,000. In addition, he feels that certain capital replacements and improvements would be necessary and this should amount to $2,000 a year for the first five years, $3,000 a year for the next five years, $4,000 a year for the next seven years, and nothing in the last three years.

Stanfield has excluded any compensation to himself from the above data.

However, should he acquire the business, he would have to leave his present job in which he earns $9,000 a year. To finance the acquisition of this business, he would liquidate his present investments with a comparable risk factor which yields a return of 10 percent before taxes.

required

1. Advise Stanfield as to whether or not it is advisable to acquire the business on the basis of the information provided. Present full details of all calculations. Ignore income taxes.
2. What additional information would you like to have had to include in your decision process?

12-22 *Three Alternatives, Effects on Inventory Investments* The Dull Company has a very stable operation that is not marked by detectable variations in production or sales.

The Dull Company has an old machine with a net disposal value of $5,000 now and $1,000 five years from now. A new Rapido machine is offered for $25,000 cash or $20,000 with a trade-in. The new machine promises annual operating cash outflows of $2,000 as compared with the old machine's annual outflow of $10,000. A third machine, the Quicko, is offered for $45,000 cash or $40,000 with a trade-in; it promises annual operating cash outflows of $1,000. The disposal values of the new machines five years hence will be $1,000 each.

Because the new machines will produce output more swiftly, the average investment in inventories will be as follows:

Old machine	$100,000
Rapido	80,000
Quicko	50,000

The minimum desired rate of return is 20 percent. The company uses discounted cash-flow techniques to evaluate decisions.

required

Which of the three alternatives is most desirable? Show calculations. This company uses discounted cash-flow techniques for evaluating decisions. When more than two machines are being considered, the company favors computing the present value of the future costs of each alternative. The most desirable alternative is the one with the least cost.

P.V. of $1 at 20% for 5 years = .40
P.V. of annuity of $1 at 20% for 5 years = 3.00
Amount of $1 at 20% for 5 years = 2.20
Amount of annuity of $1 at 20% for 5 years = 8.00

12-23 *Cost-Volume-Profit Analysis and Discounted Cash Flow* The Susan Company wants to make doughnuts for its chain of restaurants in Los Angeles. Two machines are proposed for the production of the doughnuts: semiautomatic and automatic. The company now buys doughnuts from an outside supplier at $.14 each. Manufacturing costs would be:

	SEMIAUTOMATIC	*AUTOMATIC*
Variable costs per doughnut	$.12	$.1125
Fixed costs:		
Annual cash operating outlays	$2,500	$ 3,500
Initial cost of machines	$6,000	$15,000
Useful life of machines in years	4	4
Salvage value at the end of 4 years	—	$ 3,000

required

1. The president wants to know how many doughnuts must be sold in order to have total average annual costs equal to outside purchase costs for the (a) semiautomatic machine and (b) automatic machine.
2. At what annual volume of doughnuts would the total annual costs be the same for both machines? Which machine is preferable if the volume exceeds the volume you computed? Why?
3. Assume that the sales forecast over the next four years is 400,000 doughnuts per year. The minimum desired rate of return is 10 percent. Should the automatic machine be purchased? Why? Show calculations. Ignore income taxes.

P.V. of $1.00 at 10% for 4 periods is	.7
P.V. of annuity of $1.00 at 10% for 4 periods is	3.2

Compare your answer with that in requirement 2. Do the answers differ? How? Why?

12-24 *Prediction Error* In the first example in the chapter, the original investment was $3,791, useful life five years, annual cash inflow from operations $1,000, and internal rate of return 10 percent.

1. Suppose the annual cash flow were $900 instead of $1,000. All other parameter predictions are correct. What is the cost of prediction error measured in terms of net present value, assuming a minimum desired rate of return of 10 percent?
2. Repeat (1), except assume that the annual cash flow was $1,100.

12-25 *Prediction Error* Refer to Problem 12-12. Suppose the annual cash flow were $3,200 instead of $2,800. All other parameter predictions are correct. What is the cost of prediction error measured in terms of net present value? What is the cost of prediction error if the annual cash flow of $2,800 were to last only five years instead of ten, assuming all other parameter predictions are correct?

12-26 *Sensitivity and Prediction Error* (J. Demski, adapted) Ralph is attempting to decide whether to accept (or reject) a new product proposal. He predicts that development of the project will require an initial outlay of $\$a < 0$ (cash) and will then return an end-of-period contribution of $\$b$ (cash) per unit of product produced and sold in any given period. The demand for the product is predicted to be a constant d units per period for T periods.

Letting ρ denote Ralph's minimum desired rate of return, and assuming a tax-free world, he would accept this new product proposal if and only if

$$\text{NPV}(\rho) = a + \sum_{t=1}^{T} bd(1+\rho)^{-t}$$

$$= a + bx \geq 0$$

where

$$x = \sum_{t=1}^{T} d(1+\rho)^{-t}$$

1. To be a little less abstract, let $a = \$-1000$, $b = 1$, and $x = 1200$. Then $\text{NPV}(\rho) = -1000 + 1(1200) = 200 \geq 0$. In the following graph, plot the maximum net present value associated with this decision as the contribution margin varies between $b = -1$ and $b = 5$ (given $a = -1000$ and $x = 1200$). You should clearly label the accept-reject point on your graph.

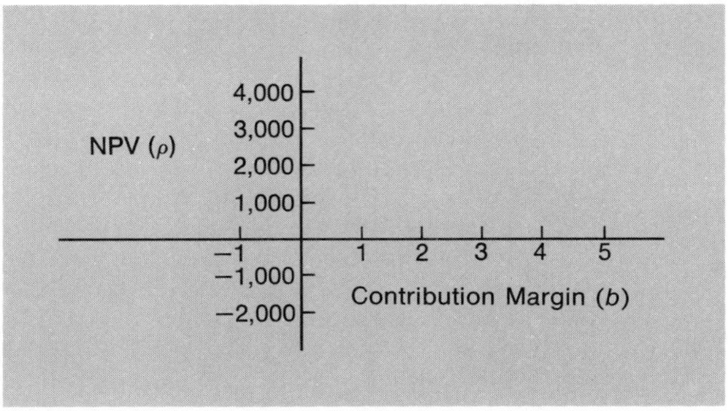

2. Suppose Ralph predicts that $b = 1.7$ given $a = -1000$ and $x = 1200$, and thus implements the project. Further suppose that the a and x parameter predictions are correct, but the contribution prediction, b, is incorrect. Plot, on a second graph, the cost of this prediction for all possible values of b in the range -1 to $+5$.
3. Suppose Ralph rejected the project because he predicted that $b = 0$. How would your graph in part 2 change?
4. Think about your graphs. What is the major lesson of this problem?

12-27 *Sensitivity to Inflation* M. Holden is considering whether to invest $200,000 in a new computer that will last five years, have $20,000 scrap value, and generate cash savings in clerical costs of $60,000 annually, using today's prices and payroll rates. It is December 31, 19_0.

The minimum desired rate of return is 22 percent per year before taxes. All analysis will be conducted on a before-tax basis.

required

1. Compute the net present value of the project.
2. Holden is concerned about how to allow for inflation, which has persisted at a 10 percent average annual rate during the past five years. He decides that the 22 percent rate embodies an element attributable to anticipated inflation. Consequently, to make the decision model consistent, the cash savings and scrap value should be adjusted upward in accordance with the 10 percent inflation rate. That is, there will be 10 percent inflation in year one. Using these assumptions, repeat requirement 1.
3. Compare your answers in requirements 1 and 2. What generalizations about the effects of inflation seem warranted?

(For more on inflation, see Problem 13-16.)

12-28 *Review of Chapters 11 and 12.* (D. Solomons, adapted) The Rainier Company sells a range of high-grade chemical products that calls for careful packaging. The company has always made a feature of the special properties of the containers used. They had a special patented lining made from a material known as GHJ, and the firm operated a department especially to maintain its containers in good condition and to make new ones to replace those past repair.

Ms. Wood, the general manager, had for some time suspected that the firm might save money and get equally good service by buying its containers outside. After careful inquiries, she approached a firm specializing in container production, Closure Inc., and obtained quotations from them. At the same time she asked Mr. Wrend, the controller, for an up-to-date statement of the cost of operating the container department.

Within a few days the quotation from Closure came in. They were prepared to supply all the new containers required—at that time running at the rate of 15,000 a year—for $300,000 per annum, the contract to run for a term of five years certain and thereafter to be renewable from year to year. If the number of containers required increased, the contract price would be increased proportionately. Additionally, irrespective of whether the above contract was concluded, Closure undertook to carry out purely maintenance work on containers, short of replacement, for a sum of $70,000 per annum on the same contract terms.

Ms. Wood compared these figures with the following cost figures prepared by Wrend covering a year's operations of the container department:

Materials		$100,000
Direct labor		175,000
Departmental overhead:		
Supervision	$50,000	
Rent	6,000	
Depreciation of machinery	30,000	
Maintenance of machinery	7,000	
Other expenses	31,000	124,000
		$399,000
Proportion of general administrative overhead		33,000
Total cost of department for year		$432,000

Wood leaned toward eliminating the department and entering into the contracts offered by Closure. However, before proceeding, she asked for the observations of the manager of the department, Mr. Spencer; at the same time, she made it clear that Spencer's own employment was not in jeopardy. Even if his department were abolished, there was another managerial position shortly becoming vacant to which Spencer could move without loss of pay or prospects.

Spencer raised a number of considerations. "For instance," he said, "what will you do with the machinery? It cost $240,000 four years ago, but you'd be lucky if you got $40,000 for it now, even though it's good for another five years at least. And then there's the stock of GHJ we bought a year ago. That cost us $120,000 and at the rate we're using it now, it will last us another three years or so. We used up a quarter of it last year. Wrend's figure of $100,000 for materials probably includes about $30,000 for GHJ. But it will be tricky stuff to handle if we don't use it up. We bought cheaply—$150 a ton we paid for it—and you couldn't buy it today for less than $180. But you wouldn't have more than $120 a ton left if you sold it, net of all handling expenses."

Wrend was present during this discussion. He said, "I don't much like all this conjecture. My figures are pretty conclusive. Besides, if we are going to have all this talk about 'what will happen if,' don't forget our problem of space. We're paying $10,000 a year in rent for a warehouse two miles away.

If we closed Spencer's department, we'd have all the warehouse space we need without renting."

"That's a good point," said Wood. "Though we should not forget that the total termination costs for the oldest employees released will amount to $14,000 annually for five years." Spencer said, "What about this $33,000 for general administrative overhead? You surely don't expect to fire anyone in the general office if I'm closed down, do you?" "Probably not," said Wrend, "but someone has to pay for these costs. We can't ignore them when we look at an individual department. If we do that with each department in turn, we shall finish by convincing ourselves that general managers, accountants, typists, stationery and the like, don't have to be paid for. And they do, believe me."

"Well, I think we've thrashed this out pretty fully," said Wood, "but I've been turning over in my mind the possibility of perhaps keeping on the maintenance work ourselves. What are your views on that, Spencer?" "I don't know," said Spencer, "but it's worth looking into. We won't need any machinery for that, and the supervision could be handled by a foreman. You'd save $30,000 a year there, say. You'd only need about one-fifth of the workers, but you could retain the oldest. You wouldn't save any space, so I suppose the rent would be the same. I don't think the other expenses would be more than $13,000 a year." "What about materials?" asked Wood. "We use about 10 percent of the total on maintenance," Spencer replied. "That is, we use about $10,000 per year on maintenance—no GHJ is required."

"Well, I've told Closure that I'd let them know my decision within a week," said Wood. "I'll let you know what I decide to do before I write to them."

required

1. Assume that the time value of money is 20 percent. Ignore income taxes. What action should be taken? Show your analysis. Prepare a clear-cut quantitative analysis. Specify your assumptions.
2. Describe any sensitivity analysis that seems particularly advisable. Without doing calculations, predict the effect of the sensitivity analysis on your final computations. For example, what would happen to your two best alternatives if the time value of money were 10 percent instead of 20 percent? State the possible influence of the nonquantified factors on the decision.

Note Problems 12-29 through 12-33 cover the accounting model, which is discussed in Appendix A of this chapter.

12-29 *Accounting Rate of Return* Refer to Problem 12-12. Using the data there, compute the accounting rate of return based on (a) average investment, (b) initial investment.

12-30 *Accounting Rate of Return* Refer to Problem 12-11. Using the data there, compute the accounting rate of return based on (a) initial incremental investment (b) average incremental investment.

12-31 *Accounting Rate of Return* Refer to Problem 12-15. Using the data there, compute the accounting rate of return based on (a) average investment, (b) initial investment.

12-32 *Accounting Rate of Return* Refer to Problem 11-23. Using the data there, compute the accounting rate of return based on (a) average investment, (b) initial investment.

12-33 *Choice of Machines; Comparison of Discounted Cash-Flow and Accounting Methods* The India Manufacturing Company is considering the purchase of a machine for their factory. Two courses are available.

(a) Machine A is being offered at a special price of \$50,000 with an estimated life of seven years and a disposal value estimated at \$1,000. The cash operating expenses would amount to \$30,000 annually. The machine would require major repairs every two years at a cost of \$5,000.

(b) Machine B is available for a price of \$75,000 with an estimated life of seven years and a disposal value of \$5,000. The cash operating expenses with this machine would amount to \$26,000 annually. Major repairs cost \$3,500 every third year.

Assume the same revenue flow in all years for both alternatives. Assume that the minimum desired rate of return is 10 percent.

required

1. Compute the average annual return on the extra \$25,000 needed to buy Machine B, using the accounting method and an "initial" investment base.
2. Using discounted cash flow, compute the present value of all future costs under both alternatives. Also compare the alternatives on an incremental basis.

answers to exercises in compound interest (problem 12-8)

The general approach to these problems centers about a key question: Which of the four basic tables am I dealing with? No computations should be made until after this basic question is answered with confidence.

1. \$8,954. From Table 1. The \$5,000 is a present value. The value ten years hence is an *amount* or *future worth.*

   $S = P(1 + r)^n$; the conversion factor, $(1 + r)^n$, is on line 10 of Table 1.

   Substituting: $S = 5{,}000\ (1.7908) = \$8{,}954$

2. \$4,997. From Table 2. The \$8,955 is an *amount* or *future worth.* You want the present value of that amount.

   $P = S/(1 + r)^n$; the conversion factor, $1/(1 + r)^n$, is on line 10 of Table 2.

   Substituting: $P = \$8{,}955(.558) = \$4{,}997.$

3. \$6,590. From Table 3. You are seeking the *amount* or *future worth* of an annuity of \$500 per year.

   $$S_n = \$500\ F, \text{ where } F \text{ is the conversion factor}$$
   $$S_n = \$500(13.1808) = \$6{,}590$$

4. \$679. From Table 3. The \$8,955 is a future worth. You are seeking the uniform amount (annuity) to set aside annually.

   $$S_n = \text{Annual deposit } (F)$$
   $$\$8{,}955 = \text{Annual deposit } (13.1808)$$
   $$\text{Annual deposit} = \frac{\$8{,}955}{13.1808} = \$679$$

5. \$2,717. From Table 4. When you reach age 65, you will get \$20,000. This is a present value at that time. You must find the annuity that will just exhaust the invested principal in ten years.

$$P_n = \text{Annual withdrawal } (F)$$
$$\$20{,}000 = \text{Annual withdrawal } (7.360)$$
$$\text{Annual withdrawal} = \frac{\$20{,}000}{7.360} = \$2{,}717$$

6. $20,019. From Table 4. You need to find the present value of an annuity for ten years.

$$P_n = \text{Annual withdrawal } (F)$$
$$P_n = \$2{,}720(7.360)$$
$$P_n = \$20{,}019$$

7. Plan B is preferable. Its present value exceeds that of Plan A by $1,038:

YEAR	P.V. FACTORS AT 6% FROM TABLE 2	P.V. OF PLAN A	P.V. OF PLAN B
0	1.000	$ 1,000	$ 5,000
1	.943	1,886	3,772
2	.890	2,670	2,670
3	.840	3,360	1,680
4	.792	3,960	792
		$12,876	$13,914

A Closer Look at Capital Budgeting

13

This chapter will consider a variety of interrelated problems of capital budgeting, including income tax factors, rationing capital, multiple alternatives, unequal lives, and cost of capital. Some readers may not wish to cover all of these topics. For example, the section on income taxes may be studied alone.

income tax factors

importance of income taxes

Income taxes are major disbursements that often have a tremendous influence on decisions. Even where tax rates and timing are the same for all alternatives, the before-tax differences between alternatives are usually heavily slashed by application of current income tax rates, so that after-tax differences become narrower. This reduction of differences often results in rejection of alternatives that are seemingly attractive on a pretax basis.

The role of taxes in capital budgeting is no different from that of any other cash disbursement. **There are two major impacts of income taxes: (a) on the *amount* of cash inflow or outflow, and (b) on the *timing* of cash flows.**

The intricacies of the income tax laws are often bewildering. This chapter will concentrate on a few pertinent provisions of the law in order to highlight a general approach to the problem. Our discussion will be confined to corporations rather than partnerships or individuals.

The applicable tax rate to be used in predicting cash flows is dependent on the income tax bracket of the taxpayer and on the type of income in question. For example, the federal rates on ordinary corporate net income in the middle 1970s were 20 percent on the first $25,000, 22 percent on the next $25,000, and 48 percent on any amount in excess of $50,000. But most states also levy income taxes, with rates that vary considerably. Thus, the combined tax effect on ordinary income in excess of $50,000 may easily exceed 50 percent.

timing and different depreciation methods

Exhibit 13-1 shows the relationship between net income before taxes, income taxes, and depreciation. Assume that a company has a single fixed asset, purchased for $90,000 cash, which has a five-year life and zero disposal value. The purchase cost, less any predicted disposal value, is tax-deductible in the form of yearly depreciation. This deduction has been aptly called a *tax shield,* because it protects that amount of income from taxation. As Exhibit 13-2 shows, the cost of the asset represents a valuable future tax deduction of $90,000. The present value of this deduction depends directly on its specific yearly effects on future income tax payments. Therefore, the present value is influenced by the depreciation method selected, the applicable tax rates, and the rate used for discounting future cash flows.

the best depreciation method

The three most widely used depreciation methods are straight-line, sum-of-the-years'-digits, and double-declining balance. The effects of the first two are shown in Exhibit 13-2. Note that the present value of the tax savings is greater if straight-line depreciation is *not* used. The accelerated depreciation methods will generally maximize present values as compared with the straight-line method. The cumulative dollar tax bills may not change, but the early write-offs defer tax outlays to future periods. The measure of the latter advantage depends on the rate of return that can be gained from funds that otherwise would have been paid as income taxes. **The general rule in shrewd income tax planning is: When there is a legal choice, take the deduction sooner rather than later.**

effects of income taxes on cash flow

The effects of income taxes on cash flow may best be visualized by a step-by-step analysis of a simple example. The following example is similar to those in Chapter 12. However, all income tax effects will now be considered and an *after-tax* hurdle rate is used.

EXHIBIT 13-1

BASIC ANALYSIS OF INCOME STATEMENT, INCOME TAXES, AND CASH FLOWS

(Data Assumed)

TRADITIONAL INCOME STATEMENT

(*S*)	Sales	$100,000
(*E*)	Less: Expenses, excluding depreciation	$ 62,000
(*D*)	Depreciation (straight-line)	18,000
	Total expenses	$ 80,000
	Income before income taxes	$ 20,000
(*T*)	Income taxes at 40 percent	8,000
(*I*)	Net income after income taxes	$ 12,000

Net after-tax cash inflow from operations is either

$$S - E - T = \$100{,}000 - \$62{,}000 - \$8{,}000 = \$30{,}000$$

or

$$I + D = \$12{,}000 + \$18{,}000 = \$30{,}000$$

ANALYSIS FOR CAPITAL BUDGETING

	Cash Effects of Operations	
(*S* − *E*)	Cash inflow from operations: $100,000 − $62,000 =	$38,000
	Income tax outflow, at 40 percent	15,200*
	After-tax effects of cash inflow from operations	$22,800
	Effect of depreciation:	
(*D*)	Straight-line depreciation: $90,000 ÷ 5 = $18,000	
	Income tax savings, at 40 percent	7,200*
	Total cash effects	$30,000†

* Net cash outflow from income taxes, $15,200 − $7,200 = $8,000.

† This can also be expressed as

$$(S - E)(1 - T) + DT = (100 - 62)(1 - .4) + 18(.4)$$
$$= 22.8 + 7.2 = 30.0.$$

example

The Lindo Company is considering replacing an old packaging machine with a new, more efficient machine. The old machine originally cost $22,000. Accumulated straight-line depreciation is $12,000 and the remaining useful life is five years. The old machine can be sold outright now for $4,000. The predicted residual value at the end of five years is $600; however, the company has not used a residual value in allocating depreciation for tax purposes. Annual cash operating costs are $50,000 per year.

Company engineers are convinced that the new machine, which costs $15,000, will have annual cash operating costs of $46,000 per year. The new machine will have a useful life of five years, with an estimated residual value of $700. Sum-of-the-years'-digits depreciation would be used for tax purposes, with no provision for residual value.

EXHIBIT 13-2

TAX EFFECTS OF TWO DEPRECIATION METHODS

				10% DISCOUNT FACTOR	PRESENT VALUE AT 10%	SKETCH OF CASH FLOWS YEAR 1	2	3	4	5
STRAIGHT-LINE DEPRECIATION										
Annual depreciation $90,000 ÷ 5 = $18,000										
Tax effect: savings in income taxes @ 40% = $7,200				3.791	$27,295	$ 7,200	$7,200	$7,200	$7,200	$7,200
SUM-OF-THE-YEARS'-DIGITS DEPRECIATION										
YEAR	*MULTIPLIER**	*INCOME TAX DEDUCTION*	*INCOME TAX SAVINGS @ 40%*							
1	5/15	$30,000	$12,000	.909	$10,908	$12,000				
2	4/15	24,000	9,600	.826	7,930		$9,600			
3	3/15	18,000	7,200	.751	5,407			$7,200		
4	2/15	12,000	4,800	.683	3,278				$4,800	
5	1/15	6,000	2,400	.621	1,490					$2,400
Tax effect: savings in income taxes			$36,000		$29,013					

* The general formula for obtaining the *denominator* of the multiplier under the sum-of-the-digits method is:

$S = n\left(\frac{n+1}{2}\right)$ when S = sum of the digits, n = number of years of estimated useful life

$$S = 5\left(\frac{5+1}{2}\right) = 5 \times 3 = 15$$

Assume that the hurdle rate, after taxes, is 10 percent. Using the net present-value technique, demonstrate which action is more profitable. Use two ways to get your answer, a total-project approach and an incremental approach. Assume that the zero residual values are acceptable for tax purposes. Assume a 40 percent tax rate.

SOLUTION See Exhibits 13-3 and 13-4 for the complete solution. The following steps are recommended. The pertinent income tax aspects are considered for each step.

Step 1. General Approach. The inclusion of tax considerations does not change the general approach to these decisions. Review Chapter 12.

Step 2. Cash Operating Costs and Depreciation. Cash operating costs and their income tax effects are separated from the tax effects of depreciation. These could be combined if preferred. However, the treatment illustrated facilitates comparisons of alternative depreciation effects and allows the use of annuity tables for the cash operating costs if they are equal per year.

In this illustration we assume that any cash flow and the related tax flow occur in the same period. For simplicity, we are neglecting the possibility that some tax payments related to the pretax operating cash inflows of year 1 may not actually occur until sometime in year 2. The analysis could be refined to account for any possible lags.

Step 3. Disposal of Equipment. In general, gains and losses on disposal of equipment are taxed in the same way as ordinary gains and losses.[1]

Exhibit 13-3 shows an analysis of the alternative dispositions of the old equipment. Disposal at the end of year 5 results in a taxable gain, the excess of the selling price over book value (zero in this case). The cash effect is the selling price less the 40 percent tax on the gain.

Immediate disposal of the old equipment results in a loss that is fully deductible from current income. The net loss must be computed to isolate its effect on current income tax, but the total cash inflow is the selling price plus the current income-tax benefit.

Step 4. Total-Project or Incremental Approach? Exhibits 13-3 and 13-4 demonstrate these approaches. Both result in the same net present value in favor of replacement. Where there are only two alternatives, the incremental approach is faster. However, the incremental approach rapidly becomes unwieldy when there are multiple alternatives or when computations become intricate.

investment tax credit

Managers have a responsibility to avoid income taxes. *Avoidance* is not *evasion.* Avoidance is the use of legal means to minimize tax payments; evasion is the use of illegal means. Because income tax planning is exceedingly complex, professional tax counsel should be sought whenever the slightest doubt exists.

[1] In this case, the old equipment was sold outright. Where the old equipment is traded in on new equipment of like kind, no gain or loss can be recognized for tax purposes in the year of the transaction. Rather, the new equipment is capitalized at the book value of the old equipment plus the cash payment. Any gain or loss is then spread over the life of the new equipment through the new depreciation charges.

Before 1962, gains from disposal of equipment were taxed at the capital-gains rate, 25 percent. Since then, the gain on sale of equipment is not considered a capital gain except in special circumstances. This complication frequently results in having part of the gain taxed at ordinary income tax rates and part at capital-gains rates. For simplicity, this chapter does not introduce the latter complication. We assume that gains on disposal are taxed at ordinary rates.

The foregoing illustration deliberately excluded many possible complications. Income taxes are affected by many factors, including progressive tax rates, loss carrybacks and carryforwards, many depreciation options, state income taxes, short- and long-term gains, distinctions between capital assets and other assets, offsets of losses against related gains, exchanges of property of like kind, and exempt income. Special tax incentives should also be considered. These come and go, as various legislation is enacted and repealed. For example, most fixed-asset purchases in the 1970s qualified for an "investment credit," which was an immediate reduction in *income taxes* of up to 10 percent of the initial cost; furthermore, the full original cost, less the predicted disposal value, was nevertheless deductible as yearly depreciation over the useful life.

Consider applying an investment tax credit of 10 percent for our Lindo Company illustration. The effect would be an immediate (ignoring any short time lags) reduction of income taxes of 10 percent of $15,000; therefore, the net present value in favor of replacement would increase by $1,500, from $2,343 to $3,843.

net present value or internal rate of return?

conflict of ranking techniques

Generally, the net present-value and the internal-rate-of-return techniques lead to the same decisions regarding the relative desirability of competing proposals. However, some crucial differences in the assumptions underlying the methods may occasionally lead to conflicting rankings of mutually exclusive investment proposals. Exhibit 13-5 illustrates this conflict. (Use tables to check your understanding of the computations in Exhibit 13-5.)

What is the essential difference between these two variations of the discounted cash-flow method? Essentially, differing assumptions are made with respect to the *rate of return on the reinvestment* of the cash proceeds at the end of the shorter investment's life. The two methods make different implicit assumptions as to the reinvestment rate of return.

The internal rate-of-return approach implicitly assumes that the reinvestment rate is equal to the indicated rate of return for the shorter-lived project. The net present-value approach assumes that the funds obtainable from competing projects can be reinvested only at the rate of the company's minimum desired rate of return.

unequal lives and reinvestment

As shown in Exhibit 13-5, where mutually exclusive projects have unequal lives, the two methods show different rankings.[2]

[2] Also, similar conflicting results can occur when the terminal dates are the same but the sizes of the investment outlays differ.

EXHIBIT 13-3

LINDO COMPANY, AFTER-TAX ANALYSIS OF EQUIPMENT REPLACEMENT: TOTAL-PROJECT APPROACH

					PRESENT-VALUE DISCOUNT FACTORS @ 10%	*TOTAL PRESENT VALUE*	*SKETCH OF CASH FLOWS* 0	1	2	3	4	5
(A) REPLACE												
Recurring cash operating costs				$46,000								
Income tax savings, @ 40 percent				18,400								
After-tax cash operating costs				$27,600	3.791	($104,631)		($27,600)	($27,600)	($27,600)	($27,600)	($27,600)
Depreciation deductions (sum of digits 1 + 2 + 3 + 4 + 5 = 15)												
YEAR	*MULTIPLIED BY $15,000*	*INCOME TAX DEDUCTION*	*INCOME TAX SAVINGS @ 40%*									
1	5/15	$ 5,000	$2,000		.910	1,820*		2,000				
2	4/15	4,000	1,600		.830	1,328			1,600			
3	3/15	3,000	1,200		.750	900				1,200		
4	2/15	2,000	800		.680	544					800	
5	1/15	1,000	400		.620	248						400
		$15,000	$6,000									
Residual value, all subject to tax because book value will be zero				$ 700								
Less: 40% tax on gain				280								
Net cash inflow				$ 420	.620	260						420
Cost of a new machine:				$15,000	1.000	(15,000)	($15,000)					

Disposal of old equipment:										
Book value now ($22,000 − $12,000)	$10,000									
Selling price	4,000	$ 4,000								
Net loss	$ 6,000									
Tax savings	×.40	2,400								
Net immediate cash effects, including tax savings		$ 6,400	1.000	6,400	6,400					
Total present value of all cash flows				($108,131)						
(B) KEEP										
Recurring cash operating costs		$50,000								
Income tax savings, @ 40%		20,000								
After-tax cash operating costs		$30,000	3.791	($113,730)		($30,000)	($30,000)	($30,000)	($30,000)	($30,000)
Depreciation deductions ($10,000 ÷ 5)	$ 2,000									
Income tax savings, @ 40%	×.40	$ 800	3.791	3,033		800	800	800	800	800
Residual value, all subject to tax		$ 600								
Less: 40% tax on gain		240								
Net cash inflow		$ 360	.620	223						360
Total present value of all cash flows				($110,474)						
Difference in favor of replacement				$ 2,343						

* Table 5 in Appendix B at the rear of the book provides a shortcut approach to computing the present value of the income tax savings from sum-of-the-years'-digits (SYD) depreciation. For a $15,000 depreciable investment at 10 percent, use the factor from the five-period row to obtain the present value of SYD depreciation: $15,000(.806) = $12,090. To get the present value of the *income tax* savings, the present value of $12,090 should be multiplied by the applicable tax rate: $12,090 × .40 = $4,836. When rounded to $4,840, this shortcut result is equal to the sum of the individual year-by-year computations in the table above: $1,820 + $1,328 + $900 + $544 + $248 = $4,840.

EXHIBIT 13-4

LINDO COMPANY, AFTER-TAX ANALYSIS OF EQUIPMENT REPLACEMENT: INCREMENTAL ANALYSIS

					PRESENT-VALUE DISCOUNT FACTORS @ 10%	TOTAL PRESENT VALUES	SKETCH OF CASH FLOWS 0	1	2	3	4	5
Analysis confined to differences between (A) and (B) in Exhibit 13-3:												
Recurring operating savings, $50,000 − $46,000				$4,000								
Income tax, @ 40%				1,600								
After-tax operating savings				$2,400	3.791	$9,098		$2,400	$2,400	$2,400	$2,400	$2,400
Differences in depreciation:												
YEAR	*REPLACE*	*KEEP*	*DIFFERENCE*	*INCOME-TAX EFFECT @ 40%*								
1	$5,000	$2,000	$3,000	$1,200	.910	1,092		1,200				
2	4,000	2,000	2,000	800	.830	664			800			
3	3,000	2,000	1,000	400	.750	300				400		
4	2,000	2,000	—	—	.680	—					—	
5	1,000	2,000	(1,000)	(400)	.620	(248)						(400)
Difference in disposal value, end of Year 5 (see Exhibit 13-3 for details): $420 − $360 = $60					.620	37						60
Incremental initial investment (see Exhibit 13-3 for details): $15,000 − $6,400 = ($8,600)					1.000	(8,600)	($8,600)					
Net present value of replacement						$2,343						

EXHIBIT 13-5

PROJECT	LIFE	INVESTMENT	ANNUAL NET CASH EARNINGS	RANKING BY INTERNAL RATE OF RETURN: RATE OF RETURN	RANKING	RANKING BY NET PRESENT VALUE: PRESENT VALUE OF EARNINGS AT 10% HURDLE RATE	NET PRESENT VALUE: AMOUNT	RANK
A	5	$2,864	$1,000	22%	1	$3,791	$ 927	3
B	10	4,192	1,000	20%	2	6,145	1,953	2
C	15	5,092	1,000	18%	3	7,606	2,514	1

Let us see how these contradictory results occur by visualizing the amount of wealth that will be accumulated at the end of fifteen years.

The original investment in Project A will accumulate to more than that in Project C under the rate-of-return method, because it is assumed that the *Project A amount at the end of the fifth year can be reinvested to earn a 22 percent rate of return:*

Project A, \$1,000 per year for five years[3] @ 22% will accumulate to 1,000 × 7.740	\$7,740	
\$7,740 invested @ 22% from the 6th through the 15th year is \$7,740 × 7.305		\$56,541

On the other hand, the net present-value method assumes that the Project A amount at the end of the fifth year can be reinvested to earn only the *10 percent minimum desired rate of return:*

Project A, \$1,000 per year for 5 years @ 22% will accumulate to 1,000 × 7.740, as above	\$7,740	
\$7,740 invested @ 10% from the 6th through the 15th year is \$7,740 × 2.5938 (the factor from Table 1)		\$20,076

As long as projects under consideration promise internal rates of return in excess of the cutoff rate, the rate-of-return method has a built-in assumption in favor of short-lived projects such as Project A, whereas the net present-value method has a built-in minimum rate of return that would favor longer-lived projects. If and when we look upon the hurdle rate of return as an approximation of the opportunity rate for reinvestment, the net present-value method should be used rather than the internal rate-of-return method.

How may we reconcile these two approaches? Ideally, the answer is to reject both assumptions as to the reinvestment rate of return and predict a

[3] The 7.740 would be the factor for the 5-period line and the 22-percent column in an expanded Table 3, the amount of an annuity. The 7.305 would be the factor for the 10-period line in Table 1. These lines and columns for the 22 percent rate are not contained in the table in this book.

EXHIBIT 13-6

ALLOCATION OF CAPITAL BUDGET: COMPARISON OF TWO ALTERNATIVES

	ALLOCATION OF $5,000,000 BUDGET							
	ALTERNATIVE ONE				ALTERNATIVE TWO			
PROJECTS[a]	INVESTMENT REQUIRED	EXCESS PRESENT-VALUE INDEX	TOTAL PRESENT VALUE AT 10%	PROJECT	INVESTMENT REQUIRED	EXCESS PRESENT-VALUE INDEX	TOTAL PRESENT VALUE AT 10%
C	$ 600,000	167%	$1,000,000	C	$ 600,000	167%	$1,000,000
A(GP)	1,000,000	140%	1,400,000				
D	400,000	132%	528,000	D	400,000	132%	528,000
				A(SP)	3,000,000	130%	3,900,000
F	1,000,000	115%	1,150,000	F	1,000,000	115%	1,150,000
					$5,000,000[b]		$6,578,000[d]
E	800,000	114%	912,000	E	$ 800,000	114%	Reject
B	1,200,000	112%	1,344,000	B	1,200,000	112%	Reject
	$5,000,000[b]		$6,334,000[c]				
H	$ 550,000	105%	Reject	H	550,000	105%	Reject
G	450,000	101%	Reject	G	450,000	101%	Reject
I	1,000,000	90%	Reject	I	1,000,000	90%	Reject

[a] Each of the specific plans for the projects listed may have been selected from alternative mutually exclusive proposals. For example, Project D may be for new Dodge trucks, selected after considering competing brands. Thus, the capital budget is the crystallization of many "subcapital-budgeting" decisions.

[b] Total budget constraint. [c] Net present value, $1,334,000. [d] Net present value, $1,578,000.

tailor-made rate of return for the time between the termination of the shorter-lived project and the termination of the longer-lived project. In other words, there is a need for a common terminal date and for explicit assumptions as to the appropriate reinvestment rates of funds. Solomon comments:

> 1. The valid comparison is not simply between two projects but between two alternative courses of action. The ultimate criterion is the total wealth that the investor can expect from each alternative by the terminal date of the longer-lived project. . . .
> 2. *If the rate of return* is to be used as an index of profitability, then the relevant rate is the per annum yield promised by each alternative course of action from its inception to a common terminal date in the future (usually the terminal date of the longer-lived project).
> 3. *If the present value* is to be used as an index of relative profitability, the expected reinvestment rate or set of rates should be used as the discounting factor. These rates will be equal to the company's present cost of capital only by coincidence.[4]

The practical difficulties of predicting future profitability on *reinvestment* are greater than those of predicting profitability of immediate projects. But

[4] Ezra Solomon, "Arithmetic of Capital Budgeting Decisions," *Journal of Business,* Vol. XXIX, No. 2, p. 127.

reinvestment opportunities should be considered where they may be foreseen and measured.

equipment replacement Equipment-replacement decisions are often complicated by unequal lives of competing equipment. One way of approaching the problem of unequal lives is to estimate the disposal value of the new equipment at the end of the remaining useful life of the old equipment. Then a comparison is made only over the remaining life of the old equipment.

Still another approach is to compare over the longer time span, including a prediction of replacement cost for the old machine at a later date. In essence, this is the approach described by Solomon above.

Of course, the crux of the problem in replacement decisions is the lack of a realistic common terminal date for both proposals. Thus, some estimate of residual value is necessary, whether the comparison is made over the remaining life of old equipment or the useful life of the new equipment. If new equipment is to last eight years and old equipment five years, a decision to retain old equipment implies that replacement will be made in five years. Therefore, if a comparison is to be made over eight years, the future replacement cost (five years hence) of the old equipment has to be predicted and also the terminal value of that replacement at the end of the eight-year span under review. This difficulty goes on and on;[5] the practical answer is to make realistic assumptions regarding residual values at a common terminal date. The common date should be as distant as can be considered with confidence.

reinvestment outlook Capital-budgeting decisions in one year have chain reactions that may affect investment opportunities and availability of capital in future years. Such diverse factors as price-level changes, technological changes, and future investment choices may strongly influence current capital-spending decisions.

For example, in Exhibit 13-5, if investment opportunities five years hence are expected to return less than 15 percent, Project C, which promises a return of 18 percent for fifteen years, may be preferable to Project A, which promises a return of 22 percent for five years. In contrast, if opportunities to invest at 22 percent or more are anticipated in five years but are not available now, the shorter-lived Project A might be more desirable than Project C, even if Project A promised only, say a 16 percent rate of return. In the latter case, Project C would require a much bigger investment than one would want committed for a prolonged period.

[5] Some writers favor handling this problem by assuming an infinitely continuous replacement cycle. Thus, alternatives are compared by using perpetuity formulas. Although this is conceptually most appealing, it is probably too unrealistic to serve as a practical technique.

applications of net present value

Chapter 12 and the preceding section indicated that the attractiveness of a capital project is best measured by discounting at the minimum desired rate of return; *any* project with a positive net present value should be undertaken. This is a general rule. Like all general rules, this is subject to qualifications. We shall now see how this rule is applied in various situations.

rationing capital

Many companies specify an overall limit on the total budget for capital spending. However, there is no conceptual justification for such a budget ceiling, because all projects that enhance long-run profitability should be accepted. This is the only decision rule that makes economic sense. To the extent that capital rationing exists, it should be a "short-run phenomenon, limiting expenditures only to the current year or two."[6]

There are no hard-and-fast rules to be found in practice regarding the selection of an overall constraint. The net present values (or some similar measure, such as internal rate of return) may strongly influence the overall budget amount. For example, a group of available projects with huge net present values would probably result in a much higher overall budget than would a group of projects that all slightly exceeded zero.

Other interrelated factors that influence the amount of total funds to be committed in a single year include:

1. Top management's philosophy toward capital spending. (Some managements are highly growth-minded, whereas others are very conservative.)
2. The outlook for future investment opportunities that may not be feasible if extensive current commitments are undertaken.
3. The funds provided by current operations less dividends.
4. The feasibility of acquiring additional capital through borrowing or sale of additional stock. Lead times and costs of financial market transactions can influence spending.
5. Period of impending change in management personnel, when the status quo is maintained.
6. Management attitudes toward risk.

excess present-value index or net present value?

The excess present-value index (also sometimes called the profitability index) is the ratio of the total present value of future net cash flows over the initial cash outflow. This index has been proposed by some writers as a means of ranking projects in descending order of attractiveness. If capital rationing does not exist, and if there are no mutually exclusive or indivisible projects, the rankings by

[6] H. Martin Weingartner, "The Excess Present Value Index—A Theoretical Basis and Critique," *Journal of Accounting Research,* Vol. 1, No. 2, p. 214.

index and by net present value will produce the same answers. That is, there is no conflict because all projects will be accepted that have an index of 100 percent or above; these will also have a net present value of zero or above.

However, as we shall now see, conflicts in decisions may be generated if proposals are mutually exclusive, or if certain conditions of capital rationing exist.

mutually exclusive alternatives and budget constraints Assume that a company is considering two projects that are mutually exclusive—that is, where the acceptance of one alternative automatically results in the rejection of the other. The company can invest in either special-purpose equipment or general-purpose equipment, as follows:

	(1) COST	(2) PRESENT VALUE AT 10% HURDLE RATE	(2) ÷ (1) EXCESS PRESENT-VALUE INDEX	(2) − (1) NET PRESENT VALUE
GP Equipment	$1,000,000	$1,400,000	140%	$400,000
SP Equipment	3,000,000	3,900,000	130%	900,000

The GP equipment promises a higher return per dollar invested; if all other things, like risk, alternative uses of funds, and the like, were equal, the GP equipment seems an obvious choice. But "all other things" are rarely equal.

Assume that $5,000,000 is the total capital budget for the coming year and that the allocation of resources, using GP equipment for Project A, is as shown under Alternative One in Exhibit 13-6.

Note that the rationing used in Alternative Two is superior to Alternative One, despite the greater profitability per dollar invested of general-purpose equipment compared with special-purpose equipment. Why? Because the $2,000,000 incremental investment in special-purpose equipment has an incremental net present value of $500,000, whereas the $2,000,000 would otherwise be invested in Projects E and B, which have a lower combined incremental net present value of $256,000:

	COST	PRESENT VALUE	INCREASE IN NET PRESENT VALUE
SP Equipment	$3,000,000	$3,900,000	
GP Equipment	1,000,000	1,400,000	
Increment	$2,000,000	$2,500,000	$500,000
Project E	$ 800,000	$ 912,000	
Project B	1,200,000	1,344,000	
Total	$2,000,000	$2,256,000	$256,000

The example above illustrates that decisions involving mutually exclusive investments of different sizes cannot be based on the excess present-value index (or the internal rate of return, for that matter). The net present-value method is the best general guide.

investment indivisibilities In general, any ranking procedure by excess present-value indexes or rates of return or net present value is an approximation because of investment indivisibilities. For example, assume that five projects are available, as follows:

(1) PROJECT	(2) COST	(3) TOTAL PRESENT VALUE	(3) ÷ (2) EXCESS PRESENT-VALUE INDEX	(3) − (2) NET PRESENT VALUE
V	$6,000	$8,400	140%	$2,400
W	3,000	4,050	135%	1,050
X	2,000	2,600	130%	600
Y	2,000	2,560	128%	560
Z	1,000	1,000	100%	—

Now, if $10,000 is available for capital spending, there are two likely combinations. There might be a tendency to select V, W, and Z and reject X and Y. But this would not yield the optimum answer (see below). Given a budget constraint, it may be wisest to accept smaller, even though less attractive, projects to use the limited funds completely in order to maximize total returns. In our example, the optimum solution rejected Projects W and Z, whose combined excess present-value index and whose combined net present values were less than those of both X and Y.[7]

		ALLOCATION OF $10,000 BUDGET					
		ALTERNATIVE ONE			ALTERNATIVE TWO		
	COST	COST	PRESENT VALUE	INDEX	COST	PRESENT VALUE	INDEX
V	$6,000	$ 6,000	$ 8,400		$ 6,000	$ 8,400	
W	3,000	3,000	4,050				
X	2,000				2,000	2,600	
Y	2,000				2,000	2,560	
Z	1,000	1,000	1,000				
Total available funds		$10,000	$13,450	134.5%	$10,000	$13,560	135.6%
Net present value			$ 3,450			$ 3,560	

[7] Integer programming would be the best attack on these difficulties. See Weingartner, "The Excess Present Value Index," p. 215. Linear programming techniques are also helpful in reaching an optimum solution when there are many variables and many constraints. See Charnes, Cooper, and Miller, "Application of Linear Programming to Financial Budgeting and the Costing of Funds," *Journal of Business,* Vol. XXXII, No. 1, pp. 20–46.

recapitulation The examples above have demonstrated the weaknesses of the internal rate of return[8] (see Exhibit 13-5) and the excess present-value index (see Exhibit 13-6, for instance). The net present-value criterion is the best general rule[9] for choosing projects, whether the complexity involves an overall budget limit, different sizes of outlays, different terminal dates, or mutually exclusive investments. This general rule should be used on an increment-by-increment basis and should be modified where there are investment indivisibilities in relation to a fixed overall capital-budget appropriation.[10]

However, despite the conceptual appeal of the net present-value model, the internal rate-of-return model is widely used in practice. Why? Probably because managers find it easier to understand and because in most instances their decisions would be unaffected by using one model or the other.

The guides above still do not provide answers to some fundamental questions. How do you consider uncertainty? How do you grapple with changes over time in desired rates of return? How do you decide on the appropriate minimum desired rate of return? These difficulties will be considered in the next section, but do not expect any fully satisfying answers. There are none. These are subjects of controversy.

minimum desired rate of return: cost of capital

importance of concept Thus far in our study of capital budgeting, a "minimum desired rate of return" has been somehow given or assumed for use in the analysis of investment proposals. It has been used either as a discount rate under the net present-value method or as a hurdle rate under the internal rate-of-return method. In any event, the minimum desired rate (k) plays a crucial role in determining the acceptability of an investment proposal.

[8] James H. Lorie and Leonard J. Savage, in "Three Problems in Rationing Capital," *Journal of Business,* Vol. XXVIII, No. 4, have demonstrated a number of weaknesses of the internal rate of return. Of special interest is the phenomenon where *two* rates of return can be calculated for *one* project; this can occur when a project, such as an oil well, may entail heavy outlays at termination date or periodically throughout the life of a project.

[9] Simon M. Keane, "Let's Scrap IRR Once For All," *Accountancy* (February, 1974), pp. 78–82, maintains that the internal rate-of-return model is never correct in principle. It is invalid not because of any implicit reinvestment assumption or because of the possibility of producing multiple yields but because a percentage is inappropriate for discriminating between projects of different sizes. And by a series of examples, Keane shows that all projects have different sizes unless they have identical initial outlays *and* cash flows. Keane criticizes the oft-used unequal-lives example because the reinvestment opportunities for the terminal cash flows of the shorter project could be financed independently; thus, they are no more relevant to selection than are the opportunities for reinvesting the intervening cash flows of either project.

[10] For a full discussion, see H. Martin Weingartner, *Mathematical Programming and the Analysis of Capital Budgeting Problems* (Englewood Cliffs, N.J.: Prentice Hall, Inc., 1963).

What is k and how should it be measured? Descriptive terms for k include minimum desired rate of return, cutoff rate, target rate, hurdle rate, financial standard, and cost of capital. The last term is probably used most frequently.

Most theorists in finance agree that the cost of capital is the rate of return on the project that will leave unchanged the market price of the firm's stock. In practice, there is little agreement regarding how to measure this cost. Nevertheless, accountants and managers cannot avoid the problem; they must choose some framework for computing the cost of capital.

complexity of measuring

Opinions differ immensely as to what cost of capital should be used for capital-budgeting purposes. A few managers erroneously cling to the notion that the cost of capital is the mere out-of-pocket interest and financing charges on any debt arising from an undertaking. This position implies that any ownership funds are cost-free, a dangerous position because it ignores the alternative earnings that could be had from the funds. Thus, a home buyer with a \$90,000, 10 percent term mortgage may regard the \$9,000 annual interest outlay as his financing charge. But the homeowner with a mortgage-free \$90,000 home also bears a real cost of capital, even though no interest outlay is involved. He could sell his home and invest the \$90,000 in 10 percent bonds or perhaps reap a bonanza on a mining stock. The sacrifice of these alternative earnings becomes his cost of capital as far as home ownership is concerned.

computation of cost of capital

There are really two basic approaches to computing the cost of capital. The piecemeal approach considers each financing as a separate problem. The other approach develops an average cost of capital.

The principal objection to the piecemeal approach is the insidious effect of low-cost debt financing on projects over a series of years. To illustrate, the cost of 100 percent financing by 10 percent bonds is only 5 percent after applying a tax rate of 50 percent, because bond interest is a deductible expense in computing corporate income subject to tax. If unlimited debt could be arranged in a given year, any project with an after-tax return of over 5 percent would be accepted. Next year, the debt limit for an optimum capital structure may already be reached, and other financing via capital stock may show a cost as high as 20 percent after taxes. This would mean that any project that could not produce such a high rate would be automatically rejected.

The reasoning underlying the calculation of a weighted-average cost of capital is complex and subject to disagreement. A thorough treatment is beyond the scope of this text. The following paragraphs summarize the framework advocated by Van Horne.[11] A prime feature of this framework is that cash dividends are the foundation for valuation of the firm.

The reasoning underlying the weighted-average cost of capital is that by financing in the proportions specified and accepting proposals that yield more than the average cost, the firm can increase the market price of its stock over the long run. Three influential factors are held constant under this framework. First, the complexion of the business risks of the firm as a whole is unaffected by the acceptance of any investment project or combination of investment projects. Second, the firm intends to maintain a constant dividend-payout ratio. Third, over time, the firm finances in the debt-equity proportions as specified in the weighting scheme for the capital structure.

debt and preferred stock

To measure the overall cost of capital, the explicit costs of specific sources of funds must first be computed. Although the historical costs of debt and stock may yield insight, we seek to *predict* the costs of new financing in the proportion that the firm intends to use over time.

The cost of debt is expressed on an after-tax basis, as pointed out above. However, the cost of preferred stock is the stated annual dividend rate. This rate is not adjusted for income taxes because the preferred dividend, unlike bond interest, is not a deductible expense in computing corporate income tax.

common stock

The cost of common stock is extremely difficult to measure. In concept, it is defined as the minimum rate of return that the firm must earn on the common-stock-financed portion of an investment project so that the market price of the stock is unaffected.

An example may clarify the fundamental approach. Suppose the required rate of return on common stock was 10 percent after taxes and that the cost of debt was 4 percent after taxes. Suppose all financing was 50 percent debt and 50 percent equity. The minimum desired rate of return on a project would be:

[11] The approach in James C. Van Horne, *Financial Management and Policy,* 4th ed. (Englewood Cliffs, N.J.: Prentice-Hall, Inc., 1977), is a widely used technique. However, disputes as to the best technique were rampant among specialists in economics and finance in the 1960s and continue to rage in the 1970s. The approach used here is that cost of capital is ultimately determined by the investors in the capital markets, not by the firm itself. Most scholars in the area agree with this concept; but there is a disagreement as to the market effects of leverage (use of debt) on the cost of capital. For a thorough discussion of the issues, see F. Modigliani and M. Miller, "The Cost of Capital, Corporation Finance, and the Theory of Investment," *American Economic Review,* Vol. XLVIII, pp. 261–97; their "Dividend Policy, Growth, and the Valuation of Shares," *Journal of Business,* Vol. XXXIV, No. 4, pp. 411–33; and their "Some Estimates of the Cost of Capital to the Electric Utility Industry, 1954–1957," *American Economic Review,* Vol. LVI, pp. 333–91.

Debt	$.5 \times .04 =$	.02
Common stock	$.5 \times .10 =$	.05
Total		.07

Consider a project costing \$1,000 with an expected after-tax return of \$70 per year forever:

Total return after taxes (.07 × \$1,000)	\$70
Less interest (.04 × \$500)	20
Return on common stock	\$50

The expected rate of return on common stock is 10 percent (\$50 ÷ \$500 portion of the total project). This just equals the rate of return required by investors. If the project failed to yield \$70 per year, the market price of the stock would decline.

How do you obtain the required rate of return on common stock? The cost of common stock is the rate of discount that equates the present value of the stream of expected future dividends per share, as perceived by investors in the market, with the market price of the stock. In general, it is inappropriate to use the ratio of earnings per share to market price as the cost of common stock. The focus should be on future dividends, which means that a growth rate must be assumed.

For example, suppose a company's expected dividend per share is \$2, the current market price is \$40, and earnings and dividends are expected to grow about 4 percent per annum. The market valuation model is:

$$P_c = \frac{D_1}{k_c - g}$$

where P_c is the market price of the common stock, D_1 is the dividend per share expected to be paid at the end of period 1, k_c is the market rate of discount (the cost of common stock), and g is the constant rate of growth.

Then:

$$P_c(k_c - g) = D_1$$

$$k_c - g = \frac{D_1}{P_c}$$

$$k_c = \frac{D_1}{P_c} + g$$

Consider the example of B Company. If the expected dividend per share at the end of period 1 is \$2, the current price is \$40, and earnings and dividends per share are expected to grow about 4 percent per annum, the company's cost of common stock is:

$$k_c = \frac{\$2}{\$40} + .04 = .09 \text{ or } 9\%$$

Van Horne points out that for k_c to be realistic, expectations in the marketplace must be such that dividends per share are thought to grow in fact at a rate g. The crucial factor, then, is measuring the growth in dividends per share as perceived by investors. As you might expect, these computations can quickly become complicated.

retained earnings There are diverse views as to how to compute the cost of financing with retained earnings.[12] The approach favored here has been called the external-yield criterion. It is the opportunity cost as determined by what the firm can obtain on external investment of funds. This return should approximate k_c, assuming equilibrium in the market between expected return and risk.

weighted-average cost of capital Suppose that the capital structure at the latest statement date is indicative of the proportions of financing that the company intends to use over time:

	*AMOUNT**	*PROPORTION*
Debt	$ 30	30%
Preferred stock	10	10
Common stock	20	20
Retained earnings	40	40
	$100	100%

* In millions.

These proportions would be applied to the assumed individual explicit after-tax costs below:

	PROPORTION	*COST*	*WEIGHTED COST*
Debt	30%	4%	1.2%
Preferred stock	10	8	.8
Common stock	20	9	1.8
Retained earnings[13]	40	9	3.6
Weighted-average cost of capital			7.4%

[12] One controversy is whether the cost should be reduced for a tax effect, because the stockholders would have to pay income taxes if they individually reinvest the retained earnings in question. That is, the company would have to declare a cash dividend in the amount of the retained earnings. In turn, the stockholders would have to pay income taxes on the dividend before the proceeds could be reinvested. See Van Horne, *Financial Management,* Chap. 5.

[13] The cost of retained earnings was based on the external-yield criterion. Van Horne would have it one percent lower than the cost of common stock because of the absence of underpricing and flotation costs associated with a new stock issue.

If measured correctly, a weighted-average cost of capital can lead to optimal capital-budgeting decisions. Van Horne stresses that the cost of capital is only a means to an end: the maximizing of the market price of the common stock. Sometimes this objective is overlooked because of the somewhat mechanical nature of the approach.

degree of risk or uncertainty

The preceding calculation of the cost of capital assumed that the acceptance of a project or projects did not change the total risk[14] complexion of the firm as a whole. Capital budgeting would be simplified if all projects bore the same degree of risk. Then a single cost of capital could be used for judging all projects. However, different investments bear different degrees of risk. If the acceptance of an investment proposal(s) alters the risk complexion of the firm, the investment community may value the company differently before and after the acceptance.

Because it is very hard to evaluate the overall risk of the firm at the operating level, the evaluation of risk is often confined to the individual proposal. Methods for allowing risk include: adjusting the minimum desired rate of return; upward calculation of the certainty equivalent of cash flows; direct analysis of the probability distributions of possible outcomes; and many others.[15] The most frequently encountered approach in practice is to boost the minimum required rate as the risk increases. For example, a petroleum company may use 8 percent for marketing facilities, 12 percent for refining facilities, and 20 percent for development facilities. (Other practical ways of allowing for risk include the use of extremely short payback periods or useful lives and the ignoring of potential salvage values.)

Of all the methods for dealing with risk, the direct use of probability distributions[16] is probably the one that will grow most rapidly in future practice. This method, which is discussed in Chapter 24, gives management a straightforward way to evaluate the dispersion of possible outcomes for an investment project. The discount rate chosen is the compensation for taking risks; it will be affected by the nature of the probability distributions.

portfolio analysis

A more penetrating analysis of risk is portfolio theory, which explicitly considers the relationship of three factors simultaneously: the investment's expected rate of return, the uncertainty of the expec-

[14] Various definitions of *risk* have been offered in the literature. Some writers like to distinguish between risk (objective) and uncertainty (subjective). As used here, risk is thought of as the probability of obtaining a future income stream. An investment in United States bonds is risk-free because the probability of getting the interest income is nearly 100 percent, whereas an investment in a single oil well is risky because the variability of prospective income is immense. Also see Chapter 24.

[15] See Van Horne, *Financial Management,* Chaps. 5 and 6, for a discussion analysis or risk for the single investment and multiple investments.

[16] David B. Hertz, "Risk Analysis in Capital Investment," *Harvard Business Review,* Vol. 42, No. 1, pp. 95–106; and his "Investment Policies That Pay Off," *Harvard Business Review,* Vol. 46, No. 1, pp. 96–108.

tation, and the other investments made by the firm. Under specified conditions, the mean-standard deviation model serves as a measure of expected return (the mean) and risk (standard deviation). The hallmark of this approach is that, for any desired rate of return, appropriate diversification of investments can quickly decrease risk.

The portfolio approach relates a given investment proposal with existing investments and with other investment proposals. Van Horne points out that if a project is highly correlated with existing investments, the total risk of the firm will increase more than if a project is added that has a low degree of correlation with others, all other things being equal. Management should be aware of the potential benefits of diversifying investments to obtain the best combination of expected net present value and risk. In short, a portfolio approach should be used to analyze the trade-off between the risk and the net present value of the total firm under varying combinations of investments.

An outgrowth of portfolio theory, the capital-asset pricing model, provides an alternative means for measuring the cost of equity capital. A discussion of this model is beyond the scope of this book.[17] The basis of the model is that the required rate of return on any asset is related to the expected rate of return on all assets in the entire economy. The key idea is that investors cannot diversfy away the entire risk. Consequently, the greater the undiversifiable portion of the risk, the greater the required return. This required return is the cost of equity capital of the firm in a market context.

SUMMARY

The uncertainty about long-run events makes capital budgeting a difficult but challenging area. The imprecision of prediction should overhang any analyst's tendency to split hairs concerning controversial aspects. However, there are a few guideposts that should help toward intelligent decisions. Some are summarized at the end of Chapters 11 and 12. Others were discussed in this chapter.

Income tax factors almost always play an important role in decision making. It is dangerous to assume that income taxes are irrelevant or insignificant.

Decisions on types of production equipment are often only remotely identifiable with cash receipts, if at all. Thus, the decision becomes one of cost minimization. A logical approach, especially if there are income tax complications and several alternative investments available, is to compare all projects, discounting each to the present and choosing the project with the least cost.

Comparisons of projects with unequal lives necessitate predictions of reinvestment of proceeds of shorter-lived projects and a comparison to the terminal date of the longer-lived project.

Two interrelated constraints for rationing capital are overall funds available and a minimum desired hurdle rate(s) of return. Capital rationing has no conceptual justification; that is, all desirable projects should be undertaken and the required funds obtained if possible. Under capital budgeting, investment indivisibilities often necessitate juggling project selections to obtain optimum overall results.

[17] William F. Sharpe, *Portfolio Theory and Capital Markets* (New York: McGraw-Hill Book Company, 1970), Chaps. 2–6. Also see Van Horne, *Financial Management,* Chaps. 3–8.

Incremental approaches are very useful in checking among multiple alternatives, to be certain that each separable investment is earning the minimum desired rate of return and that overall funds available are earning a maximum amount.

Cost of capital is used for purposes of determining the hurdle rate in the selection of projects. There is no agreement as to how to compute a magic, single-figured cost of capital. But it is agreed that recognition should be given to a "cost" of equity capital as well as debt. In practice, projects are classified by degree of risk, with different minimum hurdle rates being used for different classes of projects. Probabilistic approaches employing portfolio theory, which formally explicitly recognize the dispersion in estimated data, have just begun to be used.

SUGGESTED READINGS

BIERMAN, H., and T. R. DYCKMAN, *Managerial Cost Accounting,* 2nd ed. New York: The Macmillan Company, 1976.

BIERMAN, H., and S. SMIDT, *The Capital Budgeting Decision,* 4th ed. New York: The Macmillan Company, 1975.

GRANT, E. L., W. G. IRESON, and R. S. LEAVENWORTH, *Principles of Engineering Economy,* 6th ed. New York: Ronald Press Company, 1976.

HIRSHLEIFER, JACK, *Investment, Interest, and Capital.* Englewood Cliffs, N.J.: Prentice-Hall, Inc., 1970.

NATIONAL ASSOCIATION OF ACCOUNTANTS, *Research Report 42, Long-Range Profit Planning.* New York: the Association, 1964.

SHARPE, W. F. *Portfolio Analysis and Capital Markets.* New York: McGraw-Hill Book Company, 1970.

SOLOMON, EZRA, ed., *The Management of Corporate Capital.* New York: The Free Press, 1959.

———, *The Theory of Financial Management.* New York: Columbia University Press, 1963.

TERBORGH, GEORGE, *Effect of Anticipated Inflation on Investment Analysis.* Washington, D.C.: Machinery and Allied Products Institute, 1960.

VAN HORNE, J. C., *Financial Management and Policy,* 4th ed. Englewood Cliffs, N.J.: Prentice-Hall, Inc., 1977.

WEINGARTNER, H. MARTIN, *Mathematical Programming and the Analysis of Capital Budgeting Problems.* Englewood Cliffs, N.J.: Prentice-Hall, Inc., 1963.

PROBLEMS FOR SELF-STUDY

Review the example on the effects of income taxes on cash flow and the other illustrations.

appendix: the financial lease

Leases are frequently classified as operating or financial.[18] An operating lease is one that is cancelable or that terminates before the rental payments have

[18] See Richard F. Vancil, "Lease or Borrow—New Method of Analysis," *Harvard Business Review,* Vol. 39, No. 5, pp. 122–33; and Richard S. Bower, Frank C. Herringer, and J. Peter Williamson, "Lease Evaluation," *The Accounting Review,* Vol. XLI, No. 2, pp. 257–65, for thorough examinations of these distinctions and for consideration of income tax factors. For a comparison of a variety of approaches, see Van Horne, *Financial Management,* Chap. 22. Also see the article by Thomas A. Beechy in *The Accounting Review,* Vol. XLV, No. 4, pp. 769–73, and, Merton Miller and Charles Upton, "Leasing, Buying, and the Cost of Capital Services, *Journal of Finance,* Vol. XXXI, No. 3 (June, 1976), pp. 761–86.

repaid the purchase price. Examples are telephone equipment and monthly rentals of automobiles. For capital-budgeting purposes, the cash flows of operating leases can be analyzed just like ordinary operating cash flows.

The financial lease, according to Vancil, is noncancelable; it obligates the lessee to rentals that in total equal or exceed the purchase price of the asset leased. Examples of assets that are often subject to financial lease arrangements are jet aircraft, sports arenas, office buildings, and grocery stores. We are concerned here with the financial lease only.

example

Suppose that it is a tax-free world. A company with a weighted-average cost of capital of 10 percent is contemplating the acquisition of a machine that will save $2,400 in cash operating costs annually over its useful life of four years. The machine will have no residual value. The machine may be bought outright for $6,500 cash; it is also available on a four-year, noncancelable lease at $2,000 payable at the end of each year. Should the company buy or lease?

SOLUTION 1

The internal rate of return of leasing may be calculated as follows:

Net cash operating savings	$2,400
Lease payments	(2,000)
Net increase in cash flow per year	$ 400
Outlay at time zero	0
Internal rate of return	infinite

Something is wrong here. Intuitively, we know that this proposition does not bear an infinite rate of return.[19]

SOLUTION 2

The lease arrangement is clearly more attractive. The present value of the lease payments at 10 percent is $2,000 × 3.170 (from Table 4 in the appendix at the end of the book), or $6,340, which is less than the $6,500 purchase price. Note that the discounting of lease payments at the lessee's weighted-average cost of capital will lead to leasing rather than buying in all instances where the lessee's cost of capital exceeds the lessor's implicit contractual interest rate.

SOLUTION 3

Perplexing implications arose in the two preceding solutions because of the failure of the prospective lessee to separate the *investment* decision from the *financing* decision. The biggest pitfall is to fail to distinguish these two aspects.

The financial-lease decision is complicated because each rental payment has two components: the implicit interest charged by the lessor and the amortization of the principal sum. In effect, the lessor is a seller of an asset and a lender of money. The rent must provide him with a recovery of the selling price of the asset plus interest on the money advanced.

I. The financing decision.

Note that the decision is not whether to buy or lease, despite the fact that advertisements for leasing usually describe the decision in this way. The decision is a twofold one: (a) whether to acquire the asset or not to acquire the asset, and (b) whether to lease or borrow.

Bierman and Smidt comment on this lease-or-borrow phase as follows:

> Because the lease is presumed to require a contractually predetermined set of payments, it is reasonable to compare the lease with an alternative type of financing

[19] See Robert N. Anthony, John Dearden, and Richard F. Vancil, *Management Control Systems* (Homewood, Ill.: Richard D. Irwin, Inc., 1966), pp. 467–74 and 507–16.

> available . . . that also requires a contractually predetermined set of payments, i.e., a loan.[20]

Since the comparison is lease or borrow, the present value of the rentals should be discounted at a relatively low loan rate rather than at the weighted-average cost-of-capital rate. Therefore, the steps necessary for making the financing decision are:

a. Approximate the lowest rate at which cash could be borrowed in an amount equal to the purchase price of the equipment.
b. Discount the rentals at this borrowing rate to obtain the "cash equivalent purchase price" of the equipment. If this "equivalent purchase price" is less than the outright cash purchase cost, then leasing is desirable—provided also that the criterion described below for the overall investment decision is also met. If this equivalent price is greater than the outright purchase cost, then purchasing is desirable—again provided that the criterion below is also met.

Apply these steps to our example:

a. Approximate the company loan rate. Suppose the rate is 6 percent.
b. "Equivalent purchase price" is $2,000 at 6 percent for four years, $2,000 × 3.465 = $6,930, which exceeds the outright purchase price of $6,500. Therefore, purchase is desirable if the criterion below is met.

Note that the lessor may essentially quote two selling prices, one price for a leasing transaction and a different price for an outright sale. He may prefer to lease and thus quote a seemingly ridiculously high outright selling price, as many office equipment manufacturers do. The lessor may have many reasons for his preference for leasing rather than selling outright, including:

1. The ability to earn more in total through the selling and loaning together in the form of a lease. He may be willing to "sell" cheaper via a lease because he is assured of the implicit interest income on the rentals.

2. The lessor may have a different set of income tax considerations, which are frequently important in these cases.

II. The investment decision.

Decide whether to acquire the asset as follows:

a. Discount the operating cash inflows at the minimum desired rate of return (the weighted-average cost of capital, in this example), $2,400 at 10 percent for four years, $2,400 × 3.170	$7,608
b. Deduct the lower of the cash outright purchase price ($6,500) or the "cash equivalent purchase price" ($6,930)	(6,500)
c. Net present value	$1,108

If the net present value is positive, acquire the asset by the means indicated in Part I. In this instance, the asset would be purchased outright.

The analysis of leases can become vastly more complicated by the introduction of income taxes and residual value. To pursue this topic in more depth, study the readings cited in footnote 18.

[20] Harold Bierman, Jr., and Seymour Smidt, *The Capital Budgeting Decision,* 4th ed. (New York: The Macmillan Company, 1975), p. 216.

QUESTIONS, PROBLEMS, AND CASES

Note Compound-interest tables are at the rear of the book.

13-1 What are the two major aspects of the role of income taxes in decision making?

13-2 "It doesn't matter what depreciation method is used. The total dollar tax bills are the same." Do you agree? Why?

13-3 In general, what is the impact of the income tax on disposals of fixed assets?

13-4 "In the case of mutually exclusive investments, smaller profitability indexes may enhance overall economic returns." How?

13-5 "The crux of the problem in replacement decisions is the lack of a realistic common terminal date for both proposals." Briefly describe two practical approaches to the problem.

13-6 "Cost of capital is the out-of-pocket interest charge on any debt arising from an undertaking." Do you agree? Why?

13-7 The short-run, marginal approach considers each financing as a separate problem. What is the principal objection to the short-run approach?

13-8 Should retained earnings bear a cost of capital? Why?

13-9 "In practice there is no single rate that is used as a guide for sifting among all projects." Why? Explain.

13-10 *Recapitulation of Role of Depreciation in Chapters 11, 12, and 13* A president of a large steel company remarked, "I've read three successive chapters that have included discussions of depreciation in relation to decisions regarding the replacement of equipment. I'm confused. The first chapter said that depreciation on old equipment is irrelevant, but that depreciation on the new equipment is relevant. The second chapter said that depreciation was irrelevant in relation to discounted cash-flow models, but the third chapter indicated that depreciation was indeed relevant."

required

Prepare a clear explanation for the president that would minimize his or her confusion.

13-11 *Mining Property* (W. Crum.) Balek Company develops a mine with expected output of $5,000,000 in sales per year; expected out-of-pocket operating costs of $2,400,000 per year; planned straight-line depreciation and depletion per year of $800,000; income taxes of 50 percent per year. Original cost of the mine and improvements is expected to be $10,200,000. Compute the payback period in years. What does this mean? Compute the payback reciprocal. What does this mean?

13-12 *Taxes and Depreciation Methods* A company has just paid $42,000 for some equipment that will have a six-year life and no residual value. The minimum rate of return desired, after taxes, is 10 percent.

The president has attended a management conference luncheon where an accounting professor adamantly stated, "Not using accelerated depreciation for tax purposes is outright financial stupidity." The president has a perpetual fear of rises in income tax rates and has favored straight-line depreciation "to have greater deductions against future income when taxes are higher."

He is having second thoughts now and has asked you to prepare a financial analysis of the dollar benefits of using sum-of-the-years'-digits depreciation instead of straight-line depreciation under the following assumptions: (a) income tax rates of 60 percent throughout the coming six years; and (b) income tax rates of 60 percent for the first three years and 80 percent for the subsequent three years.

13-13 *Tax Impact of Depreciation Policies* The Mays Company estimates that it can save $2,800 a year in cash operating costs for the next ten years if it buys a special-purpose machine at a cost of $11,000. No residual value is expected. Assume that income tax rates average two-sevenths of taxable income, and that the minimum desired after-tax rate of return is 10 percent.

required

(Round all computation to the nearest dollar.)

A. Answer all questions below, assuming straight-line depreciation.
1. Payback period
2. Using discounted cash flow:
   a. Internal rate of return
   b. Net present value
3. Payback reciprocal

B. Answer all questions in Part A, assuming sum-of-the-years'-digits depreciation.

13-14 *Approach to Income Taxes and Discounted Cash Flow* The Charles Company is trying to decide whether to launch a new household product. Through the years, the company has found that its products have a useful life of six years, after which the product is dropped and replaced by other new products. Available data follow:

1. The new product will require new special-purpose equipment costing $900,000. The useful life of the equipment is six years, with a $140,000 estimated disposal value at that time. However, the Internal Revenue Service will not allow a write-off based on a life shorter than nine years. Therefore, the new equipment would be written off over nine years for tax purposes, using the sum-of-the-years'-digits depreciation and no salvage value.
2. The new product will be produced in an old plant already owned. The old plant has a book value of $30,000 and is being depreciated on a straight-line basis at $3,000 annually. The plant is currently being leased to another company. This lease has six years remaining at an annual rental of $9,000. The lease contains a cancellation clause whereby the landlord can obtain immediate possession of the premises upon payment of $6,000 cash (fully deductible for tax purposes). The estimated sales value of the building is $80,000; this price should remain stable over the next six years. The plant is likely to be kept for at least ten more years.
3. Certain nonrecurring market-research studies and sales-promotion activities will amount to a cost of $500,000 during year 1. The entire amount is deductible in full for income tax purposes in the year of expenditure.
4. Additions to working capital will require $200,000 at the outset and an additional $200,000 at the end of two years. This total is fully recoverable at the end of six years.
5. Net cash inflow from operations before depreciation and income taxes will be $400,000 in years 1 and 2, $600,000 in years 3 through 5, and $100,000 in year 6.

The company uses discounted cash-flow techniques for evaluating decisions. For example, in this case tabulations of differential cash flows would be made from year 0 through year 6. Yearly cash flows are estimated for all items, including capital outlays or recoveries. An applicable discount rate is used to bring all outlays from year 1 through year 6 back to year 0. If the summation in year 0 is positive, the project is desirable, and vice versa.

The minimum desired after-tax rate of return is 12 percent. Income tax rates are 60 percent for ordinary income.

required

Using an answer sheet, show how you would handle the data listed above for purposes of the decision. Note that you are *not* being asked to apply discount rates. You are being asked for the detailed impact of each of items 1 through 5 on years 0 through 6.

Note, too, that each item is to be considered separately, including its tax ramifications. *Do not combine your answers to cover more than one item.*

Assume that all cash flows take place at the end of each period. Assume that income taxes are due or refundable at the end of the period to which they relate.

SAMPLE ANSWER SHEET FOR PROBLEM 13-14

		NET	CASH FLOWS IN YEAR						
		PRESENT							
ITEM	*EXPLANATION*	*VALUE*	*0*	*1*	*2*	*3*	*4*	*5*	*6*
1.	*[Allow ample*								
2.	*space between*								
3.	*items]*								
4.									
5.									

13-15 *Sensitivity of Capital Budgeting to Depreciation* The president of San Juan University, Ms. Martinez, is considering whether to invest $230,000 in some power equipment that will last ten years, have zero residual value, and generate cash operating savings (mostly labor) of $40,000 annually. The minimum desired rate of return is 10 percent per year after taxes.

required

1. Compute the net present value of the project, assuming a zero income tax rate.
2. Assume that Martinez is the owner of a farm. Compute the net present value (a) assuming a 40 percent tax rate and straight-line depreciation, and (b) assuming a 40 percent tax rate, straight-line depreciation, and an investment tax credit of 10 percent.
3. Repeat requirement 2, assuming sum-of-the-years'-digits depreciation.

13-16 *Sensitivity of Capital Budgeting to Inflation* W. Hoverling, the president of a Liverpool trucking company, is considering whether to invest £110,000 in new semiautomatic loading equipment that will last five years, have zero scrap value, and generate cash operating savings in labor usage of £30,000 annually, using 19_0 prices and wage rates. It is December 31, 19_0.

The minimum desired rate of return is 18 percent per year after taxes. For simplicity, assume that this rate is applicable throughout all parts of this problem, even though it obviously would be affected by varying rates of income taxes and inflation.

required

1. Compute the net present value of the project (a) assuming a zero income tax rate and (b) assuming a 40 percent tax rate and straight-line depreciation.
2. Hoverling is positive that inflation will continue, but she is uncertain about its degree. For purposes of this analysis, she assumes that the existing rate of inflation, 10 percent annually, will persist over the next five years. Therefore, there will be 10 percent inflation *in year one*. In thinking about how to analyze inflationary effects, she decides that the 18 percent rate embodies an element attributable to anticipated inflation. Therefore, to make the decision model consistent, the cash savings should be adjusted upward in accordance with the 10 percent inflation rate. Using these assumptions, repeat requirement 1.

3. Repeat requirement 2, using an inflation rate of 6 percent. That is, for simplicity assume that the minimum desired rate of return is 18 percent per year after taxes, including the element attributable to anticipated inflation.
4. Tabulate your final results in requirements 1, 2, and 3. What generalizations about the effects of inflation seem warranted?

13-17 *Purchase of Computer* (SIA, adapted) A medium-sized manufacturing company is considering the purchase of a small computer in order to reduce the cost of its data-processing operations.

At the present time, the manual bookkeeping system in use involves the following direct cash expenses per month:

Salaries	$7,500
Payroll taxes and fringe benefits	1,700
Forms and supplies	600
	$9,800

Existing furniture and equipment are fully depreciated in the accounts and have no salvage value. The cost of the computer, including alterations, installation, and accessory equipment, is $100,000. This entire amount is depreciable for income tax purposes on a double declining basis at the rate of 20 percent per annum.

Estimated annual costs of computerized data processing are as follows:

Supervisory salaries	$15,000
Other salaries	24,000
Payroll taxes and fringe benefits	7,400
Forms and supplies	7,200
	$53,600

The computer is expected to be obsolete in three years, at which time its salvage value is expected to be $20,000. The company follows the practice of treating salvage value as inflow at the time that it is likely to be received. The company owns other assets that are in the same class for tax purposes.

required

1. Compute the savings in annual cash outflow after taxes. Assume a 50 percent tax rate.
2. Decide whether or not to purchase the computer, using the present-value method of discounted cash-flow analysis. Assume a minimum rate of return of 10 percent after taxes. Briefly explain the decision you reach.

13-18 *Comparison of Projects with Unequal Lives* The manager of the Robin Hood Company is considering two investment projects, which happen to be mutually exclusive.

The cost of capital to this company is 10 percent, and the anticipated cash flows are as follows:

		CASH FLOWS (INCOME)			
PROJECT NO.	INVESTMENT REQUIRED NOW	YEAR 1	YEAR 2	YEAR 3	YEAR 4
1	$10,000	$12,000	0	0	0
2	$10,000	0	0	0	$17,500

required

1. Calculate the internal rate of return of both projects.
2. Calculate the net present value of both projects.
3. Comment briefly on the results in 1 and 2. Be specific in your comparisons.

13-19 *Ranking Projects.* (Adapted from *N.A.A. Research Report No. 35,* pp. 83–85) Assume that six projects in the table that follows have been submitted for inclusion in the coming year's budget for capital expenditures:

	YEAR	A	B	C	D	E	F
Investment	0	$(100,000)	$(100,000)	$(200,000)	$(200,000)	$(200,000)	$(50,000)
	1	0	20,000	70,000	0	5,000	23,000
	2	10,000	20,000	70,000	0	15,000	20,000
	3	20,000	20,000	70,000	0	30,000	10,000
	4	20,000	20,000	70,000	0	50,000	10,000
	5	20,000	20,000	70,000	0	50,000	
Per year	6–9	20,000	20,000		200,000	50,000	
	10	20,000	20,000			50,000	
Per year	11–15	20,000					
Internal rate of return		14%	?	?	?	12.6%	12.0%

required

1. Rates of return (to the nearest half percent) for Projects B, C, and D and a ranking of all projects in descending order. Show computations. What approximations of rates of return for Projects B and C do you get by using payback reciprocals?
2. Based on your answer in 1, which projects would you select, assuming a 10 percent hurdle rate:
   a. If $500,000 is the limit to be spent?
   b. If $550,000?
   c. If $650,000?
3. Assuming a 16 percent minimum desired rate of return, and using the net present-value method, compute the net present values and rank all the projects. Which project is more desirable, C or D? Compare your answer with your ranking in 2. If Projects C and D are mutually exclusive proposals, which would you choose? Why?
4. What factors other than those considered in 1 through 3 would influence your project rankings? Be specific.

13-20 *Evaluating Multiple Alternatives* A retail outlet is considering extending credit to its customers for the first time in its history. A careful study of competitors' experience with a variety of credit plans shows the expected increases in net profits under various plans, as illustrated below. Which choice would you make? Why? Assume that the total $100,000 funds available can be invested in some phase of the business at 14 percent with comparable risk.

MINIMUM DESIRED RATE OF RETURN—14%

PLAN	A	B	C	D	E
Total investment in receivables	$10,000	$30,000	$50,000	$80,000	$100,000
Annual net income	500	4,200	7,800	12,120	14,320
Rate of return	5.0%	14.0%	15.6%	15.2%	14.3%
Incremental investment over preceding plan		$20,000	$20,000	$30,000	$ 20,000
Incremental net income		3,700	3,600	4,320	2,200
Rate of return on incremental investment		18.5%	18.0%	14.4%	11.0%

13-21 *Effects of Depreciation; Use of Algebra* (D. Green) The Brogan Company is in the process of acquiring a crane. The model they need is available from the factory at a price of $150,000.

An identical crane was acquired several weeks ago by a competitor. The competitor's requirements have changed and they offer to sell their crane to the Brogan Company.

The Brogan Company uses the sum-of-the-years'-digits method for computing depreciation for tax purposes, wherever the Internal Revenue Code permits. However, the code does not permit any accelerated method for assets acquired secondhand.

For the purpose of this problem, assume:

a. The two cranes are identical.
b. "Money is worth" 8 percent.
c. Income tax payments are made at the end of each year and the year-end will be 12 months removed from acquisition.
d. The cranes have a 5-year life and *no* salvage value.
e. The relevant tax rate is 40 percent for either alternative.

required

What is the highest price that Brogan can bid for the secondhand crane? (Support with calculations.)

	1	*2*	*3*	*4*	*5*
P.V. of 1 at 8%:	.93	.86	.79	.74	.68

13-22 *Capital Budgeting and Cost of Capital* (CPA, adapted) The Niebuhr Corporation is beginning its first capital-budgeting program and has retained you to assist the budget committee in the evaluation of a project to expand operations, designated as Proposed Expansion Project 12 (PEP 12).

1. The following capital expenditures are under consideration:

Fire sprinkler system	$ 300,000
Landscaping	100,000
Replacement of old machines	600,000
Projects to expand operations (including PEP 12)	800,000
Total	$1,800,000

2. The corporation requires no minimum return on the sprinkler system or the landscaping. However, it expects a minimum return of 6 percent on all investments to replace old machinery. It also expects investments in expansion projects to yield a return that will exceed the average cost of the capital required to finance the sprinkler system and the landscaping in addition to the expansion projects.
3. Under Proposed Expansion Project 12 (PEP 12) a cash investment of $75,000 will be made one year before operations begin. The investment will be depreciated by the sum-of-the-years'-digits method over a three-year period and is expected to have a salvage value of $15,000. Additional financial data for PEP 12 follow:

TIME PERIOD	*REVENUE*	*VARIABLE COSTS*	*MAINTENANCE, PROPERTY TAXES, AND INSURANCE*
0–1	$80,000	$35,000	$ 8,000
1–2	95,000	41,000	11,000
2–3	60,000	25,000	12,000

The amount of the investment recovered during each of the three years can be reinvested immediately at a rate of return approximating 15 percent. Each year's recovery of investment, then, will have been reinvested at 15 percent for an average of six months at the end of the year.

4. Assume that the corporate income tax rate is 50 percent.
5. The present value of $1 due at the end of each year and discounted at 15 percent is:

END OF YEAR	PRESENT VALUE
2 years before 0	$1.32
1 year before 0	1.15
0	1.00
1 year after 0	.87
2 years after 0	.76
3 years after 0	.66

6. The present values of $1 earned uniformly throughout the year and discounted at 15 percent follow:

YEAR	PRESENT VALUE
0–1	$ .93
1–2	.80
2–3	.69

required

1. Assume that the cutoff rate for considering expansion projects is 15 percent. Prepare a schedule calculating:
   a. Annual cash flows from operations for PEP 12
   b. Present value of the net cash flows for PEP 12
2. a. Assume that the average desired rate of return is 9 percent. Prepare a schedule to compute the minimum return (in dollars) required on expansion projects to cover the desired rate of return for financing the sprinkler system and the landscaping in addition to expansion projects. Assume that it is necessary to replace the old machines.
   b. Assume that the minimum return computed in 2a is $150,000. Calculate the cutoff rate on expansion projects.

13-23 *Cost of Capital and Common Stock* Suppose all financing is 40 percent debt and 60 percent equity. Also suppose that the required rate of return on common stock is 10 percent after taxes and that the cost of debt is 6 percent after taxes.

Consider a project costing $10,000, with an expected return that will last forever. What dollar amount must the project yield per year so that the market price of the stock will not change?

13-24 *Growth of Rate of Return on Common Stock* Suppose the expected dividend per share at the end of period 1 is $3, the current price is $50, and earnings and dividends are expected to grow about 6 percent per annum. What is the company's cost of common stock?

13-25 *Computation of Cost of Capital* Company Y expects the annual return on debt and equity before taxes to be approximately $2 million over the next few years. Annual interest on bonds will be $400,000. The market value of the bonds outstanding is $8 million; of common stock, $12 million. The book value of the bonds is $10 million; of the stock, $10 million. The company intends to finance in a proportion of 40 percent debt and 60 percent common stock.

required

Compute the effective yield on bonds, rate of return on common equity, and overall weighted-average cost of capital. Ignore income taxes.

13-26 *After-Tax Cost of Capital* Assume the same facts as in Problem 13-25. The income tax rate is 40 percent.

required

1. After-tax rate of return on common equity. Also compute the weighted-average cost of capital.
2. The company is considering investing $100,000 in a proposed project, which will increase overall return on debt and equity before taxes by $12,000. Should the project be undertaken? Show computations.

13-27 *Cost of Capital After Taxes* A company is considering a project costing $100,000. The market value of outstanding bonds is $5 million; of common stock, $5 million; this is indicative of the proportions of financing that the company intends to use over time. The coupon interest on debt is 8 percent. The required after-tax rate on equity is 10 percent. The income tax rate is 50 percent. The project is expected to yield $14,000 annually, before interest and taxes in perpetuity. Ignore depreciation. Compute:

required

1. The overall after-tax cost of capital for the company.
2. The overall after-tax cost of return on the project.
3. The after-tax rate on equity for the project.

13-28 *The Financial Lease* The Vanthony Company has a weighted-average cost of capital of 12 percent. Its basic loan rate is 6 percent. The financial vice-president is trying to decide whether to buy or lease some machinery. The purchase price is $14,000. A noncancelable lease is also available for six years at $3,000 annually. The useful life of the machine is six years; it will have no residual value. Annual cash operating savings are expected to be $4,000.

The salesman is encouraging the lease. He says, "No matter how you look at it, you can't lose by leasing. You take in $4,000 annually, pay out $3,000 annually, and make no down payment. Your rate of return is infinite."

required

Should the Vanthony Company buy or lease? Show computations. Ignore income taxes.

13-29 *The Financial Lease* An office-equipment company has offered the Dudley Company a four-year, noncancelable lease on a small computer at an annual rental of $3,000, payable at the end of each year. The Dudley Company has a weighted-average cost of capital of 10 percent. Its basic loan rate is 6 percent. The computer is expected to save $3,600 in cash operating costs annually over its useful life of four years. Because of rapid technological change, the computer will have a negligible residual value.

Carl Dudley, the president of the Dudley Company, has read some magazine articles indicating that buying is almost always better than leasing, because the implicit interest rate in the lease is almost always higher than a company's basic loan rate. He asked the salesman, "How much will we have to pay if we buy the equipment outright for cash?" The salesman was reluctant to quote a price. Finally, after checking with his sales manager, he quoted a price of $11,800.

required

Should the Dudley Company buy or lease? Show computations. Ignore income taxes.

13-30 *Addition of New Product; Sensitivity Analysis* (S. Buchin, adapted) As controller of the Buchin Company, John Northrup has just presented the president with his analysis of the proposed addition of a new product, code-named Zim. Northrup summarized his opposition as follows:

Zim should be rejected because it will not earn the minimum desired rate of return of 10 percent after taxes. We cannot sell enough units to break even, even though our marketing people insist that the product can be sold without increasing our sales force.

Zim is expected to be a highly salable product for the next ten years. Our market research department has predicted a sales volume of 45,000 units per year at a selling price of $12. But my computations indicate a breakeven volume of 50,000 units per year:

	PER UNIT
Variable costs:	
Direct material	$ 5.00
Direct labor	2.00
Variable factory overhead at 25% of direct labor	.50
Other costs (using companywide rates):	
General factory overhead at 25% of direct labor	.50
Selling and administrative costs at 1/6 selling price	2.00
Total costs per unit	$10.00

Zim will occupy space that is being vacated by our old product, Yim, which is now obsolete. The new Zim department will incur fixed costs of $100,000 annually. This sum includes $50,000 of annual straight-line depreciation on $500,000 of contemplated new equipment. The equipment is expected to have a ten-year life and zero scrap value. The other $50,000 is composed of supervision, property taxes, heat, and also a generous estimate of various incremental indirect general factory overhead and selling and administrative expenses.

The breakeven volume is $100,000 divided by $2 contribution per unit, or 50,000 units.

My computation of the breakeven point is conservative in the sense that direct labor could be looked at as being a fixed cost. A special workforce will have to be trained. These personnel will not be transferable to other departments and vice versa.

An additional $110,000 will be spent to (a) clean up the area where the new Zim department will go and (b) cover start-up and learning costs. This sum can probably be written off immediately for book and tax purposes. Because the $110,000 represents a one-shot expenditure, it has been excluded from the breakeven analysis.

Our total working capital investment will *immediately* increase by about 25 percent of Zim's sales. Because this is fully recoverable as a lump sum whenever we drop Zim from our product line, it too has been excluded from the breakeven analysis.

Last year we spent $300,000 on product development and market research for Zim. Although we have written this off immediately for both book and tax purposes, I think it should be amortized over the first five years of Zim sales. Of course, this would make the picture look even gloomier.

The after-tax effects of the above analysis would decrease Zim's attractiveness. The applicable income tax rate is 50 percent. As you know, our chairman has insisted that we use the same depreciation method for book, tax, and decision purposes because he feels it is somehow dishonest to "keep more than one set of books."

required

1. Appraise Northrup's analysis. Be specific by citing all his points with which you disagree.
2. Prepare your analysis of the attractiveness of the proposal based on an annual volume of 45,000 units.
3. What volume must be sold to make Zim a desirable investment?
4. Suppose that an investment tax credit of 10 percent of the original cost of new equipment was available at time zero. What would be your answer to requirement 3?
5. Suppose that sum-of-the-years'-digits (SYD) depreciation were used rather than straight-line depreciation. What would be your answer to requirement 3? Assume that (a) no investment tax credit is available and (b) a tax credit of 10 percent is available.

13-31 *Conflict of Models for Decisions and Evaluation of Performance* Refer to the preceding problem, part 5. Assume that sum-of-years' depreciation was used for preparing income statements for the performance evaluation of all products. Prepare a condensed income statement for the first year's performance of Zim, assuming that 45,000 units are sold. As the president, would you favor adding Zim to the product line? Why?

13-32 *Review of Chapters 7–13* (R. Jaedicke) The Heedlock Space Company produces a variety of aerospace aircraft guidance systems. The Module Division of Heedlock is faced with a modernization decision for a phase of its production process.

Production process. The entire production process in question spans three operating departments in two divisions (and involves a total of three machines). The ultimate product is a guidance module sold to customers by the Module Division. The module is used as a component for more sophisticated aircraft guidance systems.

The Module Division, which assembles the guidance module, buys a part called a setmeter from the Meter Division. The setmeter consists of a precision metal part that is produced by the Meter Division on a precision metal-cutting machine (Machine 1). This operation takes place in the Metal-Cutting Department of the Meter Division.

The setmeter is then transferred to the Adjustment Department of the Meter Division, where the setmeter is finished by performing an adjustment operation. The adjustment is partly performed by an adjustment machine (Machine 2); the machine currently in use is now five years old. Both the Metal-Cutting Department and the Adjustment Department of the Meter Division work only on setmeters. All of the output is transferred to the Module Division for use on the guidance module.

The Module Division manufactures several other components for the guidance module. After receiving the setmeters from the Adjustment Department of the Meter Division, the Module Division assembles the guidance module and ships it to customers.

The Module Division uses a highly specialized assembly machine (Machine 3) to help in the final assembly of guidance modules. This machine is now several years old and is not performing well; it is difficult to keep appropriately adjusted and therefore frequently breaks setmeters during the final assembly process. When this happens, the entire module is ruined. During the last year the breakage rate has reached an intolerable level and has prompted the modernization question.

Transfer price of the setmeter. The setmeter transfer price to the Module Division is based on full standard cost plus 20 percent profit for the Meter Division. The standard cost sheet for the setmeter is as follows:

METER DIVISION

Standard-Cost Transfer Price for Setmeter

Metal-Cutting Department:		
Raw materials (10 units @ $15)	$150	
Direct labor (20 hours @ $8 per hour)	160	
Overhead (20 hours @ $5 per hour)	100	$410
Adjustment Department:		
Direct labor (10 hours @ $6 per hour)	$ 60	
Overhead (10 hours @ $3 per hour)	30	90
Total standard cost		$500
Add 20% markup for profit		100
Transfer price to Module Division		$600

The Meter Division is able to buy raw materials on an "as needed" basis, so the raw-material cost is variable with respect to the number of setmeters produced, and currently there is no inventory of raw materials. Direct labor in both the Metal-Cutting Department and the Adjustment Department is paid on a piece-rate basis, so this cost is also variable. Variable overhead in the Meter Division consists mostly of fringe labor costs that are related to direct labor together with other variable costs that are very sensitive to direct-labor usage.

Overhead cost is allocated to the setmeter in the Meter Division by using a flexible overhead budget to determine a standard cost rate per direct-labor hour. As shown in the standard cost sheet above, the overhead rate is $5.00 per direct-labor hour in the Metal-Cutting Department and $3.00 per direct-labor hour in the Adjustment Department. The flexible budget for overhead in the Metal-Cutting Department is $150,000 fixed cost plus $2.00 per direct-labor hour. The $150,000 fixed cost budget is the straight-line depreciation on the metal-cutting machine (Machine 1). This machine has a remaining tax life of five years and is also expected to be operable for that period. The $2.00 per direct-labor hour variable overhead (as explained in the paragraph above) is composed mostly of fringe labor benefit cost on direct labor and is a variable cost. The denominator volume is 50,000 direct-labor hours in the Metal-Cutting Department.

The flexible overhead budget in the Adjustment Department used to determine the standard overhead rate of $3.00 per direct labor hour is $50,000 fixed cost plus $1.00 per direct-labor hour for the variable overhead charge. The fixed component of $50,000 is entirely composed of annual straight-line depreciation on the adjustment machine (Machine 2). This machine has a remaining tax life of five years and it is expected to be operable over that period. The denominator volume in the Adjustment Department is 25,000 direct-labor hours.

Cost situation in the Module Division. The Module Division receives the setmeters and assembles the guidance modules with the following standard costs:

MODULE DIVISION	
Guidance Module Standard Cost	
Setmeter (1 @ $600)	$ 600
Materials (15 units @ $15)	225
Direct labor (12 hours @ $10 per hour)	120
Overhead (12 hours @ $7 per hour)	84
Total standard cost of guidance module	$1,029

The cost details on the setmeter have already been explained. The other materials are purchased on an "as needed" basis, so the cost is variable and no inventory is carried. The flexible budget for overhead is $180,000 fixed plus $1.00 per direct-labor hour. The fixed portion of the overhead ($180,000) is the straight-line annual depreciation on the assembly machine (Machine 3). This machine, like the other two machines, has a remaining tax life of five years and could be operated for that period. The variable overhead of $1.00 per direct-labor hour is the fringe benefit cost on direct labor. Denominator volume is 30,000 direct-labor hours.

High breakage rate. The variance from standard cost has been high in the Module Division. This is because of the recent increased breakage rate due to the poor condition of the assembly machine. Last year, 2,500 setmeters were transferred but only 1,500 guidance modules were produced and shipped. The breakage rate, then, was about 40 percent on the setmeters. That is, 2,500 modules were put into production, but only 1,500 could be shipped because 1,000 were ruined in the Module Division. This breakage rate is very costly to the company, because it occurs at the end of the production process in the Module Division after all the cost has been incurred. Spoiled modules cannot be reused or reworked, and the cost of disposal is equal to the salvage value.

Proposed modification program. The Module Division can acquire a new, improved assembly machine, which will reduce the breakage to zero. This would allow the Module Division to meet its regular annual demand of 1,500 guidance modules without having to order 2,500 setmeters in order to obtain 1,500 guidance modules. Furthermore, the new machine would perform the adjustment function now done by the Meter Division. This would enable the Meter Division to scrap the adjustment machine (Machine 2) and reduce the direct-labor hours per setmeter in the Adjustment Department from 10 hours to 6 hours. (Since only part of the adjustment is performed by Machine 2, the department will not be completely eliminated.) The salvage value of the adjustment machine (Machine 2) is $100,000 now, but if this machine were operated for five more years, the salvage value would be zero.

The new assembly machine would also allow the Module Division to reduce its direct labor on the guidance module from 12 hours to 10 hours. The Module Division could also scrap the old assembly machine (Machine 3). This old machine has a net salvage value now of $200,000. If the old assembly machine (Machine 3) were operated for another five years, the net salvage value would equal zero.

The new assembly machine is expected to have a useful life of five years. In contrast to the straight-line depreciation being used for tax purposes on Machines 1, 2, and 3, the Heedlock Company will use sum-of-the-years'-digits depreciation on the new machine for tax purposes over the five-year period. The investment cost is $2,250,000, and the estimated salvage value five years hence is zero.

The Module Division has not been carrying an inventory of setmeters but now feels that a safety-stock inventory will have to be established if the breakage rate continues, since the breakage does not occur evenly throughout the production period. The manager of the Meter Division has indicated that 1,000 setmeters would be an appropriate level. This safety-stock inventory would be at a constant level throughout the five years, but could be sold separately for a lump sum without loss at the end of that time. If the modernization program is not undertaken, there will be no delay in normal production to produce the needed 1,000 units of safety stock. The entire plant is ordinarily shut down for a two-week Christmas vacation. However, the crews required to produce the safety stock (so as to have the inventory available at the beginning of the year) have agreed to shift the timing of their vacations. This would make it possible to use the shut-down period to produce the inventory at the ordinary production costs, thus avoiding any abnormal costs. The physical storage and handling costs of this inventory are considered negligible. Of course, if the production process is modernized, the safety-stock inventory is not necessary.

required

Prepare *a net present-value* analysis to advise the president of the Heedlock Space Company on whether to proceed with the modernization program. Use a 12 percent after-tax cost of capital and a 40 percent tax rate in your analysis. In your analysis, you may assume that all annual cash flows and their related income tax effects take place at the end of the year in question and that any investment-type cash flows take place at the beginning of the first year. You may also assume that the annual demand for guidance modules will remain at 1,500 per year for the next five years.

Inventory Planning, Control, and Valuation

14

There is an optimum level of investment for any asset, whether it be cash, physical plant, or inventories. For example, even cash balances may be too large or too small. The principal cost of having too much cash is the sacrifice of earnings; idle cash earns nothing. The principal cost of having too little cash may be lost discounts on purchases or harm to one's credit standing. For every asset class, then, there is a conceptual optimum investment that, when considered with optimum levels in other asset classes, helps to maximize long-run profits.

The major goal of "inventory control" is to discover and maintain the optimum level of inventory investment.[1] Two limits must be imposed in controlling inventory levels, because there are two danger points that management usually wants to avoid. The first danger, that of inadequate inventories, disrupts production and may lose sales. The second danger, excessive inventories, introduces unnecessary carrying costs and obsolescence risks. The optimum inventory level lies somewhere between the two danger points. Our major purpose in this

[1] Throughout this chapter, the term "inventory control" will refer to both planning inventory investment and implementing the plans.

chapter will be to see how this optimum inventory level is computed and maintained. We shall also consider the various methods of inventory valuation.

characteristics of inventories

need for inventories

If production and delivery of goods were instantaneous, there would be no need for inventories except as a hedge against price changes. Despite the marvels of computers, automation, and scientific management, the manufacturing and merchandising processes still do not function quickly enough to avoid the need for having inventories. Inventories must be maintained so that the customer may be serviced immediately, or at least quickly enough so that he does not turn to another source of supply. In turn, production operations cannot flow smoothly without having inventories of work in process, direct materials, finished parts, and supplies.

Inventories are cushions (a) to absorb planning errors and unforeseen fluctuations in supply and demand, and (b) to facilitate smooth production and marketing operations. Further, inventories help isolate or minimize the interdependence of all parts of the organization (for example, departments or functions) so that each may work effectively. For example, many parts and subassemblies may be purchased or manufactured, stored, and used as needed.

inventory records and control

Inventory records are only a means to the end of inventory control. A company may have thousands of impressive stores cards whose balances are always in precise agreement with physical counts taken in its immaculate storeroom. The requisition, purchasing, receiving, and material-handling duties may be at peak efficiency. But despite errorless paper shuffling and diligent employees, inventory control may still be inadequate. Management's major duty with respect to inventory control is not clerical accuracy. (In many cases, it is possible to attain excellent inventory control through visual inspection rather than through elaborate perpetual-inventory records.) The major inventory-control problem is to maximize profitability by balancing inventory investment against what is required to sustain smooth operations. Note that profitability can also take the form of minimizing costs in nonprofit organizations; for instance, problems of inventory investment extend to hospitals and the armed forces.

relevant costs for inventory decisions

In most instances, the total costs of an inventory policy consist of:

$$\text{Total ordering cost} + \text{Total carrying cost} + \text{Total acquisition cost}$$

The ordering costs usually consist of clerical costs of preparing a purchase order or production order and special processing and receiving costs relating to the number of *orders* processed.

The carrying costs usually consist of a desired rate of return on the investment in inventory and costs of storage space, breakage, obsolescence, deterioration, insurance, and personal property taxes.

The most obvious costs—those of *acquiring* the stock through buying or manufacturing—are usually unaffected by various inventory policies unless quantity discounts are available. For instance, whether total annual requirements of 3,000 units are purchased at $1.00 each in thirty 100-unit lots or in three 1,000-unit lots may affect the costs of ordering or carrying, but the total *acquisition* cost will be $3,000 under each alternative.

When such acquisition costs are the same for many alternatives, they are irrelevant and are often excluded from the decision model that determines inventory policy. Thus, the relevant costs are most often confined to ordering costs and carrying costs. These two costs behave in opposite ways. For example, if huge inventories are carried, ordering costs will be low and carrying costs will be high. Some of the difficulties of measuring these costs will be discussed later. First, consider the rudiments of the inventory decision.

choice of order quantity

The objective of inventory decisions is usually to minimize the total relevant costs. Two central decisions must be faced in designing an inventory control system: (a) How much should we buy (or manufacture) at a time? (b) When should we buy (or manufacture)?

how much to order?

A key factor in inventory policy is computing the optimum size of either a normal purchase order for raw materials or a shop order for a production run. This optimum size is called the *economic order quantity (EOQ)*, the size that will result in minimum total annual costs of the item in question.

example 1

A refrigerator manufacturer buys certain steel shelving in sets from outside suppliers at $4.00 per set. Total annual needs are 5,000 sets at a rate of 20 sets per working day.

The following cost data are available:

Desired annual return on inventory investment, 10% × $4.00	$.40	
Rent, insurance, taxes, per unit per year	.10	
Carrying costs per unit per year		$ .50
Costs per purchase order:		
Clerical costs, stationery, postage, telephone, etc.		$10.00

What is the economic order quantity?

SOLUTION

Exhibit 14-1 shows a tabulation of total costs under various alternatives. The column with the least cost will indicate the economic order quantity.

Exhibit 14-1 shows minimum costs at two levels, 400 and 500 units. The next step would be to see if costs are lower somewhere between 400 and 500 units—say, at 450 units:

Average inventory, 225 × $.50	= $113	Carrying costs
Number of orders (5,000/450), 11.1 × $10 =	111	Purchase-order costs
	$224	Total annual relevant costs

The dollar differences here are extremely small, but the approach is important. The same approach may be shown in graphic form. See Exhibit 14-2. Note that, in this case, the graph shows that total cost is at a minimum where total purchase-order cost and total carrying cost are equal.

EXHIBIT 14-1

ANNUALIZED RELEVANT COSTS OF VARIOUS STANDARD ORDERS

(250 Working Days)

SYMBOLS					*LEAST COST* ↓	*LEAST COST* ↓				
E	Order size	50	100	200	400	500	600	800	1,000	5,000
E/2	Average inventory in units*	25	50	100	200	250	300	400	500	2,500
A/E	Number of purchase orders†	100	50	25	12.5	10	8.3	6.7	5	1
S(E/2)	Annual carrying cost @ $.50	$ 13	$ 25	$ 50	$100	$125	$150	$200	$ 250	$1,250
P(A/E)	Annual purchase-order cost @ $10.00	1,000	500	250	125	100	83	67	50	10
C	Total annual relevant costs	$1,013	$525	$300	$225	$225	$233	$267	$ 300	$1,260

E = Order size
A = Annual quantity used in units: 5,000
S = Annual cost of carrying one unit in stock one year: $.50
P = Cost per purchase order: $10.00
C = Total annual relevant costs

* Assume that stock is zero when each order arrives. (Even if a certain minimum inventory were assumed, it has no bearing on the choice here as long as the minimum is the same for each alternative.) Therefore, the average inventory relevant to the problem will be one-half the order quantity. For example, if 600 units are purchased, the inventory on arrival will contain 600. It will gradually diminish until no units are on hand. The average inventory would be 300; the carrying cost, $.50 × 300 or $150.

† Number to meet the total annual need for 5,000 sets.

order-size formula The graphic approach can be expressed in formula form (derived via calculus).[2] The total annual relevant cost (for any case, not just this example) is differentiated with respect to order size. Where this derivative is zero, the minimum annual cost is attained. The widely used formula approach to the order-size problem may be expressed in a variety of ways, one of which follows:

$$E = \sqrt{\frac{2AP}{S}}$$

where E = order size; A = annual quantity used in units; P = cost per purchase order; and S = annual cost of carrying one unit in stock for one year.

Substituting:

$$E = \sqrt{\frac{2(5{,}000)(\$10)}{\$.50}} = \sqrt{\frac{\$100{,}000}{\$.50}} = \sqrt{200{,}000}$$
$$= 448, \text{ the economic order quantity}$$

As we may expect, the order size gets larger as A or P gets bigger or as S gets smaller.

Another widely used formula is for computing total relevant costs. The formula is applicable **at the EOQ level only.** As Exhibit 14-1 shows:

$$C = \frac{AP}{E} + \frac{ES}{2},$$

which attains its minimum value when E is set at the optimal EOQ value:[3]

[2] The formula may be derived by expressing the tabular and graphic approaches as follows:

(1) $C = \frac{AP}{E} + \frac{ES}{2}$

(2) $\frac{dC}{dE} = \frac{-AP}{E^2} + \frac{S}{2}$

(3) Set $\frac{dC}{dE} = 0$; $\frac{S}{2} - \frac{AP}{E^2} = 0$

(4) $SE^2 = 2AP$

(5) $E^2 = \frac{2AP}{S}$

(6) $E = \sqrt{\frac{2AP}{S}}$

[3] Derivation:

$$C = \frac{AP}{E} + \frac{ES}{2}$$

Multiply by $2E/2E$ to get common denominator, and combine terms:

$$C = \frac{AP(2E)}{E(2E)} + \frac{ES(2E)}{2(2E)} = \frac{2AP}{2E} + \frac{E^2S}{2E} = \frac{2AP + E^2S}{2E} \qquad (1)$$

Substitute $E = \sqrt{2AP/S}$:

$$C_{min} = \frac{2AP + \frac{2AP}{S}S}{2\sqrt{\frac{2AP}{S}}} = \frac{4AP}{2\sqrt{\frac{2AP}{S}}} = \frac{2AP}{\sqrt{\frac{2AP}{S}}} = 2AP\,\frac{\sqrt{S}}{\sqrt{2AP}} = \sqrt{2APS} \qquad (2)$$

$$C_{min} = \sqrt{2APS}$$

Substituting:

$$C_{min} = \sqrt{2(5{,}000)(\$10)(\$.50)} = \sqrt{50{,}000} = \$224$$

EXHIBIT 14-2

GRAPHIC SOLUTION OF ECONOMIC ORDER QUANTITY

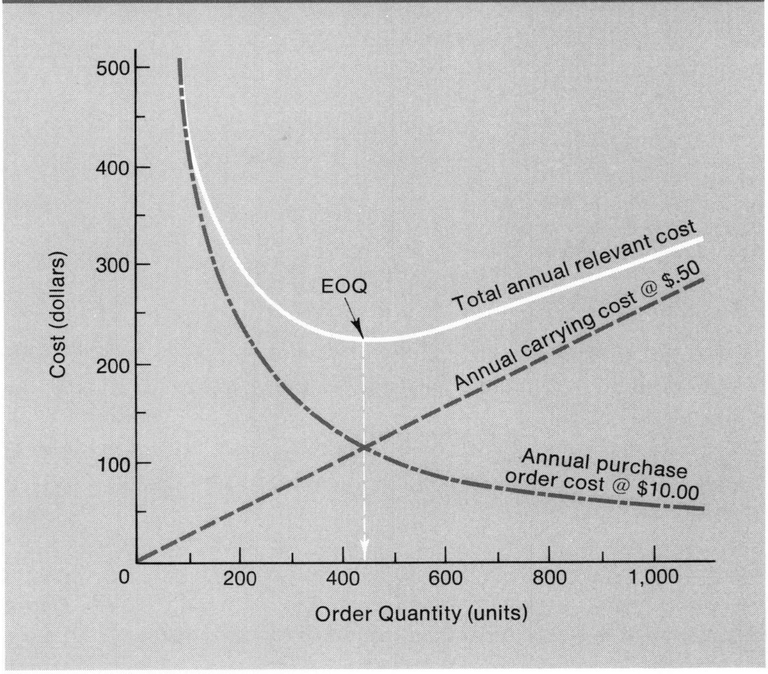

implications for accountants

cost estimates and prediction errors

The EOQ model and its variations are obviously affected by the cost estimates used. However, as Exhibit 14-2 shows, the total curve tends to flatten so that the total costs are affected very little by errors in the approximations of unit costs. Thus, a salient feature of inventory decisions is that they are rarely affected by minor variations in cost estimates. For example, suppose the carrying cost was erroneously predicted wildly at 50¢ instead of the correct cost of, say, $1.60. Even then, the cost of the prediction error would be $70, an error that is less than 18 percent of the optimal financial result of $400:

1. Original decision, given original prediction: order size of 448.
2. Results of optimal decision, given alternative parameter: order size changed from 448 to 250:[4]

$$E = \sqrt{\frac{2AP}{S}} = 250$$

$$C = \frac{AP}{E} + \frac{ES}{2}$$

$$= \frac{5{,}000(\$10)}{250} + \frac{250(\$1.60)}{2} = \$200 + \$200 = \qquad \$-400$$

3. Actual cost, given original choice of 11.1 orders of 448 units each, but using alternative cost of \$1.60 rather than \$.50:

$$C = \frac{AP}{E} + \frac{ES}{2}$$

$$= \frac{5{,}000(\$10)}{448} + \frac{448(\$1.60)}{2}$$

$$= \$112 + \$358 = \qquad -470$$

4. Cost of prediction error, item 2 − item 3: \$ 70

impact on human behavior

A fascinating aspect of inventory management is the possible conflict between what the decision model might indicate as the optimal action and what the manager might perceive as optimal. Managers are frequently governed by how their performance is evaluated, and the formal accounting system may record some inventory-related costs but ignore others, although they may be relevant.

Reconsider Exhibit 14-1. Note that if annual carrying costs were not charged to the manager in any way, he would be induced toward larger order sizes, even though they may be uneconomic from the viewpoint of the entire firm. For example, a production manager prefers longer (and less frequent) production runs because they will tend to reduce the total annual costs charged to him, although larger inventories must be carried to bridge the gaps between production runs.

Of course, the answer to this conflict is to design the performance evaluation system so that the carrying costs are charged to the appropriate manager even though all such costs are not recorded by the ordinary accounting system. Thus, we frequently see systems where an "imputed interest" charge is levied against managers for the inventories under their responsibility. This practice also inhibits managers from overbuying stocks at "bargain" prices.

[4] Or $C = \sqrt{2APS} = \sqrt{2(5{,}000)(\$10)(\$1.60)} = \sqrt{\$160{,}000} = \$400$. Again note that this shortcut formula is valid *only* at the optimum EOQ level. That is why it is not used in step 3. See the section "Cost of Prediction Error" in Chapter 3 for a fuller description of sensitivity analysis. Also see the section "Dealing with Uncertainty" in Chapter 12.

The inventory area provides another illustration of why accountants and managers must be alert to the motivational implications of failing to dovetail a performance-evaluation accounting model with the decision model that is favored by top management. The conventional accounting model is rarely made dependent on the decision model; instead, it focuses on a multiplicity of "events" or "transactions" that often simultaneously affect many programs or projects in an organization.

Note, too, that no judgment is being made here concerning this conflict of decision models and the commonly encountered accounting model. Again, we must apply the cost-benefit perspective. Is it worthwhile to redesign the conventional accounting model so that it is dependent on an assortment of formal decision models? Obviously, the resulting accounting model would be far more intricate and costly. Whether such improvements are worth their cost will clearly vary from situation to situation and organization to organization.

Of course, the point of this discussion is that accountants and managers must be alert to the differences in motivations, results, and decisions that arise from the variety of existing decision models and performance-evaluation models.

difficulties of cost estimation

As has been stated, opportunity costs often do not explicitly appear on formal accounting records. Examples are foregone quantity discounts,[5] foregone contributions to profit from sales lost because of inventory shortages, and foregone fortuitous purchases because existing stock inhibits additional acquisitions. Even if these costs were easy to identify, their measurement would be often subject to dispute. Perhaps the clearest example of this difficulty is measuring the impact of being out of stock. What is the financial impact when a disgruntled customer vows to buy elsewhere forever more?

The size of many relevant costs will differ, depending on the length of time under consideration and the specific alternative uses of resources. For example, if storage space is owned and cannot be used for other profitable purposes, differential space costs are zero. But if the space may be used for other productive activities, or if there is rental cost geared to the space occupied, a pertinent cost of space usage for inventory purposes must be recognized.

To the extent that money is invested in inventories, there is an interest cost of carrying stock. But how is this to be measured? In practice, this rate may be based on current borrowing rates, the long-run average cost of capital, or

[5] Quantity discounts affect unit prices; in general, the bigger the order, the lower the unit price. The price usually falls between brackets; within each bracket a uniform unit price prevails.

The basic formula used previously can be adapted to such situations, but its complexities will not be described further here. For our purposes the following approach will be easiest to understand.

First, compute annual basic expenses in the manner illustrated in Exhibit 14-1. Then merely add the additional expenses of *foregoing* quantity discounts. The economic order will, of course, be the one that offers the lowest total annual relevant costs.

some "appropriate" rate selected by management. The proper rate should depend on investment opportunities available to management; it may be small or large, depending on specific circumstances.

Other costs that may or may not be relevant to policy decisions include overtime premiums on rush orders that would be unnecessary if bigger inventories were carried, idle time caused by material shortages, emergency expediting, extra transportation costs (for example, air freight), extra physical-count taking, obsolescence risks, and extra moving and handling costs.

As in any policy-making situation, inventory costs that are common to all alternatives are irrelevant and may be ignored. Costs that are often irrelevant because they will not be affected by the inventory decision include salaries of stores record clerks, storekeepers, and material handlers, depreciation on building and equipment, and fixed rent.

In practice, however, for purposes of inventory planning most of the wage costs are unitized on a per-order or a per-unit-handled basis. Thus they are regarded as fully variable costs. Whether this is justified depends on specific circumstances. Surely the cost of processing 4,000 orders per period will be strikingly greater than the cost of processing 1,000 orders. The basic question is often whether in the same situation, the cost of processing 3,400 orders will be notably different from the cost of processing 3,000 orders. This is simply another example of the importance of determining what is relevant to any given decision-making situation.[6]

safety stocks

when to order?

Although we have seen how to compute EOQ, we have not yet considered another key decision: When to order? This question is easy to answer only if we know the *lead time,* the time interval between placing an order and receiving delivery, know the EOQ, and are *certain* of demand during lead time. The graph in Exhibit 14-3 will clarify the relationships among the following facts:

Economic order quantity	448 sets of steel shelving
Lead time	2 weeks
Average usage	100 sets per week

Exhibit 14-3, Part A, shows that the *reorder point*—the quantity level that automatically triggers a new order—is dependent on expected usage during lead time; that is, if shelving is being used at a rate of 100 sets per week and the

[6] It is easy to criticize various mathematical approaches to problems of inventory control on the grounds that the relevant costs are impossible to measure. But such criticisms are invalid in nearly all situations. Optimum inventory policies can be achieved without knowledge of "true costs." For an interesting discussion, see D. W. Miller and M. K. Starr, *Executive Decisions and Operations Research,* 2nd ed. (Englewood Cliffs, N.J.; Prentice-Hall, Inc., 1969), pp. 328–36.

EXHIBIT 14-3

DEMAND IN RELATION TO INVENTORY LEVELS

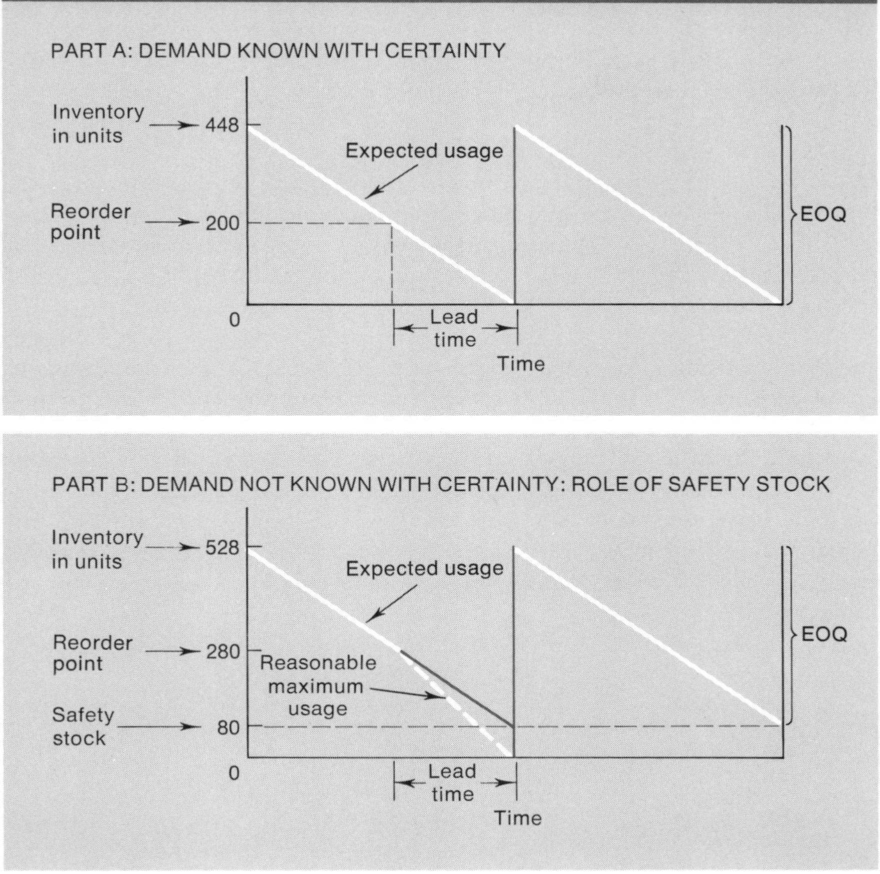

lead time is two weeks, a new order would be placed when the inventory level reaches 200 sets.

minimum inventory: safety allowance for fluctuations in demand

Our previous example assumed that 100 sets would be used per week—a demand pattern that was known with certainty. Businesses are seldom blessed with such accurate forecasting. Instead, demand may fluctuate from day to day, from week to week, or from month to month. Thus, the company will run out of stock if there are sudden spurts in usage beyond 100 per week, delays in processing orders, or delivery delays. Obviously, then, nearly all companies must provide for some safety stock—some minimum or buffer inventory as a cushion against reasonable expected maximum usage. Part B of Exhibit 14-3 is based on the same facts as Part A, except that reasonable expected *maximum* usage is 140 sets per week. The safety stock might be, say, 80 sets (excess usage of 40 sets per week × 2 weeks). The reorder point is commonly computed as safety stock plus the average usage during the lead time.[7]

computation of safety stock

In our example, we used 80 sets as a safety stock. The computation of safety stocks hinges on demand forecasts. The executive will have some notion—usually based on past experience—of the range of daily demand: what percentage of chance (probability) exists for usages of various quantities.

A frequency distribution based on prior daily or weekly changes in demand will offer data for constructing the associated costs of maintaining safety (minimum) stocks. The major relevant costs are: the *carrying costs,* which are primarily interest on investment, obsolescence write-offs, and space costs; and the *stockout costs,* which include expensive expediting, loss of contribution margins, and loss of customer goodwill. The latter costs are difficult to measure, but statisticians and mathematicians have used statistical probability techniques on this problem with some success.[8] The optimum safety-stock level exists where the costs of carrying an extra unit are exactly counterbalanced by the expected stockout costs.

For instance, suppose that the total usage over a two-week period is expected to be:

								Total Probability
Total usage	80	120	160	200	240	280	320	
Probability	.04	.06	.20	.40	.20	.06	.04	1.00

Thus, the probabilities of stockouts at four levels of safety stocks would be:

[7] This handy but special formula does not apply where the receipt of the standard order fails to increase stocks to the order-point quantity; for example, where the lead time is three months and the standard order is a one-month supply. In these cases, there will be overlapping of orders. The order point will be average usage during lead time plus safety stock *minus orders placed but not yet received.* This is really the general formula for computing the reorder point. In most cases, a simplified version is used because the last term in the general formula is zero. For elaboration, see almost any book on inventory systems.

[8] Inventory theory advances the idea that the rational entrepreneur should attempt to vary his inventory levels with the square root of sales rather than with sales. This is based on the relationships expressed in the economic-lot-size formula, discussed earlier, where the optimum lot size increased in proportion to the square root of the annual quantity used. See G. Hadley and T. M. Whitin, *Analysis of Inventory Systems* (Englewood Cliffs, N.J.: Prentice-Hall, Inc); and M. K. Starr and D. W. Miller, *Inventory Control* (Englewood Cliffs, N.J.: Prentice-Hall, Inc.).

Probability	.20	.06	.04
Total actual usage	240	280	320
Less average expected usage provided for	200	200	200
Stockouts if safety stock is:			
zero units	40	80	120
40 units	0	40	80
80 units	0	0	40
120 units	0	0	0

Suppose further that a stockout cost is estimated at $.60 per unit. Recall that the average carrying cost is $.50 per unit. Of the four safety-stock levels considered, Exhibit 14-4 shows that the total costs are minimized at $51, when a safety stock of 80 units is maintained.

The most difficult cost to determine is *stockout cost,* consisting mainly of the foregone present and future contribution to profit from losing an order because of lack of inventory:

> But if there is no demand during the period an item is out of stock, there is no lost profit, and reliable information on unfilled demand is seldom maintained. Where there is unfilled demand, but the customer is willing to wait or accept a substitute, there

EXHIBIT 14-4

COMPUTATION OF SAFETY STOCK

SAFETY-STOCK LEVELS IN UNITS	PROBABILITY	STOCKOUT COSTS: STOCKOUT IN UNITS	STOCKOUT COST[a]	ORDERS PER YEAR[b]	EXPECTED STOCKOUT COST[c]	CARRYING COST[d]	TOTAL COSTS
0	.20	40	$24	11.2	$ 54		
	.06	80	48	11.2	32		
	.04	120	72	11.2	32		
					$118	$ 0	$118
40	.06	40	24	11.2	$ 16		
	.04	80	48	11.2	22		
					$ 38	$20	$ 58
80	.04	40	24	11.2	$ 11	$40	$ 51
120	0	0	0	11.2	$ 0	$60	$ 60

[a] Stockout units × stockout cost of $.60 per unit.
[b] Annual consumption 5,000 ÷ 448 EOQ = 11.2 orders per year.
[c] Stockout cost × probability × number of orders per year.
[d] Safety stock × annual carrying cost of 50¢ per unit.

may be no immediate loss of profit. But there may be loss of future business as a result of dissatisfied customers. Because of these difficulties, most of the practical inventory-management systems specify a customer service level (percentage of items in stock) that they wish to meet rather than trying to minimize a total cost that includes stock-out cost.[9]

Instead of estimating a cost of stockouts, some managers may stipulate a maximum probability of being out of stock. In our example, a manager may choose to maintain a safety stock of 80 units, so that there would be a probability of only 4 percent of not meeting all demands.[10]

emphasis on optimality

Note that the emphasis in this chapter is on the word *optimum,* not *minimum.* Contrast this with the commonly used index of inventory management—inventory turnover, the number of times the average inventory is sold or used in a year. The traditional rule has been, "The higher the turnover, the better the inventory management." Consider the following comments:

> An infinite turnover can be achieved by carrying no inventory whatsoever. But such an inventory policy would not be a good policy because a company with no inventory would be continuously buying, expediting. . . . Turnover is worth improving, yes, but only if there is no substantial increase in ordering cost and only if there is no substantial loss of sales resulting from excessive stockouts.[11]

control classifications: the abc method

Sometimes it is difficult to comprehend the enormous number of items that companies must keep in stock—up to 50,000, and often more. An effective inventory-control system will not have all items in the inventory treated in the same manner under the same control techniques. For example, some items are often controlled by the "two-bin" system. Some companies do not bother maintaining perpetual-inventory cards; instead, two bins are kept, and after the first bin is emptied, a withdrawal from the second bin is used to signal the need for a reorder. Or physical control is exercised through having a red line painted in

[9] N.A.A. Research Report No. 40, *Techniques in Inventory Management,* p. 14.

[10] The foregoing discussion of inventory control revolved around the so-called two-bin or constant order-quantity system: When inventory levels recede to *X*, then order *Y*. There is another widely used model in practice, the constant order-cycle system. The reorder date is fixed, and the quantity ordered depends on the usage since the previous order and the outlook during the lead time.

The minimization of the total associated costs of inventories is still the prime objective, regardless of the system used. For an expanded discussion, see any book on inventory systems.

[11] Joseph Buchan and Ernest Koenigsberg, *Scientific Inventory Management* (Englewood Cliffs, N.J.: Prentice-Hall, Inc.), p. 90.

a bin at a reorder level. Another example would be keeping reorder quantities in a special package; when this package is finally opened, an attached purchase requisition for replenishment is immediately forwarded to the purchasing department.

Many companies find it useful to divide materials, parts, supplies, and finished goods into subclassifications for purposes of stock control. For example, Exhibit 14-5 shows direct materials, which are subclassified in step-by-step fashion by (a) itemizing total annual purchase cost of each item needed and (b) grouping in decreasing order of annual consumption cost. This technique is often called the *ABC method,* although it also has other labels.

The final A, B, C classification in Exhibit 14-5 demonstrates that only 10 percent of the items represent 72 percent of the total cost. In general, the greatest degree of continuous control would be exerted over these A items, which account for high annual consumption costs and correspondingly high investment in inventories. This type of control would mean frequent ordering, low safety stocks, and a willingness to incur expediting costs on A items, because the costs of placing and following up orders are relatively low in comparison with costs of carrying excess inventories. At the other extreme, where the total yearly

EXHIBIT 14-5

ABC ANALYSIS OF MATERIAL INVENTORY

Step 1. Multiply average usage times unit price to obtain total cost:

ITEM	*AVERAGE USAGE*	*UNIT PRICE*	*TOTAL CONSUMPTION COST (SEE NOTE)*
H20	10,000	$10.00	$100,000
H21	1,000	.05	50
H22	10,000	.02	200
H23	11,000	1.00	11,000
H24	110,000	.10	11,000
(and so forth)			

Step 2. Group items above in descending order of total consumption cost and then divide into three classes:

	ITEMS		*DOLLARS*	
CLASS	*NUMBER OF ITEMS*	*PERCENT OF TOTAL*	*TOTAL COST*	*PERCENT OF TOTAL*
A	5,000	10%	$14,400,000	72%
B	10,000	20%	3,800,000	19%
C	35,000	70%	1,800,000	9%
	50,000	100%	$20,000,000	100%

Note: The total annual cost of raw materials consumed is dependent on two main factors: physical quantity needed and cost per unit. It is the *total* cost rather than the *unit* cost that matters. Thus, 11,000 units @ $1.00 requires the same investment as 110,000 units @ $.10.

purchase cost is relatively low, there would be less frequent ordering, higher safety stocks, and less paper work (C items).

Type A and B items are ordered according to budget schedules prepared by a production-planning department.[12] Essentially, sales forecasts are the cornerstone for production scheduling.[13] In turn, these production schedules are "exploded" (a commonly used term for giving detailed breakdowns of data) into the various direct-material, parts, and supply components. These explosions result in purchase schedules for major items. The purchase schedules are adjusted for lead times, planned changes in inventories, and normal waste and spoilage. Purchases are made accordingly, and follow-ups are instituted by the purchasing department as needed. In other words, Type A and B items are budgeted almost on a hand-to-mouth basis, because carrying costs are too high to warrant inventories that are sizable in terms of many days' usage.

Stores cards are usually kept for Type A and B items. Such cards increasingly carry physical-unit balance only. More managements are becoming doubtful that the added clerical costs of carrying actual unit prices on stores cards are worthwhile.

the mechanics of the system

fixing responsibility

As a business becomes more complex, the interdependent problems of production planning and inventory control become imposing enough to warrant appointing an executive to assume sole responsibility for implementing a coordinated inventory-control policy. The scope of this position varies from company to company. In some firms, he may be a vice-president in charge of production planning and control. In other firms, the planning and control functions may be separated. Duties of purchasing, receiving, and storing may be the responsibility of a single executive, although day-to-day duties may be delegated to various officers, such as a purchasing agent, a receiving-room foreman, and a storeroom foreman.

An important aspect of inventory and production control systems is that they may be largely dehumanized. For example, when reorder points, economic order quantities, safety stocks, and other technicalities are calculated, the entire system may be automated with the help of a digital computer. The system can then operate with a minimum dependence on human judgment. That is why inventory-control systems are being increasingly computerized. However, human judgment cannot be eradicated altogether. The ingredients (costs,

[12] The Ford Motor Company uses four inventory classes and keeps two days' supply of A items; five days' supply of B; 10 days' supply of C; and 20 or more days' supply of D items.

[13] An effective production planning and control system is an intricate mechanism. It depends on accurate demand forecasts expressed in units of production capacity, a production budget that establishes inventory levels and production activity, and a control procedure for adjusting inventory levels when errors in the demand forecast cause inventories to exceed or fall below budget.

demand) of the model do frequently change, and a constant surveillance for the sensitivity of the model to such changes is an important, and not too automatic, part of an effective control system.

internal check Just as in production operations, inventory-control procedures should be systematized in order to promote efficiency and reduce errors, fraud, and waste. Commonly followed internal-control rules[14] should be applied in setting up an inventory system. For example, the stores record clerk should not have access to the physical storeroom, nor should the storeroom employees have access to the formal stores records.

There is a temptation at this point to discuss a typical company system in detail, including descriptions of the routing of multicopies of requisitions, purchase orders, vouchers, invoices, and receiving reports. However, we shall refrain from such a detailed study because (a) such descriptions belong in a book on accounting systems, (b) each system must be tailored to the specific needs of a company, and (c) dwelling on details of paper work often beclouds the important general concepts that need the spotlight.

purchase records The purchasing department is responsible for getting favorable prices, following up irregularities, using approved suppliers, and taking advantage of discounts. Separate, sequential records for each item may be kept by purchase lots, showing dates, source, quantity, unit price, total costs, discounts, and special remarks. Thus, all pertinent data for control are kept on a current basis at the point where control is supposed to be exercised.

The paperwork routine for purchasing and receiving is shown in Exhibit 14-6. Purchasing agents should be free to devote their energies to obtaining optimum prices, investigating sources, and studying market conditions. Their buying should be triggered strictly by purchase requisitions. In general, inventory levels and purchase requisitions are ultimately the responsibility of production planning and control, not of the purchasing department.

factory usage An effective method of controlling material usage was described in Chapter 8, but we shall summarize it here. Production-planning departments or foremen present standard bills (requisitions) of materials, including allowances for normal spoilage, to the storeroom. If standards are not met, different-colored or coded excess-materials requisitions are used to obtain additional materials. These should be routed to the foreman's superior so that immediate follow-up may be made. Any materials left over are returned to the storeroom by inspectors or foremen.

[14] For a discussion of internal control, see Chapter 21.

EXHIBIT 14-6

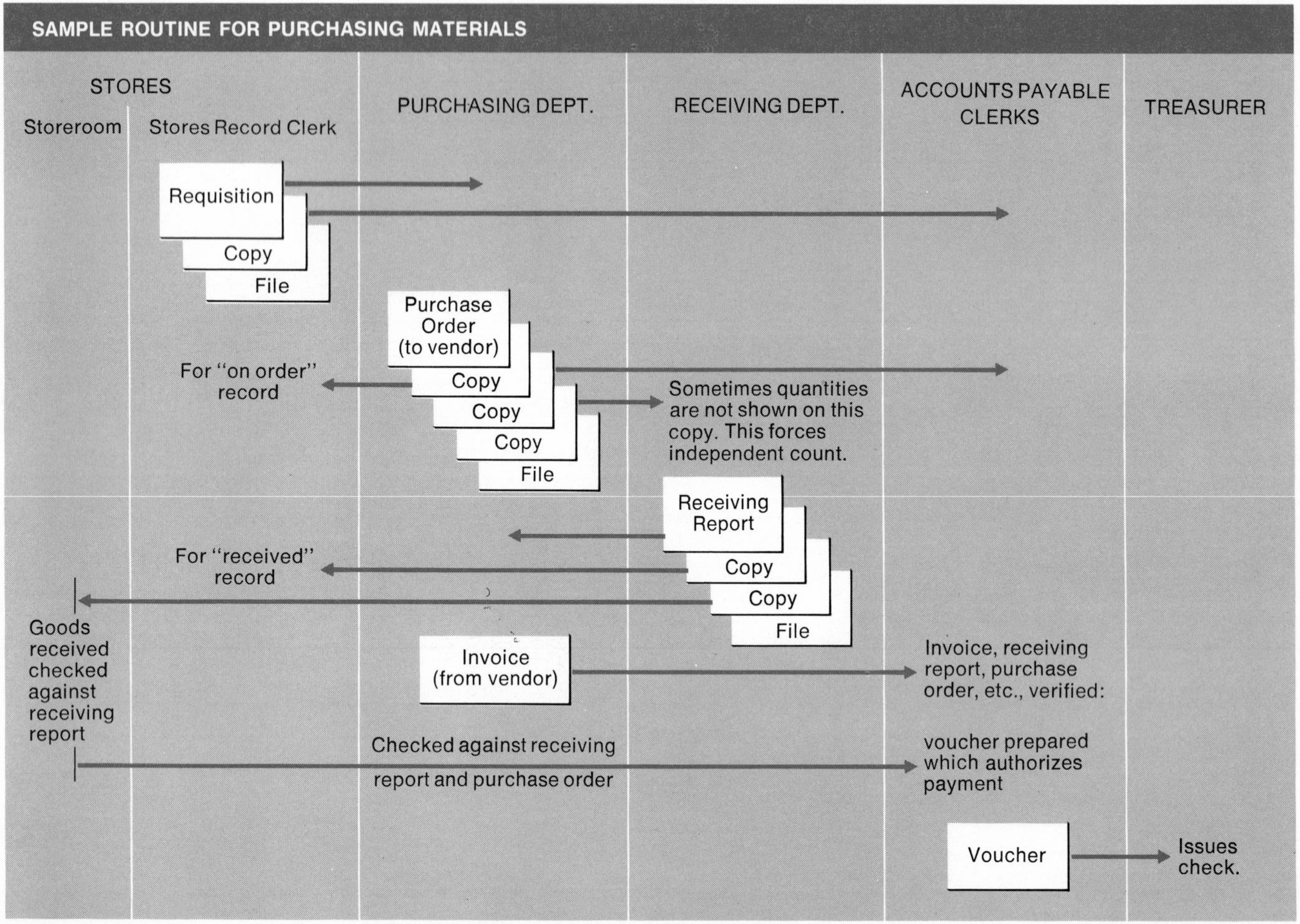

SAMPLE ROUTINE FOR PURCHASING MATERIALS
STORES
Storeroom
Stores Record Clerk
PURCHASING DEPT.
RECEIVING DEPT.
ACCOUNTS PAYABLE CLERKS
TREASURER
Requisition
Copy
File
Purchase Order (to vendor)
Copy
Copy
Copy
File
For "on order" record
Sometimes quantities are not shown on this copy. This forces independent count.
Receiving Report
Copy
Copy
File
For "received" record
Goods received checked against receiving report
Invoice (from vendor)
Invoice, receiving report, purchase order, etc., verified:
Checked against receiving report and purchase order
voucher prepared which authorizes payment
Voucher
Issues check.

inventory-valuation methods

purpose of discussion of inventory methods

Management makes policy decisions, at one time or another, regarding methods of inventory valuation. These decisions are important because they directly affect the way income will be computed.

We have already seen how price fluctuations in inventories are accounted for under standard costing. The following discussion surveys alternate approaches to valuation of identical materials acquired at various prices.[15] The intention here is to demonstrate methodology rather than to dwell on important theoretical issues of inventory valuation that are discussed at length in typical introductory, intermediate, and advanced accounting texts. Also, the influence of income taxes, which is immense, is not discussed at length here.

the question of timing

With few exceptions, the differences between inventory methods are merely ones of timing cost releases in relation to income determination.[16] In short, when do inventory costs become expenses? Where it is impractical to link inventories with specific usage or sales, some assumption is made for transferring certain costs out of inventory. The most commonly used assumption is one of the following three:

1. *First-in, first-out (FIFO).* The earliest-acquired stock is assumed to be used first; the latest-acquired stock is assumed to be still on hand.
2. *Last-in, first-out (LIFO).* The earliest-acquired stock is assumed to be still on hand; the latest-acquired stock is assumed to have been used immediately. The LIFO method releases the most recent (or last) inventory costs as cost of goods used or sold. It attempts to match the most current cost of obtaining inventory against sales for a period. As compared to FIFO, the use of LIFO will tend to result in less reported net income during periods of rising prices and more income in periods of falling prices.
3. Some version of an *average-inventory method.* An example would be the *moving-average method,* whereby each purchase is lumped with the former inventory balance so that a new average unit price is used to price subsequent issues of inventory. This method may be used with a perpetual-inventory system. A *weighted-average method* is often used with a periodic-inventory system; this average is computed by dividing the total cost of the beginning inventory plus purchases by the total number of units in those two classes. These methods are best understood through illustration.

example 2

Try to solve the problem yourself before consulting the answers that follow. (Adapted from a C.P.A. examination.) The Saunders Corporation uses raw material A in a manufacturing process. Information as to balances on hand,

[15] FIFO and weighted-average techniques under process costing are discussed in Chapters 18 and 19.

[16] Certain last-in, first-out inventory situations where base stocks are temporarily depleted call for departures from strict historical costing.

purchases, and requisitions of material A are given in the table below. You are to answer each question on the basis of this information.

RAW MATERIAL A

	QUANTITIES			DOLLARS			
Date	Received	Issued	Balance	Unit Price	Received	Issued	Balance
Jan. 1			100	$1.50			$150
Jan. 24	300		400	1.56	$468		
Feb. 8		80	320				
Mar. 16		140	180				
June 11	150		330	1.60	240		
Aug. 18		130	200				
Sept. 6		110	90				
Oct. 15	150		240	1.70	255		
Dec. 29		140	100				

1. If a perpetual-inventory record of material A is operated on a FIFO basis, it will show a *closing inventory* of:
   a. $150
   b. $152
   c. $159
   d. $162
   e. $170
   f. Answer not given
2. Assume that no perpetual inventory is maintained for material A, and that quantities are obtained by an annual physical count. The accounting records show information as to purchases but not as to issues. On this assumption, the *closing inventory* on a FIFO basis will be:
   a. $150
   b. $156
   c. $159
   d. $160
   e. $170
   f. Answer not given
3. If a perpetual inventory record of material A is operated on a LIFO basis, it will show a *closing inventory* of:
   a. $150
   b. $152
   c. $156
   d. $160
   e. $170
   f. Answer not given
4. Assume that no perpetual inventory is maintained for material A, and that quantities are obtained by an annual physical count. The accounting records show information as to purchases but not as to issues. On this assumption, the *closing inventory* on a LIFO basis will be:
   a. $150
   b. $152

c. $156
d. $160
e. $170
f. Answer not given

5. If a perpetual-inventory record of material A is operated on a moving-average basis, it will show a *closing inventory* that is:
   a. Lower than on the LIFO basis
   b. Lower than on the FIFO basis
   c. Higher than on the FIFO basis
   d. Answer not given
6. The exact closing inventory in question 5 is $____________________.
7. Assume that no perpetual inventory is maintained, and that quantities are obtained by an annual physical count. The accounting records show information as to purchases but not as to issues. On this assumption, the closing inventory on a weighted-average basis will be $____________________.

Answers and comments

1. (e) $170. Under FIFO, the ending-inventory valuation may be most easily obtained by first working back from the closing date until the number of units purchased equals the number of units in ending inventory. Then, by applying the appropriate unit purchase costs, the total dollar amount is obtained. In this example, 100 units @ $1.70 is $170.
2. (e) $170. The answer is identical under perpetual and periodic systems. Under a periodic inventory method, files must be combed for recent invoices until 100 units are tallied. In this case, the most recent invoice would suffice. In other cases, more than one invoice may be needed to cover the 100 units in the ending inventory.
3. (b) 90 units @ $1.50 plus 10 units @ $1.70 equals $152. Under LIFO, the ending-inventory valuation may generally be obtained by working forward from the beginning inventory until the total number of units equals the number of units in ending inventory. Then, by applying the appropriate beginning-inventory unit costs and the early current-purchase unit costs, the total dollar amount is obtained.

   However, under a perpetual LIFO method, a temporary reduction (September 6) below the number of units in the beginning inventory calls for the assignment of the base-inventory price to the number of units released from the base inventory.
4. (a) 100 units @ $1.50, or $150. Under a periodic LIFO method, a *temporary* reduction below the number of units in the beginning inventory will have no effect upon the valuation of the ending inventory as long as the number of units in the count of ending inventory for the year as a whole is at least equal to the beginning inventory.
5. (b) FIFO assigns earliest costs to cost of sales and latest costs to inventory. Unit prices have been rising during the period. Therefore, more of the earlier and lower-cost units will be contained in the ending inventory under the moving-average method than under FIFO.
6. $165.125. This technique requires the computation of a new average unit cost after each acquisition; this unit cost is used for all issues until the next purchase is made.

MOVING-AVERAGE

Perpetual Method

	RECEIVED			ISSUED			BALANCE		
Date	Units	Price	Amount	Units	Price	Amount	Units	Price	Amount
Jan. 1							100	$1.50	$150.00
Jan. 24	300	$1.56	$468				400	1.545	618.00
Feb. 8				80	$1.545	$123.60	320	1.545	494.40
Mar. 16				140	1.545	216.30	180	1.545	278.10
June 11	150	1.60	240				330	1.57	518.10
Aug. 18				130	1.57	204.10	200	1.57	314.00
Sept. 6				110	1.57	172.70	90	1.57	141.30
Oct. 15	150	1.70	255				240	1.65125	396.30
Dec. 29				140	1.65125	231.175	100	1.65125	165.125

Recapitulation

Costs to account for: $150 + $468 + $240 + $255 =	$1,113.000
Deduct: Issues	947.875
Ending balance	$ 165.125

7. $159. (100 units × $1.59.)

WEIGHTED-AVERAGE

Periodic Method

DATE	*UNITS*	*UNIT PRICE*	*DOLLARS*
Jan. 1	100	$1.50	$ 150
Jan. 24	300	1.56	468
June 11	150	1.60	240
Oct. 15	150	1.70	255
To account for	700		$1,113
Weighted unit cost, $1,113 ÷ 700 = $1.59			
Costs released		600 @ $1.59	$ 954
Costs in ending inventory		100 @ $1.59	159
Costs accounted for			$1,113

Note that the assumption of a weighted-average approach is subject to criticism because the October 15 purchase influences the costing of issues throughout the year, even though, strictly speaking, the cost of earlier issues would not have been affected by purchases made later in the year.

LIFO versus FIFO If unit prices did not fluctuate, all inventory methods would show identical results. Price changes appear in the financial records in different ways, depending on the specific inventory method used. LIFO ordinarily reflects current purchase prices in current operating results, whereas FIFO delays recognition of price effects. If price changes are volatile, year-to-year reported net incomes may differ dramatically between LIFO and FIFO approaches.

Balance-sheet presentations are also affected by the choice of LIFO or FIFO. LIFO usage tends to result in older and older, and hence less meaningful, prices being shown in inventory if stocks are stable or grow through the years, whereas FIFO tends to reflect more nearly current prices on the balance sheet.

If prices are rising, LIFO shows less income than FIFO, and thus it tends to postpone outlays for income taxes. Also, the periodic LIFO method permits immediate influencing of net income by timing of purchases, a feature that has not received the attention it deserves. For example, if prices are rising and a company desires to show less income in a given year because of income tax or other reasons, all that need be done is to buy a large amount of inventory near the end of the year—thus releasing higher costs to expense than ordinarily.

It should also be recognized that neither FIFO nor LIFO isolates and measures the effects of price fluctuations as special managerial problems. For example, when prices rise, FIFO buries price gains in the regular income figure, whereas LIFO excludes the effects of price changes from the income statement:

		LIFO		*FIFO*
Sales, 5,000 @ 20¢		$1,000		$1,000
Inventory, beginning	1,000 @ $.10 = $100		$100	
Purchases	5,000 @ $.15 = 750		750	
	$850		$850	
Inventory, ending	1,000 @ $.10 = 100	750	1,000 @ $.15 = 150	700
Gross margin		$ 250		$ 300

The $50 price gain (which is attributable to the 1,000 units in ending inventory @ $.05) is included without separate measurement in the $300 FIFO gross-margin figure and is ignored in the $250 LIFO gross-margin figure.

Here again we see the benefit of a standard-cost approach. When currently attainable standards are in use, standard costing automatically provides a measure of price "gains" or "losses" that can be reported separately on an income statement. This has two advantages: (a) it prevents price changes from influencing appraisals of efficiency in operations; (b) it spotlights and measures the impact of some price changes on overall company results.

SUMMARY

Inventory control is primarily concerned with optimizing inventory balances so that net income is maximized. Record keeping in itself is only one of the important phases of inventory control. Top management's task is to formulate inventory policies that will result in optimum inventory investment, will promote efficiency, and will avoid errors, fraud, and waste.

Associated costs that are affected by various inventory policies are headed by the opportunity cost of interest on investment. Other costs include quantity discounts, contribution margins on lost sales, space costs, overtime premiums, idle time, expediting, transportation, obsolescence, handling, training, learning, setup, order processing, order filling, personal property taxes, insurance, and handling. These costs are often difficult to isolate and measure, especially with regard to their differential behavior between alternatives. However, attempts at sensible measurement at least cast light on a *range* of optimum alternatives.

Different control policies may be applied to different segments of the inventory. Thus, a variety of purchase timing, storing, receiving, and recording techniques may be employed at the same time within the same company.

Modern mathematical methods, especially linear programming, have been applied on a wide front to the problems of production planning and inventory control. The complexity of inventory control is such that many consulting firms specialize in the area to the extent of studying a business's inventory problems and tailor-making a special slide rule for computing economic order quantities.

The subject matter of this chapter again shows how the field of managerial accounting spills over and invades allied fields, such as engineering, modern mathematics, and business policies. The complexities of modern business make it increasingly difficult to construct fences around technical specialities.

First-in, first-out, last-in, first-out, and various average methods of inventory valuation are used to contend with fluctuations in unit prices. However, none of these methods pinpoints a measure of price "gains" or "losses" that can be reported separately. Standard costing, on the other hand, does automatically provide helpful information about price changes.

PROBLEMS FOR SELF STUDY

PROBLEM 1 Review Example 1 in this chapter. Suppose the annual purchase-order cost was \$20 per order instead of \$10. What is the economic order quantity?

SOLUTION 1

$$E = \sqrt{\frac{2(5{,}000)\$20}{\$.50}} = \sqrt{\frac{\$200{,}000}{\$.50}} = \sqrt{400{,}000} = 633$$

Note that the higher the order cost, the higher the economic order quantity. This problem is an example of sensitivity analysis. The accountant or manager may be unsure about the "true" purchase-order cost, but in this case a doubling of the unit cost will only increase the economic order quantity from 448 to 633 units.

PROBLEM 2 Review the example that accompanies Exhibit 14-4.

SOLUTION 2 See the solution in Exhibit 14-4.

QUESTIONS, PROBLEMS, AND CASES

14-1 "There are two danger points that management usually wants to avoid in controlling inventories." Explain.

14-2 "Inventory records are only a means to the end of inventory control." Explain.

14-3 Certain costs associated with inventory policies do not appear on formal accounting records. Enumerate at least three.

14-4 "Identical space costs for inventory can be zero during some months and sizable during other months." Explain.

14-5 Define *economic order quantity.*

14-6 "The practical approach to determining economic order quantity is concerned with locating a minimum cost *range* rather than a minimum cost *point.*" Explain.

14-7 Define: *lead time, reorder point.*

14-8 What is a *safety stock?* What techniques are used to compute safety stocks?

14-9 Describe a "two-bin" inventory system.

14-10 What are the major responsibilities of the purchasing department?

14-11 Distinguish between the *moving-average* and the *weighted-average* inventory methods.

14-12 "Standard costing is superior to both LIFO and FIFO for isolating and measuring the effects of price fluctuations as special managerial problems." Why?

14-13 *Comparison of LIFO and FIFO* The Dowell Coal Co. does not maintain a perpetual-inventory system. The inventory of coal on June 30 shows 1,000 tons at $6 per ton. The following purchases were made during July:

July 5	2,000 Tons @ $7 per ton
July 15	500 Tons @ $8 per ton
July 25	600 Tons @ $9 per ton

A physical inventory on July 31 shows a total of 1,200 tons on hand. Revenue from sales of coal for July totals $30,000.

required

Compute the inventory value as of July 31, using:

1. LIFO—Last in, first out
2. FIFO—First in, first out

14-14 *Inventory Card, Moving-Average* (SIA) Steel Stores Limited is a dealer in steel products.

The company purchases its steel from various mills. Prices are f.o.b. point of shipment. On January 1, freight costs were $5 per ton; but on January 14, they advanced 10 percent. The steel industry uses the standard 2,000-pound ton.

During the month of January, the following transactions in hot rolled sheets, 60″ long and 36″ wide, took place:

Jan. 1	Inventory	10 tons at $6.00 per 100 lbs.
Jan. 2	Purchased	3 tons at $5.50 per 100 lbs.
Jan. 3	Sold	2 tons
Jan. 5	Purchased	2 tons at $5.60 per 100 lbs.
Jan. 6	Sold	3 tons
Jan. 10	Purchased	8 tons at $5.55 per 100 lbs.
Jan. 12	Sold	8 tons
Jan. 15	Purchased	2 tons at $5.55 per 100 lbs.
Jan. 16	Sold	2 tons
Jan. 30	Purchased	5 tons at $5.60 per 100 lbs.
Jan. 31	Sold	7 tons

Sales prices are determined by applying a markup of 30 percent to laid-down costs at the beginning of each month.

required

1. Show these transactions as they would appear on a perpetual-inventory card, using the moving-average cost method. Calculations should be made to the nearest cent.
2. Calculate the gross profit for the month.

3. Name two methods other than the moving-average cost method that could have been used in pricing the issue transactions above.

14-15 *Multiple Choice; Comparison of Inventory Methods* (CPA) The Berg Corporation began business on January 1, 19_4. Information about its inventories under different valuation methods is shown below. Using this information, you are to choose the phrase that best answers each of the following questions.

	INVENTORY			
	LIFO COST	FIFO COST	MARKET	LOWER OF COST OR MARKET
Dec. 31, 19_4	$10,200	$10,000	$ 9,600	$ 8,900
Dec. 31, 19_5	9,100	9,000	8,800	8,500
Dec. 31, 19_6	10,300	11,000	12,000	10,900

1. The inventory basis that would show the *highest net income for 19_4* is:
   a. LIFO cost c. Market
   b. FIFO cost d. Lower of cost or market
2. The inventory basis that would show the *highest net income for 19_5* is:
   a. LIFO cost c. Market
   b. FIFO cost d. Lower of cost or market
3. The inventory basis that would show the *lowest net income for the three years combined* is:
   a. LIFO cost c. Market
   b. FIFO cost d. Lower of cost or market
4. For the year 19_5, how much higher or lower would profits be on the *FIFO cost basis* than on the *lower-of-cost-or-market basis?*
   a. $400 higher e. $1,000 higher
   b. $400 lower f. $1,000 lower
   c. $600 higher g. $1,400 higher
   d. $600 lower h. $1,400 lower
5. On the basis of the information given, it appears that *the movement of prices* for items in the inventory was:
   a. Up in 19_4 and down in 19_6
   b. Up in both 19_4 and 19_6
   c. Down in 19_4 and up in 19_6
   d. Down in both 19_4 and 19_6

14-16 *Reconciliation of Inventory Records* As part of a test of inventory control, you examined the perpetual-inventory records of stockroom M. A full set of records (subsidiary and control) is maintained in the factory, while a controlling account is also kept in the accounting department.

You are required to set up a summarizing schedule in money amounts that simultaneously reflects the flow of materials (starting with initial inventory and ending with final inventory) and reconciles the accounting-department records with those of the factory in regard to opening inventory, receipts, withdrawals of materials, and ending inventory.

The items to be considered in preparing this schedule are as follows:

1. Receipts of materials in stockroom M, entered properly on factory records but treated by the accounting department as stockroom N, $240.
2. Correction made by the accounting department of an error in a prior period. The error was the recording of an $800 withdrawal of materials as $500. The original item had been correctly entered by the factory record clerk.

3. A shortage of item M-143, amounting to $45, which was noted and entered during the period on the factory records but information on which had not been transmitted to the accounting department.
4. An initial inventory, according to factory records, of $11,000 in stockroom M. Receipts were $14,000 and withdrawals were $13,000, according to the records of the accounting department.

14-17 *Economic Order Quantity* Compute the economic order quantity for an inventory item with the following relevant data: annual requirements, 20,000 units; ordering cost, $16; and inventory carrying cost, $.10 per unit per annum.

14-18 *Reorder Point* (SIA) Compute the reorder point in units and days, given the following.

a. A time period of 35 days in which the full inventory is used, except the safety level.
b. A safety level of 150 units.
c. A maximum inventory level of 850 units.
d. A lead time of 12 days.

14-19 *EOQ and Reorder Point* (CMA) The Robney Company is a restaurant supplier that sells a number of products to various restaurants in the area. One of their products is a special meat cutter with a disposable blade.

The blades are sold in packages of 12 blades for $20.00 per package. After a number of years, it has been determined that the demand for the replacement blades is at a constant rate of 2,000 packages per month. The packages cost the Robney Company $10.00 each from the manufacturer and require a three-day lead time from date of order to date of delivery. The ordering cost is $1.20 per order and the carrying cost is 10 percent per annum.

required

1. Calculate:
   a. The economic order quantity.
   b. The number of orders needed per year.
   c. The total cost of buying and carrying blades for the year.
2. Assuming there is no reserve (e.g., safety stock) and that the present inventory level is 200 packages, when should the next order be placed? (Use 360 days equals one year.)
3. Discuss the problems that most firms would have in attempting to apply the EOQ formula to their inventory problems.

14-20 *Quantity Discounts* (SIA) The Micro Electronic Company produces testing devices that require 12 special sockets each. Annual production is 40,000 testing devices.

Owing to the large annual usage of 480,000 special sockets, the purchasing agent approached the present supplier in an effort to reduce the current net price of $1.05 per socket.

The supplier, after some intensive studies, replied that the price could be lowered to $1.00 per socket if the company were willing to increase its present order size from 40,000 units to 120,000 units with 60 days' delivery rather than the present 30 days'.

The company estimated that additional space at $6,600 per annum would be required to stock the extra inventory. Safety stock should be increased by 10,000 units due to the greater time lag between deliveries. Inventory carrying costs are estimated at 10 percent per annum.

required

Evaluate the supplier's proposal by calculating the annual savings or losses.

14-21 *Relevant and Irrelevant Costs of Carrying* A firm is introducing an inventory-control system designed to minimize inventory costs, subject to required customer service levels that are influenced, but not completely determined, by shortage-cost estimates. A large range of products is carried, but for the purposes of this preliminary study, the following item may be taken as "average" with regard to selling price and cost structure. However, this is not necessarily a high-volume item.

CURRENT DATA FOR ONE (AVERAGE) UNIT	
Selling price	$20
Purchase-invoice cost	10
Road freight inward	1
Air freight inward	25

BUDGETS AND ESTIMATES (OTHER THAN DATA ABOVE)	
Annual sales	$1.5 million
Advertising budget	5% of sales budget
Administration	$100,000 per year
Property costs (depreciation, etc.)	$50,000 per year
Interest and insurance on inventory	30% per year
Warehouse operating cost	$2,000 per week + $10 per incoming order (bought) + $1 per unit sold. (Note: The warehouse has spare capacity.)
Clerical and other office costs	$1,000 per week + $2 per purchase order processed + $1 per unit sold. (Note: Buying lead time is about 2 weeks by road and 1 day by air freight.)

required

Estimate unit carrying and shortage (stockout) costs, and the relevant cost of a purchase order. State the assumptions necessary to support your conclusions; there may be more than one answer in some cases.

14-22 *Economic Order Quantity; Price Discounts* A medium-sized manufacturing company uses 50 barrels of soap a year in one of their plants. It costs them $1 a year to store a barrel, and a purchase order costs $10 to process.

The following discount schedule applies to the purchase price of the soap:

QUANTITY	DISCOUNT
1–9	None
10–49	$0.50 per barrel
50–99	$1.00 per barrel
100–up	$2.00 per barrel

Determine the economic order quantity, and briefly show why it is where it is.

14-23 *Make or Buy* The Gamma Company is considering the feasibility of purchasing from a nearby jobber a component that it now makes. The jobber will furnish the component in the necessary quantities at a unit price of $4.50. Transportation and storage costs would be negligible.

Gamma produces the component from a single raw material. The firm at present orders material in economic lots of 1,000 units at a unit cost of $1; average annual usage is 10,000 units. The yearly storage cost (including rent, taxes, and return on inventory investment) is computed at 50¢ per unit. The minimum inventory is set at 200 units. Direct-labor costs for the component are $3 per unit; fixed manufacturing overhead is applied at a rate of $2 per unit based on a normal annual activity of 10,000 units. In addition to these costs, the machine on which the components are produced is leased at a rate of $100 per month.

Should Gamma make or buy the component?

14-24 *Inventory Control* (SIA, adapted) A large appliance manufacturing company markets its products through a number of sales divisions. Each division is decentralized and accountable for its profit contributions. Warehousing and manufacturing, however, is centralized. Warehousing and stockkeeping costs are charged to the divisions based on average divisional inventory levels. The rate during 19_3 was 20 percent and is not expected to change during 19_4. Only over- or underapplied overhead from the manufacturing operation is charged to divisions.

A decline in divisional profits in the Residential Sales Division during 19_3 was caused by allocated charges from warehousing and from manufacturing. Apparently, the major portion of this allocated cost was incurred by one standard household product "Clean-O-Matic."

Warehousing reported that 19_3 shipments to customers totaled 250,000 units, deliveries from Manufacturing averaged 5,000 units per week, over a 50 work-week period, and that the 19_3 safety stock was 80,000 units. The unit cost is $48.00, bringing the average inventory value of this product to $3,960,000. Furthermore, the raw-material inventory included a high-value part worth $12.00, of which 2 are required to manufacture one Clean-O-Matic. Parts were purchased in lots of 30,000 during 19_3. The safety stock is 90,000 parts.

Manufacturing reported that the underapplication charged to the Residential Division was caused by high setup costs for production runs of the Clean-O-Matics. One setup, including labor testing and spoilage, amounts to $720, or $36,000 for 50 production runs during 19_3.

The divisional sales manager recommended the following changes for 19_4:

Safety stock of Clean-O Matics should be reduced gradually to 40,000 units by the end of 19_4.

Production runs should be larger to reduce total annual setup costs.

Safety stock of parts should be reduced to one average month (19_4) usage immediately, and the order size should be equal to the requirement for one production run.

Expected 19_4 sales: 280,000 Clean-O-Matics.

required

1. Compute the 19_4 economic production lot size.
2. Assuming that the sales manager's recommendations can be implemented, calculate the divisional savings of warehousing costs in 19_4 over 19_3 for finished-goods and parts inventories. Assume that production runs for 19_4 are 6,000 units each. Show your calculations.

14-25 *Reorder Point, Uncertainty, and Safety Stock* (CMA) The Starr Company manufactures several products. One of its main products requires an electric motor. The management of Starr Company uses the economic-order-quantity formula (EOQ) to determine the optimum number of motors to order. Management now wants to determine how much safety stock to order.

Starr Company uses 30,000 electric motors annually (300 working days). Using the EOQ formula, the company orders 3,000 motors at a time. The lead time for an order is five days. The annual cost of carrying one motor in safety stock is $10. Management has also estimated that the cost of being out of stock is $20 for each motor they are short.

Starr Company has analyzed the usage during past reorder periods by examining the inventory records. The records indicate the following usage patterns:

USAGE DURING LEAD TIME	NUMBER OF TIMES QUANTITY WAS USED
440	6
460	12
480	16
500	130
520	20
540	10
560	6
	200

required

1. Using an expected-value approach, determine the level of safety stock for electric motors that Starr Company should maintain in order to minimize costs.
2. What would be Starr Company's new reorder point?
3. What factors should Starr Company have considered to estimate the out-of-stock costs?

14-26 *Cost of Prediction Error* Ralph Menard has used the classic economic-lot-size model (with no stockouts) to compute an optimal order quantity for each of his raw materials and acquired parts. He initially predicts an annual demand of 2,000 units. Each unit has a supplier purchase price of $50. The incremental cost of processing an order is $40. The incremental cost of storage is $4 per unit plus 10 percent of supplier purchase price.

required

1. The total "relevant" or "associated" costs of this inventory policy.
2. Suppose that Ralph is precisely correct in all his predictions but he is wrong about the purchase price. If he had been a faultless predictor, he would have foreseen that the purchase price would have dropped to $30 at the beginning of the year and would have been unchanged throughout the year. What is the cost of the prediction error?

14-27 *Prediction Error* (J. Demski) Ralph Swash, an aggressive entrepreneur, is working on some make-or-buy decisions and a related inventory system. For one such product (and you may assume, for purposes of argument, that all such situations are independent), he decides to use the classic economic-lot-size model with *no* stockouts to determine an optimal order quantity. He initially predicts that annual demand will be 2,000 units, that each unit will cost $45, that the incremental cost of processing each order (and receiving the ordered goods) will be $67 in this case, and that the incremental cost of storage, in this case, will be $6 per physical unit per year.

1. What is the optimal order quantity?
2. What are the total relevant costs of inventory from following your policy in part 1 above?
3. Suppose that Swash is incorrect in his $67 incremental-cost-per-order prediction but is precisely correct in all other predictions. State and solve the equation to predict the maximum amount Swash should pay to dis-

cover the true incremental cost per order *if* (a) this true cost is \$33 per order and (b) in the absence of any knowledge to the contrary, Swash will implement the solution in part 1 above and will not alter it for *one* full year.

4. What happens to your answer in part 3 above if we admit that Swash has also made errors in predicting demand, price, and the cost of storage?
5. Suppose Swash implements the solution in part 1 above for *two* years. Further suppose that all of his initial predictions were (and are) correct, except that the actual incremental cost of storage is \$20 per average unit. If it costs Swash \$4 to alter his inventory policy, state the equation to determine the cost of prediction error of not changing his inventory policy at the beginning of the second year. Note: you may assume that the inventory cycle precisely repeats every year; otherwise you would have to adjust for nonintegral values.

14-28 *Performance and Motivation* Refer to Problem 14-27.

1. Assume that Ralph is approached at the beginning of the period and offered 2,000 units at \$44 each as a bargain one-shot purchase. The units will be delivered immediately and placed in Ralph's warehouse by the vendor, so Ralph's P = zero. What are the costs of this policy? Use the same approach as in 14-27, part 1.
2. Now assume that you used a "typical" standard costing system to judge performance. Suppose that the *budget* for 19_1 was based on the answer in 14-27, part 1. But on January 1 the purchasing agent chose the one-shot alternative. What variances and amounts would appear on his performance report?

14-29 *Comprehensive Study of Inventory Planning and Control* The Ward Company is trying to obtain better means of controlling inventory levels and attendant costs for an expensive part that they have been using for some time. Studies of cost behavior patterns reveal the following information:

Variable costs of placing and following up purchase orders (stationery, postage, telephone, etc.) total \$3 per order. Other clerical costs, such as salaries and related office-equipment expenses, have a step cost behavior as follows:

For every additional 200 orders processed per week, there is a \$70 increase in purchasing costs, a \$60 increase in accounting costs, and an \$80 increase in receiving costs.

Insurance and taxes on inventory are 4 percent of average inventory value per year.

The factory is rented at a cost of \$60,000 per year. It contains 100,000 square feet of floor space, of which 3,000 square feet are reserved for storing this item. Excess storage space is available in the neighborhood at 75¢ per square foot per year. Extra handling costs for using excess storage space will be $2\frac{1}{2}$¢ per inventory unit in excess storage space per year. The article requires storage space, allowing for aisles, of three square feet each and can be stacked six units high.

Breakage, obsolescence, and deterioration amount to about 2 percent of average inventory per year.

The company's average before-tax cost of capital is 10 percent per annum. The company uses this rate for inventory-investment decisions.

The Ward Company works 52 weeks a year, 5 days per week. It uses an average of 100 subassemblies per workday, but usage fluctuates from as low as 50 to as high as 150 per day. Many suppliers are available; but regardless of the source of supply and the size of the order, it will take two weeks from the time a purchase order is placed until delivery. Top management wants to keep an ordinary minimum stock of 1,500 units.

The purchasing agent is anxious to take advantage of savings in unit invoice and freight costs by purchasing in large quantities. Pertinent purchasing data are as follows:

	INVOICE COST		*FREIGHT COST*	
Lot Size	*Unit Cost*	*Total Cost*	*Unit Cost*	*Total Cost*
1,000	$55.00	$ 55,000.00	$5.00	$ 5,000.00
2,000	55.00	110,000.00	5.00	10,000.00
4,000	55.00	220,000.00	5.00	20,000.00
5,000	54.00	270,000.00	5.00	25,000.00
6,000	54.00	324,000.00	4.40	26,400.00
8,000	54.00	432,000.00	4.00	32,000.00
10,000	54.00	540,000.00	3.80	38,000.00
13,000	53.50	695,500.00	3.80	49,400.00
26,000	52.00	1,352,000.00	3.50	91,000.00

Special note Assume that the base stock is already on hand and is therefore irrelevant. The average inventory that is relevant is exclusive of the base. Assume, too, that the maximum inventory to be computed for commitments to excess storage space will be the *absolute* maximum, computed as follows: order point less minimum usage + standard order.

required

1. What order size should the Ward Company use? Support your answer by tabular analysis of the relevant costs for each lot size given above from 1,000 to 26,000.
2. What considerations other than the quantitative data may influence the decision here?
3. Comment on the cost behavior patterns in the situation. Which costs appear to be the most crucial?

14-30 *Relevant Costs of Inventory Planning; Sensitivity Analysis* (G. Feltham) The Super Corporation distributes widgets to the upper delta region of the Sunswop River. The demand for widgets is very constant and Super is able to predict the annual demand with considerable accuracy. The predicted demand for the next couple of years is 200,000 widgets per year.

Super purchases its widgets from a supplier in Calton at a price of $20 per widget. In order to transport the purchases from Calton to the upper delta region, Super must charter a ship. The charter services usually charge $1,000 per trip plus $2 per widget (this includes the cost of loading the ship). The ships have a capacity of 10,000 widgets. The placing of each order, including arranging for the ship, requires about 5 hours of employee time. It takes about a week for an order to arrive at the Super warehouse.

When a ship arrives at the Super warehouse, the widgets can be unloaded at a rate of 25 per hour per employee. The unloading equipment used by each employee is rented from a local supplier at a rate of $5 per hour. Supervisory time for each shipload is about 4 hours.

Super leases a large warehouse for storing the widgets; it has a capacity of 15,000 widgets. The employees working in the warehouse have several tasks:

a. Placing the widgets into storage, after they are unloaded, can be done at the rate of about 40 per hour.

b. Checking, cleaning, etc., of the widgets in inventory requires about one-half hour per widget per year.
c. Removing a widget from inventory and preparing it for shipment to a customer requires about one-eighth hour.
d. Security guards, general maintenance, etc., require about 10,000 hours per year.

The average cost per hour of labor is approximately \$10 (including fringe benefits). Super has developed the following prediction equation for its general overhead (excluding shipping materials, fringe benefits, and equipment rental):

$$\text{Predicted overhead for the year} = \$1{,}000{,}000 + (\$8 \times \text{Total Labor Hours})$$

The materials used to ship one widget to a customer cost \$1, and the delivery costs average out to about \$2 per widget.

The company requires a before-tax rate of return of 20 percent on its investment.

required

1. Super has decided to base its ordering policy on an EOQ model. What amount should they order each time and what should they use as the reorder point? Show all calculations.
2. If the true overhead prediction equation is

$$\$800{,}000 + (\$12 \times \text{Total Labor Hours})$$

what is the cost of the prediction error?

Cost Allocation: An Introduction

15

Cost allocation is an inescapable problem in nearly every organization and in nearly every facet of accounting. How should the costs of fixed assets be allocated to months, years, departments, and products? Accounting for depreciation is essentially a problem of cost allocation. Or, how should the costs of shared services be allocated among departments? How should the cost of a single production process be allocated to products that jointly emerge therefrom? How should university costs be split among undergraduate programs, graduate programs, and research? How should the costs of expensive medical equipment, facilities, and staff be allocated in a hospital? How should computer costs be allocated to various departments? Advertising? Central corporate staff? Personnel-department costs?

These are inevitably tough questions, so the answers often are not clearly right or clearly wrong. Nevertheless, we shall try to obtain some insights into the pervasive problem of cost allocation—at least to understand the dimensions of the problem, even if the answers seem illusory. The chances are great that you will be directly faced with this problem sometime during your career, regardless of whether you become a professional accountant or hold some other position.

A given cost allocation may be performed for one or more purposes, including: (a) predicting economic effects of decisions for planning and controlling; (b) determining income and asset valuations; (c) ascertaining a mutually agreeable price; and (d) obtaining desired motivation. These purposes will be discussed in both this and the next chapter.

We shall now examine the pervasive problems of identifying costs with cost objectives. Various books and organizations use diverse terminology to describe this tracing procedure: cost allocation, cost assignment, cost apportionment, cost reapportionment, and cost distribution. We use the term *cost allocation* here, but be on the alert to pinpoint the exact meaning of such terms in a particular organization.

By the way, note that the terms *cost application* and *cost absorption* tend to have a fairly uniform usage. They are confined to a special type of cost allocation, the tracing of costs to *products,* as distinguished from departments or divisions or cost centers.

the general process of allocation

There are essentially three facets of cost allocation:

1. Choosing the cost objective (the independent variable), which is essentially an *action.*[1] Examples are products, processes, contracts, or departments, all of which represent various actions.
2. Choosing and accumulating (pooling) the *costs* (the dependent variable) that relate to the cost objective. Examples are the material, labor, and overhead costs of making a product, as well as the nonmanufacturing expenses of selling and administration.
3. Choosing a method for specifically identifying 2 with 1. For allocating manufacturing costs, this entails choosing a cost-allocation base, which is usually direct-labor hours, machine-hours, or direct-labor cost.

The cost-allocation base is often the key means for developing a cost function that specifically links total costs with cost objectives. The ideal criterion for choosing an allocation base is a cause-and-effect relationship. In other words, the existence of the cost objective should be the dominant factor in causing the incurrence of the costs in question. This relationship is usually easy to establish for direct manufacturing costs such as material and labor.

[1] See Chapter 2 for introductory coverage of cost objectives. For a discussion of the theory of cost allocation, see J. Demski and G. Feltham, *Cost Determination: A Conceptual Approach* (Ames, Iowa: Iowa State University Press, 1976), especially Chaps. 5 and 6. Also see Y. Ijiri, *Theory of Accounting Measurement* (Sarasota, Fla.: American Accounting Association, 1975), pp. 183–86. A. Thomas, *The Allocation Problem: Part Two* (Sarasota, Fla.: American Accounting Association, 1974) is a comprehensive work on the subject.

Unfortunately, specific causes and effects of factory overhead and non-manufacturing costs are difficult to pinpoint with assurance.[2] As a practical matter, *relationships* are sought between the cost objective and the cost incurred. The preferable relationship or cost function is one that facilitates the prediction of changes in total costs, that accurately depicts persistent relationships, regardless of whether we view either the cost objective or the cost incurrence as the cause or the effect.[3]

cost pools and allocation bases

The preceding section described the general approach of using cost-allocation bases as a means of determining a cost function that relates cost objectives to cost pools. In this section, we examine the meanings of these terms and review the dimensions of the overall problem of cost allocation.

general use of pools

The term *cost pool* is often used to describe any grouping of individual costs. Subsequent allocations are made of cost pools rather than of individual costs. Costs are frequently pooled by departments, but they can also be pooled by natural categories (for example, materials-related or people-related) or by behavior pattern (for example, variable or fixed costs).

The allocation of various indirect cost pools among cost objectives is an imposing problem in theory, but it is usually solved in practice by using extremely simplified assumptions and broad averages. Whether the organization is a hospital, a government agency, a retail store, a university, or a factory, the general approach is similar. For instance, a manufacturer usually wants to somehow funnel all factory overhead costs, whether they originate in service departments or production departments, to the *production departments.* In turn, these costs are applied to *products,* using overhead rates that encompass both production- and service-department costs.

intermediate and final objectives

Sometimes cost objectives are divided into "intermediate" and "final" categories. For example, the final cost objective may be a job order. It is "final" in the sense that the accumulated costs are not allocated further except perhaps to the units of product within

[2] It is an oversimplification to say that there is a single cause-and-effect relationship between cost incurrence and the application base used. William J. Vatter, in "Limitations of Overhead Allocation," *Accounting Review,* Vol. XX, No. 2, pp. 164–65, observed: "Every cause has a number of effects; every event arises from many causes; all incidents and observations are bound together by many ties. All costs are more or less interwoven in a complex fabric; in large measure, costs are joint as to their incurrence, as well as to their associations with various costing units."

[3] For a description of how these cost functions might be chosen see Chapter 25, particularly Part One.

the job. That is, a job may cost $1,000 for 1,000 units; if 400 are sold and 600 are still held in stock, then $600 of the $1,000 would be allocated to inventory.

The overhead allocated to that job order may arrive there through a circuitous route involving many cost objectives. Consider the salary of the supervisor of the factory building maintenance department. His salary may be charged *directly* to the building maintenance department, which is only an intermediate cost objective as far as product costing is concerned. The salary usually becomes a part of a larger grouping of overhead costs—often called an *overhead pool*—that are allocated to two or more subsequent cost objectives:

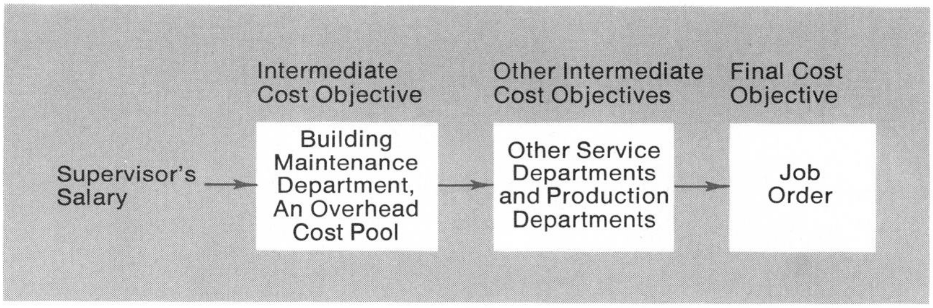

Note that an individual cost usually qualifies initially as a *direct* cost to at least one cost objective, because it can be identified specifically therewith. But the allocation process then proceeds so that costs lose their individuality. They become a part of indirect cost groups, so that subsequent allocations are made of cost *pools,* not *individual* costs. Thus, the supervisor's salary is not allocated separately to other service and production departments. Instead, the aggregated building maintenance costs are allocated as a group or pool.

cost-allocation base Given a cost objective and a total cost or cost pool, the problem is to choose a method or function that links the objectives and the costs. Reconsider the boxes illustrated above. How are we to allocate the building maintenance cost pool to other departments that consume the services represented by the pool? In turn, how are we to link the cost pools of other service departments to production departments and finally to products?

The key to the various linkages is the idea of the *cost-allocation base,* which is a systematic means of relating a given cost or cost pool with a cost objective.[4]

[4] An argument could be made that the cost-allocation base, by itself, is an intermediate cost objective. However, *allocation base* is heavily used and generally understood in our literature, although it is rarely defined. The cost-allocation base is more like an algorithm than an entity. For example, the CASB has defined many terms, including *accumulate, allocate, cost objective,* and *final cost objective*. The Board uses cost-allocation base in its pronouncements frequently, but the term is undefined. See CASB Standard 400. If you want to pursue the subject of cost allocation in more depth, begin with the CASB Standards, which are available from the Cost Accounting Standards Board, Washington D.C. Also see Appendix A at the end of this book.

The allocation base is easier to explain by example than by clearcut definition. Direct-labor time is a commonly used cost-allocation base for linking *direct* labor costs with cost objectives like departments or jobs as well as for linking *indirect* costs with cost objectives. The cost to be allocated is related to an allocation base that is a common denominator identifiable with the cost objectives in question. To illustrate, the total direct-labor cost and many indirect costs are frequently expressed in terms of the unit of the allocation base as direct-labor cost per hour or overhead cost per direct-labor hour. Then, direct-labor costs and indirect costs are allocated to departments and jobs based on the numbers of hours (the allocation base) identified therewith.

cost accounting standards board

The late 1960s and early 1970s were marked by many widely publicized disputes about the high costs of various defense contracts. In 1971, the Cost Accounting Standards Board (CASB) was formed by the U.S. Congress to establish uniform cost accounting standards, which must be used by defense contractors and federal agencies in the pricing of negotiated contracts. One of the problems that led to the formation of this board was that of how costs should be allocated among contracts and among commercial and defense products.

The CASB has published a series of standards on cost allocation. Illustrations of the Board's approach to cost allocation of home office costs are found in Exhibit 15-1, which is taken from CASB Section 403.50 (b)(1), "Allocation of Home Office Expenses to Segments." The CASB describes its approach as follows:

> The allocation of centralized service functions shall be governed by a hierarchy of preferable allocation techniques which represent beneficial or causal relationships. The preferred representation of such relationships is a measure of the activity of the

EXHIBIT 15-1

ILLUSTRATIVE ALLOCATION BASES FOR CENTRALIZED HOME OFFICE COSTS

SERVICE RENDERED	COST-ALLOCATION BASES
1. Personnel administration	1. Number of personnel, labor hours, payroll, number of hires
2. Data processing services	2. Machine time, number of reports
3. Centralized purchasing and subcontracting	3. Number of purchase orders, value of purchases, number of items
4. Centralized warehousing	4. Square footage, value of material, volume
5. Company aircraft service	5. Actual or standard rate per hour, mile, passenger mile, or similar unit
6. Central telephone service	6. Usage costs, number of telephones

organization performing the function. Supporting functions are usually labor-oriented, machine-oriented, or space-oriented. Measures of the activities of such functions ordinarily can be expressed in terms of labor hours, machine hours, or square footage.

allocation for planning and controlling

This section concentrates on the allocation of costs to aid planning and controlling. A major feature of this cost allocation is to estimate or predict the impact of various actions on the total costs of the organization. In addition, the favored cost-allocation method should promote the desired motivation.

dual allocation

Overhead pools and allocation bases sometimes are subdivided because of the difference between the behavior patterns of variable and fixed costs. The costs of power departments and computer departments provide examples. In these instances (1) variable costs are usually allocated in proportion to the short-term *usage* of the allocation base, whereas (2) fixed costs are sometimes allocated in proportion to a longer-term *availability* of the allocation base regardless of short-run fluctuations in usage. The use of separate or dual cost allocations for variable and fixed costs is an attempt to recognize some differences in cause-and-effect relationships.

Fixed costs might be allocated via a predetermined periodic lump sum for providing a fundamental *capacity to serve* based on the long-range requirements of the operating departments that justified the incurring of the fixed costs initially. This may be practical capacity or perhaps some "normal" percentage of practical capacity.

Fixed costs usually arise to provide a basic capability to serve the fundamental demands of consuming departments. Therefore, to the extent feasible, such costs might be reallocated in accordance with the plans that generated such fixed commitments. For example, what factors influence the equipping of power service departments or maintenance departments? If they are equipped with key men and machinery so that they may meet the peak needs of production departments, then the peak activity levels of the production departments should be the basis for reallocations of costs. If, on the other hand, they are equipped to meet the long-run average needs, then the "normal" level of activity in each production department should be the basis for reallocations of costs. Finally, if they are equipped because of the whims of the president, there may be no preferable base for allocation.

beware of full reallocation of actual costs

Many companies fully reallocate all service-department costs monthly on the basis of *actual* hours used in servicing the needs of the operating departments. The rate used is obtained by dividing the total actual costs of the service department by the total hours actually used by the operating departments.

To illustrate, suppose there is one service department (maintenance) plus two operating departments. The cost behavior pattern of the service department is $6,000 monthly plus $.40 per machine-hour. Assume that the total service-department capacity was originally acquired with the expected "long-run" usage of 60 percent by Department 1 and 40 percent by Department 2. Then Department 1 would bear 60 percent of $6,000, or $3,600 of the fixed costs each month regardless of monthly fluctuations in usage. Similarly, Department 2 would bear 40 percent of $6,000, or $2,400. Thus, the dual allocation rates would be:

Department 1:	$3,600 monthly + $.40 per machine-hour
Department 2:	$2,400 monthly + $.40 per machine-hour

For example, suppose the actual monthly costs of the service department are reallocated on the basis of the total machine-hours actually worked by the operating departments as shown at the top of Exhibit 15-2 for a 10,000-hour level. Each department worked 5,000 hours and would bear half the costs, or $5,000 each.

But suppose one of the operating departments worked only 3,000 hours instead of 5,000 hours. The next section of Exhibit 15-2 shows the new results.

Note that there are two basic faults in fully reallocating actual costs. First, a specific period's charges to an operating department depended on how much of the service was being consumed by the *other* operating department(s). In this example, given the same utilization of services as measured by the total labor-

EXHIBIT 15-2

REALLOCATIONS OF SERVICE-DEPARTMENT COSTS

AT A 10,000-MACHINE-HOUR LEVEL OF THE PRODUCTION DEPARTMENTS:	
Actual costs = $6,000 + $.40(10,000 hours)	= $10,000
Rate per hour = $10,000 ÷ 10,000 = $1.00	
To Department 1: 5,000 hrs. × $1.00	= $ 5,000
To Department 2: 5,000 hrs. × $1.00	= 5,000
Total reallocated	$10,000
AT AN 8,000-MACHINE-HOUR LEVEL	
Actual costs = $6,000 + $.40(8,000 hours)	= $ 9,200
Rate per hour = $9,200 ÷ 8,000 hours = $1.15	
To Department 1: 5,000 hrs. × $1.15	= $ 5,750
To Department 2: 3,000 hrs. × $1.15	= 3,450
Total reallocated	$ 9,200

hours it incurred, Department 1 had 15 percent more costs (an increase from \$5,000 to \$5,750) *solely* because Department 2's volume declined.

Second, although not illustrated by Exhibit 15-2, the amount charged is dependent on factors not directly subject to the control of the operating managers: the unit price and the efficiency of the services rendered. Frequently, operating managers do not complain so much about the allocation scheme used as they do about the total costs incurred by the service departments. If this service-department manager does not properly control his costs, his inefficiencies or high rates are routinely passed along to the producing departments.

how to allocate for planning and control

The following guidelines should help in deciding on what procedures to use for reallocating service-department or division costs:

1. Plan and control the costs of service departments or divisions just like those of operating departments or divisions. The fundamental distinctions between variable- and fixed-cost behavior should be preserved. Where feasible, use flexible budgets and standards, *not* static budgets and standards.
2. Where feasible, use a dual system that distinguishes between variable and fixed costs. That is, allocate variable and fixed costs separately.
3. To charge departments, use predetermined or budgeted unit prices or rates, *not* actual unit prices or rates. Thus, the total cost allocation would be based on actual inputs multiplied by budgeted unit prices.
4. Where feasible, in addition to using predetermined *prices,* charge on the basis of predetermined standard or budgeted *efficiency* allowed for services rendered. This is especially applicable to routine service. For example, consider the service rendered when you have your automobile repaired. The procedure is to give you a fixed total price based on the repair manager's prediction of the parts and materials to be used. In this way, the consumer is responsible for the overall output ordered, but not directly for variances in unit prices or efficiency. The total cost allocation would be based on standard allowed inputs for the outputs achieved multiplied by budgeted unit prices.
5. Do not allow short-run charges to a specific department to depend on how much of the service is being consumed by *other* departments. For example, at the start of a year (or more) various using departments would be assigned a lump-sum share of the costs of the capacity available in the service department.

These points are illustrated in the problem for self-study for this chapter.

multiple purposes of cost allocation

overlapping purposes

We noted earlier that at least four purposes may be sought by a given cost allocation:

1. *Predicting economic effects of decisions.* Estimate the impact of various actions on the total costs of the organization. Examples of such actions are decisions to add or discontinue products.

2. *Determining income and asset valuations.* Examples are product costs used for computing cost of goods sold and inventory balances.
3. *Ascertaining a mutually agreeable price.* Examples are contracts based on costs instead of market price. Hence, cost allocation can become a means of establishing a mutually satisfactory *price.* There is a subtle but important distinction here. A *cost* allocation, as a *cost* allocation, may be hard to defend on the basis of any cause-effect reasoning. However, an allocation may be a "reasonable" or "fair" *means of establishing a selling price* in the minds of the affected parties.
4. *Obtaining desired motivation.* Achieve goal congruence and incentive when other means fail. An example is charging the operating divisions for central costs such as basic research even though cause-and-effect or fairness justifications are weak. On the other hand, some top managers will insist that such allocation practices get division managers to take a desired interest in, say, central research activities. Thus, an "arbitrary" cost-allocation scheme may be chosen because the formal accounting system provides the best way to get the desired actions. These motivational aspects are discussed more fully in later sections.

Of course, the four foregoing purposes may be attained simultaneously via one cost-allocation scheme. For instance, in the rare case where cost allocations to a department can be completely based on a cause-and-effect rationale, the resulting prices may be perceived as fair, and the desired goal congruence and incentive with resulting optimal decisions will be more likely.

On the other hand, when a top manager is concerned with obtaining the "true" costs of assorted departments and products, most cost-allocation schemes can bring him only a limited distance with assurance. The cause-and-effect theme can be carried quite far with variable costs, because they are easily divisible. In contrast, the causes of fixed costs are harder to pinpoint. Decisions pertaining to fixed costs occur at a higher level in an organization and affect many subunits. Furthermore, fixed costs are lumpy (not easily divisible in any physical or engineering sense) and are often affected by long-range decisions.

Despite some flimsy assumptions, many cost-allocation systems proceed with elaborate measurements of full costs that are perceived as fair "prices" by consuming departments. Whether they lead to optimal decisions by all affected parties 50 percent, 80 percent, or 99 percent of the time is a question that each manager who is responsible for the allocation system must answer for himself. (To each, his own quagmire.)

effects on decisions

The cause-and-effect logic should be used as a frame of reference for judging various criteria for cost allocation. Wanting to know the impact of decision alternatives on costs, and faced with few instances of obvious cause-and-effect relationships, the manager is forced to rely on substitutes as approximations of these causal relationships. Hence, the fully allocated cost rather than a variable cost is often used as an approximation of "the real long-run" incremental cost.

The whole matter of reallocation is complicated by many computations. There is a misleading aura of precision, which is heightened by elaborate working papers and several decimal places. The choice of a particular reallocation method should be influenced by how sensitive the decisions are to the results of alternative reallocation methods. Again, the key question is, What difference will it make?

The crudity of some existing cost systems may be appalling. Nevertheless, the heavy use of averages and the universal tendency toward full allocations of costs are the practical means of seeking optimization. A decision to produce a given batch of product may not, by itself, be causing an increase in a particular cost at its given moment of production. But its cumulative, indirect effects do indeed cause increases in costs. Managers find that indirect costs somehow creep upward, often unobtrusively. These "creep" effects are approximated by applying average unit costs to products. The unanswered question is, How accurate are such approximations?—that is, do they provide reasonable predictions of the cumulative changes in total costs? Only specific empirical research can answer such a question.

criteria of equity, fairness, and benefits received

The imperfections of the process of cost allocation are obvious. How do you judge whether a suggested cost allocation is better than an alternative allocation? Although this chapter has emphasized cause and effect (whenever ascertainable in an economically justifiable way) as the preferable criterion for cost allocation, the literature on cost accounting has tended to favor fairness, or equity, or benefits received as preferable criteria. This section explores the interrelationships of all these criteria.

ability to bear When cause-and-effect relationships are infeasible or impossible to establish, accountants and managers often resort to arbitrary bases. An often misused base is actual sales dollars or gross margins or some other "ability-to-bear" base that often has only a most tenuous causal relationship to the costs being allocated. The costs of administrative and central corporate effort are frequently independent of the results obtained, in the sense that the costs are budgeted by management discretion or in relation to sales *targets*. Sales dollars *may* be a good substitute for establishing cause-and-effect relationships, but there should always be a serious examination of whether a better base is available, or whether *any* allocation is indeed warranted.

The use of revenue or sales as a base is a clear example of an "ability-to-bear" philosophy as contrasted with a cause-effect approach. A survey by the National Conference Board showed that 41 of 109 companies surveyed used actual sales as the sole base for allocating central expenses to divisions.[5] Sales is frequently a last resort in the search for a common denominator. The costs of efforts are frequently independent of the results actually obtained, in the sense that the costs are programmed by management, not determined by sales. Moreover, the allocation of costs on the basis of dollar sales often entails circular reasoning. That is, the costs per segment are determined by relative sales per segment. For example, examine the effects in the following situation (figures are in millions of dollars):

	PRODUCT				
YEAR 1	*A*	*B*	*C*	*TOTAL*	
Sales	$100	$100	$100	$300	(100%)
Costs allocated by dollar sales	$ 10	$ 10	$ 10	$ 30	(10%)

Assume that the dollar volume of A and B rises considerably. However, the direct costs and sales of Product C are not changed. The total costs to be allocated on the basis of dollar sales are also unchanged.

	PRODUCT				
YEAR 2	*A*	*B*	*C*	*TOTAL*	
Sales	$137.5	$137.5	$100.0	$375.0	(100%)
Costs allocated by dollar sales	$ 11.0	$ 11.0	$ 8.0	$ 30.0	(8%)

The ratio between the costs allocated on the basis of dollar sales and total sales was reduced, in the second year, to 8 percent ($30 ÷ $375), as compared with 10 percent ($30 ÷ $300) in the first year. This resulted in less cost being allocated to Product C, despite the fact that its unit volume and directly attributable costs were the same as for the first year. So the product that did the worst is relieved of costs without any reference to underlying causal relationships.

Advertising is a prime example of a cost that is typically allocated on the basis of dollar sales. Basing allocation on dollar sales *achieved* may be questionable, because the unsuccessful product or territory may be unjustifiably relieved of costs. However, there is some merit in basing allocation on *potential* sales or purchasing power available in a particular territory or for a particular

[5] *Allocating Corporate Expenses,* Studies in Business Policy, No. 108 (New York: National Conference Board), p. 13. This book has a good overall discussion of this topic. In addition, George J. Benston, "The Baffling New Numbers Game at the FTC," *Fortune,* October 1975, summarized a survey of 227 companies that showed 40 percent did not allocate common general and administrative costs to lines of business. Benston added, "The survey also showed that, on the average, common costs (excluding income taxes) equal 124 percent of net profits. . . . Most accountants and economists agree that common costs are, by their nature, not allocable at all." Also see R. K. Mautz, *Financial Reporting By Diversified Companies* (New York: Financial Executives Research Foundation), pp. 30–33 and 222–27. Mautz points out that divisional net income may be very sensitive to the allocations of common costs because such costs may be significant in relation to divisional net income even though they may be insignificant in relation to sales. The CASB reports that single general and administrative (G & A) expense pools are typically allocated on the basis of the *total costs* (exclusive of G & A) of the departments being charged (rather than on the basis of *total sales*). See CASB *Progress Report to the Congress,* published annually.

product. For example, there would be a consistent relationship between the advertising costs and sales volume in each territory, if all territories were equally efficient. If, however, a manager has poor outlets or a weak sales staff, one of the indicators would be a high ratio of advertising to sales. The usual dangers of budgetary gamesmanship also apply here; that is, there may be a temptation to underbudget sales in order to get a lighter cost allocation.

fairness for pricing When no outside market prices exist, cost allocation often serves as a means for determining a "fair" or "equitable" price. Many examples can be found in the area of government contracting, where the price is a function of the company's costs. Various costs become "allowable," whereas others are "unallowable." For example, elaborate rules promulgated by the CASB are used to help determine how costs are allocated to contracts. If cost allocations are to be used in lieu of market-based pricing, much acrimony and litigation are avoided when the allocation rules are made as explicit as is feasible in advance.

In the context of finding a substitute for a market price, equity becomes the dominant criterion for cost allocation:

> This is a concept which is easy to talk about, harder to write about except in generalities, and very difficult to apply because equity is in the mind of each individual. Yet equity is what this game is all about. Negotiations of contract price are intended to substitute for the automatic equity arising from the arm's length bargaining of the market place. The use of accounting in negotiations and settlements should ease the path to an equitable price or settlement. Accounting (or bookkeeping) form should never be permitted to get in the way of an equitable amount.[6]

fairness or equity Of particular note is the frequency with which fairness or equity is cited as a general basis for choice. For example:

> In ascertaining what constitutes cost, any generally accepted method of determining or estimating cost that is *equitable* under the circumstances may be used.[7]

> A cost is allowable if it is assignable to a particular cost objective . . . in accordance with the relative *benefits received* or other *equitable* relationships.[8]

> Any base that is chosen for proration purposes should meet two tests; it should be *equitable* and it should be *practicable.* Thus it should result in charges to each department that will be reasonable in view of the benefit the department receives, and it should not be too costly to use.[9]

[6] Howard W. Wright, "Uniform Cost Accounting Standards: Past, Present and Future," *Financial Executive* (May 1971).

[7] *Armed Services Procurement Regulations,* Sec. XV (emphasis added).

[8] *Ibid.* (emphasis added).

[9] Robert Dickey, ed., *Cost Accountants' Handbook* (New York: The Ronald Press Company, 1960), Sec. 8, p. 7 (emphasis in original).

The trouble with fairness or equity as a possible criterion is that it is so broad that other criteria must be devised to assure the existence of fairness. Equity and fairness are ethical standards that should be avoided in the building of concepts for a measurement system. In short, they are lofty objectives rather than criteria. To say that cost allocations must be fair or equitable is not an operational statement. Without specific criteria, we cannot judge how fairness conforms to overall tests of truth, justice, equity, and candor.

fairness and benefits received

The ideas of equity or fairness are indeed applicable to cost allocation in general. It is difficult to be against equity or fairness as ultimate criteria for almost any cost issue imaginable. Of course, the trouble is that equity is determined in the eyes of the affected parties, and mutual agreement regarding an equitable amount is sometimes hard to achieve. The relationships might be depicted as in Exhibit 15-3.

As the exhibit shows, the idea of "benefits received" sprouts from the fairness or equity criterion. To estimate benefits received, cause-and-effect relationships are sought. When the cause-effect logic tends to become strained, accountants often cite "benefits received" as if it were a substitute criterion. For example, the CASB will frequently say that costs should be allocated on the basis of cause and effect *or* benefits received. Such a criterion is less concrete, but it may seem convincing if it is merely another way of stating cause and effect. However, it becomes less convincing when it is used to justify allocations

EXHIBIT 15-3

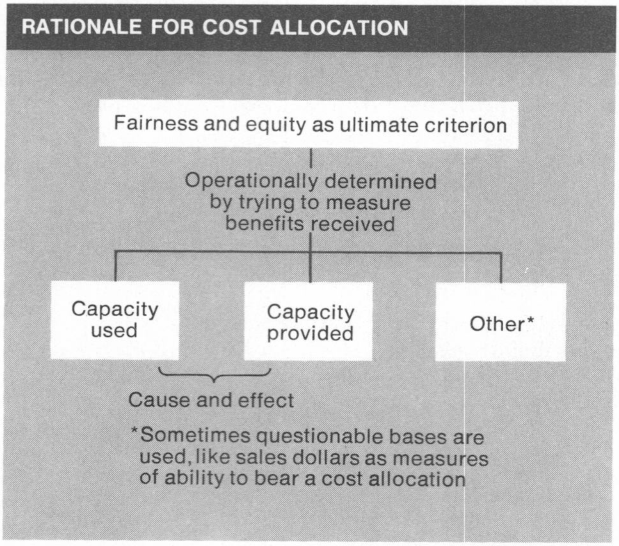

that are proportional to values added (such as the sales-dollar illustration in the earlier section). Nevertheless, such bases as sales dollars or cost of goods sold might be accepted as fair or equitable even though they come closer to being measures of ability to bear rather than measures of cause and effect.

In sum, the benefits-received criterion seems to introduce second-best logic when cause-and-effect arguments are available. For example, if the sales price is raised on a particular product line, there is little cause-effect justification for soaking that product line with a higher dose of some cost that is being allocated to products in proportion to sales dollars. If all other things are equal, the costs of the product line would be unaffected by a mere rise in selling price; yet the product line's proportionate share of central overhead costs would rise while other product lines' proportionate shares would fall—results that are hardly "fair" or "equitable."

motivation and partial or full allocation

The point has been made that motivation is often a major objective of the allocation of costs. Anthony[10] has indicated the key question: "What cost constructions are most likely to induce people to take the action that management desires?" A general answer could be: "The cost construction that best measures cause-and-effect relationships is most likely to provide information that will lead to optimum decisions."

The fully allocated versus partially allocated cost-allocation controversy illustrates the point. Some accountants favor the full allocation of costs because it makes the managers aware that the support of much of the entire organization is necessary for an individual responsibility center to run smoothly. On the other hand, some accountants maintain that some costs, such as central corporate costs, should never be allocated because no cause-and-effect relationships can be established. There can be no right answer here without knowing what decisions, if any, are affected by the cost allocations and what their differences in payoff would be.

In any event, little is known empirically about the effects on decisions of alternative cost-allocation bases. By implication, those who favor an arbitrary allocation of costs regardless of the lack of verifiable cause-and-effect relationships are saying that the danger of overstatement of costs is less than that of understatement. For example, if costs are fully allocated, managers are less likely to cut prices, to underbid, to be inefficient, to overexpand, and so on. The widespread advocacy of full cost allocations is indicative that such assertions are widely believed. But we have no evidence to support either side of the argument.

[10] *Accounting Review,* Vol. XXXII, No. 2.

Many managers insist that all costs should be fully allocated and reallocated to all departments, regardless of their controllability. Such a practice is supposed to make all managers more aware of the cost incurred and benefits offered by other parts of the organization. This practice may be desirable to the extent that this objective is reached without causing confusion in cost analysis and resentment about the methods of cost allocation.

Whether to include uncontrollable or indirect costs is a difficult question, which must ultimately be resolved in terms of how the given alternatives *influence management behavior* in a particular organization. In one organization, allocation may be desirable because it induces the desired behavior. In another organization, the same allocation procedure may cause an opposite behavioral effect. In any event, the current literature maintains that controllable and uncontrollable costs, when included in the same report, should not be commingled indiscriminately.

Are there any service departments whose costs should not be allocated even though they are clearly necessitated by the other parts of the organization? Consider the internal-auditing department or the legal department as examples. Ordinarily, where the other department managers have no discretion over their consumption of such services, the argument in favor of reallocation rests on the idea that the costs should be allocated anyway, and that managers generally do not get too concerned about such allocations as long as all departments are subject to a uniform cost-reallocation procedure. The argument against the reallocation of such costs rests on the idea that no costs should be reallocated to a manager unless he has some direct influence over their amount.

In some organizations, however, operating managers may have much leeway over their usage of such services. Charging for the auditing or legal services on the basis of the amount provided may discourage their use, even though such use may be very desirable from the standpoint of the organization as a whole. In such instances, either no charge may be made, or a flat annual fee may be charged regardless of the quantity of services consumed. For instance, a large automobile-manufacturing company does not charge for its internal-auditing services because it wants to encourage its managers to utilize such services.

As a general rule, the same objective will be attained by allocating a flat sum to the various departments regardless of actual use. It reminds the managers that the costs do exist. A possible advantage of this procedure is its retainer-fee effect, where the user feels that he is paying for the service in any event, so he had better take advantage of its availability. Of course, there is always the danger that a few managers may demand too much of what they would then regard as a "free" service. Then some priority system must be instituted, and a method of charging on the basis of services consumed may be finally adopted.

Some managers maintain that the morale effects of allocation procedures on the operating departments are given too much attention. There are also important effects on the morale of the service-department employees. That is, if the other departments are not charged with service-department costs, the service-department staff is likely to feel that it lacks the status of first-class citizenship as an integral part of the organization.

SUMMARY

Costs are allocated for multiple purposes, including: (1) predicting the economic effects of decisions, (2) determining income and valuing inventory, (3) ascertaining a mutually agreeable price, and (4) obtaining the desired motivation. When you are confronted with a cost-allocation dispute, a good place to begin your analysis is with the question: What is the purpose of the cost allocation in this instance?

There are three aspects to the cost-allocation problem: the choice of (1) a cost objective (some action or activity), (2) the pooling of costs, and (3) the cost function that relates the two. These must be considered simultaneously because they are interdependent.

Where feasible, fixed costs should be reallocated by using predetermined monthly lump sums for providing a basic capacity to serve. Variable costs should be reallocated by using a predetermined standard unit rate for the services utilized.

Fairness or equity is widely regarded as the ultimate criterion for cost allocation. Measures of benefits received are used to implement the fairness criterion, and cause and effect is usually the ideal way to establish fairness and benefits received simultaneously.

PROBLEM FOR SELF-STUDY

PROBLEM

Examine Exhibit 15-2 and the accompanying text. Suppose that the service department's fundamental readiness to serve was based on long-run expected activity of 4,000 machine-hours per month in Department 1 and 6,000 hours in Department 2. The company decided to reallocate fixed costs on a predetermined lump-sum basis and variable costs on a predetermined standard cost-per-hour basis.

a. Show the reallocations to both departments at a 10,000-hour level and an 8,000-hour level as indicated in Exhibit 15-2. Compare the results with those in Exhibit 15-2. Explain the differences.

b. Suppose the service department had inefficiencies and price and rate changes at a 10,000-hour level. The service department incurred costs of \$11,000 instead of the \$10,000 originally budgeted. How would this change the cost reallocations under the method in Exhibit 15-2 and under the alternative method? Be specific.

SOLUTION

a. Fixed costs allocated on a $\frac{4}{10}$ and $\frac{6}{10}$ basis, or (.4 × \$6,000) and (.6 × \$6,000) respectively. Variable costs allocated at 40¢ per machine-hour.

At a 10,000-hour level:

To Department 1: \$2,400 + (\$.40 × 5,000) =	\$ 4,400
To Department 2: \$3,600 + (\$.40 × 5,000) =	5,600
Total reallocated	\$10,000

At an 8,000-hour level:

To Department 1: \$2,400 + (\$.40 × 5,000) =	\$ 4,400
To Department 2: \$3,600 + (\$.40 × 3,000) =	4,800
Total reallocated	\$ 9,200

The rates used in Exhibit 15-2 were combined and not predetermined. That is, no distinction was made between variable and fixed costs, and the single combined unit rate was computed after the fact—after the actual hours used were tallied.

In contrast, a flexible budget was used in this recommended alternative analysis. Note that the charges to Department 1 do not depend on how much service is being consumed by Department 2. The $4,400 charge to Department 1 depends solely on the 5,000 hours consumed by Department 1, whereas in Exhibit 15-2, Department 1's charges went up from $5,000 to $5,750 solely because of a decrease in usage by Department 2.

b. In Exhibit 15-2, costs would go up by 10 percent for both Departments 1 and 2. Under the alternative method, the extra $1,000 would not be reallocated. The amount would remain charged to the service department as a $1,000 variance to be explained by the manager who had the most direct influence over such cost incurrence.

QUESTIONS, PROBLEMS, AND CASES

15-1 "A given cost allocation may be performed for one or more purposes." List at least three purposes.

15-2 "There are essentially three facets of cost allocation." What are they?

15-3 What is a cost pool? Give an example.

15-4 Give four examples of cost objectives.

15-5 What is the major reason for having a cost-allocation base?

15-6 For what purpose of cost allocation does equity or fairness become a dominant criterion?

15-7 "Central corporate costs should never be allocated because no cause-and-effect relationships can be established." Do you agree? Explain.

15-8 "In order to save time and effort, we use a single reallocation plan to fulfill both product-costing and control purposes." Discuss.

15-9 A prominent economist once said, "Not even Almighty God can tell a railroad the cost of moving a hundred tons of freight from Boston to New York." Do you agree? Why?

15-10 *Indirect Costs and Government Contracts* The president of a large university commented on the previous year's operations as follows:

"I should point out that, if the Congress had not recently reduced the ceiling on indirect-cost recovery in connection with research grants by the Department of Defense and the independent agencies from 25 percent, as it now is for the National Science Foundation and the National Aeronautics and Space Administration, to 20 percent, income for the next academic year would have come close to cancelling the anticipated deficit. This is another way of saying that government research grants require some sharing of the cost from general university funds, for our calculated indirect costs are about 32 percent. In other words, we recover only 63 percent of the true indirect costs."

"How do we obtain these funds? The answer is, through careful planning and hard work on the part of many people, including trustees, officers, deans, chairmen, faculty, the Development office, the Alumni Fund, and friends of the university."

For example, a research contract that formerly called for $100,000 direct costs plus $25,000, or $125,000, would now be $100,000 plus $20,000, or $120,000.

required | Evaluate the president's comments. Do you agree with his analysis? Why, or why not?

15-11 *Allocation of Advertising* (SIA) The H Company allocates national magazine advertising cost to territories on the basis of circulation, weighted by an index that measures relative buying power in the territories. Does this method give cost and profit figures appropriate for the following decisions? Indicate clearly why or why not.

1. For deciding whether or not to close an unprofitable territory
2. For deciding whether or not a territorial manager has obtained sufficient sales volume
3. For determining how efficiently the territorial manager has operated his territory
4. For determining whether or not advertising costs are being satisfactorily controlled

15-12 *Retailing and Costs for Decision Making* (CPA) You have a client who operates a large retail self-service grocery store that has a full range of departments. The management has encountered difficulty in using accounting data as a basis for decisions as to possible changes in departments operated, products, marketing methods, and so forth. List several overhead costs, or costs not applicable to a particular department, and explain how the existence of such costs (sometimes called *common costs* or *joint costs*) complicates and limits the use of accounting data in making decisions in such a store.

15-13 *Cost of Servicing a Bank Account* (CPA) A bank stated that the service charge it makes on accounts is based upon the cost of handling each account. A customer states that he does not see how it is possible to determine the cost of handling his account. Do you agree?

Discuss fully the problems involved in determining cost for such a service, including the limitations of the cost figures obtained.

15-14 *Allocation of Travel Costs* John Atherton, a graduating senior at a university near San Francisco, received an invitation to visit a prospective employer in Omaha. A few days later he received a similar invitation to visit North Platte, Nebraska. He decided to combine his visits, traveling from San Francisco to Omaha to North Platte to San Francisco.

John received job offers from both locations. Upon his return, he decided to accept the Omaha offer. He was puzzled about how to allocate his travel costs between the two prospective employers. He gathered the following data:

Roundtrip sedan service, dormitory to San Francisco airport	$ 18.00
Regular roundtrip fares from San Francisco to:	
Omaha	271.28
North Platte	241.27
Actual airfare paid	279.55

required | How much should each employer pay for Atherton's travel costs? Why? Explain. Show computations.

15-15 *Three Allocation Methods* (W. Crum) Linda Company constructed its own power plant capable of producing 6,000,000 kilowatt-hours of power per year.

It has three producing departments expected to consume power as follows: Dept. 1—3,000,000 kwh; Dept. 2—2,000,000 kwh; Dept. 3—1,000,000 kwh. During 19_5 actual consumption of power by the departments was as follows: Dept. 1—1,000,000 kwh; Dept. 2—2,000,000 kwh; Dept. 3—1,000,000 kwh. For 19_5, variable costs were $900,000; fixed costs were $800,000.

required

State how much power-department cost should be allocated to Dept. 1, using three different methods of getting your answers, one of which should be the dual-rate method. Describe each answer carefully.

15-16 *Overhead Disputes* (Suggested by Howard Wright) The Azure Ship Company works on U.S. Navy vessels and commercial vessels. General yard overhead (for example, the cost of the purchasing department) is allocated to the jobs on the basis of direct-labor costs.

In 19_3 Azure's total $150 million of direct-labor cost consisted of $50 million Navy and $100 million commercial. The general yard overhead was $30 million.

Navy auditors periodically examine the records of defense contractors. The auditors investigated a nuclear submarine contract, which was based on cost-plus-fixed-fee pricing. The auditors later claimed that the Navy was entitled to a refund because of double-counting of overhead in 19_3.

The government contract included the following provision:

> Par. 15-202. Direct Costs.
> (a) A direct cost is any cost which can be identified specifically with a particular cost objective. Direct costs are not limited to items which are incorporated in the end product as material or labor. Costs identified specifically with the contract are direct costs of the contract and are to be charged directly thereto. Costs identified specifically with other work of the contractor are direct costs of that work and are not to be charged to the contract directly or indirectly. When items ordinarily chargeable as indirect costs are charged to the contract as direct costs, the cost of like items applicable to other work must be eliminated from indirect costs allocated to the contract.

A special expediting purchasing group, the SE group, had been formed to do work (in addition to that rendered by the central purchasing group) on obtaining materials for the nuclear submarine only. Their direct costs, $5 million, had been included as direct labor of the nuclear work. Accordingly, overhead was applied to the contracts in the usual manner. The SE costs of $5 million were not included in the yard overhead costs. The auditors claimed that no overhead should have been applied to these SE costs.

required

1. Compute the amount of the refund that the Navy would claim.
2. Suppose that later the Navy also discovered that $4 million of general yard overhead was devoted exclusively to commercial engine-room purchasing activities. Compute the additional refund that the Navy would probably claim.

15-17 *Approaches to Allocation* A computer service department of a large university serves two major users, the School of Engineering and the School of Humanities and Sciences (H&S).

required

1. When the computer equipment was initially installed, the procedure for cost allocation was straightforward. The actual monthly costs were compiled and were divided between the two schools on the basis of the time used by each. In October the costs were $100,000. H&S used 100 hours and Engineering used 100 hours. How much cost would be reallocated to each school? Suppose that costs were $110,000 because of various inefficiencies in the operation of

the computer department. How much cost would be reallocated? Does such reallocation seem justified? If not, what improvement would you suggest?

2. Use the same approach as in part 1. The actual cost behavior pattern of the computer department was $80,000 per month plus $100 per hour used. In November, H&S used 50 hours and Engineering used 100 hours. How much cost would be reallocated to each school?
3. As the computer service department developed, the size and composition of the equipment was affected by a committee that included representatives of H&S and Engineering. They agreed that planning should be based on long-run average utilization of 180 hours monthly by H&S and 120 hours monthly by Engineering. In part 2, suppose fixed costs are reallocated via a predetermined monthly lump-sum based on long-run average utilization; variable costs are reallocated via a predetermined standard unit rate per hour. How much cost would be reallocated to each school? What are the advantages of this method over other methods?
4. What are the likely behavioral effects of lump-sum allocations of fixed costs? For example, if you were the representative of H&S on the facility planning committee, what would your biases be in predicting long-run usage? How would top management counteract the bias?

15-18 *Using Revenue as a Basis for Allocating Costs* The Mideastern Transportation Company has had a long-standing policy of fully allocating all costs to its various divisions. Among the costs allocated were general and administrative costs in central headquarters, consisting of office salaries, executive salaries, travel expense, accounting costs, office supplies, donations, rents, depreciation, postage, and similar items.

All these costs were difficult to trace directly to the individual divisions benefited, so they were allocated on the basis of the total revenue of each of the divisions. The same basis was used for allocating general advertising and miscellaneous selling costs. For example, in 19_3 the following allocations were made:

	DIVISIONS			
	A	*B*	*C*	*TOTAL*
Revenue (in millions)	$50.0	$40.0	$10.0	$100.0
Costs allocated on the basis of revenue	6.0	4.8	1.2	12.0

In 19_4, Division A's revenue was expected to rise. But the division encountered severe competitive conditions; its revenue remained at $50 million. In contrast, Division C enjoyed explosive growth in traffic because of the completion of several huge factories in its area; its revenue rose to $30 million. Division B's revenue remained unchanged. Careful supervision kept the total costs allocated on the basis of revenue at $12 million.

required

1. What costs will be allocated to each division in 19_4?
2. Using the results in part 1, comment on the limitations of using revenue as a basis for cost allocation.

15-19 *Cost Allocation and Variances* (H. Schaefer) The Coe Company produces its own power for use in operating Departments I and II. At denominator activity, Departments I and II consume 30,000 and 50,000 units of power monthly, making up the total monthly denominator activity of the power plant. The budgeted monthly costs of producing power at denominator activity are as follows:

Fixed costs	$6,000
Variable costs	2,400
Total	$8,400

The following data apply to operations during June:

Power fixed costs	$ 6,000
Power variable costs	1,960
Units of power consumed by Dept. I	20,000
Units of power consumed by Dept. II	40,000

In allocating power costs to Departments I and II, the Power Department spending variance is *not* distributed but the Power Department denominator variance *is* distributed.

required

Determine the allocation of power costs to Department II for June.

15-20 *Evaluating a Reallocation Method* The Daden Company has a service department that provides production departments with power. The budget for the power department was based on its normal anticipated monthly activity of providing power for 17,000 machine-hours at a total cost of $8,500, or $.50 per hour. The consuming departments had the following characteristics:

	PRODUCTION DEPARTMENT			
	A	B	C	TOTAL
Practical capacity in machine-hours	7,000	10,000	3,000	20,000
Normal activity in machine-hours	6,000	8,500	2,500	17,000
Actual activity in October—machine-hours actually used	6,000	5,000	2,700	13,700
Standard machine-hours allowed for the output produced in October	5,500	5,000	2,800	13,300

The *budget* allowance for the production departments was based on the 50-cent rate times the standard machine-hours allowed for the output produced. However, the *actual* costs incurred by the service department were fully allocated monthly to each production department on the basis of the actual hours consumed by the production departments.

The service department incurred actual costs of $8,220 in October.

required

1. Using the company's method of cost allocation, prepare a performance report for each production department, showing the amounts budgeted, the actual amounts incurred, and the variances. Use *U* or *F* to indicate whether each variance is unfavorable or favorable. Explain the meaning of the variance as reported by dividing each variance into two or more subparts in columnar fashion and commenting on the significance of your variance analysis.
2. This information should *not* be used in answering the previous part. A study of the power costs showed that efficient operation of the service department should result in total costs of $8,900 at a level of 19,000 machine-hours. Using this as well as the previous information, show how you would improve on the way the Daden Company allocates its power costs to its production departments. Give a complete illustration of how the allocations would be made for October, including a presentation of budgeted costs, actual costs, and variances by department. Explain fully why your suggested method is better.

15-21 *Cost Behavior and Cost-Allocation Alternatives* "Joe, how do you think we ought to charge ourselves for the operation and upkeep on our new airplane? It seems to me there are several ways we could decide to allocate expenses, and I don't know which is the best way.

"There must be some method which is better than others. Now that I think about it, other airplane partnerships I have heard about charge each member of the partnership a fixed monthly amount plus a variable charge depending on how much each man flies the airplane. What's wrong with doing it that way?"

"Nothing, maybe, Joe. Let me go home and take a look at the projected costs we estimated last week for our new bird. Then we'll get back and talk about it."

Jim, a recent business school graduate, had met Joe one day at the local airport after completing a local training mission with one of his students. Jim had started flying before entering the service and continued both in the service and part time while in school. Joe was a relatively new pilot who worked nearby as a sales engineer. Their conversation quickly indicated both were interested in acquiring their own airplane but that doing so alone was prohibitively expensive. The idea of a partnership of course came up and, as is often the case, the result was an agreement to jointly purchase and own, on a 50-50 basis, a high-performance light aircraft. The purchase and bank financing for the deal had been completed last week; at that time Jim and Joe had sat down to develop cost estimates for ownership and operation of the equipment.

When Jim arrived home after talking to Joe about the cost allocation question, he pulled out of the file the data he had referred to and began thinking about appropriate allocation procedures. The data follow:

Airplane purchase price	$25,000
Partner's initial capital investment (split evenly)	5,000
Amount financed	20,000
Monthly loan amortization payment (11 percent 5-year note)	430
Liability and Hull insurance, *per year*	1,200
Airport tiedown, *per year*	360
Annual inspection	432
Maintenance—*per flight hour*	10
Fuel and oil—*per flight hour*	9
Estimated *annual* usage:	
Joe 200 flight hours	
Jim 100 flight hours	

Jim knew of course that loan amortization, insurance, aircraft tiedown, and annual inspections were fixed charges in that they continued whether or not the airplane was flown. On the other hand, maintenance, fuel, and oil varied in direct proportion to flight time, as shown in the data above. At this point in their discussions Jim and Joe had agreed they both wanted to maintain 50 percent ownership of the airplane—which suggested to Jim they ought to each pay a fixed $215 monthly to cover loan amortization (and resultant equity build-up) outlays. It also was clear to Jim that the maintenance, fuel, and oil charges ought to accrue to each partner in proportion to aircraft hourly flight utilization, given the obvious direct relationship between the cost behavior for these items and flight time. The difficult question over which Jim now puzzled was how to best allocate the fixed expenses (other than loan amortization) shown in the schedule above. *He recognized that they too, along with the loan amortization expenses, could be shared equally by Joe and himself; but he wasn't convinced that would be the best way to do it. One reason he felt this way was because the fixed expenses in question were costs of operation, as opposed to basic ownership, just like the variable charges.*

At this point in Jim's deliberations Joe called and said "Listen, Jim, let's get together in an hour and settle the costing question. I want to go flying tomorrow and I want to know what its going to cost."

Jim hung up and decided to develop what he felt were two alternative ways of costing the airplane. He wanted to document the major advantages of each method so they could examine the issues and come to a conclusion that night.

required

1. Give Jim a hand. Assume that Jim and Joe will actually fly the very number of hours they have estimated. Develop the monthly bill of both Jim and Joe under each of the two alternatives implicitly suggested in the italicized part of the case (immediately before Joe's phone call).
2. If both Jim and Joe are alert in their upcoming meeting, Jim will likely favor one approach and Joe the opposite. Which is each likely to favor? Prepare a set of arguments supporting both positions. How are they going to have to settle their conflicting viewpoints?

15-22 *Dispute Regarding Fair Rate* The following series of memos recently passed through the mail of the Worldwide Enterprise Corporation. Exhibit 15-4 is an organization chart.

I. To: Tom Tumbas, Manager Plans and Controls, Palo Alto Plant
From: Clara Smith, Controller, Palo Alto Plant
Re: Direct Personnel for Eagle Project

One of the lab product managers for the Eagle Project would like to borrow some direct personnel from both the head assembly and the automated disk manufacturing functions. I'm not sure what we should charge the lab for them. Would you negotiate a meaningful rate with Mort Allen, their Controller? Cooperate, but don't let him improve his cost picture at our expense.

II. To: Mort Allen, Controller, Palo Alto Lab
From: Tom Tumbas, Manager Plans and Controls, Palo Alto Plant

Our normal procedure in temporary transfers of direct personnel is to charge the borrowing department the hourly rate used for product costing purposes in the plant department of the borrowed personnel. For the head assembly personnel this would be salary plus a burden rate of \$26/hour; for the automated disk personnel, salary plus a burden rate of \$40/hour. I trust this will be satisfactory for you also.

III. To: Tom Tumbas, Manager Plans and Controls, Palo Alto Plant
From: Mort Allen, Controller, Palo Alto Lab

How can your burden rates be so high? \$26 or \$40 is totally unrealistic; our burden rate is about \$8. Why is it that, when we last negotiated a rate, your burden rate was \$4/hour? Finally, if these people work on the Eagle project and it gets through development and turned over to manufacturing, you'll be getting back trained men and your learning costs for this new

EXHIBIT 15-4

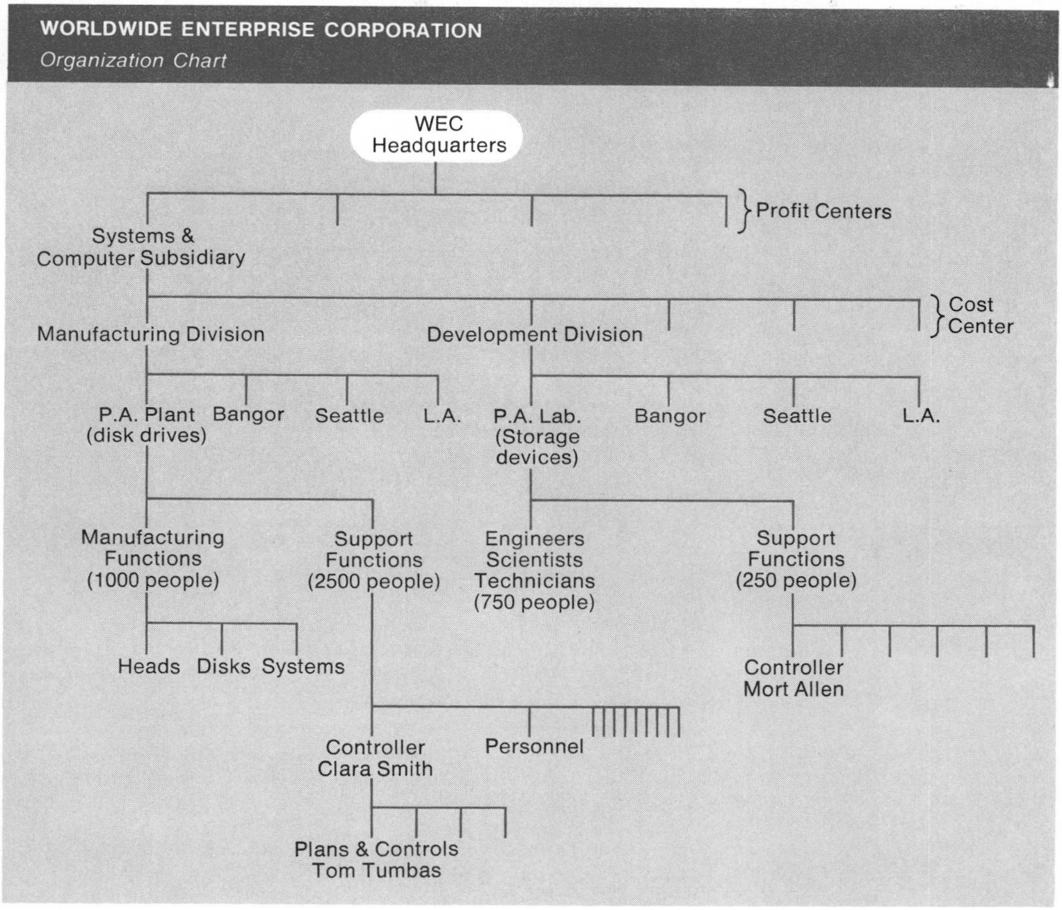

product will be reduced. Thus, you should consider giving us these people at salary.

IV. To: Mort Allen, Controller, Palo Alto Lab
From: Tom Tumbas, Manager Plans and Controls

Let me address a few of your points: no one here remembers where that old $4 burden rate came from, but we think it was "picked out of the air" as a rate that would encourage you to use our people rather than hire outside at a time when we were operating substantially below full capacity. Furthermore, if we accept a meaningless, low rate today, a precedent will continue, requiring too low a rate for future transfers.

Any potential cost gains from learning in your area are highly speculative. Those people may quit before we start building, and the project may never reach the manufacturing stage.

Our rates are higher than yours because our direct-labor personnel have a much larger support group. This support must be reflected in the cost of manufacturing the product, just as your support must be reflected in the R&D cost assigned to each product. Thus it still appears that our normal burden rate is the most meaningful for this transaction.

V. To: Tom Tumbas, Manager Plans and Controls, Palo Alto Plant
From: Mort Allen, Controller, Palo Alto Lab.

A meaningful rate would indeed be beneficial so we could make these decisions without a lot of time-consuming memo-writing. Because the people we take will be working for our managers, in our buildings, and receive primarily our support services, it would seem that a lower rate, reflecting only the costs of those services provided by you, would make the most sense. What rate would that be? Our analysis indicates that you'd be supplying only personnel department services and some accounting services, and that a rate of about $1/hour should suffice.

VI. To: Mort Allen, Controller, Palo Alto Lab
From: Tom Tumbas, Manager, Plans and Controls

Your logic is reasonable, but you suggest establishing a totally impractical precedent. We now control overhead expenses by each department within each function. We establish different burden rates for each manufacturing function so as to allocate costs to products. You appear to be suggesting that we establish different allocation rates for each department within a given function. If we did what your suggestion implies, I'd have every manufacturing department manager up here demanding a special rate for his men, since his department doesn't get full service from some other department. This would be an impossible situation, especially when a temporary transfer takes place. I could end up with hundreds of burden rates instead of the three I use now. Why don't we go with the normal rate? The difference will be a negligible part of your budget.

required

1. How can the burden rate applied to direct-labor hours be so different in these similar organizations (i.e., $40, $26, $8)?
2. Is the $40 or $26 rate a "fair" one to charge the lab?
3. Can you suggest a solution that both men might find acceptable?

15-23 *Should We Allocate?* Solve Problem 6-31, which could logically have been placed here.

15-24 *Allocation of Computer Costs* Salquist, Inc., is an international ethical pharmaceutical manufacturer that specializes in hormone research and the development and marketing of hormone-base products. The 22 different wholly owned subsidiaries and separate divisions that comprise the organization are highly decentralized, but they receive overall direction from a small corporate staff at parent-corporation headquarters in Palo Alto. The laboratories division, research division, and all corporate offices are located at the home-office site. Each of the divisional functional areas operates as a cost center. That is, labs accounting, labs production, labs sales, research accounting, and research operations are separate cost centers. Corporate purchasing, employee relations, office services, and computer (EDP) systems also function as individual cost centers, and they provide their services to Research, Labs, and the other divisions as necessary.

Until recently, no costs of the corporate service cost centers were allocated to the divisional cost centers; they were simply lumped together as central corporate overhead. Recently, however, it was decided to start charging the operating units (that is, the cost centers) for their EDP usage. Prior to this time, EDP services were simply requested as desired by the cost centers; priorities were determined by negotiations, with ultimate recourse to an EDP control committee (each cost center was represented); and all charges were absorbed as corporate overhead.

EDP systems comprise both systems programming services and computer operations. In the current "charge-back" system, the EDP director prepares a budget at the start of each quarter based upon his estimates of user demand. Using full absorption costing, he then computes an hourly charge rate, which he promulgates to the user cost centers. The users prepare their budgets utilizing his charge rate and their estimates of the services they think they will be needing. When a user desires to undertake any specific project or use EDP services, he negotiates an agreement with EDP on the hours (thus cost) that he will be charged. The user is free to reject the EDP "bid" and obtain outside services if he does not feel the EDP job estimates are reasonable. Also, since many projects last a year or more but service agreements are arranged on a quarterly basis, the user can drop a project in midstream at the end of a quarter if his overall budget should become too tight. If the actual hours needed to complete a given job exceed those contracted for, the EDP center must absorb the extra cost as an unfavorable overhead variance.

The performance of all cost centers is evaluated on the basis of how closely their actual results match budget. Thus the EDP director must not only assure that his actual expenditures coincide with those that were budgeted, but that he is able to bill other centers for all his actual charges. He must be sure that he contracts for enough projects from the users to absorb his budget.

The shift to the charge-back method was imposed by the corporate financial vice-president for the "purpose of putting control and responsibility for expenditures where the benefits are received." The VP also felt the move was necessary to avoid a "mushrooming of the EDP group" and to make users more aware of the costs they were incurring. An additional factor mentioned was an almost irresistible tide of "allocationism" prevalent in local industry because of the overpowering influence of government contracting there. He does feel he will resist allocating the other services, however, with the possible exception of printing and reproduction, which has grown to be quite costly in the last few years. The major rationale for not allocating the other services is that they are all uniform, predictable functions, whereas the EDP services are more spasmodic and project-oriented.

The head of the EDP group is strongly opposed to the new system. He believes that there is "too much lip service paid to the specialized nature of computers" and that the new system is reducing the effectiveness of the EDP group to the corporation as a whole. He and several of the user-directors believe the shift was simply a political maneuver on the part of the VP to consolidate the EDP empire under the aegis of the corporate staff. The head of the EDP group believes a nonchargeable system administered by the EDP control committee would yield better results.

required

1. What are the motivational and operational effects of this change on users, EDP group, and corporation?
2. Evaluate the impact of having coexistence of allocated and nonallocated services.
3. Evaluate the operation of this particular allocation system.

A Closer Look at Cost Allocation

16

This chapter will consider a variety of cost-allocation topics, including the contribution approach to cost allocation, service-department cost allocation, number of cost pools, and choosing allocation bases. Some of you may not wish to cover all these topics. For example, the section on the contribution approach to cost allocation may be studied alone.

the contribution approach to cost allocation

Exhibit 16-1 illustrates the contribution approach to cost allocation. This is an unusually important exhibit because it provides an overview of how accounting information may be organized to facilitate decisions and performance evaluation. The stress is on cost behavior patterns. Failure to distinguish cost behavior patterns is a big roadblock to clarity in cost analysis.

EXHIBIT 16-1

THE CONTRIBUTION APPROACH: MODEL INCOME STATEMENT BY SEGMENTS*

(In Thousands of Dollars)

	COMPANY AS A WHOLE	COMPANY BREAKDOWN INTO TWO DIVISIONS		POSSIBLE BREAKDOWN OF DIVISION B ONLY				
		Division A	Division B	Not Allocated	Product 1	Product 2	Product 3	Product 4
Net sales	1,500	500	1,000		300	200	100	400
Variable manufacturing cost of sales	780	200	580		120	155	45	260
Manufacturing contribution margin	720	300	420		180	45	55	140
Variable selling and administrative costs	220	100	120		60	15	25	20
(1) Contribution margin	500	200	300		120	30	30	120
Fixed costs controllable by division managers (certain advertising, sales promotion, salesmen's salaries, engineering, research, management consulting, and supervision costs)	190	110	80	45†	10	6	4	15
(2) Contribution controllable by segment managers	310	90	220	(45)	110	24	26	105
Fixed costs controllable by others (such as depreciation, property taxes, insurance, and perhaps the division manager's salary)	70	20	50	20	3	15	4	8
(3) Contribution by segments	240	70	170	(65)	107	9	22	97
Unallocated costs (not clearly or practically allocable to any segment except by some questionable allocation base)	135							
(4) Income before income taxes	105							

* There are two different types of segments illustrated here: *divisions* and *products*. As you read across, note that the focus becomes narrower: from the company as a whole, to Divisions A and B, to Division B only.

† Only those costs clearly identifiable to a product line should be allocated.

revenues, variable costs, and contribution margins

The allocation of revenue and of variable costs is usually straightforward, because each item is directly and specifically identifiable with a given segment of activity. The Contribution Margin, Line (1) in Exhibit 16-1, is particularly helpful for predicting the impact on income of short-run changes in volume. Changes in income may be quickly calculated by multiplying the change in units by the unit contribution margin or by multiplying the increment in dollar sales by the contribution-margin ratio. For example, the contribution-margin ratio of Product 1 is $\$120 \div \$300 = 40$ percent. The increase in net income resulting from a \$20,000 increase in total sales volume can be readily computed as $.40 \times \$20{,}000$, or \$8,000.

unallocated costs

An unallocated cost is common to all the segments in question and is not clearly or practically assignable except on some questionable basis. Examples of unallocated costs may be the salaries of the president and other top officers, basic research and development, and some central corporate costs like public relations or corporate-image advertising.

Discretionary and committed costs may or may not be allocated, *depending on the segments in question.* For example, a salesman's salary may be easily identified with a particular territory. However, if he is selling a large number of products, the allocation of his salary among such products is questionable. Consequently, there may be a limit to the allocation of a given cost in a given income statement. For instance, the Divisions in Exhibit 16-1 could be territorial. The salary of the salesman just described could be readily allocated to Division A or B (a territory), but it could not be allocated convincingly among the products. A given cost may be allocated with respect to one segment of the organization and unallocated with respect to another.

contribution controllable by segment managers

As Chapter 23 explains more fully, a distinction should be made between the performance of the segment manager and the performance of the segment as an economic investment. That distinction is keyed in the form of subtotals (2) and (3) in Exhibit 16-1. Our discussion of controllability and uncontrollability in Chapter 6 stressed how performance may be affected by factors that are subject to varying degrees of influence by a particular manager.

The reason for this distinction comes sharply into focus when you consider that many companies deliberately assign their best manager to their least-profitable divisions with the hope that improvements will be forthcoming. Unless some discrimination is made between the manager and the responsibility center as an economic entity, the skillful manager will be reluctant to accept assignments to troublesome responsibilities. Sometimes it takes a miracle worker to get a limping segment up to a minimally acceptable level of income.

What measure of income is most appropriate for judging performance by division managers or product managers? The controllable contribution, keyed as item (2) in Exhibit 16-1, should be helpful, especially when it is interpreted in conjunction with the contribution margin. This is because most top managers can influence many fixed costs, particularly *discretionary fixed costs.* (Examples of these costs are given in Exhibit 16-1.) The incurrence of discretionary costs may have interacting effects on variable costs. For example, heavier outlays for maintenance, engineering, or management consulting may reduce repairs, increase machine speeds, heighten labor productivity, and so forth. Also, decisions on advertising, research, and sales-promotion budgets are necessarily related to expected impacts on sales volumes.

Note at this stage that, although many discretionary costs may be easily traced to divisions, they may not all be directly traceable to products. Some advertising expenses for Division B may be common to all products. For example, Products 1, 2, and 3 may be consumer items that all benefit from the same advertisements, while Product 4 may be an item sold to manufacturers by a separate sales organization with its own fixed costs.

The line between controllable and uncontrollable costs must be drawn on a company-by-company basis. For example, some managements may prefer to have depreciation on some classes of plant and equipment deducted when item (2), the controllable contribution, is computed. Getting agreement as to these classifications may be bothersome, but it is not a Herculean task.

The income statement in Exhibit 16-1 has four measures of performance, ranging from contribution margin through income before income taxes. There is nothing hallowed about these four illustrative measures; some organizations may want to use only two or three such measures.

contribution by segments and income before income taxes

Contribution by segments, item (3) in Exhibit 16-1, is computed after deducting the fixed cost classified as uncontrollable by the managers in the short run. Although this figure may be helpful as a crude indicator of long-run segment profitability as an economic investment, it definitely should not influence appraisals of current performance of managers.

Income before taxes, item (4) in Exhibit 16-1, may sometimes be a helpful gauge of the long-run earning power of a whole company. However, it may be misleading to refine this ultimate measure by breaking it into segments (and still have the whole equal the sum of the parts).

It is difficult to see how segment performance can be judged on the basis of income after deductions for a "fair" share of general company costs over which the segment manager exerts no influence. Examples of such costs would be central-research and central-headquarters costs, including salaries of the president and other high officers. Unless the general company costs are clearly traceable to segments, allocation serves no useful purpose and should not be made. Therefore, income is not computed by segments in Exhibit 16-1.

This refusal to allocate some costs is the most controversial aspect of the contribution approach to the income statement. Accountants and managers are used to the whole being completely broken down into neat parts that can be added up again to equal the whole. In traditional segment income statements, all costs are fully allocated, so that the segments show final net incomes that can be summed to equal the net income for the company as a whole.

Of course, if for some reason management prefers a whole-equals-the-sum-of-its-parts net-income statement, the unallocated costs may be allocated so that the segments show income figures that will cross-add to equal the income for the company as a whole. The important point is that the contribution approach distinguishes between various degrees of objectivity in cost allocations. As you read downward in Exhibit 16-1, you become less and less confident about the cost allocations. A dozen independent accountants would be most likely to agree on how the variable costs should be allocated and least likely to agree on whether and how the unallocated costs should be accounted for.

service-department cost allocation

The costs of operating service departments ultimately find their way to user departments. Assume, for example, that a company has four departments. The two service departments are general factory administration and engineering. The two production departments are machining and assembly. Overhead costs are budgeted on a flexible basis and are accumulated by department responsibility for control purposes. For product-costing purposes, the service department costs are sooner or later reallocated to those production departments. The base for reallocation is the common denominator that best measures the services rendered to the other service and producing departments. The data for our example follow:

	SERVICE DEPARTMENTS		PRODUCING DEPARTMENTS		
	GENERAL FACTORY ADMINISTRATION	ENGINEERING	MACHINING	ASSEMBLY	
	1	2	A	B	TOTALS
Overhead costs before reallocation of service-department costs	$600,000	$116,000	$400,000	$200,000	$1,316,000
Proportions of service furnished:					
By Department 1 (based on total labor-hours):					
Total labor-hours		24,000	12,000	36,000	72,000
Proportion		2/6	1/6	3/6	6/6
By Department 2 (based on engineering-hours worked for each department):					
Engineering-hours	2,000		16,000	2,000	20,000
Proportion	1/10		8/10	1/10	10/10

direct reallocation Direct reallocation, or some similar method, is the most widely used method for reallocation of service-department costs. This method ignores any service rendered by one service department to another; it reallocates each service department's total costs directly to the producing departments. Note in Exhibit 16-2 that this method ignores the service rendered by the general factory administration department to the engineering department and also the service rendered by engineering to general factory administration. The base used for reallocation of general factory administration costs is the 48,000 total labor-hours worked in the producing departments. Distinguish between *total* labor-hours (which includes indirect hours, such as the 24,000 hours of service provided to engineering by general factory administration) and *direct*-labor hours. Total labor-hours might be used as bases for reallocations of service-department costs, whereas direct-labor hours are often used as bases for developing predetermined overhead rates in producing departments for product-costing purposes.

step method Many companies use the *step method* (sometimes called *step-down*) of reallocation, which recognizes services rendered by service departments to other service departments. This method is more complicated, because a sequence of reallocations must be chosen. The sequence typically begins with the department that renders service to the greatest number of other

EXHIBIT 16-2

DIRECT METHOD OF REALLOCATION

	DEPARTMENT				
	1	*2*	*A*	*B*	*TOTAL*
Overhead costs before reallocation	\$600,000	\$116,000	\$400,000	\$200,000	\$1,316,000
Reallocation:					
Department 1 ($\frac{1}{4}$, $\frac{3}{4}$)*	(\$600,000)		150,000	450,000	
Department 2 ($\frac{8}{9}$, $\frac{1}{9}$)†		(\$116,000)	103,111	12,889	
Total overhead of producing departments			\$653,111	\$662,889	\$1,316,000
Computation of predetermined overhead rates for product-costing purposes:					
Divide by machine-hours			40,000		
Divide by direct-labor hours				30,000	
Rate			\$ 16.328	\$ 22.096	

* Base is (12,000 + 36,000), or 48,000 hours; 12,000 ÷ 48,000 = $\frac{1}{4}$; 36,000 ÷ 48,000 = $\frac{3}{4}$.
† Base is (16,000 + 2,000) or 18,000 hours; 16,000 ÷ 18,000 = $\frac{8}{9}$; 2,000 ÷ 18,000 = $\frac{1}{9}$.

service departments; the sequence continues in step-by-step fashion and ends with the reallocation of costs of the service department that renders service to the least number of other departments. Thus, departments such as building and grounds or personnel would be reallocated earlier than would production control or product engineering.

Exhibit 16-3 shows the step method. Note that Department 1 costs are reallocated to the other service department as well as to the producing departments. Note also that, once Department 1 costs are reallocated, Department 2 costs include a share of Department 1 costs. The new total for Department 2 is then reallocated to *subsequent* departments only. **Once a service department's costs have been reallocated, no subsequent service-department costs are recirculated back to it.**

Note further that *in this case* the overhead rates for product-costing purposes are significantly different under the two methods. For example, the machine-hour rate is $16.328 under the direct method and $19.522 under the step method. Note also that Department A's rate is higher under the step method while Department B's rate is lower. If the data processing costs are not too different among allocation methods, the step method would be preferable in a case like this, because it recognizes the service rendered to engineering by general factory administration, whereas the direct method ignores this relationship. However, as always, the choice of an allocation method is a cost-benefit decision.

EXHIBIT 16-3

STEP METHOD OF REALLOCATION

	1	2	A	B	TOTAL
Overhead costs before reallocation	$600,000	$116,000	$400,000	$200,000	$1,316,000
Reallocation:					
Department 1 ($\frac{2}{6}$, $\frac{1}{6}$, $\frac{3}{6}$)	($600,000)	200,000	100,000	300,000	
Department 2 ($\frac{8}{9}$, $\frac{1}{9}$)		($316,000)	280,899	35,111	
Total overhead of producing departments			$780,889	$535,111	$1,316,000
Computation of predetermined overhead rates for product-costing purposes:					
Divide by machine-hours			40,000		
Divide by direct-labor hours				30,000	
Rate			$ 19.522	$ 17.837	

The illustrated discrepancy in product costs may have infinitesimal decision consequences in some situations, but it may have substantial consequences in situations involving pricing or product choice. Also, cost-reimbursement contracts such as those for defense industries, universities, and hospitals would obviously be affected.[1]

reciprocal services The direct method and the step method obtain approximate solutions to the third method, the reciprocal services method, via simplifying assumptions. The direct method and the step method are not theoretically accurate if service departments render services to one another reciprocally. For example, the factory administration department serves the employees of the building and grounds department, while the factory administration department occupies some floor space and has janitorial attention. If reciprocal services between service departments are significant, elaborate schemes of reallocation involving simultaneous equations may be adopted. Ordinarily, however, the step method (a simpler model) will yield final charges to the producing departments that are acceptable approximations of the results that would come from the more complex model. Consequently, the use of simultaneous equations or linear algebra is rare in practice. But digital computers now facilitate the computations, so we may expect an increasing use of linear algebra.

The use of linear algebra may make a difference in decisions upon occasion. For example, suppose that the conditions in Exhibit 16-4 exist. The repair department serves the power department and vice versa. Note that a step method of reallocation may produce significantly different answers from those by the linear algebra method, using the simultaneous equations at the bottom of the exhibit. Linear algebra is the most theoretically defensible method. For example, suppose the company had the opportunity to buy its power outside for $16,500. The step method used in Exhibit 16-4 shows a power cost of $16,000, but the linear algebra method shows a power cost of $17,391. In decisions like these, the cost-reallocation method may indeed have an influential difference.

The example in Exhibit 16-4 used only two service departments and two production departments. This required the use of two simultaneous equations. Of course, in practice, many more simultaneous equations may be required. A generalized approach for solving large systems of equations is provided by matrix algebra.[2]

[1] See the next section for a discussion of how many cost pools and cost objectives are desirable (the problem of homogeneity).

[2] See Thomas H. Williams and Charles H. Griffin, "Matrix Theory and Cost Allocation," *Accounting Review,* Vol. XXXIX, No. 3, pp. 671–78; Neil C. Churchill, "Linear Algebra and Cost Allocations: Some Examples," *Accounting Review,* Vol. XXXIV, No. 4, pp. 894–904, and Rene P. Manes, "Comment on Matrix Theory and Cost Allocation," *Accounting Review,* Vol. XL, No. 3, pp. 640–43. Robert S. Kaplan, "Variables and Self-Service Costs in Reciprocal Allocation Models," *The Accounting Review,* Vol. XLVIII, No. 4 (October 1973), pp. 738–48, stresses the decision-making implications of reciprocal services and evaluates various approaches to allocation. Also see John K. Shank, *Matrix Methods in Accounting* (Reading Mass.: Addison-Wesley Publishing Co., 1972), pp. 35–40.

EXHIBIT 16-4

COMPARISON OF STEP METHOD AND METHOD USING LINEAR ALGEBRA

(Data Assumed)

	SERVICE DEPARTMENTS		PRODUCTION DEPARTMENTS	
	Repair	*Power*	*Machining*	*Assembly**
Man-hours of repair service used		1,000	3,000	1,000
Percentage of service		20%	60%	20%
Units of power consumed	4,000		2,000	4,000
Percentage of service	40%		20%	40%
Reallocation using step method:				
Total relevant department costs before reallocation	$30,000	$10,000	$ —	$ —
Repairs (allocated first†)	(30,000)	6,000	18,000	6,000
Power department		(16,000)	5,333	10,667
Relevant costs after reallocation	$ 0	$ 0	$23,333	$16,667
Reallocation using linear algebra‡:				
Relevant costs before reallocation	$30,000	$10,000	$ —	$ —
Repairs	(36,957)	7,391	22,174	7,392
Power	6,957	(17,391)	3,477	6,957
Relevant costs after reallocation	$ 0	$ 0	$25,651	$14,349

* Heavily automated with modern equipment.

† Some companies might prefer to allocate power first. You may wish on your own to allocate power first to see how the results compare to the ''ideal'' results under the reciprocal method. More repair money is spent in the power department than vice versa ($6,000 vs. $4,000).

‡ The following equations represent the essence of the linear algebra method. In this case, two simultaneous equations are used to find the value of two unknowns:

Let R = total costs of repair department
P = total costs of power department

(1) $R = \$30{,}000 + .4P$

(2) $P = \$10{,}000 + .2R$

Substituting in (1): $R = \$30{,}000 + .4(\$10{,}000 + .2R)$

$R = \$30{,}000 + \$4{,}000 + .08R$

$.92R = \$34{,}000$

$R = \$36{,}957$[a]

Substituting in (2): $P = \$10{,}000 + .2(\$36{,}957) = \$17{,}391$[a]

[a] Instead of using equations, we could obtain the same results by using successive rounds of reducing-amount computations.

Amounts before reallocation	$30,000.00	$10,000.00
20% of $30,000		6,000.00
Total		$16,000.00
40% of $16,000	6,400.00	
20% of $6,400		1,280.00
40% of $1,280	512.00	
20% of $512		102.40
40% of $102.40	40.96	
20% of $40.96		8.19
40% of $8.19	3.28	
20% of $3.28		.66
Totals as above	$36,956.24	$17,391.25

When should linear algebra be used? If management is using the results of reallocations to make decisions on pricing products, on internal or external purchasing of services, on setting levels of output, and on related activities, the results of step-method reallocations should be periodically tested against the results obtained by the algebraic method. If the decisions are not sensitive to the results of the algebraic computations, then the simpler methods are adequate.

number of cost pools

How many cost pools and cost objectives are desirable? How should we choose the cost functions that best depict various relationships among such pools and objectives? This section explores these issues.

nature of homogeneity

The idea of aggregating or pooling costs is the result of abandoning ideal cost-allocation schemes for cost-benefit reasons. That is, instead of taking detailed costs in their most elemental form, one at a time, and deciding how they should be allocated, we aggregate them; we almost always choose one base for allocating the group (whereas individually we might choose more than one). This averaging process inevitably results in a loss of accuracy. The justification for using only one or two cost pools and only one or two cost-allocation bases is that the added cost of a more detailed cost-allocation scheme exceeds the expected benefits from getting more precise information.

This could be a testable proposition in some cases. For example, if costs directly influence pricing decisions, the effects on decisions of various cost-aggregation schemes (such as absorption and direct costing) and allocation bases could be predicted. Then, the sensitivity of the decisions to changes in the estimates would determine the degree of cost aggregation that would be optimal.

The literature contains numerous exhortations about the desirability of achieving homogeneity in the averaging process. However, homogeneity has not been sharply defined. We define it as a characteristic of any aggregated cost-allocation rate. **It is measured by comparing the costs assigned to the various cost objectives of interest, using an aggregated cost-allocation rate, with what the costs assigned would have been if disaggregated rates had been used. If there are no differences, the allocation rate is perfectly homogeneous.**[3] Note that the concept of homogeneity springs from the aggregation process. If elemental individual rates were used, no test for homogeneity would be needed.

[3] J. Demski and G. Feltham, *Cost Determination: A Conceptual Approach* (Ames, Iowa: Iowa State University Press, 1976), Chap. 6, Sec. 1.2.2, focus on regression analysis as a way to assess the degree of homogeneity: "If alternative input measures are being considered, then the evaluator may select that measure which explains the greatest percentage variation in past costs. Alternatively, if the available input measures do not explain a 'satisfactory' percentage of the variation, then the category of costs may be subdivided and different input measures considered for each subcategory."

plant-wide rate versus departmental rates

The problem of homogeneity is widespread because most factories produce more than one product. The variety of products commands varying attention and effort, different material usages, and different production routings. These situations call for refinement of overhead application by departments or cost centers so that different products may bear their related share of factory overhead.

Assume that one job is routed through two departments: machining and finishing. The machining department is heavily mechanized with costly semi-automatic and automatic equipment. The finishing department contains a few simple tools and is dependent on painstaking skilled workmanship. Overhead costs would be relatively large in machining and small in finishing.

Now consider two jobs. The first requires one hour of machining time and ten hours of finishing time. The second requires nine hours of machining time and two hours of finishing time. If a single, plantwide, blanket overhead rate based on labor-hours is used, each job would receive the same total-overhead application. But this probably would not be a sufficiently accurate measurement of the underlying relationship, because Job No. 1 made light use of overhead-incurring factors while Job No. 2 made heavy use of such services. Departmental rates, as shown in Exhibit 16-5, result in a more accurate linking of overhead with specific jobs when products do not move uniformly through the plant.

EXHIBIT 16-5

PLANTWIDE OVERHEAD RATE VERSUS DEPARTMENTAL OVERHEAD RATES

	PLANTWIDE RATE		*DEPARTMENTAL RATES*		
	Machining	Finishing	Machining	Finishing	
Budgeted annual overhead	$100,000	$ 8,000	$100,000	$ 8,000	—
Direct-labor hours	10,000	10,000	10,000	10,000	
Blanket rate per DLH:					
$108,000 ÷ 20,000	$ 5.40				
Departmental rates per DLH			$ 10.00	$ .80	
Overhead application:					
Job No. 1					
Labor time, 11 hours @ $5.40	$59.40				
or					
Labor time:					
Machining, 1 hour @ $10.00			$ 10.00		TOTAL
Finishing, 10 hours @ $.80				$ 8.00	$18.00
Job No. 2					
Labor time, 11 hours @ $5.40	$59.40				
or					
Labor time:					
Machining, 9 hours @ $10.00			$ 90.00		
Finishing, 2 hours @ $.80				$ 1.60	$91.60

To summarize, when products are heterogeneous, receiving uneven attention and effort as they move through various departments or cost centers, departmental or cost-center overhead rates are necessary to achieve more accurate product costs. In these situations, the departmental rates are frequently described as being more homogeneous than the plantwide rates.

factors affecting homogeneity

Homogeneity refers to all ingredients of the cost-allocation rate, both within and between the numerator (the cost pool) and the denominator (the cost-allocation base). That is, defects in either the numerator or the denominator can result in a nonhomogeneous average cost rate. For example, the summing of recruiting costs and data-processing costs and dividing by machine-hours is likely to be nonhomogeneous because (a) the costs in the pool have little commonality of purpose, and (b) the allocation base has no direct causal relationship to these costs.

Note especially the interdependent effects. For example, the testing for homogeneity might lead to:

1. Redefining the final cost objectives, because there may be no need to discriminate among them. Perhaps no distinction is needed between, say, Airplane 1 and Airplane 2; the cost objective should be both Airplanes 1 and 2 together.
2. Choosing a different allocation base, because in testing we discover another base (say, number of employees instead of direct-labor hours) that will yield a more acceptable[4] level of homogeneity (a better cause-effect fit).
3. Choosing different cost pools. There may be too much aggregation of, say, different classes of labor with different rates.

An advantage of testing for homogeneity is that it forces a simultaneous consideration of all three crucial factors in cost allocation: the objective, the cost pools, and the relationships or functions. Accuracy cannot be judged by looking at only one or two factors at a time.

Homogeneity is a matter of degree. At one extreme, all costs for all departments would be pooled and allocated, using a single allocation base. At the other extreme, each cost would be allocated, using individual allocation bases. In concept, the latter method is the ideal. In practice, a system approaching the former method is favored. The tendency toward the simpler, cruder methods is the result of an implicit or explicit cost-and-value-of-information decision. As already mentioned, the prevailing attitude seems to be that the additional accuracy provided by increased homogeneity will not make much difference in management decisions. Of course, this is a testable proposition that should be examined periodically in every organization—particularly those where costs directly influence pricing or product-combination decisions.

[4] The magnitude of an "acceptable" level would depend on the cost and value of the additional information that might be supplied by more disaggregation. Also see Yuji Ijiri, *Foundations of Accounting Measurement* (Englewood Cliffs, N.J.: Prentice-Hall, Inc., 1967), pp. 117–31.

intermediate cost pools The complete testing of homogeneity may be regarded as infeasible because of the difficulties of linking unaggregated costs[5] to cost objectives on a one-by-one basis. If this is the case, there may be some intermediate cost pools that can be used as a guide for tests. These intermediate pools take three forms that are not necessarily mutually exclusive nor ranked in order of importance: responsibility center, cost behavior pattern, and a natural-category orientation.

The conglomeration of various costs in massive plantwide cost pools is likely to be the antithesis of homogeneity. The first intermediate pool that can test the plantwide rate is that of responsibility centers (departments) and the use of departmental allocation rates. Because the costs attributable to responsibility centers are routinely accumulated anyway, the use of departmental rates should not overburden the cost-accounting system.

The second intermediate pool that can test any give rate or rates is based on the distinction between variable and fixed costs. Separate bases (e.g., hours used and hours available) can be developed for each, and the resulting cost allocations can be compared with those obtained via a more highly aggregated rate. Note that department costs (a cost pool) may be subdivided into two pools by using separate departmental rates for variable and fixed costs.

The third intermediate aggregation that can test any given rate is based on a natural-category orientation. Vatter[6] illustrates this idea with a classification that includes the following:

TYPES OF COSTS	*EXAMPLES*	*SUGGESTED USUAL ALLOCATION BASE*
People-oriented	Personnel department	Number of employees
Payroll-oriented	Vacation pay, payroll taxes	Payroll dollars
Materials-oriented	Storeroom costs, internal transport	Units of material, weight, size
Machine-oriented	Variable costs of power, supplies, routine maintenance	Machine-hours

Conceivably, any given aggregated allocation rate could be compared against less aggregated intermediate rates based on both variable-fixed and natural-category subclassifications within departments.

[5] Technically, in most accounting systems it is indeed difficult to find unaggregated costs in their purest form. For example, consider the travel costs that might be recorded. Usually some aggregation occurs even before recording on the source documents. Breakfasts, lunches, and dinners become "meals"; each taxi fare becomes "local transportation"; and so on.

[6] *Standards for Cost Analysis,* a research report prepared by William J. Vatter for the Comptroller General of the United States, August 1969, pp. 56–59.

different bases for different departments

Some companies use different overhead bases for different departments. Exhibit 16-5 used direct-labor hours as the base for the machining department because it was assumed that direct-labor time was proportionate to machine time. In Exhibit 16-5, if labor time was not proportionate to machine time, machine-hours would be the overhead base in the machining department whereas labor-hours would continue to be the base in the finishing department. Some machines may be almost entirely automatic; or an operator may be able to run two or three machines simultaneously on some jobs but only one machine at a time on other jobs.

Regarding homogeneity, the following general guidelines seem applicable:

1. Begin with the most detailed cost data that are economically feasible to collect. Start to form cost pools only if they are justified by the savings in clerical and other costs.
2. To obtain higher homogeneity, have more rather than fewer cost pools.

choosing allocation bases

Despite the logical attractions of using various overhead pools and various allocation bases, general practice is to use few pools and few bases. The most widely used bases are chosen after considering (a) the factors obviously associated with the individual products or jobs (for example, direct materials and direct labor), (b) necessary clerical costs and effort in application, and (c) differences in final results. Where results do not differ significantly, the easier method is used.

The logic is to relate the final cost objective to various bases and, in turn, to relate the overhead pool to the bases. Consider the data in Exhibit 16-6. The final cost objective is the product. The potential allocation bases are direct materials, direct-labor hours, direct-labor cost, and machine-hours; all these bases can be physically traced to the product. Which of the bases is best for predicting fluctuations in total overhead costs? The answer may be derived arbitrarily or by statistical regression analysis. As long as all the possible causal factors are used in the same proportions on individual jobs, each job will get the same amount of overhead.

Exhibit 16-6 illustrates the following important points:

1. Either direct-labor dollars or direct-labor time may be used as a basis for overhead application to product, as long as the direct-labor dollars and hours vary in direct proportion—that is, as long as labor rates are uniform across all jobs.

2. Where costs related to machines are the predominant overhead factor, machine-hours should be used instead of labor-hours if both do not fluctuate in

EXHIBIT 16-6

COMPARISON OF OVERHEAD APPLICATION TO PRODUCT WHEN BASES ARE USED PROPORTIONATELY

ANNUAL OVERHEAD BUDGET DATA:	*TOTAL*	*POSSIBLE RATES*
Total overhead	$100,000	
Direct-labor cost		50% of direct-labor cost
Direct-labor hours	100,000	$1.00 per DLH
Direct-material usage	$400,000	25% of direct materials
Machine-hours	20,000	$5.00 per machine-hour

			POSSIBLE OVERHEAD APPLICATION USING FOLLOWING BASES			
			DIRECT MATERIALS	*DIRECT-LABOR HOURS*	*DIRECT-LABOR COST*	*MACHINE-HOURS*
Job data:						
Job No. 1						
Direct-labor hours		5				
Machine-hours		1				
Direct materials	$ 20					
Direct-labor cost	10					
Prime cost	$ 30					
Overhead	5		.25($20) = $5	$1.00(5 hr.) = $5	.50($10) = $5	1 hr.($5) = $5
Total job cost	$ 35					
Job No. 2						
Direct-labor hours		25				
Machine-hours		5				
Direct materials	$100					
Direct-labor cost	50					
Prime cost	$150					
Overhead	25		.25($100) = $25	$1.00(25 hr.) = $25	.50($50) = $25	.5 hr.($5) = $25
Total job cost	$175					

proportion. In other words, if one operator runs one machine for a certain job and three similar machines for another job, other things being equal, the machine-hour base is more rational than a labor base.

3. If labor time has a proportionate relationship to machine time, it is unnecessary to use machine-hours because the final costs of a job will not differ.

4. Easy availability of data for a job, a department, or other cost objective is very influential. The base that is easiest and cheapest to apply is often selected, as long as individual job costs are not significantly affected. Note in Exhibit 16-6 that the final results are the same on a specific job because all bases are used *proportionately*. But if the possible bases are not used proportionately on individual jobs, certain jobs may receive relatively inaccurate amounts of overhead. This latter point is not illustrated specifically in the exhibit. However, the point can be readily seen by changing the number of machine-hours on Job No. 2 from five to six. This would change the overhead application, using a machine-hour rate, from $25 to $30.

A general discussion of the relative merits[7] of some commonly used bases follows:

1. DIRECT-LABOR HOURS Most overhead costs are more closely related to time expiration than to any other factor. Fixed costs such as depreciation, rent, taxes, and insurance relate to a given time period. Indirect labor and supply usage are most closely related to the input of hours of effort. That is why time devoted to specific products is often used for correlating overhead with products. Time is traced to specific products by using work tickets for direct labor. Predetermined overhead rates are developed by dividing predicted total overhead by predicted total direct hours. Thus, the amount of overhead applied to any given product is dependent on the amount of time devoted to an operation or product.

2. MACHINE-HOURS In these days of mechanized production, machine time is often a better predictor of overhead-cost incurrence than direct-labor time. Depreciation, property taxes, supply usage, and indirect labor are frequently more closely related to machinery utilization than to direct-labor usage. In theory, then, machine time may be the most accurate base for overhead application.

In practice, however, machine time is rarely used because of the added clerical cost and the difficulty of computing machine time on individual jobs. Machine time may be ignored where the relationship of labor time or labor costs to machine time is unchanging between jobs; that is, the final overhead application to a given type of job would not differ (for example, one direct laborer may always run two similar machines).

[7] The Cost Accounting Standards Board (CASB) has summarized the use of various allocation bases used by companies under its jurisdiction. Direct-labor dollars is by far the most widely used allocation base, and direct-labor hours is second. For example, their data bank indicated that of those operating units (346) with a manufacturing overhead pool, 254 (73 percent) use the direct-labor dollars base, 50 (15 percent) use the direct-labor hours base, and 12 percent use a variety of other bases. *Progress Report to the Congress,* published annually.

3. DIRECT-LABOR COST If labor rates are nearly uniform for every operation, the use of a labor-*dollar* base for overhead application yields the same results as using direct-labor *hours*. Otherwise, direct-labor *hours* is better in most instances, particularly where the senior and junior workers are equally efficient and therefore use the same amounts of overhead services per hour. For example, a senior worker may earn \$8 per hour while a junior worker may earn \$7.50 per hour. If a 200-percent-of-direct-labor-cost rate is in effect, the overhead cost of a given job requiring one hour of direct labor would be \$16 if the senior worker were used and \$15 if the junior worker were used. Standard or average labor rates generally prevent such ridiculous results.

Direct-labor *dollars* as an overhead base may be conceptually better than labor-*hours* where many overhead items represent fringe labor costs, which are primarily tied to direct-labor *cost* or where high-cost direct laborers make the greatest use of high-cost facilities and complex machinery.

4. DIRECT MATERIAL Unless the labor and equipment needed for material handling are a major part of overhead, the use of direct-material dollars or weights is seldom a valid base for overhead application. Again, materials may be used where the final results are the same regardless of the base adopted. Sometimes storeroom and material-handling overhead is separated from other factory overhead and is applied to jobs on the basis of direct-material weight or bulk. The remaining overhead items would be applied by using some other base.

SUMMARY

The contribution approach to the income statement and to the problems of cost allocations is accounting's most effective method for helping management to evaluate performance and make decisions. Allocations are made with thoughtful regard for the purpose of the information being compiled. Various subdivisions of net income are drawn for different purposes. The contribution approach distinguishes sharply between various degrees of objectivity in cost allocations.

Homogeneity is a frequently cited guide for deciding how many cost pools are warranted. The essence of the matter is whether final results in the form of costs and decisions will differ from the optimum as different cost bases, cost pools, and cost objectives are chosen.

The use of linear algebra provides the best theoretical answer to the allocation of costs of reciprocal services. Again, whether to use linear algebra depends on the sensitivity of decisions to the use of simpler methods.

PROBLEMS FOR SELF-STUDY

PROBLEM 1 Review the section on the contribution approach to cost allocation, especially Exhibit 16-1.

SOLUTION 1 See Exhibit 16-1.

PROBLEM 2

Consider the following case, adapted from a CPA examination:

You have been engaged to install a cost system for the Martin Company. Your investigation of the manufacturing operations of the business discloses these facts:

1. The company makes a line of lighting fixtures and lamps. The material cost of any particular item ranks from 15 percent to 60 percent of total factory cost, depending on the kind of metal and fabric used in making it.
2. The business is subject to wide cyclical fluctuations, for the sales volume follows new-housing construction.
3. About 60 percent of the manufacturing is normally done in the first quarter of the year.
4. For the whole plant, the wage rates range from \$4.25 to \$8.75 an hour. However, within each of the eight individual departments, the spread between the high and low wage rates is less than 5 percent.
5. Each of the products made uses all eight of the manufacturing departments but not proportionately.
6. Within the individual manufacturing departments, factory overhead ranges from 30 percent to 80 percent of conversion cost.

Based on the information above, you are to prepare a statement or letter for the president of the company, explaining whether in its cost system Martin Company should use:

a. A normal overhead rate or an expected-actual-activity annual overhead rate (see Chapter 10);
b. An overall overhead rate or a departmental overhead rate;
c. A method of factory-overhead application based on direct-labor hours, direct-labor cost, or prime cost.

Include the reasons supporting *each* of your three recommendations.

SOLUTION 2

Dear Sir:

From a study of the manufacturing operations of the Martin Company, it is my recommendation that, in applying its manufacturing overhead, the company use normal departmental overhead rates applied as percentages of the *direct-labor cost.*

The company should use normal rather than expected actual overhead rates because of the wide seasonal and cyclical fluctuations in its business. Expected actual rates would, owing to the large fixed-overhead expenses, make the per-unit overhead costs high in the low-production periods and low in the high-production periods. The use of normal rates would apply the same per-unit overhead costs regardless of month-to-month and year-to-year fluctuations. Both for quoting prices and for pricing inventories, it is best to use per-unit costs neither inflated by the costs of available but unused factory facilities nor deflated by the gains of better-than-normal use of the factory facilities.

The company should use departmental overhead rates because the rates obviously vary so markedly among the departments. If a blanket rate were used as an average rate, it would not be correct for any department. Because the company's overhead is a large part of the factory cost, the inaccuracy in the per-unit costs caused by the use of a blanket rate would be substantial. If all the products made used all the departments proportionately, a blanket rate would result in substantially accurate total (but not departmental) unit-overhead costs. However, in the Martin Company, the products do not use all the departments proportionately.

As the wage rates are substantially uniform within the separate departments, the labor costs in each department are closely proportionate to the labor time. Therefore, the percent-of-direct-labor-cost method of applying the factory overhead would in this case effect about as accurate an application as would the rate-per-direct-labor-hour method. The clerical expense of the percent-of-direct-labor-cost method would be low, because the method does not require accumulation of the number of direct-labor hours applicable to each job.

The percent-of-prime-cost method of overhead application is not recommended because of the wide differences in the costs of the materials that may be used to make a given lamp or fixture. Factory overhead is primarily the cost of using factory facilities. The factory facilities applied to make a lamp of silver are not more than those used to make the same lamp of copper. For this reason, the use of prime cost (because it includes material cost) would result in an excessive charge to lamps using expensive materials.

Very truly yours,

QUESTIONS, PROBLEMS, AND CASES

16-1 What is the most important criterion for selecting an overhead base?

16-2 Why are departmental overhead rates generally preferable to plantwide rates?

16-3 "Service-department costs shouldn't be reallocated." Do you agree? Why?

16-4 What are the criteria for selecting reallocation bases for service-department costs?

16-5 List at least three subtotals that might be highlighted in a contribution income statement by segments.

16-6 What is the theoretically most accurate method for reallocating service-department costs?

16-7 How is homogeneity in cost allocation measured?

16-8 What is the most frequently used cost-allocation base?

16-9 "To obtain higher homogeneity, have more rather than fewer cost pools." Do you agree? Why?

16-10 "In these days of highly mechanized production, more overhead rates should be based on machine-hours." Do you agree? Why?

16-11 "Reciprocal cost-allocation schemes are always preferable." Do you agree? Why?

16-12 *Service-Department Costs* (CPA) The Parker Manufacturing Company has two production departments (fabrication and assembly) and three service departments (general factory administration, factory maintenance, and factory cafeteria). A summary of costs and other data for each department prior to allocation of service-department costs for the year ended June 30, 19_3, appears below.

The costs of the general-factory-administration department, factory-maintenance department, and factory cafeteria are allocated on the basis of direct-labor hours, square footage occupied, and number of employees, respectively. There are no manufacturing-overhead variances. *Round all final calculations to the nearest dollar.* Choose the best answer:

1. Assuming that Parker elects to distribute service-department costs directly to production departments without interservice department cost allocation,

the amount of factory-maintenance department costs that would be allocated to the fabrication department would be
a. $0. b. $111,760. c. $106,091. d. $91,440.

2. Assuming the same method of allocation as in item 1, the amount of general-factory-administration department costs that would be allocated to the assembly department would be
a. $0. b. $63,636. c. $70,000. d. $90,000.
3. Assuming that Parker elects to distribute service-department costs to other service departments (starting with the service department with the greatest total costs) as well as the production departments, the amount of factory-cafeteria department costs which would be allocated to the factory-maintenance department would be (*Note:* Once a service department's costs have been reallocated, no subsequent service-department costs are recirculated back to it.)
a. $0. b. $96,000. c. $3,840. d. $6,124.
4. Assuming the same method of allocation as in item 3, the amount of factory-maintenance department costs which would be allocated to the factory cafeteria would be
a. $0. b. $5,787. c. $5,856. d. $148,910.

	FABRICATION	*ASSEMBLY*	*GENERAL FACTORY ADMINISTRATION*	*FACTORY MAINTENANCE*	*FACTORY CAFETERIA*
Direct-labor costs	$1,950,000	$2,050,000	$90,000	$82,100	$87,000
Direct-material costs	$3,130,000	$ 950,000	—	$65,000	$91,000
Manufacturing-overhead costs	$1,650,000	$1,850,000	$70,000	$56,100	$62,000
Direct-labor hours	562,500	437,500	31,000	27,000	42,000
Number of employees	280	200	12	8	20
Square footage occupied	88,000	72,000	1,750	2,000	4,800

16-13 *Step Method of Allocation for Product Costing* Sample Company had the following departmental factory overhead costs for a normal month (numbers reduced for simplicity):

Machining	$17,100	Factory administration	$7,800
Buildings and grounds	5,100	Assembly	3,700
Finishing	3,400	Repair and maintenance	2,460

The step method was used for allocating service-department costs to production departments. Repair costs were allocated first, based on specific services rendered, 20 percent to Buildings and Grounds, 1 percent to Factory Administration, 60 percent to Machining, 10 percent to Assembly, and 9 percent to Finishing.

Building and grounds costs were allocated next, based on square footage in each department. Factory administration was allocated last, based on direct-labor hours:

	FACTORY ADMINISTRATION	*MACHINING*	*ASSEMBLY*	*FINISHING*
Square footage	10,000	60,000	20,000	10,000
Standard direct-labor hours		24,000	3,000	3,000

required

1. Compute the total factory overhead for each production department.
2. Compute the overhead rate per standard direct-labor hour for absorption product-costing purposes.

16-14 *Departmental versus Plantwide Applications* The following are pertinent data for the Alou Company:

Budget Data for 19_7	(S1) Factory Personnel	(S2) Production Planning and Control	(P1) Machining	(P2) Assembly
Predicted overhead	$51,000	$198,500	$2,235,500	$755,000
Machine-hours			300,000	—
Direct-labor hours			40,000	500,000
Orders to be processed			8,000	2,000
Number of employees		10	30	300

Factory personnel-department costs are to be reapportioned on the basis of number of employees; production planning and control, on the basis of orders processed. The step basis is used for reapportionment.

This company produces a wide variety of products on a job-order basis. Management has always used a single, plantwide overhead application rate based on direct-labor hours.

Recently, however, customer complaints on price quotations, plus the outside auditor's criticism of the plantwide rate, has prompted management to ask you, the controller, to restudy the situation before setting rates for 19_7.

You decide that departmental overhead rates should be developed, at least as a method of attack. You think that a machine-hour rate should be used for the machining department, which contains costly automatic and semiautomatic equipment manned by a few workers who tend and control many machines simultaneously.

The workers may operate a couple of machines at a time on certain jobs, and as many as six machines or more on other jobs. Because the assembly department requires painstaking workmanship but little equipment, you think that direct-labor hours is the most proper overhead base there.

The budget data for 19_7 are little different from those for 19_6, so you pick five representative jobs worked on during December 19_6 as a basis for comparing the blanket rate with departmental rates. You keep careful records of machine-hours as well as of the direct-labor hours. The results follow:

	MACHINING		ASSEMBLY
Job Number	Machine-Hours	DLH	DLH
300	5	2	10
301	40	4	40
302	10	2	30
303	7	1	5
304	15	11	30

required

(Show and label computations)

1. Departmental overhead rates.
2. Plantwide rate.
3. A detailed summary by jobs of (a) total overhead applied, using departmental rates; (b) total overhead applied, using a plantwide rate; (c) difference between (a) and (b).
4. What is the total difference for the jobs taken together?
5. What overhead application base would you recommend? Why?

16-15 *Overhead Reapportionments Already Given; Determine Bases Used* Listed below are the Kurt Company's departmental overhead budgets for a normal activity level, overhead costs reapportioned by department utilizing predetermined rates, and a few operating and plant statistics for the period concerned. Assume that 15,000 direct-labor hours were worked in each producing department.

	Budgeted Normal Activity	REAPPORTIONED COSTS (STEP METHOD) Employment Service	General Plant Administration	Lunchroom	Storeroom	Vulcanizing Department	Assembly Department
Janitorial Service	$ 8,000	$300	$600	$ 900	$1,600	$2,300	$ 2,300
Employment Service	3,700		300	200	200	1,300	2,000
General Plant Adm.	19,100			1,000	750	8,250	10,000
Lunchroom	1,400				200	1,300	2,000
Storeroom	250					2,100	900
Vulcanizing Dept.	14,750						
Assembling Dept.	22,800						
	$70,000						

Total number of square feet	80,000
Total number of employees	200
Total number of labor-hours	40,000
Total direct-labor hours	30,000
Total number of requisitions	1,000

required

1. In tabular fashion:
   (a) Determine the most logical bases for reapportionment.
   (b) List the total costs reapportioned to each plant operation.
   (c) Compute rates for reapportionment (that is, janitorial service is 10¢ per square foot, and so on).
   (d) List the following data for *each* plant operation:
   Number of the square feet utilized.
   Number of employees assigned.
   Number of total labor-hours assigned.
   Number of direct-labor hours utilized.
   Number of requisitions initiated.
2. Compute the overhead rate per direct-labor hour for the two departments.
3. Compute a plantwide overhead application rate with direct-labor hours as the base.

16-16 *Divisional Contribution, Performance, and Segment Margins* The president of the Midwestern Railroad wants to obtain an overview of his operations, particularly with respect to comparing freight and passenger business. He has heard about some new "contribution" approaches to cost allocations that emphasize cost behavior patterns and so-called *contribution margins,* contribution controllable by division managers, and contribution by segments. Pertinent data for the year ended December 31, 19_2, follow:

Total revenue was $100 million, of which $90 million was freight traffic and $10 million was passenger traffic. Half the latter was generated by Division 1; 40 percent by Division 2; and 10 percent by Division 3.

Total variable costs were $56 million, of which $44 million was freight traffic. Of the $12 million allocable to passenger traffic, $4.4, $3.7, and $3.9 million could be allocated to Divisions 1, 2, and 3, respectively.

Total separable discretionary fixed costs were $10 million, of which $9.5 million applied to freight traffic. Of the remainder, $100,000 could not be allocated to specific divisions, although it was clearly traceable to passenger traffic in general. Divisions 1, 2, and 3 should be allocated $300,000, $70,000, and $30,000, respectively.

Total separable committed costs were $30 million, of which 90 percent was allocable to freight traffic. Of the 10 percent traceable to passenger traffic, Divisions 1, 2, and 3 should be allocated $1,800,000, $420,000, and $180,000, respectively; the balance was unallocable to a specific division.

The joint fixed costs not clearly allocable to any part of the company amounted to $1,000,000.

required

1. The president asks you to prepare statements, dividing the data for the company as a whole between the freight and passenger traffic and then subdividing the passenger traffic into three divisions.
2. Some competing railroads actively promote a series of one-day sightseeing tours on summer weekends. Most often, these tours are timed so that the cars with the tourists are hitched on with regularly scheduled passenger trains.
   What costs are relevant for making decisions to run such tours? Other railroads, facing the same general cost picture, refuse to conduct such sightseeing tours. Why?
3. For purposes of this analysis, even though the numbers may be unrealistic, suppose that Division No. 2's figures represented a specific run for a train instead of a division. Suppose further that the railroad has petitioned government authorities for permission to drop No. 2. What would be the effect on overall company net income for 19_3, assuming that the figures are accurate and that 19_3 operations are in all other respects a duplication of 19_2 operations?

16-17 *Marketing Costs* (CMA) The Scent Company sells men's toiletries to retail stores throughout the United States. For planning and control purposes the Scent Company is organized into twelve geographic regions with two to six territories within each region. One salesman is assigned to each territory and has exclusive rights to all sales made in that territory. Merchandise is shipped from the manufacturing plant to the twelve regional warehouses, and the sales in each territory are shipped from the regional warehouse. National headquarters allocates a specific amount at the beginning of the year for regional advertising.

The net sales for the Scent Company for the year ended September 30, 19_4, totaled $10 million. Costs incurred by national headquarters for national administration, advertising, and warehousing are summarized as follows:

National administration	$250,000
National advertising	125,000
National warehousing	175,000
	$550,000

The results of operations for the South Atlantic Region for the year ended September 30, 19_4, are as follows:

SCENT COMPANY

Statement of Operations for South Atlantic Region
for the Year Ended September 30, 19_4

Net sales		$900,000
Costs and expenses:		
Advertising fees	$ 54,700	
Bad-debt expense	3,600	
Cost of sales	460,000	
Freight-out	22,600	
Insurance	10,000	
Salaries and employee benefits	81,600	
Sales commissions	36,000	
Supplies	12,000	
Travel and entertainment	14,100	
Wages and employee benefits	36,000	
Warehouse depreciation	8,000	
Warehouse operating costs	15,000	
Total costs and expenses		753,600
Territory contribution		$146,400

The South Atlantic Region consists of two territories—Green and Purple. The salaries and employee benefits consist of the following items:

Regional vice-president	$24,000
Regional marketing manager	15,000
Regional warehouse manager	13,400
Salesmen (one for each territory with all receiving the same salary base)	15,600
Employee benefits (20 percent)	13,600
	$81,600

The salesmen receive a base salary plus a 4 percent commission on all items sold in their territory. Bad-debt expense has averaged .4 percent of net sales in the past. Travel and entertainment costs are incurred by the salesmen calling upon their customers. Freight-out is a function of the quantity of goods shipped and the distance shipped. Thirty percent of the insurance is expended for protection of the inventory while it is in the regional warehouse, and the remainder is incurred for the protection of the warehouse. Supplies are used in the warehouse for packing the merchandise that is shipped. Wages relate to the hourly paid employees who fill orders in the warehouse. The warehouse operating costs account contains such costs as heat, light, and maintenance.

The following cost analyses and statistics by territory for the current year are representative of past experience and are representative of expected future operations.

	GREEN	PURPLE	TOTAL
Sales	$300,000	$600,000	$900,000
Cost of sales	$184,000	$276,000	$460,000
Advertising fees	$ 21,800	$ 32,900	$ 54,700

	GREEN	PURPLE	TOTAL
Travel and entertainment	$ 6,300	$ 7,800	$ 14,100
Freight-out	$ 9,000	$ 13,600	$ 22,600
Units sold	150,000	350,000	500,000
Pounds shipped	210,000	390,000	600,000
Salesmen miles traveled	21,600	38,400	60,000

required

1. The top management of Scent Company wants the regional vice-presidents to present their operating data in a more meaningful manner. Therefore, management has requested the regions to separate their operating costs into the fixed and variable components of order-getting (for example, sales commissions), order-filling (for example, freight-out), and administration. The data are to be presented in the following format:

	TERRITORY COSTS		REGIONAL COSTS	TOTAL COSTS
	GREEN	PURPLE		
Order-getting				
Order-filling				
Administration				

Using management's suggested format, prepare a schedule that presents the costs for the region by territory with the costs separated into variable and fixed categories by order-getting, order-filling, and administrative functions.

2. Suppose the top management of Scent Company is considering splitting the Purple Territory into two separate territories (Red and Blue). From the data that have been presented, identify what data would be relevant to this decision (either for or against) and indicate what other data you would collect to aid top management in its decision.
3. If Scent Company keeps its records in accordance with the classification required in part 1, can standards and flexible budgets be employed by the company in planning and controlling marketing costs? Give reasons for your answer.

16-18 *Analysis of Channels of Distribution and Territories* The Manning Co. has three sales territories that sell a single product. Its income statement for 19_2 contained the following data:

		TERRITORY		
	Total	A	B	C
Sales: 100,000 units, @ $11	$1,100,000	$550,000	$330,000	$220,000
Cost of goods sold, including $100,000 of fixed factory overhead	$ 500,000	$250,000	$150,000	$100,000
Gross margin	$ 600,000	$300,000	$180,000	$120,000
Order-filling costs:				
Freight-out	$ 68,000	$ 34,000	$ 20,400	$ 13,600
Shipping supplies	50,000	25,000	15,000	10,000
Packing and shipping labor	50,000	25,000	15,000	10,000
Total	$ 168,000	$ 84,000	$ 50,400	$ 33,600
Order-getting costs:				
Salesmen's salaries	$ 50,000	$ 50,000		
Salesmen's commissions	26,400		$ 26,400	
Agents' commissions	11,000			$ 11,000

		TERRITORY		
	Total	A	B	C
Sales manager's salary	30,000	15,000	9,000	6,000
Advertising, local	80,000	40,000	24,000	16,000
Advertising, national	100,000	50,000	30,000	20,000
Total	$ 297,400	$155,000	$ 89,400	$ 53,000
Total marketing costs	$ 465,400	$239,000	$139,800	$ 86,600
Administrative expenses:				
Variable	$ 50,000	$ 25,000	$ 15,000	$ 10,000
Nonvariable	100,000	50,000	30,000	20,000
Total administrative expense	$ 150,000	$ 75,000	$ 45,000	$ 30,000
Total expenses	$ 615,400	$314,000	$184,800	$116,600
Net operating income	$ (15,400)	$(14,000)	$ (4,800)	$ 3,400

Territory A contains the company's only factory and central headquarters. This district employs five salaried salesmen.

Territory B is 200 to 400 miles from the factory. The district employs three salesmen on a commission basis and advertises weekly, locally.

Territory C is 400 to 600 miles from the factory. The district employs three manufacturers' agents. Local advertising costs are split fifty-fifty between the agents and the company. Cost per unit of advertising space is the same as in Territory A.

The following variable unit costs have been computed:

Freight-out, per unit		$.50, $.70, and $1.10, for Territories A, B, and C, respectively
Shipping supplies, per unit	.50	
Packing and shipping labor, per unit	.50	
Variable administrative cost, per sales order	2.00	

Territory A had 17,000 orders; Territory B, 6,000; and Territory C, 2,000. Local advertising costs were $60,000, $15,000, and $5,000, for Territories A, B, and C, respectively.

required

1. Mr. Manning asks you to recast the income statement in accordance with the contribution approach that he heard described at a recent sales convention. Assume that fixed manufacturing overhead, national advertising, the sales manager's salary, and nonvariable administrative expense are not allocated.
2. What is the contribution controllable by the segment manager per order in each territory? What clues for management investigation are generated by such a computation?
3. The salesmen in Territory B have suggested a saturation campaign in local newspaper advertising, to cost $30,000. How much must the sales volume in Territory B increase to justify such an additional investment?
4. Why does Territory A have the highest contribution-margin percentage but the lowest territorial-margin percentage?
5. On the basis of the given data, what courses of action seem most likely to improve profits? Should Territory A be dropped? Why?

16-19 *Reciprocal Cost Allocations* (D. Green) The Prairie State Paper Company located a plant near one of its forests. At the time of construction, there were no utility companies equipped to provide this plant with water, power, or fuel. Therefore, included in the original facilities were (1) a water plant, which pumped water from a nearby lake and filtered it; (2) a coal-fired boiler room that produced steam, part of which was used for the manufacturing process and the balance for producing electricity; and (3) an electric plant.

An analysis of these activities has revealed that 60 percent of the water is used for the production of steam and 40 percent is used in manufacturing. Half of the steam produced is used for the production of electric power and half for manufacturing. Twenty percent of the electric power is used by the water plant and 80 percent goes to manufacturing.

For the year 19_9, the costs charged to these departments were:

	VARIABLE	FIXED	TOTAL
Water plant	$ 2,000	$ 8,000	$10,000
Steam room	18,000	12,000	30,000
Electric plant	6,000	9,000	15,000
			$55,000

required

1. How would you allocate these costs in an absorption product-cost determination situation? Use the reciprocal method.
2. A new power company has offered to sell electricity to Prairie State for two cents a kilowatt-hour. In 19_9, the electric plant generated 600,000 kilowatt-hours. The manager of the electric plant has advised that the offer be rejected, since (he says) "our variable costs were only one cent per kilowatt-hour in 19_9." Was this the right answer? Show computations.

16-20 *Reciprocal Allocations* The Rene Company has two main products, M-4 and M-5. Each is manufactured in a separate department. Two major service departments, power (P) and material-handling (H), support the plant activities.

The energy crisis has prompted a careful analysis of all activities. The work of the service departments has been converted to "control-factor units of work used" and is distributed as follows for a typical period:

	SUPPLIER	
USER	P	H
P	—	80
H	60	—
M-4 production	80	40
M-5 production	60	80
Control-factor units	200	200

The costs of the service departments for a typical period are:

	P	H
Variable labor and material costs	$14,000	$2,000
Supervision—fixed	2,000	2,000
Depreciation and other fixed	4,000	4,000
Reallocated costs from P	—	?
Reallocated costs from H	?	—

required

1. What are the fully reallocated costs to M-4 and M-5? Allocate variable and fixed costs, using the reciprical method. Show and label all computations in an orderly way.

2. An outside power company has offered to supply all the power needed by the Rene Company and to provide all the services of the present power department. The cost will be $80 per control-factor unit. Should Rene accept? Present a comparative analysis in three parts: (a) yes or no; (b) the total cost of the units acquired from the outside company; and (c) the total variable costs if power were produced inside, assuming (perhaps unrealistically) for purposes of this analysis that only the variable costs are pertinent.

Base your decision on the quantitative data; ignore all qualitative and long run considerations.

16-21 *Choosing an Allocation Method* Refer to the preceding problem, part 1. Compute the cost allocations by the direct method and two different sequences of the step method. Do you prefer any of these methods over the reciprocal method? Why?

Joint-Product Costs and By-Product Costs

17

Nearly every manufacturing operation produces two or more products. But ordinarily, all the manufacturing costs of these multiple products are applied to a single product. For example, as cloth or metal is cut or formed, the excess is regarded as waste or scrap. The minor cost that might be applied to the waste or scrap is usually ignored, and all the production cost is applied to, say, the coat or the lamp that is eventually manufactured.

Whether the accountant applies costs individually among multiple products is dependent on their relative revenue-producing power. When a group of individual products is simultaneously produced, with each product having a significant relative sales value, the outputs are usually called *joint products.* The products are not identifiable as different individual products until a certain stage of production known as the *split-off point.* All costs incurred prior to the split-off point are called *joint-product costs.* The total of these costs is allocated carefully to individual members of the product group. A distinguishing characteristic is that no one of the products may be produced without an accompanying appearance of the other products in the joint group, although perhaps in variable proportions. Examples include chemicals, lumber, petroleum products, flour milling, copper mining, meat packing, leather tanning, soap making, gas manufacturing, canneries, and tobacco manufacturing. A meat-packing company cannot kill a pork chop; it has to slaughter a hog, which supplies various cuts of dressed meat, hides, and trimmings.

We shall see that any method of allocating truly joint costs to various units produced is useful only for purposes of inventory costing, which, of course, will affect the income statement and balance sheet. **Such allocation is useless for cost-planning and control purposes.**

The term *by-products* is usually confined to those multiple products that have very minor sales values as compared with that of the major or chief product(s).

In this chapter we shall examine (a) the methods of allocating joint costs to products, (b) the impact of joint costs on decision making, and (c) accounting for by-products.

methods of allocating joint costs to products

This section explores various ways of allocating joint costs to products for inventory-valuation and income-determination purposes *only.* The next section underscores the fact that all these cost allocations are inherently arbitrary[1] and are of no help for making decisions about product mix or whether to sell or process further.

nature of joint-product cost

Viewed broadly, joint costs plague the accountant throughout his work. However, we shall confine the term *joint-product cost* to the costs of a single process or series of processes that simultaneously produces two or more products of significant relative sales values. Joint-product costs are total costs incurred up to the point of separation of the different products. Consider Example 1:

example 1

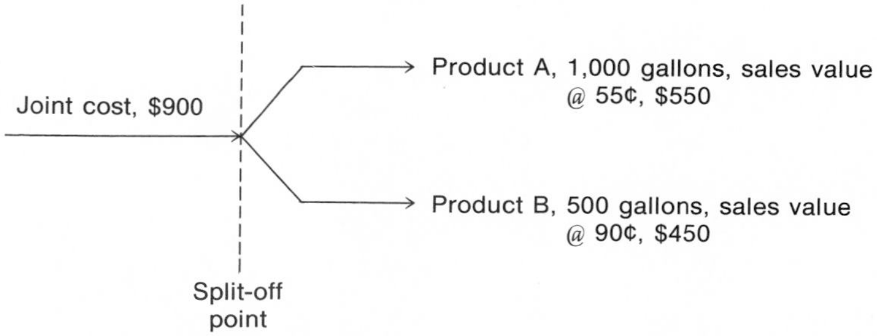

[1] Also see A. L. Thomas, *The Allocation Problem: Part Two,* Studies in Accounting Research No. 9 (Sarasota, Fla.: American Accounting Association, 1974). Thomas is an outspoken critic of allocations. Also see R. Weil, "Allocating Joint Costs," *American Economic Review,* Vol. LVIII, No. 5, pp. 1342–45.

Example 1 shows the joint costs of a chemical process that produces Products A and B; both become finished goods at the split-off point. How much of the $900 joint cost is allocable to A? How much to B? The $900 cannot be physically identified or traced to either individual product, because the products themselves were not separated before the split-off point. Yet the accountant chooses to select some systematic means of splitting the $900 between the two products so that ending inventories may be costed and income determined. Two basic approaches are commonly used, although there are many variations of both: (a) physical measures and (b) net realizable values.

physical measures In Example 1, the $900 cost produced 1,500 gallons of product on a physical-quantity basis; therefore, the unit cost is 60¢ per gallon. Costs are assigned as follows: $600 to A, $300 to B. These computations may be shown in a different manner as follows:

	PRODUCTION	WEIGHTING	COSTS ASSIGNED
A	1,000 gal.	1,000/1,500 × $900	$600
B	500 gal.	500/1,500 × $900	300
	1,500 gal.		$900

Assume that one-tenth of the output is unsold at the end of the month. A product-line income statement would appear as follows:

INCOME STATEMENT FOR JOINT PRODUCTS

For the Month Ending ________

	A		*B*		*TOTAL*
Sales	900 gals.,	$495	450 gals.,	$405	$900
Joint costs:					
Production costs	1,000 gals.,	$600	500 gals.,	$300	$900
Less inventory	100 gals.,	60	50 gals.,	30	90
Cost of sales	900 gals.,	$540	450 gals.,	$270	$810
Gross margin		($ 45)		$135	$ 90
Gross-margin percentages		(9.1%)		33.3%	10%

Note that the use of physical weighting for allocation of joint costs may have no relationship to the revenue-producing power of the individual products. Thus, if the joint cost of a hog were assigned to its various products on the basis of weight,[2] center-cut pork chops would have the same unit cost as pigs' feet, lard, bacon, ham, and so forth. Fabulous profits would be shown for some cuts, although losses would consistently be shown for other cuts.

net realizable value How do you choose the "best" method for allocating joint costs to products for inventory purposes? First, you should choose the purpose of the inventory measure. Unfortunately, there is no consensus

[2] Sometimes one joint product is a liquid while another is a solid. This situation necessitates converting all physical measures into common terms, such as pounds, gallons, square feet, and the like.

about the purpose. For example, a few accountants will contend that the purpose is merely to spread the cost in proportion to the physical units produced, as was just illustrated. The majority of accountants, however, support allocation in proportion to some measure of the relative revenue-generating power identifiable with the individual products. The most popular measure that results in a cost indicative of revenue-generating power is some approximation of net realizable value, which is commonly defined as the predicted selling price in the ordinary course of business less reasonably predictable costs of completion and disposal.

In Example 1, there are zero costs of completion and disposal, because all products are sold upon split-off at no incremental costs. Therefore, net realizable value is equal to sales value. This *net realizable-value method* is sometimes called the *relative-sales-value method:*

	NET REALIZABLE VALUE	*WEIGHTING*	*JOINT COSTS ALLOCATED*
A	$ 550	550/1,000 × $900	$495
B	450	450/1,000 × $900	405
	$1,000		$900

	A	*B*	*TOTAL*
Sales	$495.0	$405.0	$900.0
Production costs	$495.0	$405.0	$900.0
Less inventory	49.5	40.5	90.0
Cost of sales	$445.5	$364.5	$810.0
Gross margin	$ 49.5	$ 40.5	$ 90.0
Gross-margin percentage	10%	10%	10%

Compare this income statement with the previous one; note that the gross-margin percentage is the same for both products under the relative-sales-value method.

costs beyond split-off The net realizable-value method becomes more intricate when joint products are processed individually beyond the split-off point and have no ordinary markets at the split-off point. Consider Example 2 (all costs are processing costs):

example 2

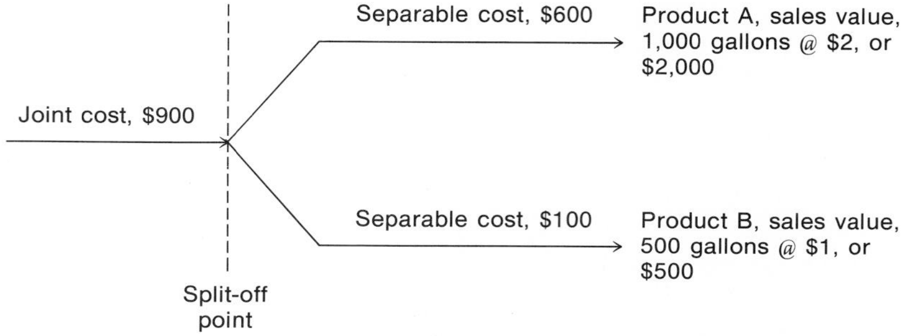

Assume the same joint costs as in Example 1, except that the products are unsalable in their stage of completion at the split-off point.

Further processing costs are needed to put the products into salable form. **This assumption is important because, when sales-price quotations (or replacement prices) at the split-off point are known or can be determined, they should be used as a basis for splitting joint costs in the way illustrated in Example 1.** That is, the best approach to assigning joint costs is the relative sales values *at the split-off point.* If these values are not explicitly available because there is no market for Products A and B at the split-off point or because the products cannot be purchased from outsiders, the *next best* alternative—for product-costing purposes only—is to take the ultimate relative sales values at the point of sale and work backward to *approximate* (computed) relative sales values at the split-off point. The conventional way of doing this is as follows:

	PRODUCTION IN TERMS OF SALES VALUES	LESS COSTS BEYOND SPLIT-OFF POINT	APPROXIMATE NET REALIZABLE VALUE AT SPLIT-OFF POINT	WEIGHTING	JOINT COSTS ASSIGNED
A (1,000 gallons @ $2.00)	$2,000	$600	$1,400	1,400/1,800 × $900	$700
B (500 gallons @ $1.00)	500	100	400	400/1,800 × $900	200
	$2,500	$700	$1,800		$900

Exhibit 17-1 shows a product-line income statement as prepared under this net realizable-value method,[3] assuming no ending inventories.

As we see later, the allocated costs demonstrated in Examples 1 and 2 should not be used for further sell-or-process decisions or for judging the performance of either the joint or the separable processes. The relative profitability of joint and separable processes must be determined by using unallocated costs and incremental analysis.

costing joint products at realizable values

The foregoing examples concentrated on allocations. Because the various schemes for joint-cost allocations are subject to so many valid criticisms, many companies refrain from the attempt entirely. Instead, they carry all inventories resulting from joint processing at sales values or at net realizable values (ultimate sales values less estimated separable costs to complete and sell). The meat-packing industry is the primary example, but the canning and mining industries provide other examples. This realizable-value approach ignores joint production costs altogether. It is difficult to criticize this approach when one compares it with the pitfalls of trying to allocate joint costs to products.

[3] A variation of this method is described in the Appendix A to this chapter.

EXHIBIT 17-1

INCOME STATEMENT
For the Month Ending ________________

		PRODUCT	
	TOTAL	A	B
Sales	$2,500	$2,000	$500
Cost of goods sold:			
Joint costs	$ 900	$ 700	$200
Separable costs	700	600	100
Total cost of goods sold	$1,600	$1,300	$300
Gross margin	$ 900	$ 700	$200
Gross-margin percentage	36%	35%	40%

However, it should be pointed out that accountants ordinarily frown on carrying inventories at net realizable values, because in this way profit is recognized before sales are made. When compared with generally accepted inventory-costing methods, the realizable-value approach results in higher profits as inventory is increased and lower profits as inventory is decreased. Using selling prices or variations thereof as bases for inventory valuation is more justifiable where differences between costs and selling prices are small and where turnover is high (for example, in the meat-packing and other food-product industries.)

Probably the most sensible method is followed by the many companies that carry their inventories at *net realizable values less a normal profit margin* to counteract the criticism that the net realizable-value method recognizes profits before goods are sold.

irrelevance of joint costs in decision making

sell or process further No technique for allocating joint-product costs should be used for managerial decisions regarding whether a product should be sold or processed further. When a product is an inherent result of a joint process, the decision to process further is not influenced by either the size of the total joint costs or the portion of the joint costs assigned to particular products.

The decision to incur added costs beyond split-off is a matter of comparing the revenue available (if any) at the split-off point with the differential income attainable beyond the split-off point. Example 2 assumed that zero revenue was available at the split-off point, whereas differential revenue for Product A ($2,000) less differential costs ($600) yields a differential income of $1,400. In other words, the company is better off by $1,400, the income that would be foregone if Product A were dumped in the river upon split-off. Similarly, if

Product B were processed beyond the split-off point, the company would be better off by \$500 − \$100 = \$400. The amount of joint costs and how they are allocated are completely irrelevant with respect to these decisions.

Many manufacturing companies constantly face the decision of whether to process a joint product further. Meat products may be sold as cut or may be smoked, cured, frozen, canned, and so forth. Petroleum refiners are perpetually trying to adjust to the most profitable product mix. The refining process necessitates separating all products from crude oil, even though only one or two may be desired. The refiner must decide what combination of processes to use to get the most profitable quantities of gasoline, lubricants, kerosene, naphtha, fuel oil, and the like. In addition, at times he may find it profitable to purchase distillates from some other refiner and process them further. Profitability depends on producing the proper product in the proper quantities at the proper time.

In serving management for these decisions, the accountant must concentrate on opportunity costs rather than on how historical joint costs are to be split among various products. The only relevant costs are the incremental costs (including the "cost" of capital) as compared with incremental revenue. In turn, these must be compared with the revenue foregone by rejecting other alternatives.

To illustrate the importance of the incremental-cost viewpoint, consider another example:

example 3

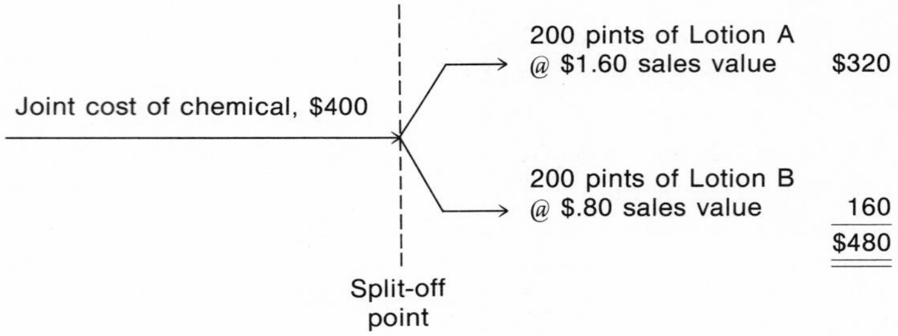

Conventional joint-cost allocations would be:

	BY WEIGHT			BY SALES VALUE		
	Pounds	Weighting	Joint Cost	Sales Value	Weighting	Joint Cost
Lotion A	200	2/4 × \$400	\$200	\$320	32/48 × \$400	\$267
Lotion B	200	2/4 × \$400	200	160	16/48 × \$400	133
	400		\$400	\$480		\$400

The manager is faced with the choice of selling the 200 pints of Lotion B at 80¢ (\$160) or bottling and perfuming the lotion as 200 bottles of Lotion C. The total additional costs of converting Lotion B into Lotion C would be \$50, while the sales price per bottle would be \$1.20 (total revenue, \$240).

Not only are conventional methods of joint-cost allocation irrelevant here, but allowing joint-cost allocations to influence the decision will yield inconsistent results. For example, the weight method would show a loss for Lotion B, whereas the net realizable-value method would show a profit:

	BY WEIGHT		BY NET REALIZABLE VALUE	
Sales, 200 pints, @ $1.20		$240		$240
Joint cost	$200		$133	
Incremental cost	50	250	50	183
Profit (loss)		$(10)		$ 57

The only approach that will give valid results is to compare the incremental revenue with incremental costs. In this case:

Incremental revenue, 40¢ × 200 bottles	$80
Incremental costs, added processing	50
Additional margin	$30

Another way of looking at the same problem:

Lotion C revenue, 200 bottles @ $1.20		$240
Costs:		
Added processing	$ 50	
Opportunity cost, foregoing of Lotion B sales (200 × 80¢)	160	210
Difference in favor of added processing		$ 30

The validity of this approach may be proven as follows:

	TOTAL INCOME COMPUTATIONS		
	Sell Lotion B	Sell Lotion C	
Sales	$480	($320 + $240)	$560
Total costs	400	($400 + $ 50)	450
Margin	$ 80		$110
Difference in margin	$ 30		

In summary, it is profitable to extend processing or to incur additional distribution costs on a joint product as long as the incremental revenue exceeds incremental explicit costs (and incremental opportunity costs of required additional capital, if any).

pricing decisions Similarly, pricing decisions generally should not be influenced by allocations of joint costs. The circular reasoning is particularly obvious under the relative net realizable-value method (prices used to set costs and costs then used to set prices). Nevertheless, regulated firms have been subjected to this reasoning as a justification for not permitting them to increase their prices. For example, many critics have claimed that shortages of natural gas have been caused by the Federal Power Commission's (FPC) approach to regulating gas prices. The FPC based prices on old competitive gas prices. Meanwhile, unregulated oil prices rose, resulting in lower and lower proportions of joint costs being allocated to gas, thus restricting gas prices and providing lesser incentives for finding natural gas.

accounting for by-products

problems of definition

The distinction among joint products, by-products, and scrap is largely influenced by the relative sales values of the products in question. However, these distinctions are not firm; the variety of terminology and accounting practice is bewildering. For example, valuable brass turnings may be called *scrap* in one company and *by-products* in another. Glycerin, which is ordinarily a *by-product* of soap manufacture, may become at least a *joint product* during wartime production. Many sewage plants that regarded their products as waste have developed the waste into joint-product stature as valuable fertilizer. Kerosene was once a major petroleum product; now it is a by-product.

The Kroehler Company, manufacturer of furniture, provides an example of the impact of technological change on importance of products. Traditionally, there has been 40 percent wastage of wood in a furniture factory. Kroehler now compresses almost all these wood scraps into cultured wood, which is used for bottoms and backs of drawers and other purposes. Previously, two-thirds of the scraps were incinerated at a cost of $2 per ton while the other third was used to fire steam boilers.

By-products are multiple products that have minor sales value as compared with that of the major or chief product(s). Examples are mill ends of cloth and carpets; cotton meal and cotton hulls in processing of cotton oil; tar, naphtha, and kerosene in gasoline production; minor chemicals, gas, and tar from coke manufacture. The distinction between scrap and by-products is often difficult to establish. A view that is sometimes helpful is that by-products (a) have relatively more sales value than scrap, (b) are often subject to additional costs beyond the split-off point, whereas scrap is usually sold outright. The basic accounting for scrap and for by-products is the same. **The net realizable values of both are best treated as deductions from the cost of the main product.** The rest of this discussion will be confined to accounting for by-products.

accounting methods for by-products

Exhibit 17-2 is a comparison of two of the many methods of accounting for by-products:

METHOD ONE Net revenue from by-product *sold* is calculated: gross revenue from by-product sold less separable costs *incurred,* such as additional manufacturing and marketing costs. This net revenue is deducted from the cost of the major product(s) *sold.*

METHOD TWO Net realizable value of the by-product *produced* is calculated: sales value of by-product produced less separable costs *applicable,* whether already incurred or to be incurred. This net realizable value is deducted from the cost of the major product(s) *produced.*

EXHIBIT 17-2

TWO ACCOUNTING METHODS FOR BY-PRODUCTS

Data for Illustration

	MAJOR PRODUCT		*BY-PRODUCT*	
	19_1	*19_2*	*19_1*	*19_2*
Beginning inventory in units	0	1,000	0	300
Production in units	10,000	0	1,000	0
Sales in units	9,000	1,000	700	300
Ending inventory in units	1,000	0	300	0
Sales revenue @ $15.00 and @ $1.50	$135,000	$15,000	$1,050	$450
Disposal costs @ $.30	—	—	210	90
Net revenue from by-product sold	—	—	840	360
Net realizable value of by-product produced: 1,000 units @ ($1.50 − $.30)	—	—	1,200	—

Partial Income Statements (In Dollars)

	METHOD (SEE TEXT FOR DESCRIPTION)			
	ONE		*TWO*	
	19_1	*19_2*	*19_1*	*19_2*
Sales revenues from major product	$135,000	$15,000	$135,000	$15,000
Cost of major product sold:				
Beginning inventory of major product		$10,000		$ 9,880
Total production costs (assumed)	$100,000		$100,000	
Net realizable value of by-product produced			1,200	
Net production costs	$100,000		$ 98,800	
Ending inventory of major product (10%)	10,000		9,880	
Cost of major product sold (gross)	$ 90,000	$10,000	$ 88,920	$ 9,880
Net revenue from by-product sold	840	360		
Cost of major product sold (net)	$ 89,160	$ 9,640	$ 88,920	$ 9,880
Gross margin	$ 45,840	$ 5,360	$ 46,080	$ 5,120
Gross margin for two years	$51,200		$51,200	

There are many methods of accounting for by-products. If the by-product is really a minor product, the differences among the methods are not worth getting excited about. Two general methods are most popular. The first takes no notice of by-products until they are sold. The second recognizes their value as they are produced. Of course, many variations and combinations of these two approaches are used.

Essentially, the first method has practical appeal, but conceptually it fails to match the value of the by-product with the cost of the major related products. For example, by-product income (that is, by-product revenue less separable costs of disposal incurred) is sometimes shown as "other income" and either (a) grouped with other sales at the top of the income statement, (b) grouped with other miscellaneous income near the bottom of the income statement, or (c) deducted from the cost of major products *sold*, as is illustrated by Method One in Exhibit 17-2. These methods (and variations thereof) are justified on the grounds that by-products are incidental and do not warrant costly accounting procedures. Unsold by-product is inventoried at zero value, although procedures may be adopted for control of physical quantities.

The second general approach tries to relate the net realizable value[4] of the by-products produced to the costs of the major products *produced*, as is illustrated by Method Two in Exhibit 17-2. This method eliminates the effect of lag between production and sales and directly matches the cost-reduction power of by-products against the production costs of the main product. The by-product inventory is carried forward at net realizable value (plus separable manufacturing costs incurred, if any).

comparison of the methods

Both methods in Exhibit 17-2 recognize that by-products somehow reduce the costs of the major products. Method Two is more precise about the timing of such cost reductions. The two periods taken together show the same income by the two methods (there being no beginning inventories for the first period and no ending inventories for the second period). The variations in methods raise some provocative theoretical problems concerning the matching of revenues and expenses. But cost-benefit comparisons in choosing among the accounting alternatives usually lead to whatever alternative seems expedient. By definition, by-products should be minor and thus immaterial.

[4] A variation of Method Two would use net realizable value *less normal profit margin* of by-products produced (plus separable manufacturing costs incurred, if any). This method is more conservative because the by-product would be valued lower than its net realizable value. Thus, the costs of major product would be higher, and a "normal profit" would be shown on the by-product as it is sold. This would shift income to a future period to the extent that the by-product in question is not sold in the current period. (For exploration of the details, solve Problem 17-18.) This method has conceptual appeal, but it implies that the by-product is important enough to warrant treatment as a separate product line. In short, the product is now a major product rather than a by-product.

The illustration in Exhibit 17-2 assumes that the separable costs of the by-product are confined to disposal costs (marketing costs). If any significant separable manufacturing costs were incurred, they would be deducted from the by-product revenue under Method One. This would be an obvious mismatching if all the separable manufacturing costs incurred were applicable to the 1,000 units produced rather than to only the 700 units sold. Under Method Two, the separable manufacturing costs applicable would be deducted in computing the net realizable value of the by-product produced. For an illustration, see Appendix B of this chapter.

by-products used internally

Sometimes by-products are used internally as fuel or even as a component of a new batch of raw materials for the main product. For example, steel companies will often remelt scrap and by-products along with purchased scrap metal as a part of producing new steel ingots. In these cases, the by-products are frequently accounted for at net realizable values or replacement values; in turn, the cost of the major product is reduced by the same amount. For instance, scrap metal would be valued at replacement cost and by-products such as gas and tar derivatives would be valued at the cost of fuel oil that would otherwise be used to yield equivalent heat units.

by-products in petroleum

The line of demarcation between joint products and by-products is fuzzy. In the petroleum industry, by-product accounting methods are often used even though the products being accounted for as by-products are important enough to warrant being called joint products. The petroleum industry uses the by-product approach for product-mix decisions even if a by-product method is not followed for inventory costing. This by-product approach views gasoline as the sole major product. The by-product proportion of production should be increased until overall profit no longer increases. In effect, this approach (which is implemented via linear programming models) computes the total incremental costs of obtaining a set of all products; the net realizable values of by-products are computed and deducted. The remainder is the cost of gasoline. For a given gasoline volume, the linear programming model increases the proportion of by-product output until profit no longer increases. Any profit increases from by-products are constantly being traded off against profits from the additional yield of gasoline that could otherwise be obtained. The model produces an optimal solution when the by-products literally break even.

Again, note that for planning and control the emphasis is on profit opportunities and comparisons of incremental profits and incremental costs. How any joint-product *costs* are allocated among the products is irrelevant, regardless of whether the products are called joint products, by-products, or scrap.

SUMMARY

Joint costs permeate accounting. Costs are joint with respect to time, facilities, and products. Accountants attempt to split joint costs among products having relatively important sales values. Where the joint product is valueless (for example, waste), all costs are applied to the major product. Where the joint product has minor value, it is often called a *by-product;* its net realizable value or income from sales is frequently deducted from the cost of the major product.

No matter what the joint-production situation, any allocation of a joint cost is useless for purposes of product-combination decisions. The only use for allocating joint-product costs is for purposes of "reasonable" inventory valuations and income determinations. The *net realizable-value method* is the technique most frequently used for assigning joint costs to products.

Only opportunity and incremental costs are relevant to the decisions on whether to incur additional separable costs beyond the split-off point. As long as the incremental revenue exceeds the incremental costs (including the opportunity costs and the appropriate cost of capital), additional cost incurrence will be warranted.

SUGGESTED READINGS

ANTON, H., "Joint Costs," *Accountants' Cost Handbook,* ed. Robert I. Dickey, 2nd ed. (New York: The Ronald Press Company, 1960), sec. 13.

BIERMAN, H. and T. DYCKMAN, *Managerial Cost Accounting,* 2nd ed. (New York: The Macmillan Company, 1976), Chap. 8.

NURNBERG, H., "Joint and By-Product Costs," in *Handbook of Cost Accounting,* ed. S. Davidson and R. Weil (New York: McGraw-Hill Book Company, 1978).

PROBLEM FOR SELF-STUDY

PROBLEM

The Alden Oil Company buys crude vegetable oil. The refining of this oil results in four products, A, B, and C, which are liquids, and D, which is a heavy grease. The cost of the oil refined in 19_9 was $27,600, and the refining department had total processing costs of $70,000. The output and sales for the four products in 19_9 were as follows:

PRODUCT	*OUTPUT*	*SALES*	*ADDITIONAL PROCESSING COST*
A	500,000 gal.	$115,000	$30,000
B	10,000 gal.	10,000	6,000
C	5,000 gal.	4,000	—
D	9,000 gal.	30,000	1,000

required

1. Assume that the net realizable value of allocating joint costs is used. What is the net income for Products A, B, C, and D? Joint costs total $97,600.
2. The company had been tempted to sell at split-off directly to other processors. If that alternative had been selected, sales per gallon would have been: A, 15¢; B, 50¢; C, 80¢; and D, $3. What would the net income have been for each product under this alternative?
3. The company expects to operate at the same level of production and sales in the forthcoming year. Could the company increase net income by altering its

processing decisions? If so, what would be the expected overall net income? Which products should be processed further and which should be sold at split-off? Assume that all costs incurred after split-off are variable.

SOLUTION 1.

SELL BEYOND SPLIT-OFF

	(A) Sales Value	(B) Separable Costs	Net Realizable Value At Split-off	(C) Allocation of Joint Costs	A − (B + C) Net Profit
A	$115,000	$30,000	$ 85,000	85/122 × $97,600 = $68,000	$17,000
B	10,000	6,000	4,000	4/122 × 97,600 = 3,200	800
C	4,000	—	4,000	4/122 × 97,600 = 3,200	800
D	30,000	1,000	29,000	29/122 × 97,600 = 23,200	5,800
	$159,000	$37,000	$122,000	$97,600	$24,400

2.

SELL AT SPLIT-OFF

	(A) Relative Sales Value at Split-off	(B) Allocation of Joint Costs	(A) − (B) Net Profit
A	500,000($ .15) = $ 75,000	75/111 × $97,600 = $65,947	$ 9,053
B	10,000($ .50) = 5,000	5/111 × 97,600 = 4,396	604
C	5,000($ .80) = 4,000	4/111 × 97,600 = 3,517	483
D	9,000($3.00) = $ 27,000	27/111 × 97,600 = 23,740	3,260
	$111,000	$97,600	$13,400

3. Note that comparing 1 and 2 in the manner computed above is irrelevant. For example, Product C's profit above is $483 or $800, despite the fact that the same amount is sold at the same price in either case. The only proper way to compare is to use an incremental approach:

	SALES BEYOND SPLIT-OFF	*SALES AT SPLIT-OFF*	*INCREMENTAL SALES*	*SEPARABLE COSTS BEYOND SPLIT-OFF*	*INCREMENTAL GAIN OR (LOSS)*
A	$115,000	$75,000	$40,000	$30,000	$10,000
B	10,000	5,000	5,000	6,000	(−1,000)
D	30,000	27,000	3,000	1,000	2,000
Increase in profit from further processing					$11,000

Based on the given data, the company income, before considering cost of capital for further processing, could be further improved by $1,000 by selling Product B at the split-off point instead of processing it further. That is, B's current incremental loss of $1,000 would be avoided by selling B at the split-off point; the overall net profit would not be otherwise affected.

appendix a: alternative to net realizable value

Speculation about the "best" method for allocating a joint-product cost is a frustrating endeavor, because any method is based on shaky assumptions. For example, the net realizable-value method contains the implicit assumption that *all* the markup or margin is attributable to the joint process and *none* of the markup is attributable to the separable costs. This is a vulnerable assumption, because profit is frequently thought to be attributable to all phases of the production and marketing functions, not just the joint process.

The *net realizable-value less overall profit-margin* method has been suggested as a way to attribute profit to the separable as well as to the joint processes. The method entails (a) deducting an *overall profit margin* from the sales values, obtaining the total costs that each product line should bear; and (b) deducting the separable costs from the total costs to obtain the joint-cost assignment. The data from Example 2 and Exhibit 17-1 would yield the following results under this *overall margin* method:

	TOTAL		A		B
Sales value	$2,500	1,000 @ $2.00,	$2,000	500 @ $1.00,	$500
Overall gross-margin percentage (from Exhibit 17-1) (36%)	900	(36%)	720	(36%)	180
Total cost	$1,600		$1,280		$320
Special processing cost	700		600		100
Joint cost	$ 900		$ 680		$220

A favorable aspect of the overall profit-margin technique is cited as follows: "Uniform markup on all products is desirable for inventory purposes. Regardless of the composition of finished goods, equal inventory values (costs) will indicate equal sales possibilities."[5]

Once this approach is understood, it is slightly easier to use than the net realizable-value method. Both techniques rest on arbitrary basic assumptions.

The vulnerability of the *overall-margin* method is the flimsy assumption that there is a uniform relationship between cost and sales value. Few companies have products bearing equal margin percentages. Clearly, accountants and managers are faced with some uncomfortable choices for allocating-joint product costs because they are fundamentally indivisible.

appendix b: by-products and separable costs

This appendix illustrates the effects of separable manufacturing costs on Method Two in Exhibit 17-2. The accounting becomes slightly more intricate because

[5] Carl Thomas Devine, *Cost Accounting and Analysis* (New York: The Macmillan Company), p. 116.

the separable manufacturing costs incurred are inventoried. Suppose the separable manufacturing costs were $1.00 per unit and the selling price were $2.50 instead of $1.50 per unit. Then the final results in Exhibit 17-2, Method Two, would be unaffected.

Some journal entries might clarify the procedure:

1. By-product inventory	1,000	
Cash		1,000
To record separable manufacturing outlays of $1.00 per unit for 1,000 units produced in 19_1.		
2. By-product inventory	210	
Cash		210
To record disposal outlays of $.30 per unit for 700 units sold in 19_1.		
3. By-product inventory	1,200	
Cost of main product produced		1,200
Net realizable value per unit, $2.50 − ($1.00 + $.30) = $1.20 for 1,000 units produced in 19_1.		
4. Cash	1,750	
By-product inventory		1,750
To record 19_1 sales of 700 units at $2.50 each.		
Note that the ending inventory would be 300 units × $1.20 or $360, the net realizable value, plus the separable manufacturing costs of 300 units × $1.00, or $300, for a total of $660. See the T-account below.		
5. By-product inventory	90	
Cash		90
To record disposal outlays of $.30 per unit for 300 units sold in 19_2.		
6. Cash	750	
By-product inventory		750
To record 19_2 sales of 300 units at $2.50 each.		

The T-account follows:

BY-PRODUCT INVENTORY

1. 1,000 @ $1.00	1,000	4. 700 @ $2.50	1,750
2. 700 @ $ .30	210	To bal. 300 @ $2.20	660
3. 1,000 @ $1.20	1,200		
	2,410		2,410
Inventory, end of 19_1: 300 @ $2.20	660	6. 300 @ $2.50	750
5. 300 @ $ .30	90		
	750		

QUESTIONS, PROBLEMS, AND CASES

Note When the term "net realizable value" is used, it refers to the conventional method illustrated in Exhibit 17-1.

17-1 "The problem of accounting for depreciation is one of joint costs." Do you agree? Why?

17-2 "Nearly every manufacturing operation produces two or more products." Do you agree? Why?

17-3 List four methods of accounting for by-products.

17-4 What is the main weakness of the relative-sales method of joint-cost allocation?

17-5 Define *net realizable value.*

17-6 "The relative-sales-value method of joint-cost allocation is the best method for managerial decisions regarding whether a product should be sold or processed further." Do you agree? Why?

17-7 *Difference Between Joint Products and By-Products* (CPA)

1. Explain the basic difference between the method of accounting for joint products and that for by-products.
2. State the conditions under which an item should be treated as a by-product rather than as a joint product.
3. Explain the two principal methods of assigning joint costs to the joint products, and state the circumstances under which each would be appropriate.

17-8 *Net Realizable-Value Method* A company produces two joint products, A and B. The joint cost is $24,000. Added processing costs: A, $30,000; B, $7,500. A sells for $50 per unit; B sells for $25 per unit.

If the company produces 1,000 units of A and 500 units of B, what is the proper amount of joint cost that should be allocated to B, assuming that the net realizable-value method of allocation of joint costs is used?

17-9 *Joint-Product Costs: Ending Inventories* The Darl Company operates a simple chemical process to reduce a single basic material into three separate items, here referred to as X, Y, and Z (all three end products being separated simultaneously at a single split-off point).

Y and Z are ready for sale immediately upon split-off without further processing or any other additional cost. Product X, however, is processed further before being sold.

The selling prices quoted below have not changed for three years, and no future changes are foreseen.

During 19_3, the selling prices of the items and the total number sold were as follows:

X—120 tons sold for $1,600 per ton
Y—340 tons sold for $1,000 per ton
Z—175 tons sold for $800 per ton

There were no beginning inventories whatsoever of X, Y, or Z.

The total joint manufacturing costs for the year were $505,000. An additional $30,000 was spent in order to finish product X.

At the end of the year, the following inventories of completed units were on hand: X, 180 tons; Y, 60 tons; Z, 25 tons. There was no ending work in process.

required

Prepare a computation of the "cost" of inventories of X, Y, and Z for balance-sheet purposes as of December 31, 19_3. Include in your presentation a summary of the cost of goods sold by product line. (The Darl Company uses the "net realizable-value" method of allocating joint costs to end products.)

17-10 *Markups and Appendix A*

1. Refer to Appendix A. Suppose that market prices were available at split-off of 70¢ for Product A and 40¢ for Product B. What is the joint cost applicable to A? to B? To what would you attribute the gross margin, the joint process or the separable process?
2. Suppose that market prices were available at split-off of 68¢ for Product A and 44¢ for Product B. What is the joint cost applicable to A? to B? To what would you attribute the gross margin, the joint process or the separable process? What is the role of bona fide market prices at split-off in management planning and control? Of computed approximate market prices?

17-11 *Introduction to Joint-Costing Techniques* The Wood Spirits Company produces two products, turpentine and methanol (wood alcohol), by a joint process. Joint costs amount to $12,000 per batch of output. Each batch totals 10,000 gallons, being 25 percent methanol and 75 percent turpentine. Both products are processed further without gain or loss in volume. Added processing costs: methanol, 30¢ per gallon; turpentine, 20¢ per gallon. Methanol sells for $2.10 per gallon; turpentine sells for $1.40 per gallon.

required

1. What joint costs per batch should be assigned to the turpentine and methanol, assuming that joint costs are assigned on a physical-volume basis?
2. If joint costs are to be assigned on a net realizable-value basis, what amounts of joint cost should be assigned to the turpentine and to the methanol?
3. Prepare product-line income statements per batch for requirements 1 and 2.
4. The company has discovered an additional process by which the methanol (wood alcohol) can be made consumable and into a pleasant-tasting alcoholic beverage. The new selling price would be $6 a gallon. Additional processing would increase separable costs 90¢ a gallon, and the company would have to pay taxes of 20 percent on the new selling price. Assuming no other changes in cost, what is the joint cost applicable to the wood alcohol (using the net realizable value basis)? Should the company use the new process?

17-12 *Net Realizable Value of Joint Products* (CPA) Miller Manufacturing Company buys zeon for $.80 a gallon. At the end of processing in Department 1, zeon splits off into products A, B, and C. Product A is sold at the split-off point, with no further processing. Products B and C require further processing before they can be sold; product B is processed in Department 2 and product C is processed in Department 3. Following is a summary of costs and other related data for the year ended June 30, 19_3.

	DEPARTMENT		
	1	2	3
Cost of zeon	$96,000	—	—
Direct labor	$14,000	$45,000	$65,000
Manufacturing overhead	$10,000	$21,000	$49,000

	PRODUCTS		
	A	B	C
Gallons sold	20,000	30,000	45,000
Gallons on hand at June 30, 19_3	10,000	—	15,000
Sales in dollars	$30,000	$96,000	$141,750

There were no inventories on hand at July 1, 19_2, and there was no zeon on hand at June 30, 19_3. All gallons on hand at June 30, 19_3, were complete as to processing. There were no manufacturing-overhead variances. Miller uses the net realizable-value method of allocating joint costs.

1. For allocating joint costs, the net realizable value of product A for the year ended June 30, 19_3, would be
   a. $30,000. b. $45,000. c. $21,000. d. $6,000.
2. The joint costs for the year ended June 30, 19_3, to be allocated are
   a. $300,000. b. $95,000. c. $120,000. d. $96,000.
3. The cost of product B sold for the year ended June 30, 19_3, is
   a. $90,000. b. $66,000. c. $88,857. d. $96,000.
4. The value of the ending inventory for product A is
   a. $24,000. b. $12,000. c. $8,000. d. $13,333.

17-13 *Christmas Trees; Allocating Joint Costs* S. Claus is a retired gentleman who has rented a lot in the center of a busy city for the month of December, 19_0, at a cost of $5,000. On this lot he sells Christmas trees and wreaths. He buys his trees by the bundle for $20 each. A bundle is made up of two big trees (average height, seven feet), four regular-sized trees (average height, five feet), and broken branches. The shipper puts in the broken branches merely to make all the bundles of uniform size for shipping advantages. The amount of branches varies from bundle to bundle.

Mr. Claus gets $2 a foot for the trees. He takes home the broken branches. He and Mrs. Claus, Donner, Blitzen, and the rest sit about the fire in the evenings and make wreaths, which Mr. Claus sells for $8 each. Except for Christmas Eve, these evenings are a time when there is nothing else to do; therefore, their labor is not a cost.

During the course of the season, Mr. Claus buys 1,000 bundles of trees and makes 2,000 wreaths. In addition to the broken branches, the wreaths contain pine cones (100 pounds, total cost $200), twine (4,000 yards @ 10¢ a yard), and miscellaneous items amounting to $400.

In 19_0, Claus sold 1,800 of the seven-foot trees, all the regular-sized ones, and half the wreaths (the local Boy Scouts were also selling wreaths). The department store next door says that they will buy the rest of the wreaths, if Claus will preserve them, for $3 each. The preservative spray costs $2,000 for enough to do the job.

required

1. What unit cost should Claus assign to each of his items?
2. What is the inventory cost on January 1, 19_1, if he doesn't sell to the department store?
3. Should he sell to the department store?

17-14 *Computation of Breakeven Point for Joint Processes* (J. March) The March-I Company processes soybeans to obtain oil, meal, and chaff. There are three processes. In the cleaning process, the chaff and foreign materials are separated from the beans. In the pressing process, soybean oil and soybean cake are produced. The oil is stored in tanks and later pumped into tank cars for shipment. In the grinding process, the soybean cake is dried and then ground into meal.

The standard yield from a ton (2,000 lbs.) of beans is 100 pounds of chaff, 800 pounds of meal, and 100 gallons of oil. The following selling prices have been chosen for the purpose of calculations: beans delivered to plant, $120 a ton; chaff, $10 a ton; oil, $1.20 a gallon; and meal, $200 a ton. Budgeted costs of processing are:

	VARIABLE COSTS PER UNIT	FIXED COSTS PER MONTH
Cleaning	10¢ per ton of beans	$ 500
Pressing	$2 per ton of cleaned beans	2,000
Grinding	$2 per ton of meal	1,500

Assume that there are no work-in-process inventories and that selling and administrative expenses are: fixed costs of $1,800 monthly; variable costs of 10 percent of dollar sales in the case of oil sales and meal sales and zero in the case of chaff sales.

required

1. Chart of physical flow.
2. How many tons of beans must be processed monthly in order to break even? Show computations clearly.

17-15 *Comparing Alternatives; Discounted Cash Flow* Pottsville Process, Inc., processes an ore that yields 60 percent product A, 20 percent product B, and 20 percent complete waste. Willo, Inc., the sole customer and a mere intermediate link in the distribution chain, purchases the entire output of products A and B.

A Pottsville company engineer has developed a process that will produce a 70 percent yield of product A from the ore—a new product A that is in a form that can be sold directly to the prime user. This will eliminate Willo, Inc., as a customer for both products; there is no other available market for product B. The required investment to provide the capital equipment and the necessary expansion is $4,000,000. These new facilities have an estimated life of 20 years, exactly the remaining life of the present equipment. This money can be obtained at a rate of 4 percent. However, the company's average cost of capital is 10 percent.

COMPARATIVE COST DATA

	PER TON
Present	
Processed: 1,000,000 tons per year.	
Cost data:	
Variable manufacturing cost	$ 5.00
Fixed manufacturing cost other than depreciation	6.00
Depreciation on equipment (straight-line)	.30
	$11.30
"New Process"	
Processed: 1,000,000 tons per year.	
Cost data:	
Variable manufacturing cost	$10.00
Fixed manufacturing cost other than depreciation	9.00
Depreciation—including new equipment (straight-line)	.50
	$19.50

PRICE DATA

Present:
- Product A—$20.00 per ton
- Product B—$ 3.00 per ton

"New Process":
- "New Product" A—$30.00 per ton

required

1. Prepare comparative annual income statements for the two alternatives.
2. Analyze the alternatives on a discounted cash-flow basis, using the present-value technique.
3. Would your decision in 2 be changed if product B in the amount produced under the present process could also be sold under the new process?

17-16 *Relative-Sales-Value Method; Discounted Cash-Flow Approach to Joint-Process Replacement*

1. The A Company produces two items, X and Y. The items first go through joint processing. Then each receives separable processing. All the production is sold, and no inventories are carried. Annual joint costs are $100,000. What is the gross margin of each product, using the net realizable-value method?

	X	Y
Yearly sales	$100,000	$300,000
Annual separable costs	50,000	150,000

2. A new joint process has been developed to replace the currently used joint process. It will reduce annual joint costs by 50 percent, but it requires an initial investment of $200,000. Its useful life is five years. Annual additional processing costs of X will be reduced by $15,000, but those of Y will increase by $20,000. Sales will not be affected. Minimum desired rate of return is 10 percent. Should the new method be adopted? (Use discounted cash-flow calculations.) How has the reallocation of joint costs affected the decision?

17-17 *Alternative Accounting Methods for By-Products* Reconsider the facts in Exhibit 17-2. Prepare a specific description of how the partial income statements for both years would be changed and how net income would be affected if the following accounting methods were used:

a. Net revenue from by-product sold shown as additional revenue.
b. Net revenue from by-product sold shown as other income near the bottom of an income statement.
c. Gross revenue from by-product sold shown as reduction of cost of major product produced.
d. Net revenue from by-product sold shown as deduction from cost of major product produced.

For methods c and d prepare a tabular comparison that is similar to Exhibit 17-2.

17-18 *Role of Normal Margins and By-Products* Refer to Problem 17-17 and to Appendix B of the chapter. Add the following method:

e. Net realizable value less normal profit margin of by-product produced deducted from cost of major product produced.

Assume that the normal profit margin on the sale of the by-product is 12 percent of selling price, or $.18 per unit. Show the effects of method (e) by adding it to the tabular comparison of c and d. How does method d differ from Method Two in Exhibit 17-2?

17-19 *Joint and By-Products* (CPA) The Harrison Corporation produces three products—Alpha, Beta, and Gamma. Alpha and Gamma are joint products while Beta is a by-product of Alpha. No joint cost is to be allocated to the by-product. The production processes for a given year are as follows:

A. In Department One, 110,000 pounds of raw material, Rho, are processed at a total cost of $120,000. After processing in Department One, 60 percent of the units are transferred to Department Two, and 40 percent of the units (now Gamma) are transferred to Department Three.

B. In Department Two, the material is further processed at a total additional cost of $38,000. Seventy percent of the units (now Alpha) are transferred to Department Four and 30 percent emerge as Beta, the by-product, to be sold at $1.20 per pound. Selling expenses related to disposing of Beta are $8,100.

C. In Department Four, Alpha is processed at a total additional cost of $23,660. After this processing, Alpha is ready for sale at $5 per pound.

D. In Department Three, Gamma is processed at a total additional cost of $165,000. In this department, a normal loss of units of Gamma occurs which equals 10 percent of the good output of Gamma. The remaining good output of Gamma is then sold for $12 per pound.

required

1. Prepare a schedule showing the allocation of the $120,000 joint cost between Alpha and Gamma using the net realizable-value approach. The net realizable value of Beta should be treated as an addition to the sales value of Alpha.
2. Independent of your answer to requirement 1, assume that $102,000 of total joint costs were appropriately allocated to Alpha. Assume also that there were 48,000 pounds of Alpha and 20,000 pounds of Beta available to sell. Prepare a statement of gross margin for Alpha using the following facts:
   a. During the year, sales of Alpha were 80 percent of the pounds available for sale. There was no beginning inventory.
   b. The net realizable value of Beta available for sale is to be deducted from the cost of producing Alpha. The ending inventory of Alpha is to be based on the net cost of production.
   c. All other cost, selling-price, and selling-expense data are those listed in A through D above.

17-20 *Joint and By-Products* (W. Crum) Miracle Company processes an ore in Department 1, out of which come two products, Product A and Product Z. Product A sells for $40 a pound. Product Z sells for $10 a pound. Product A is processed further through Department 2 at a cost of $100,000. Product Z is processed further through Department 3 at a cost of $60,000. Processing of 100,000 lbs. of ore in Department 1, at a total cost of $300,000, results in 10,000 lbs. of Product A and 30,000 lbs. of Product Z.

required

1. Prepare a cost report using the theory that A and Z are joint products, and show the costs allocated to each, as well as the cost per pound. Assume there are 1,000 lbs. of A on hand at end, and 10,000 lbs. of finished Z on hand at end; compute the ending inventory value.
2. Prepare a cost report assuming that Product Z were to be treated as a by-product, with the net realizable value being credited against the cost of Product A, after a profit of 10 percent on the selling price of Z, as well as allowance for 25 percent of the selling price for selling and administration costs. Assume the same inventories on hand as in part 1; show the cost per pound and the cost of final inventories of each product unsold.

17-21 *Joint Products and By-Products* (W. Crum) Sycamore Company mines an ore, which is crushed and processed in Dept. 1. Out of this process come two major products, Argon and Urgon, and a by-product Exgon. Exgon is processed in Dept. 4. Argon is further processed in Dept. 2. Urgon is further processed in Dept. 3. The net residual value of Exgon is to be credited against the material cost in Dept. 1, after allowing for a profit of 10 percent on Exgon, in addition to allowing for 25 percent for selling and administrative expenses and $8,000 further costs of operating Dept. 4.

Argon and Urgon are to be treated as joint products, with the net cost of Dept. 1 allocated to them on a net-realizable-value basis.

Cost statistics for the month of January 19_1 are:

Assume no beginning inventories in process.
60,000 lbs. of material costing $90,000 are processed in Dept. 1
Conversion costs of Dept. 1, $20,000
Conversion costs of Dept. 2, $10,000
Conversion costs of Dept. 3, $8,000
10,000 lbs. of Argon produced in Dept. 1
20,000 lbs. of Urgon produced in Dept. 1
10,000 lbs. of Exgon produced in Dept. 1
Argon sells for $10 per pound
Urgon sells for $5 per pound
Exgon sells for $2 per pound

required

1. Schedule showing finished cost per pound of Argon and Urgon.
2. January 31, 19_1, inventory shows 5,000 lbs. of Urgon and 1,000 lbs. of Exgon on hand. Both have been completely processed. At what inventory value would you carry the inventory in the balance sheet?

17-22 *Adding a Department* (CMA) The management of Bay Company is considering a proposal to install a third production department within its existing factory building. With the company's present production setup, raw material is passed through Department I to produce materials A and B in equal proportions. Material A is then passed through Department II to yield product C. Material B is presently being sold "as is" at a price of $20.25 per pound. Product C has a selling price of $100.00 per pound.

The per-pound standard costs currently being used by the Bay Company are as follows:

	DEPARTMENT I (MATERIALS A&B)	DEPARTMENT II (PRODUCT C)	(MATERIAL B)
Prior department costs	—	$53.03	$13.47
Direct material	20.00	—	—
Direct labor	7.00	12.00	—
Variable overhead	3.00	5.00	—
Fixed overhead:			
Attributable	2.25	2.25	—
Allocated (2/3, 1/3)	1.00	1.00	—
	$33.25	$73.28	$13.47

These standard costs were developed by using an estimated production volume of 200,000 pounds of raw material as the denominator volume. The company assigns Department I costs to materials A and B in proportion to their net sales values at the point of separation, computed by deducting subsequent standard production costs from sales prices. The $300,000 of common fixed overhead costs are allocated to the two producing departments on the basis of the space used by the departments.

"Attributable overhead" is that amount of fixed overhead that could be avoided if a given product or activity were discontinued.

The proposed Department III would be used to process material B into product D. It is expected that any quantity of product D can be sold for $30.00 per pound. Standard costs per pound under this proposal were developed by using 200,000 pounds of raw material as the denominator volume and are as follows:

	DEPARTMENT I (MATERIALS A&B)	DEPARTMENT II (PRODUCT C)	DEPARTMENT III (PRODUCT D)
Prior department costs	—	$52.80	$13.20
Direct material	$20.00	—	—
Direct labor	7.00	12.00	5.50
Variable overhead	3.00	5.00	2.00
Fixed overhead:			
Attributable	2.25	2.25	1.75
Allocated (1/2, 1/4, 1/4)	.75	.75	.75
	$33.00	$72.80	$23.20

required

1. If (a) sales and production levels are expected to remain constant in the foreseeable future, and (b) there are no foreseeable alternative uses for the available factory space, should the Bay Company install Department III and thereby produce product D? Show calculations to support your answer.
2. Instead of constant sales and production levels, suppose that under the present production setup $1,000,000 additions to the factory building must be made every 10 years to accommodate growth. Suppose also that proper maintenance gives these factory additions an infinite life and that all such maintenance costs are included in the standard costs set forth in the text of the problem. How would the analysis that you performed in part A be changed if the installation of Department III shortened the interval at which the $1,000,000 factory additions are made from 10 years to 6 years? Be as specific as possible in your answer.

17-23 *Joint and By-Products, Process Further* (CMA) Gossett Chemical Company uses comprehensive annual profit planning procedures to evaluate pricing policies, to finalize production decisions, and to estimate unit costs for its various products. One particular product group involves two joint products and two by-products. This product group is separately analyzed each year to establish appropriate production and marketing policies.

The two joint products—ALCHEM-X and CHEM-P—emerge at the end of processing in Department 20. Both chemicals can be sold at this split-off point—ALCHEM-X for $2.50 per unit and CHEM-P for $3.00 per unit. By-product BY-D20 also emerges at the split-off point in Department 20 and is salable without further processing for $.50 per unit. Unit costs of preparing this by-product for market are $.03 for freight and $.12 for packaging.

CHEM-P is sold without further processing, but ALCHEM-X is transferred to Department 22 for additional processing into a refined chemical labeled as ALCHEM-XF. No additional raw materials are added in Department 22. ALCHEM-XF is sold for $5.00 per unit. By-product BY-D22 is created by the additional processing in Department 22, and it can be sold for $.70 per unit. Unit marketing costs for BY-D22 are $.05 for freight and $.15 for packaging.

Gossett Chemical Company accounts for by-product production by crediting the net realizable value of by-products produced to production costs of the main products. The net realizable-value method is used to allocate net joint production costs for inventory valuation purposes.

A portion of the 19_5 profit plan established in September 19_4 is presented here.

Shortly after this budget was compiled, the company learned that a chemical that would compete with ALCHEM-XF was to be introduced. The marketing department estimated that this would require a permanent price reduction to $3.50 a unit for the ALCHEM-XF to be sold in present quantities. Gossett must now reevaluate the decision to process ALCHEM-X further.

The market for ALCHEM-X will not be affected by the introduction of this new chemical. Consequently, the quantities of ALCHEM-X that are usually processed into ALCHEM-XF can be sold at the regular price of $2.50 per unit. The costs for marketing ALCHEM-X are estimated to be $105,000. If the further processing is terminated, Department 22 will be dismantled and all costs except equipment depreciation, $18,400; supervisory salaries, $21,200; and general overhead, $35,200 will be eliminated.

		UNITS OF PRODUCTION	
		CHEM-P	ALCHEM-XF
Estimated sales		400,000	210,000
Planned inventory change		−8,000	−6,000
Required production		392,000	204,000
Minimum production based upon joint output ratio		392,000	210,000
By-product output			
BY-D20	90,000		
BY-D22	60,000		

	COSTS	
Budgeted Production Costs	Department 20	Department 22
Raw material	$160,000	—
Costs transferred from 20*	—	$225,000
Hourly direct labor	170,000	120,000
Variable overhead	180,000	140,800
Fixed overhead	247,500	188,000
	$757,500	$673,800

Budgeted Marketing Costs	CHEM-P	ALCHEM-XF
	$196,000	$105,000

*The cost transferred to Department 22 is calculated as follows:

		SALES VALUE OF OUTPUT	
ALCHEM-X (210,000 × $2.50)		$ 525,000	31%
CHEM-P (392,000 × $3.00)		1,176,000	69%
		$1,701,000	100%
Department 20 costs		$ 757,500	
less by-product (90,000 × $.35)		31,500	
Net costs		$ 726,000	
ALCHEM-X	31%	$ 225,000 or $1.07 per unit	
CHEM-P	69	501,000 or $1.28 per unit	
Allocated net costs	100%	$ 726,000	

required

1. Should Gossett sell ALCHEM-X at the split-off point or continue to process it further in Department 22? Prepare a schedule of relevant costs and revenues to support your answer.
2. During discussions of the possible dropping of ALCHEM-XF one person notes that the manufacturing margin for ALCHEM-X would be 57.2 percent [(2.50 − 1.07)/2.50] and 57.3 percent for CHEM-P. The normal markup for products sold in the market with ALCHEM-X is 72 percent. For the CHEM-P portion of the line the markup is 47 percent. He argues that the company's unit costs must be incorrect, because the margins differ from the typical rates. Briefly explain why Gossett's rates for the two products are almost identical when "normal" rates are not.

17-24 *Compute Maximum Price To Be Paid for Raw Materials* The Nerg Fertilizer Company buys special silt and dehydrates, sorts and bales it for sale as powerful fertilizer. The silt is separated into three grades, the separation being dependent upon the relative content of foreign matter. The three grades of fertilizer have the following list prices per ton: (1) $200, (2) $150, and (3) $125. Standards provide for 110 tons to be purchased for every 100 tons yield of baled fertilizer. Processing costs are $40 per ton of baled fertilizer and handling costs are $5 per ton of silt.

Selling and administrative expenses are 15 percent of sales; target income is 10 percent of sales.

The purchasing agent for the Nerg Company has been offered two carloads of silt at a cost of $80 per ton. Tests indicate that this silt will yield 60 percent of grade 1 and 20 percent each of grades 2 and 3; however, waste will be 10 percent higher than present levels. Should the agent accept this offer in light of the target income?

17-25 *Sell or Process Further; Allocation of Fixed Costs* The Space Parts Co. receives cold-worked steel in sheet form from a nearby steel mill. The company has a special patented machine that takes the sheet steel and produces three missile parts simultaneously. Part A is taken from the machine and further processed to make it available for sale at $3.50; the additional processing cost for part A is $495. Parts B and C are run through a vat containing a secret "dip" developed by one of the company engineers to make them heat-resistant. This dip costs 20¢ per cubic foot of product. Part B sells for $5 and part C for $8.25.

ADDITIONAL INFORMATION

Materials	$ 8,000	
Direct labor	1,600	
Maintenance and depreciation	1,200	
	$10,800	cost of running special machine for month

Month's production and sales (which is the typical product mix):

Part A	600 units
Part B	800 units
Part C	1,000 units

Part B has a volume of .50 cu. ft.
Part C has a volume of .75 cu. ft.

The vat is being depreciated at the rate of $60 per month, requires two persons for its operation at a total salary of $1,500 per month, and necessitates other operating expenses of $165 per month. All these costs are fixed.

required

1. Joint costs assignable to each part for the month's operations. Use the net realizable-value method.
2. The company has a chance to sell part B undipped at split-off at $4.70 each on a long-run basis. Should the company adopt this alternative?

17-26 *Joint Costs and Relevant Costs* The Curling Chemical Company begins all production in Department A. At the end of processing in Department A, products X and Y appear. Both can be sold immediately, but X can also be processed further in Department B, where products X-1 and X-2 appear at the end of processing. X-1 is then immediately sold; X-2 can be (a) sold in bulk to another processor, (b) packaged and sold as a consumer good, or (c) aged for one year and reintroduced as a raw material, Mysto, in Department A. One unit of aged X-2 is equal to one unit of Mysto.

Production and sales have been stable for the past few years, and the basic demand for all products does not look as though it will change for quite a few more years.

Data for the past year include the following:

Processing costs—Department A:	
Variable	$ 75,000
Fixed	45,000
Processing costs—Department B (not including transferred-in costs):	
Variable	$ 58,000
Fixed	150,000
Unit data:	

	IN UNITS	
	Production	Ending Inventories
X	220,000	20,000
Y	200,000	5,000
X-1	70,000	1,000
X-2	30,000	2,000

Selling prices per unit (unchanged throughout this year):	
X (net of separable selling expenses)	$ .20
Y (net of separable selling expenses)	.44
X-1 (after deducting $.10 variable packaging costs)	2.00
X-2 in bulk	4.30
X-2 as consumer good	5.00
Purchase costs:	
Mysto:	$4.00 per unit

5,500 units of Mysto were needed last year for production operations in Department A.

Selling costs of X-2, all variable, 10% of selling price.

Packaging costs of X-2 for consumer sales, 50¢ per unit.

The company's average cost of capital is 10%.

Packaging costs are considered as manufacturing costs by this company.

Unless otherwise stated, consider each situation below independently. State any special assumptions that you make.

required

1. The company uses "market value at split-off point" as a basis for allocating joint-production costs to products. What are the appropriate total ending-

inventory values for products X, Y, X-1 and X-2? Show computations *clearly*. For products X-1 and X-2, show a breakdown in total inventory costs between the Department A portion and the Department B portion.

2. Assume that the outside purchase cost of Mysto is going to rise. Based on the given information, how high will the price of Mysto have to go before the Curling Chemical Company should seriously consider aging X-2 and using it in Department A? Explain.
3. The company is considering adding another material at a cost of $1.00 per unit to product X-1, packaging the resulting product at a variable cost of 42¢ per unit, and selling it through manufacturer's agents at a straight commission of 10 percent of selling price. The prospective selling price will be $3.80 per finished unit. Should the company adopt this plan? Why? Show computations.
4. The company has been offered some new processing equipment for Department A. The salesman says that the new equipment will slash unit costs by 3.5¢. The new equipment will replace old equipment that has a remaining useful life of seven years, has zero disposal value now, and is being depreciated on a straight-line basis at $10,000 per year. The new equipment's straight-line depreciation would be $25,000 per year. It would last seven years and have no disposal value. The salesman pointed out that the overall unit costs now are slightly over 28.5¢ per unit of product in Department A, whereas the new equipment is being used by one of Curling's competitors at a unit cost of production of only 25¢ per unit of product, computed as follows:

Variable costs	$ 60,060
Fixed costs	76,440*
Total costs	$136,500
Divide by total units of X and Y produced	546,000
Cost per unit	25¢

* The $76,440 includes $25,000 depreciation on the new equipment in question. Curling's supervisory payroll is $6,000 less than this competitor's.

The salesman went on to point out that a saving of $3\frac{1}{2}$¢ per unit would add $14,700 to Curling's annual profits.

a. Show *specifically* how the salesman made his computations of Department A unit costs.
b. As adviser to Curling's management, evaluate the salesman's contentions and prepare a quantitative summary to support your recommendations for Curling's best course of action.

Process Costing: A Type of Product Costing

18

Process-costing techniques are used for inventory costing when there is continuous mass production of like units, in contrast to the production of tailor-made or unique goods. This chapter will cover the major *product-costing* approaches that may be used in process-cost systems. It will be concerned only incidentally with *planning and control,* because the latter techniques are discussed in other chapters and are applicable to all product-costing systems regardless of whether process costing or job-order costing is used.

general characteristics of process costing

all product costing is averaging

The most important point is that product costing is an averaging process. The unit cost used for inventory purposes is the result of taking some accumulated cost and dividing it by some measure of production. The basic distinction between job-order costing and process costing is the breadth of the denominator: In job-order costing, it is small; but in process costing, it is large.

The two polar extremes of product costing are usually labeled *job-order costing* and *process costing.* As we saw in Chapter 4, job-order costing is concerned with individual units or batches, each receiving various degrees of attention and skill. In contrast, process costing deals with the mass production of like units that usually pass in continuous fashion through a series of production steps called *operations* or *processes.* Process costing is most often found in such industries as chemicals, oil, textiles, paints, flour, canneries, rubber, steel, glass, food processing, mining, and cement.

If a company mass-produces only one uniform product, the product-costing task at first glance is simple. Obtain a unit cost by dividing the total manufacturing costs by the total units produced. Then use the resultant unit cost to compute the costs of inventories and the cost of goods sold. Indeed, it is simple, provided that (a) there are no beginning inventories of work-in-process; (b) there is no abnormal spoilage, shrinkage, or waste; and (c) the flow of all costs is a continuous and constant stream—that is, materials, labor, and overhead are assumed to be added uniformly as manufacturing progresses. However, if the foregoing conditions do not hold, the product-costing task becomes more difficult.

equivalent units: the key

example 1

First consider the following simple example:

Beginning inventory, in process	0
Units placed in process	40,000
Units completed	38,000
Units in process, end, each ½ completed	2,000
Total costs to account for	$39,000

What was the output for the period? An obvious answer would be 38,000 completed units plus 2,000 half-completed units. But we should hesitate to express the sum of the output as 40,000 units. After all, each of the partially completed units has received only half the inputs applied to the fully completed output. Instead, we express output not in terms of *physical* units, but in terms of *equivalent* units. Equivalent units is the expression of output during a given period in terms of the *doses* or *amount* of work applied thereto.

So a physical unit is viewed as a bundle of work applications, as a collection of the factors of production (material and conversion costs). Equivalent units are calculated as follows:

Units completed, full dose of cost applied	38,000
Units in process, end, each unit is ½ completed:	
2,000 × ½	1,000
Total equivalent units of output	39,000

The notion of equivalent units can be used to help judge the performance of the *department*, because it is a measure of the activity for the period. It can also be used to determine the unit costs that are the basis for applying costs to *products:*

Unit cost per equivalent unit ($39,000 ÷ 39,000)	$ 1.00
Costs to be applied:	
To completed units (38,000 × $1.00)	$38,000
To work in process (1,000 × $1.00)	1,000
Total costs accounted for	$39,000

weighted-average and FIFO

beginning inventory Product costing becomes more complicated when materials and conversion costs are used at different rates and when beginning inventories are present. The easiest way to learn process-cost accounting is probably by example. The data in Example 2 will be used. **For the time being, concentrate on the data for Department A only.**

example 2

A company has two processes. Material is introduced at the *beginning* of the process in Department A, and additional material is added at the *end* of the process in Department B. Conversion costs are applied uniformly throughout both processes. As the process in Department A is completed, goods are immediately transferred to Department B; as goods are completed in Department B, they are transferred to Finished Goods.

Data for the month of March, 19_1, include the following:

	DEPARTMENT A	*DEPARTMENT B*
Work in process, beginning	10,000 units 2/5 converted,* $7,500 (materials, $6,000; conversion costs, $1,500)	12,000 units 2/3 converted,* $21,000 (Transferred-in costs, $9,800; conversion costs, $11,200)
Units completed during March	48,000	44,000
Units started during March	40,000	?
Work in process, end	2,000, 1/2 converted*	16,000, 3/8 converted*
Material cost added during March	$22,000	$13,200
Conversion costs added during March	$18,000	$63,000

* This means that each unit in process is regarded as being fractionally complete with respect to the conversion costs of the present department only, at the dates of the work-in-process inventories.

required

Compute the cost of goods transferred out of each department. Compute ending-inventory costs for goods remaining in each department. Assume (a) weighted-average product costing and (b) first-in, first-out (FIFO) product costing. Show journal entries for the transfers to Department B.

physical flow and equivalent units

The first two steps in accounting for process costs are:

STEP 1 COMPUTE PHYSICAL FLOW Trace the physical flow of production. (Where did units come from? Where did they go?) In other words, (a) what are the units to account for? and (b) how are they accounted for? Draw flow charts as a preliminary step, if necessary. The physical flow may also be expressed as an equation:

$$\text{Beginning inventories} + \text{Units started} = \text{Units transferred} + \text{Ending inventories}$$

STEP 2 COMPUTE CURRENT OUTPUT IN EQUIVALENT UNITS Express the physical flow in terms of equivalent output for the current period. Because materials and conversion costs are applied differently, the equivalent output is usually divided into material and conversion-cost categories. For example, instead of thinking of output in terms of physical units, think of output in terms of material doses of work and conversion-cost doses of work. **Disregard dollar amounts until equivalent units are computed.**

Exhibit 18-1 illustrates Steps 1 and 2. Note that for departmental responsibility purposes, budgetary allowances for March could be built on the basis of the equivalent units.

application to products

The following steps are taken to apply the costs to the products that have been transferred out or that remain in process.

STEP 3 SUMMARIZE TOTAL COSTS Obtain the total costs to account for, classified by major categories.

STEP 4 COMPUTE UNIT COSTS Choose a cost-flow assumption and use it to determine the appropriate unit costs. Three cost-flow assumptions are in wide use in process costing: weighted-average, first-in, first-out (FIFO), and standard costing. Each will be discussed in turn in this chapter.

STEP 5 ALLOCATE AND RECONCILE TOTAL COSTS Use unit costs to determine total costs of goods completed and work in process. Be sure that total costs have been fully accounted for.

Steps 3, 4, and 5 are illustrated in Exhibits 18-2 and 18-3. Exhibit 18-2 uses the weighted average cost-flow assumption, which is explained in footnote (b) of the exhibit. Exhibit 18-3 uses FIFO, which is explained in footnote (b) of the exhibit.

As these exhibits demonstrate, there are likely to be insignificant differences in product-costing results between FIFO and weighted-average methods.

EXHIBIT 18-1

DEPARTMENT A

Computation of Output in Equivalent Units for the Month Ended March 31, 19_1

Quantities	(STEP 1) Physical Flow	(STEP 2) EQUIVALENT UNITS Materials	Conversion Costs
Work in process, beginning	10,000(⅖)*		
Units started	40,000		
Units accounted for	50,000		
Units completed and transferred out during current period	48,000	48,000	48,000
Work in process, end:	2,000(½)*		
Materials: 2,000 × 1		2,000	
Conversion costs: 2,000 × ½			1,000
Units accounted for	50,000		
Total work done		50,000	49,000
Less old equivalent units for work done on beginning inventory in previous periods:			
Materials: 10,000 × 1		10,000	
Conversion costs: 10,000 × ⅖			4,000
Remainder, new equivalent units for current period		40,000	45,000

* Degrees of completion for *conversion costs* of this department only, at the dates of the work-in-process inventories. Note that *material costs* pertaining to work in process are fully completed at each of these dates because, in this department, materials are introduced at the *beginning* of the process. The following diagram regarding conversion costs may clarify the relationships for the March work:

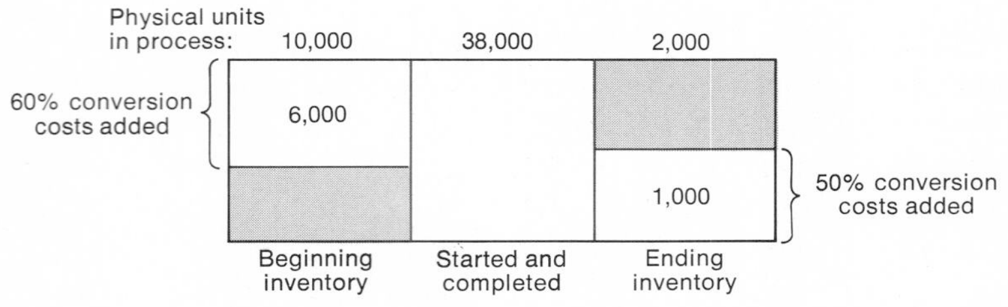

Note that the new equivalent units of conversion costs applied for the current period are 6,000 + 38,000 + 1,000, or 45,000 units.

EXHIBIT 18-2

DEPARTMENT A

Application of Costs to Products, Weighted-Average Method for the Month Ended March 31, 19_1

		(STEP 3)[a]			(STEP 4)	
		Work in Process, Beginning	Current Costs	Total Costs	Divisor Equivalent Units[b]	Average Unit Costs
	Materials	$6,000	$22,000	$28,000	50,000	$.560
	Conversion costs	1,500	18,000	19,500	49,000	.398
		$7,500	$40,000	$47,500		$.958
(Step 5)	Goods completed: 48,000 units × $.958			$45,984		
(Step 5)	Work in process, end, 2,000 units			1,518[c]		
(Step 5)	Total costs accounted for			$47,500 (rounded)		

[a] See Exhibit 18-1 for Steps 1 and 2.

[b] The divisor for computing unit costs depends on the cost flow assumption. For the weighted-average method, this is the total work done as computed in Exhibit 18-1. The equivalent units include the work completed before March on the beginning inventory as well as the work completed during March. Therefore, the beginning inventory costs are mingled with current costs as shown in the tabulation above.

[c] The cost of goods completed may simply be deducted from the total costs to obtain the cost of the ending work in process. However, it is advisable to check the accuracy of such computations by the following proof:

Materials (2,000 × $.560)	$1,120
Conversion costs (2,000 × .5 × $.398)	398
Total	$1,518

Process-cost situations usually entail mass production of a continuous nature. Beginning and ending inventories are not likely to change radically from month to month. Furthermore, conversion costs per unit are unlikely to fluctuate wildly from month to month.

If material prices are volatile, there may be significant differences in results between FIFO and weighted-average methods. In such cases the company usually will use neither method. Instead, some other technique, such as the standard costing method explained later in the chapter, is used so that the influence of price fluctuations is monitored separately.

interdepartmental transfers Now examine Department B. Most process-cost situations have two or more departments in the production cycle. Ordinarily, as goods move from department to department, related costs are also transferred. Exhibit 18-4 shows how such a transfer is handled in the computation of equivalent units.

EXHIBIT 18-3

DEPARTMENT A

Application of Costs to Products, First-in, First-out Method
For the Month Ended March 31, 19_1

			Total Costs	(STEP 4) Divisor Equivalent Units[b]	Unit Costs
	Work in process, beginning		$ 7,500		
	Current costs:				
	Materials		22,000	40,000	$.55
	Conversion costs		18,000	45,000	.40
(Step 3)[a]	Total costs to account for		$47,500		$.95
(Step 5)	Work in process, end:				
	Materials (2,000 × $.55)	$1,100			
	Conversion costs (2,000 × .5 × $.40)	400	$ 1,500		
	Completed and transferred, 48,000 units: ($47,500 − $1,500)		46,000[c]		$.95833[c]
(Step 5)	Total costs accounted for		$47,500		

[a] See Exhibit 18-1 for Steps 1 and 2.

[b] For first-in, first-out, the beginning inventory is regarded as if it were a batch of goods separate and distinct from the goods started and completed by a process within the same period. FIFO is really a step in the direction of job-order costing, because it distinguishes batches whereas the weighted-average method does not. Therefore, the divisor equivalent units for computing a unit cost are the new equivalent units for March computed in Exhibit 18-1.

[c] Note that in contrast to the weighted-average method in Exhibit 18-2, under FIFO it is easier and more direct to compute the cost of the ending work in process first and then deduct it from the total costs to obtain the cost of goods transferred. Note too that the $.95833 average unit cost of transfers under FIFO is not the same as the current $.95 cost of producing a whole finished unit. Of course, this is because the cost of the beginning inventory influences the total cost of goods transferred. If this technique is used, it is advisable to check the accuracy of the cost of goods transferred by the following proof:

Work in process, beginning, which is transferred out first	$ 7,500
Additional costs to complete: 10,000 × (1 − ⅖) × $.40	2,400
Cost of units started and completed this month: (48,000 − 10,000) × $.95	36,100
Total cost of goods completed and transferred out	$46,000

(The average cost of these is $46,000 ÷ 48,000 units = $.95833)

Transferred-in costs tend to give students much trouble, so special study is needed here. As far as Department B is concerned, units coming in from Department A may be viewed as if they were the raw materials of Department B. Costs transferred from Department A to Department B are similar to the material costs brought into Department A, although they are called *transferred-in costs* (or *previous department costs*), not material costs. That is, one might visualize the situation as if Department B bought the goods from an outside supplier. Thus, Department B's computations must provide for transferred-in costs, for

EXHIBIT 18-4

DEPARTMENT B

Computation of Output in Equivalent Units for the Month Ended March 31, 19_1

Quantities	(STEP 1) Physical Flow	(STEP 2) EQUIVALENT UNITS Transferred-in Costs	Materials	Conversion Costs
Work in process, beginning	12,000(⅔)*			
Units transferred in	48,000			
Units to account for	60,000			
Units completed and transferred out during current period	44,000	44,000	44,000	44,000
Work in process, end:	16,000(⅜)*			
Transferred-in costs: 16,000 × 1		16,000		
Materials: none				
Conversion costs: 16,000 × ⅜				6,000
Units accounted for	60,000			
Total work done		60,000	44,000	50,000
Less old equivalent units for work done on beginning inventory in previous periods:				
Transferred-in costs: 12,000 ×1		12,000		
Materials: none			—	
Conversion costs: 12,000 × ⅔				8,000
Remainder, new equivalent units for current period		48,000	44,000	42,000

* Degrees of completion on conversion costs in this department only, at the dates of the work-in-process inventories. Note that *material costs* pertaining to work in process have no completion at each of these dates because, in this department, materials are introduced at the *end* of the process. Note also that *transferred-in costs* are, of course, fully completed at each of the inventory dates.

any new material costs added in Department B, and for conversion costs added in Department B.

Exhibits 18-5 and 18-6 show how the weighted-average and FIFO methods apply Department B costs to products.

effect of transfers: modification of FIFO

In a series of interdepartmental transfers, each department is regarded as a distinct accounting entity. All transferred-in costs during a given period are carried at one unit cost, regard-

EXHIBIT 18-5

DEPARTMENT B

Application of Costs to Products, Weighted-Average Method for the Month Ended March 31, 19_1

	(STEP 3)[a]			(STEP 4)	
	Work in Process, Beginning	Current Costs	Total Costs	Divisor Equivalent Units[b]	Average Unit Cost
Transferred-in costs	$ 9,800	$ 45,982	$ 55,782	60,000	$ .9297
Materials	—	13,200	13,200	44,000	.3000
Conversion costs	11,200	63,000	74,200	50,000	1.4840
	$21,000	$122,182	$143,182		$2.7137
(Step 5) Goods completed: 44,000 units × $2.7137			$119,403		
(Step 5) Work in process, end, 16,000 units			23,779[c]		
(Step 5) Total costs accounted for			$143,182		

[a] See Exhibit 18-4 for Steps 1 and 2.

[b] This is the total work done, as shown in Exhibit 18-4.

[c] As was explained in Exhibit 18-2, the cost of goods completed may simply be deducted from the total costs to obtain the cost of the ending work in process. However, it is advisable to check the accuracy of these computations by the following proof:

Transferred-in costs (16,000 × $.9297)	$14,875
Materials	—
Conversion costs (16,000 × 3/8 × $1.484)	8,904
	$23,779

less of whether weighted-average or FIFO techniques were used by previous departments.[1]

In summary, although the so-called FIFO method is sometimes used in process-costing situations, only rarely is an application of strict FIFO ever en-

[1] Thus, although the FIFO method as used by Department A may show batches of goods accumulated and transferred at different unit costs, these goods are typically costed by Department B at *one* average unit cost, as Exhibit 18-3 demonstrates. In other words, a departmental FIFO method may be used, but in practice the strict FIFO method is modified to the extent that subsequent departments use weighted-average methods for cost transferred in during a given period. If this were not done, the attempt to trace costs on a strict FIFO basis throughout a series of processes would become too burdensome and complicated. For example, a four-department process-cost system could have at least eight or more batches, which would need separate costing by the time costs are transferred to and out of the final department. However, as goods are transferred from the last process to Finished Goods, the records of finished stock could be kept on a strict first-in, first-out method if desired. The clerical burden alone is enough to cause most process-cost industries to reject strict FIFO as a costing method. More will be said about the weakness of FIFO in the next chapter concerning spoilage. Incidentally, those readers who plan to take the CPA examination should recognize that FIFO is frequently covered on the examination, even though it is seldom encountered in practice.

EXHIBIT 18-6

DEPARTMENT B

Application of Costs to Products, First-in, First-out Method for the Month Ended March 31, 19_1

			Total Costs	(STEP 4) Divisor Equivalent Units[b]	Unit Costs
	Work in process, beginning		$ 21,000		
	Current costs:				
	Transferred-in costs		46,000	48,000	$ .95833
	Materials		13,200	44,000	.30000
	Conversion costs		63,000	42,000	1.50000
(Step 3)[a]	Total costs to account for		$143,200		$2.75833
(Step 5)	Work in process, end:				
	Transferred-in costs (16,000 × $.95833)	$15,333			
	Materials	—			
	Conversion costs (16,000 × ⅜ × $1.50)	9,000	$ 24,333		
	Completed and transferred out, 44,000 units ($143,200 − $24,333)		118,867[c]		$2.70152[c]
(Step 5)	Total costs accounted for		$143,200		

[a] See Exhibit 18-4 for Steps 1 and 2.

[b] The computation follows the same pattern as explained in Exhibit 18-3. Therefore, the divisor equivalent units are the new equivalent units for March computed in Exhibit 18-4.

[c] As was explained in Exhibit 18-3, the accuracy of the cost of goods completed and transferred out could be checked by the following proof:

Work in process, beginning, which is transferred out first	$ 21,000
Additional costs to complete:	
Materials: 12,000 × $.30	3,600
Conversion costs: 12,000 × (1 − ⅔) × $1.50	6,000
Cost of units started and completed this month: (44,000 − 12,000) × $2.75833	88,267
Total cost of goods completed and transferred out	$118,867

(The average unit cost of these is $118,867 ÷ 44,000 units = $2.70152.)

countered. It should really be called a *modified* or *departmental* FIFO method. FIFO techniques are applied within a department to compile the cost of goods transferred *out,* but goods transferred *in* during a given period usually bear a single average unit cost as a matter of convenience.

journal entries for transfers

The journal entries are:

	WEIGHTED-AVERAGE METHOD		FIFO METHOD	
Department-B—Work-in-process control	45,982		46,000	
Department A—Work-in-process control		45,982		46,000
To transfer costs from Department A. For detailed computations, see Exhibits 18-2 and 18-3.				
Finished-goods control	119,403		118,867	
Department B—Work-in-process control		119,403		118,867
To transfer costs of goods finished. See Exhibits 18-5 and 18-6.				

Sometimes a problem requires that the work-in-process account be split into Work in Process—Materials, Work in Process—Labor, and Work in Process—Overhead. In these cases, the journal entries would contain this greater detail, even though the underlying reasoning and techniques would be unaffected.

pitfalls to avoid

The solution of process-cost problems can become imposing. Building self-checks in a step-by-step solution is helpful. Such self-checks are woven into the five-step uniform approach described in this chapter.

This five-step approach is not the only or the fastest way to solve process-cost problems. Nevertheless, it is logical and has self-checks. By applying the five-step approach, you will develop confidence and comprehension. Armed with this approach, you should be able to handle adequately any process-cost situation. Shortcuts should be applied wherever feasible. But is is difficult to generalize on shortcut methods, because they differ depending upon the specific problem and the student's ability to use them.

Several pitfalls or common mistakes should be avoided:

1. Remember to include transferred-in costs from previous departments in your calculations. Such costs should be treated as if they were another kind of material cost, because each department is treated as a separate entity. In other words, when successive departments are involved, transferred goods from one department become all or a part of the raw materials of the next department, although they are called *transferred-in costs,* not raw materials.
2. Material and conversion costs (labor and overhead) are often not applied at the same rates. Special care should be used, therefore, in expressing work in process

in terms of equivalent units. For material doses, the degree of completion may be 100 percent (if all material is added at the beginning of the production cycle) for some materials and 0 percent for materials that will not be added until the end of the process. At the same time, conversion doses may be some other percentage, such as 50 percent or 75 percent.

3. In calculating costs to be transferred on a first-in, first-out basis, do not overlook the costs attached at the beginning of the period to goods that were in process but are now included in the goods transferred.
4. Unit costs may fluctuate between periods. Therefore, transferred goods may contain batches accumulated at different unit costs (see point 3). These goods, when transferred to the next department, are typically valued by that next department at *one* average unit cost.
5. Units may be expressed in terms of kilograms in one department and liters in the next. Consider each department separately. Unit costs would be based on kilogram measures in the first department and liters in the second. As goods are received by the second department, they may be converted to the liter unit of measure.
6. If the problem calls for first-in, first-out calculations, do not use the weighted-average approach, and vice versa.

standard costs and process costs

This section assumes that you have already studied Chapters 7, 8, and 9.

standards are useful Previous chapters demonstrated that the use of standard costing is completely general; that is, it can be used in job-order situations or in process-costing situations, and with absorption costing or direct costing. Standard-cost procedures tend to be most effective when they are adapted to process-costing situations. Mass, continuous, and repetitive production conditions lend themselves rather easily to setting meaningful physical standards. Price tags may then be applied to the physical standards to develop standard costs. Such standard costs would allow for normal shrinkage, waste, evaporation, or spoilage.

The intricacies and conflicts between weighted-average and FIFO costing methods are eliminated by using standard costs. Further, weighted-average and FIFO techniques become very complicated when used in industries that produce a variety of products. Standard costing is especially useful where there are various combinations of materials, operations, and product sizes. As Professor James H. March pointed out, a steel-rolling mill uses various steel alloys and produces sheets of various sizes and of various finishes. The items of raw material are not numerous; neither are the operations performed. But used in various combinations, they yield too great a variety of products to permit the averaging procedure of historical process-cost accounting. Elsewhere, similar conditions are frequently found—as, for example, in plants manufacturing rubber goods, textiles, ceramics, paints, and packaged food products.

Standard costing is growing in importance in process-costing industries. Therefore, because of its conceptual and practical appeal, standard costing deserves our study. Because we have already seen how standard costing aids planning and control, we shall concentrate on its product-costing aspects.

computations under standard costing

The facts are basically the same as those for Department A in Example 2, except that standard costs have been developed for the process as follows:

example 3

	PER UNIT
Direct materials, introduced at start of process	$ .53
Conversion costs, incurred uniformly throughout process	.37
Standard cost per unit	$ .90
Work in process, beginning, 10,000 units, ⅖ completed, (materials, $5,300; conversion costs, $1,480)	$ 6,780
Units completed during March	48,000
Units started during March	40,000
Work in process, end	2,000, ½ complete

required

1. Compute the standard cost of goods completed and of goods in process at end.
2. If "actual" material costs added during the month were $22,000 and conversion costs were $18,000, show a summary schedule of total material variance and total conversion-cost variance.

The formal solution is shown in Exhibit 18-7. Requirement 2 appears at the bottom of the exhibit. Careful study of Exhibit 18-7 will readily reveal that a standard-cost system greatly simplifies process-cost computations. A standard-cost system not only eliminates the intricacies of weighted-average versus FIFO inventory methods; it also erases the need for burdensome computations of costs per equivalent unit. The standard cost *is* the cost per equivalent unit. In addition, a standard-cost approach facilitates control.

Note that the measure of current output is the same as in Exhibit 18-1. Therefore, as Exhibit 18-7 shows, because all material is added at the beginning of the process, no equivalent units of material are added during the current period for the beginning work in process; similarly, only 6,000 units of conversion costs are added.

Incidentally, the cost-accounting literature often erroneously distinguishes among process costing, job-order costing, and standard costing as if they were mutually exclusive categories of product costing. Standard costing can be used in both process costing and job-order costing. For example, various job-order costs can be compiled using standards for all cost elements; similarly, as Exhibit 18-7 demonstrates, process costs can also be accumulated based on standard costs.

EXHIBIT 18-7

DEPARTMENT A
Standard Costs in a Process-Cost System for the Month Ended March 31, 19_1

			Total Costs	(STEP 4) Divisor Equivalent Units[b]	Unit Costs
	Work in process, beginning		$ 6,780		
	Current costs (at standard prices):				
	Materials		21,200	40,000	$.53
	Conversion costs		16,650	45,000	.37
(Step 3)[a]	Total costs to account for		$44,630		$.90
(Step 5)	Work in process, end:				
	Materials (2,000 × $.53)	$1,060			
	Conversion costs (2,000 × .5 × $.37)	370	$ 1,430		
	Completed and transferred out ($44,630 − $1,430), or (48,000 × $.90)		43,200[c]		$.90
(Step 5)	Total costs accounted for		$44,630		

	MATERIALS	*CONVERSION COSTS*
Summary of variances for current performance:		
Current output in equivalent units	40,000	45,000
Current output at standard costs applied	$21,200	$16,650
Costs charged to department for the month	$22,000	$18,000
Total variance[d]	$800 U	$1,350 U

[a] See Exhibit 18-1 for Steps 1 and 2.

[b] New equivalent units for March computed in Exhibit 18-1.

[c] *Proof:*

Work in process, beginning, which is transferred out first	$ 6,780
Additional costs to complete: (10,000)(1 − ⅖)($.37)	2,220
Cost of units started and completed this month: (48,000 − 10,000)($.90)	34,200
Total cost of goods completed and transferred out	$43,200

[d] These could be broken down further into price and efficiency variances, depending upon details that may be available.

additional aspects of process costing

estimating degree of completion

This chapter's illustrations plus almost all process-cost problems blithely mention various degrees of completion for inventories in process. The accuracy of these estimates depends on the care and skill of the estimator and the nature of the process. Estimating the degree of completion is usually easier for materials than for conversion costs. The conversion sequence usually consists of a number of standard operations or a standard number of hours, days, weeks, or months for mixing, heating, cooling, aging, curing, and so forth. Thus, the degree of completion for conversion costs depends on what proportion of the total effort needed to complete one unit or one batch has been devoted to units still in process. In industries where no exact estimate is possible, or, as in textiles, where vast quantities in process prohibit costly physical estimates, all work in process in every department is assumed to be either $\frac{1}{3}$, or $\frac{1}{2}$, or $\frac{2}{3}$ complete. In other cases, continuous processing entails little change of work-in-process levels from month to month. Consequently, work in process is safely ignored and monthly production costs are assigned solely to goods completed.

This is another example of cost-benefit analysis, whereby a simplified system is used because management decisions will be unaffected by a more elaborate cost accounting system.

overhead and predetermined rates

Labor and overhead tend to be lumped together as conversion costs for process-costing purposes. In many process-cost industries, continuous, uniform production results in little fluctuation of total factory overhead from month to month. In such cases, there is no need to use predetermined overhead rates. Of course, where overhead costs and production vary from period to period, predetermined overhead rates are used in order to get representative unit costs.

overhead and cost flow

In general, overhead is applied on a predetermined basis in the same manner as was introduced in Chapter 4. The assumption that all conversion costs are incurred uniformly in proportion to the degree of product completion is difficult to justify on theoretical grounds. For example, this implies that a wide variety of overhead-cost incurrence is directly related to labor-cost incurrence. Although such a direct cause-and-effect relationship may not exist, refinements of overhead application beyond this assumption are usually deemed too costly. When more precision is attempted, it is usually confined to developing a predetermined overhead rate to be loaded on material cost to cover such indirect costs as purchasing, receiving, storing, issuing, and transferring materials. In such cases, one overhead rate would be applied along with material costs while a separate overhead rate would be applied along with labor costs.

SUMMARY

Process-costing techniques are used for inventory costing when there is continuous, mass production of like units. The key concept in process costing is that of equivalent units, the expression of output during a given period in terms of doses or amounts of work applied thereto.

Five basic steps may be used in solving process-cost problems. Process costing is complicated by uneven flow of cost factors, by the presence of beginning inventories, and by the presence of costs transferred in from prior departments.

Two widely advocated process-costing techniques are known as the *weighted-average* and *first-in, first-out* methods. However, standard costs are the most widely used; they are simpler and more useful than other techniques for both product-costing and control purposes.

PROBLEMS FOR SELF-STUDY

Review each example in this chapter and obtain the solutions on your own. Then check your work against the solutions, which appear in the various exhibits.

QUESTIONS, PROBLEMS, AND CASES

18-1 "Standard-cost procedures are particularly applicable to process-costing situations." Do you agree? Why?

18-2 What are some virtues of standard costs as used in process costing?

18-3 "There is no need for using predetermined overhead rates for product costing in process-cost industries." Do you agree? Why?

18-4 Why should the accountant distinguish between *transferred-in costs* and *new raw-material* costs for a particular department?

18-5 What is the feature of the first two steps of the five-step uniform appraoch that distinguishes them from the final three steps?

18-6 *Introductory Process Costing: Materials Introduced at Start of Process* A certain process incurred $40,000 of production costs during a month. Materials costing $22,000 were introduced at the start of processing, while conversion costs of $18,000 were incurred at a uniform rate throughout the production cycle. Of the 40,000 units of product started, 38,000 were completed and 2,000 were still in process at the end of the month, averaging one-half complete.

In step-by-step fashion, prepare a production-cost report showing cost of goods completed and cost of ending work in process.

18-7 *Introductory Process Costs; Single Department* The following data pertain to the mixing department for July:

UNITS	
Work in process, July 1	0
Units started	50,000
Completed and transferred to finishing department	35,000

COSTS	
Material P	$200,000
Material Q	70,000
Direct labor and overhead	135,000

Material P is introduced at the start of the process, while Material Q is added when the product reaches a three-fourths stage of completion. Conversion costs are incurred uniformly throughout the process.

required

Cost of goods transferred during July. Cost of work in process as of July 31. Assume that ending work in process is one batch, two-thirds completed.

18-8 *Process Costing, Budgeting and Control* (Prepared by the author and adapted for use in a CPA examination) The Dopern Company uses departmental budgets and performance reports to help plan and control its process-costing operations. Department A has the following budget for January's contemplated production of 1,000 whole units of equivalent performance, which represents a normal month's volume.

VARIABLE AND CONTROLLABLE COSTS	
Direct materials	$20,000
Direct labor	10,000
Indirect labor	2,000
Power	200
Supplies	800
	$33,000
FIXED AND UNCONTROLLABLE COSTS	
Rent	$ 400
Supervision	1,000
Depreciation	500
Other	100
	$ 2,000
Total budgeted costs	$35,000

Direct materials are introduced at the start of the process. All conversion costs are assumed to be incurred uniformly throughout the process. Production fluctuates from month to month, so that the fixed overhead is applied on a predetermined basis at a rate of $2 per equivalent unit.

There were no beginning inventories. Eleven hundred units were started during the month; 900 were completed, and the 200 still in process at the end of the month were estimated to be three-fourths completed. There is no material shrinkage or spoilage, and no waste of materials.

The following performance report was prepared:

	BUDGET	*ACTUAL*	*VARIANCE*
Direct materials	$20,000	$22,550	$2,550 U
Direct labor	10,000	10,500	500 U
Indirect labor	2,000	2,100	100 U
Power	200	210	10 U
Supplies	800	840	40 U
	$33,000	$36,200	$3,200 U

U = Unfavorable

A total of $2,000 of fixed conversion costs were incurred during January.

required

1. Cost of goods completed during January.
2. Cost of ending work in process.
3. Amount of under- or overapplied overhead at January 31.
4. Comment on the performance report in 150 words or less. What *specific* conclusions can you draw from the performance report?

18-9 *Weighted-Average Process Costing* The following information relates to one department operating under a process-cost system: Work in process, December 1, 19_1, 1,000 units, 40 percent complete, consisting of $8,703 of materials and $5,036 of conversion costs. Production completed for December, 8,200 units; work in process, December 31, 19_1, 800 units, 20 percent complete.

All materials are introduced at the start of the process, while conversion costs are incurred uniformly throughout the process. Materials added during December were $72,000; conversion costs were $83,580.

required

Using weighted averages, show a schedule of equivalent performance, unit costs, and summary of costs. Also prepare a summary entry for the transfer of completed goods to finished stock.

18-10 *Standard Process Costs* Refer to the preceding problem. Assume standard costs per finished unit as follows: Direct materials, $8.50; Conversion costs, $10.00.

1. Compute standard costs of goods transferred and still in process.
2. Give the total variances for current performance on direct materials and conversion costs.

18-11 *Weighted Averages* The Dyer Processing Company had work in process at the beginning and end of 19_1 as follows:

	PERCENTAGE OF COMPLETION	
	Materials	Conversion Costs
January 1, 19_1—3,000 units	40%	10%
December 31, 19_1—2,000 units	80%	40%

The company completed 40,000 units of finished goods during 19_1. Manufacturing costs incurred during 19_1 were: materials, $242,600; conversion costs, $445,200. Inventory at January 1, 19_1 was carried at a cost of $10,600 (materials, $7,000; conversion costs, $3,600).

Assuming weighted average:

1. Compute new equivalent production for 19_1 for (a) materials and (b) conversion costs.
2. What is the proper cost of ending goods in process?

18-12 *Standard Process Costs* *Refer to the preceding problem.* If the standard cost for materials is $5 per finished unit and the standard cost for conversion costs is $10 per finished unit, what would be the total standard cost of work *performed during 19_1?*

18-13 *Weighted-Average Process-Costing Method* The Bright Paint Co. uses a process-cost system. Materials are added at the beginning of a particular process and conversion costs are incurred uniformly. Work in process at the beginning and end is assumed 50 percent complete. One gallon of material makes one gallon of product.

Data:

Beginning inventory		900 gallons
Materials added		9,900 gallons
Ending inventory		450 gallons
Conversion costs incurred	$18,000	
Cost of materials added	$20,000	
Conversion costs, beginning inventory	$ 800	
Cost of materials, beginning inventory	$ 1,600	

Use the weighted-average method. Prepare a schedule of output in equivalent units and a schedule of application of costs to products. Show the cost of goods completed and of ending work in process.

18-14 *Equivalent Units* (W. Crum) Walnut Company uses a process-cost system. Production and inventory data for May 19_5 are as follows:

Units put in process, 60,000.
Units completed in May, 70,000.
May 1 work in process was composed of 40,000 units with 30 percent of the material content and 40 percent of the conversion cost complete.
May 31 work in process was composed of 30,000 units with 60 percent of the material content and 70 percent of the conversion cost complete.

required

Compute the equivalent units. Using FIFO, compute the divisor for obtaining unit material cost for May, and unit conversion cost for May. Show all details.

18-15 *Equivalent Units* (CPA) The Jorcano Manufacturing Company uses a process-cost system to account for the costs of its only product, product D. Production begins in the fabrication department, where units of raw material are molded into various connecting parts. After fabrication is complete, the units are transferred to the assembly department. There is no material added in the assembly department. After assembly is complete, the units are transferred to a packaging department where packing material is placed around the units. After the units are ready for shipping, they are sent to a shipping area.

At year end, June 30, 1973, the following inventory of product D is on hand:

No unused raw material or packing material.
Fabrication department: 300 units, 1/3 complete as to raw material and 1/2 complete as to direct labor.
Assembly department: 1,000 units, 2/5 complete as to direct labor.
Packaging department: 100 units, 3/4 complete as to packing material and 1/4 complete as to direct labor.
Shipping area: 400 units.

1. The number of equivalent units of raw material in all inventories at June 30, 1973, is
   a. 300. b. 100. c. 1,600. d. 925.
2. The number of equivalent units of fabrication-department direct labor in all inventories at June 30, 1973, is
   a. 1,650. b. 150. c. 300. d. 975.
3. The number of equivalent units of packing material in all inventories at June 30, 1973, is
   a. 75. b. 475. c. 100. d. 425.

18-16 *Equivalent Units* (CPA adapted) Poole, Inc., produces a chemical compound by a unique chemical process, which Poole has divided into two departments, A and B, for accounting purposes. The process functions as follows:

1. The formula for the chemical compound requires one pound of Chemical X and one pound of Chemical Y. In the simplest sense, one pound of Chemical X is processed in Department A and transferred to Department B for further processing where one pound of Chemical Y is added when the process is 50 percent complete. When the processing is complete in Department B, the finished chemical compound is transferred to finished goods. The process is continuous, operating twenty-four hours a day.

2. No spoilage occurs in Department B.
3. In Department A conversion costs are incurred uniformly throughout the process and are allocated to good pounds produced.
4. In Department B conversion costs are allocated equally to each equivalent pound of output.
5. Poole's unit of measure for work-in-process and finished-goods inventories is pounds.
6. The following data are available for the month of October 19_4:

	DEPARTMENT A	DEPARTMENT B
Work in process, October 1	8,000 pounds	10,000 pounds
Stage of completion of beginning inventory (one batch per department)	3/4	3/10
Started or transferred in	47,500 pounds	?
Transferred out	46,500 pounds	?
Work in process, October 31	?	?
Stage of completion of ending inventory (one batch per department)	1/3	1/5
Total equivalent pounds of material Y added in Department B		44,500 pounds

required

Prepare schedules computing equivalent pounds of production (materials and conversion costs) for Department A and for Department B for the month of October 19_4 using the first-in, first-out method for inventory costing.

18-17 *Weighted Average* (W. Crum) Walden Company uses process costs, using the weighted-average-cost method. During the month of June, 1975, the cost data for Dept. 2 are as follows: 60,000 units were brought in from Dept. 1, with cost of $302,000 applied to them. Added materials of $164,920 were used in Dept. 2 in June, as well as conversion costs of $123,000. All finished product in Dept. 2 is transferred to Dept. 3. During June 70,000 units were completed in Dept. 2. Ending work in process at June 30 in Dept. 2 was composed of 10,000 units with 30 percent completion in this department.

Work in process in Dept. 2 at June 1 was composed of 20,000 units, 60 percent complete in this department, with $98,000 of Prior Dept. cost upon them, and $63,000 of materials added in Dept. 2, as well as $26,000 of conversion cost added in Dept. 2. Material in Dept. 2 is added at the halfway point. Both beginning and ending inventory are composed of a single identifiable batch of work.

required

Prepare process-cost report in good form for Dept. 2 for the month of June. Use weighted-average costs and carry all unit costs to four decimals. Be sure to show equivalents units, costs of work completed and work in process.

18-18 *Journal Entries* (W. Crum) Refer to the preceding problem. Prepare journal entries to: (a) record current additions to cost this month in Dept. 2 (omit conversion costs) and (b) record disposition of units completed this month in Dept. 2.

18-19 *Two Departments; Two Months* (W. Vatter) One of the products of this company is manufactured by passing it through two processes. The materials are started into production at the beginning of Process 1 and are passed directly from Process 1 to Process 2 without inventory between the processes. Operating data for two months are given below:

January

Process 1. No initial work in process. During the month, 800 units were put into process and $8,000 was charged to this account. Operations during the month cost $2,800. Six hundred units were finished and passed on to Process 2. The work in process at January 31 was one-half finished.

Process 2. No work in process on January 1. The work transferred from Process 1 was received and costs of $2,000 were incurred in operations to complete 300 units. At the end of the month, 300 units one-third finished remained in process.

February

Process 1. Six hundred units of material were put into process at a total price of $6,000. Other costs incurred were $2,550. At the end of the month, there were 300 units still within the process, two-thirds finished.

Process 2. Costs charged to operations in this process for February were $2,640. On February 28, there were 300 units still within the process, two-thirds finished.

There is no spoilage or shrinkage in either of the processes; all units unfinished at the beginning of the month are completed within that month.

required — Calculations of production costs for each process for each month on a weighted-average basis.

18-20 *Weighted-Average Costing* (W. Crum) The Doral Company has the following data for the month of October:

	DEPARTMENT A	DEPARTMENT B
Beginning inventory in process:	2,000 units	2,000 units
Prior department cost*	0	$4,600
Materials added last month	$2,000 (100%)	$3,200 (80%)
Conversion costs added last month	$ 900 (60%)	$ 800 (40%)
Units put in process this month	30,000	29,000
Materials added this month	$30,968	$56,580
Conversion costs added this month	$41,800	$29,803
Units completed and transferred	29,000	30,000
Ending inventory in process:	3,000 units	1,000 units
Material content	90%	50%
Conversion costs	50%	30%

* These are transferred-in costs.

required — Using weighted-average costing, prepare a production report for each department. Show the cost of goods completed and transferred and also show the cost of the ending work in process. Include a proof of your answer for the ending work in process.

18-21 *FIFO Costing* (W. Crum) Refer to the preceding problem. Using FIFO costing, repeat the requirements. Include a proof of your answer for the cost of goods completed and transferred.

18-22 *Process Costing, Weighted Average* (W. Crum) The Hickory Company manufactures a product processed through two departments. The process is lengthy, taking two weeks in Department M and ten days in Department S. Miscellaneous data include:

Dept. S, work in process, Dec. 1, 19_0—6,000 gallons, costing:

Dept. M cost in work in process	$24,000	
Materials added in S in work in process	$ 7,500	(100%)
Conversion cost added in S in work in process	$12,000	(60%)

Production brought in from Dept. M to Dept. S during month—30,000 gallons, costing—$123,000
Materials added in Dept. S in December—$18,000
Conversion costs added in Dept. S in December—$62,000
Gallons completed and transferred to finished product—32,000
On hand in process in Dept. S at Dec. 31, 19_0—4,000 gallons, bearing 80% of the material added in S, and 30% of the conversion costs of Dept. S

required

Compute for Dept. S:

1. Unit costs for December, using average-cost method, carrying unit costs to four decimals.
2. December 31, 19_0, inventory of work in process in Department S.
3. Cost of work completed in Department S in December and transferred to finished product.

18-23 *FIFO Computations* Repeat Problem 18-9, using the first-in, first-out method.

18-24 *FIFO Computations* Repeat Problem 18-13, using the first-in, first-out method.

18-25 *FIFO Computations* Repeat Problem 18-19, using the first-in, first-out method.

18-26 *Standard Costs and Equivalent Units* (CPA). The Longhorn Manufacturing Corporation produces only one product, Bevo, and accounts for the production of Bevo using a standard-cost system.

At the end of each year, Longhorn prorates all variances among the various inventories and cost of sales. Because Longhorn prices its inventories on the first-in, first-out basis and all the beginning inventories are used during the year, the variances which had been allocated to the ending inventories are immediately charged to cost of sales at the beginning of the following year. This allows only the current year's variances to be recorded in the variance accounts in any given year.

Following are the standards for the production of one unit of Bevo: 3 units of item A @ $1.00 per unit; 1 unit of item B @ $.50 per unit; 4 units of item C @ $.30 per unit; and 20 minutes of direct labor @ $4.50 per hour. Separate variance accounts are maintained for each type of raw material and for direct labor. Raw material purchases are recorded initially at standard. Manufacturing overhead is applied at $9.00 per actual direct labor hour and is not related to the standard-cost system. There was no overapplied or underapplied manufacturing overhead at December 31, 19_2.

After proration of the variances, the various inventories at December 31, 19_2, were priced as follows:

RAW MATERIAL

ITEM	*NUMBER OF UNITS*	*UNIT COST*	*AMOUNT*
A	15,000	$1.10	$16,500
B	4,000	.52	2,080
C	20,000	.32	6,400
			$24,980

WORK IN PROCESS

9,000 units of Bevo which were 100 percent complete as to items A and B, 50 percent complete as to item C, and 30 percent complete as to labor. The composition and valuation of the inventory follows:

ITEM	AMOUNT
A	$28,600
B	4,940
C	6,240
Direct labor	6,175
	$45,955
Overhead	11,700
	$57,655

FINISHED GOODS

4,800 units of Bevo composed and valued as follows:

ITEM	AMOUNT
A	$15,180
B	2,704
C	6,368
Direct labor	8,540
	$32,792
Overhead	16,200
	$48,992

Following is a schedule of raw materials purchased and direct labor incurred for the year ended December 31, 19_3. Unit cost of each item of raw material and direct-labor cost per hour remained constant throughout the year.

PURCHASES

ITEM	ACTUAL NUMBER OF UNITS OR HOURS	UNIT PRICE	AMOUNT
A	290,000	$1.15	$333,500
B	101,000	.55	55,550
C	367,000	.35	128,450
Direct labor	34,100	4.60	156,860

During the year ended December 31, 19_3, Longhorn sold 90,000 units of Bevo and had ending physical inventories as follows:

RAW MATERIALS

ITEM	NUMBER OF UNITS
A	28,300
B	2,100
C	28,900

WORK IN PROCESS

7,500 units of Bevo which were 100 percent complete as to items A and B, 50 percent complete as to item C, and 20 percent complete as to labor, as follows:

ITEM	NUMBER OF UNITS OR HOURS
A	22,900
B	8,300
C	15,800
Direct labor	800

FINISHED GOODS

5,100 units of Bevo, as follows:

ITEM	NUMBER OF UNITS OR HOURS
A	15,600
B	6,300
C	21,700
Direct labor	2,050

There was no overapplied or underapplied manufacturing overhead at December 31, 19_3.

required

Answer each of the following questions. Supporting computations should be prepared in good form.

1. What was the charge or credit to cost of sales at the beginning of 19_3 for the variances in the December 31, 19_2, inventories?
2. What was the total charge or credit to the three material price-variance accounts for items A, B, and C for the year ended December 31, 19_3?
3. What was the total charge or credit to the three material efficiency-variance accounts for items A, B, and C for the year ended December 31, 19_3?
4. What was the total charge or credit to the direct-labor price-variance account for the year ended December 31, 19_3?
5. What was the total charge or credit to the direct-labor efficiency-variance account for the year ended December 31, 19_3?

18-27 *Standard process costs and review of Chapters 9 and 10* (CPA) Norwood Corporation is considering changing its method of inventory valuation from absorption costing to direct costing and has engaged you to determine the effect of the proposed change on the 19_8 financial statements.

The Corporation manufactures Gink, which is sold for $20 per unit. Marsh is added before processing starts, and labor and overhead are added evenly during the manufacturing process. Production capacity is budgeted at 110,000 units of Gink annually. The standard costs per unit of Gink are:

Marsh, 2 pounds	$3.00
Labor	6.00
Variable manufacturing overhead	1.00
Fixed manufacturing overhead	1.10

A process-cost system is used employing standard costs. Variances from standard costs are now charged or credited to cost of goods sold. If direct costing were adopted, only variances resulting from variable costs would be charged or credited to cost of goods sold.

Inventory data for 19_8 follow:

	UNITS	
	JANUARY 1	DECEMBER 31
Marsh (pounds)	50,000	40,000
Work in process		
2/5 processed	10,000	
1/3 processed		15,000
Finished goods	20,000	12,000

During 19_8 220,000 pounds of Marsh were purchased and 230,000 pounds were transferred to work in process. Also, 110,000 units of Gink were transferred to finished goods. Actual fixed manufacturing overhead during the year was $121,000. There were no variances between standard variable costs and actual variable costs during the year.

required

1. Prepare schedules that present the computation of:
   a. Equivalent units of production for material and conversion costs.
   b. Number of units sold.
   c. Standard unit costs under direct costing and absorption costing.
   d. Amount, if any, of over- or underapplied fixed manufacturing overhead.
2. Prepare a comparative statement of cost of goods sold using standard direct costing and standard absorption costing.

18-28 *Process Costs; Standard Costs; Analysis of Variances* The Jammer Company uses standard costs and produces a chemical from a secret formula. Material A is introduced at the start of the single process, while Material B is added when the conversion process is 80 percent completed. Conversion costs are applied uniformly throughout the process.

Standard costs per finished unit:	
Materials:	
A, five gallons @ 40¢	$ 2.00
B, one pound	10.00
Conversion costs:	
Labor, 2 hours	5.00
Variable overhead*	1.00
Fixed overhead*	4.00
	$22.00

* Applied as a percentage of standard direct-labor cost.

Beginning inventory in process, July 1, 19_1, consisted of 1,000 units, all 30 percent completed. Fifty-two thousand gallons of A were added during July. Twelve thousand pounds of B were added during July. Nine thousand units were completed. Two thousand units were still in process, 90 percent completed, at the end of July.

Actual costs incurred by the production department were as follows:

Material A, $26,000
Material B, $108,000
Direct labor, 22,000 hours @ $2.50 = $55,000
Variable overhead, $10,850
Fixed overhead, $47,800

Denominator activity is 12,000 finished units per month.

required

Expression of production in terms of equivalent units for:

1. Material A
2. Material B
3. Conversion costs

Give dollar amounts and use *F* or *U* to denote whether the following variances are favorable or unfavorable:

4. Material A price variance (Assume that this company recognizes price variances for materials as they are used rather than as they are purchased.)
5. Material A efficiency variance
6. Material B price variance
7. Material B efficiency variance
8. Labor-price variance
9. Labor-efficiency variance
10. Variable-overhead spending variance
11. Variable-overhead efficiency variance
12. Fixed-overhead spending variance
13. Fixed-overhead denominator variance

18-29 *Joint Costs and Process Costs: First-in, First-out; Sell or Process Further* The Chemo Company manufactures two principal products, known as Gummo and Yummo. The company has three producing departments, A, B, and C. Raw material is started in process in Department A. Upon completion of joint processing in that department, two distinct chemicals are produced. One-fourth of the output goes to Department B, where it is made into Gummo; the other three-fourths goes to Department C, where it becomes Yummo. As Gummo and Yummo are completed, they are immediately transferred to finished stock.

The company assigns Department A costs to Gummo and Yummo in proportion to their net sales values at point of separation, computed by deducting costs to be incurred in subsequent processes from the sales value of the products.

The following information concerns the operations during May 19_1:

INVENTORIES

	APRIL 30		MAY 31
	Units	Cost	Units
Department A	None		None
Department B	500*	$10,000	700†
Department C	1,000*	11,300	700†
Finished goods—Gummo	800	19,200	500
Finished goods—Yummo	600	13,200	800

* Each unit is 1/5 completed.
† Each unit is 3/5 completed.

Twelve thousand units of output were produced in Department A.

COSTS INCURRED IN MAY

	Materials Used	Conversion Costs
Department A	$72,000	$72,000
Department B	—	$15,600
Department C	—	$12.00 per equivalent unit

SALES PRICES

Gummo	$25.00 per unit
Yummo	$22.00 per unit

Prices as of May 31 are unchanged from those in effect during the month.
The company uses first-in, first-out to cost out production.

required

1. For May production, conversion cost per equivalent unit in Department B.
2. Conversion cost per equivalent unit in Department A.
3. Total costs transferred to Department B.
4. Costs transferred from Department B to finished stock.
5. The company is considering a chance to sell the product that now goes into Department C at the split-off point, instead of processing it into Yummo. (Gummo would continue to be processed as usual.) If the long-run selling price at split-off point will be $10, should the company close down Department C and sell at split-off? Why? Answer in seventy words or less.

Spoilage, Waste, Defective Units, and Scrap

19

Problems of waste, scrap, or spoilage are found in nearly all manufacturing businesses, regardless of the specific production techniques used. Because there is a general approach to this entire area, this chapter views the problem as a whole before considering the peculiar difficulties in process-costing and job-costing situations.

The conceptual ideas of accounting for spoilage, scrap, and waste center primarily about distinguishing between abnormal and normal spoilage. Abnormal spoilage is often controllable by first-line supervision, whereas normal spoilage is not. Accounting for spoilage, defective units, and the like varies considerably in practice. This chapter will consider these matters from both product-costing and control viewpoints.

terminology

Terminology and accounting in this area are not at all precise or uniform. This chapter distinguishes between the various terms as follows:

SPOILAGE Production that does not meet dimensional or quality standards and that is junked and sold for disposal value. Net spoilage cost is the total of the costs accumulated to point of rejection less disposal value (sometimes called *salvage value*).

DEFECTIVE UNITS Production that does not meet dimensional or quality standards and that is subsequently reworked and sold through regular channels as firsts or seconds, depending on the characteristics of the product and on available alternatives.

WASTE Material that either is lost, evaporates, or shrinks in a manufacturing process, or is a residue that has no measurable recovery value; for example, gases, dust, smoke, and unsalable residues. Sometimes waste disposal entails additional costs; for example, atomic waste.

SCRAP Material residue from certain manufacturing operations that has measurable but relatively minor recovery value. For example, outlined metal from a stamping operation, shavings, filings, turnings, borings, sawdust, and short lengths from woodworking operations, and sprues, ingates, and flash from the casting operation in a foundry. Scrap may be either sold or reused.

spoilage in general[1]

management implications and factor combination

Most production processes generate some bad units along with the good ones, as an unavoidable result of the most economical combination of the factors of production. Although it may be technically possible to eliminate spoilage altogether in many instances, it may be uneconomical to do so, because the costs of lowering spoilage rates are greater than the costs of eliminating spoilage. Thus, beer bottles sometimes explode, defective castings inevitably appear, and impure as well as pure chemicals and food arise. The problem of spoilage is important from many aspects, the most important being that of managerial planning and control. Managers must first select the most economical production method or process. Then they must see that spoilage is controlled within chosen predetermined limits, so that excessive spoilage does not occur.

normal spoilage

Working within the selected set of production conditions, management must establish the rate of spoilage that is to be regarded as *normal. Normal spoilage* is what arises under efficient operating conditions; it is an inherent result of the particular process and is thus uncontrollable in the short run. Costs of normal spoilage are typically viewed as a part of the costs of *good* production, because the attaining of good units necessitates

[1] The writer acknowledges the helpful suggestions of Dean Samuel Laimon, University of Saskatchewan.

the simultaneous appearance of spoiled units. In other words, normal spoilage is planned spoilage, in the sense that the choice of a given combination of factors of production entails a spoilage rate that management is willing to accept.

abnormal spoilage *Abnormal spoilage* is spoilage that is not expected to arise under efficient operating conditions; it is not an inherent part of the selected production process. Most of this spoilage is usually regarded as controllable, in the sense that the first-line supervisor can exert influence over inefficiency. Such causes as machinery breakdowns, accidents, and inferior materials are typically regarded as being subject to some manager's influence. Costs of abnormal spoilage are the costs of inferior products that should be written off directly as losses for the period. For the most informative feedback, the Loss from Abnormal Spoilage account should appear on a detailed income statement as a separate loss item and not buried as an indistinguishable part of the cost of goods manufactured.

general accounting procedures for spoilage Before discussing debits and credits for spoiled goods, let us try to relate spoiled goods to two major purposes of cost accounting: control and product costing. Accounting for control is primarily concerned with charging responsibility centers for costs *as incurred.* Product costing is concerned with *applying* to inventory or other appropriate accounts the costs *already incurred.* Where does costing for spoiled goods fit into this framework? First, it must be made clear that the costs of both normal and abnormal spoiled goods are *product costs.* Thus, product costs can represent either good product or bad product:

	GOOD-PRODUCT COSTS—INVENTORIABLE	*BAD-PRODUCT COSTS—CHARGED OFF AS A LOSS IMMEDIATELY*
Cost of spoiled goods—normal	Yes	No
Cost of spoiled goods—abnormal	No	Yes

The existence of spoiled goods does not involve any additional cost beyond the amount already incurred.[2] Therefore, in accounting for spoiled goods, we are dealing with cost application and reallocation rather than new cost incurrence. Our objectives are:

1. To accumulate data to spotlight the cost of spoilage so that management is made aware of its magnitude.
2. To identify the *nature* of the spoilage and distinguish between costs of normal spoilage (which should be added to the cost of good units) and of abnormal spoilage (which should be written off as a loss).

[2] Where spoilage is not detected until completion of goods, spoiled units require the same effort as good units. In other words, a laborer can be performing with equal efficiency on all goods and yet turn out some spoiled units because of inferior materials, worn cutting tools, and the like. So labor efficiency may be very satisfactory, but spoilage may nevertheless be a major problem. Thus, a workman can efficiently turn out spoiled goods.

Depending on the product(s) or departments involved, there is a bewildering mass of treatments in practice, which vary from the inexcusable to the highly informative. This chapter cannot possibly cover all the theoretical and practical ramifications. It will try to contrast conceptual treatments with some methods used in practice.

A study of the conceptual entries in Exhibit 19-1 will show that, when a product is spoiled, some debit must be made to balance the necessary credit to work in process. Further, some means must be found to charge normal spoilage to good inventory and abnormal spoilage to a loss account. The entries in the conceptual treatment use a Cost of Spoiled Goods account to highlight the nature of the problem and to stress the notion that the costs applied to work in process are initially product costs that are then transferred either to Finished

EXHIBIT 19-1

GENERAL ACCOUNTING FOR SPOILAGE

Assume:		
Units worked on		1,100
Good units completed	1,000	
Normal spoilage	30	
Abnormal spoilage	70	1,100

Assume a unit cost of $10, not including any spoilage allowance. Total costs to account for are 1,100 × $10, or $11,000.

CONCEPTUAL TREATMENT

1. Work in process	11,000	
Stores, accrued payroll, applied overhead		11,000
1,100 units worked on.		
2. Cost of spoiled goods	1,000	
Work in process		1,000
100 units spoiled.		
3. Finished goods	10,000	
Work in process		10,000
1,000 good units completed.		
4. Finished goods	300	
Cost of spoiled goods		300
Normal-spoilage allowance, 30 units.		
5. Loss from abnormal spoilage	700	
Cost of spoiled goods		700
Abnormal spoilage, 70 units.		

PRACTICAL TREATMENT

1. (Same.)		
2,3,4. Finished goods	10,300	
Work in process		10,300
1,000 good units completed @ $10 plus normal spoilage of 30 units @ $10. Total costs of 1,000 good units is thus $10,300.		
5. Loss from abnormal spoilage*	700	
Work in process		700
Abnormal spoilage, 70 units.		

* In practice, abnormal spoilage is often not isolated at all. Instead, the $700 cost is erroneously lumped with the other costs to show a total cost of $11,000 and a unit cost of $11 for the 1,000 good units produced. The $700 abnormal spoilage should not be concealed as a part of the cost of the good product.

Goods or to a loss account. In practice, this account is not used, and the second set of entries in Exhibit 19-1 is more likely to be found.

process-cost accounting procedures and spoilage

distinguish between normal and abnormal spoilage

Although this discussion of process costing will emphasize accounting for spoilage, the ideas here are equally applicable to waste (shrinkage, evaporation, or lost units).

Again we must distinguish between control and product costing. For control, most companies use some version of estimated or standard costs that incorporates an allowance for normal spoilage, shrinkage, or waste in the estimate or standard. This section emphasizes product costing in so-called actual process-costing systems. A conceptual framework is stressed because it is needed to judge the many compromises necessary in practice.

As a general rule, it is sensible to trace and build the costs of spoilage separately. Then allocate normal spoilage costs to Finished Goods or Work in Process, depending on where in the production cycle the spoilage is assumed to take place. Spoilage is typically assumed to occur at the stage of completion where inspection occurs, because spoilage is recognized at this point. Normal spoilage need not be allocated to units that have not yet reached this point in the production process, because the spoiled units are related solely to the units that have passed the inspection point.

Many writers on process costing advocate ignoring the computation of equivalent units for spoilage, shrinkage, or waste. The reason cited in favor of this shortcut technique is that it automatically spreads normal-spoilage costs over good units through the use of higher equivalent unit costs. However, the results of this shortcut are inaccurate unless (a) no work-in-process inventories exist, or (b) material, conversion, *and* spoilage costs are all incurred *uniformly* throughout the production cycle. To illustrate, assume that a department has no beginning inventory. It starts 1,000 units; 500 are completed, 400 are in process, half-completed, and 100 are spoiled. The 100 units represent normal spoilage. Spoilage is detected upon completion. Material costs are $1,800 and conversion costs are $1,400. All material is introduced at the start of the process.

The solution in Exhibit 19-2 shows that ignoring spoilage lowers total equivalent units; when the latter is divided into the production costs, a higher *unit cost* results. The effective result is to load higher unit costs on work in process that has not reached the inspection point. At the same time, total charges to completed units are too low. Therefore, ending work in process contains costs of spoilage ($130 in this example) that do not pertain to such units and that properly should be charged to completed goods. Further, ending work in process that has not reached inspection undoubtedly contains some units that will not properly be recognized as spoiled until a subsequent period. Thus, work in process is being loaded now with spoilage ($130) that should instead be charged

EXHIBIT 19-2

COMPARISON OF ACCOUNTING FOR SPOILAGE

	ACCURATE METHOD: COUNT SPOILAGE			LESS ACCURATE METHOD: IGNORE SPOILAGE		
		EQUIVALENT UNITS			EQUIVALENT UNITS	
UNITS	Physical Flow	Materials	Conversion Costs	Physical Flow	Materials	Conversion Costs
Completed	500	500	500	500	500	500
Normal spoilage	100	100	100	100	—	—
In process, end (½)	400	400	200	400	400	200
Accounted for	1,000	1,000	800	1,000	900	700
		DETAILS			DETAILS	
COSTS	TOTALS	Materials	Conversion Costs	TOTALS	Materials	Conversion Costs
Current costs	$3,200	$1,800	$1,400	$3,200	$1,800	$1,400
Divide by equivalent units		1,000	800		900	700
Cost per equivalent unit		$1.80	$1.75		$2.00	$2.00
SUMMARY OF COSTS						
Units completed (500):						
Costs before spoilage	$1,775	500($1.80)	500($1.75)			
Add normal spoilage	355	100($1.80)	100($1.75)			
Total costs transferred out	$2,130			$2,000	500($2.00)	500($2.00)
Work in process, end (400):						
Materials	$ 720	400($1.80)		$ 800	400($2.00)	
Conversion costs	350		200($1.75)	400		200($2.00)
Total cost of work in process	$1,070			$1,200		
Total costs accounted for	$3,200			$3,200		

to goods later as they are completed. In effect, work in process is being doubly charged, because it is being charged with spoilage both now and also later when inspection occurs.

In summary, when spoilage occurs, trace the units spoiled as well as the units finished and in process. Compute both normal and abnormal spoiled units. Build separate costs of spoiled units. Then reallocate normal-spoilage costs to good units produced; charge off abnormal-spoilage costs as a loss. Even if no abnormal spoilage exists, it is helpful to compute normal-spoilage costs separately before reallocation. In this way, management will be constantly reminded of the normal-spoilage costs of a given process.

base for computing normal spoilage

Normal spoilage should be computed from the good output, or from the *normal* input—not from the total input. Total input includes the abnormal as well as the normal spoilage and is therefore irrational as a basis for computing normal spoilage. For example, if the normal rate of spoilage of polio vaccine is sloppily stated as 5 percent, an input of 100,000 cubic centimeters would be expected to produce 5,000 cubic centimeters of spoilage. Now, if 85,500 cubic centimeters of good units are produced, normal spoilage is not 5,000 centimeters (5 percent of 100,000), because it should have taken only 90,000 cubic centimeters of input to get 85,500 cubic centimeters of good vaccine. If normal spoilage is expressed as 5 percent of input, then good output should be 95 percent of normal input. In this case, abnormal spoilage would be 10,000 cubic centimeters and normal spoilage would be 4,500 cubic centimeters. These relationships may be clarified by the following:

			RELATIONSHIPS	
Input	100,000 c.c.			
Output:				
Good units	85,500 c.c.		95%	
Normal spoilage	4,500 c.c.	90,000 c.c.*	5%	100%
Abnormal spoilage		10,000 c.c.		
		100,000 c.c.		

* Normal input.

Thus, we could express the normal-spoilage rate more accurately either as 5 percent of *normal input* or as $\frac{5}{95}$ of good output.

weighted-average and FIFO

example 1

The costs of producing one of the B Company's products are accumulated on a process-cost basis. Materials for this product are put in at the beginning of the cycle of operations; labor and indirect costs are assumed to flow evenly over the cycle. Some units of this product are spoiled as a result of defects not ascertainable before inspection of finished units.[3] Normally the spoiled units are one-tenth of the good output.

At January 1, the inventory of work in process on this product was $29,600, representing 2,000 pounds of material ($15,000) and conversion cost of $14,600

[3] This illustration assumes inspection upon completion. In contrast, inspection may take place at some other stage—say, at the halfway point in the production cycle. In such a case, normal-spoilage costs would be reallocated to completed goods and to the units in process that are more than half completed. For a computer application to solving this process-cost problem, see Werner Frank, "A Computer Application to Process Cost Accounting," *Accounting Review*, Vol. XL, No. 4, pp. 854–62.

representing four-fifths completion. During January, 8,000 pounds of material ($61,000) were put into production. Direct labor of $40,200 was charged to the process. Indirect costs are assigned at the rate of 100 percent of direct-labor cost. The inventory at January 31 consisted of 1,500 pounds, two-thirds finished. Seventy-two hundred pounds of good product were transferred to finished-goods stock after inspection.

required

Using weighted-average and then FIFO, show calculations of:

1. Equivalent units of activity for January.
2. The dollar and unit amount of the abnormal spoilage during January.
3. Total product costs transferred to finished stock.
4. The cost of work-in-process inventory at January 31.
5. Journal entries for transfers out of work-in-process inventory.

Exhibit 19-3 presents the answer to requirement 1. Exhibits 19-4 and 19-5 present the answers to requirements 2–4, using weighted average and FIFO, respectively.

A careful study of these exhibits will show that the basic five-step procedure introduced in the preceding chapter needs only slight modification to handle spoilage. The requested journal entries follow:

EXHIBIT 19-3

B COMPANY

Computation of Output in Equivalent Units for the Month Ended January 31, 19_1

	(STEP 1)	(STEP 2) EQUIVALENT UNITS	
	Physical Flow	Materials	Conversion Costs
Work in process, beginning	2,000(4/5)*		
Units started	8,000		
Units to account for	10,000		
Abnormal spoilage	580	580	580
Normal spoilage	720	720	720
Good units completed and transferred out during current period	7,200	7,200	7,200
Work in process, end:	1,500(2/3)*		
Materials: 1,500 × 1		1,500	
Conversion costs: 1,500 × 2/3			1,000
Units accounted for	10,000		
Total work done		10,000	9,500
Less old equivalent units for work done on beginning inventory in previous periods:			
Materials: 2,000 × 1		2,000	
Conversion costs: 2,000 × 4/5			1,600
Remainder, new equivalent units for current period		8,000	7,900

* Degree of completion for conversion costs of this department at the dates of the work-in-process inventories. Note that material costs are fully completed at each of these dates, because in this department materials are introduced at the beginning of the process.

	WEIGHTED AVERAGE		FIFO	
Finished goods	139,392		139,060	
Processing department—Work in process		139,392		139,060
To transfer good units completed in January.				
Loss from abnormal spoilage	10,208		10,325	
Processing department—Work in process		10,208		10,325
To recognize abnormal spoilage in January.				

interim fluctuations in spoilage rates

There is a tendency among accountants to seize a single figure or a single rate as the standard or index of normal efficiency, when in reality the standard or norm is in the middle of a range. Thus, normal spoilage may average 10 percent of good output, but random influences may cause deviations from the 10 percent norm in a range of, say, 6 percent to 14 percent. Over an extended period—say, a year—the rate should center around 10 percent.

EXHIBIT 19-4

B COMPANY

Application of Costs to Products, Weighted-Average Method for the Month Ended January 31, 19_1

		(STEP 3)[a]			(STEP 4)	
		Work in Process, Beginning	Current Costs	Total Costs	Divisor Equivalent Units[b]	Average Unit Costs
	Materials	$15,000	$ 61,000	$ 76,000	10,000	$ 7.60
	Conversion costs	14,600	80,400	95,000	9,500	10.00
		$29,600	$141,400	$171,000		$17.60
(Step 5)	Abnormal spoilage (580 × $17.60)			$ 10,208		
	Goods completed:					
	Costs before spoilage (7,200 × $17.60)			$126,720		
	Normal spoilage (720 × $17.60)			12,672		
	Total cost of goods completed and transferred			$139,392		
	Work in process, end, 1,500 units: ($171,000 − $10,208 − $139,392)			$ 21,400[c]		
	Total costs accounted for			$171,000		

[a] See Exhibit 19-3 for Steps 1 and 2.

[b] This is the total work done, as shown in Exhibit 19-3.

[c] The accuracy of computing the cost of ending work in process may be checked:

Materials (1,500 × $7.60)	$11,400
Conversion costs (1,500 × ⅔ × $10.00)	10,000
Total	$21,400

This situation, as shown in Example 2, calls for using a predetermined 10 percent normal-spoilage cost rate for charging spoilage costs to good units produced throughout the year, regardless of actual month-to-month fluctuations within the normal range. The differences between normal-spoilage costs charged

EXHIBIT 19-5

B COMPANY

Application of Costs to Products, First-In, First-Out Method for the Month Ended January 31, 19_1

			TOTAL COSTS	(STEP 4) Divisor Equivalent Units[b]	(STEP 4) Unit Costs
	Work in process, beginning		$ 29,600		
	Current costs:				
	Materials		61,000	8,000	$ 7.625
	Conversion costs		80,400	7,900	10.1772
(Step 3)[a]	Total costs to account for		$171,000		$17.8022
(Step 5)	Work in process, end:				
	Materials (1,500 × $7.625)	$11,438			
	Conversion costs (1,500 × ⅔ × $10.1772)	10,177	21,615		
	Abnormal spoilage (580 × $17.8022)		10,325		
	Completed and transferred, 7,200 units: ($171,000 − $21,615 − $10,325)		139,060[c]		
	Total costs accounted for		$171,000		

[a] See Exhibit 19-3 for Steps 1 and 2.

[b] The divisor equivalent units are the new equivalent units for January computed in Exhibit 19-3.

[c] The accuracy of computing the cost of goods completed and transferred can be proven as follows:

Work in process, beginning, which is transferred out first	$ 29,600
Additional cost to complete:	
Conversion costs: 2,000 × (1 − ⅘) × $10.1772	4,071
Cost of units started and completed this month (7,200 − 2,000) × $17.8022	92,572
Normal spoilage (720 × $17.8022)	12,818*
Total cost of goods completed and transferred out	$139,060†

(The average cost of these is $139,060 ÷ 7,200 units = $19.3139)

* Note that a normal spoilage should really be split between the two batches of good units completed if FIFO is to be followed thoroughly. But to split spoilage costs on a pro rata basis implies that all spoilage traceable to beginning inventory is costed on the basis of full *current* costs, not past costs. This is inconsistent with the FIFO assumption, which states that past costs should be kept separate from current costs. In effect, using current costs for attaching normal-spoilage costs to beginning inventory assumes that all spoilage traceable thereto was begun and completed during the current period—an obvious contradiction of the FIFO concept. In contrast, the weighted-average method does not necessitate splitting normal-spoilage costs between two batches of good units completed, because the initial inventory is merged with the current costs to determine unit costs.

to production and those actually incurred within the normal range would rest in a temporary general-ledger account called Spoilage Random Fluctuations. It should have a zero balance by the end of a year. If a balance tends to build up, it would indicate that an erroneous normal rate of spoilage was being used.

example 2

Let us assume that a single department process produces 1,000 good units per month, but that spoilage fluctuates. Normal spoilage averages 10 percent of good output, with the normal range considered to be from 6 percent to 14 percent of good output. The company's cost behavior is such that all units are produced at an equivalent unit cost of $10. All spoilage is detected upon completion. The company uses a Spoilage Random Fluctuations account and costs completed units as if they were all accompanied by a 10 percent normal-spoilage factor. Possible situations and general-ledger entries are shown below:

	CASE			
	1	*2*	*3*	*4*
Total units completed	1,100	1,130	1,170	1,060
Good units completed	1,000	1,000	1,000	1,000
Actual spoilage	100	130	170	60
Normal spoilage	100	100	100	100
General-ledger entries:				
Finished goods	$11,000 dr.	$11,000 dr.	$11,000 dr.	$11,000 dr.
Spoilage random fluctuations	—	300 dr.	400 dr.	400 cr.
Loss from abnormal spoilage	—	—	300 dr.	—
Department—work in process	11,000 cr.	11,300 cr.	11,700 cr.	10,600 cr.

If a Spoilage Random Fluctuations account were used, abnormal spoilage would usually be recognized only when actual spoilage exceeded the top of the normal range (14 percent in this example; see Case 3 in Example 2).

The handling of subnormal spoilage is shown in Case 4 of Example 2.

SPOILAGE RANDOM FLUCTUATIONS

(2)	300	(4)	400
(3)	400		

This account should balance out to zero over a period of, say, 12 months. If it does not, the process may not be performing in accordance with expectations.

job costing and spoilage

Job-cost accounting for spoilage in practice varies considerably. Where spoiled goods have a disposal value[4] the net cost of spoilage is computed by deducting disposal value from the costs of the spoiled goods accumulated to the point of rejection.

[4] In practice, the words *scrap* and *spoilage* are sometimes used indiscriminately. Thus, *spoilage costs* may be thought of as total accumulated cost of spoiled work. Yet the spoiled goods may be "scrapped" (that is, sold for whatever can be recovered—"scrap" value). Thus, *net spoilage cost* is total spoilage cost less scrap recovery.

Where spoilage is considered to be a normal characteristic of a given production cycle, and where causes of spoilage are attributable to work done on all jobs, net spoilage cost is budgeted in practice as a part of overhead, so that the predetermined overhead rate includes a provision for normal spoilage costs. Therefore, spoilage costs are spread, through overhead application, over all jobs rather than being loaded on particular jobs only. The rationale is thus provided for the debit, to the overhead-control account, of the net spoilage cost in the following journal entry made when spoilage is considered to be normal in character:[5]

Stores control (spoiled goods at disposal value)	150	
Department factory overhead control (normal spoilage)	350	
Work in process		500

Assume that 5 pieces out of a lot of 50 were spoiled. Costs accumulated to point where spoilage was detected were $100 per unit. Salvage value is estimated at $30 per unit. Items in parentheses indicate subsidiary postings.

Another method used, where management finds it helpful for control or for pricing, is to credit specific jobs with only the resale value of spoiled units, thus forcing the remaining good units in the job to bear net normal-spoilage costs. Under this method, the predetermined overhead rate would not include a provision for normal-spoilage costs because the spoilage would be viewed as being directly attributable to the nature of particular jobs instead of being attributable to general factory conditions or processes. The journal entry, with the same data as were just used, follows:

Stores control (spoiled goods at disposal value)	150	
Work in process		150

[5] Conceptually, the prevailing treatments just described can be criticized primarily because *product costs* are being charged back to Department Factory Overhead Control, which logically should accumulate only *costs incurred,* rather than both cost incurrence and product costs. If this distinction is not maintained, Department Factory Overhead Control will include duplicate charges for overhead. For example, as both good units and those units which will eventually be spoiled are worked on, the various production costs (including applied overhead) are charged to the departmental work-in-process account. Then, when the normal spoilage is detected, the conventional treatment results in charging back these same product costs (including applied overhead), in an amount equal to the actual net spoilage cost, to the departmental overhead-control account. For an extended criticism of the duplication of charges to Department Factory Overhead Control, see Alfred P. Koch, "A Fallacy in Accounting for Spoiled Goods," *Accounting Review,* Vol. XXXV, No. 3, pp. 501–2.

A student, M. Schley, has suggested using a separate account, Cost of Spoiled Goods—Normal. All debits to it would be reallocations of costs already applied to Work in Process; all credits to it would reapply the costs to good units produced by using a predetermined application rate similar to the factory overhead application rate. (This application rate would be exactly the difference between the overhead rate used that incorporates normal spoilage and the rate that excludes normal spoilage rate.) For product-costing purposes, no difference would result. But for control purposes, Department Factory Overhead would consist only of historical costs with no duplicated charges; management would have a separate record of normal spoilage and would be reminded of the burden of normal spoilage borne by good production. (A similar line of reasoning applies to the defective units discussed in the next section.)

defective units

Defective units are subsequently reworked and transformed into units to be sold as "firsts" or "seconds." Management needs effective control over such actions, because foremen are tempted to rework rather than to junk spoiled units. If control is not exercised, foremen may rework many bad units instead of having them sold for salvage at a greater economic advantage. Rework should either be authorized by the foreman's superior or be undertaken only in accordance with prescribed operating procedures.

Unless there are special reasons for charging rework to the jobs or batches that contained the bad units, the cost of the extra materials, labor, and so on, are in practice usually charged to overhead.[6] Thus, once again we see that rework is usually spread over all jobs or batches as a part of a predetermined overhead rate. Assume that the five spoiled pieces used in our prior illustration are reworked and sold as firsts through regular channels. Entries follow:

Original cost accumulations:	Work-in-process control	500	
	Stores control		200
	Accrued payroll		200
	Factory overhead applied		100
Rework (Figures assumed):	Departmental factory-overhead control (rework)	190	
	Stores control		40
	Accrued payroll		100
	Factory overhead applied		50
Transfer to finished stock:	Finished-goods control	500	
	Work-in-process control		500

accounting for scrap

Scrap is residue from manufacturing operations that has measurable but relatively minor recovery value. There are two major aspects of accounting for scrap: control and costing. Items like metal chips, turnings, filings, and borings should be quantified by weighing, counting, or some other expedient means. Norms or standards should be determined, because excessive scrap indicates

[6] The criticisms of the practical treatment for spoiled goods are also applicable to the treatment described. The overhead-incurred and applied accounts may be padded for amounts that in themselves did not necessitate overhead incurrence. In other words, the extra materials, labor, and variable overhead may represent extra cost incurrence, but fixed overhead will not be affected. Also, any accounting entry that simultaneously involves a debit to department overhead and a credit to overhead applied tends to blur the primary purpose of the overhead-control account—that of only accumulating overhead costs *as incurred.*

Like spoiled units, defective units can be abnormal as well as normal. Applying the reasoning of the preceding footnote, rework on normally defective units should be charged to a special reallocation account and rework on abnormally defective units should be charged off as a special loss. The special reallocation account would also have its own application rate.

inefficiency. *Scrap tickets* are prepared as source documents for periodic scrap reports that summarize the amount of scrap and compare it with predetermined norms or standards. Scrap should be returned to the storeroom to be held for sale or for reuse. Scrap should be accounted for in some manner, not only from the point of view of efficiency, but because scrap is often a tempting source for theft.

There are many methods of accounting for scrap. Typically, scrap is not assigned any cost; instead, its sales value is regarded as an offset to factory overhead, as follows:

Scrap returned to storeroom:	No journal entry. (Memo of quantity received is entered on the perpetual record.)		
Sale of scrap:	Cash or Accounts receivable	xx	
	Department factory overhead control		xx
	Posting made to subsidiary record—"Sale of Scrap" column on departmental cost sheet.		

This method is both simple and accurate enough in theory to justify its wide use. A normal amount of scrap is an inevitable result of production operations. Basically, this method does not link scrap with any particular physical product; instead, because of practical difficulties, all products bear regular production costs without any particular credit for scrap sales except in an indirect manner. What really happens in such situations is that sales of scrap are considered when predetermined overhead rates are being set. Thus, the predetermined overhead rate is lower than it would be if no credit for scrap sales were allowed in the overhead budget.

An alternate method in a job-cost situation would be to trace sales of scrap to the jobs that yielded the scrap. This method is used only when it is feasible and economically desirable. For example, there may be agreements between the company and particular customers that provide for charging specific, difficult jobs with all scrap or spoilage costs and crediting such jobs with all scrap sales arising therefrom. Entries follow:

Scrap returned to storeroom:	No journal entry. (Memo of quantity received and related job made on perpetual record.)		
Sale of scrap:	Cash or Accounts receivable	xx	
	Work in process		xx
	Posting made to specific job order.		

The illustrations above assume that no inventory value is assigned to scrap as it is returned to the storeroom. However, when the dollar value is material and there is a significant time lag between storing scrap and selling it, there is justification for inventorying scrap at some conservative estimate of net realizable value so that production costs and related scrap recovery may be recognized in the same period.

Some companies tend to delay sales of scrap until the price is most attractive. Volatile price fluctuations are typical for scrap metal. In these cases, if scrap inventory becomes significant, it should be inventoried at some "reasonable" value—a difficult task in the face of volatile market prices.

comparison of accounting for spoilage, defective work, and scrap

The basic approach to the accounting for spoilage, defective work, and scrap should distinguish among the normal amount that is common to all jobs, the normal amount that is attributable to specific jobs, and abnormal amounts. The following entries recapitulate the preceding examples. Note the parallel approach to the three categories:

	SPOILAGE COSTS (NET $350)		
Normal (common to all jobs)	Stores	150	
	Departmental factory overhead control	350	
	Work in process		500
Normal (peculiar to specific jobs)	Stores	150	
	Work in process		150
Abnormal	Stores	150	
	Special loss account	350	
	Work in process		500
	DEFECTIVE WORK COSTS (REWORK COSTS OF $190)		
Normal (common to all jobs)	Departmental factory overhead control	190	
	Stores		40
	Accrued payroll		100
	Factory overhead applied		50
Normal (peculiar to specific jobs)	Same as preceding entry, except that the debit of $190 would be to Work in Process		
Abnormal	Same as preceding entry, except that the debit of $190 would be to Special Loss account		
	SCRAP VALUE RECOVERED ($100)		
Normal (common to all jobs)	Stores or Cash or Accounts receivable	100	
	Department factory overhead control		100
Abnormal (peculiar to specific jobs)	Same as preceding entry except that the credit would be to Work in Process		

some applications to standard costs

shrinkage and waste When standard-cost systems are used, allowance is made in the standard product costs for a standard shrinkage. Actual shrinkage is usually computed by working back from product output. Shrinkage in excess of standard is a material usage or quantity variance. Unlike spoilage and scrap, shrinkage cannot be tagged and traced by physical identification.

Examples of waste that are not traced and specifically costed include paint or varnish adhering to the sides of their containers, mill ends, shavings, evaporation, and so forth. Excess material consumption is usually revealed through excess-material requisitions or through standard-yield percentages for such materials as lumber, chemicals, and ores. Thus, where 15,000 gallons of raw chemicals ordinarily produce 12,000 gallons of good finished product, the standard-yield percentage could be expressed as 80 percent of normal input. On the other hand, the waste percentage could be expressed as 20 percent of normal input or as 25 percent of good output.

Note that these percentages provide a physical standard that may be used without worrying about price changes. Further, such a standard is easily understood and can be readily used as a timely index of efficiency—on an hourly or batch basis if desired.

scrap Material-usage standards usually include allowances for scrap. Although the allowance may be computed in various ways, standards are based on a careful study of the operation(s), not on historical data alone or on wild guesses. The standard cost of direct materials thus becomes (a) standard unit price times the standard input per finished unit, less (b) standard scrap price per unit times standard scrap weight loss per finished unit.

To illustrate, assume that a metal rod is fed into an automatic screw machine. About five inches (ten ounces) at the end of each 105-inch rod (210 ounces) are clutched by the chuck and cannot be used. The standard lot size is 1,000 units. The first ten units are scrapped in setting up the run. It takes five ounces of metal to produce a finished unit that weighs four ounces. Standard cost computations follow:

	OUNCES	*ASSUMED PRICE PER OUNCE*	*TOTAL COST*
Standard cost per unit:			
Finished piece	4.00		
Turnings	1.00		
Crop loss (10 oz. ÷ 40 units per rod)	0.25		
Scrap piece loss (10 units ÷ 1,000) × 5	.05		
	5.30	$.0300*	$.1590
Less credit for scrap	1.30	.0020†	.0026
Standard cost per finished unit	4.00		$.1564

* Or 48¢ per lb.
† 3.2¢ per lb.

Although standards for direct materials are built in this way for each operation, it is usually inexpedient to trace scrap to specific lots or operations. Comparisons are usually limited to monthly, or sometimes weekly, comparisons of standard costs of good work produced with the total "actual" charges to the department.[7]

spoilage In practice, allowances for net spoilage costs and for rework are often incorporated into the flexible budget for overhead. Spoiled units are removed from Work in Process at standard costs and charged to Factory Overhead. Periodic comparisons of budget allowances with actual spoilage provide summary information for managerial control. If no spoilage is allowed, the budget provided may be zero. Rework is controlled in a similar manner. Day-to-day control is aided by spoilage tags prepared at the point of inspection. These tags, or a summary thereof, are promptly shown to the foreman and other interested parties.

This procedure really spotlights spoilage and rework as special managerial problems, as opposed to, say, material-efficiency variances that are related to good units. For example, assume that the standard cost for a particular product is as follows:

Direct materials, 1 pound	$ 5.00
Direct labor, 1 hour	3.00
Factory overhead—variable	1.50
Factory overhead—fixed	1.50
Standard cost per unit	$11.00

Assume that no spoilage occurs, but that it takes 1,150 pounds of material to produce 1,000 good units:

Direct materials:	
Actual, 1,150 pounds @ $5.00	$5,750
Standard, 1,000 pounds @ $5.00	5,000
Usage variance	$ 750

Assume, instead, that 1,100 units were produced, but that 100 were spoiled because of careless machine operation. There would be two alternatives for analyzing such a variance. First consider the figures presented in the following table:

[7] For an extended discussion of spoilage and standard costs, see Stanley B. Henrici, *Standard Costs for Manufacturing* (New York: McGraw-Hill Book Company), pp. 275–80, 303–8.

	INCURRED COSTS	STANDARD COSTS— GOOD OUTPUT	TOTAL VARIANCE
*Direct materials, 1,150 lbs.	$ 5,750	$ 5,000	$ 750 U
Direct labor, 1,100 hours	3,300	3,000	300 U
Factory overhead—variable	1,650	1,500	150 U
Factory overhead—fixed	1,650	1,500	150 U
	$12,350	$11,000	$1,350 U

* Standard materials allowed for good units	1,000 lbs.
Standard materials allowed for spoiled units, which were spoiled by careless labor	100 lbs.
Excess materials used in producing 1,100 units	50 lbs.
Total	1,150 lbs.

ANALYSIS ONE Analyze variances on the basis of good output only. This is the familiar way:

Direct-material efficiency variance	$5,750–$5,000	$ 750
Direct-labor efficiency variance	$3,300–$3,000	300
Variable-overhead total variance	$1,650–$1,500	150
Fixed-overhead total variance	$1,650–$1,500	150
Total variance explained		$1,350

ANALYSIS TWO Isolate a separate variance for spoilage, $1,100, consisting of the four elements shown above. This would entail setting up a special Spoilage Variance account in the ledger. This account would represent the standard cost of spoiled work. Thus the other variance accounts would not reflect any spoilage effects:

	SPOILAGE VARIANCE	OTHER VARIANCES		TOTAL VARIANCE EXPLAINED
Direct materials	$ 500	Efficiency	$250 U	$ 750
Direct labor	300		—	300
Variable overhead	150		—	150
Fixed overhead	150		—	150
	$1,100		$250	$1,350

SUMMARY

Nearly every manufacturing company has some problems of waste, scrap, or spoilage as a consequence of management's choice of those factors of production that will render the most economic benefit. Hence, some waste, scrap, or spoilage is a normal result of efficient production. Yet there is a need to distinguish between, for example, normal and abnormal spoilage. Standards or norms must be computed so that performance may be judged and costs properly accounted for. Normal spoilage, then, is spoilage that is unavoidable under a given set of efficient production conditions;

abnormal spoilage is spoilage that is not expected to arise under efficient conditions. Laxity in setting careful standards often results in too liberal allowances for normal spoilage.

Abnormal spoilage is often controllable by first-line supervision, whereas normal spoilage is controllable only by those managers who determine the nature of products and processes.

Managerial cost accounting must distinguish between normal and abnormal spoilage, primarily for keeping management informed, but also for proper product costing.

Accounting for spoilage, defective units, and the like varies considerably. Practically, most of these net costs are allowed for in predetermined overhead rates; or, where standard costs are employed, scrap and spoilage allowances are often incorporated in the standard costs for direct materials, direct labor, and overhead.

Conceptually, some practical treatments are faulty because they muddle the distinction between product costs and costs for control by charging product costs back to Department Factory Overhead Control.

PROBLEMS FOR SELF-STUDY

Review each example in this chapter and obtain the solutions on your own. Then check your work against the solutions, which appear in the text.

QUESTIONS, PROBLEMS, AND CASES

19-1 "Management has two major planning and control problems regarding spoilage." What are the two problems?

19-2 "Normal spoilage is planned spoilage." Discuss.

19-3 "Costs of abnormal spoilage are lost costs." Explain.

19-4 "In accounting for spoiled goods, we are dealing with cost application and reallocation rather than cost incurrence." Explain.

19-5 "Total input includes the abnormal as well as the normal spoilage and is therefore irrational as a basis for computing normal spoilage." Do you agree? Why?

19-6 Explain the operation of a Spoilage Random Fluctuations account.

19-7 "The practical treatments of spoilage in job-order costing can be criticized on conceptual grounds." What is the major criticism?

19-8 Describe the general accounting for scrap where no inventory value is assigned to scrap.

19-9 How is scrap usually accounted for under standard costing?

19-10 *Two Ways of Accounting for Spoilage* (CPA) In manufacturing activities, a portion of the units placed in process is sometimes spoiled and becomes practically worthless. Discuss two ways in which the cost of such spoiled units could be treated in the accounts, and describe the circumstances under which each method might be used.

19-11 *Weighted Average and Spoilage* The Alston Company operates under a process-cost system. It has two departments, Cleaning and Milling. For both departments, conversion costs are applied in proportion to the stage of completion. But materials are applied at the *beginning* of the process in the cleaning department, and additional materials are added at the *end* of the milling process. Following are the costs and unit production statistics for May. All unfinished work at the *end* of May is one-fourth completed. All beginning inventories (May 1) were four-fifths completed as of May 1. All completed work is transferred to the next department.

BEGINNING INVENTORIES:	*CLEANING*	*MILLING*
Cleaning: $1,000 materials, $800 conv. costs	$1,800	
Milling: $6,450 previous dept. cost (transferred-in cost) and $2,450 conv. costs		$8,900
CURRENT COSTS		
Materials	$9,000	$ 640
Conversion costs	$8,000	$4,950
PHYSICAL UNITS		
Units in beginning inventory	1,000	3,000
Units *started* this month	9,000	7,400
Total units finished and transferred	7,400	6,000
Normal spoilage	500	400
Abnormal spoilage	500	0

Additional Factors

1. Spoilage is assumed to occur at the *end* of *each* of the two processes, when the units are inspected.
2. Assume that there is no other waste, shrinkage, evaporation, or abnormal spoilage than that indicated in the tabulation above.
3. Carry unit-cost calculations to three decimal places where necessary. Calculate final totals to the nearest dollar.

required

Using the weighted-average method, show for *each* department:

1. Analysis of physical flows and an analysis of equivalent performance.
2. Calculations of *unit* costs.
3. *Detailed* presentation of the *total* values assigned to goods transferred out and the total values assigned to ending work in process.

19-12 *Weighted Average* (SIA) The Easygoing Company produced a single product in a continuous process in one department.

During the month of November the company started 5,300 units and completed 3,600 good units only. Ending work in process contained 1,000 units, 50 percent completed. (Materials are all put into process at the beginning of production while labor and overhead incur uniformly throughout the process.)

Work in process, November 1:	700 units
Direct materials	$2,030
Direct labor	310
Overhead applied	215
Cost data for November:	
Direct materials	$15,970
Direct labor	15,510
Overhead applied	10,765

Spoilage is detected when the units are 90 percent completed. Normal spoilage allowance is expected to be 10 percent of normal input, or for each 10 units started the company expects to obtain a yield of 9 good units.

required

1. Compute the output in equivalent units and summarize the application of costs to products. Use the weighted-average method.
2. Journalize all cost data affecting work in process during November.

19-13 *Multiple Choice; Weighted-Average Method; Spoilage* The data that follow are to be used in answering questions 1–9, inclusive. Support your answers with a statement of production costs.

The manufacture of product XT-123 is begun in Department No. 1. From there it goes to Department No. 2, where the product is completed. Upon completion, it is sent to finished-goods storage in the warehouse. At the end of processing in each department, the units of products are inspected; only those that pass inspection are sent to Department No. 2 and to finished-goods storage, respectively. The spoiled units (both normal and abnormal spoilage) cannot be salvaged, have no scrap value, and are thrown away.

Below are listed the pertinent data regarding the production of XT-123 for the month of December 19_3:

	DEPARTMENT NO. 1	*DEPARTMENT NO. 2*
Costs applied to product:		
Materials	At the beginning of processing in the department	At 50% completion of processing in the department
Other costs	Evenly throughout entire period of processing	Evenly throughout entire period of processing
Work in process, December 1, 19_3:		
Number of units	600 units	2,000 units
Percent complete	66⅔%	25%
Accumulated cost:		
Transferred-in costs		$30,280
Department No. 1 materials	$ 2,844	—
Department No. 1 other cost	$ 3,120	—
Department No. 2 materials	—	None
Department No. 2 other cost	—	$ 6,200
Work in process, December 31, 19_3:		
Number of units	1,400 units	800 units
Percent complete	50%	75%
Normal spoilage (detected by inspection of product upon completion of processing in each department)	140 units	40 units
Abnormal spoilage:		
Number of units	60 units	None
Percent complete	100%	
Units of finished product transferred to finished-goods warehouse	—	3,960 units
December cost applied to product (exclusive of accumulated cost of work in process at December 1, 19_3):		
Materials	$19,800	$15,140
Other costs	34,260	52,860

Indicate your answer by letter.

1. The actual number of units transferred to Department No. 2 from Department No. 1 during the month was:
   a. 3,000; b. 2,760; c. 3,960; d. 2,800; e. 2,860.
2. The actual number of units begun in Department No. 1 during the month was:
   a. 4,400; b. 3,620; c. 3,520; d. 3,760; e. 3,800.

Note: Questions 3–9, inclusive, refer to answers you would secure using the weighted-average method.

3. In Department No. 1, the total equivalent "work done" for "other costs" was:
   a. 3,000; b. 3,700; c. 4,400; d. 2,800; e. 4,200.
4. In Department No. 1, the equivalent unit cost for materials was (rounded to the nearest cent):
   a. $7.71; b. $8.09; c. $5.15; d. $5.39; e. $5.22.
5. In Department No. 1, the cost of work in process at December 31, 19_3, was:
   a. $14,277; b. $18,396; c. $17,864; d. $14,616; e. $14,378.
6. The cost of goods transferred from Department No. 1 to Department No. 2 during the month of December was (rounded to the nearest dollar):
   a. $42,700; b. $43,615; c. $44,100; d. $42,010; e. $44,832.
7. In Department No. 2, the total equivalent "work done" for materials (only those materials *added* by Department No. 2) was:
   a. 4,800; b. 4,000; c. 5,000; d. 4,400; e. 4,600.
8. In Department No. 2, the equivalent unit cost for "other costs" (only those "other costs" *added* by Department No. 2) was:
   a. $14.91; b. $12.84; c. $12.30; d. $13.42; e. $12.95.
9. In Department No. 2, the total cost of units transferred to the finished-goods warehouse was (rounded to the nearest dollar):
   a. $125,294; b. $63,960; c. $63,310; d. $145,544; e. $126,567.

19-14 *Weighted Average* (SIA) The following information pertains to the operation of a processing department:

	MATERIALS	CONVERSION
Current costs	$38,600	$421,300
Beginning inventory		
1,000 Units	Complete	40% Complete
Costs	$10,000	$44,000
Units transferred—40,000 (total)		
Ending inventory		
8,000 units	Complete	25% Complete
Spoilage (detected when the units are 50% complete)		
Normal —400		
Abnormal—200		

required

1. Using the weighted-average method, determine the costs that should be allocated to:
   a. Normal and abnormal spoilage
   b. Units transferred (including spoilage costs if appropriate)
   c. Ending inventory (including spoilage costs if appropriate)
2. Discuss the reasons underlying the different treatment of abnormal and normal spoilage.

19-15 *Weighted Average and Spoilage* (SIA) The Ground Company manufactures a product MOP on a continuous-process basis through one department. The product MOP requires the following parts:

1 Subassembly "K"—beginning of process
1 Part "L"—beginning of process
2 Part "M"—when 60% completed

The subassembly "K" was formerly produced by the Ground Company in another department and then transferred in. For economical reasons, the company discontinued manufacturing the subassembly "K" a year ago and instead buys it from a a local supplier at a unit cost of $2.10.

Labor and overhead costs are added continuously throughout the process. Overhead is applied at 150 percent of direct-labor cost.

The work-in-process inventory at the beginning of April consisted of 2,500 units at a cost of $7,520 ("K"—$5,250, "L"—$1,050, conversion cost $1,220).

During April, 19_4, the following activities took place:

1. New units started: 21,000
2. Parts usage: "L"—$8,350, "M"—$10,200
3. Direct-labor cost: $18,520
4. Units completed during month: 16,000
5. An unexpected loss occurred with all the beginning work-in-process units, owing to a mechanical failure in the calibrating machine. The loss was discovered when the units were 40 percent completed. The Controller asked to show this loss separately.
6. Ending work in process consisted of 4,000 units, 50 percent completed.

The normal spoilage was as expected. Since normal spoilage is detected at the 80% completion stage, it has been the company's practice to charge this normal loss to the cost of the completed units for the month.

required

Prepare a cost-of-production report for the month of April. Show the output in equivalent units and summarize the application of costs to products. Assume that the weighted-average method is used.

19-16 *Different Ways of Accounting for Spoilage* (CPA) The D. Hayes Cramer Company manufactures product C, whose cost per unit is $1 of materials, $2 of labor, and $3 of overhead costs. During the month of May, 1,000 units of product C were spoiled. These units could be sold for 60¢ each.

The accountant said that the entry to be made for these 1,000 lost or spoiled units could be one of the following four:

ENTRY NO. 1

Spoiled goods	$ 600	
Work in process—Materials		$ 100
Work in process—Labor		200
Work in process—Overhead		300

ENTRY NO. 2

Spoiled goods	$ 600	
Manufacturing expenses	5,400	
Work in process—Materials		$1,000
Work in process—Labor		2,000
Work in process—Overhead		3,000

ENTRY NO. 3		
Spoiled goods	$ 600	
Loss on spoiled goods	5,400	
Work in process—Materials		$1,000
Work in process—Labor		2,000
Work in process—Overhead		3,000

ENTRY NO. 4		
Spoiled goods	$ 600	
Receivable	5,400	
Work in process—Materials		$1,000
Work in process—Labor		2,000
Work in process—Overhead		3,000

required | Indicate the circumstance under which each of the four solutions above would be appropriate.

19-17 *Weighted Average, Two Departments* (CPA, adapted) The Mantis Manufacturing Company manufactures a single product that passes through two departments: extruding and finishing-packing. The product is shipped at the end of the day on which it is packed. The production in the extruding and finishing-packing departments does not increase the number of units started.

The cost and production data for the month of January are as follows:

COST DATA	*EXTRUDING DEPARTMENT*	*FINISHING-PACKING DEPARTMENT*
Work in process, January 1:		
Cost from preceding department	—	$60,200
Materials	$ 5,900	—
Labor	1,900	1,500
Overhead	1,400	2,000
Costs added during January:		
Materials	20,100	4,400
Labor	10,700	7,720
Overhead	8,680	11,830
Percentage of completion of work in process:		
January 1:		
Materials	70%	0%
Labor	50	30
Overhead	50	30
January 31:		
Materials	50	0
Labor	40	35
Overhead	40	35

JANUARY PRODUCTION STATISTICS		
Units in process, January 1	10,000	29,000
Units in process, January 31	8,000	6,000
Units started or received from preceding department	20,000	22,000
Units completed and transferred or shipped	22,000	44,000

In the extruding department, materials are added at various phases of the process. All lost units occur at the end of the process when the inspection operation takes place.

In the finishing-packing department, the materials added consist only of packing supplies. These materials are added at the midpoint of the process, when the packing operation begins. Cost studies have disclosed that one-half the labor and overhead costs apply to the finishing operation and one-half to the packing operation. All lost units occur at the end of the finishing operation when the product is inspected. All the work in process in this department at January 1 and 31 was in the finishing-operation phase of the manufacturing process.
(The company uses the weighted-average method in its accounting system.)

required

1. Compute the units lost, if any, for each department during January.
2. Compute the equivalent units for the calculation of unit costs for each department in January.
3. Prepare a cost-of-production report for each department for January. The report should disclose the departmental total cost and cost per unit (for materials, labor, and overhead) of the units (a) transferred to the finishing-packing department and (b) shipped. Assume that January production and costs were normal. (Submit all supporting computations in good form.)

19-18 *Standard Process Costing; Spoilage* (S. Laimon) The Sharbill Company uses standard process costing in accounting for its cost of production. Only one product is manufactured, with standard costs *per thousand units* as follows:

Material A	15 lbs. @ 80¢		$12.00
Material B	4 lbs. @ $2.25		9.00
Direct labor	5 hours @ $3.60		18.00
Variable overhead	5 hours @ $2.00		10.00
Fixed overhead	5 hours @ $1.60		8.00
Normal spoilage	10% of Material A	$1.20	
	5% of Conversion costs	1.80	3.00
Total standard cost per 1,000 units			$60.00

The standards for materials and conversion costs are exclusive of spoilage costs. The latter costs are allowed for separately in the standard. Material A is added at the beginning of the process. Labor and overhead are added evenly throughout the process. Inspection at the 50 percent stage of completion removes all spoiled units. Normal spoilage amounts to 10 percent of all *good* units passing the inspection point. Immediately after the removal of spoiled units, Material B is added to the remaining good units, and the processing of these units is then completed.

Production data for April, 19_1, were as follows:

Beginning work-in-process inventory	400,000 units	—40% complete
Put into process during April	500,000	
Transferred to finished goods	600,000	
Spoiled units	100,000	
Ending work-in-process inventory	200,000	—60% complete

Cost Data

1. Materials: All price variances on materials are recognized at the time of purchase.
   a. Material A: Beginning inventory, 2,000 pounds
      Purchased, 10,000 lbs. @ 84¢ = $8,400
      Issued to production, 8,000 pounds

b. Material B: Beginning inventory, 1,000 pounds
Purchased, 4,000 lbs. @ $2.00 = $8,000
Issued to production, 3,100 pounds

2. Direct-labor payroll: 3,100 hours @ $3.50 = $10,850.
3. Overhead costs incurred:
   a. Variable, $6,500
   b. Fixed, $5,610
4. Budget data: Planned production for the month was 675,000 units.
5. Variance disposition: All variances are charged to the period of their incurrence.

required

1. Presentation at standard cost of:
   a. Abnormal spoilage
   b. Units transferred
   c. Ending work in process
2. Summary analysis of all variances, including detailed breakdown of direct-labor and overhead variances.

19-19 Redo Problem 19-11, using FIFO.

19-20 *First-in, First-out Process Costing; Multiple Choice* The Meara Company uses a process-cost system (first-in, first-out) in costing its sole product. Materials for the product are added at the beginning of the operating cycle; conversion costs are assumed to accrue evenly over the cycle. Spoilage is detected by inspection upon completion of the product. Normally the spoiled units are equal to one-tenth of the good output.

At January 1, the inventory of work in process was 2,000 units of product, representing an average of three-fourths complete. The cost of these units was $32,200, including $17,000 for raw materials and $15,200 for conversion cost (direct labor and indirect cost). During January, 8,000 additional units of product were begun. During January, material cost of $64,000 was requisitioned from stores and charged to operations. Direct-labor costs for the month were $38,000. Indirect costs are assigned at the rate of 100 percent of direct-labor cost.

At January 31, the work in process consisted of 1,500 units of product, two-thirds complete. During the month, 7,200 units of good product were transferred to finished-goods stock after inspection.

Select the answer that correctly completes each of the following statements (identify your answer by letter). Support your overall answer with a production-cost report.

1. Units of normal spoilage amounted to:
   a. 580; b. 1,000; c. 950; d. 800; e. 720.
2. Units of abnormal spoilage amounted to:
   a. 950; b. 580; c. 1,000; d. 720; e. 800.
3. The total "new equivalent units" for material cost were:
   a. 10,000; b. 8,500; c. 9,500; d. 9,000; e. 8,000.
4. The total "new equivalent units" for conversion costs were:
   a. 8,000; b. 9,000; c. 8,500; d. 7,000; e. 7,500.
5. The equivalent unit cost for materials was:
   a. $8.00; b. $8.50; c. $6.40; d. $8.10; e. $8.25.
6. The cost of products transferred to finished goods was:
   a. $140,184; b. $138,550; c. $127,950; d. $108,350; e. $140,550.

19-21 *Process Costs; Spoilage; FIFO and Weighted Average* (CPA) The King Process Company manufactures one product, processing it through two processes—No. 1 and No. 2.

For each unit of Process No. 1 output, 2 units of raw material X are put in *at the start* of the processing. For each unit of Process No. 2 output, 3 cans of raw material Y are put in *at the end* of processing. Two pounds of Process No. 1 output are placed in at the start of Process No. 2 for each unit of finished goods started.

Spoilage generally occurs in Process No. 2 when processing is approximately 50 percent complete.

In-process accounts are maintained for raw materials, conversion costs, and prior department costs.

The company uses FIFO basis for inventory valuation for Process No. 1 and finished goods, and average cost for inventory valuation for Process No. 2.

Data for March:

1. Units transferred: From Process No. 1 to Process No. 2 — 2,200 lbs.
   From Process No. 2 to finished goods — 900 gallons
   From finished goods to cost of goods sold — 600 gallons
2. Units spoiled in Process No. 2—100 gallons
3. Raw-material unit costs: X—$1.51 per unit; Y—$2.00 per can
4. Conversion costs: Process No. 1—$3,344; Process No. 2—$4,010
5. Spoilage recovery: $100 (treated as cost reduction)
6. Inventory data:

	PROCESS NO. 1		*PROCESS NO. 2*		*FINISHED GOODS*	
	Initial	Final	Initial	Final	Initial	Final
Units	200	300	200	300	700	1,000
Fraction complete conversion costs	½	⅓	½	⅔		
Valuation:					$13,300	
Materials	$560		0			
Conversion costs	$108		$ 390			
Prior-department costs			$2,200			

required

Journalize March entries to record the transfer of costs from Process No. 1 to Process No. 2, from Process No. 2 to finished goods, and from finished goods to cost of goods sold. Prepare schedules of computations to support your entries. Regard spoilage as normal spoilage.

19-22 *FIFO, Spoiled and Lost Units* (D. Grinnell). The Murphy Manufacturing Company manufactures a single product that is processed in five departments. The following cost data are available for Dept. 3 for the month of July, 19_5:

Opening work-in-process inventory:

Cost transferred in from Dept. 2	$19,000
Dept. 3 labor cost	3,000

Current costs:

Cost transferred in during July from Dept. 2	$105,000
Dept. 3 material cost during July	36,800
Dept. 3 labor cost during July	42,800

Material used in Dept. 3 is added to the product at the end of the Dept. 3 process. Dept. 3 conversion costs are assumed to be incurred uniformly throughout the Dept. 3 process; manufacturing overhead is applied to product on the basis of 50 percent of labor cost.

The following represents production data for Dept. 3 for the month of July, 19_5:

Work in process (July 1)	18,000 units (⅓ completed)
Units transferred in during July from Dept. 2	111,000 units
Good units completed during July	80,000
Spoiled units	12,000 units
Work in process (July 31)	28,000 units (¾ completed)

Spoiled units: Spoilage is detected by inspection upon completion of the product by Dept. 3. Normal spoilage is considered to be 10 percent of the good output. Further, normal spoilage is considered a cost of the good units completed while abnormal spoilage is written off as a loss.

Normal lost units: Units lost during processing are considered to be a normal occurrence *unless* the number of lost units exceeds 5 percent of total units accounted for (total units accounted for is equal to the sum of good units completed plus spoiled units plus units in ending inventory of work in process). The cost of normal lost units is considered a cost of total units accounted for; company accountants make no attempt to specifically determine or separately identify the cost of normal lost units (that is, the method of neglect is used in accounting for normal lost units).

Abnormal lost units: Lost units in excess of 5 percent are considered abnormal. The cost of abnormal lost units is separately identified and written off as a loss. The company accountants follow the policy of assigning only transferred-in costs to abnormal lost units.

required

1. Consistent with the *FIFO method* for treating product costs and consistent with the company's treatment of spoilage and lost units, determine the following concerning Dept. 3 operations for the month of July:
   a. Total loss (in dollars) due to abnormal spoilage.
   b. Total loss (in dollars) due to abnormal lost units.
   c. Total cost assigned to good units completed during July that is transferred out to Dept. 4.
   d. Total cost assigned to the ending (July 31) work-in-process inventory.
2. How would your answers to requirement 1 above be influenced (indicate the total dollar effect) if the spoiled units could be sold for 25¢ each?

19-23 *Weighted Average* Repeat requirement 1 of the preceding problem consistent with the *weighted-average* method for treating product costs and consistent with the company's treatment of spoilage and lost units.

Accounting for Payroll

20

The tasks of accounting for payrolls are complicated by the necessity for withholding specified amounts from employee earnings, measuring costs of employment fringe benefits, and meeting the government requirements for taxation and regulation. There are three major problems: (a) allocating labor costs to functions, departments, and products; (b) accurately computing earnings and promptly paying individual employees; and (c) computing and remitting withholdings and fringe benefits. Many of the aspects of classifying and controlling labor costs—point (a) above—have been covered previously (Chapters 4 and 8). This chapter will concentrate on other facets of payroll.

Individuals who are responsible for payroll accounting agree that, from the viewpoint of employees at least, promptness of payment and pinpoint accuracy are the foremost criteria for judging the merits of any payroll system. Whatever their educational level, be it twenty years of schooling or two, employees are excellent auditors of their own paychecks. Employees demand prompt and accurate payment, and they voice their dissatisfaction with vigor.

government impact

complexity of payroll accounting Many years ago, an employee who earned $60 per week received $60 in cash on payday. The bookkeeping problems for payroll were relatively simple. Only two parties (employer and employee) were involved.

Nowadays, the data-processing problems of accounting for payroll are staggering, and the clerical expenses for payroll accounting have soared accordingly. The rash of withholdings, fringe benefits, and incentive pay schemes requires an intricate network of accounts and supporting documents. Accounting for payroll has become so voluminous that new machine or computer installations invariably handle payroll as one of their first routine tasks.

Government requirements regarding payroll records play a big role in systems and forms design. Exhibits 20-1 and 20-2 show some of the government's impact on payroll accounting. The government has at least two major influences: (a) it requires the employer to be its collecting agent for income taxes from employees, and (b) it levies special payroll taxes on the employer.

withholding taxes The employer must withhold ordinary income taxes plus a special income tax, commonly called the *Social Security tax.* Other terms for the Social Security tax are *federal insurance contributions act tax* (F.I.C.A. tax) and *federal old-age benefits tax* (F.O.A.B. tax). The amounts and timing of these tax payments to the government are shown in Exhibits 20-1 and 20-2. The basic journal-entry pattern is as follows:

Work-in-process control	120,000	
Factory-overhead control	30,000	
Selling-expense control	40,000	
Administrative-expense control	10,000	
Accrued payroll (gross)		200,000
Accrued payroll	35,000	
Withheld income taxes payable		29,000
Withheld F.I.C.A. taxes payable		6,000
Withheld income taxes payable	29,000	
Withheld F.I.C.A. taxes payable	6,000	
Cash (or some similar credit that has this ultimate effect on cash)		35,000

The entries above show that the *gross* payroll cost is the measure of the various basic labor costs incurred by the employer. The taxes *on employees* are withheld and remitted (usually monthly) to the government. Somehow this practice tends to make the pain of the tax bite seem less severe to the employee.

EXHIBIT 20-1

U.S.A. PAYROLLS AND TAXES

TAX	*RATE*	*BASIS FOR COMPUTATION*	*DATE OF FILING FORM*	*PERIOD COVERED*
Federal income tax on employees	Depends on gross earnings and dependents	Gross earnings paid	On or before end of month following close of calendar quarter	Calendar quarters supplemented by a reconciliation at year-end
F.I.C.A. tax on employees	5.85% but increases frequently	First $15,300* of gross earnings paid to each employee	Same as above—Form 941	Calendar quarters
F.I.C.A. tax on employers	Same as above	First $15,300* of gross earnings paid to each employee	Same as above—Form 941	Calendar quarters
State unemployment insurance tax on employers†	Generally 2.7%, but may vary from .2% to 4%, depending on various state merit-rating systems for employer's labor turnover experience	First $4,200 of gross earnings paid to each employee‡	Same as above—Special state form	Calendar quarters
Federal unemployment insurance tax on employers	Generally, effective rate is .5% (3.2% nominal rate less 2.7% rate credit for state unemployment tax payments)	Same as above†	January 31—Form 940	Previous calendar year
State workmen's compensation insurance (or tax) on employers	Varies for different occupational classifications	Gross earnings paid	If insured by private company, annual premium is usually paid in advance. If taxed by state, same due-date provisions apply as for state unemployment tax.	

* The current statutory limit is tied to the increments in cost-of-living benefits since 1976, when the maximum taxable wage limit was $15,300.

† A few states also have an employee unemployment tax.

‡ Employers are not subject to tax unless they have one or more employees for at least one day a week for 20 weeks in a calendar year or pay at least $1,500 in wages in a quarter.

EXHIBIT 20-2

CALENDAR OF EMPLOYER'S OBLIGATIONS UNDER U.S.A. FEDERAL LAW

WHEN HIRING	*FORM NUMBER*
Get withholding exemption certificate	W-4
Get Social Security number. If employee has no account number, he should file application on	SS-5
WHEN PAYING	
Withhold both income taxes and F.I.C.A. taxes.	
By end of April, July, October, and January:	
File combined return for all F.I.C.A. taxes and withheld income taxes covering the quarter ending with the prior month. For example, the first calendar quarter's return must be filed by April 30.	941
By January 31 and at termination of employment:	
Give each employee a withholding statement in duplicate showing F.I.C.A. earnings and withholdings, total earnings subject to income tax withholdings, and income tax withheld.	W-2
By January 31:	
File reconciliation of quarterly returns	W-3
—plus collector's copy of all individual W-2's given to employees for prior year	W-2a
File annual return and pay unemployment tax	940

Thus, the employer does not regard withheld taxes as an employer tax; instead, the employer performs a collection-agent service for the government.[1]

other withholdings A flock of other withholdings from employees also exists. Withholdings as such are not employer costs. They are merely slices of the employee's gross earnings that are being funneled via the employer to third parties, primarily for the employee's convenience. Examples include em-

[1] Employees who have held jobs with two or more employers during a single year are entitled to a refund if excess F.I.C.A. taxes were withheld. For example, if the F.I.C.A. withholding rate is 6 percent and an employee earned $20,000 from one employer and $4,000 from another, each employer would legally have to withhold 6 percent of the first, say, $19,000 paid. Therefore, this employee would be entitled to a refund as follows:

Employer 1	.06 × $19,000 =	$1,140
Employer 2	.06 × $ 4,000 =	240
Total withheld		$1,380
Taxable limit for individual:	.06 × $19,000 =	1,140
Excess F.I.C.A. tax withheld		$ 240

His claim would be filed on his own individual income tax return. His W-2 forms would be evidence in support of his claim.

The employer is not entitled to any refund.

ployee contributions to group life insurance plans, hospitalization insurance, pension funds, employee savings plans, donations, and union dues.

fringe benefits

large size of fringe benefits

The gross earnings of employees are only nominal measures of the payroll costs really borne. The employer must not only pay payroll taxes like old-age and unemployment levies; he must also incur many more fringe costs. The following breakdown of payroll costs illustrates the general pattern:

Gross earnings of employee (Assume $15,000.)	100.00%
Federal old-age tax and hospital insurance on employers (Rate based on average employee earnings of $15,000. Tax would be, say, 6.05%.)	6.05
Federal unemployment tax (.5% of $4,200, or $21. Divide $21 by $15,000.)	.14
State unemployment tax (2.7% of $4,200, or $113. Divide $113 by $15,000.)	.75
Workmen's compensation tax (Rates vary with hazards; average rate shown.)	1.25
Vacations and paid holidays (10 days vacation and 6 holidays. Divide 16 by 260 days pay.)	6.20
Minimum total for most employers	114.39%
Add:	
Employer contributions to pension funds (average rate)	5.00
Employer contributions to health, life, and other insurance, etc. (average rate)	3.00
Employer contributions to guaranteed annual wage funds (average rate)	2.50
Total cost incurred by many employers	124.89%

These figures demonstrate that fringe costs are no longer a little dribble; their waterfall proportions have caused an increasing number of companies to recast their account classifications. Instead of treating all fringe costs as overhead, some companies add an average (that is, "equalized" or "leveled") fringe rate to the basic direct-labor rate to bring into focus a better measure of direct-labor costs. This leveled rate is computed as shown in the table above. However, perhaps because of inertia, most companies continue to treat fringe costs as a part of overhead.

timing of cost recognition

As in many other phases of accounting, there is often a time lag between incurrence and payment of various payroll fringe costs. For example, the liability for vacation payments really accrues from week to week as each employee accumulates his claim to vacation pay. Thus, many companies use an estimate to spread total vacation costs over a year instead of recognizing such costs as payments are made:

Work-in-process control (direct labor)	19,000	
Factory-overhead control (indirect labor plus $1,000 vacation pay)	7,000	
Estimated liability for vacation pay		1,000
Accrued payroll		25,000
To accrue vacation pay throughout the year because it is related to work done throughout the year. Leveled rate is 4% of Accrued Payroll. Entry here is, say, for January:		
Accrued payroll	25,000	
Estimated liability for vacation pay	300	
Cash		22,000
Withholdings payable (various)		3,300
The liability account for vacation pay is debited as actual vacation payments are made.		

Similar treatment can be given to bonus plans, holiday pay, contributions to pension funds, and contributions to guaranteed annual wage funds. The decision to adopt such leveling arrangements in accounting for fringe costs largely depends on the significance of the amounts involved and on the distortion of month-to-month costs that may arise from failure to spread charges over the year.

employer payroll taxes: theory and practice

Employers must pay old-age taxes, hospital insurance, and unemployment taxes on specified compensation paid to each employee every calendar year—up to maximum statutory taxable-wage limits that are changed by Congress from time to time. In most cases, this means that heavier tax outlays will be made in the earlier months of the calendar year than in the later months, because the employer liability diminishes as wage payments to an increasing number of employees gradually reach and pass the yearly statutory taxable-wage limit.

The problem of timing charges for employer payroll taxes raises some special theoretical questions. The employer's legal liability is ordinarily a function of wages *paid* rather than of wages *accrued.* Yet in practice, employer payroll taxes are usually accrued as wages are *earned.* Furthermore, such payroll tax accrual diminishes as months pass because more and more employees' earnings gradually surpass the maximum taxable limit.[2]

To illustrate, assume that a company has a gross payroll of $25,000 per month, $16,000 of which is direct labor, and $9,000 of which is indirect factory labor. Assume that the tax rate on employers is .5 percent for federal unem-

[2] Conceivably, in some companies, if no new workers are hired in November or December, the employer may show no payroll tax costs for these months.

ployment, 2.7 percent for state unemployment, and 5.8 percent for old-age benefits, a total payroll tax rate of 9 percent.

Early months:	Work-in-process control	16,000	
	Factory-overhead control ($9,000 plus $2,250)	11,250	
	Accrued payroll		25,000
	Employer's payroll taxes payable		2,250
	Payroll tax is .09 × $25,000 = $2,250.		
Late months:	Work-in-process control	16,000	
	Factory-overhead control	9,000	
	Accrued payroll		25,000
	Payroll is not subject to payroll tax because every employee's salary has passed the maximum taxable limits.		

In theory, employer payroll taxes (a) should be accrued as wages are earned (this practice is widely followed), and (b) should be spread over the year, using a leveled rate. Thus, payroll taxes would be handled in a fashion similar to the previous illustration on vacation pay. The reasoning in support of spreading payroll taxes over the year is that, for a going concern, the commitment to hire employees is made for a year; the payroll tax is an annual tax that is related to the year as a whole. Because it benefits the entire year's operations, such a tax should not be loaded on the early months of the calendar year. In practice, the additional clerical costs and complications often outweigh any informational advantages of this more refined approach. Therefore, early months bear the brunt of payroll tax charges.

illustration of payroll accounting

example

The Stengal Company has a gross payroll of $1,000 per day, based on a five-day, forty-hour, Monday-through-Friday workweek. Withholdings for income taxes amount to $100 per day. Payrolls for each week are paid on the following Tuesday.

Gross payrolls consist of $600 direct labor, $200 indirect labor, $140 selling expense, and $60 administrative expenses each day. The general-ledger entry to record the total of the payroll cost incurred (including accrued employer payroll fringe costs) is made on the last day of each month. Fringe costs borne by the employer are:

	PERCENT OF GROSS PAYROLL
Vacation pay	4.0%
F.I.C.A. tax	5.9%
Federal unemployment tax*	.8%
State unemployment tax*	2.3%
	13.0%

* The net federal rate depends on amounts paid to the state. The effective rates vary from state to state and are based on the individual employer's labor-turnover experience.

For our purposes, assume that the company starts business on March 3.

MARCH						
S	M	T	W	T	F	S
						1
2	3	4	5	6	7	8
9	10	11	12	13	14	15
16	17	18	19	20	21	22
23	24	25	26	27	28	29
30	31					

APRIL						
S	M	T	W	T	F	S
		1	2	3	4	5
6	7	8	9	10	11	12
13	14	15	16	17	18	19
20	21	22	23	24	25	26
27	28	29	30			

Try to solve by yourself before examining the solution. (Exhibit 20-1 contains some helpful information.)

required

1. All general-journal payroll entries for March 11, 18, 25, and 31, April 1, 8, 15, 22, 29, and 30.
2. All postings to Accrued payroll, Employees' income taxes payable, Employees' F.I.C.A. taxes payable, and Employer's F.I.C.A. taxes payable.

SOLUTION

1. Journal entries follow:

March 11	Accrued payroll (5 × $1,000)	5,000.00	
	Cash		4,205.00
	Employees' income taxes payable (assume 5 × $100)		500.00
	Employees' F.I.C.A. taxes payable (.059) × $5,000)		295.00
	To pay payroll.		

The identical entry would be repeated every Tuesday, March 18 through April 29. Note that payroll settlements are made every *payday,* regardless of when payroll costs are recognized as being incurred.

March 31	Work-in-process control (21 days × $600)	12,600.00	
	Factory-overhead control (21 × $200) + .13(21 × $200) + .13($12,600)	6,384.00	
	Selling-expense control (21 × $140) + .13(21 × $140)	3,322.20	
	Administrative-expense control (21 × $60) + .13(21 × $60)	1,423.80	
	Accrued payroll (21 days × $1,000)		21,000.00
	Estimated liability for vacation pay (.04 × $21,000)		840.00
	Employer's F.I.C.A. taxes payable (.059 × $21,000)		1,239.00
	Federal unemployment taxes payable (.008 × $21,000)		168.00
	State unemployment taxes payable (.023 × $21,000)		483.00

Such an entry is usually made and posted monthly. If desired, it could be made weekly, biweekly, or at any other interval. As contrasted with the previous entry, this entry recognizes cost incurrence rather than payment. Its measurements depend on the number of work days in a calendar month.

(Note that the entries on *paydays* are the same for April as for March.)

April 30	Work-in-process control (22 × $600)	13,200.00	
	Factory-overhead control (22 × $200) + .13(22 × $200) + .13($13,200)	6,688.00	
	Selling-expense control (22 × $140) + .13(22 × $140)	3,480.40	
	Administrative-expense control (22 × $60) + .13(22 × $60)	1,491.60	
	Accrued payroll (22 × $1,000)		22,000.00
	Estimated liability for vacation pay (.04 × $22,000)		880.00
	Employer's F.I.C.A. taxes payable (.059 × $22,000)		1,298.00
	Federal unemployment taxes payable (.008 × $22,000)		176.00
	State unemployment taxes payable (.023 × $22,000)		506.00

The entry above is based on 22 days of work done in April.

April 30	Employees' income taxes payable (3 paydays × $500)	1,500.00	
	Employees' F.I.C.A. taxes payable (3 × $295)	885.00	
	Employer's F.I.C.A. taxes payable (3 × $295)	885.00	
	Cash		3,270.00
	Payment of taxes withheld on *paydays* in March plus employer's matching of F.I.C.A. taxes withheld.		

These taxes are detailed on Form 941, a quarterly return. Legal liability arises as payroll is paid during a calendar quarter rather than as payroll is accrued. Compare, for example, the employer's F.I.C.A. taxes accrued as of March 31 ($1,239) with the amount remitted with this return ($885). This difference represents six days' cost in March ($59 per day × 6 days) that was not paid with this quarterly return. It will be paid during a subsequent period.

April 30	State unemployment taxes payable (.023 × $5,000 × 3 paydays in March)	345.00	
	Cash		345.00
	Payment to state for legal liability for first calendar quarter.		

2. Postings to selected accounts for March and April follow:

Accrued Payroll

March 11	5,000		
March 18	5,000		
March 25	5,000		
To balance	6,000	March 31	21,000
		March 31 balance, six days' gross earnings	6,000
April 1	5,000		
April 8	5,000		
April 15	5,000		
April 22	5,000		
April 29	5,000	April 30	22,000
To balance	3,000		
		April 30 balance, three days' gross earnings	3,000

Employees' Income Taxes Payable

		March 11,18,25	1,500
April 30	1,500	April 1,8, 15,22,29	2,500

Employees' F.I.C.A. Taxes Payable

		March 11,18,25	885
April 30	885	April 1,8, 15,22,29	1,475

Employer's F.I.C.A. Taxes Payable

		March 31	1,239
		April 30	1,298
April 30	885		

A study of the T-accounts above shows the following:

1. The Accrued Payroll balance at the close of business on March 31 represents the unpaid amount of *gross* earnings of employees applicable to the last six days worked in March.
2. The timing of recognition of liability for employees' and employer's F.I.C.A. taxes differs. Legally, both liabilities arise when payroll is paid. But the employer accrues his liability when he recognizes regular labor-cost incurrence, because such payroll taxes are basically related to time of *earnings* rather than to time of *payout*.

incentive plans

objective of incentives Most employees are paid a flat salary or a flat rate per hour, but wage incentive systems are widespread. Incentive plans provide extra compensation for performance that is superior to some predetermined goal or standard. The wide variety of factory incentive systems has a common objective: minimization of total costs for a given volume of production. In other words, the sweetening of the pay envelope must at least be balanced by reductions in other cost factors or by reductions in labor cost per unit. For example, assume that a worker is paid $6.00 an hour and produces 10 units in that time, resulting in an average labor cost of 60¢ per unit. He is placed on a strict piece-rate system at a rate of 55¢ per piece. His productivity may increase to 12 units per hour. His earnings would then be $6.60 per hour (12 × 55¢)—higher pay per worker and yet less cost per unit for the employer. A piece rate of 60¢ or more may even be desirable for the employer, if savings in other costs like materials, power, repairs, or other variable-overhead items can offset increased labor costs.

Incentive plans are not panaceas for problems of cost control. They add to clerical costs and may tend to increase spoilage costs and lessen quality. Yet many companies have been pleased with overall results. In any event, no incentive plan can substitute for adequate management as the most effective means of controlling labor costs.

accounting for incentive plans

Incentive plans vary widely in their details and application. The Gantt Task and Bonus Plan awards a higher piece rate, or bonus, for all production in excess of standard. The Taylor Differential Piece-Rate System applies a higher piece rate for *all* production per hour or day as long as the hourly or daily production standard is met. Incentive plans may be arranged to reward individual performance, group performance, assembly-line performance, and even plant-wide performance.

A common incentive plan is piecework coupled with a guaranteed minimum hourly rate. Thus, if the standard number of pieces per hour is not produced, pay is provided to "make up" the difference between the guaranteed rate and the piecework earnings. An example of computations follows:

*DAILY EARNINGS SUMMARY**

CLOCK NUMBER	*NAME*	*DEPARTMENT*	*OPERATION*	*UNITS PRODUCED*	*PIECE RATE*	*PIECEWORK EARNINGS*	*MAKEUP*	*TOTAL EARNINGS*
414	Atwood	4	1004	100	$.55	$55.00	$ —	$55.00
445	Barnes	4	1004	70	.55	38.50	9.50	48.00
446	Charnes	4	1004	80	.55	44.00	4.00	48.00

* Guaranteed rate is $6.00 per hour or $48.00 per day.

Makeup pay would be charged to the department as an overhead item and would be part of the department's overhead budget. The standard labor cost for the operation would be 55¢ per unit.

payroll bank account

Companies with many employees usually use a separate checking account to keep payroll checks apart from checks for other disbursements. This facilitates control, preparation, and reconciliation of vast numbers of payroll checks. The general working of a payroll bank account is as follows:

Accrued payroll	10,000	
Withholdings payable		1,500
Cash (in regular checking account)		8,500

A single $8,500 check is drawn against the company's regular checking account to cover the net payroll. The bank would then transfer $8,500 from the regular account to a special payroll bank account. Assume that there are 100 employees. One hundred payroll checks totaling $8,500 would be prepared and issued. The size, color, and numerical sequence of these checks would differ from those of the general checks. Note that, as far as this company is concerned, its payroll bank account should always have a zero balance. Any balance in the payroll account as shown by the bank represents outstanding payroll checks.[3]

SUMMARY

Payroll accounting is overwhelmed with detail, much of which is kept because of legal requirements rather than because of managerial needs.

The data-processing function is often divided between cost allocation and payouts to employees. Although electronic data processing increasingly accomplishes these objectives simultaneously, most companies allocate costs on one time basis (for example, monthly in the general ledger, daily in subsidiary records) and account for payouts on another time basis (for example, weekly).

PROBLEM FOR SELF-STUDY

Review the problem used as an illustration in the chapter.

QUESTIONS, PROBLEMS, AND CASES

20-1 "Accounting for payroll embraces plenty of big problems." Name three.

20-2 "The need for accuracy in payroll accounting is paramount." Explain.

20-3 "The government has at least two major influences on payroll accounting." What are they?

20-4 Name the major taxes associated with payrolls.

20-5 George Ripon worked for three employers during a year. His gross earnings were $1,000, $7,800, and $25,000—a total of $33,800.
a. How much of the earnings should each employer regard as subject to F.I.C.A. taxes?
b. How much of Ripon's earnings should he regard as subject to F.I.C.A. taxes?

20-6 "The Federal Unemployment Insurance Tax rate is 0.5%." Do you agree? Why?

20-7 Identify the following forms: W-4, 941, W-2, W-3, 940.

[3] The use of special bank accounts is not confined to payrolls. They can also be used for dividends, commissions, royalties, and so forth.

20-8 "Withheld taxes are taxes on employers." Do you agree? Why?

20-9 Name four common withholdings other than taxes.

20-10 "Payroll fringe costs are large enough these days to justify adding an average fringe rate to the basic direct-labor rate." Do you agree? Why?

20-11 "Leveling or averaging of vacation costs and holiday pay is used to relate them to work done throughout the year." What criteria should affect the decision to adopt such leveling arrangements?

20-12 "Conceivably, in some companies an employer may show no payroll tax costs for the last quarter of the year." Why? Explain.

20-13 Contrast the theoretical and practical accounting treatments of employer payroll taxes.

20-14 If all bookkeeping is up to date, what does the balance in Accrued Payroll represent?

20-15 "The timing of recognition of liability for employees' and employer's F.I.C.A. taxes differs." Explain.

20-16 What are incentive plans? What is their objective?

20-17 What is "makeup"? How is it accounted for?

20-18 A company uses a separate payroll bank account. Weekly wage payments are $10,000. A $1,000 minimum balance is kept to provide for salary advances, separation payments, and so forth. What cash balance should ordinarily be shown on the company balance sheets?

20-19 Briefly describe how EDP can affect conventional payroll procedures.

20-20 *Unemployment Compensation Taxes* (CPA) The cost of unemployment compensation taxes to an employer is sometimes reduced as a result of a "good" experience rating. A manufacturer negotiated with the federal government a contract that necessitated the construction of a specific plant and related facilities for the sole purpose of producing the goods called for in the contract. Because the goods were required to meet emergency needs of the government, it was possible that after the plant facilities were constructed, the employees hired, and work on the order begun, the contract would be cancelled. The ensuing termination of services of employees hired for this specific job would make the employer's experience rating worse, which in turn would increase the cost of his unemployment compensation taxes. This "possible" cost was recognized as a cost in negotiating the contract.

Describe in order of preference three alternate methods of recording in accounts and/or disclosing on the financial statements the "possible" cost during the course of operations of this emergency plant under the contract. State your reasons.

20-21 *Accounting for Idle Time* (J. March) The labor distribution of the Dunne Desk Company is made from its payroll, all the wages of its twenty shop employees, except the foreman's, being treated as direct labor. The company pays for idle time of workmen caused by material shortages, and this amounts to a substantial portion of the payroll.

For the year 19_1, the direct labor, according to the ledger, was $20,000 and the overhead $16,000. Accordingly, an overhead rate of 80 percent was used in 19_2 for the purpose of estimating costs of new products. The manager thinks that the estimates are wrong, for his income statement shows a gross margin of only $1 a desk, whereas his selling prices are at least $5 a desk above the estimated costs. He suspects that the idle-time factor is not being included in the cost estimates, and he asks you to investigate the situation.

1. How would you proceed to determine whether the manager's suspicions are correct?
2. Recompute the overhead rate for 19_1 on the assumption that $2,000 was paid for idle time that should be treated as overhead instead of as direct labor.
3. Suggest a change in the method of labor-cost allocation that would result in a more accurate accounting for idle time.

20-22 *Group Incentives* (SIA, adapted) The Smart Company of Hong Kong operates with five direct workers in its stamping department. All work is done on a job-order basis. During the week of August 15, each man worked a full 40-hour week, with output as follows:

NAME	GUARANTEED HOURLY MINIMUM	UNITS PRODUCED
Brackett, S. J.	$1.50	1,840
Emery, P. L.	1.60	1,900
Evans, E. C.	1.50	1,960
Forest, T. A.	1.70	2,050
Simmons, F.	1.50	1,650

required

1. Compute the gross earnings of each worker, assuming that a group incentive plan is in operation and that the standard output of the department is 7,200 units per week. Each member of the group receives the guaranteed hourly minimum if production is equal to or less than the standard output. The hourly rate for each worker is increased 1 percent for each 200 units per week in excess of standard production.
2. What effect does excess of "normal" or "standard" output have on the unit cost of production? Explain.
3. Assess the effectiveness of this incentive system for the Smart Company, giving reasons for your answer.

20-23 *Incentive Wage Plans* (CPA, adapted) During your audit of the accounts of the Gelard Manufacturing Corporation of Singapore, your assistant tells you that he has found errors in the computation of the wages of factory workers and he wants you to verify his work.

Your assistant has extracted from the union contract the following description of the systems for computing wages in various departments of the company. The contract provides that the minimum wage for a worker is his base rate, which is also paid for any "downtime"—time when the worker's machine is under repair or he is without work. The standard workweek is 40 hours. The union contract also provides that workers be paid 150 percent of base rates for overtime production. The company is engaged in interstate commerce.

1. *Straight piecework.* The worker is paid at the rate of $.20 per piece produced.
2. *Percentage bonus plan.* Standard quantities of production per hour are established by the engineering department. The worker's average hourly production, determined from his total hours worked and his production, is divided by the standard quantity of production to determine his efficiency ratio. The efficiency ratio is then applied to his base rate to determine his hourly earnings for the period.
3. *Emerson Efficiency System.* A minimum wage is paid for production up to 66⅔ percent of standard output or "efficiency." When the worker's pro-

duction exceeds 66⅔ percent of the standard output, he is paid at a bonus rate. The bonus rate is determined from the following table:

EFFICIENCY	BONUS
Up to 66⅔%	0%
66⅔–79%	10%
80–99%	20%
100–125%	45%

Your assistant has prepared the following schedule of information pertaining to certain workers for a weekly payroll selected for examination:

WORKER	WAGE INCENTIVE PLAN	TOTAL HOURS	DOWN-TIME HOURS	UNITS PRODUCED	STANDARD UNITS	BASE RATE	GROSS WAGES PER BOOKS
Long	Straight piecework	40	5	400	—	$1.80	$ 82.00
Loro	Straight piecework	46	—	455[a]	—	1.80	91.00
Huck	Straight piecework	44	4	420[b]	—	1.80	84.00
Nini	Percentage bonus plan	40	—	250	200	2.20	120.00
Boro	Percentage bonus plan	40	—	180	200	1.90	67.00
Wiss	Emerson	40	—	240	300	2.10	92.00
Alan	Emerson	40	2	590	600[c]	2.00	118.00

[a] Includes 45 pieces produced during the 6 overtime hours.

[b] Includes 50 pieces produced during the 4 overtime hours. The overtime, which was brought about by the "downtime," was necessary to meet a production deadline.

[c] Standard units for 40 hours' production.

required

Prepare a schedule comparing each individual's gross wages per books and his gross wages per your calculation. Computations of workers' wages should be in good form and labeled with the workers' names.

20-24 *Journal Entries for Payroll* The Stable Company operates the year around with a gross payroll of $500 a day. Withholdings for Social Security taxes and federal income taxes amount to $100 a day. The concern works five days a week, and the payroll period covers Monday to Friday, both inclusive. Payrolls for the week are paid on the following Tuesday.

Gross payrolls consist of $300 direct labor, $100 indirect labor, $70 selling expense, and $30 general and administrative expense each day. The general-ledger entry to record the total of the payroll cost incurred each month is made on the last day of the month. These totals are obtained by summarizing the Payroll Cost Recapitulation sheets. This firm uses a "leveled" percentage of 4 percent to estimate its own contribution to Social Security.

required

Using the calendar as a guide, answer the following questions:

APRIL

S	M	TU	W	TH	F	SAT
		1	2	3	4	5
6	7	8	9	10	11	12
13	14	15	16	17	18	19
20	21	22	23	24	25	26
27	28	29	30			

required

1. What is the balance in Accrued Payroll as of the close of business on March 31?
2. What journal entries should be made on:
   a. April 1? b. April 29? c. April 30?
3. What is the ending balance in Accrued Payroll as of the close of business on April 30?

20-25 *Journal Entries for Payroll* (J. March) The balance of the Accrued Wages of Kem Industries, Inc., was $12,120 on October 31, 19_1. The company has a job-order cost system. The cost accounts are in the general ledger. Time tickets for pay periods falling wholly or partly in November are summarized as follows:

PAY PERIOD	DIRECT LABOR	FACTORY OVERHEAD	TOTAL
Nov. 1–7	$8,250	$4,510	$12,760
Nov. 8–14	8,450	4,490	12,940
Nov. 15–21	8,570	4,570	13,140
Nov. 22–28	7,920	4,060	11,980
Nov. 29–Dec. 5	8,430	4,470	12,900

Of the wages earned in the pay period ending December 5, one-third is applicable to November.

Payrolls for pay periods ending in November are summarized as follows:

		DEDUCTIONS		
Pay Period Ending	Gross Earnings	F.I.C.A.	Income Tax	Net Pay
Oct. 31	$12,120	$110	$1,200	$10,810
Nov. 7	12,760	108	1,250	11,402
Nov. 14	12,940	112	1,280	11,548
Nov. 21	13,140	102	1,300	11,738
Nov. 28	11,980	95	1,200	10,685

The payroll for the period ending November 28 was paid December 2.

required

1. Journal entry for labor-cost allocation.
2. Journal entry for payrolls paid in November.
3. Postings in the Accrued Wages account.
4. Journal entry for accrual of employers' payroll taxes for the month of November at a leveled rate of 5 percent of gross earnings.
5. Answer the following questions:
   a. Theoretically, should the accrual of employers' payroll taxes be based on wages earned or on wages paid during the month?
   b. Why is the amount of F.I.C.A. deductions less than 1 percent of the gross earnings?
   c. What does the balance of Accrued Wages represent?

Journal explanations in all cases should state clearly how you arrived at your amounts.

Accounting Systems and Internal Control

21

This book has already emphasized many features of management control systems. This chapter examines some aspects of systems that are usually explored in books on general accounting systems or auditing. Such matters are included here because (a) many readers will not have a chance to study them in other courses, and (b) all managers and accountants probably benefit from an awareness of the dimensions of the problems of data processing and internal control.

As you know, accounting records are kept for many purposes. A principal purpose, of course, is to help managers conduct routine operations. The accounting system is intertwined with operating management. An individual who launches an organization inevitably learns quickly that operations would be a hopeless tangle without the paperwork that is so often regarded with disdain. For example, receivables and payables must be recorded, and cash receipts and disbursements must be traced to these and other accounts, or else confusion would ensue. The act of recording events has become as much a part of operating activities as the act of selling or buying. Even the simplest of organizations must have a minimum of records, a semblance of routine. As businesses become more complex, managers find themselves increasingly dependent on the systematic compilation of records for keeping informed and for help with planning and control.

The size of the physical handling of records is often staggering. For example, in 1977 a major oil company processed 20 million pieces of paper monthly just to handle its credit-card business. This illustrates one overwhelming feature of a total system: the voluminous data-processing procedures that tend to require a minimum of human judgment and that lend themselves to routine procedures. Other examples are check handling, payroll accounting, production scheduling, inventory control, and automated manufacturing. The accountant's everyday role in these ongoing operations is largely one of scorekeeping; however, the design of the system requires skill and care.

Recent revolutionary changes in processing business data have been so extensive that a specific system is likely to be outdated by the time its description is off the press. That is why this chapter emphasizes the general features of an internal control system that have wide applicability to a variety of organizations, regardless of their specific systems. The aim here is not to develop skills in auditing. Rather, it is to create an awareness on the part of the manager and the management accountant of the importance of the problem and of some general approaches to its solution. The prime responsibility for internal control rests with the managers themselves, not their accountants. The exploits of embezzlers are reported in the press almost each day. Still, many managers seem to take a far too casual attitude toward these risks within their own organizations.

internal control: definition

Previous chapters have covered numerous features of an accounting system, such as the need for the following: timely data; competent accounting personnel who encourage the respect, confidence, cooperation, and cost-consciousness of operating managers; and constant search for improvement of the accounting system. The feature of *internal control* has not yet received direct attention.

The auditing literature contains extensive, confusing discussions of the distinctions among internal control, accounting control, and administrative control.[1] This book has already described the features of systems and procedures that promote effectiveness and efficiency (budgets, standards, responsibility accounting, and so forth). *In its broadest sense, internal control embraces all these accounting techniques.* This chapter will highlight those aspects of internal control that minimize errors, fraud, and waste.

[1] The most authoritative discussion is presented by the Committee on Auditing Procedure, *Statement on Auditing Standards* (New York: American Institute of Certified Public Accountants, 1973), Sec. 320. In practice, the words *internal control* and *internal check* are often used interchangeably, so that many accountants regard internal control narrowly as being those characteristics of an accounting system that are designed to minimize errors, fraud, and waste.

All good systems of internal control have certain features in common. These features may be termed a checklist of internal control, which may be used to appraise any procedure for cash, purchases, sales, payroll, and the like. This checklist may sometimes be called *principles* or *rules* or *concepts.*

checklist for internal control

The following checklist is a summary of the guidance that is found in much of the systems and auditing literature.

1. COST-BENEFIT ANALYSIS Highly complex systems tend to strangle people in red tape, so that the system impedes rather than promotes efficiency. Besides, there is "a cost of keeping the costs" that sometimes gets out of hand. Investments in more costly systems must be judged in the light of expected benefits. Unfortunately, such benefits are difficult to measure. It is much easier to relate new lathes or production methods to cost savings in manufacturing than a new computer to cost savings in the form of facilitating new attacks on problems of inventory control, production scheduling, and research. Yet hard-headed efforts, as are used in making other business decisions, must be made to measure alternative costs of various accounting systems.

The relationship of costs to benefits sometimes leads to using sampling procedures. Although many companies implement more complex procedures to improve internal control, a few have taken a reverse course. They have decided that the increased costs of additional scrutiny are not worth the expected savings from catching mistakes or crooks. For example, an aerospace manufacturer routinely pays the invoice amounts without checking supporting documentation except on a random-sampling basis. An aluminum company sends out a blank check with its purchase orders, and then the supplier fills out the check and deposits it.

No framework for internal control is perfect in the sense that it can prevent some shrewd individual from "beating the system" either by outright embezzlement or by producing inaccurate records. The task is not total prevention of fraud, nor is it implementation of operating perfection; rather, the task is the designing of a cost-effective tool that will help achieve efficient operations and reduce temptation.

2. MANAGEMENT RESPONSIBILITY AND SUPERVISION The prime responsibility for internal control rests with the managers themselves, not their accountants. The system deserves surveillance to see if it is working as prescribed and if changes are warranted. In addition, appropriate overseeing and appraising of employees are essential. The most streamlined accounting system is deficient if its prescribed procedures are not being conscientiously followed.

3. RELIABLE PERSONNEL Individuals obviously should be given duties and responsibilities commensurate with their abilities, interests, experience, and reliability. Yet many employers use low-cost talent that may prove exceedingly expensive in the long run, not only from the point of view of fraud but also from the point of view of productivity. The accounting system, no matter how elaborate, is only as good as the individuals who implement it.

4. SEPARATION OF POWERS Record keeping and physical handling of assets should not be in the hands of one person. For example, the bookkeeper should not handle cash, and the cashier should not have access to ledger accounts such as subsidiary receivable records. The general-ledger bookkeeper should not have access to subsidiary records. The entire accounting function should be divorced from operating departments, so that objective, independent records may be kept, either by other operating people (for example, inspectors, not machine operators, should count good pieces) or by accounting clerks (for example, stores record clerks, not storekeepers, should keep perpetual inventory counts). This point not only better insures accurate compilation of data; it also limits the chances for fraud, which would require the collusion of two or more persons to perpetrate a fraud.

5. ROUTINE AND AUTOMATIC CHECKS In a phrase, this means doing things "by the numbers." Just as manufacturing activities tend to be made more efficient by the division and specialization of repetitive activities, so can record-keeping activities be made less costly and more accurate. Repetitive procedures may be prescribed for nonmanufacturing activities such as order taking, order filling, collating, and inspecting. The use of general routines permits specialization of effort, division of duties, and automatic checks on previous steps in the routine.

For example, disbursement-voucher systems are widely used in industry. As an illustration, see Exhibit 14-7, which diagrams a routine for purchasing materials. The essential feature of such a system is that no checks may be signed without a disbursement voucher that so authorizes. In turn, the voucher will not be prepared unless all supporting documents, such as pertinent requisitions, purchase orders, invoices, receiving reports, and freight documents, have been reviewed. Each step in the review serves as a check on previous steps.

Forms are designed so that the absence or incorrectness of key information is automatically uncovered and corrected on the spot. For example, the absence of a receiving clerk's signature on a receiving report would halt preparation of a disbursement voucher, and the omission of a foreman's signature prevents payments of overtime pay.

6. DOCUMENT CONTROL This means immediate recording, complete recording, and tamper-proof recording. This point is especially important for handling cash sales. Devices used to insure immediate recording include cash registers with loud bells and compiling tapes, private detectives, guaranteeing "rewards" to customers if they are not offered a receipt at the time of sale, and forcing

clerks to make change by pricing items at $1.99, $2.99, and $3.99 rather than at $2, $3, and $4.[2]

Complete and tamper-proof recording is encouraged by having all source documents prenumbered and accounted for, by using devices such as cash registers and locked compartments in invoice-writing machines, and by designing forms for ease of recording.

7. EMPLOYEE RESPONSIBILITY This means tracking actions as far down in the organization as is feasible, so that results may be related to individuals. It means having salesclerks sign sales slips, inspectors initial packing slips, and workmen sign time cards and requisitions. The psychological impact of fixing responsibility promotes care and efficiency; it keeps people on their toes. Individuals tend to perform better when they must explain deviations from required procedures.

8. BONDING, VACATIONS, AND ROTATION OF DUTIES Key people may be subject to excessive temptation; top executives, branch managers, and individuals who handle cash or inventories should be bonded, have understudies, and be forced to take vacations.

A facet of this idea is also illustrated by the common practice of having receivables and payables clerks periodically rotated in duties. Thus, a receivables clerk may handle accounts from A to C for three months and then be rotated to accounts M to P for three months, and so forth.

Incidentally, the act of bonding, that is, buying insurance against embezzlement, is not a substitute for vacations, rotation of duties, and similar precautions. Insurance companies will pay only when a loss is proven; establishing proof is often difficult and costly in itself.

9. INDEPENDENT CHECK All phases of the system should be subjected to periodic review by outsiders (for example, by independent public accountants) and by internal auditors who do not ordinarily have contact with the operation under review.

The idea of independent check extends beyond the work performed by professional auditors. For example, bank statements should be reconciled with book balances. The bank provides an independent record of cash. Furthermore, the monthly bank reconciliations should be conducted by some clerk other than the cash, receivables, or payables clerks. Other examples of independent checks include monthly statements sent to credit customers and physical counts of inventory to check against perpetual records.

One of the main jobs of internal auditors and outside auditors is to appraise the effectiveness of internal control; such appraisal affects the extent of the sampling of transactions needed to test validity of account balances.

[2] Historically, such pricing was originally adopted to force clerks to make change as well as for its psychological impact on potential customers.

10. PHYSICAL SAFEGUARDS Obviously, losses of cash, inventories, and records are minimized by safes, locks, watchmen, and limited access.

illustrations

McKesson & Robbins fraud: the limitations of systems

A fraud case that had a big and lasting impact on auditing procedures was the infamous McKesson & Robbins embezzlement of the 1930s. The president engineered a complicated fraud in a collusion with the assistant treasurer, the head of shipping, receiving, and warehousing, and an outside party who managed dummy companies with whom McKesson purportedly conducted business. It so happened that the partners in crime were the president's brothers. The four men did not use their real names.[3]

Essentially, the fraud involved setting up an entirely fictitious Canadian crude drug division. Pretended purchases were made from a number of Canadian vendors, who supposedly retained the merchandise in their own warehouses for the account of McKesson. Pretended sales were made by a fictitious W. W. Smith and Company, as agent for McKesson; goods were supposedly shipped to customers. Payment for goods purchased and collections from customers were pretended to have been made by the Montreal banking firm of Manning & Company—also for the account of McKesson. The actual cash embezzlement from the central headquarters of McKesson took the form of commissions paid to W. W. Smith and Company. All these transactions were supported by proper-looking but false invoices, contracts, Dun and Bradstreet credit reports, and the like.

The vastness of the fraud framework can be seen from McKesson's certified balance sheet as of December 31, 1937; it showed $87 million in assets, $20 million of which were fictitious, consisting of $10 million in receivables and $10 million in inventories, and $75,000 of cash on deposit with "Manning & Company."

The fraud, which had been conducted over a period of twelve years, was finally uncovered by Julian Thompson, controller and treasurer, when he went to Montreal to check on inventories and found none.

The president killed himself, McKesson & Robbins was taken over by a trustee in bankruptcy, and the public accounting firms were placed in a state of shock—sending their men scurrying all over the world to make sure that their clients' inventories really existed. One major change in auditing procedure that all auditing firms adopted as an outgrowth of this case was the physical testing of inventories instead of reliance on the client's word.

[3] Of course, there have been hosts of notorious frauds before and since the McKesson case. Nevertheless, this case has become the classic that seems to be cited most often by auditors.

The Securities and Exchange Commission launched a detailed investigation of the matter. A thorough investigation of the fraud was hampered by the president's suicide, but some of the figures involved are worth repeating:

1. The costs of investigation totaled $3 million
2. The public accounting firm that investigated the fraud had 300 accountants work a total of 146,000 man-hours. They found 91 bank accounts, 57 brokerage accounts, and 10 loan accounts that the president had used in the course of his twelve years at the helm of McKesson & Robbins. Ultimately, they found that the actual cash stolen was about $3,200,000.

The cost-benefit moral of this story for both managers and accountants may be best expressed by the sentence that the president underlined in a book (Morrill Goddard's *What Interests People and Why*) he had been reading shortly before committing suicide:

> The truth, which the public has never been told, is that no practical system has ever been devised by which the complicated finances of a large institution can be thoroughly checked so that every transaction is verified, except at prohibitive time and cost.

using the checklist The next illustration will show how the checklist for internal control may be used as a starting point in judging a system.

example[4] The Y Company has come to you with the following problem.

It has three clerical employees who must perform the following functions:

a. Maintain general ledger
b. Maintain accounts-payable ledger
c. Maintain accounts-receivable ledger
d. Prepare checks for signature
e. Maintain disbursements journal
f. Issue credits on returns and allowances
g. Reconcile the bank account
h. Handle and deposit cash receipts

Assuming that there is no problem as to the ability of any of the employees, the company requests that you assign the functions above to the three employees in such a manner as to achieve the highest degree of internal control. It may be assumed that these employees will perform no other accounting functions than the ones listed and that any accounting functions not listed will be performed by persons other than these three employees.

1. State how you would distribute the functions among the three employees. Assume that, with the exception of the nominal jobs of the bank reconciliation and the issuance of credits on returns and allowances, all functions require an equal amount of time.
2. List four possible unsatisfactory combinations of the listed functions. Try to answer the questions before consulting the following solution.

[4] Adapted from a CPA examination.

SOLUTION

1. Assignment of functions:
   Employee No. 1:
   a. Maintain general ledger
   b. Reconcile bank account
   c. Issue credits on returns and allowances
   Employee No. 2:
   a. Prepare checks for signature
   b. Handle and deposit cash receipts
   c. Maintain disbursements journal
   Employee No. 3:
   a. Maintain accounts-payable ledger
   b. Maintain accounts-receivable ledger
2. Undesirable combinations are as follows:
   a. Cash receipts and accounts receivable
   b. Cash receipts and credits on returns and allowances
   c. Cash disbursements and accounts payable
   d. Cash receipts and bank reconciliation
   e. General ledger and cash receipts
   f. Accounts receivable and credits on returns and allowances

The major feature of the suggested division of duties is the separation of powers so that *one individual does not have sole control over all record keeping and physical handling for any single transaction.* Not only does this limit the chances for fraud, but—probably more important—it provides for automatic checks on efficiency and accuracy.

inventory shrinkage Retail merchants must contend with a major operating problem that is often called inventory shrinkage, a polite term for shoplifting by customers and embezzling by employees. The National Retail Merchandise Association reported that in 1976, shrinkage amounted to 2.9 percent of all general merchandise sales, up from 2.0 percent in 1965. Some department stores suffered shrinkage losses of 4 to 5 percent of their sales volume; compare this to the typical net-profit margin of 5 to 6 percent.

In 1970, a management consultant firm demonstrated how widespread shoplifting has become. The firm concentrated on a midtown New York department store. Five hundred shoppers, picked at random, were followed from the moment they entered the store to the time they departed. Forty-two shoppers, or one out of every twelve, took something. They stole $300 worth of merchandise, an average of $7.15 each. Similar experiments were conducted in Boston (1 of 20 shoplifted), Philadelphia (1 of 10), and again in New York (1 of 12).

The experts on controlling inventory shrinkage generally agree that the best deterrent is an alert employee at the point of sale. But other means are also used. Retail stores have gone so far as to use tiny sensitized tags on merchandise; if not detached or neutralized by a sales clerk, these miniature transmitters trip an alarm as the culprit begins to leave the store. Macy's in New York has continuous surveillance with over fifty television cameras. Retailers must scrutinize their own personnel, because they account for 30 to 40 percent of inventory shortages.

The imposing magnitude of retail inventory shrinkage demonstrates how management objectives may differ among industries. For example, consider the grocery business, where the net income percentage on sales hovers around 1 percent. You can readily see why a prime responsibility of the store manager is to control inventory shrinkage rather than boost gross sales volume. The trade-off is clear: If the operating profit on sales is 2 percent, to offset a $1,000 increase in shrinkage requires a $50,000 boost in gross sales.

retail method of inventory control

A widely used inventory method, known as the *retail method,* is utilized as a control device as well as for obtaining an inventory valuation for financial-statement purposes. The wide variety, low unit value, and high volume of most retail merchandise prevent any economical use of a perpetual-inventory system as commonly conceived. The following is a general version of how food stores use the retail method to control grocery inventories at the store level. All merchandise is accounted for at retail prices[5] as follows:

		RETAIL PRICES
	Inventory, January 5 (by surprise count by branch auditors)	$ 15,000
	Purchases (shipments to store from branch warehouse)	101,000
	Additional retail price changes:	
	Markups	2,000
	Markdowns	(5,000)
(1)	Total merchandise to account for	$113,000
	Sales (per cash-register records)	$100,000
	Allowable shrinkage (shoplifting, breakage, etc. usually a predetermined percentage of sales)	1,000
(2)	Total deductions	$101,000
(1) − (2)	Inventory, February 11, should be	$ 12,000
	Inventory, February 11, by physical count	$ 11,100
	Inventory shortage	$ 900

If the inventory shortage is not within predetermined limits, the manager usually bears prime responsibility. There are worrisome behavioral implications here. For utmost accuracy, the retail method requires the prompt application of the directed changes in retail prices that are ordered by the branch managers. For example, to help insure a good performance regarding his control of shrink-

[5] Of course, an inventory measured at retail prices can be restated in terms of an average cost for financial-statement purposes by applying an average-cost ratio. For example, if the average gross profit is 20 percent of sales price, the $11,100 inventory would be shown at a cost of .8 × $11,100, or $8,880. Incidentally, during the mid-1970s retail food stores began to implement computerized marking, checkout, and perpetual-inventory systems. Whether these systems will be cost-effective remains to be seen. In any event, the retail method will continue to be widely used in department stores and in many food stores.

age, the store manager may be inclined to delay the entering of markdowns on price tags and may be inclined to overstate the retail prices of merchandise if possible. The branch manager typically relies on other means, such as surprise spot checks, to insure that markup and markdown directives are being followed.

effects of computers on internal check

The use of computers has both positive and negative effects on the possibilities of errors, fraud, and waste. New types of errors arise when data must be manually punched into cards or paper tape. Each step that places data into a different form boosts the probability of error. Common blunders include using the wrong magnetic tape, using an obsolete or erroneous program, processing the same data twice, and skipping a batch of data.

Computer systems also are less flexible than manual systems. Humans regularly interpret, adjust, and act upon imperfect documents that are unacceptable under the tight discipline of computer programs. The computer correction system is necessarily more complicated, more formal, and tends to be concentrated on the first run of the data.

Despite frequent horror stories to the contrary, the computer itself has very high reliability. Data are processed in strict accordance with the program, and both manual and programmed internal checks can enhance that reliability.

Although computers have generally tended to increase the efficiency and effectiveness of information systems, they sometimes have an unwarranted constraining effect on overall systems design. The attitude to avoid is "Oh, we can't do that. It won't fit on our card!"

The checklist of internal control applies to both computer and manual systems. For example, consider the separation of powers. Programmers should not be allowed to operate the computers physically. A computer consultant commented that he had immense stealing opportunities when he ran computer operations for a large bank: "I alone designed the dividend-payment operation, wrote the program for it, and ran the job on the machine. The operation was so big that it had a mistake tolerance of nearly $100,000. I could have paid at least half that much to myself, in small checks, and the money wouldn't even have been missed."

Another example of separation of powers is the necessity to keep the check-writing process out of reach of computer operators. Unless he has some way to convert his tampered machine records onto checks, he cannot operate successfully.

The rotation of duties is another characteristic of good internal check. Companies should shift operators and programmers unpredictably from machine to machine and project to project. If a tempted individual cannot depend on making substitutions in punched cards or adjusting the program for one machine, he is less likely to begin stealing.

Reliability of personnel is a check that applies to all employees, including computer personnel. It is surprising how often embezzlements are repeated by individuals who move from employer to employer. It is also surprising how often employers fail to investigate the backgrounds of newly hired personnel.

SUMMARY

The following general characteristics form a checklist that may be used as a starting point for judging the effectiveness of internal control:

1. Cost-benefit analysis
2. Management responsibility and supervision
3. Reliable personnel
4. Separation of powers
5. Routine and automatic checks
6. Document control
7. Employee responsibility
8. Bonding, vacations, and rotation of duties
9. Independent check
10. Physical safeguards

This checklist is equally applicable to both computer and manual systems.

The blizzard of paperwork continues to intensify in most organizations. Too frequently, systems and forms and reports tend to "just grow." Periodic appraisals of systems are needed to see whether they are indeed optimal under new conditions. Occasionally, managers overreact to an overwhelming number of reports and documents by deleting them entirely. The key question involves the cost and value of information: "What are the costs and benefits of alternate systems?"

Managers at all levels have a major responsibility for the success of a given system. If they do not insist on accurate documents, separation of duties, and so on, trouble is inevitable.

PROBLEM FOR SELF-STUDY[6]

PROBLEM

As a member of the controller's department, you have been asked to review the company's payroll system and procedures where all payrolls are paid in currency.

a. State what questions you would ask in your review of the system of internal control and procedures relative to payrolls.
b. Give your reasons for asking the questions, including an explanation of how you would use the questions in deciding on the effectiveness of the control over payrolls.

Formulate your own answer before examining the solution that follows.

SOLUTION

a.
1. *Costs and feasibility:* Is the overall system working efficiently and smoothly? Are there any glaring weaknesses? Is there any unnecessary routine or duplication of effort?
2. *Supervision:* Who supervises payments? Are time records approved by a timekeeper or foreman?
3. *Reliable personnel:* Who prepares payrolls? Have their past employment references been checked? What is their performance record as far as efficiency is concerned?

[6] Adapted from a CPA examination.

4. *Separation of powers:* Are hiring and firing properly authorized and reported? Are pay rates and changes properly authorized and reported? Is payroll preparation divided among employees?
5. *Routine and automatic checks:* Are receipts submitted by employees? How do employees identify themselves? How is validity of signatures checked? What procedures are used for review, approval, and reconciliation of payroll charges to various accounts?
6. *Document control:* Who has control over unclaimed pay envelopes? How are envelopes claimed after regular pay dates? Are time clocks used? Are time records properly prepared and controlled?
7. *Employee responsibility:* Who is in charge of each step in the payroll process? Do overtime hours require special approval? By whom?
8. *Bonding and vacations:* Are key payroll employees bonded? Is there rotation of payroll duties?
9. *Independent check:* Are payroll calculations independently checked before payment? Do auditors witness or perform a distribution of payroll, including control of unclaimed envelopes? Are receipts compared with payroll by somebody not engaged in payroll preparation?
10. *Physical safeguards:* Are there physical safeguards, like alarm systems, police, safes, and the like?

b. These questions were asked to determine that hiring and separation, accumulation of periodic payroll time and rate records, and payouts were handled with a minimum chance of error, fraud, and waste. The questions above are designed to discover whether duties are separated, whether adequate personnel and payroll records are kept, and whether proper authority and supervision are exercised at every step affecting payroll. The controller wants satisfactory cross-checks, physical safeguards, rotation of duties, step-by-step routines, and constant review and supervision.

appendix: factory ledgers

In this appendix, we study an example of some specialized techniques for accumulating accounting data. The purpose here is not to dwell on the intricacies of a specific system. Rather, it is to offer an overview of the immense task of effective systems design. Persons without accounting experience often find it difficult to visualize the avalanche of paper work that most companies face. It should be recognized that routine data collection and classification is the most time-consuming task of the controller's department. That is why the expenditure of time, care, and money on planning and shaping an accounting system is nearly always a worthwhile investment.

classification and coding

Any sizable company finds it convenient to classify accounts in detail and to number or otherwise code the accounts accordingly. Although an outsider may not know what the code means, accounting employees become so familiar with the code that they think, talk, and write in terms of account numbers instead of account names. Thus, if

Cash is account No. 1000 and Accounts Payable is account No. 7000, an outside auditor may find payments to creditors journalized as follows:

		MONEY COLUMNS	
#7000		125,000	
	#1000		125,000

A company usually has a chart of accounts that classifies all accounts in the entire company by name and code number. Codes differ from company to company. Each coding system is usually some variation on the following example:

GEOGRAPHIC LOCATION	GENERAL-LEDGER ACCOUNT	DEPARTMENT	SUBSIDIARY CLASSIFICATION
0	00	000	000

This classification may be used by a multiplant company with far-flung operations. It would be too cumbersome for many companies and not detailed enough for giant companies.

Assume that a company has a central plant in Chicago and branch plants in Dallas, Pittsburgh, and San Francisco. Debits for various sample transactions could be coded as shown in Exhibit 21-1.

The numbers used to code debits and credits are obtained from the company chart of accounts. These numbers are originally entered or keypunched

EXHIBIT 21-1

SAMPLE ENTRIES USING ACCOUNT CODING

		NUMBER CODE FOR DEBIT			
SAMPLE TRANSACTION	GENERAL-LEDGER ENTRY	GEOGRAPHIC LOCATION	GENERAL-LEDGER ACCOUNT	DEPARTMENT	SUBSIDIARY CLASSIFICATION
1. Requisition of supplies by a machining department in Chicago	Factory-overhead control Stores	1	91	011	112
2. Requisition of supplies by a finishing department in Dallas	Factory-overhead control Stores	2	91	015	112
3. Indirect labor incurred by machining department in San Francisco	Factory-overhead control Stores	4	91	011	202
4. President's salary	Administrative-expenses control Accrued payroll	1	98	060	801

on the source documents (requisitions, vouchers, work tickets) that are the basis for ledger entries and other analyses. For example, Chicago is coded as 1, Factory Overhead Control as 91, a machining department as 011, and supplies used as 112. The account number for such a transaction would be 1-91-011-112. What would be the complete account number for indirect-labor cost incurred by the finishing department in Chicago? The answer is 1-91-015-202.

branch ledger Many companies have branch plants sprawled all over the country and the world. Cost accumulation and analysis are most often conducted at the various geographic locations, whereas records of receivables, payables, and similar accounts may be centralized in the home office. The division of accounting between central headquarters and a branch plant calls for splitting the accounts between the two locations. At the same time, some technique must be used to ensure the dovetailing of all company accounts so that duplications, omissions, and other errors are minimized. Generally, two *reciprocal accounts* are introduced, one in the home office and one at the factory.

example

The central offices of the Homeware Company are in Chicago, but the manufacturing operations are located in Richmond, Indiana, The company uses a separate factory ledger that is maintained at Richmond for the benefit of the plant management. The factory is given credit for finished goods at cost when the goods are shipped to the central warehouses. All goods are shipped to customers from the warehouses.

The chart of general-ledger accounts for the company is as follows:

CODE	HOME-OFFICE ACCOUNTS	CODE	FACTORY ACCOUNTS
1	Cash in bank	A	Stores control
2	Accounts-receivable control	B	Work-in-process control
3	Finished-goods control	C	Factory overhead applied
4	Plant and equipment control	D	Factory-overhead control
5	Allowance for depreciation	E	Home-office-ledger control
6	Accounts payable		
7	Accrued payroll		
8	Common stock		
9	Retained earnings		
10	Factory-ledger control		
11	Sales		
12	Cost of goods sold		
13	Selling-cost control		
14	Administrative-cost control		

Below is a summary of some transactions for one month.

Indicate the accounts debited and credited in the factory ledger and in the home office ledger. Show postings and ending balances in Factory-Ledger Control and Home-Office-Ledger Control. Try to solve this problem yourself before looking at the solution.

PARTIAL LIST OF TRANSACTIONS	
1. Materials purchased on credit	$200,000
2. Direct materials requisitioned	150,000
3. Factory payroll accrued (direct labor, $130,000; other, $70,000)	200,000
4. Miscellaneous factory overhead incurred*	68,000
5. Factory overhead applied	65,000
6. Cost of goods shipped to warehouse	325,000
7. Cost of goods sold	300,000
8. Sales (on credit)	450,000
9. Cash collected on account	340,000

* Credit Accounts Payable, except for $5,000 depreciation.

SOLUTION Remember that this is only an example. The solution is shown in Exhibit 21-2. A general ledger may be split into two or more parts in any manner whatsoever, depending on practical needs. Thus, the ledger in our example could have been designed so that accounts for plant and equipment could be kept at the factory instead of at the home office. If this were done, what journal entry or entries would be changed?

Difficulties in factory-ledger accounting center around lagging or otherwise faulty communications, which result in disagreement in the balances of the reciprocal accounts. Common causes for discrepancies include transfers of inventories and cash that are in transit at the trial-balance cutoff date and failure to recognize nonroutine payments for factory costs by the office on behalf of the branch.

QUESTIONS, PROBLEMS, AND CASES

21-1 "Business operations would be a hopeless tangle without the paperwork that is often regarded with disdain." Explain.

21-2 Define *internal control.* Distinguish it from *internal check.*

21-3 "There are ten check points that I always use as a framework for judging the effectiveness of an internal-control system." Name nine of the ten.

21-4 "The words *internal control* are commonly misunderstood. They are thought to refer to those facets of the accounting system that are supposed to help prevent embezzling." Do you agree? Why?

21-5 "Internal-control systems have both negative and positive objectives." Do you agree? Explain.

21-6 Briefly describe how a bottler of soda water might compile data regarding control of finished product at the plant, where normal breakage can be expected.

21-7 The branch manager of a national retail grocery chain has stated, "My managers are judged more heavily on the basis of their merchandise-shrinkage control than on their overall sales volume." Why? Explain.

21-8 *Appraisal of Payroll System* (CPA) The Generous Loan Company has 100 branch loan offices. Each office has a manager and four or five subordinates who are employed by the manager. Branch managers prepare the weekly payroll, including their own salaries, and pay their employees from cash on

EXHIBIT 21-2

SAMPLE JOURNAL ENTRIES FOR BRANCH ACCOUNTING

TRANSACTION	HOME-OFFICE LEDGER			FACTORY LEDGER			ENTRIES THAT WOULD BE MADE IN A REGULAR, UNIFIED LEDGER		
1. Material purchases	Factory-ledger control	200,000		Stores control	200,000		Stores control	200,000	
	Accounts payable		200,000	Home-office-ledger control		200,000	Accounts payable		200,000
2. Requisitions	None			Work-in-process control	150,000		Work-in-process control	150,000	
				Stores control		150,000	Stores control		150,000
3. Factory payroll	Factory-ledger control	200,000		Work-in-process control	130,000		Work-in-process control	130,000	
	Accrued payroll		200,000	Factory-overhead control	70,000		Factory-overhead control	70,000	
				Home-office-ledger control		200,000	Accrued payroll		200,000
4. Miscellaneous overhead	Factory-ledger control	68,000		Factory-overhead control	68,000		Factory-overhead control	68,000	
	Allowance for depreciation		5,000	Home-office-ledger control		68,000	Allowance for depreciation		5,000
	Accounts payable		63,000				Accounts payable		63,000
5. Overhead application	None			Work-in-process control	65,000		Work-in-process control	65,000	
				Factory overhead applied		65,000	Factory overhead applied		65,000
6. Shipments to warehouse	Finished-goods control	325,000		Home-office-ledger control	325,000		Finished-goods control	325,000	
	Factory-ledger control		325,000	Work-in-process control		325,000	Work-in-process control		325,000
7. Cost of goods sold	Cost of goods sold	300,000		None			Cost of goods sold	300,000	
	Finished-goods control		300,000				Finished-goods control		300,000
8. Sales	Accounts-receivable control	450,000		None			Accounts-receivable control	450,000	
	Sales		450,000				Sales		450,000
9. Collections	Cash	340,000		None			Cash	340,000	
	Accounts-receivable control		340,000				Accounts-receivable control		340,000

Postings:

Factory-Ledger Control

(1)	200,000	(6)	325,000
(3)	200,000		
(4)	68,000		
		To bal.	143,000
Bal.	143,000		

Home-Office-Ledger Control

(6)	325,000	(1)	200,000
		(3)	200,000
		(4)	68,000
To bal.	143,000		
		Bal.	143,000

hand. The employee signs the payroll sheet, signifying receipt of his salary. Hours worked by hourly personnel are inserted in the payroll sheet from time cards prepared by the employees and approved by the manager.

The weekly payroll sheets are sent to the home office along with other accounting statements and reports. The home office compiles employee earnings records and prepares all federal and state salary reports from the weekly payroll sheets.

Salaries are established by home-office job-evaluation schedules. Salary adjustments, promotions, and transfers of full-time employees are approved by a home-office salary committee, based upon the recommendations of branch managers and area supervisors. Branch managers advise the salary committee of new full-time employees and of terminations. Part-time and temporary employees are hired without referral to the salary committee.

required

Based upon your review of the payroll system, how might payroll funds be diverted?

21-9 *Film Processing* (W. Crum) Write not over one page about the possible areas where internal controls should be instituted in the business described briefly below. Keep in mind the size of the business and do not suggest controls of a type impossible to set up in a firm of this sort. Make any reasonable assumptions about management duties and policies not expressly set forth below.

You have a film-developing service in Glendale, with ten men driving their own cars six days a week to contact about 40 places each, where film is left to be picked up and developed. Routes cover all parts of Los Angeles. Drivers bring film in one day, and return the processed film the second or third day later. Stores pay the route man for his charges made on film picked up at their store, less a percentage for their work as an agency. The route man then turns this cash into the Glendale office, where all film is developed and books are kept. Six to ten employees work at the office in Glendale, depending on the volume of work. You run the office and have one full-time accounting-clerical employee. Route drivers are paid monthly by mile of route covered.

21-10 *Retail Method and Internal Control* The following figures pertain to the Zenith Gift Store for the two-month period, November and December, 19_8.

Sales	$170,000	Purchases (at sales price)	$ 80,000
Additional markups	10,000	Inventory at November 1, 19_8:	
Markdowns	25,000	At cost price	105,000
Purchases (at cost price)	52,000	At selling price	160,000

required

1. What should the inventory amount to at December 31, 19_8, at retail price using the conventional retail inventory method?
2. Suppose the allowable shrinkage is 2 percent of sales. The physical inventory at retail prices at December 31 amounts to $50,000. What is the inventory shortage?

21-11 *Retail Method and Internal Control* (Suggested by W. Crum) The following data are for a ladies' clothing department in a large department store at retail selling prices:

Net sales	$1,900,000	Transfers in from other branches	$30,000
Discounts granted to employees, churches, etc.	23,500	Transfers out to other branches	12,000
Beginning inventory	900,000	Additional markups	14,000
Net purchases	2,068,000	Markdowns	79,000

required

1. What should be the ending inventory at retail prices using the conventional retail inventory method and assuming no allowances for losses (shrinkage)?
2. Suppose the estimated shrinkage is 1 percent of sales. What should be the ending inventory at retail prices? Suppose the cost ratio is 62 percent—that is, the *cost* of the ending inventory is approximated at 62 percent of retail price. What should be the ending inventory at cost?
3. The actual ending physical inventory at retail is $950,000. What is the total loss at retail? At cost? Prepare a section of the income statement through gross profit on sales. Assume that beginning inventory at cost was $580,000 and that applicable net purchases at cost were $1,280,000.

21-12 *Appraisal of Internal Control System* From the *San Francisco Chronicle,* April 3, 1971:

> The flap over missing ferry fares was peacefully—and openly—resolved at a meeting of the Golden Gate Bridge District finance committee yesterday.
>
> Only a week ago, the subject was a matter of furious dispute in which bridge manager Dale W. Luehring was twice called a liar and there were prospects of a closed meeting on personnel matters.
>
> But yesterday, after a week of investigation, the meeting turned out to be public after all, and attorney Thomas M. Jenkins revealed the full total of stolen ferry tickets equaled $26.20.
>
> The controversy began when auditor Gordon Dahlgren complained that there was an auditing "problem" and that he had not been informed when four children swiped $13.75 worth of tickets February 28. Committee chairman Ben K. Lerer, of San Francisco, ordered a full investigation.
>
> Jenkins said the situation was complicated because children under 5 have been allowed to ride the ferry without a ticket, but after May 1 everyone will have to have a ticket, allowing for a closer audit.
>
> Secondly, Jenkins explained, the "vault" in which tickets are deposited was proved insecure (resulting in two thefts totaling $26.20 worth of tickets) but has been replaced.
>
> In the future, it was decided, all thefts of cash or tickets must be reported immediately to the California Highway Patrol or the local police, the bridge lieutenant on duty, the general manager, the security officer, the auditor-controller, and the transit manager.
>
> In addition, employees must make a full written report within 24 hours to the president of the district board, the chairman of the finance-auditing committee, the auditor controller, the attorney, the bus transit manager, the water transit manager, the toll captain, and the chief of administration and security.

required

What is your reaction to the new system? Explain, giving particular attention to applicable criteria for appraising an internal-control system.

21-13 *Use of Credit Card* A business-school student used a BankAmericard for a variety of purchases. When checking his monthly bill, he compared his original copy with a duplicate copy for a gasoline purchase made at a local discount-store shopping center. The original copy showed a purchase of $4.25; the duplicate was raised to $6.25.

required

Who obtained the extra $2.00? How can the system be improved to prevent such thievery?

21-14 *Multiple Choice; Discovering Irregularities* In questions 1 through 7, you are given a well-recognized procedure of internal control. You are to identify the irregularity *that will be discovered or prevented by each procedure.* Write the numbers

1 through 7 on your answer sheet. Then place the letter of your chosen answer next to your numbers.

1. The general-ledger-control account and the subsidiary ledger of accounts receivable are reconciled monthly. The two bookkeepers are independent.
   a. The accounts-receivable subsidiary-ledger bookkeeper charges a customer with $72 instead of $74, the correct amount. The error is due to misreading the sales slip. The credit-sales summary for the day has the correct amount of $74.
   b. The accounts-receivable subsidiary-ledger bookkeeper charges a sale to Mr. Smith instead of Mr. Smithe (that is, the wrong customer). The error is due to misreading the sales slip.
   c. The employee opening mail abstracts funds without making a record of their receipt. Customer accounts are not credited with their payments.
   d. The general-ledger bookkeeper takes funds and covers the loss by charging "Miscellaneous General Expenses."
   e. When friends purchase merchandise, the salesclerk allows them an employee discount by using an employee name on the sales slip and deducting the discount on the slip. This is against company policy.
2. The voucher system requires that invoices be compared with receiving reports and express bills before a voucher is prepared and approved for payment.
   a. Unrecorded checks appear in the bank statement.
   b. The treasurer takes funds by preparing a fictitious voucher charging "Miscellaneous General Expenses."
   c. An employee in the purchasing department sends through fictitious invoices and receives payment.
   d. A cash shortage is covered by underfooting outstanding checks on the bank reconciliation.
   e. A cash shortage is covered by omitting some of the outstanding checks from the bank reconciliation.
3. Both cash and credit customers are educated to expect a sales ticket. Tickets are serially numbered. All numbers are accounted for daily.
   a. Customers complain that their monthly bills contain items that have been paid.
   b. Some customers have the correct change for the merchandise purchased. They pay and do not wait for a sales ticket.
   c. Customers complain that they are billed for goods they did not purchase.
   d. Customers complain that goods ordered are not received.
   e. Salesclerks destroy duplicate sales tickets for the amount of cash stolen.
4. The storekeeper should sign a receipt for goods received from the receiving and inspection room, and no payment should be made without his signature.
   a. Invoices are paid twice.
   b. Employees send through fictitious invoices and receive payment.
   c. Materials are withdrawn from the storeroom for personal use rather than for business purposes.
   d. Employees send through purchase requisitions for materials for personal use. After the materials are received and receiving reports are issued, employees take the merchandise for personal use.
   e. The storekeeper takes materials and charges them to company use.
5. At a movie theater box office, all tickets are prenumbered. At the end of each day, the beginning ticket number is subtracted from the ending number to give the number of tickets sold. Cash is counted and compared with the number of tickets sold.

a. The box office gives too much change.
b. The ticket taker admits his friends without a ticket.
c. The manager gives theater passes for personal expenses. This is against company policy.
d. A test check of customers entering the theatre does not reconcile with ticket sales.
e. Tickets from a previous day are discovered in the ticket taker's stub box despite the fact that tickets are stamped "Good on Date of Purchase Only."

6. In Hutchinson Commons Cafeteria, the customers enter at an *IN* door and choose their meals. Before leaving the serving rail, they are billed by a biller for the food taken. After they eat, they present their bills and make payments to a cashier. At the end of the day, cash receipts are reconciled with billings.
   a. A friend of the biller and the cashier moves through the lines and takes a free meal without being billed or paying.
   b. A customer who has been billed goes out the *IN* entrance without paying.
   c. Meat is stolen by an employee.
   d. The biller makes an error by billing an order at $1.15 instead of the correct amount, $1.35.
   e. A customer sneaks under the serving rail, takes an extra cup of coffee, sneaks back under the rail, and returns to his table.
7. The duties of cashier and accounts-receivable bookkeeper should be separated.
   a. There are two cashiers. At the end of a certain day, there is a sizable cash shortage. Each cashier blames the other. It is impossible to fix responsibility.
   b. A cash shortage is covered by overfooting (overadding) cash in transit on the bank reconciliation.
   c. A cash shortage is covered by charging it to "Miscellaneous General Expenses."
   d. Customers who paid their accounts in cash complain that they still receive statements of balances due.
   e. The accounts-receivable bookkeeper charges off the accounts of friends to "Allowance for Bad Debts."

21-15 Refer to Exhibit 21-1. State the debit number code for: (a) requisition of supplies by a finishing department in San Francisco; (b) indirect labor incurred by a machining department in Dallas.

21-16 *Factory-Ledger Fundamentals* Refer to the chart of general-ledger accounts used in the factory-ledger illustration in this chapter. Indicate the proper journal entries for the following transactions. Set up your solution in a form similar to the one illustrated in Exhibit 21-2.

1. Payments made to creditors on open account	$ 50,000
2. Cash sales	3,000
3. Depreciation on factory equipment	15,000
4. Declaration of dividend	24,000
5. Payment of payroll	105,000
6. Return of materials to vendors	2,000
7. Direct materials requisitioned	40,000
8. Factory overhead applied	30,000
9. Cost of goods shipped to warehouse	50,000
10. Cost of goods sold	25,000

21-17 *Factory Ledger* (SIA) The DEF Company uses both a factory ledger, which includes all transactions up to Cost of Sales, and a general ledger. It records its cost under a job-cost plan.

The following transactions took place during the month of March:

1. Materials purchased and delivered directly to production order No. 305—$200.
2. Depreciation on factory buildings and equipment—$5,000.
3. Finished goods returned for credit—$2,000.
4. Cost of finished goods returned—$1,200.
5. The raw-material book inventory at the end of the month amounted to $354,348. A physical inventory taken at that time showed a value of $354,148.

required

Prepare the journal entries necessary to record this information in the general and factory ledgers.

21-18 *Factory Ledger; Journal Entries* The home offices of the Splitpea Company are in Chicago, but the manufacturing operations are located in Gary. The company uses a separate factory ledger, which is maintained at Gary for the benefit of the plant management. The factory is given credit for finished goods when the goods are shipped to the central warehouses. All goods are shipped to customers from the warehouses.

Some transactions for the month of March 19_6 are summarized below:

1. Miscellaneous manufacturing expenses incurred—$10,000. The invoices for $10,000 were received.
2. Materials received by the factory (proper invoice received)—$75,000.
3. Sales to customers billed during March—$90,000.
4. Factory cost of goods sold—$70,000.
5. Direct materials placed into production—$50,000.

Questions 6–8 refer to certain discrepancies that were found upon auditing the reconciliation accounts. You are to select the entry (or entries) that *would correct* the general-ledger accounts involved.

6. Salesmen's salaries of $2,000 were incorrectly charged to Manufacturing-Expense Control
7. Machinery of $1,200 purchased by the home office for the branch was taken up in the branch books as a Stores item.
8. The machinery in 7 had been ignored in computing depreciation for one month (rate, 1 percent per month).

CODE	*HOME OFFICE ACCOUNTS*	*CODE*	*FACTORY ACCOUNTS*
1	Cash in bank	A	Material-stores control
2	Accounts receivable	B	Work-in-process control
3	Finished goods	C	Manufacturing-expense control
4	Accounts payable	D	Manufacturing expense applied
5	Accrued payroll	E	Home-office-ledger control
6	Common stock	F	Direct-labor control
7	Retained earnings		
8	Factory-ledger control		
9	Sales		
10	Factory cost of goods sold		
11	Selling-cost control		
12	Administrative-cost control		
13	Plant and equipment control		
14	Allowance for depreciation		

required

For each of the eight transactions, indicate by code the accounts debited and credited in the factory ledger and the home ledger. Use the account codes given. More than one account may be debited or credited for each entry.

Note The following two problems are from *Case Problems in Internal Auditing and Control* (Prentice-Hall, Inc.).

21-19 *Internal Audit of Inventory Differences* Superfine Supermarkets is the operator of a chain of ninety-five supermarket grocery stores. The individual stores are the familiar supermarket type, located in community shopping centers in the outskirts of a number of large cities in the Middle West. The company makes careful studies of potential locations before establishing a unit, and in general will not give consideration to any location in which the potential first-year volume is under $500,000. The result of this policy is that each of the units is a sizable operation, with volume running from $1,200,000 per year.

Control of packaged grocery items follows the customary pattern of retail inventory value. The majority of products handled in the stores are ordered by the store managers from the central warehouse, where accounting control over the stores is maintained. At the time of shipment, the store inventory account is charged with the retail sales value of the shipment. Perishable products, such as dairy items, are delivered directly to stores by suppliers. These direct deliveries are reported to the warehouse on the store report, where they are compared with billing by suppliers. On the basis of this billing, the store inventory account is charged at selling price.

When a price change is made, the store reports inventory of the products affected by the change to the warehouse, and corresponding adjustment is made in the retail inventory control value.

Fruits and vegetables are handled by a separate produce supervisor, who has authority to order according to his own judgment. Highly perishable items may be purchased locally, while semiperishables, such as potatoes and oranges, are ordered from the warehouse. In this department, the maintenance of a strict monetary control based upon units is not feasible, because much of the product is supplied in bulk for repackaging and there is considerable loss because of waste and spoilage. Consequently, inventory control over the produce department is effected by charging the produce department at cost for all shipments from the warehouse or direct purchases.

The meat department is handled on a basis similar to the produce department. The reason for this is that the large meat items, such as a side of beef, are delivered at a single overall price per pound. The butchers in the meat department then cut the meat, with the value of the final cut depending on the desirability of the meat. There is also considerable waste in bones, fat, and similar unsalable items.

To a considerable degree, the profit of the meat and produce departments will depend on the skill of the managers. The expertness of the butchering will be a most important factor in the meat department, while skill in purchasing and anticipating requirements will be a governing factor in the profitability of the produce operations. Consequently, supervisory control over produce and meat departments is through a watch of gross margin realized from sales.

So far we have been concerned with the charges to inventory controls. To summarize, packaged groceries are charged at retail, while produce and meat are charged at cost. For purposes of this problem, we will assume that all credits will come through sales (disregarding minor adjusting items such as breakage, returnable containers, and the like). Sales credits are developed when customers pass by the checking counters. The cashier-checkers, in operating their cash registers, develop separate totals for the three departments.

Thus, total sales are developed separately for packaged groceries, produce, and meat. Register totals are taken each day by the store manager and recorded on the daily report to the warehouse accounting office. Entry of these sales in the accounting records has the following results:

1. In the case of packaged groceries, total reported sales should offset original charges at retail selling price.
2. In the case of produce and meats, sales in comparison with cost will result in development of separate gross-margin figures for each of these departments.

Under company policy, internal auditors take inventories of stores every three months. Packaged-grocery inventories are taken at selling prices, so that there should be no difference if all transactions were perfectly handled, and if there had been no losses from theft by customers or for other reasons. Naturally, perfect operation does not exist, and it is usual to develop a shortage, which is written off at the time of inventory. In the produce and meat departments, the physical inventory by auditors is used to adjust the book value, which is arrived at through applying an estimated percentage of markdown to reported sales for each accounting period.

Below are shown final figures developed as the result of three inventories of the Springfield store. In the case of the packaged grocery department, a percentage of loss (shrinkage) in relation to sales for the period is shown; in the case of produce and meat, the percentage of gross margin on sales developed as a result of the inventories is the figure given.

	PACKAGED GROCERIES (SHRINKAGE)	*PRODUCE MARGIN*	*MEAT MARGIN*
January	⅔%	20%	23%
April	3% over	10%	32%
July	4% short	15%	24%

One of the control records that is maintained is a comparative record of packaged grocery inventory shrinkage and produce- and meat-department margins at all stores. In checking the January inventory, you find that all the Springfield store figures are comparable with other stores and may therefore be assumed to be correct. A further factor in considering the answer to the questions is the quantity of the average inventory. In packaged groceries, it is three weeks' sales; in produce, two days; and in meat, one week.

required

1. In the April inventory, what items merit immediate attention and follow-up? What are the possible explanations for the apparent abnormalities?
2. In the July inventory, which items appear to be out of line? What would be possible explanations?

21-20 *Analysis of Production and Shipping Control* The Cucaracha Coffee Company is a large producer of coffee for the retail market. Each day, 300,000 pounds of green coffee are roasted; this results in finished-goods production of somewhat more than 250,000 pounds, as there is a loss in roasting of from 14 to 15 percent of the original weight of the green coffee. This loss is known as "shrinkage." About one-half the production is in the most expensive coffee, Cuca Special, which is packed in vacuum cans. The remainder is in a cheaper blend that is packed in paper bags.

From the roasting plant, shipment is made by truck to fifty distributing branches, from which sale and delivery are made to 100,000 retail grocery stores.

part I From an anonymous source, a report comes to the company that the most expensive grade of coffee—the vacuum pack—is being stolen from the roasting plant and sold to retail stores. Original investigation of this report is assigned to the sales branch in the territory from which the report comes. They find that the company's Cuca brand is being offered for sale in several small stores in poorer neighborhoods at a price that is considerably lower than the usual retail price and that is even somewhat lower than the company's selling price to its smaller outlets. The branch has no record of sales to these stores, so it seems quite possible that the report of stealing is true.

As internal auditor, you are then assigned to checking the entire control plan for finished products at the roasting plant, to the end of finding out where the possibility of leakage exists and who may be responsible. As has been previously mentioned, the production is over 250,000 pounds per day, packed in shipping cases of 24 pounds; this means that over ten thousand cases clear through the production and shipping cycle each day.

You begin by observing the whole production operation, which starts with the dumping of green coffee from the bags in which it is received into mixers. Various grades and types are combined according to formulas prescribed by the coffee blenders, with a total of twenty bags being combined and mixed in a single batch. After mixing, the coffee is stored in hoppers from which it is fed to the roasters. The roasting is done in batches of about 600 pounds; after roasting, the coffee is cooled and conveyed to grinders, and then the ground coffee is fed into hoppers that feed the scales on the automatic packing lines.

The vacuum-can packing lines on which Cuca Special is produced are highly automatic and operate at a speed of about 150 cans per minute for each line. The employees on the line are principally concerned with watching for cans that may not be completely filled, damaged or defective cans, or anything else that may be wrong in the finished product or that may interrupt the operation of the line. At the end of the lines, cans are accumulated in lots of 24, which are put into corrugated cases that run through a machine that seals the cases on top and bottom. The finished cases are then stacked upon platform skids in lots of sixty cases to each skid.

The packing lines for the cheaper grade of coffee, which is packed in bags, are less automatic, because the paper bags cannot be handled in the packing equipment. On these lines, the empty bags are unfolded by hand by a girl who holds them under a scale that is set to "dump" 25 pounds a minute. This speed sets the pace for the line. After filling, the bags move on a conveyor belt past girls who fold over and seal the tops. At the end of the line, bags are packed in cases of 24 pounds each; these cases are sealed in a case sealer and then stacked on skids, also in lots of sixty cases.

To the point that the cases leave the packing line, your observation is that there is no opportunity for abstraction of finished goods. The entire flow is mechanical, down through the filling operation. Once the coffee is in containers, it is under observation by a number of employees until it is packed in cases and the cases are sealed and placed on skids.

Separate packing foremen supervise the vacuum and bag lines. As skids are loaded, the number of skids loaded is tallied before they are moved to the shipping floor. This tally is forwarded to the factory accounting department and serves to establish the original charge to the finished-goods inventory. When skids are moved to the shipping floor, the shipping clerk acknowledges the quantities received, and subsequently accounts for these quantities as shipments to branches or as stock on hand.

Shipping-floor stocks are checked by physical inventory taken by the plant accounting department every few days, and quantities reported shipped (which are the credits to inventory) are reported to the central-office accounting department where they are checked with quantities acknowledged by sales branches. You examine all the reports of production, inventory, and acknowledgement and can find only inconsequential differences for the several months that you check.

Despite the seeming indication that all is in order, you are faced with the fact that the sales-department reports indicate very definitely that coffee is being stolen. You then conclude that the only possibility is collusion within the plant. Again reviewing the established controls, you narrow the field. Your final conclusion is determined to some extent by the fact that the tally sheet of skid loads delivered to the shipping floor is a check sheet, prepared in pencil, that could readily be altered.

What would be your analysis of the situation and of the employees who must be in on any collusion? Pause and formulate your own answer before proceeding to Part II.

part II Based on your analysis of the employees who may be involved, other plant employees and outside detectives have "broken" the case, with the result that the accounting department employee who handles the production records has confessed to altering the tally sheets by one skid load (1,440 pounds) each day, and a shipping clerk has confessed to giving this extra skid load to one of the regular truckers, who in turn sold it to outside sources for about one-half the regular selling price.

Your next concern is consideration of further controls to guard against a repetition. You decide that one or two of the following four possibilities would provide greater protective control. (In your recommendation, you are concerned with the cost to the company, with the value to management, and with the capabilities of the employees who must prepare the reports.)

1. To have an additional tally sheet prepared by the operator of the lift truck who moves the filled skids from the packing lines to the shipping floor.
2. To install a cumulative, nonresettable counter on the case-sealing machine and to provide for daily counter readings, which must balance with inventory controls over production.
3. To balance the consumption of vacuum cans with production on a monthly basis, when physical inventory of cans on hand is taken. This would require the keeping of a count of cans spoiled and discarded in packing lines—which has not previously been taken.
4. To check carefully each month and inquire into any unusual variations in "shrinkage" between the weight of green coffee put into process and the weight of roasted coffee produced. As previously mentioned, this figure may vary between 14 and 15 percent normally.

required

Two of these plans you discard, and two you recommend. In recommending one of them, a factor in your recommendation is the value that the control figures will have for the plant management.

Tell which plans are discarded and why, and the reasons for recommendation of the remaining two.

21-21 *Hospital Internal Control* You have been contracted to study various means to help reduce the overall cost of running a hospital. Your first project is in the pharmacy. Upon discussing the issue of drug usage and control, various pharmacists have indicated a suspicion that a significant quantity of drugs is not accounted for. There were three possible sources of loss: (a) breakage, spillage, and wastage, (b) failure to charge patient for drugs actually delivered, and (c) theft.

The chief pharmacist estimates that the revenue value of these losses is about $120,000 per year. The three causes listed earlier probably each account for one-third of this amount. The actual invoice cost of drugs is about one-quarter of the billing price that patients pay. Drugs are ordered in bulk, and large quantities are held in inventory to minimize stockouts. Ordering and handling costs account for another 10 percent of the drug invoice cost. The remaining drug markup covers miscellaneous pharmacy overhead and contribution to hospital overhead.

Under the present system, the source document for billing purposes is the medical record sheet filled out by the nurse each time she administers medication. When the doctor prescribes a specific drug, the request is sent to the pharmacy, where the order is filled and sent up to the floor along with the rest of the drugs for that ward. The medication containers have the patients' names on them and are placed in open bins in the storeroom according to room number. The storeroom is located in the central nursing area, adjacent to the head nurse's office. The storeroom is never locked, since many different nurses and doctors use the room around the clock to prepare medication.

When the pharmacist fills the order, he includes the number of doses that will probably be required during the next three or four days. Unused portions of the order that can be reused (i.e., pills, sealed immunization ampules) are returned to the pharmacy when the patient no longer requires them. The actual number of units in the container is not tallied because it is irrelevant, as billing comes from the medical record sheet. So, if any medication is lost either through accident, neglect, or mischief, no one would really be able to trace the actual amount lost.

Two new systems have been proposed to improve the situation. One involves charging patients for all medication when the orders are filled by the pharmacist and crediting each patient for any usable returns. This "front-end-billing" is commonly used in some other hospitals. With this system, there is no lost revenue; the patient pays for all drugs that theoretically have been allocated to him. It is estimated that revenue would increase by $120,000 annually if this system were implemented. Two clerks would be needed to handle credits at a total annual cost of $16,000.

The other system involves installation of three satellite pharmacies in strategic locations in the wards. These would replace the present medication storerooms. Full-time pharmacists would be in charge of these satellites. They would be responsible for all inventory and would place exactly the needed medication for each shift in a tray for the nurse. If the pharmacist felt that a particular nurse might be neglectful in recording drug administration, he could compare her medical record sheet with his records. Since the pharmacist would be the only person to have access to the satellite inventory, and since this inventory would be accurately quantified as it left the central pharmacy and had to be completely accounted for, it was felt that losses would be almost entirely eliminated. Rescheduling of personnel and shifting of inventory from the central pharmacy would enable satellite operation at an increased annual cost of $24,000.

required

1. What is the actual current loss of net income due to the drug-control problem?
2. Of the systems being considered, which would you recommend? Explain fully.

Decentralization and Transfer Pricing

22

This chapter and the next focus on the role of accounting systems in decentralized organizations. In this chapter we examine the nature of decentralization, profit centers, and transfer pricing. The succeeding chapter concentrates on investment centers, whereby profits are related to the investments in subunits of an organization. The problems described here extend to all types of organizations, including many parts of not-for-profit organizations.

nature of decentralization

relative freedom to make decisions

As organizations grow, top managers face two continuing problems: (a) how to divide activities and responsibilities, and (b) how to coordinate subunits. Inevitably, the power to make decisions is distributed among various managers. *The essence of decentralization is the freedom to make decisions.* Decentralization is a matter of degree. Total decentralization means minimum constraints and maximum freedom for managers to make decisions, even at the lowest levels. At the other extreme of the continuum, total centralization means maximum constraints and minimum freedom.

In practice, organizations are seldom totally centralized or decentralized. Full centralization is not economic in most instances, because of the impossibility of administering the unavoidable massive volume of decisions at the top-management level. On the other hand, full decentralization implies a collection of completely separate businesses. Solomons[1] has pointed out that subunits should be more than investments. They should contribute not only to the success of the corporation but to the success of each other. They may use a common raw material and therefore permit its purchase more cheaply in bulk. They may provide complementary products (like phonographs and records), so that each division's products help to create a demand for the others'. They may share technical information about manufacturing processes or market information about various channels of distribution.

benefits of decentralization

How should top managers decide on how much decentralization is optimal? The optimal amount of decentralization is the amount that attains top management's overall objectives most efficiently and effectively. These objectives are often expressed as the maximization of short-run profits, of long-run profits, of rate of return, of net present value, or as some other measure.

Conceptually, top managers try to choose a degree of decentralization that maximizes the excess of benefits over costs. Practically, top managers cannot quantify either the benefits or the costs. Nevertheless, this cost-benefit approach helps us identify the central issues.

The claimed benefits of decentralization include the following:

1. Optimal decisions are more likely, because the manager of the subunit is in a better position to react to information about local conditions in a timely way.
2. The burden of decision making is distributed, so that the managers' collective decisions are optimized. Top managers are also likely to have more time for strategic planning than if they had to control day-to-day operations.
3. Greater freedom heightens the managers' incentives, because they have more control over the factors that affect the measures of their performance.
4. Greater freedom induces managers to check outside markets for both raw materials and finished goods more frequently. Intracompany transfers of goods or services are often based on these market prices instead of on costs. Where market-based prices are used as a part of the information system, there is a routine check on market forces that is otherwise not available. This built-in check on market prices often focuses on uneconomic activities that would not be as readily detected in a centralized system.

[1] David Solomons, *Divisional Performance: Measurement and Control* (Homewood, Ill.: Richard D. Irwin, Inc., 1968), p. 10. His Chapter 1 is a good summary of the organization of divisionalized businesses.

5. More decision making on a wide spectrum provides better training for managers as they rise in the organization.
6. Decentralization is often accompanied by the use of profit or investment centers. The managership of a profit center is somehow viewed as a higher-status position than that of a cost center and therefore may provide the psychological benefits of first-class citizenship. In other words, the profit-center structure has a more desirable motivational effect.

All these claimed advantages are "benefits" because they are supposed to result in larger gross increases in profits than would occur with a more heavily centralized organization.

costs of decentralization

The largest cost of decentralization is probably dysfunctional decision making—that is, decision making where the benefit to one subunit is more than offset by the costs or loss of benefit to other subunits. This may be caused by (a) a lack of harmony or congruence between the overall organizational goals, subunit goals, and the individual goals of decision makers, and (b) a lack of information for guiding the individual manager concerning the effects of his decisions on other parts of the organization. Moreover, the costs of gathering and processing information often increase, since decentralization is usually accompanied by more elaborate information systems. A formal information system becomes more important to top managers because it provides the principal means of obtaining goal congruence and of monitoring a collection of more independent managers. In addition, some central corporate assets, services, and administrative talent tend to be duplicated.

Transfer pricing is an example of the comparative information-gathering costs of centralization and decentralization. *Transfer prices* are the monetary values assigned to the goods and services exchanged among the subunits of an organization. A centralized system might impose transfer prices based on, say, standard costs and might require all purchases or sales of particular items to be made internally. In contrast, a decentralized system might let the managers of the selling and buying divisions negotiate their prices and might allow those managers the alternatives of buying and selling such items in outside markets—in which cases there will probably be additional costs of management time in negotiations, of friction, and perhaps of extra information gathering for making these individual decisions.

Dysfunctional decision making is most likely where the subunits in the organization are highly interdependent—that is, where the decisions affecting one part of the organization influence the decisions and performance of another part. If interdependence is great, coordination is needed to obtain optimum decisions for the organization as a whole. Subunits can rarely be completely autonomous or self-contained, so interdependence is the biggest inhibiting factor in decentralization. There are countless examples of interdependence where the performance of the receiving unit depends on the quality of the work done by the supplying unit. For instance, parts and raw materials must meet schedules and specifications; two segments of the organization may share or compete for computer services, management skills, or raw materials; they may sell in a common market (for example, Buick and Oldsmobile) in such a way that an action beneficial to one subunit may be harmful to another and to the corporation as a whole.

comparison of benefits and costs The foregoing benefits and costs must be compared by top managers, often on a function-by-function basis. For example, the controller's function may be heavily decentralized for many attention-directing and problem-solving purposes (such as operating budgets and performance reports), but heavily centralized for other purposes (such as accounts-receivable processing and income tax planning).

The patterns of benefits and costs of decentralization are shown in Exhibit 22-1. The first graph hypothesizes that, as the degree of decentralization in-

EXHIBIT 22-1

BENEFITS AND COSTS OF DECENTRALIZATION

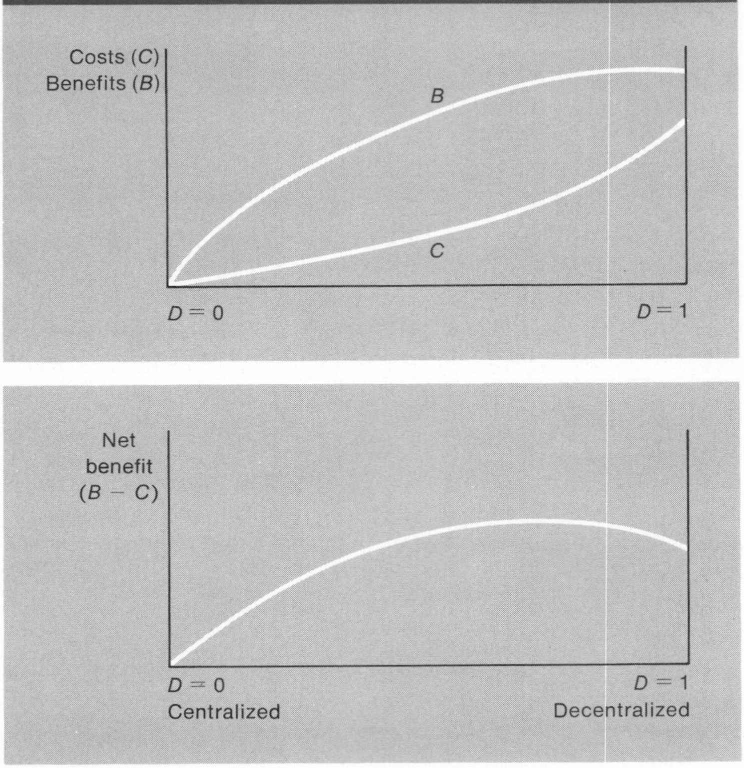

creases, the benefits (B) of decentralization will increase at a decreasing rate and the costs (C) will increase slowly at lower degrees of decentralization but then start to soar.[2]

The degree of decentralization (D) varies from zero to one. D is essentially a gauge of the freedom to make decisions. For example, it could be measured by the percentage of acquisition decisions that a division manager can make without needing top-management consent. Various attempts have been made to obtain a measure of D that might be used for comparing various organizations.[3]

Decentralization is likely to be most beneficial and least costly when the organizational units are entirely independent of each other. Then there is minimal likelihood of dysfunctional decisions. In general, a subunit is independent (self-contained) to the extent that it:

1. Does not compete with other subunits for the use of limited resources within the organization, such as capital, research services, or management skill
2. Does not compete in the same market or buy from the same sources as other subdivisions
3. Does not provide goods to other subunits or depend upon them for its own inputs
4. Can make decisions and obtain goal congruence without coordination with other subunits and without explicitly considering the objectives of the other subunits or of the organization[4]

Of course, B, C, and D in Exhibit 22-1 are impossible to determine with precision. There are indications that top managers perceive the optimum decentralization in practice as somewhere in the middle. The extent of decentralization in a particular organization is obviously affected by numerous factors.

profit centers

confusion of terms

A *profit center* is any subunit or segment of an organization that is assigned both revenues and expenses. This is a simple, straightforward definition. Note that it does not contain one word about decentralization, which was previously defined as the relative freedom to make

[2] In correspondence with the author, Professor Joshua Ronen has commented that while it is plausible to hypothesize this particular shape of the curves, there is no evident reason why B should be concave and C should be convex, except in some regions. For example, it is not unreasonable to expect the cost curve to start off being concave, owing to decreasing marginal cost of decentralization, and to become convex later on. (In fact, it should probably start being concave at the point $D = 0$ until it reaches some positive degree of decentralization.) Conversely, the benefits curve would probably start at $D = 0$ being convex, and it would start becoming concave at some positive point of decentralization.

[3] See T. L. Whisler, H. Meyer, B. H. Baum, and P. F. Sorenson, "Centralization of Organization Control: An Empirical Study of Its Meaning and Measurement," *Journal of Business*, Vol. 40, No. 1, pp. 10–26. They develop a Gini ratio of concentration, which is applied to the distribution of individual compensation within each department studied. Their rationale assumes that the way in which executive compensation is distributed reflects rather closely the way in which responsibility and control are distributed.

[4] See William T. Morris, *Decentralization in Management Systems* (Columbus: Ohio State University Press, 1968), p. 15.

decisions. **There is enormous confusion in the accounting literature and management literature because the term *profit center* is often erroneously viewed as a synonym for *decentralized subunit*. Usually this confusion is harmless, but occasionally it leads to incorrect analysis.**

Although it may seem strange at first glance, profit centers could be coupled with a highly centralized organization, and cost centers could be coupled with a highly decentralized organization. Normally, however, the profit center is the major organizational device used to implement decentralization. Still, the existence of profit centers does not necessarily mean that heavy decentralization exists. For example, a company may have many divisions called profit centers, but their managers may have little leeway in making decisions. A manager may be unable to buy or sell outside his company, he may have to obtain approval from corporate headquarters for every capital expenditure over $200, and he may be forced to accept central-staff "advice." In another company, which has only cost centers, managers may have great latitude on capital outlays and on where to purchase materials and services. In short, the labels of *profit center* and *cost center* are sometimes deceptive as clues to the degree of decentralization.

Note that decentralization may also be applied to not-for-profit organizations. Some governments, school districts, and hospitals may have enormous autonomy and not contain a single profit center.

size and number of centers

Ideas of decentralization and profit center are universal; they are not confined to large organizations. A small medical center or retail store can have several profit centers and may be either heavily decentralized or heavily centralized.

There is a tendency to jump to fallacious conclusions about the extent of decentralization in a particular company. For example, the *number* of profit centers is not a valid index of decentralization. Consider General Electric, which has over 160 subdivision managers with profit responsibility. Some of these subunits have annual sales of over $300 million. Is GE a heavily decentralized company? The answer depends on whether these individual subunits are, in turn, managed on a decentralized basis. A $300-million subdivision that is subject to autocratic rule by the division manager is surely less decentralized than a $200-million outside competitor in the same product lines that has several nearly independent subunits. Taken as a whole, General Electric may appear decentralized; however, each division may be heavily centralized when compared to its outside competitors.

three problems of systems and decentralization

After considering costs and benefits, top management may decide that heavy decentralization is desirable. By definition, this means that top management will rarely interfere with the decisions of subordinates. Therefore, the preservation of the autonomy[5] of subunit managers becomes an additional problem in the design of an accounting control system.

As Chapter 6 stressed, goal congruence and incentive are two major problems that deserve consideration when judging a particular control system. When top management is committed to decentralization, autonomy becomes the third major problem. Any accounting procedures and measures must be appraised by how they help solve these three problems in a cost-effective way.

We will relate these three problems in this chapter to the transfer-pricing issue and in the next to broader issues of subunit profit and investment measurements.

objectives of transfer pricing

Goods and services are often exchanged between various departments and divisions of a company. What monetary values (prices) should be assigned to these exchanges or transfers? Historical cost? Market price? Some version of either? The transfer-pricing question is often the most troublesome aspect of a control system.

nature of transfer prices

Transfer pricing is most often viewed in the context of one profit center's supplying a product or service to another profit center. For example, a foundry may supply castings for an assembly division; it may also sell castings to outsiders. If the foundry and the assembly division are separate profit centers, the transfer price will have an important bearing on the reported profits of each. More fundamentally, transfer-price information affects many critical decisions concerning the acquisition and allocation of an organization's resources, just as prices in the entire economy affect decisions concerning the allocation of a nation's resources. Ideally, transfer prices should guide each manager to choose his inputs and outputs in coordination with other subunits so as to maximize the profits of the organization as a whole.[6]

Of course, transfer pricing is not confined to accounting for profit centers. It takes many forms. For example, although it is rarely thought of in this way, the allocation of service-department costs to production departments is essentially a form of transfer pricing, because it is a measure of the services rendered to and received from another subunit of the organization.

[5] Joshua Ronen and George McKinney, "Transfer Pricing for Divisional Autonomy," *Journal of Accounting Research,* Spring 1970, pp. 100–101.

[6] See Kenneth J. Arrow, "Control in Large Organizations," *Management Science,* Vol. 10, No. 3, pp. 397–408, for a sweeping view of decentralization, and pp. 405–6 for an assessment of the difficulties in applying a price system to the control of an organization. He sees these difficulties as four mutually interacting types: (a) the choice of enforcement rules, (b) the complexity of the operating rules, (c) the limits on the theoretical validity of the price system, and (d) the presence of uncertainty.

choosing transfer prices

The three problems of goal congruence, incentive, and autonomy become very imposing in many transfer-pricing situations. There are few pat answers, and transfer-pricing policies tend to vary for different types of products and services within the same organization. For example, consider the stated transfer-pricing objectives of one large company:

1. To provide valid data for make-or-buy decisions.
2. To provide valid data for pricing and capital-budgeting decisions.
3. To provide corporate management with divisional performance data that appropriately reflect contribution to profit.

Note how a solution to one problem may conflict with the solution to a second problem. For example, a transfer price equal to variable cost may be appropriate to guide a short-run make-or-buy decision (problem of goal congruence), but the supplier division manager may have no motivation to sell to a consuming division at variable cost because his division's performance measure—divisional profit—will not be improved (problem of incentive). Moreover, if the manager of the supplier division is instructed by top management to transfer at variable cost, his independence is undermined (problem of autonomy).

In subsequent sections we will examine various transfer-pricing schemes in light of these three problems.[7]

market prices

appeal of market prices

For day-in, day-out use where the intermediate market is competitive and where interdependencies of subunits are minimal, market price is the most desirable transfer price because it generally leads to optimal decisions. There are no inherent conflicts in solving all three problems (goal congruence, incentive, and autonomy). The guidelines are these: (a) a market or negotiated market price should be used; (b) the seller should have the option of not selling internally;[8] and (c) an arbitration procedure should be available for settling disputes.[9] These guidelines assume that the managers of the divisions have access to perfectly competitive outside markets. Where market prices are relevant for making economic decisions, and if the costs of

[7] Joel S. Demski, "Transfer Pricing Under Uncertainty," unpublished paper, Stanford University, 1975, concludes that a transfer-pricing problem "is part of a broader, more fundamental problem of rational organization design." He maintains that "situation-specific answers" are the most that we can hope for, so we should be especially wary of generalization in this area.

[8] The reason for this option is that the seller might have more profitable alternative opportunities for using his facilities to sell *other products*.

[9] R. N. Anthony and J. Dearden, *Management Control Systems* (3rd ed., Homewood, Ill.: Richard D. Irwin, Inc., 1976).

maintaining such a system are justifiable, they are also relevant to the preservation of subunit autonomy and the maintenance of incentive (through performance evaluation).

When the market-price approach is used, the attempt is to transfer goods at a price no higher than that prevailing in an outside market at the time of transfer—that is, at the price that the receiving division would have to pay outsiders. Put another way, the market-price approach is an attempt to approximate an arm's-length, bargained, open-market price.

In most cases, internal procurement is expected where the selling division's products and services are equal to those of outsiders in quality and price. The buying division often obtains benefits such as better quality, assurance of supply, and dependable delivery.

The usefulness of a market-price method is contingent on the availability of dependable market-price quotations of other manufacturers. It is these prices that would be taken into account by parties dealing at arm's length as they establish the competitive price levels.

In sum, if a company's participation in a market has no effect on price, market prices typically establish the ceiling for transfer pricing. In many instances a lower price may easily be justified, particularly when large purchases are made, when selling costs are less, or when an advantage is obtained through an exclusive supplier contract or through a cost-plus arrangement assuring profits in all cases. These situations lead to the notion of negotiated market prices, whereby the cost savings to the firm as a whole are split between the selling and buying divisions through bargaining.

Arbitrating or umpiring is sometimes necessary. However, its frequent use indicates a step toward centralization, because it usually elevates the decision to a representative of the organization as a whole. Consequently, too much reliance on arbitration indicates the inability of the division managers to operate smoothly on a decentralized basis.

pitfalls in market prices

The use of market prices wherever possible has innate appeal for purposes of both goal congruence and incentive. Without routine checks on market prices, managers often obtain critical information only in a haphazard or tardy fashion. A frequently cited advantage of profit centers is that they compel an approximation of what revenue might be if a division were operated as a completely independent entity; in this way, the managers become more sensitive to market conditions than otherwise.

The trouble with the use of market price is either that few markets are perfectly competitive or that no intermediate market exists for the exact product or service in question. A quoted price for a product is strictly comparable only if the credit terms, grade, quality, delivery terms, and auxiliary services are precisely the same. Moreover, isolated price quotations are sometimes temporary distress or dumping prices for excess inventories that must be quickly liquidated in financial emergencies. Such prices can seldom be used as a basis for long-range planning, although they may be appropriate for monitoring short-term performance. In nearly all cases, however, temporary market prices are not applicable for repetitive, high-volume transactions, and they hurt the credibility of the so-called market transfer prices.

Many product parts are unique, a situation that causes considerable costs for preparing bids. If an outside supplier prepares a few bids and discovers that the internal supplier division always wins, the so-called resulting market prices either will not be forthcoming in the future or will be unreliable (and perhaps artificially high; after all, the bidder may submit a high price with little effort). Some companies deliberately purchase from outside suppliers to maintain alternate sources of supply and to provide a valid check on market prices.

If there is idle capacity, incongruent decisions may be caused by rigid adherence to a market price. For example, suppose Supplier Division A is a profit center that sells a variety of products inside and outside the company. Suppose further that there is idle capacity in this division and that its Product X is a component of a finished product made by Division B. There is no intermediate market for Product X. Finally, suppose the variable cost of X (in Division A) is \$1 per unit, its absorption cost is \$1.50 per unit, and Division A has an average markup on all its product of 60 percent of absorption cost.

Note the dilemma here. To benefit the organization as a whole, the supplying division should transfer the intermediate good at variable cost, because variable cost is the information needed for deciding on how many finished units should be produced by B. As the manager of the supplying division, how would you feel about such a rule? Unless you were totally generous, you probably would not be willing to transfer at a price of \$1. After all, the production of this part is essential to the overall company profit, so you are entitled to a share of that profit. In short, the transfer price of \$1 may seemingly be goal-congruent for the organization as a whole, but it may not lead to the wanted decisions because it fails to respond to the other two problems of incentive and autonomy.

Incidentally, the term *idle capacity* is used here to mean that the market will not purchase *all* of the maximum possible output at a price exceeding the incremental cost of production. The term *idle capacity* is also used to denote the presence of extra production facilities together with insufficient raw materials or labor to utilize them—but that meaning is *not* the one being used in the transfer-pricing context.

distress prices What transfer-pricing scheme should be used for judging performance if distress prices prevail? Some companies use these distress transfer prices, but others use long-run average or "normal" market prices. The decision as to which transfer-pricing basis is preferable depends on subjective judgments regarding the costs and benefits of each alternative.

If distress pricing is used, in the short run the manager of the supplier division will meet the price as long as it exceeds his additional cost. In the long run, he must decide whether disposal of some manufacturing facilities would be desirable by predicting its effect on the price in question. The danger is that managers may not take the long-range, global view and may constrict facilities to boost a short-run divisional rate of return. The resulting cut in the total industry supply may lead to a higher outside future price that may be disadvantageous to the company as a whole in the long run.

On the other hand, transfers may be based on the long-run average price. But this has the weakness of not incorporating current market prices in the information system; to the extent that transfers are forced at above-current-market prices, the short-run performance of the buying division will be hurt and that manager will be unhappy about both his performance measure and his partial loss of autonomy. However, unless the selling division's incremental costs exceed the market price, the company as a whole would benefit by an internal transfer.

If the danger of precipitous disposal of facilities is given appropriate consideration when analysis is conducted, the use of current market prices (even distress prices) is generally preferable to the use of some long-run average price. In this way, two evaluations are made. The first is a comparison of long-run predictions and current prices; this gives insights on past capital-budgeting decisions. The second entails assessing the current performance of both the buying and supplying divisions in relation to existing opportunities in the form of current prices.

general rule for transfer pricing?

outlay cost and opportunity cost

The preceding section demonstrated that market price was not a cure-all answer to the problem of setting transfer prices. The most obvious example is the nonexistence of an intermediate market for a highly specialized product component.

Is there an all-pervasive rule for transfer pricing that will lead toward optimal economic decisions? The answer is negative, because the three problems of goal congruence, incentive, and autonomy must all be considered simultaneously. If an optimal economic decision is wanted in a particular situation, the following general rule serves as a helpful first step in the analysis. **The minimum transfer price should be (*a*) the additional outlay costs incurred to the point of transfer (sometimes approximated by variable costs), plus (*b*) opportunity costs of the firm as a whole. This is the price that would ordinarily make the supplying division indifferent as to whether the output were sold inside or outside; the supplying division's contribution would be the same under either choice.**

The term *outlay cost* in this context represents the cash outflows that are directly associated with the production and transfer of the goods or services. Of course, these cash outflows do not necessarily have to be made at a particular instant, but the action of production and transfer will result sooner or later in some cash outflows that will be termed outlay costs.[10] Opportunity costs are defined here as the maximum contribution to profits foregone by the firm as a whole **if the goods are transferred internally.** These may be foregone contribution margins in some instances and even foregone net proceeds from the sale of facilities in other instances.

The distinction between outlay and opportunity costs is made here because the accounting records ordinarily record the outlay costs of the alternative selected but fail to record the opportunity costs.[11] If a perfect intermediate market exists, the opportunity cost is market price less outlay cost. A perfect market is defined as a market where the maximum available output may be sold at unchanging prices. For example, if the outlay cost is \$1 and the market price is \$4, the transfer price is \$1 + (\$4 − \$1) = \$4, which happens to be the market price. However, if no market exists for the intermediate product or alternative products that might utilize the same supplying division's facilities, the opportunity cost may be zero. In the latter case, outlay cost (perhaps approximated by variable cost) may be the correct transfer price.

To recapitulate:

Minimum transfer price	= (Outlay cost)	+ (Opportunity cost to company as a whole)	
If idle capacity exists:	= \$1	+ Possibly 0	= \$1
If no idle capacity:	= \$1	+ (Market price − Outlay cost)	
	= \$1	+ (\$4 − \$1)	= \$4

[10] Other terms, including *incremental costs, additional costs, direct costs,* and *variable costs,* were rejected as not being as sharply descriptive as is the term *outlay cost.*

[11] The jungle of terminology in this area is too dense to dwell on at length here. The "general rule" has been expressed here with the hope that it will ease the understanding of those who are more comfortable with the terminology of accountants than with that of economists. For example, some economists would examine this general rule and say that *both* (a) and (b) together are opportunity cost. That is, the outlay cost is also an opportunity cost because it measures what the firm would have saved had the outlay *not* been incurred. For an excellent discussion of cost as it is used in economics, see George Stigler, *Theory of Price,* 3rd ed. (New York: The Macmillan Company, 1966).

Other economists would say that both (a) and (b) together are the *marginal cost,* because transfer prices are usually expressed on a per-unit basis. The term *marginal cost* is avoided here because it is ambiguous in the literature. That is, some economists in some situations will use it, at any given point of production, to embrace both (a) and (b) for the last unit produced. In other situations, they will use it to represent (a) only. For example, the loss of external profits is not included in the usual economic description of marginal costs, but it must be included in one way or another for marginal cost to be appropriate as a transfer price for the cases of demand or cost dependencies. Moreover, many accountants will use *variable cost* and *marginal cost* as if they were synonymous terms.

The economist would be inclined to express the general rule slightly differently. David Solomons, in *Divisional Performance: Measurement and Control* (Homewood, Ill.: Richard D. Irwin, 1968), p. 181, points out: "Transfer prices should be set equal to the marginal cost of supply, not at just any output, but at one particular equilibrium output." This requires the matching of the outlay costs of the supplying division at different levels of output with the summation of quantities demanded at each level of additional revenue for all demands. Therefore, a general, unchanging transfer price may be appropriate only in the case of a perfect intermediate market or in the case of constant marginal costs.

imperfect markets The problems in transfer pricing would be trivial if the intermediate market were perfect. But too often the intermediate markets are nonexistent, ill structured, or imperfect. *Imperfect competition* exists when one seller or buyer, *acting alone,* can exert an influence on the market price. If the intermediate market is imperfectly competitive, additional volume can be obtained only if selling prices are lowered. This means that the existing market price at a particular volume level is no longer applicable for the decision regarding how much to produce and sell. The additions to revenue will be less than the sales of the additional units at the new selling price because the new lower price will apply to the entire volume. For example, suppose the current selling price is \$1 per unit and 80,000 units are being sold. The revenue is \$80,000. A cut in price from \$1 to \$.90 may increase unit sales to 90,000. The increase in revenue is (10,000 × \$.90) minus (80,000 × \$.10, the loss in revenue on the 80,000 units), or \$1,000. In these situations the analyses can become exceedingly complex. The optimal transfer price from the viewpoint of the corporation as a whole is different for each situation, depending on the existence of cost interdependencies and demand interdependencies. Some of these complexities are explored in the appendix to this chapter. An example of a cost interdependency is the case where the price of a certain raw material may be dependent on the total purchases by two or more divisions. An example of a demand interdependency is any vertically integrated operation where there is no intermediate market for a unique component part of a finished product. Then the total number of finished products sold is dependent on the total number of components available, and vice versa.

As we have just seen, market price is a special case rather than a universal guide. The key computation is the (b) part of the general rule above. It is easy to say, "Measure the foregone contribution from transferring goods internally." However, it is not easy to do this. For example, consider a supplier division with idle capacity and an imperfect demand in the intermediate market. Is its opportunity cost zero? Probably not. One alternative may be to cut price so as to increase demand and hope to increase overall revenue. But measuring the probable effect is difficult, so measuring the opportunity cost is also difficult. Clearly, the transfer price must be determined in relation to constantly changing levels of supply and demand. There is not a transfer price; rather, there is a schedule of transfer prices (a transfer-price function) for various quantities.

organization as a whole The foregoing general rule, although widely applicable in concept, is not a universal truth because it concentrates on the relationship of only two divisions. Transfer pricing becomes a fascinating analytical problem that must be solved on a firmwide basis in particular situations where many interdependencies exist among divisions and markets. For an expanded discussion, see the appendix to this chapter.

The proposed "general rule" provides a springboard for analysis because it often provides the solution to the problem of goal-congruent decisions under the assumption that total centralization exists. That is, the most desirable economic decision for the organization as a whole would be dictated centrally. But in real situations, where some degree of decentralization persists, the optimal transfer price dictated by economic analysis may be variable cost. Then, the manager of the supplying division must be given some incentive above that minimal transfer price in order to insure that the desired transfers do indeed occur. So transfer-pricing policies must be designed in light of the simultaneous problems of incentive and autonomy as well as goal congruence.

How do you design a performance-evaluation (incentive) scheme that induces congruence when heavy interdependencies exist? Obviously, if control systems were costless, the ideal solution would be to have a flexible (though necessarily complex) transfer-pricing policy that would insure congruent decisions. But control systems are not costless, so simple rules tend to be used for various classes of transactions. For example, market prices may be used for some transfers and cost prices for others.

Unusual cases tend to be negotiated or settled by central management. The more opportunities and interdependencies, the more likely is the desire for central control. As transfer-pricing rules become more constraining, they represent a move toward more centralization. This move is an attempt to find some intermediate point on the graph (Exhibit 22-1) that may decrease some benefits of decentralization (those arising from giving a manager more freedom of action) but that, it is hoped, will decrease to a greater extent some costs of dysfunctional decisions until some optimal point is reached.

alternatives to market prices

Sometimes market prices are either unavailable, inappropriate, or too costly to be used for transfer pricing. Let us explore other ways to set transfer prices. Nearly every version of a transfer price has some drawbacks.

full-cost bases

The use of full cost or full cost-plus is widespread. If the transfers are based on *actual* costs, the performance of the receiving divisions will bear the accumulated efficiencies or inefficiencies of other divisions not subject to their control. Transfer prices that insure recovery of actual costs often fail to provide an incentive to control costs; therefore, some version of *standard* or *budgeted* costs is better than actual costs because it gives incentive to control costs.

Full or absorption standard costs may minimize the problem of inefficiency but may still lead to suboptimal decisions. For example, Division A may supply parts to Division B at a standard cost of $5 per product unit, including a charge of $3 per unit for fixed costs based on some normal activity level. (There may also be some "plus" added in a cost-plus transfer-pricing system.) Suppose A has idle capacity and B has additional processing and selling costs of $4 per unit. B can obtain additional revenue of only $8 per unit from sales to outside customers. B will refuse to buy, because its performance would worsen at the rate of $1 per unit:

		DIVISION B PERFORMANCE
Additional revenue		$8
Additional costs:		
Transfer price from A	$5	
Additional costs in B	4	9
Additional loss		−$1

But the entity as a whole would benefit in the short run:

		ENTIRE ENTITY
Additional revenue		$8
Additional costs:		
A ($5 − $3)	$2	
B	4	6
Additional profit		$2

This is a clear example of goal incongruence that is induced by a transfer price based on so-called full or average total costs. The transfer-pricing scheme has led B to regard the fixed costs in A as variable costs. From the viewpoint of the firm as a whole, this may lead to dysfunctional decisions in the short run.[12]

cost-plus as a synthetic market price

Despite the obvious limitations of the approach, transfer prices based on full cost, or on full cost plus some markup, are in common use. A major reason for the wide use of cost-based transfer pricing is its clarity and convenience. Moreover, the transferred product or service in question is often slightly different in quality or other characteristics from that available from outside sources. As a result, cost-plus pricing is often viewed as yielding a "satisfactory" approximation of an outside market price. Therefore, the resulting synthetic market price is regarded as a good practical substitute that is responsive to problems of congruence and incentive. The alternative—getting "real" market prices—is perceived as being too costly for incorporating into a routine control system.

[12] Of course, the usual caution about the "relevant" cost for pricing—whether it should be based on the short run or long run, and whether it should be variable, absorption, or some other cost—is also applicable to transfer-pricing decisions. See Chapter 11 for a discussion.

variable-cost plus lump-sum

Top management often wants the buyer-division manager to make month-to-month purchasing decisions based on the variable costs of the supplier division. Otherwise, as the example in the preceding section showed, the buyer division may be led toward the wrong decision. One way to satisfy the needs of the two divisions and the company as a whole is to transfer at a standard variable cost. A separate predetermined lump-sum charge is made for fixed costs plus a lump-sum profit; this charge may be made annually or monthly. It is based on an *annual expectation*, not on actual purchases. In any event, the buyer's month-to-month decisions are not influenced by the supplier's fixed costs or the supplier's profit. Note that, except for the profit, this was the approach recommended in Chapter 15 for the reallocation of service-department costs to operating departments.

prorating the overall contribution

Recall the idle-capacity example in the earlier section, "Pitfalls in Market Prices." The variable cost is $1 per unit, absorption cost is $1.50 per unit, and Division A has an average markup of 60 percent of absorption cost. Suppose that Division B can use the component in a finished product that will sell for $5 and that will entail incurring other variable costs of $3 per unit. How are congruence and incentive achieved?

The interdependence of the two divisions regarding this product may be overtly recognized by making a centralized decision and imposing the $1 transfer price. In effect, this approach jettisons decentralization, at least for transactions in this product. Because most organizations are hybrids of centralization and decentralization anyway, this approach deserves serious consideration where such transfers are significant.

One popular solution is to impose a variable-cost transfer price but credit each division for a prorated share of the overall contribution to corporate profit. Suppose that 100,000 units were in question:

Sales of finished product @ $5		$500,000
Variable costs:		
Division A @ $1	$100,000	
Division B @ $3	300,000	400,000
Contribution to corporate profit		$100,000

The proration would probably be negotiated in any number of ways. Suppose that it were in proportion to the standard variable costs incurred by each division. Then Division A would get credited for $25,000 and Division B for $75,000. In this way, Division A would be willing to transfer at $1, knowing that the transfers would somehow improve its showing as a profit center. Essentially, this is a standard-variable-cost-plus transfer-pricing system; the "plus" is a function of the overall contribution to corporate profit.

dual pricing Alternatively, the seeming harshness of the foregoing authoritarian approach can be modified if organizations recognize that there is no necessity to have a *single* transfer price. The profit-center concept can be preserved more easily if one transfer price is used for one purpose (making the economic decision) and another for a second purpose (evaluation of performance). In our example, such a dual-pricing scheme could result in the transfer price to Division B being \$1, while Division A is given credit for a synthetic market price of perhaps \$2.40 (\$1.50 plus 60 percent). Under this scheme, each division's performance would be enhanced by the transfer, and the \$1 transfer price to Division B would induce the Division B manager to make the correct economic decisions from the viewpoint of the organization as a whole. Note that this dual-pricing plan essentially gives Division A a corporate subsidy. The profit for the company as a whole will be less than the sum of the divisional profits. Suppose that 100,000 units are transferred:

DIVISION A		*DIVISION B*		
Sales to B @ \$2.40	\$240,000	Sales of finished product @ \$5		\$500,000
Variable costs @ \$1.00	100,000	Variable costs:		
Contribution	\$140,000	Division A @ \$1	\$100,000	
		Division B @ \$3	300,000	400,000
		Contribution		\$100,000

Note, as computed previously, the contribution to the corporation as a whole is only \$100,000.

At first glance, dual pricing seems to be the solution to our dilemma. But it has a major weakness that may explain why it has not been used widely in practice. The trouble is that all managers in the subunits win, but the organization as a whole may lose. The supplier-division manager gets a high price, and the buyer-division manager gets a low price. The danger here is that both managers may tend to get too sloppy regarding cost controls within their subunits. Thus, the looseness of dual pricing may gradually induce unwelcome attitudes and practices.

taxes and tariffs

Previous sections have pointed out that there is seldom a single transfer price that will meet the three problems and thus induce the desired decisions. The "correct" transfer price depends on the economic and legal circumstances and the decision at hand. We may want one transfer price for congruence and a second for incentive. Furthermore, the optimal price for either may differ from that employed for tax reporting or for other external requirements.

Income taxes, property taxes, and tariffs often influence the setting of transfer prices so that the firm as a whole will benefit, even though the performance of a subunit may suffer under this set of prices. To minimize tariffs and domestic income taxes, a company may want to set an unusually low selling price for a domestic division that ships goods to foreign subsidiaries in countries where the prevailing tax rates are lower. To maximize tax deductions for percentage depletion allowances, which are based on revenue, a petroleum company may want to transfer crude oil to other subunits at as high a price as possible.

Transfer pricing is also influenced in some situations because of state fair-trade laws and national antitrust acts. Because of the differences in national tax structures around the world or because of the differences in the incomes of various divisions and subsidiaries, the firm may wish to shift profits and "dump" goods, if legally possible. These considerations are additional illustrations of the limits of decentralization where heavy interdependencies exist and of why the same company may use different transfer prices for different purposes. They are also illustrations of practices that have been criticized, sometimes justly and sometimes unjustly, on legal or moral grounds.

why profit centers?

In Chapter 7 the evolution of control systems in many organizations from physical observation to historical records to static budgets to flexible budgets was described as being based on an attempt to solve the problems of goal congruence and incentive in a cost-effective way. All of these systems are imperfect. **Given the objectives of top management, control systems are changed in a world of uncertainty with the aim of improving congruence and incentive in an economically feasible way in a specific organization.**

At this point, after studying all the weaknesses of profit centers and transfer prices, readers often jump to the conclusion that organizations should stay heavily centralized and use nothing fancier than flexible budgets. The incentive problem is a major justification for taking the step from a flexible budget to some kind of profit center. Cost centers with flexible budgets and standards have sometimes been found wanting. For instance, some cost-center managers have focused on meeting a budget and on keeping costs under control—and nothing more. When the cost centers are transformed into profit centers, managers may continue to care about costs, but they may give new attention to production schedules and important marketing factors. Top managers have sometimes found that pep talks and cajoling do not get subordinates to accept top-management goals. But giving profit responsibility works better because it crystallizes goals and provides better incentives. **That is, goal congruence may exist in a vague, half-hearted fashion, but profit centers provide the formal system that is so often the most persuasive means of communicating top management's goals and boosting incentives.**

Professors and managers can spend hours delineating the weaknesses of profit centers and transfer-pricing schemes, especially when the managers have little local autonomy. Nevertheless, despite their many defects, profit centers may often be the most cost-effective way to obtain the desired goal congruence and incentives.

accounting entries for transfers

Transfer pricing is governed by managerial objectives, including measuring divisional performance, minimizing taxes, and controlling the rate of return. These objectives often lead to transfers at prices in excess of the conventional inventory costs used for external reporting.

Accounting for market-based transfer prices provides another illustration of how current accounting systems are being designed primarily to aid managerial planning and control rather than to serve the need for external financial reports. After all, from the viewpoint of the consolidated enterprise, any goods or services transferred within the enterprise and not yet sold to outsiders should be carried at cost. Thus, although intracompany transfers may be accounted for and reported in any manner that helps achieve managerial objectives, intracompany margins must be eliminated periodically when consolidated financial statements are prepared.

The basic approach may be illustrated as follows:

Whole Company has two divisions, A and B. Goods having a manufacturing cost of $100 are transferred from A to B at a price of $135. Entries follow:

ON BOOKS OF SUPPLIER DIVISION A		
Accounts receivable—Division B	135	
Sales to Division B		135
Cost of goods sold (transferred)	100	
Inventory—Division A		100
ON BOOKS OF RECEIVING DIVISION B		
Inventory—Division B	135	
Accounts payable—Division A		135

An examination of the entries above shows that essentially the two divisions operate as separate companies. However, if the Whole Company had to prepare consolidated financial statements immediately after the transaction, the following eliminating entries would be needed:

Accounts payable—Division A	135	
Accounts receivable—Division B		135
To eliminate intracompany receivable and payable.		
Sales to Division B	135	
Cost of goods sold (transferred)		100
Intracompany gross profit—A		35
To close and recognize Division A's intracompany gross profit.		
Intracompany gross profit—A	35	
Inventory—Division B		35
To eliminate intracompany gross profit.		

SUMMARY

Transfer-pricing systems deserve careful attention if decentralization is to be established in companies whose divisions exchange goods and services. A transfer-pricing system must be judged in relation to its impact on (a) goal congruence, (b) incentive (evaluation of performance) and (c) autonomy. Some version of market price as a transfer price will usually best motivate managers toward optimal economic decisions; moreover, the evaluation of performance will then be consistent with the ideas of decentralization.

There is rarely a single transfer price that will serve all needs. Instead, there may be one transfer price for making a particular production decision, another for evaluating performance, and another for minimizing tariffs or income taxes.

Economic analysis can demonstrate that market price is not always the best guide to optimal decisions. In such instances, some centralization of control may be desired to prevent dysfunctional decisions. If so, serious thought should be given to whether profit centers and decentralization provide the optimum organizational design. Above all, the perceived costs and benefits at alternative levels of decentralization should be explicitly considered when choosing a transfer-pricing scheme.

Profit centers usually accompany decentralization, but one can exist without the other. The desirability of a profit center versus a cost center should be judged by their predicted relative impacts on decisions.

SUGGESTED READINGS

Abdel-Khalik, A., and E. Lusk, "Transfer Pricing—A Synthesis," *Accounting Review* (January 1974).

Arrow, Kenneth J., "Control in Large Organizations," *Management Science,* Vol. 10, No. 3, pp. 397–408.

Baumol, William, and Tibor Fabian, "Decomposition, Pricing for Decentralization and External Economies," *Management Science,* Vol. 11, No. 1, pp. 1–32.

Dearden, John, "Interdivisional Pricing," *Harvard Business Review,* Vol. 38, No. 1.

Dopuch, Nicholas, and David Drake, "Accounting Implications of a Mathematical Programming Approach to the Transfer Price Problem," *Journal of Accounting Research,* Vol. 2, No. 1, pp. 15–21.

Gould, J. R., "Internal Pricing in Firms When There are Costs of Using an Outside Market," *The Journal of Business,* Vol. XXXVII, No. 1, pp. 61–67.

Hass, Jerome, E., "Transfer Pricing in a Decentralized Firm," *Management Science: Application,* Vol. 14, No. 6, pp. B-310 through B-331.

Hirshleifer, Jack, "Internal Pricing and Decentralized Decisions," in *Management Controls: New Directions in Basic Research,* eds. C. Bonini, R. Jaedicke, and H. Wagner, p. 30. New York: McGraw-Hill Book Company, 1964.

Onsi, M., "A Transfer Pricing System Based on Opportunity Cost," *Accounting Review,* July 1970.

Ronen, Joshua, and George McKinney, "Transfer Pricing for Divisional Autonomy," *Journal of Accounting Research,* Vol. 8, No. 1 (Spring 1970), p. 103.

Sharav, I., "Transfer Pricing—Diversity of Goals and Practices," *Journal of Accountancy,* Vol. 137, No. 4 (April 1974), pp. 56–62.

WATSON, D., and J. BAUMLER, "Transfer Pricing: A Behavioral Context," *Accounting Review,* July 1975.

WHINSTON, ANDREW, "Pricing Guides in Decentralized Organizations," in *New Perspective in Organizational Research,* eds. W. W. Cooper, H. J. Leavitt, and M. W. Shelly (New York: John Wiley & Sons, Inc., 1964).

Also see the footnotes in this chapter. The Solomons book is particularly strong in transfer pricing.

PROBLEM FOR SELF-STUDY

PROBLEM

A transportation equipment manufacturer, the Pillercat Corporation, is heavily decentralized. Each division head has full authority on all decisions regarding sales to internal or external customers. Division P has always acquired a certain equipment component from Division S. However, when informed that Division S was increasing its unit price to $220, Division P's management decided to purchase the component from outside suppliers at a price of $200.

Division S had recently acquired some specialized equipment that was used primarily to make this component. The manager cited the resulting high depreciation charges as the justification for the price boost. He asked the president of the company to instruct Division P to buy from S at the $220 price. He supplied the following information:

P's annual purchases of component, in units	2,000
S's variable costs per unit	$ 190
S's fixed costs per unit	20

1. Suppose there are no alternative uses for the S facilities. Will the company as a whole benefit if P buys from the outside suppliers for $200 per unit? Show computations.
2. Suppose internal facilities of S would not otherwise be idle. The equipment and other facilities would be assigned to other production operations and would result in annual cash operating savings of $29,000. Should P purchase from outsiders?
3. Suppose there are no alternative uses for S's internal facilities and that the selling price of outsiders drops $15. Should P purchase from outsiders?
4. What rule would you favor for setting transfer prices in the Pillercat Corporation?
5. As the president, how would you respond to the request of the manager of S? Would your response differ according to the specific situations described in parts 1–3 above? Why?

SOLUTION

1–3. The analyses of the first three requirements are summarized below (in thousands of dollars):

	(1)	(2)	(3)
Total purchase costs from outsider	400	400	370
Total outlay costs if kept inside	380	380	380
Total opportunity costs if kept inside	—	29	—
Total relevant inside costs	380	409	380
Net advantage (disadvantage) to company as a whole from keeping inside	20	(9)	(10)

4. Of course, in part 1, if the manager of S understood cost-volume-profit relationships, and if he wanted to maximize his short-run net income, he would probably accept a price of $200. This would bring a contribution to the divisional profit of 2,000 × ($200 − $190), or $20,000.The information given indicates that the best rule might be a market price with the seller having the option to refuse to sell internally. This would have led to the correct decision from the viewpoint of both the divisions and the company as a whole.

   In situation 1, S would obtain a contribution of $200 − $190, or $10 per unit. In 2, S would lose a contribution of $10 per unit, or $20,000; but its $29,000 cost saving on other work would lead to a net saving of $9,000, or $4.50 per unit. In 3, S would lose $5 per unit, or $10,000, if the business were kept inside.

5. As president, I probably would not want to become immersed in these disputes. If arbitration is necessary, it should probably be conducted by some other officer on the corporate staff. One possibility is to have the immediate line boss of the two managers make a decision.

   If decentralization is to be strictly adhered to, the arbitrator should probably do nothing under any of the conditions described. If no forced transfer were made, P would go outside, resulting in an optimal decision for the overall company in parts 2 and 3 but not in part 1.

   Suppose in part 1 that S refuses to meet the price of $200. This means that the company will be $20,000 poorer in the short run. Should top management interfere and force a transfer at $200? This would undercut the philosophy of decentralization. Many managers would not interfere because they would view the $20,000 as the price that has to be paid for mistakes made under decentralization. But how high must this price go before the temptation to interfere would be irresistible? $30,000? $40,000? How much?

   In sum, the point of this question is that any superstructure that interferes with lower-level decision making weakens decentralization. Of course, such interference may occasionally be necessary to prevent horrendous blunders. But recurring interference and constraints simply transform a decentralized organization into a centralized organization. Indeed, the trade-offs among solving the problems of goal congruence, incentive, and autonomy may justify more centralization in many instances.

   Despite the intuitive attractions of market price, the chapter contains illustrations where market price will not lead to optimal decisions. For example, sometimes the adherence by a supplying division to a high market price despite having low variable costs may force the consuming division not to buy even though the company as a whole would benefit.

   Note that the "general rule" described in the chapter also might be applied, although it frequently might be subject to suspicion because it seems more awkward than the "market-price" rule. Also, as part 1 below shows, the goal-congruent decision may be obvious at a transfer price of $190, but the S manager has no particular incentive to favor transfer:

TRANSFER PRICE	= OUTLAY COST	+ OPPORTUNITY COST	
1.	= $190	+ 0	= $190
2.	= $190	+ ($29,000 ÷ 2,000)	= $204.50
3.	= $190	+ 0	= $190

   P would buy inside in case 1 and outside in 2 and 3; these decisions would provide goal congruence for the company as a whole.

appendix: economic analysis of transfer pricing

Transfer pricing is analyzed in depth in the literature of economics and management science. Some of these references are contained in the reading list for this chapter. A long series of individual situations may be analyzed, including various combinations of intermediate and final markets, availabilities of capacity, and interdependencies of costs and demands. This appendix will limit the discussion to two situations as examples of the analysis.

In the first example, suppose a firm has a vertically integrated operation with two divisions, manufacturing and distribution. Assume further that the two divisions are cost-independent, so that the operations of either have no effect on the cost functions of the other. Also assume that there is no market whatsoever for the intermediate product.

To optimize overall firm profits, both divisions must agree on the quantity to be produced of the intermediate product. The optimal output and price will be where firm marginal cost (*MC*) per unit of intermediate product equals marginal revenue (*MR*) per unit of intermediate product, as Exhibit 22-2 demonstrates.

MC is the sum of the marginal manufacturing cost (*mmc*) in the first division and the marginal distribution cost (*mdc*) in the second division. If the transfer price is p^*, the second-division manager will choose an output level of q_d, so

EXHIBIT 22-2

BEST JOINT LEVEL OF OUTPUT

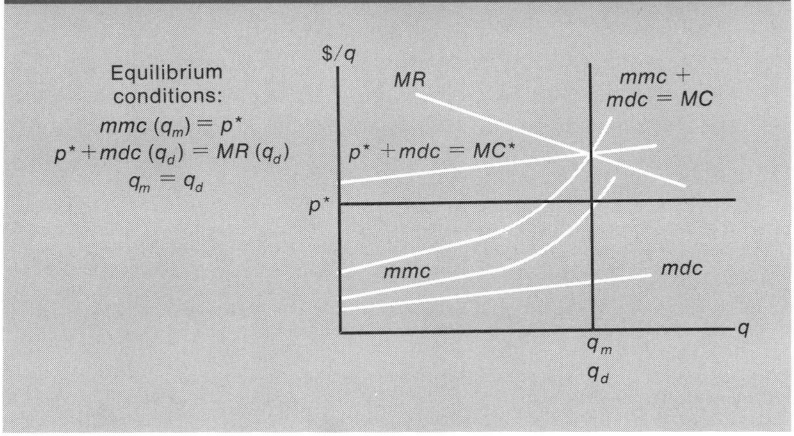

Source: This and the next exhibit are from Jack Hirshleifer, "Internal Pricing and Decentralized Decisions," in C. Bonini, R. Jaedicke, and H. Wagner, eds., *Management Controls: New Directions in Basic Research* (New York: McGraw-Hill, Inc., 1964) pp. 31, 33.

that $MR = p^* + mdc = MC^*$. In turn, the first-division manager would independently choose an output level of q_m, so that $mmc = p^*$. The transfer price p^* should, therefore, be set so that $q_d = q_m$; that is, so the two divisions operate at the same level.

Hirshleifer comments:

> There are a variety of ways in which the optimum solution might be arrived at operationally. Some device like a neutral umpire might be employed to set an initial trial p^*—after which the divisions would respond by declaring tentative outputs q_m and q_d. If q_m exceeds q_d, the p^* should be adjusted downward by the umpire, and the reverse if q_d exceeds q_m—until a p^* is found such that the planned outputs are coordinated.[13]

But coordination cannot be assured by counting on the independent decisions of the division managers. Each is in a monopolistic position. The first division is inclined to limit supply and generate more profit for itself at the expense of the overall firm. The second division is inclined to behave in the opposite way, but with a similar impact on overall profits.

Note that gamesmanship is likely. Either party may give inaccurate responses to a neutral umpire with the hope of attaining a more favorable price. The forcing of transfers at marginal cost will not be welcomed by the manager of the first division. There is an obvious conflict between the notion of what ordinarily constitutes revenue for profit centers and of what transfer price leads to optimal economic decisions. In this situation, the first division would operate at a loss at all times. Systems of subsidies or taxes have been suggested as remedies for this weakness.[14]

In the second example, assume that there is an imperfectly competitive external market for the intermediate product, so that the marginal cost of division 1, *mmc*, is less than the prevailing market price, p. Therefore, division 1 is a monopoly. Assume further that there is demand independence; that is, that additional internal sales do not affect external demands. To illustrate, in some

[13] Jack Hirshleifer, "Internal Pricing and Decentralized Decisions," in C. Bonini, R. Jaedicke, and H. Wagner, eds., *Management Controls: New Directions in Basic Research* (New York: McGraw-Hill Book Company, 1964), p. 30. Hirshleifer's work is the basis for the presentation here. Joshua Ronen and George McKinney, in "Transfer Pricing for Divisional Autonomy," *Journal of Accounting Research,* Vol. 8, No. 1 (Spring 1970), p. 103, suggest an alternative method of supplying information, which might be less restrictive than the Hirshleifer method. Also recommended is David Solomons, *Divisional Performance: Measurement and Control* (Homewood, Ill.: Richard D. Irwin, Inc., 1968), pp. 160–232.

[14] Linear programming and decomposition procedures have also been proposed as ways to insure goal congruence and incentive. Both propose elaborate models that cannot work successfully without exhaustive information about the revenue and cost functions of many divisions. All the necessary conditions lead to the conclusion that centralized decision making may be more cost effective than the use of such models. See W. J. Baumol and Tibor Fabian, "Decomposition, Pricing for Decentralization and External Economics," *Management Science,* Vol. 11, No. 1, pp. 1–32; and Jerome E. Hass, "Transfer Pricing in a Decentralized Firm," *Management Science: Application,* Vol. 14, No. 6, pp. B-310 through B-331.

cases a refinery selling unbranded gasoline to an affiliated distributor does not expect an adverse effect on the final demand for its branded gasoline. Under these conditions, the overall profit of the firm would be optimized by monopolistic exploitation of outside customers for both the intermediate and final products, but not of the internal intermediate customer.

As Exhibit 22-3 shows, the overall profit of the firm is optimized by having the prices of internal intermediate customers lower than prices for outsiders. In the exhibit, D and d are demands of outsiders and P and p are prices to outsiders. The equilibrium value for the internal price $p^* = mmc = mr$, where mr is the marginal revenue from selling to the intermediate external market. Note that the external price p exceeds p^*. A neutral umpire would set p^* so that q_m, the total intermediate quantity manufactured (which is the sum of q_s, the quantity sold to outside intermediate customers, plus q_d, the quantity incorporated in the product sold to final outside customers), provides optimal profits for the firm as a whole.

Hirshleifer comments on the analysis in Exhibit 22-3 as follows:

> The solution is found analytically by a price discrimination technique—in which *mmc* is equated simultaneously with marginal revenue, *mr*, in the external intermediate

EXHIBIT 22-3

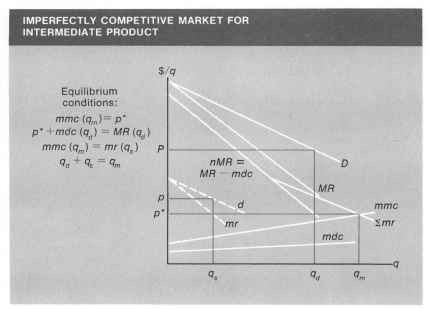

IMPERFECTLY COMPETITIVE MARKET FOR INTERMEDIATE PRODUCT

Equilibrium conditions:

$mmc\ (q_m) = p^*$

$p^* + mdc\ (q_d) = MR\ (q_d)$

$mmc\ (q_m) = mr\ (q_s)$

$q_d + q_s = q_m$

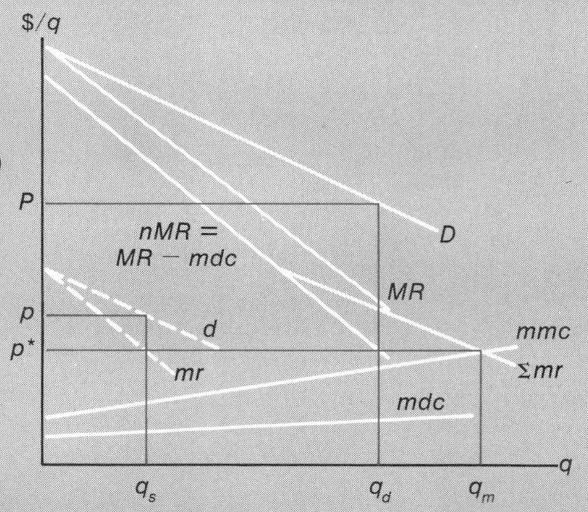

market (thus determining external intermediate sales, q_s), and with $MR - mdc$ (which we denote *net marginal revenue, nMR*) for the internal customer, thus making $mmc + mdc = MR$ and determining optimal output q_d in the final external market.[15]

QUESTIONS, PROBLEMS, AND CASES

22-1 Why are intracompany transfer prices often necessary?

22-2 What are two major bases for pricing intracompany transfers?

22-3 What is the major limitation to transfer prices based on cost?

22-4 "Company transfer-pricing policies must satisfy dual objectives." What are the objectives?

22-5 Where reliable market prices cannot be ascertained for transfer pricing, what is the impact on divisional-performance measurement?

22-6 What is the most common example in transfer pricing of a clash between divisional action and overall company profitability?

22-7 If an optimal economic decision is wanted in a particular situation, what is a general rule for transfer pricing?

22-8 What is outlay cost in the context of transfer pricing?

22-9 Why is market price as a basis for transfer pricing a special case rather than a universal guide?

22-10 What three problems regarding systems design are also applicable to transfer pricing?

22-11 "Transfer pricing is confined to profit centers." Do you agree? Why?

22-12 When does imperfect competition exist?

22-13 *Transfer Pricing in an Automobile Dealership* A large automobile dealership is installing a responsibility-accounting system and three profit centers: parts and service; new vehicles; and used vehicles. Each department manager has been told to run his shop as if he were in business for himself. However, there are interdepartmental dealings. For example:

a. The parts and service department prepares new cars for final delivery and repairs used cars prior to resale.

b. The used-car department's major source of inventory has been cars traded in as part payment for new cars.

The owner of the dealership has asked you to draft a company policy statement on transfer pricing, together with specific rules to be applied to the examples cited. He has told you that clarity is of paramount importance because your statement will be relied upon for settling transfer-pricing disputes.

22-14 *Variable Cost as a Transfer Price* A product's variable cost is \$1 and its market value is \$2 at a transfer point from Division S to Division P. Division P's variable cost of processing the product further is \$1.25, and the selling price of the final product is \$2.75.

[15] Hirshleifer, "Internal Pricing," p. 34. Later, when discussing the case of interdependent demands for the intermediate and final products, he stresses that internal transfers at marginal cost now entail loss of profitable sales at full price. "So the rule of marginal-cost pricing to internal customers no longer applies—unless marginal cost is redefined to include the loss of external profit."

required

1. Prepare a tabulation of the contribution margin per unit for Division P performance and overall performance under the two alternatives of (a) processing further and (b) selling to outsiders at the transfer point.
2. As Division P manager, which alternative would you choose? Explain.

22-15 *Transfer Pricing* The Plastics Company has a separate division that produces a special molding powder. For the past three years about two-thirds of the output has been sold to another division within the company. The remainder has been sold to outsiders. Last year's operating data follow:

	TO OTHER DIVISION		TO OUTSIDERS	
Sales	10,000 T. @ \$70*	\$700,000	5,000 T. @ \$100	\$500,000
Variable costs @ \$50		\$500,000		\$250,000
Fixed costs		150,000		75,000
Total costs		\$650,000		\$325,000
Gross margin		\$ 50,000		\$175,000

* The \$70 price is ordinarily determined by the outside sales price less selling and administrative expenses wholly applicable to outside business.

The buying-division manager has a chance to get a firm contract with an outside supplier at \$65 for the ensuing year.

required

Assume that the molding-powder division manager says that he cannot sell at \$65, because no margin can be earned. As the buying-division manager, write a short reply. Assume that the 10,000 tons cannot be sold by the molding-powder division to other customers.

22-16 *Transfer-Pricing Dispute* Allison-Chambers Corp., manufacturer of tractors and other heavy farm equipment, is organized along decentralized lines, with each manufacturing division operating as a separate profit center. Each division head has been delegated full authority on all decisions involving the sale of his division's output both to outsiders and to other divisions of Allison-Chambers. Division C has in the past always purchased its requirement of a particular tractor-engine component from Division A. However, when informed that Division A was increasing its price to \$150, Division C's management decided to purchase the engine component from outside suppliers.

The component can be purchased by C for \$135 on the open market. Division A insists that owing to the recent installation of some highly specialized equipment and the resulting high depreciation charges, A would not be able to make an adequate profit on its investment unless it raised its price. A's management appealed to top management of Allison-Chambers for support in its dispute with C and supplied the following operating data:

C's annual purchases of tractor-engine component	1,000
A's variable costs per unit of tractor-engine component	\$120
A's fixed costs per unit of tractor-engine component	\$ 20

required

1. Assume that there are no alternative uses for internal facilities. Determine whether the company as a whole will benefit if Division C purchases the component from outside suppliers for \$135 per unit.
2. Assume that internal facilities of A would not otherwise be idle. By not producing the 1,000 units for C, A's equipment and other facilities would be assigned to other production operations, and would result in annual cash operating savings of \$18,000. Should C purchase from outsiders?
3. Assume that there are no alternative uses for A's internal facilities and that the price of outsiders drops \$20. Should C purchase from outsiders?

22-17 *Transfer-Pricing Problem* Assume in the Allison-Chambers Corp. problem that Division A could sell the 1,000 units to other customers at $155 per unit with variable selling costs of $5 per unit. If this were the case, determine whether Allison-Chambers would benefit if C purchased the 1,000 components from outsiders at $135 per unit.

22-18 *Pricing and Lack of Information* Company X has more than 100 divisions, including A, B, and H. Division A wants to buy a component for its final product. Two outside bids have been received, one for $200 and one for $212. The supplier who bid $212 will in turn buy some raw materials for $30 from Division H, which has spare capacity, that will increase H's contribution to overall company profits by $20 ($30 revenue minus $10 outlay costs). The supplier who bids $200 will not buy any raw materials from Company X.

required

1. Prepare a diagram of the cash flows for both alternatives. Does the use of the external market prices lead to optimal decision for the company as a whole? Explain.
2. Suppose Division B is working at full capacity and can provide the needed part to A or to an outside buyer at the same price of $212. (For convenience, we now assume that $212 is the uniform market price.) If market price were the rule, B would have to meet the $212 bid. Assume that the outlay costs to B of filling the order were $150. Finally, assume that B, unlike the outside supplier, does not buy from H because this conglomerate organization is so large and communications are so bad that the B manager is unaware of this alternative. Will the use of $212 as a transfer price lead to optimal decisions for the firm as a whole? Apply the "general rule" as described in the chapter. Will the resulting transfer price lead to optimal decisions for the firm as a whole?

22-19 *Conflict of Interests of Profit Centers and Company as a Whole* [This and the next problem are adapted from David Solomons, *Divisional Performance: Measurement and Control* (New York: Financial Executives Research Foundation, 1965), pp. 167–79.] Division A of a company is the only source of supply for an intermediate product that is converted by Division B into a salable final product. Most of A's costs are fixed. For any output up to 1,000 units a day, its total costs are $500 a day. Total costs increase by $100 a day for every additional thousand units made. Division A judges that its own results will be optimized if it sets its price at 40¢ a unit, and it acts accordingly.

Division B incurs additional costs in converting the intermediate product supplied by A into a finished product. These costs are $1,250 for any output up to 1,000 units, and $250 per thousand for outputs in excess of 1,000. On the revenue side, B can increase its revenue only by spending more on sales promotion and by reducing selling prices. Its sales forecast is:

SALES IN UNITS	NET REVENUE PER THOUSAND UNITS
1,000	$1,750.00
2,000	1,325.00
3,000	1,100.00
4,000	925.00
5,000	800.00
6,000	666.67

required

1. Prepare a schedule comparing B's costs, including its purchases from A, revenues, and net income at various levels of output.
2. What is B's maximum net income? At that level, what is A's net income? At that level, what is the corporation's aggregate net income?
3. Suppose the company abandons its divisionalized structure. Instead of being two profit centers, A and B are combined into a single profit center with responsibility for the complete production and marketing of the product. Prepare a schedule similar to that in requirement 1. What volume level will provide the most net income?
4. Evaluate the results in 3. Why did the circumstances in requirement 1 lead to less net income than in requirement 3? How would you adjust the transfer-pricing policy to assure that overall company net income will be maximized where separate profit centers A and B are maintained?

22-20 *Transfer Prices in an Imperfect Market* Division A is the supplier division and Divisions B and C are the consumer divisions of a large company. After Division B deducts its own processing costs, the total net revenue and the marginal net revenue it derives from various quantities of intermediate product are:

DIVISION B

QUANTITY OF INTERMEDIATE PROCESSED, IN POUNDS	TOTAL NET REVENUE	MARGINAL NET REVENUE
1,000	$ 600	$600
2,000	900	300
3,000	1,100	200
4,000	1,200	100

Similarly, for Division C we have:

DIVISION C

QUANTITY OF INTERMEDIATE PROCESSED, IN POUNDS	TOTAL NET REVENUE	MARGINAL NET REVENUE
2,000	$1,200	$—
3,000	1,800	600
4,000	2,100	300
5,000	2,300	200
6,000	2,400	100

Division A, the producing division, faces the following cost conditions:

DIVISION A

QUANTITY OF INTERMEDIATE PRODUCED, IN POUNDS	TOTAL COST	MARGINAL COST
4,000	$2,000	$—
5,000	2,100	100
6,000	2,250	150
7,000	2,425	175
8,000	2,625	200
9,000	2,925	300
10,000	3,325	400

What transfer price should be set for A's output? Why?

22-21 *The Pertinent Transfer Price* The XYZ Company has two divisions, A and B. For one of the company's products, Division A produces a major subassembly and Division B incorporates this subassembly into the final product. There is a market for both the subassembly and the final product, and the divisions have been delegated profit responsibility. The transfer price for the subassembly has been set at long-run average market price.

The following data are available to each division:

Estimated selling price for final product	$300
Long-run average selling price for intermediate product	200
Outlay cost for completion in Division B	150
Outlay cost in Division A	120

The manager of Division B has made the following calculation:

Selling price—final product		$300
Transferred-in cost (market)	$200	
Outlay cost for completion	150	350
Contribution (loss) on product		$ (50)

required

1. Should transfers be made to Division B if there is no excess capacity in Division A? Is market price the correct transfer price?
2. Assume that Division A's maximum capacity for this product is 1,000 units per month and sales to the intermediate market are presently 800 units. Should 200 units be transferred to Division B? At what relevant transfer price? Assume for a variety of reasons that A will maintain the $200 selling price indefinitely; that is, A is not considering cutting the price to outsiders regardless of the presence of idle capacity.
3. Suppose A quoted a transfer price of $150. What would be the contribution to the firm as a whole if the transfer were made? As manager of B, would you be inclined to buy at $150?

22-22 *Pricing in Imperfect Markets* Refer to Problem 22-21.

1. Suppose the manager of A has the option of (a) cutting the external price to $195 with the certainty that sales will rise to 1,000 units or (b) maintaining the outside price of $200 for the 800 units and transferring the 200 units to B at some price that would produce the same income for A. What transfer price would produce the same income for A? Does that price coincide with that produced by the "general rule" in the chapter so that the desirable decision for the company as a whole would ensue?
2. Suppose that if the selling price for the intermediate product is dropped to $195, outside sales can be increased to 900 units. Division B wants to acquire as many as 200 units if the transfer price is acceptable. For simplicity assume that there is absolutely no outside market for the final 100 units of Division A capacity.
   a. Using the "general rule," what is (are) the relevant transfer price(s) that should lead to the correct economic decision? Ignore performance evaluation (incentive) considerations.
   b. Compare the total contributions under the alternatives to show why the transfer price(s) recommended lead(s) to the optimal economic decision.

22-23 *Utilization of Capacity* (J. Patell) The California Instrument Company (CIC) consists of the Semiconductor Division and the Minicomputer Division, each of which operates as an independent profit center. The Semiconductor Division employs craftsmen who produce two different electronic components, the new high-performance Super-chip and an older product called Okay-chip. These two products have the following cost characteristics:

	SUPER-CHIP		OKAY-CHIP	
Material	Parts	$ 2.00	Parts	$1.00
Labor	2 hours @ $14.00	28.00	½ hour @ $14.00	7.00

Annual overhead in the Semiconductor Division totals $400,000, all fixed. Owing to the high skill level necessary for the craftsmen, the Semiconductor Division's capacity is set at 50,000 hours per year.

To date, only one customer has developed a product utilizing Super-chip, and this customer orders a maximum of 15,000 Super-chips per year, at a price of $60 per chip. If CIC cannot meet his entire demand, the customer curtails his own production. The rest of Semiconductor's capacity is devoted to Okay-chip, for which there is unlimited demand at $12 per chip.

The Minicomputer Division produces only one product, a process-control unit, which requires a complex circuit board imported from Sweden at a price of $60. The control unit's costs are:

	CONTROL UNIT	
Material	Circuit board	$60
	Other parts	8
Labor	5 hours @ $10	50

The Minicomputer Division is composed of only a small assembly plant and all overhead is fixed at a total of $80,000 per year. The current market price for the control unit is $140 per unit.

A joint research project has just revealed that with minor modifications, a single Super-chip could be substituted for the circuit board currently used by the Minicomputer Division. The modification would require an extra 1 hour of labor by Minicomputer's staff, for a new total of 6 hours per control unit. Minicomputer has therefore asked Semiconductor to declare a transfer price at which the Semiconductor Division would sell Super-chip internally.

required

1. Minicomputer expects to sell 5,000 control units this year. From the overall viewpoint of California Instruments, how many Super-chips should be transferred to Minicomputer to replace circuit boards?
2. If demand for the control unit is sure to be 5,000 units, but its *price is uncertain,* what should the transfer price of Super-chip be to ensure proper decisions? (All other data unchanged.)
3. If demand for the control unit rises to 12,000 units at a price of $140 per unit, how many of the 12,000 units should be built using Super-chip? (All other data unchanged.)

22-24 *Transfer Pricing in Banks* The Jackson Stone National Bank is a two-branch bank servicing retail and wholesale customers in the greater Big City metropolitan area. The head-office staff consists of the president and the controller. With minor exceptions, the branch managers are permitted to conduct their affairs like the heads of two independent banks. The planning and control system centers around branch income statements prepared by the controller.

The Big City branch, located in the growing downtown area, serves primarily commercial customers. The manager, Mr. Jones, has found in recent years that while he faces a number of vigorous competitors, the principal constraint on his ability to generate new loan business is a lack of supporting deposits. The *only* alternative source of lendable funds is the purchase of Eurodollars, which are dollar deposits held in a bank outside the United States. This option is considered less than acceptable by Jones, as the 11 percent interest he would have to pay for such funds is higher than the rate he is able to charge loan customers, currently 10 percent.

The new Sun City branch, on the other hand, is located outside of town in a large and growing retirement community and is primarily a retail branch. Mr. Smith, the manager, is in his first year with the Stone Bank. In his attempts to sell the bank's services to the Sun City residents, he has found that his only success is in the area of savings deposits. Loan business, on the other hand, is both competitive and scarce. The interest rate he can charge is constrained by the fact that the manager of the local branch of the Behemoth Bank, while not actively soliciting loan business, is apparently charging rates below the prevailing Big City prime rate. Additionally, there seems to be a fundamental resistance on the part of the Sun City residents to the idea of borrowing, even at the 6 percent rates Smith has been offering. In spite of his frequent lectures on the merits of leverage, the best Smith has been able to do is to generate a few golf-cart installment and Social Security check receivable loans. As a result, he finds himself with substantial excess savings deposits on which he is paying 5 percent interest but earning nothing. Aside from the deposits, which he has to keep in the vault to satisfy the government's 20 percent (of deposits) reserve requirement, the vault additionally contains excess lendable funds equal to almost 70 percent of total savings deposits. The controller has suggested that he lend these funds to Jones at the Big City branch. This was acceptable to both managers, although some disagreement arose as to the interest rate appropriate for such a loan. The argument was finally settled by the controller, who indicated that the theoretically correct rate was the rate Smith was paying on savings deposits, 5 percent. It has been further agreed that if Smith could find additional loans, any or all of the funds lent to Jones would be returned.

required

1. Evaluate the 5 percent interbranch loan rate, and suggest appropriate changes in relation to the following criteria:
   a. Motivating managers to act in a manner consistent with the best interests of the bank as a whole.
   b. Evaluating the performance of individual *branches.*
2. Would your answer change if the Sun City loan rate were to rise to 7 percent, while all other rates, as well as the level of loan demand at Sun City, remained the same?
3. Would your answer change if all rates were the same as in part 1, except that the cost of Eurodollars dropped to 9 percent?
4. Based on your answers to the questions above, what general statements can you make about the interbranch loan rate appropriate for evaluating individual *managers?*

22-25 *Transfer Pricing to Brazil* The Amplifier Division of Cadillac Electronics, Inc., a diversified international company headquartered in New York, sells amplifier kits in the United States and several foreign countries.

The selling price for these kits is $40 in the United States, where the income tax rate is 50 percent.

The Brazilian market is one of the foreign markets in which the Amplifier Division is active. Cadillac Electronics has a 60-percent-owned subsidiary in Brazil, which buys the amplifier kits from the Amplifier Division and sells them to local wholesalers.

The total cost of the kits delivered to the Brazilian port is \$30, of which \$2 is transportation cost. Brazilian tariffs on amplifiers are 40 percent on declared value. These duties are paid by the Brazilian subsidiary and become part of its cost of inventory. There is a minimum declared value legally allowed of \$30 but no upper limit. The applicable income tax rate in Brazil is 35 percent. *There are no other restrictions or taxes affecting the transfer of funds from Brazil to the United States.*

required

1. In the past, Cadillac Electronics has transferred the kits to the Brazilian subsidiary at a declared price equal to the United States market price, i.e., \$40. Ignoring performance measurement and motivational issues, do you find the \$40 declared value a sound economic decision? If not, what declared value would you select? Explain
2. Does the transfer price you recommend suit the need for good relations with the minority shareholders of the Brazilian subsidiary? Why?

22-26 *Paper Company* (Copyright 1957 by the President and Fellows of Harvard College. Reproduced by permission.) "If I were to price these boxes any lower than \$480 a thousand," said Mr. Brunner, manager of Birch Paper Company's Thompson division, "I'd be countermanding my order of last month for our salesmen to stop shaving their bids and to bid full-cost quotations. I've been trying for weeks to improve the quality of our business, and if I turn around now and accept this job at \$430 or \$450 or something less than \$480 I'll be tearing down this program I've been working so hard to build up. The division can't very well show a profit by putting in bids which don't even cover a fair share of overhead costs, let alone give us a profit."

Birch Paper Company was a medium-sized, partly integrated paper company, producing white and kraft papers and paperboard. A portion of its paperboard output was converted into corrugated boxes by the Thompson division, which also printed and colored the outside surface of the boxes. Including Thompson, the company had four producing divisions and a timberland division which supplied part of the company's pulp requirements.

For several years each division had been judged independently on the basis of its profit and return on investment. Top management had been working to gain effective results from a policy of decentralizing responsibility and authority for all decisions but those relating to overall company policy. The company's top officials felt that in the past few years the concept of decentralization had been successfully applied and that the company's profits and competitive position had definitely improved.

In early 19_7 the Northern division designed a special display box for one of its papers in conjunction with the Thompson division, which was equipped to make the box. Thompson's package design and development staff spent several months perfecting the design, production methods, and materials that were to be used. Because of the unusual color and shape these were far from standard. According to an agreement between the two divisions, the Thompson division was reimbursed by the Northern division for the cost of its design and development work.

When the specifications were all prepared, the Northern division asked for bids on the box from the Thompson division and from two outside companies. Each division manager was normally free to buy from whichever supplier he wished, and even on sales within the company, divisions were expected to meet the going market price if they wanted the business.

In early 19_7 the profit margins of converters such as the Thompson division were being squeezed. Thompson, as did many other similar converters, bought its board, liner, or paper and its function was to print, cut, and shape it into boxes. Though it bought most of its materials from other Birch divisions, most of Thompson's sales were to outside customers. If Thompson got the business, it would probably buy the linerboard and corrugating medium from the Southern division of Birch. The walls of a corrugated box consist of outside and inside sheets of linerboard sandwiching the fluted corrugating medium. About 70 percent of Thompson's out-of-pocket cost of $400 represented the cost of linerboard and corrugating medium. Though Southern had been running below capacity and had excess inventory, it quoted the market price, which had not noticeably weakened as a result of the oversupply. Its out-of-pocket costs on both liner and corrugating medium were about 60 percent of the selling price.

The Northern division received bids on the boxes of $480 a thousand from the Thompson division, $430 a thousand from West Paper Company, and $432 a thousand from Erie Papers, Ltd. Erie Papers offered to buy from Birch the outside linerboard with the special printing already on it, but would supply its own inside liner and corrugating medium. The outside liner would be supplied by the Southern division at a price equivalent of $90 per thousand boxes, and would be printed for $30 a thousand by the Thompson division. Of the $30, about $25 would be out-of-pocket costs.

Since this situation appeared a little unusual, William Kenton, manager of the Northern division, discussed the wide discrepancy of bids with Birch's commercial vice-president. He told the vice-president: "We sell in a very competitive market, where higher costs cannot be passed on. How can we be expected to show a decent profit and return on investment if we have to buy our supplies at more than 10 percent over the going market?"

Knowing that Mr. Brunner had on occasion in the past few months been unable to operate the Thompson division at capacity, the vice-president found it odd that Mr. Brunner would add the full 20 percent overhead and profit charge to his out-of-pocket costs. When asked about this, Mr. Brunner's answer was the statement that appears at the beginning of the case. He went on to say that having done the developmental work on the box, and having received no profit on that, he felt entitled to a good markup on the production of the box itself.

The vice-president explored further the cost structures of the various divisions. He remembered a comment that the controller had made at a meeting the week before to the effect that costs that were variable for one division could be largely fixed for the company as a whole. He knew that in the absence of specific orders from top management, Mr. Kenton would accept the lowest bid, which was that of the West Paper Company for $430. However, it would be possible for top management to order the acceptance of another bid if the situation warranted such action. And though the volume represented by the transactions in question was less than 5 percent of the volume of any of the divisions involved, other transactions could conceivably raise similar problems later.

required

1. In the controversy described, how, if at all, is the transfer-price system dysfunctional?
2. As the commercial vice-president, what action would you take?

22-27 *British Television* (A. Kemble) Granada Group Ltd. was founded in the 1930s, when the present chairman opened his first movie theater in London, England. Since then the company has grown steadily and diversified throughout the leisure-communication field. Sales in 1977 exceeded £100 million and net income was £10 million.

The company has five main divisions:

DIVISIONS	*SALES IN MILLIONS*
Granada T.V. Rental	£ 40 million
Granada Commercial T.V.	37 million
Granada Cinema & Bingo	10 million
Granada Publishing	7 million
Granada Motorway Food Services	6 million
	£100 million

The managing director,[16] of each division reports to the Group Board of Directors, which approves his budgets and strategies and reviews his performance. Within this general framework the individual directors have a large degree of autonomy.

nature of divisions

Granada T.V. Rental division has a chain of over 500 television rental showrooms throughout the British Isles and rents sets to approximately one million customers. No sets are sold. (In England most people rent rather than buy T.V. sets.) The division does not manufacture its own T.V. sets but uses a wide range of domestic and foreign suppliers.

The period 1974–1977 witnessed an extraordinary explosion in demand for color T.V. sets, and the division shared in this demand. Supply throughout the industry lagged behind demand during this entire period. However, a slowdown in the growth of demand occurred in late 1976 and 1977.

Granada Commercial T.V. division holds the franchise for commercial television services in the northwest region of England. The English system is such that if a company wants to advertise on television in the northwest, it has to use Granada Commercial T.V.[17] Because of this monopoly position, there is a special tax on the profits of T.V. companies (67.5 percent as compared with the normal corporate tax rate of 52 percent).

The level of advertising revenue received by Granada Commercial T.V. is closely correlated with the state of the economy. For example, in the first half of 1976 bookings were at or very near 100 percent of available time;[18] whereas in the first quarter of 1977 there was a decline of some 20 percent in comparison with the same period in 1976.

The northwest region contains the two major urban centers of Liverpool and Manchester, so it is an important market for the other Granada divisions.

Granada Cinema & Bingo division has a chain of over 50 movie theaters and bingo clubs. Some of these are located in the northwest region.

[16] The title of "managing director" in England is equivalent to that of "president" in the U.S.

[17] Throughout England there are two parallel services—public broadcasting (BBC1 and BBC2) and commercial broadcasting.

The country is "carved up" into several regions, and a franchise is given to *one* commercial company for exclusive commercial services in that region. The BBC operates in all these regions, but there is no advertising on the BBC, so the commercial company is in a monopoly position in the franchise area.

There are five *major* commercial T.V. companies—Granada (Northwest), ATV (Midlands), Yorkshire (Northeast), Thames (London, weekdays), London Weekend (London, weekends), and a further six smaller companies in other regions.

[18] The English commercial T.V. stations, like their U.S. counterparts, are allowed to show only a certain number of minutes of advertising per hour.

Granada Publishing division publishes a wide range of material, including educational handbooks, music books, and mass-appeal paperbacks.

Granada Motorway Services division operates a chain of ten motorway (freeway) restaurant and gas-station complexes. Most of these are on the motorways that link London with the North of England.

division interaction

There is little interaction between the divisions because they are all in essentially different fields. However, there are two exceptions: Granada T.V. Rental periodically runs advertising campaigns on television. Most of its budget is spent in the London area (the biggest market) with Thames Television Ltd. or London Weekend Ltd., but about 25 percent of the budget is spent on advertising in the northwest region. Granada Commercial T.V. gives Granada T.V. Rental no discount from market price on this advertising, although the marginal cost of showing a commercial is approximately £0.

No other Granada division uses television advertising at present. However, the British industry often follows U.S. industry in advertising patterns, and there has been a recent increase in the U.S. in T.V. advertising for movies and for "best-selling" paperback books.

Granada Commercial T.V.'s head office has approximately 150 television sets for the use of executives, producers, directors, etc. (closed-circuit viewing of new material). In the past Granada Commercial T.V. has bought its sets through Granada T.V. Rental. The latter division has used its buying power to get sets for Granada Commercial T.V. at trade prices from its suppliers and has transferred these sets to Granada Commercial T.V. at this same trade price (i.e., it has made no profit on the transaction). This has been done "as a favor" for a sister division.

required

The Group Board of Directors has some doubts about the present transfer-pricing practices. You are on the corporate staff and you have been asked by the board to review the present practices and make any appropriate recommendations.

Segment Performance Measurement

23

This chapter examines the general problems of designing an accounting system for measuring segment performance. We will be especially concerned with the difficulties of relating profits to invested capital.

The preceding chapter described a profit center. An investment center goes a step further; its success is measured not only by its income but also by relating that income to its invested capital. In practice, the term *investment center* is not widely used. Instead, *profit center* is used indiscriminately to describe segments that are always assigned responsibility for revenue and expenses but may or may not be assigned responsibility for the related invested capital.

overview of problems of design

Consider the steps that must be taken by the control-system designer, who may be an accountant, a manager, or both. First, he must choose a measure of accomplishment that represents top-management objectives. This provides a conceptual structure. Should it be net income, rate of return on investment, contribution margin, sales, or some other measure? Second, whatever measure is chosen, the designer must then choose how to define such items as income or investment. Should income be based on variable or absorption costing? Should central corporate costs be allocated? Should investment consist of assets, or assets minus liabilities, or some other collection? Third, how should items be measured? Historical cost? Replacement cost? Realizable value? Fourth, what standards should be applied; should all divisions be required to earn the same rate of return on all their investments? Fifth, what timing of feedback is needed? Quarterly? Annually? Should feedback on the performance of managers be timed differently from feedback on the performance of divisions as economic investments?

These five steps are not necessarily taken sequentially. Instead, the answers to these questions are interdependent. Taken together, they produce a particular control system that is supposed to be optimal for the specific organization as a whole. In turn, as in the preceding chapter, the answers to these questions depend on predictions of how these information alternatives may solve problems of goal congruence, management incentive, and subunit autonomy in a cost-effective manner. The overlay of cost-benefit analysis is still present.

measure that represents top-management objectives

role of investment

What quantitative measure best represents top-management objectives? Income? Rate of return? Some other measure? Many managers are preoccupied with the measures of dollar sales, dollar profits, and profit margins (the ratio of profits to dollar sales). However, the ultimate test of profitability is not the absolute amount of profit or the relationship of profit to sales. The critical test is the relationship of profit to invested capital. The most popular way of expressing this relationship is by means of a rate of return on investment (ROI). The ROI approach has been used for centuries by financiers and others. Still, this technique did not become widespread in industry for judging operating performance until the early 1960s. Conceptually, ROI has innate appeal because it blends in one number all the major ingredients of profitability; the ROI statistic by itself can be compared with opportunities elsewhere, inside or outside the company. Practically, however, ROI is an imperfect measurement that should be used with skepticism and in conjunction with other performance measurements.

Companies take different approaches to the problem of measuring return on investment, differing mostly with respect to the appropriate measure of invested capital, but also differing in the measure of income.

A useful approach to the problem may be outlined by using the following relationships:

$$\frac{\text{Sales}}{\text{Invested capital}} \times \frac{\text{Net income}}{\text{Sales}} = \frac{\text{Net income}}{\text{Invested capital}}$$

or

Capital turnover × Net income percentage of sales = Return on investment

Consider the components of the relationships. One may make the following obvious generalizations: Any action is beneficial that (a) boosts sales, (b) reduces invested capital, or (c) reduces costs—while holding the other two factors constant. Put another way, there are two basic ingredients in profit making: capital turnovers and profit margins. An improvement in either without changing the other will enhance return on invested capital.

ROI as a tool for management

Assume that top management decides that a 20 percent return on invested capital is a profit target that will yield adequate rewards and yet not invite entry into the market by new competitors. How can this return be attained? Present performance (in millions of dollars) follows:

	$\frac{\text{Sales}}{\text{Invested capital}}$	×	$\frac{\text{Net income}}{\text{Sales}}$	=	$\frac{\text{Net income}}{\text{Invested capital}}$
Present	$\frac{100}{50}$	×	$\frac{9}{100}$	=	9/50, or 18%
Alternatives:					
A. Increase net income by lowering expenses	$\frac{100}{50}$	×	$\frac{10}{100}$	=	10/50, or 20%
B. Decrease assets	$\frac{100}{45}$	×	$\frac{9}{100}$	=	9/45, or 20%

Alternative A demonstrates a popular way of improving performance. Margins may be increased by reducing expenses, as in this case, or by boosting selling prices, or by increasing sales volume relative to a given amount of fixed expenses.

Alternative B shows that changes of investments in assets may also improve performance. Management has always been very conscious of the need for increasing sales and for controlling costs so that good profit margins may be attained. But control of investment has not always received conscientious managerial attention. Too often, asset balances rise without justification. Not only do operating costs have to be controlled, but investment in cash, inventory, receivables, and fixed assets must be kept to the minimum that is consistent with effective performance. This means investing idle cash, determining proper inventory levels, managing credit judiciously, and spending carefully on fixed assets. In other words, increasing asset turnover means getting the maximum mileage in sales out of every dollar invested in business resources. For example, having too much inventory is sometimes worse than having too little. Turnover decreases and goods deteriorate or become obsolete, thus dragging the rate of return downward.

ROI or residual income?

Earlier we saw that the ultimate test of profitability is the relationship of profit to invested capital. Until this point, our examples implied that the desired objective of management is the maximization of the rate of return on investment. But an investment center may be judged on what has been labeled *residual income* instead of on its rate of return. Residual income is the net income of an investment center, less the "imputed" interest on the invested capital used by the center. The choice of whether to use ROI or residual income as a management objective may induce different decisions.

Compare the calculations for two identical divisions:

	DIVISION A	*DIVISION B*
(1) Net income (after income taxes)	$ 25,000	$ 25,000
(2) Imputed interest at 16% of invested capital		16,000
(3) Invested capital	100,000	100,000
ROI [(1) ÷ (3)]	25%	
Residual income [(1) − (2)]		9,000

The objective of maximizing residual income assumes that as long as the division earns a rate in excess of the charge for invested capital, the division should expand. The manager of Division B would expand as long as his incremental opportunities earned 16 percent or more on his incremental assets.

General Electric favors the residual-income approach because managers will concentrate on maximizing a number (dollars of residual income) rather than a percentage (rate of return).[1] The objective of maximizing ROI, however, may induce managers of highly profitable divisions to reject projects that, from the viewpoint of the corporation as a whole, should be accepted. For example, the manager of Division A would be reluctant to accept a new project with a 20 percent rate even though top management regards 16 percent as a minimum desired rate of return. In contrast, the residual-income approach would charge him only 16 percent, and he would be inclined to accept all projects that exceed that rate.

There is a parallel between the discounted cash-flow methods in capital budgeting and the comparison of ROI and residual income. In Chapter 13 comparisons were made between the internal rate of return and the net present-value methods. The internal rate method is similar to the ROI method, and the net present-value method is similar to the residual-income method. Residual income changes the goal from "maximize ROI" to "maximize dollar return in excess of minimum desired ROI." In other words, ROI implies, "Go forth and maximize your *rate* of return." In contrast, residual income implies, "Go forth and maximize your *absolute amount* of income in excess of some desired minimum." As always, the choice depends on top management's preferences in light of how decisions might differ under ROI or residual income.

[1] See Robert W. Lewis, *Planning, Managing, and Measuring the Business* (New York: Financial Executives Research Foundation), p. 32.

distinction between managers and investments

role of budget

Before exploring the many facets of investment centers, consider the powerful role of the budget in all these situations. In practice, comparisons tend to be made **of actual amounts against budgeted amounts for a particular investment center.** Comparisons of income or rates of return among investment centers should be made with extreme caution, because there tend to be too many peculiarities that destroy their validity. Even for similar factories making similar products, local conditions often cause a variety of environments and costs. Therefore, a manager would usually be more appropriately judged by his performance against some budget target rather than against other investment centers.

controllable performance

As Chapters 6 and 16 stressed, a **distinction should be made between the performance of the division manager and the performance of the division as an investment by the corporation.** The manager should be evaluated on the basis of his controllable performance (in many cases some controllable contribution in relation to controllable investment). For other decisions, "such as new investment or a withdrawal of funds from the division, the important thing is the success or failure of the divisional venture, not of the men who run it."[2]

The most skillful division manager is often put in charge of the sickest division in an attempt to change its fortunes. Such an attempt may take years, not months. Furthermore, it may result in merely bringing the division up to a minimum acceptable rate of return. The division may continue to be a poor profit performer in comparison to other divisions. If top management relied solely on the absolute rate of return to judge management, the skillful manager would be foolhardy to accept such trouble-shooting assignments.

This distinction helps clarify some vexing difficulties. For example, top management may want to use an investment base to gauge the economic performance of a retail store, but the *manager* may be best judged by focusing on income and forgetting about any investment allocations. If investment is assigned to the manager, the aim should be to assign controllable investment only. Controllability[3] depends on what *decisions* managers can make regarding the size of the investment base. In a highly decentralized company, for instance, the manager can influence the size of all his assets and can exercise judgment regarding the appropriateness of short-term credit and perhaps some long-term credit.

[2] David Solomons, *Divisional Performance Measurement and Control* (Homewood, Ill.: Richard D. Irwin, Inc., 1968), p. 84.

[3] See Chapter 6 for an expanded discussion of controllability.

definitions of income and investments

contribution approach The selection of performance measures requires some concept or definition of income. The contribution approach described in Chapter 16 can help distinguish between the performance of a division and the performance of its manager. (Exhibit 16-1 shows a sample format of the contribution approach, so it won't be repeated here.)

Various measures of income and investment are possible, and companies have worked out definitions to suit their specific preferences. Almost any approach is subject to criticism, but getting agreement within a company is not an insurmountable task. For example, the definition of residual income used by General Electric is based on full allocations. That is, residual income is defined as net income (after income taxes) as ordinarily defined less an imputed interest charge on the net assets (after allocations of short-term and long-term debt). The rate of the capital charge is based on the minimum acceptable return that would justify continuance of the division.

allocating costs and assets to divisions Chapters 15 and 16 concentrated on the problems of cost allocation.[4] The points made there apply also to the problems of asset allocation. Again, the aim is to allocate in a manner that will be goal-congruent, will provide incentive, and will recognize autonomy insofar as possible. Incidentally, as long as the managers feel that they are being treated uniformly, they tend to be more tolerant about the imperfections of the allocation. For example, should cash be included under controllable investment if the balances are strictly controlled by corporate headquarters? Arguments can be made for both sides, but the manager is usually regarded as being responsible for the volume of business generated by the division. In turn, this volume is likely to have a direct effect on the overall cash needs of the corporation. Commonly used bases for allocation, when assets are not directly identifiable with a specific division, include:

ASSET CLASS	POSSIBLE ALLOCATION BASE
Corporate cash	Budgeted cash needs
Receivables	Sales weighted by payment terms
Inventories	Budgeted sales or usage
Plant and equipment	Usage of services in terms of long-run forecasts of demand or area occupied

Where the allocation of an asset (such as central corporate facilities) would indeed be arbitrary, many managers feel that it is better not to allocate.

[4] An extensive description of allocation of costs to segments is in R. K. Mautz, *Financial Reporting by Diversified Companies* (New York: Financial Executives Research Foundation, 1968).

possible investment bases

The base that is used for measuring invested capital may appropriately differ among companies and within segments of the same company. The possible alternative bases include:

1. *Total assets available.* This base includes all business assets, regardless of their individual purpose.
2. *Total assets employed.* This base excludes excess or idle assets, such as vacant land or construction in progress.
3. *Net working capital plus other assets.* This base is really the same as 1, except that current liabilities are deducted from the total assets available. In a sense, this represents an exclusion of that portion of current assets that is supplied by short-term creditors. The main justification for this base is that the manager often does have direct influence over the amount of short-term credit that he utilizes. An able manager should maximize the use of such credit, within some overall constraints to prevent endangering the company's credit standing.
4. *Stockholders' equity.* This base centers attention on the rate of return that will be earned by the business owners.

comparison of asset and equity bases

Stockholders' equity, as a possible investment base, is important to the owners, but it is not so significant to the operating manager. He is usually concerned with the management of assets, not with the long-term sources of assets. There are two major management functions: operating and financing. To the extent possible, the measurement of operating decisions (the acquisition and utilization of assets) should not be influenced by financing decisions (what long-term sources of assets were chosen).

For example, consider the following companies:

	(1)	(2)	(3)	(4)	(5)	(6)	(4) ÷ (1)	(6) ÷ (3)
		Equities					Return on Investment*	
	Assets	Liabilities	Stockholders' Equity	Income Before Interest	8% Interest	Net Income*	Assets	Stockholders' Equity
Co. A	$1,000,000	$500,000	$ 500,000	$200,000	$40,000	$160,000	20%	32%
Co. B	1,000,000	—	1,000,000	200,000	—	200,000	20%	20%

* Income taxes ignored here for simplicty.

It would be invalid to use stockholders' equity as a basis for comparing the operating performance of the managers of Company A and Company B. The 32 percent rate of return does not distinguish between the operating and the financing decisions. Company A in effect has paid 8 percent for the use of $500,000, which in turn has earned a return on assets of 20 percent. This is an example of risk taking that is often called *trading on the equity* or *using financial leverage.* It is a financing decision that results in borrowing money at a fixed interest rate with the expectation of earning a higher rate on such funds. Trading on the equity should be viewed as a separate decision and should not affect the measurement of operating performance.

For measuring the performance of division managers, one of the three other asset bases listed above is almost always superior to stockholders' equity. If the division manager's mission is to utilize all assets as best he can without regard to their financing, then base 1 is best. If top-management directives force him to carry extra assets that are not currently productive, then 2 is best. If he has direct control over the amount of the division's short-term trade credit and bank loans, then 3 is best. In practice, 1 is used most often, although 3 is not far behind.[5]

measurement alternatives for investments

How should we measure the assets that are included in the investment base? Should assets be valued at net book value, replacement cost, realizable value, or some other value? There is a propensity to have one investment measure serve many masters. Therefore, net book value[6] predominates, but its prevalence does not mean that it is necessarily conceptually correct. Of course, the relevant value depends on the decisions being affected and evaluated. Among the decision purposes are:

1. Disposal or continuance of a subunit.
2. Disposal, continuance, or expansion of a subunit.
3. Evaluation of performance as an incentive and as a basis for improving future decisions.

disposal or continuance

As Chapters 12 and 13 demonstrated, the discounted cash-flow (DCF) model needs two values for the disposal or continuance decision: total present value and current disposal (exit) value in the best alternative use. Historical cost is irrelevant except as a basis for prediction. For example, suppose there is a world of perfect certainty and there is old equipment that is expected to produce $20,000 in operating cash inflows during each of the next five years. Also suppose the disposal value today is $38,000 and five years hence is zero. The opportunity cost of capital is 10 percent. The analysis follows:

[5] John J. Mauriel and Robert N. Anthony, in "Misevaluation of Investment Center Performance," *Harvard Business Review,* Vol. 44, pp. 98–105, summarize the practice of 2,658 companies. Sixty percent, or 1,603, used investment centers. Of these, 40 percent deducted short-term external payables in arriving at the investment base.

[6] Mauriel and Anthony, *op. cit.,* report that 73 percent of the companies used net book value as their valuation measure and 18 percent used gross book value. Only 3 percent of the companies used some measure that departs from cost, such as insurance value or appraisal value.

The total present value of the alternative to continue operations, \$20,000 × 3.791 (P.V. of \$1.00 at 10% for 5 years)	\$75,820
Current disposal value, the total present value of the alternative to sell today	\$38,000

The analysis favors retention of the asset. The relevant data consisted of *both* the total present value and the current disposal value[7] in the best alternative use.

The very act of continuance implies that, as a minimum, the continuance or disposal decision has been made. Often, continuance occurs automatically, simply because disposal is so obviously economically unattractive that formal analysis is unnecessary. The decision is made unconsciously. However, the economic recession of the 1970s in the United States induced many managers to pause and explicitly analyze some activites. These analyses led to decisions to disinvest. Managers found that current disposal values were higher than the total present values of continuance in use. This illustrates the need for a periodic monitoring of both total present values and current disposal values, a monitoring that is not ordinarily incorporated in existing management control systems.

disposal or continuance or expansion

The manager often considers three basic alternatives simultaneously: disposal, continuance, or expansion. Expansion will be desirable if the alternative is more attractive than other investment opportunities. The general decision rule for adding new investments is a familiar one: Invest if the total present value exceeds the required investment so that the net present value is positive. For example, suppose additional equipment can be obtained for \$50,000 that will produce an expected annual operating cash flow of \$20,000 for five years:

Total present value at 10%, \$20,000 × 3.791	\$75,820
Required investment	50,000
Net present value	\$25,820

The analysis favors buying the asset. The relevant data consisted of both the total present value and the required investment to obtain that stream of

[7] The terms *current value* and *market value* are often used to describe disposal or sales or exit value. These general terms are avoided here because they are ambiguous in the literature and in discussions. Sometimes *current value* is used to represent total present value. At other times it is used to represent replacement cost. At still other times, it is used to represent market value. Similarly, *market value* is sometimes used to describe disposal value, but at other times it means replacement cost. The two values must be compared before an intelligent decision can be made. If the disposal value exceeds the total present value, the asset should be sold, and vice versa. Of course, linking the word "current" with some other descriptive term like "disposal" or "replacement" reduces the ambiguity. Thus, the terms "current disposal value" or "current replacement cost" are better than "current value."

cash inflows. Of course, this required investment at time zero is the acquisition cost.

To recapitulate, if the manager examines an existing investment, he often considers three decision alternatives that may be likened to investments in securities. The required data are:

DISPOSAL (SELL)	*CONTINUANCE (HOLD)*	*EXPANSION (BUY MORE)*
Total Present Value compared to Current Disposal Value	Total Present Value compared to Current Disposal Value	Total Present Value compared to Required Investment

Note that the total present value depends on a deliberate subjective assessment of expected future cash inflows: Current disposal value and required-investment values may be identical for highly marketable securities[8] (ignoring brokerage fees, markups, and income tax aspects), but they may be quite different for investments in highly specialized assets with no market values. For example, a company may invest $50,000 in new special equipment. An instant after acquisition, the replacement cost is $50,000 but the disposal value in the next best use may be only $38,000 or less. Note especially that total present value is always relevant to these decisions, whether the alternative is to reduce, continue, or expand.

evaluation of performance

As we have seen, the evaluation of performance entails a follow-up of past decisions with the hope that such an appraisal will improve incentive and future decision making. But "evaluation of performance" is a catchall term that needs subdivision before choosing the relevant investment base. For the purpose of assessing the wisdom of past investment decisions, decision by decision, using historical costs as an investment measure and compound-interest depreciation (explained later in this chapter) will provide a comparison that is consistent with the predictions made and the DCF decision model used.

The evaluation of performance is also wanted for making *comparisons* of executives as *managers* and of divisions as *economic investments* for a given time period and over a number of time periods. A fundamental rule for making comparisons of the productivity of assets is that their measurement basis be uniform. That is, you would expect assets that produce the same net cash inflows with the same risk to have the same value. For example, it would be nonsense to judge either manager performance or economic productivity on the holding of 100 shares of General Motors common stock for one year by comparing the increase in the market value of that stock (plus cash dividends) with its historical

[8] Both would be measured by quoted market prices. That is why "market value" is cited as being the relevant number for sell, hold, or buy decisions in managing a security portfolio. Historical cost is irrelevant for these decisions except as it bears on the determination of income tax aspects.

cost. If one portfolio manager bought the stock in 19_1, and another in 19_4, and another on December 31, 19_6, the comparisons of performance for holding the hundred shares during 19_7 would surely not be related to the historical costs of investments. Instead, they would be related to what the 100 shares would have cost on December 31, 19_6. In short, the relevant investment measure for the routine evaluation of performance is replacement cost, because it provides a common denominator representing the equivalent of what would have been the required investment at the beginning of any given period.

Consider another example. If one manager acquired plant and equipment in 19_1, and another manager acquired *identical* plant and equipment on December 31, 19_6 (identical in every way: appearance, technology, and expected cash-inflow productivity), the value of the investment measure for judging 19_7 performance should be identical. In a sense, every manager and every economic unit starts a new year afresh;[9] all existing assets are viewed as if they were acquired on New Year's Eve. Thus, replacement value is used as a common denominator to compare current productivity and to help predict the potential for competitive entry.

nature of replacement cost

When assets are already in use, approximations of replacement market prices often do not exist. Note that the task of approximation is *not* to obtain a price of a new asset that would in fact be used to replace an existing asset. Instead, the aim is to approximate how much it would cost to obtain similar assets that would produce the *same* expected operating cash inflows as the existing asset. The essence of the asset is its expected cash flow, not its physical or technological features. Managers rarely replace assets exactly in kind with new assets having identical operating and economic characteristics.

Approximating a replacement cost for the 1976 delivery truck in 1980 may not be too difficult, because active markets exist. But the hunt would be for prices for 1976 models in equivalent condition, not for a new 1980 model—even though in fact a 1980 model would actually be purchased if replacement occurred in 1980.

As equipment becomes more highly specialized and subject to obsolescence, the task of approximating replacement cost becomes trickier. If no market exists, either specific price indexes for similar classes of equipment or appraisal might be used. The use of indexes provides more objectivity but perhaps less relevance, because they may not be exactly applicable to the particular assets in question. On the other hand, if appraisals are used, subjectivity heightens. In many instances, the appraisal value is often obtained by discounting the expected operating cash inflows. In such cases, total present value and replacement cost may be indistinguishable. That is, the total present value is assumed

[9] Also see Yaaqov Goldschmidt, *Information for Management Decisions* (Ithaca, N.Y., and London: Cornell University Press, 1970), p. 64.

to be the best surrogate for replacement cost in the absence of an active replacement market. But the distinction, at least in concept, should be kept in mind. Total present value is a subjective appraisal of expected cash inflows, whereas replacement cost is an approximation of what investment would currently be required to obtain that expected stream.

total present value Many advocates cite total present value as the ideal investment measure for the evaluation of performance. Of course, the use of such a measure requires a concept of income (an income model) that differs from the conventional accounting model. Annual income is defined as the difference between total present values at the beginning and at the end of a year (assuming no cash dividends or additional investments). This requires an annual computation of a new total present value of the expected cash inflows. The resulting income would be affected by more than just current operating activities. Because it is dependent on a measurement of total present value at the end of the year, it would also be affected by other events and by explicit predictions of future events.

The present-value approach to measuring performance has overwhelming practical limitations because of its high degree of subjectivity. It necessitates predictions of cash flows that are uncertain and that are often interdependent with the cash flows of other assets. It also requires choosing a discount rate and perhaps changing that rate through the years. For these reasons, the use of present values for routine judging of performance of managers is rarely feasible. However, periodic attempts should be made to approximate present values in judging the desirability of assets as investments. Otherwise, managers will overlook obsolescence and investment opportunities.

Incidentally, many advocates of replacement cost favor it as an investment measure for routine evaluation of performance because, even though as a concept it is distinct from total present value, it provides answers that are reasonably objective approximations of what would be obtained under a present-value approach. In short, replacement cost is a practical surrogate for the "ideal" present value in the sense that it serves, at least usually, as a somewhat objective approximation of a *minimum* present value.

approximation of replacement cost If an old asset provides a service that is comparable to a new asset's service, the value of the assets should be based on these services. Suppose a new warehouse will cost $100,000 and will provide the same services as an existing warehouse, which yields net rents of $10,000 per year, a return of 10 percent. The old asset should be valued at $100,000—the replacement cost of an asset that will provide similar services.

But suppose the old warehouse requires maintenance costs that are $2,000 higher than those of the new warehouse. The net services provided would be

\$10,000 − \$2,000 = \$8,000. Therefore, the value of the old warehouse would be \$8,000 ÷ .10 = \$80,000. All other things being equal, management would be indifferent as to buying a new warehouse for \$100,000, paying \$10,000 in interest charges, and selling it after a year for \$100,000; or buying an old warehouse for \$80,000, paying \$8,000 in interest and \$2,000 for maintenance, and selling it for \$80,000 after a year.[10]

Suppose the old warehouse had a net book value of \$6,000 and the new warehouse a book value of \$100,000. As a manager, which warehouse would you prefer to supervise? You can readily see why in practice managers often prefer to manage the old assets if ROI computations are based on net book values. In most cases, however, replacement costs (even if crudely approximated) would probably be regarded as providing a more "equitable" or "fair" basis for performance evaluation.

Note too that in this example there is no readily obtainable market price for the old asset per se. The \$80,000 approximation of replacement cost is based on a subjective appraisal of the value of expected future cash inflows—total present value. In a practical setting, total present value is often used as an approximation of replacement cost where no market prices are available. This illustrates how present value and replacement-cost values can get blurred together even though they are essentially different concepts.

why historical cost? Although the relevance criterion is appealing, so that one or more of the foregoing investment measures seems preferable, it is not sufficient. Most important, we should recognize that the basic job of accounting systems is to supply information. Furthermore, the system is only one source of information. The issue of comparative advantage must be faced. **The acceptance or rejection of historical cost, when compared to some version of current value, would depend on the costs of each alternative set of information in light of the perceived benefits that might arise from better economic decisions, as well as on what competing sources of information are available.**

Given the defects of historical cost, why do organizations continue to use it for evaluating performance of the company as a whole and its subunits? There are several reasons. Some seem unjustifiable; others make sense. Ignorance has been cited as a likely reason. But why does this supposed ignorance persist? The routine use of some alternative value entails an extra cost of compiling data. Managers (and some investors) want *routine* data essentially as clues for deciding whether and how to seek (buy) more information. The constraints of generally accepted accounting principles are not as dominant for internal purposes. Still, most managers have regarded historical costs as good enough for

[10] Adapted from an example in Goldschmidt, *Information for Management Decisions.* For simplicity, this example uses rates of return based on infinite useful lives, but the principles are unchanged for finite useful lives.

such purposes.[11] Major internal decisions to invest or disinvest are not routine decisions. From the viewpoint of the systems designer it may be more economical to get replacement and net realizable values by conducting special studies only when the need is perceived rather than by continuous recording on a regular basis.

The implications from practice are clear. The use of "defective" data such as historical costs may often make both conceptual and practical sense—even though advocates of other approaches find the idea difficult to swallow. We can gather data on a regular basis to serve multiple needs by using a historical-cost system. Often special or supplementary data are also gathered on an irregular basis as desired.

general price-level adjustments

Some companies are exploring the use of historical cost adjusted for general price-level changes. This entails restating *historical* data in terms of current general purchasing power by use of a general index such as the gross national product implicit price deflator. General Electric has experimented with this approach for its investment centers.

In particular, as is explained more thoroughly in the literature on external reporting, note that the use of *general* price-level adjustments represents restatements of historical costs. Conceptually, restated costs are *not* the same as replacement-cost accounting, which is sometimes approximated via the use of *specific* price indexes. (However, a separate line of reasoning claims that general price-level accounting is a practical, cost-effective way of getting crude approximations of results under replacement-cost accounting.)

plant and equipment: gross or net?

Because historical-cost investment measures are used most often in practice, there has been much discussion[12] about the relative merits of using undepreciated cost (gross value) or net book value. Those who favor using gross assets claim that it facilitates comparisons among plants and divisions. If income decreases as a plant ages, the decline in earning power will be made evident, while the constantly decreasing net book value will reflect a possibly deceptive higher rate of return in later

[11] Mauriel and Anthony, "Misevaluation of Investment Center Performance," summarize the practices of 2,658 companies. Only 3 percent of the companies used some measure that departs from historical cost, such as insurance value or appraisal value. However, in 1975 and 1976 governmental bodies in the United States, the U.K., and Australia issued new external reporting requirements entailing the use of replacement costs. Therefore, we can also expect more receptivity toward using departures from historical cost as a basis for internal evaluation of performance. See U.S. Securities and Exchange Commission, *Accounting Series Release No. 190,* March 23, 1976, which deals with disclosure of replacement costs of inventory and property, plant, and equipment, and *Report of the Inflation Accounting Committee* (the Sandilands Report), September 1975, available from H. M. Stationery Office, London.

[12] *Return on Capital as a Guide to Managerial Decisions,* National Association of Accountants, Research Report No. 35, and David Solomons, *Divisional Performance,* pp. 134–42.

years. For this reason, du Pont and Monsanto use gross book value as a measure of their fixed assets when they compute rate of return. Eighteen percent of the companies surveyed[13] use gross book value.

One reason often cited for using undepreciated cost is that it partially compensates for the impact of the changing price level on historical cost. However, if a company desires to use replacement cost as a base, it should face the problem squarely by using appraisal values or specific price indexes. Reliance on gross book value is an unreliable means of approximating replacement value.

Solomons comments on the gross versus net book value debate:

> There is something inherently strange about the view that it is right to include fixed assets in a balance sheet at their depreciated value, but wrong to include them in a computation of capital at that value. The only reason for holding such a view is the irrational behavior of ROI when fixed assets are taken at book value rather than at cost. The proper remedy is to be found in the use of a compound interest method of depreciation, not in the abandonment of book value as a basis for valuing investment. If depreciation were handled in a theoretically correct manner (i.e., by the compound interest method), the decline in the book value of depreciating assets would not of itself disturb the stability of ROI.[14]

The proponents of using net book value as a measure maintain that it is less confusing because (a) it is consistent with the total assets shown on the conventional balance sheet, and (b) it is consistent with net-income computations, which include deductions for depreciation. The major criticism of net book value is not peculiar to its use for ROI purposes. The critics say that historical cost does not represent a current economic sacrifice and is useless for making decisions about allocations of resources. On the other hand, as explained in the next section, if net book value is used in a manner that is consistent with the planning model, it can be useful for auditing past decisions and it might suffice for incentive purposes.

consistency between models

Ideally, the decision model used to make a capital-investment decision and the model used to judge subsequent performance would be consistent. However, in practice we often find DCF models being used for investment decisions and the accrual-accounting models being used for performance evaluation.

This conflict of models may lead to dysfunctional decisions. Managers are sometimes reluctant to make capital outlays that are justified by DCF methods but that lead to poor performance records in the first year or two after the outlay. This is especially likely if the outlay is subject to immediate write-off

[13] Mauriel and Anthony, "Misevaluation," p. 101.

[14] David Solomons, *Divisional Performance,* p. 135. He discusses these issues at length on pp. 134–42.

(for instance, product advertising, engineering development, and process improvement costs) or to accelerated-depreciation methods.

compound interest and compatibility How can compatibility be achieved? As explained in Chapter 12, DCF methods assume a capital-recovery factor that is related to funds in use. Suppose a company is considering investing in a project with a two-year life and no salvage value. Cash inflow will be equal payments of $4,000 at the end of each of the two years. If the company paid $7,132 for the project, present-value tables would reveal its internal rate of return as 8 percent. Each cash payment consists of "interest" (rate of return) plus recovery of principal:

YEAR	*INVESTMENT AT BEGINNING OF YEAR*	*OPERATING CASH INFLOW*	*(INTEREST) RETURN, @ 8% PER YEAR*	*(DEPRECIATION) AMOUNT OF INVESTMENT RECEIVED AT END OF YEAR*	*(NET BOOK VALUE) UNRECOVERED INVESTMENT AT END OF YEAR*
1	$7,132	$4,000	.08 × $7,132 = $571	$4,000 − $571 = $3,429	$7,132 − $3,429 = $3,703
2	3,703	4,000	.08 × $3,703 = $297	$4,000 − $297 = $3,703	$3,703 − $3,703 = 0

If subsequent performance were the same as had been forecast, the income statement based on the DCF model would be as shown in the first two columns below. For comparison, the results of using other depreciation methods are also shown:

	METHOD OF DEPRECIATION					
	Compound-interest		Straight-line		Sum-of-years'-digits	
Year	1	2	1	2	1	2
Cash operating income	$4,000	$4,000	$4,000	$4,000	$4,000	$4,000
Depreciation	3,429[a]	3,703[a]	3,566[b]	3,566[b]	4,755[c]	2,377[c]
Net income	$ 571	$ 297	$ 434	$ 434	$ (755)	$1,623
Investment base—beginning balance	$7,132	$3,703	$7,132	$3,566	$7,132	$2,377
Rate of return on beginning balance	8%	8%	6%	12%	−11%	68%

[a] See preceding table for compuations.
[b] $7,132 ÷ 2 = $3,566 per year.
[c] Sum of digits = 1 + 2 = 3. Therefore, ⅔ × $7,132 = $4,755 for the first year and ⅓ × $7,132 = $2,377 for second year.

The compound-interest method results in an increasing charge for depreciation over the useful life of the asset. But it does provide for a rate of return that dovetails with the assumptions in the DCF model. The comparison above shows how the commonly used depreciation models of accrual accounting produce varying rates of return that have no relation to the DCF planning models.[15]

[15] For an elaboration of the differences, see Ezra Solomon, "Alternative Rate of Return Concepts and Their Implications for Utility Regulation," *The Bell Journal of Economics and Management Science,* Vol. 1, No. 1 (Spring 1970), pp. 65–81.

residual-income effects A residual-income approach to the compound-interest method would show:

	YEAR			
	1		2	
Cash operating income		$4,000		$4,000
Depreciation (based on original expectations)	$3,429		$3,703	
Imputed interest (at minimum desired rate)	571	4,000	297	4,000
Residual income		$ 0		$ 0

This example assumes that the 8 percent rate of return on this project is equal to the minimum desired rate that would be used in charging the division for its capital and in the computing of depreciation. Any cash flow that increased the rate of return would result in positive residual income. Assume that the cash flow was $4,500 and $3,800, respectively:

	YEAR			
	1		2	
Cash operating income		$4,500		$3,800
Depreciation (based on original expectations)	$3,429		$3,703	
Imputed interest	571	4,000	297	4,000
Residual income		$ 500		$ −200

Industry has rejected the compound-interest method of depreciation primarily because:

1. If cash flows are equal per year, they produce an increasing charge over the useful life of an asset. Intuitively, however, managers do not see the justification for an increasing charge for depreciation if cash flows remain constant.
2. The compound-interest method works clearly if projected annual operating flows are reasonably equal, but the implicit principal-recovery pattern is more difficult to compute and explain if projected cash flows differ markedly through the years.
3. The market values of particular assets do not coincide with the book values, particularly in the early years of use.

Until formal attempts are made to reconcile DCF models for planning with accrual-accounting models for control, follow-up of investment decisions must rely on the sampling of projects or on a dual planning scheme. In sampling, DCF decisions would be audited by gathering data, year by year, to see whether the specific cash-flow predictions proved accurate. In dual planning, the DCF decision would simultaneously be cast in the form of an accrual-accounting rate-of-return prediction; then the follow-up would be based on the accrual-accounting model.

choosing desired rates of return

Whatever their merits, neither the ROI nor the residual-income method avoids the question of cost of capital. The critical questions are (a) whether the same minimum rates should be used in each subunit of the organization and (b) what minimum rates to specify.

The use of different required rates for different divisions is apparently not widespread. The most extensive survey of practice in this area indicated an overwhelming tendency to use the same required rate for all divisions and for all classes of assets.[16] The use of uniform rates is probably attributable to the attitude that managers must be treated fairly (or uniformly unfairly). In this context, fairness means that the same required rate should apply to all divisions. Moreover, even the uniform use of different rates for different classes of assets (that is, one rate for investments in current assets and another rate for plant assets) may be perceived as unfair if divisions have different compositions of such assets.

Although the use of uniform companywide rates may be favored in terms of their impact on the morale of managers, more and more top managements are recognizing that the uniform approach may lead to undesirable economic decisions. Modern financial theory supports the use of different rates for different divisions. Portfolio theory provides the analytical framework for the investment decision under uncertainty. The firm would be viewed as a collection of different classes of assets whose income streams bear different risks. The minimum desired rates of return are functions of risk. Various divisions face different risks. Therefore, a different minimum desired rate should be used for each division, based on the relative investment risks of each. Indeed, if the risks are not homogeneous within a division, a case can be made for using more than one rate for investments in various classes of assets.

How should a rate be chosen for a given division? Van Horne[17] suggests trying to identify publicly traded companies that are engaged solely in the line of business of the division. For example, an electrical products division would be matched with a company engaged solely in the manufacture and sale of electrical products. Then the company's cost of capital can be regarded as an approximation of the division's appropriate cost of capital.

Van Horne warns that the use of a uniform rate for all divisions may lead a company to take larger risks over time without commensurate increases in expected return. The problem is that some "safe" projects with little systematic risks are rejected because they fail to provide a return above the company's uniform stated goal. But some of these projects may produce expected returns

[16] Mauriel and Anthony, in "Misevaluation," report that only 7 percent of the 258 respondents to this question used different rates.

[17] James Van Horne, *Financial Management and Policy,* 4th ed. (Englewood Cliffs, N.J.: Prentice-Hall, Inc., 1977), Chapter 8, gives a detailed discussion of these finance issues summarized here.

greater than the "true" divisional cost of capital. In contrast, risk-taking divisions may accept projects with expected returns higher than the uniform rate, but lower than they should earn given the systematic risk involved.

pitfalls in current practice

The problems of accounting for investment centers are dominated by goal congruence, incentive, and autonomy. ROI and residual income are subject to the usual criticisms leveled at accounting techniques. Such criticisms include:

1. Overemphasis on short-run results.
2. Overemphasis on profit and underemphasis on quality, employee relations, development of subordinates, share of the market, discovery of new products, and so on.
3. Incongruent decisions[18] because of accounting policies regarding measures of investment and policies that tend to exclude the following from the investment base: research, market development, and leased assets. For example, a manager may lease an asset even though economic analysis favors its purchase; the leased asset might be excluded from the manager's investment base, whereas the owned asset is ordinarily included.
4. Unjustifiable comparisons among divisional results, where the economic and accounting differences are significant.

Despite these weaknesses, investment centers are often the most feasible means for promoting goal congruence, incentive, and autonomy in a cost-effective way.

SUMMARY

Many techniques like ROI or residual income fall far short of the ideal goals of congruence, incentive, and autonomy. Nevertheless, in practice their conceptual shortcomings may be unimportant; often they are the best techniques available for obtaining the perceived top-management goals.

Performance reports should distinguish between the performance of the division manager and the performance of the divisional unit as an economic investment.

Although in practice the book values of assets tend to be used for ROI and residual-income purposes, many accountants believe that replacement value is a preferable multipurpose basis. If net book value is used, the compound-interest method of depreciation will be more likely to provide a basis for performance evaluation that is consistent with the past decisions being evaluated.

[18] For an interesting discussion of various investment bases and depreciation methods plus several examples of how division managers' interest can conflict with the interests of the company as a whole, see John Dearden, "Problem in Decentralized Profit Responsibility," *Harvard Business Review,* Vol. 38, No. 3, pp. 79–86. He concludes (p. 86), "It is my belief that the only completely satisfactory method for assigning values to divisional facilities is one that uses replacement values and is not tied directly into the books of account."

Despite the theoretical attractiveness of various alternative accounting methods, most managements have apparently decided that a historical-cost system is good enough for the *routine* evaluation of managers. Apparently, this crude approach provides the desired motivational effects and gives clues as to whether to invest or disinvest in a particular division. The investment decision is evidently not routine enough to justify gathering information regarding replacement costs or realizable values except as special occasions arise.

Research in modern finance favors using different minimum desired rates of returns for different divisions having different risks. In contrast, practice shows a tendency to use the same rates for all divisions.

PROBLEMS FOR SELF-STUDY

PROBLEM 1

Suppose that a division's budgeted data are as follows:

Average available assets:	
Receivables	$ 300,000
Inventories	200,000
Fixed assets, net	500,000
	$1,000,000
Fixed costs	$ 225,000
Variable costs	$5 per unit
Desired rate of return on average available assets	27.5%
Expected volume	200,000 units

a. What average unit sales price is needed to obtain the desired rate of return on average available assets?
b. What would be the expected turnover of assets?
c. What would be the net-income percentage of dollar sales?
d. What rate of return would be earned on assets available if sales volume is 300,000 units, assuming no changes in prices or variable costs per unit?

SOLUTION 1

a. 27.5% of $1,000,000 = $275,000 target net income

$$\begin{aligned} \text{Let } X &= \text{unit sales price} \\ \text{Dollar sales} &= \text{Variable costs} + \text{Fixed costs} + \text{Net Income} \\ 200{,}000\,X &= 200{,}000\,(\$5) + \$225{,}000 + \$275{,}000 \\ X &= \$1{,}500{,}000 \div 200{,}000 \\ X &= \$7.50 \end{aligned}$$

b. $$\text{Expected asset turnover} = \frac{200{,}000 \times \$7.50}{\$1{,}000{,}000} = \frac{\$1{,}500{,}000}{\$1{,}000{,}000} = 1.5$$

c. $$\text{Net income as a percentage of dollar sales} = \frac{\$275{,}000}{\$1{,}500{,}000} = 18.33\%$$

d. At a volume of 300,000 units:

Sales @ $7.50	$2,250,000
Variable costs @ $5.00	1,500,000
Contribution margin	$ 750,000
Fixed costs	225,000
Net income	$ 525,000
Rate of return on $1,000,000 assets	52.5%

Note that an increase of 50 percent in unit volume almost doubles net income. This is so because fixed costs do not increase as volume increases.

PROBLEM 2

A division has assets of $200,000 and net income of $60,000.

a. What is the division's ROI?
b. If interest is imputed at 14 percent, what is the residual income?
c. What effects on management behavior can be expected if ROI is used to gauge performance?
d. What effects on management behavior can be expected if residual income is used to gauge performance?

SOLUTION 2

a. $60,000 ÷ $200,000 = 30%
b. $60,000 − .14($200,000) = $32,000
c. If ROI is used, the manager is prone to reject projects that do not earn an ROI of at least 30 percent. From the viewpoint of the organization as a whole, this may be undesirable because its best investment opportunities may lie in that division at a rate of, say, 22 percent. If a division is enjoying a high ROI, it is less likely to expand if it is judged via ROI than if it is judged via residual income.
d. If residual income is used, the manager is inclined to accept all projects whose expected ROI exceeds the minimum desired rate. His division is more likely to expand, because his goal is to maximize a dollar amount rather than a rate.

PROBLEM 3

Using DCF analysis, the Ezra Company invested $100,000 in plant and equipment having a useful life of six years and generating $22,961 in operating cash inflows each year. At the end of six years, the assets are scrapped at zero salvage value.

a. What is the internal rate of return?
b. Suppose straight-line depreciation is used as a basis for performance evaluation. What is the ROI for the first, fourth, and sixth years if ROI is based on the initial balance (gross investment base)? On net book value at the beginning of the year?
c. How closely do the answers in part b approximate the internal rate of return? Why do they differ?

SOLUTION 3

a. The DCF factor in Table 4 in Appendix B of this book is $100,000 ÷ $22,961 = 4.355. Line 6 shows that the internal rate is 10 percent.

b.

Operating cash inflows per year	$22,961
Depreciation ($100,000 ÷ 6 years)	16,667
Net income	$ 6,294

	YEAR 1	YEAR 4	YEAR 6
ROI on initial balance (gross investment base):			
$6,294 ÷ $100,000 =	6.3%	6.3%	6.3%
ROI on net book value:			
$6,294 ÷ $100,000 =	6.3		
$6,294 ÷ $ 50,000 =		12.6	
$6,294 ÷ $ 16,667 =			37.8

c. The answers in b vary considerably from the internal rate used to guide the original investment decision. The answers differ because the DCF model was used to justify the investment and the accrual-accounting model was used to evaluate performance.

QUESTIONS, PROBLEMS, AND CASES

23-1 "Net income divided by sales is the most important single measure of business success." Do you agree? Why?

23-2 List four possible bases for computing the cost of invested capital.

23-3 "The stockholder's-equity base is the best investment base for appraising operating management." Do you agree? Why?

23-4 "The use of undepreciated cost of fixed assets as part of the investment base compensates for the impact of the changing price level on historical cost." Do you agree? Why?

23-5 Under what circumstances does the gross-asset base make most sense?

23-6 Proponents of net book value as an investment base usually cite two major reasons for their position. What are these reasons?

23-7 How should interest expense and nonrecurring expenses be considered in computing incomes that are related to investment bases?

23-8 "In recent years there has been a tendency toward corporate decentralization, accompanied by a setting of individual rate-of-return targets for corporate segments. This provides incentive because managers can operate their segments as if they were separate companies of their own." Do you agree? Why?

23-9 What income concept is likely to be most realistic for measuring performance of various corporate segments?

23-10 "The rate-of-return tool is so hampered by limitations that we might as well forget it." Do you agree? Why?

23-11 What measures besides rate of return are commonly used to judge managerial performance?

23-12 "Too much stress on rate of return can hurt the corporation." How?

23-13 *Government Contracts and Profit Margins* Spokesmen for many companies that are heavily involved in government-contract work often complain that defense work is not very profitable. They cite low-percentage profit margins as evidence. Are such contentions justified? Why, or why not?

23-14 *Analysis of Return on Capital; Comparison of Three Companies* (Adapted from *N.A.A. Research Report No. 35,* pp. 34–35)

1. Rate of return on capital is often expressed as follows:

$$\frac{\text{Income}}{\text{Capital}} = \frac{\text{Income}}{\text{Sales}} \times \frac{\text{Sales}}{\text{Capital}}$$

What advantages can you see in the breakdown of the computation into two separate components?

2. Fill in the blanks:

	COMPANIES IN SAME INDUSTRY		
	A	B	C
Sales	$1,000,000	$500,000	$ —
Income	100,000	50,000	—
Capital	500,000	—	5,000,000
Income as a percent of sales	—	—	0.5%
Turnover of capital	—	—	2
Return on investment	—	1%	—

After filling in the blanks, comment on the relative performance of these companies as thoroughly as the data permit.

23-15 *Pricing, Rate of Return, and Measuring Efficiency* A large automobile company follows a pricing policy whereby "normal" or "standard" activity is used as a base for pricing. That is, prices are set on the basis of long-run annual-volume predictions. They are then rarely changed, except for notable changes in wage rates or material prices.

You are given the following data:

Materials, wages, and other variable costs	$1,320 per unit
Fixed overhead	$300,000,000 per year
Desired rate of return on invested capital	20%
Normal volume	1,000,000 units
Invested capital	$900,000,000

required

1. What net-income percentage based on dollar sales is needed to attain the desired rate of return?
2. What rate of return on invested capital will be earned at sales volumes of 1,500,000 and 500,000 units, respectively?
3. The company has a sizable management bonus plan based on yearly divisional performance. Assume that the volume was 1,000,000, 1,500,000, and 500,000 units, respectively, in three successive years. Each of three men has served as division manager for one year before being killed in an automobile accident. As the major heir of the third manager, comment on the bonus plan.

23-16 *Using Gross or Net Book Value of Fixed Assets* Assume that a particular plant acquires $400,000 of fixed assets with a useful life of four years and no residual value. Straight-line depreciation will be used. The plant manager is judged on income in relation to these fixed assets. Annual net income, after deducting depreciation, is $40,000.

Assume that sales, and expenses except depreciation, are on a cash basis. Dividends equal net income. Thus, cash in the amount of the depreciation charge will accumulate each year. The plant manager's performance is judged in relation to fixed assets because all current assets, including cash, are considered under central company control.

1. Prepare a comparative tabulation of the plant's rate of return and the company's overall company rate of return based on:
   a. Gross (i.e., original cost) assets.
   b. Net book value of assets. Assume (unrealistically) that any cash accumulated remains idle.
2. Evaluate the relative merits of gross assets and net book value of assets as investment bases.

23-17 *The General Electric Approach* [Adapted from David Solomons, *Divisional Performance: Measurement and Control* (New York: Financial Executives Research Foundation, Inc., 1965)] Consider the following:

	(000'S OMITTED)	
	Division A	Division B
Total assets	$1,000	$5,000
Net annual earnings	$ 200	$ 750
Rate of return on total assets	20%	15%

required

1. Which is the more successful division? Why?
2. General Electric Company has chosen "residual income," the excess of net earnings over the cost of capital, as the measure of management success—the quantity a manager should try to maximize. The cost of capital is deducted from the net annual earnings to obtain residual income. Using this criterion, what is the residual income for each division if the cost of capital is: (a) 12 percent, (b) 14 percent, (c) $17\frac{1}{2}$ percent? Which division is more successful under each of these rates?

23-18 *Various Measures of Profitability* When the Coronet Company formed three divisions a year ago, the president told the division managers that a bonus would be paid to the most profitable division. However, absolute profit as conventionally computed would not be used. Instead, the ranking would be affected by the relative investments in the three divisions. Each manager has now written a memorandum claiming that he is entitled to the bonus. The following data are available:

DIVISION	GROSS BOOK VALUE AT START OF YEAR	NET INCOME AS COMPUTED FOR CONVENTIONAL EXTERNAL ANNUAL REPORT COMPILATION
X	$400,000	$47,500
Y	380,000	46,000
Z	250,000	30,800

All the assets are fixed assets that were purchased ten years ago and have ten years of usefulness remaining. The Coronet cost of capital is 10 percent. All computations of current return should be based on a balance at the start of the year.

Which method for computing profitability did each manager choose? Make your description specific and brief. Show supporting computations. Where applicable, assume straight-line depreciation.

23-19 *Discounted Cash Flow and Evaluation of Performance* John Castleman, the general manager of a division of a huge, highly diversified company, recently attended an executive training program. He learned about discounted cash-flow analysis, and he became convinced that it was the best available guide for making long-range investment decisions.

However, upon returning to his company, he became frustrated. He wanted to use the discounted cash-flow technique, but top management had a long-standing policy of evaluating divisional management performance largely on the basis of its rate of return as calculated by dividing divisional net income by the net book value of total divisional assets. Therefore, in his own best interests and in accordance with the specifications of his superiors, he had to make decisions that he felt were not really the most desirable in terms of maximizing what he considered to be the "true" rate of return (that is, the discounted cash-flow rate).

required

1. Suppose Mr. Castleman had an opportunity to invest $30,000 in some automated machinery with a useful life of three years and a scrap value of zero. The expected cash savings per year were $12,060. Compute the internal rate of return. Ignore income tax effects.
2. Show the effect on net income for each of the three years, assuming straight-line depreciation. Also show the rate of return based on the beginning balance of the net book value of the fixed asset for each year.

3. Repeat requirement 2, assuming sum-of-the-years'-digits depreciation.
4. Top management has indicated a minimum desired rate of return of 10 percent. After examining the results above, Mr. Castleman was more baffled than ever. He just could not see why he should invest in the machinery if his net income in the first year would not be at least 10 percent of the investment base. He discussed the matter with a professor at a nearby business school.

   The professor reacted: "The basic trouble is not confined to your company. Many companies now insist that their managers use discounted cash-flow techniques for appraising investment opportunities, but they use conventional accounting techniques for judging operating performance. In short, one model is supposed to be used for planning, but another model is used for control.

   "A possible solution is to use the compound-interest method of depreciation for evaluating subsequent performance. The compound-interest method is based on the same model as the discounted cash-flow technique. That is, each receipt ($12,060 in this case) consists of interest on the beginning investment balance plus the recovery of principal. For example, the $12,060 cash savings during the first year would be analyzed as consisting of 'interest' of 10 percent of $30,000, or $3,000, plus a recovery of principal ('depreciation') of $9,060."

   Repeat requirement 2, assuming the compound-interest method of depreciation.
5. Contrast the pattern of depreciation in requirement 4 with the other methods. Why is industry reluctant to use the compound-interest method of depreciation? What other means might be used to reconcile the two models described in requirement 4?

23-20 *Conflict of Accrual and DCF Models*

1. The Marples Company, a small job shop, has landed a three-year exclusive contract for 10,000 proprietary widgets per year at $2.50 each. Total variable costs, including overhead but exclusive of the machinery required, are estimated at $1.00 per unit. John Marples, the president, is considering some proposals for tooling up to meet this demand.

   One of the alternatives is the purchase of a new special-purpose machine. This would cost about $30,000 including installation and setup, and maintenance requirements would be about $310 yearly.

   Marples will introduce an entirely new line of widgets in three years. The machine is not adaptable to the new manufacturing process, and the expected salvage value at that time will barely cover removal costs. The company depreciates its tools and equipment investments on a straight-line basis, and uses 20 percent as its minimum desired rate of return on new investments.

   Ignoring income taxes, compute the internal rate of return on the initial investment. Do you recommend its purchase?
2. Marples invests in the new machine and conducts a project review at the end of one year. He evaluates product profitability on the basis of ROI on the beginning investment for the year. He uses straight-line depreciation. He finds a significant difference between the observed rate and the projected rate of return, despite the fact that all costs were kept to budgeted figures. He asks you to explain the difference, and to recommend a simple system that will eliminate this problem.

   What will you tell him?

23-21 *Soviet Approach to Return on Investment* The Soviet System is a management control and evaluation system (bonus system) that is used in much of the Soviet economy. It is used to evaluate managers and determine their bonuses, and thus (it is hoped) to motivate the individual managers to cut costs and work toward the country's goals as specified by the central planning agency. One of these goals is to modernize the country's production facilities. The stated purpose was to increase the material interest of the management and employees in the economic results of the enterprise. The new management control system was a part of sweeping economy reforms that took effect in January 1966. As stated in Bertrand Horwitz, *Accounting Controls and the Soviet Economic Reforms of 1966* (Sarasota, Fla.: American Accounting Association, 1970), p. 23:

> Prior to January 1966, when the reforms first took effect, the director of a Soviet enterprise was confronted with the requirement of satisfying numerous physical and accounting goals. The enterprise was essentially a cell in a tautly administered system which allowed the director little room for independent action because the number of physical and accounting indexes by which he could be judged highly constrained his economic actions.

The new bonus system was based on the enterprise's increase in profits and the rate of return on assets employed in the enterprise. The exact formula used to compute the total bonuses to be distributed to the enterprise's employees is as follows:

$$(1) \qquad \lambda_t = \alpha \frac{(P_t - P_{t-1})}{P_{t-1}} + \beta \frac{(P_t)}{K_t}$$

and the total amount of the bonus for the enterprise is:

$$(2) \qquad TB_t = W_t \lambda_t$$

where W_t = the wage fund for time period t, centrally determined
P_t = profit in period t that is net of explicit charges for the use of current and fixed gross assets at original cost
TB_t = total amount of enterprise bonus for period t
K_t = total average gross assets in t at original cost
α, β = coefficients that are centrally assigned norms; both are less than one and are nonnegative

The first term of equation (1) is the rate of increase in earnings over the previous year. The second term is the ROI for the enterprise based on its gross assets. The sum of these two terms gives a factor (λ_t) that, when multiplied by the enterprise's wage fund, determines the total bonus for the enterprise. Thus, the total bonus for the enterprise depends on the enterprise's increase in profit over the previous year and its ROI.

The wage fund (W_t) for the enterprise in a period is centrally determined and therefore is a given amount for purposes of computation of the bonus. The accounting profit (P_t) is the enterprise's net profit before capital charges, minus (a) charges at the rate of 6 percent of gross assets, for the use of fixed assets and normal or planned working capital; (b) fixed (rent) payments; and (c) interest on bank credit. The charge of 6 percent is essentially the enterprise's cost of capital, because the enterprise gets its fixed assets from the government. The charge is also based on gross assets. The rent payments are designed to eliminate the differences between different enterprises because of natural operating conditions. Thus, a firm with very favorable conditions would have to make rent payments, while one operating under less favorable conditions would not. The interest is for short-term loans from the central bank.

Average gross assets (K_t) is used as the investment base in order to motivate managers to replace their older, less efficient assets. The purpose is to get managers to modernize their equipment.

The coefficients α and β are centrally assigned and are set so that the resulting bonuses will be reasonable in light of the enterprise's operating conditions. This is essentially another way of equalizing the natural operating conditions of the various enterprises in the economy.

Assume that the enterprise did not have to make any rent payments and had no short-term loans from the central bank. Suppose the enterprise had the following profit (after deductions), gross assets, and wage fund, in thousands of rubles:

$$P_t = 3{,}000 \qquad K_t = 20{,}000$$
$$P_{t-1} = 2{,}800 \qquad W_t = 4{,}000$$

Also, suppose that the central planners had assigned the firm an $\alpha = .5$ and $\beta = .25$.

required

1. Compute the total bonus.
2. Compare the probable motivational effects of the Soviet method with those of ROI and residual income.

23-22 You have been hired on the controller's staff of a large motel chain that owns many motels. Your first assignment is to help the controller and executive vice-president decide whether to continue to use some of its old motels. In addition, these executives are pondering how to evaluate the performance of these motels in terms of return on investment. Prior to your employment, the executives had explored various ways of establishing a value for such motels. Net book value (based on historical costs), disposal value, and replacement value are the three alternatives now being considered.

required

1. Which of the three bases is relevant to deciding whether to dispose of an old motel? Why?
2. Which of the three bases is applicable for judging the performance of the motel and its manager? Why? Why is your answer the same as or different from your answer in requirement 1?

23-23 *What Investment Bases Should Be Used?* The president of a giant corporation has attended miscellaneous management education programs during the past few years. He has a persistent desire to keep abreast of the latest thinking regarding information for decisions and performance measurement. He greets you, a new graduate from a school of management, with the following comments and questions:

"As I read more and more on this subject and as I listen to more and more discussions, I become increasingly bewildered by the nomenclature and the concepts. Oh, I am aware of the infirmities of historical costs. What I am concerned about are such terms and concepts as market value, current value, replacement value, economic value, present value, opportunity value, disposal value, entry value, exit value, and countless similar terms.

"Consider our new processing equipment in Division A. It cost $10 million. We could sell it for perhaps $7 million. How should it be valued for measuring performance in year 1? In year 5? In year 10?

"I am not asking you to pick from the existing practices of valuation. I am asking a normative question. That is, first tell me how these assets *should* be valued to assist decisions and to evaluate performance—without regard to the practical difficulties of implementation. After you answer the question on a normative basis, then answer it again on the basis of what might be accomplished now in our organization to implement what is conceptually most desirable."

required

Prepare a memorandum in response to the president's requirements. Include definitions of the various cost terms he mentioned. You may wish to use an example to clarify your points.

23-24 *Multiple Goals and Profitability* Solve Problem 6-26, which could logically have been placed here.

23-25 *Divisional Profitability and Performance* Solve Problem 6-27, which could logically have been placed here.

23-26 *Responsibility and Control of Costs* Solve Problem 6-28, which could logically have been placed here.

23-27 *Allocation of Computer Costs* Solve Problem 15-24, which could logically have been placed here.

23-28 *Evaluation of Control System* Solve Problem 6-29, which could logically have been placed here.

23-29 *Design of Management Control System; Review of Chapters 22 and 23* Western Pants, Inc., is one of America's oldest clothing firms. Founded in the mid-nineteenth century, the firm weathered lean years and depression largely as the result of the market durability of its dominant, and at times only, product—blue denim jeans. Until as recently as 1950, the firm had never seriously marketed other products or even additional types of trousers. A significant change in marketing strategy in the 1950s altered that course, which had been revered for 100 years by Western's management. Aggressive new management decided at that time that Western's well-established name could and should be used to market other lines of pants. Initial offerings in a men's casual trouser were well received. Production in different patterns of this basic style continued, and stylish, tailored variations of the same casual motif were introduced almost yearly.

Alert planning in the early 1960s enabled Western to become the first pants manufacturer to establish itself in the revolutionary "wash and wear" field. Further refinement of this process broadened the weave and fabric types that could be tailored into fashionable trousers and still survive enough machine washings and dryings to satisfy Western's rigid quality-control standards.

With the advent of "mod" clothing and the generally casual yet stylish garb that became acceptable attire at semiformal affairs, pants became fashion items, rather than the mere clothing staples they had been in years past. Western quickly gained a foothold in the bell-bottom and flare market, and from there grew with the "leg look" to its present position as the free world's largest clothing manufacturer.

Today Western, in addition to its still remarkably popular blue denim jeans, offers a complete line of casual trousers, an extensive array of "dress and fashion jeans" for both men and boys, and a complete line of pants for women. Last year the firm sold approximately 30 million pairs of pants.

Production

For the last twenty years, Western Pants has been in a somewhat unusual and enviable market position. In each of those years it has sold virtually all its production and often had to begin rationing its wares to established customers or refusing orders from new customers as early as six months prior to the close of the production year. Whereas most business ventures face limited demand and, in the long run, excess production, Western, whose sales have doubled each five years during that twenty-year period, has had to face excess and growing demand with limited—although rapidly growing—production.

The firm has developed 25 plants in its 150-year history. These production units vary somewhat in output capacity, but the average is roughly 20,000 pairs of trousers per week. With the exception of two or three plants that usually produce only the blue denim jeans during the entire production year, Western's plants produce various pants types for all of Western's departments.

The firm has for some years augmented its own productive capacity by contractual agreements with independent manufacturers of pants. At the present time, there are nearly 20 such contractors producing all lines of Western's pants (including the blue jeans). Last year contractors produced about one-third of the total volume in units sold by Western.

Tom Wicks, the Western vice-president for production and operations, commented on the firm's use of contractors. "The majority of these outfits have been with us for some time—five years or more. Five or ten of them have served Western efficiently and reliably for over 30 years. There are, of course, a lot of recent additions. We've been trying to beef up our output, because sales have been growing so rapidly. It's tough to tell a store like Macy's halfway through the year that you can't fill all their orders. In our eagerness to get the pants made, we understandably hook up with some independents who don't know what they're doing and are forced to fold their operations after a year or so because their costs are too high. Usually we can tell from an independent's experience and per-unit contract price whether or not he's going to be able to make it in pants production.

"Contract agreements with independents are made by me and my staff. The word has been around for some years that we need more production, so we haven't found it necessary to solicit contractors. Negotiations usually start either when an interested independent comes to us, or when a salesman or product manager interests an independent and brings him in. These product managers are always looking for ways to increase production! Negotiations don't necessarily take very long. There are some incidentals that have to be worked out, but the real issue is the price per unit the independent requires us to pay him. The ceiling we are willing to pay for each type of pants is pretty well established by now. If a contractor impresses us as both reliable and capable of turning out quality pants, we will pay him that ceiling. If we aren't sure, we might bid a little below that ceiling for the first year or two, until he has proven himself. Nonetheless, I'm only talking here about a few cents at most. We don't want to squeeze a new contractor's margins so much that we are responsible for forcing him out of business. It is most definitely to our advantage if the independent continues to turn out quality pants for us indefinitely. Initial contracts are for two years. The time spans lengthen as our relationship with the independent matures."

Mr. Wicks noted that the start-up time for a new contractor can often be as short as one year. The failure rate of the tailoring industry is quite high; hence, new entrepreneurs can often walk in and assume control of existing facilities.

The Control System

"We treat all our plants pretty much as cost centers [See Exhibit 23-1]," Mr. Wicks continued. "Of course, we exercise no control whatever over the contractors. We just pay them the agreed price per pair of pants. Our own operations at each plant have been examined thoroughly by industrial engi-

EXHIBIT 23-1

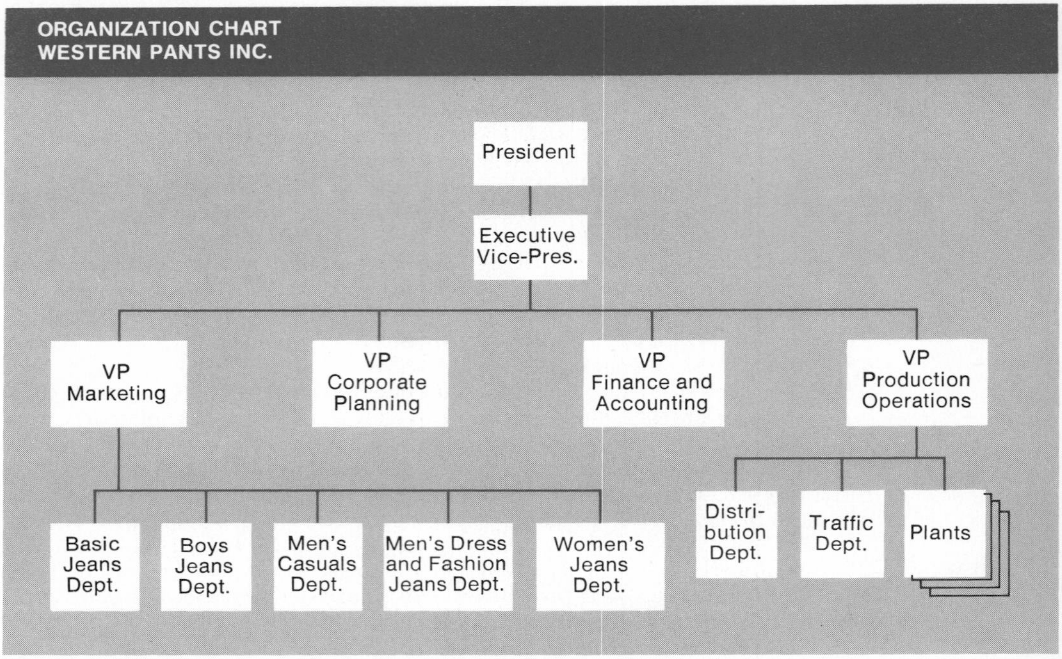

neers. You know, time-motion studies and all. We've updated this information consistently for over ten years. I'm quite proud of the way we've been able to tie our standard hours down. We've even been able over the years to develop learning curves that tell us how long it will take production of a given type of pants to reach the standard allowed hours per unit after initial start-up or a product switchover. We even know the rate at which total production time per unit reaches standard for every basic style of pants that Western makes!

"We use this information for budgeting a plant's costs. The marketing staff figures out how many pants of each type it wants produced each year and passes that information onto us. We divvy the total production up among plants pretty much by eyeballing the total amounts for each type of pants. We like to put one plant to work for a whole year on one type of pants, if that's possible. It saves time losses from start-ups and changeovers. We can sell all we make, you know, so we like to keep plants working at peak efficiency. Unfortunately, marketing always manages to come up with a lot of midyear changes, so this objective winds up like a lot of other good intentions in life. You know what they say about the road to Hell! Anyhow, it's still a game plan we like to stick to, and two or three plants making the basic blue jeans accomplish it every year.

"The budgeting operation begins with me and my staff determining what a plant's quota for each month should be for one year ahead of time. We do this mostly by looking at what past performance at a plant has been. Of course, we add a little to this. We expect people to improve around here. These yearly budgets are updated at the end of each month in the light of the previous month's production. Budget figures, incidentally, are in units of production. If a plant manager beats this budget figure, we feel he's done well. If he can't meet the quota, his people haven't been working at what the engineers feel is a very reasonable level of speed and efficiency. Or possibly absenteeism, a big problem in all our plants, has been excessively high. Or turnover, another big problem, has been unacceptably high. At any rate, when the quota hasn't been made, we want to know why, and we want to get the problem corrected as quickly as possible.

"Given the number of pants that a plant actually produces in a month, we can determine, by using the standards I was boasting about earlier, the number of labor hours each operation should have accumulated during the month. We measure this figure against the hours we actually paid for to determine how a plant performed as a cost center. As you might guess, we don't like to see unfavorable variances here any more than in a plant manager's performance against quota.

"We watch the plant performance figures monthly. If a plant manager meets his quota and his cost variances are OK, we let him know that we are pleased. I almost always call them myself and relay my satisfaction, or, if they haven't done well, my concern. I think this kind of prompt feedback is important.

"We also look for other things in evaluating a plant manager. Have his community relations been good? Are his people happy? The family that owns almost all of Western's stock is very concerned about that."

A Christmas bonus constitutes the meat of Western's reward system. Mr. Wicks and his two chief assistants subjectively rate a plant manager's performance for the year on a one-to-five scale. Western's top management at the close of each year determines a bonus base by evaluating the firm's overall performance and profits for the year. That bonus base has recently been as high as $3,000. The performance rating for each member of Western's management cadre is multiplied by this bonus base to determine a given manager's bonus.

Western's management group includes many finance and marketing specialists. The casewriter noted that these personnel, who are located at the corporate headquarters, were consistently awarded higher ratings by their supervisors than were plant managers. This difference consistently approached a full point. Last year the average rating in the corporate headquarters was 3.85; the average for plant managers was 2.92.

Evaluation of the System

Mia Packard, a recent valedictorian of a business school, gave some informed opinions regarding Western's production operation and its management control procedures.

"Mr. Wicks is one of the nicest men I've ever met, and a very intelligent businessman. But I really don't think that the system he uses to evaluate his plant managers is good for the firm as a whole. I made a plant visit not long ago as part of my company orientation program, and I accidently discovered that the plant manager 'hoarded' some of the pants produced over quota in good months to protect himself against future production deficiencies. That plant manager was really upset that I stumbled onto his storehouse. He insisted that all the other managers did the same thing and begged me not to tell Mr. Wicks. This seems like precisely the wrong kind of behavior in a firm that usually has to turn away orders! Yet I believe the quota system that is one of Western's tools for evaluating plant performance encourages this type of behavior. I don't think I could prove this, but I suspect that most plant managers aren't really pushing for maximum production. If they do increase output, their quotas are going to go up, and yet they won't receive any immediate monetary rewards to compensate for the increase in their responsibilities or requirements. If I were a plant manager, I wouldn't want my production exceeding quota until the end of the year.

"Also, Mr. Wicks came up to the vice-presidency through the ranks. He was a plant manager himself once—a very good plant manager. But he has a tendency to feel that everyone should run a plant the way he did. For example, in Mr. Wicks' plant there were eleven workers for every supervisor or member of the office and administrative staff. Since then, Mr. Wicks has elevated this supervision ratio of 11:1 to some sort of sacred index of leadership efficiency. All plant managers shoot for it, and as a result, usually understaff their offices. As a result, we can't get timely and accurate reports from plants. There simply aren't enough people in the offices out there to generate the information we desperately need *when we need it!*

"Another thing—some of the plants have been built in the last five years or so and have much newer equipment, yet there's no difference in the standard hours determined in these plants than the older ones. This puts the managers of older plants at a terrific disadvantage. Their sewing machines break down more often, require maintenance, and probably aren't as easy to work with."

required

Evaluate the management control system used for Western's plants. What changes should be given serious consideration?

23-30 *Design of Management Control System; Review of Chapters 22 and 23* (Copyright © 1964 by the President and Fellows of Harvard College. Reproduced by permission.)

Empire Glass Company was a diversified company organized into several major product divisions, one of which was the glass products division. This division was responsible for manufacturing and selling glass food and beverage bottles. Each division was headed by a divisional vice-president who reported directly to the company's executive vice-president, Landon McGregor.

Mr. McGregor's corporate staff included three men in the financial area—the controller, the chief accountant, and the treasurer. The controller's department consisted of only two men—Mr. Walker and the assistant controller, Allen Newell. The market research and labor relations departments also reported in a staff capacity to Mr. McGregor.

All the product divisions were organized along similar lines. Reporting to each product division vice-president were several staff members in the customer service and product research areas. Reporting in a line capacity to each individual vice-president were also a general manager of manufacturing and a general manager of marketing. The general manager of manufacturing was responsible for all the division's manufacturing activities. Similarly, the general manager of marketing was responsible for all the division's marketing activities. Both these executives were assisted by a small staff of specialists. Exhibit 23-2 presents an organization chart of the glass product division's top-management group. All the corporate and divisional management groups were located in British City, Canada. Exhibit 23-3 shows the typical organization structure of a plant within the glass products division.

EXHIBIT 23-2

EMPIRE GLASS COMPANY

Glass Products Division Top Management and Staff

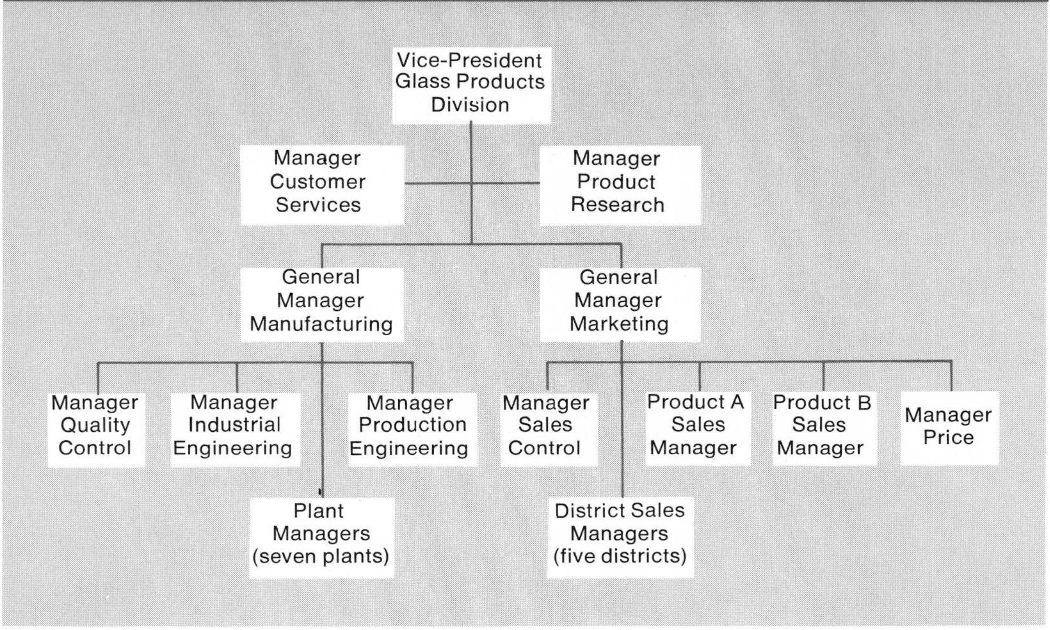

Products and Technology

The glass products division operated a number of plants in Canada producing glass food and beverage bottles. Of these products, food jars constituted the largest group, including jars for products like tomato catsup, mayonnaise, jams and jellies, honey, and soluble coffee. Milk bottles and beer and soft drink bottles were also produced in large quantities. A great variety of shapes and sizes of containers for wines, liquors, drugs, cosmetics, and chemicals were produced in smaller quantities.

Most of the thousands of different products varying in size, shape, color, and decoration were produced to order. According to British City executives, during 19_3 the typical lead time between the customer's order and shipment from the plant was between two and three weeks.

The principal raw materials for container glass were sand, soda ash, and lime. The first step in the manufacturing process was to melt batches of these materials in furnaces or "tanks." The molten mass was then passed into automatic or semiautomatic machines, which filled molds with the molten glass and blew the glass into the desired shape. The ware then went through an automatic annealing oven or lehr, where it was cooled slowly under carefully controlled conditions. If the glass was to be coated on the exterior to increase its resistance to abrasion and scratches, this coating—often a silicone film—was

EXHIBIT 23-3

EMPIRE GLASS COMPANY

Typical Plant Organization—Glass Products Division

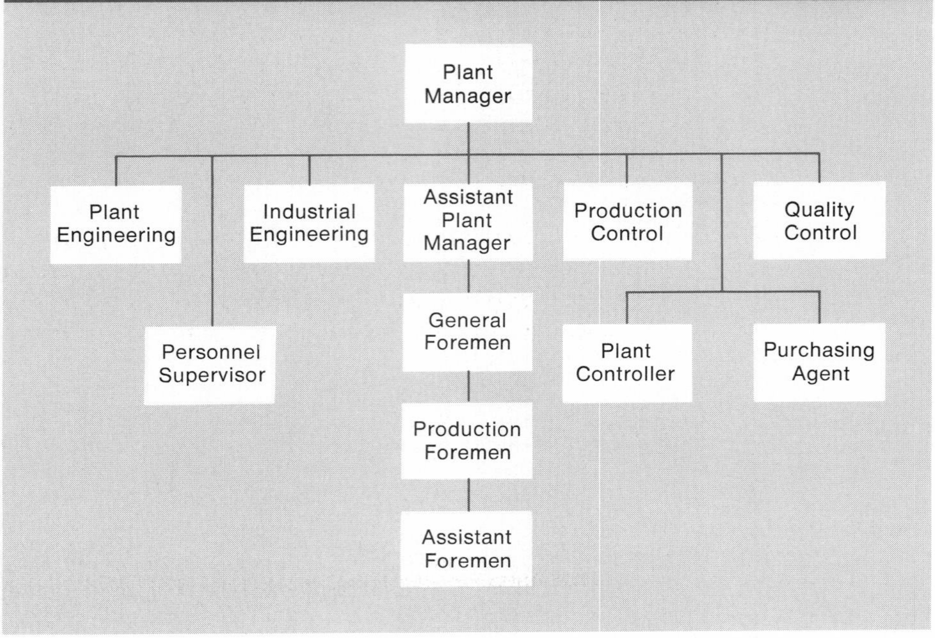

applied at the lehr. Any decorating (such as a trademark of other design) was then added, the product inspected again, and the finished goods packed in corrugated containers (or wooden cases for some bottles).

Quality inspection was critical in the manufacturing process. If the melt in the furnace was not completely free from bubbles and stones (unmelted ingredients or pieces of refinery material), or if the fabricating machinery was slightly out of adjustment, or molds were worn, the rejection rate was very high. Although a number of machines were used in the inspection process, including electric eyes, much of the inspection was still visual.

Although glassmaking was one of the oldest arts, and bottles and jars had been machine molded at relatively high speed for over half a century, the glass products division had spent substantial sums each year to modernize its equipment. These improvements had greatly increased the speed of operations and had substantially reduced the visual inspection and manual handling of glassware.

Most of the jobs were relatively unskilled and highly repetitive, and gave the worker little control over work methods or pace. The moldmakers who made and repaired the molds, the machine repairmen, and those who made the equipment setup changes between different products were considered to be the highest classes of skilled workers. Wages were relatively high in the glass industry. Production employees belonged to two national unions, and for many years bargaining had been conducted on a national basis. Output standards were established for all jobs, but no bonus was paid to hourly plant workers for exceeding standard.

Marketing

Over the years, the sales of the glass products divisions had grown at a slightly faster rate than had the total market for glass containers. Until the late 1950s, the division had charged a premium for most of its products, primarily because they were of better quality than competitive products. In recent years, however, the quality of the competitive products had improved to the point where they now matched the division's quality level. In the meantime, the division's competitors had retained their former price structure. Consequently, the glass products division had been forced to lower its prices to meet its competitor's lower market prices. According to one division executive:

"Currently, price competition is not severe, particularly among the two or three larger companies that dominate the glass bottle industry. Most of our competition is with respect to product quality and customer service. . . . In fact, our biggest competitive threat is from containers other than glass. . . ."

Each of the division's various plants shipped its products throughout Canada to some extent, although transportation costs limited each plant's market primarily to its immediate vicinity. While some of the customers were large and bought in huge quantities, many were relatively small.

Budgetary Control System

In the fall of 19_3, James Walker, Empire Glass Company controller, described the company's budgetary control system to a casewriter. Mr. Walker had been controller for some fifteen years. Excerpts from that interview are reproduced below.

"To understand the role of the budgetary control system, you must first understand our management philosophy. Fundamentally, we have a divisional organization based on broad product categories. These divisional activities are coordinated by the company's executive vice-president, while the head office group provides a policy and review function for him. Within the broad policy limits, we operate on a decentralized basis; each of the decentralized divisions performs the full management job that normally would be inherent in any independent company. The only exceptions to this philosophy are the head office group's sole responsibilities for sources of funds and labor relations with those bargaining units that cross division lines.

"Given this form of organization, the budget is the principal management tool used by head office to direct the efforts of the various segments of the company toward a common goal. Certainly, in our case, the budget is much more than a narrow statistical accounting device."

Sales Budget. "As early as May 15 of the year preceding the budget year, top management of the company asks the various product division vice-presidents to submit preliminary reports stating what they think their division's capital requirements and outlook in terms of sales and income will be during the next budget year. In addition, corporate top management also wants an expression of the division vice-president's general feelings toward the trends in these particular items over the two years following the upcoming budget year. At this stage, head office is not interested in too much detail. Since all divisions plan their capital requirements five years in advance and had made predictions of the forthcoming budget year's market when the budget estimates were prepared last year, these rough estimates of next year's conditions and requirements are far from wild guesses.

"After the opinions of the divisional vice-presidents are in, the market research staff goes to work. They develop a formal statement of the marketing climate in detail for the forthcoming budget year and in general terms for the subsequent two years. Once these general factors have been assessed, a sales forecast is constructed for the company and for each division. Consideration is given to the relationship of the general economic climate to our customers' needs and Empire's share of each market. Explicitly stated are basic assumptions as to price, weather conditions, introduction of new products, gains or losses in particular accounts, forward buying, new manufacturing plants, industry growth trends, packaging trends, inventory carry-overs, and the development of alternative packages to or from glass. This review of all the relevant factors is followed for each of our product lines, regardless of its size and importance. The completed forecasts of the market research group are then forwarded to the appropriate divisions for review, criticism, and adjustments.

"The primary goal of the head office group in developing these sales forecasts is to assure uniformity among the divisions with respect to the basic assumptions on business conditions, pricing, and the treatment of possible emergencies. Also, we provide a yardstick so as to assure us that the company's overall sales forecast will be reasonable and obtainable.

"The product division top management then asks each district manager what he expects to do in the way of sales during the budget year. Head office and the divisional staffs will give the district sales managers as much guidance as they request, but it is the sole responsibility of each district sales manager to come up with his particular forecast.

"After the district sales managers' forecasts are received by the divisional top management, the forecasts are consolidated and reviewed by the division's general manager of marketing. Let me emphasize, however, that nothing is changed in the district sales manager's budget unless the district manager agrees. Then, once the budget is approved, nobody is relieved of his responsibility without top-management approval. Also, no arbitrary changes are made in the approved budgets without the concurrence of all the people responsible for the budget.

"Next, we go through the same process at the division and headquarters levels. We continue to repeat the process until everyone agrees that the sales budgets are sound. Then, each level of management takes responsibility for its particular portion of the budget. These sales budgets then become fixed objectives."

Manufacturing Budgets. "Once the vice-presidents, executive vice-president, and company president have given final approval to the sales budgets, we make a sales budget for each plant by breaking down the division sales budgets according to the plants from which the finished goods will be shipped. These plant sales budgets are then further broken down on a monthly basis by price, volume, and end use. With this information available, the plants then budget their gross profit, fixed expenses, and income before taxes.

"The plant manager's primary responsibility extends to profits. The budgeted plant profit is the difference between the fixed sales-dollar budget and the sum of the budgeted variable costs at standard and the fixed-overhead budget. It is the plant manager's responsibility to meet this budget profit figure, even if actual dollar sales drop below the budget level.

"Given his sales budget, it is up to the plant manager to determine the fixed overhead and variable costs—at standard—that he will need to incur so as to meet the demands of the sales budget. In my opinion, requiring the plant managers to make their own plans is one of the most valuable things associated with the budget system. Each plant manager divides the preparation of the overall plant budget among his plant's various departments. First, the departments spell out the programs in terms of the physical requirements, such as tons of raw material, and then the plans are priced at standard cost.

"The plant industrial engineering department is assigned responsibility for developing engineered cost standards and reduced costs. Consequently, the phase of budget preparation covered by the industrial engineers includes budget standards of performance for each operation, cost center, and department within the plant. This phase of the budget also includes budgeted cost reductions, budgeted unfavorable variances from standards, and certain budgeted programmed fixed costs in the manufacturing area, such as service labor. The industrial engineer prepares this phase of the budget in conjunction with departmental line supervision.

"Before each plant sends its budget into British City, a group of us from head office goes out to visit each plant. For example, in the case of the glass products division, Allen Newell, assistant controller, and I, along with representatives of the glass products division manufacturing staffs visit each of the division's plants. Let me stress this point: We do not go on these trips to pass judgment on the plant's proposed budget. Rather, we go with two purposes in mind. First, we wish to acquaint ourselves with the thinking behind the figures that each plant manager will send in to British City. This is helpful, because when we come to review these budgets with the top management—that is, management above our level—we will have to answer questions about the budgets, and we will know the answers. Second, the review is a way of giving guidance to the plant managers in determining whether or not they are in line with what the company needs to make in the way of profits.

"Of course, when we make our field reviews we do not know about what each of the other plants is doing. Therefore, we explain to the plant managers that while their budget may look good now, when we put all the plants together in a consolidated budget, the plant managers may have to make some changes because the projected profit is not high enough. When this happens, we must tell the plant managers that it is not their programs that are unsound. The problem is that the company cannot afford the programs. I think it is very important that each plant manager has a chance to tell his story. Also, it gives them the feeling that we at headquarters are not living in an ivory tower.

"These plant visits are spread over a three-week period, and we spend an average of half a day at each plant. The plant manager is free to bring to these meetings any of his supervisors he wishes. We ask him not to bring in anybody below the supervisory level. Then, of course, you get into organized labor. During the half day we spend at each plant, we discuss the budget primarily. However, if I have time, I like to wander through the plant and see how things are going. Also, I go over in great detail the property replacement and maintenance budget with the plant manager.

"About September 1, the plant budgets come into British City, and the accounting department consolidates them. Then, the product division vice-presidents review their respective divisional budgets to see if the division budget is reasonable in terms of what the vice-president thinks the corporate management wants. If he is not satisfied with the consolidated plant budgets, he will ask the various plants within the division to trim their budget figures.

"When the division vice-presidents and the executive vice-president are happy, they will send their budgets to the company president. He may accept the division budgets at this point. If he doesn't, he will specify the areas to be reexamined by division and, if necessary, by plant management. The final budget is approved at our December board of directors meeting."

Comparison of Actual and Standard Performance. "At the end of the sixth business day after the close of the month, each plant wires to the head office certain operating variances, which we put together on what we call the variance analysis sheet. Within a half-hour after the last plant report comes through, variance analysis sheets for the divisions and plants are compiled. On the morning of the seventh business day after the end of the month, these reports are usually on the desks of the interested top management. The variance analysis sheet highlights the variances in what we consider to be critical areas. Receiving this report as soon as we do helps us at the head office to take timely action. Let me emphasize, however, we do not accept the excuse that the plant manager has to go to the end of the month to know what happened during the month. He has to be on top of these particular items daily.

"When the actual results come into the head office, we go over them on the basis of exception; that is, we look only at those figures that are in excess of the budgeted amounts. We believe this has a good effect on morale. The plant managers don't have to explain everything they do. They have to explain only where they go off base. In particular, we pay close attention to the net sales, gross margin, and the plant's ability to meet its standard manufacturing cost. Incidentally, when analyzing the gross sales, we look closely at the price and mix changes.

"All this information is summarized on a form known as the Profit Planning and Control Report No. 1 [see Exhibit 23-4]. This document is backed up by a number of supporting documents [see Exhibit 23-5]. The plant PPCR No. 1 and the month-end trial balance showing both actual and budget figures are received in British City at the close of the eighth business day after the end of the month. These two very important reports, along with the supporting reports (PPCR No. 2, PPCR No. 11) are then consolidated by the accounting department on PPCR-type forms to show the results of operations by division and company. The consolidated reports are distributed the next day.

"In connection with the fixed-cost items, we want to know whether or not the plants carried out the programs they said they would carry out. If they have not, we want to know why they have not. Here, we are looking for sound reasons. Also, we want to know if they have carried out their projected programs at the cost they said they would.

"In addition to these reports, at the beginning of each month the plant managers prepare current estimates for the upcoming month and quarter on forms similar to the variance analysis sheets. Since our budget is based on known programs, the value of this current estimate is that it gets the plant people to look at their programs. We hope they will realize that they cannot run their plants on a day-to-day basis.

"If we see a sore spot coming up, or if the plant manager draws our attention to a potential trouble area, we may ask that daily reports concerning this item be sent to the particular division top management involved. In addition, the division top management may send a division staff specialist—say, a quality control expert if it is a quality problem—to the plant concerned. The division staff members can make recommendations, but it is up to the plant manager to accept or reject these recommendations. Of course, it is well known throughout the company that we expect the plant managers to accept gracefully the help of the head office and division staffs."

EXHIBIT 23-4

EMPIRE GLASS COMPANY

Profit Planning and Control Report No. 1

MONTH			Ref.		YEAR TO DATE		
Income Gain (+) or Loss (-) From		Actual			Actual	Income Gain (+) or Loss (−) From	
Prev. Year	Budget					Budget	Prev. Year
			1	Gross Sales to Customers			
			2	Discounts & Allowances			
			3	Net Sales to Customers			
%	%		4	% Gain (+)/Loss (-)		%	%
				DOLLAR VOLUME GAIN (+)/ LOSS (-) DUE TO:			
			5	Sales Price			
			6	Sales Volume			
			6(a)	Trade Mix			
			7	Variable Cost of Sales			
			8	Profit Margin			
				PROFIT MARGIN GAIN (+)/ LOSS (-) DUE TO:			
			9	Profit Volume Ratio (P/V)			
			10	Dollar Volume			
%	%	%	11	Profit Volume Ratio (P/V)	%	%	%
		Income Addition (+)			Income Addition (+)		
			12	Total Fixed Manufacturing Cost			
			13	Fixed Manufacturing Cost-Transfers			
			14	Plant Income (Standard)			
%	%	%	15	% of Net Sales	%	%	%
		Income Addition (+) Income Reduction (−)			Income Addition (+) Income Reduction (−)		
%	%	%	16	% Performance	%	%	%
			17	Manufacturing Efficiency			
		Income Addition (+)			Income Addition (+)		
			18	Methods Improvements			
			19	Other Revisions of Standards			
			20	Material Price Changes			
			21	Division Special Projects			
			22	Company Special Projects			
			23	New Plant Expense			
			24	Other Plant Expenses			
			25	Income on Seconds			
			26				
			27				
			28	Plant Income (Actual)			
%	%		29	% Gain (+)/Loss (−)		%	%
%	%	%	30	% of Net Sales	%	%	%
			36A				
Increase (+) or Decrease (-)				EMPLOYED CAPITAL	Increase (+) or Decrease (-)		
			37	Total Employed Capital			
%	%	%	38	% Return	%	%	%
			39	Turnover Rate			

__________ Plant   __________ Division   __________ Month 19___

Sales-Manufacturing Relations. "If a sales decline occurs during the early part of the year, and if the plant managers can convince us that the change is permanent, we may revise the plant budgets to reflect these new circumstances. However, if toward the end of the year the actual sales volume suddenly drops below the predicted sales volume, we don't have much time to change the budget plans. What we do is ask the plant managers to go back over their budgets with their staffs and see where reduction of expense programs will do the least harm. Specifically, we ask them to consider what they may be able to eliminate this year or delay until next year.

EXHIBIT 23-5

EMPIRE GLASS COMPANY

Brief Description of PPCR No. 2–PPCR No. 11

	INDIVIDUAL PLANT REPORTS
Report	Description
PPCR No. 2	Manufacturing expense: Plant materials, labor, and variable overhead consumed. Detail of actual figures compared with budget and previous year's figures for year to date and current month.
PPCR No. 3	Plant expense: Plant fixed expenses incurred. Details of actual figures compared with budget and previous year's figures for year to date and current month.
PPCR No. 4	Analysis of sales and income: Plant operating gains and losses due to changes in sales revenue, profit margins, and other sources of income. Details of actual figures compared with budget and previous year's figures for year to date and current month.
PPCR No. 5	Plant control statement: Analysis of plant raw material gains and losses, spoilage costs, and cost reduction programs. Actual figures compared with budget figures for current month and year to date.
PPCR No. 6	Comparison of sales by principal and product groups: Plant sales dollars, profit margin, and P/V ratios broken down by end-product use (i.e., soft drinks, beer). Compares actual figures with budgeted figures for year to date and current month.
	DIVISION SUMMARY REPORTS
Report	Description
PPCR No. 7	Comparative plant performance, sales, and income: Gross sales and income figures by plants. Actual figures compared with budget figures for year to date and current month.
PPCR No. 8	Comparative plant performance, total plant expenses: Profit margin, total fixed costs, manufacturing efficiency, other plant expenses, and P/V ratios by plants. Actual figures compared with budgeted and previous year's figures for current month and year to date.
PPCR No. 9	Manufacturing efficiency: Analysis of gains and losses by plant in areas of materials, spoilage, supplies, and labor. Current month and year to date actuals reported in total dollars and as a percentage of budget.
PPCR No. 10	Inventory: Comparison of actual and budget inventory figures by major inventory accounts and plants.
PPCR No. 11	Status of capital expenditures: Analysis of the status of capital expenditures by plants, months, and relative to budget.

"I believe it was Confucius who said, 'We make plans so we have plans to discard.' Nevertheless, I think it is wise to make plans, even if you have to discard them. Having plans makes it a lot easier to figure out what to do when sales fall off from the budgeted level. The understanding of operations that comes from preparing the budget removes a lot of the potential chaos and confusion that might arise if we were under pressure to meet a stated profit goal and sales declined quickly and unexpectedly at year-end, just as they did last year. In these circumstances, we don't try to ram anything down the plant managers' throats. We ask them to tell us where they can reasonably expect to cut costs below the budgeted level.

"Whenever a problem arises at a plant between sales and production, the local people are supposed to solve the problem themselves. For example, a customer's purchasing agent may insist he wants an immediate delivery, and this delivery will disrupt the production department's plans. The production group can make recommendations as to alternative ways to take care of the problem, but it's the sales manager's responsibility to get the product to the customer. The salesmen are supposed to know their customers well enough to judge whether or not the customer really needs the product. If the sales manager says the customer needs the product, that ends the matter. As far as we are concerned, the customer's wants are primary; our company is a case where sales wags the rest of the dog.

"Of course, if the change in the sales program involves a major plant expense that is out of line with the budget, then the matter is passed up to division for decision.

"As I said earlier, the sales department has the sole responsibility for the product price, sales mix, and delivery schedules. They do not have direct responsibility for plant operations or profit. That's the plant management's responsibility. However, it is understood that sales group will cooperate with the plant people wherever possible."

Motivation. "There are various ways in which we motivate the plant managers to meet their profit goals. First of all, we promote only capable people. Also, a monetary incentive program has been established that stimulates their efforts to achieve their profit goals. In addition, each month we put together a bar chart that shows, by division and plant, the ranking of the various manufacturing units with respect to manufacturing efficiency.* We feel the plant managers are 100 percent responsible for variable manufacturing costs. I believe this is true, since all manufacturing standards have to be approved by plant managers. Most of the plant managers give wide publicity to these bar charts. The efficiency bar chart and efficiency measure itself is perhaps a little unfair in some respects when you are comparing one plant with another. Different kinds of products are run through different plants. These require different setups, etc., which have an important impact on a position of the plant. However, in general, the efficiency rating is a good indication of the quality of the plant manager and his supervisory staff.

"Also, a number of plants run competitions within the plants, which reward department heads or foremen, based on their relative standing with respect to a certain cost item. The plant managers, their staffs, and employees have great pride in their plants.

"The number one item now stressed at the plant level is *quality.* The market situation is such that in order to make sales you have to meet the market price and exceed the market quality. By quality I mean not only the physical characteristics of the product but also such things as delivery schedules. As I read the company employee publications, their message is that if the company is to be profitable, it must produce high-quality items at a reasonable cost. This is necessary so that the plants can meet their obligation to produce the maximum profits for the company in the prevailing circumstances."

* Manufacturing efficiency $= \dfrac{\text{Total actual variable manufacturing costs}}{\text{Total standard variable manufacturing costs}} \times 100\%$

The Future. "An essential part of the budgetary control system is planning. We have developed a philosophy that we must begin our plans where the work is done—in the line organization and out in the field. Perhaps, in the future, we can avoid or cut back some of the budget preparation steps and start putting together our sales budget later than May 15. However, I doubt if we will change the basic philosophy.

"Frankly, I doubt if the line operators would want any major change in the system; they are very jealous of the management prerogatives the system gives to them.

"It is very important that we manage the budget. We have to be continually on guard against its managing us. Sometimes the plants lose sight of this fact. We have to be made conscious daily of the necessity of having the sales volume to make a profit. And when sales fall off and their plant programs are reduced, they do not always appear to see the justification for budget cuts—although I do suspect that they see more of the justification for these cuts than they will admit. It is this human side of the budget to which we have to pay more attention in the future."

required

Comment on the strong points and the weak points in the management control system of the Empire Glass Company. What changes, if any, would you suggest? (Assume that sales districts cannot match up perfectly with manufacturing plants.)

Decision Models, Uncertainty, and the Accountant

24

The first part of Chapter 1 concentrated on the role of information in management, i.e., in choosing among various future actions. As Exhibit 1-1 showed, the accountant must visualize the entire decision process before choosing an accounting information system. Essentially, the interdependent steps are: (a) predict the set of data or signals that will be generated by alternative accounting systems; (b) predict the actions that will be induced; (c) predict the resultant expected values[1] (for example, net incomes or cash flows) associated with each set of actions; and (d) select the accounting system that will maximize the net expected values. Net expected value must reflect the costs of accumulating, reporting, and understanding the accounting data.

This chapter explores this decision process in more depth by examining the role of risk or uncertainty. Before proceeding, you may wish to review the first part of Chapter 1.

[1] Throughout this chapter we imply that expected monetary values represent the general case. However, decision theory regards the use of expected monetary values as a special application of the general approach, which uses utility values. In particular, the use of expected monetary value ignores aversion to risk. See the brief discussion at the end of the chapter.

characteristics of uncertainty

As Chapter 1 explained, a decision model is a conceptual representation that measures the effects of alternative actions. The models that are expressed in mathematical form usually have the following characteristics:

1. An organizational objective that can be quantified. This objective can take many forms. Most often it is expressed as a maximization (or minimization) of some form of profit (or cost). This quantification is often called a *choice criterion* or an *objective function.* This objective function is used to evaluate the courses of action and to provide a basis for choosing the best alternative.
2. A set of the alternative courses of action under explicit consideration. This set of *actions* should be collectively exhaustive and mutually exclusive.
3. A set of all the relevant *events* (sometimes called *states* or *states of nature*) that can occur. Because this set should also be collectively exhaustive and mutually exclusive, only one of the events will actually occur. Examples of events include success or failure, rain or no rain, war or peace, and so on.
4. A set of *probabilities* that shows the likelihood of each event's occurring.
5. A set of *outcomes* (often called *payoffs*) that measure, in terms of the objective function, the consequences of the various possible combinations of actions and events. Each outcome is conditionally dependent on a specific course of action and a specific event.

Several examples in this chapter will clarify these essential ingredients of a formal decision model.

decisions under certainty

Decisions are frequently classified as those made under certainty and those under uncertainty. Certainty exists when there is absolutely no doubt about which event will occur, and hence there is a single outcome for each possible action. Exhibit 1-1 showed such a comparison where complete certainty was assumed; that is, there would be only one possible event for the two possible actions: "Do nothing" at a future labor cost of $2.00 per product unit for, say, 100,000 units, or "rearrange" at a future labor cost of $1.80 for 100,000 units. A decision table (sometimes called a *payoff table*) would appear as follows:

	EVENT: SUCCESSFUL IMPLEMENTATION
Probability of event	1.0
ACTIONS:	
Do nothing	Outcome, 100,000($2.00) = $200,000
Rearrange	100,000($1.80) = $180,000

Note that there is only one column in the decision table because there is only one possible outcome for each action. The decision obviously consists of choosing the action that will produce the most desirable outcome (least cost). However, decisions under certainty are not *always* obvious. There are often countless alternative actions, each of which may offer certain outcomes. The problem is then finding the best one. For example, the problem of allocating twenty different job orders to twenty different machines, any one of which could do the job, can involve literally *billions* of different combinations. Each way of assigning these jobs is another possible action. This decision table would have only one *column,* because the costs of production using the various machines are assumed to be known; however, it would have $2\frac{1}{2}$ quintillion *rows.* This demonstrates that decision making under certainty can be more than just a trivial problem.[2]

When an event is certain, the prediction is a single point with no dispersion on either side. There is a 100 percent chance of occurrence; the probability is 1.0. For example, the expected cash inflow on a federal Treasury note might be, say, \$4,000 for next year. This might be graphed as follows:

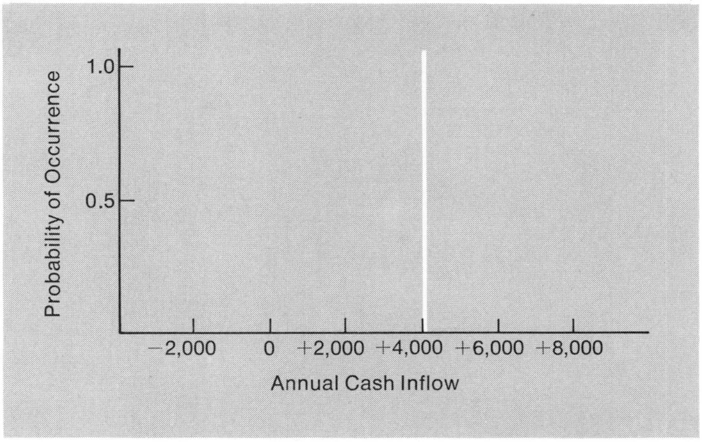

decisions under risk or uncertainty

Of course, the decision maker must frequently contend with uncertainty rather than certainty; he faces a number of possible events. The distinction among various degrees of uncertainty centers on how probabilities are assigned. The probabilities may be assigned with a high degree of confidence.[3] That is, the decision maker may know the probability of occurrence of each of the events because of mathematical proofs

[2] See D. W. Miller and M. K. Starr, *Executive Decisions and Operations Research,* 2nd ed. (Englewood Cliffs, N.J.: Prentice-Hall, Inc., 1969), pp. 104–5. Their distinctions among certainty, risk, and uncertainty are used here.

[3] This is sometimes called decision making under risk, as distinguished from decision making under uncertainty. See Miller and Starr, *op. cit.,* p. 105. The distinction between risk and uncertainty in the current literature and in practice is so blurred that the terms are used interchangeably here.

or the compilation of historical evidence. For example, the probability of obtaining a head in the toss of a symmetrical coin is .5; that of drawing a particular playing card from a well-shuffled deck, $1/52$. In a business, the probability of having a specified percentage of defective units may be assigned with great confidence based on production experience with thousands of units.

If the decision maker has no basis in past experience or in mathematical proofs for assigning the probabilities of occurrence of the various events, he must resort to the *subjective* assignment of probabilities. For example, the probability of the success or failure of a new product may have to be assessed without the help of any related experience. This assignment is subjective, because no two individuals assessing a situation will necessarily assign the same probabilities. Executives may be virtually certain about the *range* of possible events or outcomes, but they may differ about the likelihoods of various possibilities within that range.

The concept of uncertainty can be illustrated by considering two investment proposals on new projects.[4] The manager believes that the following discrete probability distribution describes the relative likelihood of flows for the next year (assume that the useful life of the project is one year):

PROPOSAL A		PROPOSAL B	
Probability	Cash Inflow	Probability	Cash Inflow
0.10	$3,000	0.10	$2,000
0.20	3,500	0.25	3,000
0.40	4,000	0.30	4,000
0.20	4,500	0.25	5,000
0.10	5,000	0.10	6,000

expected value and standard deviation

Exhibit 24-1 shows a graphical comparison of the probability distributions. One approach to this problem is to compute an expected value[5] for each probability distribution.

The expected value of the cash inflow in Proposal A is

$$\overline{A} = 0.1(3{,}000) + 0.2(3{,}500) + 0.4(4{,}000) + 0.2(4{,}500) + 0.1(5{,}000) = \$4{,}000$$

[4] James C. Van Horne, *Financial Management and Policy,* 4th ed. (Englewood Cliffs, N.J.: Prentice-Hall, Inc., 1977), Chapter 2.

[5] An expected value is an arithmetic mean, a weighted average using the probabilities as weights. The formula is

$$\overline{A} = \sum_{x=1}^{n} A_x P_x$$

where A_x is the outcome or payoff or cost or cash flow for the xth possible event or state of nature, P_x is the probability of occurrence of that outcome, and $\overline{A}$ is the expected value of the outcome.

EXHIBIT 24-1

COMPARISON OF PROBABILITY DISTRIBUTIONS

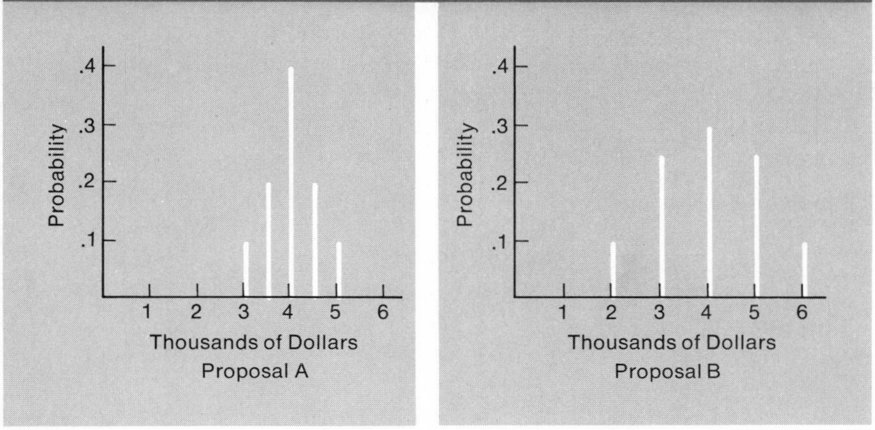

The expected value for the cash inflow in Proposal A is also \$4,000:

$$\overline{A} = 0.1(2{,}000) + 0.25(3{,}000) + 0.3(4{,}000) + 0.25(5{,}000) + 0.1(6{,}000) = \$4{,}000$$

Incidentally, the expected value of the cash inflow in the federal Treasury note is also \$4,000:

$$\overline{A} = 1.0(4{,}000) = \$4{,}000$$

Note that mere comparison of these \$4,000 expected values is an oversimplification. These three single figures are not strictly comparable; one represents certainty, whereas the other two represent the expected values over a range of possible outcomes. The decision maker must explicitly or implicitly (by "feel" or hunch) recognize that he is comparing figures that are really representations of probability distributions; otherwise the reporting of the expected value alone may mislead him.[6]

To give the decision maker more information, the accountant could provide the complete probability distribution for each proposal. However, often

[6] For example, how would you feel about choosing between the following two investments? First, invest \$10 today with a probability of 1.0 of obtaining \$11 in two days. Second, invest \$10 today with a probability of .5 of obtaining \$22 in two days and .5 of obtaining \$0. The expected value is \$11 in both cases. Also see the final section of this chapter on expected monetary value and utility.

that course means flooding the manager with too much data for his comprehension. Therefore, a summary measure of the underlying dispersion is often supplied. The conventional measure of the dispersion of a probability distribution for a single variable is the standard deviation. The standard deviation is the square root of the mean of the squared deviations from the expected value:

$$\sigma = \sqrt{\sum_{x=1}^{n} (A_x - \bar{A})^2 P_x}$$

The standard deviation for Proposal A is smaller than that for Proposal B:

For A: $\sigma = [.1(3{,}000 - 4{,}000)^2 + .2(3{,}500 - 4{,}000)^2 + .4(4{,}000 - 4{,}000)^2 + .2(4{,}500 - 4{,}000)^2 + .1(5{,}000 - 4{,}000)^2]^{1/2}$
$= [300{,}000]^{1/2} = \$548$

For B: $\sigma = [.1(2{,}000 - 4{,}000)^2 + .25(3{,}000 - 4{,}000)^2 + .3(4{,}000 - 4{,}000)^2 + .25(5{,}000 - 4{,}000)^2 + .1(6{,}000 - 4{,}000)^2]^{1/2}$
$= [1{,}300{,}000]^{1/2} = \$1{,}140$

For the Treasury note: $\sigma = \sqrt{1.0(4{,}000 - 4{,}000)^2} = 0$

A measure of relative dispersion is the coefficient of variation, which is the standard deviation divided by expected value. The coefficient for Proposal B is 1,140 ÷ 4,000 = .29; for A it is 548 ÷ 4,000 = .14; and for the Treasury note it is 0 ÷ 4,000 = 0. Therefore, because the coefficient is a relative measure of risk or uncertainty, B is said to have a greater degree of risk.[7]

the accountant and uncertainty

Many accounting practitioners and businessmen shudder at the notion of using subjective probabilities to quantify things that are supposedly "intangible" or "unmeasurable" or "qualitative" or "unquantifiable." However, this position is weak, simply because decisions *do* have to be made. The attempts by statisticians, mathematicians, and modern accountants to measure the unmeasurable is an old and natural chore that scientists have performed for centuries. The use of subjective probabilities merely formalizes the intuitive judgments and hunches that managers so often use. It forces the decision maker to expose and evaluate what he may have done unconsciously for years.

We should distinguish between *cost estimation,* which is an attempt to measure historical costs, and *cost prediction,* which is an attempt to measure

[7] As most widely defined, risk is the dispersion described above. However, to many individuals risk is not dispersion by itself; rather, it is the possibility of downside deviations from the expected value. As Van Horne and others have pointed out, an investor does not consider upside deviations undesirable. A measure of downside risk may be helpful, but the mathematical complexities are imposing for anything beyond the simplest situations. Moreover, the riskiness of a single investment should be related to its role as a part of a portfolio of investments. Some risk can be diversified away by investments in independent projects. For an expanded discussion, see Van Horne, *Financial Management and Policy,* Chapters 6–8.

expected future costs. Almost all accounting data are subject to uncertainty, whether the data are predictions or are historical. Too often, managers and accountants regard historical accumulations as precise calibrations rather than as approximations. The estimates (the measures of the effects of past events) should be marked by less uncertainty than are the predictions. Still, we must recognize that the accounting process deals with the real world, a world marked by uncertain predictions and uncertain estimates about what really happened.

Many statisticians and accountants favor presenting the entire probability distribution directly to the decision maker. Others first divide the information into a threefold classification of optimistic, middle, and pessimistic categories. Still others provide summary measures of dispersion, such as the standard deviation or the coefficient of variation. In any event, we are likely to see the accountant's formal recognition of uncertainty and probability distributions in his reporting. In this way, the information will portray underlying phenomena in a more realistic fashion instead of portraying a world of certainty.

coping with uncertainty

general approach to uncertainty

Our plant-rearrangement example in Chapter 1 will be used to demonstrate the general approach to uncertainty. Suppose the manager is faced with equal likelihoods of success or failure regarding the rearrangement. Success will bring one set of outcomes; failure will bring another set. Then the one-column decision table introduced earlier becomes a two-column decision table, as shown in Exhibit 24-2.

Assume the choice criterion is that the expected savings from rearrangement must equal or exceed $11,000. Given this model, the decision maker would rearrange, because the expected value of the rearrangement costs is $20,000 less than the other option.

EXHIBIT 24-2

DECISION TABLE

	EVENTS		
	Success	Failure	
Probability of event	.5	.5	Expected
	Cost	Cost	Value of Costs[a]
ACTIONS:			
Do nothing	$200,000	$200,000	$200,000
Rearrange	100,000	260,000	180,000

[a] If do nothing, $\bar{A}$ = $200,000(.5) + $200,000(.5).
If rearrange, $\bar{A}$ = $100,000(.5) + $260,000(.5).

The accountant often provides many of the data that are included in these decision models. His understanding of the nature of decision models should have a direct effect on how he designs a formal information system.[8]

buying perfect information

Even though the expected value of the costs is $20,000 lower under "rearrange," the manager is nervous. His performance would look bad if the actual cost were $260,000. His present cost-analysis staff is overloaded with other work, but he can hire an expensive consultant who, after studying the data, has clairvoyance in these matters. What would be the maximum amount he would be willing to pay for the consultant's wisdom?

Note that the basic decision here is whether to purchase advance revelation (perfect information) without knowing what the revelation will be. The general approach is to first compute the expected value, assuming that the manager will be told the event and outcome in advance with absolute certainty. A *decision table with perfect information* would appear as in Exhibit 24-3.

Reflect on what Exhibit 24-3 reveals. If the manager knew in advance that the rearrangement were going to succeed, he would rearrange and incur costs of $100,000. Similarly, if he knew in advance that the rearrangement were going to fail, he would do nothing and incur costs of $200,000. But he cannot be sure of what particular prediction he will receive. Because the perfect information that he is considering buying will contain one of two predictions, the expected value with perfect information will be .5($100,000) + .5($200,000) = $150,000. Consequently, the maximum price the manager should be willing to pay for perfect advance information would be the difference between the expected values with *existing* information and with *perfect* information, $180,000 − $150,000, or $30,000. This top price has been called the *expected value of perfect information.*

buying imperfect information

Obviously, perfect information is generally unobtainable (except in textbooks), but imperfect information may still be worth buying. Suppose a consultant offers to conduct an accounting analysis that would affect the manager's assessments of probabilities of success of failure. The consultant is expected to produce one of three possible reports: neutral, optimistic, or pessimistic. The neutral report would not change the original decision table in Exhibit 24-2. The optimistic and pessimistic reports would change the decision table, because they would change the manager's assessments of probabilities of success or failure. Exhibit 24-4 shows the effects of each report.

[8] For a more rigorous approach to this topic, see G. Feltham and J. Demski, "The Use of Models in Information Evaluation," *The Accounting Review,* Vol. XIV, No. 4.

EXHIBIT 24-3

DECISION TABLE WITH PERFECT INFORMATION

	EVENTS		
	Success	Failure	
Probability of event	.5	.5	Expected Value of Costs
	Cost	Cost	
ACTIONS:			
Do nothing		$200,000	$100,000
Rearrange	$100,000		50,000
			$150,000

EXHIBIT 24-4

EFFECTS OF CHANGES IN PROBABILITY

	EVENTS		
	Success	Failure	
Optimistic report:			
Probability of event	.8	.2	Expected Value of Costs
	Cost	Cost	
ACTIONS:			
Do nothing	$200,000	$200,000	$200,000
Rearrange	100,000	260,000	132,000[a]
Pessimistic Report:			
Probability of event	.2	.8	
	Cost	Cost	
ACTIONS:			
Do nothing	$200,000	$200,000	$200,000
Rearrange	100,000	260,000	228,000[b]

[a] $100,000(.8) + $260,000(.2) = $132,000

[b] $100,000(.2) + $260,000(.8) = $228,000

Should the manager hire the consultant to make the accounting analysis? That depends on what type of report the manager foresees. The trouble is that he is unsure. He assesses a probability of .4 neutral, .3 optimistic, and .3 pessimistic. He then proceeds to determine the top price to pay for this imperfect information.

First, Exhibits 24-2 and 24-4 showed that the expected values with the imperfect information (the reports) would be:

If neutral, rearrange	.5($100,000) + .5($260,000) =	$180,000
If optimistic, rearrange	.8($100,000) + .2($260,000) =	$132,000
If pessimistic, do nothing		$200,000

The foregoing may be placed in a decision table (that is similar to the table with perfect information in Exhibit 24-3):

	EVENT (TYPE OF REPORT)			
	Neutral	Optimistic	Pessimistic	Expected Value of Costs
Probability	.4	.3	.3	
ACTION:				
Do nothing			$200,000	$ 60,000[a]
Rearrange	$180,000	$132,000		111,600[b]
				$171,600

[a] .3($200,000) = $60,000

[b] .4($180,000) + .3($132,000) = $111,600

The maximum price that should be paid for the report is the difference in the expected value of costs with the report ($171,600) and the expected value of costs with the existing information ($180,000), or $8,400.

cost-benefit is paramount

Reconsider the preceding example. There were two choice problems: First, should a report be acquired? Second, what action should be taken regarding the plant rearrangement? The first problem is merely an example of possible accounting alternatives, such as what accounting system to employ, what cost estimate to use, and so on. Note that the choice among accounting alternatives is critical only when they are perceived as inducing different economic decisions. Furthermore, the "costs of obtaining the cost estimates" are an ingredient of the decision of how much information to buy.

The second problem, the action choice, affects how the first problem, the accounting system or data choice, is resolved. That is, the preferred accounting system, data, or report is not a single, absolute truth. Rather, it is any of a *set* of several alternatives that helps induce the preferred economic decision (subject to cost of the system or data). For example, when should we care whether an overhead rate is "truly" $2.00 per labor-hour or $1.00 per labor-hour? Sometimes we may care a lot, but other times we may be indifferent. Our degree of concern depends strictly on whether the action choice is going to be altered because of that specific cost estimate. That is, to be "useful," accounting data must be capable of altering the recipient's probabilities sufficiently to affect his selection of an action.

The cost-benefit approach provides a philosophical overview, but it becomes difficult for us to apply in concrete fashion when choosing among alternative accounting systems. The trouble is that systems must be designed to accommodate a multitude of routine decisions; an appraisal of costs and benefits must be made in light of their collective effect. Therefore, even though given data may have little or no value in a particular decision situation, the system that provides such data may nevertheless be economically justifiable in a collective sense. For example, a discounted cash-flow model may be part of an accounting system that supports capital-budgeting decisions. For any specific decision, a simpler model may be good enough because the data provided by the discounted cash-flow model would not change the action choice. Therefore, the data or models may be valueless for a particular decision, but the models or systems may still be economically justifiable when their impact on the entire class of decisions is predicted.

expected monetary value and utility

In most business cases, expected monetary value is a useful guide to action; that is, the manager chooses the act that will bring the greatest expected financial advantage. However, there are instances where expected monetary profit will not be governing. For psychological reasons—perhaps fear of bankruptcy—managers may have *personal* evaluations that do not coincide with monetary evaluations.

For example, suppose that each of two managers has an opportunity to prepare a proposal at a cost of \$10,000. There is a 50-50 chance that the proposal will be accepted, in which case there would be a \$25,000 net profit (after deducting all associated costs, including the \$10,000 proposal cost). The table and the computation of an expected monetary value of \$7,500 for making the proposal follow:

	EVENT	
	GET CONTRACT	*DO NOT GET*
Probability	.5	.5
ACTION:		
Make proposal	\$25,000	−\$10,000
No proposal	-0-	-0-

$$\bar{A}\text{ (Make proposal)} = .5(25{,}000) + .5(-10{,}000) = \$7{,}500$$
$$\bar{A}\quad\text{(No proposal)} = 0$$

But the two managers may have very different attitudes toward the situation. The attractiveness of the proposal to each may depend on his own financial position. If one of the managers may be easily bankrupted by the loss of the \$10,000 proposal cost, he may decide to forego this opportunity. The other manager may have adequate working capital and may make the proposal. What must be decided is simply whether it is worth taking a 50 percent risk of losing \$10,000 in order to have an even chance of a \$25,000 profit. This decision depends on a direct expression of personal preference.

Thus, where the amounts at stake are large, an expected value of one dollar may not be worth a dollar to the manager; that is, an expected dollar may have an expected *utility value* of only, say, 70 cents (a direct expression of personal preference). Strict money value then will not be a valid guide to action. The approach to the decision will be the same, but in these special cases *dollar values* will no longer coincide with *utility values,* and so the latter will replace dollar values in the evaluation.

Traditional accounting approaches work with expected *monetary* values and therefore ignore risk. If expected *utility* values are introduced, the risk-aversion characteristics of the decision maker are contained in his utility function. Then maximizing expected utility does explicitly make trade-offs between levels of risk and return.[9]

SUMMARY

The accountant must be acquainted with the entire decision process. He must focus on decision objectives, prediction methods, decision models, and alternative outcomes.

Formal decision models are used increasingly, because they replace or supplement hunches and implicit rules with explicit assumptions and criteria. The decision maker must choose the decision model to use. Both the choice criterion or objective function and the complexities of the decision situation affect the choice of model. What information is to be compiled depends on the chosen prediction method and the decision model.

Managers and accountants are often prone to regard quantification as precise just because numbers are somehow supposed to be accurate. However, almost all data, whether they depict the past or the future, are subject to uncertainty. Accounting reports for decision making are aimed increasingly toward the formal, explicit recognition of uncertainty. Cognizance of probability distributions is often essential to providing information for decisions, and the use of utility values provides a systematic way for measuring risk-return trade-offs.

SUGGESTED READINGS

AMERICAN ACCOUNTING ASSOCIATION, "Report of the Committee on Managerial Decision Models," *Accounting Review* (Supplement), Vol. XLIV, 1969. Also see the reports of other committees on related topics in the annual Supplements in succeeding years.

BALL, R., and P. BROWN, "Portfolio Theory and Accounting," *Journal of Accounting Research,* Autumn 1969.

BEER, S., *Decision and Control.* New York: John Wiley & Sons, Inc., 1966.

DEMSKI, J. S., *Information Analysis.* Reading, Mass.: Addison-Wesley Publishing Co., Inc., 1972.

DEMSKI, J. S. and G. A. FELTHAM, *Cost Determination: A Conceptual Approach.* Ames, Iowa: Iowa State University Press, 1976.

[9] See H. Raiffa, *Decision Analysis: Introductory Lectures on Choices Under Uncertainty* (Reading, Mass.: Addison-Wesley Publishing Co., Inc., 1968) and L. Savage, *The Foundation of Statistical Inference* (New York: John Wiley & Sons, Inc., 1962).

FELTHAM, G. A., *Information Evaluation.* Sarasota, Fla.: American Accounting Association, 1973.

HERTZ, D. B., "Investment Policies that Pay Off," *Harvard Business Review,* January–February 1968.

———, "Risk Analysis in Capital Investment," *Harvard Business Review,* January–February 1964.

MILLER, D. W., and M. K., STARR, *Executive Decisions and Operations Research,* 2nd ed. Englewood Cliffs, N.J.: Prentice-Hall, Inc., 1969.

MORRIS, W. T., *Management Science: A Bayesian Introduction.* Englewood Cliffs, N.J.: Prentice-Hall, 1968.

RAIFFA, H., *Decision Analysis: Introductory Lectures on Choices Under Uncertainty.* Reading, Mass.: Addison-Wesley Publishing Co., Inc., 1968.

SCHLAIFER, ROBERT, *Analysis of Decisions Under Uncertainty.* New York: McGraw-Hill Book Company, 1969.

Books of readings on management accounting topics published since 1970 include:

ANTON, HECTOR R., and PETER A. FIRMIN (ed.), *Contemporary Issues in Cost Accounting,* 2nd ed. Boston: Houghton Mifflin Company, 1972.

BENSTON, GEORGE J., *Contemporary Cost Accounting and Control.* Belmont, Cal.: Dickenson Publishing Company, Inc., 1970.

DECOSTER, D., K. RAMANTHAN, and G. SUNDEM (eds.), *Accounting for Managerial Decision Making.* Los Angeles: Melville Publishing Company, 1974.

LIVINGSTONE, JOHN LESLIE (ed.), *Management Planning and Control: Mathematical Models.* McGraw-Hill Book Company, 1970.

RAPPAPORT, ALFRED (ed.), *Information for Decision Making: Quantitative and Behavioral Dimensions,* 2nd ed. Englewood Cliffs, N.J.: Prentice-Hall, Inc., 1974.

ROSEN, L. S. (ed.), *Topics in Managerial Accounting,* 2nd ed. McGraw-Hill Ryerson, Ltd., 1974.

SCHIFF, MICHAEL, and ARIE Y. LEWIN (eds.), *Behavioral Aspects of Accounting.* Englewood Cliffs, N.J.: Prentice-Hall, Inc., 1974.

THOMAS, W., (ed.), *Readings in Cost Accounting, Budgeting and Control,* 4th ed. Cincinnati: South-Western Publishing Co., 1973.

PROBLEMS FOR SELF-STUDY

Review the examples by trying to compute your own solutions, particularly for the examples on standard deviation and the expected value of perfect information.

QUESTIONS, PROBLEMS, AND CASES

24-1 Define *decision making.*

24-2 "Determining the problem is the key to successful decision making." Comment.

24-3 A fire has destroyed a factory. As the company manager, list as many alternative actions as you can formulate.

24-4 "Taking no action must always be listed among alternative courses of action." Discuss.

24-5 "The management consultant is happy when he finds that his client has wholeheartedly accepted a beautiful decision program that is the consultant's brainchild and the product of weeks of analysis." Later, the consultant's joy often becomes sadness when he finds that the decisions were never transformed into action. What is the probable reason for the apparent failure of the consultant's plans?

24-6 "The wisdom of a decision can never really be measured until the future becomes the past." What are the merits and weaknesses of a postdecision audit?

24-7 Distinguish among *risk, certainty,* and *uncertainty.*

24-8 Define *expected value.*

24-9 What steps should be taken in computing expected value?

24-10 Many businessmen refuse to accept marginal business at cut prices under any circumstances. They say that acceptance of such orders will hurt the industry price structure and thus boomerang to the detriment of "unmeasurable" future profits. Does the businessman base such decisions on quantitative, tangible factors? Explain.

24-11 What is the major benefit of using subjective probabilities in forecasting?

24-12 What is *utility value?*

24-13 *Assessment of Subjective Probabilities* Both Sears, Roebuck and Montgomery Ward faced the same general economic conditions in the decade after World War II. Ward's policy was to keep a relatively large proportion of its assets in liquid form, whereas Sears invested heavily in expansion of operations.

required | Comment on the influence of subjective probabilities on the chief executives.

24-14 *Size of Inventory* Once a day, a retailer stocks bunches of fresh-cut flowers, each of which costs 40¢ and sells for $1. The retailer never cuts his price; leftovers are given to a nearby church. He estimates demand characteristics as follows:

DEMAND	*PROBABILITY*
0	.05
1	.20
2	.40
3	.25
4	.10
5 or more	.00
	1.00

How many units should he stock in order to maximize profits? Why?

24-15 *Perfect Information* Refer to the preceding problem. Compute the most he should be willing to pay for a faultless prediction concerning the number of units to be sold on any given day.

24-16 *Choosing a Selling Price* (CPA, adapted) Management wants to determine the best sales price for a new appliance, which has a variable cost of $4 per unit. The sales manager has estimated probabilities of achieving annual sales levels for various selling prices as shown in the following chart:

SALES LEVEL (UNITS)	SELLING PRICE			
	$4	$5	$6	$7
20,000	—	—	20%	80%
30,000	—	10%	40%	20%
40,000	50%	50%	20%	—
50,000	50%	40%	20%	—

Prepare a schedule computing the expected incremental income for each of the sales prices proposed for the new product. The schedule should include the expected sales levels in units (weighted according to the sales manager's estimated probabilities), the expected total monetary sales, the expected variable costs, and the expected incremental income. Which price should be chosen?

24-17 *Selection of Production Plan* (Adapted from Malcom Pye, "Reasons, Probabilities, and Accounting Principles," *Accounting Review,* Vol. XXXV, No. 3, pp. 440–41.) Assume that the XYZ Company manufactures the Gadget, in which a Gismo is installed. The Gismo costs $10, but when a Gadget is returned because of a defective Gismo, the replacement cost of the Gismo will be $25 because of special handling and the necessary dismantling of the Gadget. Prior to the installation of the Gismo, these alternatives are available to management:

1. If the Gismos are tested by random sampling, quality can be controlled so that only 3 percent of the installed Gismos will be defective. The average cost of such sampling, per Gadget, is $.10.
2. All Gismos can be tested and no replacements will be necessary. The average cost of sampling is $1.50.
3. The manufacturer of the Gismo will guarantee that 92 percent will be good. The cost of replacing Gismos in excess of this 8 percent level will be borne by that manufacturer. However, the price per Gismo will be $10.25.

required

Assume that annual production is 100,000 units. Select an alternative. Show computations.

24-18 *Buying Equipment* The board of directors is faced with a decision on buying special equipment for a new product. The wisdom of the decision is ultimately dependent on total sales volume. Labor and associated variable costs per unit will be much less with the more elaborate equipment. Assume zero disposal values for the equipment:

EQUIPMENT	TOTAL ORIGINAL COST	VARIABLE COSTS PER UNIT OF PRODUCT
M-1	$40,000	$4
M-2	95,000	3

Marketing executives believe that this highly specialized product will be salable only over the next year. They are very uncertain about sales prospects, but their best judgment of sales potential at $5 per unit is as follows:

TOTAL UNITS	TOTAL SALES	PROBABILITY
30,000	$150,000	.2
50,000	250,000	.4
60,000	300,000	.2
70,000	350,000	.2

required

Prepare an analysis to guide the board's action.

24-19 *Evaluation of Degree of Risk: Standard Deviation and Coefficient of Variation* Suppose that you are the manager of a bottling company. You are trying to choose between two types of equipment, F and G. The proposals had the following discrete probability distributions of cash flows in each of the next four years:

PROPOSAL F		PROPOSAL G	
Probability	Net Cash Inflow	Probability	Net Cash Inflow
.10	$3,000	.10	$1,000
.25	4,000	.25	2,000
.30	5,000	.30	3,000
.25	6,000	.25	4,000
.10	7,000	.10	5,000

required

1. For each proposal, compute (a) the expected value of the cash inflows in each of the next three years, (b) the standard deviation, and (c) the coefficient of variation.
2. Which proposal has the greater degree of risk? Why?

24-20 *Expected Value, Standard Deviation, and Risk* Suppose the Van Horne Company is planning to invest in a common stock for one year. An investigation of the expected dividends and expected market price has been conducted. The probability distribution of expected returns for the year, as a percent, is:

PROBABILITY OF OCCURRENCE	POSSIBLE RETURN
.05	.284
.10	.224
.20	.160
.30	.100
.20	.040
.10	−.024
.05	−.084

required

1. Compute the expected value of possible returns, the standard deviation of the probability distribution, and the coefficient of variation.
2. Van Horne could also earn 6 percent for certain on federal bonds. What is the standard deviation and coefficient of variation of such an investment?
3. Relate the computations in part 1 with those in part 2. That is, what role does the coefficient of variation play in determining the relative attractiveness of various investments?

24-21 *Standard Deviation and Comparisons* Freund, a salesman of industrial chemicals, made sales of $15,000 in April; Williams, a salesman of office supplies, made sales of $6,250. Sales in April by salesmen of industrial chemicals and of office supplies had, respectively, means of $13,000 and $5,000 and standard deviations of $2,000 and $500.

required

1. How many standard deviations above the mean were the sales of Freund and Williams? Who rated higher in their respective groups?
2. Which group of sales had higher dispersion?

24-22 *Effects of Variability on Decisions to Analyze Operations* A plant manager is trying to determine when to analyze operations. He does not have a standard-cost system, but he has accumulated a great deal of data. He finds that the cost of Process A per week per thousand units is $76,000 with a standard deviation of $22,000. Last week the cost was $109,000. Process B has a cost per week per thousand units of $26,000 with a standard deviation of $4,000. Last week the cost was $38,000.

required

Suppose the costs of investigation are identical for each process, and the plant manager has decided to investigate only one of the two processes. Which process should be investigated? Which process is more variable?

24-23 *Setting Prices and Uncertainty* Assume that the unit cost of a product is known with certainty to be $1.60. The top executives are trying to decide whether to set a selling price of $2.00 or of $2.20. The top price has been $2.00 for the past 30 months. Average monthly sales are forecast as follows:

AT A PRICE OF $2.00

Units	Probability
1,050	.05
1,000	.90
950	.05

AT A PRICE OF $2.20

Units	Probability
800	.10
750	.60
700	.30

required

Which is the optimal price? Show computations.

24-24 *Measuring Dispersion* Refer to the preceding problem. Compute, for the two alternative prices, the expected monthly sales in units, their standard deviation, and their coefficient of variation.

24-25 *Weather Predictions and Profitability* (CPA) Food Products, Inc., posed the following problem and requested guidelines that can be applied in the future to obtain the largest net income.

A Food Products plant on the coast produces a food product and ships its production of 10,000 units per day by air in an airplane owned by Food Products. The area is sometimes fogbound, and shipment can then be made only by rail. The plant does not operate unless shipments are made. Extra costs of preparation for rail shipment reduce the marginal contribution of this product from 40¢ per unit to 18¢ per unit, and there is an additional fixed cost of $3,100 for modification of packaging facilities to convert to rail shipment (incurred only once per conversion).

The fog may last for several days; Food Products normally starts shipping by rail only after rail shipments become necessary to meet commitments to customers.

A meteorological report reveals that during the past ten years, the area has been fogbound 250 times for one day, and that fog continued 100 times for a second consecutive day, 40 times for a third consecutive day, 20 times for a fourth consecutive day, and 10 times for a fifth consecutive day. Occasions and length of fog were both random. Fog never continued more than five days and there were never two separate occurrences of fog in any six-day period.

required

1. Prepare a schedule presenting the computation of the daily marginal contribution (ignoring fixed conversion cost):

a. When there is no fog and shipment is made by air.
b. When there is fog and shipment is made by rail.

2. Prepare a schedule presenting the computation of the probabilities of the possible combinations of foggy and clear weather on the days following a fogbound day. Your schedule should show the probability that, if fog first occurs on a particular day,
a. The next four days will be foggy.
b. The next three days will be foggy and day 5 will be clear.
c. The next two days will be foggy and days 4 and 5 will be clear.
d. The next day will be foggy and days 3,4, and 5 will be clear.
e. The next four days will be clear.

3. Assume you determine it is probable that it would be unprofitable to start shipping by rail on either the fourth or fifth consecutive foggy day. Prepare a schedule presenting the computation of the probable marginal income or loss that should be expected from rail shipments if they were started on the third consecutive foggy day, and the probability that the next two days will be foggy is .25; the probability that the next day will be foggy and day 5 will be clear is .25; and the probability that the next two days will be clear is .50.

24-26 *Cost-Volume-Profit under Uncertainty* (J. Patell) In your recently won position as supervisor of new product introduction, you have to decide on a pricing strategy for a specialty product with the following cost structure.

Variable cost per unit = \$50
Fixed cost of production = \$200,000

The units are assembled upon receipt of orders, so the inventory levels are insignificant. Your market research assistant is very enthusiastic about probability models and has presented the results of his price analysis in the following form.

a. If you set the price at \$100/unit, the probability distribution of total sales dollars is uniform between \$300,000 and \$600,000.
b. If you lower the price to \$70/unit, the distribution remains uniform, but it shifts up to the \$600,000 to \$900,000 range.

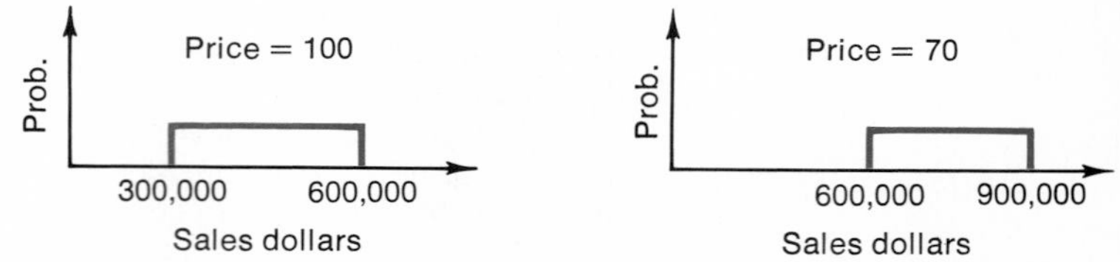

1. This is your first big contract and, above all, you want to show a profit. You decide to select the strategy that maximizes the probability of breaking even or earning a positive profit.
   a. What is the probability of at least breaking even with a price of \$100/unit?
   b. What is the probability of at least breaking even with a price of \$70/unit?
2. Your assistant suggests that maximum expected profit might be a better goal to pursue. Which pricing strategy yields the higher expected profit?

24-27 *Uncertainty and Cost-Volume-Profit Analysis* (This and the next problem are adapted from Robert K. Jaedicke and Alexander A. Robichek, "Cost-Volume-

Profit Analysis under Conditions of Uncertainty," *The Accounting Review,* Vol. XXXIX, No. 4, pp. 917–26) The Jaedicke and Robichek Company is considering two new products to introduce. Either can be produced by using present facilities. Each product requires an increase in annual fixed expenses of $400,000. The products have the same selling price and the same variable cost per unit—$10 and $8, respectively.

Management, after studying past experience with similar products, has prepared the following subjective probability distribution:

EVENTS (UNITS DEMANDED)	PROBABILITY— PRODUCT A	PROBABILITY— PRODUCT B
50,000	—	0.1
100,000	0.1	0.1
200,000	0.2	0.1
300,000	0.4	0.2
400,000	0.2	0.4
500,000	0.1	0.1
	1.0	1.0

required

1. What is the breakeven point for each product?
2. Which product should be chosen? Why? Show computations.
3. Suppose management was absolutely certain that 300,000 units of Product B would be sold. Which product should be chosen? Why? What benefits are available to management from the provision of the complete probability distribution instead of just a lone expected value?

24-28 *Uncertainty, Choice of Product, and Cost-Volume-Profit Analysis* You are a division manager of the K Company. You have conducted a study of the profit potential of three products:

	PRODUCTS		
	1	2	3
Expected profit	$450,000	$450,000	$ 450,000
Standard deviation of profit	$500,000	$681,500	$1,253,000
The probability of:			
At least breaking even	.816	.745	.641
Profit at least $250,000	.655	.615	.564
Profit at least $600,000	.382	.413	.456
Loss greater than $300,000	.067	.136	.274

The expected contribution per unit for each product is $1,250, and the expected fixed expenses per year are $5,800,000, so each product has the same breakeven quantity, 4,640 units.

required

Which product would you choose? Explain fully, including comparisons of the relative riskiness of the three products.

24-29 *Inventory Levels and Sales Forecasting* The owner of a small bakery must decide on how many of a new kind of sweet roll to bake each day. He estimates it will cost him 15¢ each to bake the new rolls, which can then be sold the same day for 35¢. And any rolls not sold during the day on which they are baked, the baker is certain, can be sold the next day for 10¢ each. Although he has never sold this type of roll before, his experience leads him to assess probable demand as follows:

FIRST MONTH

Demand (Per Day)	Probability
Less than 3	.00
3	.10
4	.25
5	.45
6	.20
7 or more	.00

SECOND MONTH AND THEREAFTER

Demand (Per Day)	Probability
Less than 3	.00
3	.00
4	.15
5	.35
6	.40
7	.10
8 or more	.00

required

How many rolls should he bake each day for the first month? The second month?

24-30 *Value of Perfect Information* In the previous problem, assume that the local witch goes into a trance every night and forecasts the exact demand for sweet rolls for the next day. What would be the baker's expected profit per day? How much would the baker be willing to pay the witch for this information? Answer for both time periods referred to above.

24-31 *Cost and Value of Information; Using Decision Trees* (Adapted from "Report of Committee on Managerial Decision Models," *Accounting Review,* Supplement to Vol. XLIV) An oil well driller, George Davis, is thinking of investing $50,000 in an oil well lease. He estimates the probability of finding a producing well as .4. Such a discovery would result in a net gain of $100,000 ($150,000 revenue − $50,000 cost). There is a .6 probability of not getting any oil, resulting in the complete loss of the $50,000.

required

1. What is the net expected value of investing?
2. Mr. Davis desires more information because of the vast uncertainty and the large costs of making a wrong decision. There will be an unrecoverable $50,000 outlay if no oil is found; there will be a $100,000 opportunity cost if he does not invest and the oil is really there. What is the most he should be willing to pay for perfect information regarding the presence or absence of oil? Explain.
3. Although perfect information is seldom obtainable, some additional information is usually available at some price. Mr. Davis might consider a geological test of the subsurface. His decision tree would then appear as in Exhibit 24-5.

   The geological testing company might advise the wildcatter that if there is oil on the land, the test results will be favorable (positive) three-quarters of the time and unfavorable (negative) one-quarter of the time. In other words, the test is not perfect. Similarly, if there is no oil, the test will give unfavorable results two-thirds of the time but will be (falsely) favorable one-third of the time. (These probabilities will be referred to as conditional probabilities.)

EXHIBIT 24-5

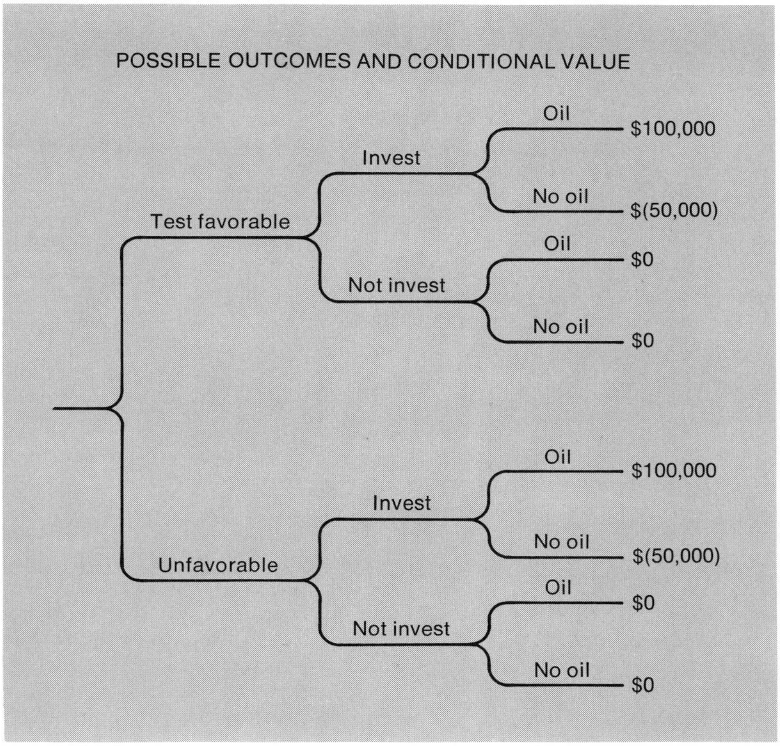

The wildcatter wants to know the probability of finding oil, given the result of the test. These revised conditional probabilities are found by weighing the prior subjective probabilities by the appropriate likelihoods:

PROBABILITIES OF STATES, GIVEN A FAVORABLE OR UNFAVORABLE TEST RESULT

EVENT (E)	*(1) PRIOR P (E)*	*(2) CONDITIONAL PROBABILITIES OF FAVORABLE TEST*	*(1) × (2) PROBABILITIES OF TEST OUTCOME AND EVENT*	*PROBABILITIES OF EVENTS GIVEN THE TEST OUTCOMES*
If the test if favorable:				
Oil	.4	¾	.3	.3 ÷ .5 = .6
No oil	.6	⅓	.2	.2 ÷ .5 = .4
Probability of favorable test			.5	1.0
If the test is unfavorable:				
Oil	.4	¼	.1	.1 ÷ .5 = .2
No oil	.6	⅔	.4	.4 ÷ .5 = .8
Probability of unfavorable test			.5	1.0

The computations of conditional probabilities show that the probability of finding oil is 0.6, given a *favorable* test. However, if the test is *unfavorable*, the probability of finding oil is only .2. With this knowledge, construct a payoff table for Mr. Davis. How much should he be willing to pay for the test? Explain.

24-32 *Uncertainty and Discounted Cash Flow* (CPA, adapted) Vernon Enterprises designs and manufactures toys. Past experience indicates that the product life cycle of a toy is three years. Promotional advertising produces large sales in the early years, but there is a substantial sales decline in the final year of a toy's life.

Consumer demand for new toys placed on the market tends to fall into three classes. About 30 percent of the new toys sell well above expectations, 60 percent sell as anticipated, and 10 percent have poor consumer acceptance.

A new toy has been developed. The following sales projections were made by carefully evaluating consumer demand for the new toy:

CONSUMER DEMAND FOR NEW TOY	CHANCE OF OCCURRING	ESTIMATED SALES IN		
		Year 1	Year 2	Year 3
Above average	30%	$1,200,000	$2,500,000	$600,000
Average	60	700,000	1,700,000	400,000
Below average	10	200,000	900,000	150,000

Variable costs are estimated at 30 percent of the selling price. Special machinery must be purchased at a cost of $860,000 and will be installed in an unused portion of the factory that Vernon has unsuccessfully been trying to rent to someone for several years at $80,000 per year and that has no prospects for future utilization. Fixed expenses (excluding depreciation) of a cash-flow nature are predicted at $50,000 per year on the new toy. The new machinery will be depreciated by the sum-of-the-years'-digits method with a predicted salvage value of $110,000 and will be sold at the beginning of the fourth year. Advertising and promotional expenses will be incurred uniformly and will total $100,000 the first year, $150,000 the second year, and $50,000 the third year. These expenses will be deducted as incurred for income tax reporting.

Vernon believes that state and federal income taxes will total 60 percent of income in the foreseeable future and may be assumed to be paid uniformly over the year income is earned.

required

1. Prepare a schedule computing the probable sales of this new toy in each of the three years, taking into account the probability of above-average, average, and below-average sales occurring.
2. Assume that the probable sales computed in part 1 are $900,000 in the first year, $1,800,000 in the second year, and $410,000 in the third year. Prepare a schedule computing the probable net income for the new toy in each of the three years of its life.
3. Prepare a schedule of net cash flows from sales of the new toy for each of the years involved and from disposition of the machinery purchased. Use the sales data given in part 2.
4. Assuming a minimum desired rate of return of 10 percent, prepare a schedule of the present value of the net cash flows calculated in 3. The following data are relevant:

YEAR	PRESENT VALUE OF $1 DUE AT THE END OF EACH YEAR DISCOUNTED AT 10 PERCENT	PRESENT VALUE OF $1 EARNED UNIFORMLY THROUGHOUT THE YEAR DISCOUNTED AT 10 PERCENT
1	.91	.95
2	.83	.86
3	.75	.78

24-33 *Judging Risk of Investment* Refer to the preceding problem. Suppose the project is abandoned if the sales at the end of the first year are below average.

1. Compute the total loss if the salvage value at the end of the first year is $385,000.
2. Compute the total loss if the project is abandoned at the end of the second year because the sales continue to be below average throughout the two years. Assume that the salvage value at the end of the second year is $235,000.
3. When should the project be abandoned? Why?
4. In your view, is the project very risky? Why?

24-34 *Relevant Costs, Probabilities, Discounted Cash Flow, and Pricing* The Vang Construction Company is bidding on a construction contract. If the bid is accepted, work will begin in a few days, on January 1, 19_1. Ten thousand units of material X will be needed at that date. The company currently has 10,000 units of this material in stock, originally costing a total of $10,000. The current purchase cost of material X is $1.20 per unit. The company could sell material X now for $.80 per unit after all selling costs.

If this current contract is not landed, material X could be used on another job to begin in one year, on January 1, 19_2. Then the company would not need to buy a substitute material at $1.02 per unit.

If it is not used in either of these ways, material X would be of no use to the company and would be sold a year hence, probably for $.80 per unit, net. The president estimates that the probability of using material X on the other job is .7.

The president of the construction company is puzzled about the appropriate total cost of material X to be used in bidding on the current contract. He has assembled the following data:

	TOTAL COSTS
Miscellaneous materials	$ 40,000
Material X, 10,000 units	?
Direct labor	60,000
Relevant overhead	30,000
	$xxx,xxx

Competition is intense and markups are thin. He asks you to suggest the appropriate total-cost figure for material X. Show all computations, carefully labeled, and state all assumptions made. The minimum desired rate of return is 10 percent per annum; assume that the present value at 10 percent of $1 to be received one year hence is .900.

24-35 *Perfect Information and Inventory Control* (J. Demski) This problem assumes that you are familiar with Chapter 14.

Ralph is a consultant. His client uses the economic-order-quantity model (with no stockouts). A particular raw-material item is presently under study. The annual requirement is 40,000 units. The item costs $40 per unit, and delivery costs average $10 per unit. Processing an order requires 3 hours of labor and consumes $5 of miscellaneous materials. Labor costs $8 per hour; in addition, variable overhead averages $7 per hour of labor. No storage costs other than the opportunity cost of 8 percent per year are involved.

1. Determine the optimal order quantity *and* the minimum relevant annual cost associated with optimal policy.
2. Ralph questions the variable overhead rate. In consultation with the client, he decides that the variable overhead rate is either $5 per labor-hour, $7 per labor-hour, or $9 per labor-hour. Assuming each value to be equally probable, compute the expected value (per annum) of discovering the actual variable overhead (per labor-hour) *before* the policy in part 1 above is implemented.

24-36 *Risk Aversion and Utilities* Reconsider the initial data of the plant rearrangement example in the chapter. Suppose the decision maker was risk averse so that the expected monetary values are reexpressed as utility values or utiles that are not linear:

MONETARY VALUES	*UTILES*[a]
$100,000	− .4623
200,000	−1.1598
260,000	−1.7183

[a] Derived from an exponential utility function, where the expected value of the cost = $1 - e^{c/260}$, where c represents cost. Tables of exponential functions are not included in this book.

required

1. If the decision maker minimizes expected costs expressed in utiles instead of in monetary values, will his decision change? Show calculations.
2. Suppose that the utiles for $260,000 were −1.90 instead of −1.7183. Would the decision change? Show calculations.

24-37 *Buying Imperfect Information* The following problem (as in many real situations) contains some simple assumptions that are made to underscore some fundamental points:

Linda Knight manages a factory that is in the midst of processing a large order to make thousands of newly designed portable stereo record players. Several serious production problems have been encountered.

Knight is concerned whether the units will be of acceptable quality. If they are acceptable, the factory will have a net gain (revenue less cost) of $800,000. If the units have unacceptable quality, legal problems, warranty repair outlays, and unfavorable publicity will result in a net loss of $500,000. However, Knight could add an intricate inspection procedure so that all defective units would be discovered and repaired before the product left the factory; alas, the cost of this fail-safe procedure would be $830,000.

required

1. Formulate Knight's problem as a "decision table" or "payoff table," showing actions, events, and outcomes.

2. Suppose that both events are equally likely and that Knight bases her decision strictly on expected monetary return. Which action will Knight prefer?
3. Suppose Knight could obtain a consultant's special accounting analysis that would affect her assessments of probabilities of acceptable or unacceptable quality. The consultant is expected to produce one of three possible reports: neutral, optimistic, or pessimistic.

   The neutral report would not change the original decision in part 2. The optimistic report would change Knight's assessments of probabilities to .7 acceptable and .3 unacceptable. The pessimistic report would have the reverse effect, changing the probabilities to .3 acceptable and .7 unacceptable.

   Knight assesses probabilities of receiving various reports as follows: .3 that the report will be neutral, .3 optimistic, and .4 pessimistic. What is the top price that Knight should pay for the report?

24-38 *Imperfect Information and Special Order* (J. Demski and C. Horngren) Consider a decision of whether to accept or reject a special order for 1,000 units of a product that is a unique variation of a firm's regular output. Acceptance of this order will not interfere with regular sales, now or in the future. The incremental revenue will be $20,000, and production will require raw materials costing $5,000 plus 800 direct-labor hours from department A and 200 hours from department B. The special order will be accepted if it has a positive expected contribution margin. Thus, if the expected incremental cost of labor and overhead is less than $15,000 (20,000 − 5,000), the decision maker will accept the offer.

The accounting system currently uses a *plantwide rate* to assign labor and variable overhead costs to production. The rate for the preceding period was $16 per hour, and, without additional information, the decision maker will use this rate to predict the incremental labor and overhead cost for the special order. Hence, in the absence of additional information, he will reject the offer: $20,000 − $5,000 − $16(800 + 200) = −$1,000.

Consider the question of whether this choice can be improved. The accountant is concerned about the quality of the data to be used in the decision. In particular, the $16 rate is based on the regular use of an equal number of hours from the two departments, and the accountant suspects that the rates for the two departments are not identical. A special analysis could be conducted to determine the departmental rates. The question, then, is whether the accountant should conduct this analysis and report the resulting data to the decision maker. The outcome of the analysis is not presently known, but the accountant feels that one of three findings will materialize: the rates for departments A and B will be, respectively, $12 and $20, $14 and $18, or $16 and $16. The respective contribution margins will then be:

	ANALYSIS OUTCOME		
Departmental rates (A and B)	$12 and $20	$14 and $18	$16 and $16
Expected incremental revenue	$20,000	$20,000	$ 20,000
Expected incremental costs			
Raw materials	$ 5,000	5,000	5,000
Labor and variable overhead			
Dept. A (800 hrs.)	9,600	11,200	12,800
Dept. B (200 hrs.)	4,000	3,600	3,200
Total	$18,600	$19,800	$ 21,000
Expected contribution margin	$ 1,400	$ 200	$−1,000

Moreover, the accountant perceives that if he learns and reports the actual rates, the decision maker will employ those rates in his decision. Hence, the offer will be accepted by the decision maker only if the rates of $12 and $20 or $14 and $18 are reported.

The accountant, then, has two alternatives: (1) do not perform the analysis, which guarantees an incremental gain to the firm of $0; (2) perform the analysis, which guarantees an incremental gain to the firm of $1,400, $200, or $0, less the cost of the analysis. Choice between them will, of course, depend on his risk attitudes, his beliefs concerning how likely the three cost figures will be, and how costly the analysis is. Suppose that he is risk neutral and assigns respective probabilities of .2, .2, and .6 to the three events.

required

1. Compute the expected contribution margin if the special analysis is conducted (before considering the cost of the special analysis). Compute the most that the accountant or decision maker should be willing to pay for the analysis.
2. Repeat part 1, but assume that the decision maker will not accept the special order unless its expected contribution margin is at least $500.
3. The accountant could present all the data in the problem together with the probabilities. If so, what is the expected contribution margin? Why does he not consider this as a feasible alternative presentation to the decision maker at the outset?
4. Suppose the probabilities were .2, .6, and .2. What would be your answers to items 1 and 2 above?
5. What is the principal lesson of the above computations?

Determination of Cost Behavior Patterns

25

How do costs fluctuate? What is the relationship between various decisions and the level of costs? We have seen again and again throughout this book that various predictions of costs under assorted alternatives can have a significant influence on decisions—decisions such as these: What products should we manufacture or sell? When? How much? What inputs should be used? How? When should the inputs be acquired? In what quantities?

A knowledge of how costs behave under a variety of influences is essential to intelligent predictions, decision making, and performance evaluation. This chapter will explore the complex problem of how to determine cost behavior patterns (cost functions) so that predictions are as accurate as is desired.

Because this is a long chapter, it is divided into two distinct parts. Part One provides a general overview. Part Two covers the interpretation of the results of simple and multiple regression; it assumes knowledge of regression, which is surveyed in the chapter appendix.

PART ONE

cost estimation and cost prediction

Ther term *cost estimation* is often used to describe the measurement of historical costs for the ultimate purpose of facilitating the prediction of expected costs for decision purposes. Many people are inclined to regard historical costs as "actual" or "true" costs, even though the accounting measures of costs are permeated by many assumptions, including those of the ubiquitous average. Consequently, some accountants and statisticians distinguish between *cost estimation,* which in their minds is an attempt to measure historical costs, and *cost prediction.* This distinction is not universal; many often use *estimated cost* and *cost estimation* to describe forecasts or predictions. Consequently, be wary when you encounter the term. Make sure of its meaning in a specific situation.

general approach to approximating cost functions

independent and dependent variables

Chapter 8 introduced the problem of flexible budgeting for overhead costs, which is essentially a problem of determining cost behavior patterns. The manager must make three basic decisions. First, he must choose the cost to be predicted, which is the *dependent* variable, usually called y. Second, he must choose an *independent* variable, usually called x. The latter is sometimes termed the *controllable* or *decision* variable, because the choice—for example, to travel a particular number of miles—is within the specific influence of the decision maker. The dependent variable—say, cost of gasoline—may be expressed as a function of the independent variable—that is, $y = f(x)$. Third, he must choose a relevant range of activity, the range where the relationship expressed by the cost function is valid.

The function may be either linear or nonlinear. The general formula for a straight line is $y = a + bx$, where y is the computed value of y for any specified value of x. The constant a is the intercept, defined as the value of y when x is zero; b is the slope, defined as the amount of increase in y for each unit increase in x. The values of a and b are each called *coefficients.* Note that a is equal to zero when a cost is proportionately variable.

Which of the possible independent variables should be chosen? Among the typical possibilities are:

units of product	direct-labor dollars
weight of materials	dimensions of materials
dollar sales volume	machine-hours
direct-labor hours	miles driven

Should only one of these, or more than one, be picked? Very often—perhaps too often—only one independent variable is chosen. The analyst tries to select the independent variable that is likely to have the most influence on total cost incurred (the dependent variable), which is typically some type of material, labor, or other input.

When the independent variable is chosen and a decision is made to employ a simple linear equation, the remaining tasks are the determinations of the appropriate slope and intercept coefficients. To approximate cost functions, plausible *relationships* are sought between the actions and the costs incurred. The preferable cost function is one that facilitates the prediction of changes in costs, that accurately depicts persistent relationships, regardless of whether particular causes or effects can be established with assurance. The cost function is developed on the basis of some theory that supports the relationships between the dependent and independent variable—not on the basis of observed statistical relationships only. Physical observation, when it is possible, probably provides the best evidence of a relationship.

scatter diagrams

The scatter diagram or chart is often used to analyze cost variation. As Exhibit 25-1 shows, past monthly behavior of individual costs at different volumes is plotted on separate charts. Scrutiny of the scatter of points will indicate the degree of relationship between cost and volume (often called *correlation*). A clear pattern of behavior of the points is indicative of a high degree of correlation. A widely dispersed arrangement of points is indicative of low correlation.

If the position of the plotted points indicates that cost follows volume, a line is either visually located or is fitted to the points by statistical methods. This line indicates the specific dollar cost to be budgeted at different volumes. If cost behavior is irregular, so that it is difficult to fit the data to a formula, the graph is used as a basis for assigning costs at different activity levels directly to a department budget.

EXHIBIT 25-1

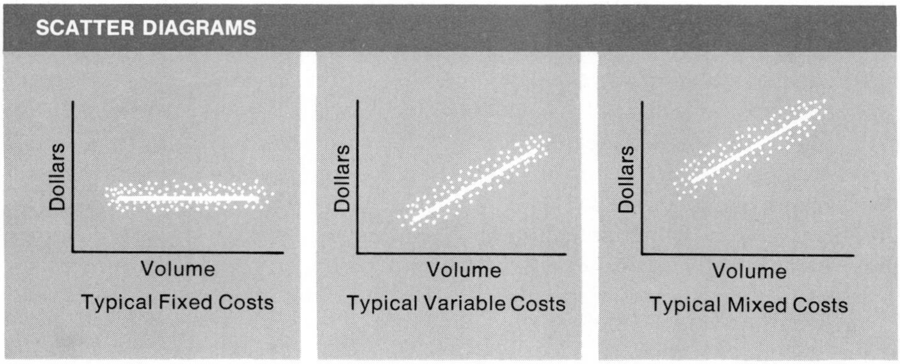

One of the dangers in overreliance on the statistical analysis of past cost behavior is the tendency to ignore other important factors. *Concern with the past is justified only insofar as it helps prediction.* Management wants to plan what costs should be, not what costs have been.

objectives provide the framework

The subject of determining cost functions should be viewed from the perspective of the sensitivity of the results to the decision. Ideally, the decision maker wants to know the "real" or "exact" impact of a variety of actions and states (such as events) on costs. In the vast majority of instances, that impact cannot be known with certainty. Instead, the statistician or accountant provides some cost function (for example, $y = bx$) that is a simplification of the underlying relationships. The discussion in this chapter will often be couched in terms of obtaining more accuracy, as if more accuracy were always desirable. But keep in mind that obtaining more accuracy is often too expensive.

The central question is whether the resulting approximation, which is nearly always a linear function, is good enough for the purpose at hand. The answer to that question is often difficult to establish with much confidence. Nevertheless, it is a cost-and-value-of-information question that cannot be avoided. By the very act of using the cost function, the manager has made an information decision. He may have faced the decision squarely and explicitly by saying, "Yes, I can use this cost function for my prediction rather than a simpler or more complicated cost function." Or he may have reached the same conclusion implicitly, by proceeding with the given function with no questions asked. For example, when a manager uses an overhead rate of $2 per direct-labor hour as a part of the accumulation of costs for a pricing decision—even though he knows that overhead is affected by labor-hours, machine-hours, weight of materials, dimensions of materials, and weather conditions—he has made an information decision. He has decided that the simple $2 cost function is good enough for his purpose. In his mind, his pricing decision would not be sufficiently affected by a more complicated cost function to justify its added cost.

Two common simplifications are widely used in the determination of cost functions. First, a common assumption is that cost behavior can be sufficiently explained by one independent variable (such as labor-hours) rather than by more than one (for instance, labor-hours, machine-hours, and dimensions of materials). Second, linear approximations to cost functions are "good enough," even though nonlinear behavior is more likely. We will investigate these two simplifications later in this chapter. Of course, whether these simplifications provide sufficiently accurate approximations of underlying relationships is a question that can be answered only in actual situations, on a case-by-case basis.

linearity and cost functions

Almost without exception, accountants and managers use linear cost functions to approximate the relationships of total costs to a given range of inputs or outputs. There are several assumptions that are sufficient conditions for linearity to exist when total costs are related to output:

1. The technological relationships between inputs and outputs must be linear; for example, each unit of finished product must contain the same amount of raw materials.
2. The inputs acquired must equal the inputs used; for example, each worker hired must be fully utilized.
3. The cost of acquiring each input must be a linear function of the quantity acquired; for example, the unit price of raw materials must be identical regardless of the amount purchased.

As Exhibit 25-2 shows, **the relevant range of output under consideration may permit a linearity assumption within specified limits of output.** Outside this range the cost of production may increase much faster or slower than the assumed linear rate.

EXHIBIT 25-2

COST BEHAVIOR, NONLINEAR

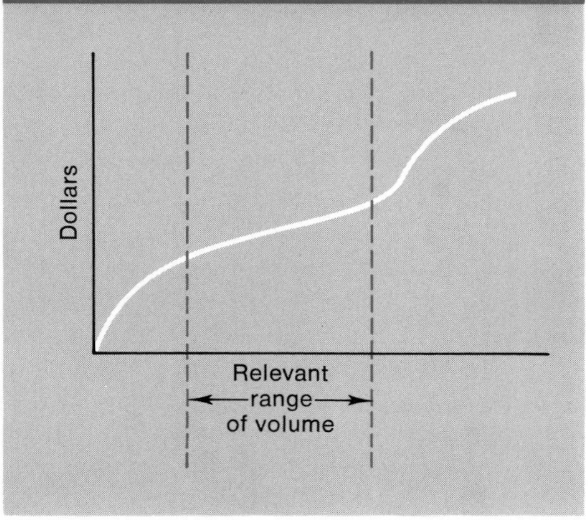

nonlinearity and cost functions

As Chapter 8 indicated, variable and fixed costs must be viewed as generic terms. In their purest sense, they represent polar ends of a spectrum of various existing cost functions. We now refine distinctions among costs to include an assortment of behavior patterns.

examples of nonlinearity

Nonlinear cost behavior can be caused by a variety of circumstances, for example, economies or diseconomies of scale. An illustration of nonlinear functions is the upward-sloping supply curve for a raw material, where the purchase price soars as the desired quantity increases, as in Exhibit 25-3. Another example is the availability of quantity discounts, as in Exhibit 25-4, where the cost per unit falls as each price break is reached.

step-function costs

Few costs are variable in the strict sense of fluctuating in exact proportion to changes in volume. Many raw-material costs provide examples of this proportionately variable cost behavior, as shown in the first graph in Exhibit 25-5.

The second graph in Exhibit 25-5 exemplifies a step-function cost, whereby the cost of the input is constant over various small ranges of output, but it in-

EXHIBIT 25-3

EFFECTS OF UPWARD-SLOPING SUPPLY CURVE

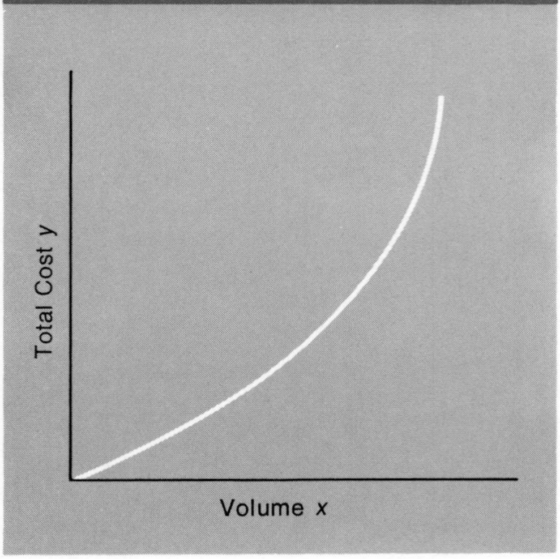

creases by discrete amounts as activity moves from one range to the next. This steplike behavior occurs when the input is acquired in discrete quantities but is used in fractional quantities. For example, labor costs of all sorts—direct or indirect, manufacturing or administrative—often represent step-variable costs.

EXHIBIT 25-4

EFFECTS OF QUANTITY DISCOUNTS

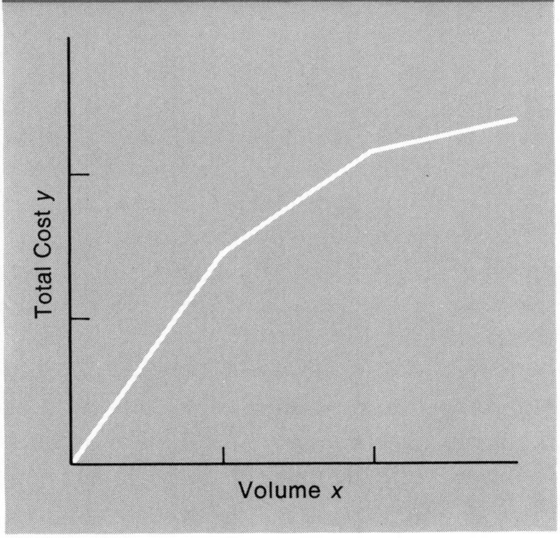

EXHIBIT 25-5

VARIABLE COST BEHAVIOR

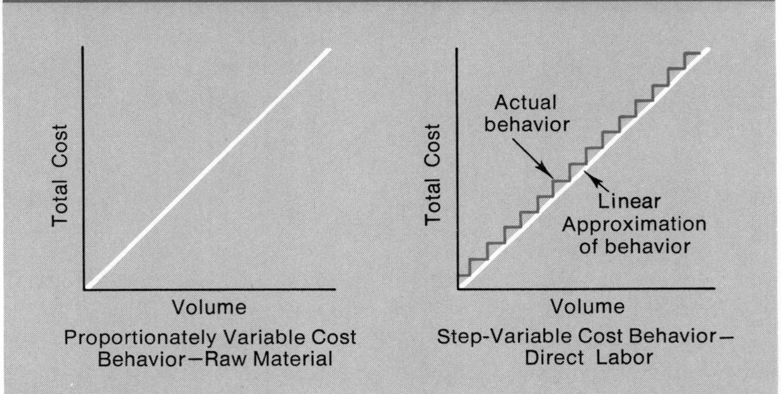

These increase or decrease abruptly at intervals of activity because their acquisition comes in indivisible chunks. Labor services cannot be stored for future use and are either utilized or lost as the workday ebbs away. They cannot be turned on or off like a faucet.

The popular objective in the planning and control of step costs is usually to attain activity or utilization at the highest volume for any given step. This will maximize returns for each dollar spent, because the services involved will be fully utilized and their unit cost will be least. That is why a "linear approximation" of the step-variable cost behavior often takes the form of a proportionately variable cost for budgetary control purposes, as the second graph in Exhibit 25-5 shows.

width of steps

The problems of measurement are much more difficult for step-variable costs than for proportionately variable costs. The need for a unit of raw material is easy to determine, but the measurement of direct labor, indirect labor, administrative labor, and selling labor becomes progressively more difficult. In practice, secretaries, stock clerks, file clerks, and others are frequently subject to uneven work pressures. They may be able to work intensively or leisurely for various spurts of time.

The width and height of the steps may vary among the types of labor services. For instance, the number of hours worked by each direct laborer may be closely geared to production. The use of overtime, part-time help, or short workweeks may cause the direct-labor-cost steps to be very narrow and very small so that they approximate a proportionately variable cost behavior pattern. On the other hand, failures to use part-time help, to gear the workweek to current needs, and to use overtime tend to widen and heighten the labor-cost steps.

Of course, as the steps widen, a so-called step-variable cost may become a "step-fixed" or even a "fixed" cost. Exhibit 25-5 shows how direct labor may be regarded as a variable cost, because only a small error is caused by using a straight line instead of a step function. On the other hand, Exhibit 25-6 demonstrates how supervision costs may have wider steps, so that a fixed-cost approximation would be more accurate than a variable-cost approximation for the bulk of the relevant range under consideration.

industrial-engineering approach

Subsequent sections of this chapter will discuss seven means of approximating cost functions: (a) industrial-engineering approach, (b) account analysis, (c) high-low points, (d) representative incremental cost, (e) visual fit, (f) simple regression, and (g) multiple regression. The engineering method may be used in conjunction with one or more of these other means, each serving as a check on the other. For example, the industrial engineer may use multiple regression

EXHIBIT 25-6

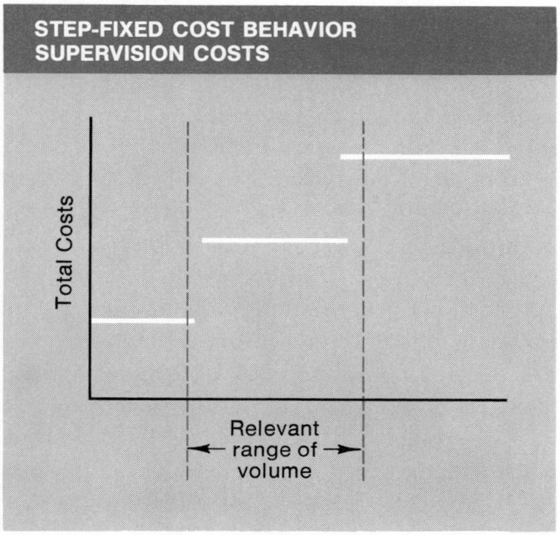

as an integral part of his techniques. The point is that each of these other means is insufficient by itself; they are only first steps to solving the problem of cost prediction. In contrast, the engineering approach, appropriately applied, is the most complete attack on the problem because it draws on all available tools.

Although the industrial-engineering approach to determining cost functions usually gets little attention in books on accounting and statistics, its importance should not be overlooked. It is a frontal assault on the problem of cost prediction, because it takes a normative—what costs *should* be—stance. The engineering approach systematically attempts to find the most efficient means of achieving the wanted output. The approach looks forward rather than backward, so it provides a good philosophical approach as well as a practical technique in operational settings that are marked by frequent changes in workers, skills, materials, machines, processes, and products. The watchword is to avoid placing too much weight on what has happened, as if it were almost the only basis for prediction. Estimates of historical cost functions are usually just a part of the basis for predicting future costs.

The engineering approach searches for the most efficient means of achieving wanted output. It entails a systematic review of materials, labor, services, and facilities used to accomplish objectives. Time and motion studies and evaluation of workers and materials are essential. The industrial-engineering staff works in conjunction with those people responsible for budgets. Engineers express requirements in terms of physical measures—hours of labor, tons of material, number of supervisors, and so forth. Then the physical measures are transformed into dollar budgets by the application of appropriate unit prices.

Standard costs are determined for direct materials and direct labor. If they reflect current price levels, these standard costs are usually used in building the budget for materials and labor. Other costs are studied separately. To illustrate, indirect labor is divided into its components, such as janitorial, clerical, supervisory, inspection, and so forth. Each individual labor duty is reviewed in the setting of the budget. The duty is examined with respect to its characteristics and objectives. The number of employees needed for each duty at two or more volumes is then determined. When converted into dollar cost, these data compose the basis for the flexible budget. Similar procedures are used in budgeting other costs.

The engineering approach has been used increasingly in recent years. For example, clerical, shipping, warehousing, order filling, and stocking have become subject to formal work measurement. Even though the work-measurement approach is expensive at first glance, its growth in nonmanufacturing as well as in manufacturing activities is evidence that in many places its perceived benefits exceed its costs.

Engineering approaches are particularly suitable for determining the technical relationships for materials, supplies, many labor operations, and many machine-related inputs. Any input-output relationship that is physically observable is an obvious candidate for this approach. **However, the engineering approach falters when costs cannot be directly traced to inputs or outputs, or when relationships are not easy to observe or tally on an individual basis.** Examples are relationships between indirect costs and output. Then other cost-prediction tools, such as regression analysis, may be desirable.

analysis of accounts

a necessary first step

The analysis of accounts, which facilitates cost estimation (for example, compiling the costs of jobs in process at the end of the year) and cost prediction (for example, establishing a predetermined overhead rate for the coming year), is the first of the six other methods of linear approximation of cost functions that will be described. These six methods may be viewed as increasingly complex ways of determining cost functions. The first method may be good enough in simple situations. However, in many organizations each of these six methods is used in succession over the years as the desirability of more accurate approximations becomes evident.

One way to approximate cost functions is to pick the independent variable(s) and the relevant range. Then the cost analyst proceeds through the accounts, one by one, and classifies each into one of three categories: variable, fixed, and mixed (often called semivariable). In so doing, he may use his past experience intuitively and nothing else. However, many analysts will at least study how total costs behave over a few periods before making judgments.

An examination of the accounts is obviously a necessary first step, no matter whether cost functions are approximated via simple inspection of the accounts or via multiple regression. Familiarity with the data is needed to avoid analytical pitfalls. The study of the accounts should alert the analyst to how closely the cost records comply with some technical requirements for the determination of cost functions by statistical methods. Let us look at some of these requirements.

1. LENGTH OF TIME PERIODS. The time periods should be long enough to permit the recording procedures to link output produced with the cost incurred because of that production. For example, allowance should be made for lags in recording costs.[1] The recording of production in one period and related costs such as supplies or indirect labor in another will obscure the true underlying relationships.

The time periods should be short enough to avoid the averaging of fluctuations in production within a period. Averages also tend to hide the true relationship between cost and output. For example, month-to-month comparisons may overlook some important week-to-week changes in production within particular months.

2. SEPARATE SPECIFICATION OF FACTORS. All factors that influence costs should be identified separately as far as is feasible. Other factors besides output that influence costs include changes in technology, periods of adjustment to new processes or products (learning time), seasonal differences, inflationary effects, and unusual events. These factors must often be separately specified as independent variables.

3. ERRORS IN MEASUREMENT. In addition to detecting clerical errors, the analyst must be on guard against the tendency to allocate fixed costs as if they were variable. For example, such costs as depreciation, insurance, or rent may be allocated on a per-unit-of-output basis. The danger is to regard these costs as variable rather than fixed. They may seem to be variable because of the accounting methods used. However, there is no point in including these costs in the dependent variable if they really do not vary with the independent variables.

As we said previously, the account-analysis method, which implies that mere inspection of the accounts will be sufficient for determining cost functions, is merely a first step in any serious attempt to determine costs.

high-low method

A major disadvantage of the account-classification method is its inherent subjectivity. The high-low method is a slightly less subjective method, in that it at least employs a series of samples and relies on two of their results.

[1] George J. Benston, "Multiple Regression Analysis of Cost Behavior," *Accounting Review*, Vol. XLI, No. 4, p. 663.

The high-low method is described in Chapter 8, so an extensive description will not be repeated here. This method necessitates the plotting of two points, representing the highest cost and the lowest cost, respectively, over the *contemplated relevant range.* The slope of the line that connects the two points is regarded as the variable cost per unit of volume. Whether the resulting line is an acceptable approximation of the cost function depends on the decisions at hand and on the behavior of that function over the entire relevant range. The high-low method may provide only a loose approximation, as the following diagram indicates:

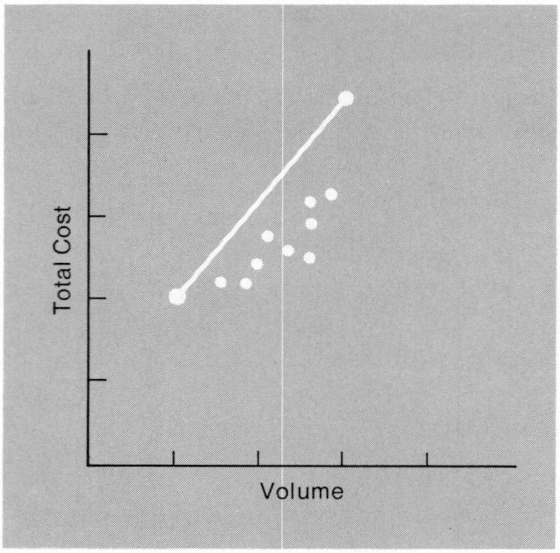

The graph illustrates the need to plot the data and not rely on picking the highest and lowest cost. Note in this case that the high-low method overstates the variable-cost component of the total cost function. Furthermore, the high-low method is statistically inefficient. For example, if 36 data points were available, the high-low method would use only 2 and would disregard the other 34. Because of the obvious danger of relying on extreme points, which often represent abnormal rather than normal situations, the high-low method is not recommended.[2]

representative marginal or incremental cost

Another approach is to choose, within the relevant range, an activity level that is perceived to have a marginal or incremental cost representative of that range.

[2] Professor Joel Demski has suggested, "If you don't want to use the high-low method, you may want to use the next-high, next-low method or the next-next-high, next-next-low method."

If the actual cost function is continuous and differentiable in the region of the representative activity level, then differential calculus can be used to compute the marginal cost.[3] Again, this method depends on the judgment of the analyst and so is regarded as too subjective for widespread use. Either method, of course, relies on one or two sample points, disregarding all others. A more inclusive procedure would recognize all sample points.

visual fit

An advantage of visual fit is that all sample points are used in determining the cost function. To avoid the use of more formal procedures, sometimes a visual fit is applied by drawing a straight line through the points on a scatter diagram. This procedure may provide more accurate estimates than the previous methods described. Nevertheless, there are no objective tests to assure that the line is the most accurate representation of the underlying data. Moreover, visual fit ignores information that may be valuable about the quality of the fit.

PROBLEM FOR SELF-STUDY

PROBLEM Suppose a linear approximation is used for flexible budgeting as shown in the accompanying graph. The "true" cost function is the nonlinear function as shown.

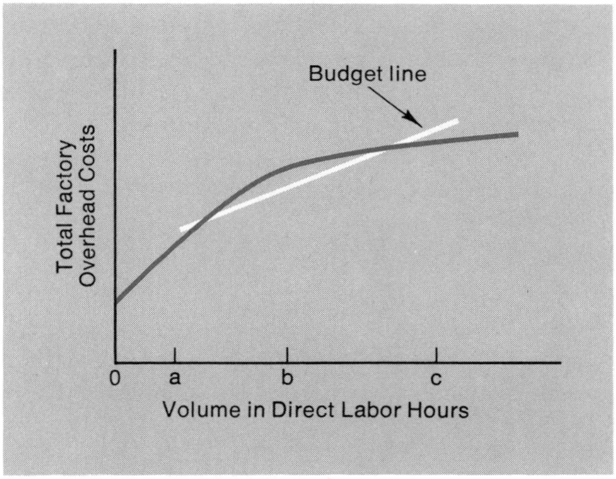

required Will the flexible budget be higher or lower than what the budgeted "true" costs would be at *Oa*, *Ob*, and *Oc*? What are the decision implications of using the linear approximations at each point?

[3] The marginal cost is an estimate at any given *point* of activity and only at that point. If differential calculus is applicable, the incremental cost over a *range* of activity may be approximated by expanding the function into a Taylor series around the nominal marginal cost.

SOLUTION

Budgeted factory overhead costs will be higher at *Oa* and *Oc* and lower at *Ob*. The decision implications depend heavily on the particular situation and organization. The linear approximation may be good enough in the vast majority of cases in the sense that, for example, the more accurate approximation will not result in changing any decisions regarding pricing or choice of product lines. In terms of the credibility of budgets and their motivational effects, the use of linear approximations may influence the attitudes and beliefs of managers regarding this part of the accounting system or the system as a whole. In other words, a little inaccuracy, by itself, may be unimportant in one decision situation or with respect to one class of costs. But more accuracy may be preferable to less when the system as a whole is judged in relation to a host of decisions and attitudes that might be affected.

PART TWO

The term "regression analysis" refers to the measurement of the *average* amount of change in one variable that is associated with unit increases in the amounts of one or more other variables. When only two variables are studied, the analysis is called *simple regression;* when more than two variables are studied, it is called *multiple regression.*

When all its assumptions are met, and when *analysis* rather than just mechanical curve fitting is conducted, regression is a powerful technique. When the assumptions hold, regression analysis is superior to other techniques because it produces measures of probable error. Moreover, specification analysis can be performed to test the assumptions, and regression can be applied where there are several independent variables instead of just one.

The remainder of this chapter assumes that you are already familiar with the rudiments of both simple and multiple regression. **Therefore, before reading on, if you need a review, consult either the appendix to this chapter or any elementary book on statistics.**

presentation of results

Regression analysis fundamentally entails using a *sampling* of past cost behavior to formulate an estimation of how the entire *population* of costs truly behaves. The equation of the least-squares line is often presented as follows, where y' is the estimated total cost.

$$y' = a + bx$$

The following is the result of the simple regression described in the chapter appendix, where y' is the direct-labor cost and x is batch size.

$$y' = \underset{(15.70)}{24.43} + \underset{(.81)}{10.53}x$$

$$r^2 = .9557$$

where the numbers in parentheses are the standard errors of the regression coefficients. The *t*-values may or may not be presented.

Alternatively, a digital computer will often present the results of regression analysis in the following format:

VARIABLE	COEFFICIENT	STANDARD ERROR	T-VALUE	
Intercept	24.43			
2	10.53	.81	13.00	
Value of *R*-Square is				.9557

choosing among regressions

Often the accountant or the manager is confronted with a choice among various possible regressions that use different independent variables or combinations thereof. For example, one regression may use direct-labor hours as the independent variable, another may use machine-hours, and another some combination thereof. How does the decision maker pick from among these alternatives? My colleague, Joel Demski, has suggested that for regression to be helpful at all, the following three criteria should be met:

1. The regression equation should be plausible. It should make economic sense intuitively to both the accountant and the operating manager.
2. The *goodness of fit* should be acceptable. The r^2 (coefficient of determination) should be "high." The *t*-values (the regression coefficient of each independent variable divided by its standard error) should be "respectable"—say, at least 2.0.
3. *Specification analysis* should be conducted so that various statistical pitfalls are guarded against or allowed for. This analysis includes tests of the basic assumptions underlying regression analysis. Digital computer programs are widely available for the routine performance of these tests.

If the accountant decides that regression analysis is indeed appropriate, he may then use the results to pick one or more independent variables. For instance, in choosing between direct-labor hours and machine-hours as a base for overhead application, he would ordinarily run three regressions using (a) labor-hours, (b) machine-hours, and (c) labor-hours *and* machine-hours as independent variables. **He would then pick the regression equation that fitted the data the best.[4] This judgment is often based on the equation having the highest r^2, assuming that the *t*-values of the coefficients were sufficiently high, that both independent variables were logically defensible, and that no specification difficulties were apparent.**

[4] Various tests of goodness of fit may be appropriate, depending on the size of the sample and other characteristics. Some analysts may want to use the coefficient of correlation (*r*), the standard error of the estimate (s_e), or F distributions. The coefficient of correlation (*r*), coefficient of determination (r^2), and standard error of the estimate (s_e) are related measures of goodness of fit. They all try to measure the scatter and thus measure how well the independent variable accounts for the variability in the dependent variable.

criterion 1: economic plausibility

The first criterion, economic plausibility, places regression analysis in perspective. Does a high correlation between two variables mean that either is a cause of the other? Correlation, by itself, cannot answer that question; x may cause y, y may cause x, x and y may interact on one another, both may be affected by z, or the correlation may be due to chance. High correlation merely indicates that the two variables move together. No conclusions about cause and effect are warranted. For example, church attendance and beer consumption correlate over the years, but this does not mean that attending church makes one thirsty or that drinking beer incites piety; they both simply increased with population growth.[5]

But high correlation coupled with economic plausibility is desirable. Thus, if a factory overhead cost had a high r^2 in relation to advertising space committed, you might doubt the plausibility of the relationship. But if a factory overhead cost had a high r^2 in relation to direct-labor hours worked, you might have greater confidence in the plausibility of the relationship. Our knowledge of cost behavior and the production function confirms the latter relationship; in contrast, there is no theoretical basis to support the first.

The point is that qualitative correlation, which implies causality in a logical sense, should ideally be coupled with quantitative correlation, which uses formal statistical means to determine the extent to which a change in one factor was accompanied by a change in another.

If the decision maker cannot resort to physical identification to establish a basis for prediction, he may use regression analysis to help identify a reliable relationship. But first he uses his prior knowledge of operations to choose a particular relationship that may be so intuitively satisfying that formal regression is unnecessary (as in allocating power on the basis of related machine-hours). Of course, where it is applicable and feasible, such intuition should be buttressed by regression analysis.

criterion 2: goodness of fit

use of tests The accountant and manager use tests of goodness of fit for personal reassurance about their choice of a plausible cost function. They look at r^2 because it is a ready interpretation of the extent to which the independent variable accounts for the variability in the dependent variable. They look at t-values for the slopes—that is, the b's—because they seek reliable slope coefficients for predicting how costs change over a range of volume.

The t-value for a is seldom important, because regression is rarely concerned with ascertaining the value at the y-intercept. Instead, the major objec-

[5] W. Spurr and C. Bonini, *Statistical Analysis for Business Decisions,* rev. ed. (Homewood, Ill.: Richard D. Irwin, Inc., 1973), p. 483.

tive is to predict how costs behave as activity changes over a relevant range of activity, which seldom encompasses zero activity.

An example may clarify why the *t*-value of *a* may be unimportant. Suppose a company had a nonlinear cost function but used a linear approximation over the relevant range of activity, as in Exhibit 25-7.

Notice that *a* has a high *t*-value, but *a* is negative! How can a cost be negative at zero activity? It is virtually impossible, but who cares? The cost analyst should be unconcerned, because he wants a reliable basis for prediction within the relevant range; the *t*-value for *b* is critical for this purpose. Its extremely high value of 25 indicates that great confidence can be placed in *b* as a predictor *only within the relevant range.* Thus, in this case of a nonlinear cost function, the cost analyst would find the linear approximation offered by regression analysis very comforting.

Of course, if a cost function is expected to be linear from zero to a very high level of activity, the *t*-value of *a* would help in judging goodness of fit. For example, the negative intercept shown in Exhibit 25-7 would (a) lead to the rejection of that cost function because negative costs are not "conceptually" possible or (b) lead to a closer look as to whether linearity indeed exists over such a wide range of activity. Moreover, in cases where a cost function is hypothesized to be wholly variable, an insignificant *a* coefficient (*t*-value less than 2)

EXHIBIT 25-7

INTERPRETATION OF INTERCEPT

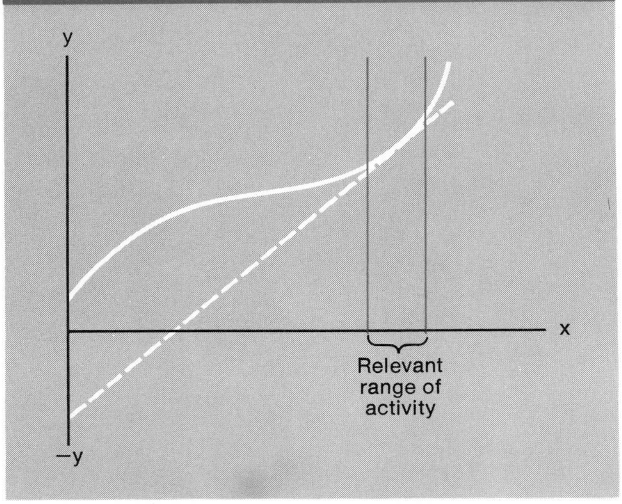

Note: Assume that the intercept is \$−48,000 and that its t-value is 12.
Assume also that the t-value for b, the slope within the relevant range, is 25.

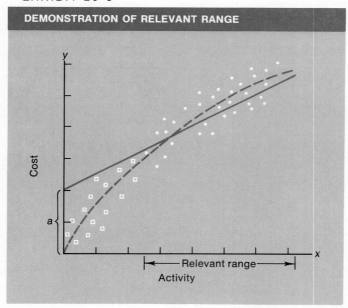

would be expected. To illustrate, direct-material costs would be expected to have an *a* coefficient of zero.

fixed-cost component The foregoing example illustrates why the oft-called "fixed-cost" component of a total-cost function should be carefully interpreted and labeled.

As is seen in Exhibits 25-7 and 25-8, which should be examined now, a cost function that is estimated for a mixed (semivariable) cost may yield a good approximation to the actual cost function over the relevant range. However, that relevant range rarely includes zero activity. *Therefore, rather than thinking of the intercept (the fixed component) as a fixed cost, think of it as merely the intercept at* $x = 0$. For example, see Exhibit 25-8. Note that *a* would be a valid estimate of fixed cost if the actual observation included the point where activity was zero and the relationship between activity and output was linear. If more observa-

EXHIBIT 25-8

DEMONSTRATION OF RELEVANT RANGE

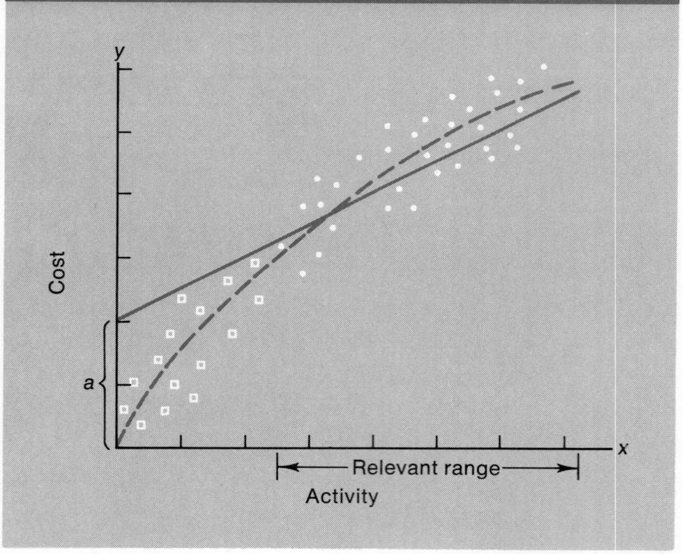

a is the *y* intercept at $x = 0$
Actual observations • • •
Regression line ———
Additional observations □ □ □
Newly fitted curve — — — —

Source: Adapted from George J. Benston, "Multiple Regression Analysis of Cost Behavior," *The Accounting Review*, XLI, No. 4, p. 662.

tions were available, perhaps the dashed curve would be a better approximation and a would be zero. Therefore, the value of the constant term, a, is *not* the expected cost at zero activity; it is only the value that is computed as a result of the regression line calculated from the available data. Too often, cost analysts unjustifiably extrapolate beyond the range of the data upon which the regression equation was estimated.

criterion 3: specification analysis

Although regression analysis can be a helpful tool for predictions and decisions, it can be easily misused. There is no shortcut or substitute for the scrutiny of a particular situation to assure that the assumptions of regression analysis are applicable to the data. Too often, regression is conducted mechanically, using canned computer programs and invalid assumptions about the pertinence of the statistical tools to the data being analyzed. The reading of one chapter on regression does not qualify a person to apply regression analysis in practice. Professional help from statisticians is vital for any successful application.

Probably the most important limitation of regression analysis is the assumption that the relationships will persist—that there is an ongoing, stable relationship between cost and the independent variable or variables used to estimate the cost. That is why regression analysis is usually confined to repetitive operations.

To make valid inferences from sample data about population relationships, four assumptions must be satisfied: (1) linearity, (2) constant variance, (3) independence, and (4) normality.[6]

The inherent appeal of regression is that computer programs usually have tests that may be systematically applied to see whether these and other assumptions hold. These tests are often referred to as *specification analysis.* When these assumptions are satisfied, the sample values a and b are the best available efficient, unbiased estimates of the population values A and B.[7]

linearity and relevant range

First, linearity must exist between x and y in the population. The hypothesized relation is

$$y = A + Bx + u$$

[6] Spurr and Bonini, *Statistical Analysis,* pp. 469–70.

[7] One way to appreciate these assumptions is to construct a set of data that are consistent with them. To illustrate, suppose the actual relationship is

$$y = 10{,}000 + 25x + u$$

where u is normally distributed about a mean of zero with a variance of 100. For each value of x in the sample, the corresponding value of y will then be 10,000 + $25x$ *plus* a random draw from the indicated normal distribution.

and we assume $E(u) = 0$. This leads to

$$E(y) = A + Bx$$

where A and B are the true (but unknown) parameters of the regression line. The deviation of the *actual* value of y from the true regression line is called the *disturbance term u* (also called the *error term*), which is defined as $y - y'$. The average or expected value of u is zero. When there is one independent variable, the presence of linearity can be checked most easily by studying the data on a scatter diagram—a step that often is unwisely skipped.

The role of the relevant range is paramount in interpreting the scatter diagram. In the present context, the relevant range can be defined as the span of activity or volume that encompasses the observed relationships. As Exhibit 25-8 shows, the top set of dots indicates that a linear relationship exists. A regression line might be calculated from these data that would provide an accurate fit for the relevant range.

But suppose that a new relevant range enveloped all activity from zero to the maximum shown. The additional observations are portrayed by the square dots, and the round dots plus the square dots would be better approximated by the newly fitted curve. In other words, the linearity assumption must hold for the relevant range that the analyst is concerned about. As always, it is risky to extrapolate beyond the relevant range.

constant variance The second assumption is that the standard deviation and variance of the u's is constant[8] for all x, that the u's are drawn from the same population. It is the same for all values of x. This indicates that there is a uniform scatter or dispersion of points about the regression line. Again, the scatter diagram is the easiest way to check for constant variance; this assumption is valid for the first chart, but not the second, of the following:

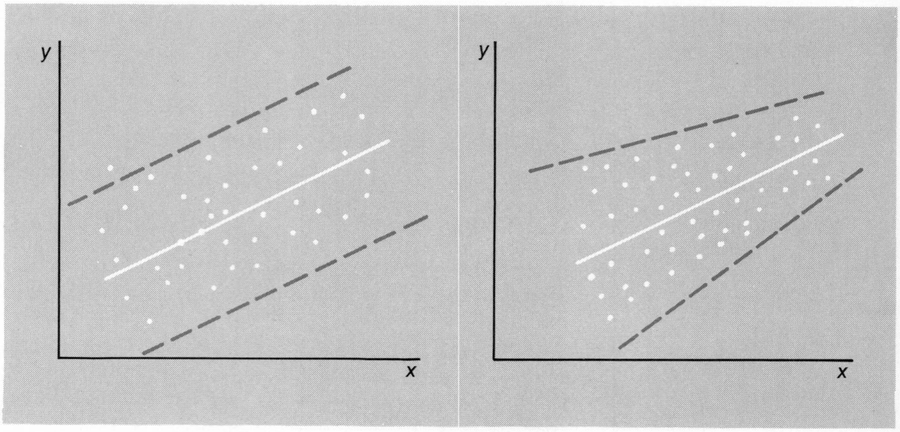

[8] Constant variance is known as *homoscedasticity* (but let us refer to it as constant variance). Violation of this assumption is called *heteroscedasticity*.

If the constant-variance assumption does not hold, the accuracy of the b coefficient is open to question. Violation of this assumption is likely in many cost-volume situations; the higher the volume, the higher the probability of higher scatter for higher x's than for lower x's.[9]

independence The third assumption is that the u's are independent of each other. That is, the deviation of one point about the line (its u value, where $u = y - y'$) is unrelated to the deviation of any other point. If the u's are not independent, the problem of *serial correlation* (also called *autocorrelation*) is present.

To illustrate, when observations are taken in successive time periods, the disturbances that arose in a period t may not be independent from those that arose in previous periods $t - 1$, $t - 2$, and so on. One cause of serial correlation is the tendency of costs to be "sticky." That is, costs may rise in response to increases in volume over time but may not decline in the same way as volume declines.

When serial correlation exists, (a) the standard errors of the regression coefficients are seriously underestimated, (b) the sampling variances of the coefficients will be very large, and (c) the predictions of cost made from the regression equations will be more variable than is ordinarily anticipated from least-squares estimation.[10] The computation of standard errors is based on n independent observations. If observations are not independent, there simply are not enough observations in the sample. Fortunately, computer programs usually have tests for serial correlation.[11]

normality The fourth assumption is that the points around the regression line are normally distributed. That is, the u values are normally distributed. This assumption is necessary concerning inferences about y', a, and b. For example, the normality assumption is necessary to make probability statements using the standard error of the estimate. In addition, the rule of thumb that the t-values must be equal or greater than 2 is based on the normality assumption.

[9] Spurr and Bonini, *Statistical Analysis,* p. 469, point out that if the scatter tends to be a constant *percentage* of the independent variable X, then the use of log Y makes the deviations about the regression line more uniform. For an expanded discussion of this and similar transformations, particularly when applied to multiple regression, see R. Jensen, "A Multiple Regression Model for Cost-Control—Assumptions and Limitations," *Accounting Review,* Vol. XLII, No. 2, pp. 265–73. Also see J. Johnston, *Econometric Methods,* 2nd ed. (New York: McGraw-Hill Book Company), p. 216, which shows the effects when the variance of the disturbance term is proportional to the square of x.

[10] Benston, "Multiple Regression Analysis," p. 668.

[11] The degree of first-order serial correlation is tested by the Durbin-Watson statistic. If the statistic approaches a value of 2, there is no serial correlation. The statistic will tend to be small for positively autocorrelated series and large for negatively autocorrelated series. See Johnston, *Econometric Methods,* pp. 251–52. In dealing with problems of serial correlation, analysts often search for a new variable that will explain the systematic pattern of the u's. Also, they often try to work with lags or differences in the data.

no multicollinearity A fifth assumption, the absence of multicollinearity, is applicable only to multiple regression, which is discussed in the chapter appendix. In multiple regression there are two or more independent variables—for instance, two or more product lines. When the independent variables are highly correlated with each other, the net regression coefficients may be unreliable. For example, when marginal costs are computed, we would prefer to estimate the marginal cost of each class of product manufactured in a multi-product firm. Consider the manufacturer of major home appliances. If the demand for all appliances is highly correlated, the number of refrigerators, dishwashers, and clothes dryers produced will move together. Then it is impossible to use multiple regression to disentangle the marginal cost of making refrigerators from the marginal cost of making dishwashers and clothes dryers. However, the computed regression can provide accurate predictions of *total* costs if the past relationships of production among the different outputs are maintained. Still, the analyst is often concerned about the reliability of the individual coefficients; in other words, he wants to know the separate effects of each independent variable on Y. If multicollinearity is present, estimates of coefficients become very sensitive to particular sets of sample data, and the addition of a few more observations can substantially shift some coefficients.[12]

The presence of multicollinearity can be tested by examining the correlation between the independent variables. As a rule of thumb, if a correlation exceeds, say .8, the less important of the two independent variables should be dropped from the estimating equation.

SUMMARY

Predictions of how costs will behave in response to various actions usually have an important bearing on a wide number of decisions. The cost function used to make these predictions is usually a simplification of underlying relationships. The choice of a cost function is a decision concerning the cost and value of information.

Two common assumptions are widely used in cost analysis. First, cost behavior can be sufficiently explained by one independent variable. Second, linear approximations to cost functions are "good enough" for most purposes.

The engineering approach, which may be expensive and which concentrates directly on the future, is recommended as the best practical and philosophical approach to approximating cost functions. This approach may encompass all kinds of techniques, from time and motion studies to multiple regression. However, in all cases the techniques should serve as checks on one another. The following guides for cost estimation and prediction should be used:

1. To the extent that physical relationships are observable, use them.
2. To the extent that relationships can be implicitly established via logic and knowledge of operations, use them—preferably in conjunction with 3.

[12] Johnston, *Econometric Methods,* p. 160. Multicollinearity is also suspected if the model has a high r^2 but insignificant t-values for two or more x's. Also see Benston, *op. cit.*

3. To the extent that relationships can be explicitly established via regression analysis, use them. The use of 3 is a check on 2. This step should never be taken before step 2 is performed.

Regression analysis is the most systematic approach to cost estimation. Unlike other approaches, it has measures of probable error and it can be applied when there are several independent variables instead of one. Nevertheless, regression has many assumptions and pitfalls, so professional help should be sought when it is applied.

SUGGESTED READINGS

ASSOCIATION OF AMERICAN RAILROADS, *A Guide to Railroad Cost Analysis.* Washington D.C.: Bureau of Railway Economics, The Association, 1964.

BENSTON, GEORGE, "Multiple Regression Analysis of Cost Behavior," *Accounting Review,* Vol. XLI, No. 4, pp. 657–72.

FREUND, J., and B. PERLES, *Business Statistics: A First Course.* Englewood Cliffs, N.J.: Prentice-Hall, Inc., 1974.

JENSEN, ROBERT, "Multiple Regression Models for Cost Control—Assumptions and Limitations," *Accounting Review,* Vol. XLII, No. 2, pp. 265–72.

JOHNSTON, J., *Econometric Methods,* 2nd ed. New York: McGraw-Hill Book Company, 1972.

———. *Statistical Cost Analysis.* New York: McGraw-Hill Book Company, 1960.

SPURR, WILLIAM A., and CHARLES P. BONINI, rev. ed. *Statistical Analysis for Business Decisions.* Homewood, Ill.: Richard D. Irwin, Inc., 1973.

PROBLEMS FOR SELF-STUDY

PROBLEM 1

You are trying to predict the cost of overhead. You have decided to choose one of the following independent variables: labor-hours or machine-hours. A computer program has been used to analyze the past behavior of overhead over eighteen months in relation to each independent variable:

VARIABLE	*COEFFICIENT*	*STANDARD ERROR*	*T-VALUE*	*R-SQUARED*
Intercept	30,000	5,000	6.00	
2 (Labor-hours)	1.50	.30	5.00	
				.907
Intercept	10,000	4,000	2.50	
3 (Machine-hours)	.50	.15	3.33	
				.658

Which base should be used to predict overhead cost incurrence? Why?

SOLUTION 1

Both are equally plausible. Labor-hours would be chosen as the basis for the application of overhead, because they explain a higher percentage of the past variations in overhead than did machine-hours (r^2 of .907 versus .658). The t-values are significant in both cases; the higher t-value for labor-hours reinforces the choice of labor-hours in preference to machine-hours.

PROBLEM 2

In the preceding problem, you also decided to analyze the overhead in relation to the two independent variables simultaneously:

VARIABLE	COEFFICIENT	STANDARD ERROR	T-VALUE	R-SQUARED
Intercept	21,000	10,000	2.10	
2	2.00	1.20	1.67	
3	.25	.40	.63	.942

CORRELATION COEFFICIENTS

Variable	2	3
2	1.000	.917
3	.917	1.000

Does the use of both independent variables together improve your confidence in your prediction of overhead cost incurrence? Why?

SOLUTION 2 If your intent is *solely* to predict overhead cost, then the higher r^2 indicates that the multiple regression gives a better fit—as long as the past relationships of machine-hours and labor-hours are maintained. However, note the deterioration of the t-values of the individual coefficients. These lower t-values are the results of high multicollinearity. Thus we have much less confidence about the *individual* coefficients; it is risky to disentangle the marginal or variable overhead effect on overhead costs of adding one more labor-hour versus one more machine-hour. The latter is often a central question of cost analysis.

PROBLEM 3 In Problem 1, suppose that the regression model had a negative intercept. An industrial engineer informs you that the actual overhead cost in any month of zero activity would be about $14,000. There were no months of zero activity during the previous eighteen months. Does this additional number alter your decision in Problem 1? Why?

SOLUTION 3 No data in Problem 1 covered zero activity. The 30,000 or 10,000 intercepts in Problem 1 or the possible negative intercept suggested here are *not* estimates of overhead cost when activity is zero. These intercepts are merely the intercept of the estimation model for the *range spanned by the data.* For additional explanation see the sections in this chapter on goodness of fit and the fixed-cost component.

appendix: regression analysis

least squares Although an experienced statistician can visually fit a straight line to a scatter diagram with remarkable accuracy, the surest, most exact fit is obtained by two major steps. First, inspect the scatter chart to detect any unusual features that warrant further investigation. For example, one or two points may be obviously awry. Investigation may reveal clerical errors that need correction. Perhaps an unusual situation (such as a strike or a storm that disrupted the usual relationships between, say, machine-hours and direct-labor costs) may justify removing isolated or extreme cases from the data.

Second, apply the mathematical method of least squares. This assures an objective, precise fit, and it can be easily performed with widely available, inexpensive standardized computer programs.

To illustrate regression analysis,[13] suppose that a manufacturer is troubled by fluctuations in labor productivity and wants to determine how direct-labor

[13] This illustration and analysis is adapted from John E. Freund and Frank J. Williams, *Elementary Business Statistics: The Modern Approach,* 2nd ed. (Englewood Cliffs, N.J.: Prentice-Hall, Inc., 1972), pp. 299ff.

costs are related to the various sizes of batches of output. The workers in question set up their own jobs on complex machinery. The following data show the results of a random sample of ten batches of a given kind:

BATCH SIZE x	*DIRECT-LABOR COSTS* y
15	$180
12	140
20	230
17	190
12	160
25	300
22	270
9	110
18	240
30	320

Note that the data are paired. For example, the next-to-last sample consists of a batch size (independent variable) of 18 with an *associated* direct-labor cost (dependent variable) of $240.

The scatter diagram of these ten points in Exhibit 25-9 indicates that a straight line should provide a reasonable approximation of the relationship between labor costs and size of batch that prevailed during the sample history. The least-squares criterion is the most widely used means of judging whether a line drawn through the points provides the best possible fit. That is, the sum of the squares of the vertical deviations (distances) from the points to the line must be smaller than they would be from any other straight line. Note especially that, as the graph in Exhibit 25-10 shows, the deviations are measured vertically. The deviations are *not* perpendicular to the regression line.

The object is to find the values of a and b in the predicting equation $y' = a + bx$, where y' is the calculated value as distinguished from the observed value y. We wish to find the numerical values of the constants a and b that minimize $\Sigma\,(y - y')^2$, the difference between the actual y and the y' value predicted by the equation relating y to changes in x. This is accomplished by using two equations, usually called *normal equations:*[14]

[14] These normal equations can be derived through elementary calculus. Let

$$q = \sum_{i=1}^{n} (y_i - a - bx_i)^2$$

where n is the number of paired observations in the sample.

The objective of least squares requires the estimates of a and b to minimize q. Therefore, a and b should be values that make

$$\frac{\partial q}{\partial a} = 0 \quad \text{and} \quad \frac{\partial q}{\partial b} = 0$$

These partial derivatives are

$$\frac{\partial q}{\partial b} = -2 \sum_{i=1}^{n} (y_i - a - bx_i)$$

$$\frac{\partial q}{\partial b} = -2 \sum_{i=1}^{n} x_i(y_i - a - bx_i)$$

The normal equations are then obtained by setting the partial derivatives equal to zero and performing the indicated summations. (The discerning student would check second-order conditions here to insure that a minimum is being attained.)

EXHIBIT 25-9

SCATTER DIAGRAM AND POSSIBLE LINEARITY

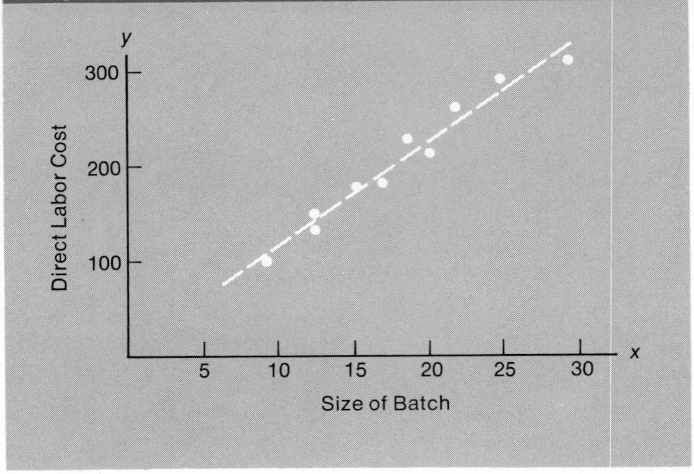

EXHIBIT 25-10

LEAST-SQUARES CRITERION

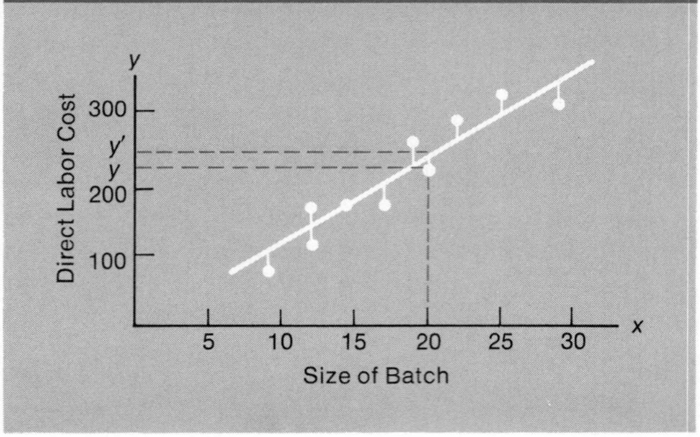

$$\Sigma y = na + b(\Sigma x)$$
$$\Sigma xy = a(\Sigma x) + b(\Sigma x^2)$$

where n is the number of pairs of observations, Σx and Σy are, respectively, the sums of the given x's and y's, Σx^2 is the sum of the squares of the x's, and Σxy is the sum of the products obtained by multiplying each of the given x's by the corresponding observed value of y.

EXHIBIT 25-11

COMPUTATIONS FOR LEAST SQUARES

BATCH SIZE x	DIRECT-LABOR COSTS y	x^2	xy
15	$ 180	225	$ 2,700
12	140	144	1,680
20	230	400	4,600
17	190	289	3,230
12	160	144	1,920
25	300	625	7,500
22	270	484	5,940
9	110	81	990
18	240	324	4,320
30	320	900	9,600
180	$2,140	3,616	$42,480

Using our numerical illustration, we obtain the ingredients of our normal equations from the table in Exhibit 25-11.

Substituting into the two simultaneous linear equations, we obtain:

$$2{,}140 = 10a + 180b$$
$$42{,}480 = 180a + 3{,}616b$$

The solution is $a = 24.43$ and $b = 10.53$, which can be obtained by direct substitution if the normal equations are reexpressed symbolically as follows:

$$a = \frac{(\Sigma\, y)(\Sigma\, x^2) - (\Sigma\, x)(\Sigma\, xy)}{n(\Sigma\, x^2) - (\Sigma\, x)^2}$$
$$b = \frac{n(\Sigma\, xy) - (\Sigma\, x)(\Sigma\, y)}{n(\Sigma\, x^2) - (\Sigma\, x)^2}$$

and for our illustration we now have:[15]

$$a = \frac{(2{,}140)(3{,}616) - (180)(42{,}480)}{10(3{,}616) - (180)^2} = \frac{91{,}840}{3{,}760} = 24.43$$
$$b = \frac{10(42{,}480 - (180)(2{,}140)}{10(3{,}616) - (180)^2} = \frac{39{,}600}{3{,}760} = 10.53$$

[15] Another way of obtaining the values is often used. First, b is calculated as above. Then its value is substituted into the first of the two normal equations to obtain a:

$$2{,}140 = 10a + 180(10.53)$$
$$a = 24.46$$

Placing the amounts for a and b in the equation of the least-squares line, we have:

$$y' = 24.43 + 10.53x$$

where y' is the predicted labor cost for any given batch size. A prime is placed on the y to distinguish between the value of y that was actually observed for a specified value of x and the corresponding value obtained with the use of the equation of the line.

If we apply the equation, we would predict, for example, that a lot size of 20 would have labor costs on average of $24.43 + 10.53(20) = \$235$. See Exhibit 25-12, an enlarged version of the graph in Exhibit 25-10, for the graph at this lot size.

Because the points in Exhibit 25-9 are somewhat dispersed, we know that our predictions for any given lot size x will be subject to error. The regression

EXHIBIT 25-12

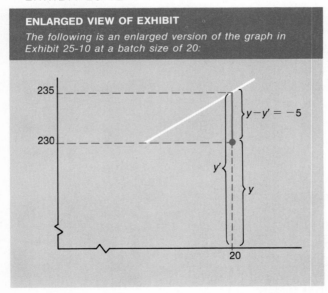

ENLARGED VIEW OF EXHIBIT

The following is an enlarged version of the graph in Exhibit 25-10 at a batch size of 20:

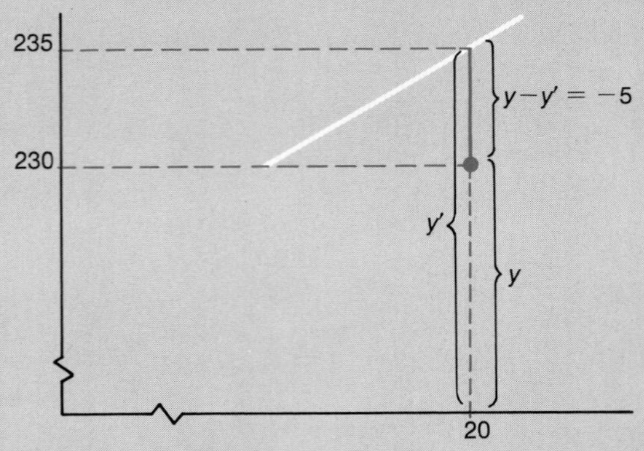

Example, batch size of 20:

$$y' = 24.43 + 10.53\,(20) = \$235$$
$$y = 230$$
$$y - y' = -5$$

line represents an *average* relationship; it is an estimation of the average values of y for different batch sizes.

correlation

How much of the total variation of the y's can be attributed to chance? How much can be attributed to the relationship between the two variables x and y? The coefficient of correlation (r) is a measure of the extent to which the independent variable accounts for the variability in the dependent variable. Note in Exhibit 25-13 that the total deviation of the dependent variable y from its mean $\bar{y}$ (that is $y - \bar{y}$) can be divided into two parts: first, the deviation of the value on the line (y') from the mean $\bar{y}$, or ($y' - \bar{y}$), which is explained by the given value of x; and second, the deviation of y from the regression line ($y - y'$), which is not explained by x.

The measure of the closeness of fit of a regression line is made by comparing $\Sigma (y - y')^2$ with the sum of the squares of the deviations of y's from their mean $\Sigma (y - \bar{y})^2$. Using our illustration from Exhibit 25-11, $\Sigma y = 2{,}140$ and $\bar{y} = 2{,}140 \div 10 = 214$. Therefore,

$$\Sigma (y - \bar{y})^2 = (180 - 214)^2 + (140 - 214)^2 + \cdots + (240 - 214)^2 + (320 - 214)^2 = 43{,}640$$

EXHIBIT 25-13

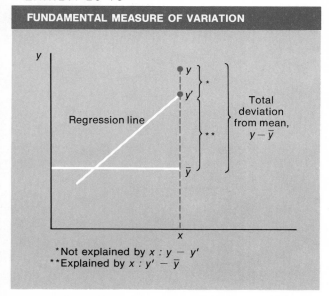

FUNDAMENTAL MEASURE OF VARIATION

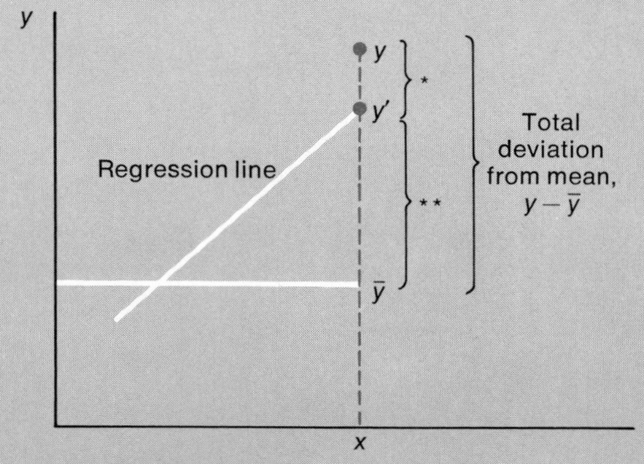

*Not explained by x : $y - y'$
**Explained by x : $y' - \bar{y}$

Chance variation is measured by the deviations of the points from the regression line, by the quantity $\Sigma (y - y')^2$. If all the points actually fell on a straight line, $\Sigma (y - y')^2$ would equal zero. To compute this quantity for our illustration, the predicted values y' must be calculated by substituting the given values of x into the least-squares equation

$$y' = 24.43 + 10.53x$$

Therefore, we obtain $y' = 24.43 + 10.53(15) = 182.38$ for the first batch, $y' = 24.43 + 10.53(12) = 150.79$ for the second batch, and so on. Substituting these values and the observed y's into $\Sigma (y - y')^2$, we get

$$\Sigma (y - y')^2 = (180 - 182.38)^2 + (140 - 150.79)^2 + \cdots + (320 - 340.33)^2 = 1{,}934$$

Therefore,

$$\frac{\Sigma (y - y')^2}{\Sigma (y - \bar{y})^2} = \frac{1{,}934}{43{,}640} = .0443 = 4.43\%$$

of the variation in the cost of the batches can be attributed to random variation (chance) and the effect of other variables not explicitly incorporated in the model. The remaining 95.57 (100 − 4.43) percent of the variation in the costs is accounted for by differences in the size of the batch.

The coefficient of determination is often called r-square (r^2). It indicates the proportion of the variance, $(y - \bar{y})^2$, that is explained by the independent variable x. The coefficient of determination is also more informatively expressed as 1 minus the proportion of total variance that is not explained:

$$\begin{aligned} r^2 &= 1 - \frac{\Sigma (y - y')^2}{\Sigma (y - \bar{y})^2} = 1 - \frac{\text{Unexplained variance}}{\text{Total variance}} \\ &= 1 - \frac{1{,}934}{43{,}640} = 1 - .0443 = .9557 \end{aligned}$$

The square root of the proportion .9557 (that is, the proportion of the total variation in costs that is accounted for by differences in the size of the batches) is called the coefficient of correlation, r:

$$r = \pm \sqrt{1 - \frac{\Sigma (y - y')^2}{\Sigma (y - \bar{y})^2}}$$

The sign attached to r is the sign of b in the predicting equation:

$$\begin{aligned} r^2 &= .9557 \\ r &= + \sqrt{.9557} = .978 \end{aligned}$$

In this illustration, the least-squares line provides an excellent fit, so there is indication of a strong relationship between the costs of the labor and the size of the batch. The coefficient of correlation is a relative measure of the relationship between two variables, varying from zero (no correlation) to ± 1 (perfect correlation).

Note that the coefficient of correlation may indicate a higher degree of explanation than is warranted. For instance, if 60 percent of the variance in y is explained by x, $r^2 = .60$, but $r = \sqrt{.60} = .775$.

standard error of estimate

How accurate is the regression line as a basis for prediction? We are using a sample of historical events. Obviously, if we duplicated that sample using different data, we would not expect to obtain the same line. The values for a and b would be different for each sample taken. What we really want to know is the true regression line of the entire population,

$$y = A + Bx$$

where A and B are the true coefficients. The values of a and b are estimates based on samples. Therefore, they are subject to chance variation like all sample statistics.

In Chapter 24, we saw that data are often expressed as averages. A standard deviation and a coefficient of variation were computed to help indicate the relative degree of dispersion about the mean. Similarly, the line we obtained with the method of least squares, $y' = 24.43 + 10.53x$, is only an *estimate* of the true regression line.

To judge the accuracy of the regression line, we examine the dispersion of the observed values of y around the regression line. A measure of this dispersion will assist us in judging the probable accuracy of a prediction of the average labor cost of a batch of, say, 20 units. The measure of the scatter of the actual observations about the regression line is termed the *standard error of estimate.* The standard error of estimate for the population may be calculated from a sample in linear regression, as follows:

$$s_e = \sqrt{\frac{\Sigma\,(y - y')^2}{n - 2}}$$

where n is the size of the sample.[16]

[16] The standard error of the estimate for the sample itself is $\sqrt{\Sigma\,(y - y')^2/n}$. The use of $n - 2$ represents the degrees of freedom around the regression line. It is $n - 2$ because two constants, a and b, had to be computed first on the basis of the original data. Moreover, computer programs will frequently provide for an r^2 that is "adjusted" or "corrected" for the degrees of freedom. The unadjusted R^2 will never decrease as additional explanatory variables are added to a regression, but it is possible for the adjusted r^2 to decline if an additional variable produces too small a reduction in $(1 - r^2)$ to compensate for an increase in $(n - 1)(n - k)$, where k is the number of coefficients (including the constant term, the intercept). See Johnston, *Econometric Methods,* p. 130.

As will be demonstrated in more detail later, the sum of the squared deviations, $\Sigma\,(y - y')^2$, is that portion of the total variation in y's that can be attributed to chance.

When a linear regression has been fitted by least squares, a simpler computation is

$$s_e = \sqrt{\frac{\Sigma\, y^2 - a\,\Sigma\, y - b\,\Sigma\, xy}{n - 2}}$$

Consider our illustration. All the data are from Exhibit 25-11, except for $\Sigma\, y^2$, which happens to be 501,600.

$$s_e = \sqrt{\frac{501{,}600 - 24.43(2{,}140) - 10.53(42{,}480)}{10 - 2}}$$

$$s_e = 15.8$$

If the four assumptions underlying regression analysis (linearity, independence, constant variance, and normality) are satisfied, we can use the standard error to help gauge our confidence in our predictions. For instance, if no sampling error exists, then approximately two-thirds of the points should lie within the band measured $y' \pm 15.8$. Therefore, management can predict that a batch size of 20 would result in costs of \$235 ± \$15.80, or between \$219.20 and \$250.80, with two chances out of three of being correct.

sampling errors and regression coefficients

testing for significance of a relationship

Does a significant explanatory relationship exist between x and y? For example, the regression coefficient of x of 10.53 implies a change in cost of \$10.53 for each additional unit in a batch. The regression coefficient 10.53 is an estimate of a population parameter. A particular sample may indicate a relationship, even when none exists, by pure chance. If there is no relationship, then the slope B of the true regression line would be zero. A hypothesis can be set up that $B = 0$. If the sample value b is significantly different from zero, we would reject the hypothesis and assert that there is a definite relationship between the variables.

To test this hypothesis, we need to calculate the standard error of the b regression coefficient:

$$s_b = \frac{s_e}{\sqrt{\Sigma\,(x - \bar{x})^2}}$$

It may also be expressed as:

$$s_b = \frac{s_e}{\sqrt{\Sigma\, x^2 - \bar{x}\,\Sigma\, x}}$$

where s_e is the sample standard error of the estimate, and the denominator describes the dispersion of x values around their mean. The value s_b is a measure of the amount of sampling error in b. The s_b for our example is

$$s_b = \frac{15.8}{\sqrt{3{,}616 - 18(180)}} = \frac{15.8}{\sqrt{3{,}616 - 3{,}240}} = \frac{15.8}{\sqrt{376}} = \frac{15.8}{19.4} = .81$$

The procedure[17] for deciding whether a positive relationship exists between batch size and labor costs is this:

Null hypothesis: $B = 0$ (no relationship)
Alternative hypothesis: $B \neq 0$ (labor costs increase as batch sizes increase)

The value of b is 10.53. If the null hypothesis is true, $B = 0$, and b is 10.53 units from B. In terms of its standard error, this is $10.53 \div .81 = 13.0$. Therefore, b is 13 standard errors from $B = 0$. A deviation of more than two standard errors is usually regarded as significant. Therefore, the chance is infinitesimal that a deviation as large as 13 standard errors could occur by chance. Consequently, we reject the null hypothesis and accept the alternative hypothesis that there is a significant relationship between the variables.

The amount of 13.0 standard errors just computed is called the *t-value* of the regression coefficient:

$$t\text{-value} = \frac{\text{Coefficient}}{\text{Standard error of the coefficient}} = \frac{10.53}{.81} = 13.0$$

High t-values enhance confidence in the value of the coefficient as a predictor. Low t-values (as a rule of thumb, under 2.00) are indications of low reliability of the predictive power of that coefficient.[18]

confidence intervals and *t*-values

The standard error of the regression coefficient and the t-value permit us to assess a probability that the "true" B is between specified limits. These limits are usually called confidence intervals. The 95 percent confidence interval is computed with the use of the appropriate t-value from the table in Exhibit 25-14.

[17] Spurr and Bonini, *Statistical Analysis,* pp. 566–68.

[18] For reasons explained in the body of this chapter, we have concentrated on the t-value of b rather than the t-value of a, which is computed as follows:

$$s_a = s_e\sqrt{\frac{1}{n} + \frac{\bar{x}^2}{\Sigma(x - \bar{x})^2}}$$

$$s_a = 15.8\sqrt{\frac{1}{10} + \frac{324}{376}} = 15.8\sqrt{.962}$$

$$s_a = 15.8(.981) = 15.70$$

$$t\text{-value}_a = 24.43 \div 15.70 = 1.56$$

EXHIBIT 25-14

VALUES OF *t*

d.f.	$t_{.100}$	$t_{.050}$	$t_{.025}$	$t_{.010}$	$t_{.005}$	*d.f.*
1	3.078	6.314	12.706	31.821	63.657	1
2	1.886	2.920	4.303	6.965	9.925	2
3	1.638	2.353	3.182	4.541	5.841	3
4	1.533	2.132	2.776	3.747	4.604	4
5	1.476	2.015	2.571	3.365	4.032	5
6	1.440	1.943	2.447	3.143	3.707	6
7	1.415	1.895	2.365	2.998	3.499	7
8	1.397	1.860	2.306	2.896	3.355	8
9	1.383	1.833	2.262	2.821	3.250	9
10	1.372	1.812	2.228	2.764	3.169	10
11	1.363	1.796	2.201	2.718	3.106	11
12	1.356	1.782	2.179	2.681	3.055	12
13	1.350	1.771	2.160	2.650	3.012	13
14	1.345	1.761	2.145	2.624	2.977	14
15	1.341	1.753	2.131	2.602	2.947	15
16	1.337	1.746	2.120	2.583	2.921	16
17	1.333	1.740	2.110	2.567	2.898	17
18	1.330	1.734	2.101	2.552	2.878	18
19	1.328	1.729	2.093	2.539	2.861	19
20	1.325	1.725	2.086	2.528	2.845	20
21	1.323	1.721	2.080	2.518	2.831	21
22	1.321	1.717	2.074	2.508	2.819	22
23	1.319	1.714	2.069	2.500	2.807	23
24	1.318	1.711	2.064	2.492	2.797	24
25	1.316	1.708	2.060	2.485	2.787	25
26	1.315	1.706	2.056	2.479	2.779	26
27	1.314	1.703	2.052	2.473	2.771	27
28	1.313	1.701	2.048	2.467	2.763	28
29	1.311	1.699	2.045	2.462	2.756	29
inf.	1.282	1.645	1.960	2.326	2.576	inf.

The *t*-value describes the sampling distribution of a deviation from a population value divided by the standard error.

Degrees of freedom (*d.f.*) are in the first column. The probabilities indicated as subvalues of *t* in the heading refer to the sum of a one-tailed area under the curve that lies outside the point *t*.

For example, in the distribution of the means of samples of size $n = 10$, $d.f. = n - 2 = 8$; then .025 of the area under the curve falls in one tail outside the interval $t \pm 2.306$.

For instance, with a sample size of 10, we find the row in Exhibit 25-14 with $n - 2 = 8$ degrees of freedom and the column $t_{.025}$ (for one-tail) to find the confidence interval:

$$b \pm t_{.025}(s_b)$$

This is

$$\begin{aligned} &10.53 \pm 2.306(.81) \\ = &10.53 \pm 1.87 \end{aligned}$$

If all the pertinent assumptions hold, the accountant could assess a probability of .95 that the "true" marginal cost (B) is between \$8.66 and \$12.40. Similarly, he could assess a probability of .80 that the interval is between \$9.40 and \$11.66. The latter is computed by using $t_{.100}$ instead of $t_{.025}$: 10.53 $\pm$ 1.397(.81) = 10.53 $\pm$ 1.13.

multiple regression

improving accuracy

In many cases, satisfactory predictions of a cost may be based on only one variable, such as labor-hours. Nevertheless, there are instances where accuracy can be substantially improved by basing the prediction on more than one independent variable. The most widely used equations to express relationships among more than two variables are linear equations of the form[19]

$$y = a + bx_1 + cx_2 + dx_3 + \cdot \cdot \cdot + u$$

where y is the variable to be predicted, x_1, x_2, and x_3 are the independent variables on which the prediction is to be based; a, b, c, and d are unknown constants; and u is the "disturbance term" that includes the net effect of other factors. For cost predictions, there may be two, three, or more independent variables such as labor-hours, labor cost, machine-hours, weight, dimensions,

[19] These equations may be expressed in many alternate forms. For instance:

$$y = b_0 + b_1x_1 + b_2x_2 + b_3x_3 + \cdot \cdot \cdot$$

A general form is:

$$Y_i = A_0 + \sum_{j=1}^{m} X_{ij}A_i + u_i \qquad i = 1, \ldots, n$$

where the Y_i are the independent variables, the X_{ij} are the independent variables, and the u_i are the residual (error) terms. The u_i is the sum of the unspecified factors, the disturbances, that are assumed to be normally distributed with a zero mean and constant variance.

temperature, types of machines, types of labor skill, and so forth. For example, the weekly cost of labor in a shipping room may be more accurately predicted by the equation

$$y = \$180 + \$.80\text{ (units shipped)} + \$.30\text{ (weight of units shipped)}$$

than by basing the prediction on either units shipped or weight of units shipped alone.

The terms b, c, d, . . . are the *net regression coefficients.* Each measures the change in y per unit change in the particular independent variable while holding the other independent variables constant. In the example above, the 80¢ rate per unit shipped indicated how much cost will rise for units of the same weight.

The major difficulty in fitting a linear equation having more than two unknowns to a given set of data is that of finding the constants a, b, c, d, . . . , so that the resulting equation will yield the best possible predictions. As in the two-variable case described in a previous section, this problem is generally solved by using the method of least squares.

Fundamentally, the problem of finding predicting equations of the form $y = a + bx_1 + cx_2 + dx_3 + \cdots$ does not differ from that of fitting lines of the form $y = a + bx$. Moreover, the widespread availability of suitable computer programs makes the use of multiple regression feasible. Least-squares equations having 25 or more variables can be solved in a matter of seconds on a fast digital computer.

illustration of technique

The details of multiple regression are beyond the scope of this text. However, the following example will show how regression may be used for cost analysis.[20] Suppose a firm manufactures electronic circuit boards and other products in which the services of several departments are used. In the assembly department, two types of circuit boards are produced, *nenex* and *denex.* The nenex are assembled in batches, but the denex are assembled singly. Weekly observations on cost and output are taken and punched on cards. Graphs are prepared, and it appears that a linear relationship is present. Furthermore, the cost of producing nenex is not believed to be a function of the production of denex or other explanatory variables. Therefore, the following regression is computed:

$$\begin{aligned} y = {} & 110.3 + 8.21n - 7.83b + 12.32d + 235s + 523w - 136a \\ & (40.8) \quad (.53) \quad (1.69) \quad (2.10) \quad (100) \quad (204) \quad (154) \\ r^2 = {} & .892 \text{ (the coefficient of multiple determination)} \end{aligned}$$

[20] Adapted from Benston, "Multiple Regression Analysis," pp. 670–71. Also see Robert Jensen, "Multiple Regression Models for Cost Control—Assumptions and Limitations," *Accounting Review,* Vol. XLI, No. 4, pp. 265–72.

where the number of observations is 156 and

y = expected cost
n = number of nenex
b = average number of nenex in a batch
d = number of denex
s = summer dummy variable, where s = 1 for summer, 0 for other seasons
w = winter dummy variable, where w = 1 for winter, 0 for other seasons
a = autumn dummy variable, where a = 1 for autumn, 0 for other seasons

As before, the numbers in parentheses beneath the coefficients are the standard errors of the regression coefficients. For example, the regression coefficient for n is 8.21 with the other factors affecting costs "held constant" or "accounted for." The regression coefficient 8.21 is an estimate of the population parameter. The sampling error associated with this estimate is called the *standard error of the regression coefficient.* If the underlying assumptions of regression are satisfied, the standard error of the coefficient, .53, permits us to assess a probability of 0.67 that the "true" marginal cost is between 7.68 and 8.74(8.21 ± .53) and of 0.95 that it is between 7.15 and 9.27 (8.21 ± 1.06) for large n.

Moreover, we can use the t-value to test whether the presence of the independent variable contributes significantly toward explanation of the movements in the dependent variable. For example, the t-value of n is 8.21 ÷ .53 = 15.68. Such a high t-value enhances confidence in the value of the coefficient as a predictor.

The regression might be used for flexible budgeting and the analysis of performance. For example, suppose the following for one week: n = 532; b = 20, d = 321; and s = summer = 1. If this week is like an average of the experience for past weeks, total costs would be

$$110.3 + 8.21(532) - 7.83(20) + 12.32(321) + 235.3(1) = 8{,}501$$

With the help of a computer program, the standard error of the estimate can be computed so that the budget can provide a range of $8,501 ± the standard error. The actual costs can then be compared to this expected amount. With these figures, management can judge how unusual the actual production costs are in light of past experience.

QUESTIONS, PROBLEMS, AND CASES

Problems for Part One

25-1 Distinguish between *cost estimation* and *cost prediction.*

25-2 What two common simplifications are used in determining cost functions?

25-3 Describe three assumptions that are sufficient conditions for linearity.

25-4 To make valid inferences from sample data about population relationships, what four assumptions must be satisfied?

25-5 "High correlation between two variables means that one is the cause and the other is the effect." Do you agree? Why?

25-6 Why does regression analysis offer a means of cost estimation that other methods do not?

25-7 *High-Low Method* Examine Exhibit 25-11. Compute the cost equation using the high-low method. How does your answer compare with the equation produced by the method of least squares? Does this comparison enhance or detract from your confidence in the high-low method as a means of estimating cost behavior? Why?

25-8 *Interpretation of Regression Coefficient* A manager learned about linear regression techniques at an evening college course. He decided to apply regression in his study of repair costs in his plant. He plotted 24 points for the past 24 months and fitted a least-squares line, where

$$\text{Total repair cost per month} = \$80{,}000 - \$.50x$$

where x = number of machine-hours worked

He was baffled because the result was nonsense. Apparently, the more the machines were run, the less the repair costs. He decided that regression was a useless technique.

required

Why was the puzzling regression coefficient negative? Do you agree with the manager's conclusion regarding regression? Explain.

25-9 *Account Analysis and Cause and Effect* The costs of maintenance of way and structures (M of W & S) are incurred by a railroad to continue in usable condition the fixed facilities employed in the carrier's railway operations. These costs are usually very material in relation to revenue and net income. A substantial portion of M of W & S costs is incurred on a cyclical program. For example, the costs are influenced by the tonnage that moves over the road for periods of up to or more than ten years. The costs are also influenced by management policy decisions and other nontraffic factors.

required

1. What are likely to be heavy influences (the influential independent variables) on the M of W & S costs for any given year? Be as specific as possible.
2. If M of W & S costs were estimated by simple regression using a measure of traffic (such as train-miles or gross ton-miles) as the independent variable, will the variable-cost portion (the b-coefficient) tend to be too high or too low? Why?

25-10 *Nonlinear Behavior* (J. Demski, adapted) Ralph Thurow is manager of logistics for the Cortex Pharmaceutical Company. He has become increasingly uneasy about his cost predictions with respect to the transportation of assorted vaccines. Ordinarily, a transportation cost factor is added to the overall cost of the vaccines by a predetermined formula based on "average" transportation costs for all products. No attempt has ever been made to identify particular transportation costs with particular product lines. Transportation costs depend on units shipped, weight, whether company-owned equipment or outside shippers are used, and so on.

Top management has launched a three-year "profit-search" plan whereby all managers have been urged to "rethink your methods and costs to enhance profitability." Thurow has conducted a fine-toothed investigation of cost behavior; he has uncovered the following nonlinear cost curve, where x denotes thousands of units of vaccine shipped an average of 500 miles:

$$TC(x) = \tfrac{1}{3}x^3 - 8x^2 + 65x + 260$$

1. Plot $TC(x)$ for $0 \leq x \leq 10$.
2. Determine Ralph's fixed and marginal cost.
3. Consider the range $4 \leq x \leq 8$. Determine Ralph's cost at $x = 4$ and $x = 8$, and then construct a linear approximation to $TC(x)$ by drawing a line between these two points. [Specifically, the *slope* will be $TC(8) - TC(4)/(8 - 4)$.]
   a. Plot this approximation on your graph in part 1 above.
   b. Determine, using this "local linear approximation," Ralph's fixed and variable cost.
   c. Can you think of another method of approximating $TC(x)$?

25-11 *Linear Approximations* Suppose that the following situation existed:

VOLUME LEVEL IN DIRECT-LABOR HOURS	TOTAL ACTUAL OVERHEAD COST BEHAVIOR
30,000	$340,000
40,000	400,000
50,000	435,000
60,000	477,000
70,000	529,000
80,000	587,000

required

1. Compute the formula for the flexible budget line, using only two "representative" volumes of 40,000 hours and 70,000 hours, respectively.
2. What would be the predicted cost for 50,000 labor-hours using the flexible budget developed in part one? Using a nonlinear flexible budget equal to the "actual cost behavior" curve? For 80,000 hours? Plot the points and draw the flexible budget line and the "actual cost behavior" curve.
3. The manager had a chance to accept a special order that would have boosted production from 40,000 to 50,000 hours of activity. Suppose the manager, guided by the linear flexible budget formula, rejected a sales order that would have brought a total increase in contribution of $38,000 less the predicted increase in total overhead cost. What is the cost of the prediction error of the decision to reject?
4. Repeat part 3, except assume that the minimum acceptable increase in contribution (after deducting the predicted increase in total overhead cost) is $6,000.
5. If you were an operating manager responsible for budgetary control of overhead, would you regard the linear budget allowances at 50,000 hours and at 80,000 hours as too tight or too loose as compared to the nonlinear budget? Why?
6. Does the intercept of the flexible budget line represent the fixed overhead costs? Why?
7. In your own words, summarize the major lessons of this problem.

25-12 *Nonlinear Cost Behavior* Solve Problem 8-27, which could logically have been placed here.

25-13 *Two Independent Variables* Suppose the cost behavior pattern of overhead is linear but two-dimensional. That is, cost incurrence depends on two independent variables, direct-labor hours, x_1, and machine-hours, x_2. For example, there may be two subdepartments, one heavily automated and one extremely labor-intensive. Therefore, the actual cost behavior pattern is:

$$\text{Total overhead} = a + bx_1 + cs_2$$

where a = fixed costs, b = rate per direct-labor hour, and c = rate per machine-hour.

Using the traditional approach, the controller has examined the cost behavior of total overhead in relation to x_1 and x_2. He has decided to compute a budgeted-overhead function that is based on direct-labor hours:

$$\text{Budgeted total overhead} = a + bx$$

The results for the most recent reporting period appear on the following graph:

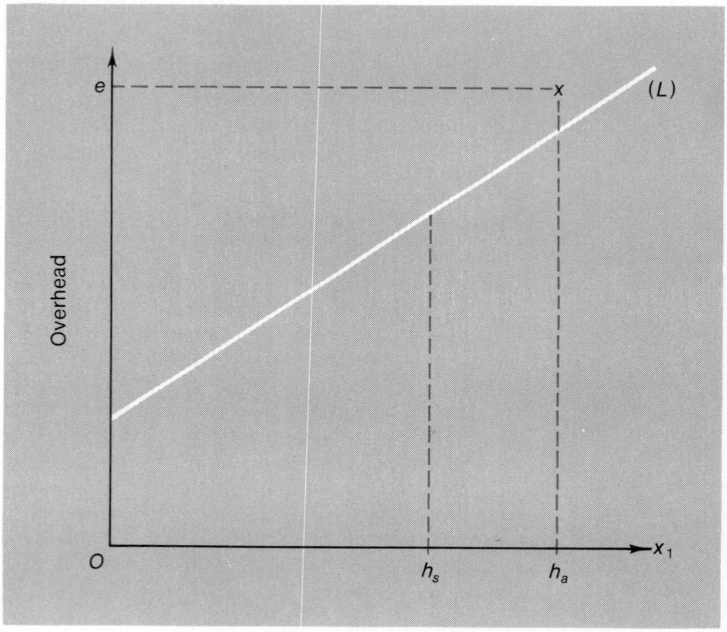

The budget is based on line (L). At the end of the period, actual hours are Oh_a, the standard hours allowed for the work done are Oh_s, and actual overhead is Oe. Smith controls direct labor, James controls machine-hours, and Johnson is responsible for total overhead.

required

1. Use the graph to measure the amount of the spending variance (call it *ge*), the efficiency variance (call it *gh*), and the budget variance (*he*). Which of the three managers is ordinarily held responsible for each variance?
2. What are the likely effects on the attitudes of the three managers if line (L) is used as a basis for budgeting?

25-14 *Various Cost Behavior Patterns* (CPA, adapted) Select the graph below that matches the numbered factory-cost or expense data. You are to indicate by letter which of the graphs best fits each of the situations or items described.

The vertical axes of the graphs represent *total* dollars of expense and the horizontal axes represent production. In each case the zero point is at the intersection of the two axes. The graphs may be used more than once.

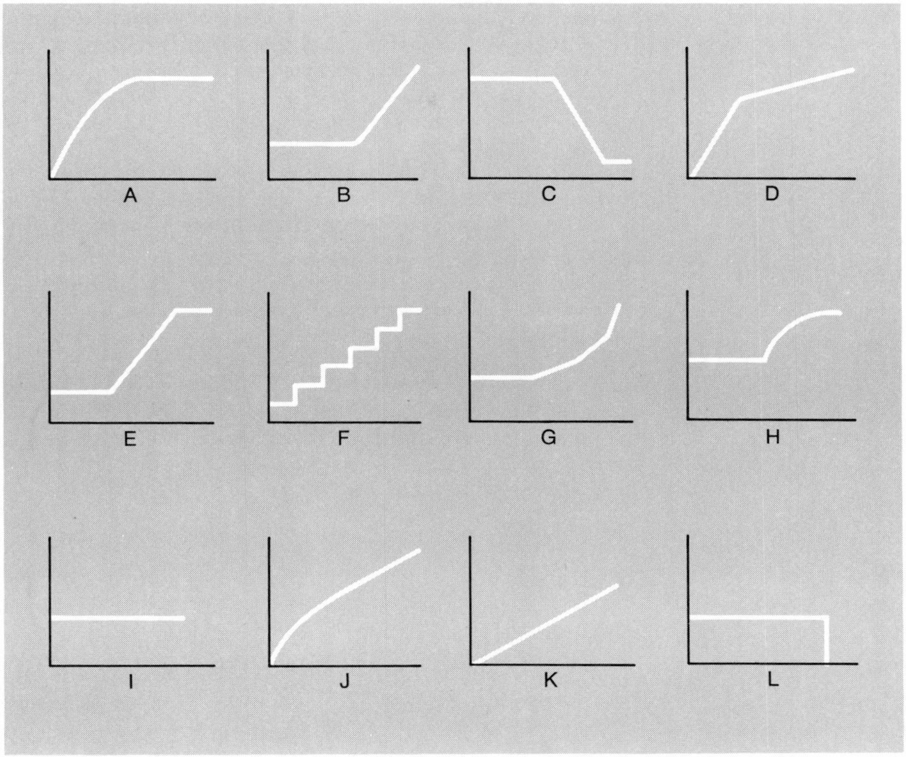

1. Depreciation of equipment, where the amount of depreciation charged is computed by the machine-hours method.
2. Electricity bill—a flat fixed charge, plus a variable cost after a certain number of kilowatt hours are used.
3. City water bill, which is computed as follows:

First 1,000,000 gallons or less	$1,000 flat fee
Next 10,000 gallons	.003 per gallon used
Next 10,000 gallons	.006 per gallon used
Next 10,000 gallons	.009 per gallon used
etc.	etc.

4. Cost of lubricant for machines, where cost per unit decreases with each pound of lubricant used (for example, if one pound is used, the cost is $10; if two pounds are used, the cost is $19.98; if three pounds are used, the cost is $29.94) with a minimum cost per pound of $9.25.
5. Depreciation of equipment, where the amount is computed by the straight-line method. When the depreciation rate was established, it was anticipated that the obsolescence factor would be greater than the wear-and-tear factor.

6. Rent on a factory building donated by the city, where the agreement calls for a fixed-fee payment unless 200,000 man-hours are worked, in which case no rent need be paid.
7. Salaries of repairmen, where one repairman is needed for every 1,000 machine-hours or less (that is, 0 to 1,000 hours requires one repairman, 1,001 to 2,000 hours requires two repairmen, and so forth).
8. Federal unemployment compensation taxes for the year, where labor force is constant in number throughout the year (average annual salary is $6,000 per worker). Maximum salary subject to tax is $4,200 per employee.
9. Cost of raw materials used.
10. Rent on a factory building donated by county, where agreement calls for rent of $100,000 less $1 for each direct-labor hour worked in excess of 200,000 hours, but minimum rental payment of $20,000 must be paid.

25-15 *Matching Graphs with Descriptions of Cost Behavior* (D. Green) Given below are a number of charts, each indicating some relationship between cost and another variable. No attempt has been made to draw these charts to any particular scale; the absolute numbers on each axis may be closely or widely spaced.

You are to indicate by number which of the charts best fits each of the situations or items described. Each situation or item is independent of all the others; all factors not stated are assumed to be irrelevant. Only one answer will be counted for any item. Some charts will be used more than once; some may not apply to any of the situations. Note that category 14, "No relationship," is not the same as 15, "Some other pattern."

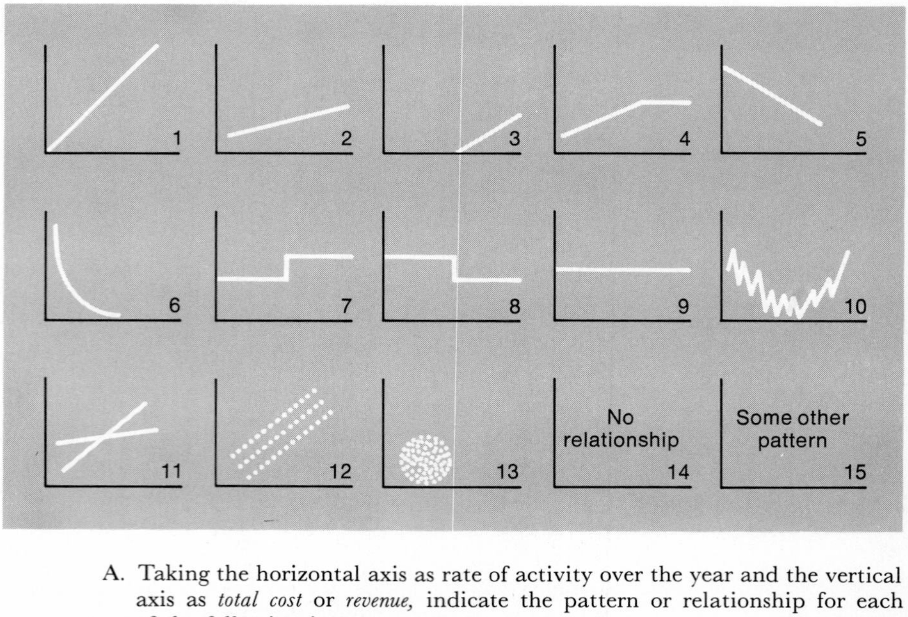

A. Taking the horizontal axis as rate of activity over the year and the vertical axis as *total cost* or *revenue,* indicate the pattern or relationship for each of the following items:
   1. Direct-material cost.

2. Federal Social Security tax, as legally assessed, per worker, with workers earning over $15,300 per year, which is the maximum subject to tax.
3. Foremen's salaries.
4. A breakeven chart.
5. Total average unit cost.
6. Mixed costs—for example, electric power *demand charge* plus usage rate.
7. Average versus marginal cost.
8. Depreciation of plant, computed on a straight-line, time basis.
9. Data supporting the use of a variable-cost rate, such as $2 per direct labor-hour.
10. Vacation pay accrued for all workers in a department or plant.
11. Data indicating that an indirect-cost rate based on the given activity measure is spurious.
12. Variable costs *per unit* of output.
13. Incentive bonus plan, operating only above some level of activity.
14. Interest charges on money borrowed to finance acquisition of plant, before any payments on principal.

B. Taking the horizontal axis to represent a time series of weeks during a year and the vertical axis as representing *total cost per week,* match the following items with the relationship shown by the charts:

15. Direct-labor cost under stable production.
16. Direct materials purchased in small quantities during a period of widely fluctuating prices (inventory held at zero).
17. Effect of declining production volume over the year.
18. Result of a shutdown because of vacations, a serious casualty, or complete failure of demand. The shutdown continues to the end of the year.
19. Under- or overapplied factory overhead, taken weekly over the year, when a volume varies widely and the cost rate is assumed to be correct.
20. Seasonal fluctuation in the use of fuel for heating the plant building over the year.

C. Taking the horizontal axis to represent a time series of weeks or months during a year, but the vertical axis to represent *unit-product cost* as determined by conventional methods, that is, by using indirect-cost rates, match the charts with each of the following items:

21. Upward revision during the year of the variable indirect-cost rate, because of changes in price, or other factors, expected to be permanent.
22. Indirect materials acquired for immediate use in small quantities at fluctuating prices.
23. Unusual repair charges caused by careless operation of the machinery.
24. A downward revision of the fixed indirect-cost rate because of greater volume than was anticipated; the higher volume is expected to continue over the rest of the year.

Problems for Part Two

25-16 *Fundamentals of Least Squares* (Adapted from *Separating and Using Costs As Fixed and Variable, N.A.A. Bulletin,* Accounting Practice Report No. 10) Assume that nine monthly observations of power costs are to be used as a basis for developing a budget formula. A scatter diagram indicates a mixed cost behavior in the form $y = a + bx$. The observations are:

MONTH	MACHINE-HOURS	TOTAL MIXED COST
1	22	$ 23
2	23	25
3	19	20
4	12	20
5	12	20
6	9	15
7	7	14
8	11	14
9	14	16
	129	$167

required

Using least squares, compute the equation for the budget formula.

25-17 *Rudiments of Least-Squares Regression Analysis* (H. Nurnberg) ABC Corporation wishes to set flexible budgets for each of its operating departments. A separate maintenance department performs all routine and major repair work on the corporation's equipment and facilities. It has been determined that maintenance cost is primarily a function of machine-hours worked in the various production departments. The actual machine-hours worked and maintenance cost incurred during the first four months of 19_1 are as follows:

	MACHINE-HOURS	MAINTENANCE COST
January	800	$350
February	1,200	350
March	400	150
April	1,600	550

(This example simply illustrates the methods that can be used for determining similar information. If, as in this instance, the number of observations is small, additional analysis should be performed to determine whether the results are reliable.)

required

1. Draw a scatter diagram.
2. Compute variable maintenance cost per machine-hour and fixed maintenance cost per month, consistent with the high-low method.
3. Compute variable maintenance cost per machine-hour and fixed maintenance cost per month, consistent with least-squares regression analysis.
4. Compute the coefficient of determination, the r^2.
5. Compute the standard error of estimate, the s_e. Assume that 1,100 machine-hours are budgeted for May. Compute a point estimate and a prediction interval of maintenance cost for May. Use 95 percent confidence coefficient.
6. The maintenance manager of ABC Corporation questions your computation of variable maintenance cost per machine-hour computed as part of part 3. He argues that maintenance cost per machine is a discretionary fixed cost. Test the validity of his argument. Use 95 percent confidence coefficient.

25-18 *Simple Regression* [Adapted from an illustration in Benjamin Perles and Charles Sullivan, *Freund and Williams' Modern Business Statistics* (Englewood Cliffs, N.J.: Prentice-Hall, Inc., 1969), pp. 288ff.] A random sample of various batch sizes and of recorded direct-labor costs follows:

SIZE OF BATCH	DIRECT-LABOR COST
48	$312
32	164
40	280
34	196
30	200
50	288
26	146
50	361
22	149
43	252

required

1. Prepare a scatter diagram.
2. Using least-squares analysis, compute the equation of the line.
3. Compute the coefficient of determination.
4. What is the level of fixed costs at zero activity? Explain fully.

25-19 *Simple Least Squares* (SIA) The annual sales of the Major Department Store, Limited, are being analyzed for sales-forecasting purposes.

Results for the past six years are:

	$ MILLIONS
19_4	8
19_5	11
19_6	9
19_7	10
19_8	11
19_9	12

required

Estimate the sales expected in 19_0 by the least-squares method.

25-20 *Perform Least-Squares Analysis* (SIA, adapted) The GH Manufacturing Company makes a product called Z. Some of the manufacturing expenses are easily identified as fixed or directly variable with production. The cost accountant of the company is confronted with the problem of preparing a flexible budget for the coming year and wishes to determine the fixed and variable elements of the semivariable manufacturing expenses.

The following details are provided for the first ten months of the past year:

MONTH	NUMBER OF UNITS PRODUCED	SEMIVARIABLE MANUFACTURING OVERHEAD
1	1,500	$ 800
2	2,000	1,000
3	3,000	1,350
4	2,500	1,250
5	3,000	1,300
6	2,500	1,200
7	3,500	1,400
8	3,000	1,250
9	2,500	1,150
10	1,500	800

required

Determine by simple regression the fixed and variable elements of the semi-variable manufacturing overhead based on the first ten months of the past year.

25-21 *Least-Squares Estimate of Sales* (SIA, adapted) Sales of the Popular Manufacturing Co., Ltd., for the past 11 years have been:

	SALES (IN THOUSANDS OF DOLLARS)
19_8	30
19_9	40
19_0	60
19_1	70
19_2	70
19_3	90
19_4	100
19_5	110
19_6	120
19_7	140
19_8	140

required

By the method of least squares, determine the annual trend equation of sales for the company.

Hint: Let the origin be the midpoint in time, 19_3. Then 19_2 is -1 and 19_4 is $+1$, and so on. The values of x in the first half of the series offset the positive values in the second half. In this way, the normal equations to be solved become

$$\Sigma y = na \qquad \text{and} \qquad \Sigma xy = bx^2$$

25-22 *Forecasting Sales at Different Locations* (SIA, adapted) Sellman Department Stores Ltd. have 40 retail outlets across Canada. Studies covering stores in cities with a population of 10,000 to 400,000 show a definite relationship between sales and population.

The following data have been developed:

1. y (annual sales) = \$200,000 + $5X$, where X is the population
2. s_e = \$20,000
3. r = .85

Market surveys have been made in two cities in which the company does not have stores, and you have been asked to forecast potential sales for each of the proposed locations. The population in City A is 200,000; in City B, 500,000.

required

1. What sales would you anticipate in City A with 95 percent confidence in your results?
2. Forecast the sales for City B and state what degree of reliability you would put in these results.

25-23 *Explaining a Multiple-Regression Equation* (G. Benston) Assume that a cost recorded in a week is a function of such specified factors as x_1 = units of output, x_2 = number of units in a batch, and x_3 = the ratio of the number of luxury units to total units produced. The expected cost for any given week is $C = 100 + 30x_1 - 20x_2 + 500x_3$.

required

1. What is the marginal cost of producing an additional unit of output?
2. The coefficient for x_2 is negative. Why? Explain fully.

25-24 *Predicting Cash Balances* (CMA) Jackson Co. is experiencing cash-management problems. In particular, they have been unable to determine their temporary cash needs on a timely basis. This has increased the cost of borrowing, because they have often been unable to obtain desirable terms. Borrowing in advance would give them better terms at a lower cost. A review of the cash flows indicates that all factors can be adequately predicted except the expenditures for hourly payroll and certain other expenditures. The cash receipts can be accurately determined, because Jackson's customers are all reliable and pay on an identifiable schedule within the two calendar months following the sale. The payments for raw materials are similarly predictable, because they are all paid in the calendar month subsequent to the purchase. Disbursements for monthly fixed obligations, such as lease payments, salaried personnel, etc., are known well in advance of the payment dates.

In an attempt to better forecast cash changes for the next month, the company conducted a statistical analysis of many possible variables that might be suitable as a basis for forecasting the expenditure for payroll and other items. This analysis revealed a high correlation between the advance sales orders received in a month and those expenditures in the next month. The following relationships useful for cash forecasting have been identified (n = the forecast month):

1. Collections on account:

$$C_n = .9S_{n-1} + .1S_{n-2}, \qquad \text{where } S = \text{sales}$$

2. Disbursements for raw-material purchases:

$$D_n = R_{n-1}, \qquad \text{where } R = \text{raw-material purchases}$$

3. Monthly fixed obligations:

$$F_n = \$400{,}000$$

4. Payroll and other expenditures:

$$P_n = .25A_{n-1} + \$70{,}000, \qquad \text{where } A = \text{advance sales orders}$$

Coefficient of correlation	= .96
Standard error of the estimate	= 10,000
Standard error of the regression coefficient of the independent variable	= .0013
t-statistic for 95% confidence interval	= 2.07

required

1. Estimate the change in the cash balance for July 19_5 using the relationships specified above and the following data:

	SALES (S)	*RAW-MATERIAL PURCHASES (R)*	*ADVANCE SALES ORDERS (A)*
April	$1,300,000	$300,000	$1,225,000
May	1,200,000	400,000	1,050,000
June	1,000,000	350,000	1,400,000

2. Revise your estimate of the change in cash to recognize the uncertainty associated with the payroll and other expenditures.
3. How could management use this information to study alternative plans to reduce the short-term borrowing costs?

25-25 *Choosing a Prediction Method* (CMA, adapted) The Ramon Co. manufactures a wide range of products at several different plant locations. The Franklin Plant, which manufactures electrical components, has been experiencing some difficulties with fluctuating monthly overhead costs. The fluctuations have made it difficult to estimate the level of overhead that will be incurred for any one month.

Management wants to be able to estimate overhead costs accurately in order to plan its operation and financial needs better. A trade association publication to which Ramon Co. subscribes indicates that, for companies manufacturing electrical components, overhead tends to vary with direct-labor hours.

One member of the accounting staff has proposed that the cost behavior pattern of the overhead costs be determined. Then overhead costs could be predicted from the budgeted direct-labor hours.

Another member of the accounting staff suggested that a good starting place for determining the cost behavior pattern of overhead costs would be an analysis of historical data. The historical cost behavior pattern would provide a basis for estimating future overhead costs. The methods proposed for determining the cost behavior pattern included the high-low method, the scattergraph method, simple linear regression, and multiple regression. Of these methods Ramon Co. decided to employ the high-low method, the scattergraph method, and simple linear regression. Data on direct-labor hours and the respective overhead costs incurred were collected for the previous two years. The raw data follow:

	19_3		19_4	
	DIRECT-LABOR HOURS	OVERHEAD COSTS	DIRECT-LABOR HOURS	OVERHEAD COSTS
January	20,000	$84,000	21,000	$86,000
February	25,000	99,000	24,000	93,000
March	22,000	89,500	23,000	93,000
April	23,000	90,000	22,000	87,000
May	20,000	81,500	20,000	80,000
June	19,000	75,500	18,000	76,500
July	14,000	70,500	12,000	67,500
August	10,000	64,500	13,000	71,000
September	12,000	69,000	15,000	73,500
October	17,000	75,000	17,000	72,500
November	16,000	71,500	15,000	71,000
December	19,000	78,000	18,000	75,000

Using linear regression, the following data were obtained:

Coefficient of determination	.9109
Coefficient of correlation	.9544
Coefficients of regression equation	
Constant	39,859
Independent variable	2.1549
Standard error of the estimate	2,840
Standard error of the regression coefficient for the independent variable	.1437
True *t*-statistic for a 95% confidence interval (22 degrees of freedom)	2.074

required

1. Using the high-low method, determine the cost behavior pattern of the overhead costs for the Franklin Plant.
2. Using the results of the regression analysis, calculate the estimate of overhead costs for 22,500 direct-labor hours.
3. Of the three proposed methods (high-low, scattergraph, linear regression), which one should Ramon Co. employ to determine the historical cost behavior pattern of Franklin Plant's overhead costs? Explain your answer completely, indicating the reasons why the other methods should not be used.

25-26 *Analysis of Regression Results* (J. Demski) Ralph's Division (RD) is, for your convenience, a two-product, two-department firm. The two departments are code-named I and II, and the two products are designated A and B. Ralph's first problem is to determine a satisfactory production schedule; in thinking about this problem, he decides to analyze the firm's overhead structure. The accountant tells him that manufacturing overhead averages "about $9 per *direct-labor hour.*" The accountant also supplies Ralph with the following data for the ten most recent *quarters.*

RD OVERHEAD AND VOLUME DATA

Period	DL hours in Dept. I	Overhead in Dept. I	DL Hours in Dept. II	Overhead in Dept. II	Total DL Hours	Total Overhead
1	984	$12,600	1,841	$13,200	2,825	$25,800
2	967	11,500	2,143	17,000	3,110	28,500
3	710	9,200	1,980	15,500	2,690	24,700
4	1,040	11,900	1,610	11,200	2,650	23,100
5	1,015	11,650	1,485	10,600	2,500	23,250
6	940	11,200	2,160	17,300	3,100	28,500
7	950	11,000	1,600	11,100	2,550	22,100
8	640	8,400	2,100	16,900	2,740	25,300
9	680	8,600	1,940	15,400	2,620	24,000
10	1,018	11,980	1,567	11,200	2,585	23,180

A computer program has been used to analyze these data. The results are:

DEPENDENT VARIABLE	*INDEPENDENT VARIABLE*	*COEFFICIENT*	*STANDARD ERROR*	*T-VALUE*	*ADJUSTED* R^2
6	1	8.51	1.40	6.1	
	3	10.09	.83	12.1	
	Intercept	−1,357	2,471	−.6	
					.94
Std. error of estimate,		538			
2	1	9.47	.85	11.1	
	Intercept	2,337	777	3.0	
					.93
Std. error of estimate,		392			
4	3	10.59	.49	21.6	
	Intercept	−5,579	915	−6.1	
					.98
Std. error of estimate,		382			
6	5	10.03	.87	11.5	
	Intercept	−2,617	2,404	−1.1	
					.94
Std. error of estimate,		565			

A correlation matrix shows:

VARIABLE	*1*	*2*	*3*	*4*	*5*	*6*
1	1.00	.97	−.56	.61	.05	−.06
2	.97	1.00	−.47	.54	.13	.03
3	−.56	−.47	1.00	.99	.81	.85
4	−.61	−.54	.99	1.00	.76	.82
5	.05	.13	.80	.76	1.00	.97
6	−.06	.03	.85	.82	.97	1.00

required

1. After surveying these results, Ralph picks the model relating total manufacturing overhead to total direct-labor hours. State (indicating intercept and slope values and independent variable) the model Ralph is proposing to use and give a *one-sentence* interpretation of the coefficients.
2. Ralph, filling with confidence, calls an accounting friend to show him this model. Regardless of your answer to (a), suppose Ralph submits a model having a negative intercept. The friend inquires about the negative intercept, and Ralph (being none too confident) is subsequently shattered when he is informed (by technical personnel) that actual manufacturing cost for any quarter with zero production will be approximately \$4,000. How, in *one sentence,* do you reconcile (or compare) the \$4,000 datum with the negative regression intercept?
3. Suppose Ralph now obtains relevant data and runs a regression relating the cost of direct material *in A* to units of Product A. The results are

$$\widehat{(\text{DM Cost})}_A = \underset{(98.2)}{-407.8} + \underset{(1.01)}{3.14A} \qquad R^2 = .83$$

Provide Ralph with a *one-sentence* interpretation of the negative intercept.

25-27 *Analysis of Regression Results* (J. Demski) Ralph's Sauna, Ltd., is a manufacturer of custom electronic instruments and analog computer components. All "jobs" are manufactured to customer specification; the firm is, in fact, a classic example of the job shop. The firm has become interested in its cost function and is in the process of attempting to estimate its manufacturing overhead cost. A single manufacturing department was focused on and the following data were obtained (for the most recent 16 months):

TOTAL DEPARTMENTAL OVERHEAD	*TOTAL DIRECT-LABOR HOURS*	*MATERIAL UNITS*	*ORDERS PROCESSED*
\$25,835	878 hours	970 Units	88 Orders
27,451	1,088	934	100
28,611	1,281	667	108
32,361	1,340	1,243	110
28,967	1,090	964	90
24,817	1,067	903	67
29,795	1,188	876	88
26,135	928	820	28
31,361	1,319	984	19
26,006	790	933	90
27,812	934	966	93
28,612	871	940	87
22,992	781	518	81
31,836	1,236	1,017	236
26,252	902	881	92
26,977	1,140	751	140

A computer program has been used to analyze these data. The results are:

DEPENDENT VARIABLE	INDEPENDENT VARIABLE	COEFFICIENT	STANDARD ERROR	T-VALUE	ADJUSTED R^2
1	2	8.50	1.93	4.4	
	3	6.95	2.21	3.2	
	4	6.59	7.19	.9	
	Intercept	12,052	2,286	5.3	
					.76
Std. error of estimate,		1,281			
1	2	8.88	1.87	4.7	
	3	7.06	2.19	3.2	
	Intercept	12,190	2,267	5.4	
					.76
Std. error of estimate,		1,273			
1	2	10.98	2.27	4.8	
	Intercept	16,310	2.421	6.7	
					.60
Std. error of estimate,		1,646			
1	3	10.68	3.26	3.27	
	Intercept	18,277	2.98	6.14	
					.39
Std. error of estimate		2,027			

A correlation matrix shows:

	OVERHEAD	LABOR	MATERIAL	ORDERS
OVERHEAD	1.0000			
LABOR	.7913	1.0000		
MATERIAL	.6580	.3489	1.0000	
ORDERS	.3253	.2420	.1324	1.0000

required

1. (a) Develop, (b) present, and (c) defend what you think is the most "reasonable" estimate of the recently experienced manufacturing overhead cost function.
2. Interpret the coefficients and independent variable (or variables) in your above answer.
3. Do you think your answer in part 1 would also provide a "useful" prediction of the manufacturing overhead that might be experienced next month?
4. For what purposes do you think management might use your answer in part 1?

25-28 *Selecting an Order* (Prepared by J. Demski) Z Company has excess production capacity. The manager is trying to decide between two orders, one for 300 units of Product G at $38 each and the second for 200 units of Product H at $54 each. The cost predictions per unit are:

	DIRECT MATERIALS	DIRECT LABOR	FACTORY OVERHEAD	TOTAL
G	$20	$6	$12	$38
H	30	8	16	54

Five hundred machine-hours of capacity are going to be idle next year, so they could be utilized for producing one of these products. Factory overhead is applied at a rate of $8 per machine-hour. Nonmanufacturing costs will not be allocated to either order. Freight costs will be borne by the purchaser.

Further examination of the accounting indicates that the $8 per machine-hour is a firmwide rate that reflects allocations of central management overhead. Listed below are data relating to actual overhead expenditures for the particular producing facilities concerned. The underlying relationships and levels of expenditures are expected to remain essentially the same during the coming period.

TOTAL FACTORY OVERHEAD EXPENDITURES	*PRODUCTION OF G*	*PRODUCTION OF H*	*MACHINE-HOURS*
$12,935	169 units	41 units	1,279 hrs.
25,918	306 units	366 units	4,559 hrs.
31,821	371 units	453 units	5,947 hrs.
26,367	270 units	480 units	5,045 hrs.
20,513	375 units	166 units	3,486 hrs.
31,736	258 units	513 units	5,737 hrs.

required | Which order should be accepted? Explain, showing computations.

25-29 *Special Order and Breakeven Analysis* (Prepared by G. Feltham) The Holman Company manufactures a synthetic fiber that can be sold in its raw state or chemically impregnated and manufactured into cloth. The demand for the cloth has been spotty in the past, but Holman's prime customer (and usually the only one) has offered to sign a contract for 9,000 bolts per month at a price of $160 per bolt. This would be a 12-month contract, and if Holman does not accept it, the customer will go elsewhere. The Holman Company must decide whether to accept this contract and has accumulated the following information:

a. The demand for fiber has been weak during the past year, but the marketing manager believes that the company can sell 20,000 units per month at $80 per unit during the coming year. (A unit of fiber is the amount required to produce one bolt of cloth.)
b. The company has two production facilities, and each has a 10,000-unit capacity. The standard cost of a unit of fiber in each of these facilities is given below:

	A	*B*
Materials	$20	$20
Labor	10	12
Overhead (300% of labor)	30	36
Total	$60	$68

c. Facility B may be used to produce cloth instead of fiber. If B is used to produce cloth, the capacity is 10,000 bolts and the standard cost of a bolt of cloth is:

Cost of fiber produced in Facility A	$ 60
Additional materials	10
Additional direct labor	15
Overhead	45
Total	$130

Facility B will be used to produce either fiber or cloth, but not both.

d. The overhead rate is based on the labor costs and overhead incurred during the previous year. The monthly data plus the total production (units of fiber plus bolts of cloth) are given below:

MONTH	TOTAL OVERHEAD (THOUSANDS)	TOTAL PRODUCTION (THOUSANDS)	LABOR COST (THOUSANDS)
1	$ 585	19	$ 208
2	515	13	160
3	535	15	166
4	590	18	225
5	570	17	215
6	545	14	150
7	585	20	220
8	530	16	200
9	540	16	178
10	495	10	125
11	505	13	138
12	565	17	205
Total	$6,560	188	$2,190

required

1. Will acceptance or rejection of the contract yield the highest profits? Present the analysis that supports your answer.
2. What level of sales is required to break even if only fiber can be sold?
3. What level of sales is required to break even if only cloth can be sold?

25-30 *Predicting How Costs Will Vary* (J. Demski) You are to determine a set of equations that will be useful for predicting the manner in which certain costs will vary. Listed below are three costs—production overhead, direct production, and marketing—along with five possible independent variables. Determine a "satisfactory" prediction model for each of the three costs. Determine each one separately, and defend your selection. (Note that labor quantity and production quantity are highly correlated; also, marketing is totally separate from production.)

	(1) OVERHEAD	(2) DIRECT	(3) MARKETING	(4) DIRECT-LABOR INPUT	(5) PRODUCTION QUANTITY	(6) SALES QUANTITY	(7) PRODUCTION LESS PRODUCTION LAST PERIOD	(8) PRODUCTION LESS PRODUCTION LAST PERIOD, THE QUANTITY SQUARED
1	$11,719	$1,035	$604	81.9	76	100	−24	576
2	11,190	1,071	582	85.5	79	95	3	9
3	11,860	871	565	65.1	70	70	−9	81
4	19,225	1,756	735	132.3	136	136	66	4,356
5	12,876	1,618	591	127.9	125	109	−11	121
6	11,922	1,725	387	130.3	128	91	3	9
7	12,261	1,698	622	124.9	125	105	−3	9
8	11,747	1,804	355	143.8	133	83	8	64
9	11,747	1,725	696	135.1	124	122	−9	81
10	12,057	1,699	609	126.6	129	113	5	25
11	12,771	1,477	636	120.1	115	94	−14	196
12	12,575	1,060	748	83.1	84	104	−31	961
13	11,034	1,088	666	90.9	84	92	0	0
14	14,316	1,597	551	122.4	122	91	38	1,444
15	13,380	1,148	537	89.1	90	100	−32	1,024

25-31 *Choosing from Among Independent Variables* (J. Demski) Data relating overhead cost to possible independent variables have been collected for the ten most recent periods and are presented below. Determine an equation that you feel would be useful in predicting the dependent variable (overhead cost) for the coming period. Your answer should contain the equation and the reason you feel it is the most appropriate alternative.

PERIOD	*OVERHEAD COST*	*PRODUCTION (UNITS OF A)*	*PRODUCTION (UNITS OF B)*	*PRODUCTION (UNITS OF C)*
1	$7,792	8	67	45
2	1,514	0	16	45
3	1,189	12	11	57
4	6,670	5	70	64
5	3,912	12	37	31
6	3,313	12	30	44
7	7,857	5	98	65
8	1,810	6	20	66
9	8,435	1	76	76
10	2,671	13	24	53

25-32 *Effects of Overtime* (J. Demski) Ralph Larutan produces a natural food product, consisting mainly of prunes and pig hocks, that is nationally marketed under the tradename Natural (which is Larutan spelled backwards). A highly placed government official has asked Ralph to produce 100 bushels of a special blend of new Natural to be used in a special government program. This extra quantity will not alter Ralph's present demand, and the only issue is whether the offered price of $5,000 is sufficient for Ralph to accept the offer.

Ralph collects the following production-cost data:

Standard material cost per bushel	= $20
Standard labor cost (at $10/hour) per bushel	= $10
Overhead	= $20
Standard cost per bushel	$50

Where the overhead standard is based on recent monthly experiences of overhead averaging about $20 per labor-hour (at an average of about 1,000 labor-hours per month). Selling costs average about $10 per bushel, but these will not be incurred if the government's offer is accepted.

Ralph is relatively certain of the material- and labor-cost components but is bothered by the overhead. In particular, he realizes that the $20 datum is but an average that may be far removed from actual incremental shifts. Moreover, he also knows that this particular order, if accepted, will have to be produced on an overtime schedule, necessitating time and one-half labor payments.

One question, then, concerns predicting the cost of processing this order for 100 bushels of new Natural. Ralph feels that a linear approximation to the overhead cost function is sufficiently accurate for analysis of this decision; he also feels that labor-hours is a defensible independent variable. Hence, he collects the monthly data displayed in the accompanying table (from the 15 most recent months) and obtains the following regression result:

$$\widehat{\text{OUHD}} = \underset{(2{,}902)}{12{,}475} + \underset{(2.7)}{8.2}\ (\text{DL hrs}) \qquad R^2 \text{ adj} = .38$$

These results are somewhat disappointing, because Ralph expected a better fit; and he thought that the actual overhead rate was closer to (a slope of) $10 per DL hour.

RALPH'S RECENT OVERHEAD DATA

Total Overhead	Total DL Hours	Regular-time DL Hours	Overtime DL Hours
$21,358	976	879	97
18,747	1,038	951	87
22,114	1,194	1,049	145
23,275	1,187	1,091	96
19,416	983	927	56
23,009	1,418	1,320	98
21,229	1,059	950	109
24,664	1,162	1,079	83
20,952	833	781	52
21,445	1,132	1,013	119
21,254	1,107	1,021	86
23,864	1,202	1,138	64
20,397	1,153	1,056	97
20,155	873	735	138
17,617	911	846	65

required

1. What is the literal interpretation of the regression coefficients in the above equation?
2. What, using these predictions, is the full absorption cost and the direct (variable) cost per bushel of Natural?
3. What is the literal interpretation of each datum given in part 2? A two-sentence answer will suffice.
4. What is the predicted incremental gain to Ralph if he accepts the government's offer?
5. At this point, Ralph begins to stop placing so much faith in his accounting data. In particular, he knows that overtime premiums are generally lumped into overhead. (Check the data again.) Assuming this to be the case, would the 8.2 regression coefficients be biased? If your answer is yes, you should also state the *direction* of the bias.
6. Ralph also feels that other additional costs—besides the labor premium—are incurred by overtime production. Diseconomies in maintenance provide an example. Are the data consistent with Ralph's hypothesis? Give a one-sentence answer in support of your position.
7. Do you think Ralph's hypothesis (in part 6 above) is incorrect? Why?

Variances: Mix, Yield, and Investigation

26

A principal function of comparing results with plans is to help explain what has happened. In this way, the user improves his or her comprehension of the impact of key variables on the actual results and acquires some feeling about areas that deserve more investigation. In short, the user may employ variance analysis to decide what additional information, if any, to buy. For example, a large variance may indicate a high probability that there will be a net benefit from conducting an investigation and gathering more data.

This chapter surveys some major areas of the analysis of accounting variances that have been covered only briefly, if at all, in earlier chapters. Three subjects are discussed: (a) the analysis of sales-mix variances, (b) the analysis of production-yield variances, and (c) the problem of when to investigate variances. Each subject can be studied independently, so the chapter is divided into three major parts.

PART ONE: SALES-MIX VARIANCES

Most organizations produce more than one product or service. Therefore, overall plans for revenue usually specify some combination (often called *mix*) of products to be sold. Managers often want help in tracing deviations from original plans. We are already familiar with how price, efficiency, and volume variances assist in this regard for *individual* products or services. Now we explore the complications that may arise at the individual and aggregate levels when the mix differs from the original plan.

The accounting literature on variance analysis in multiple-product situations is sizable and bewildering.[1] Every author and every organization seems to have a pet way of attacking the problem. Therefore, the first point is: be on guard whenever you see the terms "mix variance" or "yield variance." In any situation be sure that all parties discussing such variances agree regarding definitions of all variances.

product-by-product analysis

Consider the analysis of budgeted and actual results in Exhibit 26-1. As a manager, you have prepared a budget; inevitably, the actual net income differs from the budget. This total variance between budgeted and actual net income is explained in a variety of ways in practice. The simplest, most informative analysis usually concentrates on a product-by-product analysis that has three components: price, efficiency, and volume variances. Brief definitions follow:

> *Price variance*—the difference between budgeted unit prices and actual unit prices for goods sold (or goods or services acquired).
>
> *Efficiency variance*—the difference between the actual inputs and the inputs that should have been allowed (budgeted) *for any actual output,* multiplied by some standard price.
>
> *Volume variance*—the difference between some initial or original budgeted or expected output and the *actual output,* multiplied by some standard price.

A major purpose of computing price variances is to exclude the often confusing effects of price fluctuations from other variances. Both the above definitions of efficiency and volume variances have a major underlying assumption in common. *All unit prices are standard, budgeted, or predetermined prices.*

All the variances in Exhibit 26-1 can be labeled as being caused by changes in sales *volume;* in brief, they are volume variances. There are no price or efficiency variances.

[1] For an excursion into chaos, see the suggested readings on mix and yield variances at the end of this chapter, or see Chapter 26 of the third edition of this book. Note that nearly everyone begins from the same place: total variance = actual costs minus some version of budgeted costs, or $v = a - b$. But disagreement arises rapidly when $(a - b)$ is factored so that:

$$(a - b) = (a - a') + (a' - b') + (b' - b)$$

Consensus is hard to obtain regarding how and where a' and b' should be defined.

EXHIBIT 26-1

COMPARISON OF ORIGINAL BUDGET AND ACTUAL RESULTS

	PRODUCT								
	A			*B*			*TOTAL*		
	Budget	Actual	Variance	Budget	Actual	Variance	Budget	Actual	Variance
Sales in units	120,000	110,000	10,000 U	40,000	50,000	10,000 F	160,000	160,000	—
Sales @ \$5 and @ \$10	\$600,000	\$550,000	\$50,000 U	\$400,000	\$500,000	\$100,000 F	\$1,000,000	\$1,050,000	\$50,000 F
Variable costs @ \$4 and @ \$3	480,000	440,000	40,000 F	120,000	150,000	30,000 U	600,000	590,000	10,000 F
Contribution margin @ \$1 and @ \$7	\$120,000	\$110,000	\$10,000 U	\$280,000	\$350,000	\$ 70,000 F	\$ 400,000	\$ 460,000	\$60,000 F

use by managers Consider the appropriate variance analysis at three levels of management: (1) the individual product manager, (2) the manager of the two-product line consisting of A plus B, (3) higher management in a vast company that markets numerous product lines.

The individual managers of Products A and B will be primarily concerned with why their volume levels differed from their individual budgets. We have discussed this type of variance analysis before (Chapter 8).

The manager of the A-B product line may concentrate on the "total" columns. In particular, notice that the total columns offer the manager only an analytical beginning. First, note that the budgeted and actual aggregated physical units were equal. So what? Adding physical units together often offers a summed hodgepodge. For example, Product A may be shaving lotion and Product B may be shampoo. The point is that as we move beyond a one-product situation, aggregated physical units fail to provide a common denominator for measuring overall volume. Instead, physical units are converted into monetary equivalents such as sales dollars. But we should not lose sight of the fact that the fundamental inputs and outputs of organizations are physical goods or services.

Second, the aggregated dollars give an overall picture of the product line, but decisions typically must focus on individual products. The variances in the total columns are merely the sums of the individual product volume variances.

Third, there is enormous confusion in practice regarding the $50,000 and $60,000 total variances. Taken together, the **total volume in units** was unchanged, but the original proportions or mix changed. That is why this total variance is sometimes called something else, or some of it is called a mix variance while the remainder is called a volume variance. No matter what the label, the fundamental explanation is that the physical volumes of individual products deviated from what was expected. Obviously, if the original budget in total units is attained, but a larger proportion of higher-margin products are sold than was specified in the original mix, higher profits will ensue.

Fourth, if the product-line manager really wants a full explanation, he must buy more information. That is, he must get the individual product analyses contained in the other columns. This is not a trivial point. Many accounting systems do not routinely prepare current reports by individual products, so the manager may have to work with only the totals in dollars (not even including the total physical units).

higher managers Higher managers usually receive summary monetary figures rather than being flooded with too much detail. Occasionally, using the summary signals generated by variance analysis, higher managers will buy more information by requesting the underlying disaggregated analyses.

Thus, higher managers would probably receive only the dollar totals (not the physical units) in the total column in Exhibit 26-1.

What does higher management learn from such numbers? All variances are favorable. That is comforting! But why? Did physical volume of each product rise by 5 percent? Or did the sales of higher-margined items soar while the lower-margined items merely met targeted levels? Again, the higher managers will never know unless they obtain a product-by-product breakdown. Of course, higher managers frequently may be satisfied with the aggregated data as shown; they may prefer to have subordinates conduct the detailed follow-up.

mix and quantity variance Thus far, we have suggested that the $60,000 should be labeled a volume variance. If we insist on splitting the volume variance into subdivisions of mix and quantity, the rationale shown below has some appeal. For the moment, concentrate on the contribution margin. (The same analysis can be performed in terms of sales dollars; the principles are unaffected.)

Quantity variance = (Actual volume − Budgeted volume in units) × Budgeted average contribution margin per unit

For A:	= (110,000 − 120,000) × $2.50	=	$25,000 U
For B:	= (50,000 − 40,000) × $2.50	=	25,000 F
Total			$ 0

Mix variance = Difference in units (as above) × (Budgeted individual contribution margin per unit − Budgeted average contribution margin per unit)

For A:	= (110,000 − 120,000) × ($1.00 − $2.50)	=	$15,000 F
For B:	= (50,000 − 40,000) × ($7.00 − $2.50)	=	45,000 F
Total			$60,000 F

For *quantity-variance purposes,* observe that this method weights all physical units at a single overall weighted-average budgeted contribution margin per unit. For a given change in physical volume, the total contribution margin would be expected to change at the rate of the average unit margin ($400,000 ÷ 160,000 units, or $2.50 in the example).

However, for *mix-variance purposes,* this method measures the impact of the deviation from the budgeted average contribution margin per unit associated with a change in the quantity of a particular product. The actual mix produced a weighted-average unit contribution of $2.875:

	UNITS SOLD	BUDGETED UNIT CONTRIBUTION MARGIN	ACTUAL CONTRIBUTION AT BUDGETED MARGINS
A	110,000	$1.00	$110,000
B	50,000	7.00	350,000
	160,000		$460,000

Weighted average = $460,000 ÷ 160,000 = $2.875

Therefore, the unit margins attained were \$.375 higher than the \$2.50 budgeted. Thus, the mix variance would be 160,000 units at \$.375 each, the same \$60,000 computed above.

If the original mix were maintained, but physical volume increased by 5 percent, there would be no mix variance, only a quantity variance. The actual sales would be 126,000 units of A and 42,000 of B. The quantity variance would be:

For A:	= (126,000 − 120,000) × \$2.50 =	\$15,000 F
For B:	= (42,000 − 40,000) × \$2.50 =	5,000 F
		\$20,000 F

This would be consistent with the idea that, given an unchanging mix, a 5 percent increase in physical volume should produce a 5 percent increase in sales dollars and a 5 percent increase in contribution margin. The budgeted contribution margin would increase from \$400,000 to \$420,000, or the \$20,000 increase calculated above.

Of course, various combinations can be tested so that both quantity and mix variances would be positive. But this author sees little analytical advantage in subdividing the volume variance into quantity and mix components as described above. The details of the volume variance tell the manager the full story in a more straightforward manner:

Volume variance = Difference in units × Budgeted individual contribution per unit

For A:	= (110,000 − 120,000) × \$1.00 =	\$10,000 U
For B:	= (50,000 − 40,000) × \$7.00 =	70,000 F
Total		\$60,000 F

Thus, if higher managers want more details about the \$60,000 variance, they can be given the product breakdown as a start. It tells them that less A was sold than budgeted, causing the total contribution margin to be \$10,000 lower than budgeted. On the other hand, as shown above, the higher-margined B more than made up for A's shortfall.

sales mix and p/v charts

Reconsider Exhibit 26-1. Suppose that the total fixed costs were \$300,000. What would be the breakeven point? The usual answer assumes that the budgeted mix will not change—that is, that volume is measured in units that consist of a combination of $\frac{120}{160}$ of A and $\frac{40}{160}$ of B, or 3 A for every 1 B. As the last columns of Exhibit 26-1 show, the contribution to income of each "unit" averages \$400,000 ÷ 160,000, or \$2.50. Therefore, the breakeven point is:

\$300,000 ÷ \$2.50 = 120,000 units (consisting of 90,000 A and 30,000 B)

But the breakeven point is not a unique number. It obviously depends on the composition of sales volume. For example, suppose only A (its unit contribution margin is $1) were sold:

$300,000 ÷ $1.00 = 300,000 units (consisting exclusively of A)

Similarly, if only B (its contribution margin is $7) were sold:

$300,000 ÷ $7.00 = 42,857 units (consisting exclusively of B)

These breakeven relationships are shown in Exhibit 26-2, which is a P/V chart (a profit-volume graph):

1. The vertical axis is net income in dollars. The horizontal axis is volume, which may be expressed in units or in sales dollars.
2. At zero volume, the net loss is $300,000, the total fixed costs.
3. A net-profit line will slope upward from the −$300,000 intercept at the rate of how many dollars are contributed to income by each unit increase in volume.

The top graph shows the income effects of A, sold alone, with its contribution to income of $1.00 per unit and a breakeven point of 300,000 units. The middle graph shows the similar effects of B, taken alone. The bottom graph highlights the basic assumption of what "volume" means when plans are based on a specified combination of products. **Then volume, whether expressed as units or as sales dollars, is assumed to fluctuate without changing the assumed combination or mix of the components.** The dashed line is based on a contribution margin for each "package" of product (3 A plus 1 B), which provides 3($1) + 1($7), or $10. The average contribution per unit of product would be $10 ÷ 4 units in each package = $2.50.

In sum, cost-volume-profit analysis must be done carefully, because so many initial assumptions may not hold. When the assumed combinations change, the breakeven point and the expected net incomes at various volume levels also change. Of course, the breakeven points are frequently incidental data. Instead, the focus is on the effects on net income under various production and sales strategies.

PROBLEM FOR SELF-STUDY

PROBLEM

Review Exhibit 26-1. Suppose that 113,000 units of Product A and 41,000 units of Product B were sold. Consider the contribution-margin line only. Compute the volume variances for each product and in total. Subdivide the volume variance into quantity variances and mix variances.

SOLUTION

Volume variance = Difference in units × Budgeted individual contribution margin per unit

For A:	= (113,000 − 120,000) × $1.00 =	$7,000 U
For B:	= (41,000 − 40,000) × $7.00 =	7,000 F
Total		0

EXHIBIT 26-2

P/V CHARTS, PRODUCT COMBINATIONS

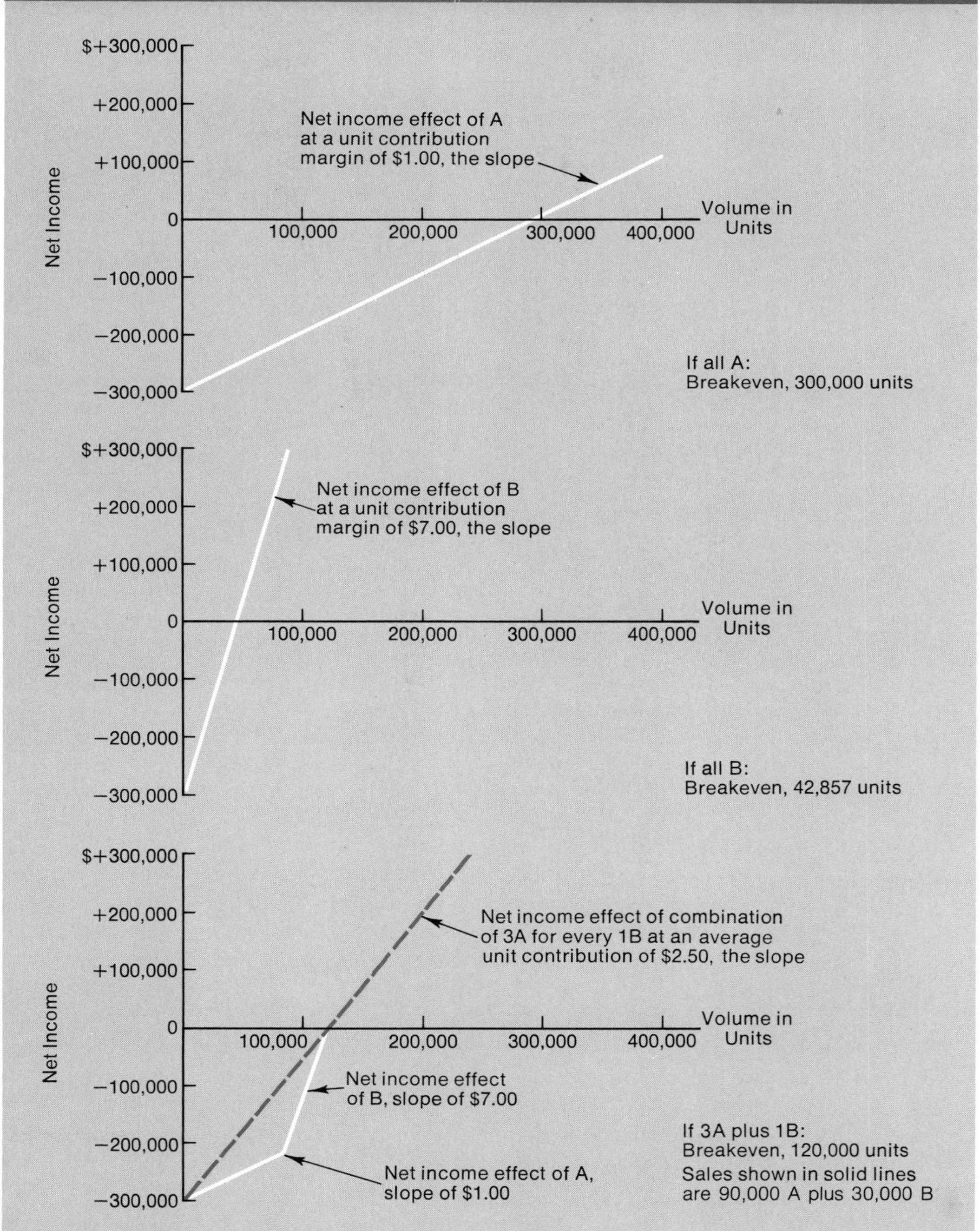

$+300,000
+200,000
+100,000
0
−100,000
−200,000
−300,000
Net Income
Volume in Units
100,000
200,000
300,000
400,000
Net income effect of A at a unit contribution margin of $1.00, the slope
If all A: Breakeven, 300,000 units
Net income effect of B at a unit contribution margin of $7.00, the slope
If all B: Breakeven, 42,857 units
Net income effect of combination of 3A for every 1B at an average unit contribution of $2.50, the slope
Net income effect of B, slope of $7.00
Net income effect of A, slope of $1.00
If 3A plus 1B: Breakeven, 120,000 units
Sales shown in solid lines are 90,000 A plus 30,000 B

Quantity variance = Difference in units × Budgeted average contribution margin per unit

For A:	= (113,000 − 120,000) × $2.50 =	$17,500 U
For B:	= (41,000 − 40,000) × $2.50 =	2,500 F
Total		$15,000 U

Mix variance = Difference in units × (Budgeted individual contribution margin per unit − Budgeted average contribution margin per unit)

For A:	= (113,000 − 120,000) × ($1.00 − $2.50) =	$10,500 F
For B:	= (41,000 − 40,000) × ($7.00 − $2.50) =	4,500 F
Total		$15,000 F

The weighted average unit contribution was $2.5974:

	UNITS SOLD	BUDGETED UNIT CONTRIBUTION MARGIN	ACTUAL CONTRIBUTIONS AT BUDGETED MARGINS
A	113,000	$1.00	$113,000
B	41,000	7.00	287,000
	154,000		$400,000

Weighted average = $400,000 ÷ 154,000 = $2.5974

Therefore, the unit margin attained was $.0974 higher than the $2.50 budgeted. This produced a mix variance of $15,000, which could be computed by multiplying 154,000 units by $.0974.

Also ponder the meaning of the quantity variance. Given an unchanging mix, a failure to attain the budgeted unit quantity of 160,000 units would produce an unfavorable quantity variance of 160,000 − 154,000, or 6,000 units multiplied by the average unit contribution of $2.50, for a total of $15,000.

PART TWO: PRODUCTION-YIELD VARIANCES

the production setting Manufacturing processes often entail the combination of a number of different materials to obtain a unit of finished product, or the use of a single material to produce several joint products. Chemicals, plastics, lumber, fruit, vegetables, rubber, and fabrics, for example, can sometimes be combined in various ways without affecting the specified quality characteristics of a finished product.

What is usually meant by the terms mix and yield? The meaning of each should be pinpointed in a particular setting. In general, *mix* refers to the relative proportion or combination of the various ingredients of direct materials or of the components of a finished product line. *Yield* refers to the quantity of finished output produced from a predetermined or *standard combination and amount of inputs* such as direct material or direct labor.

When we initially discussed material and labor variances in Chapter 7, we pointed out that trade-offs sometimes are made between price and efficiency variances. For example, a cheaper grade of leather may be used if the potential price savings exceed the potential excessive waste (inefficiency). Sometimes humidity, temperature, molecular structure, or other physical characteristics can dramatically affect output; similarly, deliberate changes in combinations of raw materials may be made to save costs. How may we trace these variations in inputs and outputs? As in the case of sales-mix analysis, production-yield analysis is not uniform. Again, be sure of your definitions in a particular situation.

expectations as a frame of reference

Consider a specific example of multiple inputs and a single output. Suppose a company has the following standards:

5 gallons of Material F at	$ .70	=	$3.50
3 gallons of Material G at	1.00	=	3.00
2 gallons of Material H at	.80	=	1.60
10			$8.10 for 10 gallons of standard mix, which should produce 9 gallons of finished product at a standard cost of $.90 ($8.10 ÷ 9) a gallon.

Suppose, for simplicity, that no inventories of raw materials are kept. Purchases are made as needed, so that all price variances relate to materials used. Actual results show that 100,000 gallons were used during a certain period:

45,000 gallons of F at actual cost of	$ .80	=	$36,000
33,000 gallons of G at actual cost of	$1.05	=	34,650
22,000 gallons of H at actual cost of	$ .85	=	18,700
100,000			$89,350
Good output was 92,070 gallons at standard cost of $.90			$82,863

A production manager may want to know why actual results (100,000 gallons of input, 92,070 gallons of output, and a cost of $89,350) deviated from expectations. Therefore, the amount of variance analysis to be conducted depends on what is meant by "expectations."

As a start, suppose the manager is merely interested in nothing more than the usual price and efficiency variances. That is, "expectations" are geared to the output produced. Given any output, a specified level of costs is anticipated.

Using the framework of Chapter 7, we see that the total material variance is analyzed by this twofold distinction.

MATERIAL	ACTUAL INPUTS × ACTUAL PRICES	ACTUAL INPUTS × STANDARD PRICES	STANDARD INPUTS ALLOWED × STANDARD PRICES
F	45,000 × $ .80 = $36,000	45,000 × $ .70 = $31,500	51,150 × $ .70 = $35,805
G	33,000 × $1.05 = 34,650	33,000 × $1.00 = 33,000	30,690 × $1.00 = 30,690
H	22,000 × $ .85 = 18,700	22,000 × $ .80 = 17,600	20,460 × $ .80 = 16,368
Total	$89,350	$82,100	$82,863

Price variance, $7,250 U | Efficiency variance, $763 F

Total variance, $6,487 U

First, concentrate on the total variance. Note that it is computed in the usual way: (actual inputs × actual prices) − [(good output, or standard inputs allowed) × standard prices]. Moreover, the usual way of computing the price and efficiency variances provides a supplementary explanation of where these numbers arose:

The price variances are computed in the usual manner:

Price variance = Difference in unit price × Actual product quantity
For F: = ($ .70 − $ .80) × 45,000 = $4,500 U
For G: = ($1.00 − $1.05) × 33,000 = 1,650 U
For H: = ($ .80 − $ .85) × 22,000 = 1,100 U
$7,250 U

The efficiency variances may also be computed in the usual manner. The differences in inputs are:

MATERIAL	DETAILED COMPUTATIONS FOR COLUMN (1)	(1) BUDGETED OR STANDARD QUANTITY OF INPUTS ALLOWED	(2) ACTUAL QUANTITY OF INPUTS USED	(1) − (2) DIFFERENCE
F	(.5 × 102,300)	51,150	45,000	+6,150
G	(.3 × 102,300)	30,690	33,000	−2,310
H	(.2 × 102,300)	20,460	22,000	−1,540
Total	(10/9 × 92,070)	102,300*	100,000	2,300

* Note that the budgeted input must be that standard combination normally needed to produce 92,070 gallons, or 92,070 ÷ .9, or 102,300 gallons. Material F's budgeted share would be .5 × 102,300, or 51,150 gallons; G's, .3 × 102,300, or 30,690; and so on.

The dollar amounts are:

Efficiency variance[2] = Difference in inputs × Standard price
For F: = +6,150 × $ .70 = $4,305 F
For G: = −2,310 × $1.00 = 2,310 U
For H: = −1,540 × $ .80 = 1,232 U
$ 763 F

[2] In this context the efficiency variance might also be viewed as a mix variance and might be labeled as such. Note that the deviations from the standard combination of allowed material inputs for any given output may be viewed as a change in mix, because the relative proportions are no longer constant. But the input-output relationships of individual materials, considered

meaning of the usual analysis There is little new here, except that three materials are being analyzed simultaneously. The frame of reference is an output standard—that is, the amount of F, G, and H that should have been consumed to obtain the 92,070 gallons of output. If less F is used than expected, given the output, the variance represents a cost saving. The manager may know why less F was used. But he may not know, and he may want to invest in more analysis to discover whether less F was used because of superior controls, quality characteristics, inherent chemical variation, deliberate substitutions, assorted random causes, and so on.

more elaborate analysis The preceding analysis was a typical flexible budgeting and standard costing approach, whereby expectations are a function of good output, whatever it may be. Suppose the manager is not satisfied because the foregoing analysis is incomplete. He wants a more exhaustive analysis, beginning from his initial expectations.

Suppose his initial schedule called for producing 99,000 gallons by introducing 110,000 gallons of inputs. However, because several sales orders were cancelled, only 100,000 gallons were introduced, and expectations were adjusted to 90,000 gallons of output. Actual production, however, was 92,070 gallons at a total material cost of $89,350.

Now, "expectations" can take many forms. They began with a static concept, a target of 99,000 gallons, based on inputs of 110,000 gallons; they were adjusted to 90,000 based on inputs of 100,000; and they were later determined to be 92,070 based on inputs of 102,300. In particular, note that the measure of volume is expressed in two equivalent ways: (a) a gallon of finished product or (b) a *standard combination* of inputs for a gallon of finished product. A graph of these relationships is in Exhibit 26-3.

Exhibits 26-3 and 26-4 underscore a modification of the definition of volume that is usually unnecessary when we analyze production of single raw materials or single products. When various combinations of inputs can affect the total physical volume of output, volume is usually measured by assuming a constant predetermined standard combination of inputs in relation to outputs.

Of course, an elaborate analysis that traces all these relationships can be prepared, as Exhibit 26-4 shows. Because the analysis of direct labor is similar to that for direct materials, it is introduced here—but let us focus first on the materials.

Consider Exhibit 26-4, step by step. Concentrate on the bottom analysis of materials, which splits the entire picture into the familiar price, efficiency, and volume variances. The price and efficiency variances for materials were discussed earlier. Note that the direct-material price and efficiency variances in

one by one, are typically considered as measures of efficiency, because there is no mix concept on a one-by-one basis. Consequently, the term efficiency variance is used throughout this section, because it is more descriptive and it is applicable to both individual-material and multiple-material situations.

columns (1) through (3) are unchanged. We are merely introducing the volume variance in an attempt to show the manager how he got from his initial expectations (column 5) to actual output (column 3). For instance, as shown in both Exhibits 26-3 and 26-4, our initial direct-material budgeted costs of $89,100 fell to $82,863 because volume fell from the targeted 99,000 gallons to the 92,070 gallons produced.

Further, the manager's frame of reference for judging performance may be inputs rather than outputs. That is, if 100,000 *inputs* are placed in process, he expects to get 90,000 outputs. If so, his expectations are shown in column (4). He may gain insight from comparing columns (3) and (4). The *yield variance* for direct materials is $1,863, which also happens to be the vertical distance between $82,863 and $81,000 on the graph in Exhibit 26-3. This *yield variance* is anchored *to the basic assumption that the standard combination of inputs remains unchanged. Given this assumption, it may be defined as the anticipated change in expected cost because output deviated from that expected for the total actual inputs.*

In the case of direct materials, if a standard combination of 100,000 gallons is introduced, the expected material costs are $81,000, because 90,000 gallons of output are expected. If 92,070 gallons of output are produced, the standard combination of inputs would have been 102,300 gallons. Therefore, costs would be expected to be higher.

The "order adjustment variance" is labeled as such in this case to describe the remaining major reason why the initial expectations were not fulfilled. In

EXHIBIT 26-3

RELATIONSHIPS OF INPUTS AND OUTPUTS

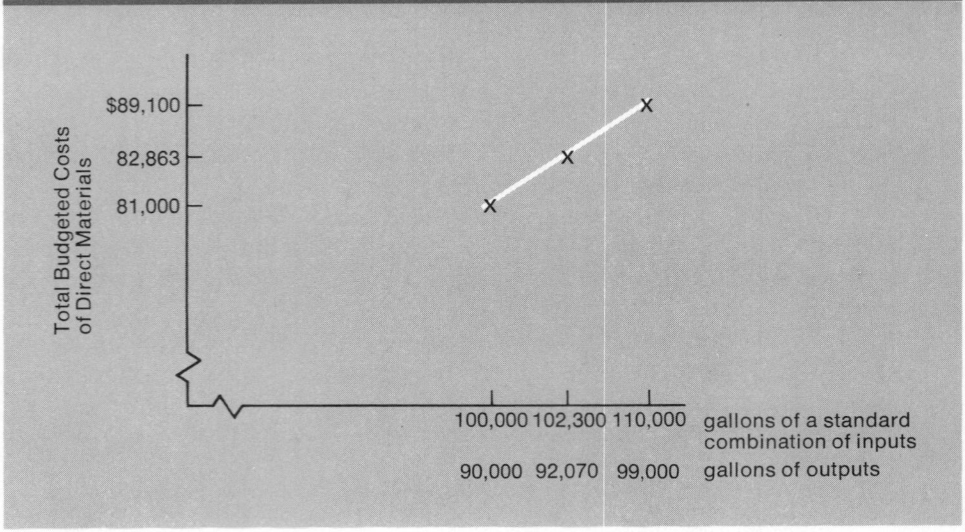

EXHIBIT 26-4

VARIANCE ANALYSIS OF DIRECT-MATERIALS AND DIRECT-LABOR COSTS

	(1) Actual Inputs for Actual Output at Actual Prices	*(2)* Actual Combination of Inputs for Actual Output at Standard Prices	*(3)* Standard Combination of Inputs for Actual Output at Standard Prices	*(4)* Adjusted Expectations: Given Standard Combination of Actual Inputs	*(5)* Initial Expectations: Given Standard Combination of Inputs for Scheduled Outputs
Direct materials:	$89,350	$82,100	92,070 × $.90 or 102,300 × $.81 = $82,863	90,000 × $.90 or 100,000 × $.81 = $81,000	99,000 × $.90 or 110,000 × $.81 = $89,100
	Price variance, $7,250 U	Efficiency variance, $763 F	Yield variance, $1,863 U	Order adjustment variance, $8,100 F	
	Price variance, $7,250 U	Efficiency variance, $763 F	Volume variance, $6,237 F		
Direct labor:	10,000 × $4.10 = $41,000	10,000 × $4.00 = $40,000	9,207 × $4.00 = $36,828	9,000 × $4.00 = $36,000	9,900 × $4.00 = $39,600
	Price variance, $1,000 U	Efficiency variance, 793 hrs. × $4.00 = $3,172 U	Yield variance, 207 hrs. × $4.00 = $828 U	Order adjustment variance, 900 hrs. × $4.00 = $3,600 F	
	Price variance, $1,000 U	Efficiency variance, $3,172 U	Volume variance, $2,772 F		

Note: Columns (3) through (5) are at standard weighted-average unit prices and a standard combination of inputs.

those instances where the initial expectations are never adjusted, columns (4) and (5) will be the same.

The variances for direct labor are computed in the same basic way as the variances for direct materials. The direct labor for processing these materials had the following characteristics, as indicated in Exhibit 26-4: standard price, $4.00 per hour, or $.40 allowed per gallon of output at the standard allowance of 1 hour for every 10 gallons of output. Therefore, for instance, in column (3), the standard allowed hours were 92,070 × .1 hour per gallon, or 9,207 hours; the standard allowed cost for the output would be 9,207 × $4.00, or $36,828. The actual price was $4.10 per hour.

PROBLEM FOR SELF-STUDY

PROBLEM

Review the example on direct-material yield variances. Suppose that 40,000 gallons of G and 15,000 gallons of H were actually used. Compute the total price and total efficiency variances. Explain why the efficiency variance is no longer $763, favorable.

SOLUTION

MATERIAL	*ACTUAL INPUTS × ACTUAL PRICE*	*ACTUAL INPUTS × STANDARD PRICE*	*STANDARD INPUTS ALLOWED × STANDARD PRICE*
F	45,000 × $ .80 = $36,000	45,000 × $ .70 = $31,500	51,150 × $ .70 = $35,805
G	40,000 × $1.05 = 42,000	40,000 × $1.00 = 40,000	30,690 × $1.00 = 30,690
H	15,000 × $ .85 = 12,750	15,000 × $ .80 = 12,000	20,460 × $ .80 = 16,368
	$90,750	$83,500	$82,863

↑ Price variance, $7,250 U* ↑ Efficiency variance, $637 U ↑

* Coincidentally, the price variance of $7,250 is the same as the $7,250 in the original example. This is because both G and H have unfavorable unit-price variances of $.05, and the same total quantities of these were used in each example (55,000).

The efficiency variance of $763, favorable, has become $637, unfavorable, a $1,400 move in the wrong direction, because the new actual combination is less economical than the old actual combination:

INPUTS USED

	Old Combination	New Combination	Difference
F	45,000 × $ .70 = $31,500	45,000 × $ .70 = $31,500	$ 0
G	33,000 × $1.00 = 33,000	40,000 × $1.00 = 40,000	7,000 U
H	22,000 × $ .80 = 17,600	15,000 × $ .80 = 12,000	5,600 F
	100,000 $82,100	100,000 $83,500	$1,400 U

Note that the yield variance would be unaffected; only the combination of inputs has changed, and yield variances are based on an assumption of no change in the standard combination of inputs.

PART THREE: THE DECISION TO INVESTIGATE

Given feedback in the form of routine reports of cost variances, when should managers investigate a process? These variances may lead to investigation or no investigation. In turn, investigation may prompt correction or no correction.

The accounting system often plays a part in these decisions, but it is not an exclusive source of information. Managers obviously do not investigate every variance that arises, line by line. As usual, the decisions are based on layers of simplifications, assumptions, and incomplete knowledge about the relative costs and benefits. This section explores the dimensions of this investigation decision.

types of deviations

Suppose feedback—such as a cost variance—prompts a decision maker to investigate the process. One or more of five separate deviations (that is, sources of variances) might have contributed to this variance between actual and predicted costs: implementation, prediction, measurement, model, and random.[3] These types of deviations are discussed in sequence. Note that each may call for different corrective actions.

1. An *implementation* deviation is a human or mechanical failure to achieve a specific obtainable action. For example, consider the economic-lot-size inventory model, which was discussed in Chapter 14. Perhaps because of improper motivation or instruction, a clerk or worker may order the wrong quantity or produce the wrong size of batch. The economic lot size is assumed to be obtainable, given whatever events may have occurred. Consequently, there is a strong likelihood that the deviation can be immediately suppressed once its existence is determined.

The optimal correction requires that we compare the cost of suppression (which is likely to be minimal) with the resultant saving (benefit). If no other deviations are present, this net saving indicates the expected amount of net benefit (per future period, if this deviation is likely to persist) that will be saved by correction.

2. A *prediction* deviation is an error in predicting a parameter value in the decision model. For example, in an economic-lot-size model, the cost of storage, the cost of a setup, or the total amount of production or materials required in a time period may be incorrectly predicted. (Another example is a discounted cash-flow model for capital budgeting, where perhaps the useful life or the annual cash inflows may be incorrectly predicted.)

Optimal correction in the economic-lot-size model again requires that we compare the cost of adjusting the optimal lot size with the resultant cost saving

[3] Joel S. Demski, *Information Analysis* (Reading, Mass.: Addison-Wesley Publishing Co., Inc., 1972), Chapter 6.

per period. Sensitivity analysis will help the manager to decide the potential net benefits from maintaining a routine monitoring of possible prediction deviations.

3. A *measurement* deviation is an error in measuring the actual cost of operating a process. For example, a worker may incorrectly count the ending inventory, resulting in an erroneous measure of total costs. Note the distinction made here between the prediction of a future cost and the measurement of a past cost. Improper classification, counting, or recording produces such measurement deviations.

Optimal correction usually centers on the problems of obtaining accurate documentation by individual employees as a part of their everyday work habits. As Chapter 6 points out, this is an especially troublesome problem of systems design and motivation that permeates all types of organizations. For example, employees are sometimes encouraged to falsify time records so that the true variances from standards on particular operations are masked.

4. A *model* deviation is an erroneous functional representation or formulation in the decision model. That is, the objective function, variables, or constraints may be incorrectly identified. For example, the failure to include a constraint for maximum storage space may be an error in the formulation of an inventory model. Another example would be the failure to provide for salvage value or interest in a capital-budgeting model.

Note that a model error is not the same as a prediction error. The former pertains to an incorrect functional relationship, while the latter pertains to an incorrect parameter prediction.

Deciding to correct a model error usually necessitates a comparison of the cost of correction with the benefits over many future time periods. In contrast, the decision to correct a parameter prediction involves a similar analysis but typically relates to a shorter time period, because these predictions are updated more frequently.

5. A *random* deviation is a divergence between actual cost and (statistically) expected cost arising from the stochastic operation of some correctly specified random parameter. For example, the raw-material input per unit of output in a chemical process may fluctuate because of random variations that are inherent in the process. By definition, a random deviation per se calls for no corrective action affecting the existing process. However, as we shall see in later sections, to distinguish random deviations from other types is a helpful step in deciding whether and when to investigate any deviations.

The idea of randomness is rarely formally recognized by accounting systems. Instead, standard costing systems view a standard as a *single* acceptable measure. Practically, the accountant (and everybody else) realizes that the standard is a *band* or *range* of possible acceptable outcomes. In other words, the performance (and costs) ought to be generated by a well-behaved underlying process. If the process is not behaving acceptably, it may be economical to intervene to make it behave better. For example, a foreman may expect a machine operator to produce an average of 100 bearing brackets per hour. If he notices that 105 are being turned out the first hour, 98 the second, 103 the third, and 95 the fourth, he may consider such a variation in performance to be *random.* However, if the performance falls to 85 and then jumps to 120, he may consider the performance *nonrandom* and worth investigating.

The distinctions among the five deviations above formalize and make explicit the complexities that decision makers face. The manager should be alert for these five sources of variances because they focus on his assumptions about his prediction methods, his decision models, and his implementation. In contrast, the traditional view of a cost variance tends to focus almost wholly on implementation deviations.

difficulties in analysis of variances

Ideally, managers would like to have an information system that pinpoints the deviations just described into five mutually exclusive categories and that indicates a sequence of investigation that will maximize net payoff, the excess of benefit over cost. Unfortunately, the state of the world is complex and the state of the accountant's and the mathematician's art in this area is primitive and simple. The overall problems can be delineated, sometimes with rigor.[4] However, the interdependences are manifold and the difficulties of ascertaining the costs and benefits of investigation are imposing. For example, the five sources of variances described above may not be independent. The time needed for investigation of each source may also not be independent. Furthermore, the net savings associated with each alternative of when, how, and where to investigate a deviation will depend on the state of each process subject to investigation. Neither the processes, investigations, nor time periods are necessarily independent.

When a manager is deciding whether to investigate a deviation, he must consider the nature of the search. For instance, the time needed for investigation will differ for each form of deviation. An implementation-deviation search may require interviewing a specific worker or his supervisor. A model-deviation search may focus on discussions with the appropriate engineer or mathematician. Of course, the expected costs of these investigations must be compared with their expected savings before investigation is launched.

comparison of costs and benefits

The essential nature of the decision to investigate is best illustrated by a simple example. Consider the two-state, two-action situation depicted in Exhibit 26-5.[5] Examine the exhibit carefully so that the facts are clear.

[4] See Demski, *Information Analysis,* Chapter 6; T. R. Dyckman, "The Investigation of Cost Variances," *Journal of Accounting Research,* Vol. 7, No. 2, pp. 215–44; and H. Bierman, Jr., and T. R. Dyckman, *Managerial Cost Accounting,* 2nd ed. (New York: The Macmillan Company, 1976), Chapter 2, and the Kaplan paper described in a later footnote.

[5] The example is based on one in Bierman and Dyckman, *op. cit.,* pp. 36–40. As they point out (p. 35), there are several implicit assumptions, including the following: The decision maker is willing to act on the basis of expected values; incurred costs are reported on a periodic basis, so a do-not-investigate action implies that an activity is continued at least until the next cost observation is available; and an investigation always detects the cause of an out-of-control situation that can and will be immediately corrected.

EXHIBIT 26-5

DECISION TABLE

	STATES: θ_j	
Actions: a_i	θ_1: In Control	θ_2: Out of Control
a_1: investigate	$C = \$2{,}000$	$C + M = \$\ 5{,}000$
a_2: do not investigate	0*	$L = \$15{,}000$

where

C = \$2,000, the cost of investigation; M = \$3,000, the cost of correction if an out-of-control process is discovered; L = \$15,000, the present value of the extra costs over the planning horizon, which may be either the time until the process is expected to go out of control again or the time until a routine intervention is scheduled. Clearly, the amount of L depends on expected future actions.

* All other amounts in this table are incremental in relation to this action and state.

Suppose the probability of the process being in control (θ_1) is .82 and the probability of its being out of control (θ_2) is 0.18. Then the expected costs (E) are:

If investigate,[6]

$$E(a_1) = C(1 - p_{\theta_2}) + (C + M)p_{\theta_2}$$
$$E(a_1) = \$2{,}000(.82) + \$5{,}000(.18) = \$2{,}540$$

If do not investigate,

$$E(a_2) = \qquad Lp_{\theta_2}$$
$$E(a_2) = \$0 + \$15{,}000(.18) = \$2{,}700$$

Therefore, investigation is the optimal action, because the expected costs are \$160 less than the alternative of no investigation.

role of probabilities The foregoing computation illustrates the critical role of the assessment of probabilities in the decision of whether or not to investigate. A low probability, say .10, of the process being out of control will change the desirability of conducting an investigation:

[6] This equation may also be expressed as

$$E(a_1) = C + Mp_{\theta_2}$$
$$E(a_1) = \$2{,}000 + \$3{,}000(.18) = \$2{,}540$$

If investigate,

$$E = \$2{,}000(.90) = \$\ 5{,}000(.10) = \$2{,}300$$

If do not investigate,

$$E = \$0 \qquad\qquad + \$15{,}000(.10) = \$1{,}500$$

Of course, the level of the critical probability will depend on the relative costs and benefits in a particular situation. In our example, it can be computed as follows. The point of indifference (sometimes called the breakeven point) is where the expected costs of each action are the same:

$$\text{Let } p_{\theta_2} = \text{level of probability where } E_{a_1} \text{ and } E_{a_2} \text{ are equal}$$
$$E_{a_1} = E_{a_2}$$

Substituting:

$$\begin{aligned}
C(1 - p_{\theta_2}) + (C + M)p_{\theta_2} &= Lp_{\theta_2} \\
C - Cp_{\theta_2} + Cp_{\theta_2} + Mp_{\theta_2} &= Lp_{\theta_2} \\
C + Mp_{\theta_2} &= Lp_{\theta_2} \\
C &= Lp_{\theta_2} - Mp_{\theta_2} \\
p_{\theta_2} &= \frac{C}{L - M} \\
p_{\theta_2} &= \frac{\$2{,}000}{\$15{,}000 - \$3{,}000} = .17
\end{aligned}$$

Therefore, in this example, investigation is desirable only if the probability of being out of control exceeds .17.[7]

Note especially that variances provide the information for assessing these critical probabilities. However, the measurements of the costs and benefits are unlikely to be provided by the variances. For example, the table in Exhibit 26-5 does not contain the cost variance itself, but the size of the cost variance may be crucial in assessing the probabilities of .82 and .18.

practical approach Again and again we have seen that managers use simple decision models in complex situations. In the area of variance analysis, they use judgments that generally grow from the experience and know-how of the executives involved. For some items, any tiny variance from budget or standard may spark scrutiny. For other items, 5, 10, or 25 percent variances

[7] Prior probabilities, based on past performance, are subject to revision by means of current sample evidence and Bayes' Theorem to provide posterior probabilities for use in revising expected costs. See Dyckman, "Investigation of Cost Variances," pp. 222ff.

from standard may be necessary to spur follow-ups. Rules of thumb are frequently developed that focus either on the absolute size of the variance or on some percentage obtained by dividing the cost variance by the budgeted or standard cost.

Of course, when rules of thumb or intuition are used to decide whether to investigate, the manager has at least implicitly proceeded through the decision process illustrated in our example. He has combined costs, benefits, and probabilities in such a way that the rules of thumb are equivalent to go/no-go points of indifference.

statistical quality control

In practice, the standard cost variances are simple signals that do not neatly trace back to one of the five types of deviations described earlier. Nevertheless, because the costs and benefits of investigation differ, depending on the type of suspected deviation, managers are faced with the problem of at least implicitly classifying the likely deviations. As a first step in deciding whether to investigate variances, managers frequently attempt to distinguish random deviations from all other types.

A whole field of statistical quality control (SQC) has been developed to pinpoint random deviations in industrial processes and other repetitive operations. Control charts are frequently used, whereby the means of small samples are successively plotted. Statistical tables of the normal distributions are used to formulate upper and lower control limits. Only the observations beyond these limits ordinarily are regarded as nonrandom and worth investigating. These observations have usually been measured in engineering terms (such as times, material usage, rejects, and so on) rather than economic terms (such as dollars of cost). The biggest weaknesses of traditional SQC are that (a) its rules for setting the control limits have not explicitly considered costs and benefits and (b) its monitoring procedures do not allow for prior observations.[8]

Although there are some obvious similarities between traditional SQC and accounting variances, fundamental differences limit the usefulness of traditional SQC procedures in an accounting setting.[9] SQC provides frequent

[8] To pursue this subject in more depth, begin with Robert S. Kaplan, "The Significance and Investigation of Cost Variance: Survey and Extensions," *Journal of Accounting Research,* Vol. 13, No. 2 (Autumn 1975). Kaplan surveyed the accounting, statistics, and management-science literature dealing with the significance and investigation of variances, including the other references footnoted elsewhere in this chapter. He is critical of the statistical quality-control chart that is often favored in the accounting literature. Kaplan says, "Despite the widespread use of quality-control techniques in industry the application of these ideas in actual standard cost accounting settings can generously be characterized as minimal." He favors processing current data along with all prior observations in the form of a cumulative-sum (cusum) procedure coupled with cost-benefit analysis. As more experience is gained, he would try to model the underlying stochastic process directly.

[9] *Ibid.* Incidentally, some accountants favor using statistical regression for developing budgets and standards and then using confidence intervals in conjunction with judgment to make the decision of whether to investigate variances. For discussions of some pros and cons, see W. Ferrara and J. Hayya, "Toward Probabilistic Profit Budgets," *Management Accounting* (October, 1970), pp. 23–28 and S. Buzby, "Extending the Applicability of Probabilistic Management Planning and Control Models," *Accounting Review,* Vol. XLIX, No. 1 (January 1974), pp. 42–49.

observations (sometimes hourly or more frequently), but accounting reports rarely are prepared more often than weekly.

Furthermore, the out-of-control physical processes discovered under SQC can frequently be placed back into control with the manipulation of a dial or a similar procedure. Consequently, the benefit from investigation can be measured by the almost certain return to the in-control state.

In contrast, the investigation of cost variances contains no similar assurance that performance will be restored to its original standard. For instance, prices may have changed or operating procedures developed that may be difficult or impossible to reverse. The underlying processes for which costs are being aggregated are often not as easily identifiable as those processes for which SQC controls are typically exercised. Thus, the benefits from investigations of cost variances are more uncertain. The difficulty of measuring likely benefits may be the major barrier to the implementation of formal decision models for this purpose.

SUMMARY

Accounting variances are a means of communicating what has happened. By this and other means, the manager enhances understanding and decides whether specified areas deserve more investigation.

Mix and yield variances sometimes aid comprehension, but they are supplements to the basic price, efficiency, and volume variances that were covered in previous chapters.

The decision to investigate variances is often one of minimizing expected costs. It requires consideration of the profitable states of the process, the costs of investigation and correction, and the present value of the net savings. Because these factors are difficult to quantify, rules of thumb are often used in practice for deciding when to investigate.

PROBLEM FOR SELF-STUDY

PROBLEM

Refer to the example in Exhibit 26-5. Suppose that C, the expected cost of investigation, were \$4,000 instead of \$2,000, with the probability of being in control unchanged. What would be the expected costs of investigation and of no investigation? What level of probability would exist of the process's being out of control where the expected costs of each action would be the same?

SOLUTION

If investigate, $E = \$4,000(.82) + \$\ 7,000(.18) = \$4,540$
If do not investigate, $E = \$0 + \$15,000(.18) = \$2,700$

Therefore, do not investigate. The level of probability of being out of control where the expected costs would be the same is

$$p_{\theta_2} = \frac{\$4,000}{\$15,000 - \$3,000} = .33$$

PROOF

If investigate, $E = \$4,000(.67) + \$\ 7,000(.33) = \$5,000$ (rounded)
If do not investigate, $E = \$0 + \$15,000(.33) = \$5,000$

SUGGESTED READINGS

For Parts One and Two

CHUMACHENKO, NIKOLAI G., "Once Again: The Volume-Mix-Price/Cost Budget Variance Analysis," *The Accounting Review,* Vol. XLIII, No. 4, pp. 753–62. This is an exhaustive article by a Soviet author on the alternative ways of analyzing sales-mix variances.

HASSELDINE, C. R., "Mix and Yield Variances," *The Accounting Review,* Vol. XLII, No. 3, pp. 497–515. This article concentrates on alternative ways of analyzing mix and yield of various combinations of direct materials in a production context.

HOBBS, JAMES R., "Volume-Mix-Price/Cost Budget Variance Analysis: A Proper Approach," *The Accounting Review,* Vol. XXXIX, No. 4, pp. 905–13.

MALCOM, R. E., "Sales Variances; A Further Look," *Management Advisor,* March–April 1971, pp. 948–53.

MANES, RENE P., "In a Seminar on Budget Mix Variances," *The Accounting Review,* Vol. XLIII, No. 4, pp. 784–87.

WOLK, H. I., and HILLMAN, A. D., "Material Mix and Yield Variances—A Suggested Improvement," *Accounting Review,* Vol. 42, No. 3, pp. 549–53.

For Part Three

BATHER, J. A., "Control Charts and Minimization of Costs," *Journal of the Royal Statistical Society,* Series B, Vol. XXV, No. 1 (1963), pp. 49–80.

BIERMAN, H., and T. R. DYCKMAN, *Managerial Cost Accounting,* Chapter 2. New York: The Macmillan Company, 1971.

DEMSKI, JOEL S., *Information Analysis,* Chapter 6. Reading, Mass.: Addison-Wesley Publishing Co., Inc., 1972.

DUVALL, R. M., "Rules for Investigating Cost Variances," *Management Science,* Vol. 13, No. 10, pp. 631–41.

KAPLAN, R. S., "Optimal Investigation Strategies with Imperfect Information," *Journal of Accounting Research,* Vol. VII, No. 1 (Spring 1969), pp. 32–43.

——— "The Significance and Investigation of Cost Variances: Survey and Extensions," *Journal of Accounting Research,* Vol. 13, No. 2 (Autumn 1975).

LEV, B., "An Information Theory Analysis of Budget Variances," *Accounting Review,* Vol. XLIV, No. 4, pp. 704–10.

LUH, F. S., "Controlled Cost: An Operational Concept and Statistical Approach to Standard Costing," *Accounting Review,* Vol. XLIII, No. 1, pp. 123–32.

OZAN, T., and T. R. DYCKMAN, "A Normative Model for Investigation Decisions Involving Multi-Origin Cost Variances," *Journal of Accounting Research,* Vol. 9, No. 1.

RONEN, JOSHUA, "Nonaggregation versus Disaggregation of Variances," *Journal of Accounting Research,* Vol. 9, No. 1.

QUESTIONS, PROBLEMS, AND CASES

26-1 Define *mix variance.*

26-2 Define *quantity variance.*

26-3 "The breakeven point is not a unique number." Do you agree? Why?

26-4 Distinguish between *mix* and *yield*.

26-5 Define *yield variance*.

26-6 Define a *sample*. Is sampling more accurate than a 100 percent count? Why?

26-7 Name five statistical applications to business situations.

26-8 What are some common difficulties in the analysis of variances?

26-9 Contrast the accountant's and the statistician's concept of the word *standard*.

26-10 Describe the basic approach of statistical quality control.

26-11 What does the word *quality* mean as it is used in *statistical quality control?*

26-12 What is the *state of statistical control?*

26-13 "When a process is in control, it is beyond change or improvement." Comment.

Problems for Part One

26-14 *Breakeven for Multiple Products* (CPA) The Dooley Co. manufactures two products, baubles and trinkets. The following are projections for the coming year:

	BAUBLES		*TRINKETS*		
	Units	Amount	Units	Amount	Totals
Sales	10,000	$10,000	7,500	$10,000	$20,000
Costs:					
Fixed		$ 2,000		$ 5,600	$ 7,600
Variable		6,000		3,000	9,000
		$ 8,000		$ 8,600	$16,600
Income before taxes		$ 2,000		$ 1,400	$ 3,400

Choose the best answer for each question:

1. Assuming that the facilities are not jointly used, the breakeven output (in units) for baubles would be
   a. 8,000; b. 7,000; c. 6,000; d. 5,000.
2. The breakeven volume (dollars) for trinkets would be
   a. $8,000; b. $7,000; c. $6,000; d. $5,000.
3. Assuming that consumers purchase composite units of four baubles and three trinkets, the composite unit contribution margin would be
   a. $4.40; b. $4.00; c. $1.33; d. $1.10.
4. If consumers purchase composite units of four baubles and three trinkets, the breakeven output for the two products would be
   a. 6,909 baubles; 6,909 trinkets
   b. 6,909 baubles; 5,182 trinkets
   c. 5,000 baubles; 8,000 trinkets
   d. 5,000 baubles; 6,000 trinkets
5. If baubles and trinkets become one-to-one complements and there is no change in the Dooley Co.'s cost function, the breakeven volume would be
   a. $22,500; b. $15,750; c. $13,300; d. $10,858.
6. If a composite unit is defined as one bauble and one trinket, the composite contribution margin ratio would be
   a. 7/10; b. 4/7; c. 2/5; d. 19/50.

26-15 *Breakeven and Sales-Mix Assumption* Refer to Exhibit 26-1. Fixed costs are $300,000. The chapter showed three possible breakeven points, one for all A, one for all B, and one for a combination of 3 A and 1 B. Suppose that plans changed so that the budget was going to be 100,000 A and 60,000 B. Compute the new budgeted income and the new breakeven point. Are they better than the original combination of 120,000 A and 40,000 B?

26-16 *Basic Product Mix and Breakeven* The multiplicity of products is exemplified by women's (or men's) clothing stores. Consider an oversimplified illustration in Exhibit 26-6, where there are only three product lines and the variable expenses consist only of the costs of the products plus sales commissions.

required

1. Suppose the fixed costs applicable to the store were $7,000 per month. What would be the breakeven point in dollar sales based on the budgeted mix? Based on the actual mix?
2. Suppose that actual sales for May were $40,000, consisting of dresses, $25,000; shoes, $8,000; and blouses, $7,000. There have been no changes in unit prices, unit variable costs, or the mix within each of the three product lines. Compute the variance in total contribution margin and total contribution-margin percentage. If this mix persists, what is the new breakeven point?
3. Breakeven points are often incidental to the study of cost-volume-profit relationships. As the manager of this store, how would you react to the analysis in requirement 2?

26-17 *P/V Chart and Sales Mix* The Bannister Company has three products—A, B, and C—having contribution margins of $3, $2, and $1, respectively. The president is planning to sell 200,000 units in the forthcoming period, consisting of 20,000 A, 100,000 B, and 80,000 C. The company's fixed costs for the period are $255,000.

EXHIBIT 26-6

MULTIPLE-PRODUCT ANALYSIS
For the Month Ended May 31, 19_1

	BUDGET FOR MAY			ACTUAL FOR MAY		
	Sales	Contribution Margin	Contribution-Margin Percentage	Sales	Contribution Margin	Contribution-Margin Percentage
Dresses	$20,000	$ 8,000	40.0%	$10,000	$4,000	40.0%
Shoes	10,000	3,000	30.0	10,000	3,000	30.0
Blouses	10,000	2,000	20.0	10,000	2,000	20.0
Total	$40,000	$13,000	32.5%	$30,000	$9,000	30.0%

Budget variances (the differences between budgeted and actual outcomes):

Variance in sales	$10,000 U
Variance in total contribution margin	4,000 U
Variance in total contribution-margin percentage	2.5% U

U = Unfavorable

required

1. What is the company breakeven point in units, assuming that the given sales mix is maintained?
2. Prepare a P/V chart for a volume of 200,000 units. Have a broken line represent the average contribution margin per unit and have solid lines represent the net income effects of each product by showing their unit contribution margins as the slopes of each line. What is the total contribution margin at a volume of 200,000 units? Net income?
3. What would net income become if 20,000 units of A, 80,000 units of B, and 100,000 units of C were sold? What is the new breakeven point if these relationships persist in the next period?
4. Refer to requirement 3. Prepare a comparison for each product (and all products in total) of the original budgeted total contribution margin and the actual total contribution margin. Show the variances.
5. The differences between budgeted and actual results in requirement 4 are sometimes called volume variances. Split the volume variance into its quantity and mix components. As a manager, would you gain more insights from this split? Why?

26-18 *Breakeven Analysis and the Product-Mix Assumption* Suppose that the Blanton Company has the following budget data for 19_1:

	PRODUCT		TOTAL
	X	Y	
Selling price	$3	$6	
Variable expenses	1	2	
Contribution margin	$2	$4	
Total fixed expenses	$100,000	$120,000	
Number of units to be sold to break even	?	?	?
Number of units expected to be sold	30,000	50,000	80,000

required

1. Compute the breakeven point for each product.
2. Suppose that Products X and Y were made in the same plant. Assume that a prolonged strike at the factory of the sole supplier of raw materials prevented the production of X for all of 19_1. Suppose also that the Blanton fixed costs were unaffected.
   a. What is the breakeven point for the company as a whole, assuming that no X is produced?
   b. Suppose instead that the shortage applied so that only X and no Y could be produced. Then what is the breakeven point for the company as a whole?
3. Draw a breakeven chart for the company as a whole, using an average selling price and an average variable expense per unit. What is the breakeven point under this aggregate approach? What is the breakeven point if you add together the individual breakeven points that you computed in requirement 1? Why is the aggregate breakeven point different from the sum of the individual breakeven points?

26-19 *Change in Sales Mix* Refer to the preceding problem. Suppose that actual results showed that 100,000 units were sold, consisting of 35,000 X and 65,000 Y. No price changes occurred.

required

1. Prepare a comparison for each product, and for all products in total, of the original budgeted total contribution margin and the actual total contribution margin. Show the variances.

2. The variance in part 1 is sometimes called the volume variance. Split the variance into its quantity and mix components. As a manager, would you gain insight from the split? Why?

26-20 *Quantity and Mix* Consider the following budget:

	PRODUCT X			PRODUCT Y			TOTAL		
	Units	Price	Total	Units	Price	Total	Units	Price	Total
Sales	1,000	$10.00	$10,000	9,000	$2.50	$22,500	10,000	$3.25	$32,500
Variable costs	1,000	6.00	6,000	9,000	2.00	18,000	10,000	2.40	24,000
Contribution margin	1,000	$ 4.00	$ 4,000	9,000	$ .50	$ 4,500	10,000	$ .85	$ 8,500
Contribution margin percentage		40%			20%			26.15%	

Suppose that 7,000 units were actually sold—2,000 of X and 5,000 of Y:

	PRODUCT X			PRODUCT Y			TOTAL		
	Units	Price	Total	Units	Price	Total	Units	Price	Total
Sales	2,000	$10.25	$20,500	5,000	$2.50	$12,500	7,000	$4.71+	$33,000
Variable costs	2,000	6.00	12,000	5,000	2.00	10,000	7,000	3.14+	22,000
Contribution margin	2,000	$ 4.25	$ 8,500	5,000	$ .50	$ 2,500	7,000	$1.57+	$11,000
Contribution margin percentage		41.46%			20%			33.33%	

Prepare a complete explanation of why the contribution margin is $2,500 more than originally budgeted. Include a detailed variance analysis of price changes per unit and changes in volume. Also subdivide the volume variance for the contribution margin into changes in quantities and changes in mix.

26-21 *Sales-Mix Variances for Motorboats* Suppose a motorboat distributor planned on selling only two models, Storms and Thunderheads. He expected to sell the following during a given year:

	STORMS			THUNDERHEADS			TOTAL		
	Units	Price	Total	Units	Price	Total	Units	Price	Total
Sales	4,000	$4,000	$16,000,000	1,000	$6,000	$6,000,000	5,000	$4,400	$22,000,000
Variable costs	4,000	3,200	12,800,000	1,000	4,500	4,500,000	5,000	3,460	17,300,000
Contribution margin	4,000	$ 800	$ 3,200,000	1,000	$1,500	$1,500,000	5,000	$ 940	$ 4,700,000

Suppose that 5,100 units were actually sold:

	STORMS			THUNDERHEADS			TOTAL		
	Units	Price	Total	Units	Price	Total	Units	Price	Total
Sales	3,700	$4,000	$14,800,000	1,400	$6,000	$8,400,000	5,100	$4,550	$23,200,000
Variable costs	3,700	3,200	11,840,000	1,400	4,500	6,300,000	5,100	3,558	18,140,000
Contribution margin	3,700	$ 800	$ 2,960,000	1,400	$1,500	$2,100,000	5,100	$ 992	$ 5,060,000

The dealer is astounded to learn that he reached his target unit selling prices, unit costs, and unit contribution margins. He realizes that his unit sales were not on target, and he has asked you to analyze the figures in more depth so that he may get more insight into his problems.

required

1. Prepare an explanation of why the actual total contribution margin differed from the budgeted margin, using (a) only a volume variance and (b) a quantity variance and a mix variance.
2. Which of the two variance analyses in part 1 did you prefer? Explain fully.

26-22 *Sales Analysis* (CMA, adapted) The Arsco Co. Makes three grades of indoor-outdoor carpets. The sales volume for the annual budget is determined by estimating the total market volume for indoor-outdoor carpet, and then applying the company's prior year market share, adjusted for planned changes due to company programs for the coming year. The volume is apportioned between the three grades based upon the prior year's product mix, again adjusted for planned changes due to company programs for the coming year.

Given below are the company budget for 19_3 and the results of operations for 19_3.

BUDGET

	Grade 1	Grade 2	Grade 3	Total
Sales—units	1,000 rolls	1,000 rolls	2,000 rolls	4,000 rolls
Sales—dollars (000 omitted)	$1,000	$2,000	$3,000	$6,000
Variable expense	700	1,600	2,300	4,600
Variable margin	$ 300	$ 400	$ 700	$1,400
Traceable fixed expense	200	200	300	700
Traceable margin	$ 100	$ 200	$ 400	$ 700
Selling and administrative expense				250
Net Income				$ 450

ACTUAL

	Grade 1	Grade 2	Grade 3	Total
Sales—units	800 rolls	1,000 rolls	2,100 rolls	3,900 rolls
Sales—dollars (000 omitted)	$810	$2,000	$3,000	$5,810
Variable expense	560	1,610	2,320	4,490
Variable margin	$250	$ 390	$ 680	$1,320
Traceable fixed expense	210	220	315	745
Traceable margin	$ 40	$ 170	$ 365	$ 575
Selling and administrative expense				275
Net income				$ 300

Industry volume was estimated at 40,000 rolls for budgeting purposes. Actual industry volume for 19_3 was 38,000 rolls.

required

1. Prepare a comparison for each product, and for all products in total, of the original budgeted total contribution margin and the actual total contribution margin (holding unit prices constant). Show the variances.
2. What is the dollar impact on profits (using budgeted variable margins) of the shift in product mix from the budgeted mix? That is, split the variance in part 1 into its quantity and mix components.
3. What portion of the variance, if any, can be attributed to the state of the carpet market?

Problems for Part Two

26-23 *Review of Chapter Illustration on Yield Variances* Review the chapter illustration that is summarized in Exhibit 26-4. Suppose the manager's initial schedule called for producing 87,300 gallons by introducing 97,000 gallons of inputs.

However, many extra sales orders occurred, which caused 100,000 gallons to be introduced.

required

1. Compute the volume variances and the order-adjustment variances for direct material and direct labor.
2. Suppose that 48,000 gallons of F, 30,000 gallons of G, and 22,000 gallons of H were actually used. Furthermore, 11,000 actual direct-labor hours of input were used. Compute the price, efficiency, and yield variances for direct materials and direct labor. (You may wish to use the same summary format as in Exhibit 26-4.)

26-24 *Material Yield and Mix* A company has the following standards for producing a special gasoline additive:

50	gallons of petroleum concentrate G-101 @ $.10 =	$ 5.00
50	gallons of petroleum concentrate G-177 @ $.30 =	15.00
100	gallons of standard mix @ $.20 =	$20.00

Every 100 gallons of input should yield 80 gallons of PST, the finished product.

The production manager is supposed to make the largest possible amount of finished product for the least cost. He has some leeway to alter the combination of materials within certain wide limits, as long as the finished product meets specified quality standards.

Actual results showed that 400,000 gallons of PST were produced during the previous week. The raw materials used in this production were 280,000 gallons of G-101 and 240,000 gallons of G-177.

No price variances were experienced during the period.

required

Comment on the performance of the manager. Include a presentation of yield and efficiency variances.

26-25 *Material-Mix and Yield Variances* A company has the following standards:

50 pounds of Material C at	$1.40 =	$ 70.00	
30 pounds of Material D at	2.00 =	60.00	
20 pounds of Material E at	1.60 =	32.00	
100 pounds of standard mix at	1.62 =	$162.00	should produce 90 pounds of finished product at a standard cost of $1.80 per pound ($162.00 ÷ 90).

No inventories of raw materials are kept. Purchases are made as needed, so that all price variances relate to materials used. Actual results showed that 50,000 pounds were used during a period.

26,000	pounds of C at actual cost of $1.20 =	$31,200
16,000	pounds of D at actual cost of 2.10 =	33,600
8,000	pounds of E at actual cost of 1.90 =	15,200
50,000		$80,000

Good output was

40,000 pounds at standard cost of $1.80 =	72,000
Total material variance to be explained =	$ 8,000 U

What are the efficiency, yield, and price variances?

26-26 *Conversion-Cost-Rate, Efficiency, and Yield Variances* Suppose that in Problem 26-25, the following direct-labor and variable-overhead factors were combined in a single conversion-cost analysis:

1. Standard rate per hour	= $ 7.20
2. The conversion of 10 pounds of raw materials into 9 pounds of finished product should take 30 minutes, so that the standard rate per pound of output should be $7.20 ÷ 18 pounds per hour	= $ .40
3. Standard cost of 40,000 pounds of output	= $16,000
4. Actual rate per hour (averaged)	= $ 7.50
5. Total actual costs	= $18,000
6. Actual hours	= 2,400
7. Standard hours allowed for 40,000 pounds of output (40,000 ÷ 18)	= 2,222

What are the conversion-cost-price, efficiency, and yield variances?

26-27 *Variances and Joint Products* A cannery buys raw fruit and processes it into three products: fancy, choice, and seconds. The standard pounds of output expected per 100 pounds of input are 60 fancy, 30 choice, and 10 seconds at market values per pound of $1.50, $1.00, and $.50 respectively. The standard cost per pound of raw fruit is $.40. Direct labor has a standard price of $10 per hour and its standard output is 100 pounds per hour.

Your immediate superior prepared a static budget for this product (based on the acquisition and processing of 10,000 pounds of raw fruit) as follows:

		FANCY	CHOICE	SECONDS	TOTAL
Sales		$9,000	$3,000	$500	$12,500
Joint costs identified:					
Raw fruit	$4,000				
Direct labor	1,000				$ 5,000
Contribution to all other costs and profit					$ 7,500

The 10,000 pounds of fruit were processed, and the output consisted of 6,200 pounds of fancy, 2,800 choice, and 500 seconds. All actual unit prices were the same as standard prices. Actual direct labor used amounted to 120 hours.

required

Prepare a comparison of actual results with the static budget. Your boss is familiar with mix and yield variances and wants you to incorporate them in your analysis.

26-28 *Relating Sales-Mix and Production-Yield Variances* This problem relates Parts One and Two of the chapter. Reconsider the first illustration in the chapter; also study Exhibit 26-4. You are going to analyze the sales variance (not the contribution-margin variance). If you were forced to place either $1,000,000 or $1,050,000 in each of the five columns in Exhibit 26-4, what amounts would you put in each column? What would be the amounts of price, efficiency, yield, order adjustment, and volume variances? How do the variances in Part One overlap with Exhibit 26-4? Why?

Problems for Part Three

26-29 *Types of Deviations* The chapter described five possible kinds of deviations as sources of a variance between actual and predicted costs: (a) implementation, (b) prediction, (c) measurement, (d) model, and (e) random. Below are listed some examples of deviations. Use one of the letters (a) through (e) to identify the most likely type of deviation being described.

1. A foreman gets a year-end bonus that is really attributable to overtime that he worked seven months previously. The bonus is charged to overhead at year-end.
2. Costs of supplies are charged to overhead as acquired rather than as used.
3. Costs of setting up printing jobs are consistently pegged too low when bids are made.
4. The salvage value of scrap from production is forecast incorrectly.
5. Normal spoilage in a food-processing plant amounts to 5 percent of good output.
6. The salvage value of scrap from production is ignored completely.
7. A worker is inefficient because of daydreaming.
8. A worker is inefficient because he is new at his job and is just learning how to do the work.

26-30 *Decision to Analyze Operations* Solve Problem 24-22, which could logically have been placed here.

26-31 *Decision to Investigate a Variance* A semiautomated process is rarely out of control. The cost of investigation is $300. If a process is discovered to be out of control, its cost of correction is $1,000, and gross savings are the equivalent of $2,500 received at the end of each year for three years.

required

1. Suppose the minimum desired rate of return is 12 percent per annum. The manager has examined a cost variance that makes him assess a probability of .05 that the process is out of control. Should the process be investigated? Show computations.
2. At what level of probability will the manager be indifferent about whether to investigate?

26-32 *Decision to Investigate a Variance* When a process is investigated in an automated department, the costs of investigation are $1,000. If an out-of-control process is discovered, the cost of correction is $1,500. The manager is always indifferent about conducting an investigation when there is a probability of .60 that the process is in control.

required

How large must the present value of the cost savings be to warrant an investigation?

26-33 *Statistical-Control Limits and Investigation Decision* Traditionally, control limits, using the techniques of statistical quality control, have been set a ± 2 sigmas in British countries and ± 3 sigmas in the United States. Consider the 2-sigma limits, which imply that the probability is .05 of observing a nonrandom deviation when the dollar amount of the variance is within the 2-sigma limits.

required

1. Suppose C is $100, M is $800, and L is $5,800. Would you investigate deviations that lie within the 2-sigma limits? Why?
2. In the decision of whether to investigate, what is the role of the size of the variance in relation to the standard cost? In relation to the potential savings?

26-34 *Decision to Investigate a Variances* You are the manager of a manufacturing process. A variance of $10,000 in excess material usage has been reported for the past week's operations. You are trying to decide whether to investigate.

You feel that if you do not investigate and the process is out of control, the present value of the cost savings (L) over the planning horizon is \$3,800. The cost to investigate is \$500. The cost to correct the process if you discover that it is out of control is \$1,000. You assess the probability that the process is out of control at .30.

required

1. Should the process be investigated? What are the expected costs of investigation and of no investigation?
2. What level of probability that the process is out of control would exist where the expected costs of each action would be the same?
3. If the cost variance is \$10,000, why is L only \$3,800?

26-35 *Decision to Investigate* (CPA) The Folding-Department foreman must decide each week whether his department will operate normally the following week. He may order a corrective action if he feels the Folding Department will operate inefficiently; otherwise he does nothing. The foreman receives a weekly Folding-Department efficiency-variance report from the Accounting Department. A week in which the Folding Department operates inefficiently is usually preceded by a large efficiency variance. The graph below gives the probability that the Folding Department will operate normally in the following week as a function of the magnitude of the current week's variance reported to the foreman:

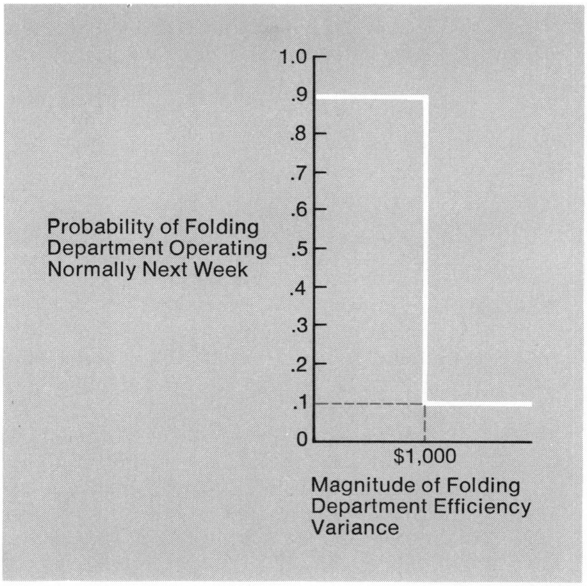

Choose the best answer for each of the following:

1. An efficiency variance of \$1,500 this week means the probability of operating normally the following week is
   a. 0%. b. 10%. c. 90%. d. 100%.
2. What are the possible relationships between the current efficiency variance and next week's operations?

a. Large variance followed by normal operation, large variance followed by inefficient operation, small variance followed by normal operation, and small variance followed by inefficient operation.
b. Large variance followed by normal operation, small variance followed by inefficient operation, and small variance followed by normal operation.
c. Large variance followed by inefficient operation, small variance followed by normal operation, and small variance followed by inefficient operation.
d. Large variance followed by 90 percent of normal operation, small variance followed by 10 percent of normal operation, large variance followed by inefficienct operation, and small variance followed by inefficient operation.

3. If the foreman can determine for certain whether the Folding Department will operate normally next week, and the cost of corrective action is less than the extra cost of operating the Folding Department inefficiently, then the best decision rule for the foreman to follow is
a. If normal operations are predicted, do *not* take corrective action; if inefficient operations are predicted, take corrective action.
b. Regardless of the current variance, do *not* take corrective action.
c. If normal operations are predicted, take corrective action; if inefficient operations are predicted, do *not* take corrective action.
d. Regardless of the current variance, take corrective action.

4. The following cost information is relevant to the Folding-Department foreman in deciding whether corrective action is warranted:

$500 = cost of corrective action that will assure normal operation of Folding Department for the following week.
$3,000 = excess cost of operating Folding Department inefficiently for one week.

The foreman receives a report that the Folding Department efficiency variance is $600. The expected cost of *not* taking corrective action is
a. $0. b. $300. c. $2,700. d. $3,000.

26-36 *Navy Rework* (C. Oleson) The Naval Air Rework Facility (NARF) at Alameda, Calif., is one of several facilities throughout the U.S. that has as its main function the overhaul and repair of naval aviation weapons systems. These include aircraft, missiles, engines, electronics, and other miscellaneous systems.

The NARF operates like civilian organizations that have a profit/loss responsibility. "Sales" are made to project managers in Washington who have overall accountability for the maintenance of specified weapons systems. Because the government is generally nonprofit, the price does not include a "profit" but is based solely on standard absorption costs.

To motivate efficiency, the Navy holds each NARF responsible for attaining standards. This is accomplished by measuring the NARF's performance in meeting a zero-profit objective while pricing on the basis of standards, called norms, which are derived from historical data and engineering estimates. If costs exceed norms, the NARF suffers a loss. If costs are less than norms, the NARF derives a profit. Either situation represents a deviation from the desired objective. The first situation is deemed to result from inefficiency; the second, from loose standards.

Norms for any given work are determined immediately prior to the quarter in which the work starts; the price is negotiated accordingly with the Washington project manager. At this time, the exact condition of the units (say aircraft) is unknown. Predictions must be based on known general characteristics such as age, number of flight hours on the unit, and the type of work to be done. Although the average cost per unit may be accurately predicted from such characteristics, the cost for a particular unit may vary widely from the average because its exact condition is unknown when the predictions of cost are made. One aircraft, for example, may have excess corrosion from having been outside near the ocean spray. Another may have been abused by a careless crew. Thus, the norm set at the planning conference represents the mean of a distribution with some standard deviation.

Although the resultant profit would be zero over a long period that included many production units where norms were being met on the average, the controller was concerned that for a period as short as a year these random deviations between actual and expected costs might have a significant effect on fiscal-year operating results (profits). He decided to study the problem in more detail.

Data on unit actual and expected (norm) costs were gathered over a three-year period from 19_1 through 19_3. The resulting distribution of actual less expected costs had a small negative mean, indicating that on the average norms had been beaten (or set somewhat loosely). It was then assumed that setting this mean to zero would result in the distribution of random deviations caused by differences in unit condition. This distribution was then used in a model that simulated product flow and the accounting system by quarters throughout a fiscal year. One thousand iterations of this model resulted in a distribution of probable outcomes of fiscal-year profits if norms were met on the average. The distribution was approximately normal with a mean of zero, as expected, and standard deviation of $350,000.

required

1. What are the implications of this study for the manager of the NARF? For his superior in Washington?
2. A cost-benefit analysis showed that the cost of investigating a *negative* deviation from zero profit (a loss) was $3,650, the cost of correcting the average out-of-control process was $7,000, and the present value of cost savings over the planning horizon from correcting an out-of-control process was $12,000. Determine the level of loss at which the NARF manager would be indifferent to investigating. (Use Table 1.)

TABLE 1

NORMAL DISTRIBUTION WITH STANDARD DEVIATION OF $350,000

X ($)	PROBABILITY OF DEVIATION ≤ X (≥ |X|)
0	.50
−105,000	.38
−210,000	.27
−315,000	.18
−420,000	.12
−525,000	.07
−630,000	.04
−735,000	.02
−840,000	.01
−945,000	.004
−1,050,000	.001

Probability of being in control = Probability of deviation ≤ *X*

Cost Accounting and Linear Programming

27

As management decisions have become more closely studied, mathematical models have become more widely adopted; examples discussed in previous chapters include discounted cash-flow models for capital-budgeting decisions, control models for inventory decisions, and multiple-regression models for estimating cost behavior patterns. To avoid groping in the dark, accountants and managers must be able to interpret the inputs, outputs, assumptions, and limitations of these models. The ultimate usefulness of these decision models depends on their key ingredients—which are often accounting data. In particular, users should be conscious of the effects of measurement errors on decisions.

Linear programming (hereafter often referred to as LP) will be the last formal decision model discussed in this book. Our basic approach is not altered. We examine the model and explore its implications for accounting systems and measurements. Our cost-benefit theme persists; the worth of formal models and more elaborate systems ultimately depends on whether decisions will be collectively improved.

The rudiments of LP are discussed, but the focus is on the interpretation of the solutions, not on the procedures for obtaining the solutions. Of course, books on mathematics or quantitative methods should be consulted if you wish to develop a solid grasp of resource allocation models like LP.

the linear-programming model*

Although the LP model may be used in a variety of decision contexts, its most widespread use is as a short-run allocation model. All such short-run models assume that a fixed set of resources is available that generates a specified level of fixed costs. The objective is to decide on what types and amounts of products or services to produce or sell in the face of revenue and cost behavior regarding the given set of resources. Practical examples of LP applications include blending gasoline, designing transformers, scheduling flights, formulating shipping schedules, and setting production schedules.

single constraint

Chapter 11 pointed out that the choice of what product to emphasize is not dependent on contribution margins alone. That is, the most profitable product is not necessarily the product with the highest gross profit or contribution margin per unit of *product.* Instead, the preferable product is that which produces the largest contribution per unit of the scarce resource or constraining factor, such as total available machine-hours.

The basic idea propounded in Chapter 11 still holds, but in practice there is usually more than one constraint. Therefore, the problem becomes one of maximizing total contribution, given many constraints. The LP model is designed to provide a solution to such problems.

building the model

All of us are familiar with linear equations (for example, $X + 3 = 9$). We also know that simultaneous linear equations become progressively more difficult to solve with pencil and paper as the number of equations (and unknowns) increases. LP essentially involves: (a) constructing a set of simultaneous linear equations and inequalities, which represent the model of the problem and which include many variables; and (b) solving the equations with the help of the digital computer.

The formulation of the equations—that is, the building of the model—is far more challenging than the mechanics of the solution. The model aims at being a valid and accurate portrayal of the problem. Computer programmers can then take the equations and process the solution.

As a minimum, accountants and managers should be able to recognize the types of problems in their organizations that are most susceptible to analysis

* If you are familiar with linear programming, skip these sections and jump to the section, "Implications for Managers and Accountants."

by linear programming. They should also be able to help in the construction of the model—that is, in specifying the objective, the constraints, and the variables. Ideally, they should understand the mathematics and should be able to talk comfortably with the operations researchers who are attempting to express their problem mathematically. However, the position taken here is that the accountant and the manager should concentrate on the formulation of the model and not worry too much about the technical intricacies of the solution. The latter may be delegated to the mathematicians; the feasibility of delegating the former is highly doubtful.

Consider a company that has two departments, machining and finishing. This company makes two products, A and B, each of which requires processing in each of two departments, machining and finishing. There are 200 hours of machining capacity and 120 hours of finishing capacity available per day. Product A requires 1 hour of machining time per unit and 1 hour of finishing time per unit. Therefore, the daily capacities for A are 200 product units for machining and 120 for finishing. However, Product B requires 2 hours of machining time per unit, but only .6 hours of finishing time per unit. Therefore, the daily capacities for B are 200 ÷ 2 = 100 product units for machining and 120 ÷ .6 = 200 for finishing. These and other relevant data are summarized as follows:

	CAPACITIES (PER DAY) IN PRODUCT UNITS		
Products	Dept. 1 Machining	Dept. 2 Finishing	Contribution Margin per Unit
A	200	120	$2.00
or			
B	100	200	$2.50

Severe material shortages for Product B will limit its production to a maximum of 90 per day. How many units of each product should be produced each day to obtain the maximum profit?

The LP approach has the following basic pattern, although variations and shortcuts are available in unique situations:

1. Determine the objective. Usually this takes the form of either maximization of profit or minimization of cost. Technically, this objective is called an *objective function,* a figure of merit, or a measure of effectiveness.
2. Determine basic relationships in the situation, especially the constraints (which specify the available or *feasible* alternatives).
3. Compute the optimum solution. Techniques may vary here. In uncomplicated situations, the graphic approach is easiest to see. However, algebraic approaches are more widely used in practice.

Using our example, let's apply these steps.

1. *Determine the objective.* The objective here will be to find the product combination that maximizes *total* contribution margin. This can be expressed in equation form

EXHIBIT 27-1

LINEAR PROGRAMMING—GRAPHIC SOLUTION

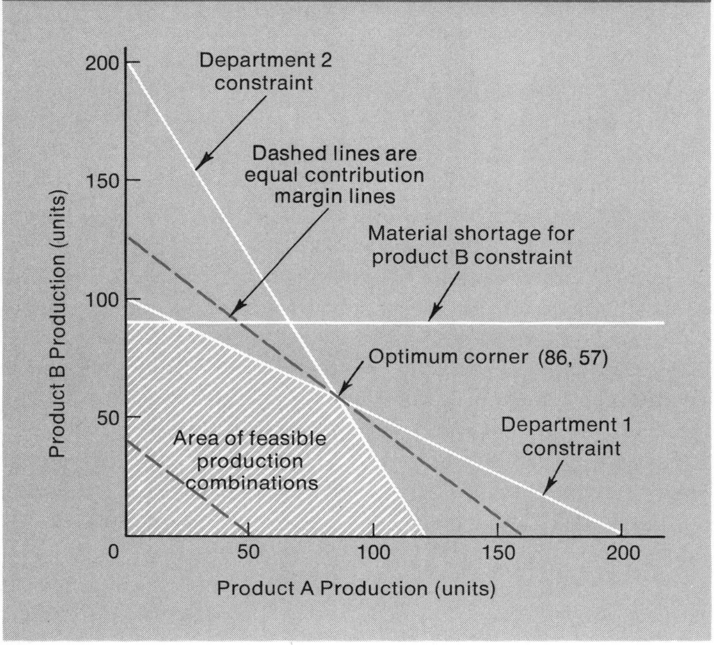

as follows: \$2.00A + \$2.50B = Total contribution margin, where A equals the number of A product units and B the number of B product units. We want to maximize this objective function.

2. *Determine basic relationships.* The relationships here can be depicted by inequalities as follows:

Department 1:	$A + 2B \leq 200$	
Department 2:	$A + .6B \leq 120$	
Material shortage for Product B:	$B \leq 90$	
Because negative production is impossible,	$B \geq 0$	and $A \geq 0$

The three solid lines on the graph in Exhibit 27-1 will aid visualization of the existing constraints for Departments 1 and 2 and of the material shortage.[1] The feasible alternatives are those that are technically possible. We do not want to bother with useless computations for impossible alternatives. The shaded area in Exhibit 27-1 shows the boundaries of those product combinations that are feasible—that is, combinations of quantities of A and B that satisfy all the constraining factors.

[1] As an example of how the lines are plotted in Exhibit 27-1, assume for Department 1 that $B = 0$; then $A = 200$. Assume that $A = 0$; then $B = 100$. Connect those two points with a straight line.

3. *Compute optimum solution.* In step 2 we have concentrated on physical relationships alone. Now we return to the economic relationships expressed as the objective in step 1.

graphic solution In the graphic solution, the optimum solution must lie on one of the corners of the "area of feasible product combinations."

Why must the best solution lie on a corner? Consider all possible combinations that will produce an equal total contribution margin, say, a total contribution margin of \$100 ($\$2.00A + \$2.50B = \$100$). This is a straight dashed line through (50, 0) and (0, 40). Other equal total contribution margins can be represented by lines parallel to this one. The equal total contribution margins increase as the lines get further from the origin. The optimum dashed line is the one furthest from the origin that has a feasible point on it; this happens at a corner (86, 57). This will become apparent if you put a ruler on the graph and move it outward from the origin and parallel with the \$100 line. In general,[2] the optimal solution lies at the corner where the dashed line intersects an *extreme point* of the area of feasible combinations.

The slope of the objective function (the dashed line representing the equal total contribution margin, *TCM*) can be computed from the equation:

$$TCM = \$2.00A + \$2.50B$$

To find the slope (the rate of change of B for one additional unit of A), divide by the coefficient of B and transfer B to the left-hand side of the equation:

$$\frac{TCM}{\$2.50} = \frac{\$2.00}{\$2.50}A + B$$

$$B = \frac{TCM}{\$2.50} - \frac{\$2.00}{\$2.50}A$$

Therefore, the slope of the objective function is a negative \$2.00/\$2.50 or $-\frac{4}{5}$.

trial and error The same result can be accomplished by trial and error, usually by working with the corners of the polygon delineated by the constraints. The steps are simple:

a. Start with a possible combination.
b. Compute the profit.

[2] An exception occurs if the dashed line has the same slope as a constraint line. Then any combination along the intersection of the dashed line and constraint line would provide the same maximum total contribution margin.

c. Move to another possible combination to see if it will improve the result in *b*. Keep moving from corner to corner until no further improvement is possible.[3]

These computations, corner by corner, are summarized as follows:

		COMBINATION		
Trial	Corner	Product A	Product B	Total Contribution Margin
1	0,0	0	0	\$2.00(0) + \$2.50(0) = \$ 0
2	0,90	0	90	2.00(0) + 2.50(90) = 225.00
3	20,90	20	90	2.00(20) + 2.50(90) = 265.00
4	86,57	86	57	2.00(86) + 2.50(57) = 314.50*
5	120,0	120	0	2.00(120) + 2.50(0) = 240.00

* Optimum.

substitution of scarce resources

At the outset of this example, the reader may have jumped to the conclusion that production of Product B, which promises the most margin *per unit,* should be maximized. Then any remaining productive capacity should be devoted to Product A. This is fallacious reasoning, because the scarce factor is productive capacity. The key to the optimum solution rests in the relative rates of substitution and profitability per unit (hour or day) of *productive capacity.* This point becomes clearer if we examine the graph. Moving from corner (20, 90) to corner (86, 57) implies that the company is transferring the scarce resource (productive capacity) between the products. In Department 1, each productive hour devoted to one unit of Product B may be given (sacrificed or traded) for two units of Product A. Will this exchange add to profitability? Yes, as shown below:

Total contribution margin at corner (20, 90)		\$265.00
Added contribution margin from Product A:		
66 units @ \$2.00	\$132.00	
Lost contribution margin, Product B:		
33 units @ \$2.50	82.50	
Net additional contribution		49.50
Total contribution margin at corner (86, 57)		\$314.50

[3] This is a simplified version of the *simplex* method, which is described later in this chapter. Note that the optimum point (86, 57) can be solved algebraically by solving the two pertinent constraint inequalities as simultaneous equations:

$$(1)\quad A + 2B = 200$$
$$(2)\quad A + .6B = 120$$

Subtract (2) from (1):

$$2B - .6B = 200 - 120$$
$$1.4B = 80$$
$$B = 80 \div 1.4 = 57$$

Substitute for B in (1):

$$A + (2)(57) = 200$$
$$A = 200 - 114 = 86$$

This approach is not recommended. It provides a solution that maximizes the total number of physical units, but it ignores the critical role of the *contribution per unit.*

As we move from corner (20, 90) to (86, 57), we are contending with the Department 1 constraint. There is a net advantage of trading two units of A for one unit of B; such substitution will add $1.50 to the total contribution (receive two times $2.00, or $4.00, instead of one times $2.50). The increase in total contribution, as shown above, is $49.50.

But the advantage of substituting A for B reverses when the Department 2 constraint takes effect. As we move from corner (86, 57) to corner (120, 0), the rate of substitution may be stated as follows: Each productive hour devoted to one unit of Product B may be devoted to .6 of a unit of Product A. This would entail giving up $2.50 contribution margin in exchange for .6($2.00) or $1.20 contribution margin, a decrease of the total contribution margin of $1.30 for each unit of Product B given up. Therefore, corner (86, 57) is the optimum solution.

Note again that the heart of the substitutions discussed above is a matter of swapping a given contribution margin per unit of *scarce resource* for some other contribution margin per unit of *scarce resource;* it is not simply a matter of comparing margins per unit of *product.*

implications for managers and accountants

Like all formal decision models, LP models are subject to measurement errors and other limitations that often have important implications for managers and accountants.

sensitivity analysis

What are the implications of a faulty estimate of the revenue, cost, or technical coefficients[4] used in the LP model? **These accounting and engineering measurements inevitably affect the slope of the objective function, the equal-contribution line in our example, and also affect the feasible set.** Questions about measurement errors are frequently explored via sensitivity analysis, as we have done in previous chapters.

Errors in approximations of costs and revenues per unit may reduce or increase unit-contribution margins, but may not tilt the slope of the equal-contribution line enough to alter the optimal solution. That is, the slope of the equal-contribution line may change, but when the line is pushed outward from the origin, the extreme corner can be the same as before. Thus, the optimal decision about product mix may be unchanged, even though the total contribution is affected.

Reconsider the material costs for Product A in our illustration. Management is concerned that its material costs for A will be, say, $10.00 instead of the $9.50 used in computing the $2.00 contribution appearing in the original solution. What is the cost of the prediction error?

[4] The coefficients of the constraints are often called *technical coefficients.* For example, in Department 1 the technical coefficient of A is 1 hour and the technical coefficient of B is 2 hours.

The contribution margin for A would become \$1.50 instead of \$2.00. The new optimal solution can be found by either graphic means or by corner computations, as before. The slope of the equal-contribution line, the objective function, would change from the $-4/5$ in Exhibit 27-1 to $-3/5$.[5] The new optimal solution would be unchanged,[6] so the cost of the prediction error would be zero (that is, the decision would be the same regardless of this particular error.)

The next obvious question is how much measurement error can be tolerated before the optimal choice would change? That is, what is the critical value, the value where the (86, 57) combination is no longer optimal? Concentrate on the constraint for Department 1. If the slope of the objective function is the same as that constraint, optimal solutions will be identical all along that constraint as long as it is binding. For example, if the contribution of Product A falls to \$1.25, the objective function will be \$1.25*A* + \$2.50*B*, which is the same slope as the constraint for Department 1. Then the total contribution would be the same for corners (20, 90) and (86, 57):

CORNER	*TOTAL CONTRIBUTION MARGIN*
20, 90	\$1.25(20) + \$2.50(90) = \$250
86, 57	1.25(86) + 2.50(57) = 250

Suppose the material cost were \$.90 higher than originally expected. Then the contribution margin for A would become \$1.10 instead of \$2.00. The slope of the objective function would change from $-4/5$ to $-11/25$. The new optimal solution would be different. If you put a ruler on the graph and move it outward from the origin using a $-11/25$ slope, the optimum corner will now be (20, 90), providing a contribution of \$247. The cost of the prediction error[7] would be:

(1) Original decision, given original prediction: (86, 57)	
(2) Results of optimal decision, given alternative parameter, \$1.10(20) + \$2.50(90)	\$247
(3) Results of original decision (using alternative parameters), \$1.10(86) + \$2.50(57)	237
(4) Cost of prediction error, (2) − (3)	\$ 10

effects of other costs

In the illustration above, the original solution is relatively insensitive to errors in predicting material costs. Of course, other complexities could be introduced. For example, the material costs of both A and B might change simultaneously. Moreover, a change in labor productivity would affect both the contribution margins and

[5] The computation of the slope shown earlier would be altered by substituting \$1.50 for the \$2.00 used in the original computation.

[6]

CORNER	*TOTAL CONTRIBUTION MARGIN*
20, 90	\$1.50(20) + \$2.50(90) = \$255
86, 57	1.50(86) + 2.50(57) = 272*

* Optimum

[7] Chapter 3 describes how to compute the cost of a prediction error.

the technical coefficients. You can easily imagine more complicated situations where heavy interdependencies (many constraints and many products) might make the action choices very sensitive.

Regardless of what decision model is used, the impact of sensitivity analysis is usually the same. If the prediction errors may prove costly, more resources may be spent initially to enhance the accuracy of the predictions before an action choice is made. Also, once the choice is made, extra efforts may be made to implement the choice so that the predicted outcomes (for example, costs or production volumes) are achieved. Of course, such endeavors are economically justifiable when the costs of prediction errors are sufficiently alarming. Indeed, when optimal actions are very sensitive to measurement errors, the formal model can be linked to the accounting control system.[8]

shadow prices

The output of computer programs frequently provides *shadow prices,* which are measures of the contributions foregone by failing to have one more unit of scarce capacity in a particular situation. Thus, a shadow price of $1 for machining means that the total contribution of the firm would increase by $1 if machining capacity were increased by one unit. Therefore, shadow prices facilitate the computation of the possible changes in contribution from expansion of capacity.

Despite their ready availability, shadow prices should be interpreted cautiously. They are valid quantifications of opportunity costs provided that the basic solution (the chosen types of products and idle facilities) does not change. For example, the shadow prices would not change as long as some A, some B, and some idle facilities were present. But the shadow prices would change if either all A or all B became the optimal solution.

assumptions and limitations

Among the major assumptions underlying the LP model are:

1. All relationships are linear. (For a discussion of linearity, see Chapter 25.)
2. All constraints and coefficients are stated with certainty—that is, are known magnitudes. (However, probabilities may be used to forecast the specific magnitudes that are used in the construction of the LP model.)
3. Solutions in fractional units are permissible. (Otherwise, rounding is performed; or integer programming may be desirable, whereby only integer solutions are allowed.)

Few actual situations completely satisfy these assumptions. Therefore, the user must be on guard that the approximations of the LP model are simplifications that are tolerable in relation to their impact on the particular decisions

[8] See J. Demski, "Variance Analysis Using a Constrained Linear Model," in D. Solomons, ed., *Studies in Cost Analysis* (Homewood, Ill.: Richard D. Irwin, Inc., 1968), pp. 526–40.

faced. The key question is whether some costly blunders may be made as a result of choosing the wrong decision model or as a result of various measurement errors.

simplex method

The fundamental problem of linear programming is to discover the specific set of variables that satisfies all constraints and maximizes (or minimizes) the objective sought. Although graphical methods aid visualization and are useful for two or possibly three variables, they are impractical where many variables exist. The *simplex method*, a general technique for solving any linear-programming problem, is an iterative, step-by-step process that is very effective, especially when a digitial computer performs the calculations. Basically, the simplex method proceeds by solving sets of simultaneous equations where the number of unknowns in each set is equal to the number of constraints. Although it is much too detailed to be described here, the simplex method essentially starts with a specific feasible alternative and algebraically tests it by substitution to see if the solution can be improved. These substitutions continue until no further improvement is possible, and thus the optimum solution is produced.

Computer programs can accommodate a large number of variables and constraints. Therefore, users such as accountants or managers should concentrate on the construction of the model and on the validity of its inputs—the statement of the objective function, the constraints, the estimation of all magnitudes employed. For example, are plant capacities and product-contribution margins accurately measured?

SUMMARY

The linear programming model is a widely used formal decision model for deciding how to optimize the use of a given set of scarce resources in the face of interdependencies and constraints. Accountants and managers should be especially alert to the sensitivity of the LP solution to possible measurement errors of all parameters of the model—the technical coefficients (resource required per unit), constant terms (total capacities) in the constraint equations, and the coefficients (e.g., contribution margin per unit) of the objective function.

SUGGESTED READINGS

Bierman, Harold, and Thomas R. Dyckman, *Managerial Cost Accounting,* 2nd ed. New York: The Macmillan Company, 1976.

Demski, Joel S., *Information Analysis.* Reading, Mass.: Addison-Wesley Publishing Co., Inc., 1972.

FELTHAM, GERALD A., *Information Evaluation.* Sarasota, Fla.: American Accounting Association, 1972.

LIVINGSTONE, JOHN LESLIE, ed., *Management Planning and Control: Mathematical Models.* New York: McGraw-Hill Book Company, 1970.

MILLER, D. W., and M. K. STARR, *Executive Decisions and Operations Research,* 2nd ed. Englewood Cliffs, N.J.: Prentice-Hall, Inc., 1969.

STOCKTON, R. STANSBURY, *Introduction to Linear Programming.* Homewood, Ill.: Richard D. Irwin, Inc., 1971.

WAGNER, HARVEY M., *Principles of Operations Research with Applications to Managerial Decisions,* 2nd ed. Englewood Cliffs, N.J.: Prentice-Hall, Inc., 1975.

PROBLEM FOR SELF-STUDY

PROBLEM

Reconsider the illustration in the chapter. Suppose the production rate for Product A in Department 1 will be 400 per day instead of 200. The relevant labor and overhead for Department 1 regarding Product A in the original solution was assumed to be $1,600 per day, which was $8.00 per product unit. The total labor and overhead cost of $1,600 per day is unchanged. What is the cost of the prediction error?

SOLUTION

The labor and overhead cost for Product A would be reduced from $8.00 per unit to $1,600 ÷ 400 = $4.00 per unit. Thus, the contribution margin for A would be increased from $2.00 to $6.00 per unit. In addition, the machining time for Product A would be reduced to 200 ÷ 400 = .5 hour per product unit. Therefore, the objective function and the constraint for Department 1 would change:

$$\text{Total contribution margin} = \$6.00A + \$2.50B$$
$$\text{Department 1:} \quad .5A + 2B \leq 200$$

The new relationships are shown in Exhibit 27-2. Note that the new slope of the objective function is −6.00/2.50 or −2.4, which is steeper than the slope of the Department 2 constraint. This means that as you push the equal-total-contribution line outward from the origin, the most extreme feasible point will be (120, 0), providing a contribution of $6 × 120 units, or $720.

The cost of the prediction error is:

(1) Original decision, given original prediction: (86, 57)	
(2) Results of optimal decision, given alternative parameters	$720
(3) Results of original decision, using alternative parameters:	
$6.00(86) + $2.50(57) or $516 + $143	659
(4) Cost of prediction error, (2) − (3)	$ 61

QUESTIONS, PROBLEMS, AND CASES

27-1 Define *linear programming.*

27-2 Give five examples of business applications of linear programming.

27-3 What is an *objective function?* A *feasible* alternative?

27-4 What are the four basic steps in linear programming?

27-5 What are *technical coefficients?*

27-6 What are *shadow prices?*

EXHIBIT 27-2

LINEAR PROGRAMMING—REVISED GRAPHIC SOLUTION

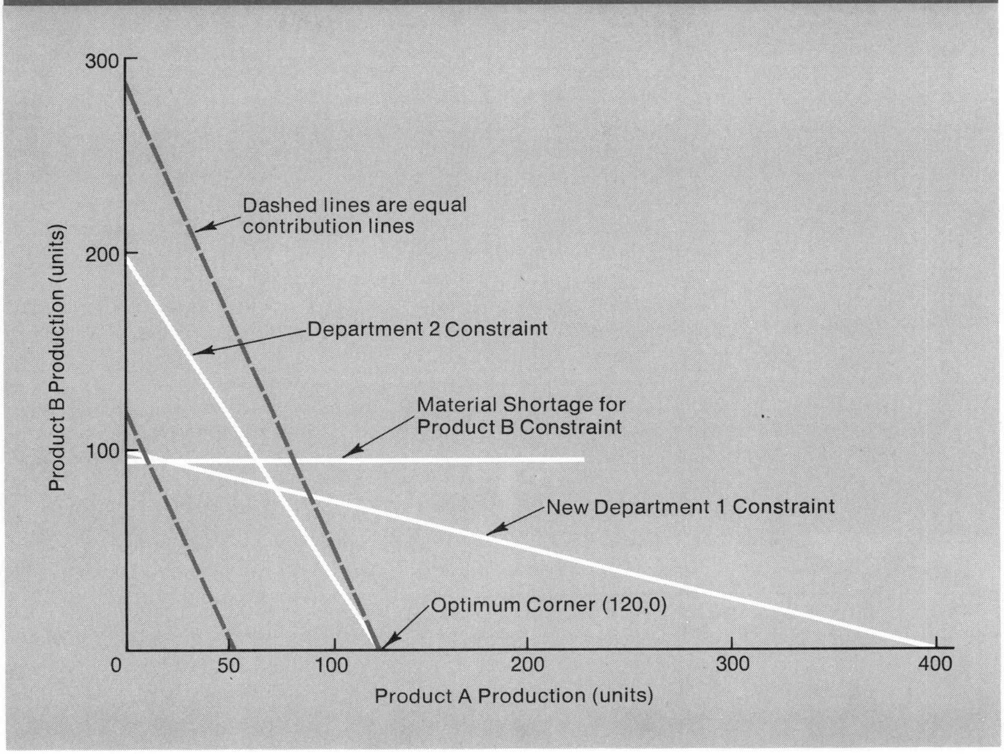

27-7 List three assumptions underlying the LP model.

27-8 Describe the *simplex method.*

27-9 *Allocation of Machine Time* Machine 1 has 24 hours available time and Machine 2 has 20 hours for processing to two products. Product X yields a contribution margin of \$2 per unit; Product Y, \$1 per unit. These products must be sold in proportions such that the quantity of X will be equal to or less than the quantity of Y. X requires 6 hours' time on Machine 1 and 10 hours' time on Machine 2. Product Y requires 4 hours' time on Machine 1 only.

required

Using graphic techniques, determine which product combination will maximize profit. Express the relationships in mathematical form.

27-10 *Finding Optimal Mixture for Box of Chocolates* (Adapted from Miller and Starr, *Executive Decisions and Operations Research,* pp. 217–22.) A candy manufacturer is attempting to find the optimal mixture for a box of chocolates. There are two kinds of candy that he wants in the box, C_1 and C_2. The following are the characteristics of the candy and the box:

	C_1	C_2	BOX
Number of pieces	x	y	35 or greater
Weight per piece (oz.)	1.6	0.8	32 or more
Space per piece (sq. in.)	2.0	1.0	65*
Cost per piece	$.02	$.01	$.60 maximum

* Maximum. By the use of fillers, the box can range from 40 square inches to 65 square inches.

required

Find the optimal mixture (least cost) by graphic means.

27-11 *Adding Another Constraint* Assume the same facts and requirements as in 27-10 except that at least 10 pieces of C_1 must be in the mixture.

27-12 *Linear Programming and Minimum Cost* The local agricultural center has advised Sam Bowers to spread at least 4,800 pounds of a special nitrogen fertilizer ingredient and at least 5,000 pounds of a special phosphate fertilizer ingredient in order to increase his crops. Neither ingredient is available in pure form.

A dealer has offered 100-pound bags of VIM at $1 each. VIM contains the equivalent of 20 pounds of nitrogen and 80 pounds of phosphate. VOOM is also available in 100-pound bags, at $3 each; it contains the equivalent of 75 pounds of nitrogen and 25 pounds of phosphate.

Express the relationships as inequalities. How many bags of VIM and VOOM should Bowers buy in order to obtain the required fertilizer at minimum cost? Solve graphically.

27-13 *Formulate Objective Function* (SIA) Z LTD. produces two products, A and B. Product A sells for $50 per unit and requires 3 hours of direct-labor time to produce. Product B sells for $30 per unit and requires 2 hours of direct-labor time. Assume, for simplicity, that direct labor is the only variable production cost. The cost of direct labor is $7 per hour.

Fixed costs of Z LTD. are $500 per period.

Owing to the specialized nature of Z LTD's direct-labor requirements, the amount of direct labor available for production cannot be varied in the short run. For next period the maximum number of direct-labor hours available is 120 hours.

Z LTD's marketing expert advises that the maximum number of units that could be sold next period is 30 units of A and 45 units of B.

required

1. Z LTD. must decide how many units of A and B to produce next period in order to maximize its profit. To assist in this decision problem you are asked to formulate it as a linear programming problem—i.e., set up the objective function and the constraints. You are not required to solve the problem.
2. A linear programming problem is an example of a *deterministic* model; i.e., the various numbers and relationships within the model are assumed to be known with certainty. Given, however, that most firms operate in an uncertain environment, do you think that it is wise to ignore uncertainty in decisions such as this? Why?

27-14 *Automobile Profit Analysis* (D. Green and G. Miller) The *Wall Street Journal* reported in February 1970 on the Chrysler Corporation's performance for the year 1969. Among other items, the story pointed out that Chrysler had boosted its market share from 10 percent in 1962 to 18 percent in 1968. In 1969, however, countermeasures by Ford and General Motors plus a 10 percent decline (that is, 1 million units) in total industry sales created severe problems for Chrysler. In its (unsuccessful) efforts to maintain its market share and protect its profitability, Chrysler cut prices and increased advertising allowances, which reduced contribution by an average of $100 per unit compared to 1968. Working toward internal economies, cutbacks in technical and administrative staff permitted a 20 percent reduction in fixed costs for 1969 relative to 1968. Nonetheless, 1969 pretax profits were only $80 million on sales of 1.4 million units, whereas 1968 pretax profit was $300 million.

required

From these fragments, answer the following questions. *Notice:* It is not hard to solve this by trial and error.

1. What was the fixed cost in 1968?
2. What was the fixed cost in 1969?
3. What was per-unit contribution in 1968?
4. What was per-unit contribution in 1969?
5. List major assumptions you have made and discuss them briefly.

27-15 *Formulate Objective Function* (CMA, adapted) The Tripro Company produces and sells three products, hereafter referred to as Products A, B, and C. The company is currently changing its short-range planning approach in an attempt to incorporate some of the newer planning techniques. The controller and some of his staff have been conferring with a consultant on the feasibility of using a linear programming model for determining the optimum product mix.

Information for short-range planning has been developed in the same format as in prior years. This information includes expected sales prices and expected direct-labor and material costs for each product. In addition, variable and fixed overhead costs were assumed to be the same for each product, because approximately equal quantities of the products were produced and sold.

PRICE AND COST INFORMATION (PER UNIT)

	A	B	C
Selling price	$25.00	$30.00	$40.00
Direct labor	7.50	10.00	12.50
Direct materials	9.00	6.00	10.50
Variable overhead	6.00	6.00	6.00
Fixed overhead	6.00	6.00	6.00

All three products use the same type of direct material, which costs $1.50 per pound. Direct labor is paid at the rate of $5.00 per hour. There are 2,000 direct-labor hours and 20,000 pounds of direct materials available in a month.

required

1. Formulate and label the linear-programming objective function and constraint functions necessary to maximize Tripro's contribution margin. Use Q_A, Q_B, Q_C to represent units of the three products.
2. What underlying assumptions must be satisfied to justify the use of linear programming?

27-16 *Effects of Regression Analysis* Refer to the preceding problem. The consultant, upon reviewing the data presented and the linear-programming functions developed, performed further analysis of overhead costs. He used a multiple linear-regression model to analyze the overhead cost behavior. The regression model incorporated observations from the past 48 months of total overhead costs and the direct-labor hours for each product. The following equation was the result:

$$Y = \$5{,}000 + 2X_A + 4X_B + 3X_C$$

where Y = monthly total overhead in dollars
X_A = monthly direct-labor hours for Product A
X_B = monthly direct-labor hours for Product B
X_C = monthly direct-labor hours for Product C

The total regression has been determined to be statistically significant, as has each of the individual regression coefficients.

Reformulate the objective function for Tripro Company using the results of this analysis.

27-17 *Multiple Choice* (CPA) A company markets two products, Alpha and Gamma. The marginal contributions per gallon are \$5 for Alpha and \$4 for Gamma. Both products consist of two ingredients, D and K. Alpha contains 80 percent D and 20 percent K, while the proportions of the same ingredients in Gamma are 40 percent and 60 percent respectively. The current inventory is 16,000 gallons of D and 6,000 gallons of K. The only company producing D and K is on strike and will neither deliver nor produce them in the foreseeable future. The company wishes to know the numbers of gallons of Alpha and Gamma that it should produce with its present stock of raw materials in order to maximize its total revenue.

1. The objective function for this problem could be expressed as
   a. $f_{max} = 0X_1 + 0X_2 + 5X_3 + 5X_4$
   b. $f_{min} = 5X_1 + 4X_2 + 0X_3 + 0X_4$
   c. $f_{max} = 5X_1 + 4X_2 + 0X_3 + 0X_4$
   d. $f_{max} = X_1 + X_2 + 5X_3 + 4X_4$,
   e. $f_{max} = 4X_1 + 5X_2 + X_3 + X_4$
2. The constraint imposed by the quantity of D on hand could be expressed as
   a. $X_1 + X_2 \geq 16{,}000$
   b. $X_1 + X_2 \leq 16{,}000$
   c. $.4X_1 + .6X_2 \leq 16{,}000$
   d. $.8X_1 + .4X_2 \geq 16{,}000$
   e. $.8X_1 + .4X_2 \leq 16{,}000$
3. The constraint imposed by the quantity of K on hand could be expressed as
   a. $X_1 + X_2 \geq 6{,}000$
   b. $X_1 + X_2 \leq 6{,}000$
   c. $.8X_1 + .2X_2 \leq 6{,}000$
   d. $.8X_1 + .2X_2 \geq 6{,}000$
   e. $.2X_1 + .6X_2 \leq 6{,}000$
4. To maximize total revenue, the company should produce and market
   a. 106,000 gallons of Alpha only
   b. 90,000 gallons of Alpha and 16,000 gallons of Gamma
   c. 16,000 gallons of Alpha and 90,000 gallons of Gamma
   d. 18,000 gallons of Alpha and 4,000 gallons of Gamma
   e. 4,000 gallons of Alpha and 18,000 gallons of Gamma
5. Assuming that the marginal contributions per gallon are \$7 for Alpha and \$9 for Gamma, the company should produce and market
   a. 106,000 gallons of Alpha only
   b. 90,000 gallons of Alpha and 16,000 gallons of Gamma
   c. 16,000 gallons of Alpha and 90,000 gallons of Gamma
   d. 18,000 gallons of Alpha and 4,000 gallons of Gamma
   e. 4,000 gallons of Alpha and 18,000 gallons of Gamma

27-18 *Product Mix* (SIA) The Carter Company currently enjoys a strong demand for its Standard Product so that, in effect, it can be sold in unlimited quantities at the list price of $1.70 per unit. However, the long-term market trend appears to be toward more "trading up" among buyers. As a consequence, the initial product and process specifications have just been completed for a new deluxe model, which would be priced initially at $1.80 per unit.

The firm is now planning its weekly output for the next quarter. Because the company does not wish to expand its investment in plant and equipment, no changes in capacity are contemplated during this period. However, an arrangement has just been made with a local foundry to provide additional castings, if needed, during the period.

There has been some disagreement over the "correct" product mix for the quarter. While he agrees it is not critical, the sales manager would like to have some production of the deluxe items. The production manager is being pressed by the new foundry supplier for a preliminary estimate of volume for the quarter.

Late yesterday, agreement was reached that an analyst would be asked to evaluate the problem and to present his findings this morning. The following ground rules for the analysis were established:

1. Because profit conditions were so favorable, the mix must maximize return on investment over the quarter.
2. If justified on the above basis, limited production of up to as many as 1,500 units of the deluxe item could be produced per week.

The relevant cost estimates, process times, and planned capacities are shown below:

	STANDARD	DELUXE	CAPACITY AVAILABLE
Costs (dollars per unit):			
Purchased casting	.40	.60	
Casting operation*	.40	.60	
Machining operation	.25	.15	
Assembling operation	.30	.25	
Time (minutes per week):			
Machining operation	8	4	8,000
Assembling operation	4	3	6,000

* Exclusive of fixed overhead costs. Purchased castings skip the casting operation.

required

Assume you are the analyst. Your work should demonstrate your knowledge of the following:

1. Set up the problem for solution by linear programming and develop an initial solution. Explain each variable and constraint.
2. Develop an objective function.
3. Is the objective function of your model consistent with that stated by management? How would the fixed overhead costs in our casting department be treated in the analysis?
4. Would your approach to part 1 above have been different if the agreement had been that exactly 1,500 deluxe units must be produced next quarter? Why?
5. If both standard and deluxe units are to be produced, it is quite likely that some down-time will be necessary in the machining department to change machinery over from one product to another. Have you included, or could you include, this fact in your analysis?

6. What specific kinds of information would you hope to be able to provide for management from the optimal solution?

27-19 *LP and Matrices* (CPA, adapted) This problem assumes knowledge of simplex tableaus, which are not covered in the chapter. Select the best answer for each of the following items.

1. If there are four activity variables and two constraints in a linear-programming problem, the most products that would be included in the optimal solution would be
   a. 6. b. 4. c. 2. d. 0. e. None of the above.
2. Assume the following data for the two products produced by Wagner Company:

	PRODUCT A	PRODUCT B
Raw-material requirements (units)		
X	3	4
Y	7	2
Contribution margin per unit	$10	$4

   If 300 units of raw material X and 400 units of raw material Y are available, the set of relationships appropriate for maximization of revenue using linear programming would be

   a. $3A + 4B \geq 300$; $7A + 2B \geq 400$; $10A + 4B$ MAX
   b. $3A + 7B \geq 300$; $4A + 2B \geq 400$; $10A + 4B$ MAX
   c. $3A + 7B \leq 300$; $4A + 2B \leq 400$; $10A + 4B$ MAX
   d. $3A + 4B \leq 300$; $7A + 2B \leq 400$; $10A + 4B$ MAX
   e. None of the above.
3. A final tableau for a linear-programming profit-maximization problem is shown below:

	X_1	X_2	X_3	S_1	S_2	
X_1	1	0	4	3	−7	50
X_2	0	1	−2	−6	2	60
	0	0	5	1	9	1,200

   If X_1, X_2, and X_3 represent products, S_1 refers to square feet (in thousands) of warehouse capacity, and S_2 refers to labor-hours (in hundreds), the number of X_1 that should be produced to maximize profit would be
   a. 60. b. 50. c. 1. d. 0. e. None of the above.
4. Assuming the same facts as in item 3, the contribution to profit of an additional 200 hours of labor would be
   a. 9. b. 2. c. 1. d. −7. e. None of the above.
5. Assuming the same facts as in item 3, an additional 1,000 square feet of warehouse space would
   a. Increase X_1 by 3 units and decrease X_2 by 6 units.
   b. Decrease X_2 by 6 units and increase X_1 by 2 units.
   c. Decrease X_1 by 7 units and increase X_2 by 2 units.
   d. Increase X_1 by 3 units and decrease X_2 by 7 units.
   e. Do none of the above.
6. The following is the final tableau of a linear programming profit maximization problem:

	X_1	X_2	S_1	S_2	
X_1	1	0	−5	3	125
X_2	0	1	1	−1	70
	0	0	5	7	500

The marginal contribution to profit of 5 for each added resource unit S_1 can be maintained if the added resource units do not exceed

a. 125. b. 100. c. 70. d. 25. e. None of the above.

7. Assume the following per-unit raw-material and labor requirements for the production of products A and B.

	PRODUCT A	*PRODUCT B*
Pounds of lead	5	7
Hours of labor	3	4

Assuming that 13,400 pounds of lead and 7,800 hours of labor are available, the production of products A and B required to use all the available lead and labor hours is shown in the following final Gaussian tableau.

$$\begin{matrix} 1 & 0 & -4 & 7 & 1{,}000 \\ 0 & 1 & 3 & -5 & 1{,}200 \end{matrix}$$

If the available amounts were increased to 15,000 pounds of lead and 8,800 hours of labor, the matrix operation to perform to determine the production schedule that would fully utilize these resources would be

a. $\begin{pmatrix} 5 & 7 \\ 3 & 4 \end{pmatrix} \begin{pmatrix} 15{,}000 \\ 8{,}800 \end{pmatrix}$ c. $\begin{pmatrix} -4 & 7 \\ 3 & -5 \end{pmatrix} \begin{pmatrix} 1{,}000 \\ 1{,}200 \end{pmatrix}$

b. $\begin{pmatrix} 15{,}000 \\ 8{,}800 \end{pmatrix} \begin{pmatrix} -4 & 7 \\ 3 & -5 \end{pmatrix}$ d. $\begin{pmatrix} -4 & 7 \\ 3 & -5 \end{pmatrix} \begin{pmatrix} 15{,}000 \\ 8{,}800 \end{pmatrix}$

e. None of the above.

8. The following schedule provides data for Product A, which is processed through processes 1 and 2, and Product B, which is processed through process 1 only:

	PRODUCT A	*PRODUCT B*
Raw material cost per gallon	$ 4	$ 9
Process 1 (500-gallon input capacity per hour):		
Processing cost per hour	$60	$60
Loss in processing	30%	20%
Process 2 (300-gallon input capacity per hour):		
Processing cost per hour	$50	
Loss in processing	10%	
Selling price per gallon	$20	$40

If the objective were to maximize profit per eight-hour day, the objective function of a profit-maximizing linear-programming problem would be

a. $20A + 40B - 4A - 4B$

b. $20A + 40B - 4A - 4B - 60(A + B) - 50A$

c. $20(.63A) + 40(.80B) - 4(.63A) - 9(.8B)$
$-60\left(\frac{A + B}{500}\right) - 50\left(\frac{.7A}{300}\right)$

d. $20(.63A) + 40(.80B) - 4A - 9B$
$-60\left(\frac{A}{500} + \frac{B}{500}\right) - 50\left(\frac{.7A}{300}\right)$

e. None of the above.

9. Assuming the same facts as in item 8, a constraint of the problem would be

a. $.63A \leq 2{,}400$ d. $.9A \leq 4{,}000$

b. $.8A \leq 2{,}400$ e. None of the above.

c. $.7A + .8B \leq 4{,}000$

27-20 *Choosing a Product Mix* Brian Jones has just received a university degree in management. He has taken the position of assistant to the president of a fairly small company in South Africa that manufactures tungsten carbide drill steels for the gold-mining industry.

Two types of drill steels are manufactured. One has a steel rod of $\frac{3}{4}$-inch diameter and the other a diameter of 1 inch. The manufacturing takes place in three departments. In the tip-fabricating department, tungsten carbide tips are manufactured from powdered wolfram. In the steel-forging department, the steel rods are slotted and prepared for the insertion of the tips. The assembly department puts the tips and steel rods together in a brazing process.

Each department has severe capacity limits. The first constraint prohibits further capital expenditure because of a very weak liquid position arising from past losses; the second is the labor situation in South Africa, which makes the hiring of more labor or the working of overtime virtually impossible. The capacity of each department is as follows:

Tip fabricating (Dept. A)	240,000 hours
Steel forging (Dept. B)	180,000 hours
Assembly (Dept. C)	180,000 hours

The treasurer has just completed the budget for the forthcoming year. Because of the renewed confidence in gold, the company is expected to produce at full capacity.

The treasurer has produced the following profit analysis of the two products, on which a major production decision was based:

	¾″	1″
Selling price	$5.00	$6.00
Direct materials		
Tungsten carbide	$ .75	$1.00
Steel	1.45	2.05
	$2.20	$3.05
Direct labor		
Department A	$ .60	$ .30
Department B	.20	.30
Department C	.20	.15
	$1.00	$ .75
Prime costs (from above)	$3.20	$3.80
Factory overhead	.80	.60
Selling and administration	.50	.60
Total costs	$4.50	$5.00
Profit	$ .50	$1.00

The market survey performed by the sales manager showed that the company could sell as many of either type of rod as it could produce. However, the sales manager urged that the needs of three of the big gold mines must be satisfied in full, even though this meant producing a large number of the $\frac{3}{4}$-inch rods that had only half the profit of the 1-inch rods. The quantities required by these three gold mines amounted to 270,000 $\frac{3}{4}$-inch rods and 540,000 1-inch rods.

As the 1-inch rods have twice the profit of the $\frac{3}{4}$-inch rods, the treasurer suggested that the remaining capacity be used to produce two 1-inch rods for every $\frac{3}{4}$-inch rod. This would mean producing an additional 135,000 $\frac{3}{4}$-inch rods and 270,000 1-inch rods. Department B would then be working at full capacity and would be the constraint on any further production.

The treasurer then produced the following budgeted income statement for the forthcoming year. Sales are expected to occur evenly throughout the year.

	¾″	1″
Sales (in units)	405,000	810,000
Sales (in dollars)	$2,025,000	$4,860,000
Direct materials	891,000	2,470,500
Direct labor	405,000	607,500
Factory overhead	324,000	486,000
Selling and administration	202,500	486,000
Total costs	$1,822,500	$4,050,000
Profit	$ 202,500	$ 810,000

Jones, as his first assignment, is asked by the president to comment on the budgeted income statement. Specifically, the president feels that capacity might be better utilized with a different sales mix. He wants to know just how much it is costing the company in lost profits by supplying the full needs of the three big gold-mining customers. He feels it might be more profitable to produce only the 1-inch rods.

Jones gathers the following additional information before making his recommendations:

Wolfram is purchased at $10 per kilogram (1,000 grams). The $\frac{3}{4}$-inch tips use an average of 75 grams and the 1-inch tips 100 grams. The special alloy steel costs $2,000 per 2,000 pounds. The $\frac{3}{4}$-inch rods use 1.45 pounds and the 1-inch rods 2.05 pounds.

Direct-labor costs per hour follow:

Department A	$2.40
Department B	1.80
Department C	1.50

Tip fabricating (Department A) is a skilled process. The smaller tips require twice as much detailed work. Owing to the nature of the work, most of the labor is considered fixed because it would be difficult to replace. Approximately 200,000 hours per annum in Department A are considered fixed. In the steel-forging process, the bigger rods require more time because of the handling difficulties. In the assembly department, the smaller rods again take more time because of the intricacies of the operations. However, this is not skilled work.

Factory overhead in the budgeted income statement is considered 50 percent fixed. It has been allocated to the products on the basis of direct labor.

Fixed selling and administrative expenses have been allocated on the basis of the number of units sold. Variable selling expenses are predicted to be 10¢ per unit sold of either size.

required | If you were Jones, what would be your recommendations to the president?

27-21 *Sensitivity Analysis* Refer to the basic illustration in the chapter. To what amount must the unit contribution of Product B rise so that the present optimal product combination of (86, 57) no longer applies?

27-22 *Meaning of Total Contribution* Consider an objective function:

$$\max.\quad \$1A + \$2B + \$4C$$

The optimum solution is $A = 100{,}000$, $B = 200{,}000$, $C = 300{,}000$.

$$\text{Net profit} = \text{Total contribution margin} - \text{Other costs}$$
$$= \$1{,}700{,}000 - \$400{,}000 = \$1{,}300{,}000$$

Additional investigation of cost behavior revealed that the unit contributions should have been $1.10, $2.80, and $4.30, respectively. Despite the better cost approximations that provided the more accurate unit contributions, the optimal decision of 100,000, 200,000, and 300,000 units was unchanged.

required

Would the change in unit contributions affect the net profit? Why? By how much? What is the cost of the prediction error?

27-23 *General Review, Prediction Error* (J. Demski and C. Horngren) Mary Demhorn is the manager of a company that produces two products in two departments. She has great confidence in her cost accounting data regarding direct material and direct labor, but she is less sure about the manufacturing overhead. She has been using a plantwide total factory overhead prediction equation of:

$9,000 per month + $4 per direct-labor hour.

Mary is considering whether to produce either product alone or some combination of the two products. The available alternatives are:

ALTERNATIVES	*PRODUCE AND SELL PRODUCT*	
	X	Y
a_1	0	0
a_2	200	400
a_3	0	500
a_4	250	0

Mary collects the following, price, cost, and technical data:

	PRODUCT	
	X	Y
Selling price per unit	$114	$149
Incremental selling cost per unit sold	$ 4	$ 8
Direct material per unit	$ 20	$ 30
Direct-labor hours per unit:		
Machining	1	2
Finishing	4	3

The wage rate is $7 per hour in machining and $9 per hour in finishing. In addition, miscellaneous (all fixed) nonmanufacturing costs for the company as a whole are $12,000 per month.

required

(Show computations)

1. Which action should Mary select?
2. What are the per-unit (a) variable costs and (b) absorption costs that each product would be valued at as finished-goods inventory? Use a "denominator" volume of 3,000 hours.

3. The day after she has made an irrevocable decision in part 1, Mary is presented with some impeccable regression analysis of the manufacturing overhead costs in each department:

Machining overhead = \$6,000 per month
+ \$3.00 per machining direct-labor hour

Finishing overhead = \$3,000 per month
+ \$5.00 per finishing direct-labor hour

She is convinced that these prediction models give a "truer" or "more accurate" picture than the plantwide model that she used. What is the cost of using the wrong model (akin to the cost of prediction error)?

27-24 *Comprehensive Review* (J. Demski) This problem includes linear programming and the regression analysis that was discussed in Chapter 25. Access to a computer is necessary for its solution.

In November 19_1 the Bayshore Manufacturing Company was in the process of preparing its budget for 19_2. As the first step it prepared a proforma income statement for 19_1 based on the first ten months' operations and revised plans for the last two months. This income statement, in condensed form, was as follows:

Sales		\$3,063,000
Materials	\$1,105,000	
Labor	343,000	
Factory overhead	858,000	
Selling and administrative	459,000	2,765,000
Income before income taxes		\$ 298,000

These results were better than were expected and operations were close to capacity, but Bayshore management was not convinced that demand would remain at present levels and hence had not planned any increase in plant capacity. Its equipment was specialized and made to its order; over a year lead time was necessary on all plant additions.

Bayshore produces three products; sales have been broken down by product, as follows:

100,000 of Product A @ \$20.63	\$2,063,000
40,000 of Product B @ 10.00	400,000
20,000 of Product C @ 30.00	600,000
Total sales	\$3,063,000

Management has ordered a profit analysis for each product and has available the following information:

	A	*B*	*C*
Material	\$ 6.00	\$ 4.00	\$17.25
Labor	2.33	1.00	3.50
Factory overhead	5.83	2.50	8.75
Selling and administrative	3.09	1.50	4.50
Total costs	\$17.25	\$ 9.00	\$34.00
Selling price	20.63	10.00	30.00
Profit	\$ 3.38	\$ 1.00	\$ (4.00)

Factory overhead has been applied on the basis of direct-labor cost at a rate of 250 percent; management feels that approximately a quarter of the overhead is variable and that it varies primarily with labor cost. Selling and administrative costs have been allocated on the basis of sales at the rate of 15 percent; approximately one-half of these costs are variable, and they vary primarily with sales in dollars.

As the first step in the planning process, the sales department has been asked to make estimates of what it could sell; these estimates have been reviewed by the firm's consulting economist and by top management. They are as follows:

A	130,000 units
B	50,000 units
C	50,000 units

Production of these quantities is impossible. Each product requires the use of machines in each of two departments; department 1 has a practical capacity of 75,000 hours and department 2, 60,000 hours. The industrial engineering department has concluded that these capacities cannot be increased without the purchase of additional equipment. The production rates for the two departments are:

	PRODUCT		
	A	B	C
Department 1	2 per hour	4 per hour	4 per hour
Department 2	3 per hour*	8 per hour	$\frac{4}{3}$ per hour

* Thus, it takes .333 hours to process Product A in Department 2, *not* .33 or .3333. In this problem your answer is extremely sensitive to rounding, so for uniformity use .333.

These solutions to the limited-production problem have been rejected: (1) subcontracting the production out to other firms is considered to be unprofitable because of problems of maintaining quality, (2) operating a second shift is impossible because of shortage of labor, (3) operating overtime would create problems because a large number of employees are "moonlighting" and would therefore refuse to work more than the normal 40-hour week. Price increases have also been rejected; although they would result in higher profits this year, the long-run competitive position of the firm would be weakened, resulting in lower profits in the future.

The treasurer then suggested that Product C had been carried at a loss too long and that now was the time to eliminate it from the product line. If all facilities were used to produce A and B, profits would be increased.

The sales manager objected to this solution because of the need to carry a full line. In addition he maintained that there was a group of customers who had provided and would continue to provide a solid base for the firm's activities and these customers' needs must be met. He provided a list of these customers and their estimated purchases (in units), which totaled as follows:

A	80,000
B	32,000
C	12,000

It was impossible to verify these contributions, but they appeared reasonable, and they served to narrow the bounds of the problem so that the president concurred.

The treasurer reluctantly acquiesced, but maintained that the remaining capacity should be used to produce A and B. Because A produced about 3.4 times as much profit as B, he suggested that the production of A (in excess of the 80,000 minimum set by the sales manager) be 3.4 times that of B (in excess of the 32,000 minimum set by the sales manager).

The production manager made some quick calculations and said that this would result in budgeted production and sales of approximately

A	122,000
B	44,000
C	12,000

The treasurer then made a calculation of what profits would be, as follows:

A	122,000 @ $3.38	$412,360
B	44,000 @ $1.00	44,000
C	12,000 @ ($4.00)	(48,000)
		$408,360

As this would represent a substantial increase over the current year, there was a general feeling of self-satisfaction. Before final approval was given, however, the president said he would like to have his new assistant check over the figures. Somewhat piqued, the treasurer agreed, and at that point the group adjourned.

The next day the above information was submitted to you as your first assignment on your new job as the president's assistant. *Prepare an analysis showing the president what he should do.*

Exhibit 27-3 presents additional cost-related data that are available in the accounting records.

27-25 *Sensitivity Analysis* (J. Demski) Refer to the preceding problem. The managers of Bayshore are uncertain about some of the predictions they made in arriving at their production plans for 19_2. You are to determine the cost

EXHIBIT 27-3

ACCOUNTING INFORMATION FOR THE FIRST TEN MONTHS OF 19_1.

	LABOR COST			OVERHEAD				
Month	Dept. 1	Dept. 2	Total	Dept. 1	Dept. 2	Total	Sales Revenue	Selling & Administrative Expense
1	14,000	14,600	28,600	31,512	34,638	66,150	275,000	39,900
2	13,500	12,500	26,000	29,825	33,487	63,312	240,000	37,400
3	12,200	11,800	24,000	29,450	33,133	62,583	230,000	36,950
4	13,200	13,800	27,000	31,025	33,854	64,879	260,000	38,800
5	13,800	13,200	27,000	31,437	34,381	65,818	270,000	39,700
6	12,300	11,700	24,000	29,675	32,962	62,637	230,000	37,200
7	11,500	11,500	23,000	29,325	32,321	61,646	220,000	36,200
8	14,500	13,500	28,000	31,400	34,208	65,608	270,000	39,050
9	12,000	13,000	25,000	30,950	33,591	64,541	255,000	38,750
10	11,700	11,300	23,000	29,262	32,485	61,747	220,000	36,300
Total	128,700	126,900	255,000	303,861	335,060	638,921	2,470,000	380,250

of the following possible prediction errors if they were to occur and if the production plans were based on the predictions in the preceding problem. The errors in each section are to be analyzed separately. You should assume, however, that any production-rate changes systematically affect the respective product's labor cost.

1. The selling price of Product A may actually be \$21.63 instead of the predicted magnitude of \$20.63.
2. The material cost of producing Product B may actually be \$5.00 instead of the predicted magnitude of \$4.00.
3. The production rate in Department 1 for Product C may actually be 3 per hour instead of the predicted magnitude of 4 per hour.
4. The production rate in Department 2 for Product C may actually be 2 per hour instead of $4/3$ per hour.
5. Major repairs to the machinery in Department 2 may reduce its capacity to 55,000 hours.

If the planned production is infeasible, Bayshore's production staff usually cuts back the production with smallest profit (*as calculated in the first profit analysis in the preceding problem*) subject to the restriction that the production of any product must be sufficient to satisfy the demands of the customers whose needs must be met.

Cost Accounting in Professional Examinations

28

Many readers may eventually take the Certified Public Accountant examination or the Certified Management Accountant[1] examination. This chapter will discuss how to prepare for the cost accounting topics in these examinations. It will also consider some major alternative approaches in general-ledger treatments, standard costs, and spoilage. This book includes numerous questions and problems extracted from past CPA and CMA examinations.[2]

Cost accounting and income taxes are the two most important topics in the Practice section of the CPA examination. Of special note is the increasing

[1] The CMA program was established in 1972 by the National Association of Accountants to recognize educational attainment and professional competence in management accounting. For more information, write the Institute of Management Accounting, 570 City Center Building, Ann Arbor, Mich. 48108.

[2] These are designated in this book as "(CPA)" and "(CMA)." The Society of Industrial Accountants of Canada administers a set of annual examinations on accounting. There are various sections with graduated levels of difficulty. The problems designated "(SIA)" in this book have been taken with permission from the society's examinations. Some of these problems have been adapted to bring out particular points in the chapter for which they were chosen. Several additional problems have been taken from the examinations of the Certified General Accountants Association of Canada (CGAA). Examinations are also given by the Institute of Internal Auditors. For a comparison of curricula and the content of professional examinations, see the report of the Committee on Professional Examinations, *Accounting Review,* Supplement to Vol. XLXI, 1976.

emphasis in recent years on the management decision-making purposes of cost accounting rather than the inventory and income-determination purposes. Topics covered include standard costs, flexible budgets, analysis of variances, cost-volume-profit analysis, direct costing, relevant costs for special decisions, and discounted cash-flow analysis. Each recent examination has included quantitative methods and techniques, including mathematics, statistics, and probability analysis (see Chapters 24 and 25 for examples). Problems on product costing emphasize process costs, including spoilage, and joint costs.

The CMA examination covers the same cost accounting topics as the CPA examination. In addition, it emphasizes budgeting, and it contains many more questions on internal accounting than the CPA examination.

review for examinations

The candidate faces an imposing task of review. In addition to preparing for probable cost accounting topics, he or she must recognize two special characteristics of a national examination. First, accounting terminology is not uniform. Second, alternative solutions are possible for many accounting problems.

divergent terminology

Variations in terminology will inevitably appear in a national examination that is drawn from many sources. Likely questions and problems are contributed by individual accounting practitioners, public accountants, accounting teachers, and employees of the relevant professional association. They are stockpiled and used as needed.

Thus, the candidate should be familiar with the variety and interchangeability of many cost terms.[3] For example, *factory overhead* is usually interchangeable with the following terms: *indirect manufacturing costs, manufacturing expenses, factory burden,* and *manufacturing overhead. Cost of goods sold* is often called *cost of sales.*

alternative solutions

Alternative solutions can arise because (a) there are slight variations in practical accounting procedures or techniques, and (b) there are different schools of thought on certain cost matters, such as ledger designs, analysis of variances, and accounting for spoilage. Thus, the candidate must anticipate problem situations that do not exactly coincide with either the text treatments that he knows or the cases that he has encountered in practice.

The associations take elaborate steps to insure equitable grading of examinations. The graders recognize and give full credit to all alternative solutions that are reasonable. Therefore, the candidate should not be discouraged if in

[3] Eric Kohler, *Dictionary for Accountants,* 5th ed. (Englewood Cliffs, N.J.: Prentice-Hall, Inc., 1975) is a helpful reference.

the course of his review he finds published solutions[4] that do not precisely agree with his favorite approach or the approach that he learned when he took a cost accounting course. The associations have found it impracticable to publish a large collection of alternative solutions, so they usually confine their "unofficial answers" to one widely accepted approach.

Problems are designed to be straightforward. Requirements should be taken at face value. Special assumptions are rarely necessary. Sometimes a candidate still feels that an assumption must be made. If so, the assumption should be stated, together with the reasons therefor. *Such reasons should include a statement as to why a possible alternate assumption is being rejected.*

In summary, although the candidate does not have to worry about the acceptability of alternate solutions to a given problem, he or she should have an awareness of divergencies in accounting practice and terminology. As a minimum, his terminology should coincide with that given in the problem. He should also know what areas of cost accounting tend to have alternative treatments. In these areas especially, he should take particular pains with his answer so that it will be clear to all graders.[5] We shall examine these areas in the remainder of this chapter.

alternate general-ledger treatments

The text has generally shown one technique for cost accumulation in the general ledger. Obviously, there are alternative methods, some of which have been briefly described (Chapters 4 and 7). Comparisons of a few alternative techniques are shown in Exhibit 28-1. The first and third columns show the methods used throughout this book; the second and fourth columns show alternate techniques that are preferred by many accountants for reasons of convenience or feasibility. For example, consider the problem of when to isolate a material-efficiency variance. In concept, it should be isolated as quickly as possible for control purposes (see column 3). Yet often the efficiency variance is impossible to calculate until the work is completed. Consequently, in these cases, the method shown in the fourth column is used.

standard costs

Standard costs may be integrated into the general ledger in a number of ways, depending on the preferences of the person who is setting up the standard-cost

[4] Divergences in practice and terminology creep not only into the examination but also into the "unofficial answers" that are published subsequent to the examination dates. These published answers are neither official nor necessarily the only acceptable solutions. Yet many students and teachers have the mistaken belief that the published solutions are *the* only acceptable answers.

[5] The candidate can be confident that the *proper* use of the specific techniques he has learned will be given full credit. However, in some instances, he can strengthen his solution by pointing out important aspects that might receive alternative treatment.

EXHIBIT 28-1

ALTERNATIVE GENERAL-LEDGER DESIGNS

TRANSACTION	*NONSTANDARD COST ACCOUNTING*						*STANDARD COST ACCOUNTING*					
	Col. 1			Col. 2			Col. 3			Col. 4		
Direct-material usage	Work in process	xx		Direct material used	xx		Work in process	xx		Work in process	xx	
	Stores		xx	Stores		xx	Efficiency or usage variance	xx		Stores		xx
							Stores		xx			
				Work in process	xx					Finished goods	xx	
				Direct materials used		xx				Efficiency or usage variance	xx	
										Work in process		xx
Payroll accounting	Work in process	xx		Direct labor	xx		Work in process	xx		Direct labor	xx	
	Department overhead	xx		Department overhead	xx		Direct-labor price variance	xx		Department overhead	xx	
	Accrued payroll		xx	Accrued payroll		xx	Direct-labor efficiency variance	xx		Direct-labor price variance	xx	
							Department overhead	xx		Accrued payroll		xx
							Accrued payroll		xx			
				Work in process	xx					Work in process	xx	
				Direct labor		xx				Direct labor		xx
										Finished goods	xx	
										Direct-labor efficiency variance	xx	
										Work in process		xx
Overhead accounting	Department overhead	xx		(Similar methods to those shown at the left.)								
	Various accounts		xx									
	or											
	(a) Depreciation	xx										
	Repairs	xx										
	Supplies used	xx										
	Various accounts		xx									
	(b) Department overhead	xx										
	Depreciation		xx									
	Repairs		xx									
	Supplies used		xx									

system. The candidate should be familiar with alternative methods, because the ledger procedure described in a given problem will influence a solution. No computations or entries should be prepared until the given general-ledger procedure (and specific types of variance analysis called for, if any) is fully comprehended. Problems on standard costs usually emphasize general-ledger entries and variance analysis. A key account, Work in Process, could appear in any one of three alternative ways, depending upon the system employed:

(ALTERNATIVE 1) WORK IN PROCESS

Actual quantities × Actual prices	Standard quantities × Standard prices

(ALTERNATIVE 2) WORK IN PROCESS

Actual quantities × Standard prices	Standard quantities × Standard prices

(ALTERNATIVE 3) WORK IN PROCESS

Standard quantities × Standard prices	Standard quantities × Standard prices

As explained in Chapter 7, the terminology for variances and the timing of the isolation of material, labor, and overhead variances will be influenced by the specific system employed.

Although the computations of material and labor variances are usually the same regardless of the standard-cost system used, the computations of overhead variances are by no means uniform in practice. The methodology described in Chapter 9 is generally superior to other methods, but published solutions have shown a number of alternative approaches. Moreover, a single overhead application rate, composed of both variable and fixed elements as described in a section of Chapter 9, is often used. These alternative solutions are described below, using the following basic data:

Budget formula for monthly overhead: \$100,000 fixed overhead
+ (\$1.00 × direct-labor hours)

Denominator volume, which is more often called normal or standard volume: 400,000 hours

Combined-overhead rate for product costing: $\frac{\$100,000 + (400,000 \times \$1.00)}{400,000} = \$1.25$

Month of August:

Actual direct hours	450,000
Standard direct hours allowed for work done	430,000
Actual overhead, including \$103,000 of fixed costs	\$570,000
Applied overhead, 430,000 × \$1.25	\$537,500
Total variance, \$570,000 less \$537,500	\$ 32,500

ALTERNATIVE 1 The recommended approach as described in Chapter 9. Budget based on standard hours allowed.

	ACTUAL	BUDGET—ACTUAL HOURS	BUDGET—STANDARD HOURS	APPLIED
		$100,000 + $1(450,000)	$100,000 + $1(430,000)	
V	$467,000	$450,000	$430,000	$430,000
F	103,000	100,000	100,000	107,500
	$570,000	$550,000	$530,000	$537,500

Spending Variance, $20,000 U

Efficiency Variance, $20,000 U ($1.00 × 20,000 hours)

Volume Variance,[6] $7,500 F ($.25 × 30,000 hours)

Budget Variance, $40,000 U

Volume Variance

Underapplied Overhead, $32,500 U

ALTERNATIVE 2 The pertinent budget level for measuring volume variance is considered to be actual hours rather than standard hours as in Alternative 1. Also, fixed factory overhead shows an efficiency variance (sometimes called an *effectiveness variance*), measured like other efficiency variances. This supposedly gives a measure of the efficient or inefficient utilization of facilities.

	ACTUAL	BUDGET—ACTUAL HOURS	ACTUAL HOURS × OVERHEAD RATE	APPLIED
V	$467,000	$450,000	$450,000	$430,000
F	103,000	100,000	112,500	107,500
	$570,000	$550,000	$562,500	$537,500

Budget Variance, $20,000 U

Volume Variance, $12,500 F (450,000 − 400,000) × $.25

Efficiency Variance:

Variable	$20,000 U
Fixed	5,000 U
	$25,000 U

COMPARISON OF ALTERNATIVES 1 AND 2: EFFICIENCY VARIANCE FOR FIXED OVERHEAD? Note that the efficiency variance is a subpart of the budget variance under Alternative 1, whereas it could be considered a subpart of the volume variance under Alternative 2. Let us compare these two alternatives more closely.

Alternative 1: Budget variance consists of both spending and efficiency variance.
Alternative 2: Budget variance is the same as the "spending" variance under Alternative 1.

The efficiency variance for variable overhead is the same under both alternatives.

Under Alternative 2, the fixed-overhead analysis differs considerably from that in Alternative 1. Basically, however, all that is done is to take the volume variance of $7,500 computed in Alternative 1 and subdivide it further as follows:

[6] The term "volume variance" is more likely to be encountered than the term favored in this book, "denominator variance." So be on special guard for the volume variance. That is why "volume variance" will be used throughout this chapter instead of "denominator variance." See Chapter 10 for additional discussion.

Volume variance in Alternative 1		$7,500 F
Breakdown in Alternative 2:		
Fixed-overhead efficiency variance, $.25 × 20,000 hours	$ 5,000 U	
True "volume" variance (actual hours worked minus denominator hours) × rate (50,000 hours × $.25)	12,500 F	$7,500 F

The efficiency variance for fixed overhead is a misnomer; it would be better to call it an effectiveness variance. It should be distinguished sharply from the efficiency variances for materials, labor, and variable overhead, because efficient usage of these three factors can affect actual cost incurrence, whereas short-run fixed-overhead cost incurrence is not affected by efficiency. Thus, a better label for the fixed-overhead "efficiency" variance would be "effectiveness" variance, a sort of rough-and-ready measure that may have some psychological value as a reminder to the department head that his efficiency has an impact on effective utilization of facilities.

This writer sees little merit in this computation except where ineffective utilization of facilities means a loss of sales. For instance, if maximum capacity is 500,000 standard hours, and the sales department can obtain orders in excess of 500,000-hour capacity, the inefficient use of facilities involves an opportunity cost that is properly chargeable to the foreman. The best measure of this cost would often be the lost contribution margins on the orders not filled. In lieu of this measure, the use of the effectiveness variance could be a crude attempt to quantify the foreman's performance. Hence, if an efficiency or effectiveness variance is employed, its weakness should be recognized.

Thus, the volume variance in Alternative 1 would be chargeable to someone other than the foreman. It might be traceable to the sales manager, to the head of production control, or to random outside influences. Under Alternative 1, the foreman would not ordinarily be considered explicitly responsible for efficient use of facilities.

ALTERNATIVE 3 This is a hybrid of Alternatives 1 and 2. It demonstrates that overhead-variance analysis can be conducted in a great number of ways. Here the budget is based on standard hours allowed, but the efficiency variance is computed by using a combined $1.25 rate rather than attributing efficiency to variable-overhead control only.

ACTUAL	*BUDGET STANDARD HOURS ALLOWED*	*APPLIED*
$570,000	$530,000	$537,000
↑ Budget Variance, $40,000 U	↑ Volume Variance, $7,500 F	↑

Subdivide the budget variance as follows:

Efficiency variance is $1.25 × 20,000 hours	$25,000 U
Remainder is spending variance	15,000 U
Budget variance	$40,000 U

ALTERNATIVE 4 This is the most miserable alternative of all, because the flexible-budget concept is not employed. Instead, the appropriate budget is considered to be the one based on the planned activity level used to set the overhead rate for product costing (normal or standard volume), regardless of the actual level of activity that ensues. The resulting variance analysis seems more confusing than it is worth; yet it is shown here because several CPA solutions through the years have presented this approach.

ACTUAL	*BUDGET— DENOMINATOR ACTIVITY*	*ACTUAL HOURS × OVERHEAD RATE*	*APPLIED*
$570,000	$500,000	$562,500	$537,500

Budget Variance,*	Volume Variance,†	Efficiency Variance,
$70,000 U	$62,500 F	$25,000 U

* Note that this compares actual cost incurrence with a budget based on activity entirely different from the actual activity level.

† The volume variance's main weakness is the use of a combined rate rather than the fixed-overhead rate, which is pertinent to the measure of a volume variance.

spoilage

The alternate ways of accounting for spoilage in process costing were discussed in Chapter 19. Many published solutions ignore the computations of equivalent units for spoilage, shrinkage, or waste. The reason cited in favor of this shortcut technique is that it automatically spreads spoilage costs over good units through the use of higher equivalent unit costs. However, the results of this shortcut are questionable in many cases, as was shown in Chapter 19. If the candidate faces a spoilage problem, he should solve it in the conceptually correct manner but make a special note to describe his approach and to state that alternative approaches ignore computations of equivalent units for spoilage, shrinkage, and waste.

SUMMARY

The candidate needs to be aware of which cost-accounting topics are most likely to appear on a professional examination. An analysis of the five to ten most recent examinations provides the best clues.[7]

He also should have a general knowledge of what areas in cost accounting are marked by divergent accounting terminology and techniques. These include general-ledger design, analysis of overhead variances, and accounting for spoilage.

[7] For example, see J. Harris and J. Krogstad, "A Profile and Index of the CMA Examination," and M. Usry, "Cost Accounting in the CPA Examination—Updated," both in *Accounting Review*, Vol. LI, No. 3 (July, 1976), pp. 633–42.

Careful study of appropriate topics in this book will fortify the candidate with sufficient background for success in the cost accounting phases of the professional examinations. Chapters 7–13 and 17–19 should be particularly helpful.

SUGGESTED READINGS

HORNGREN, CHARLES T., and J. ARTHUR LEER, *CPA Problems and Approaches to Solutions,* 4th ed. Englewood Cliffs, N.J.: Prentice-Hall, Inc., 1974.

MILLER, HERBERT E., and GEORGE MEAD, eds., *CPA Review Manual,* 5th ed. Englewood Cliffs, N.J.: Prentice-Hall, Inc., 1977.

QUESTIONS, PROBLEMS, AND CASES

28-1 What are the two special characteristics of the national professional examinations in accounting that the candidate must recognize?

28-2 "We should be careful to review the solutions to past professional examinations in accounting so that we learn the official answers." Do you agree? Why?

28-3 *Four Methods of Analyzing Overhead Variances* The Signe Company uses a combined-overhead rate of $4.00 per hour for product costing under a standard-cost system. Denominator activity is 10,000 hours, or 5,000 finished units. At that level the overhead budget is: variable, $30,000; fixed, $10,000.

Actual level of activity: 8,700 hours and 4,400 units produced
Actual overhead incurred: variable, $28,000; fixed, $9,700

required

Show at least four different methods of analyzing overhead variances. Include one method in which the appropriate budget is considered to be one based on denominator activity regardless of the actual activity that ensues; that is, assume that the flexible-budget concept is not employed.

28-4 *Standard Costs, Alternate Analysis of Variances* (CPA) The Dearborn Company manufactures Product X in standard batches of 100 units. A standard-cost system is in use. The standard costs for a batch are as follows:

Raw materials	60 lbs. @ $ .45 per lb.	$ 27.00
Direct labor	36 hrs. @ $2.15 per hr.	77.40
Overhead	36 hrs. @ $2.75 per hr.	99.00
		$203.40

Production for April 19_0 amounted to 210 batches. The relevant statistics follow:

Denominator output per month	24,000 units
Raw materials used	13,000 lbs.
Cost of raw materials used	$ 6,110.00
Direct-labor cost	$16,790.40
Overhead cost	$20,592.00
Average overhead rate per hour	$2.60

The management has noted that actual costs per batch deviate somewhat from standard costs per batch.

required Prepare a statement that will contain a detailed explanation of the difference between actual costs and standard costs.

Note: **Additional problems from professional examinations are found for nearly every chapter in this book, designated as (CPA), (CMA), or (SIA).**

Appendixes

SECTION FOUR

Cost Accounting Standards Board

A

Many organizations have had an influence on the development of cost accounting. In particular, the National Association of Accountants has published many research studies through the years. For a list of their publications, write to their headquarters at 919 Third Avenue, New York. The Financial Executives Institute, 50 West 44th Street, New York, also has many research publications on cost accounting.

The most influential organization of all will probably be the Cost Accounting Standards Board (CASB). In response to complaints about inconsistent accounting practices, the Board was created as an agent of Congress by a law passed in 1970 (Public Law 91-379):

> The Board shall from time to time promulgate cost accounting standards designed to achieve uniformity and consistency in the cost accounting principles followed by defense contractors and subcontractors under Federal contracts.

The Comptroller General of the United States is chairman of the CASB. He appoints the four other members; there must be two members from the accounting profession, one representative of industry, and one from a department of the Federal Government. The Board serves part time, but there is a full-time professional staff of approximately 25.

The magnitude of the CASB influence on accounting can become very great indeed. Over $100 billion is spent annually by the Department of Defense alone. Moreover, all negotiated contracts in excess of $100,000, defense and nondefense, are subject to CASB regulations. "Negotiated" means that the price is tied to costs rather than to competitive bidding. Some state and local governments also use the standards.

The topical coverage of the following CASB standards indicates the breadth of coverage. The standards are largely concerned with definitions, uniformity, and consistency. The standards begin with Number 400:

400 Definitions.
401 Cost accounting standard—consistency in estimating, accumulating and reporting costs.
402 Cost accounting standard—consistency in allocating costs incurred for the same purpose.
403 Allocation of home office expenses to segments.
404 Capitalization of tangible assets.
405 Accounting for unallowable costs.
406 Cost accounting standard—cost accounting period.
407 Use of standard costs for direct material and direct labor.
408 Accounting for costs of compensated personal absence.
409 Depreciation of tangible capital assets.
410 Allocation of general and administrative expenses.
411 Accounting for acquisition costs of material.
412 Composition and measurement of pension cost.
413 Adjustment of historical depreciation costs for inflation (withdrawn).
414 Cost of money as an element of the cost of facilities capital.
415 Deferred compensation costs.

Above all, the purpose of the standards is to obtain a "fair" price for both buyer and seller. That is, the standards focus on ways of using a "cost accounting pricing system" as a substitute for the "free market pricing system." Therefore, the applicability of the standards for other purposes, such as external reporting, is subject to challenge. For example, Standard #414 provides for allocating imputed interest on contractors' investments. Contractors are to use the "Renegotiation Board Rate," which is based on the interest rate on new private commercial loans maturing in five years. This rate is applied to the average investment in tangible capital assets and amortizable intangible capital assets. Nevertheless, the imputing of interest on capital is not a generally accepted accounting principle for reports to stockholders.

The Board's action will be worth monitoring, especially to see if CASB regulations sooner or later affect financial accounting standards. The Board will necessarily deal with topics pertaining to financial accounting, even though the CASB's primary focus is pricing.

The CASB publications are obtainable from the Board at 441 G Street, N.W., Washington, D.C. 20548.

Notes on Compound Interest and Interest Tables

B

interest

Interest is the cost of using money. It is the rental charge for funds, just as rental charges are made for the use of buildings and equipment. Whenever a time span is involved, it is necessary to recognize interest as a cost of using invested funds. This applies even if the funds in use represent ownership capital and if the interest does not entail an outlay of cash. The reason why interest must be considered is that the selection of one alternative automatically commits a given amount of invested funds that otherwise could be invested in some other opportunity. The measure of the interest in such cases is the return foregone by rejecting the alternative use.

Interest is often unimportant when short-term projects are under consideration, but it looms large when long-run plans are being considered. Because of this, the rate of interest in question is of telling import. The rate used will often influence the ultimate decision. For example, $100,000 invested now and compounded annually for ten years at 3 percent will accumulate to $134,392; at 7 percent, to $196,715.

interest tables

Four basic tables are used for computations involving interest. Tables 2 and 4 are the most pertinent for our purposes.

table 1—amount of $1 Table 1 shows how much $1 invested now will accumulate to in a given number of periods at a given compounded interest rate per period. The future proceeds of an investment of $1,000 for three years at 8 percent compound interest could be sketched as follows:

Accumulate →

$1,000 × $(1.08)^3$ or $1,000 × 1.2597* (from Table 1) = $1,259.70

0 1 2 3

Present Value ← Discount — Amount

* To minimize discrepancies from rounding, the four-place factor (1.2597) is used here instead of the three-place factor (1.260) shown in Table 1.

TABULAR CALCULATION

YEAR	INTEREST PER YEAR	CUMULATIVE INTEREST, CALLED COMPOUND INTEREST	TOTAL AT END OF PERIOD
0	$ —	$ —	$1,000.00
1	80.00	80.00	$1,080.00
2	86.40	166.40	1,166.40
3	93.30	259.70	1,259.70

Note that what is really being done in the tabular presentation is a series of computations that could appear as follows:

$$S_1 = 1{,}000(1.08)$$
$$S_2 = 1{,}000(1.08)^2$$
$$S_3 = 1{,}000(1.08)^3$$

The formula for the "amount of 1," often called the "future value of 1," can be written:

$$S = P(1 + r)^n$$
$$S = 1{,}000(1 + .08)^3 = \$1{,}259.70$$

S is the *amount,* the future worth; P is the present value, $1,000 in this case; r is the rate of return; n is the number of periods.

Fortunately, tables make key computations readily available, so that a facility in selecting the *proper* table will minimize computations. Check the accuracy of the answer on the preceding page against Table 1, page 910.

table 2—present value of $1

In the previous example, if $1,000 compounded at 8 percent per annum will accumulate to $1,259.70 in three years, then $1,000 must be the present value of $1,259.70 due at the end of three years. The formula for the present value can be derived by reversing the process of *accumulation* (getting the amount) that we just finished. Look at the earlier sketch to see the relationship between accumulating and discounting.

If
$$S = P(1 + r)^n$$

then
$$P = \frac{S}{(1 + r)^n}$$
$$P = \frac{\$1{,}259.70}{(1.08)^3} = \$1{,}000$$

Use Table 2, page 911, to check this calculation.

When accumulating, we advance or roll forward in time. The difference between our original amount and our accumulated amount is called *compound interest.* When discounting, we retreat or roll back in time. The difference between the future amount and the present value is called *compound discount.* Note the following formulas (where $P = \$1{,}000$):

$$\text{Compound interest} = P[(1 + r)^n - 1] = \$259.70$$

$$\text{Compound discount} = P\left[1 - \frac{1}{(1 + r)^n}\right] = \$259.70$$

table 3—amount of annuity of $1

An (ordinary) *annuity* is a series of equal payments (receipts) to be paid (or received) at the *end* of successive periods of equal length. Assume that $1,000 is invested at the end of each of three years at 8 percent:

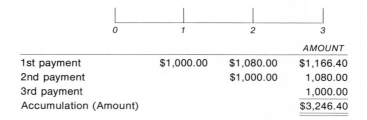

			AMOUNT
1st payment	$1,000.00	$1,080.00	$1,166.40
2nd payment		$1,000.00	1,080.00
3rd payment			1,000.00
Accumulation (Amount)			$3,246.40

The arithmetic shown above may be expressed algebraically as the amount of an ordinary annuity of \$1,000 for three years = $\$1{,}000(1 + r)^2 + \$1{,}000(1 + r)^1 + \$1{,}000$.

We can develop the general formula for S_n, the amount of an ordinary annuity of \$1, by using the example above as a basis:

1.	$S_n = 1 + (1 + r)^1 + (1 + r)^2$
2. Substitute:	$S_n = 1 + (1.08) + (1.08)^2$
3. Multiply (2) by $(1 + r)$:	$(1.08)S_n = 1.08 + (1.08)^2 + (1.08)^3$
4. Subtract (2) from (3): Note that all terms on right-hand side are removed except $(1.08)^3$ in equation (3) and 1 in equation (2).	$1.08S_n - S_n = (1.08)^3 - 1$
5. Factor (4):	$S_n(1.08 - 1) = (1.08)^3 - 1$
6. Divide (5) by $(1.08 - 1)$:	$S_n = \dfrac{(1.08)^3 - 1}{1.08 - 1} = \dfrac{(1.08)^3 - 1}{.08}$
7. The general formula for the amount of an ordinary annuity of \$1 becomes:	$S_n = \dfrac{(1 + r)^n - 1}{r}$ or $\dfrac{\text{Compound Interest}}{\text{Rate}}$

This formula is the basis for Table 3, page 912. Look at Table 3 or use the formula itself to check the calculations.

table 4—present value of an ordinary annuity of \$1

Using the same example as for Table 3, we can show how the formula of P_n, *the present value of an ordinary annuity,* is developed.

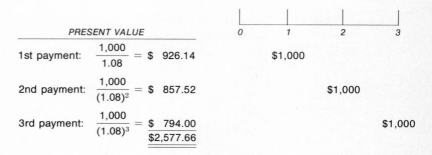

	PRESENT VALUE		0	1	2	3
1st payment:	$\dfrac{1{,}000}{1.08}$	= \$ 926.14		\$1,000		
2nd payment:	$\dfrac{1{,}000}{(1.08)^2}$	= \$ 857.52			\$1,000	
3rd payment:	$\dfrac{1{,}000}{(1.08)^3}$	= \$ 794.00				\$1,000
		\$2,577.66				

For the general case, the present value of an ordinary annuity of \$1 may be expressed:

1. $$P_n = \frac{1}{1 + r} + \frac{1}{(1 + r)^2} + \frac{1}{(1 + r)^3}$$

2. Substituting, $P_n = \frac{1}{1.08} + \frac{1}{(1.08)^2} + \frac{1}{(1.08)^3}$

3. Multiply by $\frac{1}{1.08}$: $P_n\frac{1}{1.08} = \frac{1}{(1.08)^2} + \frac{1}{(1.08)^3} + \frac{1}{(1.08)^4}$

4. Subtract (3) from (2): $P_n - P_n\frac{1}{1.08} = \frac{1}{1.08} - \frac{1}{(1.08)^4}$

5. Factor: $P_n\left(1 - \frac{1}{1.08}\right) = \frac{1}{1.08}\left[1 - \frac{1}{(1.08)^3}\right]$

6. or $P_n\left(\frac{.08}{1.08}\right) = \frac{1}{1.08}\left[1 - \frac{1}{(1.08)^3}\right]$

7. Multiply by $\frac{1.08}{.08}$: $P_n = \frac{1}{.08}\left[1 - \frac{1}{(1.08)^3}\right]$

The general formula for the present worth of an annuity of $1.00 is:

$$P_n = \frac{1}{r}\left[1 - \frac{1}{(1 + r)^n}\right] = \frac{\text{Compound Discount}}{\text{Rate}}$$

Solving,

$$P_n = \frac{.2062}{.08} = 2.577$$

This formula is the basis for Table 4, page 913. Check the answer in the table. The present-value tables, Tables 2 and 4, are used most frequently in capital budgeting.

Note that the tables for annuities are not really essential. That is, with Tables 1 and 2, compound interest and compound discount can be readily computed. Then it is simply a matter of dividing either of these by the rate to get values equivalent to those shown in Tables 3 and 4.

table 5—present value of SYD depreciation

As Chapter 13 explains more fully, depreciation is a deductible item that reduces income-tax cash outflows. Assume that some equipment has an original cost of $6,000, a useful life of three years, and a terminal scrap value of zero. Table 5, the *Present Value of Sum of the Years Digits' (SYD) Depreciation*, is developed for $6,000 depreciable investment at 8 percent:

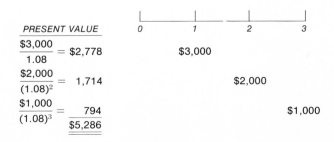

PRESENT VALUE	*0*	*1*	*2*	*3*
$\frac{\$3{,}000}{1.08} = \$2{,}778$		$3,000		
$\frac{\$2{,}000}{(1.08)^2} = 1{,}714$			$2,000	
$\frac{\$1{,}000}{(1.08)^3} = 794$				$1,000
$5,286				

Compare this result with the factor from the third-period row of Table 5: \$6,000(.881) = \$5,286.

To get the present value of the *income-tax* savings, the present value of SYD depreciation should be multiplied by the applicable tax rate. If the tax rate were 40 percent, the present value of the associated tax savings would be \$5,286 × .40, or \$2,114.

Consider another example of new equipment having a depreciable cost of \$100,000 and being depreciated on an SYD basis for eight years. The present value at 10 percent of the associated tax savings would be \$100,000 × (.740) × the income-tax rate. If the tax rate were 40 percent, the present value of the tax savings would be \$100,000(.740)(.40) = \$29,600.

TABLE 1

COMPOUNDED AMOUNT OF \$1.00

$S = P(1 + r)^n$. In this table P = \$1.00.

PERIODS	*4%*	*6%*	*8%*	*10%*	*12%*	*14%*	*20%*
1	1.040	1.060	1.080	1.100	1.120	1.140	1.200
2	1.082	1.124	1.166	1.210	1.254	1.300	1.440
3	1.125	1.191	1.260	1.331	1.405	1.482	1.728
4	1.170	1.263	1.361	1.464	1.574	1.689	2.074
5	1.217	1.338	1.469	1.611	1.762	1.925	2.488
6	1.265	1.419	1.587	1.772	1.974	2.195	2.986
7	1.316	1.504	1.714	1.949	2.211	2.502	3.583
8	1.369	1.594	1.851	2.144	2.476	2.853	4.300
9	1.423	1.690	1.999	2.359	2.773	3.252	5.160
10	1.480	1.791	2.159	2.594	3.106	3.707	6.192
11	1.540	1.898	2.332	2.853	3.479	4.226	7.430
12	1.601	2.012	2.518	3.139	3.896	4.818	8.916
13	1.665	2.133	2.720	3.452	4.364	5.492	10.699
14	1.732	2.261	2.937	3.798	4.887	6.261	12.839
15	1.801	2.397	3.172	4.177	5.474	7.138	15.407
16	1.873	2.540	3.426	4.595	6.130	8.137	18.488
17	1.948	2.693	3.700	5.055	6.866	9.277	22.186
18	2.026	2.854	3.996	5.560	7.690	10.575	26.623
19	2.107	3.026	4.316	6.116	8.613	12.056	31.948
20	2.191	3.207	4.661	6.728	9.646	13.743	38.338
30	3.243	5.744	10.063	17.450	29.960	50.950	237.380
40	4.801	10.286	21.725	45.260	93.051	188.880	1469.800

TABLE 2

PRESENT VALUE OF $1.00

$P = \frac{S}{(1+r)^n}$. In this table S = $1.00.

PERIODS	*4%*	*6%*	*8%*	*10%*	*12%*	*14%*	*16%*	*18%*	*20%*	*22%*	*24%*	*26%*	*28%*	*30%*	*40%*
1	.962	.943	.926	.909	.893	.877	.862	.847	.833	.820	.806	.794	.781	.769	.714
2	.925	.890	.857	.826	.797	.769	.743	.718	.694	.672	.650	.630	.610	.592	.510
3	.889	.840	.794	.751	.712	.675	.641	.609	.579	.551	.524	.500	.477	.455	.364
4	.855	.792	.735	.683	.636	.592	.552	.516	.482	.451	.423	.397	.373	.350	.260
5	.822	.747	.681	.621	.567	.519	.476	.437	.402	.370	.341	.315	.291	.269	.186
6	.790	.705	.630	.564	.507	.456	.410	.370	.335	.303	.275	.250	.227	.207	.133
7	.760	.665	.583	.513	.452	.400	.354	.314	.279	.249	.222	.198	.178	.159	.095
8	.731	.627	.540	.467	.404	.351	.305	.266	.233	.204	.179	.157	.139	.123	.068
9	.703	.592	.500	.424	.361	.308	.263	.225	.194	.167	.144	.125	.108	.094	.048
10	.676	.558	.463	.386	.322	.270	.227	.191	.162	.137	.116	.099	.085	.073	.035
11	.650	.527	.429	.350	.287	.237	.195	.162	.135	.112	.094	.079	.066	.056	.025
12	.625	.497	.397	.319	.257	.208	.168	.137	.112	.092	.076	.062	.052	.043	.018
13	.601	.469	.368	.290	.229	.182	.145	.116	.093	.075	.061	.050	.040	.033	.013
14	.577	.442	.340	.263	.205	.160	.125	.099	.078	.062	.049	.039	.032	.025	.009
15	.555	.417	.315	.239	.183	.140	.108	.084	.065	.051	.040	.031	.025	.020	.006
16	.534	.394	.292	.218	.163	.123	.093	.071	.054	.042	.032	.025	.019	.015	.005
17	.513	.371	.270	.198	.146	.108	.080	.060	.045	.034	.026	.020	.015	.012	.003
18	.494	.350	.250	.180	.130	.095	.069	.051	.038	.028	.021	.016	.012	.009	.002
19	.475	.331	.232	.164	.116	.083	.060	.043	.031	.023	.017	.012	.009	.007	.002
20	.456	.312	.215	.149	.104	.073	.051	.037	.026	.019	.014	.010	.007	.005	.001
21	.439	.294	.199	.135	.093	.064	.044	.031	.022	.015	.011	.008	.006	.004	.001
22	.422	.278	.184	.123	.083	.056	.038	.026	.018	.013	.009	.006	.004	.003	.001
23	.406	.262	.170	.112	.074	.049	.033	.022	.015	.010	.007	.005	.003	.002	
24	.390	.247	.158	.102	.066	.043	.028	.019	.013	.008	.006	.004	.003	.002	
25	.375	.233	.146	.092	.059	.038	.024	.016	.010	.007	.005	.003	.002	.001	
26	.361	.220	.135	.084	.053	.033	.021	.014	.009	.006	.004	.002	.002	.001	
27	.347	.207	.125	.076	.047	.029	.018	.011	.007	.005	.003	.002	.001	.001	
28	.333	.196	.116	.069	.042	.026	.016	.010	.006	.004	.002	.002	.001	.001	
29	.321	.185	.107	.063	.037	.022	.014	.008	.005	.003	.002	.001	.001	.001	
30	.308	.174	.099	.057	.033	.020	.012	.007	.004	.003	.002	.001	.001		
40	.208	.097	.046	.022	.011	.005	.003	.001	.001						

TABLE 3

COMPOUNDED AMOUNT OF ANNUITY OF $1.00 IN ARREARS*

$$S_n = \frac{(1 + r)^n - 1}{r}$$

PERIODS	*4%*	*6%*	*8%*	*10%*	*12%*	*14%*	*20%*
1	1.000	1.000	1.000	1.000	1.000	1.000	1.000
2	2.040	2.060	2.080	2.100	2.120	2.140	2.200
3	3.122	3.184	3.246	3.310	3.374	3.440	3.640
4	4.247	4.375	4.506	4.641	4.779	4.921	5.368
5	5.416	5.637	5.867	6.105	6.353	6.610	7.442
6	6.633	6.975	7.336	7.716	8.115	8.536	9.930
7	7.898	8.394	8.923	9.487	10.089	10.730	12.916
8	9.214	9.898	10.637	11.436	12.300	13.233	16.499
9	10.583	11.491	12.488	13.580	14.776	16.085	20.799
10	12.006	13.181	14.487	15.938	17.549	19.337	25.959
11	13.486	14.972	16.646	18.531	20.655	23.045	32.150
12	15.026	16.870	18.977	21.385	24.133	27.271	39.580
13	16.627	18.882	21.495	24.523	28.029	32.089	48.497
14	18.292	21.015	24.215	27.976	32.393	37.581	59.196
15	20.024	23.276	27.152	31.773	37.280	43.842	72.035
16	21.825	25.673	30.324	35.950	42.753	50.980	87.442
17	23.698	28.213	33.750	40.546	48.884	59.118	105.930
18	25.645	30.906	37.450	45.600	55.750	68.394	128.120
19	27.671	33.760	41.446	51.160	63.440	78.969	154.740
20	29.778	36.778	45.762	57.276	75.052	91.025	186.690
30	56.085	79.058	113.283	164.496	241.330	356.790	1181.900
40	95.026	154.762	259.057	442.597	767.090	1342.000	7343.900

* Payments (or receipts) at the *end* of each period.

TABLE 4

PRESENT VALUE OF ANNUITY OF $1.00 IN ARREARS*

$$P_n = \frac{1}{r}\left[1 - \frac{1}{(1+r)^n}\right]$$

PERIODS	4%	6%	8%	10%	12%	14%	16%	18%	20%	22%	24%	25%	26%	28%	30%	40%
1	0.962	0.943	0.926	0.909	0.893	0.877	0.862	0.847	0.833	0.820	0.806	0.800	0.794	0.781	0.769	0.714
2	1.886	1.833	1.783	1.736	1.690	1.647	1.605	1.566	1.528	1.492	1.457	1.440	1.424	1.392	1.361	1.224
3	2.775	2.673	2.577	2.487	2.402	2.322	2.246	2.174	2.106	2.042	1.981	1.952	1.923	1.868	1.816	1.589
4	3.630	3.465	3.312	3.170	3.037	2.914	2.798	2.690	2.589	2.494	2.404	2.362	2.320	2.241	2.166	1.849
5	4.452	4.212	3.993	3.791	3.605	3.433	3.274	3.127	2.991	2.864	2.745	2.689	2.635	2.532	2.436	2.035
6	5.242	4.917	4.623	4.355	4.111	3.889	3.685	3.498	3.326	3.167	3.020	2.951	2.885	2.759	2.643	2.168
7	6.002	5.582	5.206	4.868	4.564	4.288	4.039	3.812	3.605	3.416	3.242	3.161	3.083	2.937	2.802	2.263
8	6.733	6.210	5.747	5.335	4.968	4.639	4.344	4.078	3.837	3.619	3.421	3.329	3.241	3.076	2.925	2.331
9	7.435	6.802	6.247	5.759	5.328	4.946	4.607	4.303	4.031	3.786	3.566	3.463	3.366	3.184	3.019	2.379
10	8.111	7.360	6.710	6.145	5.650	5.216	4.833	4.494	4.192	3.923	3.682	3.571	3.465	3.269	3.092	2.414
11	8.760	7.887	7.139	6.495	5.938	5.453	5.029	4.656	4.327	4.035	3.776	3.656	3.544	3.335	3.147	2.438
12	9.385	8.384	7.536	6.814	6.194	5.660	5.197	4.793	4.439	4.127	3.851	3.725	3.606	3.387	3.190	2.456
13	9.986	8.853	7.904	7.103	6.424	5.842	5.342	4.910	4.533	4.203	3.912	3.780	3.656	3.427	3.223	2.468
14	10.563	9.295	8.244	7.367	6.628	6.002	5.468	5.008	4.611	4.265	3.962	3.824	3.695	3.459	3.249	2.477
15	11.118	9.712	8.559	7.606	6.811	6.142	5.575	5.092	4.675	4.315	4.001	3.859	3.726	3.483	3.268	2.484
16	11.652	10.106	8.851	7.824	6.974	6.265	5.669	5.162	4.730	4.357	4.033	3.887	3.751	3.503	3.283	2.489
17	12.166	10.477	9.122	8.022	7.120	6.373	5.749	5.222	4.775	4.391	4.059	3.910	3.771	3.518	3.295	2.492
18	12.659	10.828	9.372	8.201	7.250	6.467	5.818	5.273	4.812	4.419	4.080	3.928	3.786	3.529	3.304	2.494
19	13.134	11.158	9.604	8.365	7.366	6.550	5.877	5.316	4.844	4.442	4.097	3.942	3.799	3.539	3.311	2.496
20	13.590	11.470	9.818	8.514	7.469	6.623	5.929	5.353	4.870	4.460	4.110	3.954	3.808	3.546	3.316	2.497
21	14.029	11.764	10.017	8.649	7.562	6.687	5.973	5.384	4.891	4.476	4.121	3.963	3.816	3.551	3.320	2.498
22	14.451	12.042	10.201	8.772	7.645	6.743	6.011	5.410	4.909	4.488	4.130	3.970	3.822	3.556	3.323	2.498
23	14.857	12.303	10.371	8.883	7.718	6.792	6.044	5.432	4.925	4.499	4.137	3.976	3.827	3.559	3.325	2.499
24	15.247	12.550	10.529	8.985	7.784	6.835	6.073	5.451	4.937	4.507	4.143	3.981	3.831	3.562	3.327	2.499
25	15.622	12.783	10.675	9.077	7.843	6.873	6.097	5.467	4.948	4.514	4.147	3.985	3.834	3.564	3.329	2.499
26	15.983	13.003	10.810	9.161	7.896	6.906	6.118	5.480	4.956	4.520	4.151	3.988	3.837	3.566	3.330	2.500
27	16.330	13.211	10.935	9.237	7.943	6.935	6.136	5.492	4.964	4.524	4.154	3.990	3.839	3.567	3.331	2.500
28	16.663	13.406	11.051	9.307	7.984	6.961	6.152	5.502	4.970	4.528	4.157	3.992	3.840	3.568	3.331	2.500
29	16.984	13.591	11.158	9.370	8.022	6.983	6.166	5.510	4.975	4.531	4.159	3.994	3.841	3.569	3.332	2.500
30	17.292	13.765	11.258	9.427	8.055	7.003	6.177	5.517	4.979	4.534	4.160	3.995	3.842	3.569	3.332	2.500
40	19.793	15.046	11.925	9.779	8.244	7.105	6.234	5.548	4.997	4.544	4.166	3.999	3.846	3.571	3.333	2.500

* Payments (or receipts) at the *end* of each period.

TABLE 5

PRESENT VALUE OF SUM-OF-THE-YEARS'-DIGITS DEPRECIATION ON $1.00 OF INITIAL INVESTMENT*

PERIODS	*8%*	*10%*	*12%*	*14%*	*16%*	*20%*
3	.881	.855	.831	.808	.786	.745
4	.860	.830	.802	.776	.751	.706
5	.839	.806	.775	.746	.719	.670
6	.820	.783	.749	.718	.689	.637
7	.801	.761	.725	.692	.661	.606
8	.782	.740	.701	.667	.635	.578
9	.765	.720	.680	.643	.610	.552
10	.748	.701	.659	.621	.587	.528
11	.731	.683	.639	.600	.565	.506
12	.715	.665	.620	.581	.545	.485
13	.700	.648	.602	.562	.526	.465
14	.685	.632	.585	.544	.508	.447
15	.671	.616	.569	.527	.491	.430
16	.657	.601	.553	.511	.475	.414
17	.644	.587	.538	.496	.460	.400
18	.631	.573	.524	.482	.445	.386
19	.618	.560	.510	.468	.432	.373
20	.606	.547	.497	.455	.419	.360
30	.504	.442	.393	.353	.320	.269
40	.428	.369	.323	.287	.257	.213

* *The quantity tabulated is equal to*

$$\sum_{n=1}^{N} \frac{2(N - n + 1)}{N(N + 1)(1 + r)^n}$$

Author Index

f

g

h

i

j

k

l

m

n

o

r

s

Subject Index

b

c

d

e

f

g

j

l

m

n

q

r

s

t

u

v